Letters of

Louis D. Brandeis

Letters of
Louis D. Brandeis

Volume V (1921–1941): *Elder Statesman*

EDITED BY MELVIN I. UROFSKY
AND DAVID W. LEVY

ALBANY, NEW YORK, 1978

STATE UNIVERSITY OF NEW YORK PRESS

First Edition

Published by State University of New York Press,
99 Washington Avenue, Albany, New York 12210
© 1978 State University of New York. All rights reserved
Printed in the United States of America
Designed by P.J. Conkwright

Library of Congress Cataloging in Publication Data

Brandeis, Louis Dembitz 1856–1941

Letters of Louis D. Brandeis.

CONTENTS:

Vol. I. 1870–1907: Urban reformer.
Vol. II. 1907–1912: People's attorney.
Vol. III. 1913–1915: Progresssive and Zionist.
Vol. IV. 1916–1921: Mr. Justice Brandeis.
Vol. V. 1921–1941: Elder statesman.

E664.B819A4   1971   347'.7326'34   73–129640
ISBN 0–87395–330–4 (v. 5)

For
Susan Linda Urofsky
and
Lynne Hunt Levy
with love and gratitude for their help,
their encouragement, and their
patient forebearance.

Contents

Illustrations   ix

Acknowledgements   xi

Note on Volume V   xv

Chronology, 1921–1941   xvii

Cumulative Key to Letter Source Citations   xxiii

Editorial Markings   xxxi

Letters of Louis D. Brandeis, 1921–1941   3

Additional Letters of Louis D. Brandeis,
1881–1920   656

Cumulative Index, Volumes I–V   661

Illustrations

Mr. Justice Brandeis   FRONTISPIECE
University of Louisville Law School

ILLUSTRATION SECTION FOLLOWING PAGE 386

Oliver Wendell Holmes, Jr.
Harvard Law School Library

The United States Supreme Court in 1929
Library of Congress

Franklin Delano Roosevelt
Franklin D. Roosevelt Library

Felix Frankfurter
Harvard Law School Library

LDB and Alfred Brandeis
Elizabeth Brandeis Raushenbush

Robert Szold
Zionist Archives and Library

Solomon Goldman
Zionist Archives and Library

Emanuel Neumann
Zionist Archives and Library

LBD, Alice Brandeis and grandchildren, Chatham, 1938
Elizabeth Brandeis Raushenbush

LDB and Fannie Brandeis
Elizabeth Brandeis Raushenbush

LDB at Chatham, 1931 (two pictures)
Elizabeth Brandeis Raushenbush

Paul, Walter, and Elizabeth Raushenbush, 1932
Elizabeth Brandeis Raushenbush

Acknowledgements

O ver the past ten years, we have accumulated substantial debts to many individuals and institutions. We have tried to thank them as we have gone along, and their names appear in the first four volumes. But we wish to acknowledge once again the financial support extended by the National Endowment for the Humanities, which, with a bravery rarely matched in the annals of modern bureaucracy, funded the wild-eyed scheme of two young scholars, and then continued its aid through a series of successive grants to help bring this project to completion. We shall ever be grateful for that bravery and that faith.

We also owe a debt beyond measure to members of the Brandeis family who have been a constant source of encouragement and information. Our admiration of Paul and Elizabeth Brandeis Raushenbush knows no bounds, and we are proud to be able to call Eric and Mary K. Tachau our friends.

We were deeply saddened, during the preparation of this final volume, by news of the death of two women close to the project from its inception. Pearl Von Allmen, for so long the devoted guardian of the Brandeis manuscripts in Louisville, had been untiring in her aid and we will always remember her personal kindnesses to us. Susan Brandeis Gilbert, the Justice's elder daughter, offered an encouragement and moral support which we (inadequately) attempted to acknowledge in our dedication to the second volume. We hope that our labors have been worthy of their confidence and help.

For assistance extended primarily in the preparation of this volume, we wish to thank Erika Chadbourn of the Harvard Law School Library and James R. Bentley, secretary of the Filson Club in Louisville, both of whom have been of invaluable aid throughout our work. We also thank Professor Herbert Aptheker; Ms. Andrea Gillis of the Harvard University Archives; Dr. Philip D. Lagerquist, chief archivist of the Harry S. Truman Library; Mrs. Ruth W. Lester, assistant editor of the Thomas Jefferson Papers; Mrs. Sylvia Landress, director of the Zionist Archives and Library in New York, and her staff; Bernard A. Bernier, Jr., head of the Reference Section of the Library of Congress Serial Division; Professor Emmet V. Mittlebeeler of American University; Dr. Michael Heymann, director of the Central Zionist Archives in Jerusalem; Martha B. Katz-Hyman of the American Jewish Historical Society; Mrs. Fannie Zelcer of the American Jewish Archives; Mr. Benjamin S. Kirsh, former law partner of Susan Brandeis Gilbert; Mrs. Mary E. Carver, registrar of the J. B. Speed Museum in Louisville; Prof. John J. Weisert of the University of Louisville; Dr. Arnold Schuetz, formerly of Virginia Commonwealth University; and Malcolm L. Call of the W.E.B. DuBois Papers. In addition we also want to thank Professor Alpheus T. Mason, now professor Emeritus of Princeton University; Mr. Philip Slomovitz, editor and publisher of the *Detroit Jewish News;* the late Hyman Parker and his son, Dr. Philip J. Parker, of Detroit, Michigan; Mr. Irving J. Dilliard of St. Louis; and Mr. Robert Szold of New York. We also received assistance from Professor Arthur S. Link, editor of the Woodrow Wilson Papers; not only has his work been a model for our own, but he has been unfailingly courteous and supportive of the project from the beginning.

Mr. William LaPiana served as research assistant on this volume, together with Thomas L. Owen, who rendered conspicuous service throughout the life of the project; Ms. Betty Leviner typed part of the manuscript, as did Alexis Rodgers and Cathye Woody. The cumulative index was prepared with the devoted assistance of Steven Elliott Brown, C. B. Clark, Stephen Gens, Francis Gosling, and Terry Hammons. The editors wish to gratefully acknowledge two generous grants from the Research Council of The University of Oklahoma, which made the preparation of the cumulative index a much lighter task.

Again, we wish to acknowledge the work of Mr. Thomas L. Davis, III, who has been copy editor for all five volumes, and who has done so much to assure the accuracy and consistency of the annotation. We hope that the faith and high hopes expressed by Mr. Norman Mangouni, director of the State University of New York Press, nearly a decade ago have not been disappointed. His help and support have been invaluable.

Finally, it is impossible to describe how much we owe to our wives, Susan Linda Urofsky and Lynne Hunt Levy, who for so many years had to share their lives, and frequently their homes, with a man named Louis Brandeis, whose papers could be found in every room, on every table, in every nook. Their patience held up–at least most of the time; their humor rarely failed; and their love encouraged and sustained us always. The dedication of this volume is but a small token of all they have done, and of how much they mean to us.

We can now say to them, and to all those many others who helped us so generously, "We have finished."

Richmond, Virginia
Norman, Oklahoma

Note on Volume V

IN our introduction to the first volume of these letters we attempted an assessment of what made Louis Dembitz Brandeis such a towering figure, not only in his own time, but in the broader sweep of American history. Largeness of spirit, intelligence, integrity, thoughtfulness and energy all combined to make this man a leading reformer in the progressive era, the synthesizer of a uniquely American Zionism, and one of the great jurists to occupy a seat on the United States Supreme Court. We confidently predicted that this edition of his letters would amply demonstrate all of these qualities, and to us at least that original estimate of the man, his character and his accomplishments has grown as this work has progressed. "The trait called greatness is an elusive one," Arthur M. Schlesinger, Sr. wrote in his memoirs, "but if it comprehends humility, moral majesty, faith in the common folk, deep human compassion, and constancy of purpose – in short, the quality of having made the world better for having lived in it – then Brandeis alone of the men I have known fulfilled the requirements."

This volume, which opens after the great schism in the Zionist movement and closes with Brandeis's death, depicts him trying, in a variety of ways to make the world a better place. Once again, the scope of his interests and the intensity of his involvement is astounding. Zionism, Palestine, the liberal press, economics, the University of Louisville, family affairs, Savings Bank Life Insurance, the Harvard Law School, unemployment compensation, prohibition enforcement, civil liberties – all engaged him to some extent, even while he struggled with Holmes and Stone and Cardozo to keep alive the liberal tradition on the bench. Some of these ventures were new, such as his commitment to making the University of Louisville a first rank local institution, while others, such as the Harvard Law School and Savings Bank insurance, had been the beneficiary of his interest for decades.

There are two areas of his life during these years for which the letters do not give a full portrait. First, there is the work of the

Supreme Court; except for some tantalizing comments in his important and extensive correspondence with Felix Frankfurter, Brandeis never wrote about his work on the Court. He had a purist's notion of the sanctity and confidentiality of the Court's business, which he guarded with as much zeal as his own privacy. Second, Brandeis's involvement with New Deal affairs is far greater than is indicated in these letters. The reason in this case is not any unwillingness to talk about it, but rather because in the thirties Brandeis delivered opinions and advice, for the most part, orally and directly to the many government officials–from newly minted lawyers in obscure agencies on up to cabinet members and even to the president himself–who sought the benefit of his wisdom and experience. He was, in a full and rich sense, the "elder statesman" of humane liberalism during the New Deal.

On the eve of Brandeis's sixtieth brithday Oliver Wendell Holmes had passed him a note scribbled on Supreme Court stationery. "My dear Brandeis," Holmes wrote. "You turn the third corner tomorrow. You have done big things with high motives– have swept over great hedges and across wide ditches, always with the same courage, the same keen eye, the same steady hand. As you take the home stretch the onlookers begin to realize how you have ridden and what you have achieved. I am glad that I am still here to say: Nobly Done." The "home stretch" for Brandeis, as for Holmes, was not a period of relaxation or reminiscence. Indeed, some of his finest and most enduring work, the preservation of a constitutional heritage open to flexibility and innovation and the protection of individual rights and privileges, took place during these years, and Brandeis had the good fortune to see some of his great dissents later become the law of the land.

This volume depicts the creativity and accomplishments of that "home stretch," and a cumulative index to all five volumes will hopefully make it easier for students and scholars to trace the various threads that were woven together in the quite remarkable life of this one man.

Chronology, 1921–1941

1921 July 16–17, Conference to reorganize Brandeis–Mack forces after Cleveland convention

July 27–August 9, LDB vacations in Canada with Susan Brandeis

September 1–14, Twelfth Zionist Congress in Carlsbad Czechoslovakia

November 12, Washington Naval Conference opens

December 14, Nahum Sokolow attempts to reconcile LDB and WZO

December 19, LDB dissents in *Truax* and *American Lumber* cases

1922 January, Solomon Rosenbloom goes to Palestine for PDC

February 23, LDB sets forth reform creed at Federal Council of Churches meeting

February 27, Supreme Court, through LDB, upholds women suffrage

April 1, Coal strike begins

April, Susan Brandeis opens New York law office

June 5, *Coronado* case

July 1, Railroad strike begins

July 24, League of Nations confirms British mandate over Palestine

September 4, Coal strike ends

September 13, Railroad strike ends

1923 February 19, *New England Division* cases

April 9, Supreme Court invalidates minimum wage law in *Adkins* case

August 2, Warren G. Harding dies; Calvin Coolidge becomes president

1924 February 3, Woodrow Wilson dies

February 17, Preliminary conference on Jewish Agency convened by Louis Marshall

May 20, Senator Wheeler cleared of influence peddling charges

July 4, Robert M. LaFollette launches third-party campaign

September 24, LDB begins program to build up University of Louisville

November 4, Coolidge defeats John W. Davis and LaFollette for presidency

1925 January 5, Harlan Fiske Stone nominated to Supreme Court

February 13, Congress passes Court Jurisdiction Act

April 20, Elizabeth Brandeis engaged to Paul Arthur Raushenbush

June 18, Robert Marion LaFollette dies

July 2, Elizabeth Brandeis marries Paul Raushenbush

October 5, Susan Brandeis becomes first woman to argue case before United States Supreme Court

December 30, Susan Brandeis marries Jacob Gilbert

1926 March 8, Oliver Wendell Holmes's 85th birthday

October 25, *Myers v. United States*

November 2, LDB's first grandchild, Louis Brandeis Gilbert, born

November 3, Republicans lose heavily in congressional elections

November 13, LDB is 70 years old

December 2, LDB meets with Chaim Weizmann for first time since 1921 fight

1927 February 25, Coolidge vetoes McNary-Haugen bill

April 6, Massachusetts Supreme Judicial Court denies new trial to Sacco and Vanzetti

April 11, *Bedford Cut Stone* case

April 26–27, Wigmore-Frankfurter exchange over Sacco and Vanzetti

May 16, LDB dissents in *Whitney* case

May 21, Lindbergh flies solo across the Atlantic

June 2, Governor Fuller appoints three-man advisory board on Sacco and Vanzetti case

July 8, Henry Ford publicly apologizes for his anti-Semitic campaign

August 4, Governor Fuller finds Sacco and Vanzetti received a fair trial

August 22, LDB turns down last minute appeal; Sacco and Vanzetti executed

November 2, William J. Burns accused of jury tampering in Sinclair trial

1928 March, proposed restrictions on SBLI defeated in Massachusetts legislature

May 14 LDB's granddaughter, Alice Gilbert born

May 28, LDB dissents in *Quaker City Cab* case

June 4, LDB dissents in *Olmstead* case

June 11–13, temporary but sharp drop in stock market

June 13, birth of Walter Raushenbush

June 28, ZOA convention opens; first major challenge to Lipsky regime

August 8, Alfred Brandeis dies

November, Herbert Hoover defeats Alfred Smith for the presidency

1929 March 9, Establishment of Wickersham Commission

August 7, Zionist Congress ratifies Jewish Agency agreement

August 23, Arab riots erupt in Palestine

September 11, Louis Marshall dies

October 9, LDB meets with Ramsey MacDonald

October 23, First break in bull market

October 28, Wall Street stock market crash

November 1, Boston Five Cents Savings Bank joins SBLI

November 24, LDB makes first public Zionist appearance since 1921

1930 February 3, William Howard Taft resigns as Chief Justice; Charles Evans Hughes nominated to replace him

March 6, ZOA committee approaches LDB for reconciliation

March 8, William Howard Taft dies

March 31, Shaw Commission report

May 22, Brandeis–Mack group issues its terms for reassuming ZOA leadership

July 1, ZOA elects Robert Szold and Brandeis–Mack slate

July 12, LDB surrenders on retaining Jacob deHaas in ZOA leadership

October 21, Hope-Simpson Report and Passfield White Paper issued

1931 June 30–July 15, Seventeenth Zionist Congress meets in Basle; ousts Weizmann from presidency of WZO

November 13, LDB is 75 years old

1932 January 12, Oliver Wendell Holmes retires from Supreme Court

February 15, Benjamin Cardozo named to succeed Holmes

March 21, LDB dissents in *New State Ice Company* case

July 1, Democratic Party nominates Franklin D. Roosevelt for president

November 8, Roosevelt defeats Hoover for presidency

1933 January 17, Emanuel Neumann and King Abdullah agree on Zionist option for land in Transjordania

January 30, Adolf Hitler becomes Chancellor of Germany

March 4, Roosevelt inaugurated, "Hundred Days" begin

1934 April 19, Alice Grady dies

June 7, LDB meets with Roosevelt on unemployment compensation bill

August 2, Hitler assumes full dictatorial power in Germany

1935 March 6, Oliver Wendell Holmes dies

May 6, Supreme Court declares Railroad Retirement Act unconstitutional

May 27, Black Monday; Court strikes down National Recovery Act and Frazier-Lemke Act

August 15, Roosevelt signs Social Security act

August 24, Roosevelt signs Public Utility Holding Company act, marking start of Second New Deal

September 7, Revisionists secede from WZO

1936 January 6, Court declares Agricultural Adjustment Act unconstitutional

March 7, Hitler reoccupies Rhineland

April 17, Arab riots break out in Palestine; martial law declared

May 18, Court strikes down Guffey Coal Act and New York Minimum Wage law

July 20, Peel Commission named

November 3, Roosevelt elected to second term

November 13, LDB is 80 years old

1937 February 5, Roosevelt proposes Court reorganization plan

March 21, Jacob deHaas dies

July 7, Peel Commission report

September 26, Edward A. Filene dies

December 20, Supreme Court, in *Nardone* case, adopts LDB's views on wiretapping

1938 January 5, Herbert Lehman proposes SBLI for New York

March 16, New York legislature passes SBLI law

September 28, Hitler, Mussolini, Daladier and Chamberlain meet at Munich

November 9, Woodhead Commission report

November 9–10, *Kristallnacht* in Germany

1938 January 5, Roosevelt nominates Felix Frankfurter to Supreme Court

January 30, Frankfurter takes seat on Court

February 7, St. James Conference opens in London

February 13, LDB resigns from United States Supreme Court

March 20, William O. Douglas nominated to fill LDB's seat on the Supreme Court

May 17, MacDonald White Paper

August 23, Molotov-Ribbentrop agreement

September 1, Germany invades Poland; start of Second World War

December, publication of Lowdermilk study of Palestine

1940 May 25, Harold Ickes publishes defense of Richard A. Ballinger

July 1, Brandeisists elect Edward Kaufmann president of ZOA

October, Weizmann seeks to make peace with American Zionists

November 5, Roosevelt elected to third term

1941 June 13, Roosevelt nominates Harlan Fiske Stone to succeed
     Hughes as Chief Justice
     October 1, LDB suffers heart attack
     October 5, Louis Dembitz Brandeis dies
1945 October 12, Alice Goldmark Brandeis dies

Cumulative Key to Letter Source Citations

Alderman MSS Edwin Anderson Alderman Papers, University of Virginia Library, Charlottesville, Virginia

Antitrust Hearings United States Senate, Committee on Interstate Commerce, *Hearings on Control of Corporations, Persons, and Firms Engaged in Interstate Commerce*, 62d Congress, 2d Session (3 vols., Washington, D.C., 1912)

Baker MSS Ray Stannard Baker Papers, Manuscript Division, Library of Congress, Washington, D.C.

Bayard MSS Thomas Francis Bayard Papers, Manuscript Division, Library of Congress, Washington, D.C.

Berlin Office Records of the Central Zionist Office, Berlin (Zionistisches Zentralbureau), Record Group Z3, Central Zionist Archives, Jerusalem, Israel

Billikopf MSS Jacob Billikopf Papers, American Jewish Archives, Hebrew Union College-Jewish Institute of Religion, Cincinnati, Ohio

Brandeis MSS Louis Dembitz Brandeis Papers, University of Louisville Law Library, Louisville, Kentucky; letters and numbers refer to specific files

Brodie MSS Israel Benjamin Brodie Papers, Record Group A251, Central Zionist Archives, Jerusalem, Israel

Carnegie MSS Andrew Carnegie Papers, Manuscript Division, Library of Congress, Washington, D.C.

Chafee MSS Zechariah Chafee, Jr. Papers, Harvard Law School Library, Cambridge, Massachusetts

Chandler MSS William Eaton Chandler Papers, New Hampshire Historical Society, Concord, New Hampshire

Commerce Dept. General Correspondence Files, Office of the Secretary, Department of Commerce Records, Record Group 40, National Archives, Washington, D.C.

Cooke MSS Morris Llewellyn Cooke Papers, Franklin D. Roosevelt Library, Hyde Park, New York

Copenhagen Office Records of the Provisional Zionist Office at Copenhagen, Record Group L6, Central Zionist Archives, Jerusalem, Israel

deHaas MSS Jacob deHaas Papers, Zionist Archives and Library, New York, New York

Dilliard   Letters provided through the courtesy of Irving Dilliard, St. Louis, Missouri

Douglas MSS   Douglas Family Papers, Missouri Historical Society, St. Louis, Missouri

DuBois MSS   William Edward Burghardt DuBois Papers, Library of the University of Massachusetts, Amherst, Massachusetts

EBR   Letters provided through the courtesy of Mrs. Elizabeth Brandeis Raushenbush, Madison, Wisconsin

Ehrmann MSS   Herbert Brutus Ehrmann Papers, Harvard Law School Library, Cambridge, Massachusetts

Eliot MSS   Charles William Eliot Papers, Harvard University Archives, Cambridge, Massachusetts

Ernst MSS   Morris Leopold Ernst Papers, University of Texas Library, Austin, Texas

Ettinger MSS   Jacob Akiba Ettinger Papers, Record Group A111, Central Zionist Archives, Jerusalem, Israel

Evans MSS   Elizabeth Glendower Evans Papers, Women's Archives, Schlesinger Library, Radcliffe College, Cambridge, Massachusetts

Fannie Brandeis   Letters provided through the courtesy of Fannie Brandeis, Louisville, Kentucky

Farber   Letters provided through the courtesy of J. Eugene Farber, Toledo, Ohio

Fetter MSS   Frank Fetter Papers, University of Indiana Library, Bloomington, Indiana

Filene MSS   Edward Albert Filene Papers, Bergengren Memorial Museum Library, World Council of Credit Unions, Inc., Madison, Wisconsin

Flexner MSS   Bernard Flexner Papers, Zionist Archives and Library, New York, New York

Fola LaFollette   Letters provided through the courtesy of Fola LaFollette, Washington, D.C.

Foreign Office   Records of Her Majesty's Government Foreign Office, Public Records Office, London, England

Frankfurter MSS-CZA   Felix Frankfurter Papers, Record Group A264, Central Zionist Archives, Jerusalem, Israel

Frankfurter MSS-HLS   Felix Frankfurter Papers, Harvard Law School Library, Cambridge, Massachusetts

Frankfurter MSS-LC   Felix Frankfurter Papers, Manuscript Division, Library of Congress, Washington, D.C.

Friedenwald MSS   Harry Friedenwald Papers, Record Group A182, Central Zionist Archives, Jerusalem, Israel

Friendly   Letters provided through the courtesy of Henry Jacob Friendly, Washington, D.C.

Goldmark MSS Pauline Goldmark Papers, Manuscript Division, Library of Congress, Washington, D.C.

Gottheil MSS Richard James Horatio Gottheil Papers, Record Group A138, Central Zionist Archives, Jerusalem, Israel

Grady MSS Correspondence between Alice Harriet Grady and Louis Dembitz Brandeis, Goldfarb Library, Brandeis University, Waltham, Massachusetts

Gray MSS John Chipman Gray Papers, Autograph Collection, Houghton Library, Harvard University, Cambridge, Massachusetts

Griswold MSS William Edward Schenk Griswold Papers in the United States Railroad Securities Papers, Sterling Library, Yale University, New Haven, Connecticut

HLS Louis Dembitz Brandeis Autograph Collection, Harvard Law School Library, Cambridge, Massachusetts

Hand MSS Learned Hand Papers, Harvard Law School Library, Cambridge, Massachusetts

Hildegarde Nagel Letters provided through the courtesy of Ms. Hildegarde Nagel

Holmes MSS Oliver Wendell Holmes, Jr. Papers, Harvard Law School Library, Cambridge, Massachusetts

House MSS Edward Mandel House Papers, Sterling Library, Yale University, New Haven, Connecticut

Howe MSS Mark deWolf Howe Papers, Harvard Law School Library, Cambridge, Massachusetts

Huebsch MSS Benjamin W. Huebsch Papers, Manuscript Division, Library of Congress, Washington, D.C.

Hurwitz MSS Henry Hurwitz Papers, YIVO Institute for Jewish Research, New York, New York

Hurwitz MSS-AJA Henry Hurwitz Papers, American Jewish Archives, Hebrew Union College-Jewish Institute of Religion, Cincinnati, Ohio

Interior Department Hearings *Investigation of the Department of the Interior and of the Bureau of Forestry*, Senate Document 719, 61st Congress 3rd Session (13 vols., Washington, D.C., 1910)

Kallen MSS Horace Meyer Kallen Papers, American Jewish Archives, Hebrew Union College-Jewish Institute of Religion, Cincinnati, Ohio

Kellogg MSS Paul Underwood Kellogg Papers, Goldfarb Library, Brandeis University, Waltham, Massachusetts

Kesselman MSS Robert D. Kesselman Papers, Record Group A168, Central Zionist Archives, Jerusalem, Israel

Kirsh Letters provided through the courtesy of Benjamin Sollow Kirsh, New York, New York

LaFollette MSS Robert Marion LaFollette Papers, Manuscript Division, Library of Congress, Washington, D.C.

Laski MSS Harold Joseph Laski Papers, Yale University Law Library, New Haven, Connecticut

Lehman MSS Herbert Henry Lehman Papers, School of International Affairs Library, Columbia University, New York, New York

Levinthal MSS Louis Edward Levinthal Papers, privately held, Philadelphia, Pennsylvania

Lief *Guide* Alfred Lief, editor, *The Brandeis Guide to the Modern World* (Boston: Little, Brown and Company, 1941)

Lloyd MSS Henry Demarest Lloyd Papers, The State Historical Society of Wisconsin, Madison, Wisconsin

London Office Records of the London Office of the World Zionist Organization/Jewish Agency for Palestine, Record Group Z4, Central Zionist Archives, Jerusalem, Israel

McAdoo MSS William Gibbs McAdoo Papers, Manuscript Division, Library of Congress, Washington, D.C.

McCarthy MSS Charles McCarthy Papers, The State Historical Society of Wisconsin, Madison, Wisconsin

McClennan Memorandum Edward F. McClennen, "Louis D. Brandeis as a Lawyer," 33 *Massachusetts Law Quarterly* 1 (1948)

McReynolds MSS James Clark McReynolds Papers, University of Virginia Library, Charlottesville, Virginia

Mack MSS Julian William Mack Papers, Zionist Archives and Library, New York, New York

Magnes MSS Judah Leon Magnes Papers, Central Archives for the History of the Jewish People, Hebrew University, Jerusalem, Israel

Marshall MSS Louis Marshall Papers, American Jewish Archives, Hebrew Union College-Jewish Institute of Religion, Cincinnati, Ohio

Mason *Brandeis* Alpheus Thomas Mason, *Brandeis: A Free Man's Life* (New York: Viking Press, 1946)

Mason *Brandeis Way* Alpheus Thomas Mason, *The Brandeis Way* (Princeton: Princeton University Press, 1938)

Middleton MSS George Middleton Papers, Manuscript Division, Library of Congress, Washington, D.C.

Mitchell MSS John Mitchell Papers, Catholic University Library, Washington, D.C.

Mittlebeeler Letters provided through the courtesy of Emmet Vaughn Mittlebeeler, Washington, D.C.

Moore MSS William Underhill Moore Papers, Special Collections, Columbia University Library, New York, New York

Morgenthau MSS Henry Morgenthau, Sr. Papers, Manuscript Division, Library of Congress, Washington, D.C.

Motzkin MSS Leo Motzkin Papers, Record Group A126, Central Zionist Archives, Jerusalem, Israel

Murdock MSS Victor Murdock Papers, Manuscript Division, Library of Congress, Washington, D.C.

Neumann MSS Emanuel Neumann Papers, privately held, New York, New York

New Haven *Returns* Massachusetts House of Representatives, Document 1175, *Report of Board of Railroad Commissioners on Annual Returns of New York, New Haven & Hartford Railroad Company* (Boston, 1908)

Nomination Hearings United States Senate, *Hearings before the Subcommittee of the Committee of the Judiciary . . . on the Nomination of Louis D. Brandeis to be an Associate Justice of the Supreme Court of the United States*, 64th Congress, 1st Session (2 vols., Washington, 1916)

Palestine Office Records of the Palestina Amt at Jaffa, Record Group L2, Central Zionist Archives, Jerusalem, Israel

Palmer MSS Paul A. Palmer Papers, Sterling Library, Yale University, New Haven, Connecticut

Parker Letters provided through the courtesy of Hyman Parker, Detroit, Michigan

A. Pinchot MSS Amos Richard Eno Pinchot Papers, Manuscript Division, Library of Congress, Washington, D.C.

G. Pinchot MSS Gifford Pinchot Papers, Manuscript Division, Library of Congress, Washington, D.C.

Political Department Records. Records of the Political Department of the World Zionist Organization/Jewish Agency for Palestine, Record Group S24, Central Zionist Archives, Jerusalem, Israel

Pound MSS Roscoe Pound Papers, Harvard Law School Library, Cambridge, Massachusetts

Powell MSS Thomas Reed Powell Papers, Harvard Law School Library, Cambridge, Massachusetts

Redfield MSS William Cox Redfield Papers, Manuscript Division, Library of Congress, Washington, D.C.

Report of Organization Harvard Law School Association, *Report of*

the Organization and of the First General Meeting at Cambridge, November 5, 1886 (Boston: Privately printed, 1887)

Rice   Letters provided through the courtesy of William G. Rice, Jr., Madison, Wisconsin

Richards MSS   Bernard Gerson Richards Papers, privately held, New York, New York

Richberg MSS   Donald Randall Richberg Papers, Chicago Historical Society, Chicago, Illinois

Roosevelt MSS   Franklin Delano Roosevelt Papers, Franklin D. Roosevelt Library, Hyde Park, New York

Rosenthal MSS   Albert Rosenthal Papers, Historical Society of Pennsylvania, Philadelphia, Pennsylvania

SBLI   Division of Savings Bank Life Insurance Archives, Boston, Massachusetts

Schiff MSS   Jacob Henry Schiff Papers, American Jewish Archives, Hebrew Union College-Jewish Institute of Religion, Cincinnati, Ohio

Seligman MSS   Edwin Robert Anderson Seligman Papers, Special Collections, Columbia University Library, New York, New York

Silver MSS   Abba Hillel Silver Papers, Archives of Temple Tifereth Israel, Cleveland, Ohio

Sokolow MSS   Nahum Sokolow Papers, Record Group A18, Central Zionist Archives, Jerusalem, Israel

Speed MSS   Hattie Bishop Speed Papers, J.B. Speed Museum, University of Louisville, Louisville, Kentucky

State Department Records   Records of the United States Department of State, Record Group 59, The National Archives, Washington, D.C.

Steffens MSS   Lincoln Steffens Papers, Special Collections, Columbia University Library, New York, New York

H. Szold MSS   Henrietta Szold Papers (private), Record Group A125, Central Zionist Archives, Jerusalem, Israel

R. Szold MSS   Robert Szold Papers, Zionist Archives and Library, New York, New York

Taft MSS   William Howard Taft Papers, Manuscript Division, Library of Congress, Washington, D.C.

Tannenbaum MSS   Frank Tannenbaum Papers, Special Collections, Columbia University Library, New York, New York

Thompson MSS   Huston Thompson Papers, Manuscript Division, Library of Congress, Washington, D.C.

VanDevanter MSS   Willis VanDevanter Papers, Manuscript Division, Library of Congress, Washington, D.C.

Wade MSS   Wade Family Papers, Sterling Library, Yale University, New Haven, Connecticut

Wald MSS   Lillian D. Wald Papers, Special Collections, Columbia University Library, New York, New York

Walsh MSS   David Ignatius Walsh Papers, Manuscript Division, Library of Congress, Washington, D.C.

Warren MSS   Charles Warren Papers, Manuscript Division, Library of Congress, Washington, D.C.

Wehle MSS   Louis Brandeis Wehle Papers, Franklin D. Roosevelt Library, Hyde Park, New York

Weizmann MSS   Chaim Weizmann Papers, Library of Yad Chaim Weizmann, Rehovot, Israel

White MSS   William Allen White Papers, Manuscript Division, Library of Congress, Washington, D.C.

Whitlock MSS   Brand Whitlock Papers, Manuscript Division, Library of Congress, Washington, D.C.

Wilson MSS   Woodrow Wilson Papers, Manuscript Division, Library of Congress, Washington, D.C.

Wingate MSS   Charles Wingate Papers, Autograph Collection, Houghton Library, Harvard University, Cambridge, Massachusetts

Wise MSS   Stephen Samuel Wise Papers, Library of the American Jewish Historical Society, Waltham, Massachusetts

Wise MSS-AJA   Stephen Samuel Wise Papers, American Jewish Archives, Hebrew Union College-Jewish Institute of Religion, Cincinnati, Ohio

Woolley MSS   Robert W. Woolley Papers, Manuscript Division, Library of Congress, Washington, D. C.

YIVO   Miscellaneous Collections, YIVO Institute for Jewish Research, New York, New York

EDITORIAL MARKINGS

[   ]   Words, letters or punctuation added by the
          editors. When brackets appear in the editorial
          heading, except for the manuscript source, it
          signifies that the information enclosed is
          not certain, but merely the best estimate
          we can make.

[*]   Indecipherable or illegible word; each asterisk
          indicates one word.

To Felix Frankfurter

July 6, 1921 Woods Hole, Mass. [Frankfurter Mss–HLS]

DEAR FELIX: [1] 1. Re Warner's letter enclosed. Couldn't you appropriately, in your survey of C[leveland].,[2] refer as one of the enduring causes of crime to crime in high places, i.e. such lawlessness as the American Legion & Ku Klux Klan?

"If gold rusteth, what should iron do?" [3]

2. I have written Mack [and] deH[aas] urging all kinds of preparedness so as to enable us to get off the Congress statement etc. immediately after our July 16–17 conference.[4]

3. Mack feels quite deeply about B[ernard]. Flexner's not making good on things undertaken. Did he talk with you about it? [5]

And shouldn't he be definitely communicated with? I wrote JWM & DeH. to send BF immediately a report on our doings.

Hope you found Marion in good form.

Emma Erving & Selma [6] had motored over for yesterday & today.

1. Persons identified in Volumes I—IV are not identified again in Volume V.

2. Felix Frankfurter and Roscoe Pound, eds., *Criminal Justice in Cleveland* (Cleveland, 1921). For the background of the Cleveland survey, see LDB to Frankfurter, 12 January 1921; see also LDB to Frankfurter, 29 September 1921.

3. Geoffrey Chaucer, *The Canterbury Tales*, "Prologue," l. 496.

4. See LDB to Frankfurter, 6 September 1921, n. 7.

5. In an attempt to reorganize forces after the mass resignation at Cleveland (see LDB to Julian W. Mack, 3 June 1921), there was considerable confusion among LDB's supporters as to who would do what work. Bernard Flexner had previously been responsible for several financial projects, and the confusion here appears to concern his responsibility to follow through on them.

6. Emma Erving was a Washington, D.C. orthopedist and a close personal friend of LDB and his wife; Selma was her daughter.

To Alfred Brandeis

July 12, 1921 Woods Hole, Mass. [Brandeis Mss, M 4–4]

DEAR AL: Yours of 9th with interesting data on milling has come. I have thought during the past weeks often of your remark that "corn thrives only in weather unfit for man." Elizabeth arrived Sunday with dire reports of Washington weather & Miss [Alice H.] Grady & [George W.] Anderson, who came Friday (& left Saturday), give even worse for Boston. Here it has been uniformly comfortable.

Miss Grady reports a recent dinner with [Bernard J.] Rothwell devoted to a rhapsody on you.

Two Misses Cochrane, daughters of Robert C. of Louisville are here, also Washington Flexner [1] family; and your nephew S[*](?) (Edith is at Wellesley for a few days.) S. says Walter reports business so dead that he will close shop & clear out soon.

Hoover is certainly having opportunity to test any & all his powers as economic leader. I guess the law of supply & demand still holds sway, despite the Republican monopoly of prosperity.

The determination of the Administration to lend the RR. $500,000,000 seems to me wise.[2] Ultimately the govt will have to take over the RRs & it is just as well to do it piecemeal in this way. To let them default generally in their bonds would spell widespread disaster, which may properly be averted under the circumstances. But it is silly to put out this talk that this will start business on the upgrade. Humphrey (?) Marshall's friend would have known better.

I expect to be in N.Y. Sat & Sunday & possibly Monday on Zionist affairs, but trip may be postponed.

Your Tachau cousins etc. are gathering.[3] Hannah has come also. Says Harry [Wehle] dined with her the evening before she left N.Y.

1. Washington Flexner (1870–1943) was the youngest child of the nine in the distinguished Flexner family. He headed printing and engraving companies in New York and Chicago.

2. American railroads, which had been returned to private ownership after the war by the Esch-Cummins Act in February, 1920, were caught in the major recession of 1921. Despite strong pressure to "nationalize" the system, President Harding was expected to request as an alternative that the War Finance Corporation be empowered to relieve the railroads of their debts.

3. Alfred's daughter Jean had married Charles Tachau of Louisville. See LDB to Alfred Brandeis, 4 June 1925, n. 1.

To Alfred Brandeis

July 19, 1921 Woods Hole, Mass. [Brandeis Mss, M 4-4]

DEAR AL: Returned this morning from N.Y.

Susan says one Joffe is bragging that his brother worked with you in Food Administration.

Saw Lewis Straus[s], who was, as always, agreeable. But I am rather confirmed by his looks that he isn't as fine as he was.

Perhaps it is merely deterioration incident to aging, which is discernible also in other Jews.

I note Pullman Co. says it has never experienced such a dearth of commercial travellers. There have been times when their absence would have seemed a blessing.

Alice tells me your niece Edith & husband called.

Gruesse,

To Alfred Brandeis (Fragment)

July 21, 1921 Woods Hole, Mass. [Brandeis Mss, M 4-4]

DEAR AL: One Beckden (lumber dealer) St Louis is here. Says he thinks C[harles] N[agel] is in much better shape than earlier, & that he took a very active (losing) part in mayoralty campaign.[1]

Your niece Edith tried to raise me in the estimation of her son yesterday, by disclosing that I am your brother. He dei[g]ned to say, like Herbert White, "I see".

Eliz[abeth]. is to be here until the 31st, so don't dare to go to Washington before that date. I think you had better postpone this oft postponed trip until September.

1. In April, St. Louis voters reelected Mayor Henry W. Kiel. He defeated James W. Byrnes, a local businessman.

To Alfred Brandeis

July 27, 1921 Toronto, Canada [Brandeis Mss, M 4-4]

DEAR AL: Susan and I arrived 9:40 this morning & our train to the Tegamini Lakes does not go out until 8:45 P.M. We did a bit of leisurely sightseeing this morning afoot, dropping into shady nooks or seats in parks or university grounds. It was warm but there was a virile North West wind which made the degree of heat enjoyable.

A Toronto steel merchant who "occurred to me" in the breakfast car says business is literally dead—like one complete [*] off orders. Everybody using up what stock he has on hand, even if not exactly appropriate. He spoke feelingly of a wagon & sleigh concern organized in 1852, which had never before shut down completely & spoke generally as one who had struck a new kind of terror, an ogre of the mythical age.

Still we had an interesting time at Niagra [*sic*] in 1865 which came vividly to mind this morning.

To Alfred Brandeis

August 9, 1921 New York, N.Y. [Brandeis Mss, M 4-4]

DEAR AL: Glad to get your letter here. We had a most satisfactory outing in Canada, & I enjoyed much having a solid fortnight uninterruptedly with Susan. Hadn't seen so much of her for ten years.

Sunday afternoon we spent at Niagra [*sic*]. The old International is still in ruins after the fire, & the Cataract House is just as it was in 1865 apparently except for the natural wear, which is great. It seemed strange to find any where in America such a survival of the early ages. The only fine hotel at Niagra [*sic*] appears to be the Clayton on the Canadian side.

But the falls are still fun, despite obstructions for power which are discernible.

We went under the falls from the Canadian side, through a tunnel built in 1904. Susan & I had been in Niagra [*sic*] in 1909, & I not since. You will recall I was there with Alice in 1903.

I am off by the New Bedford Boat this PM for Woods Hole.

Gruesse,

To Alfred Brandeis

August 19, 1921 Woods Hole, Mass. [Brandeis Mss, M 4-4]

DEAR AL: Enclosed from Louisville please return.

Mrs. Elizabeth Glendower Evans' friend, Mrs. Hodder, who has just returned from revisiting Italy brings interesting account of agricultural development there—throughout the South. She says the former swamplands are being converted into flourishing market gardens & described particularly the region between Salerno & Paestum. She spoke also of wheat culture there flourishing.

I note Chicago grain markets moving downward, particularly in corn & oats. I don't see where Europe gets the money to buy so much wheat from us.

The Sears Roebuck story is interesting. A year ago Julius Rosenwald advised Abe Flexner to buy the stock at 165 & Abe did.[1]

Mrs. [David O.] Ives & daughter leave us for So. Yarmouth today. We are sorry to have them go.

Your relatives here are in good health.   Gruesse,

1. July sales for Sears Roebuck and Co. were down 35 percent from a year before; on August 19, 1921, the stock was quoted at 63⅜.

To Felix Frankfurter

August 25, 1921 Woods Hole, Mass. [Frankfurter Mss—LC]

F.F. Some industrial researchers should determine and make clear to consumers how much of the high cost of some necessaries e.g. clothing and shoes is due to mere change of styles.

The wasteful cost of such change appears at every stage in the processes of manufacture and distribution. It is an important factor in irregularity of employment, since it prevents production & storing of articles otherwise staple. It introduces an undesirable speculative element into both production and merchandising, resulting i.a. in demoralizing bargain sales.

The long period of enforced economy ahead of us offers an opportunity of enabling those who desire this stability to resume in a measure their sometime freedom of purchasing what they had come to desire, thus saving money & effort, and escaping the flightiness of fashion which is inconsistent with the dignity of man.[1]

And be it remembered, the changes in style deprive us also of that best, the most beautiful or most useful, with which chance or labor sometime blesses us.

In a reactionary world it should be possible to get some con-

verts to the doctrine that change is not necessarily improvement.
Let those who want to buy it pay the price.

1. Cf. LDB to Alice Goldmark, 26 February 1891.

To Julian William Mack, Jacob deHaas, Stephen Samuel Wise, Felix Frankfurter, and Abba Hillel Silver

August 26, 1921 Woods Hole, Mass. [Mack Mss]

JWM—DEH—SSW—FF—AHS: Re JWM's of August 24, 23 and 25

1. I am strongly of the opinion that Miss Szold should stay in Palestine and should not return to America in any eventuality or for any purpose, even for a short visit.[1]

Our supreme task is the moral regeneration of the Palestinians, new and old. That task and not the Medical Unit was the reason why Miss Szold's going there was significant. Miss Kallen's letter to her brother has shown that we did not exaggerate the seriousness of the evils or the difficulties which confront us. Our meagre forces on the firing line should be strengthened by other women of the right calibre as soon and so far as this is possible. But under no circumstances should we weaken our position there, and Miss Szold's return, even for a brief visit, would be a serious weakening.

Leading [sic] for the Hadassah forces in America should be found in the governing Seven or some new leader for America should be found by them who will rise to the responsibilities.[2] If the Seven cannot hold the 16,000 they must hold as many as they can. But surely the summons to support Miss Szold on the firing line should be a mighty weapon or rallying cry.

"When could they say, till now, that talked of Rome,
That her wide walls encompassed but one man?"[3]

2. The decision as to Mrs. Danziger can await the receipt of report on the Congress.

As to S.S.W.—Aug. 19

3. I think it would be wiser not to send any greeting to the

Congress. America is represented by the delegates. We are represented by the Statement [4] and our Resignation.

4. I can arrange to be in New York on September 11 or probably any other time in September. But would it not be wiser to fix some later day so that we could have (a) fuller reports of the Congress before us, and (b) Ben Flexner present, and (c) Rosenbloom of course. And should we not arrange for a session, not of one, but of two or three days, of uninterrupted consideration of the Simon's matter to be passed upon.

If and so far as we are certain of the men we want and can get for the Palestine Development Council trustees we should begin their education by having them present at some of our sittings.

5. Has the money subscribed at Pittsburgh been collected.

6. Are the two concerns incorporated.

1. Henrietta Szold had originally gone to Palestine to supervise the Medical Unit's operation and had planned to return to the United States after the war. Upon the urging of LDB and others, however, she agreed to stay in Palestine and eventually assumed greater roles in the administration of the Yishuv's social welfare system.

2. With Miss Szold's removal to Palestine, her close friend and associate, Alice Seligsberg, assumed the presidency of Hadassah, supported by a strong executive board dominated by pro-Brandeis women, including Irma Lindheim, Zip Szold, and Rose Jacobs. Although Miss Szold reassumed the presidency in name only from 1923 to 1926 and would remain the unquestioned moral leader of Hadassah until her death, LDB managed to convince Hadassah leaders that it was their obligation to let Miss Szold stay in Palestine. He maintained that they not only should, but could, assume the burdens of leadership and administration.

3. William Shakespeare, *Julius Caesar*, act 1, sc. 2, lines 154–55.

4. The Mack-Brandeis group decided that, at the least, they would present their side of the dispute with Chaim Weizmann (see letters in Volume IV, especially those for January through June 1921) to the Twelfth Zionist Congress scheduled to meet in Carlsbad, Czechoslovakia, at the beginning of September 1921. At the congress, the American position was presented by Julius Simon, and a copy of the statement can be found in Simon, *Certain Days* (Jerusalem, 1971), 114–16. See LDB to Felix Frankfurter, 6 September 1921.

To Alfred Brandeis

September 3, 1921 Washington, D.C. [Brandeis Mss, M 4–4]

DEAR AL: Yours re farmer legislation confirms impressions I had—that this was another instance of distributing gold bricks.

Susan is here for the week end & labor day—Elizabeth is off for a hiking party on the Potomac canoeing for the same period.

The Senator & Mrs. LaFollette are to dine with us to meet Miss Susan B[randeis].

We have had canoeing each day since return & morning drives (with a repainted carriage) & were to go canoeing this afternoon. But the rain is on for the moment.

The British must have shadenfreude [1] to note Irish conditions in Mingo & Logan Counties. How near is this to Bell Co? [2]

1. "Malicious pleasure."

2. In connection with the coal strike there, these two West Virginia counties had experienced a summer of violent labor disorders and armed confrontations (see LDB to Felix Frankfurter, 20 May 1921, n. 6). Bell County, Kentucky, is in the southeast corner of the state, on the border with Tennessee and West Virginia. See Daniel P. Jordan, "The Mingo War: Labor Violence in the Southern West Virginia Coal Fields, 1919–1922," in Merl E. Reed and Gary M. Fink, eds., *Essays in Southern Labor History* (Greenwich, 1977).

To Alfred Brandeis

September 6, 1921 Washington, D.C.
[Brandeis Mss, Unmarked Folder]

DEAR AL: 1. I entirely agree with you as to our Foreign Trade. Because some or most European countries need it, we foolishly pursue it, like the lady who wanted a mortgage on her house, as all the neighbors had one. Hoover had much that view once—talked with me in 1919 at length on the folly of increasing our manufactures etc.

2. I am sorry to say, your impression as to Hoover is shared by many here who have been watching affairs this summer. They speak of "his insatiable and absurd graspingness" and "insane longing for publicity"; & it is said this is common talk among newspaper men.

3. I had not noticed Nat Myers' death, but judging from what I saw of him during the war, I think he should have been glad to go.[1]

4. The LaFollettes were in good form—the Senator looks finely, & is in great fighting trim. He & his friends are giving the administration severe headaches. He says, in substance, that the President is an automaton worked by the Old Guard, & that these constant statements of what the President wants are all prepared feed, put out to effectuate their purpose.

5. Susan returned to N.Y. last night & is to start out in her own office (140 Nassau St.) today. She has good courage.

Gruesse,

1. Nathaniel Myers (1848–1921) had died on 31 August. He had risen from a job as messenger boy in St. Louis to become a leading New York City corporation lawyer. He was very active in Jewish charitable work and was considered the founding spirit behind the Federation of Jewish Philanthropic Societies in New York. He was particularly noted for his work with the Hebrew Technical School for Girls.

To Felix Frankfurter

September 6, 1921 Washington, D.C. [Frankfurter Mss—LC]

DEAR FELIX: 1. Re yours of 3rd concerning [Roscoe] Pound, whose letter is returned herewith. I talked to Norman [Hapgood]. He will write nothing now, will confer with you before writing anything. Had planned to say something about Pound & you when your Cleveland Survey [1] is published. He had letters from Pound & from Chafee recently.

He apparently know[s] nothing of the real developments (of course I said nothing to him), but he remarked, the other day, that the enemy is gunning primarily at Pound, think they can brush you & Chafee away when P. shall have been disposed of.[2]

It will be wise later, after you see Pound, to consider whether fighting publicly may not be a necessary course.[3] Norman leaves for Petersham tomorrow.

2. I am much relieved that operation on Mack does not appear to be imminent. If he could be frightened into careful diet, that might serve.[4]

3. I am interested in John Walker's plan to study, but hope he will be very careful not to lose full touch with his labor friends. Roger Baldwin [5] suggested recently that there was danger of his doing so, & this was before his proposed study period.

4. After Dean [Acheson]'s visit I am sure I can add nothing to your & Marion's knowledge of Washington affairs. But I may add, that I have not discovered that any progress has been made since June. My father would have said: "Nichts Erfreuliches." [6]

5. I note we are being much discussed at Carlsbad.[7]

6. Villard's [8] article on the Times is admirable. I did not think he could do anything as good.[9]

1. See LDB to Frankfurter, 12 January and 6 July 1921.

2. Although conservatives opposed to the liberal philosophy of the Harvard Law School faculty had been defeated in their attack on Zechariah Chafee (see LDB to Chafee, 19 May 1921), they still hoped to force the resignation of Pound. Staunch support from President A. Lawrence Lowell as well as some of the more prominent law school alumni thwarted the conservatives' plans.

3. Hapgood did not write anything about the difficulties at Harvard.

4. Mack had been troubled for several years by diabetes and complications arising from the condition, including phlebitis; he did not undergo surgery at this time.

5. Roger Nash Baldwin (b. 1884), after several years work with juvenile courts, had been a founder of the American Civil Liberties Union in 1917, and was its director from 1917 to 1950. During his long life Baldwin has been a constant crusader for numerous causes involving civil rights and liberties.

6. "Not very pleasant."

7. At the Zionist Congress in Carlsbad, Julius Simon had presented the Brandeis-Mack justification of their position (see LDB to Mack *et al.*, 26 August 1921). Following Simon's talk, a number of delegates attacked Weizmann for his alienation of the Brandeis group; but Weizmann was firmly in control of the situation. The best that his opponents could do was suggest that the executive try to make peace with the disaffected Americans, a proposal that Weizmann completely ignored. After the Congress, Weizmann went over to Simon, embraced him and said: "This was the speech of a decent opposition, not a lawyer's brief like those of Mack and Frankfurter." Both men, together with LDB, had of course taken part in drafting the statement.

8. Oswald Garrison Villard (1872–1949), the grandson of the great abolitionist William Lloyd Garrison, had been editor and publisher of the New York *Evening Post* from 1897 to 1918, and afterwards was editor and owner of the influential weekly, *The Nation*. One of the founders of the National Association for the Advancement of Colored People, Villard wrote widely on a number of liberal causes. See his autobiography, *Fighting Years: Memoirs of a Liberal Editor* (New York, 1939).

9. In "Adolph S. Ochs and His *Times*," *The Nation* 113 (31 August 1921): 221–22, Villard had praised Ochs for transforming the paper in twenty-five years into the country's most reliable purveyor of news. However, he attacked Ochs for ignoring news that did not support his own narrow-minded opinions, and for fostering much race hatred. Ochs, according to Villard, also ignored the needy. "For not even the Jews, Mr. Ochs's race, has [the paper] pleaded as ardently as have others, apparently for fear lest it be further decried and criticized as a Jew paper; how else can one explain its refusal to print the British report on the Polish pogroms save as paid advertising?"

To Alfred Brandeis

September 16, 1921 Washington, D.C. [Brandeis Mss, M 4–4]

MY DEAR AL: Re. yours of 14th.

1. Yes, that is an uncommonly satisfactory report on Hildegarde & a nice letter altogether from Charlie. I am very glad he got so much out of his visit to you. The remark about "thinking aloud" is pathetic.[1]

2. As to the check for Annette: I enclose Otto's letter and mine to him, which letter please return after perusal. In it I have answered for the present about Lincoln [Dembitz]'s family.[2] I suggest that you might find out through the commercial agencies if available to you, something about the West family circumstances.[3] I will make enquiries if opportunity offers from some Washington folk.

3. I am sorry to learn that you and Otto sent the $350 to Annette last spring without letting me know. I think you had better let me take care (through you) of any amounts which may be required for the relatives hereafter—be they Brandeis, Dembitz or Wehle. And if you will let me know any regular amounts you are now sending to any of the relatives & the dates, I will have the quarterly (?) checks which are now being sent you by the Boston office on like account, increased by the amount of your own present contributions. You must remember that you have four daughters and I only two.

4. The President made another "strich durch die Rechnung"[4] as to my dining with Hoover. I guess H. must be suffering like a [*] on this play voyage with the President.[5] I am quite sure Bridge, Whist, and escorting Mrs. Harding while the President plays golf isn't Hoover's favorite sport. I spent the evening with

Adolf Caspar Miller pleasantly enough chatting on things political & economic, but can't recall any additions to my knowledge which you would be enriched by.

5. We leave for N.Y. this afternoon. Hope to see Frank T[aussig] before we go.   Gruesse,

If DeHaas has not sent you a copy of the statement of the outgoing Zionist administration (127pp), write him to 31 Union Square, R1103, to send you a copy.[6]

1. Nagel had written to Alfred: "I remember with so much pleasure our visit with you. It means something to be once more where you can feel and think aloud."

2. The death of LDB's cousin, Abraham Lincoln Dembitz, occasioned a continuing discussion between LDB, Alfred Brandeis, and Otto Wehle over who should provide financial assistance to needy members of the family. Annette was the sister of Lincoln Dembitz.

3. Lincoln Dembitz had been married to Sara West.

4. "disruption of plans."

5. Hoover was accompanying President Harding on his Chesapeake Bay cruise aboard the U.S.S. *Mayflower*.

6. See preceding letter, n. 7, and LDB to Mack *et al.*, 26 August 1921.

To Alfred Brandeis

September 19, 1921 Washington, D.C. [Brandeis Mss, M 4-4]

DEAR AL: Returned from N.Y. this AM. Alice will stay day or two at Scarsdale. Susan & I took supper at Louis [B. Wehle]'s at Tuckahoe Saturday. He is certainly making every effort to build up a practice & the report he gave of matters on hand & possibilities seems to me very promising. And there must be some substance there, as I have not had a call for funds since the $500 middle of August.

Among his matters was one concerning Export of Coal from Harlan County which disclosed this interesting fact: His clients had an offer (?) from War Finance Corp. to lend up to the amount of cost here (at Tidewater) plus insurance & freight from Tidewater to Genoa, provided the insurance & freight were in American insurance companies and in American vessels. But the cost of freight & insurance in American concerns was $5 a ton as against $3.50 a ton in foreign bottoms & insurance companies, so the credit offered was of no use. I think he said that is in the law. Are the credit possibilities provided by the Bullion Credit & the War Finance Co. to the farmers similarly limited?

Adolph Miller said he saw the old cart & mule doing considerable work again on Western farms—also more women in the fields than formerly.

To Felix Frankfurter

September 20, 1921 Washington, D.C. [Frankfurter Mss—LC]

FF: Our merchant marine presents, perhaps, the most difficult of our purely economic problems. At the moment, attention is being directed to Shipping Board deficits.[1] These can end only when all the vessels have been disposed of. But if disposed of to be used by Americans in foreign commerce, a most serious expenditure is threatened. They cannot be operated in competition with foreign bottoms, British, Dutch, Norwegian, Greek, Japanese, without a subsidy. And the tonnage is so large that the subsidy, aside from other objections, would be burdensome in amount. The demand for a subsidy of those vessels [which] are held privately will doubtless be irresistible.

We ought to have a large ocean tonnage, e.g. as a protection in case of war. But we could utilize a large ocean tonnage in coastwise trade, protected by our shipping monopoly. If we did this wholeheartedly in connection with our inland water navigation and short land hauls, we could provide for that great increase in transportation facilities which will be required in the near future without much new development of our railroad facilities. As to railroads the law of diminishing returns is largely applicable. Speaking generally, any large increase of their traffic will tend not to lower but to higher costs on railroad operation.

Would it not be worthwhile to have some good man look into this for the N[ew]. R[public].; and if upon enquiry this view seems sound, put forth the suggestion in a commanding article.[2]

1. The United States Shipping Board had been established by Congress in September 1916 in order to fill the vast need for merchant shipping created by the war. The board had subsidized the purchase and building of large numbers of bottoms, and then helped maintain them. During the war

there had been no question but that the operation would require vast amounts of money, but by 1921 the crisis was over, although the board still operated at a deficit in excess of $5,000,000 monthly, and there were increasing demands that it curtail its operations. The directors of the board promised that it would be able to end activity sometime in 1922.

2. See E. J. Clapp, "The American Transportation System," *The New Republic* 30 (15 March 1922): 72–75.

To Julian William Mack

September 20, 1921 Washington, D.C. [Mack Mss]

J.W.M. Re yours 19th concerning B[enjamin].V.C[ohen].

Your (1.) — I leave to you & Felix to handle as experts

Your (2.) — I think B.V.C. wrong.[1] Of course, he is right in principle. I wish it were possible to so limit loans in practice; & hope we shall have a man in Palestine who is so impressed with that idea, & so capable of impressing it on the community that he will be able to decline all, or most, applications for individual loans.

But to disable ourselves from making individual loans & publish that to the Palestinian world would, I think, be a mistake. Beware of constitutional limitations in Social Economic Experimentation.

Now that Coop Co. has been organized, for loan purposes, can you not arrange to transfer to it the orange etc. loans to be held as a surplus.[2]

I am asking Felix to send you S[amuel] J.R[osensohn]'s letter re mandate.

1. Cohen had advocated that the Palestine Development Corporation be prohibited from making any individual loans, restricting its financial activities only to cooperatives or business firms.

2. During the early years of the war a number of loans were made to the orange growers in Palestine whose markets had been cut off.

To Harold Joseph Laski

September 21, 1921 Washington, D.C. [Laski Mss]

MY DEAR HAROLD: Your "Foundations of Sovereignty" is fine.[1] You have presented the essential problem of democracy, and a challenge to those who harbor hopes of a great civilization. The Preface alone affords texts for a thousand sermons.

America has not been averse to social-political experimentation. But there has been a twofold lack of study and care in developing and adjusting inventions; and a lack of both patience and persistence in applying them. Few of our political inventions have had, therefore, a fair test. But the most potent causes of our failures have been our unbounded faith in the efficacy of machinery and our worship of the false god Bigness.

I hope you will develop further the cult of the unit of greatest efficiency and spread further the truth that progress must proceed from the aggregate of the performances of individual men—and that each is a wee thing, despite the aids and habiliments with which science, invention and organization have surrounded him. When once these truths are widely recognized we shall, I believe, have vision, wisdom and ingenuity enough to adjust our institutions to the wee size of man and thus render possible his growth and development.

Felix is doing fine work on the Cleveland Survey.[2] I hope to see him soon in New York where we are to discuss again Jewish Affairs. And I am looking forward to the return here of Justice Holmes, our veritable fountain of Eternal Youth. Our best to Frieda,   Most cordially,

1. Harold Laski, *The Foundations of Sovereignty and Other Essays* (New York, 1921). The book was dedicated to Roscoe Pound.
2. See LDB to Felix Frankfurter, 12 January and 6 July 1921 and the next letter.

To Felix Frankfurter

September 29, 1921 Washington, D.C. [Frankfurter Mss—LC]

MY DEAR FELIX: I have just finished Parts I and II of the Survey.[1] The work is done ably and thoroughly, with dignity and discrimination. It is well-planned & effectively edited. And the conclusions are sound. With increased insistence, however, comes the question: "What will he do with it?"

What should be done is made clear. But can the forces be aroused to the kind of persistent, unostentatious detailed effort which is essential to the attainment of results worth while? They are obviously possible, if only the community will care, or even a small part of it will care enough.

There is little more that outsiders can do, unless it be this: Have the [Cleveland] Foundation arrange now that through the same investigators and directors, it will have annually, say for ten years, a survey of the progress made during the preceding year. That would give notice both that it is in earnest & that the job is one in which time is a necessary element & continuity of effort indispensable.[2]

1. See LDB to Frankfurter, 6 July 1921.
2. There was no follow-up on the Cleveland survey.

To Julian William Mack, Stephen Samuel Wise, Abba Hillel Silver, Jacob deHaas, Felix Frankfurter, Robert Szold, Solomon Rosenbloom, and Nathan Straus, Jr.[1]

October 6, 1921 Washington, D.C. [R. Szold Mss]

JWM, SSW, AHS, DeH, FF, RS, SR, NS, JR.: Referring to JWM's memo of 4th

I am not disturbed by James Rosenberg's J.D.C. mission.[2] If we are to succeed, it will be by what we do, not by what other groups do for us, whether it be A[merican]. P[alestine]. Co. or J.D.C. or Z.O.A. as now constituted.

There is room for all. What we are to do is to do our work well here & abroad. It cannot be shifted to others. And of course what we do abroad in P[alestine]. will necessarily depend upon what the Central Com[tee] [3] directly & indirectly enable us to do. The immediate task is theirs.

The work to which all effort should be directed now is completing the $250,000 cash so that Sol Rosenbloom may start for P.[4] Then the task will be, while he is away, to raise the next $250,000 or more.

1. Nathan Straus, Jr. (1889–1961), a writer and editor, had been elected in 1920 to the New York State Assembly, where he served until 1926. He

became interested in public housing and was a member of the New York City Housing Authority (1936) and head of the United States Housing Authority from 1937 to 1942. He later established a chain of public service radio stations.

2. James Naumburg Rosenberg (1874–1970), a lawyer, was in 1921 chairman of the Joint Distribution Committee's European task force. During the 1920s and 1930s he was involved in several projects that attempted to relocate Russian and Eastern European Jews in places other than Palestine. His obvious anti-Zionist sentiments worried the Brandeis group, but as LDB assumed, there was a great deal of relief work to be done both in Europe and Palestine, and the J.D.C. could not effectively interfere with any Zionist work then under way.

3. of the Palestine Development Council.

4. The Palestine Development Council was designed not only to serve as an outlet for the activities of the Brandeis–Mack group in Palestine but also to prove to the European Zionists that private capital could serve useful purposes in building up the Jewish homeland. The P.D.C. had decided to raise $500,000 initially, and as soon as half of that was actually in hand, to send Pittsburgh businessman Solomon Rosenbloom to Palestine to explore the most effective avenues for utilizing the money. Rosenbloom left on his mission in January 1922.

To Julian William Mack and Bernard Flexner

October 6, 1921 Washington, D. C. [Mack Mss]

JWM—BF: I have Kligler's [1] Anti-Malaria Report for May-June '21, and think the results he reports most satisfactory. Fundamental work—ably, conscientiously and economically done—by one who seems to be thinking only of his job and its relation to the great work in hand.

The Migdal-Digania-Kinnereth region were a hotbed of malaria in 1919.[2]

It would be an unalloyed pleasure to work for Palestine if we could feel that our efforts were being similarly reflected in other fields of activity.

1. Israel Jacob Kligler (1889–1944), a Russian-born bacteriologist, had gone to Palestine in 1920 with the Hadassah Medical Unit, and the following year he undertook a special antimalaria project (see next note). From 1926 to 1944 he was head of the hygiene department at the Hebrew University and chairman of the health services department of the Va'ad Le'umi, the shadow government of the Yishuv.

2. After failing to convince Weizmann and the Zionist Executive of the

need to eradicate malaria in Palestine (see LDB to Jack Mosseri, 24 September 1919, n. 1.), LDB privately financed an experimental project through Hadassah, which Kligler directed. In areas in the Galilee and surrounding Lake Kinnereth (Tiberias), malaria had decimated the Jewish settlements, with the incidence rate running at better than 95 percent of the workers in 1919. LDB provided $10,000 for the purpose of planting eucalyptus trees and securing pesticides to kill the mosquito larvae. Kligler's report for 1921 showed that the incidence rate had been cut drastically, with many settlements reporting no cases at all. Hadassah and the Joint Distribution Committee continued to finance the antimalaria work until 1926, with Kligler heading the project.

To Alfred Brandeis

October 8, 1921 Washington, D.C. [Brandeis Mss, M 4-4]

DEAR AL: Yours of Thursday has come. It was a long time between letters.

Home is a pretty good place these days, as you say. The grain section may be even bluer than you found it, in view of the drop since you left Chicago.

Yesterday's corn was a long way below 1913–1914, particularly when freight rates are considered; & I suppose oats must be also. I don't think the folk here have any idea that they can help the unemployment situation now. Their real notion is, either to build for the future by reducing irregularity of employment in normal times, or to talk for political effect—particularly to get the load off the administration by referring the problem to the local communities for solution. I don't think there is any serious thought of lending any govt money to the communities. The govt hasn't any, & is likely to have less hereafter instead of more. With ships & RRs on its hands, it doesn't crave additional parasites.

Very cheerful reports from Susan, who is being generally congratulated on her courage.[1]

1. in opening a New York law office.

To Alfred Brandeis

October 11, 1921 Washington, D.C. [Brandeis Mss, M 4–4]

DEAR AL: We have sold the Dedham house to Maynard who buys for his son Haskell & will alter it, making the front door on the side facing the Maynard house.

Price, $11,875, which is $2125 less than I was offered 2½ years ago & about $1000 less than the cost 22½ years ago, plus alterations then & cost of additional strip of land about 9 years ago. Still considering other shrinkages from 1919 & the customary ones on residences, it is not very bad. We have not even painted it since some years before 1916.

Dedham by reason of cutting of RR train service, the increased trolley fares & the opening up of wider suburban country through the auto, is less valuable real estate than it was.

Alice is planning a cottage on Cape Cod.[1] Sadie and Bessie Evans are to take care of the house contents for us, some of which we shall sell, some store & the books have brought here. Alice was entirely ready to sell; Elizabeth sighed but would never go near it. Susan not yet heard from. But when she was in B[oston] last May, did not, I think, go out to Dedham.

As to your enquiry about Chinese loan—"Kann dienen."[2] The Pacific development took its bonds at 81. They haven't sold any & are likely to go into receiver's hands (confidential). The Continental I guess took the bonds at about the same figure. It seems that there is much Chinese & international politics in this & that the Chinese bankers are financing the Southern Republic & are ready to have the Pekin government go broke.[3]

I thought I would politely called [sic] Eugene Meyer's bluff [4] & asked him (1) for a list of loans to farmers by states and (2) how much cash he had advanced to Cooperatives. The press bureau data I am sending under another cover. His letter enclosed bears out your views.

Elizabeth's party had to change their objective. And they started at 3:30 AM today on the train to Linden Va, in the day coach. Das zeigt dass es ja noch Kinder gebt.[5]

Enclosed from Louis B. W[ehle] will show that he is not yet out of the woods.[6]

1. See LDB to Alfred Brandeis, 26 July 1924.

2. "can serve."

3. In late 1921, the financial structure of the Chinese Republic seemed gravely imperiled by the civil war raging there. Rumors circulated that the government would default on its obligations around 1 November, and on that date, it did default on a $5.5 million loan from the Continental and Commercial Trust Company of Chicago. The Chinese were able to pay the interest but not the principal on a similar loan from the Pacific Development Corporation. Rumors also reached the United States that the Bank of China would no longer honor the checks of the Peking government unless funds were deposited to cover them. See also LDB to Alfred Brandeis, 23 October and 5 November 1921.

4. Meyer, as head of the War Finance Corporation, had been boasting about how loans from the corporation had aided farmers and cattle raisers. See *New York Times*, 2 October and 8 October 1921.

5. "This shows they are still children."

6. See LDB to Alfred Brandeis, 8 December 1921.

To Alfred Brandeis

October 15, 1921 Washington, D.C. [Brandeis Mss, M 4-4]

DEAR AL: 1. John Dudley seems to be as expert in making commercial reports as in providing eggs. We are getting another customer for him (Senator Bristow) if he has products available. I guess Otto wont miss this particular chance for worry, when the factory is working day & night shifts.

2. The ham has come. Sorry it didn't arrive a few days earlier, so as to have been shared with Hoover who dined with us the other evening. He was in good form, talkative and interesting. The net result was that "Every prospect pleases only man is vile" [1]—or rather inexpressibly stupid.

Among his specifications were:
The worst outlook is attributable to the coal situation. He had been trying to get some agreement between operators & men— in vain. Says that a strike April 1 is probable [2] & that in a month business will get its preliminary jolt, because no one will be able to know that he can get coal to carry through building projects etc etc. He says union coal operators (bituminous) haven't earned 4% on cash invested during the last 10 years, on the average, & that they are about desperate. Very many are losing money now, with the mines operating on small tonnage, & that the men are not

getting more than 2 days a week work &, in the year, 140 days.

On the other hand the 20% who are not union are running 6 days a week & the miners at $4 a day are earning $24 a week as against $14 ($7 a day) in union mines.

There are now 80% of the miners unionized as against 70% a short time ago. A majority of these want nationalization of mines & their leaders do not represent the men's wishes & hence are afraid to stand up for reduction in wages, although they really believe in it. The operators would be content with a strike because they think this is a good time to fight to a finish. The men because they want to show what a rumpus they can make. Hoover hopes that fear of a strike April 1 will induce consumers to stock up meanwhile.

1. Reginald Heber, "Missionary Hymn," stanza 2.

2. Hoover, who would be making this prediction publicly by January 1922, was accurate. John L. Lewis issued the strike order in late March. See LDB to Felix Frankfurter, 4 September 1922.

To Alfred Brandeis

October 23, 1921 Washington, D.C. [Brandeis Mss, M 4-4]

DEAR AL: The guests at your ham dinner were Senator & Miss Burton,[1] Mr. & Mrs. Jesse Adkins & Mr. Justice Clarke. They were duly appreciative.

Herbert White was here Thursday, looking hale & hearty. He reports Pacific Development Co. affairs in better shape,[2] mainly due to rise in cotton, & in silver, which affects the stock in China & business there. He says they have recently sold to China, machinery (complete) for five cotton mills. I asked Hoover about Chinese cotton manufacture. He says they (the Chinese manufacturers) are merely taking care of the increased demand & that our (& others') imports of cotton goods have not been lessened. He also says that the Chinese cant [sic] manufacture cheaper than we because they are incapable of division of labor & they do only about 1/5 of the work per man that we do in higher grades of manufacture & not more than 1/2 as much in unskilled labor. He ought to know, but I found in my mind a lingering doubt.

Is the cut in western grain rate enough to help? Ray Stevens, formerly of the Shipping Board, turned up Thursday also. He was about as much broken up by his experiences on the board as the rest of those associated with it. He had, for nearly a year, a pretty bad case of nervous prostration.

Weather lovely here. We have been on the river the last three Sundays—today & last week we lunched al fresco.

Susan writes that she hoped to have Maidie at dinner last evening.

Your enquiry about German currency I wont [sic] venture to answer.[3] It's hard enough to have to guess what is to become of the RRs.[4]

We expect the LaFollettes for dinner this evening.

Gruesse,

---

1. There was no senator named Burton serving in 1921. Probably LDB had entertained former Senator Theodore Elijah Burton (1851–1929) of Ohio. Burton had been a member of the Senate from 1909 to 1915, but at this time was a member of the House of Representatives. He would be elected again to the Senate in 1928.

2. See LDB to Alfred Brandeis, 11 October 1921.

3. Postwar reconstruction, worldwide economic conditions, the burden of reparation payments, and the frantic issuing of new paper currency had all combined to plunge the value of the German mark catastrophically. The mark, which had already declined to 150 to the dollar by 16 October, fell to 300 to the dollar only two weeks later.

4. See LDB to Alfred Brandeis, 12 July 1921.

To Alfred Brandeis

October 27, 1921 Washington, D.C. [Brandeis Mss, M 4–4]

DEAR AL: Your letter about grain prices & freight rates are [sic] illuminating. Even if wages were reduced (which seems now less likely), lower grain rates would probably not be remunerative to the RR. I am sure that the 1913 grain rates were in large measure unremunerative.

Would it be possible to consume more of the corn nearer the farms? [1]

Senator & Mrs. LaFollette dined with us Sunday. He is in fine form & spirits. I have not seen him in such good condition, all things considered, since the spring of 1911—in the fall of that year his presidential [*] began.

Young Bob [LaFollette] is well again—was in last evening for Elizabeth's dinner party. Fola & [George] Mid[dleton] are flourishing. Mary married & Phil engaged.[2]

Eliz[abeth]. has invited Hildegarde [Nagel] to come here for her week end hike.

I wrote Rauch.[3] Sent him $25 & told him I would underwrite further to the extent of $75.

It looks to me as if the Labor Board had put the worst possible crimp into the RRs.[4]

Ford's interview was fine.[5]

1. See LDB to Alfred Brandeis, 5 November 1921.

2. Mary La Follette had married Ralph G. Sucher, a friend of her brother Phil, on 15 June. After a long engagement, Phil married Isabel Bacon on 14 April 1923.

3. Rabbi Joseph Rauch (1881–1957) was the leader of Louisville's Adath Israel Congregation, and he became an important religious and philanthropic leader in that city. Rauch, who served his congregation for forty-four years, would be associated with LDB in their mutual concern for the University of Louisville (see LDB to Adele Brandeis, 24 September 1924) and the J. B. Speed Memorial Museum.

4. The Railway Labor Board had authorized wage cuts to railroad workers, a decision that contributed to labor dissatisfaction and helped provide fuel for the widespread and crippling railroad strikes in the fall of 1921.

5. Henry Ford was interviewed by William A. DuPuy of *The Nation's Business* on the topic of the railroads, and he offered a series of opinions on how to make them operate more profitably. Ford said he would eliminate "unproductive stockholders," stop dealing with banks, fire unnecessary employees (particularly lawyers), and install new and more efficient road equipment.

To Julian William Mack and Stephen Samuel Wise

October 28, 1921 Washington, D.C. [Mack Mss]

JWM, SSW: A few days ago I had a call from Mintz [1] and Dr. Dunn(?) of New Britain, Conn. They had been in Baltimore, as I understood, in the interest of the Keren H[ayesod]. & as old Zionists, came over here in the hope of getting the opportunity of telling me "from the people" how hopeless the state of Zionism is without the old leaders leading them. Mintz is, as I recall, one of my earliest Zionist acquaintances whom I met in 1914 when he was active in Worcester. They said that they couldn't raise any money "without my name" etc., that they thought we were right & that the people would not have voted as they did had they understood. They wanted to know what to do. I told them in gentle tones what we had felt obligated to do, & what we were trying to do. I told them that what we should succeed in doing depended wholly on the support we should receive. I made no suggestions, except that I thought Dr. Wise would doubtless be willing to see them. I thought S.S.W. might learn, for the Central Com[tee] some things from them first-hand, & that possibly they might conclude to work for the P[ales-tine] Dev[elopment]. Leagues. They seemed to me of interest as coming from what I have been told is distinctly enemy's country.

I hope that the Central Com[tee] is making good progress & that we shall soon have on hand the $250,000 cash & S. Rosenbloom's passage engaged.[2]

1. Samuel Mintz (1884–1954), was head of the urological clinic at the Massachusetts General Hospital.
2. See LDB to Mack *et al.*, 6 October 1921, n. 4.

To Alfred Brandeis

October 31, 1921 Washington, D.C. [Brandeis Mss, M 4-4]

DEAR AL: We are delighted that the new ham is coming. The anticipations are inviting the Bob Woolleys, the Fred Delanos & George Rublee for Friday.

Hildegarde couldn't come for Elizabeth's hike, so another niece of yours, Catherine T[aussig] joined the party.

Can you tell me what the spread between

      Wheat on the farm & flour at retail—say in N.Y.,
      Boston & Washington

             and between

   Corn on the farm & ham in N.Y. Boston or Washington
was at the period before the war when present farm prices for wheat & flour prevailed?

I think it is the excessive in between costs which is "grinding the poor."

Deutsch was a much better fellow than those in whose neigh-borhood he was fated to live.[1] The decay of the Queen City is one of the saddest of American hopes.

Tomorrow 49 years ago on the Hassarenberg.[2] Looked down on a happier Austria.   Gruesse

1. Gotthard Deutsch (1859–1921), a professor and administrative officer of the Hebrew Union College in Cincinnati, died on 14 October. Deutsch's funeral received some national attention because of the elaborate instructions he left; he prohibited any eulogy or even any mention of his own name and directed that money that would have been given for flowers be given instead to charitable causes.

2. A reference to the Brandeis family's European trip of 1872. See LDB to Adolph Brandeis, 1 November 1889, n. 4.

To Julian William Mack and Stephen Samuel Wise

November 3, 1921 Washington, D.C. [Mack Mss]

JWM–SSW: Since writing JWM this morning I have his of 2d.

First: As to DeH[aas], I assume you will agree that this is a matter as to which Silver, as chairman of Central Com[tee], has the prime responsibility. SSW wrote me about the situation more or less a month ago. I then assumed (without expressing any opinion) that I should acquiesce in any decision in which you two, Silver & Felix agree. I thought then, and think now, that I ought not express any opinion for two reasons:

1. DeH. is Exec. Secy. of the Central Com[tee] which has assumed the task of raising the money [1], & the raisers of the money ought not to be hampered in any way by those not on it. Full power should go with the responsibility.

2. I had opposed formation of the Com[tee], or any agency which should in any way relieve our vertrauen männer [2] in the several communities from the responsibility for achievement, because I feared the creation of such a national body would retard instead of stimulating effort. Therefore, I have sedulously refrained from making suggestions as to the conduct of the Com[tee] work.

If DeH. should conclude to sever the connection with the Com[tee] with the purpose of taking his family to Palestine and settling permanently there, prepared to make sacrifices (so called) involved with simpler living involved in building up the country, I should be ready now (as I offered a year and a half ago) to make a very substantial contribution to a fund which would make that possible. He has deserved so well of his long service to the cause, that if he still wants to settle with his family, we ought to aid him in every possible way.[3]

Second: As to the 2% commission [4] I am reluctant to express an opinion as it, also, is a Central Com^tee matter.

After the $250,000 cash is in hand, I shall have, as I wrote you earlier, some suggestions to make on this & other matters.

It certainly would be a declaration of insolvency to offer any such inducement now; & I fear it would prove a boomerang. If there are not a large number of persons who really care to do what we want to see done, those present at the Friday meeting in N.Y. & at the Pittsburg meeting deceived themselves & us. If there are a large number who really care, there will be no difficulty in raising large amounts, in the aggregate, by voluntary efforts guided by the Central Com^tee.

1. See LDB to Mack *et al.*, 6 October 1921, n. 4.
2. "trustworthy men"
3. With the reorganization of both the Zionist Organization of America as well as of the Brandeis-Mack group, Jacob deHaas found himself wielding considerably less power than he had commanded from 1914 to 1921. Moreover, many of the members of the Central Committee of the Palestine Development Council were unwilling to put up any longer with deHaas's abrasive personality. As a result, he began to talk about moving to Palestine. See LDB to Robert D. Kesselman, 26 October 1924.
4. As an inducement to raising their initial capital of $500,000, the committee briefly toyed with the idea of paying a 2 percent commission to fund raisers. The idea was never adopted.

To Alfred Brandeis

November 5, 1921 Washington, D.C. [Brandeis Mss, M 4-4]

DEAR AL: The Burlings & Carl Weston had to be substituted for the Delanos and Rublee as your dinner guests with the Bob Woolleys, but did well. R. Walton Moore,[1] who might a [*sic*] learnt a thing or two about Louis [B. Wehle], was prevented by a political engagement from joining us.

When I suggested the corn growers utilizing more of the crop at home,[2] I had in mind, not only hog raising, but also packing. The only escape from the packing monopoly has seemed to me to lie in many packing plants distributed, through cooperatives like the Danish, over the farming region.

I notice Minneapolis patent at $6.90 yesterday.[3] I remember a Boston case when they were selling by the carload at $4.50.

How much of the wheat is still in farmers' hands & where? i.e. in what states.

Herbert White was in yesterday. He was here again on Pacific Development Co. matters. They have also a $5,000,000 Chinese loan which is likely to have on Dec 1 the same fate that the Continental & C[ommercial] B[an]k of Chicago's had. Herbert is having ample insight into the ways of the great international bankers. Pawn brokers are a "Hund dagegen."[4]

Yes, Susan was very happy over her appointment.[5] I don't know where it originated. But I think not from among her friends. "The office sought the woman." Podell, the Asst. U.S. Att[orne]y, came to Posner (her former employer) supposing she was still there.

Susan is free to continue with her private practice. The U.S. is only one of her clients. She is "special Asst." in certain cases only. Thanks to her many little receiverships and her modest living & offices expenses she is paying her way now & had been before this new opportunity came.

Bob Woolley told interesting tales of the Democratic Nat[ional]. Com[mit]tee meet at St Louis & how their McAdoo party captured the chairmanship.

1. Robert Walton Moore (1859–1941) was a Democratic Representative from Virginia. In 1933, he joined the State Department.
2. See LDB to Alfred Brandeis, 27 October 1921.
3. After the general drop in wheat prices, high-grade patent flour had dropped below $7.00 a barrel for the first time in more than five years.
4. "a dog by comparison." See LDB to Alfred Brandeis, 11 October 1921.
5. Susan Brandeis had been appointed a special assistant to David Louis Podell (1884–1947), a distinguished New York trial lawyer, who had just become a special assistant attorney general in the southern district of New York in charge of antitrust cases. Podell became an expert on antitrust law and wrote on the subject. Susan Brandeis's special responsibility in Podell's office was to be investigating building trade monopolies.

To Woodrow Wilson

November 8, 1921 Washington, D.C. [Wilson Mss]

MY DEAR MR. WILSON: Let me thank you for the noble and penetrating note enclosed with yours of yesterday.[1]

I am sending a copy to Mr. Colby.   Most Cordially,

1. Former President Wilson had enclosed a suggestion for possible inclusion in "The Document," which was being prepared by Thomas Chadbourne, Bainbridge Colby, and LDB (see LDB to Wilson, 25 June 1921). Wilson's suggestion dealt with the slogan "America first," which he claimed was being defined narrowly and selfishly by the Republicans, but which ought to be defined in a way to illustrate America's responsibility to the international community.

To Felix Frankfurter

November 9, 1921 Washington, D.C. [Frankfurter Mss—LC]

MY DEAR FELIX: 1. Mack was in last evening for dinner. There is a little movement, but the progress seems painfully slow in Zionist affairs. Today I have enclosed from DeHaas.

2. The report on the Jaffa riots seems to me very sensible & fair in what it says of responsibility of Zionist leaders. It is what we sought in vain to impress upon our associates.[1]

3. I am glad Villard approved the Ray Stevens suggestion.[2]

Wouldn't it be worth while (if W.D. Lane is not already writing for the Nation) that V. get him to write. The Nation, the N[ew]. R[epublic]. & the Survey ought to avail of his knowledge of the coal problem already acquired, & make it possible for him to develop the authority on the subject & see it through. It's a long pull. But we need such experts on fundamental problems, and there ought to be such cooperation of publications.[3]

4. I am glad [Harvard Law] School matters are solving themselves so well.[4]

1. In order to exert pressure on the Allies and prevent the awarding of a mandate recognizing a Jewish home in Palestine, Arabs in the area had rioted in 1920 and again in the spring of 1921. The official British report of the riots blamed the Arabs but also noted that large-scale Jewish immigration exceeded the country's economic capacity to absorb the new ar-

rivals. The Brandeis group, of course, had been arguing all along that proper economic, medical, and social preparations had to be made prior to immigration.

2. LDB had been urging his old friend Stevens to write on shipping board matters, but no signed article by Stevens appeared.

3. The *Survey* published three articles by Winthrop Lane on coal problems: "Miners in Distress," 47 (18 February 1922): 786–87; "Breaking the Miners," (4 March 1922): 887; and "Black Avalanche," (25 March 1922): 1002–6.

4. See LDB to Frankfurter, 6 September 1921, n. 2.

To Horace Meyer Kallen

November 11, 1921 Washington, D.C. [Kallen Mss]

MY DEAR KALLEN: My thanks for your "Zionism and World Politics." [1] It is good to have the story and the essentials told, and told so well. I wish we could make sure that it will be read, and not only with the eye, but understood.

I have been thinking much of the "Vita Nueva" for which we long. For its attainment the first step must be to appreciate what is really worthwhile in life; the next to realize that the sanctity of humans is imperative. And as I think over these essentials, I become more and more convinced that we can accomplish in Palestine something significant only by having there a group who feel as we do and feel so deeply and convincingly. That is why I was so eager to have your sister remain there, and why I think that our few worthy representatives there should be supported by newcomers who will help to keep the light burning, and spread its rays.

These years of Katzenjammer [2] after the great men should make men and women realize how false have been, in large measure, the tests of achievement recently applied and how mistaken the avenues pursued in search of happiness.

I trust you are really getting your strength [back] & will not overtax yourself.   Cordially,

1. Horace M. Kallen, *Zionism and World Politics* (New York, 1921).
2. "Hangover"

To Alfred Brandeis

November 13, 1921 Washington, D.C. [Brandeis Mss, M 4-4]

MY DEAR AL: Following Mother's example I am writing you on my birthday to hers.

Your greetings came in due time, and the ham has arrived.

Both daughters are off for the week end. Susan to Long Island hoping for a long walk, but laden, as she writes, with 300 type-written pages of testimony to be studied before going into a case with her chief on Monday.[1] She is much elated over a remark of the chief repeated to her by one of his assistants: "It was a good move to get that girl."

I enclose some more Meyer literature.[2]

Secretary Hughes was fine yesterday & has showed the "Allied and Associated Powers" how to "let go" on armaments, which they want to do. He will do well if he can find the formula for their letting go of their Asiatic grabs, which they are less anxious to do.[3]

As you were much interested 40,000 years ago, in discovering (thru the Concordance) how the Lord shaved with a hired razor, I am sending you Marcou's article on what the Aztecs did in their time.[4]   Gruesse,

1. See LDB to Alfred Brandeis, 5 November 1921, n. 5.

2. See LDB to Alfred Brandeis, 11 October 1921, n. 4.

3. In recognition of the growing naval armaments race between Japan and the United States, Senator William Borah had amended the 1921 Naval Appropriations Act to request the President to invite Great Britain and Japan to discuss naval disarmament. Secretary of State Charles Evans Hughes opened the conference in Washington on 12 November 1921, and boldly proposed that the large powers agree to a ten-year "holiday" in the construction of battleships. Moreover, in order to achieve a measure of balance, all of the big powers should be willing to scrap some of their existing ships. Negotiations proceeded smoothly over the next few months, and Hughes secured a number of treaties, but the most important provisions established a ratio of parity of capital ships at five each for the United States and Great Britain and three for Japan, and recognized Japan's "special interests" in the Pacific. See Thomas H. Buckley, *The United States and the Washington Conference* (Knoxville, Tenn., 1970). See also the next two letters.

4. See Isaiah 7:20: "In that day the Lord will shave with a razor which is hired beyond the River. . . ." Philip Marcou, "Procédé des Aztèques pour la Taille par Éclatement des Couteaux ou Rasoirs d'obsidienne," *Société des Américanistes de Paris Journal*, 13 (1921): 17–24.

To Felix Frankfurter

November 13, 1921 Washington, D.C. [Frankfurter Mss—LC]

MY DEAR FELIX: It is good to have your and Marion's [birthday] greeting.

Hughes has done an admirable job. His persuasive business-like, determined manner was appropriate to the proposal, which almost took on the character of a command without its form. Of course, this part is relatively easy. But the elan of initial success may carry him far.[1]

My own belief is that we westerners might as well recognize that we have established that we lack the character & intelligence which alone would justify our controlling Asia and that we should begin an orderly retreat. When we shall have evacuated, it will be China and India, not Japan, that dominates.

My real concern is about America. Will there develop here a worthy civilization? Success in this international situation, where all the nations are anxious to have us help them "let go" may turn our heads further & divert us again from a consideration of our own shortcomings.

We have seen the [Loring] Christies, the [Alfred] Zimmerns and [H.G.] Wells, and Regina.[2]

My greetings to Marion,

1. See preceding letter and also following letter.
2. The Englishmen were in Washington for the naval conference.

To Susan Goldmark

November 13, 1921 Washington, D.C. [EBR]

MY DEAR SUSIE: The tie bringing your good wishes gleams with beauty as if to celebrate the long step forward made yesterday through Secretary Hughes admirable practical proposal.[1] It was a master stroke, presented with simple directness and simplicity, impressive and persuasive almost to the point of demonstration. One felt that it left to "the Allied & Associated Powers" hardly an option. In form a proposal, it was in substance a command.

Of course curtailment of armament is what each nation wants; because it is for all an imperative domestic need. And men readily find a way of doing that which they desire. The more difficult task will come when the Far Eastern problem is approached, and the nations are urged to do what they really deem a sacrifice— though erroneously. For it would be best for all the Westerners to commence now the orderly retreat from their Asiatic excursions. The East has been awakened from its sleep. The doubt of our wisdom and of our superior virtue is widespread, as is the conviction that we are not invincible. And I fancy it is not Japan but China and India which will be standard-bearers of Asiatic civilizations. Japan's strength is that borrowed from the West, in large part, and to be rejected.

You see how the calm even of anticipated disarmament stimulates speculation.   With much love,

1. See two preceding letters.

To Alfred Brandeis

November 24, 1921 Washington, D.C. [Brandeis Mss, M 4–4]

DEAR AL: Anna Bird dined with us Saturday & enquired very particularly about you & your family.[1] She is here as member of the Advisory Com[mit]tee of Disarmament Conference. You doubtless know that she has become a leading Republican in Mass[achusetts]. She threw herself into this & other activities, so as to control & occupy herself after her son Billy's death. Her husband seems to be more immersed in business than ever. Has mills in Chicago, Canada, R.I., Walpole & perhaps at other places. "Narr ist er." [2]

Joseph Teele [sic] is coming in for the Thanksgiving dinner. Sorry we cant give our guests one of your hams—a fine one has just arrived. But even we are slaves to the turkey convention.

Poor Louis Wehle is not over his troubles as you will see from enclosed.[3]

Mrs. William Allen White, who was in last week, says she is from Nicholasville [Kentucky] & Judge Hardison (of the D.C. Municipal Court),[4] whom I met last evening, claims that he is from Logan County. Do you know them?

Mary Henderson was in Monday, looking finely but almost too fat—as Belle [LaFollette] would say.   Gruesse,

1. Anna Child Bird (1856–1942), the wife of Massachusetts politician Charles S. Bird (see LDB to Alfred Brandeis, 10 July 1912), was active in the women's movement and in organizing women within the Republican Party.

2. "He is a fool."

3. See next letter.

4. Robert Hardison was judge of the Washington D.C. Police Court.

To Alfred Brandeis

December 8, 1921 Washington, D.C. [Brandeis Mss, M 4–4]

DEAR AL: I have yours re Louis [Wehle]. Enclosed from him (actually 12/3) was written before the others of 3d which I sent you Sunday. Today I had a partial financial statement, the balance is to come in a few days. The outstanding debts were not as bad as I feared.[1] About $750 personal & household (including $167.66 insurance) bills now payable, led me to send him $1000 more today. Will send you the data in full when I get them.

His bad financial habits were revealed by $300 borrowed in 1919–20 still outstanding. Is that due you?

On the whole I was relieved to find things no worse.

Sunday evening we dined with Anna Bird & found there C. S. Barett [sic] the farmers's chief, who is on the Peace Advisory Com[mit]tee.[2] I suppose you know him. He seems to me a good jollier & quite entertaining but doesn't impress me as a great leader for half the nation; or very trustworthy in his information.

The remedy for your Illinois farmer who got 2% on his $300 an acre farm, is to count his land worth $125. It ought to come down to near that.

Barrett considers the War Finance [Corporation] merely a temporary aid.

Alice met a Cap. Chambers U.S.N. who said he was a classmate of yours.[3] Was he?

1. On 3 December LDB had written his brother: "I am disturbed by his [Wehle's] being 'beset by bills'. He has had from me $2000 in 30 days— and a month earlier $500—in all $6250. Of course, it doesn't do me any harm; but I am much troubled about him and his future." See LDB to Alfred Brandeis, 27 May 1926.

2. Charles Simon Barrett (1866–1935) was elected president of the National Farmers' Union every year from 1906 to 1928.

3. Frank Taylor Chambers (1870–1932), a career naval officer who became a rear admiral in 1927, had graduated from the Louisville Male High School in 1888.

To Woodrow Wilson

December 8, 1921 Washington, D.C. [Wilson Mss]

MY DEAR MR. WILSON: I am very glad to have your two letters with enclosures.[1] Copies of the letter I am sending today to Mr. [Bainbridge] Colby.

The hope which you brought to an agonized world is reviving and making possible Christmas cheer and confidence that happier years will come.

With every good wish,   Most cordially,

1. Wilson had sent two more suggestions for "The Document" (see LDB to Wilson, 25 June 1921), one dealing with equal access to raw materials and energy supplies, the second with the unhappy condition of the merchant marine. Wilson wrote LDB on 6 December: "I hope that it will not seem to you that I am firing these things at you with inconsiderate frequency and rapidity; they form themselves somewhere in the hidden recesses of my system and I am uneasy until I get them out."

To Julian William Mack, Stephen Samuel Wise, and Jacob deHaas

December 14, 1921 Washington, D.C. [Mack Mss]

J.W.M., S.S.W., DEH. Note enclosed from Sokolow. He and daughter called, stayed about 40 minutes.[1] We talked of U.S. Supreme Court, then of the Arbitration Court in Jerusalem, of the objections Mizrachis thereto.[2] Then S. wanted my advice as to study at [Hebrew] University of Jewish law with a view to ultimate use in P[alestine]. I suggested he should confer with [David] Amram etc. There was some talk of Agudath Israel[3] activities, then of obstacles to getting mandate through, of French obstacles and intrigue.[4] He spoke of his desire to get something from American Administration (Dept. of State) to help.[5] Just as he was leaving he dropped a gentle word about my help—I didn't pick it up. I talked then of [Emile] Berliner's fine qualities. Escorted S. and daughter to the elevator.

And lo and behold—all was over. A joyous interview and no harm done.

He said Otto Warburg was coming here to see some one in the Agricultural Dept. and sent me greetings.[6] (said also a great obstacle to reconstituting the experiment station is debts alleged to be outstanding). Aaronsohn[s] claim huge sum—perhaps 150,000 francs.

He also spoke of Goldstein having been in the U.S. S[upreme]. Court. I passed it over without comment.

1. Nahum Sokolow, who had four daughters, had arrived in the United States on 12 November at the head of a high-level Palestinian mission to raise money and discuss conditions in Palestine.

2. Traditional Jews within the Zionist movement had always envisioned a reconstituted Jewish state governed by the religious law (Halakah), and a major reason for the organization of Mizrachi had been to push this Orthodox viewpoint. The British government, on the other hand, was establishing a court system based primarily on English common law, and the Mizrachi feared the impact such secular law would have upon a Jewish society.

3. Agudath Israel was a political and religious organization that maintained the Torah and the commentaries on the Torah were the only legitimate codes of law binding upon the Jews as individuals and on the Jewish people as a whole. The group's attitude toward Zionism and the restoration of Palestine had been ambivalent ever since its founding in 1912. Some of the more moderate factions were sympathetic to Zionism and cooperated closely with Mizrachi; other groups viewed Zionism as contradicting the divine will, and not until after the Second World War did they come to support the idea of a Jewish state in Palestine.

4. See LDB to Sokolow, 24 July 1922.

5. With the change of administrations, the Zionists found themselves cut off from official agencies in Washington. The State Department, which had been anti-Zionist even in Wilson's administration, now felt that it could safely ignore the movement without fear of recrimination. During the 1920s the Zionists received little more than an occasional symbolic word of encouragement from the Republican administrations.

6. See LDB to Mack et al., 23 December 1921. Otto Warburg was also a member of the Sokolow mission (see note 1, above).

To Julian William Mack

December 16, 1921 Washington, D.C. [Mack Mss]

MY DEAR JUDGE MACK: I understand you are assured that before Jan 8/22 the Palestine Development Council will have received as donations or for investment at least two hundred and fifty thousand (250,000) dollars in cash (beside the amount contributed for its administrative fund).

I also understand that the Central Com^tee of the Palestine Development Leagues has set itself the task of raising before July 1, 1922 the additional sum for the Council of two hundred and fifty thousand (250,000) dollars in cash.

If the Council shall have received the first $250,000 before Jan 8/22 and shall also receive before July 1/22 at least two hundred and twenty five (225,000) of the second $250,000 to be raised as above stated, I will contribute to the Council as a donation the sum of twenty five thousand (25,000) dollars on or before July 1, 1922.   With best wishes,

To Julian William Mack, Stephen Samuel Wise and Jacob deHaas

December 23, 1921 Washington, D.C. [Wise Mss—AJA]

JWM–SSW–DEH: As I wrote you, Prof O[tto]. Warburg was in yesterday 1¼ hours. We discussed at length experiment stations in P[alestine]. including the Aaronsohn one, agriculture in Palestine, University Building and other university plans and American agriculture etc. for fully ¾ hours. Then he came out flatfooted, saying he had not come officially but he wanted to know whether some treaty of peace could not be negotiated etc. by laying down (through a committee) what the principles of action hereafter should be etc. etc. that the Congress was now passed [1] and we ought to be able to agree on some plan. I could not avoid the question and concluded that it would be [in]advisable to refuse to talk to him. So I told him of the moral problems involved, honest finance etc. and the impossibility of avoiding recurrence of past deviations under present conditions; discussed Ussishkin's failings and our attempt to keep him from the position of infinite harmfulness to the cause which he has occupied for more than two years.[2] Of our attempt in 1919 to put Bob Szold, the ideal man, in charge and that if those in power had feared half as much British and Arab, as they did U[ssishkin]. it would have been done; for W[eizmann]. and others agreed with us as to what was desirable. I endeavored otherwise to make him understand our position, that we had done and would do nothing to prevent their success and that we, on the other hand, were trying to do what little we could to help in the cause. But we could not take the responsibilities incident to a position which would involve in effect our recommending people to put their money into the hands of those whose administration we could not trust. I discussed again the desirability of eliminating the Commission from Palestine and the wrong being done to [Sir Herbert] Samuel and the British as well as to the cause. Told him Sol Rosenbloom in whom we have much confidence was leaving soon for Palestine.[3] He answered that our failure to approve the K[eren]. H[ayesod]. was hindering them and pleaded that we should, at least, do what Benderly had done.[4] I indicated rather than said that we could not. All very friendly. But I gave him no encouragement.

1. See LDB to Felix Frankfurter, 6 September 1921.
2. Menachem Ussishkin (1863–1941) had been the most vociferous of the anti-Brandeis group in the fight earlier in 1921 and had consistently thwarted each and every attempt at compromise between Weizmann and Mack, just as in 1903 he had bitterly attacked Herzl for even considering the East Africa offer. Ussishkin was head of the Jewish National Fund in Palestine, responsible for the purchase of land, and he often effected deals without first checking to see if there were sufficient financial resources in Zionist coffers. Robert Szold reported that he once remonstrated with Ussishkin about spending without having the money in hand, to which Ussishkin replied that what he did was necessary and that Zionists would have to find the money. He then charged Szold, who was as economically conservative as LDB, with being a "gezunter goy" (a "healthy gentile") while he, Ussishkin, was a "kronker yid," (a "sick Jew"), implying that Szold had no real feeling for Jewish matters.
3. See LDB to Mack, 6 October 1921, n. 4.
4. Samson Benderly (see LDB to Mack et al., 8 January 1921, n. 3), the organizer of much of Jewish education in the United States, had supported the Brandeis-Mack group in its dispute with the World Zionist Organization. Afterwards, however, he had made a sort of peace with the Weizmann group. He did not work for it, but he did not oppose it, either.

To Woodrow Wilson

December 28, 1921 Washington, D.C. [Wilson Mss]

MY DEAR MR. WILSON: You were so deeply interested in the labor provisions embodied in the Clayton Act that I am venturing to send you the recent opinions in the Truax Case.[1]

Possibly you may care to see also the opinions in the Duplex Case enclosed.[2]

With every good wish to you and Mrs. Wilson for the New Year.   Most cordially,

1. *Truax* v. *Corrigan*, 257 *U.S.* 312 (1921). A restaurant owner in Arizona was being picketed. He applied for an injunction, but an Arizona law, restricting the use of the labor injunction, made that course impossible to follow. He contended that he had been deprived of property without due process, and Chief Justice Taft, for the majority, struck down the Arizona anti-injunction law. As historian Paul Murphy has written: "The ruling left no doubt that to Taft business was property and any infringement upon the way it was conducted was a potential infringement of property rights." Even Mr. Justice Pitney, whose lower-court rulings had been antilabor, was surprised: "I can find no ground for declaring that the State's action is so arbitrary and devoid of reasonable basis that it can be called a deprivation of liberty or property without due process of law. . . ." See Murphy, *The Constitution in Crisis Times* (New York, 1972): 48, 75–76. LDB filed a massive dissent holding that the Constitution should not be interpreted so as to stifle social experimentation, and Frankfurter was so angered by the Chief Justice's opinion that he attacked it in the *New Republic* (see "The Same Mr. Taft," reprinted in Archibald MacLeish and E. F. Prichard, eds., *Law and Politics: Occasional Papers of Felix Frankfurter* [New York, 1939], 44). For an analysis of the case and the various dissents, see Konefsky, *The Legacy of Holmes and Brandeis*, 124–29.
2. See LDB to Felix Frankfurter, 4 January 1921, n. 1.

To Felix Frankfurter

December 31, 1921 Washington, D.C. [Frankfurter Mss—LC]

MY DEAR FELIX: Thank you for the interesting enclosed returned herewith.

1. Your letter to Freund is admirably put and absolutely sound. I am glad Farrand is so comprehensive in his assent. But I think the memo. of conference with Freund & Stone indicates a pur-

pose of taking up far more subjects than can possibly be well done at one time.[1]

Couldn't they limit themselves to a single state. Perhaps Illinois, where Freund is, would be the most convenient. It surely would present problems galore. After that has been fully explored there would be time to go elsewhere with the light gained by that experience in research.

2. I am enclosing letter from Will Hays' secretary.[2] He is apparently not doing what I talked over with you & suggested to him. Won't you talk this over with Chafee & let me have his formulated suggestions to send to Hays?

3. The A[ttorney]. G[eneral].'s [3] & President's actions re Debs has been inexpressibly bad.[4]

4. I am glad you like the Lumber dissent. I was waiting for a chance to say some of those things. There is a touch of humor in the [*] of the two other dissenters in my last paragraph.[5]

5. About Pitney's virtues I will tell you more when we meet.[6]

6. Yes, we shall have now the test of American International Statesmanship.[7] My grave concern is on the National. As I said to you, prosperity of the status quo ante will not go far toward satisfying any of us; and we are not likely to have even that for a long time to come. We really have problems ahead that can't be lied away by "loyal optimism."

7. Was glad to see [Calvert] Magruder yesterday.

Every good wish to you and Marion for the New Year.

1. Ernst Freund was proposing a study on administrative law and practice which he hoped would be financed by the Commonwealth Fund. Frankfurter was advising both Freund and Max Farrand (1869–1945), the well known Yale historian, who was a director of the Commonwealth Fund. Freund's project did not receive financial support.

2. George Walbridge Perkins, Jr. (1895–1960), son of the Morgan partner and financial angel of the Roosevelt Bull Moose campaign, was serving in 1921 as executive secretary to the Postmaster-General, William H. Hays. Perkins later became assistant secretary of state for European affairs in 1949 and after that served as American representative to the North Atlantic Treaty Organization. The matter under discussion here probably involved the restoration of mailing privileges to radical groups that had been suspended during the war and in the Red Scare that followed the Armistice.

3. Harry Micajah Daugherty (1860–1941), a Columbus, Ohio, attorney and a close friend of Warren Harding, had been named Attorney General

in the Republican administration. He was forced to resign that office on 28 March 1924, and he was later indicted, but acquitted, of charges to defraud the government. His version of the scandals can be found in his *Inside Story of the Harding Tragedy* (New York, 1932).

4. On 23 December 1921, Warren Harding had commuted Eugene V. Debs's prison sentence, and Debs had been released from the Atlanta penitentiary on Christmas Day. In the memorandum prepared by Daugherty (reprinted in full in *New York Times*, 31 December 1921), Debs was considered undeniably guilty of sedition, and his commutation was seen as an act of charity which would also soften some criticism from civil liberties groups. Because Harding merely commuted the sentence, and did not pardon Debs, the Socialist leader did not regain his citizenship.

5. LDB had written a strong dissent in an antitrust case brought against an association of hardwood manufacturers. The majority of the Court held that the agency was in violation of the law, but LDB argued that the dealers were legitimately trying to impose some rationality upon a chaotic industry that had been ravaged by cutthroat competition. His jibe at the majority consisted of reminding his brethren that in the steel case, where U.S. Steel controlled fifty percent of the market, and in the shoe machinery case, where the accused controlled nearly all of the market, the Court had found against the government. Why, then, did they find the lumber dealers, who controlled between them about one-third of the market, in violation of the law? LDB was joined by McKenna and Holmes. See *American Column & Lumber Co. et al. v. United States*, 257 *U.S.* 377 (1921). LDB's dissent is at 413.

6. See preceding letter, n. 1.

7. See LDB to Alfred Brandeis, 13 November 1921, n. 3.

To Rufus Daniel Isaacs

January 8, 1922 Washington, D.C. [Steffens Mss]

MY DEAR LORD READING: Lincoln Steffens goes to India at the instance of my good friend Norman Hapgood, who has recently become the editor of Hearst's International Magazine.

You doubtless know Steffens by reputation. He has long been one of our best known journalists. He is high-minded, serious, fearless. A generous lover of liberty and justice, with faith in democracy. He has been a persistent progressive in politics and is often called a radical, by his opponents. The enclosed sketch of Jack Reed, which came with the Christmas mail indicates the character of his heart and mind.

Whether he has views on India I do not know. But I know him

to be a searcher after knowledge. And I think you will wish him to have trustworthy sources of information. Hence this letter of introduction.   With cordial greetings,

To Julian William Mack

January 12, 1922 Washington, D.C. [Frankfurter Mss—LC]

JWM: Re yours of 8 concerning your donation funds and F.F.

I am entirely clear (1) that F.F. ought not to accept anything from either of your funds or from Mrs [Mary] Fels

(2) that anything which he should accept from anyone should come from me.

And, of course, anything that I can do for Felix, which is best for him and for the causes he so generously serves, I am more than glad to do.[1]

My doubt is as to what it is best to do. You know my apprehensions of "easier ways" and the removal of financial limitations; also my belief in the saving grace of what many call drudgery.

But I think it may be consistent with what is best to put $1000. into his hands this year to pay expenses incident to his public work, and I shall write him to that effect.

1. See LDB to Frankfurter, 24 September 1925. See also letters to Frankfurter, 19 and 25 November 1916.

To Felix Frankfurter

February 3, 1922 Washington, D.C. [Frankfurter Mss—LC]

DEAR FELIX: 1. It would be a great mistake not to make a wholly new index covering 1–35 H[arvard] L[aw] R[eview]. The new index would give new opportunity for selling whole sets, & it would greatly widen & deepen the influence of the Review for the future.[1]

If the H.L.R. trustees funds will not permit, friends of the School should be called on for contributions. I shall be glad to contribute. Give the Law School Assn. something to do. Let them raise money.[2]

2. The matter of accuracy & thoroughness should be definitely taken up by the faculty. Next to knowing how to think legally, they are the most important requirements of lawyers. The graduates' actual knowledge is necessarily limited. But they ought to be guaranteed intellectually trustworthy. High ability, resourcefulness, imagination, the essentially legal mind, come, like kissing, by favor of the gods (although there is much in the way of development that training may do in them). But accuracy & thoroughness is [*sic*] possible for everybody who is worthy of being graduated by the H.L.S. It means banishing indolence & carelessness & teaching that being occupied—called working—is not taking pains.

3. I am glad that my next secretary looks promising & interesting.[3]

4. Your Dr. Metz and Aaron Sapiro [4] were both in. The latter is a most engaging person, with all the hopefulness & exhilaration of the days when the world was young. I approve of his going ahead regardless; but I think he is underestimating

> (a) the danger which inheres in not having also cooperative credit institutions to supply the needed money,
>
> (b) the danger of the cooperative producers squeezing the consumers.

5. You have doubtless heard from Wise of our Balfour visit,[5] & from DeHaas of his visit Wednesday. Mrs. Fels was here today, Mendel Berlis yesterday, & from Mack daily communications; so there is no danger of forgetting Jerusalem.[6]

My greetings to Marion,

1. A comprehensive index was not published until 1937, and it covered the first fifty volumes of the *Review;* there had been earlier indexes for volumes I–X and I–XXV.

2. See LDB to Frankfurter, 23 April 1922.

3. William Edward McCurdy (1893–1967) served as LDB's secretary during 1922–23 and then returned to a lengthy teaching career at Harvard. After the Second World War, McCurdy was associate director of Allied legal units in occupied Germany.

4. In 1922 Aaron Sapiro (1884–1959) was gaining a reputation as one of the country's outstanding experts on cooperative marketing, but he was to be best known as the man who stopped Henry Ford's anti-Semitic campaign in the 1920s. In 1927, Sapiro sued Ford for $1 million, charging that his libels against the Jews had affected Sapiro's own legal practice (see LDB to Frankfurter, 9 July 1927). In the 1930s, Sapiro's name was often

linked with Al Capone and other mobsters, and although he was acquitted of charges of racketeering, Sapiro was eventually disbarred.

5. Arthur Balfour was in the United States as a British delegate to the Disarmament Conference (see LDB to Alfred Brandeis, 13 November 1921). Although he limited his public appearances, Balfour had met with a group of American Zionists and reaffirmed his faith in the Zionist movement. He repeated this pledge privately to several of LDB's associates.

6. *Psalms*, 137:5.

To Felix Frankfurter

[February 15, 1922] Washington, D.C. [Frankfurter Mss—LC]

FF: Mr. W[ilson] was remarkably improved.[1] His voice was natural, his face also, & he seemed mentally as well as physically invigorated. He is following much more keenly current events.

1. LDB had gone to see the former president on the afternoon of 15 February.

To Robert Walter Bruere

February 25, 1922 Washington, D.C. [Frankfurter Mss—HLS]

MY DEAR BRUERE: I fear I was far from helpful to your fellows. Perhaps I should, at least, have lessened the chances of misunderstanding, if I had made of views vaguely stated or left to be implied, this summary: [1]

Refuse to accept as inevitable any evil in business (e.g. irregularity of employment). Refuse to tolerate any immoral practice (e.g. espionage). But do not believe that you can find a universal remedy for evil conditions or immoral practices in effecting a fundamental change in society (as by State Socialism). And do not pin too much faith in legislation. Remedial institutions are apt to fall under the control of the enemy and to become instruments of oppression.

Seek for betterment within the broad lines of existing institutions. Do so by attacking evil in situ; and proceed from the individual to the general. Remember that progress is necessarily slow; that remedies are necessarily tentative; that, because of varying conditions, there must be much and constant enquiry into facts (like that being made by your Bureau) and much experimentation; and that always and everywhere the intellectual, moral and spiritual development of those concerned will remain an essential—and the main factor—in real betterment.

This development of the individual is, thus, both a necessary means and the end sought. For our objective is the making of men and women who shall be free—self-respecting members of a democracy—and who shall be worthy of respect. Improvement in material conditions of the worker and ease are the incidents of better conditions—valuable mainly as they may ever increase opportunities for development.

The great developer is responsibility. Hence, no remedy can be hopeful which does not devolve upon the workers' participation in, responsibility for the conduct of business; and their aim should be the eventual assumption of full responsibility—as in cooperative enterprises. This participation in and eventual control of industry is likewise an essential of obtaining justice in distributing the fruits of industry.

But democracy in any sphere is a serious undertaking. It substitutes self-restraint for external restraint. It is more difficult to maintain than to achieve. It demands continuous sacrifice by the individual and more exigent obedience to the moral law than any other form of government. Success in any democratic undertaking must proceed from the individual. It is possible only where the process of perfecting the individual is pursued. His development is attained mainly in the processes of common living. Hence, the industrial struggle is essentially an affair of the Church and is its imperative task.

Possibly I have again failed to help.   Most cordially,

1. LDB had spoken informally to a group connected with the Department of Research and Education of the Federal Council of Churches in America. Fearing that he had been unclear, he summarized his remarks in this famous letter. Professor Mason calls it "his creed in essence" (Mason, *Brandeis*, 584–85).

To Woodrow Wilson

March 3, 1922 Washington, D.C. [Wilson Mss]

MY DEAR MR. WILSON: I am very glad that you are turning your thoughts to the railroad problem.[1] The need of constructive action is becoming daily more manifest.

The wisdom of the principle of "safety first" finds confirmation; for Colby had not sent me a copy of your statement.[2]

Let me thank you also for sending me Prof. Ford's suggestive memorandum returned herewith.[3] I am particularly impressed with his proposals in regard to water transportation. A high development of coastwise and inland transportation is essential to an adequate system.

You had so large a part in giving us woman suffrage that you may care to see these opinions which establish the Nineteenth Amendment as a part of our Constitution.[4]

And possibly you may be interested also in the Lemke case, where a promising effort of a state to protect itself met its doom.[5]

Most Cordially,

1. Wilson had sent LDB a statement on railroads for possible inclusion in "The Document" (see LDB to Wilson, 25 June 1921).

2. The former president had written that the statement may "have already reached you through [Bainbridge] Colby, but I do not know that it has and am acting on the principle of 'safety first',—a rule of practice not unknown to lawyers though of little practical interest to a member of a court of final resort."

3. Wilson had also sent another memorandum on transportation, prepared at his request by Henry Jones Ford (1851–1925). Ford had moved from an early career in journalism to teaching political science, first at Johns Hopkins and then at Princeton during Wilson's presidency there. At the end of his second term as President, Wilson appointed Ford to the Interstate Commerce Commission, and he served during 1920 and 1921.

4. On 27 February the Supreme Court easily brushed aside two last-ditch attacks on the Nineteenth Amendment; LDB spoke for a unanimous Court in both cases. In *Lesser* v. *Garnett*, 258 *U.S.* 130 (1922), a Maryland citizen contended that Maryland's constitution stipulated male suffrage only and that Maryland never ratified the amendment. Lesser also raised other technical objections, none of which persuaded the high court. In *Fairchild* v. *Hughes*, 258 *U.S.* 126 (1922), a New Yorker contended that the ratification proclamation was unconstitutional since the Nineteenth Amendment contradicted the principles of the U.S. Constitution.

5. In the important case of *Lemke* v. *Farmers' Grain Co.*, 258 *U.S.* 50 (1922), the Court struck down a North Dakota statute that attempted to provide for the inspection of grain. Since the grain was almost all destined for interstate shipment, the Court ruled that North Dakota had no power to regulate. LDB wrote a short dissenting opinion in which he was joined by Justices Holmes and Clarke. For an incisive discussion of the case, see Alexander M. Bickel, *The Unpublished Opinions of Mr. Justice Brandeis* (Chicago, 1967), 167–70; Bickel calls the decision an instance of "the Court's

robbing the country of the fruits of federalism by pointless expansion of exclusive federal power. . . ."

To Oliver Wendell Holmes, Jr.

March 8, 1922 Washington, D.C. [Holmes Mss]

To my comrade in arms and The Man. Every good wish.[1]

1. This note was written on LDB's card; it was passed to Holmes on his eighty-first birthday.

To Felix Frankfurter

April 2, 1922 Washington, D.C. [Frankfurter Mss—LC]

FF: Why does the Law School discriminate so against Federal Law? Doubtless many rich federal nuggets lie concealed beneath the many general titles in the Programme of Instruction. But no aggregate of uncoordinated parts can supply the needed treatment.

Is this seeming neglect a survival of the days when the School was provincial, the federal functions few and the Military rules received more discussion than the Constitution?

What we need is comprehensive consideration of the respective fields of federal and state law, civil and criminal, and not merely jurisdiction, procedure and the so-called federal common law.

And the course should be one for undergraduates.[1]

1. In 1924–25, Frankfurter introduced a course in "Jurisdiction and Procedure of the Federal Courts," which soon became a standard part of the undergraduate curriculum at Harvard. Contrast with LDB to Christopher C. Langdell, 30 December 1889.

To Harold Joseph Laski

April 2, 1922 Washington, D.C. [Laski Mss]

MY DEAR HAROLD: I should have written you long ago.

First, to thank you for the Karl Marx.[1] It is admirable, on the whole—perhaps your best writing.

Second, to congratulate you on the Irish and the Egyptian settlements.[2] These do the British great credit, and furnish new evidence that they are the leading statesmen of the world. Such performances are a reservoir of hope.

Please give my congratulations particularly to Lord Milner when you see him.

Judge Holmes at 81 is at his best, as his opinions will testify. He speaks of you always with deep affection.

We are hoping to have Felix and Marion here at Easter, and shall talk often of you and Frida, to whom our best greetings.

Most cordially,

1. Harold J. Laski, *Karl Marx, An Essay* (London, 1922).
2. The tension between England and Ireland during and after the war resulted in negotiations in late 1921. On 6 December an agreement was reached which provided for the Irish Free State, to include twenty-six of Ireland's thirty-two counties. This awarding of dominion status was ratified by the British Parliament on 16 December 1921 and by the Parliament of Southern Ireland, henceforth "Eire," on 15 January 1922. Then, on 1 March 1922, England announced that Eygpt was henceforth independent, and the wartime protectorate over her was terminated.

To Benjamin Sollow Kirsh

April 5, 1922 Washington, D.C. [Kirsh Mss]

MY DEAR MR. KIRSH: [1] To the new firm our best wishes.[2]

May its members experience in generous measure the joys of a great profession nobly pursued.

With thanks for your thoughtful letter.   Most cordially,

1. Benjamin Sollow Kirsh (b. 1898), a New York attorney, had been chairman of the Trucking Commission of the Labor Board during the war and, like Susan Brandeis, a special assistant to the United States attorney in New York for the prosecution of antitrust cases. Kirsh has written on the legal aspects of various economic questions, including a book, *Automation and Collective Bargaining* (Brooklyn, 1964).
2. Kirsh, Samuel Rosenman, and LDB's daughter Susan had just formed Kirsh, Rosenman & Brandeis, a new law firm with offices in the Woolworth Building in New York.

To Felix Frankfurter

April 8, 1922 Washington, D.C. [Frankfurter Mss—LC]

DEAR FELIX: I was immersed in Court work which delayed correspondence & now find so much to say about interesting enclosures returned herewith, that I think it best to await our discussion orally next week. Holmes J. was beset with a cold & did not attend the Conference.[1] He is merely housed, not abed. He is enthusiastic over Walter's Public Opinion.[2]

The Conference seemed dreary without him.

1. The weekly Saturday conference of the Court for the discussion and assignment of pending opinions.

2. Walter Lippmann had just published *Public Opinion* (New York, 1922), an analysis of the forces that molded public attitudes on various questions, as well as the obstacles to wide dissemination of knowledge. In this very influential work, Lippmann also introduced a discussion of the power of prejudices and stereotypes on the public mind and criticized the press for its failure to provide sufficient information for the people to exercise their judgment intelligently. Reviewing the book in the *New Republic*, John Dewey wrote: "To read the book is an experience in illumination. . . . The manner of presentation is so objective and projective, that one finishes the book almost without realizing that it is perhaps the most effective indictment of democracy as currently conceived ever penned."

To Felix Frankfurter

April 23, 1922 Washington, D.C. [Frankfurter Mss—HLS]

MY DEAR FELIX: I trust you understand that I shall be glad to contribute to any or all of the small Law School funds which we discussed.

I consider these current needs a distinct asset of the School which may be made to serve an important purpose. They may be used to bind successful graduates and others to the School, by keeping them alive to its growth and problems, and it may serve also to awaken and develop, through them, the bar, by acquainting them with the growth of legal education. For the present it would be undesirable to have the needs met either (a) from income of a general endowment, or (b) from gifts of the whole amount from single individuals, or (c) from funds derived through increasing tuition fees. That is, the recurrent need must be preserved, for it is desirable that the School should have to call on its graduates, justifying itself from year to year; and it is likewise desirable for the graduates that they should be called on for support.[1]

It was good to have you & Marion here.

1. See LDB to Frankfurter, 3 February 1922.

To Nathan Straus

April 25, 1922 Washington, D.C. [R. Szold Mss]

MY DEAR MR. STRAUS: I have now your letter of the 21st.[1] The thought you suggest has been much in my mind for some time; and I hope to discuss the matter with you soon. This, however, I deem to be clear; until Mr. Sol Rosenbloom returns from Palestine, no decision should be made and no action of any kind should be taken which deviates in the slightest degree from the course laid out by us last summer. We asked Mr. Rosenbloom to go to Palestine to represent us; asked him to examine carefully the field; to determine the needs and the possibilities there; and to ascertain what the situation in the organization is; to confer with our friends in Europe and on his return to advise us.[2] We have confidence in Mr. Rosenbloom's judgment as well as in his character. We should not be justified in changing in any respect the status of our work and our relations to the organization until we have the benefit of his advice and the conclusion reached after painstaking inquiry.

With best wishes and cordial greetings,

1. In his letter, Straus had urged LDB that the time might now be ripe for reconciliation between their group and the current leaders of the movement. LDB received numerous letters of this kind, as well as several visits from Zionists who wanted the Mack-Brandeis faction to return to an active role in the Z.O.A.

2. See LDB to Rosenbloom, 25 June 1922.

To Donald Randall Richberg

May 22, 1922 Washington, D.C. [Richberg Mss]

MY DEAR MR. RICHBERG: [1] It was good of you to send me your book.[2]

It presents questions which may well occupy a lawyer's serious, as well [as] his idle hours. And the best judge in my family paid it the compliment of sitting deep into the night to finish the book.[3]   Cordially,

1. Donald Randall Richberg (1881–1960) was an important liberal lawyer in Chicago, specializing in public utilities and labor matters. He was already an experienced political hand, having helped to organize the Bull Moose Party in 1912, and he was to be active in the Progressive Party campaign in 1924. But his most important political service came in the 1930s. Richberg followed his law partner, Harold L. Ickes, to Washington and became a high level figure in the New Deal—counsel for the NRA and then executive director of the National Emergency Council. See his engaging autobiography, *My Hero: Memoirs of an Eventful but Unheroic Life* (New York, 1954).

2. Richberg had sent his latest novel, *A Man of Purpose* (New York, 1922).

3. Richberg replied that "your designation and my designation of the best judge in your family may not be the same."

To Felix Frankfurter

June 16, 1922 Chatham, Mass. [Frankfurter Mss—HLS]

My dear Felix: 1. We look forward to the 23rd. Our telephone is Chatham 13 Ring 2 (the W. T. Sears house). I assume you and Marion will prefer an afternoon train. I think there are two now (since the change on June 12).

2. The examination papers are interesting. Perhaps it is fortunate that we JJ. don't have to pass annual exams.

3. I wish someone would produce something effective, for constant quotation, on the cowardly pretence of rejecting able men, on the ground that their judgment is unsound.

4. Pound hasn't overcome all his anti-Bolshevism yet.

5. Charles Warren's USSC. in History of US. interests me intensely.[1] It seems to me better than Beveridge's Marshall.[2] And it suggests to me this re Child Labor decision: [3]

About every really important decision (at least in the early days), gave rise to some proposal of the disappointed class to amend the Constitution.

If one of your young men would gather the data (Warren furnishes much) an interesting article might be written, as bearing on recent proposals, including LaFollette's & Mrs. Kelley's.[4]

6. I hope Marion has written Elizabeth about California.

1. See next letter.

2. Albert J. Beveridge, *The Life of John Marshall*, 4 vols. (Boston, 1916–19).

3. In 1918, the Supreme Court had struck down the first federal Child Labor Act as unconstitutionally exceeding the power to regulate interstate commerce (*Hammer* v. *Dagenhart*, 247 *U.S.* 251). Congress then passed a second Child Labor Act, relying on the taxing power rather than the interstate commerce clause. Once again the Court struck the statute down, declaring that Congress had abused its power. Speaking for the majority of the Court, Chief Justice Taft differentiated between a tax and a penalty, in that the latter was used merely to disguise the real purpose of regulating labor in plants that the Court had already held were local in nature. See *Bailey* v. *Drexel Furniture Company*, 259 *U.S.* 20 (1922). It was to be almost two decades before the Court finally—and unanimously—upheld a federal child labor law in *United States* v. *Darby*, 312 *U.S.* 100 (1941). Shortly after the Court handed down the *Bailey* decision, LDB wrote to Frankfurter on 16 May: "The N.R., the Survey & like periodicals should not be permitted to misunderstand yesterday's decisions on the Child Labor and Board of Trade cases, & should be made to see that holding these invalid is wholly unlike holding invalid the ordinary welfare legislation. That is, that we here deal (1) with the distribution of functions between State & Federal Governments [and] (2) with the attempt at dishonest use of the taxing powers."

4. In the light of such cases as *Bailey* and the antilabor attitude evinced by the Court in other cases (see LDB to Frankfurter, 31 August 1922), a number of progressives urged revision of the Constitution to limit the Court's power to nullify laws. Addressing the American Federation of Labor convention in Cincinnati, Senator Robert M. LaFollette on 14 June 1922 had attacked Chief Justice Taft and the "judicial oligarchy" for the child labor and antiunion decisions. LaFollette, to the loud cheers of the delegates, proposed a constitutional amendment that would have prohibited lower federal courts from invalidating legislation and would have allowed the Congress to override a Court decree regarding specific legislation by the simple expedient of repassing the measure. On the same platform, Mrs. Florence Kelley, LDB's former ally from the National Consumers League, had endorsed the Wisconsin senator's proposal. See LDB to Frankfurter, 19 September 1922.

Whether or not Frankfurter himself took up LDB's suggestion, Charles Warren did so in an address to the Massachusetts Bar Association on 14 October 1922 entitled "The Early History of the Supreme Court of the United States in Connection with Modern Attacks on the Judiciary."

To Charles Warren

MY DEAR WARREN: You have performed an important public service.[1]

A better understanding of the functions of our Court is an essential of political and social health; and your book will prove a great aid in education.

It is of commanding present interest; and research, judgment and style combine to give it enduring value.

My personal debt to you is heavy. Since I joined the Court no book has given me so much instruction or more pleasure.

Much having makes me hunger more. Have you ever thought of writing on the lower Federal courts? A consideration of their functioning in the past would be interesting and it would help in determining their province for the future. My impression is that it should be abridged—particularly in criminal cases.[2]

Most cordially,

1. LDB had just received Warren's classic three-volume study, *The Supreme Court in United States History* (Boston, 1922). See preceding letter.
2. Despite LDB's persistent urging (see LDB to Warren, 24 October 1924), Warren never took up the study of the lower court system.

To Solomon Rosenbloom

June 25, 1922 Chatham, Mass. [Frankfurter Mss—HLS]

MY DEAR MR. ROSENBLOOM: Your letter of May 28th brings us much encouragement in its report of the selection of the bank managers, the assurance that you will remain in Palestine until operations are begun, the projects for an intensive plan of money raising upon your return. The purpose to confer with leaders in Germany and elsewhere and the confirmation of your opinion that the course adopted by us in relation to work for Palestine is the right one.

As you may imagine there has been pressure from many quarters to induce us to change our course;[1] but we have adhered steadfastly to that adopted at Pittsburgh on July 4, 1921.

Of recent happenings and particularly of our conference in New

York last week re Rutenberg project [2]—I am asking Mr. deHaas to report fully.

Since receipt of your letters of 28th Ult., we have your cable stating that you will remain in Palestine until late in July. I trust this means, among other things, that you and the ladies are restored to health. It will certainly be of great service to the cause to have you prolong your stay as long as possible. The resultant gains there and ultimately here, will be large.

With every good wish,

1. See LDB to Nathan Straus, 25 April 1922.

2. Pinhas Rutenberg (1879–1942) was a Russian-born irrigation engineer who had settled in Palestine in 1919. Rutenberg worked out a plan to harness the waters of the Jordan River in order to generate electrical power, and in 1921 he secured a concession from the British government to implement his scheme. He was unable to secure the necessary funding at first (see LDB to Julian Mack, 22 January 1924) but in 1923 he established the Palestine Electric Corporation, Ltd. The project proved to be enormously successful, and ultimately it became the Israel Electric Corporation, Ltd.

To Norman Hapgood

July 24, 1922 Chatham, Mass. [Brandeis Mss, SC 6–1]

MY DEAR NORMAN: I enclose letter from Sen. Reed & copy of my reply.[1]

You will recall our meeting at your apartment, and how handsomely he behaved after that. I hope you will promptly make the statement he desires.[2]

Please return enclosures & let me have copy of what you say.

1. Senator James A. Reed had written that rumors were circulating in Missouri that he had opposed LDB's confirmation on the grounds of LDB's religion and that he was, therefore, an enemy of the Jewish people.

2. See LDB to Hapgood, 1 February 1916, n. 1. LDB replied to Reed that he could not enter the controversy personally, but that he was requesting Hapgood to issue a statement. On 27 July, Hapgood telegraphed Reed: "It gives me pleasure to state of my absolute knowledge that far from opposing Mr. Brandeis on the ground of race prejudice you gave most attentive hearing to all points brought forward by the opposition, and after such full hearing used your influence strongly and valuably in favor of confirmation."

To Oliver Wendell Holmes, Jr.

July 24, 1922 Chatham, Mass. [Holmes Mss]

O.W.H. Your letter to Felix furnishes the required best evidence that—sixty years after—you have again bested the surgeons.[1]

With this new birth, we may expect from your eighties drainage of legal swamps, more important than the Paduan achievement of Luigi Cornaro.[2]

You timed the event with great consideration for the Court.

With much affection,

1. On 13 July Holmes underwent surgery, but he recovered quickly. The reference is to his Civil War experience when the young Holmes was wounded three times.

2. Luigi Cornaro (1475–1566) was a Venetian nobleman and a student of hydraulics. He moved to Padua and devoted some of his energies to swamp drainage. Cornaro was most famous, however, for his dietary experiments, which, he claimed, saved him from severe illness and preserved his life and health.

To Nahum Sokolow

July 24, 1922 Chatham, Mass. [Sokolow Mss]

MY DEAR MR. SOKOLOW: It was very good of you to send me the glad tidings which have just come.[1]

With this great task accomplished, that of Palestine upbuilding should proceed more rapidly. May each year mark increasing progress.   With most cordial greetings,

1. On this date, the Council of the League of Nations confirmed the British mandate over Palestine that had been granted at the San Remo conference on 25 April 1920. For details and the text of the mandate, see the *Encyclopedia of Zionism and Israel* 2: 749–60.

To Felix Frankfurter

August 31, 1922 Chatham, Mass. [Frankfurter Mss—HLS]

FF: I think you have let off [*] too gently. I think he is wrong almost in every respect (except that the op[inion]. should have been so clear that he couldn't have [*]). His "legal logic" with which you say you "agree" is faulty:

Every entity, unless it enjoys immunity, is liable for its wrongs. A natural person, a firm, an association, a corporation, in some states even the sovereign, is so liable. The unions, in effect, claimed for themselves immunity. The court denied the immunity.[1]

But even where no immunity exists, liability for an alleged wrong can be enforced, only if:

1. The defendent is properly before the court. This involves
    (a) going before a court with jurisdiction over subject matter and party
    (b) joining proper necessary parties
    (c) adequate error
2. The plaintiff is proven to have suffered a legal wrong.
3. The defendent is proven to have committed a legal wrong.
4. The pleadings are appropriate to recovery for the wrong proven.

The Courts having held the Unions do not enjoy (as a matter of substantive law) immunity for wrongs committed, had to decide (as a matter of procedure) whether the unions had been legally brought into court. And it properly decided this (namely 1. above) before taking up any other question. If it had decided that unions have an immunity as a matter of substantive law, like the sovereign ordinarily, or if it had decided that the unions were not legally before the Court, it would have gone no further. But holding that the unions were not immune and that they were legally before the Court, it necessarily proceeded to the determination of the other three questions. It found, then, that the plaintiffs had suffered legal wrongs; that the International Union had committed no wrong whatsoever; that the District and local union had committed wrongs; but that these wrongs proved were not those sued on; that is, were not violations of the federal law.

To have proceeded first to the determination of questions 2, 3 or 4 supra would have been, at least, bad judicial practice; for the Court should not have enquired into them, unless it had decided that unions were not immune as matter of substantive law and were, as matter of procedure, properly before the Court.

The liability sought to be enforced was not the joint and several liability of the members of the union. It was the liability of the unions as entities. If the judgment below had been affirmed, no person would have been liable *qua* member. Only the property of the entity, present and thereafter to be acquired could have been reached to satisfy that judgment. There were joined as defendents 66 natural persons, but not *qua* members. As to these only questions 2, 3 and 4 actually arose.

If the judgment had been affirmed and had not been satisfied by, or out of property of the Union, a question might have arisen whether by any proceeding the individual members could be made to satisfy the judgment. That is, whether there is a members' liability akin to a stockholders' liability; and also whether there is, otherwise, an individual liability for the wrongs proven. But no such question could arise or was discussed in that case.

It is not true that a union can be liable only if every member authorized or ratified the alleged wrong deed or that a union cannot be liable unless every member is liable. Entities are often liable for acts which were neither actually authorized nor ratified, as a railroad for the conductor's negligence or wanton act. And, of course, a person who is a member may be liable, although the union is not. To hold that a union could be liable only if every member authorized or ratified the act would involve treating the union not as entity but merely as the joint agent of the several members. That a labor union is an entity was certainly not new law.

1. The first *Coronado* case, which the Court had decided on 5 June 1922, stirred up a great deal of controversy, and much of the debate centered on what the decision actually meant for the rights of unions. In an effort to break the local mineworkers' union, some coal operators had locked out union workers in western Arkansas. Violence inevitably followed, leading to destruction of several mines. The operators sued the union for treble damages under the Sherman Act; and in the original jury trial, the local judge directed the jurors to find for the owners. The decision, for $600,000 plus costs, was affirmed by the Circuit Court of Appeals, and then it was appealed to the Supreme Court in October 1920, where Charles Evans Hughes argued the case for the union. The Court divided in conference, five to four, against the union; but before a decision could be handed down, Chief Justice White died, and the case was rescheduled for new argument after Taft took his seat.

LDB in the meantime had prepared a dissent against the original majority decision, in which he argued that the Court had to be consistent. In earlier cases, notably *Hammer* v. *Dagenhart*, the Court had placed a narrow interpretation on what constituted interstate commerce; certainly the effect upon interstate commerce of the output of these Arkansas mines was no greater than the merchandise in the Hammer case. Although Chief Justice Taft originally had favored finding against the union, according to Professor Alexander Bickel, LDB managed to win him away from that position. Instead, the Court's decision, delivered by Taft, overturned the award, holding that the Sherman Act was inapplicable here; instead, a new trial was ordered, and the Court declared, much to LDB's satisfaction, that unions could be sued under common law for damages.

It was this part of the decision that confused many people, since it appeared to open the door to all sorts of actions against unions. But while there would undoubtedly be harassments, the real question was not whether unions could be sued, but what they could be sued for. This not only imposed some social responsibility upon the unions but also gave them a new status before the courts, and it was this issue which LDB had recognized. Taft's having delivered the opinion for a unanimous Court elicited a later comment from LDB to Frankfurter: "They [the conservatives] will take it from Taft but wouldn't take it from me. If it is good enough for Taft, it is good enough for us, they say—and a natural sentiment."

See *United Mine Workers* v. *Coronado Coal Company*, 259 *U.S.* 344 (1922). For a discussion of the case and of the content of LDB's undelivered dissent, see Bickel, *The Unpublished Opinions of Mr. Justice Brandeis*, ch. 5; see also Felix Frankfurter, "The Coronado Case," *The New Republic* 31 (16 August 1922): 328-30.

To Felix Frankfurter

September 4, 1922 [Washington, D.C.] [Frankfurter Mss—LC]
What to Do

FOR F.F. When the coal and rail strikes are ended,[1] a rational people should begin to think how a recurrence of like situations can be prevented. Clearly it is not by prohibiting strikes by compulsory arbitration or by crippling trade unions. It is not by physical force or by legal coercions. As long as these industries are privately owned or operated strikes in them must be permitted; and, even if publicly owned and operated, their employees must be free to join the unions. The promise of better conditions lies in industrial sanitation, not dosing.

First: Trade unionism should be frankly accepted and all war upon it, direct and indirect, by employers must cease. Unions should be free, at all times and under all circumstances, to use any form of persuasion (as distinguished from coercion) upon other workers to join their unions. Non-union workers should be protected against coercion; but never by or through the employer, or by any act or proceeding brought or done in his interest. Protection may be afforded unto the non-union man only by action or proceeding instigated and conducted by himself or on his behalf by the state.

Second: The employment by the employer of the private detectives and of the private armed guards, and the employers [*sic*] resort to the injunction must be discontinued. It should be recognized that such remedies can lead only to more war. Civil redress by the employer should be had only through action for damages; and violations of the criminal law should be vigorously prosecuted. Even on behalf of the State (or Nation) the injunction should never be used as a remedy for or for the prevention of acts which are criminal. Like most "easier ways" the use of the injunction in this connection is fraught with evil. The resources of the State are ample in the criminal law if it be made effective. There may, however, conceivably be instances where the non-union man should have protection by injunction for his personal rights against trade-union oppression; but the occasions for intervention by injunction would certainly be few.

Third: Such enlargement of the rights of unions and discontinuance of the use of armed guards, detectives and injunctions would appear to involve great damages to property and great loss and inconvenience to the public. In fact the loss would probably be at once much less than it is now. For the withdrawal of the present delusive protection against labor union excesses and this enlargement of their rights would tend:

(1) To remove the all pervading, irritating causes of discontent; the general conviction that the powers of the government are perverted by and in aid of the employers; and the deep sense of injustice suffered even in the Courts. It is of the essence that the curb upon trade union action should be administered by Court only by proceedings in which disputed facts are determined by juries. If trade unions are convicted of wrongful acts—by laymen—the belief in the impartiality of courts may be restored.

(2) To effect on the part of the employer to ascertain and to remove, or minimize, the substantive causes of discontent. The existence of the present delusive protection operates as a strong

incentive to arbitrariness and inconsiderateness and as a discourager of constructive thought. Nine-tenths of the injustices of which workers complain in the country could be removed by persistent application of the inventive mind to the situations involved in the relation of Employer & Employee. But for the delusive "easier way," necessity would again prove itself the mother of social-industrial invention.

(3) To the creation of conditions which would leave the employer and the community less exposed to serious loss by arbitrariness on the part of the unions. The delusive present protections leads [sic] employers and the community to expose themselves without insurance to such arbitrariness, and thereby encourages it.

(4) Ordinarily we insure ourselves against every conceivable bodily accident, error, or the wrongdoing of others. We provide not merely for money indemnity, but for insurance in kind, the spare part or tire, the factor of safety in bicycle or bridge, the safety-deposit box and the registered bond. But we fail to store adequate commodities, duly distributed, of coal and pig iron as to keep in adequate repair an ample supply of cars and locomotives, so that a relatively short interruption of work prove [sic] embarrassing.

(5) Investors of ordinary prudence have learned to insure against accident, error and wrongdoing by not putting all their eggs into one basket. But our unreasoned passion for bigness and for integration has led us to disregard in social-industrial life that wise warning. Safety lies in diversity, in decentralization, financial and territorial, with protective federations, in maintaining independent supplies of substitutes. Some restrictions against arbitrariness on the part of coal barons or miners may be found in hydro-electric power light and heat and oil or natural gas. Some protection against arbitrariness of railworkers, in water transportation, the trolley, the auto and the air service. And the existence of such ways is a mighty curb on arbitrariness.

Fourth: If the all pervading, irritating causes of discontent and the specific unnecessary injustices due to inconsiderateness and want of thought on the employer's part are removed as above indicated, the field of necessary conflicts of interest between employers and employes will be narrowed to relatively small and hence manageable proportions, and the temper of the parties will be such that reasonable adjustment will ordinarily be possible. If, in the exceptional case, adjustment as a result of negotiation proves not to be attainable, the remedy lies not in force, physical or legal, but in passive resistance. The remedy for the arbitrary demand of an excessive price for an article or service is doing without. Employers and consumers must have courage and must exhibit their powers of endurance when emergencies arise. Walls, mercenaries and laws have never succeeded in affording for long protection to a fear-ridden, comfort-loving people. Employer and consumer must show that they love justice and independence more than they do goods or ease. In the exercise of these qualities, the true preparedness indicated above, and vigorous enforcement of the criminal law if need be, lies the democratic way out.[2]

1. Both strikes were over within a matter of days. The anthracite coal strike ended with the miners winning their fight to avert a wage reduction, after President Harding, Secretary of Commerce Hoover, and both Pennsylvania senators brought all of their influence to bear on the operators. On 4 September the unions ratified an agreement that kept in effect the wage rates prevailing on 31 March 1922, until 31 August 1923. Both the union and the operators also agreed to ask for the creation of an Anthracite Coal Commission to mediate future disputes. On 13 September the national strike by railroad shop workers collapsed in the face of a court injunction. The shop workers had originally walked out in protest against a Labor Board decision that reduced their wages; at the end of the strike they finally accepted the original proposals of the board.

2. The substance of this letter appeared as an unsigned article, "What To Do," *The New Republic* 32 (4 October 1922): 136–37.

To Felix Frankfurter

September 6, 1922 Washington, D.C. [Frankfurter Mss—LC]

FF: To saddened Americans seeking the light which shall lead them from the slough of despond, the N[ew]. R[epublic].'s advertisement of the "three special numbers"—Sept. 27, "The teaching of English Literature"; Oct. 25, "Educational number"; Nov. 22, "Fall Literary Number" must bring disheartenment. It sounds like a comfortable, bourgeois, self-supporting, Mid-Victorian "Home and Fireside." Mrs. Straight's enlightened beneficence should give us a clarion call; and its essentials are:

1. Distinction—in thought and form. Thought bears on knowledge, the fruit of research. Quality as distinguished from quantity. Articles one cannot afford to miss.
2. Direction. The pathfinder must possess and exercise insight, judgment, decision. There must be neither deviation nor dissipation, no pleasing "abstecher"[1] to explore interesting ruins, to gather rare flowers, or even to kill a noxious animal, however large the variety. Every article must follow the same general direction. And the direction must be pursued without change.
3. Movement—unbroken movement. That is an essential of holding both interest and confidence. There must be no stop for meditation or consideration, and no thinking aloud. The thinking of leaders must be done at midnight in the cave, while the followers, without, sleep; and doubts must be suppressed.
4. Militancy—Courage, resourcefulness, aggressiveness, dash. Man—and woman too loves the fighter. They turn from the querulous and even from the wise critic. The gallant and the bold seem brilliant; and they are always interesting.

The editor must seek to hold the readers' interest, not by diversions, but by skillful presentation of the varieties of experience of the pilgrims plodding the weary way. To the knowing, every rock and every grain of sand, the trees and the flowers mark the watershed. So each day's wisdom sustains and the memories of a richly-stored past may be used as indicating that the trail followed is the right one. And while all roads lead to Rome, the greatest joy of the traveller is in the unexpected glimpse of the Holy City far away. And the Journal of distinction, direction, movement & militancy will never be mistaken for propaganda.

1. "diverting excursion."

To Felix Frankfurter

September 19, 1922 Washington, D.C. [Frankfurter Mss—LC]

F.F. Enclosed article of Buell[1] is much saner than all the La-Follette-Gompers talk,[2] but it shows the urgent need of Scott's article on dicta, the Constitution & the USSC.[3]

The remedy for the prevailing discontent with USSC must be sought:

1. In refraining from all constitutional dicta.

2. In refusing to consider a constitutional question except in "cases" or "controversies"—"initiated according to the regular course of judicial procedure"

3. In refusing to pass on constitutional questions if the case can be disposed of on any other

4. In refusing to hold an act void unless it clearly exceeds powers conferred etc.[4]

1. Raymond Leslie Buell (1896–1946) was in 1922 an instructor in government at Harvard. He later gained renown as a writer and lecturer on foreign affairs. In "Reforming the Supreme Court," *The Nation* 114 (14 June 1922): 714-16, he had listed some of what he considered the Court's recent abuses of the power of judicial review; and after discounting such drastic methods as impeachment or constitutional amendment, he suggested that all cases invalidating state or federal laws require at least a two-thirds majority.

2. See LDB to Frankfurter, 16 June 1922, n. 4.

3. Austin Scott did not publish any articles on this subject either in the popular press or in any legal periodicals.

4. For a discussion of this policy of "judicial restraint," see Konefsky, *The Legacy of Holmes and Brandeis, passim.*

To Felix Frankfurter

September 24, 1922 Washington, D.C. [Frankfurter Mss—LC]

DEAR FELIX: Enclosed memo on transportation is not for publication. But I should like you to study it. The N[ew]. R[epublic]. should declare soon a definite policy on transportation.[1]

And it should make its readers understand (what most Americans fail to realize) that to social-political reform there are three essentials:

1. Ascertaining what it is best to do

2. Getting the consent of the community to doing it

3. Actually doing it, after consent is given

We have developed only -2.-   We have become, in many fields, masters of "selling" ideas as well as material things. Any old idea will do. And the poorer the idea, the greater the skill of the salesman & hence his emoluments.

A conference is a coming together to determine the means by which, or to develop the motive power for, putting things over. Of course, only to get consent, and then "what ought to be done will be considered as done."

We plan to go to N.Y. Tuesday & to be there (Alice in Scarsdale) at City Club, Wednesday, Thursday, Friday.

1. See LDB to Frankfurter, 4 and 30 September 1922.

To Felix Frankfurter

September 25, 1922 Washington, D.C. [Frankfurter Mss—LC]

F.F.: Re Prohibition

Among the questions on which the N[ew]. R[epublic]. should take promptly a clear & virile stand, to be pursued persistently, is that of *concentrating* all Federal effort on performing the essentially federal function of excluding smuggling of liquor from foreign countries or interstate, and *leaving* to the States all intra-state violations of the law.[1]

Certainly this would tax to the utmost federal capacity for achievement.

There should be no attempt to change the Volstead Act. If there is any change of legislation needed, it should be limited to the appropriation, i.e. confining the appropriation to use in the essentially federal field.

I have not overlooked the recent article [2] in the N.R. taking, on the whole, this view. But it was egregiously what a N.R. article on the subject should *not* be.

It was weak, wooly, apologetic, ineffective.

1. See LDB to Frankfurter, 24 October 1923.
2. "The Enforcement of Prohibition," *The New Republic* 32 (13 September 1922): 59–60.

To Felix Frankfurter

September 30, 1922 Washington, D. C. [Frankfurter Mss—HLS]

F.F.: Re N[ew]. R[epublic]. policies I am enclosing as my last will & testament before opening of term memo as follows—of course not for publication—but for your study or consideration:

(1) On Prohibition
(2) On Capitalism
(3) On the spread
(4) On Fear
(5) On transportation (supplemental)
(6) Labor Saving devices [1]

What to do about Capitalism

We recognize the evils and abuses of Capitalism. But we do not believe in Communism; we do not believe in State Socialism; and we do not believe in Guild Socialism. We do believe in consumer cooperation. But we also believe that private capital has now and at least for a long time to come must have an important part to play in the best development of America and its ideals. We believe that the part of private capital may be a beneficent one and should be confined in a sphere which is desirable or necessary. What shall be the limitations? To curb its power; and to remove the abuses lest the propular wrath against private capital [———].[2]

First: Consumer cooperation should be encouraged in every field of commerce, industry, finance or service, where it is or may hereafter become feasible. So far as it can, from time to time, supersede privately owned businesses, it should be encouraged to do so. It is essentially democratic. It gives the consumer the ultimate control of what is actually his, but. . . . It puts upon the consumer the ultimate responsibility for its proper conduct; and in so doing develops the consumer. If properly conducted, consumer cooperatives [———]. will eliminate wastes & particularly the excessive spread between cost of production and the price to the consumer.

Second: Producers' cooperatives should be encouraged. They limit the power of the capitalists and of the middle man, and lessen the abuses common in the use of private capital. They do this by enabling small private capitalists, like the consumers, to help themselves. The producers' cooperatives are also democratic. They distribute the responsibility, as well as the right to the profits, among those directly interested as producers. Hence, they develop the producer. Ultimately, the producers' cooperatives to a large extent, merge into consumers' cooperatives, that is, the consumers through their cooperatives should become also producers, as they already are to a considerable extent

Third: Cooperative banks & credit unions should be encouraged. Like producing cooperatives, the credit unions lessen the menacing power of the finance, high and low, by [——]. And like consumers' and producers' cooperatives, credit unions are essentially democratic. The direct gains from the capital go to those whose capital is used. The owners of the capital have the ultimate responsibility for its proper use. And the responsibility develops those upon whom it rests.

Fourth: The sphere of private capitalistic control is now and will necessarily be, from time to time, further narrowed, through the assumption by the nation, state or municipality of functions which the public or community concludes cannot properly be performed by or be entrusted to private ownership or management. Such are now the municipally owned water, gas, electric light and power services, and tramways, motor busses, ferrys and wharves—and the gradual substitution of the modern state highway for the privately owned toll-pike.

Fifth: In order that such extension of the government functions may really limit capitalistic control it is essential that the government—national, state and municipal—should free themselves from the need of banker intervention in securing the necessary capital (see "Other Peoples Money"—"Where the Banker is Superfluous").

Sixth: The further limitations upon capitalistic power must be sought through tax legislation which will limit the rate, or amount, of income or accumulation of the individual, and the size of the financial or individual units through which business is done, i.e.

(a) Super—that is, graduated—income taxes, state and national (Here is the best field for curtailing accumulation)

(b) Graduated inheritance taxes—state & national

(c) Super corporation taxes—national—that is making the larger corporation pay a higher prorate on capital or profits, in recognition of bigness as a curse, because of the menace, social and economic, which inheres in size by reason of its dominant position and its power of endurance.

The failure of the anti-trust laws is due largely to

(a) To its failure to recognize size as the danger and aiming only at combinations.

(b) To its adoption of prohibition & the criminal penalty. Illegal combination was inherently difficult to prove. Furthermore, it was not deemed by the community a wrong. Size should not be prohibited, should not be treated as criminal, but should be discouraged by supertaxes & by being thus made less profitable. The equalitarian argument will appeal to many as requiring the handicap, so as to produce a square deal.

Seventh: The special danger of tax exempt capital should be met wherever it exists, by national super-inheritance (estate) taxes.

Eighth: Whether the business be private capitalistic, cooperative or public, the labor union is the essential. Employees must have that protection. On the other hand, consumer cooperation is the best curb on trade union as on capitalistic employer excesses.

Ninth: When the principle of unsolicited life insurance (as promoted by Savings Bank Ins.) becomes widely accepted, but not before, life insurance will be the simplest and most appropriate sphere for governmental (preferably state) activity. If the state does the life insurance business—

(a) the large accumulation of liquid capital now represented by life insurance investment will be (in part) ended

(b) the huge requirements of the governments (which do the insurance) can be met without the issue of bonds, i.e. the insurance reserves will consist of direct obligations of the govt to pay the insurance, instead of indirect obligations to pay the bond which secures payment through the proceeds when sold or paid.

(For working of life insurance in this respect see Business a Profession insurance articles.)

The impoverishing spread

This subject is pre-eminently one for the N.R. because

(1) To treat it properly, it is essential that there be much careful, and some strictly pioneer, investigation.

(2) It will be necessary to attack advertising as practiced, of which that in magazines (see clipping annexed) [3] is only a small part.

Investigation will, I think, confirm that for say ¾ of a century prior to 1900, invention & development in the fields of production and transportation resulted (with temporary interruptions) in a fairly steady trend toward lower costs of production and lower costs to the consumer.

It was a period in which lessening of the cost of production and of transportation was engaging the best minds and offering the largest rewards. And the advances in production and transportation, being directed to the field of the necessaries of life, the standard of living could rise without the cost of living rising.

Since say 1900 the cost of production of transportation has tended to rise. The progress in reducing specific costs in these arts has been small. It has been mainly (a) in reducing costs of production through the elimination of skilled labor, a process socially injurious & tending to a great increase of the contribution of capital clamoring for a return, or (2) in lessened cost in new articles (like the auto) which are largely luxuries. Such reduction in costs on early stages [——] Ford is a genius & a "sport", the exception which tends to prove the rule.

Thus, in general, the cheapening the costs to the consumer of the necessaries of life has not only ceased, but was followed by a tendency to a fairly steady rise, and both the inventive mind and the emoluments of business have gone to the distributor, including in this term the selling department of the manufacturer who, to a greater and greater degree, has assumed the functions of distributor.

Distribution, in its development, should have been attended by reduction in costs & expense similar to the earlier lessening of the cost of production.

Unlike the progress in manufacturing methods which resulted in lower costs, the progress in distributive methods have resulted mainly in greater & wider distribution of particular brands. This expense rate (when all distribution costs are reckoned) has tended to rise. The greater profits are made, not in the main by a larger profit per unit, but by largely increasing the number of units sold by the particular concern.

Essentially the only elements in distribution in which costs have been apparently lessened are

A. By the parcel post. And this has been due, in part

(1) At the expense of the railroads, who were, for a considerable time, and perhaps still are underpaid, and

(2) At the expense of the taxpayer, parcel post being run
at a loss by the P[ost]. O[ffice]. Department.

B. By the Cash & Carry stores, where, in fact, it is the service
which has been lessened:

1. No credit—hence no loss on credits & no bookkeeping
2. No delivery costs &
3. Practically no returns & no exchanges.

From the consumer's standpoint, the legitimate sphere of advertising (in any form) is limited

(a) To creating a volume of demand sufficiently large to secure
the lowest costs of production & distribution.

(b) To introducing a new—useful or enjoyable—article.

(c) To ensuring sale of that which is of deserved quality.

The selling methods pursued, in so far as they entail greater costs,
are not only anti-social, but tend [to] ever increasing extortion
from the consumer (in that they fail to give value) & tend to ever
greater mechanization of industrial life. The nationally advertised
branded goods make the retailer practically an automatic machine,
instead of an expert to whom the consumer pays, in profits, compensation for expert service & trustworthiness. Every brand becomes, in effect, a profit making "fighting brand," & the great
selling expense is, as to the consumer, mere waste. Some chain
stores, notable A & P, are eliminating this waste by establishing
their own brands. If they give to the public the saving [——]
attempt toward proper distribution.

In a large part of the field there is no social justification for the
national widespread market for very many of the trademarked
articles. The distribution costs, notably unnecessary transportation & advertising, should be discouraged.

In this investigation of the wastes, much data may be found in
the recent

(a) "Report of Joint comtee of Agricultural Enquiry"
                67 Cong. 1st Session, Rep. 408

(b) In Federal Commn Reports & Cases

(c) & in Fed. Court Trademark & Unfair Competition Cases,
but there *must be much original* investigation in order that the
facts may be properly ascertained & presented.

The merits of labor saving devices

The funds available to N[ew]. R[epublic]. for research should be applied in part to an attempt to ascertaining [*sic*] whether prevailing tendency toward labor saving is really cost saving. The tendency toward substitution of machine-tenders for skilled operatives etc. is certainly anti-social. I doubt whether (except in factories like Ford's) it is not, in large measure, also uneconomic. That is, whether the limit of machinery & organization efficiency in substitutions for human labor may not have been exceeded, just as the limit in size of greatest efficiency has been, involving as it does

(1) A greatly increased plant charge, of
    (a) interest
    (b) repairs
    (c) depreciation
        obsolescence   and often
    (d) failure of continuous use
(2) Increased organization, supervision expense

And isn't the capitalist and white collar man thus silently exploiting & undermining the overall producer?

1. Of the six memoranda referred to, copies were found in the Frankfurter collections only of the ones dealing with "Capitalism," "On the Spread," and "Labor Saving devices." For LDB's suggestions on "Prohibition," see his letter to Frankfurter, 25 September 1922, and for "Transportation," the one for 24 September.

2. Unfortunately, the only copy of this lengthy memorandum is a poor photocopy of the original draft, with many crossed-out lines, and several completely illegible passages, indicated in this letter by [——].

3. Attached to this memorandum was an article from the *New York Times* of 27 September 1922 dealing with the distribution of more than $95 million in advertising in 1921, placed in seventy-two magazines. Although this figure represented a drop from the $132 million spent in 1920, it was still well above the 1915 figure of nearly $39 million.

To Felix Frankfurter

October 2, 1922 Washington, D.C. [Frankfurter Mss—HLS]

FF: 1. Re N[ew]. R[epublic]. & yours of 30th.

A heavy term begins today and I must jettison all thoughts on N.R. & its policies. It was with this in view that I sent you the various memoranda.[1] My purpose was not to have them submitted to H[erbert]. C[roly]. & the board, but to clarify my own mind as to what was desirable, & to have you take over to yourself the thoughts if, and so far as, they seemed to you sound. I should, therefore, think it inadvisable to send the transportation, or any other of the memoranda, to H.C. in their present form. If, and so far as, you may deem the views expressed valuable and you have the opportunity to present them personally at any meeting of the N.R. board which you may at any time attend, I have of course no objection to your doing whatever your judgment dictates.

2. I have no doubt that H.C. wishes to fight. Possibly he has the will to do so. But I think he would suffer from inhibitions like those to which JWM[ack]. is subject; and that he lacks the fighting force. He really doesn't know how. He is essentially the philosopher, and as indicated in "America as the Promised Land," [2] it is the crying need of a national policy with which he is filled. He does not see, or feel, the greater all pervading problems which Raymond Fosdick [3] presents so forcibly in his Wellesley address,[4] nor does H.C. really feel that the national problems must be tackled by dealing with the myriad of single problems which our so-called civilization has cast upon us.

3. I think the proposed letter to Davis re injunctions is a bit of evidence of H.C. not knowing how. The letter proposed re W.Z. Foster [5] presented a clear case of lawlessness, the Chicago injunction, confirmed by W. after long hearing & about [to be] appealed would furnish J.W.D[avis]. the best possible material for a step back.

4. Re J.H. Clarke's letter, I am reminded of

"Wenn ich ein Künstler wär ich mahlte traun nur hübsche mädchen interessante Frauen" [6]

Holmes J. would have a different opinion of the "unimportant cases."

5. The Ormsby-Gore letter presents unfortunate truths which we must not permit to stay in our Palestinian activities.

6. No, I have not seen E.B. Whitney's brief in the Debs case.

1. See LDB to Frankfurter, 24, 25, and 30 September 1922.
2. LDB probably meant Croly's *The Promise of American Life* (New York, 1909).

3. Raymond Blaine Fosdick (1883–1972) was a New York lawyer and public official who undertook many governmental assignments during his life. See LDB to Frankfurter, 8 November 1925.

4. See "Our Machine Civilization," *Current Opinion* 73 (September 1922): 362–67.

5. William Z. Foster (1881–1961) had been a labor organizer for the American Federation of Labor, and had come to national prominence in the steel strike of 1919. In 1921 he joined the Communist Party of the United States, which he later headed as national chairman from 1932 to 1957. He wrote numerous books and pamphlets dealing with the working classes and with communism.

6. "If I were an artist, I would paint only pretty girls and interesting women." The letter might have been the one, soon to be published, where Mr. Justice Clarke explained his resignation from the Supreme Court. Clarke, sixty-five, enlisted in the cause of the League of Nations.

To Felix Frankfurter

October 19, 1922 Washington, D.C. [Frankfurter Mss—LC]

FF: 1. I delayed writing you about Holmes J. because I wanted to make up my mind. I now think he is in good form & able to carry the load. He looks well, has attended throughout all sessions & conferences and has written opinions with customary speed. He has been often tired physically & at times mentally; but I think this has been due mainly to the unfortunate fact that he has not been able to work as usual in his study because the repairs incident to elevator construction at 1720 [1] are not yet completed. The annoyance of living at the Powhatan & travelling to & from, necessarily by carriage, has put much strain upon him. He should work easily when he gets back to 1720, & has the rest which the next recess will make possible.

2. I humbly withdraw my suggestion for a law periodical index, [2] and suggest instead a society for instructing judges & practitioners in tools of the trade. I had not known of the quarterly index, in existence for 15 years. It is not just what I had in mind; but it is clearly adequate to meet our needs. Of Jones' book I had known, indeed, had bought it a quarter century ago. It had slipped my mind; but, as I now recall, it seemed to me rather poor, perhaps because of the then paucity of material.

3. Rosenbloom's letter of Sept. 28 saying that he would be

here for the proposed Thanksgiving conference is the most encouraging event in recent Palestinian affairs.[3]

4. JWM[ack] may have sent you copy of my letter about [Ferdinand] Fohs. He was here Sunday & I am trying to get him to take a continuous part in P[alestine]. D[evelopment]. C[ouncil]. councils.

5. Our greetings to Marion & best wishes for 37 River St.

1. Holmes lived in Washington at 1720 I Street. Throughout the 1920s, there were frequent expressions of concern from both Frankfurter and LDB over Holmes's physical ability to continue the heavy workload of the Court. Holmes, then eighty-one years old, continued on the Court for another decade before he finally bowed to old age. See LDB to Holmes, 8 December 1922.

2. On 10 October, LDB had suggested to Frankfurter the advisability of establishing an index to legal periodicals so that both bench and bar would have knowledge of the advances in legal theory being expounded in the various law journals. Frankfurter evidently had advised LDB that such an index already existed. In the latter part of the nineteenth century, Leonard A. Jones had published *An Index to Legal Periodical Literature* (Boston, 1888) covering the years up to 1886, and in 1899 he produced a second volume covering 1887–1899. Frank E. Chipman then continued the series, and ultimately five additional volumes appeared irregularly until 1938. In 1928, however, a more comprehensive index began to appear on a yearly basis published by the American Association of Law Librarians. That journal, still in use, is entitled *Index to Legal Periodicals*.

3. See LDB to Julian W. Mack, *et al.*, 6 October 1921, n. 4.

To Felix Frankfurter

October 23, 1922 Washington, D.C. [Frankfurter Mss—HLS]

F. 1. It is fine to have your cases under the I.C.C. Act with a gracious inscription.[1] A furtherwise contribution is made in to-day's decision in the Waste Merchants Case. The decision of the Court of App. of the district (Robb) [2]—and the C[hief]. J[ustice]. dissenting was monstrous.[3]

2. [William] McCurdy will send you extra copy of my ops. as requested. I have not tried him out fully, but think he will measure up to your expectations.

3. As to next year's secretary,[4] I shall leave your discretion to act untrammelled. Wealth, ancestry, and marriage, of course, create presumptions; but they may be overcome.

4. Enclosed by Senator Walsh of Mont. you may not have seen. I am confirmed in the belief:

   (a) that the only effective remedy for U[nited]. S[tates]. S[upreme]. C[ourt]. actions in holding statutes unconstitutional is to change the attitude of judges in approaching the allowed function. Statute-Killers when confronted with an objectionable law say: How can I manage to hold it void?

     Constitutionalists say—How can I manage to sustain it?

   (b) That it was a great mistake to hold that corporations were citizens entitled to sue in Federal Courts on the grounds of citizenship.

5. I wrote E.O. Poole as suggested.

6. I wrote Ben F[lexner]. some time ago and had acknowledgement from him, which indicated that the operation was a serious matter.

7. Had not heard of Deedes' resignation.[5] That is, indeed, serious, and I suppose changes at home may bring other difficulties.

8. That's a very interesting letter of Harold A.

9. [*] are pretty disappointing.

10. Glad Phillips found Louis W[ehle]. helpful.

11. Your talk to the women must have been impressive.

12. I am not impressed at Fosdick's and Manly [Hudson's] report on [*].

13. Yes, Hoover is tired & disappointed. He is doing neither country or himself much good by the talk. He will be happier when he goes West in Nov[ember]. to his River problems.[6]

Our greetings to Marion,

1. Frankfurter had sent the new edition of his *A Selection of Cases Under the Interstate Commerce Act* (Cambridge, 1922). The work was originally published in 1915.

2. Charles Henry Robb (1867–1939) had been a justice of the Court of Appeals for the District of Columbia since 1906.

3. A suit had been brought against the Interstate Commerce Commission by New York waste paper dealers to force a change in the rate schedule through the New York harbor. The I.C.C. had held investigative hearings before turning down the request, and the Supreme Court of the District of Columbia had dismissed the merchants' suit. The Court of Appeals, however, had reversed the commission. In a short opinion for a unanimous Court, LDB reversed the appellate court, holding that the I.C.C. had proper

jurisdiction, it had investigated, and its findings were not subject to court review. *Interstate Commerce Commission* v. *United States* ex rel. *Members of the Waste Merchants Association of New York*, 260 U.S. 32 (1922).

4. See LDB to Frankfurter, 17 June 1923.

5. Sir Wyndham Henry Deedes (see LDB to Julian W. Mack, *et al.*, 28 June 1920, n. 4) had just resigned as civil secretary in Palestine.

6. Hoover convened the Colorado River Commission on 9 November at Sante Fe. The difficult negotiations (see Hoover, *The Memoirs of Herbert Hoover: The Cabinet and the Presidency, 1920–1933* [New York, 1952], ch. 17) paved the way for what later became Hoover Dam.

To Susan Goldmark

November 14, 1922 Washington, D.C. [EBR]

MY DEAR SUSIE: The tie is charming—and even aged I may give myself the pleasure of wearing it—evenings—when off duty.[1]

We had a cheering gathering of friends for Alice's first Monday afternoon yesterday, but it was hard to do without Pauline [Goldmark] and the Norman Hapgoods to whom we had acquired almost a vested right for such occasions.

There was, of course, much talk of the elections.[2] Gov. Allen of Kansas[3] (who happily has less chances now for presidential nomination) said cleverly: "Discontent seeks another sacrifice."

The last two years prove that it is easier to put an administration out, than to keep [one] in. The problems of government have become so difficult, and the progress in solving them is so slow— if any is made—that even wished for overthrows do not satisfy. But there is satisfaction in quite a number of defeats (Kellogg, Beveridge, Calder et al.[4])—and in the election of Al. Smith as essentially a Goldmark possession.[5]   Much love,

1. 13 November had been LDB's sixty-sixth birthday.

2. The Republicans watched helplessly during the 1922 congressional elections, as the majority of seven million won by Warren Harding in 1920 was wiped out by a remarkably strong Democratic resurgence. The Democrats picked up seventy-five seats in the House of Representatives and half-a-dozen in the Senate. The election was widely interpreted as a crippling blow, both to the Republican program and to President Harding's chances for reelection in 1924.

3. Henry Justin Allen (1868–1950) was a popular and colorful Kansas politician. The leader of the Bull Moose element in the state, Allen had placed Roosevelt's name in nomination in 1912 and then led the Kansas

walkout at the Republican convention. While serving in France in 1918, he was elected governor of the state by the largest majority ever recorded in Kansas history up to that point. In 1920 he declined the offer to run on the Harding ticket as the candidate for vice president.

4. Senator Frank B. Kellogg, the Republican senator from Minnesota, lost by 80,000 votes to the Farmer-Labor candidate, Henrik Shipstead. The veteran Indiana Republican Albert Beveridge had been defeated by the Democratic candidate, former Governor Samuel M. Ralston. In New York, William Musgrave Calder (1869–1945), a Republican who had served in one or the other house of Congress since 1905, was defeated by Democrat Royal S. Copeland.

5. Alfred Emanuel Smith (1873–1944) was probably in 1922 at the height of his personal popularity in New York politics. A poor boy from the Lower East Side, Smith had risen through machine politics to the speaker-ship of the state assembly. But from 1911 (the date of the tragic Triangle Shirtwaist Company fire) he became associated with an important group of New York social workers, intellectuals, and reformers—chief among them being the Moskowitzes, the Goldmarks, Frances Perkins, and Florence Kelley. With wide public support, he won the governorship in 1918 but was defeated in the Republican landslide of 1920. In 1922, Smith swept the state with a 390,000-vote majority, and he won again in 1924 and 1926. As governor he compiled an enviable record as a progressive, and in 1924 he was nominated for the presidency by Franklin Roosevelt, who coined in that speech the enduring characterization of Smith as "the Happy Warrior." In 1928, Smith became the first Roman Catholic nominated by any major party for the presidency of the United States, but President Hoover easily defeated him by more than six million votes. While Smith's Catholicism, antiprohibitionism, and big-city image doubtless played a part in his defeat, most historians now feel that it was unlikely any candidate could have overturned Hoover in view of the wave of prosperity sweeping over the United States. After 1928, Smith became increasingly conservative; he broke with his long-time friend Roosevelt, opposed him for the Democratic nomination in 1932, and became a vociferous and increasingly harsh critic of New Deal liberalism in the mid-1930s. Toward the end of the decade, however, he was again reunited with Roosevelt when he backed the President's fight against isolation. There are a number of biographical studies, the best probably being Matthew and Hannah Josephson, *Al Smith: Hero of the Cities* (Boston, 1969) or Oscar Handlin, *Al Smith and His America* (Boston, 1958). See also David M. Burner, *The Politics of Provincialism: The Democratic Party in Transition, 1918–1932* (New York, 1968). Two of LDB's friends also collaborated on a biographical appreciation: Norman Hapgood and Henry Moskowitz, *Up from the City Streets: Alfred E. Smith* (New York, 1927).

To Oliver Wendell Holmes, Jr.

December 8, 1922 Washington, D.C. [Holmes Mss]

For O.W.H.

Twenty years after—
Still the dash of a D'Artagnan.[1]

1. On 4 December 1902, Holmes had taken his seat on the Supreme Court

To Felix Frankfurter

December 14, 1922 Washington, D.C. [Frankfurter Mss—LC]

My dear Felix: Re yours of 7th & 12th

1. You and Pound know from my letter of last term how, in my opinion, Law School needs should be financed, and why. There are special reasons why funds for Criminal Law & Legislation chair should be raised by a fairly wide appeal to the successful & influential alumni and friends of legal education. If the School adopts a plan on those general lines for raising the money, I shall, of course, be glad to contribute, and should be disposed to subscribe such sum as you and Pound think would be most helpful in inducing a fairly wide participation.[1] If, however, the School concludes to pursue the "easier way" and appeal to Foundations for the whole or part of the funds needed, my disposition would be to do nothing but regret the lost opportunity.

2. I think it would be better for you *not* to write the C[hief]. J[ustice]. about the report of your action re P.B. Your letter to his son [2] ought to have done all that can properly be done to set matters right.

3. Opinions in the Cave in Case [3] have gone to you today (also copy of the record & briefs which please return). I shall be glad to hear what you & Pound think of this.

4. Enclosed copy of War Department letter of 5th (which came after opinions were delivered) may interest you and show that adherence to Ct Claims procedure has practical value.

5. I see (through driving home via Charles) more of H[olmes] than heretofore, but there is nothing I can say on the subject you suggest & have in mind.

6. When C.J. is in minority, the senior associate who is not is supposed to assign case, but, in fact, the C.J. is apt to do so.

7. I had not known of offer to Miller. I am told our Clerk's office says M.C.J. will be nominated.[4]

8. I fear little is to be hoped from Governors' Conference.[5]

9. Ernst Freund will be disappointed about Ill[inois]. Constitution vote, but I am not.[6]

10. Vernon Kellogg says W.A. White is to write on some economic subject

Tell him to postpone that & write on Free Speech.[7]

11. Those Mass. Child Labor figures are pretty bad.
Enclosed Shipping Board articles, cowritten by Dean, seem to me very clever.[8] Could you get him to write on Pitney. It might educate the bench & it would be an act of Justice to Pit.[9]

1. See next letter.

2. Robert Alphonso Taft (1889–1953), son of the Chief Justice, was in 1922 practising law in Cincinnati and serving his first term in the Ohio House of Representatives, of which body he was to be speaker in 1926. In 1930 he was elected to a single term in the Ohio Senate, and in 1938 he began his fifteen-year tenure in the United States Senate. By 1945, Taft was the acknowledged leader of the conservative wing of the Republican Party, although he was far from being the reactionary some of his critics made him out to be. He was far less flexible in foreign affairs than in domestic matters, and was a critic of the United Nations, foreign aid, and many of the postwar alliances. A man of strong convictions, he reaped widespread criticism for his opposition to the Nuremberg Trials of Nazi leaders—he claimed that there was no precedent for such action in international law. Taft tried unsuccessfully to gain his party's presidential nomination in 1944, 1948, and 1952. See James T. Patterson, *Mr. Republican: A Biography of Robert A. Taft* (Boston, 1972). The "P.B." referred to is probably Pierce Butler (see LDB to Frankfurter, 3 January 1923, n. 5).

3. A Pennsylvania state law requiring a certain percentage of coal deposits to be left in place so as to avoid mine cave-ins had been challenged as violating a contract that predated the passage of the law—the contract allowed full exploitation of the mineral resources. Holmes, speaking for the Court, said that the state had exceeded the limits of its police power in voiding the contract. LDB dissented and argued that "coal in place is land; and the right of the owner to use his land is not absolute." See *Pennsylvania Coal Company* v. *Mahon*, 260 *U.S.* 393 (1922); LDB's dissent is at 416.

4. Speculation on a replacement for Justice Pitney (see n. 9 below).

5. On this day a special Governors' Conference on Law Enforcement opened in White Sulphur Springs, West Virginia. Despite numerous speeches against prohibition by individual participants, the conference ultimately is-

sued a mild statement promising support to the federal government in enforcing prohibition.

6. A special constitutional convention had been called in Illinois in 1920 to revise the existing document, which dated from 1870. The revision, in which Ernst Freund had a hand, would have done much to streamline the administration of the state government and courts, but it included two controversial provisions: one opening the way for state income tax and the other reducing the influence of Cook County (Chicago) in the state legislature. On these issues the proposed constitution was defeated by more than 700,000 votes on 12 December.

7. William Allen White (1868–1944) had purchased the Emporia (Kansas) *Daily and Weekly Gazette* in 1895 and had made it into one of the most widely read and quoted country papers in the nation. In 1896 he had gained national fame with his attack on Populism in the editorial "What's the Matter with Kansas?" White published a number of books of short stories and essays, and he was a frequent contributor to the periodical press. In 1913 he won a Pulitzer Prize. White backed Theodore Roosevelt in the Bull Moose split of 1912 and he became a national committeeman of the Progressive Party. In 1923 he ran as an independent candidate for governor in Kansas on an anti-Ku Klux Klan platform. See his *Autobiography* (New York, 1946).

8. No articles on the shipping situation by Acheson were published.

9. Pursuant to a special act of Congress, Mahlon Pitney had just sent in his resignation from the Supreme Court. Acheson did not write on Pitney. To succeed Pitney, Harding named Edward Terry Sanford (1865–1930), a District Court Judge from Tennessee.

To Felix Frankfurter

December 19, 1922 Washington, D.C. [Frankfurter Mss—LC]

MY DEAR FELIX: Re yours of 17th

I understand that you and Pound have under consideration the plan of raising for the Law School, a fund of twenty thousand (20,000) dollars a year for ten years, of which $10,000 yearly shall be for a chair in Criminal Law and $10,000 for a chair in Legislation; and that all shall be raised by contributions from members of the bench and the bar.

If this fund is so raised, I shall be glad to contribute, of that amount, one thousand (1000) dollars a year for the period of ten years, that is, annually five hundred (500) dollars for the chair in Criminal Law and five hundred (500) dollars for the chair in Legislation.[1]

1. In his report for the academic year 1923–24, Roscoe Pound called for the establishment of professorships at the Harvard Law School in criminal law and legislation, but he was evidently successful only in his bid for the former. By the beginning of the 1928 school year, Harvard had established an Institute of Criminal Law, headed by Professor Francis Bowes Sayre. A number of years later this post was converted into the Roscoe Pound Professorship of Criminology. There is no record of any endowed chair in legislation, although a course was introduced in that field. See LDB to Frankfurter, 2 April 1922.

To William Howard Taft

December 26, 1922 Washington, D.C. [VanDevanter Mss]

MY DEAR CHIEF JUSTICE:

No. 86 [1]

I agree with you that V[anDevanter]'s [2] changes will make our record more consistent with the statute than the opinion as written. But they also make clearer that the proper course for us would be to send the case back to the Commission to make further findings, so that they can, if they wish, hear additional evidence.

The Com[missio]n should get at the same time a scolding for not making fuller findings of fact.

I hope you can effect other more radical change in the opinion.

Cordially,

Papers returned herewith.

1. In *Federal Trade Commission* v. *Curtis Publishing Co.*, 260 *U.S.* 568 (1922), the Court upheld an F.T.C. ruling prohibiting the Curtis Company from enforcing a wholesalers' agreement under which only Curtis publications could be handled. But while agreeing with the Commission's ruling, the Court chastised the F.T.C. for impinging upon the court's domain in determining what is fair or unfair competition. Taft and LDB entered a "doubting" opinion, not a dissent, questioning just how far the Court would be willing to go in questioning F.T.C. functions.

2. Willis VanDevanter (1859–1941) had first practiced law in his native Indiana before moving to Cheyenne in the Wyoming territory. There he served in the territorial legislature, and as chief justice of the new state's Supreme Court. From 1897 to 1903 he was assistant attorney general of the United States, and then went on to the Court of Appeals; in 1910 Taft had elevated him to the United States Supreme Court. Although a member of the conservative bloc, he and LDB maintained cordial relations. VanDe-

vanter was the first of the conservative justices to retire after the Roosevelt court packing affair in 1937.

To Woodrow Wilson

December 27, 1922 Washington, D.C. [Wilson Mss]

MY DEAR MR. WILSON: The year now closing brought you, after much sorrow, the satisfaction which came with the reawakening of the American people. May the years to come bring you and others the happiness which would attend the realization of your ideals.   Most cordially,

To Alfred Brandeis

January 3, 1923 Washington, D.C. [Brandeis Mss, M 4–4]

DEAR AL: Re yours 29.

The Hadassah is all right—but the Keren H[ayesod]. is all wrong and I think, as they combine the two, you may properly decline.[1]

Alice is delighted to hear that Fanny has also discovered the Goldmark Concerto. We did, two months ago through the Victor catalogue.[2]

I can't understand where all this (and other) money comes from.[3] We are certainly not earning it as a nation. I think we must be exploiting about 80 percent of Americans, for the benefit of the other 20 percent. And that all the new bonds—national, state, and municipal—are simply a mortgage held by the few on the many.

· 1. Alfred Brandeis had asked his brother whether or not he should contribute to a joint Keren Hayesod and Hadassah fund-raising drive in Louisville.

2. Probably a recording of the well known Violin Concerto in A Minor, by Karl Goldmark (1830–1915), the distinguished German composer.

3. LDB had enclosed a newspaper clipping announcing huge production increases in automobiles for 1922. In eleven months, production had reached over 2.3 million, compared to 2.2 million for all of 1920, the record year to that point. In November 1922, twice as many cars had been produced as in November 1920.

To Felix Frankfurter

January 3, 1923 Washington, D.C. [Frankfurter Mss—LC]

F.F.: 1. The letter to Cobb[1] is most effective. I wish he would ask leave to publish it.

Possibly Norman H[apgood]. could make him see the need of attaching a good lawyer to the World. As you know, H. and I spoke of Dean [Acheson] for the job. Dean could act specifically on Supreme Court decisions.

2. Holmes J. felt so perky yesterday that he insisted on getting out of the carriage yesterday to walk with me from 12th & H home. And he said today that he felt better for the walk.

3. As to Cave-in etc.[2] there are indications that Benjamin is accentuating the tendency of age to conservatism.

4. Isn't Baker really something of a Toto [*]? What does Marion say?

5. At the Chief's dinner of the Circuit Judges Friday, I was surprised to find (a) that Gilbert,[3] the old gent, reads the Nation, is keen against suppression of free speech and for amnesty. (b) that Baker J.[4] is really a polite reactionary, the kind that reads Puck, and thinks he is progressive.

6. That clipping about Wheeler gives me great joy. I return it, so that you can use it when you introduce him to a Boston audience.

7. Talk with the Circuit Judges far more than confirms the guess that, with the exception of N.Y. & one or two other states, the appointment of new judges was wholly unjustifiable & that some of the prospective appointments are mere pork.

8. Pierce Butler makes a good impression.[5]

9. The Bulletin of A.A.U.P. goes to you under another cover. It is a fearful story which, I hope, will be written up not only for the American people but in some English magazine.[6] I think Butler and his ilk would appreciate their crime better if it were discussed in England than through any American comment.

1. Frank Irving Cobb (1869–1923), for many years an insider in progressive circles, was the editor of the *New York World*.

2. See LDB to Frankfurter, 14 December 1922, n. 3.

3. William Ball Gilbert (1847–1931) had practiced law in Portland, Ore-

gon, before becoming a federal district judge in 1892; in 1912 Taft had elevated him to the Circuit Court of Appeals.

4. Frank Elisha Baker (1860–1924) had been a judge on the Indiana Supreme Court when he was named to the Court of Appeals in 1902.

5. Pierce Butler (1866–1939), a Minnesota lawyer, had been named to the
Supreme Court in November 1922; he had taken his seat on the day previously, and soon was aligned with the Court's conservative faction.

6. Under the title "Columbia University vs. Professor Cattell," the *AAUP
Bulletin* 7 (November 1922): 433–53, published documents relating to the
wartime dismissal of Professor James M. Cattell. President Nicholas Murray
Butler and the Columbia trustees had fired Cattell in 1917 for "treason,"
"sedition," and "opposition to the enforcement of the laws of the United
States." The celebrated case, in which the AAUP issued a severe censure
to Columbia, resulted in Charles Beard's resignation from the University
and the AAUP's publication of *Academic Freedom in War Time* (in the
February–March *Bulletin* for 1918). The documents reprinted here dealt
with Professor Cattell's attempt to secure his pension after twenty-six years
of continuous service at Columbia. See Richard Hofstadter and Walter P.
Metzger, *The Development of Academic Freedom in the United States*
(New York, 1955): 499–502.

To Felix Frankfurter

January 4, 1923 Washington, D.C. [Frankfurter Mss–LC]

F.F.: *First:* Here is my answer to Big Business & High Finance
with their Stock Dividends and Anti-trust decisions & their repeal
of Excess Profits & Reduction of Super income tax laws.[1]

Put on all corporations (except utilities including railroads) a
supercorporation tax, progressive in rate

(1) Base it on all values over $1,000,000

(2) Include in values bonds as well as stocks & surplus & un-
divided profits

3) Make the rate very low at $1,000,000, but in the higher
stages quite accute [*sic*].

4) Life insurance should be included, but have more favored
treatment. The argument:

The only justification to the big unit is supposed greater efficiency. If they have it, they can afford to pay the greater tax,
making it a sort of excess profits tax. (See every prospectus of
proposed or effected consolidations.) If they are not earning
more, than [*sic*] they have no justification for existence.

This tax would eliminate the judicial factor of the Sherman

Law Cases, the constitutional quibbles, the accountants' juggling, the [Justice] department's shortcomings. It is for all practical purposes, certain in amount.

Second: My answer to the State & Municipal Tax Exempt Bonds (really resulting, so far as Federal taxation goes, from Evans v. Gore) [2] is not the propose[d] amendment [3] (which would in large part paralyze development through State, as distinguished from federal control) but a super inheritance tax, progressive in rate, on tax exempt securities, held at or within 5 years of death. See Watson case, 254 U.S. 122.[4]

1. See LDB to Frankfurter, 20 November 1923.

2. In *Evans* v. *Gore,* 253 *U.S.* 245 (1920), a United States District Judge had claimed that, insofar as his federal salary was concerned, the federal income tax following upon ratification of the Sixteenth Amendment (1913) violated that part of the Constitution prohibiting the reduction of judges' compensation while in office (Art. III, Sec. 1). In the majority opinion, Justice VanDevanter concluded that since the tax had been created after the judge had taken office, it could not apply to his salary. Both Holmes and LDB dissented, and Holmes argued (at 264) that the constitutional clause did not apply in this case, since it did not single out the judiciary for any specific threatening purpose. Moreover, in Holmes's and LDB's opinion, the Sixteenth Amendment creating the income tax justified its imposition.

3. State and municipal bonds were normally exempt from federal income taxes. As a result, many wealthy people were able to avoid taxation by investing their capital in such bonds. During the 1920s there were several proposals, including one to amend the constitution, to restrict the issuance of tax-free securities by local and state governments.

4. New York law distinguished between property in an inheritance that had been taxed during the owner's lifetime and property that had not yet borne such taxation, and the state levied a heavier inheritance tax on the latter. In a case challenging this law as discriminatory, LDB had delivered the Court's decision in a three-page opinion that held the law to be reasonable. See *Watson* et al. v. *State Comptroller of New York,* 254 *U.S.* 122 (1920).

To Learned Hand

January 7, 1923 Washington, D.C. [Hand Mss]

MY DEAR HAND: It was good of you to tell me of your assents to the dissents.

We are sorry to learn that there is no probability of your and

Mrs. Hand's coming soon. There are many things that need dis-cussion. It's a great pity that he in authority doesn't summon you to come and stay. That would help much.[1]　　Most cordially,

1. Learned Hand's name came up for practically every vacancy on the Supreme Court for nearly thirty years. In this case, no doubt, LDB's wish that Hand be appointed was occasioned by the fact that no successor had yet been chosen for retired Justice Pitney (see LDB to Frankfurter, 14 December 1922, n. 9).

To Woodrow Wilson

January 22, 1923 Washington, D.C. [Wilson Mss]

MY DEAR MR. WILSON: Some passages in your admirable "What is Progress?" leads me to send you enclosed opinions on the Cave-in law.[1]　　Cordially,

1. See LDB to Felix Frankfurter, 14 December 1922, n. 3. Wilson replied: "I do not happen to remember having published anything under the title 'What is Progress', but I am none the less pleased that you should have been struck by anything I have written. . . ." See next letter.

To Woodrow Wilson

January 26, 1923 Washington, D.C. [Wilson Mss]

MY DEAR MR. WILSON: Herewith "What is Progress?"
Now will you confess?[1]　　Most cordially,

1. The piece that LDB sent to Wilson on 26 January is not to be found in either the Brandeis or Wilson collections. On 28 January the former president replied: "I can't 'confess', because I still do not admit having written an essay 'What Is Progress'. I can only conjecture that what you have sent me was extracted or compiled out of some extemporaneous address which I have forgotten. . . . Fortunately I subscribe to the sentiments expressed in the paper, and am free to hope that it will at least do nobody any harm."

To William Howard Taft

January 27, 1923 Washington, D.C. [Taft Mss]

MY DEAR CHIEF JUSTICE: Re 585.[1] Opinion returned herewith.
I think the decision clearly right, the argument on the merits sound and persuasive, indeed unanswerable.

But I think it would be very unfortunate to decide that Barton et al., as individuals, could, under any circumstances, be enjoined from expressing their opinions on a matter which they believe is properly before them.

I think the Board qua board is suable—perhaps an injunction or prohibition may lie to prevent the board from exceeding its jurisdiction. But we ought not to say that it may not publish its opinion, and we don't have to do so, to approve the judgment below.

I hope we can talk this over.

1. *Pennsylvania Railroad Co.* v. *United States Railroad Labor Board*, 261 *U.S.* 72 (1923). The Railroad Transportation Act of 1920 had given the Labor Board the right to make findings and recommendations in labor disputes, but not the power to enforce them; the intention of Congress had been that the weight of public opinion would lead the railroads to accept the board recommendations. The Pennsylvania Railroad had sued to prevent the board from publishing its findings, and challenged the right of Congress to create such an agency. Taft, speaking for a unanimous Court, upheld the right of Congress to create the board and to invest it with its designated functions.

To Alice Goldmark Brandeis

February 4, 1923 Washington, D.C. [EBR]

DEAREST: It was good to get your letter—and, later, to know from Eliz[abeth]'s telephone that you are to have another day at Annapolis & together.

I have practical solitude, save a call on Holmes J. this afternoon. (He has finished for the printer his introduction to John Wigmore's book & read it to me.[1] It is really good) and he seems in good form. I rode on his beautiful elevator which reminds of the sacred precincts of a safe deposit vault.

Met Senator [Atlee] Pomerene while walking this AM. Not a great man. He is to talk on ship subsidy next week.

For dinner, breakfast, luncheon company I have had John Morley, an interesting chap.[2]   Lovingly,

1. John Henry Wigmore (1863–1943) was the dean of the Northwestern University Law School for nearly three decades. A prolific writer on legal topics, Wigmore was particularly noted for his work on evidence. The book for which Holmes wrote the introduction was Wigmore and Albert

Kocourek, eds., *The Rational Basis of Legal Institutions* (New York, 1923).

2. LDB no doubt meant that he was engaged in reading one of John M. Morley's many biographies of public figures. The prolific Morley (1838–1923) was one of LDB's favorite writers.

To Felix Frankfurter

February 19, 1923 Washington, D.C. [Frankfurter Mss—LC]

DEAR FELIX: One of the most important cases set for 28th was reassigned today. The list is so uncertain that I think you had better have the Clerk wire you Friday, and perhaps again on Saturday.[1]

Holmes' Arkansas Case today is a satisfaction.[2]

I am enclosing the galley of the New England Divisions Case which you may care to see speedily.[3]

1. Frankfurter was scheduled to argue before the Court in the federal minimum wage case; see next letter.

2. Arkansas sought to impose a 5 percent "occupation tax" on a Missouri-based company doing business in Arkansas in order to equalize rates with the higher-priced Arkansas firms. The Court, speaking through Holmes, voided the lien as being not a true tax but an exaction. *St. Louis Cotton Compress Co.* v. *Arkansas*, 260 U.S. 346 (1922).

3. The Transportation Act of 1920 gave the Interstate Commerce Commission power to establish rate zones, to consider the needs of particular carriers in setting rates, and to divide returns in different ratios among joint carriers. LDB delivered the unanimous opinion of the Court upholding the law and the I.C.C. powers, declaring that the rate division was not in violation of the due process clause. See *New England Divisions Case*, 261 U.S. 525 (1923).

To Felix Frankfurter

March 5, 1923 Washington, D.C. [Frankfurter Mss—HLS]

DEAR FELIX: It is good to know that Marion & you think well of Chatham for the summer.

Elizabeth fears she must miss your Minimum wage argument.[1] Friday she was operated on—appendicitis—after 36 painful hours. She is doing finely & is comfortable at the Emergency Hospital. We were fortunate in having her here, with Dr. Mitchell & Dr.

Parker at hand. Six days earlier she was in the snow-covered
Mountains of Maryland & Pennsylvania.

It is a relief to have Congress adjourn, & the President away. Of
him I hear even worse things.[2]

1. A statute adopted by Congress in 1918 authorized the Minimum Wage
Board in the District of Columbia to establish wage minimums sufficient "to
women workers to maintain them in good health and to protect their
morals." LDB disqualified himself from this case, since his daughter Elizabeth was secretary of the board, but as Samuel Konefsky notes, his dissent
would probably have borne a great resemblance to the "Brandeis brief"
filed by Frankfurter, who defended the statute on behalf of the National
Consumers' League. (See Felix Frankfurter and Francis H. Stephens, *District of Columbia Minimum Wage Cases. Briefs* . . . , 2 vols. [New York,
1923]). The case was heard on 14 March 1923 and on 9 April the Court
handed down a five-to-three ruling invalidating the statute. Mr. Justice
Sutherland dismissed the many authorities cited by Frankfurter in support
of such legislation and claimed that such evidence had no relevance to the
Court. Holmes wrote a forceful dissent, and even Chief Justice Taft could
not support Sutherland's "Spencerian edict." See *Adkins* v. *Children's Hospital*, 261 *U.S.* 525 (1923). A brilliant exposition of the case is Thomas
Reed Powell, "The Judiciality of Minimum Wage Legislation," 37 *Harvard
Law Review* 545 (1924). Not until 1937 did the Court again uphold wage
legislation, in *West Coast Hotel* v. *Parish*, 300 *U.S.* 379 (1937), where Chief
Justice Hughes relied heavily upon the reasoning in Holmes's 1923 dissent.

2. The administration of Warren G. Harding was beginning to crumble,
and the President himself left the Capitol for a vacation in Florida. Although no major scandals had yet erupted, the capital was rife with rumors
about corruption in the Cabinet and in high offices generally, rumors that
would ultimately coalesce into the so-called Teapot Dome Scandal; several
members of the administration were indicted for attempted bribery in order
to lease oil-rich government lands to private companies. The best exposition of the entire situation is Burl Noggle, *Teapot Dome: Oil and Politics
in the 1920's* (Baton Rouge, 1962).

To Alice Harriet Grady

April 1, 1923 Washington, D.C. [Grady Mss]

AHG: Your report on the C. H. Jones talk with Loring is fine.
He'll have to succumb on the Infantile Policies.

You remind of Antaeus—only they never throw you to the
ground; and Hercules would have had a hard time throttling you
on high.

I am eager for the March report on [Savings Bank Insurance] business written.

To Felix Frankfurter

April 6, 1923 Washington, D.C. [Frankfurter Mss—HLS]

F.F.: 1. I had a good talk with Mack whom you will be seeing these days. Yes, DeHaas is doing good thinking. I assume he is sending you carbons of his letters to me.

2. I hope, in the readjustment of courses, you may be able to shift "Restraints of Trade" to one who would enjoy it more, & yourself get on to state & federal jurisdictions. There is [a] fair bit of work to be done there and great need. Some of the re-working of state jurisdiction which our western Courts of Appeal have been guilty of I will talk to you of later.

3. I should be surprised if the business boom does not break in time to help the Democrats in the 1924 campaign. The RR program proclaimed by the Executives is positive evidence of their folly.[1] The equipment is undoubtedly needed. But they should have ordered it 1–2½ years ago when prices were low & business slack. It is just 50 years this spring since I witnessed the Vienna Bankrott [2] which preceded the crash of '73.

4. Mrs. [Elizabeth Glendower] Evans writes that Marion wants to know whether there are cooking possibilities in the Annex [in Chatham]. As I understand, No. It is strictly a "Season sale," bedrooms, garage or woodshed, etc. There may be possibilities of leasing for her mother & sisters nearby. But I guess nothing can be done about that till we are on the spot.

5. I hope you will let Marion compare, as manifestation of culture, the Harvard Club 25th Annual Meeting leaflet with the Amalgamated 1923 Almanac.

6. Alice is, I think, gaining, but still slowly. Eliz[abeth]. is gradually regaining her strength.

I thought Marion might like to preserve this in her strong box.[3]

Marion will find, in the Webb's "Decay of Capitalistic Civilization" [4] much support for her views on advertising.

---

1. The railroads had recently announced that they would spend over $700 million during 1923 for new equipment and improvements, an increase of more than $200 million over their normal expenditures.

2. "bankruptcy."

3. LDB enclosed a clipping in which a number of Republicans had urged President Harding to hire a press agent so he could better "sell himself" to the people.

4. Sidney and Beatrice Webb, *The Decay of Capitalist Civilization* (New York, 1923).

To Woodrow Wilson

April 15, 1923 Washington, D.C. [Wilson Mss]

MY DEAR MR. WILSON: I enclose, as you requested, a statement of the proposition which we discussed;[1] also the opinion in the Vigliotti case to which I referred.[2]

The attainment of our American ideals is impossible unless the States guard jealously their field of governmental action and perform zealously their appropriate duties.   Most cordially,

1. LDB enclosed a short statement which attempted to divide authority for prohibition enforcement between state and federal officers. The position taken in the memorandum is identical to that taken in LDB to Felix Frankfurter, 25 September 1922 and 24 October 1923. The editors wish to thank Arthur S. Link for his help in identifying this memorandum.

2. *Vigliotti* v. *Commonwealth of Pennsylvania*, 258 *U.S.* 403 (1922). The Supreme Court upheld the conviction of Vigliotti under the Brooks Law, a Pennsylvania statute for enforcing prohibition. The defendant had erroneously claimed that the Pennsylvania law, which required licenses, was rendered null by the Volstead Act. The court, speaking through LDB, held that the state law was an appropriate exercise of the state's police powers.

To George Henry Soule [Draft]

April 22, 1923 Washington, D.C. [Brandeis Mss, SC 6–2]

MY DEAR SOULE:[1] Yes, the paper interests me much.[2]

Your conclusion that labor's share is less[en]ing confirms my impressions.

I guess that in agriculture the increased share went not to man, but to property & to the machinery & the cost of maintaining it. We have not only greatly increased value of the land, but greatly increased cost of equipment repairs, [*] supplies, fertilizer & depreciation charges & taxes. With the gross proceeds of wheat per acre at $14.10 in 1922, as reported, I don't see how more than $7 per acre can be left for man

I guess also that those who "live by owning" got a larger share of the increased product than your statement suggests—although not necessarily a larger percentage of return on current value. Because present value represents partly unearned increment and partly ploughing of operating expenses creating good will, trademark etc.

Distribution took of course the main increase. For a quarter of a century it has absorbed an ever increasing percentage of the brains & the profits of business. And it represents largely social waste. In Distribution we have created a body of tax farmers more oppressive, because insidious & efficient, than those of old. I guess the only remedy lies in educating the public. Here is the job for Stuart Chase.[3]

Teach the public

1. To buy through consumers cooperatives [4]
2. To refuse to buy any nationally advertised brand & to look with suspicion upon every advertised article
3. Start a buyers' strike at any rise in price of any staple article of common consumption.

The Consumer is servile, self-indulgent, indolent, ignorant.

Let the buyer beware.

1. George Henry Soule (b. 1887) had been one of the bright young men associated with the *New Republic* since 1914; he went on to be an editor of the journal from 1924 to 1947. Soule had a distinguished career as a social investigator and writer on economic topics. His best known works are *The Ideas of the Great Economists* (New York, 1952) and *Prosperity Decade: From War to Depression 1917–1929* (New York, 1947).

2. Probably Soule's paper before the American Economic Association, "Productivity Factor in Wage Determinations," published in *The American Economic Review* 13 (March 1923): suppl. 129–40. For a condensation and summary, see Soule's article, "What the Worker Doesn't Get," *New Republic* 35 (30 May 1923): 12–13.

3. Stuart Chase (b. 1888) was a popular writer on economic and social topics, known for his incisive wit. One of Chase's primary interests was consumer affairs, and he was a founder of Consumers' Research, Inc.

4. See LDB to Felix Frankfurter, 30 September 1922.

To Alice Goldmark Brandeis

May 8, 1923 Washington, D.C. [EBR]

DEAREST: Your Sunday letter has come with its glorious report. Even Vandy [1] would be satisfied.

My friendly relations with my "brethren" took a new advance yesterday, when I asked McR[eynolds] to write the dissent in a case in which we two are unable to concur with the majority. He seemed greatly pleased at being asked.[2]

Next Saturday has been specifically assigned for the exclusive consideration of my elaborate memo;—so you see we are very friendly.

I plan to send Louis Wehle a signatured copy of the Court (which you would spurn).

At this rate, you will outwork me at Chatham.

Hayes Robbins is coming in to dine.　　Lovingly,

1. Willis VanDevanter.
2. Perhaps for the case of *Pennsylvania* v. *West Virginia*, 262 *U.S.* 553. The case involved a 1919 West Virginia law prohibiting the sale of natural gas to other states until West Virginia's needs had been fully met. Pennsylvania alleged that the law constituted entrance by a state into the reserved arena of interstate commerce; and the Court upheld Pennsylvania. LDB and McReynolds (who, in the end, filed separate but similar dissents) argued that the Court had no jurisdiction in the case and that, as there was no real "controversy" and no real "parties," this was hardly a case at all. Holmes dissented on an interpretation of whether the untapped gas being controlled was actually in interstate commerce. See LDB to Felix Frankfurter, 17 June 1923 and 20 November 1923.

To Felix Frankfurter

May 14, 1923 Washington, D.C. [Frankfurter Mss—LC]

F.F.:

1. I hope Guthrie has favored you with his book of addresses & that you have read the one on the Lusk Laws.[1]

In this connection read:
- (a) Editorial Comm[ercial]. & Fin[ancial]. Chronicle, May 12/23, p. 2049 [2]
- (b) Mahaffy, Greek Life & Thought, pp. 143 [3]

2. Glad to see the Harv[ard]. Law Review performing in May issue its function of enlightened public opinion on U.S.S.C.[4] With 20 such organs, & the service continued throughout 10 years, we may hope to see some impression made. There must be persistence.

Who wrote the article on Portsmouth Case? [5] It is very well done.

3. I will bring full set U.S.S.C. reports to C[hatham]. Do you want anything else?

4. When you have Mahaffy in hand read also:
    (a) On old men in government pp. 3–5
    (b) On courage p. 55 [6]

5. Hope Pound is really out of Filene Foundation.

5/15   6. What you say of Alfred Cohen [7] & Rockefeller Foundation is very interesting.

7. A pretty sad note of Massingham.

8. I shall be glad to see E. Angell.[8]

9. Yes. [*] tax case is good. Will tell you about that & others some day, with some reflections on the ultimate.

Greetings to Marion,

---

1. William Dameron Guthrie (1859–1935) had just retired as Ruggles Professor of Constitutional Law at Columbia and had published *The League of Nations and Miscellaneous Addresses* (New York, 1923), The so-called Lusk Committee investigated "Bolshevism" in New York state during the Red Scare. Guthrie's book contains two essays on the Lusk Committee, both of them justifying the expulsion from the New York Assembly of five Socialist members (see LDB to Learned Hand, 20 January 1920).

2. The *Chronicle* had commended several new organizations that had been established to foster greater respect in the United States for law, order, and the Constitution. Among these were the Liberal League, founded by Nicholas Murray Butler, Bishop Manning and others, and the Minute Men of the Constitution, headed by Charles G. Dawes, former Director of the Budget.

3. Sir John Pentland Mahaffy, *Greek Life and Thought from the Age of Alexander to the Roman Conquest* (London and New York, 1887). On page 143 Mahaffy described the attempt of the ancient Greeks to control thought. The effort "made by the extreme democratic party" was to prohibit the keeping of any philosophic school without the permission of the council and popular assembly. There followed "a great exodus of philosophers," and the law was repealed within a year.

4. Manley O. Hudson, "The Turntable Cases in the Federal Courts," 36 *Harvard Law Review* 826 (1923), dealt with two recent Supreme Court cases, *United Zinc & Chemical Co.* v. *Britt,* 258 *U.S.* 268 (1922), and *New*

York, New Haven & Hartford R.R. Co. v. *Fruchter*, 43 *Sup. Ct. Rep.* 38 (1922). Hudson argued that the decisions weakened liabilities of land occupiers for injuries to small children who inadvertently came on to the land. Holmes wrote the majority opinion in the first case, in which he was joined by LDB.

5. In the same issue appeared an explicatory note on *Portsmouth Harbor Land & Hotel Co.* v. *United States*, 250 *U.S.* 1 (1919), which had been reargued at 260 *U.S.* 326 (1922). In both instances the Court, speaking through Mr. Justice Holmes, held that the discharge of artillery on government firing ranges did not constitute damages to neighboring property interests. LDB dissented from the opinion, arguing that the attendant noise and discomfort did constitute damages. As usual, these notes, written by law students, were unsigned, and there is no copy of a reply from Frankfurter indicating the identity of the author.

6. Mahaffy described the sad state of Grecian politics at the death of Alexander as having been due to the rule of elderly men in nearly all of the city-states. "If the laws were not obsolete, the politicians were so. It is one of the most signal of the many instances in history of the vast mischief done by the government of old men." The reference to courage dealt with Demetrius Polioiketes (337–281 B.C.), who aroused the valor of his men by his own personal example and used his intelligence to create an aura of leadership.

7. Alfred Morton Cohen (1859–1949) was a distinguished Cincinnati attorney and a leading figure in B'nai Brith.

8. Ernest Angell (1889–1973), a Harvard Law School graduate, was in 1923 a New York lawyer. During the 1930s he worked with the Securities Exchange Commission, and he was later a leading figure in the American Civil Liberties Union.

To Felix Frankfurter

May 20, 1923 Washington, D.C. [Frankfurter Mss—LC]

DEAR FELIX: 1. Let me know what records & brief[s] of this term you want, so that they may be segregated before the shipment goes to the University of Chicago.

2. I am glad of your letter in the Nation. M.O.H. deserved a jog.[1]

3. The Challenge to Hoover in the latest N[ew]. R[epublic]. is admirable.[2] It has all the qualities I plead [*sic*] for last September, — i.a. notable distinction.[3]

The writer should collect material from Hoover's occasional addresses, May 1922 to May 1924, for an article to appear May 1924 entitled

"But the World's Wise are not Wise"
& make him swallow then his voluminous prophecies.

The article on China is also very good.[4]

4. I expect to send you by parcel post tomorrow some [*] Case brief & other material for use at Harvard & other law schools, as you deem best.

5. Recent numbers raise N.R. to a higher level. If Bruce Bliven[5] has done this, he has accomplished much in very short time.

Alice was looking forward to a visit from Marion & you yesterday.

1. In "The Liberals and the League," *The Nation*, 116 (4 April 1923): 383–84, Manley O. Hudson had criticized American liberals for failing to support the League of Nations and for not working to secure American entry. In his answer to Hudson's article (published on page 571 of the 16 May 1923 issue), Frankfurter argued that the whole issue of American involvement was not simple. The idea of the League was certainly good, but no one had yet determined what would be the conditions, the responsibilities, or the rights involved in membership. Frankfurter pointedly noted that while it was true that the United States was part of the world, the country was not a part of Europe; and the League seemed preoccupied with European problems.

2. In what the anonymous author called "a friendly challenge" to Hoover, he urged that the Secretary of Commerce turn his attention to ironing out the fluctuations of the business cycle. See "An Open Letter to Mr. Hoover," *New Republic* 34 (23 May 1923): 334–35.

3. See LDB to Frankfurter, 6 September 1922.

4. In "China and the Powers" (in the same issue of the *New Republic*), the editorialist presented an astute and straightforward analysis of internal Chinese politics and urged that other powers not interfere in internal Chinese matters.

5. Bruce Bliven (1889–1977) had been a newspaperman before joining the *New Republic* in 1923; he directed its editorial policy until his retirement in 1955. See his autobiography, *Five Million Words Later* (New York, 1970).

To Alfred Brandeis

June 2, 1923 Washington, D.C. [Brandeis Mss, M 4–4]

DEAR AL: 1. The 2 days with the Zionists were, unexpectedly, very gratifying.

2. I have sent to Judge Seymour & to Otto the photos.

3. I entirely agree with you about an essay in foreign shipping. We should limit ourselves to coastwise & inland waters.[1]

4. You can't escape auto statistic[s]. Here are some more.[2]

I too can't figure where the money we are spending comes from. But I fancy it is:

(a) Partly exhaustion of natural resources (timber, natural gas & oil, which should be largely charged against the nation's capital account)

(b) "Kiting checks'

We have practically mobilized all our wealth, converting it into bonds & notes. The farms are now being blown in, following in inverse order:

Mercantile, manufacturing, mining, public utilities, national, state & municipal loans.

And through the banks all m[erchan]d[i]se. That is, deposits means largely debts *due* the banks. When we established the Federal Reserve System, we came pretty near doubling the possible loans.

Thus we have endless securities. But I can't see great additions to wealth. That would have to be evidenced either

(1) By large investments (solvent) abroad

(2) Additions to property here, or

(3) Facilities of some kind for increased production.

I don't see them in large volume.

Eliz[abeth] plans to go to Boston on Tuesday's Federal & to take Alice to Chatham Wednesday.

1. See LDB to Alfred Brandeis, 6 September 1921 and to Felix Frankfurter, 20 September 1921.
2. See LDB to Alfred Brandeis, 3 January 1923, n. 3.

To Thomas Reed Powell

June 8, 1923 Washington, D.C. [Powell Mss]

MY DEAR MR. POWELL: [1] Again my thanks for your review of our constitutional cases.[2]

I incline to think that the law schools and their journals will ultimately furnish the most effective means for recall of erroneous judicial decisions.   Cordially,

1. Thomas Reed Powell (1880–1955) was professor of law at Columbia and an authority on constitutional law. He moved to the Harvard Law School in 1925 and remained there until his retirement.

2. Probably LDB was commenting on Powell's continuing series, "The Supreme Court's Adjudication of Constitutional Issues in 1921–22," 21 *Michigan Law Review* 290, 437, 542.

To Felix Frankfurter

June 17, 1923 Chatham, Mass. [Frankfurter Mss—LC]

DEAR FELIX: 1. As to Maslon.[1] I told McCurdy I should want him some time in Sept., probably from the middle to the time he must go to Harvard,[2] & that I want him to have, at the end of that period, time to show Maslon the ropes. Except for this I do not think I shall need Maslon before Oct. 1. He had better keep in touch with McCurdy. Of course, McC. could give him this instruction at any time, so far as I am concerned.

2. As to super-power. W. Va. case [3] was evidently decided largely on ground that natural gas had been made an article of interstate com[merce], inviting large investment & reliance upon its continued supply. What would happen in the absence of these elements [*].

I do not see how a State e.g. N[ew]. H[ampshire]. could let its power enter into interstate com. without danger of robbery unless it got federal protection, either:

(a) through a fed. interstate com. law & Com[mission]., or

(b) through an application of the doctrine of the Webb-Kenyon law (Clark Dist. Co. case) [4]

Of course you will recall the limitations therein stated, which might prevent extension of the doctrine, as well as the criticism of the doctrine (see Minnesota Law Rev. articles) [5] and nothing would be safe.

My own opinion has been that it was wise (1) to treat the constitutional power of interstate Com. as very broad & (2) to treat acts of Congress as not invading State power unless it clearly appeared that the federal power was intended to be exercised exclusively (3) to rectify the tendency to hold federal power exclusive by applying the Webb-Kenyon doctrine.

Shall talk over Ben [*] when you come here. Things are going well here. Alice seems to be gaining pretty steadily. We have canoed some and walked considerably.

1. Samuel Henry Maslon (b. 1901), had emigrated to the United States from Russia as a child. He clerked for LDB during the 1923–24 term and then settled in Minneapolis to practice law. Maslon has been a director of several corporations.

2. William McCurdy, who had been LDB's secretary during 1922–23, returned to the Harvard Law School to begin his long teaching career there in the fall of 1923.

3. See LDB to Alice G. Brandeis, 8 May 1923, n. 2.

4. The Webb-Kenyon Act of 1913 (37 *U.S. Statutes* ch. 90: 699), passed over Taft's veto, provided federal support for state laws regarding prohibition and, exempting liquor from normal protections of interstate commerce, controlled the traffic between "wet" and "dry" states. This law was upheld in *Clark Distilling Co.* v. *Western Maryland R.R. Co.*, 242 *U.S.* 311 (1917).

5. Noel T. Dowling, "Concurrent Power Under the Eighteenth Amendment," 6 *Minnesota Law Review* 447 (1922).

To Elizabeth Brandeis

August 7, 1923 Chatham, Mass. [EBR]

DEAREST ELIZABETH: I have yours of 4th.

I think the combination of law and economics is a good one. If you pursue economics as a teaching career, or otherwise, I shall look forward to your doing important work someday, for which your abilities fit you.[1] And, whether it be in teaching, in writing or in administration, knowledge of the law, and of its processes, is almost an indispensable for first class work. Perhaps some day you may conclude to do for the Massachusetts textile industry—with its Lowell and Lawrence and Fall River—what the Hammonds have done in "The Town Labourer,"—an admirable book,—or the Webbs in The Cooperative Movement.[2] If you go into research, it should be on your own account, not as part of a machine, but to enable you to present the results of your own thinking in the best possible form.

I have no doubt that the Wisconsin Law School is good enough for your purposes, and I should think it probable that you would find economics instruction—and, doubtless, other conditions more sympathetic there than at Yale. The next few years are apt to be tinged with a radical hue; and it will be particularly satisfying to live in an atmosphere which breathes LaFollette's air.

It is good to think of Susan being with you today.

With much love,

---

1. Elizabeth Brandeis worked as secretary of the District of Columbia Minimum Wage Board until that agency was declared unconstitutional by the Supreme Court. In the summer of 1923 she moved to Madison, Wisconsin to study law and in the fall, she shifted from law to economics—studying under John R. Commons (see LDB to Commons, 27 May 1913).

2. John L. and Barbara Hammond, *The Town Labourer* (London, 1917). Beatrice (Potter) Webb, *The Co-operative Movement in Great Britain* (London, 1891); the work was published with Mrs. Webb's name alone.

To Felix Frankfurter

September 16, 1923 Washington, D.C. [Frankfurter Mss—LC]

F.F.: My greetings to you & Marion on the homecoming. Es war ein schönes Zusammensein.[1]

1. Potter Com[missione]r[2] dined with me Thursday. Says Richberg's[3] argument in the recent valuation motion (as to original costs) was a beautiful piece of advocacy, as fine in tack and method as in substance.[4]

2. John R. Commons dined with me Friday. He was very enthusiastic over Bill Rice, says he did an extraordinarily good job in connection with the drafting of unemployment bill & considers him a distinct gain for Wisconsin.

Commons talked himself out on present-day economic & social-industrial problems. He has a fine spirit, an open mind & a happy freedom from classic economic theories. But his vision is narrow & his thinking not deep.

3. I think Van Vleck should include in his immigration survey[5] a thorough study of the cancellation of naturalization cases.

4. Maslon is here & I have set him to work.

5. The Palestine days in N.Y. were busy ones. DeH[aas]. and B[ernard]. F[lexner]. (in his field) have done thinking. I have arranged in divers ways to take care of DeH. Administration Fund requirements.[6]

Walton Hamilton[7] is to dine with us today.

1. "It was a nice get-together."

2. Mark Winslow Potter (1866–1942) was a New York attorney. He had been a member of the Interstate Commerce Commission since June, 1920.

3. Donald Richberg was general counsel of the National Conference on Valuation of American Railroads (see next note) and worked closely with the railway unions in defending a number of progressive laws, including the Railway Labor Act, of which he was the principal drafter.

4. In 1914, Senator Robert M. LaFollette had sponsored legislation authorizing the Interstate Commerce Commission to evaluate all railroad property as the basis for determining rates. A decade later, the I.C.C. began issuing its tentative findings, which pleased neither consumer groups nor the railroads. LaFollette then helped establish the National Conference on Valuation of American Railroads, which attacked the methods utilized by the I.C.C. in reaching its estimate of $20 billion as the value of all American railroad properties. The conference, using the "original cost" methods, estimated the value at $12 billion; the railroads, using "reproduction cost," declared the value to be in excess of $40 billion. Richberg, as general counsel of the conference, had unsuccessfully argued before the I.C.C. that all valuation matters be returned to the Bureau of Valuation for recomputation according to the "original cost" method.

5. William Cabell Van Vleck (1885–1956) had received a Doctor of Juristic Science degree at Harvard in 1921. He taught law and served as dean of the George Washington University Law School for forty years and was an expert on law relating to aliens. In 1923 he was at work on *The Administrative Control of Aliens* (New York, 1932).

6. On 6 September LDB had met with members of the Palestine Development Council in New York to chart the future work of the group. At the urging of Jacob deHaas, the P.D.C. agreed to establish local leagues to recruit members and raise money for work in Palestine. Reports of the meeting and of LDB's speech (which emphasized the need for new members) can be found in *The Palestine Progress,* 1 (1 October 1923): 9–11. See also LDB to Jacob deHaas, 29 December 1923.

7. Walton Hale Hamilton (1881–1958), an economist and lawyer, was teaching at the Brookings Institution in 1923. In 1928 he began a lengthy tenure at the Yale Law School. He wrote several treatises on both legal and economic problems.

To Adolph Augustus Berle Jr.

September 28, 1923 Washington, D.C. [Brandeis Mss, SC 6–2]

To BERLE: The hall-mark of the prospective client [1] does not [*] verity, and I should not think it desirable to become its General Counsel. But its money cannot properly be designated "tainted" and I think there is no adequate reason why you should decline to perform for it specific professional work otherwise attractive.

1. Berle had written LDB on 26 September asking whether he should accept an offer from the National Industrial Conference Board to prepare an independent evaluation of the antitrust laws. The paper would not be published, but would be for the internal consideration of the group. Berle knew little about the Board, and wrote "there are groups whose money is so tainted that acceptance of it is not to be considered; and there are people with whom any dealing is unwise."

To Julian William Mack (fragment)

October 20, 1923 Washington, D.C. [R. Szold Mss]

I understand that Israel N. Thurman [*sic*] has retired from the laundry business, having sold out for a "fortune". I suggest that you send for him and put up strongly to him his duty to himself and to the cause. He had eight years ago a fine Zionist spirit and expected to do much for the cause. As late as four years ago he registered a vow in Heaven and on earth that as soon as he was financially able, he would make large contributions and give much time to the cause.[1] He had in him promising qualities, moral and intellectual. He must, to save his soul, combat greed; and I think it would do even more for him than for the cause to make him realize what his self-respect demands and that we have in mind his failure to make good. I have no objection to your telling him orally what I have written you as being my opinion, etc.—But don't mention my name in any letter you may write him.

1. Although Thurmin remained active in general Jewish causes, including Zionism, he never assumed the leadership role that LDB had in mind for him.

To Felix Frankfurter

October 24, 1923 Washington, D.C. [Frankfurter Mss—LC]

F.F.: 1. Holmes J. closed our first 3 weeks sitting in fine shape physically & mentally. He walked with me from the John Paul Jones statue to 1720. His mind is in much better condition than at any time during the 1922 term & quite as good as at any time during the 1921 term.

2. Have you seen R[oscoe]. P[ound].'s endorsement of the Community Trust?

3. The [Charles F.] Amidon letter is fine. I have written him.

4. The President (C[alvin]. C[oolidge].) seems to be quite in harmony with your paper on liquor.[1] The answer to Stimson should be:

Do not change the Volstead Law in any respect. Leave the percentage of alcohol where it is. Merely provide in the annual appropriation bills that the prohibition money shall be used for protection against smuggling from abroad & from one state or territory into another, and the suppression in the District of Columbia & any government reservation, etc.

5. I had a good talk with Mack Saturday. In answer to enclosed letter, I have written him that I do not think the C[hief]. J[ustice]. believes he is shirking etc.[2]

7[sic]. I think Alice is gradually regaining what she had lost since the early days of August in Chatham.

9[sic]. There is one bit of Palestine work which I should like to have you undertake if you see no objection. You know that for years I have believed that an appropriate letter should go to a select body of Jewish lawyers calling attention to the possibility (now through the P[alestine]. D[evelopment]. C[ouncil]. or P[alestine]. E[ndowment]. F[und].) of bequests for Palestine.[3] There were 5 years of delay before anything was done. Then it was left to DeHaas to send out some letters. I don't know how much he has done of this. But whatever it was, it was nothing. The letter should have gone from our distinguished lawyers in distinguished form. I think one signed by you as chairman etc or something would be most effective.

You will know what to say, to whom to send it, who else should sign, etc. But this idea, which may win us much money & open the way to other support, should be appropriately followed up.

Glad Marion found the [*] so interesting.

1. In an address before the American Academy of Political Science, Frankfurter had argued against Henry L. Stimson's call for full national enforcement of prohibition. Frankfurter noted that although he personally disagreed with prohibition, the policy had been adopted as the law of the land after much deliberation. There were now three courses open: repeal, nullification (by making believe the law did not exist), or enforcement. The first two options were dangerous, and only the third was honest. But, he maintained, the best method would be to have the states enforce local laws, with the federal government concentrating on fighting smuggling, both from outside

the country and from one state to another. See Frankfurter, "A National Policy for Enforcement of Prohibition," *Annals of the American Academy of Political Science*, 109 (September 1923): 193–95. See also LDB to Frankfurter, 25 September 1922.

2. With LDB refusing to take any public role in Zionist affairs, the burden of work had fallen upon Julian Mack, who was also involved in many non-Zionist causes. A conscientious man, he was worried that others might feel his work on the Court of Appeals was suffering.

3. See LDB to Frankfurter, 7 October 1919.

To Julian William Mack

October 30, 1923 Washington, D.C. [R. Szold Mss]

J.W.M.: Lewis Straus [*sic*] (bringing Jim Becker [1] of Chicago) called on me to talk Palestine. They wanted me to talk on Weizmann which I didn't do. On leaving Lewis asked me whether there was "anything he could do for me". I answered "See Judge Mack & get to work under his orders." He said something indicating a willingness, but a doubt as to his effecting anything.[2]

I wish you would send for him *at once* & give him a talking to. Also take from him money; $5000 cash would not be too much.

There was much I should have said to him but for Becker's presence. I urged B. to go to Palestine soon.

1. Probably James Herman Becker (1894–1970), a Chicago businessman and philanthropist. For Becker's Jewish charitable work, see Edgar Siskin, "Chaim Weizmann and James H. Becker: The Story of a Friendship," *American Jewish Archives* 27 (April 1975): 32–50. According to Siskin, Weizmann hoped that Becker would develop into a Louis Marshall of the West.

2. Strauss did not get involved in Zionism again, choosing to concentrate his energies in the financial field as a partner in Kuhn, Loeb & Co.

To Felix Frankfurter

November 20, 1923 Washington, D.C. [Frankfurter Mss—HLS]

F.F.: 1. In connection with the Japanese Alien Land Cases,[1] following matter arising incidentally should receive separate appropriate comment—

The Jap. get ½ the crop—only;

The owners get ½ for furnishing, practically, only the land (paying taxes thereon)

I think throughout history you probably could not find such rack-renting as we have made common in America.

The church took $\frac{1}{10}$th. (I think even of its [*] lands)

The Attica tenants thought 5 per cent to the landlord was high.

2. In connection with the Craig Contempt case,[2] this point arising incidentally should receive separate treatment.

The absurdity of the running of a municipal utility being committed for years to a Federal Court, in a state which is the financial center of America & where probably nearly all the utility's securities are held.

3. I suppose you have noticed the interesting fight by N. Dak. etc. to insure its supply of Lignite coal.[3]

4. The W. Va. natural gas cases were argued, if possible, more badly than ever before.[4] The questions of substantive constitutional law and of procedural constitutional law involved are as important as any now conceivable. Neither the bar, the public or the interests great or small indicated in any way that they cared in the least. Charles Warren, who was present, could tell a strange tale of the lack of interest as compared with that which he described as having been taken on similar occasions a century & less ago. The court room was empty, even the lawyers awaiting later assigned cases not being in attendance. One might have supposed that a default judgment was being entered in a police court on the promissory note of an insolvent. No Atty. Genl or other person appeared as amicus. No member of the S.C. peeped.

5. Replying to your enquiry re Mellon tax reduction plan.[5] I am wholly contra.

(a) I don't think there will be any appreciable surplus in 1925, unless there are heavy cuts in War & Navy appropriations, which is not to be expected.

(b) The classes & individuals who are now suffering from the tax burden would not benefit appreciably. Those who would benefit are the rich & big business. They have been the beneficiaries of the excess war profits tax removal.

And of course, I am agin taking from the States their tax exemption on bonds.

I am deep again in early Italian history, now in the thirteenth century from which much modern wisdom may be deduced.

1. On 19 November 1923, the Supreme Court handed down two decisions relating to the California Alien Land Law of 1920, which forbade aliens who were ineligible for citizenship (namely Japanese) to own land or enter into any contracts, such as sharecropping, which would give them the benefit of the land. The legal question was whether the California law could go further in limiting the rights of aliens than the 1911 treaty between the United States and Japan. Mr. Justice Butler delivered the opinion of the Court, which upheld the statute. LDB and McReynolds believed there were no justicable questions involved and that the cases should have been dismissed. See *Webb* v. *O'Brien*, 263 *U.S.* 313 (1923) and *Frick* v. *Webb*, 263 *U.S.* 326 (1923).

2. In October 1919 the New York City Comptroller had published a letter to the state's Public Service Commission critical of a federal judge's actions taken in receivership. At the behest of the judge, the United States District Attorney had charged the comptroller with contempt; upon being jailed, the latter had sought a writ of *habeus corpus* in proceedings of error. Mr. Justice McReynolds, writing the majority opinion, had declared that the means sought for relief were not proper and had dismissed the suit; Chief Justice Taft had concurred in a separate opinion. Holmes, joined by LDB, had dissented, charging that not only was the relief sought proper, but the lower court judge had abused his power. See *Craig* v. *Hecht*, 263 U.S. 255 (1923).

3. North Dakota was protesting new rail rates that increased freight costs of native lignite coal by 40 to 60 percent. The state's governor blamed the increase on eastern rail and coal interests, which had long battled against use of the cheaper lignite fuel.

4. See LDB to Alice G. Brandeis, 8 May 1923, n. 2.

5. On 11 November 1923, Secretary of the Treasury Mellon had proposed a $323 million tax reduction. The major cuts were in the upper brackets, with the surtax reduced on incomes over $100,000 from 42 to 25 percent.

To Jacob deHaas

December 29, 1923 Washington, D.C. [Frankfurter Mss—HLS]

deHaas: Yours of the 28th reached me after my talk with JWM. The talk was sadd[en]ing in the extreme. He has suffered much in all this.

You and FF had not succeeded in making him understand—as he thought—how I felt about this matter. And he said the purpose of his coming was mainly to find out and report to our associates. I hope he understands now.[1] To make sure that there should be no misunderstanding, I wrote him after (immediately)

he left, special delivery, and asked him to send you and Felix a
copy.

I hope you will get now the full cooperation. But I am sure it
will be very difficult for others as well as yourself.

                                    With every good wish,

Please send FF a copy of this.

    1. In 1923 Julian Mack visited Palestine for the first time, and he was
deeply moved by what he saw there of Jewish work on the land. He returned to America hoping that some sort of compromise might be worked
out that would heal the breach opened at Cleveland in 1921 but found that
LDB was still adamant in his opposition to cooperation with Weizmann
and his group. The particular issue over which LDB and Mack differed was
a plan created by deHaas to establish local chapters of the Palestine Development Council and allow investors to pick out smaller projects to support
in Palestine, with all of the funds channeled through the national P.D.C.
Mack did not think the plan would work (in fact, it never even began),
and he wanted to seek closer relations with the non-Zionist Marshall group
being cultivated by Weizmann. See next letter, as well as LDB to deHaas,
14 February 1924.

To Julian William Mack

December 31, 1923 Washington, D.C. [R. Szold Mss]

JWM: I have yours of yesterday and am returning it and also
yours of 24th so that copies can be made as you suggest.

"Ich kann nicht anders." [1] I, too, am sad and sorry—very. And
particularly for you who have given to the cause without reserve;
and with singleness of purpose and purity of motive, which are
rare in this carnal world.

I still hope that 1924 will bring surcease of sorrow.

And to you, in every way, much happiness.

    1. "I can do no other," Martin Luther's famous cry at the Diet of Worms
in 1521. See preceding letter.

To Alfred Brandeis

[?], 1924 Washington, D.C. [Brandeis Mss, M 4–4]

DEAR AL: Miss [Henrietta] Szold is a very fine woman. She has
been called the Jane Adamms [sic] of our Jewish world—and not
without reason. Her father was a great friend of Uncle Lewis

[Dembitz]. You and the family might be interested in what she is able to tell of Palestine. You might, if Jennie felt disposed, invite her to take a meal at Ladless, and if in line with your custom, invite [Rabbi Joseph] Rauch and/or some other German Jew to join you.

But I see no reason why you should, contrary to inclinations, accede to the request of Miss Isaacs et al., and attempt to interest the German Jews in Palestine. It would, judging from experiences elsewhere, probably be a futile proceeding. Moreover, the Russian Jews who really care about Palestine for its own sake, and for relatives whom they hope will find a refuge there, are old enough in America to stand alone in this matter. There is no chance of help from practically any German Jew, unless he has been in P. One sight of the country usually makes a convert of him.

Gruesse,

To Julian William Mack

January 4, 1924 Washington, D.C. [R. Szold Mss]

J.W.M.: 1. As I wrote B[en].V.C[ohen]. yesterday, you must not permit yourself to run any risk by departing tomorrow. Do not go, unless you are entirely "hergestellt." [1] You have been under severe strain, and nothing, Zionist or judicial, is as important as that you should take the best possible care of yourself.[2]

2. I wired you that I agree with Felix that it is imperative that you should act now on your own judgment. This, of course, includes not only the matter of the proposed Jan. 13 meeting and the proposed conference with [Harry F.] Fischel et al. referred to in your (3) [3]; but also all other matters arising in this connection. In saying this I mean, of course, your own deliberate judgment—whatever it is—not the adoption of the judgment of others.

3. As to my own position, I cannot depart from, or, indeed, add to, what was expressed in our talk of the 29th & in my letter to you of that date. You know how highly I value B[ernard]. F[lexner].'s work, also my high opinion of him & the others. But I, in turn, cannot abdicate my judgment. And I am strengthened in my doubts by knowledge of the fact that probably none of them have quite the same view as I have of what is really worthwhile. Or, perhaps, to put it more accurately, how much of the

worthwhile one should sacrifice or risk, in order to make more rapid progress in matter[s] immediately in hand. I must keep myself free to act as events may hereafter indicate is proper.[4]

Be assured that whatever you decide is wise in the present emergency, my affection and admiration will in no way be affected. You have made your record by years of rare devotion.

Please show this to DeH[aas]. and send Felix and me each a copy.

1. "restored."
2. Mack had been suffering from a severe laryngitis and had been ordered by his doctor to rest.
3. There was increasing pressure on the Mack-Brandeis group to rejoin the Zionist movement, and to participate in a number of cooperative efforts with the Joint Distribution Committee in the rebuilding of Palestine. Mack from the beginning had been open to overtures of reconciliation, but he had never pushed for their consideration in the light of LDB's intransigence.
4. LDB is here referring to the various maneuvers that ultimately coalesced into the Jewish Agency; see LDB to Jacob deHaas, 14 February 1924.

To Felix Frankfurter

January 6, 1924 Washington, D.C. [Frankfurter MSS—LC]

F.F.: I had an interesting, harmonious and surprisingly intimate hour's talk with [Victor] Morawetz. It may well lead to his making important contributions, intellectual and financial, to legal education & specifically to Harvard L[aw]. S[chool].

The immediate manifestation is a promise that he will ask you to call on him when you are next in New York. He, like [William] Guthrie, has confidence in you. He, more in you than in Pound, whom, he fears, may be a bit "metaphysical."

It came about in this way: You know we were together at C[ambridge]. 2 years. When he entered, I said: "Now before we talk about our business, tell me about yourself." With astounding directness he said, as he sat down, and started giving an account of himself: "I haven't made as good use of my life as you have." Then, he recounted the vapidness of his achievements re Acheson [*sic*] & Norfolk & Western,[1] & his mistake in paying no heed "to the human" until it was too late; said he had tried to do something in foreign affairs, & economics, & legal education, but without much success.

Then he took up German reparations, told of his futile attempt to influence Hughes etc. In all his views on this subject we were in accord. Then, he took up the Institute,[2] told of early plans he had had, went into detail on the matter I had heard from Guthrie, & asked me whether I could recommend the needed young men. He still believes the task is a possible one, but he knows now the difficulties & I think sees my reasons for apprehensions. As to the manner & means by which alone, the task could possibly be performed, we agreed fully.

Finally, I told him that he ought to eschew all other things, & devote his mind & special talents & rich experience solely to legal education, pictured to him what he might accomplish, & laid before him my old idea of drafting for the Law School the young men, 10 at a time, etc. He was enthusiastic, said he had had just such a thought about legal & economic research work; & had, some years ago, told Dr. Pritchett[3] that he would himself finance three.

Finally I clinched the situation by advising he talk matters over with you. He promised he would ask you to come. He has, of course, some heretical views: —

Is eager for Foundation aid (Abe Flexner) & clings to American Institute ideas. But he is in fine mood & good health; & far finer than he was 40 years ago.

I really enjoyed the hour; & think you may be able to lead him where he can be of great service. His mind is of rare clarity, & I think he wants to do. In all he said he was merely dissecting himself. There was not even a suggestion of the morbid.

1. Morawetz was counsel in the reorganizations of both the Atchison, Topeka and Sante Fe, and the Norfolk & Western railroad companies.
2. Morawetz, together with Elihu Root and George W. Wickersham, helped to found the American Law Institute.
3. Perhaps Henry B. Pritchett of the Carnegie Foundation.

To Felix Frankfurter

January 11, 1924 Washington, D.C. [Frankfurter Mss—HLS]

DEAR FELIX: (1) I am glad you found it possible to consent to help DeHaas at Buffalo.[1]

(2) Mack seems to have recovered his balance & some of his cheer. I suspect that what contributed most to his collapse was discovering that he had been led into a disloyalty of secrecy as against DeHaas.

(3) Prof. Heinrich [*] of Berlin, here on National Palestine Library, will doubtless call on you soon. I found him an engaging party.

(4) *Re* Amidon's letter. I guess from what N.D. told me, Baker was formerly no other than he is.

(5) You gave Walter L[ippmann]. much good advice. I begin to believe again (as I did in my younger days) that no man without legal training is to be trusted in American public affairs.[2]

(6) I saw Hoover at White House yesterday. He was downcast. Thinks defeat of Cummins on Interst[ate]. Com[merce]. Com[tee] [3] destroys his (Hoover's) plan for consolidating RRs on which he has been hard at work for 6 months; that his plan would otherwise have gone through; & that it would have solved the RR problem within 5 years; also that it was 5 RR presidents who did the killing.[4]

Marvellous credulity.

1. Jacob deHaas had been on a speaking tour for the Palestine Development Council.

2. See LDB to Leonard Augustus Jones, 8 May 1905, n. 2.

3. On 9 January, Senator Robert M. LaFollette and five of his supporters sided with the Democrats to defeat Albert Cummins's bid for reelection as chairman of the important Senate Committee on Interstate Commerce. LaFollette, who had long opposed Cummins, was thus able to demonstrate that he and his independents controlled the swing vote in the Senate. The new chairman of the committee was Ellison D. Smith of South Carolina.

4. In his annual report for 1921, Hoover had called for consolidating America's railroads into larger systems, in order to gain the benefits recognized during the government's operation of the entire rail network during the war. Hoover, however, wanted the new groupings to be privately owned. He would have received strong support from Cummins, who was coauthor of the 1920 Transportation Act, which did encourage the consolidation of competing lines. Among the railroad operators, the larger and more profitable roads opposed Hoover's scheme, while the smaller ones showed a greater receptivity to the idea.

To Julian William Mack

January 22, 1924 Washington, D.C. [R. Szold Mss]

J.W.M.: Yours of 20th rec'd.

I am, as I wrote [Julius] Simon on Jan. 1, entirely ready to contribute to the Ruttenberg [*sic*] project.[1] But it does not seem to me wise to inject myself into this morning's conference by telegraphing.

I do not criticize or blame any of our active associates. But I must form a judgment on facts. One of these indisputable facts is that they distrust DeH[aas]. DeH. could not, under very trying conditions, work effectively with or for those who do not trust him or his judgment. If the R[eorganization]. Com[tee] concludes that DeH. can't raise the money;—he surely can't. If they think there is a way to raise it, they are free, as they always have been, to raise it in such way as they think best.

In reaching these conclusions I am profoundly impressed by the fact that some of the most honorable men I have ever know[n] deemed it necessary to withhold from DeH. all knowledge of the contemplated consolidation.[2]

1. In 1923, Pinhas Rutenberg set up a small diesel plant in Tel Aviv to supply the electric needs of that city, and he soon began extending his operations to other parts of the Yishuv (see LDB to Solomon Rosenbloom, 25 June 1922, n. 2). Much of the money for the project was subscribed in the United States, and it was a sign of the weakness of the Palestine Development Council that this group did not have the resources necessary to underwrite Rutenberg's scheme. Nearly all of the funds came from sources affiliated with the Joint Distribution Committee. Eventually, the Rutenberg project came to supply electricity for all of Israel; for the record of its growth, see the article in the *Encyclopedia of Zionism and Israel*, 1:586–87.

2. See LDB to Jacob deHaas, 14 February 1924.

To Harry Friedenwald

February 3, 1924 Washington, D.C. [Friedenwald Mss]

MY DEAR DR. FRIEDENWALD: By the same mail which brings your letters, comes one from deHaas with an enclosure which I am sending you.

So far as I am personally concerned, the fact that I couldn't attend the conference, and that we are not asked, seems conclusive.[1] But I, too, have grave doubts of solving our problems by a consolidation.

If our group were in the position, that we were in 9 years ago, where we could fight for control, in order to establish our views as to what is worth while in Palestine and how to attain it, there ought or might be much to be said in favor of attending the conference and fighting vigorously with the determination to win. But as it is, I see only a probability of our being caught in traps and compromised. There is plenty of work for us to do, primarily holding high our banner, working along the lines you and others laid out in 1921, with faith and perseverance.

There is a chance of my seeing Mack soon, and of course, we shall weigh carefully what you and Edgar [Friedenwald] say.

Cordially,

1. See LDB to Jacob deHaas, 14 February 1924.

To Edith Bolling Wilson

February 4, 1924 Washington, D.C. [Wilson Mss]

MY DEAR MRS. WILSON: To an imperiled world Mr Wilson brought courage and hope. It sorrows now. Someday, bettered by his high striving, it will enjoy the happiness for which he gave his life.[1]

With our deep sympathy,   Cordially,

1. The former president had died in his sleep the day before. See LDB to Edwin A. Alderman, 11 May 1924.

To Elizabeth Brandeis

February 8, 1924 Washington, D.C. [EBR]

DEAREST ELIZABETH: Yours of the 6th has come.

My advice is to accept the job at Smith.[1] Pres[iden]t Neilson [2] evidently wants you. He is one of the finest of college presidents. And if you do as well as I expect you to do in the Labor course you would give, there is pretty sure to be a call by him to more & higher service.

Moreover, if it should happen that a distinctly more desirable opportunity offers elsewhere, before the summer, I have no doubt that Pres[iden]t Neilson—being what he is—will be glad to release you.

Smith seems to me not at all an undesirable place—in spite of being a girls college. It is in a beautiful country—a small place which you like—near enough Amherst to be in touch with men folk. And it has a reputation which would make it a good stepping-stone to another job.

What I am eager for you is to have next year the opportunity of showing somewhere what you can do;—which, *I* think, is unusually good work.

Mother is quite prepared to have you take an immediate job anywhere in the United States. She approved my talking with Mr. [Joseph N.] Teal about the University of Oregon, and I think wrote you to write Clara [Goldmark] about the University of California. She has asked Dr [*] to write Pres[iden]t Comstock about Radcliffe; [3] & I think has written Bessie [Evans] & Pauline [Goldmark] about Bryn Mawr. So you see [she] is bent on having you make the trial this fall. [4]   Lovingly,

1. Elizabeth Brandeis was completing her M.A. degree in economics at the University of Wisconsin. She was also looking for a job for the following year, and there had been some suggestion of being hired at Smith.

2. William Allan Neilson (1869–1946) was a scholar and professor of English who assumed the presidency of Smith in 1917. He retained the office until 1939. Throughout his life, Neilson was involved in many liberal and civil rights causes. He also published many studies of English literature.

3. Ada Louise Comstock (1876–1973) had been a dean at Smith when she was called to the presidency of Radcliffe in 1923. She was a member of President Hoover's "Wickersham Commission" (see LDB to Felix Frankfurter, 13 March 1929, n. 1). In 1943, Miss Comstock left Radcliffe to marry Professor Wallace Notestein (see LDB to Frankfurter, 26 September 1929, n. 8).

4. Elizabeth Brandeis remained at Madison as a graduate student and teaching assistant.

To Jacob deHaas

February 14, 1924 Washington, D.C. [Weizmann Mss]

MY DEAR MR. DEHAAS: I assume you will attend the conference on the 17th.[1] Please say this for me:

The happenings of the last four years have strengthened my conviction that the resettlement of Palestine by Jews offers the only promising road toward the solution of the Jewish Problem; that there are in Palestine economic opportunities which, if availed of, will afford to at least many hundreds of thousands the means of leading lives worthy of the high Jewish traditions; that there rests upon the Jews of America the duty of aiding in the upbuilding by making careful studies of these opportunities, by necessary capital outlays and by efficient leadership, and that with such aid we may hope for great advance in the economic, social and cultural development of the country.

1. Ever since the fight between the rival groups of Zionist leaders at Cleveland in 1921, Chaim Weizmann had been attempting to create an organization that would bring the wealthy non-Zionists to support restoration work in Palestine and thus fill the gap left by the departure of the Brandeis group. After nearly three years of negotiations with Louis Marshall and Felix Warburg, Weizmann had worked out the tentative structure of what would ultimately be called the Jewish Agency. At Louis Marshall's behest, a preliminary conference composed primarily of non-Zionists had been called for 17 February 1924 in New York. Over 150 prominent American Jews not directly affiliated with the Z.O.A., including LDB and Julian Mack, were invited; Weizmann alone represented the Zionist Executive.

At the meeting, Marshall declared that all Jews, regardless of their attitude toward Zionism, had the obligation to work for the rebuilding of Israel. In words that could have been uttered by LDB, Marshall said: "As loyal American citizens, therefore, we have the right to consider the question as to what, if anything, we shall do with regard to Palestine and its development, and as loyal Jews we have the duty to take action with regard to this all important subject, and to define ourselves, our thoughts, our ideas and our intentions, with regard to Palestine. We have no right to be indifferent." Both Marshall and Weizmann carefully avoided the morass of political ideology, and not one word at the conference was uttered about nationalism or a Jewish state. But a common ground was carefully delineated in which the non-Zionists could share in the economic and cultural rebuilding of the Holy Land.

It was to take more than five years of further negotiation between the Zionist Executive and the non-Zionists, as well as among the participants on both sides, before the so-called "pact of glory" was signed at Geneva in

1929. Weizmann had to convince his colleagues to give the non-Zionists 50 percent of the seats in the Agency, and to cede greater authority to the Agency than to the Congress, a proposal far surpassing LDB's 1921 plan to involve non-Zionists. Marshall and Warburg had to assure American non-Zionists that working for Palestine had no connection with Jewish nationalism and that it did not affect their status and loyalty as Americans. Much of the groundwork for this, of course, had been done by the Mack-Brandeis group prior to 1921, and Marshall had been well along in his conversion thanks to the negotiations between the American Jewish Committee and the Z.O.A. following promulgation of the Balfour Declaration.

For details of negotiations leading to the Agency, its accomplishments and its ultimate transformation into a completely Zionist organ, see Melvin Urofsky, *American Zionism from Herzl to the Holocaust*, ch. 8, and Sam Z. Chinitz, "The Jewish Agency and the Jewish Community in the United States" (M.A. essay, Columbia University, 1959).

To Felix Frankfurter

February 25, 1924 Washington, D.C. [Frankfurter Mss—HLS]

DEAR FELIX: 1. J[ulian].W.M[ack]. & DeH[aas]. will report to you on the Thursday conference. I think it was helpful.[1]

2. Pepper is showing the same lack of political sense which characterized his Ballinger performance— [2]

1.a. I am informed by high authority that he is gunning for the Presidency.

3. [Walton] Hamilton brought Meickeljohn [3] in last Wednesday & this Wednesday they (and Prof. Dodge) [4] are coming in to dine.

4. I am glad you & Scott thought the admiralty opinion worthwhile.[5] It involved [*] more work than appears. There seemed to be nowhere available the data needed & the search was a long one. It is that kind of thing that Scott ought to do, I felt many times while the task was in hand.

5. Today's dissent re Jensen case will interest you. I thought this a good occasion to let the law journal contributors know that they are helping.

6. C[alvin]. C[oolidge]. wanted Charles Choate to prosecute [7] and & [*sic*] he would have done so, had not his partners had in the past 2 retainers from Sinclair.

7. Have had long talk with Elwood Mead.[8] He confirms all & even more about the possibilities economically of Palestine. Its all up to the Jews who go there.

1. See preceding letter.

2. In an article in the *New York Times* the preceding day, Pennsylvania Senator George Wharton Pepper had seemingly placed the blame for the unfolding oil scandal not on the men involved, but on the post-war situation, which had engendered widespread corruption throughout the country. See also LDB to Norman Hapgood, 27 February 1910, n. 3.

3. Alexander Meikeljohn (1872–1964), the well known educational philosopher, was president of Amherst College in 1924, but two years later he founded his famous Experimental College at the University of Wisconsin.

4. Robert Elkin Neil Dodge (1867–1935) was professor of English and chairman of that department at the University of Wisconsin.

5. On this date the Court handed down its decision in *Washington* v. *Dawson*, combined with *California* v. *Rolph*, 264 *U.S.* 213, in which state workmen's compensation laws were held to be inapplicable to longshoremen, since those workers were destined to be covered by the interstate and foreign maritime laws. LDB filed an elaborate dissent (at 228) in which he traced various aspects of both admiralty and state compensation laws; he saw no reason why the state laws would not be valid.

6. In the majority opinion (see n. 5 above), Mr. Justice McReynolds upheld the doctrine enunciated in *Southern Pacific Co.* v. *Jensen*, 244 *U.S.* 205 (1916), in which a New York workmen's compensation law had been found to infringe upon the domain of maritime law. LDB argued that *Jensen* was wrong to begin with and buttressed his dissent with copious citations of recent articles in various law journals dealing with the problem.

7. The government decided to appoint a special prosecutor to deal with the Teapot Dome scandals (see LDB to Frankfurter, 5 March 1923). Eventually the government named Harlan Fiske Stone and Owen J. Roberts to do the work; both men were ultimately to sit with LDB on the Supreme Court.

8. Elwood Mead (1858–1936) was an agricultural engineer, pioneering in irrigation work. He undertook a number of Palestinian projects and became an authority on that country

To Julius Simon

February 26, 1924 Washington, D.C. [Frankfurter Mss—HLS]

MY DEAR SIMON: My thanks for your letter of 25th. I think you have made an error in judgment. But, in my opinion, the right to be wrong is of the essence of liberty.[1]   Most cordially,

1. There is no copy of Simon's letter in either the Brandeis, Frankfurter, or Simon collections, but its contents probably concerned Simon's support of the Jewish Agency proposal (see LDB to Jacob deHaas, 14 February 1924).

To Felix Frankfurter

March 3, 1924 Washington, D.C. [Frankfurter Mss—HLS]

F.F.: 1. Your letter to Walter [Lippmann] re receiverships is bearing good fruit.

2. We are delighted with Meikeljohn. Alice & Emma Irving have quite lost their hearts & Holmes J. was warm in his & [Walton H.] Hamilton's praise.

3. Hamilton, who was in yesterday, doesn't agree with Keynes [1] on the gold menace.[2]

4. Enclosed No. 489 may interest your class. The ICC performance was again shocking. If that Comm isn't reorganized they will drive us to Gov't ownership.[3]

1. John Maynard Keynes, later First Baron of Tilton (1883–1946) first gained international fame as an economist with his devastating critique of the Paris peace treaty in *The Economic Consequences of the Peace* (London, 1920). Keynes had attended the conference as the principal representative of the British Treasury. During the 1920s and 1930s Keynes taught at King's College, Cambridge, and developed the new monetary theories that were ultimately published as *A General Theory of Employment, Interest and Money* (London, 1936), in which he attacked the classical economic beliefs of *laissez-faire* and proposed that the national government assume a positive role in managing a country's economy.

2. Keynes had recently noted with disapproval that the United States, which was accumulating much of the world's gold reserves, was maintaining the price of that commodity at an artificially high level. He urged the United States to stop buying gold and allow the metal to find its natural price level—a policy that, he insisted, would not devalue the dollar. See J. M. Keynes, "Gold in 1923," *The New Republic*, 38 (27 February 1924): 10–11, and a follow-up article, "The Prospects of Gold," *Ibid.*, 38 (12 March 1924): 66–67. In 1924 Keynes also published a book on monetary reform.

3. On this day LDB delivered the opinion of the Court in the *Chicago Junction Case*, 264 *U.S.* 258. The Interstate Commerce Commission in 1922 had authorized the New York Central Railroad to buy a terminal line within the Chicago district, a line that handled the bulk of the area's switching work. The Central's major competitors had opposed the purchase, and now they sought to void it after the lower courts had upheld the commis-

sion's ruling. In a six-to-three decision, the Supreme Court reversed the ruling, and LDB severely chastised the I.C.C. for its entire handling of the matter.

To Alice Harriet Grady

March 5, 1924 Washington, D.C. [Grady Mss]

A.H.G.: 1. I entirely agree with you that Dean Lord's [1] proposition should be accepted.

His appreciation of the value of State reports leads me to add that when he enlarges the available shelf-space to take in all the reports & current numbers, I will, through you, add to his University's collection, the collection which I now have of the Mass[achusetts]. Labor Reports—as they should be in constant use; whereas I use them only occasionally & can get copies of (most at least) from the Congressional Library.

2. I am glad to know that a new edition of "Business—A Profession" is contemplated.

Ernest Poole may be in N.Y. But I do not think he should be asked to supplement his own introduction. He could not do it without great labor; would not (because of other interests) do it very well; and really would not wish to do so. Prof. Felix Frankfurter, on the other hand, knows most of the facts which should be stated, understands fully, and could, with little labor, write all that is desirable.

If the Small, Maynard [Company] would care to do so, a few addresses made between 1914 and June 1916 could be added— e.g. "True Americanism,"—"The Living Law" & possibly "The Jewish Problem"—On this, also, Prof. Frankfurter's advice would be most useful.[2]

Judging from requests of me, there would probably be quite a demand for the book.

3. Mrs. Brandeis has borne her mother's death better than I fear[ed]. She thanks [you] for your message.

4. Mrs. C. P. Hall is to call today.

5. Donald Wilhelm called recently.[3] He now lives at Madison, Conn[ecticut]. & seems fully engaged in writing for Sat[urday] Ev[ening] Post, Collier's, et al. I think if he ever can serve you for S[avings]. B[ank]. I[nsurance]. he will gladly do so.

1. Undoubtedly the reference concerns Everett William Lord (1871–1965), who organized the Business College of Boston University and served as its dean from 1913 to 1941. Probably Lord had suggested to Miss Grady that various state reports dealing with insurance be deposited at Boston University.

2. A second edition of *Business—A Profession* appeared in 1925. Ernest Poole's introduction was allowed to stand, but "Supplementary Notes" were added by Frankfurter. Both "True Americanism" (see LDB to Norman Hapgood, 23 June 1915) and "The Living Law" (see LDB to George Rublee, 28 December 1915) were included in the new edition; "The Jewish Problem" was omitted.

3. Donald Wilhelm (1887–1945) was a free-lance writer for many newspapers and magazines. He had also served as Herbert Hoover's secretary in 1922–23. He did not write on Savings Bank Insurance.

To Felix Frankfurter

March 8, 1924 Washington, D.C. [Frankfurter Mss—HLS]

F.F.: 1. O[liver] W[endell] H[olmes] seemed happy on his birthday & was thoroughly alert at the Conference.

2. Beware of V.—High authority who has seen him recently says he is mentally unbalanced.

3. I should think Jos. Cotton might feel a bit uncomfortable at the disclosures.

4. To my mind, as you know, the most disreputable & blameworthy part of the Harding Administration was the association with, & influence of McLean.[1] That was worse than occasional grafting even in high places, because it expresses decadence. I think to make the country realize how leaders have fallen, it should know what McLean is, which now only those familiar with Washington life do. It is proper that all who have touched that pitch should be shown up as defiled. B[ernard]. Baruch's endearing telegram is not to his credit.[2]

5. I am sorry for Nicely's decision.[3] He is so good a fellow that the regret is apt to come "twenty years after."

6. The fall of the franc is encouraging.[4]

1. Edward Beal McLean (18[?]–1941) was the publisher of the *Washington Post*. In 1921 McLean had lent Albert B. Fall, Harding's Secretary of the Interior, $100,000, allegedly to permit Fall to enlarge his ranch holdings in New Mexico. During the entire Harding Administration McLean

had been in close contact with many of the figures later touched by scandal, and he had wielded quite a bit of influence.

2. The Senate committee investigating the oil scandals had uncovered a number of telegrams sent in code by McLean. One of them referred to Bernard Baruch and implied that Baruch, who thought highly of McLean, was intending to put in a good word for the publisher with Senator Thomas J. Walsh.

3. James Mount Nicely (1899–1964) had graduated from Harvard Law School in 1923, and was then clerking, upon the recommendation of Frankfurter, for Mr. Justice Holmes. The decision evidently refers to Nicely's desire to enter a commercial law firm, which he did in 1925, rather than to pursue an academic vocation.

4. The long depreciation of the French franc had by this time threatened the economic stability of France and the continued existence of the Poincare government. At the beginning of the year the franc had been worth 5¢; on this day it had slipped to 3.42¢. The French government finally stabilized the franc at 5.1¢ with the help of an American loan, an action that trapped many speculators.

To Oliver Wendell Holmes, Jr.

March 8, 1924 Washington, D.C. [Holmes Mss]

OWH: Like Odofredus,[1]
"Mundi sensus, jurisque profundi lux, foedus pacis, doctorum flos" [2]
and much besides.   With every good wish,

1. Odofredus (d. 1265) was an eminent Italian jurist and commentator on Roman law. He taught at Bologna from 1228 until his death.

2. "Sense of the world, light of profound justice, compact of peace, ornament among teachers." The note was sent to Holmes on his eighty-third birthday.

To Felix Frankfurter

March 17, 1924 Washington, D.C. [Frankfurter Mss—HLS]

1. I think the public has a pretty general conception of the impropriety of ex-officials practicing promptly before the Departments; & will know more when the returns come in in response to the Norris Resolution.[1] An article from you would, of course, be illuminating. But I think at the moment what is more needed

is an article on the text of your letter to C[harles].C.B[urling-ham].—re dereliction of Amer. Bar Ass. J.W. Davis and C.E. Hughes, as ex Presidents should be particularly addressed.

If there hadn't been in the Dept. of Justice during Palmer's [2] and Daugherty's Administration a single criminal act, the obvious demoralization of the Dept. would have aroused any fearless body of lawyers capable of indignation & with a sense of professional duty. The decadence was so obvious as not to escape detection even by the blind. They were bent on suppression of knowledge. Among the elect in high places there is now no indignation except at the exposure. It is only over [Frederick M.] Kerby speaking [3] that vested interests rise in denunciation.

Bob Woolley, Ned Lowery [sic] & Frank Lyons [sic] are talking Carter Glass for Pres[ident].

1. On 26 February 1924 the Senate had unanimously adopted resolutions introduced by Senator George W. Norris (see LDB to Frankfurter, 8 February 1927, n. 3.) calling upon various government departments to supply the names of any Congressman or Cabinet member who, within two years of their leaving government service, appeared in connection with any claim against the government, or who belonged to any law firm making such appearances.

2. Alexander Mitchell Palmer (1872–1936), a Pennsylvania attorney, served in the House of Representatives from 1909 to 1915. During the war he was Alien Property Custodian, and in 1919 Wilson named him Attorney General. It was during Palmer's tenure in that office that the United States underwent the Red Scare hysteria. See Stanley Coben, *A. Mitchell Palmer: Politician* (New York, 1963).

3. See LDB to Knute Nelson, 21 March 1910, n. 1.

To Harold Joseph Laski

March 30, 1924 Washington, D.C. [Laski Mss]

MY DEAR HAROLD: You are a marvel—and a most commendable one.

I am delighted that you have done the "Defence of Liberty"; and "The Position of Parties" brings needed illumination.[1]

To be in England, and of it as you now are, must bring joys like the Elizabethan days when the world was young and hope was on its springing board.[2] We are watching the Labor Government with admiration and eagerness.

Our own deplorable exhibition is not without its compensa-
tions.[3] This letting in of light upon dark places must ultimately
lead to health; unless we are much further gone in rottenness than
I believe.

Holmes J. is in fine form—very much better than at the last
term. I think President [Charles W.] Eliot's ninetieth Birthday
has erected for the judge a new goal. He talks some of age. But
his enjoyment of things worthwhile has in no way lessened.

With best to Frieda [sic],   Most cordially,

1. Laski had written the introduction to Herbert Languet (Junius Brutus),
*A Defence of Liberty Against Tyrants, A Translation of the Vindiciae
Contra Tyrannos* (London, 1924). He had also completed "The Position of
Parties and the Right of Dissolution," Fabian Tract No. 210 (London, 1924).

2. On 22 January 1924, Ramsay MacDonald became Prime Minister of the
first Labour cabinet in British history.

3. A reference to the unfolding Harding scandals.

To Felix Frankfurter

April 6, 1924 Washington, D.C. [Frankfurter Mss—LC]

1. Marion is dead right about J. W. Davis—in every word she
says. J.W.D.'s acts & omissions during the last 3 years have been
thoroughly in harmony with the judgment which she expresses.[1]

2. Your review of the St. Louis Administrative Law volume
is admirable in every respect.[2] I am eager, as [Thomas Reed]
Powell is, to have your Due Process of Law book appear in due
time & to have it followed by one specifically on Administrative
Law.[3] But I cannot regret that you have devoted to other tasks a
part of your time during the last 5 years. The sum total of good to
the community—pre-eminently through your teaching inspiring
writing—has been fully as great as it could have been through the
book. And the book will be, as the country as well[,] all the better
for what you have so generously done in stimulating & aiding the
efforts of others.

3. C[harles]. N[agel].'s appreciation of a kind word—since his
war & postwar experiences—is almost pathetic.[4]

4. I will try to get hold of VanVleck[5] & see how he has grown
qua Dean [of George Washington University Law School].

5. Daugherty's answer to Pepper is a ripper.[6] P. has about as much political sense as Hoover, and is as little of a statesman.

6. I am glad you think well of Stone. I am sure some would like to make a vacancy for him on the Court. But, even if one came, it is question[able] whether he, as a Morgan man, could get the votes before Nov[.], or after if C[alvin] C[oolidge] is beaten.[7]

7. Powell's article in M[ar]ch. issue should open eyes & cannot fail to help.[8] Such shots continued a few years may revolutionize attitudes. He talks English, & you may see in Monday's journal entries some reflex. Some might say, "He talks turkey."

8. I think Wheeler (despite Eastern newspaper yapping) is doing an uncommonly good job.[9] I hope his uncoverings will make Stone & others realize

"Quid latet apparebit
Nil in ultum remanebit." [10]

9. Walter L[ippmann]. will need a lot of education before he will be competent to guide public opinion on American affairs.[11]

10. Of course I shall be glad to see Amberg.[12] I should have better hopes—if it were his wife.

11. Can't E.P. Costigan [13] be lured away from his worse than [*] job to some law school. His labors are a monumental exhibition of "Time elaborately thrown away."

1. On 1 April 1921, after resigning as ambassador to the Court of St. James, John W. Davis had become the head of the prestigious Wall Street law firm of Stetson, Jennings & Russell, which later became Davis, Polk & Wardwell. The firm's clients included J. P. Morgan & Company, Standard Oil, and United States Steel; and Davis argued a number of big-business cases, winning most of them and developing a reputation as a leading defender of large-scale capitalism in this country. LDB, who had thought highly of Davis during the latter's tenure as solicitor-general, had told him in London in 1919 that he hoped someday to see him on the Supreme Court. In 1923, Davis had been sounded out to see if he would accept the appointment that ultimately went to Sanford, and he had turned it down. Now, of course, Davis was a leading contender for the Democratic presidential nomination. See William H. Harbaugh, *Lawyer's Lawyer: The Life of John W. Davis*, chs. 12–13.

2. Frankfurter reviewed Ernst Freund, Robert V. Fletcher, Joseph E. Davies, Cuthbert W. Pound, John A. Kurtz, and Charles Nagel, *The Growth of American Administrative Law* (St. Louis, 1923), in 37 *Harvard Law Review* 638 (1924). The six essays delighted Frankfurter in that some

attention was finally being paid to administrative law; more important to him, its very existence was being recognized. Frankfurter paid handsome compliments to the essay by LDB's brother-in-law, Charles Nagel, on federal departmental practices, and on Nagel's own interpretation of administrative law while he was secretary of commerce and labor.

3. Felix Frankfurter and J. Forrester Davison published *Cases and Materials on Administrative Law* (New York, 1932), which soon became a standard text on that subject; Frankfurter never did get around to publishing a book on due process.

4. See n. 2 above; Nagel had evidently dropped Frankfurter a note of appreciation.

5. See LDB to Frankfurter, 16 September 1923, n. 5.

6. On 3 April 1924, Senator George Wharton Pepper had told a Portland, Maine, political convention that the appointment of Daugherty as attorney general had been "a grave error in judgment." Daugherty attacked the speech, which most people assumed had Coolidge's endorsement, and accused Pepper of trying to put the blame for the Republican Party's troubles on the dead Harding. The former attorney general attacked Pepper directly, but by implication he hit out at those Republicans who had convinced Coolidge to oust Daugherty from the Cabinet.

7. On 4 April 1924, President Coolidge had named Harlan Fiske Stone (1872–1946) as attorney general. Stone, who was then dean of the Columbia Law School, was also a member of the firm of Sullivan & Cromwell, which handled a number of large business clients including, on occasion, J. P. Morgan & Company. As it turned out, a vacancy on the Court did occur with the resignation of Joseph McKenna (1843–1926) on 4 January 1925, and Coolidge within a few weeks named Stone to the Court. In June 1941, President Roosevelt elevated Stone to the chief justice's chair. Despite Stone's connections with Wall Street and business, he became a close ally of LDB's while on the bench, and during the 1930s especially he could be counted among the liberals on the Court. See Alpheus T. Mason, *Harlan Fiske Stone: Pillar of the Law* (New York, 1956).

8. Thomas Reed Powell, "The Judiciality of Minimum-Wage Legislation," 37 *Harvard Law Review* 545 (1924) was a devastating critique of the majority reasoning in the Washington minimum wage case (see LDB to Frankfurter, 5 March 1923).

9. Burton Kendall Wheeler (1882–1975) served as a Democratic Senator from Montana from 1922 to 1947. In 1924 he was Robert M. LaFollette's running mate on the Progressive Party ticket, but his greatest fame came in the late 1930s when he headed the isolationist bloc in Congress opposed to Franklin Roosevelt's efforts to involve the United States in fighting fascism. After 1947 Wheeler practiced law in Washington, D.C.

10. "What is hidden will be apparent; nothing will remain unpunished." From the hymn "Dies Irae," attributed to Thomas A. Celano, lines 17–18.

11. Upon the death of Frank Cobb in 1923, Walter Lippmann left the *New Republic* to take over the editorial page of the *New York World*. He stayed there until the *World* merged with the *Telegram* in 1931, when he

began writing his widely syndicated column "Today and Tomorrow." At his death in 1974, Lippmann was acclaimed by many as the most distinguished political analyst of his time and, LDB's judgment notwithstanding, as one who had certainly "guided public opinion on American affairs."

12. Probably Julius Houseman Amberg (1890–1951), a Michigan attorney who had been Frankfurter's special assistant during the war.

13. Edward Prentiss Costigan (1874–1939), a Denver attorney involved in numerous progressive causes, had been named to the United States Tariff Commission in 1917. Despite the high hopes of its sponsors, the commission never became a powerful instrument of foreign and economic policy, and its members had little to do. Costigan finally resigned in 1928, and three years later he was elected for a single term as United States Senator from Colorado.

To Felix Frankfurter

April 23, 1924 Washington, D.C. [Frankfurter Mss—HLS]

1. Thanks for the correction in 662. The error would not have gotten by in Pitney's day.[1]

2. I fear W[alter]. L[ippmann]. is hopeless. We shall have a test.

I didn't answer his letter. But his aid—Arthur Krock [2]—came in yesterday. He is a Louisville boy, long on the Courier-Journal & was correspondent at time of Ballinger investigation. I talked Dutch to him. Walter is to be [here] on 26th & I shall probably have occasion to repeat the dose.

K. saw J.W. Davis, who wholly approves of the plan. So does Hughes, who mustn't be quoted. And so in substance, he says, do Borah, Stanley & even Pat Harrison.

3. To fully appreciate the rent decision,[3] recent Congressional record & files of Washington papers on proposed extension of law to 1926 must be consulted.

4. I think you will conclude that 94 is worse even than Lochner & Adams.[4]

1. In a case decided on procedural grounds, LDB had delivered the opinion of the Court regarding whether a suit begun before Mexico had been recognized by the American government could be continued afterwards. The case was transferred to the Court of Appeals on technical grounds. *Oliver Company* v. *Mexico*, 264 *U.S.* 440 (1924).

2. Arthur Krock (b. 1887) had worked his way up to editor-in-chief of the *Louisville* (Ky.) *Times* before becoming assistant to the president of

the *New York World* in 1923. He later joined the *New York Times* in 1927 as its Washington correspondent, and from 1953 until his retirement in 1967 he wrote a very influential column for the *Times*. He won the Pulitzer Prize three times; see his *Memoirs: Sixty Years on the Firing Line* (New York, 1968).

3. Two days earlier Holmes had delivered the opinion of the Court in voiding the District of Columbia Rent Act of 1919, the same act that the Court, also speaking through Holmes, had upheld three years earlier (see LDB to Frankfurter, 19 April 1921, n. 2). In this instance, Holmes reasoned that the act had been passed as an emergency war measure; that emergency now being over, it could not be used to continue to justify the regulation of rents. *Chastleton Corp.* v. *Sinclair,* 264 *U.S.* 543 (1924).

4. Nebraska had passed a law regulating not only the minimum size of bread loaves, but the maximum as well; and the Court, speaking through Mr. Justice Butler, held the statute, insofar as it concerned maximum size, to be unreasonable. LDB, joined by Holmes, entered an extensive dissent in which he described the entire history of such regulatory legislation to justify its reasonableness. He consulted numerous trade journals and wrote: "Much evidence referred to by me is not in the record. Nor could it have been included. It is the history of the experience gained under similar legislation, and the result of scientific experiments made, since the entry of the judgment below. Of such events in our history, whether occurring before or after the enactment of the statute or of the entry of the judgment, the Court should acquire knowledge, and must, in my opinion, take judicial notice, whenever required to perform the delicate judicial task here involved." He went on to cite, among other cases, to support his view, *Muller* v. *Oregon,* in which he had first managed to get the Court to consider experience in its decision. See *Burns Baking Co.* v. *Bryan,* 264 *U.S.* 504, 533 (1924).

To Edwin Anderson Alderman

May 11, 1924 Washington, D.C. [Alderman Mss]

MY DEAR PRESIDENT ALDERMAN: [1] Norman Hapgood has shown me his letter to you. With the views which he has expressed I agree, in the main.

This may be added:

1. Perhaps the most extraordinary achievement of Mr. Wilson's first administration was dissipation of the atmosphere of materialism which had enveloped Washington for at least forty years, and probably since Lincoln's days. The rich man—the captain of industry—was distinctly at a disadvantage. One breathed the pure, rarified air of mountain tops.

2. Mr. Wilson knew not fear.

3. He should be judged by what he was and did prior to Aug. 4, 1918, the date of the paper justifying the attack on Russia. That was the first of his acts which was unlike him;—and I am sure the beginning of the sad end.[2]

It is better that *I should not be quoted*.[3]

Some day when you are in Washington, I hope you will let me have the pleasure of seeing you.   Cordially,

1. Edwin Anderson Alderman (1861–1931) was the distinguished president of the University of Virginia. Alderman had been a close adviser to Woodrow Wilson during the war, and he had just been invited to make a memorial address on Wilson before the joint houses of Congress on 15 December 1924. He had solicited LDB's opinion of Wilson to incorporate in his address.

2. See LDB to Alice G. Brandeis, 13 June 1919.

3. For Alderman's address, see *Woodrow Wilson: Memorial Address. . . .* (Washington, D.C., 1925).

To Alfred Brandeis

May 11, 1924 Washington, D.C. [Brandeis Mss, M 4-4]

DEAR AL: Greetings to Father's birthday—cold & rainy here.

Henry Goldmark was in town Friday for meeting of War Airship Committee (of which he is chairman) & dined with us. He is one of the relatively few people who improve with age & is an uncommonly fine specimen of a civilized society. Modest, cultured, hardworking at his profession for which he is zealous, enjoying the little pleasures of life & taking them in a worthy way, with commendable delight in his children.   Gruesse,

To Felix Frankfurter

May 11, 1924 Washington, D.C. [Frankfurter Mss—HLS]

DEAR FELIX: 1. This is very good. I doubt that I have any suggestions unless it be to make more pointed our practices—(a) to hold acts unconstitutional "as applied"—and (b) to let them stand, except at the instance of a party who can show that the Act hurts him.

That M[anley]. O. H[udson]. should be willing to support advisory opinions, so obviously bad in American affairs, to help his international striving, discloses a new danger in these foreign missionaries.[1]

2. I suppose you have seen Haine's article in Apr/24 Texas Law Review, a very creditable piece of work.[2]

3. The McAdoo article in this weeks N[ew]. R[epublic]. is fine.[3]

4. C[alvin]. C[oolidge]. will be up against vetoing or acquiescing this week & later which will test his mettle & judgment.[4]

1. In an article in the *Harvard Law Review*, Hudson had presented a generally favorable view of the practice of courts providing advisory opinions to legislatures and to contesting parties prior to adjudication. See "Advisory Opinions of National and International Courts," 37 *H.L.R.* 970 (June 1924). In a "Note" appended at 1002, Frankfurter had added a caveat in which he held it "dangerous to encourage extension of the device of advisory opinion to constitutional controversies."

2. Charles Grove Haines, "Judicial Reviews of Legislation in the United States and the Doctrines of Vested Rights and of Implied Limitations on Legislatures," 2 *Texas Law Review* 257, part II at 387 (1924).

3. "Money and Government," *The New Republic* 38 (14 May 1924): 299–300. The unsigned editorial was a denunciation of William G. McAdoo for allowing personal materialism to interfere with public service.

4. Within the next few days Coolidge vetoed a soldiers' bonus bill, a generous federal pension bill, and a postal salary increase, but he did not veto the tax reduction bill. The soldiers' bonus veto was easily overridden by Congress.

To Susan Goldmark

May 13, 1924 Washington, D.C. [Goldmark Mss]

DEAR SUSIE: *My father's birthday.*

It was good of you to think of my Palestine interest when you found the Frankl.[1]—That cause has suddenly become popular among the Jews, and the task from now on will be rather to guide the interest than to stimulate it—as in many other causes which it was difficult to make fashionable. Unwisely applied interest has a way of harming unpleasantly often.

We plan to reach Chatham on June 10, and shall hope that a stay there will be among your summer project[s]. If the climate suits you, there would be much that would bring joy in its simple loveliness.

We had a nice evening with Henry [Goldmark].[2] He is one who improves with age, and is an altogether civilized man—unsullied by the barbarism which surrounds.

1. Probably one of the works of Ludwig August Frankl (1810–1894), an Austrian poet, scholar, educator, and editor who wrote widely about Jewish topics. Frankl founded a school in Jerusalem in the middle of the nineteenth century.

2. See LDB to Alfred Brandeis, 11 May 1924.

To Felix Frankfurter

May 28, 1924 Washington, D.C. [Frankfurter Mss—LC]

1. We had Senator & Mrs. Wheeler in Sunday. He has been terribly hard hit by the indictment, & that the A[ttorney]. G[eneral]. won't order it dismissed despite the Borah report.[1] The long strain of continuous hard work, immeasurably increased by the criminal proceedings, has worn on his strength & he needs all the cheering up which can come through appreciation. A personal word from you, in addition to your fine "piece" in the N[ew]. R[epublic]. (which he had not then seen) will help.[2] And I hope you can gently suggest to Pound & to Z[echariah]. Chafee that a letter (promptly sent) would be in order.

2. Ben Dinard [*sic*] (Minneapolis) was in yesterday.[3] He seemed quite depressed (a) by the difficulty of getting a living through practice (b) by the very engrossing work necessary to do it, which compels exclusion of contemplation & all things otherwise appealing. I suspect his brother's blindness adds much to the burden, & that his salary is a bit meagre. He did not complain of that however; rather of the exhausting quantity of the grind. There ought to be a place at some law school for as attractive a fellow as he appeared to me.

1 On 8 April, Burton Wheeler had been indicted by a grand jury in Great Falls, Montana, on charges of accepting retainers to use his influence to obtain gas and oil permits from the Interior Department. A special Senate committee, headed by William E. Borah, reported on 20 May that the entire

episode looked like a frame-up, that there was not a single bit of hard evidence to support the charges, and that people of high standing in the community who had knowledge of Wheeler's law practice had testified that there was no violation of the law. Wheeler had been head of the committee that uncovered evidence leading to Harry Daugherty's ouster from the Cabinet (see LDB to Frankfurter, 6 April 1924), and it later emerged that Daugherty, while he was attorney general, had sent the then head of the Federal Bureau of Investigation, William J. Burns, to discover "evidence" against Wheeler. After the Borah report was delivered, the charges were finally dropped; Burns himself left government service to establish the well known detective agency.

2. "Hands Off the Investigation," *The New Republic* 38 (21 May 1920): 329-31; see next letter, n. 2.

3. Benedict Spinoza Deinard was the son of a Minneapolis rabbi. He had done post-graduate work at Harvard in 1922 and returned to Minneapolis where he continued to practice law.

To Felix Frankfurter

June 3, 1924 Washington, D.C. [Frankfurter Mss—LC]

FF.: 1. Sen. Ashurst [1] told me with much satisfaction of inserting your article in the Congr. Record.[2]

2. You cornered the A[ttorney]. G[eneral]., and I don't think he helped himself by attempting what Hough J.[3] call[s] a hurdle. He hasn't stood the acid test.

3. The Child Labor resolution brings new dangers.[4] I guess we'll have to remember that our first instalments from women suffrage are this & the prohibition amendment. One would think that the Hull Housers would occasionally think of Chicago conditions. Mrs. Medill McC[ormick]. is eloquent on the almost unbelievable corruption (political) there. Interesting as coming from Mark Hannah's [*sic*] daughter.[5]

4. In the Frank tragedy it is, at least, a mercy that the victim was a Jew.[6]

5. Read the House Immigration Report. Whatsoever one may think of the policy, all must recognize that it is a very weak legislative presentation. The N[ew]. R[epublic]. might appropriately say this about July 1.[7]

6. You will find some things of interest in yesterday's opinions.[8]

7. Holmes J. is in fine form again, and seems to have had the joy of a child in yesterday's honors.[9]

8. LaFollette has again exhibited his political skill.[10]

There will be much to talk over at Chatham.

The [Walton H.] Hamiltons were in Sunday in fine form & very happy over the developments at the School here.

1. Henry Fountain Ashurst (1874–1962) had been a member of Arizona's territorial assembly and then served as the first Senator from that state from 1912 to 1941.

2. Frankfurter's article, "Hands Off the Investigation" (see preceding letter), had been inserted at Ashurst's request into the *Congressional Record*, 68th Cong., 1st Sess. (Washington, 1924), 9080–82.

3. Charles Merrill Hough (1858–1927), after ten years on the federal District Court, had been elevated by Wilson in 1916 to the United States Circuit Court of Appeals in New York.

4. On 2 June 1924, the Senate passed the proposed child labor amendment and sent it on to the states for ratification. Foes of the proposal gained some satisfaction in that the Senate did not allow for the special ratifying conventions in the states, but left the matter to the more conservative legislatures.

5. Ruth Hanna, the daughter of the conservative Republican leader Marcus Alonzo Hanna (1837–1904), had married Joseph Medill McCormick (1877–1925). The liberal McCormick had been a leader of Illinois progressivism; in 1924, he was serving his only term in the Senate.

6. See LDB to Roscoe Pound, 27 November 1914.

7. During 1924 Congress had again dealt with the explosive issue of immigration, and both houses had come up with measures severely limiting immigration. The "report" was the conference committee report on the Johnson bill, which established national-origin quotas and excluded the Japanese completely. The report and bill were adopted on 15 May, and President Coolidge signed the measure into law on 26 May 1924. For the *New Republic's* comments, see "Corollaries of the Immigration Law," *New Republic* 39 (11 June 1924): 61–62.

8. On 2 June the Court handed down seven opinions. LDB wrote one majority opinion in *United States* v. *American Railway Express Co.*, 265 U.S. 403, upholding the power of the Interstate Commerce Commission to set certain routes. He also entered one dissent, in which he was joined by Holmes, in *Pacific Gas & Electric Co.* v. *San Francisco*, 265 U.S. 393—he differed from the Court's interpretation of how public utility rates should be set. Here LDB was following the line he had set out in the *Southwestern Bell* case.

9. The day before, President Coolidge had presented Mr. Justice Holmes with the Roosevelt Memorial Association medal. In part the citation read: "In peace and in war, as a soldier and as a jurist, you have won the gratitude of a nation by your uniformly gracious and patriotic devotion of great talent to its service. One can but well feel very confident that President Roosevelt would have been peculiarly gratified to know that this distinction was to be conferred upon you."

10. On 28 May, Senator LaFollette had released a letter declaring he would be ready to lead a third party unless both major parties cleaned house. He attacked the communists and warned progressives that the communists were seeking to dominate the Farmer-Labor-Progressive convention scheduled to take place in St. Paul, Minnesota, on 17 June. See LDB to Alfred Brandeis, 19 July 1924.

To Paul Underwood Kellogg

June 9, 1924 Washington, D.C. [Kellogg Mss]

MY DEAR KELLOGG: In the heyday of prosperity, Americans never think. In suffering, they sometimes do. Business depression is apt to bring much suffering within a twelvemonth. I suggest that the Survey Graphic avail [itself] of the probable thinking period, by three issues—each to be devoted *exclusively* to one of the three following subjects:

1. Irregularity of Employment—the cause of Unemployment. The crime (in this respect, of highly organized monopolistic business[)] is expressed in the steel production fluctuations.[1]

The crime of the chaotic business, largely in coal production figures.

It is by tackling irregularity, instead of in musing on trade-cycles, that we are to find the way out.

Robert Bruere and M[orris]. L. Cooke can handle this issue.

2. Preserving our Timber Supply & Planting of trees.

On this, urge strongly state and municipal action. Massachusetts is setting a fine example. (Notably in the town movement.) Even Congress is waking up.

3. Soil preservation. In Albert J. Mason's[2] notable papers in which M. L. Cooke is well versed. He could lead with Mrs. Bruere's cooperation. She who so loves the land.

The three matters are fundamental, demanding attention from Economic Statesmen. Our social, industrial, political look ahead calls for a different vision than that of stock-broker patriots.[3]

Cordially,

1. LDB had enclosed in this letter an article from the 9 June *Washington Post* entitled "Steel Output in U.S. Fluctuates Rapidly." The article pointed out that from December to April 1924, ingot production shot forward 40 percent and then dropped off 19 percent.

2. Albert John Mason (1857–1933) had come to America from Australia in 1881. He retired from a profitable career as a mining engineer to devote himself to the study of soil erosion. LDB had met Mason earlier in the year when Morris Cooke brought him to Washington.

3. *The Survey* never devoted special issues to these topics.

To Julian William Mack

July 2, 1924 Chatham, Mass. [R. Szold Mss]

JWM: To you and Mrs. Mack every good wish, and for us, your safe return.[1]

I am enclosing a line to Edmund Benedikt, who, Redlich said, is one of the leading lawyers of Vienna & with whom we were in close relations in 1872–3.[2] His mother was my mother's best friend. I have not seen him since.

1. The Macks were going to Palestine.

2. Edmund Benedikt (1851–1929) was editor and publisher of the influential *Juristische Blatter* and author of numerous works on the law, including *Die Advokatur Unserer Zeit* (Berlin, 1912). Although the Austrian jurist was Jewish, he was not active in either Jewish or Zionist affairs.

To Alfred Brandeis

July 19, 1924 Washington, D.C. [Brandeis Mss, M 4–4]

DEAR AL: Here are some of the N[ew]. R[epublic]. editorials. There will be more. The Senator will have (if he keeps his health) a grand fight. If I had several watertight compartment lives, I should have liked to be in it. The enemies are vulnerable & the times ripe.[1]

The Chicago consolidation doesn't look to me very promising for the farmers.[2]

Will return the Cal[ifornia] wires from Reece later. I think I remember Miss R.

1. After weeks of rumor, Senator Robert M. LaFollette announced his candidacy for the presidency of the United States on a third-party ticket. On 4 July the new Progressive Party, meeting in convention at Cleveland, nominated him and, as his running mate, Senator Burton K. Wheeler. La-

Follette immediately won the endorsement of disaffected groups all over the country. Labor unions, the Socialist Party, the Farmer-Labor organizations, and the liberal periodicals all joined in announcing their support for him. His platform, in some ways a distant echo of the campaign of 1912, called for the whole catalogue of traditional liberal demands. See Kenneth C. McKay, *The Progressive Movement of 1924* (New York, 1947). The *New Republic*, badly disappointed by the Democratic choice of John W. Davis, warmly supported LaFollette, and there were many articles and editorials on him throughout the campaign.

There had been persistent reports that LaFollette wanted LDB as his running mate, and as early as March the rumors reached the attention of the press (see the *New York Times*, 18 March 1924). Throughout the summer the speculation continued (see the *New York Times* 3, 14, and 19 July 1924). LaFollette never discussed the matter directly with LDB, but he did send Gilson Gardner to Chatham to explore the possibility. LDB, preferring his life on the bench, refused as he had refused the leadership of the World Zionist Organization three years before. See LaFollette and LaFollette, *Robert M. LaFollette* 2: 1115–16. See also LDB to Felix Frankfurter, 7 November 1924.

2. On 16 July several of the leading grain companies in Chicago merged to form the Grain Marketing Company. Farm organizations were quick to condemn the merger, despite the proposal's being presented as a "cooperative" enterprise to be owned and controlled by farmers themselves. Even the spokesman for the Farmers' Cooperative Marketing Association called the consolidation an attempt to fool the nation's farmers. See next letter.

To Alfred Brandeis

July 22, 1924 Chatham, Mass. [Brandeis Mss, M 4–4]

DEAR AL: Re yours on grain [1]

It is not conceivable to me that the farmers will, or can, put up the $26,000,000. I don't understand the situation. But I cant believe that is "the way out."

Nor can I believe that short U.S. crops will be a blessing to the country. The short cotton crop certainly hasn't been, in the long run. The idle textile mills tell a terrible story. If prices go too high, the "Ersatz" comes in, & there is a wide margin in the irreducible necessary consumption & the possible maximum in food also—though not to the same degree.

I should suppose this would be particularly true of a short corn crop as to its being undesirable. I fancy the Lord has subtler ways than the boll-weevil to work out our destiny.

I think LaFollette has made a great gain in getting Wheeler for second place.[2] The fact that he is a Democrat, has such wide publicity, is young & fearless are great attributes.   Gruesse,

1. See preceding letter, n. 2.
2. See preceding letter, n. 1.

To Alfred Brandeis

July 26, 1924 Chatham, Mass. [EBR]

DEAR AL: The parents engagement day.

The hog meat has come. Thanks.

Your letters & enclosures about the grain deal are all interesting. It simmers down to: "I don't know what to think." Frank [Taussig] is coming over next week to talk it over. The further Minneapolis offer adds to the [*] of nations.[1]

Fate is making us the owner of this estate.[2] The owner concluded to sell, had an offer, and we had to buy to "protect the home". The papers have been signed (subject to Miss Malloch's scrutiny to be made) & we think fate dealt kindly with us. At all events, as Father said to Aunt Julie: "Ich füge mich in mein Schicksal." [3]

The price is only $15,000—the acreage $12\frac{1}{10}$ (twelve). Now we enjoy nearer twelve hundred, stretching out over the unoccupied land North, South, East & West of us on either side of Oyster Road. As the village is a mile and half away, we shall hope other folk will be slow in buying.

Emma Erving was here yesterday. She is always a great comfort in need & a joy when there is none. Fortunately Alice seems to be gaining pretty steadily.

The talk of the household is largely of politics, with Mrs. Evans high in national duties, Felix Frankfurter very active in writing & thinking & the rest of us hardly less keen in our interest.[4] Wheeler has helped much in taking the second place. Bob ought to make a fine fight & a great beginning for the future tussle.

If Davis gets the licking which the Democrats deserve for hitching their horse in Wall St.,[5] we may get the country divided on these new lines of Conservative & Progressive & get some honest thinking into our political & social problems.

Susan is due here today to stay until Monday P.M.
I hope things go well with Jennie.

1. Thirty-six additional grain companies in the Northwest offered to
sell their holdings to the American Farm Bureau Federation on 22 July. See
LDB to Alfred Brandeis, 19 July 1924 and preceding letter.

2. LDB, after summering in rental properties on Cape Cod for a number of years, finally bought a large, rambling house overlooking Oyster
Pond in Chatham. Eventually his daughter and son-in-law, Susan and Jacob
Gilbert, built a summer house of their own a few hundred yards away. For
the next seventeen years, dozens of public officials, writers, and Zionist
leaders found their way to Chatham every summer to give LDB information
and to seek his advice. In August 1974, the National Parks Service declared
the Chatham house a national historic landmark.

3. "I succumb to my fate."

4. Elizabeth Glendower Evans was a member of the executive committee
of women organized for LaFollette. Frankfurter's efforts provided an article,
"Why I Shall Vote for LaFollette," *The New Republic* 40 (22 October
1924): 199–201.

5. See LDB to Frankfurter, 6 April 1924, n. 1.

To Felix Frankfurter

September 6, 1924 Chatham, Mass. [Frankfurter Mss—HLS]

FF: Since our talk on conspiracy, I have looked at the cases in
U.S.S.C. & at those in the Fed. Rep. since 196. We have over half
a century of experience with J.C. § 37 (R.S. 5480).[1] There are
available data on which the careful and sagacious might determine
the usefulness of this form of prosecution & eliminate the abuses.

The enquiry shows, among other things, to what extent

(1) The field of state function has been invaded.

2. The proceeding has been used to secure trial at a jurisdiction
deemed more favorable to the Govt.

3. The conspiracy count has been joined to those for the substantive offence (as the indictments have been consolidated)
in order to secure admission of evidence which would have
otherwise been excluded wholly or as against certain defendants.

4. Injustice has been done by including in a single proceeding
many issues in part distinct & involving many defendants.

5. The discretion of the trial court has been abused by admit-

ting evidence of declarations as against alleged coconspirators before the fact of conspiracy has been clearly established.

The survey has been painful & has confirmed my conviction of the need of a fundamental enquiry into the causes of prevalence of crime in America. I don't think we can get far in cures until the diagnosis shall have been made.

1. Chapter 37 of the Judicial Code dealt with questions of jurisdiction. Section 5480 of the Revised Statutes dealt with conspiracy to commit mail fraud. LDB had often contended that mail fraud cases, within the federal jurisdiction, were one of the chief causes for the clogged federal judiciary.

To Adele Brandeis

September 24, 1924 Washington, D.C. [Brandeis Mss, M 15-1]

MY DEAR MAIDIE: I am very glad to have your letter and those of Prof. Ware [1] and the Dean.[2] Three cases of books (two large and one small) were shipped yesterday. The bill of lading is enclosed. A fourth case (large) should go within a few days. Later, from time to time, some small lots will be sent.[3] A note to Prof. Ware is also enclosed.

For such of the books as I possessed before removing to Washington, a card catalogue existed, which will be sent, if still available. It was prepared with reference to my peculiar needs & to be used only by my Secretaries. Hence, it is not such as Prof. Ware would require; but it may be helpful. Next week, I will send you a check for $1000 to defray the immediate expenses to be incurred by you and Prof. Ware in the preparation of an adequate catalogue, the binding and shelving; and the purely clerical expenses incident to efforts to complete and supplement (otherwise than by purchase) the sets of official and other periodic reports and publications which I deem the most valuable part of the collection—i.e. those issued by the Federal Government, state and foreign governments and organizations such as trade unions. By intelligent and persevering application to the publishing body or to those to whom these reports were distributed free, most of them can be readily obtained. E.g. Kentucky Congressmen and Senators can secure all hereafter published, by the Federal Government; and any heretofore published would doubtless be found, untreasured, in other libraries or in those of their predecessors or be otherwise procurable by them.

My collection was not planned as a library on Sociology; nor for comprehensive study. It is merely an aggregation of units acquired in connection with specific practical tasks which I had undertaken. Some parts of the collection had already been given to others who I thought might be aided in like work. If after familiarizing himself with the contents of the four cases sent, Prof. Ware finds that he lacks the books immediately required by his classes, I shall be glad to send a further check to be expended in purchasing such books as he and you deem desirable.

Please send me the catalogue of the University or Programs of Instruction.

Answering your enquiry: the gift may be announced at such time as you and the Dean think would be most helpful.

1. Norman Joseph Ware (1886–1949), who was a professor of economics and sociology at the University of Louisville between 1919 and 1926, was already embarked upon his notable career as a public servant and historian of the labor movement. In addition to his two most important works, *The Industrial Worker, 1840–1860* (Boston, 1924) and *The Labor Movement in the United States, 1860–1895* (New York, 1929), Ware would serve on a number of federal and state boards dealing with economic questions.

2. Warwick Miller Anderson (1872–[?]) was a Louisville native. After doing graduate work at Johns Hopkins and Chicago, he returned to the University of Louisville to teach physics. In 1924 he was named dean of the College of Liberal Arts.

3. In the fall of 1924, LDB began to interest himself in a matter which occupied his thoughts throughout the 1920s: the improvement of the University of Louisville. He entered this effort with the same energy and enthusiasm, and the same attention to detail, as were characteristic of his earlier social and economic crusades; but this time, because of judicial duties and the handicap of distance from the scene, he operated through intermediaries. These intermediaries were both University of Louisville officials and, principally, members of Alfred Brandeis's family resident in Louisville—particularly, after Alfred's death, LDB's niece, Fannie Brandeis. The effort to create a high-quality institution of higher learning in Louisville began, as in this letter, with personal donations of books, reports, and government documents. Within a few months, however, LDB concentrated the work largely toward an improvement of the University libraries and the University Law School. In the end, as following letters in this volume will reveal, LDB thought that the most productive initial step would be to establish a number of specialized library collections and from that base create a research and education center which would attract superior faculty and stu-

dents. For the most complete statement of LDB's underlying philosophy in undertaking the task, see his letter to Alfred Brandeis, 18 February 1925; for details on the various libraries, see the letter to his brother on 4 June 1925, and other letters to Adele and Fannie Brandeis and to Frederick Wehle and Charles and William Tachau.

It should be noted that LDB's work on behalf of the University of Louisville was intimately tied to his fear of the over-centralization of American life and his increasingly passionate belief that if America was to be saved, salvation would come from the diversity of its various locales. For LDB this meant encouraging local experiments in social and political life and local centers of cultural and educational significance. For that reason, he always insisted that the primary responsibility for building a great university would always remain with the faculty and administration of the University of Louisville and with the citizenry of the city.

For the details of LDB's involvement, see the thorough monograph by his friend and associate, Bernard Flexner, *Mr. Justice Brandeis and the University of Louisville* (Louisville, 1938). See also the brief summary of LDB's efforts in Mason, *Brandeis*, 588–93.

To Adele Brandeis

September 29, 1924 Washington, D.C. [Brandeis Mss, M 4–4]

MY DEAR MADIE: I wrote you on 24th enclosing bill of lading, freight prepaid, for the first three cases of books. Now, I enclose, bill of lading, freight prepaid, for the fourth (a much larger one). Among the books sent, are quite a number of which the value consists merely in showing how that longing for social justice may induce people to write who have nothing to offer save vapidities or irrationalities. But as Dr. Hagen said long ago: "Das Studium des menschlichen verirrungen hat auch werth." [1]

Included in the box is a small package (containing some reports & catalogues) which I thought the General Librarian might care to have; also a small package with two books & two pamphlets which seemed appropriate for the Library of the Scientific School.

When this fourth case is unpacked, please search vigilantly for the following books—which, cherishing as daily companions, we took to Chatham & back & which I fear the faithful Poindexter mistakenly put into this case—probably in the upper third. If found, kindly return them promptly & relieve an aching void.

Livingston's "What the Greek Genius Means to Us."

The Legacy of Greece.

Gilbert Murray's Translation of Euripides, "The Bacchae etc."
A volume of Plutarch's Lives
Some like minded books which I do not recall may be in the same package. If so, please return them also.

1. "The study of human error also has value." Johannes Georg Hagen (1847–1930) was an Austrian priest and a well known astronomer. In 1888 he moved to Washington, D.C. and became the director of the Georgetown University Observatory. He later became the director of the Vatican Observatory.

To Felix Frankfurter

September 29, 1924 Washington, D.C. [Frankfurter Mss—HLS]

That Oct. 1 article is a rip-snorter.[1] Of course C[alvin]. C[oolidge]. won't understand. But J[ohn]. W. D[avis]. can and will; and some others high in authority may get an inkling. I hope it will receive its due of comment;—approval or attack, it matters not which. What will Mr. George Rublee say?

Would it not be possible to get some one to write (say for the Atlantic, i.e.) a comparison of the actual security of life & property in U.S.—and on the other hand in Britain, Canada, Australia, New Zealand, South Africa? Could Harold Armstrong do it, or Loring Christie or Phil Kerr or Lionel Curtis?[2]

The Higgins are coming in this evening, & we have asked Father Ryan[3] to meet them.

1. In an unsigned editorial (obviously by Frankfurter), "The Red Terror of Judicial Reform," *New Republic* 40 (1 October 1924): 110–13, the journal attacked both Coolidge and Davis for their stands on judicial reform. Both men, in speeches delivered only hours apart, defended the Supreme Court majority in nearly identical terms. In his attack, Frankfurter listed areas in which the majority on the High Court may have been guilty of "slaughtering of social legislation on the altar of the dogma of 'liberty of contract.'" Among other changes, the editorial suggested that "due process" litigation under the Fourteenth Amendment ought not to be considered by the Supreme Court.

2. None of these writers produced any articles along the lines suggested by LDB. The suggestion was provoked by Frankfurter's assertion (see n. 1, above) that life, liberty, and property are not less protected by other constitutional arrangements in the English-speaking world.

3. John Augustine Ryan, S.J. (1869–1945) was a professor of moral theology and industrial ethics at Catholic University and a leader in the Catholic social justice movement. He wrote numerous books on the ethical demands of an industrial society, and in 1933 Pope Pius XI elevated him to the rank of domestic prelate. Noted for his political liberalism, Father Ryan was an important factor in smoothing Catholic-Protestant relations in twentieth-century America, and one of the most important leaders in American Catholicism.

To Zechariah Chafee, Jr.

October [?], 1924 Washington, D.C. [Chafee Mss]

MY DEAR CHAFEE: Thank you for the alluring book.[1] I'd like to enter the course.

The swelling numbers should enable Harvard to develop soon a body of worthy teachers willing to develop the law schools. For of law schools, also, it is time that: "In der Beschränkung zeight sich Erst der Meister."[2]   Cordially,

1. Probably Zechariah Chafee, ed., *Cases on Equitable Relief Against Torts* (Cambridge, Mass., 1924).

2. "It is in restraint that the master primarily reveals himself." The quotation is from Goethe's play, "Was Wir Bringen," Scene 19. For LDB's meaning here, see the letter to Felix Frankfurter, 9 October 1924.

To Alfred Brandeis

October 3, 1924 Washington, D.C. [Brandeis Mss, M 4–4]

DEAR AL: An Ala[bama]. judge speaking of Italian immigration in his region told me yesterday that land-owners have imported (?) quite a large number a few years ago, were delighted with them as tenant-farmers, but found that, in a few years, every Italian had saved enough money to buy himself a farm & quit his tenancy, & that there was no use counting on Italians.

We plan to serve to [*sic*] your ham to Professor [John A.] Hobson & wife (of London), Circuit Judge Woods[1] of South Carolina, Grace Abbot [*sic*][2] & Dr. Ernest Gruening[3] of N.Y. They ought to know a good thing.

We were on the Potomac yesterday & today. Fortunately we have a bit of heat occasionally.

1. Charles Albert Woods (1852–1925) had been judge of the fourth Circuit Court since 1913.

2. Grace Abbott (1878–1939) had been trained in social work by Jane Addams during a nine-year residency at Hull House. Miss Abbott developed into a leading figure in numerous civic and industrial reforms, but is best known for her work in the United States Children's Bureau. She succeeded Julia C. Lathrop as chief of the bureau in 1921.

3. Ernest Gruening (1887–1974) was at the height of his journalist career in 1924, serving as managing editor of *The Nation* and also as LaFollette's publicity director for the presidential campaign. A distinguished second career was still before him. In the 1930s he moved to Alaska and became the territorial governor in 1939. He remained governor until 1953, and in 1956 he became the territory's provisional senator. When Alaska became a state, Gruening was chosen her Senator, serving from 1958 to 1969. A leading liberal in Congress and an outspoken early critic of the Vietnam War, Gruening retired in 1969. See his *Many Battles: The Autobiography of Ernest Gruening* (New York, 1973).

To Felix Frankfurter

October 9, 1924 Washington, D.C. [Frankfurter Mss—LC]

1. Pound has doubtless told you of his letter to me of 10/6 about the L[aw]. S[chool]. building plans, and of my reply which was:

"Thank you for letting me know about the plans under consideration.

Do let me talk with you when you are next here. I have grave apprehensions and want to suggest an alternative."

Entre nous, the alternative is roughly this:

Make frank recognition of the fact that numbers in excess of 1000, and the proposed 350 seats lecture halls & lectures, are irreconcilable with H.L.S. traditions & aims. Instead, make frank avowal of a purpose to aid in building up the lesser schools. Then aid in placing H.L.S. resources at their disposal so far as possible, i.a., create a new kind of exchange-professorships—i.e., H.L.S. professors who will go out, as legates, temporarily to aid in developing lesser schools & there teach and take in exchange the local professors who shall come for a year or so to H.L.S. to *learn*.

Also arrange that picked students from such lesser schools may enter, not only postgraduate H.L.S. classes, but the higher undergraduate classes. Of course, I see the difficulties of putting such an alternative scheme into operation. But it is "constructive—not destructive." Be the mother church for the new & worthy legal education & legislation.[1]

2. It is fine to hear of Marion on the stump.[2]

3. "   "   "   "   " Herman A. in perfect health again.

4. Guthrie's partner H. was not happy when I last saw him.

5. Who wrote the World editorial?

6. S. Adele Shaw [3] is able enough to understand even if she doesn't heed.

1. As the popularity and prestige of the Harvard Law School increased, its physical facilities, dating back to the nineteenth century, became severely overcrowded. Pound was considering a number of ways of dealing with the situation, and the one he had presented to LDB involved a large-scale expansion of the school's physical plant, faculty, and student body. On 21 October Pound named a committee chaired by E.H. Warren, which included Frankfurter, to consider plans for a new building. Despite Pound's expansionist ideas, the committee, probably under Frankfurter's prodding, recommended that the law school be more selective in its admissions rather than less, and that it seek $4.2 million in additional endowment funds for program purposes. Eventually, Pound announced a drive to raise $5.4 million for building and endowment, but the effort yielded only slightly more than $2.3 million. See Sutherland, *The Law at Harvard*, 262–70; see also LDB to Frankfurter, 25 October 1924.

2. In support of Robert LaFollette's independent presidential bid.

3. S. Adele Shaw had been the youngest member of the famed Pittsburgh survey, and then joined the Survey Associates. Married to Jonathan Freeman, she was active in Pittsburgh civic affairs.

To Fannie Brandeis

October 20, 1924 Washington, D.C. [Brandeis Mss, M 4–4]

MY DEAR FANNY: Until the University of Louisville shall be equipped to promote the study of the fine arts and music, one of its important functions must remain unperformed. Doubtless many years will elapse before adequate provision for this can be made. But it is not too early to begin, now, to dream what might be; and to plan what shall be. Moreover, any concrete steps toward realization taken now, however modest they be, will, as overt acts, manifest the purpose of the University, and may be the means of securing from others needed cooperation. I hope you will care to do some of this planning and will undertake the small beginnings which I want to suggest.

First. The beginning of a departmental library. The University gives now some instruction in Greek and Latin and in Ancient history. Obviously, the earlier civilizations cannot be understood without full appreciation of their contributions to the fine arts. Access to the rich and ever growing fruits of archeological exploration is essential to an intimate knowledge of the life of the older peoples. Thus, books on ancient arts and archaeology are primal needs of instructors who seek to awaken in students an interest in the achievements of a great past and to feed the hope for a greater future.

If the University authorities approve, Aunt Alice and I will be glad to place at your disposal, from time to time, funds to be applied in the purchase, for this purpose, of such books as you and the appropriate members of the faculty deem necessary; and for the attendant expense of shelving, binding, and cataloguing. We should expect also to help, through you, in like manner, in the acquisition of the books on art required for an adequate study of the Renaissance and the later period; and eventually to lay a wee corner-stone for a library of music. To learn modern history implies understanding of the culture of the several peoples and knowledge of such contributions as each has made to civilization.

Second. The beginning of an art collection. Living among things of beauty is a help toward culture and the life worthwhile. But the function of the University in respect to the fine arts is not limited to promoting understanding and appreciation. It should strive to awaken the slumbering creative instinct, to encourage its exercise and development, to stimulate production. There is reason to think that Kentuckians have, among their many gifts, imagination and creative power. There seems to me no reason why this should not express itself in the fine arts. The Brenner which your Aunt Hattie and Mr. Speed generously gave me is an example of Kentucky art, finely achieved.[1] With her approval, I should be glad to give it to the University, through you, as an encourager of effort in others.

These are functions of the University which would have made the strongest appeal to your two grandmothers and your Aunt Fannie. They must interest deeply also your mother, Maidie and

Jean. And I am sure your cousin Harry would be ever ready to give his expert advice.[2]   Your uncle,

1. See LDB to Alfred Brandeis, 10 July 1912.
2. LDB's nephew, Harry Wehle, worked at the Metropolitan Museum of Art in New York City.

To Charles Warren

October 24, 1924 Washington, D.C. [Warren Mss]

MY DEAR WARREN: It was good of you to send me your valued Princeton lectures.[1] The burden of our indebtedness to you grows, but with each success on your part, also increasing obligation. So I venture to express again the hope that your studies for the history of the lower federal courts are progressing.[2]

Most cordially,

1. Warren's Stafford Little lectures at Princeton University were published as *The Supreme Court and Sovereign States* (Princeton, 1924).
2. See LDB to Warren 23 June 1922.

To Felix Frankfurter

October 25, 1924 Washington, D.C. [Frankfurter Mss—HLS]

F.F.: Re yours 21

1. I talked with S.[1] about H[arvard]. L[aw]. S[chool]. as suggested. He knew nothing of conditions, did not know there was a problem, &, of course, had not thought on the subject. His reaction was wholly toward our view, thought larger numbers irreconcilable with proper teaching of the case-system to which he is wedded. He realized that he had not thought on the subject; later suggested it was a matter which ought to be thoroughly discussed by and in the faculty; & said he would think further himself. He asked about Williston [2] and [Joseph H.] Beale, would be much influenced probably by Williston's views, possibly by B.'s. I should doubt whether he would stand adamant against P[ound]'s insistence & whether it would be desirable to arrange an interview.

I suppose you have reason to think that S.['s] opinion would carry large weight with P. I don't see why.

2. As to use of my alternative suggestion.[3] Do with it what you please. Disclose or withhold authorship—appropriate it; modify it; or any other treatment you deem helpful. I should think you, with Williston, would be more potent in argument than anyone else could be with P.

3. As to method of limitation: I think there should be strong insistence that in consideration of the subject, the questions should be definitely segregated:

    (a) whether limitation to, say, 1000 is desirable.

    (b) if so, the mind of man may be then put solely upon devising or selecting the best, or least objectionable means.

    (c) if not, the mind should proceed to devise the means which will make numbers least harmful.

S. began by asking for means & method of limitation, before expressing an opinion. But I convinced him of the wisdom of rejecting that method of approach, & he then agreed that we must limit, & having determined on that, find the best method of applying the limitation.

I have no definite views as to methods of selection. A field for wide research & inventive thought is open. A few things seem clear:

    (a) Limitations must *not* be effected by raising tuition fees.

    (b) The method must ensure national representation, geographically & in respect to colleges.

    (c) Provision must be made for star men (undergraduates) of other law schools.

    (d) Provision must be made for teachers of or those definitely preparing for teaching at other law schools.

1. Probably Harlan Fiske Stone, who had been dean of the Columbia Law School.

2. Samuel Williston (1861–1963) had taught at the Harvard Law School since 1890, had been Weld Professor of Law from 1903 to 1919, and then was Dane Professor until his retirement in 1938. He was an authority on contracts, and in 1929 he received the first gold medal of the American Bar Association for "conspicuous service to American jurisprudence."

3. See LDB to Frankfurter, 9 October 1924.

To Robert D. Kesselman

October 26, 1924 Washington, D.C. [Kesselman Mss]

MY DEAR KESSELMAN: It was good to get your greetings, and to know through DeHaas' reports that things are going well with you.

I am sure DeHaas' settling in Palestine will bring happiness and encouragement to you and others, and aid in efforts spiritual as well as economic. His keen analysis has never lessened his own enthusiasm, and it tends to make his fellows remember what is the life and striving worth-while.[1]

With every good wish,   Cordially,

1. Jacob deHaas was on an inspection tour of Zionist work in Palestine. Although he spoke many times of settling in the Holy Land, he never actually did so. See LDB to Julian Mack, 3 November 1921.

To Frederick Wehle

October 28, 1924 Washington, D.C. [Brandeis Mss, M 4–4]

MY DEAR FRED: [1] The World War has wrought epochal changes. Every phase and incident of the stupendous struggle and of the efforts at readjustment will become the subject of special research and of interpretation. To understand the causes of the war, its conduct and its consequences will hereafter be essential to statesmanlike conduct of our public affairs. To study them will be a necessary part of a liberal education. Opportunity for this study must be afforded Kentuckians if they are to be fitted for tasks which await them. The ambition of the University of Louisville should rest even higher. It should seek to become truly a seat of learning; a place where historical research may be pursued and histories be written. It is only by affording facilities for such study and research that it may hope to attract to its faculty, and retain, men and women who will bring to students not instruction merely, but inspiration; teachers through whom, indirectly, history is made.

To this end the University must possess an adequate library of the war and the post-war period. This library must include not merely the tools necessary for undergraduates, but so far as possible, also the mass of publications which constitute the new material for historical research. Most of the unpublished papers bearing upon the period will necessarily remain in the official archives of belligerents or neutrals, or will be made available only through the world's greatest libraries. But the materials which most concerns [*sic*] Americans is not of that unique character. We shall learn most by unprejudiced, painstaking study of our own strengths and weaknesses; by enquiries into our own achievements and shortcomings. It is thus that we may best learn how great are the possibilities of high accomplishment in the future; and what are the real dangers with which we shall be confronted. The rich material for these enquiries may be obtained by the University, if the members of its department of history and political science care enough to build up such a library to be willing to make the necessary effort. For the publications required for this purpose—partly official, partly private in origin—were widely circulated in the United States. Copies of most of these are still procurable. And probably copies could be obtained from some sources without resort to purchase.

My own collection of such books and papers might serve as the nucleus for such a library of the war and post-war period. It is quite large; and is comprehensive. It includes a fair number of books on the causes of the war, its conduct and its results; on the birth of the new nations; on the proposals for ending war. It includes publications of the numerous war-agencies established or utilized by our Government in the prosecution of the war and in the adjustments made after the Armistice; publications emanating from foreign Governments or their nationals which were circulated in this country; and publications of societies or individuals seeking to advance our interests in the war, a satisfactory solution of foreign problems, or the World peace. But my collection would serve as a skeleton merely. It is, in no respect, complete. For there has been no conscious effort on my part to build a library. What I possess of this character is an aggregation of books and papers which I procured, from time to time, because I was interested in the general subject or was called upon to advise in respect to some specific matter. Some of these publications came to me unsolicited—indeed many of them.

In order to develop my aggregation of books and papers into a worthy library on the war and the post-war period, much work would have to be done. The files of publications which I have must be completed. Of other publications, not represented in my collection, the full files would have to be sought. Publications soon to appear must be obtained when issued. To this end members of the faculty would have to familiarize themselves with the existing and available material, and to enquire into and consider carefully the sources from which such material could be obtained without purchase. If the task of obtaining such material is entered upon promptly and efforts are pursued unremittingly, Kentuckians within and without the State can be counted on for furnishing such aid as may prove to be needed.

If the University authorities approve of making such a collection, if the appropriate members of the faculty are willing to assume the task suggested, and if you care to aid them in it, Aunt Alice and I will be glad to give the University now my collection of books and published papers on the war and post-war period, together with sums required to defray the expense of cataloguing, binding and shelving and the purely clerical disbursements incident to the immediate efforts to complete and supplement the files of publications as indicated. At a later time we should expect to give to the University some unpublished documents relating to the war which seem to have historic interest, but should, for the present, be treated as Confidential.

Your father's life-long study of history and government leads us to hope that he will join you in lending aid to the faculty in this task. We hope, also, that some day Fred Jr.[2] and his cousins will, as students at the University, find valuable the material which you will bring to it.　　Your Uncle,

1. Frederick Wehle (1896–1973) was the third child of LDB's sister Amy and Otto Wehle, hence LDB's nephew. He was the only one of the Wehle children to remain in Louisville.

2. Frederick Wehle, Jr. (b. 1919) is the eldest son of Frederick Wehle. He has worked in various companies around Louisville for thirty-five years.

To Felix Frankfurter

November 3, 1924 Washington, D.C. [Frankfurter Mss—LC]

F.F.: 1. I suppose you have seen the straw vote in the Nov. 1 New Student.[1] That is the most discouraging feature in our life. It means that youth has its eye on the main chance, almost to the exclusion of other things. It is just what we of Public Franchise League experienced a quarter of a century ago.

2. Alice bids me say, as to Marion's article, that quite apart from the merits of the argument, there is in it undeniably literary quality, that it has atmosphere & style.

3. I guess the British Labor defeat will hurt us considerably.[2]

1. There were several student polls taken at this time, and all of them showed college students supporting Coolidge overwhelmingly. In most cases, Coolidge had twice as many straw votes as his opponents, John W. Davis and Robert M. LaFollette, combined.

2. On 8 October, Ramsay MacDonald's Labour Government had suffered a stinging vote of no confidence over its handling of the prosecution of a Communist writer. MacDonald resigned shortly after, and on 4 November the king asked Stanley Baldwin to form a new cabinet.

To Felix Frankfurter

November 7, 1924 Washington, D.C. [Frankfurter MSS—LC]

F.F. 1. As to Austin W,—Ask Nutter and McClennen who know much more of his worst than I do. My impression is that he has the intellectual quality & some acuteness of mind, but is not an A1 man. Moreover, he seems to be doing good work where he is and should be left in C.

2. Tuesday's events constitute a dismal deluge of surprises.[1] But there are some rays of sunshine peeping through the clouds:

    (a) It looks as if extension of federal functions had rec'd an important check. Billy Hard says C[alvin]. C[oolidge]. is strong against it (with the education bill a strange exception) & that Sen. Wadsworth & Ogden Mills who are against extension of federal functions will be his chief advisors legislatively.[2] Hard says also that J[ohn]. W. Davis's own strong feeling (largely suppressed) was against federal assumption of state powers.

    (b) It looks as if we should have practically no federal leg-
islation (except appropriations bills at the short session)
before 1926. That closed season, with Washington free
of legislators, would be something to be thankful for.
Meanwhile the community might be induced to think.

    (c) Davis & the like are, I suppose, not likely to reappear as
Democratic nominees for another generation.

3. However bad the Tuesday showing is, I think we may say
that it reflects truly the American attitude. I can't imagine a fairer
election. Every party was amply heard orally & in the press. Without more than the inevitable fallacious or unwise misrepresentation
in argument. It was a time of calm, economically — neither boom
nor depression. There was no undue excitement political or otherwise for any cause; no hysteria; nothing abnormal or unusual to
deflect the judgment. The vote is a representative precipitate of
American life, with its virtues and its shortcomings. It should lead
one to think. I don't believe in "the slush fund" theory.

4. Alice thinks your conversion of J.W.M[ack]. is a notable
achievement.

5. We are to have the Wheelers, the Costigans & Laura Thompson in to dine tomorrow.[3]

6. That's a good memo of yours re dormitories [at Harvard].

7. Poor N[ewton]. D. B[aker].

8. Enclosed re Zinovief letter [4] would afford a good text for a
sermon on detectives, or a dime novel, "The Biter Bitten."

9. What do you know of the qualities & antecedents of Mark
Sonnheim?

I suppose Dave Walsh will try it again—for Lodge's place.[5]

Send the explanation of the Mass[achusetts] Child Labor
Amendment vote.[6]

England with Birkenhead in and [*] has dangers ahead,—But
it's good to see Eustace Percy get a chance.[7]

1. On 4 November, Calvin Coolidge buried both John W. Davis and
Robert M. LaFollette under an avalanche of 15.7 million votes (LaFollette
was able to garner only about a sixth of the popular vote); and the Republicans captured complete control of both houses of Congress.

2. James Wolcott Wadsworth, Jr. (1877–1952), a New York Republican,
had served in the Senate since 1915. Ogden Livingston Mills (1884–1937),

another New York Republican, served in the House of Representatives from 1921 until his defeat in the New York gubernatorial contest of 1926. Thereupon Coolidge appointed him Undersecretary of the Treasury; Hoover appointed him Secretary of the Treasury for the last year of his administration.

3. Laura A. Thompson (1877–1949) worked for the Children's Bureau; she later became librarian for the Department of Labor.

4. One of the factors involved in the defeat of England's first Labour government (see preceding letter, n. 2) was the so-called Zinoviev letter. Allegedly written by Grigori Evseevich Zinoviev (1883–1936), the leading Bolshevik and Chairman of the Executive Committee of the International, the letter instructed the British Communist Party on subversive activity. Its publication caused widespread comment and a reaction against the Labourites. Zinoviev, who was later executed in the Great Purge, denied having written the letter.

5. David I. Walsh was defeated for reelection to the Senate; but within a week of the writing of this letter, Henry Cabot Lodge died. In 1926, Walsh was elected to fill the vacancy (see LDB to Frankfurter, 28 October 1926, n. 5) and he served there until 1946—when he was defeated, ironically, by Henry Cabot Lodge, Jr.

6. Massachusetts voters defeated the Child Labor Amendment, instructing the state legislature to vote against it; the Amendment lost by over 400,000 votes.

7. Frederick Edwin Smith, 1st Earl of Birkenhead (1872–1930) reconciled his differences with the Conservatives and accepted the position of Secretary of State for India. LDB's and Frankfurter's old friend Eustace Percy was named president of the Board of Education. See LDB to Frankfurter, 10 January 1926.

To Frederick Wehle

November 19, 1924 Washington, D.C. [Brandeis Mss, M 4–4]

MY DEAR FRED: I have yours of 16th.

I assumed that the University is poor in possessions—including the instructors. What I aim to do is to make them rich in ideals and eager in the desire to attain them. I want the authorities to dream of the University as it should be; and I hope to encourage this dreaming by making possible the first steps toward realization. The only assurance I care to exact is that a desire for high standards is felt, and that an effort will be made to carry out the project as suggested. Teachers are largely a meek, downtrodden, unappreciated body of men. To know that others believe in them, consider them capable of high thinking and doing, and are willing to help them rise—may enable them to accomplish more than even they think possible.   Your Uncle,

To Felix Frankfurter

November 20, 1924 Washington, D.C. [Frankfurter Mss—HLS]

F.F.: 1. Your article on Injunctions & the S[upreme]. C[ourt]. is in every way admirable.[1]

2. Glad you had so satisfactory a talk with C[harles]. W[illiam]. E[liot]. Isn't he extraordinary? But Holmes J. gives promise of doing likewise. He has not been in better form these 8 years.

3. T.W. Gregory was in to dine yesterday with Dodd and the Hamiltons.

4. T.W. Gregory was in Sunday. Most enthusiastic over Manley Hudson's performance at Geneva,[2] and heartsick over moral decadence in Texas where he is now living. (Houston)

5. I don't see that there is anything I can suggest for the N[ew]. R[epublic]. that you & I haven't talked over.

6. The Dept. of Justice says the A[ttorney]. G[eneral]. is slated for the S[upreme]. C[ourt].;[3] Dick for England (unless it be Hoover); & Hoover for Secretary of State (if not to England).[4]

1. In an unsigned article, "Injunctions and Contempt of Court," *The New Republic* 40 (19 November 1924): 287–89, Frankfurter had written approvingly of the Supreme Court's sustaining the right of trial by jury in criminal contempt cases.

2. Hudson had attended the recent Geneva meetings of the League of Nations and had participated in a number of committee sessions as a representative of the Non-Partisan Association for the League, headed by former justice John H. Clarke.

3. On 5 January President Coolidge nominated Attorney General Harlan Fiske Stone to succeed Joseph McKenna on the Court.

4. Frank Billings Kellogg had been recalled from the Court of St. James to replace Charles Evans Hughes, who had resigned as Secretary of State following the 1924 election. To replace Kellogg, Coolidge nominated Alanson Bigelow Houghton (1863–1941) as the new ambassador to Great Britain on 13 January 1925. Herbert Hoover remained as Secretary of Commerce.

To Learned Hand

December 3, 1924 Washington, D.C. [Hand Mss]

MY DEAR HAND: I am glad—for the law, for our Court and for yourself.[1]   Most Cordially,

1. Coolidge had nominated Hand to fill a vacancy as judge for the 2nd U.S. Circuit Court. He was speedily confirmed and began his distinguished service on 20 December.

To Felix Frankfurter

January 1, 1925 Washington, D.C. [Frankfurter Mss—HLS]

Our best wishes for 1925 to you & Mrs.

1. A[ugustus]. N. Hand[1] called Sunday, was evidently anxious to talk H[arvard]. L[aw]. S[chool]. for he called twice, I having been out when he came first. [Joseph H.] Beale had visited him, & set forth his plans to H. & to [Charles M.] Hough (whom H. invited for the evening). H. set forth his views. He is entirely of our way of thinking. When he got through I told him in detail why I concurred with him.[2]

You were not mentioned by either of us in this connection. He said Beale said that (practically?) everybody except [Samuel] Williston was for the plan, which contemplated doubling the faculty in numbers, etc.

H. is to be in Cambridge on the 16th.

2. Had you thought of making an attempt now to start Malcolm Sharp at teaching law somewhere?[3] I understand that he is disappointed at not having any work with L & S in labor controversies. He might now be more ready to go at teaching.

3. You will recall our asking John M. Nelson (with E. Keating) to dine to talk over election results.[4] I set forth to him my views (a) the need of a general staff of thinkers, who shall be divorced from office & the political task of putting things over. (b) the need of developing a body of doers, by setting men to the accomplishment of local tasks within their capacities.

He stated as to (a) at this time his favorable inclination, as he had himself thought vainly about what he ought to put through if, by chance, the Progressives succeeded. Last week he tele-

phoned for a[n] appointment, said he was wholly convinced of
(a), that he had been talking over the whole situation with two
men of high character & public spirit in the House. One a good
Republican, the other a good Democrat. That he was pretty sure
that they could form, in the next Congress, a coalition which
could control the House & that they (the three) wanted to develop the (a) project etc., Nelson putting himself & associates in
the background. He wanted me to pick out men for the general
staff whom he could call on etc. after March 4. I told him of you
(of course confidentially) & that I would ask you to think up the
men to ask. It seems to me that we ought to be able to find a
group of men willing to be the politico-economic thinkers, who
would, in privacy, think out what it is wise to do, why & how.[5]

4. A. N. Hand told me of Charles Howland's[6] reaction to
Meicheljohn [sic] which is very unpromising & may, I fear, stand
in the way of any help from the N.Y. source. If you start H. on
C.H. you will doubtless hear the same story.

5. The [*] verdict is indeed a strong argument for juries.

6. A. N. Hand said that Beale & others at the H.L. School admit that the quality of the graduates is worsening. H. is quite convinced that the School is already too large & is prepared to see
evidence like this in support.

7. Mack was in today. We talked H.L.S. a little. Told him I
wanted not a bigger H.L.S., but 20 Harvard Law Schools & told
him what Hand had said. I did not develop my ideas either to
him or to A.N.H.

8. Hermann Blumgart was in. A fine fellow & a terrible tragedy.[7] He told us of your wonderful reception at the Union.

9. I am glad to hear what you write about Landis.[8]

10. Mack will tell you of our talk as to his own future.

11. The talk now is that the A[ttorney]. G[eneral]. will be the
next choice for the U.S.S.C.[9]

12. Tell your mother that Estelle is looking well.

13. I am venturing to increase the amount of the check enclosed, so as to more nearly defray the disbursements of our joint
adventure.[10]

1. Augustus Noble Hand (1869–1954) had been named by Wilson to the
United States District Court in 1914, and in 1927 Coolidge would elevate

him to the Court of Appeals, where he served until 1953. During his career he was active in the Harvard Law School Association.

2. See LDB to Frankfurter, 9 October 1924.

3. Malcolm Pitney Sharp (b. 1897) had graduated from the Harvard Law School in 1923, and in 1925 was in private practice. He returned to Harvard for graduate work during the 1926–27 year and afterwards joined the faculty of the University of Wisconsin. In 1933 he began his long service as a professor of law at the University of Chicago.

4. John Mandt Nelson (1870–1955) was a LaFollette Republican from Madison, Wisconsin. He served in the House of Representatives from 1906 to 1919, lost the 1918 election, and then returned for the period 1921 to 1933. Edward Keating (1875–1965) was a Democrat from Colorado, who served in the House from 1913 to 1919. Upon his defeat, he stayed in Washington, D.C. and edited *Labor*, the magazine of the railroad brotherhoods.

5. During the early 1930's, Frankfurter became involved in just such an informal advisory group, which the popular press dubbed Roosevelt's "Brains Trust."

6. Charles Prentice Howland (1869–1932), a graduate of the Harvard Law School, had been in partnership with LDB's old friend Victor Morawetz before opening his own office in New York. He was active in a number of educational programs, including the Rockefeller Foundation and the General Education Board.

7. Hermann Ludwig Blumgart (b. 1895) was a Boston physician and a professor of medicine at Harvard; he was a close friend of Frankfurter's.

8. James McCauley Landis (1899–1964), still a young law student at Harvard, would become one of the leading figures in American legal education. Frankfurter had arranged for Landis to clerk for LDB during the 1925 term, but Landis and Frankfurter were then involved in research that would ultimately lead to several important articles (see LDB to Frankfurter, 2 June 1925). LDB therefore offered to give up Landis's services if Frankfurter felt that the research work would be more important. Finally Landis did clerk for LDB during the 1925–26 term, after which he returned to teach at Harvard until 1933. Franklin Roosevelt appointed him to the Federal Trade Commission and then to the new Securities and Exchange Commission, where he was named chairman. In 1937 he returned to Harvard as dean of the Law School. In 1946 he resigned to pursue a variety of assignments both in governmental work and in private practice.

9. Four days later President Coolidge did nominate Attorney General Harlan Fiske Stone (see LDB to Frankfurter, 6 April 1924 n. 7.) to fill the vacancy created by the resignation of Justice Joseph McKenna. Stone was confirmed by the Senate on 5 February and took his seat on 2 March 1925.

10. See LDB to Frankfurter, 19 and 25 November 1916.

To Frederick Wehle

January 13, 1925 Washington, D.C. [Brandeis Mss, M 4–4]

MY DEAR FRED: I am glad to have yours of 9th & will write you at length as soon as time serves.

Meanwhile:

1. Let me know when it will be convenient for the U[niversity] to receive the books & papers. I presume they will prefer to have nothing come until this brick building is available to receive books, at least for storage.

2. Have you talked this over fully with the members of the History Department? And have you shown them my original letter to you, so that they may know what is expected of them and of you? [1]

3. If the University is to become a worthy institution, it must be *through* its faculty and officers. They are to build up a library. You and I are to help them. And, of course, your part will be an important and continuous one, and it is my purpose to keep on helping them to build up the Department.

Your Uncle,

1. See LDB to Wehle, 28 October 1924.

To Albert Rosenthal

January 18, 1925 Washington, D.C. [Rosenthal Mss]

MY DEAR MR. ROSENTHAL: [1] I hope you will not consider me ungracious. But I am averse to any portrait of myself except the official one customarily taken after each change in the membership of the Court.

With high appreciation of your courteous offer,   Cordially,

1. Albert Rosenthal (1863–1939) was a well known American artist who had done portraits of many Supreme Court judges.

To Felix Frankfurter

January 31 and February 3, 1925 Washington, D.C.
[Frankfurter Mss—HLS]

1. The first cert[iorari] involving Act of Oct 29/19 c[hapter] 9 41 St[atutes]. 324 and the first case on const. of Esch (transporting stolen autos in interstate comm.) have reached us.[1]

I think amendments of the act are pending or have been passed.

With the awakened sense of the dangers of centralization wouldn't it be well to begin the campaign for freeing the federal courts of unnecessary burdens. Could Landis find time for this?

2. We reached today No 300—entered Feb 26/24, & adjourned early on two days this week because no case was ready. A large number were continued to next term as a result of our speed.

2/3

3. I have yours re doubts re R[oscoe]. P[ound].[2] We are, I guess, of one mind as to this. The press and folk seem to think that the matter is not yet settled. But today came a statement that he had definitely declined Wisconsin. I guess it was you alone who achieved this.

I understand [John R.] Commons says, "Damn the lawyers" (in this connection).

4. Emory Buckner has the abilities and the experience which will make of him a [*] U.S. atty, provided he has the spirit, and can keep his eye steadily on that job instead of thinking of the next.[3]

5. How did the men do on your Labor Exam?

Morris Cohen's was an uncommonly good letter.

1. The act, which became law without President Wilson's signature, stipulated a fine of up to $5,000 or prison for not more than five years for anyone knowingly shipping or receiving stolen automobiles.

2. Erroneous stories had reached the press that Pound had accepted the presidency of the University of Wisconsin Law School.

3. Buckner (see LDB to Charles R. Crane, 17 May 1916) had been nominated for the position of United States District Attorney for the Southern District of New York. He was confirmed by the Senate on 10 February and began serving on 2 March.

To Felix Frankfurter

February 6, 1925 Washington, D.C. [Frankfurter Mss—HLS]

Our jurisdiction bill will doubtless become a law within a few days.[1] When it does, this story, with a moral, may well be written:

U.S.S.C.—venerated throughout the land.

Despite the growth of population, wealth and governmental functions, & development particularly of federal activities[,] the duties of the Court have, by successive acts passed from time to time throughout a generation, been kept within such narrow limits that the nine men, each with one helper, can do the work as well as can be done by men of their calibre, i.e. the official coat has been cut according to the human cloth.

Congress, Executive Depts., Commissions & lower federal courts.—All subject to criticism or execration. Regardless of human limitations, increasing work has been piled upon them at nearly every session. The high incumbents, in many cases, perform in name only. They are administrators, without time to know what they are doing or to think how to do it. They are human machines.

1. The Jurisdictional Act was passed by Congress on 13 February and became effective on 13 May 1925; a copy can be found at 266 *U.S.* 687.

To Felix Frankfurter

February 7, 1925 Washington, D.C. [Frankfurter Mss—HLS]

1. As to Emory Buckner[1] & Prohibition Cases, I agree. But he does not need any legislation of any kind, if he will formulate this plan & keep his mouth, & that of his underlings, resolutely shut.

A. Examine all prohibition cases now in & coming in. Divide them into two classes: (a) those involving smuggling from abroad or bringing in from other states; (b) those involving violations wholly intra-state.

B. Then, give the preference in trials (without saying so) to cases in class (a). That will take up all the ability of the office; all the capacity of available judges; and all the appropriation available for prohibition. If & when there is any surplus capacity, etc., he can take up (b). Parallel lines are said to meet in infinity.

2. I wrote J.W.M[ack]., suggesting, as a means of tackling crime in America & his individual problem, that he secure his assignment for a long period in the Criminal Sessions in N.Y. He says that he agrees fully & had talked with Gus Hand & will again about this.

3. That letter from Edison is fine. It gives me a different opinion of him than I have ever had. And E.A. [Filene]'s service (unintended) in getting it is the best of his achievements in a decade.

4. Do you think the naive Solicitor Gen[2] will appreciate [Thomas] R. P[owell].'s skit?

5. Norman H[apgood]., the Keatings & the Donald Richbergs are coming in tomorrow for dinner to discuss the state of Progressivism.

1. See LDB to Frankfurter, 31 January and 3 February 1925, n. 3.
2. James M. Beck.

To Fannie Brandeis

February 14, 1925 Washington, D.C. [Brandeis Mss, M 15–1]

MY DEAR FAN: We are delighted to hear of Aunt Hattie's gift.[1] In honor of it, Aunt Alice is sending you today by Amer. Ry Express (receipt enclosed) a piece of old Japanese lacquer, which we are told is of large value artistically and financially.

Its ancient history we cannot, at the moment give you. Doubtless you will divine it, after you have mastered those "uncut leaves."

The recent history is this: It was given us by Percival Lowell (brother of A. L[awrence]. L[owell].) who, as your father will remember, was, nearly half a century ago, the secretary of the mission of Japan to the United States. (P.L. wrote three books on Japan.)

Aunt Alice and I, in our ignorance, gave this piece what we thought was a place of honor in our Boston home. Denman Ross saw it there & was shocked at the sacrilege—told us of its value and that it should be exhibited only under glass.

So it has been carefully preserved awaiting the day when Aunt Alice should send it to you for the University.[2]   Affectionately, I hope to answer your letter tomorrow.

1. Hattie Bishop Speed had donated the J. B. Speed Memorial Museum to the University of Louisville.
2. See also LDB to Hattie Speed, 9 October 1927.

To Fannie Brandeis

February 17, 1925 Washington, D.C. [Brandeis Mss, M 4–5]

MY DEAR FAN: Your letter gave Aunt Alice and me much pleasure.

1. "The Fine Arts Library of the University of Louisville" seems to us admirable for the book plate. Do not let the Louis D. Brandeis name creep in there or in the Museum, as Aunt Hattie has so generously suggested. We have been willing that it should be used in the publicity solely because, in view of my official position, it appeared to be effective as a lever to move others to aid. But any use of the name in a more permanent way would tend to defeat the purposes we have in mind. We want to stimulate action, and to this end it is important that others have the memorials. This is of particular significance because of other plans we have in mind about which I am writing your father.[1]

2. Aunt Alice & I think it would be better for you to write Mr. Currall for the Journal & the Bulletin. A letter written by you on University paper would doubtless be effective.

We hope that the express package arrived safely.[2]

Your Uncle,

1. See next letter.
2. See preceding letter.

To Alfred Brandeis

February 18, 1925 Washington, D.C. [Brandeis Mss, M 4–4]

MY DEAR AL: What has been started through Maidie and Fanny, and what was attempted through Fred [Wehle], are but parts of a larger plan to lay broad and deep the foundations of the Univer-

sity. It is a task befitting the Adolf Brandeis family, which for
nearly three-quarters of a century has stood in Louisville for culture and, at least in Uncle Lewis [Dembitz], for learning. For
this undertaking conditions seem favorable now. It would be fine
if all the grandchildren could take an active part. But six of them
are disqualified, for the present, by non-residence; and Fred has
declared himself ineligible for another reason. So the task devolves
upon your family—yourself, Jennie, the girls and the sons-in-
law—and upon Alice and me. If we elders can have ten years to
work in, the preliminary work will have been done. The rest can
be left wholly to your descendants and the Centuries.

Money alone cannot build a worthy university. Too much
money, or too quick money, may mar one; particularly if it is
foreign money. To become great, a university must express the
people whom it serves, and must express the people and the community at their best. The aim must be high and the vision broad;
the goal seemingly attainable but beyond the immediate reach. It
was with these requisites in mind that I made the three essays
referred to. To indicate, through the Department of Sociology,
the purpose to influence the life of the State socially and economically. To indicate, through a Department of Fine Arts and of
Music, the purpose to provide that development which is comprised in the term culture. To indicate, through the proposal concerning the World War history, the purpose, not only to encourage research and learning, but to influence the political life of
the State and the nation by a deep and far-reaching study of history, an enquiry into the causes and consequences of present ills,
and a consideration of the proper aspirations of the United States
and of the functions of the State. History teaches, I believe, that
the present tendency toward centralization must be arrested, if
we are to attain the American ideals, and that for it must be substituted intense development of life through activities in the several states and localities. The problem is a very difficult one; but
the local university is the most hopeful instrument for any attempt
at solution.

Our university can become great, and serve this end, only if it
is essentially Kentuckian—an institution for Kentuckians, developed by Kentuckians. For this reason, everything in the life of
the State is worthy of special enquiry. Every noble memory must

be cherished. Thus, the detail of Kentucky history, political, economic and social, become factors of ultimate importance. The biographies of its distinguished sons and daughters, including as such, Kentuckians who have lived and achieved elsewhere, are matters of significance. The University library should grow rich in Kentuckiana. It should become a depositary of unpublished manuscripts and like possessions associated with the life of the State and the achievements of Kentuckians.

Growth cannot be imposed upon the University. It must proceed mainly from within. The desire for worthy growth must be deeply felt by the executive officers and members of the faculty. It must be they who raise the University to standards and extend its usefulness. But the desire may be stimulated by suggestion; and achievement may be furthered by friendly aid. Thus, there is a large field for the efforts of those outside the University whose capacity, experience and position gives them a wider view and bolder vision; whose position enables them to secure for the University's projects the approval and support of the community; and whose means enable them to furnish financial aid. From them may come also the encouragement without which few achieve and that informed, friendly supervision, without which few persevere in the most painstaking labors.

If the development is to be both sound and fine, it is essential that the growth be gradual, continuous and manifold. Every department must be improved; some expanded, some divided. From time to time, new departments must be added and the functions of the University must be enlarged. This can be accomplished, in part, by single acts—specific gifts of buildings or the establishment of endowments, general or special. The recent Speed gifts are sure to be followed by similar ones from other persons.[1] Alice and I think that the Adolf Brandeis family is equipped to promote the development of the University by a continuous service which, while less conspicuous, will be no less useful and should prove of enduring value. It is to take the part of the ever helpful sympathetic friend who, with thought, tact and patience, will awaken aspiration and encourage effort on the part of officers and members of the faculty; and also those without the University who may join in advancing the high purposes of the University. The family service which we have in mind is, in its general character, similar to that which is already being performed by Fanny and Maidie. If you and your angehörigen [2] are willing to extend your operations, Alice and I will be glad to aid with our suggestions and with such part of our surplus income as may be wisely applied in the undertaking. The money required will doubtless increase with the expanding functions and intensive character of the work. But in this connection the service of money will resemble that of water in agriculture, always indispensable, always beneficent to the point where it becomes excessive, but of little avail unless the soil be rich, naturally or through fertilizers, unless there be appropriate cultivation, and unless the operations be conducted with good judgment.

This letter has grown so long that I must leave for another letter some suggestions which we wish to make for immediate activities. [3]

1. See LDB to Fannie Brandeis, 14 February 1925.
2. "relations."
3. See LDB to Alfred Brandeis, 4 June 1925.

To Felix Frankfurter

February 21, 1925 Washington, D.C. [Frankfurter Mss—HLS]

1. It would be fine to have you & Marion here for a week. When may it be?

2. I think if you would write (& have Pound as well as yourself sign) a request to the C[hief]. J[ustice]. to have (a) our Reporter include annually in the reports the judicial statistics, & (b) to lay the matter before his Council of Judges at his Sept. meeting for similar action by the Cir. & Dist. courts—for publication in the Federal Report—he would be disposed to comply. [1]

I suppose you could get the Deans etc. of Yale & other law schools to join in the request. That would help. Also indirectly, it would tend to make the Fed. judges realize a bit more that they are being watched throughout the country & that there is being developed an enlightened public opinion which will judge the judges.

3. What you report about [Emory] Buck[ner] is fine. [2] If he can be induced to be steadfast at his job 4 full years so as to show

real results, for which at least that period is essential, he can create by his conspicuous position an example that will be potent through the country.

4. I told J. M. Nelson that you would be ready to see him after March 4 & he will write you for an appointment.[3]

5. I am glad you talked with Croly about Child Labor. I assume you will now put it up to Julia Lathrop[4] et al. to get to work in the States. By the way, what does her Illinois do—on paper & otherwise. What Miss [Florence] Kelley's N.Y.? What Grace Abbot's [sic] Nebraska? etc.

I note yesterday's note in [*]. It should arouse the Men-folk to work at home.

6. The Am. Woolen Report of $6 million deficit should teach folk again that Southern competition is not the trouble with the textile industry.[5] I suppose the woolen mills in the South are an obviously negligible quantity.

But to see textile wages go down 10% & living costs go up nearing 10% should make [*] Brown & the like give themselves up to thinking.

7. Is Croly getting any data on that Verona, Miss. schoolmaster story from Collier's? [6]

8. Louis Levine has done a fine job on the Int. Garment Workers Union history.[7]

1. Beginning in the October 1930 term, the Supreme Court expanded slightly its own statistical reporting, indicating for the previous three years the nature of its cases (original jurisdiction or appelate) and the number of cases disposed of. No information for lower courts was included.

2. See LDB to Frankfurter, 31 January and 3 February, and also 7 February 1925.

3. See LDB to Frankfurter, 1 January and 2 June 1925.

4. Julia Clifford Lathrop (1858–1932) had long been associated with Jane Addams at Chicago's Hull House, and was a leading figure in various child welfare reforms; she was also the first director of the Children's Bureau in the Department of Labor.

5. For the company's report, see *New York Times*, 19 February 1925.

6. LDB had uncovered a story about a Verona, Mississippi school teacher who had trained a large number of distinguished pupils—civic, political, and economic leaders. The *New Republic* did not run such a story, but *Collier's* picked up the item later.

7. Louis Levine, *The Women's Garment Workers* (New York, 1924).

To Felix Frankfurter

March 1, 1925 Washington, D.C. [Frankfurter Mss—HLS]

F.F.: 1. You & Landis may care for enclosed copy of the Jurisdiction Act.[1]

2. George Soule still lacks due repentance. He, Julia Lathrop & others are in danger of not seeing the woods because of the trees; and are establishing a strange mechanistic view of life. Child Labor is pretty bad, even in America. But if the "broken lives" they & Miss Kelley talk about are to [be] eliminated they must look much deeper.[2] A study of the Juvenile, the divorce and the criminal courts, and some thought of the upper ten might help to a more balanced view [of] social evils.

3. Josephine [Goldmark] who is for the Amendment (but doesn't pretend to know very much about N.Y. conditions) is under the impression that in N.Y. both the child labor & the enforcement are satisfactory.

4. The Van Vlecks came in Friday. He has grown considerably through his new responsibilities.[3]

1. See LDB to Frankfurter, 6 February 1925.
2. See LDB to Frankfurter, 3 June 1924.
3. William C. Van Vleck (see LDB to Frankfurter, 16 September 1923 n. 5). had just become dean of the law school at George Washington University.

To Felix Frankfurter

March 6, 1925 Washington, D.C. [Frankfurter Mss—HLS]

FF: 1. Not even an Edgar Allan Poe could have imagined how terrible would be Dawes' V.P. address.[1]

2. I hope the humorists wont overlook this in C[alvin]. C[oolidge]'s Inaugural:

"Mindful of these limitations, the one great duty that stands out requires us to use our enormous powers to trim the balance of the world." [2]

3. Yes, the C[hief]. J[ustice], like the Steel Corporation, is attaining old time production records. He has no intention of

yielding to C[harles]E[vans]H[ughes] (who told me that he will take six months vacation.) [3]

Miss Grady reports that your Sunday address at Ford Hall was "Superb!"

1. Charles Gates Dawes (1865–1951) had been active in Republican politics since the 1890s. He returned from World War I a much decorated hero and entered government service. Author of the famous "Dawes plan" for relieving the German reparation burden by means of private loans, he was nominated for the vice-presidency in 1924, was elected, and served in that office through Coolidge's administration. He then was named ambassador to England. Dawes shocked the Senate in his 1925 inaugural address by ignoring the normal pleasantries and launching a vigorous attack on the body and its antiquated rules. The *New York Times* wrote: "Some Senators looked aghast. Others leaned forward, amazement in their faces. Others took it humorously, and a few put their hands over their mouths as if to stifle laughter." The text of the address can be found in the *Times* for 5 March.

2. The quotation, which is accurate, appears near the end of Coolidge's address. LDB is amused at the word "trim," which of course can mean to cheat. The text of the President's remarks are also in the *New York Times* for 5 March.

3. For reasons never altogether clear, Hughes resigned as Secretary of State in January. Perhaps rumors were afloat that Taft would resign from the Court and Hughes be appointed Chief Justice. Actually, Hughes did succeed Taft as Chief Justice, but not until 1930.

To Alfred Brandeis

March 9, 1925 Washington, D.C. [Brandeis Mss, M 4–4]

DEAR AL: Glad to have yours of 4th & 7th.

I heard recently that Ford has in mind making a "drive" for Endowments, at some time.[1] Before he settles upon any plan for this, I hope there will be a chance of my talking with him.

I am particularly desirous of preventing Louisville from taking foreign money, notably not from "foundations." If we are to have a worthy Kentucky institution, it should be through Kentuck support. The other is the "easier way"—but like most "easier ways"—apt to defeat the best development.

There are other things also about the "drive" I should want to discuss with him; but I thought you might mention the above to Dr. Ford when you see him (if you think it wise) so that he wont have committed himself before I have a chance to talk with him.

Sorry I cant report on any Simon-pure Kentuckians today. But I had a call last week from Bob Wool[l]ey's and Louis W[ehle]'s friend Henry M. Waite who married John Mason Brown's daughter.[2]

It is fine that you have such good reports from Martinsville.

1. Arthur Younger Ford (1861–1926), a Kentucky journalist and business-man, had assumed the presidency of the University of Louisville in 1922.

2. Henry Matson Waite (1869–1944) was a railroad and industrial engineer, once the city manager of Dayton, Ohio. He was married to Mary Brown, daughter of prominent Louisville lawyer John Mason Brown and sister of the famous literary and drama critic, John Mason Brown, Jr.

To Alfred Brandeis

March 26, 1925 Washington, D.C. [Brandeis Mss, M 4–4]

DEAR AL: We celebrated Maidies's visit by running off late this afternoon for our first paddle of the season.

Maidie will tell you of the LaFollettes with whom we had a very pleasant evening Sunday, they dining with us alone. He is in good form, but does not bear his years as well as you do.[1]

I am glad that you refused Owen Young[2] plea to head the Page drive.[3] I rather think most can be done for Louisville by tending to its home affairs; & especially in money matters, by teaching them to spurn foreign money. As Father used to say: "Italia farà da se."[4]

The Frankfurters are here for a few days—Felix to talk at the Graduate School.   Gruesse,

1. Senator LaFollette died ten weeks later, on 18 June. On 20 June, LDB wrote to Frankfurter: "Yes, LaFollette died fittingly. He had put all there was in him into the great fight—never sparing himself. And he knew not fear."

2. Owen D. Young (1874–1962) was chairman of the board for General Electric and honorary chairman for the Radio Corporation of America. He frequently advised people in government on social and economic prob-lems, and was probably best known for the "Young plan" of 1929, reducing German reparation payments.

3. Young was heading the fund-raising drive to establish the Walter Hines Page School of International Relations, in connection with Johns Hopkins University.

4. Cavour: "Italy will take care of herself."

To Felix Frankfurter

April 2, 1925 Washington, D.C.[Frankfurter Mss—HLS]

FF.: Your and Marion's visit was all too short. There is much more to talk over.

1. Re curtailing jurisdiction on ground of diversity of citizenship.[1] Why should a plaintiff ever be permitted to sue in a federal court of the District of which he is a citizen & resident? Why should he be entitled to sue an alien in a federal court? Why should a consolidated & domesticated corporation ever have a right (under the diversity of citizenship provision) to enter or removed [sic] to the federal court?

2. The N[ew]. R[epublic]. editorial treatment of the Colorado treaty is plumb silly.[2] Opponents of the Child Labor amendment are not proposing dissolution of the union or abrogation of federal powers. Those who cherish the promise of American life[3] should remember that time & patience are indispensable factors in its realization. And as to speed in federal action, they should not forget Muscle Shoals.[4]

3. Have you heard from Max L. & [Malcolm P.] Sharp?

4. Do you recall Shiras J. in DeArnaud, No. 151 U.S. 488, 493:[5]

"We are relieved from considering whether the newfangled term "military expert" is only old "spy" writ large".

1. The phrase "diversity of citizenship" refers to questions of the proper jurisdiction of the federal courts. The Constitution provides that citizens of different states, engaged in litigation, may enter the federal court system. LDB wanted to limit the use of federal courts as much as possible. See Henry J. Friendly, "The Historic Basis of Diversity Jurisdiction," 41 *Harvard Law Review* 483 (1928).

2. In "An Interstate Compact Fails," *New Republic* 42 (1 April 1925): 144–45, the editor denounced the attempt of seven western states to arrive at a sensible agreement on the use of the waters of the Colorado River. The negotiations over the Boulder Dam project, he said, provided ample evidence that state control is unworkable. Narrow local interests were not able to settle the difficult technical questions of irrigation *vs.* power; only

the federal government could provide the expertise and objectivity required. "Doctrinaire antifederalism in such a situation is little less than absurd."

3. A reference to *New Republic* editor Herbert Croly's book of that title.

4. During World War I, the federal government had constructed a dam and two nitrate plants on the Tennessee River at Muscle Shoals, Alabama, performing the work so quickly that the plant was in operation by mid-1918. During the 1920s, Senator George W. Norris (see LDB to Frankfurter, 8 February 1927, n. 3.) led a battle to expand the Muscle Shoals facilities to serve as a yardstick for the measurement of private power company performance. Although Norris twice secured congressional approval, the idea was vetoed first by Coolidge and then by Hoover. During the 1930s, Muscle Shoals became the pilot plant of the enormous Tennessee Valley Authority. The best sources for the Muscle Shoals fight in the 1920s are Richard Lowitt, *George W. Norris: The Persistence of a Progressive* (Urbana, 1971), and Preston J. Hubbard, *Origins of TVA: The Muscle Shoals Controversy, 1920–1932* (Nashville, 1961).

5. Charles de Arnaud had claimed that the federal government owed him $100,000 for his services as a "military expert" employed by John C. Frémont. The Supreme Court dismissed his claim and, in the opinion Justice George Shiras, Jr. (1832–1924), supplied the phrase quoted by LDB here. *De Arnaud v. United States*, 151 *U.S.* 483 (1894).

To Willis VanDevanter

April 29, 1925 Washington, D.C. [VanDevanter Mss]

MY DEAR VAN: I hope that your good judgment, which is so generously used for the protection of others, will lead you to take a fortnight off—far from briefs, records and your associates.

Three weeks, with your mind refreshed by the rest, will leave ample time for all the work needed of you before the end of the term.

To Felix Frankfurter

May 13, 1925 Washington, D.C. [Frankfurter Mss—HLS]

FF: 1. With old Boston vital on Free Speech & arrayed, would it not be well to try to start the move for abolishing speaking licenses for the [Boston] Common?

2. With Mass. excited about the Alpha Cement decision,[1] could not H. L. Shattuck [2] (aided by ex ass[istan]t Att[orne]y

Gen[era]l Hitchcock, who is learned on taxes) — start the Webb
Kenyon idea [3] as to Foreign Corp[oration]s? La. with the Texas
Transport,[4] Mo. with the [**] Line decisions, & many more communities dismayed at amendment of their license fee taxation,
would surely be glad to join & with the Back to the State Movement on the rise, Congress might do some work on these lines.

3. I am returning [to] you Jim Wilson letter & enclose one
from a very different Texas District Judge — please return it.

4. Will you kindly send Alice a list of any persons (and addresses) here or abroad, whom you or Marion think we might
be likely to forget in making up our list for Elizabeth's wedding
announcement.[5]

1. *Alpha Portland Cement Co.* v. *Massachusetts,* 268 *U.S.* 203. The Court,
with LDB in dissent, declared illegal a Massachusetts tax on a "foreign" corporation that was dealing exclusively in interstate commerce. The decision
was handed down on 4 May.

2. Henry Lee Shattuck (1879-1971) was a prominent Boston attorney. He
served in the state legislature and was active in Harvard University affairs.
Shattuck had strong banking and insurance connections and was an inveterate
foe of Savings Bank Insurance (see LDB to Frankfurter, 9 February 1928).

3. See LDB to Frankfurter, 17 June 1923, n. 4. William Harold Hitchcock
(1874-19[?]), a Boston lawyer, served as assistant attorney general of Massachusetts from 1915 to 1920.

4. *Texas Transport & Terminal Co., Inc.* v. *New Orleans,* 264 *U.S.* 150.
The Court, with LDB and Holmes dissenting, once again restricted the
power of the state to tax, through licensing, a corporation engaged in interstate commerce exclusively. The case was decided on 18 February 1924.

5. On 20 April 1925, LDB's younger daughter Elizabeth announced her
engagement to Paul Arthur Raushenbush (b. 1898). The two were colleagues in the Economics Department of the University of Wisconsin. He
was the son of the illustrious social gospel minister and theologian Walter
Rauschenbusch.

To Oliver Wendell Holmes

May 18, 1925 Washington, D.C. [Holmes Mss]

O.W.H.: Noblesse Oblige.

You have "no right to retire".

You are now the most useful man on the bench, and should

resist all attempts of the ignorant or the designing to push you from your seat.[1]

1. Since January 1925 rumors had circulated about Justice Holmes's imminent retirement. On 15 January, LDB wrote to Felix Frankfurter: "OWH is not in the least disturbed about the newspaper items re his retirement. He believes them to be inspired, and as [Melville W.] Fuller, C[hief]. J[ustice]. said: 'I don't propose to allow myself to be paragraphed out of my job.'" See the *New York Times,* 10 January 1925, for one such rumor. Along with this note LDB sent a clipping of 18 May entitled "Holmes' Retirement from Court Rumored." Holmes was not to retire until 1932.

To Oliver Wendell Holmes

May 19, 1925 Washington, D.C. [Holmes Mss]

O.W.H.: What do you say to this clipping? [1]

It looks as if the game of imagining the king's death were in full play.

1. LDB had enclosed a clipping from this date's *Washington Post*. The headline read "Justice Brandeis Leaves Sanitarium" and the article contained the preposterous claim that LDB "has been a patient at the Hinsdale sanitarium for a week, it was learned today. He left the institution last night and came to Chicago. Attendants at the sanitarium say Justice Brandeis, who is 69 years old, displayed great recuperative power and in eight days built himself up to normal condition from a state of exhaustion. He returned to Washington at noon today." Holmes replied, ". . . . If anything should happen to you the Court and I both would lose an eye." And LDB jotted a reply: "How do you account for this 'news'—it's too early for dog day stories."

To Learned Hand

May 25, 1925 Washington, D.C. [Hand Mss]

MY DEAR HAND: With trepidation, I send you the opinion in Benedict v Ratner in which we are boldly reversing you and your C[ircuit]. C[ourt of] A[ppeals]. on a question of New York law.[1]

It is situations like this (here of course unavoidable) which I had in mind in our talk about U[nited] S[tates] S[upreme] C[ourt] and state law.   Cordially,

1. The case involved a complex question of New York bankruptcy law. A carpet company had given Ratner, a creditor, book accounts for his collection as collateral for loans. Subsequently the company declared bankruptcy and the receiver collected the accounts of the company. Ratner demanded the proceeds and Benedict, the receiver, refused to hand them over because of a provision of New York law that declared such a conveyance void. Hand's court upheld Ratner, but LDB, speaking for a unanimous Court, reversed the judgment. 268 *U.S.* 353. See next letter.

To Felix Frankfurter

June 2, 1925 Washington, D.C. [Frankfurter Mss—HLS]

1. Your and Landis' papers go back today. Receipt herewith. This is a most promising piece of work.[1] Thank you.

2. I guess [Thomas R.] Powell is right about your Yale L.J. article.[2]

3. Your questions re B. v. R.[3] are in order: (1) Case heard early in '23 term, assigned to V[an Devanter]. Recently reassigned to me to equalize burdens. (2) Court may not know as well at time of considering pet[ition]. for cert[iorari], whether question involved is a state question, as it does later. (Sometimes it doesn't know later, the Salem Trust Co. & Mfrs Finance Co, 264 US 152).[4] (3) In Hooker and Estave cases, the question dealt with was a federal question. Hence it was permissible to use the appropriate language discarding old terms. Here question was a state question; the inappropriate language was hallowed by state use; and, in laying down the state law, it seemed obligatory to use "the language of the country."

4. That's a fine report you are making to Nelson.[5]

5. C[alvin]. C[oolidge]. is doing good work for us on state functions. Note the enclosed by Rogers. What poor statesmanship & politics the Democrats have been guilty of, omitting to grasp this issue.

6. George Soule was in last week & I talked to him on this subject & particularly on cutting public jobs to fit the human cloth available.

7. We gave Fred Delano a deserved tribute yesterday in closing the Texas-Okl. receivership.[6]

8. The U.S.S.C. is probably 100 cases worse off than last year at terms end. We have disposed of the usual number of cases & certs, but the inflow seems very large now.

9. Magnes probably told you of his talk with me, I hope accurately. It was an entirely harmonious talk.[7]

10. The Hough book has not come yet.[8]

11. O[liver]. W[endell]. H[olmes]. in resplendent form.

12. Your telegram re Peelis came dramatically while I was talking with Ford & Miller. I have made it clear to both that you are the Supreme Adviser, & that Miller comes through you. M. will doubtless go to Louisville within a fortnight for the first conference with Alex Humphrey, Helm Bruce et al. More of this when we meet.[9]

13. I think you will find Stone's Trade Assn. op[inion]s. his best work.[10]

1. Frankfurter and James M. Landis had just published "The Business of the Supreme Court—A Study in the Federal Judicial System, Part I: The Period Prior to the Civil War," 38 *Harvard Law Review* 1005 (1925). Four more sections subsequently appeared and two years later the five pieces were published as a book, *The Business of the Supreme Court* (New York, 1927); see LDB to Frankfurter, 1 August 1927, for LDB's final evaluation.

2. Again collaborating with Landis, Frankfurter published "The Compact Clause of the Constitution: A Study in Interstate Adjustments," 34 *Yale Law Journal* 685 (1925).

3. *Benedict* v. *Ratner;* see preceding letter.

4. The Salem Trust case had been in and out of federal courts for several years; the sticking point was which courts had jurisdiction in establishing bankruptcy rules and procedures. For final disposition, see 280 *Fed. Rep.* 803 (1925).

5. See LDB to Frankfurter, 1 January and 21 February 1925.

6. In another bankruptcy case, the Supreme Court had to make final decisions on the disbursement of the assets of a mineral-exploiting company doing business in two states. *Oklahoma* v. *Texas,* 268 *U.S.* 472 (1925). There is no mention in the record of Fred Delano acting for either party, although he may have served as an officer of the Court itself.

7. See LDB to Julian W. Mack, 13 June 1925.

8. Charles M. Hough, ed., *Report of Cases in the Vice-Admiralty of the Province of New York* . . . (New Haven, 1925).

9. In a long conference with the University of Louisville's president, Arthur Y. Ford (see next two letters), it was agreed that the Alfred Brandeis

family would concentrate its activities on the University's library. But the upbuilding of the Law School would be directed by Frankfurter, operating through his classmate from Harvard (1906) Robert Netherland Miller (1879–1968). Miller was a tax lawyer with offices in both Louisville and Washington, D.C. He had been born in Louisville and had taught in the law school there.

10. The day before, the Supreme Court had decided two important anti-trust cases: *Maple Flooring Manufacturers Association* v. *United States,* 268 *U.S.* 563; and *Cement Manufacturers Protective Association* v. *United States,* 268 *U.S.* 588. Harlan Fiske Stone had written the opinions in both cases, which were decided by 6–3 votes. The government had attacked both trade associations as being in violation of the Sherman and Clayton acts. Both groups collected and disseminated information, and while no overt price fixing took place, the government held that the statistical services led to an informal price maintenance. Stone, echoing arguments that LDB had used over a decade earlier, took pains to draw a distinction between illegal acts that restrained trade and legal but cooperative endeavors that supported free trade.

To Alfred Brandeis

June 4, 1925 Washington, D.C. [Brandeis Mss M 4–4]

MY DEAR AL: In my talks with Pres[iden]t [Arthur Y.] Ford, concerning the development of the University, I explained to him my fundamental purpose and the objective, the scope and direction of the aid which I purposed giving, and the method and means which it seemed wise to pursue for the attainment of these ends. What I proposed seemed to meet his approval; and I think we may go forward with the work, assured of his cooperation. The plan covers:

First: The Law School—this I need not trouble you with, at least for the present. Robert N. Miller (suggested by his class-mate Felix Frankfurter) has this special task in hand.

Second: The University Library—the instrument for raising the standards of the Institution now and for all time, the means of stimulation to instructor and student—I want to feel is wholly the task of your family, and yourself, through:

    (a) Maidie—in the Department of Sociology and Economics.

    (b) Fanny—for Archeology, Art and Music

    (c) Charles and Billy [1] and their wives—for War History and Generally American History and Government

    (d) Kentuckiana. I look to you personally.

The all-embracing character of the desired Kentuckiana I indicated to you in an earlier letter.[2] With a view to having some knowledge of existing available material I applied for information to the Congressional Library. They referred me to the bibliography in McElroy's "Kentucky in the Nation's History" (1909 Moffat-Yard & Co.), a most interesting book which you should know—for other reasons. The Library's Chief Bibliographer also prepared at my request, the enclosed bibliography of publications in the Congressional.

Some day, Louisville should have the best collection of Kentuckiana also on these lines. But it seems wise not to make that our special concern for the present. What we should now direct our attention to is not histories, biographies or the like, but the raw material out of which these are made, namely, among other things:

  I. The official reports and other publications of the State issued by or through the several departments and bureaus.
 II. Like reports and publications of Louisville, of Jefferson County and other municipalities and counties, including their ordinances, by-laws, etc.
III. Annual reports and publications of institutions, not Governmental, but of a public nature. Such as educational, philanthropic, religious, and particularly such as are located in or have specific relation to Louisville.
 IV. Reports and publications of businesses; particularly the Public Service Corporations and Banks, but including also private business concerns which make annual or other reports; also such reports and other publications of business organizations like the Board of Trade.

It is in publications of this nature, largely uncopyrighted and usually treated as being of ephemeral, if of any, value, that the real history of the Community is recorded. By their close and continuous study the important facts, political, economic, and social will evolve. And it is through an adequate study of such sources that the experience, which is to become our teacher, is to be gained.

There has been, in America, in general a failure hitherto to recognize the value of such material, or at all events, a failure to make a systematic collection of it. Even the Congressional Library which is rich in its collection of American copyrighted material, is very poor in the collection of such uncopyrighted matter; as the enclosed bibliography will show you. The reason is that the collection of the uncopyrighted involves far more knowledge, imagination and effort. The volumes of the copyrighted books come to the Congressional by operation of law—and to other libraries through the publishers' lists and solicitation. To get the uncopyrighted publications requires the kind of knowledge which you have, the thought which you will give, and the eternal watchful interest without which a really valuable collection cannot be built up. It must be the work of an individual who really cares.

My suggestion is, that you commence—by attempting to make a fairly complete collection of all such publications issued in the year 1925. After that is done, work forward and backward—that is, make a note that we get such publications issued in 1925 and later years, and work towards securing the publications in each field of activity for the years before 1925, the aim will always be approximate completeness. To attain it will not be possible in the relatively few years which you and I are likely to live, but what we are to think of is the library as it will be 25 or 100 years hence—bearing always in mind that the value of the collection will increase in geometrical ratio as it approaches completeness in any of these departments.

The greater part of the material is not on sale, and much of it never will be. In regard to this material, particularly that of the earlier years, the University will have to rely upon the gift of these publications from Kentuckians who have the desired publications in their possession, and either do or do not value them. Much will, I feel sure, come—as soon as the University makes an appropriate announcement of its determination to make a complete collection. More will come when the University is able to announce overt Acts indicating progress. Those who value material which they have will be moved by the announcement that funds are assured for cataloging, shelving and necessary binding and care of all publications received. Others who have not recognized the potential value of such publications in their libraries or attics, and have even thought of them as food for the ash heap, will yield to the suggestion of sending them to the library. But much of the material can be secured only by thinking, who, among Kentuckians, would be likely to have what is wanted and asking such for it. And the personal application will bear rich fruit. It will make everyone who gives, a friend of the University Library, and will secure from him, in some measure, thought of its interest. Eventually, it ought to secure, also, for the University, original manuscripts of historic value; for which a University Library is the appropriate resting place. There is much of this character, among the unpublished material in the archives of Kentucky families. The effect of the making and the existence of such a collection upon the instructors and students is obvious, but the effect in developing love of, and interest in, the State will be widespread.

I am confident that Judge [Robert W.] Bingham will be only too glad to aid you in any way by his papers. In answering the other day an inquiry from him on a very different subject, I added a request that he let me see him when he is next here, so that I can confer with him about the University.

I, of course, expect to pay for the cataloging, binding and shelving involved, and also any incidental expenses, clerical or otherwise. If there should develop opportunities here and there, of making purchases that seem wise, I shall also be glad to supply funds for that. My idea is that I should send you, as I did Maidie and Fan, a check for deposit in a special account to be drawn on by you when needed. This course seems for many reasons wiser than to send the money direct to the University. I talked to Ford of this among other things. As soon as you can use any money, let me know.

1. Charles Gabriel Tachau (1892–1955) was born in Louisville and lived there his entire life. His father, Emil, was LDB's second cousin; and in 1921, Charles Tachau married Jean Brandeis, Alfred's youngest daughter. William G. Tachau (1875–1969) was the youngest of Emil Tachau's eight siblings. An architect, he eventually left Louisville and practiced in New York City. He designed the Central Park band shell.
2. See LDB to Alfred Brandeis, 18 February 1925.

To Charles Gabriel Tachau

June 5, 1925 Washington, D.C. [Brandeis Mss, M 15–2]

MY DEAR CHARLES: 1. While [Arthur Y.] Ford was here last week I considered fully with him my suggestions concerning the future of the University, the objective, the lines of attack, and the means to be pursued to that end. I think that in respect to these matters we are entirely in accord. As the field is too broad for discussion in a letter, and [as] I have had no chance of talking the matter over with you, I asked him to tell you of our talk (other than that relating to the Law School in which you have no special interest.) If he has not yet done so, I hope you will make the opportunity.

2. As to completing the set of the Congressional Records;—I think we cannot rely upon Ford and/or his subordinates to do the necessary work. It requires thought and imagination to get at the present owners of the volumes lacking. Moreover, the by-product, making friends for the University, will be lost, if this task is undertaken by a subordinate. Ford himself has too many things to do, to supply the thought and care. It will need you and such member or members of the faculty in American History and Government as you can interest and develop thereby & by the other collections ahead.

3. Ford told me that the University would be ready for the War Collection in July. I do not expect to make any shipment before September. The work which John Dudley has undertaken in this behalf is stupendous in its proportions; and it cannot possibly be completed before then—although it is already fairly under way. There are over 40 departments, bureaus or the like, of the Federal Government which have in some way (and many of them in many ways) been the origins of publications relating to the war and war activities. These are being carefully enquired into separately in order to ascertain, in the first place, what we should try to get. Then comes a checking up of what I have in my own collection; and pursuit of other documents to their lairs. What I have is a very small part of the desired.

In regard to these documents, as with the Congressional Records, it will be necessary, doubtless, ultimately, to put individual issues through the second hand dealers; and I shall be ready to provide funds for this, when the time comes. But it is important, for other reasons also than economy, not to avail of that resort, until and except so far as, other means prove futile.

To Robert Netherland Miller

June 8, 1925 Washington, D.C. [Brandeis Mss, Notebook]

MY DEAR MILLER: I am glad to have your letter of yesterday.

In thinking over what we might do now—an overt act, making clear our intention to build a law school of distinction, it occurred to me that it would be desirable to secure for the Library of the Louisville School annually a full set of the records and briefs of all cases disposed of by our Court. Harvard has, for many years, secured such collection, through Justice Holmes; the University of Chicago has the collection through me (my daughter Susan graduated there); [1] Minnesota has it from Justice Butler; the Instute [sic] at New York through the present Chief Justice and his predecessors. Learning that Mr. Justice Sanford had not pledged his set, I applied to him, hoping that he would be specially interested as coming from the Sixth Circuit. I am happy to say that he was—and is—as enclosed letter of his to me (with copy of his letter to the clerk) shows.

Will you kindly see that enclosed letter is appropriately acknowledged direct to him by President Ford. You doubtless know that Harvard considers the Supreme Court records & briefs among its proudest possessions.

It is not clear whether the Clerk of the Court [2] has still on hand the full set for the 1924 Term of all Judge Sanford's records etc. I think you had better get all you can, even if you cant get the set complete. I understand that for some years the recipients of the Chief Justice's set, and of one other, have arranged with one of the assistants of the Clerk to attend to the work of collecting and shipping these papers and to pay for this extra-official service $50 (fifty dollars) a year. I think it would be advisable to arrange through Justice Sanford (who will be in Washington at least a week or ten days longer) to have the Clerk's assistant get together at the University's expense the 1924 Term papers. (It is possible that with Judge Sanford's approval he would do the same for the '23 Term, also:—the Justice did not come to the bench until the middle of the '22 Term.)

What arrangement it will be best to make for getting shipped the records for the 1925 Term & hereafter I will discuss with you when we meet. It may be desirable to ask Justice Sanford to have the Secretary & messenger attend to the matter (as mine do for the University of Chicago), beginning with the 1925 Term.

Kindly acknowledge receipt of this to me at Chatham, Mass., so that I may be sure that these valuable papers reach you promptly. It is obviously valuable for our Cause, in other ways, that Justice Sanford—another Harvard man—is interested in furthering the project.   Cordially,

1. See LDB to James P. Hall, 23 October 1916.
2. William R. Stansbury.

To Julian William Mack

June 13, 1925 Washington, D.C. [Frankfurter Mss—HLS]

J.W.M.: 1. At Felix' suggestion I had 1¾ hours with Dr. Harry E. Fosdick [1] today. F. thought it would be valuable as F[osdick]. is going to Palestine this summer. We had 1¼ hours of Zionism & Jews then half an hour on the state of America. We are to have another talk after his return on both subjects. I think the talk will prove to have been helpful. F. thought it was.

2. Magnes may have told you that we had a harmonious time. I told him that I agree entirely with his general outline of University aims & plans as he detailed them,[2] but that I deem it essential that the University authorities bear in mind

> *First.* that the paramount achievement of the Jews is in the realm of human conduct, in contradistinction to intellectual prowesss & that character building, morality in its larger sense must be both the cornerstone of the edifice & the keystone of the arch.
>
> *Second.* That for the development of a university, as in that of an individual, it is essential to abiding worthy results that the process be that of a gradual, slow unfolding.

He said that he agreed.

1. In 1925 Harry Emerson Fosdick (1878–1969) was already an important and controversial minister. His modernist views, his liberal interpretation of the Bible, and his insistence that narrow dogmatic creeds from the past inhibited Christianity were making him a storm center of theological controversy. He assumed the leadership of what became the Riverside Church

in New York City and devoted his life to liberal preaching and to the writing of numerous books on Christianity and its social responsibilities.

2. Magnes was preparing to take up his position as the first president of Hebrew University.

To Alfred Brandeis

July 25, 1925 Chatham, Mass. [Brandeis Mss, M 4–4]

DEAR AL: Nothing from you since your first day at Blowing Rock. You will recall your explanation to mother, who was worried about lack of news from Fanny & Charles [Nagel] who were summering at the Mount Adams House, White Mountains: "You must remember at that elevation the air is rarified."

Miss Grady, with Judge [George W.] Anderson are [*sic*] due for their annual visit, motoring from Boston. Your new ham will be sacrificed for the occasion.

Enclosed letters of yours may make the past more vivid.

Gruesse,

To Harold Joseph Laski

August 3, 1925 Chatham, Mass. [Laski Mss]

MY DEAR HAROLD: It is a great satisfaction to have your "Grammar" of politics and of much else which man should be thinking about in a state which hopes to attain or to preserve liberty.[1]

The possession of men who think hard and through, as you do, is a great asset to any country. And the fact that England has bred such able, fearless ones, gives me confidence that she will grapple successfully with the many serious problems which now beset her and emerge both strengthened and purified.[2]

You probably know from both Holmes J. and Felix how finely the former has borne himself, in the struggle against Father Time. There is no impairment of his working powers; and he retains equally his keen senses for the enjoyment of things worth while.

The year has been for Felix, also, one of happy usefulness, with an ever widening appreciation of his rare qualities. His students are becoming teachers. Given another twenty years of such activity, and he will have profoundly affected American life.

Mrs. Brandeis bids me send her warm greetings—to you, Frida and the infants.   Cordially,

1. Harold J. Laski, *A Grammar of Politics* (London, 1925).
2. See LDB to Felix Frankfurter, 8 November 1925.

To Felix Frankfurter

August 15, 1925 Chatham, Mass. [Frankfurter Mss—HLS]

FF: 1. That's a grand report which O[liver]. W[endell].Holmes]. gives of himself, & it carries much of promise for the 1925 Term. He may be interested to be reminded that one B[enjamin]. Franklin read Port Royal's "Art of Thinking"—at the age of 16.[1] Despite the obvious differences, the new portrait of Goethe which his "Italienische Reise" [2] brought me, led me to think oftener of OWH. than of any other person—in some of the finest intellectual qualities.

2. The A[merican]B[ar]A[ssociation] is obviously one of the carefully planned acts.[3] You will find evidence of another in the enclosed letter which please return.

3. That's a cheering report of R[oscoe].P[ound]'s.

4. I guess [Sidney] Hillman must feel hard hit by the Injunction, & to be otherwise a bit worried.[4]

5. It looks as if real disaster were inpending for the Coal Union —disaster more nearly attributable to obvious unwisdom than most which affect humans.[5]

6. I hope there will be some chance of you & Paul [Raushenbush] getting better acquainted before he & E[lizabeth] go West about Labor Day. He seems a rare find.

1. Antoine Arnauld and Pierre Nicole, of [the Jansenist community at] Port Royal, *Logic: or The Art of Thinking* (English translation, London: 1687). Franklin mentions reading the book, along with John Locke's work, in the first section of his *Autobiography*.

2. Probably LDB was reading the new Alfred Kuhn edition of the *Italian Journey* (Munich, 1925).

3. The American Bar Association meetings were to open in Detroit on 3 September.

4. On 13 August the New York Supreme Court granted an injunction prohibiting picketing of the International Tailoring Company by members

of the Amalgamated Clothing Workers. Hillman called the decision "an open invitation to employers to start sweat shops in the city under the protection of the courts."

5. Talks had been under way since early July in an attempt to avert a threatened nationwide coal strike. The central issues were higher wages and the "check-off" system. In August the discussions were deadlocked, despite deep public concern and official offers to mediate. Then on 31 August John L. Lewis issued the strike order, and over 150,000 workers at more than 800 mines walked off their jobs.

To Felix Frankfurter

September 1, 1925 Chatham, Mass. [Frankfurter Mss—HLS]

F.F.: 1. I think you should pay Alice royalty for the Curio-book reading. It was she, as I recall, who brought it to Hermann's attention.

2. Not much light can be gained from our action on the orders in Bankruptcy enquired about.[1] It was agreed, at the outset, that our Com^{tee} should act merely as a com^{tee} on third readings. The subject has been much threshed out by a special com^{tee} of the Judicial Council in conjunction with representatives of several associations of credit men & lawyers, & the C[hief]. J[ustice]. had participated in these earlier functions. Still, considerable time was spent by Sanford on this job (time he could ill afford) & quite a little by the C.J. I spent only a few hours.

3. In the Roman survey, Duruy (English translation presided over by J.P. Mahaffy) was my piece de resistance, Ferrero (Zimmern's translation) was my entree.[2] I plan to read Cicero's letters & some Tacitus, but I guess it is pretty clear that Toynbee[3] put an appropriate estimate upon the Roman contribution and that Wells[4] is, in substance, not far wrong. The Romans had the great advantage of controlling the publicity agents, and of having their writings survive. The value of these writings as a means was undoubtedly great; & as their influence much greater than their value. On the whole I should put the Romans first as a quarry for warnings. Of course, they serve also as a base base [sic] for precious metals. They shine most in their performances in the period prior to the Punic War. The decline began at the end of the first Punic War.

4. I have not seen the Keynes statement on centralization.[5]

5. I think Mrs. LaFollette (who will continue the LaFollette's Magazine) would like to publish this note of [Loring] Christie's on Furuseth and that there could be no objection on L.C.'s part if his identity were concealed. She would, besides, appreciate it much as evidence of your interest in the continued publication.[6]

5[sic]. Paul & Elizabeth have no very good impression of [*]. Eliz. sampled his course on Const. Law & then fled to the Law School course. Both say he is "terribly conservative" & "popular."

6. P[aul]. & E[lizabeth]. leave probably next Saturday, possibly not until Labor Day. We are to leave possibly as early as Friday Sept. 10 & not later than Monday the 14th; & plan to spend a day (possibly two) at the Bellevue. We hope that your obstinate knee will not prevent our seeing you before we leave Mass. for Washington.

The household's greeting to Marion.

P. & E. think highly of Mason.[7]

1. A special committee of the American Bar Association had met with LDB, Chief Justice Taft, and Justice Sanford to draw up a model bankruptcy bill, which they hoped Congress would adopt to replace the antiquated statute then on the books.

2. Jean Victor Duruy, *History of Rome, and of the Roman People, from Its Origin to the Invasion of the Barbarians*, 8 vols. (Boston, 1883), trans. by M.M. Ripley and W.J. Clarke, ed. by J.P. Mahaffy; Guglielmo Ferrero, *The Greatness and Decline of Rome*, 5 vols. (New York, 1907–09), trans. by Alfred E. Zimmern and H.J. Chaytor.

3. Arnold Joseph Toynbee (1889–1975) had served with the British Foreign Office during World War I and had been with the Middle Eastern section at the Paris Peace conference. In 1925 he had already begun to earn fame as a historian, although his reputation would reach its peak with *A Study of History*, a twelve-volume *magnum opus* that he published intermittently from 1934 to 1961.

4. Wells's *The Outline of History*, 2 vols. (London, 1919–20), provided a rather critical view of Roman society.

5. John Maynard Keynes had issued a number of statements, mainly in connection with his attack on the fiscal policies of the British government (see LDB to Frankfurter, 8 November 1925). Only a few days earlier he had again called for central control of the currency.

6. "Andy Has Undertaken a Big Job," *LaFollette's Magazine* 17 (June 1925): 83. The article recounts Furuseth's plans to go to Europe to persuade governments to undertake reforms similar to those he and LaFollette had

achieved in the famous law of 1915 in the United States. See LDB to Robert M. LaFollette, 5 March 1915.

7. In 1925 Alpheus Thomas Mason (b. 1899) was at the beginning of his teaching career at Princeton, from which he retired in 1968 as McCormick Professor of Jurisprudence. According to Professor Mason, at the time of this letter LDB may have been aware of his book, *Organized Labor and the Law, with Special Reference to the Sherman and Clayton Acts* (Durham, N.C., 1925), a topic that would certainly have been of interest to LDB. Within a few years Mason began a lengthy study of LDB's career, with books on savings bank life insurance, the New Haven struggle, the judicial philosophy, and finally a semiauthorized biography, *Brandeis—A Free Man's Life* (New York, 1946).

To Felix Frankfurter

September 24, 1925 Washington, D.C. [Frankfurter Mss—HLS]

F.F.: 1. I am glad you wrote me about the personal needs and I'll send the $1500 now or in installments as you may prefer. Your public service must not be abridged. Marion knows that Alice and I look upon you as half brother, half son.

2. R[oscoe]. P[ound].'s university address is a masterpiece. Abe F[lexner]. and [Raymond] Fosdick are right about the pusillanimous ending. This ending, like his acceptance of the arbitration duty, discloses his weaknesses. I guess he knew what advice he would have gotten from his associates had he asked for advice.

3. I am sending the address to Alfred [Brandeis], with the suggestion that he give it to [Arthur Y.] Ford, for daily reading.

4. You doubtless include Glenn Frank's [1] editorials in your daily reading

"Ach Gott, Ach Gott, Ach Gotte
Ich Schäm mich vor der Lotte" [2]

5. Alice & I want much to see & hear Alfred Cohen if he & wife come to Washington, but hardly feel justified in asking him to come solely for our education.

6. Robert Miller has doubtless told you (or will) about his engagement to Judge Frederic Dodge's daughter. I think he, too, should have R.P.'s University address.

7. You packed much good advice in the letter to Fosdick. But I guess serving God and Mammon remains as difficult as of yore.

1. Glenn Frank (1877–1940) had worked for E. A. Filene, performing research on Filene's civic and social welfare projects. From 1919 until 1925 he wrote editorials for the *Century Magazine*. In 1925 Frank was called to the presidency of the University of Wisconsin, where he helped to build a distinguished center of learning. He was forced out of office by the LaFollettes in 1937, and he died three years later in an automobile accident while campaigning for the Republican nomination to the United States Senate.

2. "Oh God, Oh God, oh God
   I am ashamed in front of Lotte."

To Robert Netherland Miller

September 25, 1925 Washington, D.C. [Brandeis Mss Notebook]

MY DEAR MILLER: 1. When you take up in Louisville the matter of binders for the U[nited].S[tates].S[upreme].C[ourt]. records and briefs, it will be desirable for you to confer with Charles G. Tachau (husband of my niece Jean.) He is helping me in developing for the University a worthy library of the World War etc; and in this connection, will have occasion to provide binding for many pamphlets etc.

2. I am sending you herewith, for the Law School, photo and an autographed copy of our 1920 Court. I think if this is hung properly framed, at the time the first years records are put in place, it will help to make the School realize its obligations.

Cordially,

To Felix Frankfurter

October 5, 1925 Washington, D.C. [Frankfurter MSS—HLS]

F.F.: 1. Apropos "The Strategy of the Progressives" & much else in the N[ew]. R[epublic].[1] I think the fundamental error in the political science of the philosophic editor is that he fails to realize that in government, as in other spheres of human activity, happiness is usually attained, if at all, as a bi-product [*sic*]; and that, because of our finite wisdom, and the infinite possibility of error in judgment, we are more likely to be right in turning our thoughts primarily to the simpler problem of means than directly to hoped for ends. He talks of enacting progressive legislation. What? As Holmes used to say: "State your proposition and I'll deny it." Lindsay Rogers [2] has made a very practical suggestion. It would take a very few Wisconsins to make anything hopeful, possible in politics.

2. The C[hief].J[ustice]. has written upon Swan's insistence an article on the new stat. and the rules for the Yale L.J.! It will doubtless appear in the Oct. issue.[3] He is apparently in the same relatively good condition that he was last term.

3. I suppose we shall begin the term with 800 cases on the list, of course most of the recent ones pet[ition]s for cert[iorari]s.

4. I shall send for the Demosthenes Private Orations to which Max R. refers. Lionel Curtis was in for an hour today.[4] I found some points of complete agreement, to which the talk was confined.

Bureau of Labor Statistics et al give recent prices (cost of living) at 173+ as compared with 1913. Irving Fisher [5] et al. give wholesale prices at 153+ as compared with 1913.

Is the 20 point difference due to relatively increased retail distribution costs? And how much has been the increase of wholesale distribution costs? Ask your N.R. economists & others.

Dr. Leon Reich [6] (whom you will recall from Paris) was in & talked i.a. of your "Uncle Henry".[7]

1. "The Strategy of Progressive Politics," *New Republic* 44 (7 October 1925): 163–65. The long editorial is an attack upon the contention of Lindsay Rogers (see next note), whose article "Progressive Half-Preparedness," appeared in the same issue (pp. 169–72). Rogers argued that progressives must give up the attempt to elect presidents and concentrate instead upon consolidating local pockets of progressive sentiment.

2. Lindsay Rogers (1891–1970) was a professor of political science at Harvard until 1929, when he moved to Columbia. He wrote numerous books and articles on political topics.

3. William Howard Taft, "The Jurisdiction of the Supreme Court under the Act of February 13, 1925," 35 *Yale Law Journal* 1 (1925). The article explored the changes resulting from the new law. Thomas Walter Swan (1877–19[?]) was in 1925 dean and professor of law at the Yale Law School. In 1927 he was named judge for the Second U.S. Circuit Court.

4. Lionel George Curtis (1872–1955) was a British author and adviser on colonial affairs. A leading advocate of the "federation" of former colonies, Curtis was in the United States in 1925, at the Institute of politics at Williams College.

5. Irving Fisher (1867–1947) taught economics and statistics at Yale for nearly half a century and was for many years considered one of America's premier authorities on economics. He wrote numerous articles and monographs on the cost-of-living indices and related subjects.

6. Leon Reich (1879–1929) was a Polish Zionist leader.

7. Perhaps Henry Morgenthau, Sr.

To Fannie Brandeis

October 18, 1925 Washington, D.C. [Brandeis Mss, M 4–5]

MY DEAR FAN: I am glad you plan to talk with Mr. Ford about the librarian. A good librarian is an essential to worthy achievement in each of the family's projects: to the sociological, the world war, and the Kentuckiana collections, as well as to those on Art and Music. To be a good librarian one must love books, reverence them, and have the passion for collecting, all of which the present incumbent seems to lack. With the right person installed, your knowledge and enthusiasm and the welcome which will be accorded to your personal efforts, will doubtless make of the Art and Music corner a living place for those who love these things.

You may conclude that some of these books should be put into cases—and kept under lock and key. Mr. Robert Miller suggested this to Mr. Ford in respect to some irreplacable [*sic*] books which I have secured for the Law Library.

Aunt Alice is very glad to hear of your Furtwanglers [1] and is watching eagerly the growth of your collection.

And sends her love.

1. Probably Fannie Brandeis had acquired for the proposed art library some of the works of Adolf Furtwängler (1853–1907), the German authority on Greek art and sculpture.

To Felix Frankfurter

October 20, 1925 Washington, D.C. [Frankfurter Mss—HLS]

F.F.: 1. Since writing you yesterday of W[alter]. L[ippmann].'s book [1] I have your letter. With the specific things which you say

I agree entirely. But I think it is a remarkable book with the classic quality in thought and expression. The defects are the inevitable ones due to his qualities and lacks which we have often discussed. "Denn der Sonne Busen ist liebeleer" [2] Still, I think his book will be distinctly helpful to those who try to think on political science; & that this helpfulness will more than outweigh the misuse which the Industrial Conference et al. will make of his statements. Walter's criticisms should compel others who feel and care as we do, to come to grips with the difficulties instead of closing their eyes and "just grabbing" as Mr. Starts suggested.

W.L. has a definite art as a mind, and a pen. For the rest we must look elsewhere.

2. Those are good letters from & on Gottlieb [3] & the Research Fellowships.

3. Alice asks whether you have seen Toynbee. If he is coming here we want, of course, to see him.

1. Lippmann had just published *The Phantom Public* (New York, 1925), which was a sequel to his *Public Opinion* (New York, 1922). In his new work Lippmann questioned the very idea of whether a "public" exists. In fact, he argued, there is no such thing, but rather a number of competing factions. Most people are totally uninformed on public issues, he wrote, with only a handful truly concerned about the great questions of the times.

2. "For the sun's bosom is without love."

3. Leo Gottlieb was a young attorney who was assisting Emory Buckner (see LDB to Frankfurter, 31 January and 3 February 1925). His application for membership in the American Bar Association was in jeopardy ostensibly because of the methods he had used in gathering evidence against violators of the prohibition law. The attempt to block Gottlieb was interpreted generally, by LDB and other friends of Gottlieb, as being inspired by corrupt lawyers and others resentful of Buckner's crackdown. Judge A. N. Hand issued a statement saying that Gottlieb's methods were perfectly legal and proper. In a letter to Frankfurter on 19 October, LDB had written: "The Leo Gottlieb episode is illuminating. Merely a new edition of an old story."

To Julian William Mack

November 6, 1925 Washington, D.C. [R. Szold Mss]

MY DEAR JUDGE MACK: Confirming our talk on the 2nd: I will continue for the calendar year 1926 my payment to you as trustee for Miss [Henrietta] Szold of one thousand (1000) dollars, payable in quarterly installments as heretofore.¹   Cordially,

1. See LDB to Mack, 11 March 1916.

To Felix Frankfurter

November 8, 1925 Washington, D.C. [Frankfurter Mss—HLS]

1. Your compact clause proposition is doing effective work.¹

2. It would be fine to have Ray Stevens landed in Siam.²

3. Keynes may or may not be right in his "Economic Consequences of Mr. Churchill." ³ But a country which can produce men who think as vigorously, write as effectively, and speak out as fearlessly, as he does, has a good chance of winning out against all comers.

4. Our Courts project should receive hearty support from all opponents of U.S. entering the League [of Nations].

5. Alice & I called on the R[oscoe]. P[ound].s. He was not in but she was. She has developed much since they dined with us at Otis Place. Alice took her Friday to make the Ambassadorial calls.

6. The customary P[er]. C[urium]. is, in most cases, inadequate. I suggested that instead, brief op[inion]s. be written like my Davis v. Henderson, 266 U.S. 92, a form that seems to me better than the N.Y. C[ourt]. of A[ppeals]. memos.⁴ The suggestion didn't prevail. But there is other ineffectual grumbling at the defects of the P.C. The [*] P.C. was intentionally blind. The reasons, later.

7. J[ulian].W.M[ack]. reported for 2 hours on international and national Jewish matters. "Nichts Erfreuhliches" ⁵ as my father used to say.

8. Have just rec'd Raymond Fosdick's Colgate address.⁶ He is one of the most disappointing of men. He sees, but he doesn't do. If instead of putting up the job vaguely to the "young," he would, having arrived, strike out boldly from his pinnacle, some things would be started—and at least the "young" inspired to action. He is teaching them the charms of hot air.

9. Ripley's remedy isn't very promising. But its something to

have a man speak out.[7] Could not others be induced to think? And then have men who want to think together, but not in public, come together in a small group to consider the economic state of the nation. It's clear, I think, that the gentle enslavement of our people is proceeding apace—politically, economically, socially—& that the only remedy is via the individual. To make him care to be a free man & willing to pay the price. There is, of course, [no] mechanism possible to promote the desire & when existing to make it effective. But we need now a diagnosis i.a.

10. Morris Cohen is weekending with Jerome Michael [8] & they are coming in this afternoon.

11. It will be interesting to see H[arold].J.L[aski].

12. You will soon see L.D.'s individual portrait in the press.

13. Keynes Point III is very fine.

14. The Judd Welliver incident was an example of our most dangerous enslavement—the intellectual.[9] The interests have made great strides in this line.

15. The Sacco-Vanzetti expense a/c is a terrible indictment of our criminal justice.[10]

1. See LDB to Frankfurter, 2 June 1925, n. 2.

2. Stevens served as special adviser to Siam (now Thailand) from 1926 to 1935.

3. (London, 1925); the American edition of this 32-page pamphlet had the title *The Economic Consequences of Sterling Parity* (New York, 1925). In it Keynes attacked the policy of the Chancellor of the Exchequer, Winston Churchill, in forcing the resumption of the gold standard, which Britain had deserted after World War I. Keynes blamed the inflation and high unemployment of the 1920s on the government policy, and he called for a centralized currency control which could avoid both inflation and depression.

4. A majority of the cases appealed to the Supreme Court were and are dismissed "per curiam," literally "by the court" with no explanation. In the Davis case, LDB had written a very brief statement summarizing the major issues and also the reasons why the Court had chosen not to act. The comparable New York method, mentioned by LDB, failed to provide the litigants with sufficient information regarding the reasons for the court's disposal of a case.

5. "Nothing very pleasant."

6. Fosdick (see LDB to Frankfurter, 2 October 1922, n. 3) was advocating United States participation in the League of Nations (he was a League undersecretary), and Colgate University had just awarded him an honorary degree.

7. William Z. Ripley (see LDB to Ripley, 13 June 1908) had just issued a warning against the control of big business by bankers because of the diffusion of stock ownership. His remarks came at the meeting of the Academy of Political Science. See *New York Times*, 29 October 1925.

8. Jerome Michael (1890–1953) was a special assistant to the Attorney General of the United States. In 1927 he began a long tenure as professor of criminal law at Columbia University.

9. Welliver (see LDB to Alfred Brandeis, 21 July 1910) had just resigned from his position as chief clerk at the White House to accept a public relations job for the American Petroleum Institute.

10. In 1920, a robbery in South Braintree, Massachusetts, had resulted in the murder of a payroll guard. Two immigrants, Nicola Sacco and Bartolomeo Vanzetti, were arrested and charged with the crime and after a hasty trial were convicted and sentenced to death. The case caught the imagination and sympathies of liberals all over the country, who claimed that the two men were really convicted of being radicals, that the trial had been a travesty of justice in which the judge demonstrated bias and the prosecution distorted evidence. The furor led to the appointment by the governor of Massachusetts of a special commission which included the presidents of both Harvard and the Massachusetts Institute of Technology. Ultimately the commission found no irregularities in the trial procedure to warrant either pardon or commutation of the defendants' sentences. Frankfurter was one of the leaders in the liberal crusade to free Sacco and Vanzetti, and his vigorous attacks on the system that allegedly condemned men because of their political ideas soon stirred up a hornets' nest among the conservative alumni of the Harvard Law School. Although there have been dozens of books on the case, which ultimately ended with the execution of the two men in 1927, the best contemporary account is Frankfurter's *The Case of Sacco and Vanzetti* (Boston, 1927). While LDB sympathized with the men, he disqualified himself from acting on their appeal to the Supreme Court, both because of his friendship with Frankfurter and because members of his family were involved in efforts to free the two accused. The reference in this letter is to the report of the Sacco and Vanzetti defense committee issued 4 October. The committee announced that over $282,000 had already been spent on legal and related costs and that only $4,500 was left on hand.

To Julian William Mack

November 22, 1925 Washington, D.C. [R. Szold Mss]

J.W.M.: Re yours of 20th & 21st

1. As to Novomesky [*sic*] enterprise.[1] As to the facts, I have no opinion. As you know, my test of a business investment in Palestine is not the payment of dividends, or making of profits,

but conduct, in a businesslike manner, of a business enterprise which will advance the economic and social life of the Jewish community & ultimate Zionist aims.

If N's enterprise promises, after reasonable enquiry, that format, and the P[alestine]. E[conomic]. C[orporation]. has a surplus, I should think it would be a justifiable investment, although you expect it may not or will not pay dividends.

2. I shall probably have to wire you & B[ernard]. F[lexner]. Tuesday that the conference suggested for Friday must be deferred. I don't know just what B.F. wants to talk over. If it is generally the future activities, attitudes, etc. of our group, I should think it undesirable to have the conference without you, Bob Szold, [Julius] Simon and Sam Rosensohn (at least) being present. And possibly also some of the others who attend[ed] the conference on May 4, 1924 (when we assented to B.F.'s projects) ought to have the opportunity of attending.

1. Moshe Novomeysky (1873–1963) was a Russian-born chemist and engineer. He first became interested in Palestine and Zionism in 1906 at Otto Warburg's instigation, and a few years later he went to Palestine to do analyses of the mineral-laden Dead Sea waters. Novomeysky settled in Palestine in 1920 and began a decade-long struggle to win a franchise from the United States to finance the enterprise. He finally succeeded and in 1929 established Palestine Potash, Ltd., which later became the Dead Sea Works Company. The story has been told in his autobiography in Hebrew, *Given to Salt: The Struggle for the Dead Sea Concession* (Jerusalem, 1958).

To Felix Frankfurter

November 29, 1925 Washington, D.C. [Frankfurter Mss—HLS]

FF: 1. We are relieved by what you write and others tell us of the operation.[1] Take very good care of yourself. There is much work that only you can do—until your disciples have taken their proper places.

2. What you write about the [Harvard Law School] Faculty, Ray Stevens and Page is, indeed, cheering. (By the way, it was Alice who started the thought which places Ray at Siam.) [2]

3. Mack reports B[ernard]F[lexner] & himself happy over the P[alestine].E[conomic].C[orporation] adjustment, and himself & others happy over the [*] adjustment & harmony at Baltimore.[3]

For me, the outcome is saddening. Of course Palestine will get some needed material aid. But spiritually, it will suffer by the depreciation of Zionist activity into charity-drive materialism. And for America it is a defeat or submergence, of what I had hoped from the Zionist movement. My [*] Hall address of Sept. 1914 and the democratic idealism of [the] 1915 Zionist Convention & meetings are indeed out of date.

4. I know [*]. "He comes from Sheffield."

5. We are asking the [*] for Wednesday evening for a quiet talk, & shall get the Carl Beckers to join us.[4]

1. Frankfurter had been having trouble with his knee and had undergone an operation to correct the difficulty.

2. See LDB to Frankfurter, 8 November 1925, n. 2.

3. Despite LDB's reluctance to become involved with the enlarged Jewish Agency (see LDB to Jacob deHaas, 14 February 1924, n. 1), it had become obvious that the Palestine Economic Corporation just did not possess the resources necessary for the type of economic and social investment it hoped to make in Palestine. With Bernard Flexner serving as the go-between, negotiations had been begun which ultimately led to the P.E.C.'s being enlarged and absorbed under the framework of the Jewish Agency. LDB, while personally opposed to this development, realized that he could do little to stop it. See Urofsky, *American Zionism*, ch. 8.

4. Carl Lotus Becker (1873–1945) was one of the most productive and influential American historians of the twentieth century. His most important work examined American ideas and American life in the eighteenth century, but he was also well known for his views on the philosophy of history. At the time of this letter, he had been at Cornell for eight years (and Frankfurter had met and had been impressed with him when he visited Cornell earlier in 1925). Becker was elected president of the American Historical Association in 1931. See Cushing Strout, *The Pragmatic Revolt in American History* (New Haven, 1958), or Burleigh T. Wilkins, *Carl Becker: A Biographical Study in American Intellectual History* (Cambridge, Mass., 1961).

To Felix Frankfurter

December 11, 1925 Washington, D.C. [Frankfurter Mss—HLS]

FF: 1. It is grand to have had three letters from you—the best evidence in itself that all goes well.[1] And that just received tells of your homegoing today. Take very good care not to overdo.

2. What you write of the [Harvard Law School] Faculty dis-

cussions & attitude is most encouraging. I guess R[oscoe]P[ound] will have to fall into line. It's fatal for a man who has kinks to go away & let his associates coagulate.

3. Susan is making an unambitious marriage upon which we look hopefully.[2] She is very sure of herself. And the year of their acquaintance has been unquestionably the year of her best development.[3]

4. George Rublee was in yesterday in great happiness over Ray [Stevens]'s appointment.[4]

5. Carl Becker said apropos R.P. & the Wisconsin presidency: [5] "When a man writes a good book, they want to make him keep books."

Our congratulations to Marion.

1. See preceding letter, n. 1.

2. LDB's daughter was engaged to Jacob H. Gilbert (1883–1966), a young lawyer whom she had met in New York when the two were on opposite sides of a minor litigation. They were married at the end of December.

3. During the year Susan Brandeis had argued a case before the United States Supreme Court (her father, naturally, absenting himself from the bench and from any deliberation regarding the case); she thus became the first woman in American history to accomplish this feat.

4. See LDB to Frankfurter, 8 November 1925, n. 2.

5. See LDB to Frankfurter, 31 January and 3 February 1925, n. 2.

To William and Charles Gabriel Tachau

December 14, 1925 Washington, D.C. [Brandeis Mss, M 15–2]

MY DEAR BILLY AND CHARLES: 1) In view of the important part the League of Nations has already played in World History, and the greater part it is likely to play in the future, I have deemed it important to secure for our World War Library (while they are still available) copies of all its publications and records for the full period of its existence. To this end, I took up the matter with Prof. Manley O. Hudson, the Professor of International Law at Harvard Law School. His action is expressed in his letter to me of Nov. 30th & the copies of the letters of that date to Mr. Symons and to the World Peace Foundation all of which I enclose.

2) Today, I am [in] receipt from the World Peace Foundation of their memo, dated Dec. 4, covering the 1925 publications

shipped to the Library & calling for the years subscription of $100.

3) I am enclosing check to you two—"Special University of Louisville World War Lirbary" for one thousand (1000) dollars, which please deposit, subject to your check, in the same account in which you deposited the $1000 sent Oct 12, 1925—and from this account please pay over this $100. to the World Peace Foundation, and later the amounts which will become payable for the publications of the earlier years as per Prof. Hudson's letters.

As soon as you have shown Prof. Hudson's letters to Dean Anderson, (and take copies) please return it to me; and let me know that this bill has been paid, and later, any payments made hereafter.

4) You will recall that I suggested earlier the desirability of enlisting the special interest in the World War Library of some member of the faculty, of course, after consultation with Dean Anderson. In talking, a few days ago with Prof. Carl Becker of Cornell (one of the finest minds devoted to American History) he chanced to mention Prof. Gottschalk, a former student of his, and spoke of him as a man of ability and promise.[1] Perhaps you and Dean Anderson may think it wise to enlist Prof. G's cooperation now.

5) Have you received the R. C. Ballard Thruston Congressional Records etc.,[2] and what progress have you made in getting from others the missing volumes?

6) Last year Maidie had sent me U of L Bulletin Vol. XVIII No. 1. Please have Mr. Ford send me all issues of Bulletins since that date (May 24th).

1. Louis Gottschalk (1899–1975) took all three academic degrees at Cornell. He taught at the University of Louisville from 1921 to 1927, and in the latter year he began his distinguished career as a professor of European history at the University of Chicago. Gottschalk was at the center of a controversy at the University of Louisville which directly involved the Brandeis family; see LDB to Alfred Brandeis, 23 January 1927, n. 2.

2. Rogers Clark Ballard Thruston (1858–1946), a geological engineer, was active in Louisville philanthropic, patriotic, and historical activities. He served as president of the Filson Club after 1923. LDB had met with Thruston in Washington and had induced him to donate his extensive collection of issues of the *Congressional Record* to the University of Louisville libraries. See LDB to Alfred Brandeis, 16 January 1927.

To Felix Frankfurter

January 6, 1926 Washington, D.C. [Frankfurter Mss—HLS]

0. I found nothing worthy in Hale's article except the reference to Philip P. Wells' article.[1]

1. The recent interstate commerce cases lead me to suggest again that a state bloc in Congress be educated to the necessity of a quasi Wilmot Proviso [2] on all legislation involving the debateable ground between state & federal powers.

2. Your Economist friends should comment on:

A. Hoover's solicitude to protect auto manufacturers & users from excessive rubber costs [3] —of material necessarily imported. Although in 1913, rubber per pound cost 57 cents per pound

in 1926 [4] rubber per pound cost only 38½ cents while

B. He makes no comment on the increased cost of other articles also used.

(a) steel billet in Nov 1913 $23.50 per gross ton
    (open hearth [*]) Oct '26   35.00
(b) oil (Kans. Okla) Oct, '13 $1.03 per barrell [*sic*]
             Oct, '26   2.37

Articles produced in this country; also

(c) coal (Bitum.) Oct '13 $1.40 per ton
            Oct '26   2.25

3. Our materialistic friends have expanded the greeting of wishes for a happy new year, to "Happy & Prosperous New Year."

We are giving ever new evidence that
"Nichts ist schwerer zu ertragen
Als ein Reihe von schönen Tagen." [5]

1. Frankfurter may have sent LDB an early draft of Robert Lee Hale's "Regulation of Electric Rates," which would appear in *New Republic* 47 (26 May 1926): 22–25, and which was extremely critical of the Supreme Court's intervention in regulatory rate-making processes; Philip Patterson Wells, "Power and Interstate Commerce," *Annals of the American Academy of Political and Social Science* 118 (March 1925): 163–67, had also dealt with this theme.

2. The Wilmot Proviso of 1846 was intended to prohibit slavery in all newly acquired U.S. territory. It never became law.

3. Hoover entered into a long campaign of criticism against the price of imported rubber and, particularly, the control of the supply by the British. See, for example, his testimony before the House Committee on Interstate and Foreign Commerce, summarized in the *New York Times*, 7 January 1926.

4. LDB apparently meant "1925" here and throughout the letter.

5. "Nothing is harder to endure than a series of beautiful days."

To Felix Frankfurter

January 10, 1926 Washington, D.C. [Frankfurter Mss—HLS]

FF: 1. Alice hopes you have seen something of Auntie B.[1] She was hard hit by her sister Eugenia's death—although to Eugenia the passing was a great mercy.

2. Alice sends enclosed about Eustace Percy. The lot of those who practice economy in government is not an easy one.[2]

3. The most important advice one can give [Emory] Buckner is to persist—not only in the course taken, but in office.[3] He should take (internally) the vow not to quit before the end of the four years. Time is the great factor in real achievement.

4. [Au]Gus[tus] Hand should be led to have gathered the statistic—of time spent by his Court, say in the last 5 years, on cases under #215 (Postal frauds). He spoke to me of this burden —especially great because of the length of the trials. If & when his data is worked up, he, or someone, ought to get them from the other districts. The law is bad as criminal legislation. If we can get rid of the postal fraud cases, we shall get rid also of one of the largest & most pestilential body of detectives, masquerading under the title of inspectors.

5. Hoover's talk on foreign monopolies (rubber et al) [4] is more mischievous even, and less justified, than his anti-bolshevist scare. His statistics would do honor to a [Max] Nordau.

Note in this connection clipping on Philippine hemp monopoly enclosed.[5]

6. When [Thomas R.] Powell gives us his annual reflections on the performances of U[nited]S[tates]S[upreme]C[ourt], he will doubtless have something to say of recent developments re stare decisis re hearings & dissents.

7. Wont Landis be able to do some of the things you hoped for in their vacation times[?] [6]

1. Elizabeth Glendower Evans.

2. Eustace Percy was serving as president of the national board of education in Britain. In response to the retrenchment efforts of the Baldwin government, he issued a circular directing the restriction of funds for local educational development. The resulting outcry was intense and bitter, and it came both from radicals (who saw the attempt as limiting the educational prospects of poor children whose parents could not afford private schooling) and from large numbers of conservatives as well, who argued that England's future was intimately tied to educational excellence. Percy withdrew the circular as a result of this dual pressure.

3. See LDB to Frankfurter, 31 January and 3 February 1925.

4. See preceding letter.

5. General Leonard Wood, governor of the islands, had just approved a law prohibiting the exporting of abaca seeds from the Philippines, thereby assuring the continuance there of a virtual monopoly on hemp. See *New York Times*, 6 January 1926.

6. James M. Landis, having finished his term as LDB's clerk, accepted a professorship at Harvard Law School. On 1 January, LDB wrote Frankfurter: "My congratulations on securing Landis already next year. I think it wiser for him not to wait. He is so mature that he has less need than the ordinary teacher for a preliminary bout at the bar."

To Charles Gabriel Tachau

January 15, 1926 Washington, D.C. [Brandeis Mss, M 15–2]

MY DEAR CHARLES: Re yours of 13th:

I am glad to know that the offer from Mr. Costigan has come and has been accepted.[1] I suggested to him that he make this gift, mainly for the following reason:

In my opinion, an effort should be made to develop the library on Economics in a manner similar to that undertaken through Prof. [Norman J.] Ware for the library on Sociology. There is a large amount of very valuable material in the official federal and state reports, in the reports of corporations and trade organizations, and in other papers and periodicals which should be collected currently; and there are many files of back numbers which are important, which can probably be compiled now, but cannot be later. I have some such on my shelves which I have planned should go to the University, and some material on Economics was included in the shipments made of the collection on Sociology. Prof. Ware would doubtless be glad to have his special library freed of this material, through transfer to the library on Economics.

I have heard much good of Miss Ethel B. duPont.[2] If it will be agreeable to her to undertake to develop the economics collection, in occasional conference with you, and the project has the approval of Dean Anderson and Prof. Belknap,[3] I shall be glad to aid the Economics collection in the same way as I have done others, and will place at the disposal of Miss DuPont and yourself a fund for cataloguing, binding and shelving and necessary purchases.

It seemed to me appropriate that this special effort to develop a collection of Economics should be inaugurated by a gift of the Tariff Commission publications, in view of the connection with that body of Jean's Uncle Frank [Taussig].

Please send me a copy of this letter, and copies also to Dean Anderson and Jean's father [Alfred Brandeis].

Aunt Alice and I look forward to your coming on the twenty-second.

1. Edward P. Costigan had agreed, at LDB's request, to supply the University of Louisville with the various publications of the United States Tariff Commission. LDB's request to Costigan was typical of dozens which he addressed to various governmental and civic organizations, asking for contributions of their publications for the University.

2. Ethel B. DuPont was a Louisville member of the famous and wealthy family, but was something of an exception in her politics. For many years a labor columnist for the Louisville *Times*, Miss DuPont on one occasion placed newspaper advertisements supporting G.M. strikers in 1945–46. According to Gerard Colby (*DuPont: Behind the Nylon Curtain* [Englewood Cliffs, New Jersey, 1974], 581), "Zadie and Ethel are the only DuPonts in the family's 170-year history to have ever supported a work stoppage by labor."

3. William Burke Belknap (1885–1965), a member of the prominent Louisville family, had been chairman of the Economics Department at the University since 1916. He also served in the Kentucky House of Representatives, and was active in horse-breeding farms and the family hardware business.

To Felix Frankfurter

January 24, 1926 Washington, D.C. [Frankfurter Mss—HLS]

FF: 1. The coincidence of dropping the Wheeler prosecution & the shame of Daugherty ought not to pass without scathing rebuke of C[alvin].C[oolidge] & the Department of Justice.[1]

2. As to Wheeler. He ought to be induced to vow that he will devote himself unreservedly to stamping out the spy system in the federal government. That, with due aid, should be his task. It would be potent as ladder & pedestal; and it will, if accomplished, be a worthy movement.

3. The N[ew].R[epublic] & the [New York] World should not let pass the farmers' surplus agitation without uncovering a fundamental cause of the farmers' plight—the gross overvaluation of the land. It is not only the most wide-spread of all causes, but is far reaching in its consequences. I think the farm economists would have to admit that (excluding the war years) farms in the last 25 yrs have not earned anything like a fair return on their selling price in the rich territory of the midwest. Iowa lands today could easily earn a fair return on say $75 to $100 an acre. The cry is that it doesn't on $300 to $400. Many owners (of the equity) have paid that much. Many others have leased on that basis. Carl Vrooman admitted to us that on his Iowa or Illinois lands he is getting 50% of the crop & furnishing only the land with improvements tax free. That means, of course, that every tenant must support, in effect, two families. The overvaluation has promoted the evil of tenancy.[2]

The indirect effects of the overvaluation are i.a. the heavy burdens incurred for taxation & other things, which never would have been dreamed of, but for the land inflation.

The common answer is that farmers have gotten their pay for a generation largely in the increment of value. That is—in plain English—that the farms have produced a very small income & hence are not worth anything like the selling values. There is little probability that any real & permanent improvement can come without rectifying the fundamental situation. Of course, it is very, very difficult. But there ought to be at least a peep hole into the truth.

4. The other fundamental need is integrating agriculture, thus

letting people move to the producing territory instead of expecting miracles in cheap transportation. Manufactures etc. should
move to the raw material.

5. You certainly have done much effective work through the
World.

6. I am not surprised at what you say of R[oscoe].P[ound].

7. I hope your Social Science Research Council wont "formulate" anything until after a long period of secret conference a la
Fed[eral] Const[itutional] Convention.

8. *Who* are the Milton Research Fund? I should think Mas-
s[achusetts]. a peculiarly fit place for such a survey [3]—because
the difficulties inherent in getting at causes would probably be
less there than in any large community in the U.S. But I guess
that only a very small part of the causes are technical or professional; and that one will have constantly to bear in mind

"Sie sprechen eine Sprache, die ist so lieb [*sic*], so schön,
Doch keine der Philologen kann diese Sprache verstehen." [4]

9. The proposal to publish R.P. papers would now meet with
greater favor with [*]—in view of his new trend.

10. That is a fine letter from the Boston Carmen's Union &
does them great credit.

11. I hope C. W. Pound will realize how much work is required of him if the judicial statistics are to be of much value.[5]
Some of his opinions indicate that he does not realize the value
of hard work in that field.

12. You did well to bring to the [New York] Herald Gus
Hand's views on Registration.

13. O[liver]W[endell]H[olmes] enters his 4th week of the
sitting in quite as good shape as he did any. His work in Court &
in Conference has never been better.

14. I am glad to see your article in the latest H[arvard]L[aw]
R[eview].[6]

15. Some political science man with a historical sense & style
should use the interesting parallel afforded by the recent Mass[a-
chusetts] movement to protect by state action the small cities
from financial irregularities of officials and the limitation of local
expenditures—with the control gradually assumed by the Imperial
Prussian Govt (in the time of the good Emperor) on account of
the dishonesties & extravagancies over the finances of the many

city states—and the gradual emasculation of the local civic & political life, and thereby the destruction of the great training ground for political etc. leaders.

Duruy's "Rome" has many interesting passages on this.[7]

1. There were two developments in ongoing political scandal investigations within the same week: the Department of Justice announced that it would not appeal the decision of the Washington, D.C. Supreme Court, which voided the indictment against Wheeler for defrauding the government (see LDB to Frankfurter, 28 May 1924, n. 1), and former Attorney General Harry M. Daugherty was cited for contempt of court for refusing to answer questions before the Federal Grand Jury. The "scathing rebuke" which LDB called for here, actually came from Wheeler himself in a Senate speech on 4 February. In that speech he denounced the administration of the Department of Justice and the attitude of President Coolidge who, Wheeler argued, seemed more interested in shielding the Department than in seeing justice done.

2. See next letter.

3. Frankfurter was about to embark upon another crime survey, modeled, in part, on the work he and Pound had done at Cleveland. This one was to examine Boston, and it was designed to examine the "effect of legal control on the restraining of crime and the efficacy of the law's treatment of criminals." LDB would make numerous suggestions to Frankfurter regarding the work. The Boston crime survey was never completed, but three volumes did appear in 1934. See Liva Baker, *Felix Frankfurter*, 109–11.

4. "They [the stars] speak a language so majestic, so beautiful, and yet no linguist can understand this speech." LDB misquoted, substituting "lieb" (lovely) for "reich" in the original. The quotation is from Heine's *Buch der Lieder* of 1851.

5. Cuthbert Winfred Pound (1864–1935) had served as a judge on the New York Supreme Court for the Eighth Judicial District and, in 1915, he was appointed to the New York Court of Appeals. When Cardozo was elevated to the Supreme Court, Pound succeeded him as chief justice of the New York court.

6. The article was another instalment of the series "The Business of the Supreme Court of the United States: A Study in the Federal Judicial System." 39 *Harvard Law Review* 325.

7. See LDB to Frankfurter, 1 September 1925.

To Felix Frankfurter

January 26, 1926 Washington, D.C. [Frankfurter Mss—HLS]

FF: Enclosed from Ripley and Harrigan requires your attention. I wrote Ripley that I don't remember.[1] Please write Harrigan also.

If your agricultural economist is historical minded,[2] I hope he will tell us whether history records any dirt farmer who has rendered unto the landlord as much as 50% of the gross product. And note the Iowa tenant referred to supplied really a part of the plant—i.e. the agricultural implements as well as supplies to run them & the seed. My impression is that the temple slaves of Asia, the Prussian tenants, the tenants of the monastery lands & even the French peasants before the Revolution—though worse off in fact—did not yield to their landlords any such part of the product of the land.[3]

1. William Z. Ripley, who was writing about both railroads and banks during these months, wanted the source for a quotation by LDB.
2. See preceding letter.
3. See LDB to Frankfurter, 14 March 1926.

To Alfred Brandeis

February 6, 1926 Washington, D.C. [Brandeis Mss, M 4–4]

DEAR AL: Glad to hear such good report of Jennie and Frank [Taussig].

I guess you are right about Iowa banks. Eugene Meyer told me some years ago that blue-sky investments [1] had so crippled them (holding hundreds of millions) that they would have failed in 1920–21, bringing down some large Chicago banks, but for War Corporation help.

Elwood Mead was strong on Iowa over-valuation as a cause of farm troubles there; and Alvin Johnson says its [sic] true of his native state, Nebraska. He says his father's farm, valued in his youth at $25 an acre, is really worth only $75 now (based on earning power)—but was sold a few years ago at $250 an acre. He says, however, that nobody wants to foreclosure[sic], although mortgages are badly in default & that if the farms were deflated, the whole of the North & Middle West territory would go broke. [Carl S.] Vrooman admitted as much.[2]

I wish to record my utter inability to understand why a lot of other folk dont go broke. These consolidations, & security floatations—plus the building boom, beat my comprehension—unless there is a break coming within the year.

1. Fraudulent or unwise investments.
2. See LDB to Felix Frankfurter, 24 January 1926.

To Felix Frankfurter

February 12, 1926 Washington, D.C. [Frankfurter Mss—HLS]

FF: Isn't there among your economists some one who could make clear to the country that the greatest of social-economic troubles arise from the fact [that] the consumer has failed absolutely to perform his function? He lies not only supine, but paralyzed & deserves to suffer like others who take their lickings "lying down".

He gets no worse than his deserts. But the trouble is that the parallelogram of social forces is disrupted thereby. It destroys absolutely the balance of power & lets producers and distributors "trim the balance of the world" as C[alvin] C[oolidge] would say.[1]

Ripley showed cleverness & courage as well as discernment in his recent essay.[2] But no real good can come from it. The curse of bigness rests upon such endeavor.

But consumers—if they did their duty—could be as effective continuously as they were momentarily in 1920 by the Buyers' Strike.[3]

As for the [National] Consumers' League—lucus a non lucendo— [4] usurping functions not theirs.

1. See LDB to Frankfurter, 6 March 1925.
2. See LDB to Frankfurter, 8 November 1925.
3. Beginning in the late spring of 1920, a nationwide nonbuying movement had been deemed successful in lowering prices on selected commodities.
4. "A grove [lucus] is so called because it excludes the light [lux]"—that is, a ridiculous appellation, a misnomer.

To Charles Gabriel Tachau

February 20, 1926 Washington, D.C. [Brandeis Mss, M 15–2]

MY DEAR CHARLES: Re yours of 16th.

I wired you yesterday: "I approve. Glad to see Miss Flexner at nine thirty any day before March first." [1]

On that day our Court reconvenes & its work will be engrossing. I approve of all save your expression "your libraries." Alice and I will aid. But if the libraries attain the worth we dream of, the achievement will be the work of the Louisville family—work which we hope will go forward long after we shall have passed away.

1. Miss Flexner, sister of LDB's friend Bernard, was considering assuming the duties of special librarian at the University of Louisville. See next letter.

To Charles Gabriel Tachau

February 25, 1926 Washington, D.C. [Brandeis Mss, M 15–2]

MY DEAR CHARLES: Re yours of Feb 22/

You are entirely right in assuming that I approved generally of the plan for a special librarian, and that my approval was not conditioned upon acceptance by Miss Flexner.[1]

I am sorry she did not accept; because aside from her purely personal qualities, she possesses two qualifications of which, at least the first, seems almost essential to the achievement of what we have in mind. *First* she has the local knowledge. Some knowledge of Kentucky and Kentuckians will be required at almost every turn. *Second* She is a woman; and my experience in this kind of works leads me to think that we are more likely to get the results for an enduring task from a devoted woman than from the men who would ordinarily be available for work of this character. However, I am content to leave wholly to you and Dean Anderson the selection of the special librarian. So you will consider what I have said merely as suggestions—not as conditions.

1. See preceding letter.

Oliver Wendell Holmes

March 8, 1926 Washington, D.C. [Holmes Mss]

O.W.H.: The top of the morning—To him who is top of the heap.[1]

1. This note was passed to Justice Holmes on his eighty-fifth birthday. See next letter.

To Felix Frankfurter

March 14, 1926 Washington, D.C. [Frankfurter Mss—HLS]

FF: 1. O[liver]W[endell]H[olmes] bore his birthday week in the pink of condition physically & mentally and in the most joyous spirits—despite heavy court work and nearly 100 letters answered. Your beautiful piece in the N[ew]R[epublic] will add to his happiness.[1]

2. Newton Baker made an admirable argument in Wisconsin v. Illinois & the Chicago Sanitary District.[2] It was not only good in advocacy, it revealed grasp, vision and intellectual power of a high order. OWH & I agreed entirely on this. Pity B. has not the supporting character. He might, if he had, do great things.

3. That lack of character, of this strength, is our greatest weakness, impressed me more & more. I thought of it again last evening when a telegram from George C. Lee advised me of Storrow's death.[3] S. might have been the first citizen of Boston—even of the old grand manner. He had ample ability & in station, means and perception of a changing world would have been competent to deal with almost any situation. But whenever the supreme test came—he wasn't there.

4. A newspaper item says Mass[achusetts] has gained in farm population about 30,000 since 1920—a very large percentage compared with a total of 150,000; also that the new farmers are individual owners of the farms, presumably small farms and cheap land. If the item is true, it may have great significance. Isn't there some economist who can think as well as plod, who will look into the matter & interpret it?

5. As bearing on my enquiry of some months ago, of our Western and Southern rapacious farm rack-renting,[4] I suppose you noticed in Hirst's Jefferson [5] p. 217, that in France the rents of the agricultural laborers were "about half" of the produce and "English rents about a third." But neither English or French tenants provided expensive plant like the modern agricultural machinery.

6. Who wrote "Governors as State Bosses" in N.R? The con-
cluding paragraph is particularly wise.[6] I fear this is another reform of "the easier way" kind. In this article it is always the last
steps "that cost". The first are easy & seemingly bear good fruit.

7. The "Nickel Plate Decision" is also discerning.[7]

8. Buckner's talk on "Light Wines & Beer" is being much criti-
cised by some of his one time ardent friends.[8]

9. The McCamant episode, of which the N.R. brought me the
first detail, must be disturbing to Canny Cal[vin Coolidge], particularly after the Woodlock turn down.[9] Ad interim appointments to such offices are indefensible.

10. J[ohn]H[aynes]Holmes dies hard. But he learns a bit while
protesting.

11. Elizabeth & Paul had Meikeljohn in with the Phil LaFollettes for supper & the talk did not break up until midnight. Phil
& wife were tremendously impressed. Eliz. who heard M's first
session with 70 students says he is a wonder.

12. Yes the U.S. Daily is a bright, valuable publication.[10] I have
had the U. of Louisville subscribe & preserve the file.

13. Your report of Friendly & others of your students is
cheering.[11]

14. The Boston Criminal survey should bear rich fruit.[12]
I should think it perhaps the most promising of all fields for such
an enquiry.

15. I wish to record my doubt as to the wisdom of A[lfred E.]
S[mith]'s housing plan.[13]

1. See preceding letter. Frankfurter's tribute took the form of an unsigned editorial, "Mr. Justice Holmes," *New Republic* 46 (17 March 1926):
88–89: "The fruit of his wisdom has become part of the common stock of
civilization. Wherever law is known, he is known."

2. Baker, representing the state of Ohio, made his argument on a motion
to dismiss, on 10 March 1926. The dispute was referred on 22 March to a
special master, Charles Evans Hughes.

3. George Cabot Lee (1871–1950) was a Boston banker closely associated
with James J. Storrow in the Lee Higginson Company. Storrow (see LDB
to Alice H. Grady, 16 November 1906) died 13 March 1926. See also LDB
to Alfred Brandeis, 28 March 1926.

4. See LDB to Frankfurter, 24 and 26 January 1926.

5. Francis W. Hirst, *The Life and Letters of Thomas Jefferson* (New
York, 1926).

6. The unsigned editorial, *New Republic* 46 (17 March 1926): 85–87, was a balanced and intelligent examination of the report of the Hughes Commission on the reorganization of the New York state government. While generally favorable ("it embodies a genuine advance in the art of state political administration"), the writer raised questions about centralizing power in the hands of the governor.

7. *Ibid.:* 87–88. The editorial discussed the refusal of the Interstate Commerce Commission to approve the Nickel Plate Railroad merger. The disapproval came, not on the grounds of economic feasibility, nor of public desirability, but on the basis of the questionable way the deal had been promoted.

8. Buckner's speech before the Economic Club of New York on 3 March advocated experimentation with the prohibition on light wines and beer.

9. Raymond Clapper, "Portrait of a Federal Judge," *New Republic* 46 (17 March 1926): 96–98. Clapper's article was a slashing attack on Wallace F. McCamant (1867–1944). McCamant, who had nominated Coolidge for the vice-presidency in 1920, was given an interim appointment as judge of the Circuit Court of Appeals for the Ninth Circuit. When the time arrived for his confirmation by the Senate, Hiram Johnson revealed that McCamant held some unusually bizarre opinions. Once, in a speech, for example, McCamant had called LDB an "avaricious mountebank." He also had labelled Theodore Roosevelt "un-American" for favoring recall of judicial decisions. The nomination was referred back to the Judiciary Committee and it failed of confirmation. Thomas Francis Woodlock (1866–1945) was an Irish immigrant who rose to become a prominent journalist, associated for many years with the *Wall Street Journal*. Because he was a specialist in railroad affairs, Coolidge nominated him for the Interstate Commerce Commission. Woodlock's nomination was confirmed, but only after an adverse committee recommendation, a protracted Senate debate, and rumors of a "deal" with President Coolidge.

10. The new newspaper had begun publication on 4 March, under the editorship of David Lawrence.

11. Frankfurter's praise of Henry Jacob Friendly (b. 1903) was well founded. After serving as LDB's law clerk, 1927–28, Friendly went on to a distinguished career as a lawyer and, after 1959, as a Circuit Court justice and chief justice. In 1926 Friendly was in the process of planning his career, and he and his parents appealed to LDB and Frankfurter for advice; see LDB to Frankfurter, 28 October and 9 November 1926.

12. See LDB to Frankfurter, 24 January 1926, n. 3.

13. Governor Smith had transmitted a comprehensive housing plan to the legislature in late February, involving, among other proposals, destroying outmoded tenements and replacing them with model housing. See *New York Times*, 23 February 1926. See also LDB to Frankfurter, 21 March 1926.

To Alfred Brandeis

March 20, 1926 Washington, D.C. [Brandeis Mss, M 4-4]

My DEAR AL: Today our birthday wishes go to you. I hope the day may bring joyous zusammensein.[1]

My recollection is that we left Vienna between 9 & 10 AM on March 20 [1872], arrived in Gratz [*sic*] that evening, spent the night there, started, between 8 & 10 AM Mch 21 and arrived in Trieste about 5 PM. Spent March 22 mainly in visit to Miramar. Took the steamer before supper, having supper on board, and arrived off Venice after 6 AM March 23. & land[ed] there before 8 AM.

I am glad Hattie [Speed] is getting so much recognition for her U of L[ouisville] gifts.[2] Also that the Jews are becoming active givers.

1. "Gathering." Alfred was seventy-two.
2. See LDB to Fannie Brandeis, 14 February 1925.

To Felix Frankfurter

March 21, 1926 Washington, D.C. [Frankfurter Mss–HLS]

FF: 1. I think I have never seen O[liver].W[endell].H[olmes]. so joyously playful as now. He said yesterday at luncheon that the last 15 years—"his old age"—had been unquestionably the happiest period of his life.

2. Enclosed editorial from J[ournal] of C[ommerce] (which appeared since I wrote you) touches on the objections to Smith's housing plan which I had in mind.[1] I stated the objection to Alfred Bettman who (with wife) were [*sic*] with us Friday evening.[2] I think both in this matter & in his state reorganization [Smith] shows the qualities of a social minded, enlightened, efficient administrator—but not of a far-seeing statesman.

3. No 10. was argued by Walter Pollock[*sic*]. Noscitur a sociis.[3]

4. A trustworthy lawyer from the South who was in yesterday said his rich clients had said in 1924—"we hope Coolidge will be elected, but, of course, we cant vote for him." I think there may be more dangerous reactions from rich southerners, who have

gotten so without much effort, than has attended the more laborious process in the North.

5. Anti-Court and Anti League Senators are having some "schadenfreude".[4]

6. The Journal of Commerce has data from Milan confirming N[ew]. R[epublic] Italian debt views & suggesting that the "balanced budget" is faked.[5]

7. I wonder who is carrying the French, Belgian & Italian loans to stabilize the currency, which J. P. Morgan & Co. made.

1. See LDB to Frankfurter, 14 March 1926, n. 13. The *Journal of Commerce* editorial of 16 March, entitled "Congestion and Housing," raised questions about the concentration of workers' housing in a central, overcrowded, congested area. The editorial argued that it would be preferable to spread out the population more evenly.

2. Alfred Bettman (1873–1945) was a Cincinnati attorney, extremely active in civic affairs. He had worked with Frankfurter on the Cleveland Survey, and he went on to accept many governmental assignments in the area of city planning and urban problems.

3. "He is recognizable from his associates." Walter Heilprin Pollak (1887–1940) was a Harvard Law School graduate and a New York attorney. He later helped to defend the Scottsboro defendants. Case #10 was an early stage of the landmark *Whitney* v. *California*. For this stage of the proceeding, see 269 *U.S.* 530, 538. For the outcome, see LDB to Frankfurter, 20 May 1927, n. 4. Pollak's "associates" at this stage in the Whitney case were Walter Nelles and John F. Neylan.

4. "malicious pleasure." On 27 January 1926, the Senate voted to join the World Court but coupled their action with reservations. The irreconcilables chose to capitalize on a relatively minor issue to reopen the entire League debate in the Senate. Ambassador Alanson Houghton was reported to have returned from England with damning and pessimistic reports on the League and on European politics generally; when word of Houghton's alleged report was leaked to the press, a furious European reaction ensued. See *New York Times*, 22 and 23 March 1926.

5. "The Dishonest Italian Settlement," *New Republic* 46 (24 March 1926): 132–34.

To Alfred Brandeis

March 23, 1926 Washington, D.C. [Brandeis Mss, M 4–4]

DEAR AL: Your greetings came by the morning's mail.

You seem to remember the Italian days [of 1872] so well, perhaps you can say definitely:

(a) How long we had Mueller as guide & where

(b) How long & where Buchler was with us.

Frank [Taussig] called today. We were sorry to miss him & to find that he had "checked out" of the Cosmos [Club] before we could telephone there.

I called at Dudley's office & was very glad to find him there at 4PM &, as he says, in better shape than at any time in 2 years—due to "transfusion" treatment, ultimately tried by the Johns Hopkins folk. I saw his wife also (and a child) who had come for him in the car.

Alice bids me tell you that Washington Flour, which she uses religiously under your instructions, is not obtainable anywhere in the city.

The terrific fluctuations in grains lead me to enquire whether the world has really gotten much benefit from the International Institute of Agriculture & other statistic-collecting agencies. It was said that knowledge so derived would prevent speculation & bring stability of prices.

To Alfred Brandeis

March 28, 1926 Washington, D.C. [Brandeis Mss, M 4-4]

MY DEAR AL: I was interested in Gov. Bramwell's message—and am glad to hear of Judge Kerr.[1] Will try to get into touch with him, but will leave the matter of Librarian out of our talk, as this is for Charles [Tachau] & Dean Anderson.

Herbert White blew in the other evening. He is looking finely —much younger than recently, not so fat.

He told us much of [James J.] Storrow[2] (who he thinks amassed a fortune of $40,000,000). From his estate, Herbert is to have Storrow's half of the boat & an endowed fund to cover the expense of running it.

Herbert was South with Storrow this winter—a part of the time at a small rich-man's club in No. Carolina (60,000 acres) and then visiting a friend in South Carolina (30,000). Lucullus was ein Hund dagegen.[3] Father would have said: "Nichts erfreuh-liches".[4] It is evident, you & I are relics of a past world—which I prefer.

Herbert is quite his old good self, not visibly affected by his rich associations (& no riches himself)—But he is also quite the same unregenerate boy whom I met 30 years ago.

The Frank Lyons are coming in to dine. He has won a great I[nterstate].C[ommerce].C[ommission]. victory before the I.C.C. re Canal traffic and transcontinental rates.

[Edward F.] McClennen & wife turned up 10 days ago, having motored down from Boston. He argued a case in N.Y. En route & was to argue one here but our Court recessed before it was reached. We sent them back via Gettysburg & they were delighted with the trip.

1. Charles Kerr (1863–1950) was a Kentucky lawyer who served as judge of a Kentucky circuit court. Harding appointed him judge of the district court of the Canal Zone. He had a long interest in Kentucky history and edited a five-volume history of the state.
2. See LDB to Felix Frankfurter, 14 March 1926, n. 3.
3. "a dog by comparison."
4. "not very pleasant."

To Elizabeth Brandeis Raushenbush

April 8, 1926 Washington, D.C. [EBR]

DEAREST ELIZABETH: It is three weeks since your letter came.

1. Harold Laski has been in Monday, Tuesday & Wednesday. We have had considerable talk & find him one of the few surviving who hold Felix's & my views on current American problems. He further ingratiated himself with me by bringing a copy of the Hammonds' "Rise of Modern Industry," [1] & by speaking most enthusiastically of your Eileen Power.[2] He says she is as beautiful and charming as she [is] talented & learned; & dresses uncommonly well. Her great book, he says, is the volume on the nunneries.[3]

You & Paul and Phil & Isen [LaFollette] will be interested to learn (what I suppose, is quasi-confidential) that the Faculty of London University declined—almost unanimously—an offer from the Rockefellers of 8 new professorships & provision for research work. Harold is almost as skeptical about the value of research endowments as I am. You & Paul, who are confronted with

American niggardliness in university salaries, may be able to tell those in authority that poor England pays Harold 1000 pounds a year. Harold says that the University is determined to restrict numbers to 2500. There is more of his talk that must await Chatham.

2. While Harold was with me Tuesday Sidney Hil[l]man came in & we three had an hour together. Of the S.H. attitude, I shall have much to tell when we meet. He is not as democratic as I had supposed.

3. I had a further talk with Mr. [Walton H.] Hamilton. I then told him of your urgent call for teachers as against researchers. He expressed himself definitely of that opinion, favoring research largely as a means of training & educating teachers.

4. I should think an employment insurance plank would be a more appealing campaign for the workers than cheap life insurance. But I suppose Mr. Eckern [sic] might fear the interests' opposition.[4] Of course, cheap life insurance is about the easiest way of saving money conceivable. But the "interests" fight strenuously against it. Miss [Alice H.] Grady has had a running feud on her job these six months, but it looks as if the enemy would have a large casualty list. She is a wonderful fighter. Quite equal to Allan Breck.[5]

The enclosed statement shows the rapid rate of growth in recent years.[6] The current year's growth is even better. In March the premium income gained 42 percent over last year.

It is my hope, however, that *no* other state will try anything very like Savings Bank Insurance for some years to come.[7] It will be better for all that Mass[achusetts]. should have become thoroughly permeated with S.B.I. before it is tried anywhere else.

Lovingly,

1. John L. and Barbara Hammond, *The Rise of Modern Industry* (London, 1925).

2. Eileen Edna Power (1889–1940) was an English historian whose special field was the economic and social history of late medieval and early modern England. After 1921 she was associated with the London School of Economics.

3. *Medieval English Nunneries, c. 1275 to 1535* (Cambridge, England, 1922).

4. Herman Lewis Ekern (1872–1954) was a Wisconsin lawyer and political figure. At one point Speaker of the Wisconsin House of Representatives

(in 1907), Ekern was a leading progressive, involved in various unemployment and insurance agencies.

5. The hero of Robert Louis Stevenson's *Kidnapped*.

6. In 1920, four banks were writing Savings Bank Insurance policies, and there were 30,834 policies in effect; in 1926, ten banks were participating, and there were 55,822 policies.

7. It was not until 1938, that a second state, New York, adopted the Savings Bank Life Insurance plan.

To Stella and Emily Dembitz

April 22, 1926 Washington, D.C. [Brandeis Mss, M 4–4]

MY DEAR STELLA AND EMILY: [1] In discussing, last year, with President [Arthur Y.] Ford the project of developing at the University [of Louisville] a worthy World War Library, I made the following suggestion which seemed to impress him deeply.

The liberation of lesser nationalities is prominent among the hopeful results of the War, and yet, their independence was won less by arms than by the slow process of education. It was largely the work of far seeing, patient, persistent, devoted men and women, who awakened in the rising generation an interest in the language, the literature, the traditions of their people, and, through the acquisition of knowledge, developed the striving for liberty and opportunity and the fuller life. This is true of the liberation of Czechs, Slovaks and Yugoslavs; of the Finns, Letts, Esthonians and Lithuanians; of the Irish and the Poles; and of other peoples. In these victories of ideas, America had an important part. Our War of Independence was an inspiration and an encouragement. And, throughout long years, there came from men and women of these nationalities living in happier America, money and other supplies for these campaigns of education. Finally when the war came, committees of these nationals, formed in America, lent, in many ways, important aid.

These struggles, rich in heroic incident and noble achievement, present material for some of the most promising chapters in the [history] of mankind. The University should have in its library, not only the books in which the events are summarized, but, so far as possible, the contemporary publications which were themselves acts in the process of liberation, or which record in detail events of importance. Louisville has among its citizens men and women of many of the liberated nationalities; and among these, doubtless, some who aided materially in their struggles for independence. That the University purposed making such collections and desired their cooperation to that end, of these of its citizens, when announced, [would] be an event of civic significance. It would indicate the breadth of Louisville's hospitality; its appreciation of all contributions to civilization, regardless of the nationality of those who made them, and that what was noble and fine in the tradition of all the peoples of which its population is composed, is to be cherished as a subject for generous study. Thus would be made clear that the University is the University of all, regardless of race, or creed, and however recent their migration to America; and that all should endeavor to work through it for the City's finest development.

Among the peoples to whom the war brought the opportunity of liberty and development are the Jews of Eastern Europe and of other lands of oppression. Through the Balfour Declaration, the ages long dream of the Jewish Homeland became possible of realization. Through my connection with the Zionist movement during the last fourteen years, I chance to have made a collection of the publications in which, to a considerable extent, the ideas and events are recorded which have led to the Rebirth of Palestine. These, with some unpublished documents of historic value I purpose offering to the University; and also funds to provide for the necessary cataloguing binding, shelving and purchases to supplement the collection. All would be an appropriate addition to the books on Jewish life and thought which the generous gift of Adath Israel Congregation is bringing to the University. The collection would surely be enriched, in course of time, by many valuable contributions of other volumes and documents. And it is reasonable to expect that these gifts will lead Louisvillians of other nationalities to aid similarly in the efforts of the University to develop a worthy World War Library.

I should like that this offer to the University be made through you, with the suggestion that if it is accepted, you will share the burden of supervision by associating with yourselves some member of the faculty, or other member of the community, having special interest in this subject.[2] That the offer should be made through you seems peculiarly fitting for the following reason. To your father the recent growth of the University would have given great joy. To those of my generation he was a living university. With him, life was unending intellectual ferment. He grappled eagerly with the most difficult problems in mathematics and the sciences, in economics, government and politics. In the diversity of his intellectual interests, in his longing to discover truths, in his pleasure in argumentation and in the process of thinking, he reminded of the Athenians. He loved books as a vehicle of knowledge and an inciter to thought; and he made his love contagious. It is appropriate that his influence should be remembered in the library where he would have worked. A collection of books is the memorial for which he would have cared most. And the collection which tells of Palestine's rebirth seems the most appropriate.

For the deepest of his studies were those allied to the Jewish religion. He was orthodox. He observed the law. But he was not satisfied with merely observing it. He sought to understand the law. And to find its reason, he studied deeply in the history of the Jewish people. His was not the drive of intellectual curiosity with the realm of dead knowledge. He recognized in the past the mirror of the future—a noble and glorious one for his people. It was natural that he should have been among the first in America to support Herzl in his effort to build a New Palestine.

If it will be agreeable to you to aid in this undertaking, I shall send you later the details as to the collection, and some suggestions for supplementing it.   Your cousin,

1. Stella and Emily Dembitz were the daughters of LDB's favorite uncle, Lewis N. Dembitz (see LDB to Frederika D. Brandeis, 7 September 1870, n. 11).

2. Rabbi Joseph Rauch (see LDB to Alfred Brandeis, 27 October 1921, n. 3) agreed to serve in this capacity.

To Julian William Mack

April 25, 1926 Washington, D.C. [R. Szold Mss]

J.W.M.: Pam was in & will tell you of our talk of today.[1]
I proposed the following—with which he seemed well satisfied.

The full amount (about $47,000) net, to be paid into Palestine Endowment Fund, to be supplied towards making possible carrying out the Ruttenberg [*sic*] project [2] (presumably by investment with P[alestine]D[evelopment]C[ouncil] & J[oint]D[istribution] C[ommittee] funds, as junior securities, through P[alestine]E[conomic]C[orporation]). The securities rec'd by P.E.F. to be used (or proceeds) for the Hebrew University & to be used for the fitting of Palestinian youth for the Palestine public service.

This we thought consistent with the purpose of the trust & the presumed views of the Testator. Thereby, we *as trustees*, would have fully performed our trust when payment made to P.E.F. & that course seemed to me consistent with my purpose to keep out of every office except Associate Justice U[nited]S[tates]S[upreme]C[ourt].

1. LDB and Hugo Pam were named as trustees in the will of a Zionist who had left $47,000 to the cause.

2. See LDB to Solomon Rosenbloom, 25 June 1922, n. 2 and to Julian W. Mack, 22 January 1924.

To Alfred Brandeis

May 2, 1926 Washington, D.C. [Brandeis Mss, M 4-4]

MY DEAR AL: Alice shipped her nurse yesterday 8 PM & we celebrated today with two hours on the Potomac in heavenly weather.

Ben Flexner's report on Palestine was encouraging. Relations with Arabs so friendly that there is at present no Arab problem. The English army has been withdrawn & there is only a very moderate police force in the country. The budget of the Mandate territory is, I understand, balanced. Malaria situation eminently satisfactory. Immigration about 2500 a month. That is quite as large as it should be, making a percentage addition to the Jewish population of about 20 to 25 percent a year.

I have written Jessie C[ochran] as James Speed desired.

I saw your friend Judge Kerr today, & Walker Hines the day before. H. looks blooming.   Gruesse,

To Felix Frankfurter

May 2, 1926 Washington, D.C. [Frankfurter Mss—HLS]

I am inclined to think that the most copious & futile of the single wastes of our Court's efforts have been in the Federal Liability Cases both (a) before the Sept 6, 1916 Act, on writ of error and (b) since, in granting certioraris.[1] It might be worthwhile to put one of your jurisdiction sharps on that enquiry.

1. Section 2 of the law permitted the Supreme Court to reexamine and reverse decisions from the highest state courts, just as if the cases had risen through the federal system. The same section also permitted the Court, by certiorari, to require reviews of such decisions in the state court systems. 39 *U.S. Statutes*, Ch. 448 (1916).

To Alfred Brandeis

May 19, 1926 Washington, D.C. [Brandeis Mss, M 4-4]

DEAR AL: Here's a nice letter from Lydia.

As you don't like the French, I guess we shed no tears over the drop of the franc yesterday to 2.73. The decline is at a pretty rapid pace now.

Are you trying to equal Otto [Wehle] on walking and T[homas] Jefferson on riding?

We modestly keep to the river.

To Willis VanDevanter

May 19, 1926 Washington, D.C. [VanDevanter Mss]

MY DEAR VANDEVANTER: My thanks for yours of 17th.

The ground you recommend was not the one on which I voted "no"—But I think that, as a matter of policy, you are clearly right; and I am engaged in redrafting the opinion on that line.[1]

May I trouble you to formulate the rule of law, which you think should be established? And I should be very glad to have any authorities or arguments in support of the construction recommended.   Cordially,

1. It is not possible to know to which opinion LDB referred.

To Alfred Brandeis

May 22, 1926 Washington, D.C. [Brandeis Mss M 4-4]

DEAR AL: Glad to have your two letters reporting satisfactory telephone talks with Stella [Dembitz].[1] Shall doubtless have report of your meeting at office in your next.

I had not seen the Hoover propaganda. I guess you are right as to his chances—1928 is pretty far off and it is not beyond the possibilities that Chambers of Commerce & their officers will be in less public favor by that time.

We are diligently pursuing our Potomac sport. Weather has been perfect. The rarest days of the year.

Alice had a fine letter from your Fan which she will answer soon.

Vernon Kellogg is coming in for dinner tomorrow. Possibly he may say something about Hoover.[2]

1. See LDB to Stella and Emily Dembitz, 22 April 1926.
2. See next letter.

To Alfred Brandeis

May 27, 1926 Washington, D.C. [Brandeis Mss, M 4-4]

DEAR AL: Alice bids me say Please send the ham to Chatham to arrive after Sept 10.[1] We are due there that day. Except Mrs. [Elizabeth Glendower] Evans to be there at the start, and Felix Frankfurter to arrive on the 12th for 8 or 9 days.

Vernon Kellogg did not say anything about Hoover's running.[2] But his talk with Norman Hapgood on Coolidge & the essentials of a President who could meet bad times etc. convince me that he was thinking of H. for the place.   Gruesse,

Louis Wehle, who for some months has been making payments on account, sent today a check *wiping out the balance*—principal and interest.[3]

1. LDB meant to write "June 10."
2. See preceding letter.
3. See LDB to Alfred Brandeis, 19 September and 8 December 1921.

*

To Alice Harriet Grady

June 5, 1926 Washington, D.C. [Grady Mss]

AHG: We still plan to leave Monday on the Federal.[1]

Of course we want Tal. at the luncheon if he is available.[2] Mrs. Brandeis has sent your Transcript article to Susan Goldmark, the literary member of the family.

I took my seat on U[nited]S[tates]S[upreme]C[ourt] 10 years ago *today*.

1. For Chatham.
2. Talmadge Grady was Alice Grady's brother. He became a field worker for the Savings Bank Insurance system.

To Fannie Brandeis

June 11, 1926 Chatham, Mass. [Brandeis Mss, M 15–1]

MY DEAR FANNY: Aunt Alice and I suggest, if it meets with your and Dean Anderson's approval, that the collection of scores be called the "Hast Collection".[1]

It is to this romantic German piano-teacher that Louisville owes the beginnings of its appreciation of the great chamber and orchestral music. In lofty enthusiasm he formed the quartette and quintette clubs. With untiring devotion he guided them. Courageously he organized an amateur orchestra. Thus he afforded the opportunity of gaining knolwedge and understanding through doing. And the joy of the doing was experienced.

1. Louis Henry Hast (1822–1890) had come to Louisville around 1850 and, according to Bernard Flexner, "for fully forty years was the leader in all musical effort in Louisville." *Mr. Justice Brandeis and the University of Louisville*, 21. LDB himself had played the violin in one of Hast's orchestras in 1875, with Henry Waterson as another of the young musicians. The Hast Library, founded by LDB, was aided by Hast's daughters and by Morris B. Belknap and Mrs. S. Thruston Ballard. It developed into an extensive collection of musical manuscripts and books.

To Felix Frankfurter

June 22, 1926 Chatham, Mass. [Frankfurter Mss—HLS]

FF: Thanks for the British works which shall go to Louisville. I have been re-reading Chafee's Freedom of Speech with ever growing admiration of his head, his heart and his character.[1]

What has become of McCurdy's enquiry into the P[ublic].A[dministration].[2] & Van Vleck's into the Immigration Dept?[3]

Couldn't you get started through your men a series for the H[arvard]L[aw]R[eview] covering the danger of arbitrariness etc. in the several federal Depts & Bureaus? The impending change re naturalization & deportation suggests thought & may suggest preventive remedies.[4]

In 1819, Jefferson wrote in acknowledging a copy of the No[rth] Amer[ican] Review: "I see with pride that we are ahead of Europe in Political Science."[5]

And in the same year this: "And if Caesar had been as virtuous as he was daring and sagacious, what could he, even in the plenitude of his usurped powers have done to lead his fellow citizens into good government? I do not say to *restore it*, because they never had it from the rape of the Sabines to the ravages of the Caesars."[6]

1. Zechariah Chafee, *Freedom of Speech* (New York, 1920).
2. McCurdy, LDB's former clerk now teaching at Harvard, published nothing on the subject.
3. See LDB to Felix Frankfurter, 16 September 1923, n. 5.
4. Both houses of Congress were considering modifications in both deportation rules (increasing the number of those deported and the reasons for deportation) and naturalization (with an eye to speeding the process).
5. Jefferson to John Adams, 19 January 1819.
6. Jefferson to John Adams, 10 December 1819.

To Felix Frankfurter

June 23, 1926 Chatham, Mass. [Frankfurter Mss—HLS]

FF: I omitted to ask you what progress is being made in the effort to reduce the appropriations for spies in the public service. It may take a generation to rid our country of this pest, but I think it probably can be done, if the effort is persistent and we are prepared for action when, in the course of time, "the day" comes. The temper of the public at some time in conjunction with some conspicuous occurrence will afford an opportunity & we should be prepared to take advantage of it. Knowledge—detailed & put into effective usable forms is the foundation onto which to build. The machinery for collecting the data must be perfected.

For the process of nibbling at appropriations, the next years may afford promise—on the one hand, the wets indignant at prohibition practices; on the part of anti-administration forces, the policy of pin-pricks; and on that of the administration the policy of Economy.

The subject is so closely allied to evidence that possibly you could interest Maguire or Morgan, if they are likeminded with us.[1] And, if so, some among their students could be enlisted, who could, i.a. make the work undertaken, at the Brookings School a bit effective. Or possibly you might stir up some one in the Political Science department at Harvard to work with the H[arvard]L[aw]S[chool]. And/or this subject could (locally) be appropriately pursued in connection with the Milton enquiry into Criminal Administration in Boston.[2]

1. John MacArthur Maguire (b. 1888) taught at Harvard from 1923 to 1957. Edmund Morris Morgan (1878–1966) had come from Yale's law school in 1925, and he remained at Harvard until 1950. Both were specialists in the law of evidence.

2. See LDB to Frankfurter, 24 January 1926, n. 3.

To Felix Frankfurter

June 25, 1926 Chatham, Mass. [Frankfurter Mss—HLS]

FF: 1. Would it not be desirable to let follow, after your article on overruled etc. cases of U[nited]S[tates]S[upreme]C[ourt],[1] one on cases reversed, in effect, by Congressional action—distinguishing between (a) cases where Congress apparently undertook to correct what it deemed our erroneous construction, from (b) those where its presumed actual intent was not made effective either because (1) of a casus omissus [2], or (2) other inadvertence or want of precision in drafting the statute.

You will recall that I dealt with this matter somewhat in the Weitzel case [3] & later.

The recent Washington Quarantine case & legislation is in point.[4]

2. Wouldn't it be possible to interest Bohlen and Dickinson [5] directly & through them students, to make the necessary investigation & present in the [Harvard] Law Review articles bearing on the redress for the invasion of civil and political rights through arbitrary etc. governmental action, by means of civil suits?

I think the failure to attempt such redress as against government officials for the multitude of invasions during the war and post-war period is also as disgraceful as the illegal acts of the government and the pusilanimous action of our people in enacting the statutes which the states and the nation put on the books.[6] Americans should be reminded of the duty to litigate. Dickinson, at least, ought to have a hereditary concern about liberty.

I hope the N[ew]R[epublic] will pay its respects to "Pepper, the Consistent" and "Mellon, the Honorable".[7]

1. Another installment of the series by Frankfurter had just appeared: "The Business of the Supreme Court of the United States," 39 *Harvard Law Review* 1046 (1926).

2. A case not provided for, in this instance, by a particular statute.

3. *United States* v. *Weitzel*, 246 *U.S.* 533 (1918). Weitzel was appointed receiver of a Kentucky bank. He was charged with embezzlement under a law that mentioned "every president, director, cashier, teller, clerk, or agent," but did not mention "receivers." LDB, for a unanimous Court, ruled that "statutes creating and defining crimes are not to be extended by intendment because the court thinks the legislature should have made them more comprehensive."

4. The state of Washington, plagued by a dangerous alfalfa weevil, promulgated a quarantine order which prohibited the transportation, into Washington, of alfalfa. The Oregon-Washington Railroad shipped some alfalfa anyway. The railroad contended that although states can issue such quarantines, they cannot do so when Congress has acted in the matter. The railroad argued that a law of 1912 gave the Secretary of Agriculture responsibility for preventing the spread of infectious plants and animals. The Supreme Court, speaking through Chief Justice Taft, agreed with the railroad (Sutherland and McReynolds dissenting), and overturned the Supreme Court of Washington, which had allowed the quarantine. Congress, in response, immediately took up an examination of the law with an eye to permitting states to issue such protective quarantines against infected or diseased plants. *Oregon-Washington Railroad & Navigation Co., plaintiff in*

error, v. *State of Washington* 270 *U.S.* 87 (1926). The case was decided on 1 March.

5. Francis Herman Bohlen (1868–1942) taught law at the University of Pennsylvania Law School from 1898 to 1938; from 1925 to 1928, however, he was Langdell Professor of Law at Harvard. John Dickinson (1894–1952) had come to Harvard in 1925 from a law partnership with William G. McAdoo. Dickinson, a descendant of the Revolutionary publicist of the same name, left Harvard in 1927 for Princeton and the University of Pennsylvania. He held a number of important governmental positions, and in the mid-1930s was Assistant Attorney General.

6. See LDB to Frankfurter, 16 July 1926.

7. George Wharton Pepper had just been defeated in Pennsylvania's Republican primary for reelection to the Senate. He lost in spite of huge financial contributions and vocal campaign support from Secretary of the Treasury Andrew Mellon. The defeat was followed by allegations, on both sides, of financial wrongdoing and excessive spending; in 1930, the Senate denied William Scott Vare (1867–1934), the man who had beaten Pepper, his seat on account of campaign excesses.

To Felix Frankfurter

July 2, 1926 Chatham, Mass. [Frankfurter Mss—HLS]

1. Cobbett (Cole's Life of C[obbett],[1] p. 208) said (1816): "A reformed Parliament would . . . want no secret service money"; it would sweep away the hosts of "horrid scoundrels" and informers; there would be none of this "disgraceful spy-work".

2. I am glad to see that the announcement of your criminal survey is out.[2]

I suggest that, as an incident of the current survey, special care be taken to ascertain and record:

(a) The character (ethical) of the evidence through which it is sought to obtain a conviction—e.g. to what extent it is of the character held legal in Burdeau v McDowell 256 U.S. 465,[3] & the many cases where fed[eral] crimes were prosecuted in U.S. courts with evidence illegally procured by state officials.

(b) The instruments through which the evidence [is] introduced—e.g. by policemen & (1) to what extent detectives & undercover men & (2) ordinary policemen, inspectors etc.

(c) The extent to which there are convictions due to transactions which involve participation of police or detectives, even where they fall short of entrapment.

(4) [*sic*] The attitude, demeanor & conduct of the representatives of the government: policemen, jail officials, court officials, prosecuting officers & judges—all engaged in the function of enforcing & administering the law.

I have grave doubt whether we shall ever be able to effect more than superficial betterment unless we undertake to deal fundamentally with the intangibles; and succeed in infusing a sense (A) of the dignity of the law among a free, self-governing people and (B) of the solemnity of the function of administering justice. Among the essentials is that the government must, in its methods, & means, & instruments, be ever the gentleman. Also we must recognize the fallacy of the [***] that the function of Courts is to settle controversies. This view seems to me a bit of that finite 19th century wisdom of the Militarians which has brought so much evil as well as good. There are times of ease & prosperity when the pressing danger is somnolence rather than litigiousness.

I think that, in respect to evidence as in other respects, there is a limit to what can be accomplished by the mercenary alone. There must be some point at which the ability of the citizen to shift the burdens of government upon the paid expert—be he policeman or executive—ends.

Your survey should note particularly the limits of the mala prohibited, as distinguished from the mala in se.[4] It seems to me we were rather presumptuous in brushing away the distinction—another bit of really shallow rationalization; that there is, moreover, an essential difference between a crime and a delict;[5] & that there are few acts or omissions which ought to be treated as crimes which do not arouse righteous indignation. For these some other solution should be found than existing penalties.

1. G. D. H. Cole, *The Life of William Cobbett* . . . (London, 1924).

2. See LDB to Frankfurter, 24 January 1926, n. 3.

3. In this June 1921 decision, evidence was fraudulently obtained and used against the defendant. McDowell was dismissed from his job for fraud; his company dispatched another employee to Pittsburgh and this employee took over McDowell's office, blasted open two safes containing private papers, and turned over the evidence he found there to company

officials. Justice William R. Day, speaking for the majority, argued that McDowell's later conviction was legal because the government itself did not do an illegal act in obtaining the evidence.

4. The distinction between an act prohibited by law and an act morally wrong.

5. A "delict" is an act by which a person causes damage to another.

To Felix Frankfurter

July 16, 1926 Chatham, Mass. [Frankfurter Mss—HLS]

FF: 1. Wouldn't it be possible to have some one in Congress move for a Claims Commission to make reparations to American citizens for the outrages incident to the Jan 20 Palmer raids?[1] An article on the Sedition law reparations would prepare the way. And the move for appointment of the Commission might lead to diplomatic representations by foreign nations who have settled their debts & by Russia, when it is recognized. Americans ought not to be allowed to forget their Sicilian Vespers.[2] We need a John Quincy Adams to persistently press forward the right to free speech.[3]

2. It is fine that Nicely appreciates his association with Holmes J. & that he wants something other than he has.[4] Couldn't he be "saved from the burning?"

3. Every N.Y. lawyer I meet speaks highly of Thatcher [sic].[5]

4. The C[hesapeake] & O[hio] and the Illinois Central, to whom my brother wrote about the [University of Louisville] R[ail]R[oad] library, has promised hearty cooperation.

5. I should think young Walter Fisher would like that job.[6]

1. See LDB to Frankfurter, 25 June 1926. The Palmer raids of 1920 involved the government's rounding up over four thousand suspected radicals and eventually deporting 556 of them. The raids were authorized by Attorney General A. Mitchell Palmer.

2. The terms "Sicilian Vespers" refers to a popular uprising in 1282 by Sicilians against their French rulers, during which many Frenchmen were murdered. The signal for the revolt was the ringing of the vesper bell in Palermo.

3. A reference to the effort of former President Adams to protect free speech in his battle, in the House of Representatives during the 1830s, to debate the slavery issue, despite the House's "gag rule" on the subject.

4. James Mount Nicely had served as Holmes's secretary in 1924–25; see LDB to Frankfurter, 8 March 1924.

5. Probably Judge Thomas Day Thacher (1881–1950), who had worked with Frankfurter in Henry L. Stimson's office twenty years earlier. In 1925 he was named judge for the Southern District of New York, and President Hoover appointed him U.S. Solicitor General in 1930. After another term in private practice, Governor Thomas E. Dewey appointed him, in May 1943, to the New York Court of Appeals.

6. Walter Taylor Fisher (b. 1892) was the son of Walter L. Fisher, former Secretary of the Interior and an occasional associate of LDB's. The son was a Chicago lawyer. He did serve in some public offices, but not during the mid-1920s.

To Felix Frankfurter

July 25, 1926 Chatham, Mass. [Frankfurter Mss—HLS]

1. This, from Arthur Young's "Thoughts on the Establishment of a Chamber of Manufacturers" pp. 452–3 ed. 1785, may interest friends of "The Chambers" & of the Hoover boom: "Now the union of all sorts of manufacturers, not for the improvement of their fabricks, but for the conversion of themselves into politicians to watch with kindling jealousy the motions of the legislature; . . . ; to quicken, alarm, and give alacrity to apprehensions; to array private feeling in the garb of public needs; . . . to give facility to discontent, and vigour to resistance—an institution that does all this, is wonderfully different from the combination of talents for the purpose of improvement which might have done honour to the projector; it may become, instead of a society of arts, a den of politicians".

2. Re yours of 23rd about [James M.] Landis. I had heard nothing of this cheering event—from him or otherwise: [1]—and, of course, know nothing of the facts, on which to form an opinion as to whether it would be wise for him to borrow. If it is wise for him to incur an indebtedness, I much prefer that the loan should be made by me than by someone else. If upon talking the matter over with him, you and he conclude that it is desirable for him to borrow, I shall be glad to lend the two thousand ($2000) which you name.

3. This, attributed by Murray to Sir John Fortescue's "On the Governance of England" (1471), is interesting in connection with

present French finances: "he contrasts the readiness with which the taxes are paid in England with the "grudging" they call forth in France."

4. We expect Elizabeth & Paul on Tuesday via Rochester.

1. Landis had announced his engagement to Miss Stella G. McGehee.

To Robert Netherland Miller

August 10, 1926 Chatham, Mass. [Brandeis Mss, M 15–3]

MY DEAR MILLER: Among the tasks of the Law School of the University of Louisville is that of developing in its students the desire for mastery of the federal law. To this end easy access to the sourcebooks will be an aid; and a reminder of the contributions made by Kentuckians to this branch of the law may prove an inspiration.

It is just a century since Thomas Todd, the first Kentuckian to sit upon the Supreme Court of the United States closed twenty years (1807–1906) of honorable service there. He was followed by Robert Trimble (1826–1828) and much later by John M. Harlan (1877–1911). If it is agreeable to the faculty, I shall be glad to provide funds for completing the school's set of the reports of our court—the present and all future volumes to bear, as an appropriate memorial, the names of these three men.[1]

Distinguished service in the federal law was rendered by Kentuckians in two other capacities—as Federal District Judges and as Attorneys General. If it is agreeable to the faculty, I shall be glad to complete similarly the school's set of Federal Cases—as a memorial to the following District Judges. Harry Innes (1789–1816); Robert Trimble (1817–1826); John Boyle (1826–1834); Thomas B. Monroe (1834–1861); Bland Ballard (1861–1879); William H. Hays (1879–1880); John W. Barr (1880–1899).

And as a memorial to the Attorneys General—

John Breckenridge (1805–1806); John J. Crittenden (1841 and 1850–1853); James Speed (1864–1866), I shall be glad to supply funds for securing a set of the volumes containing the Opinions of the Attorneys General.

If these suggestions meet with your approval, I shall be glad to have you send a copy of this letter to Dean Lewis,[2] and to my brother Alfred.   Cordially,

1. See also LDB to Miller, 3 November 1926.
2. Leon Patteson Lewis (1878–1932), a Louisville native, returned to teach in the School of Law in 1908. Lewis served as dean of the School from 1925–1930.

To Felix Frankfurter

August 11, 1926 Chatham, Mass. [Frankfurter Mss—HLS]

1. Would it not be useful to have the Commonwealth or other Foundation undertake a comprehensive study of lawyers fees— with special regard to contingent fees, ambulance, tax return and other chasing, and what court rules and/or legislation should be adopted to stay the evils? Among the subjects for special consideration would be what the fee provisions should be where the claim is against the Federal or a State government; also what should be the special protections if any, where payments are made from other people's money.

2. Norman talked too much at Williamstown yesterday.[1]

3. We are looking forward to seeing you two and the Cohens on Monday.

1. Norman Hapgood was a participant in the sessions of the Institute of Politics at Williams College.

To Alfred Brandeis

September 11, 1926 Washington, D.C. [Brandeis Mss, M 4–4]

DEAR AL: Our trip was carried through per schedule. Reached the [Hotel] Bellevue [Boston], 7:15 Thursday, Miss Grady meeting us at station—and the Frankfurters & Hermann Blumgart for dinner that evening.

Friday AM Elizabeth & Paul arrived from their glorious camping (river [*], rapid shooting canoe trip). At luncheon Friday, they, Walter Child, Felix Frankfurter & Miss Grady were with us; and at 6:35 Miss Grady went with us from South Station to Back Bay.

I was at 161 Devonshire all morning where i.a. Herbert White came in & told of his great trip off Labrador to 54° from which he had returned (in Cachil of N[ova]S[cotia]) two days before. He sailed for 400 miles along the iceberg lane, & saw at one time 20. He is his old self.

Walter Child spends his time mainly at E[ast].Walpole now. With Anna, keeping up his spirits, etc. Charles Bird has been sick for 18 months & probably wont live long.[1]

At the Bellevue, on Thursday evening I had a meeting which should "ring bells" for you. Do you remember Otto Michaels, the handsome soldier boy who was at Uncle Gottlieb's courting Bertha [2] & who showed his strength by tossing me into the air? Was it in 1862 or in 1864? His son George Michaels reminded me of seeing him 30 years ago.

We are in our new apartments,[3] the living apartment No. 505 — my study No. 601, above it. We hope you will come & see them soon. The 505 you will like; & the lady would like to see you.

Sadie came here in August to move to 505 (with Poindexter's help); and the latter moved my office effects into 601; so there is only rearranging for me to do, and Alice too, will not have overmuch to do to get us into rights below.

As you may infer, 505 is on the fifth floor; 601 on the sixth.

Eliz. & Paul are spending today in N.Y. with Susan & Jack, and with Paul's sisters & brothers & are then to settle for 6 months in Philadelphia, where studies are to be made for their PhD's.[4]

Gruesse,

1. Charles Bird, Anna Child's husband (see LDB to Alfred Brandeis, 10 July 1912, n. 4) died in October 1927.

2. Gottlieb Wehle (1802–1881) was related to LDB in several ways; most directly he was Alice Brandeis's grandfather. Bertha was one of his ten daughters.

3. At Florence Court West (California St., N.W.). LDB confided to Julian W. Mack on 3 September: " 'Improvements' have at last driven us from Stoneleigh."

4. See LDB to Felix Frankfurter, 21 November 1927.

To Ray Stannard Baker

September 17, 1926 Washington, D.C. [Brandeis Mss, NMF 86-1]

MY DEAR BAKER: Re yours of 15th: [1]

1. Mr. Wilson's letter of May 5, 1916 was given wide publicity.[2] When you are next in Washington I can show you the collection of newspaper clippings made by my then secretary Miss Alice H. Grady, (now Deputy Commissioner of Savings Bank Insurance, State House, Boston.) Judge Geo. W. Anderson, Norman Hapgood and my then partner Edward F. McClennen, 161 Devonshire St., Boston, can tell you about the genesis of the letter.

2. I called on Mr. Wilson at his home during the summer of 1912 and had a long talk with him on trusts. Later, at Norman Hapgood's request I wrote a number of articles on trusts for Collier's—many of which appeared over my name; some were adopted by Norman as editorials. I can show these to you when you come to Washington, as these also were collected by Miss Grady. The articles were carefully studied during the campaign by Wilson as his then aid Dudley Field Malone told me. Several appear in my "Business—A Profession."

I cannot now recall my letter of Sept. 30 [1912] to Mr. Wilson; but I will send your letter to Miss Grady who has access to my papers in Boston. She will be glad to look the matter up, but probably cannot do so for a month or two.

Mrs. Brandeis bids me send warm greetings.   Cordially,

1. Baker had requested information from LDB about his relations with Woodrow Wilson, for the biography of the former president.
2. See LDB to Edward F. McClennen, 10 May 1916, n. 1.

To Alfred Brandeis

September 18, 1926 Washington, D.C. [Brandeis Mss, M 4-4]

DEAR AL: I think you have the steamboat gent nailed to the mast on Great Eastern electric lights. Of course there was an arc-lamp long before the incandescent—but not in the early days of the Great Eastern; & I doubt whether at any time before 1875.

I can't aid you as to date of seeing either Great Eastern or Great Western.

But I am sure were [*sic*] went East in 1861 & 1862 (both at Long Branch)—1864 & 1865, both at Newport. In 1862 we came back over the Erie line (broad guage) with Mr. Tachau & we four children & his feet occupied one seat on the day coach.

Alice bids me enclose this of Edna Ferber's book on River traffic[1]—it was Edna F. who introduced a "Fanny Brandeis" in a book, 10 years or so ago.[2]

Under another cover Alice sends a play of Fulda's[3] which she thinks Jennie may enjoy.

1. *Show Boat* (Garden City, N.Y., 1926).
2. "Fanny Brandeis" was the steamboat operated by Adolph Brandeis's business.
3. One of the works of the prolific German dramatist and translator, Ludwig Fulda (1862–1939).

To Felix Frankfurter

October 15, 1926 Washington, D.C. [Frankfurter Mss—HLS]

1. Do you hear anything under-ground about Daugherty-Miller disagreement?[1]

2. Jack Gilbert says that Mack's charge was the fairest charge he has ever heard in a criminal case.[2] Altogether JWM seems to have given further evidence that his service & reputation can best be furthered by sticking to the Criminal Session, and with Criminal law the chief centre of interest at the moment, he could hardly do better, for many reasons.

3. The H[arvard]L[aw]R[eview] should not miss, or fail to treat adequately No. 230, Industrial Com[missio]n v. Terry & Tench Co., in which we reversed N.Y. C[ourt of].A[ppeals]. (Cardozo) in a P[er].C[uriam]—!![3] The significance of the decision, in connection with some other recent ones on the same general subject might be made clear.

The Amer[ican] Hebrew is properly forgetful.

1. The jury had reported hopeless disagreement after sixty-five hours of deliberation in the government's conspiracy case against former Attorney General Harry Daugherty and the codefendant, Col. Thomas Woodnut Miller.

2. Mack's charge in the Daugherty case came on 9 October and required

an hour and forty-five minutes to deliver. See *New York Times*, 9 October 1926.

3. *State Industrial Board of the State of New York* v. *Terry & Tench Co., Inc. and United States Fidelity & Guaranty Co.*, 273 U.S. 639 (1926). The case was decided on 11 October. It involved a worker injured while employed on a floating raft, repairing a pier. Cardozo (for a unanimous New York Court of Appeals) reversed an original award on the ground that maritime law should apply and that the state law (the New York Workmen's Compensation Act) should not interfere. The outrage here expressed, and also expressed in 40 *Harvard Law Review* 485–91 (1926–27). was not due so much to the ultimate decision as to the fact that the Supreme Court would reverse so distinguished a state court *per curiam*, without even delivering an opinion.

To Alfred Brandeis

October 18, 1926 Washington, D.C. [Brandeis Mss, M 4-4]

DEAR AL: Ben & Miss Flexner were in this morning & send you greetings. They were in good form. Ben wanted to discuss Palestinian problems, but we talked some on American ones also. He is quite as flabbergasted as we are by the manifestations of business & says that, never in his life, has he felt himself so helpless— so unable to cope with tides about him. And like some others of his generation he doesn't like it at all. Unlike most of his business associates he does not think that the prosperity will last.

He says no one can form a conception of the tearing down of houses & rebuilding now going on in lower New York & that no where except in the devastated regions of France, has he seen such devastation.

He reports Abe [Flexner] in better health than for 2 years & that his book on medical education is having a great reception.[1] It is now being translated into Czech. Simon [Flexner] also is in good health. Was in Edgartown with his family last summer.

1. Abraham Flexner, *Medical Education: A Comparative Study* (New York, 1925).

To Fannie Brandeis

October 21, 1926 Washington, D.C. [Brandeis Mss, M 15-1]

MY DEAR FANNY: I hear that Professor Patterson has retired from the Chancellorship and has become the head of the Greek Department.[1] This should prove helpful in the development of that department, and, among other things, in the study of art and archaeology, in which you are particularly interested. Recently, Dr. Carrol Wight has proved at Johns Hopkins that enthusiasm for the study of the language may become contagious; and Prof. [Alexander] Meiklejohn has made the faculty at the University of Wisconsin realize the educational value of Greek culture.

Aunt Alice and I think we may be able to aid Prof. Patterson by providing a fund upon which he and his associates may call, from time to time, for the purchase of such books as may be needed. Our thought is to start a strictly departmental library;— to be housed in the class room, visible and accessible to the students; and to be under the fostering care of the Greek faculty. If this project meets with Prof. Patterson's approval, and it is agreeable to you, I will send you, as in other connections, a check to be deposited at interest in a special account and to be drawn upon by you, from time to time, for the purchase of the books and bookcases and incidental expenses.

I hope you will be able to see Prof. Patterson soon.[2]

Your uncle,

1. John Letcher Patterson (1861–1937), a former Greek teacher in Kentucky high schools, had come to the University of Louisville in 1908 and had served as chancellor there from 1922 to 1926. He was acting president in 1928–29.

2. See LDB to Fannie Brandeis, 7 December 1926.

To Felix Frankfurter

October 28, 1926 Washington, D.C. [Frankfurter Mss—HLS]

FF: 1. Telegram rec[eive]d. I mailed you yesterday (first class) the Myers op[inion] [1] and also under separate cover the Dorchy [2] & a letter. This incident should help awaken interest in political science. Some of the majority are not happy.

2. The N[ew].R[epublic]. editorial on the N.Y. candidates was a fine bit of work.[3]

3. I am glad of the temporary arrangement W[alter].L[ippmann]. has made.

4. The N.R. & the [New York] World should not fail to face Hoover with his inconsistencies. The attack on the British. Rub-

ber restriction policy etc.[4] vs. the encouragement of the cotton restriction policy. H. said to a friend of mine that he thought he could not only withdraw the 4,000,000 bales now, but could reduce acreage 25%; because 80 percent of the crop is raised on borrowed money & the U.S., by means of Fed[eral].Res[erve]. B[oar]d & banks could compel compliance with conditions next year.

5. Mass[achusetts]. with its Butler-Coolidge campaign is the centre of national interest. It would be grand if Walsh should win.[5] I have been hearing inside about Coolidge administration and am inclined to think that it is in some ways worse than Harding's. There are exceptionally well advised folk here who are glad of the Daugherty disagreement,[6] because worse sinners are still high in office in the odor of sanctity. Among other things, the prohibition end is said to be more corrupt, and all with C[alvin] C[oolidge]'s connivance.

6. Mr. & Mrs. Friendly were in for an hour. Their misapprehensions as to facts & relative values of Practicing Lawyer v. Professor of Law, are many.[7] Most of the time, after their recital, was spent in disabusing their minds.

(a) The only definite advice I gave them was to leave their son alone; to let him make up his own mind & not merely to say so, but let him see & know that they will be happy in whatever decision he makes. I put this as strongly as I could; & I think they understood me.

(b) I definitely refused to transmit through them any advice to the son. They wanted specifically to know whether I advised him to take a post graduate year at C[ambridge]. I said I would not advise on that unless I talked with the son etc. And I agreed that I would see him, if he comes here Christmas week.[8]

7. Thanks for I[nterstate].C[ommerce].C[ommission] memo.

8. You may care, during the Crime survey, to carry in the back of your mind, Tolstoi's views on Crime & Punishment. The father of E.A. Goldenweiser wrote an essay on "Resurrection" under the title "Crime a Punishment and Punishment a Crime" which was translated & published by the son in Washington in 1909.[9]

9. Holmes J. was downed by a head cold, caught from Butler J. & absent from C[our]t yesterday on that account.

1. *Myers* v. *U.S.*, 272 *U.S.* 52 (1926). This important case centered around Woodrow Wilson's removal of Frank Myers, a postmaster. Wilson discharged Myers without requesting the Senate's consent, thereby reopening a question of removal power as old as the republic itself. Myers sued and in this case the Supreme Court confirmed the removal. Chief Justice Taft (speaking with the authority of an ex-President) delivered a seventy-one page opinion supporting a president's power to remove not only cabinet officers but lower federal officials as well. Such power, he contended, was a necessary tool in the exercise of executive responsibilities. LDB, Holmes, and McReynolds dissented separately, and Taft exploded in anger, calling the dissenters men "that have no loyalty to the Court and sacrifice almost everything to the gratification of their own publicity. . . ." On the case, see Edward S. Corwin, "Tenure of Office and the Removal Power Under the Constitution," 27 *Columbia Law Review* 353 (1927). Instead of creating the precedent that many feared, including the destruction of the Civil Service system, the decision had little impact and was reversed in *Humphrey's Executor* v. *U.S.*, 295 *U.S.* 602 (1935), when the Court struck at Roosevelt's growing power by denying the right to discharge a Federal Trade Commissioner. See William E. Leuchtenburg, "The Case of the Contentious Commissioner: Humphrey's Executor vs. U.S.," in Harold M. Hyman and Leonard W. Levy, eds., *Freedom and Reform* (New York, 1967), 276–312.

2. *Dorchy* v. *Kansas*, 272 *U.S.* 306 (1926). The case was decided on the same day as *Myers*. Dorchy, vice-president of the mine workers' union, called a strike in violation of Kansas law. He was convicted in Kansas courts. The purpose of the strike was to force payment of back wages to an aggrieved worker. LDB, for a unanimous Court, upheld the conviction: "But a strike may be illegal because of its purpose, however orderly the manner in which it is conducted. To collect a stale claim due to a fellow member of the union . . . is not a permissible purpose."

3. *New Republic* 48 (27 October 1926): 256–57. The editorial pointed out that the issues being raised by Republican candidates were irrelevant and that New Yorkers would cast their votes on the basis of two questions— prohibition and whether the presidential ambitions of Governor Smith ought to be furthered.

4. See LDB to Frankfurter, 6 January 1926.

5. The Massachusetts Senatorial campaign saw LDB's old friend, David I. Walsh (see LDB to James P. Munroe, 15 May 1901, n. 3) pitted against the Republican William Morgan Butler (1861–1937). Butler (whom the *New Republic* described as "the President's avuncular friend") was running with the strongest possible support from Coolidge, Hoover, and Charles Evans Hughes. His campaign was taken to be a measurement of support for the administration, especially as he was serving as Republican National Chairman at the same time. Walsh defeated Butler by a substantial margin.

6. See LDB to Frankfurter, 15 October 1926, n. 1.

7. See LDB to Frankfurter, 14 March 1926, n. 11.

8. See LDB to Frankfurter, 9 November 1926.

9. Emanuel Alexandrovich Goldenweiser (1883–1953) was an economist and statistician who specialized in monetary questions. His father's book was Aleksandr Solomonovich Gol'denveizer, *Crime a Punishment and Punishment a Crime: Leading Thoughts of Tolstoi's "Resurrection"* (Washington, 1909).

To Alfred Brandeis

November 1, 1926 Washington, D.C. [Brandeis Mss, M 4-4]

MY DEAR AL: Enclosed may interest you as showing how live the revived Hebrew language is.

Elizabeth was in New York two days to attend R[ail]R[oad] wage conference meetings. But, like that gent who watched our billiard playing at Silvaplana [in 1872], she writes: "Na, Da Kann man nicht viel lehrnen." [1]

I feel more interest in politics than for many a year. The Massachusetts situation was made significant by the President's throwing his popularity into the breach; and there seems to be much Mass. opinion that it will prove to be of no effect for Butler & that C[alvin].C[oolidge]. will come out of the fray badly bruised.[2]

And the [Boston] Transcript of Saturday (which Miss Grady sent me) says it is considered that C.C. "has made his first major political mistake".

Vedremmo.[3] I hope Kentucky will down Ernst.[4]

The C[hief].J[ustice] said he thought that would be the result. And Basil Manly [*] with moot prognostication that the Rep[ublican]s will lose the Senate.

1. "One can't learn much there." A board of arbitration was established to hold hearings over the demands of eastern railway employees for higher wages. The meetings began on 29 October; in early December a wage increase was granted.

2. See preceding letter, n. 5.

3. "We shall see."

4. Richard Pretlow Ernst (1858–1934), the incumbent, was defeated for reelection to the Senate by a narrow vote.

To Robert Netherland Miller

November 3, 1926 Washington, D.C. [Brandeis Mss, Notebook]

MY DEAR MILLER: In arranging for the gift to the University of Louisville Law School of the set of reports of our Court, please include the name of Samuel F. Miller. He is a Kentuckian who rendered most distinguished service as Associate Justice. He was so closely associated in later years with Iowa that it slipped my mind, when I wrote you last summer, that Justice Miller was a native of Kentucky, lived there until he was 34, and made there his preparation for the bar.[1]   Cordially,

My Vol. 34 of the Opinions of the Attorney General is still available if you want it for the Law School.

1. See LDB to Miller, 10 August 1926. Samuel Freeman Miller (1816–1890) served on the United States Supreme Court from 1862 until his death.

To Felix Frankfurter

November 4, 1926 Washington, D.C. [Frankfurter Mss—HLS]

FF: 1. Tuesday's election will lift a great weight from many a depressed American.[1] It is fine to think that C[alvin].C[oolidge]. "lost on errors." That's how most games, in war and in peace, are lost. I think from all one reads & hears in W[ashington] that there is many a Republican who feels malicious joy & will begin to talk that C.C. is a liability instead of an asset. Basil Manly says, he hasn't a friend in the Senate, now that Butler is out.[2]

2. It will, indeed, be fine if you can get Charles P. Howland to devote himself to the [Crime] Survey. He couldn't make better use of his time, and I am sure he would feel immense satisfaction in the work.

3. Stoughton Bell's list on Administrative Law is a fine tribute to your course.[3]

I suppose you and Marion have heard from Auntie B. that Susan's son is a strapping fellow & that all goes well with them.[4]

It's a great thing to have Morton Prince & his ilk take a hand in S[acco].V[anzetti].[5]

1. The elections were a victory for anti-administration forces. The Republican majority was cut in both houses of Congress, and it appeared that Progressives and Democrats could control the Senate if they could cooperate on issues.

2. See LDB to Frankfurter, 28 October 1926, n. 5.

3. Stoughton Bell (1874–19[?]) had graduated from the Harvard Law School in 1899, after which he entered private practice in the Boston area. He was active for a short time in local Cambridge politics.

4. LDB's first grandchild, Louis Brandeis Gilbert, was born on 2 November 1926.

5. On 2 November, Prince (see LDB to Arthur A. Maxwell, 10 May 1900, n. 6) had attacked the denial of a new trial for Sacco and Vanzetti. See *New York Times*, 3 November 1926.

To Alfred Brandeis

November 5, 1926 Washington, D.C. [Brandeis Mss, M 15–1]

MY DEAR AL: I am told that the University[of Louisville]'s collection of books relating to the German language and literature is meagre, and entirely inadequate. The importance of German, culturally and as aid to scientific research, can hardly be overestimated. Alice and I wish to make available to students and the German faculty such books as the faculty may, from time to time, deem desirable. For this purchase and the expense of appropriate shelving etc. I enclose check to your order for $1000—to be deposited in a special account at interest and drawn upon by you as needed.

It is our thought to start a strictly Departmental Library; to be housed in the class room, or otherwise visible and accessible to students; and to be under the special and fostering care of the German faculty.

More than half a century ago William N. Hailmann [1] made important contributions to education in Louisville. Through his German-American Academy he rendered two special services. He introduced there, in some measure, the new methods of pedagogy which had been developed in Germany; and he opened a path to the rich treasures of German literature and science.

If it is agreeable to the University, I suggest that Prof. Hailmann's name be associated with this collection of books to be made by the German Department. [2] There must still be living in

Louisville a number of his pupils who will be glad to have his services to education remembered. Perhaps the University is now enjoying indirectly through some of its instructors, the fruits of Dr. Hailmann's labors.   Your brother,

1. William Nicholas Hailmann (1836–1920) was the leader in the kindergarten movement in the United States. Born in Switzerland, Hailmann arrived in Louisville in 1852 and became an important figure in the educational life of the city. He later directed German-American Academies in Milwaukee and Detroit and served in various pedagological positions in many cities. G. Stanley Hall called him "by far the most eminent of all men in this country devoted to the interests of the kindergarten."

2. The University Librarian, Evelyn Schneider, informed Hailmann's daughter, then living in California, of LDB's project. She objected to the idea of her father's name being associated with things German, and requested LDB to drop the idea, which he did.

To Felix Frankfurter

November 9, 1926 Washington, D.C. [Frankfurter Mss—HLS]

1. The C[hief].J[ustice]. is incorrigible re Certioraris. But I guess we are over the worst of it for this season. He stands alone in his irresistible appetite.

2. That's fine about C.P. Howland. I hope you will arrange to keep him fully employed.[1]

3. I suppose you will have someone to present the Community's responsibility. You will recall my tale of the surprise of the Kentucky giant that his young son used less words. We must remember "The wages of sin is death." I doubt whether any system of criminal administration can grapple successfully with our crime problem, unless the American can be made to modify his tests of success—of the worthwhile. That vice infects means and ends alike. And I think probably the most fruitful result of your work will be to make that appear. As I ponder over the problem, this admonition came ever ominously like the motif in the Wagner opera.

4. John Mason seems to be experiencing religion.

5. I think it clear that I had better not broach the subject of H[arvard]L[aw]S[chool] to Page.[2] But rather let him come to me if he wants to. If you plan coming here to ask him, couldn't

you arrange for some day after Nov. 14 & before Nov 22, when Court reconvenes. I suppose you might not think it wise to be here on Nov. 21 when [Henry J.] Friendly is to be & possibly not to be here at all until after his visit. His father seemed to think the son was being subjected by you and J.W.M[ack]. to "undue influence."

I am glad the parents understood me.[3]

6. I judge that the [Boston] Globe has followed the Hermes suit,[4] from what I read in A.F. of L. news bulletin.

7. Landis did notable work on the Myers case.[5]

8. I'll send you tomorrow an address of J[oseph]. B. Eastman's on relative expenditure for regulation etc., which you may care to see & the N[ew].R[epublic]. may find of value in some connections.

1. See LDB to Frankfurter, 4 November 1926.

2. LDB's clerk for 1926–27 was Robert Guthrie Page (1901–1970). Despite his being urged to return to Harvard Law School (see LDB to Frankfurter, 30 November 1926), Page went into private practice in New York City. In 1947 he became president of the Phelps Dodge Corporation. See LDB to Frankfurter, 13 October 1929.

3. See LDB to Frankfurter, 14 March and 28 October 1926; see also LDB to Frankfurter, 13 October 1929.

4. The steamship "Hermes" had collided with another steamer in New York's East River, and its owners had sued the other line, claiming that under the harbor's navigation rules, the "Hermes" was clearly in the right and the other ship had failed to heed correct signals. In July 1927, the Circuit Court awarded damages to the "Hermes" owners, 21 F.(2d) 314; the Supreme Court shortly afterwards denied certiorari, 275 *U.S.* 569.

5. See LDB to Frankfurter, 28 October 1926, n. 1.

To Julian William Mack

November 14, 1926 Washington, D.C. [R. Szold Mss]

MY DEAR JUDGE MACK: Let me thank you—and through you the good friends whom you name—for their gracious gift to the Harvard Law School, which touches me deeply.[1]

I assume that you have assured yourself that the gift will be agreeable to the Faculty.   Most cordially,

1. In honor of LDB's seventieth birthday, celebrated the day before this letter, a group of his friends presented a gift of $50,000 to the Harvard Law School. The gift went to establish the Brandeis Research Fellowship.

To Edward Albert Filene

November 14, 1926 Washington, D.C. [Filene Mss]
MY DEAR E.A.: It was good of you to send me again your good wishes bearing memories of the good days when we were working side by side.

To Felix Frankfurter

November 15, 1926 Washington, D.C. [Frankfurter Mss—HLS]

FF: For your letter and Marion's greeting warm thanks, and also for the Rostovtzeff.[1] As you knew, it deals with a subject of intense interest to me; and I am glad to have this access to the fruits of later studies and discoveries.

Tell me what you know about R.[2]

The day went off well, and it brought from O.W.H. a few beautiful lines.[3]

That was a beautiful thought of my friends to which Mack gave expression in announcing to me the gift to H[arvard]L[aw] S[chool].[4]

1. Mikhail Ivanovich Rostovtsev, *The Social and Economic History of the Ancient World* (Oxford, 1926).

2. Rostovtsev (1870–1952) had been born in Russia but migrated to the United States during the 1917 revolution. He taught ancient history at Wisconsin until 1925 but moved to Yale where he taught for twenty years. He is recognized as a pioneer social historian of the ancient world.

3. Holmes had written: "You turn the third corner tomorrow. You have done big things with high motives—have swept over great hedges and across wide ditches, always with the same courage, the same keen eye, the same steady hand. As you take the home stetch the onlookers begin to realize how you have ridden and what you have achieved. I am glad that I am still here to say: Nobly done."

4. See LDB to Julian W. Mack, 14 November 1926.

To Hildegarde Nagel

November 15, 1926 Washington, D.C. [H. Nagel]

MY DEAR HILDEGARDE: Your grandmother Brandeis' birthday. Only your presence could have gladden[ed] the [birth]day more than your letter. You would have looked well at dinner with Aunt Do and Elizabeth, Jack, and Paul.

It was a joyous day. And on the next we took our guests, not only to the tow path to which you were trailed, but on that noble Potomac irresistible in its sunny calm. Remember that, while the lure of New York is upon you.

Still I am glad Susan and Jack have you near; and I hope their boy will appreciate the blessing.[1]   With much love,

1. See LDB to Felix Frankfurter, 4 November 1926, n. 4.

To Harry Friedenwald

November 19, 1926 Washington, D.C. [Friedenwald Mss]

MY DEAR DR. FRIEDENWALD: To Mrs. Friedenwald, you and the children, warm thanks.

The Zionist cause has brought me much of what I value most in life and among its cherished joys is your friendship.

Most cordially,

To Edward Albert Filene

November 23, 1926 Washington, D.C. [Filene Mss]

MY DEAR E.A.: I have not heard of the incident except through your letter.[1]

Do not let it give you any concern. I understand fully.

1. Filene had written to explain his action regarding a contribution to the Harvard Law School in honor of LDB (see LDB to Julian W. Mack, 14 November 1926). Filene's Boston department store had been appproached by Mack to contribute to the fund, and the management voted to give $10,000—with only Filene dissenting. He felt compelled to vote against making the contribution, he explained, only because he thought it improper to

use corporate funds for that purpose—making customers give to a cause they knew nothing about. Filene hoped that LDB, who had often complained about the high cost of doing business, would understand and approve the stand Filene had taken.

To Felix Frankfurter

November 30, 1926 Washington, D.C. [Frankfurter Mss—HLS]

1. When your "Business of lower federal courts" is developed, it would be well to have made clear to the states, how they could avoid in tax cases the enjoining of their tax collections through suits in federal court—by removing the possibility of the claim there is no adequate remedy in the state courts, if the tax is paid etc. There ought to be a whole article devoted to this subject, so that even those who need the Kindergarten course could understand. And copies of the Review should go to the high state taxing officials & the Att[orne]ys General etc.

2. I think there ought to be worked out also an article showing how, by appropriate changes in state criminal administration, the excuse for going into federal Equity courts for injunction because of claim of irreparable damage, due to multiplicity of suits & oppressive penalties, before the final adjudication of validity, could be obviated.

3. By careful work on these & cognate lines, with state cooperation which seems now procurable, the whole illegitimate brood of such resorts to equity & the federal courts could be stamped out.

4. In 87 etc. I have endeavored to make clear, as a matter of statutory construction, the "occupying the field" doctrine.[1] I think the states could be taught, by a similar ABC article that, if they wish to preserve their police power, they should, through the "state block" in Congress, see to it in every class of Congressional legislation that the state rights which they desire to preserve be expressly provided for in the acts.

5. Page has not referred to the Professorship matter again—although he has had chances to do so.[2]

6. I hope you will have recd before this last week's op[inion]s.

7. As to Harlan [F. Stone]'s liberalism—wait.

8. Miss Grady quotes you as saying that I am to be asked for suggestions for subjects re. Research Fund.[3] If I am, I shall submit them to you for consideration before sending anything in.

9. Could the [New York] World be stimulated to enter upon a persistent attack upon [Andrew] Mellon tax plans & prophecies —to be conducted throughout the session, to avert further Democratic blunders? E.g. urge "Debt Payment the best Preparedness." Hardy's book on the surtaxes would doubtless help.[4]

10. I was glad to see the Lefkowitz editorial in N[ew].R[epublic].[5] That is a vital subject which the World should also campaign for & the recent [*] incident in Washington in which Gen[era]l Fries was downed should afford lovers of free speech & thought some encouragement.[6]

11. I am glad there are prospects for Wells.

12. The Brewster Gould incident should help.[7]

13. There was meat in N.R.'s "Inertia" editorial.[8]

---

1. No. 87 was *Napier* v. *Atlantic Coast Line Rrd Co.*, 272 *U.S.* 605 (1926). For a unanimous Court, LDB struck down a state law requiring automatic doors on locomotive fire boxes as a safety device. The grounds given were that the Boiler Inspection Act had "occupied the field" of regulating locomotive equipment on interstate highways and that the states were precluded from such activity.

2. See LDB to Frankfurter, 9 November 1926.

3. See LDB to Julian W. Mack, 14 November 1926.

4. Charles Oscar Hardy, *Tax-Exempt Securities and the Surtax* (New York, 1926).

5. Abraham Lefkowitz was a New York teacher who had been denied a promotion because of his radical opinions and activities outside the classroom. The editorial "Are School Teachers Citizens?" *New Republic* 49 (1 December 1926): 28–31, was a ringing denunciation of such attempts to coerce mindless conformity and stifle true education.

6. Apparently LDB is referring to an incident which began in March 1923. Brigadier General Alfred Amos Fries, head of the Chemical Warfare Service of the Army, defended the use of poison gas in the next war. He was vigorously attacked by the National Council for the Prevention of War (Alice Brandeis was an officer of the group) and by other antiwar and women's organizations. In response, Fries and other elements within the War Department issued a series of violent denunciations, all trying to link the pacifists with the Bolshevik menace. The response to the militarists' attacks was strenuous and, after a meeting between representatives of various liberal groups and Secretary of War John W. Weeks, the latter warned his officers against unjustified remarks. See Paul L. Murphy, *The Meaning of*

Freedom of Speech: First Amendment Freedoms from Wilson to FDR
(Westport, Connecticut, 1972): 191–92.

7. Arthur Robinson Gould (1857–1946) had just been elected to the
United States Senate as a Republican from Maine. It emerged, however,
that in 1911 he had paid a $100,000 bribe to the Premier of New Brunswick
for railroad favors. The governor of Maine, Ralph Owen Brewster (1888–
1961), had assailed Gould for excessive campaign expenditure—a charge
that brought a countercharge from Gould, namely that Brewster was in
league against him with the Ku Klux Klan. After investigation by the Senate, Gould was allowed to take his seat.

8. "Inertia as a Patriotic Ideal," *New Republic* 49 (24 November 1926):
4–5. Taking the occasion of the U.S. retreat, once again, from joining the
World Court, the editorial contended that the prevailing mood in American
politics was to equate inertia and true patriotism. The marriage between the
two, the writer maintained, accounted for the steady abandonment of any
political position which smacked of genuine progressivism. The editorial
was probably written by Herbert Croly.

To Felix Frankfurter

December 2, 1926 Washington, D.C. [Frankfurter Mss—HLS]

FF: Yesterday PM. my secretary had telephone enquiring whether
Dr. [Chaim] Weizmann could see me that evening. He answered
for me impossible. W. asked whether he could come this AM,
and 10 AM. was fixed for his call. He stayed 50 minutes. On entering the room he offered his birthday congratulations "though
late". I immediately asked him when he had last been in Palestine
& of conditions there. He reported fully. Then I asked him about
the Pritchett incident.[1] This we discussed fully. He reported that
he would answer further on Sunday at Carnegie Hall. I advised
that he do not answer in form, or refer, in any way to Pritchett,
but that he make a clear and comprehensive statement of facts,
emphasizing i.a. the Surplus Govt revenues, the small army &
police as well as economic development.

Then he reported fully on political conditions, his talks with
Briand [2] Amery [3] etc; and, finally, as to his project for a comprehensive survey to be undertaken by Elwood Mead (with the
assent of our Govt) with non-Jewish aids who shall remain a year
in Palestine. I asked whether he had talked this over with [Ber-
nard] Flexner. He said no—not to anyone yet, except Mead.
I asked whether any reason why he should [not] talk it over

with F. He answered emphatically no reason; & said he would do so. He thinks that with the kind of report which he expects would come from the American experts, it would be possible to raise $10,000,000 a year for 10 years; & thus during these 10 years to settle 25,000 persons a year in Palestine. His statements throughout were conservative & I told him I thought that his project was sound & should be capable of achievement, provided provisions were made for proper spending, as well as raising of the money.[4]

The talk was calm & friendly throughout; no mention by me whatsoever of our past relations; and none by him except in a parenthetical clause, to the effect that he was aware of our differences but I must admit he had stuck to the job.

He said as he was leaving that he thought it would be advisable to spend a few days here to get into touch with some of those high in authority here [5] & that he planned to come back before or after Christmas for this purpose. I agreed that it would be & that Elwood Mead would be an advisable avenue. Nothing was said definitely by me or by him about his seeing me when he came again, or about my aiding him.

I had told him that Flexner et al. could, if they approved, doubtless help both in securing assent that Mead make the survey & also in financing.

1. Dr. Henry Smith Pritchett (1857–1939), a prominent educator and a trustee of the Carnegie Foundation, had just returned from a trip to the Middle East. He presented a report to the foundation contending that Zionism was bound to fail. The movement was "unfortunate and visionary," Pritchett said, because of the poverty of the land and the brooding hostility of the native Arab population. The full text of the report can be found in the *New York Times,* 29 November 1926. Naturally, Pritchett's views sparked angry replies from many Zionists, including Stephen Wise, Bernard Rosenblatt, Emanuel Neumann, Emanuel Cellar, David de Sola Pool, and Weizmann himself.

2. Aristide Briand (1862–1932), the distinguished French statesman, was currently his country's minister for foreign affairs.

3. Leopold Charles Maurice Stennett Amery (1873–1955) was serving as England's secretary of state for the colonies; he was a longtime student of British colonial affairs.

4. See LDB to Frankfurter, 15 February 1927.

5. Weizmann had been received by President Coolidge on 2 November, a few days after his arrival; on 2 December he conferred with Vice-President Dawes and Secretary of State Kellogg.

To Felix Frankfurter

December 5, 1926 Washington, D.C. [Frankfurter Mss—HLS]

1. In connection with the new threat of a McNary Haugen bill,[1] Francis Parkman's dramatic story of the first attempt to deal with surplus production in America—the tale of the beaver skin crop (told, I think, in his "Old Regime in Canada") should be revived.[2]

2. Ask Auntie B. about [*] She has or had all the clippings & should be able to give you the full story. The most encouraging event re free speech for many a year.[3]

3. I am glad you corrected Basil Manly's step.

4. Allyn Young[4] uses the term "speculation" in a very narrow sense. What is occurring is a wholly new kind of speculation— the boom is not in prices, because it is in production capacity coupled with credit to consumers. It is true that there is nothing "mathematical" in the cycles. But I am inclined to think they are "inevitable" because they are result of the lack of self-control & of foresight in Man; as well as other qualities. I think your Rostostzeff[5] would be a good course for economists.

5. Others, I know, agree with your judgment as B. Hand's comments on me.

5. [sic] As to Rostostzeff—he is very illuminating on futile attempts of the Roman Emperors to deal [with] the problem of farm surpluses despite their power to legislate for the whole of their world.

6. Newt[on] Baker is his charming clever self.

Tell Allyn Young that when he comes here next I should be glad to see him.

1. The McNary-Haugen Bill was designed to meet the problem of agricultural surplus. It stipulated that the government buy surplus crops at a relatively high price and sell them abroad at the world price; farmers would pay an "equalization fee" to compensate the government's loss. The bill had a long and difficult legislative history. It was first introduced in January 1924, and after a number of rejections by the House it finally passed in early 1927. But President Coolidge vetoed it on 25 February.

2. Parkman described the French attempts in Canada, around 1700, to control the surplus of beaver skins being trapped and traded. The experiments ended in disaster, with more than half of the accumulated skins being burned. The difficulty was caused by a government-guaranteed price, regardless of the conditions of demand. The measure sent large numbers of

trappers and traders into the wilderness and resulted in an intolerable surplus of pelts. See Francis Parkman, *The Old Regime in Canada*, 2 vols.
(Boston, 1897 edition) 2: 104–08.

3. See LDB to Frankfurter, 30 November 1926, n. 6.

4. Allyn Abbott Young (1876–1929) was a leading economist; he had been
a professor of economics at Harvard since 1920.

5. See LDB to Frankfurter, 15 November 1926.

To Fannie Brandeis

December 7, 1926 Washington, D.C. [Brandeis Mss, M 4–5]

MY DEAR FANNY: I have yours of 5th enclosing Pres[iden]t Colvin's [1] letter of Dec. 3rd and Prof. Patterson's of Nov. 24th. Please
say this to them:

Aunt Alice's and my purpose is to promote the study of Greek
and Latin culture, and specifically to aid Prof. Patterson in that
connection.[2] We are entirely willing to leave to him the placing
as well as the selection of the books. The fact that the Greek
language is not being taught at the moment, we do not deem of
importance. We have confidence that with the development of
the University there will be an irresistible call for it.

I am returning the letters.

1. George Colvin (1875–1928) was a former lawyer who served as state
superintendent of education for Kentucky. In 1926, he assumed the presidency of the University of Louisville. Within weeks of his taking office the
campus was caught up in an immense controversy over his administration;
see LDB to Alfred Brandeis, 23 January 1927.

2. See LDB to Fannie Brandeis, 21 October 1926.

To Julian William Mack

December 11, 1926 Washington, D.C. [R. Szold Mss]

JWM: 1. I will send you at the end of this month $500 for the
Margolin Fund. If you have with this enough subscribed for the
two years, use $250 this year & 250 next. If you should not get
enough for the two years, you have liberty to use the whole
amount during the first year with liberty to apply next December
for a like amount.

2. Your message re recent opinion was referred to the C[hief]. J[ustice]. Watch the orders entered. By this means changes in opinions are made & recorded.

3. I enclose memo re Weizmann interview.[1] Please return it.

4. As to Mrs. Rosenbloom gift:[2] Magnes letter has the 'statesmanlike quality. Mrs. R's expresses with more than usual accuracy the substance of my views as given her. They still seem to me sound. Of course, I do not know how much of the $500,000 will be needed for purposes 1, 2, and 3, nor specifically whether anything is needed for 3, in view of gifts for that same purpose already made or promised by others. But I think Mrs. R. should assure herself that the fund for instruction will be adequate. And I should think that the income of $250,000 plus $32,500 increment, plus $25,000, would not be adequate, unless other income were also assured. In the long run the say $325,000 could not be expected to yield more than $15,000 income.

5. Can't you get [James H.] Becker & some other of your millionaire friends—particularly some of the new rich—to give to Dr. Tchernowitz's Talmud project?[3] The lawyers particularly ought to realize the significance of the Talmud. A body of laws which for so many centuries has governed a people living scattered and dispersed under most varying conditions. There is nothing to equal it in the Western World, & we have yet to be shown that the Orient cant produce such extraordinary efficacy in the law. Moreover, it is to the study of the law that much of your Jewish lawyer's success is due. Make it clear to these N.Y. lawyers & raise for T. the balance of the $100,000 needed.

1. See LDB to Felix Frankfurter, 2 December 1926.
2. To Hebrew University.
3. Chaim Tchernowitz (1871–1949) was a Talmudic scholar and author who had come to the United States in 1923 and was teaching Talmud at the Jewish Institute of Religion in New York.

To Charles Gabriel Tachau

December 14, 1926 Washington, D.C. [Brandeis Mss, M 15–2]

MY DEAR CHARLES: In answer to your telegram, have just wired you: "Glad to see [President George] Colvin Monday twentieth.

Think it important you should accompany him. Am sending some suggestions by letter."

1. I think it important that you should come with Colvin, among other reasons, because:

(a) You will have an uninterrupted time to educate him while en route. I dont think he understands our plan and purpose; and I am sure it will take more than his interview with me to get it into his system.

(b) I want you to be present at our interview, to hear what I say, to hear what he says; and to take such part as will suggest itself.

(c) You will also have an uninterrupted time on the way back to talk over things, which may prove important. The education must be continued after the interview.

2. I suggest that before the trip you make sure, by conferring with Alfred, that you have a complete file of all the letters to the several members of the family in which I endeavored to set forth what we proposed to do, how it was to be done, and why in that way; and that you make a careful study of these letters before you meet him on the train; that you take this file with you; and that in your discussions on the train you make such use of passages in those letters to help Colvin's understanding of our project, as may seem to you wise.

3. I think you, Fanny and others ought to confer with Alfred fully on this situation before you start, and you may deem it wise to have Dr. [Joseph] Rauch present at the conference, or some part of it. He has been very helpful and is deeply interested.

4. I judge from what Alfred wrote me that Judge [Robert W.] Bingham's gift of $50,000 was the result of Dr. Rauch's talk to him about our project. If this is so, it might help a good deal to have Colvin hear from Judge Bingham that this is so.

Please send me a copy of this letter, and also hand copies to Alfred and to Fanny.

I suppose you will arrive Monday early, so that our Conference can begin at 9AM. or soon thereafter.[1]

1. See LDB to Alfred Brandeis, 23 December 1926.

To Felix Frankfurter

December 21, 1926 Washington, D.C. [Frankfurter Mss—HLS]

FF: 1) Roberts [1] made an uncommonly good impression on our Court. In case of doubt, I should accept his judgment as to advisability of trial of a case.

2. Thanks for references to your articles. Are you able to give me the data as to our overruling ourselves in cases under the Commerce Clause?

3. If you have some economist & government men, willing to look a little ahead, have them get some coming PhD write on the danger of tax exemption of educational, philanthropic, religious etc. institutions, e.g. foundations. That will prove a much greater point before long than tax exempt state securities. The latter is largely a question of wise or unwise state financing, particularly with the decline of federal taxation.

1. Owen Josephus Roberts (1875–1955), a former professor of law at the University of Pennsylvania, had been appointed by President Coolidge as one of the special prosecutors in the Teapot Dome investigation in 1924. In 1930, Hoover named him to the Supreme Court, where he served until 1945. During the court tests of New Deal measures in the mid-thirties, Roberts proved the swing vote in an evenly divided court. From 1948 to 1951, he returned to the University of Pennsylvania as dean of its law school.

To Alfred Brandeis

December 23, 1926 Washington, D.C. [Brandeis Mss, M 4–4]

DEAR AL: 1) Thanks for the Trimble report, which has gone to [Robert N.] Miller.

2) Our guests enjoyed your latest ham Tuesday. (2 Germans, 3 recent visitors to Germany & Grace Abbot [*sic*])

3) Alice says you didn't seem as enthusiastic about Dr. [*]'s daughter as she would have expected from one of your age.

4) Re. yours 21st. re [President George] Colvin.

Our talk (other than on Law School matters at which Miller also was present) occupied 2¼ hours.[1] The first hour was occupied by an uninterrupted talk by me—setting forth our purpose, the means I thought it desirable to employ, and the why of both purpose & means. At the close of the hour he said he was in entire accord. He said also that he had read my letters which Charles [Tachau] had shown him en route. Then Colvin talked about ½ hour, somewhat interrupted by me. The remaining ¾ was occupied with discussion of points of detail—Charles making a brief statement of his views, etc.

It was agreed that Charles would prepare a memo embodying our agreement as to modus operandi; that he would submit the memo to yòu, Fanny, Maidie, Billy & Amy for revision; would then submit it to Colvin; and that after all these had made sure that it covered the situation satisfactorily, it would be sent to me for consideration.

The points on which Colvin made requests or reservations related solely to preserving the discipline of the faculty, and the etiquette towards the governing body. These involved

a) that no members of the faculty should be on our committees; but it was expressed that we should be absolute[ly] free to get their suggestions & confer with them.

b) that our special communications, enquiries, or requests otherwise should go through the librarian; and it was expressly agreed that we must have a competent librarian (which the present one is not) and that I would bear a share of the greater expense involved.

He assented unreservedly to the necessity of lending aid—material, intellectual & moral—to the faculty from without; and I made the need of this very clear, if we are to get & keep good instructors & develop those in the University, from time to time, to give all that is in them. He assented specifically to the desirability of small class-room libraries on various subjects, under the control of the several faculty members, as well as the general library. And I assented, to the propriety of the necessary division of general library books, between those in the Reading room (about 9,000 volumes) and those in the stacks (where there would be room for nearly 80,000 volumes). He admitted—from a reading of my letters—that I had carefully observed the etiquette towards the officers of the University in making every proposed gift "if agreeable to the authorities" etc. And he indicated (but did [not] say in terms) that the fault lay rather in Dean Anderson who had usurped authority in respect to the library. He seemed not to have a very high opinion of the Dean, in this connection.[2]

I made it very clear to him that no librarian, however competent, could develop the various special collections which we have started; that this might conceivably be possible if one had, like the Congressional Library, a score of expert special librarians, one at the head of each department, like Dr. Sapiro [*sic*] [3] at the head of the Semitic section with its 26,000 Hebrew books, etc—; but, that in the absence of such, we must have the thinking, for the several special collections, done partly by outsiders, partly by the members of the faculty specifically versed or interested.

Little was said in regard to the Post Graduate courses, beyond what he had stated in his letter to Charles. He repeated that the Post Graduate department was an essential, that it would not be abandoned; but stated that he could not for the present undertake to develop it; and thought that they should be frank in saying so. The need of post graduate work, as an essential of developing, attracting & keeping the proper professors & instructors for undergraduates was emphasized by me; and assented to by him.

At the end of the 2¼ hours, I took Colvin & Charles to see Alice, leaving them with her until Miller (who had been telephoned for) should arrive. He came in about 20 minutes. Then Colvin, Charles & I had about 45 minutes on specifically Law School matters. Colvin agreed fully to our plan. I made it absolutely clear that if members of the Kentucky bar (including Kentuckians resident, like myself, elsewhere) would give ⅔ of the money necessary to start this as a worthy Law School, I would give the remaining ⅓ in 10 annual installments; that the sum needed might, for a part of a period of 10 years, be $20,000 to $30,000 a year, beginning with a smaller sum, rising to that named & later falling off as increased tuition fees gradually became sufficient to defray the sums needed. I had told him that a Law School—unlike other departments of the U.—might become a money maker, as the Harvard Law School had. Colvin said we must have a full time Dean & might have to pay him $10,000 a year. (I told him I thought this higher than necessary). He rather suggested that if we got a fund for a year or two, with such a man, he could do much toward educating the bar to give the funds necessary. I was emphatic that this would not do; that the right man wouldn't come unless he could know, in advance, that there were funds provided which would ensure his having the opportunity to make a success. Colvin assented to all this; then said that he expected the current drive to end in May; & after that would take up this problem, meanwhile giving it such thought as he could; & that he would talk to Helm Bruce etc.

I was clear that I would give nothing toward running the [Law] School unless the Kentucky bar did twice as much—except that I might do more of the sort of thing for the law library which I have been doing.

Miller & Charles went off with Colvin & Miller writes me that he had a satisfactory talk with Colvin about plans for the immediate future, about which Miller will probably write you.

Please send me a copy of this letter.

Alice & I plan to go to New York Monday morning to view the grandson et al., returning here Wednesday afternoon.

1. See LDB to Charles Tachau, 14 December 1926.
2. See LDB to Alfred Brandeis, 23 January 1927.
3. Israel Schapiro (1882–1957), a Russian immigrant and scholar, had been head of the Semitic Division of the Library of Congress since 1913. In 1950 Schapiro moved to Israel.

To Felix Frankfurter

January 1, 1927 Washington, D.C. [Frankfurter Mss—HLS]

Our best to you and Marion.

1. I hope you will protect [Benjamin N.] Cardozo from all this Jewish pressure [1]—local, national & international. He will serve the Jewish people best by conserving his health and calmness of spirit in order to do his judicial job as well as he can do it. With his frail health and unfamiliarity with tribal warfare, this course seems imperative. You can make this clear to him.

2. Weiz[mann] is welcome to Marshall. But he wont get me for his new Commission.[2] And I shall refrain from giving him any money for this undertaking lest he represent that it is (in part) my Commission. I understand that he has already done some tall talking of that nature to the Jewish Press.

3. Alice bids me tell you that Dick Child is so forsaken that he sent us a Xmas card.[3]

4. We are glad to hear that the S[acco].V[anzetti] article is so far advanced.[4]

5. Who is David Cecil?

6. Ellery Sedgewick's approach is interesting.[5]

7. Have [Josef] Redlich let us know when he is to be here so that we can arrange a dinner for him.

O[liver]W[endell]H[olmes] is in good form. I called on him today as he didn't go to the White House.

1. To become active in Jewish and Zionist affairs.

2. One of Weizmann's purposes in visiting the United States was to make peace between Zionists and wealthy non-Zionists like Louis Marshall. He courted Marshall openly, offering a tribute to the American leader at a dinner honoring his seventieth birthday (12 December 1926). By 23 January, Marshall was publicly praising the "peace" between the two groups. The "Commission" referred to in this letter was originally designed to serve as a successor to the defunct Zionist Commission; but it never served that purpose, being notable instead as a stage in the long negotiations leading (with Marshall's support) to the establishment of the Jewish Agency.

3. Probably Richard Washburn Child. Perhaps LDB was making a reference to Child's much publicized divorce case.

4. Felix Frankfurter, "The Case of Sacco and Vanzetti," *Atlantic Monthly* 139 (March 1927): 409–32. For the amusing story of the publication of this article, see *Felix Frankfurter Reminisces*, 213–15.

5. Ellery Sedgwick (1872–1960) had been editor of the prestigious *Atlantic Monthly* since 1909.

To Felix Frankfurter

January 7, 1927 Washington, D.C. [Frankfurter Mss—HLS]

FF: An uncommonly interesting batch of enclosures returned herewith.

C. P. Howland shows that he is taking hold of the essential things.

The [New York] World has done a fine job on Nicaragua. I hope it will continue relentlessly. The Pres[iden]t & State Dept are behaving as badly as man could conceive—it is amazing to me that Congress lets them.[1]

Will R[oscoe]. P[ound]. let the World publish his letters to R.W.C.?

1. President Coolidge had withdrawn the U.S. Marines from Nicaragua in 1925. Within months, that country was torn by a civil war that pitted a liberal, anti-American rebel force against the conservative Diaz regime,

friendly to the United States. In 1926, Coolidge sent the marines back to Nicaragua, justifying his action in terms of the protection of American property, including a proprietary interest in a potential canal that might be built in Nicaragua. As 1927 began, Coolidge's policies came under heavy attack, especially by Senate Democrats and isolationists. Ultimately Coolidge sent a personal envoy, Henry L. Stimson, who was able to negotiate a settlement between the contestants—but the settlement depended upon the presence of American forces in Nicaragua until 1931.

To Felix Frankfurter

January 7, 1927 Washington, D.C. [Frankfurter Mss—HLS]

FF: Pursuant to request, I mailed you complete file, 1916–1925 Terms of synopses, first class mail spec. delivery. I think there is nothing in the synopses which you cant use (you will know if there is). But, of course, the source of the synopses should not be mentioned publicly.

[*] (Louis Levine) mentioned last evening, as if it were an encouraging sign, that there was a heavy trend among Columbia students to study of philosophy & that Will Durant's book was a "Best Seller".[1] I think some one should make clear to the public that this is a very bad sign.

Philosophy is rather the cyclone cellar for finer souls. As it was in the declining days of Greece, and as the monastery was in the so called Dark Ages.

In our Democracy, the hopeful sign would be recognition of politics & government as the first of the sciences & of the arts.

1. Will Durant, *The Story of Philosophy: The Lives and Opinions of the Greater Philosophers* (New York, 1926).

To Alfred Brandeis

January 14, 1927 Washington, D.C. [Brandeis Mss, M 4–4]

DEAR AL: Since the Jackson Day Dinner, the spirit of hope seems to have entered Democratic ranks. The whole situation, selection of Houston [1] & the course of the dinner, leads to the view that Al Smith's high political sense has been operating & that his influence is being widely felt. Even McAdoo seems to have yielded & considering his feelings, he behaved remarkably well.   Gruesse,

1. Houston, Texas, was to be the site of the 1928 Democratic National Convention.

To Alfred Brandeis

January 15, 1927 Washington, D.C. [Brandeis Mss, M 4–4]

MY DEAR AL: I have yours of 11th, 12th and 13th, and hope to get time to write you fully on the several matters tomorrow. But I want to say today that I am not in the least discouraged by any of the events or attitudes to which you refer. The difficulties are inherent in the situation.[1] Largely because I recognized that they must exist, I adopted the particular method of approach and form of helping the University to develop which has been pursued during the last two and a half years. There is no obstacle, so far as I see, that cannot be overcome with the requisite thinking, tact and persistence. Some opposition is rather to be desired as an incentive to our and others' thinking; and as a means of stirring up interest. But, of course, we must be sure that we set the right course & maintain it.

1. See next two letters.

To Alfred Brandeis

January 16, 1927 Washington, D.C. [Brandeis Mss, M 4–4]

MY DEAR AL: I have the copy of your letter to [President George] Colvin of 12th, an excellent summary, and also your typewritten letters of 12th & 13th to me, which give just the information I wanted. Supplementing my note of yesterday:

A. As to the Trustees' preoccupation in the Drive, their indifference & "Herrsucht".[1]

1. Preoccupation. The need of the money is great and urgent. The value of money as a means of achieving things is familiar to them. The drive, as a means of raising money is a prevailing fash-

ion. To devote themselves to the obvious need, and to pursue familiar ways is natural. It doesn't require thinking or vision. I do not criticize it. I accept it as a fact. While I recognize it as an obstacle, I am convinced that it is not an insuperable one; and in some respects is only temporary in its intensity. It is in other respects permanent, and inevitable probably in any board of trustees charged with the duties of administrative supervision. Arthur Allen [2] might have saved us much trouble, but probably he would have been less interested in administration.

But even if the Trustees were really interested in the things we are, and understood them, it would have been impossible for them and the President to do the thinking necessary to carry out the purposes we have in mind. No matter what one's background, that takes time, and if one has not the background, it takes a great deal of time. Moreover, the necessary thinking cannot be done by those who govern. It must be done by others;—primarily by those charged with the special responsibility like the members of your family; largely by others of the community who may become interested through them or indirectly through dissemination of their ideas or whose latent interest may be ignited by some spark dropped through newspaper publicity; and to a great extent it must come from the customarily downtrodden members of the faculty, who should be encouraged & taught to overcome their meekness.

The enthusiasm for the Law School project, as compared with our more subtle projects for the College of Arts, illustrates what I have stated above. The miserable state of the Law School is visible. Every lawyer—including Colvin—recognizes it. To give the school essential tools of trade, and a decent work room is satisfying an obvious need. To make the gift in honor of persons—partly members of the Trustees' families or fellow members of their profession is a compliment easily understood. And when this is coupled with our offer of as much as $10,000 a year for ten years—well "money talks".

The obstacles I had foreseen. The character, the number, and the method of the gifts were all part of the plan of overcoming the foreseen obstacles. If our thought, things and money had been concentrated on a single narrow department, we might have built more quickly and without opposition a monument, not without value; but by that course it would not be possible to influence fundamentally the character of the University and, through it, ultimately the character of the people of the city and the state.

When I said our project is "irresistible," I didn't mean that obstacles would vanish in the winking of an eye, and walls tumble before the blowing of the horn. "This sort of thing takes a deal of trimming," of patience, persistence and tact. But with these, and time, I am convinced there is good reason to expect a worthy achievement.

2. Indifference. Of course they are in the main indifferent. If they weren't they would have set in motion before this forces which would have relieved us of the necessity for effort. With the exception of Arthur Allen there is probably not one of them who sympathizes deeply with anything we are trying to do for the College of Arts, and I should guess that even Arthur Allen's interest would not extend to the whole field. Jouett [3] cares for the R[ail] R[oad] library, but not broadly as we do. I do not consider this indifference insuperable. I guess that by appropriate treatment each one of the trustees can be made not only to see, but to feel, the worthwhileness of at least one of the many things we are trying to further. There is in most Americans some spark of idealism which can be fanned into a flame. It takes sometimes a divining rod to find what it is; but when found—and that means often, when disclosed to the owners—the results are often most extraordinary. The goods we have to offer are so varied, and the stock so large, that there is in fact probably included the particular fly to which the particular trout would rise. The experiments require "time, and the place, and the loved one all together". It requires the opportunity for uninterrupted, intimate talk—something different than a business meeting. That's why I suggested inviting one at [a] time—and at the appropriate time—to your house. What was proposed was all a part of making them understand.

3. Herrsucht. I do not underrate the attitude. It's common among men, and particularly among governing boards. Because of the quality and its narrowing effects, it seemed to me inadvisable to put funds at their disposal. But because of it also, I think they can be won by making great glories talked of, the University in their charge—"by putting it on the map"—and making them feel that we are helping them to do what they are made to think they want to do. For this reason, among others, we were glad to send

them money for the librarian's salary & for the curator of the Art Museum salary; and to have you and the others get the books which the University Committee reported that it needed in the several departments. Tact has been defined as the art of making another do what you want in the way that he wants. And I think you have mastered the art.

B. As to the memo. I have Billy [Tachau]'s suggestions; Alice had a letter from Maidie; and yesterday one came to her from Fanny. Fan will stop off here on her way home; and formulation of the memo had better await her return. But I hope thinking on it will continue meanwhile. The formulation of the modus operandi should, in my opinion, be worked out in conference of your family with [Joseph] Rauch, if that is agreeable to the others. Billy, Amy and Fanny ask each whether I agreed to some specific detail. Of course, no such detail was dealt with in the conference with Colvin.[4] What we agreed upon (as I wrote you in the account of our interview) was (a) He agreed unreservedly to our general purpose, plans and means. (b) I agreed to his request that the work be done in such a way (1) that the proper authority of & deference due the Trustees be observed (2) that no course be pursued inconsistent with the maintenance of proper discipline on the part of the faculty. (3) that the Librarian should be a medium through which work should be co-ordinated. On the other hand, it was fully agreed that no obstacles should be put in the way of our going forward on the various lines through our individual thought & effort and i.a. that we should be absolutely free to consult with and promote the interest etc. of the individual members of the faculty as we saw fit; except that no faculty member should be put on any of our committees.

As there must be a *modus operandi* of which each of our workers fully approves it seems to me necessary that the details be worked out by you & the others in conference so that all possible needs & situations be foreseen & provided against. It was for this reason, among others, that I suggested Charles [Tachau] taking up the memo with the family before he sent it to me (and, as so approved, before it would go to Colvin).

C. The excitement of Temple Bodley [5] & that created by him, is all to the good. Of course, I had no thought of a "Brandeis" Library of Kentuckiana, and certainly none of competing with the

Filson Club.[6] My purpose was that stated in the letter to you on the subject—which, as a matter of fact, was awaiting consideration & action for nearly two years. Its purpose was to deal with matters in which, certainly in the main, the Filson Club has now no interest,—that is contemporary, or nearly contemporary material. And the purpose of my Kentuckiana was (1) to make the University Kentuckian in character, (2) to make Kentuckians gain interest in the University through aiding in collecting. It was part of the plan of making this a people's University; interesting every class, section & kind of people in it. Some through their sociological interest, some through their art or music, some through their nationality, some through their war interest, some through their ancestors, some through local and state interest. The collections were designed largely as a means to an end. I made this clear, I hope, to Colvin—that I would not create a collection—but to fashion & employ an instrument; that the library must be not a static thing but a dynamic force.

Indeed, I think Ballard Thruston [7] should have understood this as to the proposed Kentuckiana, for I talked to him some on these lines when he came to Chatham. You suggested my seeing him, after I had written you on this subject in June 1925.

Of course, it would be desirable to knit the Filson Club closely to the University. I talked this also with Ballard Thruston. He thought the Club's functions (& such a collection) not within a University's purview. But perhaps he might feel differently now; & particularly when he sees what we are attempting. The value of the Kentuckiana for University purposes is manifested by the fact that it caught [Judge Robert W.] Bingham's fancy & fired him to activity without any solicitation from anyone on this line, so far as I have heard. It is just such prairie fires which I had hoped to set (unwittingly) by the broadcasting.

I entirely approve of your talking with Temple Bodley & of your showing him my 1925 letter embodying the Kentuckiana idea if you deem it wise. At the same time you can educate him generally on the University projects as we see them.

D. As to R.R. Library. If Jouett et al are too busy to think of this now, their part of the work can rest & we can go ahead with our thinking & collecting without them, for the present.

Confidential. I have (quietly) started (1) the RR labor end

(through Edward Keating, a former Congressman & a good friend, the able and financially successful editor of "Labor") to gather all the documents on the development of the [Railway] Brotherhoods.

(2) I have asked Otto Beyer [8] (who has of all men contributed most—beginning with the B & O) to effect efficiency & cooperation between labor & management, to gather his data covering the last five years.

(3) I have talked to [Joseph B.] Eastman, to send I[nterstate]. C[ommerce].C[ommission]. books, and

(4) I am beginning to collect the Congressional documents on the last 40 years of endeavor at regulation etc. through I.C.C. operations.

We shall want i.a. (5) to get the material of the Traffic Associations & Leagues & when you are ready to do that, I guess you will get a lot of valuable material.

Thus, we'll have a lot ready for the University by the time they & Jouett are ready to act. Of course, the Drive (set for May) will be over some time; & when it is, I suppose Jouett et al will be more interested in this particular project.

E. Re German & English collections.

I am very glad you and Billy are turning to Lubschutz to get the books, and I hope you will mention this to Charles, Fanny and Maidie. It will save, in course of time a lot of money. And it is also important as developing a home industry. Booksellers & Bookbinders, "to the University" are all a part of the necessary equipment. In connection with purchasers of larger volume from publishers it may be well for them to bear in mind what I am writing Charles in enclosed note.

F. As to my letters of which Colvin has (or has seen) copies, I entirely agree with you that at the appropriate time & in the appropriate manner, these should be submitted to the Trustees—unless there be something in one or the others of them that should be deleted. I am glad you will talk with Barr [9] or others as to this.

As to my going to Louisville. This is not feasible. And I am pretty sure it is not desirable, at least at this time. I shall of course, be glad to talk to any one of them who comes here. I saw Helm Bruce [10] in Court the other day (he didn't argue) and if he had given me any suggestion that he wanted to see me, I should have arranged a conference.

But while I am glad to see any or all Trustees here, as I did Colvin, I think they should feel that it is you & the other members of the family and Rauch who are carrying out Alice's & my wishes or ideas in conjunction with your own; and that it is not I, so much as you & the others who are doing the job. I am sure that your many friends & your standing in Louisville fit you eminently for the task.

1. "thirst for power"

2. Arthur Dwight Allen (1879–1949) was a man of diverse interests and talents. He was a leading Louisville businessman, active in civic and philanthropic work, and was also a painter and a composer. Allen was a trustee for the University of Louisville.

3. Edward Stockton Jouett (1863–19[?]) was a Louisville attorney and counsel for the Louisville & Nashville; Jouett served as chairman of the board for the University of Louisville.

4. See LDB to Alfred Brandeis, 23 December 1926.

5. Temple Bodley (1852–1940) was a retired Louisville lawyer who had turned to writing on Kentucky's history. He was active in city affairs and in the Filson Club (see next note).

6. The Filson Club was founded in May 1884 for the purpose of preserving the records of the history of Louisville and Kentucky. The Club still publishes the *Filson Club History Quarterly* and maintains an extensive and invaluable repository of historical material.

7. Thruston (see LDB to William and Charles G. Tachau, 14 December 1925, n. 2) was the moving spirit behind the Filson Club at this time. His private library was the core of the Club's collection, and he served as its president for many years.

8. Otto Sternoff Beyer (1886–1948) was a construction engineer who became an authority on labor–management relations in transportation. He served in a number of high ranking positions during the New Deal and World War II.

9. John Watson Barr, Jr. (1863–1941) was another trustee of the University of Louisville. He was a prominent lawyer and businessman, serving on many boards of directors.

10. Helm Bruce (see LDB to Alfred Brandeis, 17 December 1914, n. 2) was also a trustee of the university.

To Alfred Brandeis

January 23, 1927 Washington, D.C. [Brandeis Mss, M 4–4]

DEAR AL: I. Replying to yours of 13th (Seligman) and of 17th; and your note of 20th.

The management of the Louisville end rests wholly with you

and your family—aided by [Joseph] Rauch. What Alice & I have said and may say hereafter is to be treated merely as suggestions, not even as recommendations. You, with them, must exercise the judgment when to rest, when to move forward; what the field of action at a particular time; and what the method to be pursued. You and we are wholly agreed on the end to be sought and on the general plan. All other matters are left to your and your family's decision.

II. I enclose copy of Colvin's letter to me of Jan 20th.[1] Please show this to Charles [Tachau] and send a copy to Rauch.

III. Despite Colvin's letter and what you report from Charles in your note of 20th, I am convinced that Colvin's personality, his character, and perhaps lack of it, is a very serious factor, which will ever demand on our part keen circumspection both in shaping our course, from time to time, and in pursuing it; and will constantly impose difficulties in operation.[2] From several sources I had been warned, some months ago, that he is meanly ambitious and is untrustworthy. Charles in his recent interview referred frankly (although only in passing) to this opinion, entertained by some, and showed that he did not share it. His letter to me of Jan 14 (which see) indicated to me, when read in the light of his other letters since Colvin's appointment (which also see) that he discovered that he had been deceived in and by a close friend. I hope you showed Charles my letter to you containing a report of the interview.

But whether Colvin is untrustworthy or not, I am clear from his own remarks at the interview that he is the slave of qualities which unfit him for the office for which he was selected. His ideas of discipline smack of reformatory institutions, of earlier ages, now discarded by the best penologists. He is not only arbitrary, he is ungenerous and envious. A competent executive, even of an industrial establishment, seeks to encourage, and stimulate effort on the part of those under him & to magnify their importance in the eyes of the world. Colvin's course in the interview (in the passing remarks) tended not only to belittle Dean Anderson & one or more of the professors, but to hold them up to contempt.[3] His aggrandizement of power in himself by removing Dean Anderson from the glory giving function of presiding over the growth of the Library, his interference with my effort to rehabilitate Prof.

[John L.] Patterson in his own self-respect after the humiliation of his contemptuous demotion [4] & his attitude toward [Louis] Gottschalk & others, are all acts directly in conflict with what he knows, intellectually, are essentials to the development of teachers and indispensable to a great university.

IV. What I have said about Colvin does not modify, in the least, what in earlier letters I have said of the possibility of carrying out our purpose and plan. It imposes, however, eternal vigilance & much otherwise unnecessary thinking and work; and it makes imperative intensive cultivation (in a tactful way, of course) of the Trustees and the teaching force.

V. I enclose copy of my letter of Jan 18 to [Robert N.] Miller. When he saw me on the 19th he knew not that [John W.] Barr was chairman of the Com[mi]tee, had heard nothing from him and had no reply to one or more letters he had written Colvin. Please show Charles the copy of my letter to Miller.

1. President Colvin's letter was an acknowledgement of a shipment of books from LDB on Czechoslovakia and an assurance that all "misunderstandings" between the university and the family were now cleared up (see next note).

2. The administration of President George Colvin was short and controversial. Beginning in early 1927, a storm of controversy swept through the entire community, engulfing the Brandeis family in its wake, and for all practical purposes causing a hiatus in LDB's attempts to improve the institution. The battle raged over the conduct of President Colvin and the ten trustees. Colvin, in a case involving the angry resignation of Louis Gottschalk (see LDB to Charles and William Tachau, 14 December 1925, n. 1), was charged with arbitrary administrative actions, favoritism, abolishing tenure, anti-Semitism, and lying. The controversy exploded into the press, and soon there was a war of pamphlets. The most rational account of the difficulties was the report of the American Association of University Professors, completed in October. That report was critical of both Colvin and the trustees; see *AAUP Bulletin* 13 (1927): 429–69. Only the death of Colvin in 1929 and the selection of Dr. Raymond A. Kent as his successor (see LDB to Joseph Rauch, 23 September 1929) permitted the active resumption of the work of the Brandeis family.

3. See LDB to Alfred Brandeis, 23 December 1926.

4. Patterson (see LDB to Fannie Brandeis, 21 October 1926, n. 1) had been demoted from chancellor; he returned to teaching Greek.

To Alfred Brandeis

January 30, 1927 Washington, D.C. [Brandeis Mss, M 4–4]

MY DEAR AL: [William G.] McAdoo's letter, which please return, may interest you. I guess he hasn't a much better chance than Hoover. There is considerable talk here now of Jim Reed. After timid, safe and sane Cal, the country may fly to courageous, emphatic, erratic Jim. Certainly Coolidge is making a pitiable mess of our foreign policy. He was on safe ground when "tun nichts, sag nichts" [1] was his practice. He was of those "That therefore only are reputed wise for saying nothing" [2]

Gruesse,

1. "do nothing, say nothing."
2. *The Merchant of Venice*, I, 1: 97.

To Felix Frankfurter

February 8, 1927 Washington, D.C. [Frankfurter Mss—HLS]

1. I am convinced that ineptitudes & worse of our State Dep[artment]. are such that there is great danger, with Mexico, Nicaragua & China active, in going 8 months with[out] a Congress sitting. I think the [New York] World ought to use all its influence to force an extra session.

2. I heard the inside of K[ellogg]'s China doing—they show a shiftiness equal to his otherwise inadequacy.[1] Moreover, I heard of action by the Navy Dep. (in an entirely different connection) which reminds of the worst in the Dreyfus Affair.[2] My information comes from a very reliable source.

3. This of Norris'[3] is good, but is wholly inadequate.[4] Moreover, request should be directed also to Commerce Dep & to Federal Reserve Bd who have less occasions for "incompatible with the public interest." [5] We ought to know how many people, how much property & specifically what large U.S. interests are being "protected".

4. There ought to be a general onslaught of the long established practice of State Dep not to publish annual or other reports.

5. Would the Herald join the World in #4?

1. In the face of threatening antiforeign demonstrations in China, the United States tried desperately to define a workable Chinese policy. Secretary of State Kellogg enunciated a version of that policy on 27 January. The secretary insisted upon the maintenance of the "open door" but was willing to make tariff concessions to the Chinese. There was much talk, during these months, about the possible use of force in order to protect American nationals in China, and doubtless that sort of speculation made LDB nervous about the future. For his views on Nicaragua, see LDB to Frankfurter, 7 January 1927.

2. See LDB to Roscoe Pound, 27 November 1914, n. 2.

3. George William Norris (1861–1944), by any standard one of the most influential statesmen of the twentieth century, had represented Nebraska in Congress since 1903, and he continued to do so until 1942. A crusading liberal throughout his career, Norris was an acknowledged expert on farm policy and on water power development. His expertise in the latter field was demonstrated in the effort to save Muscle Shoals and to establish the TVA. The best biographical study of Norris is a two-volume (to this point) study by Richard Lowitt, *George W. Norris: The Making of a Progressive, 1861–1912* (Syracuse, 1963); and *George W. Norris: The Persistence of a Progressive 1913–1933* (Urbana, 1971).

4. LDB had enclosed a clipping reporting the Senate's unanimous passage of a resolution by Norris calling upon Secretary of State Kellogg for all information concerning oil concessions held by Americans in Mexico.

5. The Norris resolution (note 4) contained the usual proviso, "if not incompatible with public interest."

To Felix Frankfurter

February 15, 1927 Washington, D.C. [Frankfurter Mss—HLS]

1. Too bad R[oscoe].P[ound]. is so.

2. I think you had better do the suggesting to J.W.M[ack] of abstention during the oil trial; & perhaps write him before to prevent his burdening himself.

3. I shall have considerable to say to him re Zionist affairs. I presume you have had through him & deH[aas], theirs & my interchange of letters.

4. Pritchett correspondence returned herewith.[1] I guess he will subside.

5. Weizmann impressed me more than ever with his ability, resourcefulness & Mephistophelian quality. I rather think M "was ein Hund dagegen." [2] When with him, I felt like the good Christians who grasped at the Cross for protection.

6. What does not appear by correspondence sent you is that his operations here are greatly disturbing the British.

7. He has completely transformed the character of the proposed survey [3]—so that it is now pre-eminently a political instrument, besides being propaganda to win the American bankers.[4]

1. See LDB to Frankfurter, 2 December 1926, n. 1.
2. "a dog by comparison."
3. See LDB to Frankfurter, 2 December 1926.
4. See LDB to Frankfurter, 1 January 1927, n. 2.

To Felix Frankfurter

February 26, 1927 Washington, D.C. [Frankfurter Mss—HLS]

1. There are rumors of a S[acco]. V[anzetti]. article in the forth-coming March Atlantic to which we are looking forward.[1]

2. So far as I can recall, there are now no questions pending on the construction of the 1925 Jurisdiction; that under 238 and 266 as amended having been disposed of by my recent opinion & that of Stone putting the limitation of the right to appeal where it should be.[2]

3. Hughes argued the Los Angeles case poorly.[3] Other recent arguments of his show likewise (as do [John W.] Davis') the evil of understanding too much.

The RR brief in the Los Angeles case was, however, a very good one. Find out when you have occasion, who did it. The I[nterstate]. C[ommerce]. C[ommission]. didn't challenge the jurisdiction. I have not heard just why. I guess they foolishly wanted our Court to decide all their difficulties for them.

4. You cannot conceive how painful, distressful & depressing it was to listen (officially) to Cal [Coolidge]'s Washington's Birthday address.[4] I think the purpose of those behind (who must have prepared the address) was to confiscate the whole of G[eorge]. W[ashington]'s good will for Big Business, by showing that we owe everything we value to the qualities of business efficiency, commercial courage & vision & thrift & that these were G.W.'s dominating qualities fitting him for the greatest of the World's achievements. Even his religion was of the efficient business type, as described. I have been told from all high that the purpose of the

talk being made now was to set the "key note for the next five years of talk". There is no man in [the] U.S. [who] could have so perfectly—by looks, voice & action—have [*sic*] deprived G.W. of every idealistic aim or emotion.

When I tried to recall the next most depressing & distressful experience of a lifetime, I had to go back to 1894, when in preparing for the Public Institutions Hearings,[5] I went to Long Island (Boston Harbor) Poor-House hospital & passed through the syphilitic ward. I had a like sense of uncleaness. Alice administered music as a restorative. And happily Bob Bruere came in to dine with us alone.

5. I saw much of [Stephen S.] Wise & of Mack Saturday & Sunday, but it will take all of the six weeks (of the Boston oil case) for you to wipe out of Mack's mind his deep reverence for the magnificent potency of money in Jewish affairs. He seemed surprised & stunned when I urged upon him that there were two things Jews needed more than money in their great problems:

1. Thought
2. Compelling high conduct in carrying out their plans & projects.

6. I learn from Kohler via Wise that [Benjamin N.] Cardozo's physician has prohibited his making any more speeches.

7. I am glad to hear of Roger Foster's going to H[arvard]. L[aw]. S[chool].[6]

8. [*] Robert Fritz was in yesterday. Spoke with enthusiasm of your course at Columbia.

9. About the Ky declaratory judgment case, more when we meet.[7]

10. It was news to me that [John] Hay had as Sec[retar]y of State made an annual report.[8]

Holmes J. is in superb form.

1. See LDB to Frankfurter, 1 January 1927, n. 4.

2. Actually, both cases involving these sections of the 1925 Jurisdiction Act had opinions written by Harlan Stone. In *Waggoner Estate* v. *Wichita County*, 273 *U.S.* 113 (1927), the Supreme Court upheld section 238 which provided for appeals of substantive constitutional questions directly from the District Courts to the Supreme Court; in *Smith* v. *Wilson*, 273 *U.S.* 388 (1927), the Court approved section 266, which allowed that a final hearing on preliminary injunctions did not require a full three-judge court if the

plaintiff did not press the issue. In both cases, the Court established rules that limited the right to appeal on procedural issues.

3. *United States* v. *Los Angeles & Salt Lake Railroad Co.*, 273 *U.S.* 299 (1927), involved a suit challenging the power of the Interstate Commerce Commission to value property for rate decisions under the 1922 act. Hughes acted as counsel for the railroad, and put forward an interpretation of the commerce clause that even a conservative court had rejected years earlier. LDB spoke for a unanimous court in upholding the law.

4. On 23 February LDB had written his brother: "The President's address yesterday, which I attended reluctantly (in robes) was one of the most painful experiences of a lifetime." For the text of the message, which was also broadcast widely by radio, see *New York Times,* 23 February 1927.

5. See LDB to Amy Brandeis Wehle, 1 February 1895, n. 1.

6. Roger Sherman Foster (b. 1900) taught law at Harvard until 1929, when he moved to Yale. He became an attorney for the Securities and Exchange Commission after 1935.

7. *American Railway Express Co.* v. *Kentucky,* 273 *U.S.* 269 (1927). A declaratory judgment is one that declares the rights of the parties without ordering anything to be done. In this case the courts affirmed that the American Express Company was responsible for the debts, in Kentucky, of its predecessor firm, the Adams Express Company.

8. See LDB to Frankfurter, 8 February 1927.

To Oliver Wendell Holmes

March 8, 1927 Washington, D.C. [Holmes Mss]

OWH:

"Ed egli a me: Nessun tuo passo caggia;
Pur su al monte dietro a me acquista, ...
Certo, Maestro mio, diss'io, unquanco
Non vid'io chiaro si, com'io discerno.
Là dove mio ingegno parea manco; . . . ." [1]

1. "And he to me: 'Let no step of thine descend;
Ever up the mount behind me win thy way. . . .'
'Of a surety, Master mine,' said I, 'never
saw I so clearly as I discern, there where my
wit seemed at fault. . . .'"

Dante, *Purgatorio,* Canto 4, lines 37–38, 76–77. This note was sent to Holmes on his eighty-sixth birthday.

To Felix Frankfurter

March 9, 1927 Washington, D.C. [Frankfurter Mss—HLS]

1. O[liver]W[endell]H[olmes]'s birthday went off most happily. He circulated on the morning an excellent opinion—in [a] case which was assigned to him Saturday evening, & which he wrote Sunday AM. Sunday PM he spent in rollicking laughter at "The Black Pirate" (Douglas Fairbanks). Monday he delivered with much joy the Negro primary opinion.[1] He was never more eager in pursuing the early spring flowers & birds—and carried me off to the Duncan Phillips Gallery the other day, after Court, to see an Egyptian head for which we both care much.

2. I wrote you Sunday asking for the S[acco].V[anzetti]. book. Monday it came.[2] It will prove an event of importance with bench & bar; perhaps a turning point.

3. Do you know Wachtell,[3] a young Jewish lawyer from N.Y., who argued the Wiener bank case[4] the other day against C.E. Hughes? W. made a strong impression on the Court—in every way a fine presentation—much better than his distinguished opponent.

4. I am glad Brewster is so intelligently active, and

5. Also of Reynold's [sic] letter. Where did he get his Webb-Kenyon suggestion?

6. [Horace M.] Kallen report etc. enclosed at Mack's request.

7. J.W.M[ack] seems ever more eager to support Ch. W[eizmann].[5]

1. Holmes, speaking for a unanimous Court, struck down a Texas law providing for an all-white primary for the Democratic Party. See *Nixon* v. *Herndon et al.,* 273 *U.S.* 536 (1927).

2. Felix Frankfurter, *The Case of Sacco and Vanzetti: A Critical Analysis for Lawyers and Laymen* (Boston, 1927). This widely noticed and extremely controversial book appeared five months before the two men were executed; it persuasively stated the view that the trial Sacco and Vanzetti had received was filled with irregularities and apparent injustices. For the story of how the book came to be written, see *Felix Frankfurter Reminisces*, ch. 20.

3. Samuel Robert Wachtell (1886–1943), an immigrant born in Austria-Hungary, practiced law in New York City for thirty years. He specialized in the law of international finance, particularly as it pertained to Austria and Hungary. In the 1930s, Wachtell devoted nearly all of his efforts to rescuing Jewish refugees from Europe. See also LDB to Frankfurter, 22 February 1928.

4. The property of the Austrian Wiener Bank-Verein had been seized during the war, and some of its Austrian creditors had sued, under provisions of Austrian law, to recapture the assets from the Alien Property Office; the bank claimed that under American law, it should not have to pay. Although Wachtell evidently presented the bank's case well, the Court ruled in favor of the creditors. *Zimmerman* v. *Sutherland*, 274 *U.S.* 253 (1927).

5. On the 4th, Mack had written LDB, asking for a chance to come to Washington to discuss Weizmann's proposed "survey" (see LDB to Frankfurter, 2 December 1926 and 15 February 1927); LDB replied that he would be glad to see Mack, "but I should add that I have reached the conclusion as to W's Survey after careful consideration & am not likely to change it."

To Felix Frankfurter

March 29, 1927 Washington, D.C. [Frankfurter Mss—HLS]

1. That's a fine lot of letters, & the [Boston] Herald has done well re S[acco]V[anzetti]. The Rudolph Albrocchi letters ought to be reproduced somewhere.

2. I am not surprised at either the Union Club, the Back Bay or the Boston bar.[1] If C[harles].N[agel]. writes for the American Bar Asso[ciatio]n Journal, let me know.[2]

3. As to the 3 U.S. S[upreme]. C[ourt] Justices on [the] H[arvard].L[aw].S[chool]. [fund-raising] Drive: O[liver]W[endell] H[olmes] talked with me about the constant requests, which the mail brings, a month or two ago, and was much relieved when he heard my views. I doubt whether he would wish to give, even if the objections which I have to the scheme did not exist.[3]

[Edward T.] Sanford also talked with me. He also was relieved on hearing my views, largely because he has calls from his Tennessee Educational Institutions (which he was & in part still is connected) & which are making drives.

But, I think, both O.W.H. and Sanford feel as I do that the School is going all wrong in its bigness. I should be glad, at the proper time, to aid further in research work under your direction. But I should think it unwise to give until the Drive is well in the background. I don't want any inference drawn, from anything I do, that I favor it. Of course I remain silent, unless asked.

3. [*sic*] That's a fine quotation from Spinoza. And I was de-

lighted with Morris Cohen's paper on S. in the N[ew].R[public].[4]

4. R. Walton Moore, who is wholly of our view re Mexico & Nicaragua,[5] tells me confidentially that Dwight Morrow [6] is very much troubled about Mexico & the possibilities of our intervening; also that C[alvin]. C[oolidge]. would like to get rid of K[ellogg]., but doesn't know how to do it or whom to substitute.[7] Of course, C.C. hasn't the courage. He is showing up his nothingness.

5. As to China, I am less troubled. Of course, we are doing terrible things.[8] But the 400 millions there & the distance make it pretty certain that all occidentals will be wiped out soon, as they deserve to be. And it would not be surprising if that were the beginning of the end of the whites in Asia.

6. We had a fine evening with Abe Flexner.

1. The debate over the Sacco and Vanzetti case raged through the spring and summer of 1927; and it arrayed the traditional forces of American conservatism against radicals, liberals, intellectuals, and labor.

2. Charles Nagel did not write for the *ABA Journal*, but he had his say on Sacco and Vanzetti in a laudatory review of Frankfurter's book; see 40 *Harvard Law Review* 1031 (1927).

3. See LDB to Frankfurter, 25 May 1927.

4. Morris R. Cohen, "Spinoza: Prophet of Liberalism," *New Republic* 50 (30 March 1927): 164–66. "It is because he so well exemplifies the faith that the way to human salvation is through reason and enlightenment that Spinoza may well be considered the philosopher-prophet of liberalism."

5. See LDB to Frankfurter, 7 January and 8 February 1927.

6. Dwight Whitney Morrow (1873–1931), after a decade with J. P. Morgan & Co. and a distinguished wartime service in shipping and supply, was named U.S. ambassador to Mexico.

7. Frank Kellogg remained as Secretary of State through the conclusion of President Coolidge's administration.

8. See LDB to Frankfurter, 8 February 1927.

To Felix Frankfurter

April 6, 1927 Washington, D.C. [Frankfurter Mss—HLS]

1. The S[acco]. V[anzetti]. decision came quick & of course was not unexpected by you.[1] It will perhaps heighten the already great impression your book has made.

2. Gooch, who was in this afternoon for tea, says [President A. Lawrence] Lowell told him that "its publication stopped dead the Law School drive." [2] I hope it is so. At all events the arrest is a fortunate thing for the School.[3]

3. Please say to Prof. Whitehead [4] that we shall be very glad to have him, Mrs. Whitehead and Prof. Woods [5] (& the others if any) take a cup of tea with us on Sunday April 17th at say 5 P.M. at Florence Court.

4. We are awaiting Al Smith's declaration with eagerness.[6] You have given him (via Belle [Moskowitz]) good advice.

5. Glad to see the spirit of Ky even in a banker.

6. It's good to hear that young [David] Amram is doing worthy things.

7. Alice was particularly interested in Hans Zinsser article.[7] His grandfather was a revolutionary associate of Dr. Goldmark.[8]

1. On this date the Massachusetts Supreme Judicial Court handed down its verdict, denying a motion for a new trial for Sacco and Vanzetti.

2. It was frequently alleged that Frankfurter's "radicalism" cost the Law School contributions from its alumni; for Frankfurter's view, see Sutherland, *The Law At Harvard*, 262.

3. See preceding letter.

4. Alfred North Whitehead (1861–1947), the renowned British philosopher and mathematician, joined the faculty at Harvard in 1924. He remained in Cambridge until his retirement in 1937.

5. Perhaps James Haughton Woods (1864–1935), Whitehead's colleague in Harvard's Philosophy Department. Woods had taught at Harvard since 1891.

6. For all practical purposes, Al Smith had announced his presidential candidacy at his inaugural as governor, back on 1 January. The "declaration" LDB refers to here is undoubtedly Smith's famous reply to C. C. Marshall. In April 1927, Marshall, an Episcopal lawyer, raised the issue of the suitability of a Roman Catholic for President, through a letter to the *Atlantic Monthly*. Smith decided to meet the issue directly and he published, in the May issue, a reply which defined his views and asserted the absolute separation of church and state. See Edmund A. Moore, *A Catholic Runs for President: The Campaign of 1928* (New York, 1956), ch. 3, for an account of the Marshall exchange.

7. Hans Zinsser (1878–1940) was a leading bacteriologist. He achieved a kind of popularity with his *Rats, Lice and History* (Boston, 1935). The article referred to may have been "The Perils of Magnanimity," *Atlantic Monthly* 139 (February 1927): 246–50.

8. Alice Brandeis's father, Dr. Joseph Goldmark (see LDB to Alfred Brandeis, 28 June 1878).

To Felix Frankfurter

April 11, 1927 Washington, D.C. [Frankfurter Mss—HLS]

Opinion in No. 412 herewith.[1]

If anything can awaken Trade Unionists from their lethargy, this should.

And perhaps it needs a jolt of this kind to arouse them in this era of friendly cooperation.

1. *Bedford Cut Stone Co.* v. *Journeymen Stone Cutters' Assoc.,* 274 *U.S.* 37 (1927). The case involved a group of peaceful stonecutters who refused, in accord with their constitution, to "finish" limestone cut by non-union cutters. The company sought an injunction; and although they were refused by two lower courts, the Supreme Court granted their request. Paul Murphy calls the ruling, "the high point in the trend toward utilizing the antitrust structure to curb labor activity" (*Constitution in Crisis Times,* 62). Organized labor was furious and the decision occasioned much comment (see LDB to Frankfurter, 26 April 1927, for example). Holmes joined LDB in a strong dissent.

To Alfred Brandeis

April 14, 1927 Washington, D.C. [Brandeis Mss, M 4–4]

DEAR AL: Yours of 12th recd. I suppose letter of 13th may bring clippings galore, or whispered reports.

Telephone from McAdoo yesterday, which opened with reference to your letter.[1] He came up after dinner, was with me nearly an hour & a half. Was full of his fight in California in which he beat first, the [James D.] Phelan wet crowd in the primaries, and then (in the general election, I think) the effort to repeal the Wright (state enforcement) law.

Of course, he has hankerings for the Presidency still, is full of fight, but uncertain what to undertake.

He will use your Worcester quotation[2] as key-note for a commencement address he must give in Georgia in June.

We expect Paul & Elizabeth tomorrow late. They plan to bring Mrs. Rauschenbusch[3] to show her Washington—& us.

1. In late January, LDB had sent his brother an advance copy of a speech to be made by McAdoo in Toledo. The speech argued the moral necessity

of enforcing the law on prohibition. Alfred Brandeis, on 2 February, wrote McAdoo praising the sentiment and pledging his support for 1928. Alfred Brandeis opposed national prohibition, but believed that the matter of enforcing existing laws was crucial.

2. Alfred had written McAdoo (see preceding note): "Over the entrance to the County Court House, in Worcester, Mass., are carved the words: 'Obedience to law is true liberty.' "

3. Pauline Rother Rauschenbusch, Paul's mother.

To Elizabeth Brandeis Raushenbush

April 24, 1927 Washington, D.C. [EBR]

DEAREST ELIZABETH: Your and Paul's triumphal march to Madison has laid the foundation for much of the happiness which I wish you two.[1]

Before abdicating the office of Educational Adviser recently assumed I venture to suggest this:

Confine your labor course or courses to American labor. Use your growing knowledge of English labor merely as an enriching background to enable you to understand and elucidate American conditions. Do not profess to teach about English or other foreign labor.   Lovingly,

1. Paul and Elizabeth Raushenbush returned from Philadelphia, where they had been working on their PhD theses, and were offered jobs at the University of Wisconsin for the coming academic year. Elizabeth was hired in the Economics Department; Paul, part time in Economics and part time in the new Experimental College which was to open in the fall of 1927.

To Felix Frankfurter

April 26, 1927 Washington, D.C. [Frankfurter Mss—HLS]

1. All of the Court, I think, realize how great a loss is suffered in Hough's death.[1]

2. The batch of letters & clippings returned herewith show how much more valuable to Massachusetts & the country the S[upreme]. J[udicial]. C[ourt]. has made your work by its denying relief.[2]

3. The widespread upswing is a tribute to the American people

as well as to the quality of your publications. This is the first event (other than the war) for many years which has made a deep rift in Boston's upper ten, & seems really to have stirred those with the faculty for being right, in many parts of the country. Coming after the protest against Kellogg's Latin American policies it is indeed heartening.

4. Your 'Reminds of Involuntary Servitude" is a stirring document.[3] It looks as if the A.F. of L. were really alive to the danger.

5. The poverty of the British Labor Party in lawyers, reminds of the old time difficulties of Whig Chancellors in finding men fit to be judges.

6. Poor R[oscoe]. P[ound]. I guess he will dissolve through sheer lack of vertebrae.

7. That the Epicurean C. C. Burlingham should have become a S[acco]. V[anzetti]. protagonist is a remarkable manifestation of the power in your story & the deep down possibilities for Americans.[4] Ellery Sedgwick's rising to the opportunity & Burr's support of the Bishop [5] in his tilt are also very significant.

8. Alice bids me ask you for the Rev. Gordon's "impudence" letter.[6] It is truly great to have smoked him out.

9. Will Charles Nagel write the Amer[ican] Bar Asso[ciatio]n Journal? [7]

10. Auntie B. must have great joy in Harry Taber's fire.

11. When we meet, remind me of "law review criticisms of the courts".

We were glad to see the McNeils and Calvert.

1. Judge Charles M. Hough (see LDB to Frankfurter, 3 June 1924, n. 3) died on 23 April.

2. See LDB to Frankfurter, 6 April 1927, n. 1.

3. " 'Reminds of Involuntary Servitude,' " *New Republic* 50 (27 April 1927): 262–64. This anonymous article, obviously written by Frankfurter, is a denunciation of the Supreme Court's decision in the Bedford stonecutters' case (see LDB to Frankfurter, 11 April 1927). The title is part of a sentence in LDB's dissent. Frankfurter reviewed both the case and also conditions in the stonecutting industry, asserting that labor should be alerted by the decision to shake itself free of the "siren propaganda of 'prosperity.' " Referring to LDB's dissent, Frankfurter wrote: "The only consolation about the Bedford Cut Stone case is that the moral judgment upon the decision has already been authoritatively uttered as part of the decision."

4. Burlingham spoke out in a letter to the *New York Times*, 20 April 1927.

5. Bishop William Lawrence appealed to Governor Fuller for a full and impartial review of the Sacco and Vanzetti case. See *New York Times*, 22 April 1927.

6. Rev. George Angier Gordon (1853–1929), the long-time minister of Boston's Old South Church, denounced Bishop Lawrence's letter (see preceding note) as "impudent." Massachusetts judicial officials, Gordon argued, were perfectly capable of handling the matter without interference from outside authorities.

7. See LDB to Frankfurter, 29 March 1927, n. 2.

To Alfred Brandeis

April 27, 1927 Washington, D.C. [Brandeis Mss, M 4–4]

DEAR AL: Yours of 25th with newspaper matter of the 24th recd.

I am glad you got Callahan,[1] and am not surprised at the abstentions of the likeminded, who abstained from fear & particularly for "business reasons". My own experience with would have been supporters was ample on this line & McAdoo told me much in the same line about present Los Angeles conditions.

I fear "business as usual" is undermining the native courage of Americans. I had rather expected that Kentuckians, who had rather more of courage & manliness than most, would have shown less of the weakness. But I guess Goethe's wisdom is of universal application:

"Nichts ist schwerer zu ertragen
Als ein Reihe von schoenen Tagen." [2]   Gruesse,

1. The letter from Alfred Brandeis is lost, but undoubtedly the Brandeis family had gained the support, for University of Louisville work, of Patrick Henry Callahan (1866–1940), a local varnish-company executive who was extremely active in philanthropic and civic affairs.

2. "Nothing is harder to endure
Than a series of beautiful days."

To Felix Frankfurter

April 27, 1927 Washington, D.C. [Frankfurter Mss–HLS]

Your telegram reached me at Court. Your letter with the Wigmore blast & your answer did not come to me until late this afternoon.[1] I talked personally to Holmes J., & he is fully prepared for any rabid attack by Wigmore on any one, through W's attacks on him.

W's attack on the Senate in the April Illinois Law Review[2] & other performances are evidence of an unbalanced mind.

The enclosed from Graham Wallas to Alice will be good evidence for Marian as to how W's ploy strikes the intelligent layman.

I agree with you, W's performance, however sad & unpleasant, will not affect the results—indeed, it should help, however painful[ly], to the ultimate end sought. S[acco].V[anzetti]. is only an incident in a long battle line.

I will return the other clippings later.

1. On 26 April, the *Boston Transcript* ran a full, front-page article under the headline "Wigmore Attacks Frankfurter." Dean John H. Wigmore (see LDB to Alice G. Brandeis, 4 February 1923) had accused Frankfurter of inaccuracies and bias in his work on Sacco and Vanzetti. Frankfurter responded immediately and at length in the next morning's *Boston Herald* (the editor, Frank Buxton, holding publication until the reply from Frankfurter arrived). For Frankfurter's exciting version of the incident, see *Felix Frankfurter Reminisces*, 215–17. The telegram from Frankfurter to LDB read: "Holmes may hear at second hand about Wigmore attack and be troubled by it. Please assure him not slightest reason for concern. Quite contrary have had nothing but commendation from important lawyers and others on my reply. Nothing but condemnation and pity expressed for Wigmore." See next letter.

2. Wigmore had written an editorial, "Every Senator a Legislative Dictator," 21 *Illinois Law Review* 804 (1927); it was an intemperate attack on the way any one irresponsible Senator could obstruct legislation.

To Felix Frankfurter

April 29, 1927 Washington, D.C. [Frankfurter Mss—HLS]

The morning papers & mail from Miss Grady bring good news. The respite given Maderos[*sic*][1], and the request of Pound[2] et al for the Review, coming after the Wigmore article,[3] appear at the most effective time conceivable.

With your crushing reply to Wigmore, those responsible for his intercession should feel humiliated—if their prejudices have not made them proof against emotions as well as ideas.

Your copies of Wigmore & the reply returned herewith.
Beveridge's death is sad.[4] I had not realized that he was so old.

1. Celestino F. Madeiros, a professional highjacker and a member of the
notorious Morelli gang, had confessed to the South Braintree, Massachusetts,
robbery and murder; but he insisted that Sacco and Vanzetti were not involved in the crime. Madeiros had been convicted of murder and was due
to be executed—he had already been removed to death row. But on 28 April
he received a stay of execution.

2. The day before, Roscoe Pound joined others in petitioning Governor
Fuller for a review of the Sacco-Vanzetti case, See *New York Times,* 27
April 1927.

3. See preceding letter.

4. Albert Beveridge died on 27 April at the age of sixty-four.

To Felix Frankfurter

May 2, 1927 Washington, D.C. [Frankfurter Mss—HLS]

1. O[liver].W[endell].H[olmes]. closed yesterday's sitting (our
last argued case) in fine form & eager spirit—with all his cases
written. (Save such as the C[hief].J[ustice]. may give him to
help out other jjs.)

2. The award of the Pulitzer prize for "We Submit" comes
at an opportune time.[1]

3. One of the important by-products of your S[acco].V[an-
zetti]. stunt is the assertion by Law School professors of the Law
Schools' prerogative as guardians of law & justice. The performance of Yale's Dean & Associates is a notable event.[2] I had
hoped (and still hope) that C.C.B[urlingham] will stir Columbia
& the other N.Y. Schools to similar action. Is there not hope of
something similar from the Cornell men? Wigmore's sad performance should really help much in this connection, and [it] is
almost a noblesse oblige for others who disagree with him. A rare
opportunity is afforded the Law Schools to amplify their jurisdiction. F.W.T.[3] gave, I think, poor advice to C.C.B.

4. It was natural that the Transcript should ressurect the Roosevelt letter. I had been thinking of the Mooney case & wondering
whether your S.V. action might not lead some able, courageous
man who cares, to write up the terrible Mooney story.[4] It is all
of a piece with what I see of the California judiciary & bar.

1. "We Submit" was the 26 October 1926 editorial in the *Boston Herald*. The piece was written by F. Lauriston Bullard (see LDB to Frankfurter, 15 June 1928, n. 2), and it urged a new trial for Sacco and Vanzetti. Bullard's editorial had just been awarded the Pulitzer Prize for the best editorial of 1926.

2. Yale's Acting Dean Robert M. Hutchins (see LDB to Frankfurter, 28 April 1929, n. 2) spoke along with Frankfurter at a mass meeting of the Yale Liberal Club on behalf of Sacco and Vanzetti. On 6 May LDB added: "Your S.V. should yield also this important by-product: Students may realize now that a law school professorship affords an admirable pedestal for participating in the practical affairs."

3. Perhaps Frank W. Taussig.

4. For the Mooney case, see LDB to Alice G. Brandeis, 13 June 1919, n. 4. The "Roosevelt letter" that was resurrected was the ex-President's rebuke to Frankfurter, 19 December 1917, for Frankfurter's reports on the Mooney case and on the Bisbee deportations. Roosevelt's letter is an hysterical denunciation of such "Bolsheviki of America" as LaFollette and Amos Pinchot. For the text, see E. E. Morison, ed., *The Letters of Theodore Roosevelt*, 8: 1262–65.

To Felix Frankfurter

May 21, 1927 Washington, D.C. [Frankfurter Mss—HLS]

1. It's good to see the U. of P[ennsylvania]. fall into line.[1] I trust the contagion is spreading among the Law Schools.

2. My congratulations to you and Patterson on No. 1. of Harvard Studies in Administrative Law. It is fitting that No. 1. should be "The Insurance Commission[*sic*]"—& fortunate that it should be written by a professor of a university other than Harvard.[2]

3. When will No. 2. appear? [3]

4. I had sent copies of the Whitney opinion [4] to Laski, Learned Hand, [*], Villard & Morris Cohen; & after your letter sent copies to Chafee and Justice Higgins.[5]

5. Enclosed from Borah is, I suppose, to make amends for 1916.[6]

6. Alvin Johnson was in yesterday. That is a terrific job which he is undertaking with Seligman.[7]

7. Lowell Mellett [8] (editor, Scripps-Howard newspapers 1322 N.Y. Ave, Washington) undertook the Espionage campaign at my suggestion & finally put it into the hands of Ruth Furness, a very competent young woman who produced a series of 11 arti-

cles of value. I think it would encourage Mellett, if you write
him & ask for a copy of the articles.

    1. In the effort to get a new trial for Sacco and Vanzetti.

    2. Edwin Wilhite Patterson, *The Insurance Commissioner in the United
States* (Cambridge, Mass., 1927). Patterson (1889–1965) taught law at
Columbia.

    3. The second volume was John Dickinson, *Administrative Justice and
the Supremacy of Law in the United States* (Cambridge, Mass., 1927).

    4. *Whitney* v. *California*, 274 *U.S.* 357 (1927). Anita Whitney was con-
victed under California's Criminal Syndicalism Act of 1919 while helping to
organize the Communist Labor Party in that state. The Supreme Court,
speaking through Justice Sanford, upheld the conviction. Sanford argued
that the California legislature had determined that certain activities constituted the necessary "clear and present danger" which permitted the limitation of speech. The legislature's definition was not unreasonable, he maintained, and it was entitled to be given very great weight. LDB, with Holmes
joining, wrote a long concurring opinion which Samuel Konefsky calls
"unusually eloquent." LDB held that the Court could decide upon different
criteria in different cases on "clear and present danger" and that it was not
obliged to accept California's definition. LDB made clear his personal definition (particularly on the ground of the "imminence" of the danger in Anita
Whitney's speech) would have resulted in overturning the conviction. LDB
concurred in the opinion, apparently, because there was not opportunity to
"inquire into errors now alleged," and also because the Court had never
clearly fixed the meaning of the "clear and present danger" formula. Konefsky writes of LDB's opinion: "But even if Brandeis had not essayed so
searching an examination of the meaning of 'clear and present danger,' his
opinion would have been notable for another reason. In it is to be found one
of the most moving expositions of America's heritage of freedom. The passages in which he states his libertarian creed do indeed reveal him to be, in
Professor Chafee's phrase, one of the 'strongest conservators of Americanism.'" For Konefsky's illuminating discussion of the Whitney case, see *The
Legacy of Holmes and Brandeis*, 209–13.

    5. Henry Bournes Higgins (1851–1929) was a distinguished judge of
Australia's High Court and a longtime chief judge of the Federal Court
of Conciliation and Arbitration. He was in close contact with Frankfurter
from 1910 until his death.

    6. The enclosure is unknown; the reference, of course, is to Borah's op-
position to LDB's confirmation in 1916.

    7. Alvin Johnson and E. R. A. Seligman began work in 1927 on the
monumental *Encyclopedia of the Social Sciences*. The preparation stretched
from 1927 to 1933, and publication of the volumes extended from 1930 to
1935. See Alvin Johnson, *Pioneer's Progress*, ch. 29.

    8. Lowell Mellett (1884–1960) remained a Washington journalist until
1937. He then went into government service and worked as an administrative assistant to President Franklin Roosevelt from 1940 to 1944.

To Alice Harriet Grady

May 22, 1927 Washington, D.C. [Grady Mss]

AHG: If the W[omen's].C[ity].C[lub]. goes wrong, it will at least be easier for you to decline the Vice Presidency.

I suppose evidences of bad business & unemployment must be whispered in Mass[achusetts], in view of C[alvin].C[oolidge]'s instructions. It would be "unpatriotic" to suffer otherwise than in silence.

Have you heard the N.Y. mot: "Massachusetts—Thayer she stands".[1]

I have a huge mass of seventieth Birthday clippings. If it is agreeable to you, I will send them to you by mail or express, so that they can be mounted & bound as supplement to my library of LDB clippings which you provided.

I suppose we might get E. D. P[eabody]. to do the work during the summer office days.

1. A reference to Massachusetts trial judge Webster Thayer (1857–1933), who presided over the Sacco and Vanzetti trial and also over the hearings for new trials—all of which motions he denied.

To Felix Frankfurter

May 25, 1927 Washington, D.C. [Frankfurter Mss—HLS]

1. I note Gov. Fuller's [1] "Italia fara da se".[2]

2. Before Lindbergh [3] gets off the front page, the N[ew].R[epublic]. should draw the lesson of his heritage. His father—farmer-labor insurgent. The dignity & sense for the worthwhile of his mother.[4] His Scandinavian ancestry—which gave us also Andrew Furuseth. Moral courage—self-reliance—individuality.

Enclosed from "Labor" on these lines.

3. After you have seen Ruth Finney's [*sic*] stuff, it would be fruitful probably to advise Mellett to have her go to N.Y. to go over thoroughly the material of the Amer[ican]. Civil Liberties League.[5]

4. Has Ellery Sedgwick made any progress with "Life, Leisure & Pleasure"? He might follow such an article with "The Midas Touch—Our Curse?"

5. Saw O[liver]W[endell]H[olmes] today. He is in fine shape. He confessed to me that, importuned by Cochran, he had sent the H[arvard]L[aw]S[chool] fund $100. (One hundred).[6]

6. Things are in a pretty bad way in England.

7. We are expecting to see Morris Cohen Sunday.

1. Alvan Tufts Fuller (1878–1958), a former Massachusetts Congressman, was serving as governor of the state.

2. "Italy will take care of herself." Fuller was under heavy pressure to appoint a high-level commission, preferably composed of outsiders, to investigate the Sacco and Vanzetti trial. On 25 May, however, he announced that he intended to keep the investigation in his own hands. Within a week he changed course and appointed an "advisory committee" to help inform his decision on whether or not to grant clemency. See LDB to Frankfurter, 2 June 1927, n. 2.

3. In 1927, Charles Augustus Lindbergh, Jr. (1902–1974) was, by any standard, the premier hero of the hour. On 21 May 1927 he completed the first solo transatlantic flight in *The Spirit of St. Louis* and so was thrust into a world of constant public attention. His later marriage to Anne Morrow, the kidnapping and murder of their small son, his comments on Nazi Germany and his work for neutrality before Pearl Harbor—all were exposed to the gruelling searchlight of unrelenting public attention. For the attempt to read a symbolic meaning into his flight and to "draw lessons" (as LDB does here) from his personality, see John W. Ward, "The Meaning of Lindbergh's Flight," *American Quarterly* 10 (1958): 3–16.

4. Charles Augustus Lindbergh (1859–1924) was a liberal Congressman from Minnesota between 1906 and 1916. He is credited with having introduced the resolution which led, in 1913, to the establishment of the Pujo Committee to investigate the "money trust"—a phrase that Lindbergh used as freely as LDB. In 1901, he married Evangeline Lodge Land.

5. For research on federal espionage. See LDB to Frankfurter, 21 May 1927.

6. See LDB to Frankfurter, 29 March 1927.

To Alfred Brandeis

May 26, 1927 Washington, D.C. [Brandeis Mss, M 4–4]

DEAR AL: You have handled U. of L. matters with so much wisdom & skill that I have no suggestions to make except one—on that I have had half-a-century of experience and you none.

Alice's & my plans for the University extend over the next ten years. We don't want to lose our managing partner. It's just 50 years since my eyes gave out.[1] Since then, there has never been a time that I haven't had to bear in mind physical limitations of some sort. The walls curbing activity were always in sight; and I had to adjust my efforts. Your superb constitution relieved you from that necessity. But age is a fact that may not be ignored. It has added to the limitations to which I have been subject, and there is not a day when I am not reminded of it.

Your constitution is better than mine. But you are nearly three years older. Remember that—and Act Accordingly.   Gruesse, Alice thinks enclosed on Educationals Sir Anthony Absolute's Elsewhere may interest you & Jennie.[2]

1. See LDB to Amy B. Wehle, 20 January 1877, n. 2.
2. Sir Anthony Absolute was a character in Sheridan's *The Rivals.*

To Alfred Brandeis

June 2, 1927 Washington, D.C. [Brandeis Mss, M 4–4]

DEAR AL: It's fine to hear from Mrs Gross that you are making good progress.

About the time enclosed on Eugene Meyer came in, he called. M. says he has no fear in regard to confirmation, & the "charges" are the old ones which were exploded long since.[1]

He told me much of interest about the Farm Loan Board & the banks. The record is a pretty terrible one—much pettifogging political corruption, particularly in employing incompetents & also financial corruption in many places.

He says that 2 billion in mortgages are outstanding. He attributes much of the farm land market demoralization to the conduct of the banks, first in boosting loan values, then in unwise foreclosures, and in unwise disposing of farms bought in. He instanced one case, of the Minnesota bank, which foreclosed 400 mortgages, then sold the 400 farms bought in, to a speculator for 50 percent of the amount of the loan. So that the speculator got his farms at about 25 percent of the loan value (?)

We plan to leave here Monday PM for Boston.

1. President Coolidge had appointed Meyer Farm Loan Commissioner on a recess appointment. The position involved administering banks and loan associations in an effort to aid agriculture. Meyer was opposed for the

position by agricultural spokesmen and Senators from agricultural districts on the grounds that his appointment would introduce "Wall Street influence" into agricultural affairs. After performing creditably on the interim appointment and helping to reorganize the badly administered Farm Loan Board, he was confirmed by the Senate on 3 February 1928.

To Felix Frankfurter

June 2, 1927 Washington, D.C. [Frankfurter Mss—HLS]

1. Yours of 31st just received. I am deeply chagrined at my oversight in not having Miss Malloch make the deposit of $2000 on Jan 1st/27. I am writing her by this mail & asking her to advise you immediately on making the deposit. Until further notice, it is my intention that $1500 shall be deposited Oct 1, and $2000, Jan 1 during each year for our joint endeavors through you.[1] If, by any chance, the deposit is not regularly made please enquire of Miss Malloch or let me know.

I have realized that S[acco].V[anzetti]., inter alia, must have made heavy demands for incidental expense, as well as time, & meant to ask you when we meet whether an additional sum might not be appropriate this year. Let me know.

2. Fuller's advisory board is not as good as the one you intimate as possible.[2]

3. We are doing some heavy reversing of 8th Circuit [Court] & 2d. Some note should be made how the Circuits fare.

I am asking [James M.] Landis & his Mrs. to join us Tuesday evening.

1. See LDB to Frankfurter, 19 and 25 November 1916; and 24 September 1925. See also LDB to Julian W. Mack, 12 January 1922.

2. See LDB to Frankfurter, 25 May 1927, n. 2. On 2 June Governor Fuller announced that his advisory committee on the Sacco and Vanzetti matter would consist of three distinguished Massachusetts citizens: A. Lawrence Lowell, president of Harvard; Judge Robert Grant (1852–1940), for many years a probate judge but best known as a novelist; and Samuel Wesley Stratton (1861–1931), physicist, former director of the National Bureau of Standards, and since 1923 the president of the Massachusetts Institute of Technology.

To Jacob deHaas

June 5, 1927 Washington, D.C. [Frankfurter Mss—HLS]

DEH: You understand and must make clear to Israel Goldberg, Zeldin and all others, the severe limitations upon my participation in the task ahead.[1] I have not only the same heavy judicial work, but I am seven years older than when I last took an important part in Zionist affairs. To the right management I should be happy to give moral support, and also financial support, such as I gave from 1914 to 1921. In the vacation time I should be glad to lend such aid by exercise of judgment and occasional conference with those in charge on serious general problems, in so far as that can be done at Chatham.[2] But I have been made conscious of the great difference which five years make after 65. It would be impossible for me to do at any time anything which smacks of executive determinations, the exercise of judgment in minor matters, or participation in conferences to straighten out dissentions or controversies; and during eight months of the year, there would have to be largely a closed season for me, with only the possibility of those infrequent conferences in Washington, such as have [been] had with you and others during the past year.

These necessary limitations upon my participation should be made clear by you not only to Israel Goldberg, Zeldin, Bob Szold, but to all others, who might otherwise think that I can exercise something like the control and participation which they may recall from 1917 to 1921. I cannot take any office—even an honorary one.

As to the possibility of our friends regaining control, the immediate aim, and the essential of any effective participation, must be unfettered control of the American Organization, and through it of all American money raising; there can be no compromise with Lipsky or any of his ilk. All must get out, if our friends are to go in.

No attempt should be made by our friends to take possession, unless they have secured assurance of unreserved support from the Hadassah.[3] The Hadassah have the votes. They hold their convention before the Z[ionist].O[rganization]. does, and what they do there and before, will enable our friends to know whether unreserved support of the Hadassah can be had.

If our friends can control the American Organization and the money raising I think they would have to work in the World Organization with and through Weizmann.

1. The year 1927 marked the start of the expulsion of the Louis Lipsky regime from Zionist affairs. Everywhere one looked in American Zionism (except Hadassah), chaos seemed to reign. Membership continued to fall disastrously. Fund raising, which had become almost the sole function of the American organization, fell off to such an extent that important commitments in Palestine were left without financial support. Allegations of mismanagement tore the fabric of the movement. Under these circumstances, many Zionists—even those who had once supported Lipsky and Weizmann—came to feel that only a return of the so-called "Americanized" leadership of LDB and Mack could save the Z.O.A. These Zionists assumed that, once the old leadership was restored, LDB himself would take active command as in the period 1914 to 1921. One of those was Israel Goldberg (1889–1964), better known by his pen name, Rufus Learsi. Goldberg, who had been an official in the controversial Keren Hayesod, went so far as to lead the opposition to Lipsky on the floor of the 1927 Z.O.A. convention. After failing to unseat the Lipsky regime, he resigned his post and concentrated on Jewish education and upon his writing.

2. See LDB to Joshua Bernhardt, 9 July 1930, n. 2.

3. Hadassah had always been strongly pro-Brandeis-Mack in the Zionist disputes. The organization was naturally sympathetic to LDB's Palestine development ideals, to his emphasis on financial accountability, and to his attempt to harmonize Zionism and Americanism. For the role of Hadassah in the internal disputes within American Zionism, see Urofsky, *American Zionism*, 341–46.

To Felix Frankfurter

June 5, 1927 Washington, D.C. [Frankfurter Mss—HLS]

1. I trust you have received 'ere this word from Miss Malloch that the check has been deposited.[1]

2. There should be in "Business of U[nited]S[tates]S[upreme] C[ourt]" or elsewhere, a full exposition of the methods & practices of our Court, which have been large factors in its relatively good performance as compared by the Supreme Courts of the States, i.a.

    A. Encouragement of oral argument. Discouragement of oratory. Socratic method at argument applied through the judges. We have almost no cases submitted in briefs, and those few are either a first for us or a surrender.

B. Assignment of cases to the J[ustice]s by the C[hief]. J[ustice]. after discussion and vote at conference.

C. Distribution of opinions in print, and consideration at subsequent conference. Ample time thereafter for writing dissents & at conference for suggestion & then recirculation of revised opinion.

D. Consideration of every case, certiorari & motion by every judge before the conference & action thereon at the conference.

E. Limiting, by means of certiorari, the number of cases by the human limitation of 9 judges' working time.

F. Discouraging rehearings.

G. Importance of length of service, as distinguished from method of selection of judges.

H. Team play, encouraging individual enquiry (and dissent) as distinguished from subservient ignorant unanimity.

I. Tradition.

J. The play of public opinion upon the Court's performance.

These factors play probably a larger part than elevation of status, high responsibility & greater ability incident to wider selection.

K. And the extraordinary service through longevity & loyalty in the Clerks & Marshal's offices are also to be considered.

The above elements & others which will occur to you, should be made the basis of a campaign in the several states through the Law Schools & the Law Reviews for bettering the state tribunals. In the main, their product is shocking. And their methods are perhaps more so.

3. Your memo on graduate students embodies much wisdom persuasively presented.

1. See LDB to Frankfurter, 2 June 1927.

To Jacob deHaas

June 6, 1927 Washington, D.C. [Frankfurter Mss—HLS]

DEH: It seems to me clear that our friends cannot wisely assume control for the future if it means shouldering the huge indebtedness of the several organizations and institutions.[1] Payment of these must be independently provided for. If the proposed new management should assume these staggering burdens they would become slaves instead of masters—followers instead of leaders. Some arrangement must be worked out for dealing independently with the hang overs of the past six years. The new management will have all it can handle to deal adequately and honestly with future demands.

You will recall the passage in Herodotus about the Persians. They considered lying the greatest of sins. And the next greatest was running into debt. For debts made men lie.

1. The Lipsky administration of Z.O.A. had run large deficits, totalling around $140,000. See LDB to deHaas, 5 June 1927.

To Felix Frankfurter

June 16, 1927 Chatham, Mass. [Frankfurter Mss—HLS]

1. Alice & I hope that in planning your busy summer you will leave some break for idle days at Chatham.

2. Your Governor seems to be very diligent.[1] Let us hope that knowledge may be accompanied by wisdom.

3. If the Va Law Register is at hand, look at Major A.S. Lanier's strange performance. He publishes his rejected brief in the Coast Guard Case.[2] Perhaps in search of fame as great as has attended "Rejected Addresses".

4. I am reading The Federalist with amazement that such lofty, closely reasoned arguments should have been vote-getters in 1787–1788.[3]

5. Hope you will have satisfactory dinner tomorrow, & that after it you will have a talk with deH[aas]. on Zionist affairs. He is very sad over the dashing of his hopes.[4]

1. Governor Fuller spent much of June 1927 investigating the Sacco and Vanzetti case. On 15 June, for example, he had interviewed members of the jury that had convicted Vanzetti of another crime prior to the South Braintree highjacking.

2. Alexander Sidney Lanier published his brief in 12 *Virginia Law Register* 747 (1927). Lanier had been on the losing side in *Maul* v. *United States*, 274 *U.S.* 501 (1927), a complicated case involving a Coast Guard seizure of a

ship beyond the twelve mile limit. The ship, the *Underwriter*, had violated
several laws, including sailing without a license, failing to get proper clear-
ances, and engaging in trade for which she was not licensed, all of which
made her forfeit for seizure. The owners did not dispute the charges, but
through Lanier argued that the Coast Guard had no powers to seize the
boat on the high seas. Justice Van Devanter wrote the court's opinion, and
tracing the law back to colonial times, upheld the seizure. LDB, joined by
Holmes, entered a concurring opinion (at 512) agreeing with Van Devanter's
conclusions, but not with his reasoning; in a typical LDB opinion, the reasoning was buttressed by extensive footnoting.

3. During the ensuing month, LDB sent Frankfurter numerous short quotations from the *Federalist Papers*.

4. See LDB to Jacob deHaas, 5 June 1927. DeHaas had hoped that if LDB
returned to active leadership in American Zionist affairs, he would elevate
deHaas to his former position of power and influence.

To Alfred Brandeis

June 19, 1927 Chatham, Mass. [Brandeis Mss, M 4–4]

DEAR AL: Letter from Walter Child enclosed. His reference to
[*] means his annual tramp there in the swamps in search of
orchids.

He is one of the men who, opportunities and obstacles considered, made the most of life. He overcame the inherited appetite for drink. He bore & lived down the terrible misfortune inherent in his wife, and he functioned in business despite his lack
of business ability. His happiness he earned through pursuit of art
& the history which went with it; and the pursuit of orchids &
the science which attended it; and took perhaps equal pleasure in
the cultivation of a few worthy friends.

There are only a few of our friends who have excelled in the
art of living. I count him & Denman Ross, and Prof. [Ephraim]
Emerton preeminent among the number.   Gruesse,

To Felix Frankfurter

July 9, 1927 Chatham, Mass. [Frankfurter Mss—HLS]

1. Cardozo has done an uncommonly good job in Campbell vs
City of N.Y. by showing how Connally v Gen[eral]. Const[ruc-
tion] Co. can be avoided & its poison delimited.[1]

2. Have any of the city planners proposed a special municipal excise tax, a progressive super tax, based (a) upon percentage of area covered (b) upon height of building, over the standard. Thus, fixing as standard, say ½ of the area and as height say 60 feet & 15 feet cellar?

Such a law, plus division of railroad freight charges into terminal & line haul—with terminal representing not less than actual cost of service—would go far toward solving the excessive growth of cities & congestion of traffic.

3. Sam Morrison[*sic*] [2] will be good at anything. But I rather wish he had limited himself to a narrower subject. e.g.

    (a) To a history of the departures in practice from the American ideals of liberty & equality, or

    (b) To non-Anglo Saxon contributions to American ideals of civilization.

    (c) To American intolerances to ideas later embraced with avidity.

He is particularly fitted to do such a job for freedom.

4. Henry Ford made a handsome retraction.[3]

5. I hope the Hamiltons found you & Marion yesterday.

6. That's good about [*].

7. We shall bear Parrington in mind.

---

1. Both Oklahoma and New York had statutes which stipulated that workers hired to do public work had to be paid at the "prevailing rate" by the state. In *Connally* v. *General Construction Co.*, 269 *U.S.* 385 (1926), the Supreme Court held that the Oklahoma law was unconstitutionally vague and obscure—insufficient, in short, to sustain a criminal prosecution. But in *Campbell* v. *City of New York*, 244 *N.Y.* 317 (1927), Cardozo deftly upheld the "prevailing rate" stipulation and attempted to show why the Connally case did not apply to the New York situation.

2. Already in 1927 Samuel Eliot Morison (1887–1976) was an important historian of America. He was early recognized as one of the foremost practitioners of the discipline in the United States, and during his long career he received many major prizes and honorary degrees as the author of numerous important studies in the history of American life and culture. Morison had come to Harvard in 1908 as an undergraduate; and his association with the institution did not end until his death, although his formal teaching duties came to a close in 1955.

3. On 8 July Henry Ford publicly apologized for his long campaign of anti-Semitism. He issued orders to the *Dearborn Independent* to end its attacks on Jews and moved to settle, out of court, a libel suit brought against

him by Aaron Sapiro (see LDB to Frankfurter, 3 February 1922, n. 4). The formal apology came in the form of a letter to Louis Marshall, after a series of meetings between Ford's representatives and Marshall.

To Felix Frankfurter

July 22, 1927 Chatham, Mass. [Frankfurter Mss—HLS]

Re yours of 20th.

1. The enclosures returned herewith are interesting. I was particularly glad of your reply to [*].

2. As to your going before the Commission or the Governor. If by their wholly spontaneous action you are called, you must of course go—But I think it would be unfortunate to have (a) anyone interested in S[acco].V[anzetti]. stimulate a call from either the Gov. or the Comm., or (b) to have you go before either under such circumstances.

3. Auntie B. came back Tuesday evening physically fatigued,[1] but in joyous spirits, which have [*] since.

4. I have found since our talk on Communism a passage once quoted by me from Achad [*sic*] Ha-Am which indicates that the remarkable quality of living for the future salvation of the class— as distinguished from the individual—is a Jewish trait.

1. Elizabeth Glendower Evans was very active on behalf of Sacco and Vanzetti. Indeed, Frankfurter credited her with awakening his own interest in the case. See *Felix Frankfurter Reminisces*, 209-10. See also LDB to Frankfurter, 5 August 1927.

To Felix Frankfurter

July 28, 1927 Chatham, Mass. [Frankfurter Mss—HLS]

1. We are glad to know that you & Marion plan to be here again before Aug. 15. Elizabeth & Paul are due here August 1st & I am sure E. will be eager to talk with you about the course on Labor Legislation which, to her joy, [John R.] Commons has asked her to give, as well as other things.

2. Was J.R.'s S[acco].V[anzetti] ch[ec]k spontaneous? [1] Or did J.W.M[ack] promote it?

3. Syracuse L[aw].S[chool]. was thinking of W. G. Rice Jr. a few months ago. Do you know whether they asked him? [2]

4. That['s] good of Lippmann on S.V.

5. Has any adequate study been made of the exercise of the Pardoning Power in the United States? Could the Commonwealth Fund be induced to put the appropriate man on an intensive study of its exercise by the President—with special reference to the grounds; i.a. miscarriage in court proceedings? If that were done, it might be easier to get like studies started for each of the states, which should follow.

6. Some one, with the competence, ought to be put also into the job of collecting American causes celebres—miscarriages of justice as evidenced by pardons or otherwise. Such a collection would make much easier the S.V. struggles of the future.

7. Elizabeth writes that Prof. Commons says he remembers my having used in some writing something like the phrase, "Reasonable value is welfare economics." Did I, & if so, where? Commons wants to use it as a motto for his new book.[3]

1. Probably a contribution to the defense fund by Mack's friend, the philanthropist Julius Rosenwald.

2. LDB's former law clerk remained at the University of Wisconsin.

3. The only book Commons published in 1927, a revision of his earlier work with John B. Andrews, *Principles of Labor Legislation* (New York, 1927), appeared without a motto from LDB.

To Felix Frankfurter

August 1, 1927 Chatham, Mass. [Frankfurter Mss—HLS]

Upon reading your & [James M.] Landis' Business, the sense of its significance is deepened. The appearance of the book with an adequate index will be an event of importance in American law.[1] The story is so interestingly told that it will be read. It brings together, for the first time, the facts necessary to an understanding of what is; and it is fertile in suggestion of what should be. The disclosure of sources consulted carries proof of imagination as well as thoroughness. The influence of the book, direct & indirect will be widespread. It must induce many to try and do likewise. And it sets the pace. When it is supplemented by the further studies which it suggests we shall really begin to know how the administration of our law can be bettered.

I assume No. 100 39 H[arvard]L[aw]R[eview]. pp 57–8 has been modified by Holmes J. sitting in Boston & the C[hief].J[ustice]. in Norfolk a few years ago.

Do you recall Abbe [*]'s definition of eloquence—"The art of saying Everything without going to the Bastille."

1. *The Business of the Supreme Court.* See LDB to Frankfurter 2 June 1925, n. 1.

To Felix Frankfurter

August 5, 1927 Chatham, Mass. [Frankfurter Mss—HLS]

Wednesday's action came as a complete surprise to all of us except Jack [Gilbert], who had felt sure, from his experiences, that the decision would be what it has proved.[1] Auntie B. telephones that she will not be here again before Monday Aug. 15th—I assume you also will be bound up with S[acco].V[anzetti]. for the immediate future & must postpone Marion & your visit to Chatham. But we shall hope that there will be merely a short postponement. Let us know.

You & Auntie B. have played noble parts.[2]

Samuel Rubin's address is 111 No. Charles St. Baltimore.

1. Governor Fuller announced his findings on 4 August. His view was that Sacco and Vanzetti had received a fair trial and that their execution must be carried out. The date was set for 10 August, but it was later postponed until 22 August.

2. See LDB to Frankfurter, 22 July 1927, n. 1. Hours before the execution on 22 August, the defense lawyers appeared in Chatham to ask LDB to issue a stay. He met them on the porch of his summer home and told them that, for personal reasons, he could not agree to have any part of the case. Probably he was led to this conclusion by the fact that both Alice and Susan Brandeis were active in the controversy, as were his close friend Frankfurter and his frequent houseguest Mrs. Evans—all arrayed on the side of the defense. Such intimate connection with one side of the case, LDB felt, precluded any sort of judicial determination on his part. See the front page story in the *New York Times*, 22 August 1927.

To Jacob deHaas

August 23, 1927 Chatham, Mass. [Brodie Mss]

DEH: I have just finished your Herzl.[1]

To what I said the other day,[2] this should be added: You have told a great story in the grand manner. It has dignity and self-restraint—the majesty of truth. It has high dramatic quality. One shares the exaltation and senses the hastening doom. It is the Jewish Tragedy.

1. Jacob deHaas, *Theodor Herzl*, 2 vols. (Chicago, 1927).
2. LDB had received the book on 18 August, and after reading a few chapters he wrote deHaas: "Your task has been nobly performed. In style it is your best. It manifests grasp and penetration. It carries conviction. It is informing. And (so far as I have gone) always interesting."

To Felix Frankfurter

August 24, 1927 Chatham, Mass. [Frankfurter Mss—HLS]

1. To the end, you have done all that was possible for you.[1] And that all was more than would have [been]possible for any other person I know. But the end of S.V. is only the beginning. "They know not what they do".

2. When you and Marion shall have read deHaas' "Herzl"—let me know whether I am wrong in thinking that it is a great biography.[2] I had no conception that he could do it.

3. When we meet, remind me to tell you of my talk with [James M.] Nicely about his future.

4. Re Criminal Survey: I forget whether I wrote you: the testimony of State's evidence accomplices should go into the discard with the twin abominations—spies and third degree.

5. Be sure now to take all the rest you can before Term begins.

6. If we do not see you & Marion here before then (and in any event) bear in mind that we plan to leave here on Sept. 8. And shall hope you two can dine with us at the Bellevue that evening. Our plan is to leave Boston for Washington the next evening (Friday).

7. All your enclosures have gone to the Law School with a "Please do not forward".

1. Sacco and Vanzetti were executed on 22 August 1927.
2. See preceding letter.

To Alfred Brandeis

September 20, 1927 Charlottesville, Va. [Brandeis Mss, M 4–4]

DEAR AL: Alice was so enterprising as to bring me up here today, mostly in order to see Monticello tomorrow

We look out upon it from this room, three miles away, over the lovely rolling country which you know.

I have just been rambling about the town, with its old houses like, or a little better than, Louisville's near-best of half a century ago; with some old men & women quite of that time—and their young girls and boys indistinguishable from those of their own age in the North.

In all that is old here there is a distinction—quiet dignity and assurance that they are of the best. And I had a touch of the old time hospitality, being invited into a club, before which I was gazing upon a table[t] recording the Revolutionary exp[l]oit of a Jouett.[1]

The hotel is amidst the court buildings; & it is good to see the old time law offices from which even the omnipresent typewriter cannot remove the inherent calm.[2]

1. The tablet commemorated John Jouett (1754–1822), who galloped forty miles to warn Jefferson and the Virginia legislature of the approaching British in 1779.
2. See next letter.

To Alfred Brandeis

September 22, 1927 Washington, D.C. [Brandeis Mss, M 4–4]

DEAR AL: 1. I hope Davis' hesitations will be overcome. It is just the people who have a realization of the requirements of the office of Trustee, and a conscience as to performing the duties, that we need.[1]

2. We are looking forward to the ham.

3. I am sending your bookseller's card to deHaas, so that he can make sure that his actual & potential wants are satisfied.

4. Returned home last evening with deepest conviction of T[homas].J[efferson].'s greatness.[2] He was a civilized man.

5. I had at Charlottesville some glimpses of old Louisville, i.a. a whitewashed coal shed with a linden tree beside it which visibly recalled our First Street House. Dust-laden scattered court papers in inadequate book cases with broken panes of glass & forbidding plastered walls in the entrance to the Court House, which were [sic] the replica of much in Louisville 50 years ago. But with few exceptions, public as well as private buildings have cleanliness & up-to-dateness. I know of no American city which has so well retained the fine in its character despite growth in recent years.

6. Enclosed from Berea may interest you.

1. No one named Davis was appointed to the Board of Trustees for the University of Louisville during this period.

2. See preceding letter. On this date, LDB wrote Felix Frankfurter: 'Alice & I have spent a day at Charlottesville to see Monticello & the University. It is strong confirmation that T.J. was greatly civilized. Washington, Jefferson, Franklin, Hamilton were indeed a Big Four."

To Alice Harriet Grady

September 22, 1927 Washington, D.C. [Grady Mss]

AHG: Yes, the loss of a group insurance project is not very serious.

This month's figures are impressive—in time these results will prove irresistible. As President [Charles W.] Eliot said: "It takes a generation to introduce a new idea into most men's heads".

Some of your fellow citizens could be guaranteed to wear even longer than that.

Mrs. Brandeis & I went for a day to Charlottesville to pay homage (at Monticello & the University) to Thomas Jefferson. He would have had no difficulty in appreciating S[avings].B[ank]. I[nsurance].

Your ad. was admirable, and should add many policies.

To Alfred Brandeis

September 26, 1927 Washington, D.C. [Brandeis Mss, M 4–4]

DEAR AL: 1. It's fine to have such good reports from you & Jennie.

2. Alice has wanted us to make a trip to Charlottesville ever since the Sesqui[1] accentuated interest in Jefferson. Last week weather & other conditions were so favorable that even you could not have invented an excuse.

3. The John Sharp Williams item is a strong ad. for the preservative qualities of whiskey.[2]

4. Yes—I was at Great Falls several times in 1913–14.

5. Alice & I were on the canal above Chain bridge again yesterday, for a paddle & longer stay, lunching al fresco near a bubbling brook over which mother would have been in raptures.

6. You seem to be having a great demand for farm products. Weather perfect here.

1. The 150th anniversary of American independence had been celebrated in 1926 with a variety of events.

2. The former Mississippi Senator was seventy-three and about to celebrate his fiftieth wedding anniversary.

To Felix Frankfurter

September 26, 1927 Washington, D.C. [Frankfurter Mss—HLS]

These Chinese cases present food for Civil Liberties Ass[ociatio]n activity.[1] Some steps should be taken, through Chinese minister, consuls or otherwise, to help Chinese to better counsel.

Some way should be pursued to make the Federal official suffer for such illegal acts. And to make sure, through Congress or otherwise that illegalities such as here condemned do not go unnoticed.

Re Lawrence Brooks.[2] G.W.A[nderson]. should talk to him.

1. There were a number of cases involving Chinese, many of them centering on questions of admission into the United States (275 *U.S.* 475 [1927]) or the rights of naturalized citizens of Chinese descent (275 *U.S.* 78 [1927]). Unfortunately it is impossible to tell to which cases LDB refers, or even whether these particular cases were before the Supreme Court.

2. Perhaps Lawrence Graham Brooks (1881–19[?]), the son of John

Graham Brooks, the sociologist. Lawrence Brooks was a Massachusetts lawyer; in 1928 he accepted appointment as a special justice of the first district court of eastern Middlesex County.

To Hattie Bishop Speed

October 9, 1927 Washington, D.C. [Speed Mss]

MY DEAR MISS HATTIE: With your consent, Alice and I wish to give to the University and place in its Museum,[1] as an example of Kentucky art, the Brenner which you and Mr. Speed gave us.[2]

We are also giving to the University, and wish to place in the Museum, some examples of ancient and foreign art and craftsmanship which, in the long years, have come to us through like generosity. Alice is enclosing the list.[3] All are now at Ladless;[4] and with them data as to origin.

We are glad to think that we may have some association with your noble gift to the University and hope that you will deem ours a worthy contribution.　Most cordially,

1. The museum was a gift of Mrs. Speed, in memory of her husband. See LDB to Fannie Brandeis, 14 February 1925.
2. See LDB to Alfred Brandeis, 10 July 1912, n. 6.
3. LDB and his wife gave the J. B. Speed Museum six items, besides the Brenner painting. They ranged from a 14th-century Japanese sword to two volumes of Plutarch.
4. "Ladless" was Alfred Brandeis's farm in Louisville.

To Alfred Brandeis

October 15, 1927 Washington, D.C. [Brandeis Mss, M 4–4]

DEAR AL: 1. Enclosed postal, will interest Jennie, Fanny & Jean. It represents a manuscript recently discovered in Central Europe & secured by the Congressional Library—the earliest, I think, of musical mss., & has been deciphered by Dr. [*] whom Fanny will remember. Tell her to keep it for the homecoming.

2. Charlie N[agel]. made a brief argument in our Court yesterday. He has been in & out of the Court room most of the week. He is in fine form—& in appearance, manner, mannerisms, walk, clothes and attitudes is exactly the C.N. of 50 years ago.

There is really little sign of aging except the grayness in hair & moustache. Yetti Hegman would have said: "Er sieht sich selbst lächerlich ähnlich." [1]

3. Have had no time yet to give consideration to the list of historical books submitted by Colvin.[2]

4. In the St. Louis case one Theodore Rassieur, presumably a son of Leo, made an uncommonly good argument.[3] He is a better lawyer than Leo as I remember him.

5. You can tell Otto [Wehle] that his cousin Godfrey Goldmark,[4] also was before our Court yesterday & that he is an uncommonly good lawyer.

1. "He looks comically like himself." See n. 3 below.

2. President George Colvin had submitted a list of books which the University of Louisville Library badly needed.

3. Leo Rassieur (1844–1929) was a Russian immigrant who settled in St. Louis. After private practice in the law, he served a term as probate judge. Theodore Rassieur made his argument in *State of Missouri, ex rel. St. Louis Brewing Association* v. *Public Service Commission of Missouri and Union Electric Light and Power Company* on 14 October. This was one of a series of related cases—it was in one of the others that Charles Nagel made his appearance. The Court dismissed all for lack of jurisdiction. See 275 *U.S.* 489 (1927).

4. Godfrey Goldmark (1880–1968) was the son of Ida Wehle and Adolf Goldmark. He was a New York City corporation lawyer.

To Felix Frankfurter

October 29, 1927 Washington, D.C. [Frankfurter Mss—HLS]

1. Norman H[apgood] was in last evening & seems ready to write on S[acco].V[anzetti]. if Ehrmann [1] will cooperate.[2]

2. Our four weeks of hearings has made a deep cut into the general list. We have reached the July 1, '26 filings. At this rate we ought be hearing Oct-Nov/27 entries on [*sic*] April & May.

3. Cert[iorari]s have been so demanding that we set apart this Friday afternoon & that of the previous weeks for certs., leaving the Saturday conference for argued & submitted cases. We shall carry about 95 certs into the recess & plan to have conferences each Saturday during the recess so as to clean up the lot by Nov. 21.

4. You will note from the P[er].C[uriam]. that quite a number of the Certs. in 1925–6, appear to have been improvidently granted. Some day you must have an article in H[arvard]L[aw] R[eview]. reviewing the Cert. work since Feb 13, 1925 act, and another article on the P.C.'s.

5. I am glad Arthur Hill has declined pay in the S.V. case.[3]

6. Holmes is in fine shape.

1. Herbert Brutus Ehrmann (1891–1970), like LDB himself, was born in Louisville, graduated from Harvard Law School, and set up practice in Boston. Also, like LDB he interested himself in labor policy and arbitration. He was associated with William G. Thompson (see LDB to Frankfurter, 28 January 1928, n. 3) in the defense of Sacco and Vanzetti, as junior counsel. He was active in the American Jewish Committee, eventually becoming its president.

2. No signed article by Hapgood appeared. However, Ehrmann (see preceding note) wrote about the case in two books. The first, *The Untried Case* (New York, 1933), was written at the instigation of Hapgood (see p. xi), and it concentrates on the aspect of the trial concerned with the Madeiros confession (see LDB to Frankfurter, 29 April 1927, n. 1) and the Morelli gang. The second book, *The Case That Will Not Die: Commonwealth* v. *Sacco and Vanzetti* (Boston, 1969), was written after Ehrmann's retirement from active practice; it covers the entire case.

3. Arthur Dehon Hill (1869–1947) had become chief counsel for Sacco and Vanzetti after the resignation of William G. Thompson in 1927.

To Alfred Brandeis

October 31, 1927 Washington, D.C. [Brandeis Mss, M 4–4]

DEAR AL: 1. Yours of 29th with enclosures brings interesting material re U[niversity]. of L[ouisville]. I had seen nothing of the Report on Colvin, as I do not read the N.Y. Times regularly here.[1]

2. If you care to feed your hostility to France re debts to U.S., you can read in Claude Bowers' account of "The Party Battles of the Jackson Period", of France's behavior concerning the agreed payment on account of French spoliation claims.[2] But that book may pain you by its account of Henry Clay's performances.

3. I am sending you weekly the Editorial Research Reports, which are to go always to Elizabeth when you have finished with them.

4. Susie Goldmark is still with us & in better form, I think, than she has been for a quarter of a century.

5. Norman Hapgood was in yesterday with Milton[3] of the Chattanooga Sentinal & much talk on politics. Norman's Life of Smith is to appear Nov 3 (Up from the City Streets).[4]

1. There is no mention of either Colvin or the University of Louisville in the *New York Times Index* for these months.

2. Claude G. Bowers, *The Party Battles of the Jackson Period* (Cambridge, Mass., 1922), ch. 14.

3. Probably George Fort Milton (1894–1955), who was editor of the *Chattanooga News* from 1919 to 1939. Milton was perhaps best known for his historical studies of the Civil War and Reconstruction.

4. Norman Hapgood and Henry Moskowitz, *Up From the City Streets: Alfred E. Smith, A Biographical Study of Contemporary Politics* (New York, 1927).

To Alfred Brandeis

November 2, 1927 Washington, D.C. [Brandeis Mss, M 4-4]

DEAR AL: 1. Susan, Jack, Louis and Britta (the nurse) arrive in due time. This is the young man's first birthday.[1]

2. Susie Goldmark left at 11. this morning.

3. Hapgood will be glad to see Barrett's letter.

4. I note that you expect to have meeting with Laurent soon & will send AAUP Report soon.[2]

5. If O'Neal is elected,[3] it will do much toward clearing the University situation.   Gruesse,

I assume you thought as much yesterday of our trip to the Husarrenberg as I did.[4] The 55 years make a difference in us as well as in things external.

You and Jennie will be interested in reading this letter of Miss Grady which shows what a rawboned high school girl earning $10 a week 33 years ago has developed into. Wheeler's Point is in Gloucester. Talmage [*sic*] is her brother.

1. Louis Brandeis Gilbert was LDB's first grandson.

2. See LDB to Alfred Brandeis, 23 January 1927, n. 2.

3. Joseph Thomas O'Neal (1881–1944) did win election as Louisville's mayor, defeating W. B. Harrison. O'Neal was a graduate of the University of Louisville Law School.

4. See LDB to Alfred Brandeis, 1 November 1889, n. 4.

To Alfred Brandeis

November 5, 1927 Washington, D.C. [Brandeis Mss, M 4–4]

DEAR AL: 1. Re proposed letter to [E. S.] Jouett. I think it unwise either to write to him or to talk with him on this subject, unless he initiates the subject. His term expires, as I recall, in March/28. If O'Neal is elected on Tuesday,[1] it will probably be wise to supplant Jouett when there is an opportunity. He certainly is not a friend of our projects.

2. I hope you are wrong on your Alf. E. Smith guess. I can't believe that Ky or other southern states (except possibly Tenn) will vote against him if he is the Democratic nominee.[2] I "yearn" to live through another Democratic administration.

3. I have recd from Dean Anderson the [*] Com[mit]tee Report. It is comprehensive & complete consideration of G[eorge]. C[olvin]. & his Board.

1. See preceding letter.
2. Alfred Brandeis's prediction was correct. In 1928 Al Smith carried most of the deep South but lost the border states, including Kentucky (59% to 41%) and Tennessee (55% to 45%).

To Felix Frankfurter

November 5, 1927 Washington, D.C. [Frankfurter Mss – HLS]

1. It is eminently appropriate that copies of "Business" be sent to the C[hief].J[ustice]. & Van[Devanter].[1] [Edward Terry] Sanford is interested in production & would no doubt appreciate the courtesy. As to [Harlan F.] Stone, you will know what your relations suggest.

2. I suggest your sending a copy to Ex Senator [William E.] Chilton who did service in 1916, as chairman of the Subcommittee.[2] He called on me last week & I found he had developed finely in these years of aging. He & his sons have a very profitable & enterprising paper at Charleston West Va or Wheeling;[3] & he would doubtless give the book due notice there besides appreciating the attention.

3. That's good about Paul Mazur & Karl Llewellyn.[4]

4. Your letter to Mack re [Thomas] Nelson Perkins is excellent.

5. George Rublee was in. He is keen for Mexico & plans to leave for there next week.[5]

6. You will doubtless hear from JWM[ack] & from deH[aas] about our "conference" this AM. Sam Rosensohn, [Norvin R.] Lindheim, Berenson, Bob Szold, [Abraham] Tulin & [Israel B.] Brodie were also present. [Rabbi Stephen] Wise promised to come, but didn't.

1. See LDB to Frankfurter, 1 August 1927.

2. The subcommittee that held hearings on LDB's nomination; see LDB to Norman Hapgood, 1 February 1916, n. 2.

3. The *Charleston Gazette*.

4. Paul Myer Mazur (b. 1892) was a New York investment banker. He also wrote several books analyzing America's economy. Karl Nickerson Llewellyn (1893–1962) left private practice in 1922 to teach law first at Yale and then for extended periods at Columbia and the University of Chicago as well. Llewelyn was probably best known for his contributions to legal philosophy, particularly his defense of judicial "realism." See his "Some Realism About Realism," 44 *Harvard Law Review* 1234 (1931).

5. Rublee (see LDB to Norman Hapgood, 27 February 1910, n. 5) served as legal advisor to the American embassy in Mexico City, 1928–1930.

To Henrietta Szold

November 10, 1927 Washington, D.C. [H. Szold Mss]

My dear Miss Szold: You know that my good wishes attend you.[1] I write solely to repeat this: You will serve our great cause best by keeping yourself most fit—keeping your head as clear as your heart. Resolve each day to avoid fatigue. Refrain from concerning yourself with detail. Consult, in case of doubt, those staunch, honest Americans whom you have found ever faithful.

1. Miss Szold, who had been visiting the United States, was about to return to Palestine.

To Felix Frankfurter

November 13, 1927 Washington, D.C. [Frankfurter Mss—HLS]

1. My thanks to you & Landis for "Business"—an impressive volume, which came on the birthday eve;[1] and to you & Marion for the greeting which came this morning.

2. Upton Sinclair, who was here Friday & Norman [Hapgood], who was here a week earlier, will both help to keep S[acco]. V[anzetti]. alive.[2]

3. The Burns-Sinclair incident [3] should make it easier to induce Sen. Tom Walsh and Sen. [Burton] Wheeler to take up the detective abuse [4] and for the [New York] World to push it. I suppose Hitz [5] told you about Burns['s] attempt to get at the file at Dep. of Justice during [Thomas W.] Gregory's administration & the disappearance of the papers incriminating B. in the Oregon matter, during the Daugherty regime.[6]

4. As to Certiorari in Goodman et al. Holmes J. is incorrigible when there is an opportunity of curbing the power & province of a jury.[7] And the worst is yet to come.

5. I have asked [Henry J.] Friendly to send to [you] from time to time instances of P.C.'s & of Certs. granted or denied that deserve study.

6. O[liver]W[endell]H[olmes] is in his best form. Yesterday (& it was after a 4½ hour conference i.e. until 5 PM): "I found some years ago that I began to puff on walking, but I have not observed yet that I get more fatigued in work or using my mind." He was never more fresh in conference.

7. Sutherland is reported better,[8] but the Chief thinks he should make up his mind not to come back to work before spring. His wife is sicker than he is now. And Van Devanter has had a stroke which bears heavily upon him. But his work in conference is unimpaired.

8. Weiz[mann]. got up a grand dinner to Lord Balfour, which has some advantages to the cause. But the Jewish multitude is beginning to catch on.

1. See LDB to Frankfurter, 1 August 1927; 13 November marked LDB's seventy-first birthday.

2. Upton Beall Sinclair (1878–1968), the famous muckraking novelist whose *The Jungle* (New York, 1906) won him enduring fame, continued to turn out topical novels. His book on the Sacco and Vanzetti case was *Boston, A Novel* (New York, 1928).

3. The newspapers were suddenly full of a new scandal in the aftermath of the Teapot Dome frauds. It was revealed on 2 November that the notorious W. J. Burns Detective Agency had been employed by Harry F. Sinclair to tamper with the jury in the trial. The judge immediately declared a mistrial, and the grand jury began examining the jury tampering charges.

4. See LDB to Frankfurter, 24 January 1926.

5. William Hitz (1872–1935) graduated from Georgetown University Law School in 1900 and practiced in Washington, D.C. In 1914 he worked for the Justice Department, and two years later he began a fifteen year service on the Supreme Court of the District of Columbia. In 1931 he was named a justice of the Court of Appeals for Washington, D.C.

6. In 1909 Burns had probably tampered with another jury in Oregon, in a land fraud case. The man thereby convicted, one Willard N. Jones of Portland, was pardoned after an investigation of Burns's activities by Attorney General Wickersham in 1911. Under Daugherty, Burns had been appointed head of the secret service.

7. The Goodman case involved the death of a man who had driven a truck across a railroad crossing, and been struck by a speeding train. The jury had awarded damages to the widow, and the railroad had appealed on the basis that the man had been negligent, thus contributing to his own death. Holmes, speaking for the Court, reversed the jury decision, finding for the railroad. *Baltimore & Ohio Railroad* v. *Goodman*, 275 *U.S.* 66 (1927).

8. Sutherland had fallen ill at the beginning of October; he did not return to the Court until 3 January 1928.

To Alice Harriet Grady

November 18, 1927 Washington, D.C. [Grady Mss]

A.H.G.: 1. Do you know Mr. Bang. Judging from what LaFollette's says he ought to be one who would not only appreciate S[avings].B[ank].I[nsurance]., but might become an effective ally.

2. Mr. Nesbit [1] was in Tuesday & it was a real pleasure to see him. He seems young again & vigorous—a real renaissance.

Mr. Phillips might enjoy this, re admission of applicant to the G[eorgi]a bar.

Examination oral. 3 questions:

1. (An abstruse one on real property)
2. (One on the law of contracts)
3. What was your mother's maiden name.

The rule required that 2 out of 3 be answered correctly.

Applicant answered:

1. Wrong
2. I don't know
3. Margaret Richardson.

The examiner found that he answered 2 & 3 correctly & therefore admitted him.

1. Perhaps Charles Francis Nesbit (1867–1934), an insurance expert and adviser of Washington, D.C. Nesbit served the government in several advisory capacities and also was a consultant, on insurance matters, to several labor unions.

To Felix Frankfurter

November 21, 1927 Washington, D.C. [Frankfurter Mss—HLS]

1. 67 & 68 enclosed will interest you & Landis.[1]

2. The N[ew].R[epublic]. has properly taken Al. Smith to task in his attitude toward Estate tax.[2] It is strangely doctrinaire. How did it happen.

3. Lovett has not done the Herzl credit.[3] I hope Norman [Hapgood] will do better in the Nation.[4]

4. I am glad to see N.R. paying its respects to Burns.[5]

5. We clean up today all cert[iorari]s. presented prior to day [sic]. Some have been denied which should not have been. Some expansions in the orders will interest you.

6. John Dewey on the Lowell report [6] reminds of Ben Butler's interjection when a Harvard Medical School Prof. was being qualified as an expert in a will case: "So you are a professor at the Harvard Medical School. We hung one of those for murder not long ago."

7. Louis Glavis, who was in today, says there is a lot of stuff on Burns in N.Y. where there was an effort 7–8 years ago to take away his state license.

8. It's fine to hear of Thompson's expedition & the happy results.

9. We had Gardner Jackson's sister in to dine yesterday.[7]

10. Harlan F. S[tone]. says that the incriminating report was in the Dep. of Justice in his day, was read by him, that thereupon he fired Burns and 30 of his henchmen who had "criminal records"—which I understand means, had been sentenced for some cause.

Tell Marion that Elizabeth is now a PhD. There is much enthusiasm at Madison about her thesis.[8]

1. No. 67 was *City of Hammond* v. *Schappi Bus Line, Inc.*, 275 U.S. 164 (1927); and No. 68 was *City of Hammond* v. *Farina Bus Line & Transpor-*

tation Co., 275 *U.S.* 173 (1927). Two bus companies contended that a Hammond, Indiana, city ordinance discriminated against them. For a unanimous Court, LDB returned the case to a lower court for further proceedings on the grounds that the matter was "not yet ripe for decision" by the Supreme Court.

2. The editors condemned Smith for joining those who were attempting to repeal the federal estate tax. Smith argued that such a tax was properly within the sphere of state power. The editors contended that such a line of reasoning was designed to help millionaires avoid taxes in inheritance-tax-free states, like Florida. "It is a pity that the Governor's first essay in national politics should commit him to the support of such an unprogressive and shabby cause." *New Republic* 53 (23 November 1927): 3.

3. For Robert Morss Lovett's review of deHaas's biography of Herzl, see "A Leader of Zion," *New Republic* 53 (23 November 1927): 21–22.

4. Norman Hapgood, "A Hero of the Jews," *The Nation* 125 (7 December 1927): 645–46.

5. *New Republic* 53 (23 November 1927): 1–2. "If the latest charges against him are upheld, Mr. William J. Burns . . . will have forfeited all claim to the respect of honest Americans." The editorial was a thorough denunciation of Burns's activities in the Sinclair jury-tampering case (see LDB to Frankfurter, 13 November 1927).

6. John Dewey, "Psychology and Justice," *New Republic* 53 (23 November 1927): 9–12. In the essay, Dewey attempted to explore the state of mind of the three members of Governor Fuller's advisory committee in the Sacco and Vanzetti case.

7. Gardner Jackson (1897–1965) was a newspaperman and a sometime public official. The son of wealthy parents, he graduated from Harvard in 1921 and went to work for the *Boston Globe*. He quit his job in order to work full time for Sacco and Vanzetti. In President Franklin Roosevelt's first administration, Jackson accepted a job in the Agricultural Adjustment Agency but left after a quarrel with Henry Wallace. His sister was Edith Banfield Jackson (b. 1895), a noted pediatrician.

8. "The Wage-Earner and the Common Rule—A Study in the Employer-Employee Relation." The degree was awarded in 1928.

To Robert D. Kesselman

November 27, 1927 Washington, D.C. [Kesselman Mss]

MY DEAR KESSELMAN: Re yours of Nov 2.

It was good of you and the family to send birthday greetings.

I am pained to know that the general depression in Palestine has affected you personally so severely.[1] A talk with Miss Szold, shortly before she sailed,[2] brought me the first word of this; and what she told of the arrangement with Price, Waterhouse &

Co led me to believe that the immediate situation had been taken care of. I hope that her arrival has helped to overcome the obstacles to which you refer.

I am calling the matter to the attention of our New York friends; and am asking deHaas to speak of your affairs to Israel Brodie who is to sail shortly. I think it desirable that you should discuss the matter frankly with him. He shares our views as to Palestine development and has shown himself wise in many ways.

It would be a misfortune to Palestine as well as to yourself for you to leave after these many years of service on the firing line. You are among the few significant human contributions which America has made to the force for upbuilding; and there will be great need of your aid in the trying time immediately before us, and the brighter days, which I am confident, lie only a little beyond. Miss Szold will, from what she told me, turn much to you for counsel and aid; and I hope will be able also to aid in securing for you work which you are so well fitted to do. Show her this letter, if you care to do so; and also to Mohl [3] and Nathan Kaplan. I hope the latter will have fully recovered his strength before this reaches you.

There is this consolation in the present lamentable condition: It would have been more disastrous to the future development of Palestine and our great cause, if prosperity had come under an administration [4] which combined with self-seeking, dishonesty, unwisdom and incompetence.   Most cordially,

1. Kesselman (see LDB to Benjamin Perlstein, 30 July 1915) was an accountant; he had moved to Palestine in the early 1920s.

2. See LDB to Henrietta Szold, 10 November 1927.

3. Emanuel N. Mohl (1883–19[?]), an American-trained engineer, was the officer in charge of the Palestine Industrial Survey. He later held several advisory positions in the Palestine administration.

4. of the Zionist Organization of America.

To Alfred Brandeis

November 29, 1927 Washington, D.C. [Brandeis Mss. M 4–4]

DEAR AL: Re yours of 25th

1. I think the decisions on these matters submitted had better be deferred until you & I shall have had full talk on U[niversity].

matters when you come here for Christmas holidays. I suggest, therefore, that you say nothing definitely, either way, to anyone connected with the U.—answering tactfully that you will discuss the matter with me then.

2. I have only this to add: Don't be too discouraged. The future has many good things in store for those who can wait, and have patience and exercise good judgment. There are likely to be fortunate as well as unfortunate accidents. There is nothing more probable than that some improbable things, or even the seeming impossible, will happen. "My faith is great in time, and that which shapes it to its perfect end". And men in a fight should remember that Napoleon's Old Guard "never resigned and seldom died". If Arthur Allen had held his place, we should be in much better fix today.[1]

3. I enclose letter to Charles [Tachau], which please mail after reading & making copies.

As you may not have seen Charles to me of 11/26 I am enclosing same. Please return it.

1. See LDB to Alfred Brandeis, 16 January 1927, n. 2.

To Felix Frankfurter

December 6, 1927 Washington, D.C. [Frankfurter Mss—HLS]

1. No. 169 will interest you.[1] Enclosed.

2. Among yesterday's shower of P[er].C[uriam].s are several worthy of H[arvard].L[aw].R[eview]. notes—and one, Standard Oil Co v. City of Lincoln, which should be blazoned in an article.[2]

The C[our]t has gone the whole hog on State & municipal trading. Properly used this decision may put to shame the State Courts which have narrowed the function.

In view of the grip of big business & the Ct's limitations on public utilities regulation, this way out should be opened wide. The threat of State & municipal action may develop curbs on greed which the regulative power is prevented from applying.

3. What do you know of Albert Jay Nock? His Jefferson is a worthy contribution.[3]

4. I suppose you have seen the irrepressible Judge Wade on S[acco].V[anzetti].[4]

5. We had Henry W. Edgerton in yesterday.[5]

1. No. 169 was *Bothwell et al. v. Buckbee Mears Co.*, 275 *U.S.* 274 (1927). This was a complex case involving an insurance company and the interstate commerce regulations. LDB wrote the opinion for a unanimous Court.

2. *Standard Oil Co. and Claude E. Sharp* v. *City of Lincoln*, 275 *U.S.* 504 (1927). The case involved the attempt by the city of Lincoln, Nebraska, to establish a municipal gas station which would dispense gas at cost. For the arguments, see 114 *Neb.* 243. The *Harvard Law Review* did not deal with the case or with the High Court's handling of it *per curiam.*

3. Albert Jay Nock (1870–1945) had come up through muckraking journalism and *The Nation* to found his own magazine, *The Freeman*, in 1920. After 1924, he devoted himself to writing books, and chief among them, perhaps, was *Jefferson* (New York, 1926). Nock was a believer in weak central government, agrarian virtues, and Henry George's single tax theories. See his autobiography, *Memoirs of a Superfluous Man* (New York, 1943).

4. Perhaps Martin Joseph Wade (1861–1931), a U.S. District Court judge for Iowa since 1915.

5. Henry White Edgerton (1888–1970), a graduate of the Harvard Law School, practiced in Boston before joining the faculty of the George Washington Law School in 1921. In 1938 he began thirty years of service as Circuit Court of Appeals judge for Washington, D.C.

To Felix Frankfurter

December 11, 1927 Washington, D.C. [Frankfurter Mss—HLS]

1. To your good mother you have been a good son, and a never-failing source of happiness. Give her our love. To my mother came the same affliction and at the same age.[1]

2. O[liver]W[endell]H[olmes]. closes this sitting in fine form and with practically no work ahead for the next three weeks.

3. Sutherland says he will return to the job Jan 3.[2]

4. When you see No. 559—Hunter v. State of Louisiana in the Journal of cases argued, and decided, bear in mind that it was entered in our Court Oct. 26 & argued last week.[3]

5. I was told by an insider, that his associates, railroad & business men, who were eager to have the Sherman Law liberalized were advised by William [*sic*] Gordon Merritt [4] to let it alone

as it is the only means of curbing labor & that since then they
have been quiescent.

1. Emma Winter Frankfurter died on 10 January 1928, at the age of
seventy-four.
2. See LDB to Frankfurter, 13 November 1927, n. 7.
3. *Henry Hunter* v. *State of Louisiana*, 275 *U.S.* 508 (1927).
4. Undoubtedly Walter Gordon Merritt (1880–1968), a New York lawyer specializing in labor relations. See his *Destination Unknown: Fifty Years
of Labor Relations* (New York, 1951).

To Felix Frankfurter

December 20, 1927 Washington, D.C. [Frankfurter Mss—HLS]

Your article will give O[liver].W[endell].H[olmes]. much joy.
It is far in advance of its two predecessors.[1] And its luminous
quality will make it an effective instrument of education.

When we meet, let me tell you of a talk yesterday with
G[eorge].S[utherland]. on conservatism & liberalism in members
of the Court—a subject introduced by G.S. who did the talking.

What is the status of the Injunction Article? [2]

Gifford Pinchot has imported Wells [3] to Washington & is full
of fight.[4] The North Carolina Senators are true to the Mellon
form.[5]

[Walton Hale] Hamilton has his formal appointment at the
Yale L[aw].S[chool].

1. "Mr. Justice Holmes and the Constitution," 41 *Harvard Law Review*
121 (1927). The "two predecessors" were earlier attempts by Frankfurter:
"The Constitutional Opinions of Justice Holmes," 29 *Harvard Law Review*
683 (1916) and "Twenty Years of Mr. Justice Holmes' Constitutional Opinions," 36 *Harvard Law Review* 909 (1923).
2. Felix Frankfurter and Nathan Greene, "The Labor Injunction and
Federal Legislation," 42 *Harvard Law Review* 766 (1929).
3. Perhaps Gifford Pinchot's close adviser on conservation matters, Philip
P. Wells (see LDB to Pinchot, 11 June 1910, n. 1).
4. Probably Pinchot's combativeness related to hearings involving the rate-
making power of the electrical utilities; there were also some rumors about
his running for the Senate from Pennsylvania and even a few about his
trying to capture the Republican nomination for the Presidency.

5. A reference to the views of North Carolina's Senator Furnifold Mc-Lendell Simmons (1854–1940). He served thirty years in the Senate and was the coauthor of the Underwood-Simmons tariff. Simmons's remarks on taxation policy came during the consideration of the Federal Tax Reduction Bill and they carried particular weight since Simmons was the ranking Democrat on the Senate Finance Committee. See *New York Times*, 17 and 18 December 1927.

To Felix Frankfurter

January 12, 1928 Washington, D.C. [Frankfurter Mss—HLS]

1. Yesterday No. 500, Casey v U.S. (Criminal Case) was argued.[1] Petition for cert[iorari]. filed Sept 1/27. Certiorari granted Nov 21, 1927. also

No. 600 Nigro v U.S. (Criminal)—certificate filed Oct 31/27.[2]

Both, as I recall, had been set for the December sitting & were postponed to Jan. because of the important questions involved (Harrison Act) [3] for which the J.J. wanted time.

2. When S[acco].V[anzetti]. fears subside & the appreciation of Civil Liberty revives, possibly interest can be aroused in our project of speaking on Boston Common without a license.[4] Then, it may be well to bear in mind—for those who fear disturbances—what was said in Beatty v. Gillbanks, 15 Cox's C[riminal] C[ases] 138, 146: [5]

"The present decision of the justices amounts to this, that a man may be punished for acting legally if he knows that his so doing may induce another man to act unlawfully—a proposition without any authority to support it."

Thank you much for the Montaigne.

1. *Casey* v. *U.S.* 276 *U.S.* 413 (1928). The case involved a Seattle attorney who was convicted of selling narcotics to prisoners who were his clients. The issue was entrapment because of the use of a federal agent to apprehend the attorney. The case is notable in part because of the revealing difference between Holmes's view and LDB's. Holmes wrote the Court's opinion, upholding the conviction; LDB dissented, not to protect Casey, but to "protect the Government. To protect it from illegal conduct of its officers. To preserve the purity of its courts." (at 425). Samuel J. Konefsky, *The Legacy of Holmes and Brandeis*, 241.

2. *Nigro* v. *U.S.*, 276 U.S. 332 (1928). Another drug-related case, *Nigro* broadened the interpretation of the Harrison Anti-Narcotic Act (see next

note) by prohibiting "any person," and not merely those listed in § 1 of the law, from selling drugs without a written order.

3. The Harrison Anti-Narcotic Act of 1914, 38 *U.S. Stat.* 785, ch. 1.

4. See LDB to Frankfurter, 13 May 1925 and 2 September 1928.

5. This English case of 1882 defined the right of peaceful assembly in an incident involving the Salvation Army.

To Alice Harriet Grady

January 22, 1928 Washington, D.C. [Grady Mss]

A.H.G.: When you have a fight on, one never knows whether to be glad or sorry. Somehow you make the enemies of S[avings]. B[ank].I[nsurance]. pay tribute & we come out a peg or two ahead.[1] And your statement enclosed (to Oct 31/27), gives the best pedestal for ultimate success, which, so far as I recall, we have ever had. "Total expenses 5.54% of the premiums received during the year"—is an admirable record.

I guess Mr. [George L.] Barnes will let you fight now without gloves. And despite absences of old allies, you will enlist a mighty army.

I am very glad you captured Mr. [James L.] Richards.

1. The Savings Bank Life Insurance scheme had to regularly fight off attempts by private insurance companies to cripple it. Usually these attacks took the form of attempting to get the Massachusetts legislature to limit the size of the policy permissible for SBLI. In 1927 the attempt to limit policies to $2,000 and annuities to $400 had been beaten. The fight shaping up for 1928 involved the system reimbursing to the state of Massachusetts all amounts expended by the SBLI Division. It too was defeated.

To Felix Frankfurter

January 28, 1928 Washington, D.C. [Frankfurter Mss—HLS]

1. Do you recall this from Xenophon's Memorabilia?
"Should I be more serviceable to the State, if I took an employment, where function would be wholly bounded in my person, and take up all my time, than I am by instructing everyone, as I do, and in furnishing the Republic with a great number of citizens who are capable to serve her?" [1]

2. As to Goldsmith.[2] Act as usual on your own good judgment. Of course, other things being equal, it is always preferable to take some one whom there is reason to believe will become a law teacher.

3. By the way, if ever you have a first class man available whom H[arvard].L[aw].S[chool]. wont take, let me know. I may find him a desirable berth in some other law school.

4. What do you know of Gregory H[*], who is doing the Legal Research Bureau for the press, as to our opinions?

5. Glad to see the Thompson interview is reproduced in N[ew]. R[epublic].[3]

6. We are very sorry Marion has not been well & glad to know she is well on the mend.

It's rather surprising that the Herald published the Mencken.[4]

1. Bk. 1, ch. 6, par. 15.

2. Irving Baer Goldsmith (b. 1902) had been selected to serve as LDB's next law clerk. After a year in Washington, Goldsmith went into private practice in Chicago. He also lectured at the Northwestern Law School. For LDB's less-than-satisfactory relations with Goldsmith, see LDB to Frankfurter, 7, 12, and 15 October 1928.

3. William Goodrich Thompson (1864–1935) had graduated from Harvard Law School in 1891 and had practiced law in Boston ever since. He frequently taught courses at Harvard and in the 1890s served as Assistant United States Attorney. He was the chief counsel for Sacco and Vanzetti until his resignation in 1927. The article, "Vanzetti's Last Statement," *New Republic* 53 (1 February 1928): 294–96, was reprinted from the *Atlantic Monthly*'s February issue. It recounted a last visit to Vanzetti on the day of his execution.

4. Henry Louis Mencken (1880–1956), "the sage of Baltimore," was at the height of his popularity and influence. A caustic critic of American life, its false standards, and its tawdry politics and cheap literature, Mencken achieved a vogue in the 1920s that he had never previously enjoyed; but his great popularity vanished with the Great Depression. His best outlets were two magazines, *The Smart Set* and, after 1924, *The American Mercury*. The *Boston Herald* had published a piece by Mencken under the title, "Ghosts of Sacco, Vanzetti Sure to Plague Courts." In the article Mencken asserted that despite the hopes of the "Boston Babbitts," the case would not disappear; indeed "the plain fact is that the Sacco-Vanzetti uproar, in its sweetest and worst forms has yet to begin."

To Felix Frankfurter

February 9, 1928 Washington, D.C. [Frankfurter Mss—HLS]

1. When I called on O[liver].W[endell].H[olmes], on the 5th, he seemed more brilliant—sprudelst [1]—than I have seen him for years—ranging with a perfect memory over wide fields of literature. He keenly enjoys now his recesses, which are in the main vacations.

2. I expect to see J.W.M[ack]. tomorrow, en his route to Cincinnati. B[ernard].F[lexner]. was coming here today from Baltimore, but found he [sic] Jonas [Friedenwald] wanted him there all of today.

3. You have not mentioned what I consider the worst of [Charles E.] Hughes' retainers. His effort to set aside the Swift Armour consent decree.[2] Das war gemeins.[3]

4. You spoke last summer of the possibility of getting Evans Clark to write for the N.Y. Times an article on Savings Bank Insurance.[4] With the growing success, Miss Grady is encountering ever more intense opposition in the Legislature, with Henry Lee Shattuck as the devil in chief. If you think you can get Evans Clark to write, you might ask Miss Grady whether she would like that now. King should quickly do his best. Cook gave her a good editorial.

5. [Henry L.] Stimson was very grateful (wrote me from France) for what I had done for him there, but I can't recall what it was.

6. What say you to this, re Chicago crime: "Rich men look sad, and ruffians dance and leap; The one in fear to lose what they enjoy, the other to enjoy by rage & war." Richard II. Act II, Sc. 4.

I am glad of what you wrote [Charles] Merz. We must have official liquidators & receivers.

1. "bubbling, sparkling"
2. In the summer and fall of 1919 the Federal Trade Commission had held hearings over the extent of monopolization in the meat packing industry. Under heavy pressure, Attorney General A. Mitchell Palmer promised speedy prosecution under the antitrust law. But in late 1919 and early 1920 a consent decree issued, which all parties agreed to. It provided that the big companies would divest themselves of many of their operations (cold storage warehouses, retail stores, railroad terminals, market news-

papers) not directly related to meat production. Before long, however, the big meat packers were attempting to set aside some of the provisions of the decree. See Lewis Corey, *Meat and Man: A Study of Monopoly, Unionism and Food Policy* (New York, 1950), ch. 5; see also J. Donald Fewster, "The Packers' Consent Decree," *Harvard Business Review* 8 (April 1930): 346–53.

3. "That was common, vulgar."

4. Evans Clark (1888–19[?]) had come up through journalism, editing several industrial magazines. Between 1925 and 1928 he was a feature writer for the *New York Times*, contributing stories on various business and industry topics. From 1928 until 1953 Evans headed the Twentieth Century Fund. He did not write an article on Savings Bank Insurance for the *New York Times*.

To Felix Frankfurter

February 11, 1928 Washington, D.C. [Frankfurter Mss—HLS]

1. The Margold [1] papers are interesting & sad. If M. concludes not to remain at Harvard, dont let him tie himself up with an agreement to return to practice, until I shall have had an opportunity to suggest his name for a teaching job I have in mind. (Not Louisville.)

2. Senator [Henrik] Shipstead was in last evening. His Anti-injunction bill is the result of his intimacy with Andrew Furuseth who almost lives at the Shipsteads.[2] If the injunction bill (which I haven't seen) is not drawn as it should be, you can doubtless get it changed, as you deem wise. For the subcommittee of the judiciary consists of Tom Walsh, [George W.] Norris and Blaine.[3] Furuseth is also intimate with the LaFollettes—breakfasts there every Sunday.

3. Senator Blaine was in the other day. I took occasion to talk to him and Sen LaFollette jointly on restricting federal jurisdiction whenever they saw a chance. Blaine seemed entirely in accord. I guess it would be a good idea for you to write him a line accompanying "Business".[4]

4. Learned Hand didn't go into detail on diversity of citizenship jurisdiction.[5] But he left the impression that he thought it ought to [be] restricted wherever possible & that he hoped you would tackle the job.

5. As far as I can foresee, I shall not need [Irving B.] Goldsmith before Oct 1. My idea would be to have [Henry J.]

Friendly come here toward the middle or end of September—if
as is usual, there is then some work to be done, & I should like
to have him break in Goldsmith for a day or two. G. will have
a hard time as the successor to F.[6]

Hope Marion's good progress continues.

6. What do you think of the work (Industrial & political) of
the Federal Council of the Churches of Christ. They have lost
their angel & are appealing for help. Should we send them some
money?

1. Nathan Ross Margold (1899–1947) was a Rumanian immigrant who
had come to Frankfurter's attention when he was a student at Harvard.
From 1925 to 1928 he was an instructor at the law school; but he left in
1928 to undertake a wide variety of professional and governmental positions—he worked for the New York City Transit Commission, the Department of Interior, and the NAACP. In 1942 he was appointed judge of the
District Court for Washington, D.C.

2. The Shipstead anti-injunction bill was introduced on 12 December 1927
(S. 1482). Hearings were held in February and March, and they revealed
widespread dissatisfaction with the bill. It was drawn, as LDB indicates, principally by the self-taught seaman Andrew Furuseth, and many Congressmen
who were sympathetic with his aims decided they could not support the
bill. Finally, in May 1928, the judiciary subcommittee called in Frankfurter
and other legislative experts, and they all consulted in isolation until a proper
bill was completed. The measure was reintroduced by George Norris on
29 May 1928, and the new version provided the basis for the legislation that
eventually was enacted. See the very helpful discussion in Irving Bernstein,
The Lean Years: A History of the American Worker, 1920–1933 (Boston,
1960), ch. 11.

3. John James Blaine (1875–1934), former Wisconsin attorney general and
governor, was serving his only term in the Senate.

4. See LDB to Frankfurter, 1 August 1927.

5. See LDB to Frankfurter, 2 April 1925 and 4 and 16 March 1928.

6. See LDB to Frankfurter, 7, 12, and 15 October 1928.

To Felix Frankfurter

February 22, 1928 Washington, D.C. [Frankfurter Mss—HLS]

1. Yes, Laughlin did well.[1]

2. Exhibit B. should earn for [Thomas R.] Powell absolution
for all past sins.

3. Was your talk with R[oscoe].P[ound]. before he had received Powell's letter? & what next?

4. I don't recall the alleged clash with Lowell of fifty years ago. Still it may have occurred. I recall that [C.C.] Langdell considered that A. L[awrence]. L[owell]. & Frank C.J. had committed an unpardonable sin by not staying for the third year. The clash may have occurred in connection with the H[arvard].L[aw]. S[chool]. Ass[ociatio]n celebration in 1886, when undoubtedly I had the say. I have no recollection.

5. Both Harold [Laski] and the Massies told us of [Loring] Christie's being with the Hydroelectric Com[missio]n.

6. You will recall your & my vain enquiries to learn something of one Samuel R. Wachtel[l] who argued so well the Wiener Bank Case against [Charles Evans] Hughes.[2] "Tout vient a qui sait attendre".[3] A week ago a Mrs. Wachtel[l] (who had called previously at the Court & found we were not in session) sent up her name at Florence Court. Having neither Friendly nor Poindexter available, I bade the elevator boy have her come up. A comely youngish woman appeared. The enclosed letter tells the rest. Except the first of my cross-examination. S.R. came to America from Crackow at the age of 13; had a very hard boyhood & youth; got his education at Cooper's Union; intended first to be an engineer; later went into the law; studied law at N.Y. Law School; was admitted 17 years ago; was in the office of Mr. or Judge Mannheim or Manheimer, is now head of the firm of Wachtel, Manheim(er) (son of the judge); & is now 43; has quite a number of foreign clients. Comes home tired after the day's work & loves best music which his wife supplies on the piano. It was quite a sentimental journey episode.

7. An editor of the N[ew].R[epublic]. ought to know better the needs of this democracy than to say: "Next to being corrupt, complacency & inertia in the face of corrupt[ion] is the unforgivable offence" etc. (Feb. 22 issue p. 4) It is much *above* being corrupt. Some corruption will happen among fallibles. But complacency is the Seven Deadly Sins heaped into one.

8. This Administration is debauching the judiciary with inexcusable political appointments. The latest is Green of Iowa.[4] A man in his 72d year [5] for the Court of Claims. He has been in Congress since 1911. Before that he was a petty Iowa lawyer; then a petty state district judge until 1911. Alf. A. Wheat had been urged for the place, but he is without political support.[6] This was

a most unpardonable offense as there was no need to consider the wishes of local Senators. Some one in Al Smith's interest & that of the law, ought to make a study of Cal's enormities in this line—a long one.

1. James Laurence Laughlin (1850–1933) was a distinguished economist and professor of political economy. He left Harvard in 1888 and in 1892 assumed the chairmanship of the Department of Political Economy at the brand new University of Chicago. He wrote many books on economic topics, particularly on monetary policy. On 20 February, Laughlin published a letter in the *New York Times* condemning the Carnegie Foundation for abolishing its chair of historical research in Washington (a position held with important results by J. Franklin Jameson, for twenty years). What probably appealed to LDB, however, were Laughlin's remarks about the recent shake-up of the Brookings Institution, which had sent Walton H. Hamilton to Yale Law School (see LDB to Frankfurter, 20 December 1927). A strong indication that LDB or Frankfurter may have prompted the Laughlin letter is Laughlin's having quoted, in his piece, the very lines from Xenophon which LDB had shared with Frankfurter (see LDB to Frankfurter, 28 January 1928).

2. See LDB to Frankfurter 9 March 1927, n. 3.

3. "Everything comes to one who waits."

4. William Raymond Green (1856–1947) had been a judge before coming to Congress. His new appointment to the Court of Claims involved service from 1928 to 1942.

5. Interestingly, Green was born less than a week before LDB himself.

6. Alfred Adams Wheat (1867–1943) had extensive experience arguing cases before the Supreme Court (for the Department of Justice). In 1929, President Hoover appointed him to the Supreme Court of the District of Columbia, and in 1930 he became chief justice of that court. See next letter also.

To Felix Frankfurter

February 29, 1928 Washington, D.C. [Frankfurter Mss—HLS]

1. O[liver].W[endell].H[olmes]'s lack of an opinion on Feb 20 was not due to lack of readiness on his part. He also distributed Tuesday opinion assigned to him last Saturday.

2. OWH. has been absent this week, because of a cough (not serious) but his new MD (the old one died) has ordered him to stay indoors. His recuperative powers are as amazing as ever; & the MD. says his arteries are as of a man of 40.

3. The Coolidge debauch of the Judiciary continues apace.[1] You have noticed appointment of Peyton Gordon to S.C. of the District.[2] You will have heard from Hitz how the Court had twice endeavored to prevent Gordon's reappointment as Dist. Atty. The bar wanted [Jesse C.] Adkins for the J.P. of the District, & he would have accepted at a considerable financial sacrifice. Alfred Wheat would have been glad to get either that judgeship or the one on the C[our]t of Claims; & would make a good judge.

4. The Senate Com[mit]tee is doing a very serious thing in the treatment of Esch.[3] Such action is bound to destroy morale & independence in action. Of course it would have been better not to have appointed Esch originally, but for a very different reason.

5. Alice sends you enclosed passage from Bacon which will interest also Chafee if he doesn't know it.

6. Would Margold prefer Columbia to Yale?[4] Those were good letters from the faculty members.

7. Estelle, who was in Monday told us of your conquest of Vassar.

Ex A[ttorney].G[eneral]. [Thomas W.] Gregory was in yesterday & is strong for Al Smith.

1. See preceding letter.
2. Peyton Gordon (1870–1946) had had a series of District of Columbia appointments since 1901; he was named District Attorney for Washington, D.C., by President Harding in 1921 and then was reappointed by President Coolidge in 1926. He served as an associate justice of the District's supreme court until 1941.
3. John Jacob Esch (1861–1941) had served in Congress, representing Wisconsin, for more than twenty years, until 1921. His best known legislation was the Transportation Act of 1920, written with Cummins of Iowa. Esch then was appointed to the Interstate Commerce Commission. In 1928, his term expired and Congress refused to act on Coolidge's renomination. The Senate Committee on Interstate Commerce questioned his judgment and the full Senate rejected his confirmation on 17 March.
4. See LDB to Frankfurter, 11 February 1928.

To Felix Frankfurter

March 4, 1928 Washington, D.C. [Frankfurter Mss—HLS]

1. R. Walton Moore is an "old Virginian of the best type"—now in his fifth term in Congress—formerly commerce counsel for the

Southern carriers. When he dined with us Thursday, he volunteered the suggestion that the diversity of juris citizenship jurisdiction should be abridged.[1] That led to my telling him I would
ask you to send him your "Business"[2] & his saying that with a
little pushing (which he was ready to give) he thought a bill or
bills could be put through, raising the jurisdictional amount &
otherwise bringing abridgement. In the course of the talk, it was
suggested that you & associates might be willing to draw the desirable bills.

I suggest now that you merely send him "Business" with a letter saying that you do so at my suggestion. I think he will answer,
asking you to draw some bills etc. & furnish data. When the time
comes for work on your part, [Henry J.] Friendly can, I think,
be drafted by you. He has become keenly interested in jurisdictional matters.

2. Alice thinks enclosed from William James on teachers will
interest you.

3. I hope the opposition press will put to full use the recent oil
disclosures.[3] To do so, they must be brought home skillfully to
C[alvin].C[oolidge]. & his Cabinet. Not only the doctrine of
noscitur a sociis;[4] but as an explanation of the persistent silence &
attempt at suppression which has gone forward for 4½ years, despite Daugherty & Fall iniquities. The high-ups must have known.
And Hoover should not be permitted to escape, because of his
personal sanctity, & the immoral acts must be brought home to
the leaders of the party of moral ideas by insinuation & more.

4. Experienced Republicans realize that the Scandals, & particularly Will Hays' last disclosure,[5] has made things very difficult for
the party—if the Democrats don't make fools of themselves. One
of those experienced Republicans said to me in private: "I am sure
Smith will be nominated. And then, if he is, it will be an even
bet which party wins."

If the Democratis can find & utilize some men as politically wise
and as loyal as Amos Kendall, Frank Blair and Isaac Hill,[6] there
should be an extremely good chance of putting Smith into the
White House, and now that the prosperity bubble is bursting and
unemployment is in the public eye.

5. Your diary entry is a terrible indictment of R[oscoe].
P[ound]. It is fine to see Calvert [Magruder] rise to full height &
Landis's courage. Redlich talked well.

6. Glad the Judiciary matter is being taken up. Who are the 27 Madison Ave. men?

7. With good men following Reading, I am reminded of Edmund Benedikts "Gott, was hab die Familie aber unglück".[7]

On regular docket, we reached last week the first of the Cert[iorari]s filed Oct 10/27 & have passed the last day of 1926 term's entries.

1. See LDB to Frankfurter, 2 April 1925, n. 1., and 16 March 1928.
2. See LDB to Frankfurter, 1 August 1927.
3. See note 5 below.
4. "He is recognizable from his associates."
5. The Senate investigating committee, doggedly pursuing the oil scandals of the Harding administration, had uncovered what appeared to be more fraudulent sales of the Teapot Dome reserves. While attempting to trace the profits of that sale, it was disclosed that some of the money might have come to the Republican Party's campaign fund. On 2 March, Will Hays (see LDB to Frankfurter, 2 June 1921) admitted before the Senate committee that Harry Sinclair had given him $260,000. Hays claimed that he returned $100,000 of the sum.
6. Amos Kendall (1789–1864), Francis Preston Blair (1791–1876), and Isaac Hill (1789–1851) were all members of President Andrew Jackson's "Kitchen cabinet."
7. "God, what does the family have but misfortune." Perhaps a reference to the impeachment hearings for Massachusetts' Republican attorney general Arthur K. Reading, for financial irregularities while a lawyer. He resigned his office on 7 June.

To Alice Harriet Grady

March 9, 1928 Washington, D.C. [Grady Mss]

A.H.G.: Of course you have been having a horrid time. But you will win. You have only to live and keep your health, and decline all compromise—always being tactful in manner. If anyone doesn't want you present at a conference, it is merely a dodge because he fears you.

I don't wonder that the Savings fund project is putting the companies other than life behind Merle Summer's fight.[1] Not only the accident companies—the fire companies also have a record as shameful as the Metropolitan. The expense rate of all is about 40 per cent—many of them more. They are fighting for their scandalous "vested right" to commissions & high salaries despite the public interest.

Your February record is fine. Letters like yours to the Post should make March show up well also.

1. Merle G. Summers was the legislative sponsor of the bill requiring the return to the state of money spent by the SBLI Division (House 808). See LDB to Miss Grady, 22 January 1928.

To Paul Underwood Kellogg

March 11, 1928 Washington, D.C. [Kellogg Mss]

MY DEAR KELLOGG: Private.

Now that unemployment has been forced upon public attention, would it not be possible for the Survey to take up vigorously and persistently the musts of Regularity in Employment?

That is the fundamental remedy. All others are merely palliatives. The right to regularity in employment must be raised above the right to dividends. It must be given an equality with rent, interest and taxes. Regularity of employment would go far toward eliminating business cycles, in this country. It is essential to the emancipation of labor.   Cordially,

To Felix Frankfurter

March 16, 1928 Washington, D.C. [Frankfurter Mss—HLS]

1. Isadore Levine [*sic*] made a most creditable appearance in our Court—well prepared, dignified, tactful.[1] With experience added, he should do much.

2. I hope next year your Seminar will produce an article demonstrating the futility of our Grants of Certiorari's in Federal Em[ployer]. Liability Cases (1916–1927 terms).

3. Hasn't the time come for legislation bringing the RR's under compensation acts? If so this simple device might be suggested to John B. Andrews. Have Congress pass an act making it optional for RRs in any state that has the requisite compensation law, to elect to come under it in respect to its interstate operations; &

wherever it does elect, make the state aid apply to all accidents happening within the state.

4. R. W. Moore writes me that he has written you asking for draft of bill or bills. (See 7).[2]

5. DeHaas was here Wednesday (with [*] of Chicago Chronicle) & Mrs. Lindheim, Zip [Szold] & Miss Franklin (of Chicago) were here yesterday. The revolt is growing.[3] If only Mack & Wise were resolute!

6. Your S[acco].V[anzetti]. has done well. What is total number sold to date?

7. I should think limiting diversity of jurisdiction: [4]
   (a) By raising the limit to $10,000—might escape serious opposition.
   (b) By excluding foreign corporations which have a usual place of business within the state (excepting interstate RR, telegraph & telephone companies) might get reasonable support. I make the exceptions only in order not to have the combined opposition of the utilities.

What amendments are prepared, ought to be each by a separate bill & each bill as short as possible.

I assume you will write Friendly.[5] I shall not say anything to him.

8. Alice is much pleased with the Herald review of the Karl Goldmark.[6] Did you have it inserted? And who did it?

9. Alice is sending Elizabeth the Brailsford article.

10. Yes, Charlie Merz has done well.

11. Alice sends you the clipping from Madison, which Elizabeth sent to show that there are some free speakers there.

12. That enquiry into Civil Service is a bit different from Cal[vin Coolidge]'s performances.

13. I have seen nothing of moment in the press about the Shipping Board Scandal. (Still, I understand there is another member about as guilty, who it was expected would go before this.) [7] The fact is that Cal. is willing to appoint men to office in reckless disregard of character & despite warnings.

14. The Review of "Business" is a worthy one.

1. Isadore Sandler Levin, a Fall River, Massachusetts attorney, had graduated from Harvard Law School in 1920. On 7 and 8 March he argued

the case of *Hemphill* v. *Orloff* 277 *U.S.* 537. The case involved the attempt of a "foreign" corporation, doing business in Michigan, to collect a promisory note although the corporation had not complied with Michigan law.

2. See LDB to Frankfurter, 4 March 1928.

3. See LDB to Jacob deHaas, 5 June 1927. Pearl Franklin (1885–1958) was a lawyer and a lifelong leader of Hadassah. She was the president of the Chicago chapter from 1921 to 1930 and thereafter its honorary president.

4. See LDB to Frankfurter, 2 April 1925, n. 1.

5. See LDB to Frankfurter, 4 March 1928.

6. Alice G. Brandeis had just published her translation of *Notes from the Life of a Viennese Composer* (New York, 1927), the memoir of Karl Goldmark (see LDB to Alfred Brandeis, 3 January 1923).

7. A federal grand jury was investigating a loan of $15,000 to W. S. Hill, a former member of the Shipping Board. The loan was made by Joseph L. Bley, of the West Coast Shipping interests. Within weeks, Philip S. Teller, another member of the Board, also resigned his position.

To Alice Harriet Grady

March 16, 1928 Washington, D.C. [Grady Mss]

AHG: Yours of 14th & 15th recd. The fight seems to be on in real earnest.

I know you are a "bonnie fighter"—& with the right, for which you always battle, on your side—even the legions of the Evil ones cannot beat you.

To Alice Harriet Grady

March 25, 1928 Washington, D.C. [Grady Mss]

A.H.G.: 1. Your four month's statement is fine—the advertising has been obviously effective.

2. The country banks & the North End have given you good cooperation.

3. Your victory [1] ought to be celebrated by our undertaking a campaign for the next nine months which will make attacks upon S[avings].B[ank].I[nsurance]. in 1929, still more improbable of success, even if undertaken with increased forces and virulence.

To this end I suggest for your consideration:

A. An effort through publicity to increase the monthly growth in outstanding insurance to One Million Dollars.

B. A renewal of tactful efforts to increase the number of SBI banks.[2]

C. An educational campaign which shall make folk realize:

    (a) That other than the working people are entitled to have insurance—a necessary of life—as cheap as possible.

    (b) That economy & efficiency—the essential of Massachusetts' holding its own—is not consistent with an unnecessary waste of 24 percent on every dollar spent for premiums hereafter, on new business.

    (c) That it is essential to Mass.' holding its own in the competition with other states, and for the easy financing of strictly Mass. enterprises whether in Mass. or elsewhere, that it should have in its local institutions, the management of the huge sums accumulated from insurance premiums.

As to A. This campaign of publicity could be carried out:

    (1.) within the confines of the Savings Bank—

        (a) By signs conspicuously posted

        (b) By attaching or inserting into the Bank books, (not pasting on) each time they come in for posting, a slip bearing, for instance, a digest like Exhibit X, or one more dignified.

    (2) In the press. By advertising.

I realize the absurd objection which individual Treasurers make to (1)—But would it not be possible to induce one or more of the progressive minded of the 10 S.B.I. Treasurers or of the near 100 Agency Treasurers to make the start?

As to C. My thought on this would be to try to get some speaking—not only by you & Tal [Grady], Mr. [George L.] Barnes & J[udd].D[ewey].,[3] but by John H. Fahey, Mr. [Charles H.] Jones, Mr. [Bernard J.] Rothwell, Mr. [Fred S.] Elwell, Labor men & others, before organizations like the Economic Club, Chambers of Commerce or local boards of trade—something like our campaign of 1906–1907.

We dealt then in prophecy. This "Twenty Years After" furnishes the [*] facts.

More important than anything stated above, is, however, that you should not overtax in any way your strength.

All that is needed to have this a huge success is time. Even if we go on as now, provided you keep your health *and live*.[4]

Under another cover I am sending you some credit news literature, thinking it still possible that cooperation may come from
that source.

1. The defeat of the Summers proposal in the Massachusetts legislature
(see LDB to Alice Grady, 22 January and 9 March 1928).

2. In 1928 ten banks across Massachusetts were dispensing Savings Bank
Life Insurance policies.

3. Judd Ellsworth Dewey (1882–1961) graduated from Harvard Law
School in 1913. He went into private practice in Boston after World War I.
He was intensely interested in Savings Bank Life Insurance and succeeded
Miss Grady as deputy commissioner of the system.

4. Miss Grady died on 19 April 1934 (see LDB to Leila Colburn, 22 August 1934).

To Felix Frankfurter

March 29, 1928 Washington, D.C. [Frankfurter Mss—HLS]

1. O[liver]W[endell]H[olmes] is in fine form. Daily, for the last
five days he has called me spontaneously—propria persona [1] on
the telephone. On four days, to talk opinions. In one case, he read
me one on the telephone—a whole opinion. Yesterday, the call
was solely to tell me that he had beat me to it, & has discovered
the first dandelion on the wall of Potomac basin.

2. Last year or earlier, you told me E. H. Warren had doubt
whether on the whole business corporations had been a blessing
or a damage to America—(as distinguished from unincorporated
businesses).[2] Has he written anything on the subject, or has any
other person? [3] And who has written on the dangers, social, economic & political, incident to our business being absorbed by corporations.

Please let me have as soon as you can any references available.

3. I suppose you saw the Federal Dist. Court jurisdiction bill
reported by Senate Judiciary (in U.S. Daily of yesterday or Tuesday).[4]

4. That's good about the Outlook.

5. I do not understand fully the reference to R. L. O'Brien.

6. Those are great stuff in N.Y. World on Republican honesty.

7. I hope the N.Y. World, N[ew].R[epublic]. & Nation will
not fail to make the most of Sec[retar]y of Labor's report on unemployment & prevent his misleading the public by misinterpret-

ing the facts gathered by Ethelbert Stewart.[5] They are really worse than I supposed. If his guess of near 1,900,000 shrinkage in employment since 1925 is correct, the number of unemployment must be at least 4,000,000—possibly much more. (He assumes N.Y. fairly represents the U.S. and manufacturing & railroading fairly represent all employments). For

> (a) The number employed in N.Y. factories in Jan, 1925 was about the same as in Jan, 1914. Think of (a) growth in population by natural growth & immigration, (b) gain in employables through trek to cities.

The A.F. of L. report their average unemployed at 18 percent— rising to 30 in Phila[delphia].

I guess that means about 20 percent skilled & unskilled. 20% of 23,000,000 = 4,600,000.

8. Is John Dickinson going to H[arvard].L[aw].S[chool]. for the Chair on Legislation? [6]

9. What has happened with [Nathan R.] Margold's Columbia prospect?

10. That's an interesting report of Columbia L[aw].S[chool].

1. "in one's own proper person," a legal phrase.

2. Edward Henry Warren (1873–1945) had taught law at Harvard since 1904. He was the only member of the faculty to oppose LDB's confirmation to the Supreme Court in 1916 (see LDB to Frankfurter, 3 April 1916).

3. Edward H. Warren, *Corporate Advantages Without Incorporation* (New York, 1929).

4. S. 3151 was not acted upon during the session.

5. Ethelbert Stewart (1857–1936) served as a statistician in various governmental agencies. From 1920 to 1932 he was commissioner of labor statistics. Secretary of Labor James J. Davis reported on national unemployment to the Senate. See *New York Times*, 27 March 1928.

6. Dickinson (see LDB to Frankfurter, 25 June 1926) never returned to the Harvard Law School in any capacity.

To Clarence Henry Howard

April 1, 1928 Washington, D.C. [Brandeis Mss, SC 8–1]

My dear Mr. Howard: [1] Strictly private.

The humane, wise and farseeing planks in the Commonwealth Plan leads me to suggest another which would make you the leader in American industry:

"For the Commonwealther who "is steady in his work," there shall be steady work. The right to regularity in employment is co-equal with the right to regularity in the payment of rent, in the payment of interest on bonds, in the delivery to customers of the high quality of product contracted for. No business is conducted successfully which does not perform fully the obligations incident to each of these rights. Each of these obligations is equally a fixed charge. No dividend should be paid unless each of these fixed charges has been met. The reserve to ensure regularity of employment is as imperative as the reserve for depreciation; and it is equally a part of the fixed charges to make the annual contribution to that reserve. No business is socially solvent which cannot do so." [2]   Cordially,

1. Clarence Henry Howard (1863–1931) was the president of the Commonwealth Steel Co. of St. Louis. He had sent LDB a booklet outlining industrial policies.

2. This letter was published in the April 1929 issue of the *Survey Graphic*.

To Felix Frankfurter

April 10, 1928 Washington, D.C. [Frankfurter Mss—HLS]

Holmes's dissent in the Black & White Taxi Cab Case will stand among his notable opinions.[1] It was delivered with fervor.

Galloway [2] did a good job.

1. *Black & White Taxi Co.* v. *Brown & Yellow Taxi Co.*, 276 U.S. 518 (1928). The case was an extremely complex one involving two competing taxi companies in Louisville, Kentucky. The Brown & Yellow Co. enjoyed a monopoly arrangement with the Louisville & Nashville railroad for servicing the Louisville station. The Black & White, knowing that such an arrangement would be declared illegal by Kentucky law, invaded the business. But, to evade the Kentucky *state* court judgment, the Brown & Yellow had itself chartered in Tennessee and brought suit in the Kentucky *federal* court instead. Under the old rule enunciated by Justice Story in 1842 (*Swift* v. *Tyson*, 16 Pet. 1 [1842]), the federal court was not bound by the state court's monopoly rule. The evasion worked, and six members of the Supreme Court supported the contention of the Brown & Yellow Co. Holmes was joined in his dissent by LDB and Stone. The case illustrated perfectly the imperfections of the existing doctrine on "diversity of jurisdictions." See LDB to Frankfurter, 21 April 1928.

2. Perhaps Herman Jamison Galloway (b. 1890), the Assistant Attorney General in the Coolidge administration.

To Jacob Gilbert

April 18, 1928 Washington, D.C. [Wise Mss]

Answering your inquiry re: Dr. Wise.[1] The World War has taught us how "Allied and Associated Powers" may cooperate with success. Exploit to the full the individual initiative; but avoid all diversions, physical, intellectual or emotional, which may embarass the pursuit of the common immediate objective. As stated before, I think that even the slightest reference by Dr. Wise, either to Dr. Weizmann, the Jewish Agency, the delinquencies of the World Organization or the Russian agricultural undertakings would be harmful, if made at any time before the close of the ZOA convention. Let the next two months and a half be devoted to "turning the rascals out" of the American Organization. There is a long future after that.

You will recall what John Morley said of John Stuart Mill: "The only fear he ever knew was fear lest a premature or excessive utterance should harm a good cause. He had measured the prejudices of men, and his desire to arouse this obstructive force in the least degree compatible with effective advocacy of any improvement, set the single limit to his intrepidity."

1. During the spring of 1928, a growing tension surfaced between Rabbi Stephen S. Wise and the rest of the Brandeis-Mack group. A series of meetings were held in New York between the principals and in smaller groups in order to air the disagreements and attempt a repair. As it emerged there were several matters bothering Wise. He was lukewarm toward deHaas and felt that LDB was making loyalty to deHaas a criterion of orthodoxy; he was willing to follow LDB, if LDB would agree to assume more visibility. But above all, Wise was firmly convinced that the coming attack should not be restricted to Lipsky and the American administration, but that it should embrace Weizmann, the Jewish Agency, and World Organization's flirting with the "Crimea Plan" for settling Jews in Russian agricultural districts. LDB and the others, as LDB here instructs his son-in-law, thought the attack should be narrow at first and focussed on Lipsky.

To Felix Frankfurter

April 21, 1928 Washington, D.C. [Frankfurter Mss—HLS]

1. Answering your enquiry: I think it would be an excellent idea to draft a bill to correct the alleged rule acted on as to general

law in the Black & White taxi case.[1] The draft bill should go to Sen. Tom Walsh. He sat through the reading of the opinions, seated in a front seat, & seemed much interested.

2. Another bill should be drawn, correcting the court's error in construction of the Fed Statutes as to what is a fraud on its jurisdiction. Such action as was taken in the Black & White Case, ought to be prohibited whether strictly a fraud or not. That bill should go to Judge [R. Walton] Moore.

3. Another bill should be drafted to put an end to removals, where there is a several controversy.[2] That provision is being construed as removing the whole cause—an obvious injustice to those defendants who want to remain in the State Court, & to the pl[ainti]ff. That bill also should go to Judge Moore.

4. I was asked by the C[hief].J[ustice]. to go with him & Van-[Devanter] (for obvious reasons) to Sen. Norris (& T.J. Walsh) to get them to put through the amendment (enclosed) to the ridiculous appeal act (Jan 31/28) which the Amer. Bar Assn had ignorantly put through.[3] I told Walsh that I had heard that his Boston speech was fine. This pleased him.

5. Glad to hear of your talk on unemployment. Yes Beveridge gave Ethelbert Stuart [*sic*] what was coming to him.[4] Who wrote "Laid Off." [5]

6. If the Atlantic got the real stuff on Lawyer's Ethics it would be helpful.[6] But you cant & others wont give it.

7. Is the Law Quarterly article out? [7]

8. I wont believe the $2,000,000 Filene tale without a certificate of the trustees, duly countersigned.

9. R[oscoe].P[ound]. on this was naive, as to Margold.

10. Perhaps the Donnelley decision was *because* of certain views as to prohibition.[8]

We are due in Boston June 5. Hope you & Marion will reserve that evening. And that we may see you two at Chatham at the weekend & thereafter.

1. See LDB to Frankfurter, 19 April 1928.
2. Simply, a case which involves several separable and distinct questions.
3. The new law (45 *U.S. Statutes*, ch. 14 [1928]) abolished the writ of error and ordered that all relief heretofore obtainable by a writ of error should now be possible through appeal. The act was approved 31 January 1928. The amendment which LDB, Taft, and Van Devanter urged, was passed on 26 April as 45 *U.S. Statutes*, ch. 440 (1928); it permitted the writ of error at the appeal level.

4. Sir William Henry Beveridge (1879–1963) was on the threshold of a distinguished career as a political scientist and a political thinker. He was already an authority on insurance and unemployment and was director of the London School of Economics. During the early 1940s Beveridge was asked by the British government to prepare an outline for the future "welfare state." In 1946 he became Baron of Tuggal. The reference here is to his slashing attack on Ethelbert Stewart's unemployment report (see LDB to Frankfurter, 29 March 1928), which appeared as a communication, "The British Know," *New Republic* 54 (11 April 1928): 247–49.

5. The article, *New Republic* 54 (11 April 1928): 236–39, was signed by Anne W. Armstrong.

6. Perhaps a reference to George W. Alger, "Cleaning the Courts," *Atlantic Monthly* 141 (March 1928): 403–11.

7. Felix Frankfurter and Nathan Greene, "Use of the Injunction in American Labor Controversies," 44 *Law Quarterly Review* 164 (1928). This was the first of a series; it appeared in April.

8. John Donnelley was the prohibition director of Nevada. He had been convicted and fined $500 for ignoring a violation of the Volstead Act. He appealed his conviction on the grounds that enforcement officers have discretion to ignore some cases and prosecute others. The Supreme Court (including LDB) upheld the conviction by a vote of 7–2. See *Donnelley* v. *U.S.*, 276 *U.S.* 505 (1928).

To Alice Harriet Grady

May 9, 1928 Washington, D.C. [SBLI]

A.H.G.: 1. I think I laid yesterday a solid foundation on which you can build a powerful ally. John H. Fahey, whom I probably had not talked to for 10 years, telephoned to enquire whether he could see me. I had been thinking of him for S[avings].B[ank]. I[nsurance]. & eagerly assented. For an hour I expounded to him the past & the present situation & our campaign projected for the future & told him what he could do.—(1) With his Worcester paper (2) by public speaking (3) otherwise. I expounded to him specifically the importance for Mass[achusetts]. of the financial end—i.e., (a) keeping the premiums in Mass. to be invested by Mass. men (b) available for Mass. industries & enterprises (c) in small units—through many Savings Banks, thereby putting life into the moribund banks & communities & developing many men.

He goes west from here; is due back in Boston week after next & promised to see you promptly after his return. (Mr. Fahey resurrected recently the Public Franchise League.) [1]

2. As to Bergengren's letter.[2] You & I have no illusions about E.A.F[ilene]. But I am inclined to think that he may be made serviceable in the coming campaign & the way is open (which he invited) for you to have a full talk with him. Convey, if you do, your & my thanks for his aid. I will write him a line myself of thanks. My reason for thinking he may be ready to aid is largely based on the following:

You know he is bitterly at odds with A.L.[Filene], Mr. [Louis E.] Kirstein & Frost. E.A. thinks (says) that he is a "failure"—because his great aim was to reduce to the smallest possible point, the spread between the cost to the retailer and that to the customers. The Filene spread has risen constantly, & with it huge profits for the business.

S.B.I. in its small operating cost, achieves his lamented ideal. And if this is put to him (of course [*] without refrence in any way to his lamented failure), he may possibly be ready to take hold. Of course I realize that (like some others) his aid has to be used with circumspection. His help might hurt in some places. But there are things he can do & you will know when, where & how.

His Twentieth Century Foundation (which he says will have $150,000 to spend this year) might possibly give something for advertising. John Fahey, Bruce Bliven &, I think, Judge [George W.] Anderson are among the trustees.

He might (which is more important) induce Mr. Bergengren to try to get the Credit Unions to become active agencies for S.B.I.

He might influence some people of weight our way.

3. You did a handsome job in the Globe for the Senators. I guess I had better not write them, or see them, when in Boston, lest the cry goes out that I am "lobbying".

4. You might tell Sen. Kidder that someone says he needn't fear reelection.[3] The men who will have occasion to fear are those who oppose S.B.I. Tell him of our experience in 1906–7. How with only one vote ([George L.] Barnes) among the 15 members of the Recess Ins[urance] Com[mit]tee, we got a unanimous report;[4] & how we overcame the enemy in the Great and General Court.[5]

5. In talking to Mr. Fahey, I mistakenly said that the $2,800,000

was written in 3 months, whereas it appears to have been in 4. But I guess May or June will bring us near the million a month that I told him was imminent.

6. I agree that Mr. Barnes should be the first visitor & Mr. [Bernard J.] Rothwell next.[6] We must remove their defeatist thoughts. When you have time, see what the Com[mit]tee expends for similar purposes in other connections without reimbursement.

7. Suspending the usual luncheon will (a) save the limited vitality of L.D.B., and (b) will show our friends that we mean business.

1. Fahey (see LDB to John H. Fahey, 22 December 1910, n. 1) became active in Savings Bank Insurance, and served as a director of the Savings Bank Insurance League.

2. Roy Frederick Bergengren (1879–1955) devoted his life to the furtherance of the credit union movement in the United States. Together with E. A. Filene, Bergengren supervised the gradual expansion of the Massachusetts credit union system into the Credit Union National Association (CUNA) in 1934. See J. Carroll Moody and Gilbert C. Fite, *The Credit Union Movement: Origins and Development, 1850–1970* (Lincoln, Nebraska, 1971).

3. Senator Clarence P. Kidder was chairman of the Massachusetts Senate's Ways and Means Committee.

4. See LDB to Henry Beach Needham, 14 January 1907.

5. See LDB to various correspondents throughout June 1907.

6. As LDB passed through Boston on the yearly trip to Chatham, he customarily met with those involved in Savings Bank Insurance, and Miss Grady arranged these meetings.

To Alice Harriet Grady

                    May 13, 1928 Washington, D.C. [SBLI]

AHG.: I. Tell your doubting firends:

"One man with a conviction is more powerful than 99 who have only interests" (John Stuart Mill).

II. Isn't it terrible to think that Mass[achusetts]. by her public schools is interfering with the business of private schools?

And how terrible that it should have built the Commonwealth dock, when there were so many unused private docks.[1]

III. Consider the possibilities of inaugurating for the fall & early winter a campaign of joint debates with the Ins[urance]. folk like we had 22 years ago.

Are the Economic Club & J.W. Beatson still functioning?

Could H. W. Kimball be trusted & induced to talk in Men's Church Clubs & the like.[2] (His parishioners, Mr. & Mrs. Wilkinson (insurance agent) introduced themselves to me in the Court corridor recently).

IV. What (under present system of taxation & mortality) would Mass. get in taxes for the next 10 years—if each year $10,000,000 of the premiums which now leave the Com[monweal]th should remain in S[avings].B[ank].I[nsurance]. banks?

1. The state had constructed the Commonwealth pier just to the east of the South Boston flats. The pier was served by the New Haven tracks. LDB, of course, was trying to counter the arguments, reported by Miss Grady, that Savings Bank Insurance was wrong because it put the state in competition with private enterprises.

2. Rev. Harry W. Kimball had been an activist for Savings Bank Insurance up until 1917. He served simultaneously as secretary for the trustees of the General Insurance Guaranty Fund and also as field secretary for the League.

To Alice Harriet Grady

May 16, 1928 Washington, D.C. [SBLI]

A.H.G.: 1. Your engagement with the teachers on June 7th is the best possible use of your time.[1]

I hope that, before then, you may have a chance to talk privately with some of your audience & that thereby a foundation may be laid for prompt cooperative action on their part.

2. Your letter to Mr. Wingate tells an excellent story. May should give us even better results. When the Boston Five [Cent Savings Bank] gets going in June [2] we should have a good story to celebrate our Twentieth Anniversary with.

3. Are there not some small city agencies that want to stimulate their banks?

4. I asked Mr. [Charles F.] Nesbit to come in today in order to secure his cooperation to mobilize the labor forces in Mass[achusetts]. He has promised help; will write you preliminarily for

information, formally; and will see you in June & July when he plans being in Mass. again. I suggested his getting his folk to work on Central Labor Unions & others—to get resolutions, speeches etc.

Susan's daughter Alice was born May 14—a fine child.[3]

1. LDB had long been interested in making teachers, on all levels, aware of Savings Bank Insurance. See LDB to Edwin F. Gay, 25 September 1929, for example.

2. See LDB to Felix Frankfurter, 14 July 1928.

3. Alice Brandeis Gilbert Popkin (b. 1928) was LDB's third grandchild and only granddaughter; she later became a Washington lawyer.

To Alice Harriet Grady

May 18, 1928 Washington, D.C. [SBLI]

AHG.: 1. Thanks to Miss Colburn for the 6 months' report.[1] The next 6 months should show much better.

2. I am particularly glad to see the Waltham advertisement. It will be a step in what I hope may be a systematic test of the relative value of small town newspaper advertising as compared with the city ads.

It *may* prove that the small town paper produces largely [*]:

(a) Display ads at small costs

(b) Read more leisurely by the folks at home with less distraction of news & other ads

(c) develops a local interest

(d) develops in the newspaper an interest in S[avings].B[ank]. I[nsurance].

(e) develops the interest in Savings bank officials & trustees.

If these possible advantages prove realities, it may be desirable for the League to stimulate the advertising campaign, by bearing part of the cost.

3. A. L. Filene writes me that sometime this month he expects to take up at Weston with Henry Dennison, John H. Fahey, Harry Kimball & J. L. McElwain, an unemployment matter about which I spoke with him. (You are not supposed to know this.) But I hope before then, you may have your talk with Mr. Fahey & he be so filled with S.B.I., that he will spill over on that occasion.[2]

4. Let me know what the present attitude & what the past has been, of the Springfield Republican on S.B.I. My impression is that we got little help from them in 1906–7 & that the local insurance interests made Springfield a black spot for us.

I have in mind the possibility of getting the Springfield Republican interested (through friends) in your June 7 talk.[3]

Have you any newspaper support there?

1. Miss Leila E. Colburn was the Chief Clerk of the Massachusetts Savings Bank Life Insurance system. After Miss Grady's death, in 1934 (see LDB to Miss Colburn, 22 August 1934), LDB's correspondence regarding the daily details of S.B.I. was done with her.
2. See LDB to Miss Grady, 9 May 1928.
3. See preceding letter.

To Julian William Mack

May 21, 1928 Washington, D.C. [R. Szold Mss]

JWM: Rabbi Max Heller called on me today, having written me from Cincinnati for an appointment. He told me frankly, when he came in, that he had had 1½ hours or more talk with you, & that despite it he was inclined to go with [Louis] Lipsky for reasons detailed which seemed to me pretty illogical. I talked with him ¾ hours—obviously uselessly—telling a small part of the reasons why he should not support the present management.

The discussion did not disprove my opinion of the clerical life as a preparation for the exercise of sound judgment or the development of ethical practice. But it made me the more glad that the fight is on in good earnest.

To Charles Gabriel Tachau

May 27, 1928 Washington, D.C. [Brandeis Mss, M 15–2]

My dear Charles: Replying to yours of 16th, enclosing President Colvin's letter of that date:

1. I had supposed that Miss Lavin was to devote herself to the work of cataloguing the World War Library. If she was competent for the job, I can't quite see why so much remains to be done, and think we should have an accurate knowledge of what

has been accomplished in quantity and quality before we commit ourselves to further expenditures.

2. As to the salary for the coming year. I think we had better wait before deciding. As you know, my thought has been to develop the University through the library and not merely to build up a storehouse of books. In this development the individual members of the faculty are essential factors. They, in their several fields, must help individually to build up the library. The library, through that cooperation will develop them. And through them, the students are to be inspired. Moreover, the library is to become dynamic also in respect to the Community. Its needs are to awaken interest and make friends for the University. I do not see how this plan of development can be carried out, if the faculty members are to be excluded from active participation in the work of building up the libraries of peculiar value in this work. The ablest librarian, with all available technical knowledge, cannot supply the needs of the situation, unless conditions are such that the cooperation of the faculty members in the manner indicated is not only tolerated, but welcomed; and unless conditions are such that we may feel reasonably sure that it will be given.

To Felix Frankfurter

June 15, 1928 Chatham, Mass. [Frankfurter Mss—HLS]

It was good to have had the weekend talk.[1]

1. Glad to hear Bullard will see Miss Grady.[2]

2. Al Smith should be able to beat Hoover, depressed by a stock market smash.[3] Vare should help neutralize Tammany.[4]

3. Now that state taxation is becoming confessedly burdensome & the federal taxes growing ever lighter, might it not be possible to get through Congress legislation which permitted equal taxation of intrastate and interstate commerce, & do away with the court-made tax discrimination against intrastate commerce? Isn't there somewhere a lawyer who could draw the bill & with or without economist's aid, present the supporting argument? Powell's articles would furnish a collection of the legal material.[5] It would probably take years to get the legislation, but the idea set agoing would win converts steadily.

4. Elizabeth has a son, Walter,[6] born on the 13th—which seems to be a favorite day in the Brandeis family—my father's, my own, & Louis Wehle's.

I suppose some reviewer of the wire tapping decision will discern that in favor of property the Constitution is liberally construed—in favor of liberty, strictly.[7]

1. LDB had spent a few days in Boston en route to Chatham.

2. Probably Frederic Lauriston Bullard (1866–1952), the editorial writer whose Sacco and Vanzetti editorial won the Pulitzer Prize for 1926 (see LDB to Frankfurter, 2 May 1927). LDB was anxious to encourage favorable publicity for Savings Bank Life Insurance, and no doubt he urged Frankfurter to arrange a meeting between Miss Grady and Bullard.

3. In mid-June stock prices on Wall Street fell dramatically in a series of record trading days. See New York Times, 29 May and 12–14 June 1928. The break in prices was temporary, of course, and the "smash" was not a factor in the election of 1928.

4. William S. Vare (see LDB to Frankfurter, 25 June 1926, n. 7), then under a cloud because of campaign expenses (he was rejected by the Senate in December 1929), endorsed Hoover at the 1928 Republican National Convention (12–13 June 1928). He stampeded the Pennsylvania delegation for Hoover and thus was a key factor in securing the nomination for the Secretary of Commerce. Democrats, of course, hoped that this taint would serve to balance the taint of Al Smith's long association with Tammany Hall.

5. Thomas R. Powell published a two-part article on the subject: "Contemporary Commerce Clause Controversies over State Taxation," 76 University of Pennsylvania Law Review 773, 958 (1928).

6. Walter Brandeis Raushenbush (b. 1928) graduated from Harvard in 1950 and from the University of Wisconsin Law School in 1953. After the Air Force and three years of private practice, he joined the faculty at Wisconsin. His special interest is real estate law.

7. Olmstead v. United States; McInnis v. United States; Green v. United States, 277 U.S. 438 (1928). Chief Justice Taft, speaking for a majority of 5 to 4, argued that convictions for prohibition-related crimes, even though obtained by wiretap evidence, should be allowed to stand. Taft ruled that wiretap evidence did not constitute "search and seizure" within the meaning of the Fourth Amendment. LDB fired off an eloquent dissent which the New York Times called "one of the most sharply worded opinions from the bench in years" (5 June 1928). Calling wiretapping worse than tampering with the mails, LDB warned that "the greatest dangers to liberty lurk in the insidious encroachment by men of zeal, well meaning but without understanding." And, in one of his most often quoted passages, he said: "Our government is the potent, the omnipresent teacher. For good or ill, it teaches the whole people by its example. Crime is contagious. If the government becomes a law-breaker, it breeds contempt for the law; it invites

every man to become a law unto himself; it invites anarchy." Justice Holmes, writing that LDB had summed up his own opinion, added another famous word: "We have to choose, and for my part I think it less evil that some criminals should escape than that the government should play an ignoble part." In 1934, Congress registered agreement with the dissenters and passed a law prohibiting wiretapping.

To Alice Harriet Grady

June 24, 1928 Chatham, Mass. [SBLI]

A.H.G.: 1. I talked over the Cambridge Savings Bank situation with Mr. [Edward F.] McClennen & found he takes more interest in his bank than the usual trustee. He will think over what can be done & after the Boston Five [Cents Savings Bank] starts its agency [1] will probably make some gradual approaches.

2. I enclose letter from Mr. Pelham. If, at some time it seems desirable, the way is opened for an approach.[2]

3. I should think Judge [George W.] Anderson must have friends in some of the Savings Banks; & at a session between him, J[udd].D[ewey]. and you with the list of trustees available, some specific task could be imposed on him. We hope to have him here sometime; but I don't know when that will be possible. I suppose you & J.D. don't need any help from me in this. If you do, let me know.

4. I am glad there are only 78 of the Sav[ings]. Banks now agencies. That leaves us more of the world to conquer & make tribute bearers.

5. At your convenience, let me see your sheet showing the 10 years expenses (other than commissions) of the [commercial life insurance] companies & of S[avings].B[ank].I[nsurance].

At your convenience let me know:

6. Do you find that our lapse rate is diminishing?

7. And do you know where the strictly over the counter business shows the lower rate?

1. See LDB to Felix Frankfurter, 14 July 1928.
2. Thomas W. Pelham was general counsel and head of the legal department of the Gillette Safety Razor Company. He had written a cordial letter to LDB.

To Julian William Mack

July 5, 1928 Chatham, Mass. [R. Szold Mss]

J.W.M.: — for the group.

deH[aas]'s night letter, July 3, has come (as yet I have not seen even a newspaper report of the officers elected other than Lipsky).

The fight was a grand one.[1] And the result one in which all of us should feel much satisfaction. In view of facts disclosed by the Convention's performance, the result is more fortunate than victory would have been. For it discloses the depth of the degradation to which Lipsky & his ilk have carried Zionists. At least another year will be necessary for even a slight realization by the members of the demoralization into which they have fallen. It took forty years of wilderness to shake off the effects of servitude after the chains had been broken. And alas, the priests have played their wonted part.[2]

The need of our effort has had complete demonstration. And the Hadassah achievement is memorable.

What is Hermann [Blumgart]'s mail address. And what his telephone?

1. The 1928 Zionist Convention opened in Pittsburgh on 28 June. It was a bitter and controversial meeting. The atmosphere was clouded by continuing charges of Lipsky's mismanagement and possibly even corruption. A special committee of five judges, appointed by Weizmann to investigate the charges, reported that while no "criminal" activity had occurred, the Lipsky administration was guilty of mismanagement and irregularities. The committee recommended that no one of the old administration be reelected. In addition, Hadassah had taken the unprecedented step of denouncing the Lipsky regime (by an action of the executive board) a few days before the opening of the convention. Nevertheless, Louis Lipsky was chosen again as president by a substantial majority of the convention (398 to 159). Various reasons have been given. Apparently the administration tampered with credentials and delegate allocation so as to deny Hadassah approximately a hundred delegates, most of whom would certainly have supported the Brandeis-Mack group. In addition, the Brandeis-Mack opposition could offer the convention no outstanding leader who was willing to assume the rigors of office. Finally, the delegates seemed to have been moved by the belief that Lipsky and his followers were the more "Jewish" of the two groups and that the Americanized, Brandeis-Mack faction were un-Jewish, even

"Nordic." See Shapiro, *Leadership of the American Zionist Organization*, ch. 8; and Urofsky, *American Zionism*, ch. 9.
    2. See LDB to Julian W. Mack, 21 May 1928.

To Felix Frankfurter

July 14, 1928 Chatham, Mass. [Frankfurter Mss—HLS]

1. Unless Max Lowenthal's study is to cover the subject, would it not be profitable to have one of your seminars consider the establishment of official reviewers as a means of freeing the Fed Courts of patronage & also of diminishing the duties practically of the Judges? [1]

2. Many thanks for the data for Miss Grady. The Boston Herald of today announces the Boston Five Cents Savings agency.[2]

3. Should not Walter L[ippmann]. be reminded of Von Jhering's statement in Der Kampf ums Recht,[3] that it is a greater social crime or sin to suffer silently the doing of wrong than to commit the wrong?

4. [Alfred E.] Smith has by his appointment of Raskob,[4] achieved assurance of three things: (1) an effective organization of the campaign; (2) adequate funds; (3) silencing of "Business views with alarm". His chore now should be to secure the Progressive vote. For that he should (a) stress his Water power views & efforts [5] (b) make the most of the Federal Trade Com[missio]n public utility disclosure.[6] That is not mudslinging. He must not ignore moral indignation. Much of what Norris said in statemnt (N.Y. Times yesterday) should be met by Smith's action & utterances.[7] And Labor should be reminded soon of his views on unemployment.

5. Cook & Beard should not be dormant too long.

6. Chafee has sent me "The Inquiring Mind" doubtless at your suggestion.[8] I am glad of it.

1. Lowenthal did not publish a full study of court patronage, but in his *The Investor Pays* (New York, 1933), an examination of a railroad bankruptcy and subsequent court receivership, he touched upon some questions of court patronage. See also, LDB to Frankfurter, 4 February 1929.
    2. The Boston Five Cents Savings Bank was the largest in New England, and its announcement (9 July) of the establishment of a Savings Bank Insurance agency marked an important victory for the system.

3. Rudolph von Jhering, *Der Kampf Ums Recht* (Vienna, 1873).

4. John Jakob Raskob (1879–1950) was a leading financier and business-man who had left General Motors in order to become the chairman of the Democratic National Committee.

5. From the beginning of his political career, Al Smith had opposed turn-ing over New York's waterpower sites to private companies. His view was that a public corporation should be formed that would sell power to the "power barons" who ran the private utilities.

6. Throughout the spring of 1928, hearings before the Federal Trade Commission revealed a concerted nationwide plan to fight the public owner-ship movement. Private utilities raised large sums of money, fought un-favorable legislation in various states, and even attempted to influence opin-ion in schools by spreading propaganda among children.

7. In a statement issued to reject the presidential nomination of the Farmer-Labor Party, George W. Norris, the leading authority on public power in the Senate, condemned both parties for apparently avoiding the public power issue.

8. (New York, 1928). The book was a collection of essays on judicial, free speech, and industrial problems.

To Jennie Brandeis

August 8, 1928 Chatham, Mass. [Fannie Brandeis]

MY DEAR JENNIE: In these days Alice and I have talked of Al-fred's beautiful, gladsome life.[1] He brought happiness ever to parents, wife, children, grandchildren; help to individuals, the community, his country; joy to all who shared in his activities or with whom he came into contact. From others he received, in large measure, love, friendship, appreciation. Thus he experi-enced the happiness and satisfaction of a radiant, generous nature.

The long years seem short because each brought so richly of these gifts and youth remained in body, mind, spirit. To all of us there is the comfort that to the end the beauty was unmarred, undimmed.

Frank and Catherine [Taussig] [2] are coming to us tomorrow.

1. On this date LDB's brother Alfred died in Louisville, at the age of seventy-four.

2. Catherine Taussig was Frank's daughter, Jennie's niece.

To Jennie Brandeis

August 14, 1928 Chatham, Mass. [Fannie Brandeis]

MY DEAR JENNIE: Alfred's will was the natural expression of his confidence in you and his reliance upon you. I do not recall a word of his which could guide your discretion.

Alice and I are very glad that you summoned Louis Wehle. His help in legal and business matters will relieve you much; and no son could have loved more.

I have been reliving early days, aided by a file of old family letters which had escaped destruction. Alfred was always the same—generous, considerate, discerning, wise, joyous, charming. You may care to have these which refer to you in pre-engagement days. The girls and Alfred McCreary will appreciate the one which announces the firm, A. Brandeis & Son. That was a gift of happiness to Father and Mother for the rest of their days.

Please thank Fan and Jean for their letters. Fan's we shall share with Christine and Susie Goldmark.

Alice is much occupied with her grandchildren.

The enclosed from Felix Frankfurter's letter to me shows his discernment.

To Henry Jacob Friendly

September 1, 1928 Chatham, Mass. [Friendly Mss]

H.J.F.: I enclose opinion Ct. of App[eals]. M[arylan]d in West v. United Railways & El[evated]. Co.[1]

On Aug 30 counsel for the Commission, saying they proposed to file petition for cert[iorari]. on ground of rule as to method of fixing annual depreciation as an item in operating expense— applied to me for stay of judgment of the Ct. App. It appears that the Co[mmission] has already taken an appeal to our Court.

I raised the questions:

1. Whether there is a final judgment from which an appeal or cert. can be taken.[2]
2. Whether Commission's remedy, if any, is not by cross appeal.
3. Whether there is any jurisdiction of its complaint in view of the Pawhuska-Trenton cases.[3]

The Comm's Counsel asked time to consider these questions. This I granted, saying I expected to reach Washington not later than Sept 12 (possibly on 10th) & would hear them (both sides) then & that meanwhile the Co was free (so far as I was concerned) to take any appropriate action.

I wish that you would, by Sept 11, let me have at Washington, memo on above questions, returning to me the enclosed opinion. Also I wish you would consider the merits on the question of depreciation—the same question being raised in the United Fuel Gas Cases; [4] & let me have all there is on the subject. For that there is nothing, logically where rule of Smyth v. Ames applies,[5] rule adopted by Maryland Court should perhaps apply. But we are not slaves to logic. And I think a decided effort should be made to limit the evil of the Smyth v. Ames rule by applying to depreciation, when considered as an annual charge, the fixed percentage on cost which will retire the property within its life, the rule of practice adopted by every utility in its accounting.[6]

Of course, this rule would in no way interfere with fixing value or rate base by observed depreciation as applied to reproduction cost etc.

We expect to leave here Friday Sept 7th or Sat. the 8th; & then spend about two days in Boston (Hotel Bellevue).

I trust you have had an enjoyable vacation.

If not inconvenient, I should like to have you reach Washington Wednesday Sept 12th; but if you have already made plans for that week which would be interfered with by reaching there earlier than the 15th, the latter date will do.

1. 155 *Md.* 572; and 157 *Md.* 70. The Public Service Commission of Maryland permitted a raising of rates, but not one satisfactory to the United Railways, who sought an injunction against the new rates. The Maryland court sustained the order of the Commission. One issue in the controversy was over the proper method for assessing depreciation.

2. Actually in the first appearance of this case before the Supreme Court (278 *U.S.* 567), the appeals were dismissed on precisely the grounds that the decree sought to be reviewed was not yet a final one. But the case was reintroduced in October 1929 (280 *U.S.* 234). At that time the majority reversed the Maryland Court of Appeals and found for the Railway. LDB entered a thirty-three page dissent, in which he was joined by Justice Holmes, while Justice Stone dissented separately. LDB's dissent was highly technical and explored fully the matter of figuring depreciation.

3. *Pawhuska* v. *Pawhuska Oil & Gas Co.*, 250 *U.S.* 394; and *Trenton* v. *New Jersey*, 262 *U.S.* 182. Both cases held that the state's power to regulate utilities was unrestrained by the contract clause of the Constitution.

4. *United Fuel Gas Co., et al.* v. *Raliroad Commission of Kentucky, et al.*, 278 *U.S.* 300; and *United Fuel Gas Co.* v. *Public Service Commission of West Virginia*, 278 *U.S.* 322. Both cases were decided in January, 1929.

5. *Smyth* v. *Ames*, 169 *U.S.* 466 (1898) boldly asserted the right to the judicial review of utility rate-fixing by state legislatures. It was an attempt to assure a "fair return" for companies despite the "populistic" tendencies of certain legislatures. The case also laid down a "rule" for determining a fair return, but it was vague enough to leave wide discretion to the courts. See Mason, *Brandeis*, 548–50.

6. This was the line of argument which LDB took in his dissent. See 280 *U.S.* 277ff.

To Felix Frankfurter

September 2, 1928 Chatham, Mass. [Frankfurter Mss—HLS]

1. I hope some Democrats will make clear to the Harding-Coolidge-Hoover pseudo-drys how close is the connection between Chicago, Philadelphia bootleggerism & Crime.

2. That's promising fee news from Cardozo.

3. R[oscoe].P[ound]. seems to have his mind on one job.

4. Yes. The Kallen episode is helpful.[1] And should make easier the task of freeing the [Boston] Common.[2] George Anderson will help on that if called upon, provided there is anything he can do.

5. I knew you would join in my schadenfreude[3] over A.L.L.'s recent notoriety.[4] The shrewd man of business will begin to question his views on S[acco]. & V[anzetti].

6. The N[ew].R[epublic]. and the Nation on [Alfred E.] Smith should help dispel the defeatism of our friends. And also such talk as Sen. [John J.] Blaine's.[5] But the disease of defeatism is widespread. I found it in George Anderson.

7. The recent Worcester Case of mistaken conviction should help.

1. In a bizarre incident, Horace M. Kallen was charged with blasphemy in Boston. In an address to a Sacco and Vanzetti memorial meeting, Kallen remarked that if the two men had been anarchists, then so were Jesus,

Socrates, and others. The law under which he was charged dated from 1697. Kallen said that he welcomed a trial, but the charges were quickly and quietly dropped. See *New York Times*, 28 and 30 August 1928.

2. See LDB to Frankfurter, 13 May 1925 and 12 January 1928.

3. "malicious pleasure."

4. The newspapers revealed that a federal investigation had uncovered an immense land fraud that cheated many New England investors. Harvard's president, A. Lawrence Lowell (who had headed Governor Fuller's advisory committee in the Sacco and Vanzetti case [see LDB to Frankfurter, 2 June 1927]) had lost a reported $70,000.

5. Blaine, while campaigning for LaFollette in Wisconsin, roundly denounced the Harding-Coolidge record but stopped short of endorsing Smith. Blaine finally endorsed Smith, bolting from his own party, in October.

To Oliver Wendell Holmes, Jr.

September 10, 1928 Boston, Mass. [Holmes Mss]

O.W.H.: We are homeward bound. I write merely to tell you that Washington will be a much more attractive place when you reach it.

To Felix Frankfurter

September 13, 1928 Washington, D.C. [Frankfurter Mss—HLS]

1. Will the Bar Ass[ociatio]n act? [1]

2. I suppose you noticed the copious pictures in the press of John Coolidge, accompanied to & from his new job at the New Haven, by a Secret Service man. The World, N[ew].R[epublic]. & Nation should explode.

"Can such things be,
    And overcome us as a summer cloud
    Without our special wonder?" [2]

3. Walter L[ippmann]. might have added to Republican Phila-[delphia] & Chicago etc. as crime centers, Republican Washington under Coolidge-appointed Commissioners & Prosecuting Attorney & under his eyes. Note this editorial from today's Post.[3]

1. LDB had enclosed a clipping reporting that Max David Steuer (1870–1940), a noted criminal lawyer, had been fined $5,251 for concealing un-

declared goods in his luggage. He and his wife had just returned from Europe. Steuer had defended Harry M. Daugherty from a charge of conspiracy to defraud the government.

2. *Macbeth*, III, 4: 110. John Coolidge, the President's twenty-two-year-old son, had taken a job on 8 September with the New York, New Haven & Hartford Railroad.

3. The unsigned editorial, "Police Reform Needed," demanded that "the Police Department muddle" be straightened out and advocated thoroughgoing reform of the department.

To Felix Frankfurter

September 23, 1928 Washington, D.C. [Frankfurter Mss—HLS]

1. Poor R[oscoe].P[ound].

2. Gardner Jackson has pasted the appropriate label on Richard Walden Hale in the Nation.[1]

3. Jos Lee is fine. I guess he would join Zach Chafee in freeing the Common.[2]

4. Lowell Mellet, who is personally for Smith, was in last evening. He was enthusiastic over the Omaha speech, but says Al did a very poor job in Oklahoma.[3] (He listened to both over the radio). It was the performance he criticized; as he approved of both the subject & the place. I.a. he says Al's evidence as to participation of the Republi[can]. Nat[ional]. Com[mit]tee in Klu [*sic*] Klux propaganda was woefully insufficient.

5. Mrs. Burt Wheeler who was also in & has been in Minn[esota]., says Dem. chances (Al) there are very good & Shipstead's chances are also.[4]

6. I was amazed to find Leo Rowe (who was in Friday) a Hoover man & a wholly unthinking one.[5] He was for H. because he was "internationally minded" and because he (R.) thinks the gains socially through National Prohibition are large.

7. Jim Landis should write H[enry].J.F[riendly].

8. Hoover isn't getting yet all he deserves on labor.

9. Walter [Lippmann] did a neat job on Max Steuer—[*] is *collosal*.[6]

1. Gardner Jackson, "The Way of Boston," *Nation*, 127 (26 September 1928): 297–98. In his article Jackson recounted the difficulty in getting a

place to hold the memorial meeting for Sacco and Vanzetti (see LDB to Frankfurter, 2 September 1928, n. 1). The first choice of the organizers was the Old South Church's meeting house, and Jackson and others asked Richard W. Hale (see LDB to Cornelia L. Warren, 10 March 1900, n. 3) if the hall could be used. According to Jackson, Hale declared himself in favor of the meeting, but after checking with other trustees denied the use of the facility to the group. Jackson went on to describe similar refusals all over Boston.

2. See LDB to Frankfurter, 13 May 1925, and 12 January and 2 September 1928.

3. Smith spoke at Omaha on 18 September, emphasizing farm policy and also fielding some questions on prohibition; his speech in Oklahoma City, on 20 September, was a direct attack on the Ku Klux Klan and an attempt to connect the Klan with Republicanism.

4. Henrik Shipstead won reelection to the Senate in Minnesota; but Smith suffered a substantial (59% to 41%) defeat.

5. Leo Stanton Rowe (1871–1946) was a leading authority on Latin American affairs and a director of the Pan American Union.

6. See preceding letter, n. 1.

To Felix Frankfurter

October 1, 1928 Washington, D.C. [Frankfurter Mss—HLS]

1. Hoover "in the hands of his friends" verily cuts a pitiable figure. The Caldwell letter, atop Mrs. Willebrand [sic] will take a deal more of denials to obliterate the effect.[1]

"Spiele noch mit [*], etc."

These are severe blows to women in public life.

2. Alice suggests as Philadelphia director of the Nation, Bob Bruere's friend Morris Leeds.[2] Or would Morris L. Cooke do better? Neither is just Oswald V[illard]'s kind. But either, if he accepted, would add much to the Nation and to his own education.

3. Too bad about Jane Addams.[3] Will she stomach the bigotry campaign? Couldn't she be headed off?

4. The Keatings were in (& Father Ryan) last evening. All thought Smith would surely be elected if it weren't for anti Catholicism; & all feared his defeat.

5. What will R[oscoe].P[ound]. do about Ruggles? [4] If he comes in our peers should holler about the Business School's subsidy from the utilities.

6. It's fine to learn how the students respondent [*sic*] to your Fed[eral]. Jur[isdiction]. & Adm[inistrative]. Law courses & that you must reject half of the applicants.

The World editorial page is doing a good job.

1. The Republican National Committeewoman from Virginia warned, in a letter secured by the *Washington Post* and then widely disseminated, that Al Smith's election would result in America's becoming "Romanized and rum ridden." Hoover quickly and unequivocally repudiated the letter. Earlier, but during the same week, Mrs. Mabel Walker Willebrandt, the Assistant Attorney General of the United States, assailed Smith in Ohio, before a Methodist conference, for his views on prohibition and also for certain deficiencies of "character."

2. Morris Evans Leeds (1869–1952) was a Philadelphia manufacturer and inventor who was involved in a great many civic and social activities.

3. Miss Addams had apparently made it clear that she was about to endorse Hoover. The formal endorsement did not come, however, until 18 October in conjunction with the endorsement of twenty-eight prominent social workers.

4. Clyde Orval Ruggles (1878–1958) did leave his position as dean of the business college at Ohio State University in order to become professor of public-utility management and regulation at Harvard. He taught at Harvard for twenty years.

To Alice Harriet Grady

October 5, 1928 Washington, D.C. [Grady Mss]

A.H.G.: Re yours of 3rd.

1) The offer made by Governor Fuller is very flattering and will, if rejected, prove very helpful to Savings Bank Insurance and your future work.[1] To accept it would, in my opinion, be harmful to S.B.I. and otherwise unwise for you.

2) If there is anyone in whom you have full confidence fitted for the Commissionership whom you could, in response to the Governor's invitation, suggest for the office, it would of course, be highly beneficial to S.B.I. to have such a person appointed through you.

3) I think it true that the Governor really has respect for my opinion. When he was wrestling with the Boston Elevated problem and summoned Jos. Eastman to advise him, he was glad to have Eastman confer with me on the situation.

4. I don't assent to your modest disclaimer of being "big enough for the job". But I feel very sure that you can serve S.B.I. much better in your present position. All that is essential for S.B.I. now is to press forward. For that two things are needed: (a) that you should be able to think as hard & as much on the subject as you have been doing heretofore; (b) that to this end you should be able to devolve upon an understudy much of the executive work which now occupies so much of your time & energy, and which must be well & thoroughly done, if the system is to have its full measure of success.

5. Aside from the needs of S.B.I., I think the office of Com-[missione]r. (despite the higher salary & greater worldly honor) far less desirable for you than your present job. (a) the work of the Comr. is necessarily largely executive. For a person who can think, the occupation of thinking is far preferable to that of engrossing executive direction, (b) in your present office, you have the satisfactions incident to mastery of your subject. No one could gain mastery of all branches of insurance, unless it be after a long series of years of study. (c) for the near future the Office of Commissioner will be one subject to much political attack; and it is by no means certain that merit will, in the immediate future, triumph.

6. The contests of the future are likely to be to put an end to most of the agents' commissions in most lines of insurance. The waste (& graft) in fire, accident liability, etc. insurance is perhaps as serious as in life insurance. The recent automobile insurance rumpus is an indication of what is to come. I am convinced that the wiser insurance men see this & that their determined attacks on S.B.I. are motivated in part by the fear that it will become a precedent. If you were Comr., your judgment on the impending issues on the other lines of insurance would be suspected and attacked as prejudiced & being the result of S.B.I. prejudice and practice. On the other hand, if, keeping free from all entanglements with the attacks on the other lines, we can calmly go forward with S.B.I. success, we shall ultimately be recognized as the pioneer to insurance at necessary cost in all lines.

7 I suggested recently to Mr. [George R.] Nutter that (as Busi[ness]. Ass[ociatio]n head) he advocate putting an end to all actions for auto accidents, & substitute insurance by the state,

the cost to be paid out of an addition to the gasoline tax. Mr. Nutter's reply herewith.[2]

Your letter of 3rd returned herewith.

1. Governor Alvan Fuller had suggested that Miss Grady leave her position as deputy commissioner for Savings Bank Life Insurance and become the insurance commissioner for the state of Massachusetts. Miss Grady chose to remain in her old position.

2. In his letter LDB's former law partner noted that there had been considerable talk about such a proposal, although LDB's suggestion that it be funded out of a gasoline tax was new. Although he promised to look into the matter, Nutter wrote: "I am frank to say, however, that I have several irons in the fire which I should like very much to drop. . . . I agree with your remarks about the years of service ahead. Unfortunately the things that ought to be done seem to increase in inverse ratio with the years in which to do them!"

To Felix Frankfurter

October 7, 1928 Washington, D.C. [Frankfurter Mss—HLS]

1. It looks at the moment as if [Irving B.] Goldsmith would prove himself impossible—and that soon. I spoke to him frankly yesterday after the second grave offense.

The task of introducing him to his work, I left to [Henry J.] Friendly's oral instructions and demonstration and his explicit written memo. My supplement was to tell him, with the utmost brevity:

(a) that he must report at the office each day at 9AM.
(b) that whatever he sees, hears or infers is to remain confidential as to everyone, now & forever after.

He started work Monday Oct 1. Wednesday he did not appear until noon (after I had left for Conference); could not be reached by telephone at his hotel ([*] Park[)]). There was specific work for him to do for the Conference—as he knew. When I returned late in the afternoon, he expressed himself as most sorry & explained his default thus: that he had been poisoned by seafood; had been awake until the early hours, and that the hotel telephone clerk had omitted to wake him at 8 as directed; that he was accustomed at home to be awakened (by a servant); would buy an alarm clock & that this would not happen again.

Saturday, he again did not appear before I left for Conference & sent no word. I left a memo on his desk at 9:15 to see me as soon as he came in. He knew that there was specific work to do for the Conference. On returning from the Conference, I went immediately to my office, before going to the apartment. When I started to talk with him he asked whether I had seen his note on my desk [*]. As I had not we talked at once. He said the telephone clerk had failed to awake him. He did not claim to have been sick, but said he had been very tired (from hard work during the last few days & perhaps unduly hard work in Chicago to finish up there); and that he had gone to bed at 11 P.M. His note, which I found later, was of the same tenor substantially.

I made clear to him the needs of his position as aid. He was explicit in his regrets & that it shouldn't happen again.

His excuses are barely plausible. I suspect his habits are bad—the victim of drink or worse vices. I have a sense of his being untrustworthy; and something of the sense of uncleanness about him.

Do you know of anything which might bear upon the situation?

He appears to have a legal sense & to know the law; and his judgment so far as evidenced in his memos on Certioraris & other matters, seemed good.[1]

Holmes J. is in great shape & evidently relieved in having survived Oct 4. He talks now of what he will do on certs. next summer—if he is alive. More soon on other matters.

1. See next two letters.

To Felix Frankfurter

October 12, 1928 Washington, D.C. [Frankfurter Mss—HLS]

Yours of 9th re Goldsmith reached me Wednesday P.M. & your telegram about Shulman yesterday noon.[1] If I had felt free to consult only my own preference, I should have made the switch to Shulman. But making the change would be a severe blow to G. and might impair his future success for an appreciable time, so I concluded to talk further frankly with Goldsmith, to see

whether he was, with full knowledge of all the restrictions and
burdens involved, prepared to undertake the task of making good.
He assured me that he was willing and anxious & felt that he had
the will power to carry out the program, which involves total
abstinence from drink and generally keeping himself in such
training as will give him his maximum working capacity.

I should have kept him under observation a little longer before
talking with him on the subject—if an accident had not put him
into possession of the contents of your telegram before I saw it:
the Marshal opened it & telephoned it to my office, while I was
out and Goldsmith there. It seemed necessary, therefore, to take
up the matter with G. at once.[2]

1. See preceding letter. Frankfurter, who of course selected LDB's clerks
each year, wrote back immediately. The conduct of Goldsmith was intolerable, he sympathized, and LDB should not have to be bothered with
such a problem. He promised to look into possible alternatives. On 11 October he telegraphed that the research fellow at Harvard was available if
LDB cared to make the switch. This was Harry Shulman (1903–1955).
Shulman was a Russian immigrant who did, in fact, become LDB's law
clerk for the year 1929–30. Upon leaving Washington, Shulman went to
Yale where he taught until 1954, the year he became Dean of the Yale Law
School. In addition, he engaged in considerable governmental work, especially during World War II, and also in various efforts at labor-management
conciliation.

2. See next letter.

To Felix Frankfurter

October 15, 1928 Washington, D.C. [Frankfurter Mss—HLS]

1. Your power article is of more than temporary significance.[1]
Whatever the issue of the campaign, the struggle for government
ownership must become widespread and persistent. For the decisions and attitudes of the Supreme Court have made public ownership the only way out;—and banker rapacity has made the fight
urgent. The intensity of this campaign should serve to put an
end to the pernicious era of good feeling between the parties.
Americans may again realize that fighting, politically & economically, is the price of liberty & life, and weapons long hang-
ing "in monumental mockery"[2] should be repaired & furbished

for use. There are good days ahead for the lawyer, the economist and the political scientist if they can be awakened from lethargy.

2. I suppose you saw Harlan's statement on Ottinger in the N.Y. Times of the 11th (?).[3] Remind me of the incident when we meet.

3. Goldsmith has certainly had the [*] and scare of his life and seems determined to make good. Still, it is a comfort to think of Shulman as a possible reserve. If he is not permanently attached in N.Y., perhaps you may have him in mind for next year.[4]

4. I am glad at your dig at My Lord.

5. Harold's Bookman article seemed to me less valuable than most of his.[5]

6. The next 3 weeks should show constant gains for Al Smith.

1. Felix Frankfurter, "Mr. Hoover on Power Control," *New Republic* 56 (17 October 1928): 240–43. The article reviewed the contradictions in various statements on public power that Hoover had issued since 1923. "One thing is clear: instead of Mr. Hoover educating the electrical industry, the power interests have educated Mr. Hoover."

2. *Troilus and Cressida*, III, 3: 153. On 21 October LDB wrote Frankfurter: "Al Smith's offensive is refreshingly Napoleonic. He is reminding us what a political opposition is for; and the gain now & hereafter should be great."

3. Albert Ottinger (1878–1938), a New York lawyer and former state attorney general, was about to be defeated for the governorship there by Franklin D. Roosevelt. The *New York Times* reported that Harlan F. Stone, LDB's colleague, wrote Ottinger a letter congratulating him warmly on his nomination and wishing him success in the campaign.

4. See two preceding letters. Goldsmith remained as LDB's clerk for the full year; Shulman succeeded him in 1929. See LDB to Frankfurter, 29 September 1929.

5. Harold Laski, "Crisis in the Modern State," *Bookman* 68 (October 1928): 182–87.

To Felix Frankfurter

November 6, 1928 Washington, D.C. [Frankfurter Mss—HLS]

1. You have earned in the resuscitated Democratic Party a position as thinker, which should enable you to exert much influence hereafter. If this day's voting goes wrong,[1] the urgent task will

be to devise ways and means by which Smith may, without loss of the momentum, become the recognized leader of a militant opposition to the Republican rule. If that function can be exercised by him he will be able to render a service politically almost as great as if he were President, and in some ways, may do perhaps more than a President could.

2. Brandt (of the St Louis Post Dispatch), one of the very best, was in yesterday.[2] I asked him about Borah's $1000 per.[3] He was greatly surprised at the rumor, says he would put the question directly to Borah. I am not surprised. I think I must have written you after he was robbed of $400 and his secretary of $300 cash the night after his speech at Omaha—that I could conceive of no explanation of his having that amount of cash except (a) that he was paid for his speech; (b) that he had engaged in a successful poker game; or (c) that he was in league with the bootleggers.

3. Hughes does not surprise me either.[4]

Nearly all Washington folk, though Smithites, are defeatists.

1. See next letter.
2. Raymond Peter Brandt (b. 1896) returned from Oxford and joined the Washington bureau of the *Post Dispatch* in 1923. He became chief of the bureau in 1934 and remained in that position until 1961.
3. Perhaps a rumor that Borah received that much money for making speeches.
4. On 2 November, Charles Evans Hughes made a speech denouncing Smith's stands on prohibition, water power, and the tariff. He said that Smith had "delusions of grandeur."

To Felix Frankfurter

November 8, 1928 Washington, D.C. [Frankfurter Mss—HLS]

We have nothing to regret but the result.[1] What did it—the women mainly or the great god Prosperity?

New York City is the most disturbing. Even more so than the State. Why should Copeland have run so far ahead.[2] One of the unworthy?

The big cities in New York State and elsewhere are generally disappointing. Did labor go wrong? Did foreigners go wrong? What did the Catholics do? And what the bootleggers?

Stocks went up yesterday. Wheat and Cotton down. As for the farmers, I am reminded of Sir Toby:

"God give wisdom to those who haven't, and those that are fools, let them use their talents." [3]

Massachusetts has redeemed herself.[4] Gov. Fuller to the newspaper men was amusing.

1. Hoover decisively defeated Smith, 21.4 million (58.8%) to 15.0 million (41.2%). The electoral vote was 444–87.

2. Royal Samuel Copeland (1868–1938), an ophthalmologist, went to the Senate from New York in 1923. He had just won reelection with a large plurality, leading Smith and the other Democratic candidates.

3. Sir Toby Belch. *Twelfth Night*, I, 5: 14.

4. David I. Walsh was reelected to the Senate from Massachusetts; and Frank Gilman Allen (1874–1950), a Republican, was elected governor.

To Felix Frankfurter

November 14, 1928 Washington, D.C. [Frankfurter Mss—HLS]

1. Thanks for your birthday best wishes.[1] To the happiness and usefulness you have, throughout long years, contributed very much.

2. If I should chance to see Franklin Roosevelt, I should not hesitate to talk with him about my two requests.[2] But I think it entirely unnecessary that I should see him. If he can be induced to take up these matters, I am sure that the request from you will accomplish what we desire.

3. Would it not be possible, in aid of the militant Democratic opposition, to organize, from Smith's recent aids & others, a sort of general staff & expert body, which would supply thought and research for the men on the firing line, and have them always supplied with ammunition when the opportunities for attack arise?[3] They are sure to be numerous.

I mentioned this project to Ben Flexner. He thought it would be valuable, and said: "There will be no difficulty in getting the money needed." Some will, of course, be needed; but the unpaid thinking & help such as you have given is essential, if the project is to succeed.

3. [*sic*] The sadness over Smith's defeat is widespread; and encouraging. S[amuel]. E[liot]. Morrison[*sic*]'s letter is fine.

4. O[liver].W[endell].H[olmes]. is in fine form. He seemed like one of 67 at last week's conference.

5. We had a delightful evening Sunday with Alfred Cohen.

6. Emma Erving spoke of a joyous visit with you & Marion.

1. On 13 November, LDB was seventy-two.

2. On 4 November, LDB had written to Frankfurter: "If, as I expect, Roosevelt is elected [governor of New York], I should like through you to put in early two requests: (a) Far reaching attack on 'The Third Degree', (b) Good counsel in N.Y.'s cases before our Court."

3. Cf. LDB to Frankfurter, 1 January 1925.

To Harold Joseph Laski

November 29, 1928 [1] Washington, D.C. [Brandeis Mss, M 18–3]

My Dear Harold: I am glad of your "Recovery of Citizenship." [2] You have dealt with a much neglected field, and perhaps the most important of all, economically and politically. What you say of the consumer is most discerning. And I am cheered by your references to recent successes of the Cooperatives.

In most instruments of social-economic advance the credits have set against them debits—sometimes heavy ones. In the Cooperatives there are only credits;—and the problem is merely one of occupying the field, and of overcoming defects, of perfecting the instrument.

We have suffered a grievous disappointment that Al. Smith should have been so badly beaten—even in his own State. [3] Felix has doubtless written you. We have nothing to regret except the result. Such mistakes as were made were negligible. Smith's fine qualities and performance—and his large popular vote—show that no mistake was made in nominating him. Many prejudices combined to compose his defeat. I fancy our most formidable opponent was prosperity. We were routed by "the villainy of our fears" [4]—the fears of the prosperous.

Felix did for this campaign, as for very much else, service of the greatest value. He seems to me clearly the most useful lawyer in the United States.

Judge Holmes is in great shape—in mind and spirit—and also in body—save his posture and walk. He is a constant joy. Our best to you and the lady,

1. This letter was apparently misdated by LDB as "Nov. 29, 1929."
2. Harold J. Laski, *The Recovery of Citizenship* (London, 1928). The book is a study of the cooperative movement.
3. See LDB to Felix Frankfurter, 8 November 1928.
4. *Cymbeline*, V, 3: 13.

To William Allen White

December 29, 1928 Washington, D.C. [White Mss]

MY DEAR WILLIAM ALLEN WHITE: It was very good of you to send us your book—with so generous an inscription.[1]

Shall we have soon another "Great Rebellion"?[2] Mrs. Brandeis bids me say that she hopes you and Mrs. White will answer that enquiry orally—early in the New Year.

For all of it, our best wishes.   Cordially,

1. William Allen White, *Masks in a Pageant* (New York, 1928).
2. "The Great Rebellion" was the title White gave the chapter of his book dealing with Theodore Roosevelt, William Howard Taft, and Woodrow Wilson. On 12 January White replied: "You ask 'Shall we soon have another "great rebellion"?' Probably not I should say. We shall probably have a slow evolutionary adjustment of the blessings of prosperity, an evolutionary movement toward justice in which greed shall be overtaken; righteousness not in what you might call criminal action but in equity. I hope with all my heart that the Hoover administration will mean just this for I see no other immediate hope."

To William Edward Burghardt DuBois

January 10, 1929 Washington, D.C. [DuBois Mss]

MY DEAR MR. DUBOIS:[1] To my regret, judicial duties preclude compliance with your courteous request.

I recall with pleasure our meeting at Mrs. Glendower Evans' house many years ago and have watched ever since your work on behalf of your people.   Cordially,

1. William Edward Burghardt DuBois (1868–1963) was one of the foremost leaders of American Blacks in the twentieth century and also one of the leading intellectuals. The first Black to be awarded a Ph.D. degree from Harvard (1895), DuBois poured forth a stream of books, articles, novels, editorials. Most of his writings concerned the problems of Black people

in America, but he also maintained a deep interest in African affairs. He broke with Booker T. Washington early in the twentieth century and became identified as the leader of the most aggressive and politically active wing of the Black protest movement. He founded the Niagara Movement in 1905 and was one of the moving spirits behind the NAACP. For a quarter century he edited that organization's journal, *Crisis;* and it was in this connection that he wrote LDB, asking for a contribution to the magazine. DuBois's career led into ever more radical paths, and at the age of ninety-three he joined the Communist Party and settled in Ghana, where he became a citizen. See Francis L. Broderick, *W. E. B. DuBois, Negro Leader in a Time of Crisis* (Stanford, 1959); and August Meier, *Negro Thought in America, 1880–1915* (Ann Arbor, 1963), ch. 11. The editors wish to thank Malcolm L. Call for calling this letter to their attention.

To Felix Frankfurter

February 4, 1929 Washington, D.C. [Frankfurter Mss—HLS]

1. Kent is all wrong.

2. I was much interested in your correspondence re [Charles Evans] Hughes & agree entirely with all that you say. By an odd coincidence Learned Hand (with [William] Hitz) called on the afternoon of the day your letter arrived. The talk on the N.Y. receivership scandal [1] gave occasion to discuss the ethics of the bar & generally crime. I aired, with perhaps unseemly vehemence, my views on the leaders—saying i.a., that a single one does more harm etc. than a thousand shysters, & there was considerable discussion of Hughes. L.H. (as well [as] I) may have had you in mind as the discussion proceeded, but no mention of you or of the views of any other person was made. The pursuit of the "golden fleece" was the theme.

3. Mark Potter has an interesting mind. There are blind spots which keep him near the interests. But it must always stand to his credit (a) that we probably owe [Joseph B.] Eastman's appointment to him, and (b) that it was he to whom I recommended Otto Beyer & he who grew so enthusiastic that he opened Beyer's way to Dan. Willard.[2]

4. Miss Grady has new evidence of H. L. Shattuck's shortcomings.[3]

5. I guess we shall see a strong trend toward public ownership before long. I understand Hoover fears the P[ublic].U[tilities]. Co's folly is hurrying it on.

1. New York was in the midst of a scandal involving corruption and bribery in the "bankruptcy business"—the Grand Jury handed down the first indictments the day after this letter. Beginning with the case of David Steinhardt (who had been granted 126 receiverships since 1923), investigations revealed numerous cases of lawyers running bankrupt firms in their own interest or in the interest of their friends—sometimes even in the interest of the bankrupt himself. The continuing investigation uncovered numerous instances of the fraudulent passing out of receiverships. A good discussion of the legal issues is a feature article, *New York Times*, 20 January 1929, IX: 10. More and more creditors, judges, and members of the bar were moving to the position long held by LDB: that professional full time public receivers should be appointed and not private attorneys. For LDB's further views, see letter to Frankfurter, 21 February 1929.

2. See LDB to Alfred Brandeis, 16 January 1927.

3. See LDB to Frankfurter, 9 February 1928.

To Felix Frankfurter

February 4, 1929 Washington, D.C. [Frankfurter Mss—HLS]

Boni should have sent you copies of his letter to me & of my reply.[1] He wrote, "the name which strikes me most favorably (to undertake the task) is Felix Frankfurter. Before approaching anyone regarding the undertaking I should [want] to know whether this would meet with your approval."—I answered in substance: "If the project should ever become desirable no one would be more competent than Prof. Frankfurter. But I know that now he has work on hand of *far greater importance*"—which I affirm again.

1. Albert Boni (b. 1892), the publisher, had suggested a collection of LDB's legal decisions, and proposed Frankfurter as a likely editor for such a volume.

To Felix Frankfurter

February 21, 1929 Washington, D.C. [Frankfurter Mss—HLS]

1. My brother would have said: "That is just like Marshall Bullitt." [1]

2. I hope F.D.R. appreciates what you said of Owen Young.

3. C. C. Burlingham came here Tuesday re N.Y. judicial scandal.[2] After Conference with the C[hief].J[ustice]. and Har-

lan [F. Stone] & with John Davis, he called on me, being really puzzled as to what to do & much concerned, & seeking advice. I told him:

(a) that they must eliminate possibility of patronage in either bankruptcy or equity receiverships, by appointing official receivers & liquidators, & meanwhile standing resolutely against any large fees to any one in judicial proceedings. The money-changers must be excluded from the Temple.

(b) that they must put an end to the fake diversity of citizenship jurisdiction,[3] particularly in receivership cases.

(c) generally reduce federal jurisdiction, so that there be no increase & eventually a reduction in number of judges, so that the honor of office will revive.

(d) Take the judicial offices out of politics, so that we can get men of proper calibre.

He said he agreed with everything, except as to the possibility of getting official receiverships for all the Circuits & Districts through Congress, & told of (1) [*]'s effort (? in 1924) to do this via Congress & (2) via the D[istrict].J[udge].s when all were willing except Winslow & Bondy.[4] I told him to take this up

You may not have seen the report of the Bar Com[mit]tee on present scandalous condition. I enclose copy which please treat as confidential & return after perusal.

C.C.B. told me that the recent appointment of the Circuit Judge (from Vt) was the worst yet.[5]

I advised him to stop passage of the present bill for 3 more D[istrict]. J[udge].s which has passed the House, so as not to let C[alvin]. C[oolidge]. make another appointment.[6] He said he would see Wagner about that.[7]

4. Apropos our recent orders of reargument. I think there should again be brought prominently before the bar—its inadequate presentations (to which you called attention in your article on the Worcester Labor Case)—This week's batch present striking instances of the bar's failures, in

(a) Harlan's Danish Treaty case [8]

(b) The Oklahoma Coop. gin case [9]

(c) The income tax (B & M-Old Colony & Co. cases) [10]

5. Bickle [11] made an excellent argument in the Lake Cargo cases.[12]

6. I shall be delighted to see Cuthbert Pound. I hope he can come during a recess when there will be no difficulty in arranging adequate time.

5. [*sic*] Hope you wrote T.J. Walsh on the Stolen Property Bill.[13] See U.S. Daily Feb 20, p. 3.

6. Glad you have satisfied Boni.[14]

7. Did Maston's first wife die? If so when?

1. William Marshall Bullitt (1873–1957), a Louisville attorney, had been Solicitor General of the United States in the last year of the Taft administration, and had later served as counsel to the United States Shipping Board and Emergency Fleet Corporation. A leading constitutional lawyer, he wrote a number of treatises on various aspects of the law.

2. See LDB to Frankfurter, 4 February 1929, n. 1.

3. See LDB to Frankfurter, 2 April 1925, n. 1.

4. Francis Asbury Winslow (1866–1932) had been appointed by President Harding in 1923 to be a judge for the Southern District of New York. Winslow was heavily implicated in the current scandals and was under investigation both in Washington, D.C., and New York. Bowing to heavy pressure he resigned his office in April. William Bondy (1871–1964) had been appointed to the same court in the same year.

5. Harrie Brigham-Chase Chase (1889–1969), a Battleboro attorney, had been a justice of the Superior Court and of the Supreme Court of Vermont. Coolidge had just named him judge of the U.S. Court of Appeals for the Second District. He became chief judge in 1953.

6. The bill was passed by the Senate and signed by Coolidge on 27 February. But most of his judicial appointments were stalled in the Senate and left for President Hoover to make.

7. Robert Ferdinand Wagner (1877–1953) of New York was one of the powerful members of the United States Senate, where he served from 1926 to 1949. Born in Germany, Wagner worked his way through law school and New York state politics. During the New Deal Wagner drafted and passed many important pieces of legislation. The National Labor Relations Act (1935), known popularly as the Wagner Act, was probably the culmination of his achievement.

8. *Nielson* v. *Johnson*, 279 *U.S.* 47, decided on 18 February 1929, declared that treaties with foreign countries, in this case Denmark, involving tax agreements, took precedence over any conflicting state laws.

9. Cattle owners in Oklahoma had formed a marketing cooperative to sell their livestock, and found that the commercial dealers declared a boycott against the cooperative. The Secretary of Agriculture petitioned for an end to the boycott, on grounds that it restrained trade, and the Court, speaking through Holmes, granted the request. *United States* v. *American Livestock Commission Co. et al.*, 279 *U.S.* 435 (1929).

10. The two cases involved similar questions. In *Old Colony Trust Co. et al.* v. *Commissioner of Internal Revenue*, 279 *U.S.* 716, the question was

whether, when a company paid the income taxes on any of its executives' salaries, the men had to declare the amount of the taxes as additional income. In *United States* v. *Boston & Maine Rail Road*, 279 *U.S.* 732, a parent company paid the taxes for a subsidiary. Did the subsidiary have to declare that amount as income? In both cases, Chief Justice Taft affirmed the government's contention that the taxes should be considered as additional income.

11. Henry Wolf Bikle (1877–1942) was general counsel of the Pennsylvania Rail Road and professor of law at the University of Pennsylvania.

12. See 279 *U.S.* 812 (1929). The four cases were found to present moot points, and the Supreme Court reversed the lower court and dismissed the original bill of complaints.

13. The bill, H.R. 10287, prohibited sending or receiving stolen property through interstate and foreign commerce. The measure was reported out, but not acted on during the session.

14. See preceeding letter.

To Felix Frankfurter

March 1, 1929 Washington, D.C. [Frankfurter Mss—HLS]

I hope the [New York] World, the N[ew].R[epublic]. & the Nation will not fail to make clear the full significance of Mitchell's appointment as A.G.[1]

It is the most hopeful event in the legal-judicial sphere in half a century; and at no time was there as great a need.

To have attained this post by sheer merit—despite party label, because of (a) his legal ability
(b) high professional standards
(c) absolute courage & independence

With the prospect of thereby cleaning the Department & securing hereafter at least, respectable federal judges, is a matter of supreme public importance. If Hoover will stand by him (I think he intends to do so), there should soon be a marked change in the professional attitude that will pervade even NY City & Chicago.

And a large premium is added to the appointment by the incidental riddance of Donovan from administrative circles.[2] I understand D. has behaved very badly.

I don't think Mitchell is a "liberal"—But he is a gentleman and intelligent & pure minded.

He was as S[olicitor].G[eneral]. incomparably better than even John W. Davis.

1. Confirming rumors that had been circulating for nearly a week, President Hoover announced that his choice for Attorney General would be William DeWitt Mitchell (1874–1955). Mitchell, a Minnesota lawyer, had been appointed Solicitor General by President Coolidge in 1925. He served as Attorney General through Hoover's administration. Mitchell was later chief counsel to the congressional committee investigating the attack on Pearl Harbor.

2. William Joseph Donovan (1883–1959), a highly decorated officer during World War I, served as assistant to the Attorney General from 1925 to 1929. His name had been whispered as the likely successor since mid-January, but in the end Hoover declined to appoint him to any cabinet position (Donovan was a "wet" and a Roman Catholic). During World War II, Donovan became director of the Office of Strategic Services and was appointed a major general.

To Felix Frankfurter

March 6, 1929 Washington, D.C. [Frankfurter Mss—HLS]

1. I am glad you wrote Bob Szold as you did. I had received enclosed from Bob Miller on the same day; and immediately requested Harlan [F. Stone] to work against Buchanan's appointment, which he is doing.¹ B. is making a drive a la modern business, determined to overcome sales resistance. He was here Monday & tried to see [William D.] Mitchell, who declined to see him, sending word that he is still Solicitor General. Urgent appeals to the Chief [Justice] & others are coming in his behalf from different parts of the Union. He is certainly making a bad impression upon members of our Court by his methods.

It is lamentable that men like Bob Szold and Bob Miller haven't a better sense of the public interest.

2. What you say to C.C. [Burlingham] about the judges is true. Neither Woolsey nor Wheat are more than respectable.² They are that, and, perhaps, considering what the N.Y. districts have become, that is a good deal.

3. Hoover has made a good start in putting law observance first in his message.³ I have asked Harlan to get him (a) to give to the foreign embassies the tip that liquor should not be served

to Americans, (b) to get his Cabinet to refuse to go to dinners where liquor is served.

3. [*sic*] I agree with you that it is important that you get out a case book on Federal jurisdiction, and if Turrentine is available to you as aid, I shall be glad to provide for that purpose the Twenty five hundred (2500) Dollars.[4]

4. I suppose H. L. Shattuck's passing into the Treasuryship will deprive the Com[monweal]th of his services as legislator.[5]

1. John Grier Buchanan (b. 1888) was a Pittsburgh attorney whose name had been mentioned as a possibility to replace Mitchell (see preceding letter) as Solicitor General. He did not get the nomination.

2. Alfred A. Wheat (see LDB to Frankfurter, 22 February 1928, n. 6) and John Munro Woolsey (1877–1945), a New York lawyer, had been named to federal judgeships by President Coolidge, but their nominations had not been acted upon by 4 March, when Coolidge left office. Both men's names were resubmitted for judicial offices by President Hoover, and both were confirmed by the Senate. Wheat went to the Supreme Court of the District of Columbia; Woolsey became judge of the District Court for the Southern District of New York.

3. See next letter, n. 2.

4. The book was eventually coedited by Frankfurter and Wilber G. Katz (see LDB to Frankfurter, 20 September 1929, n. 6). *Cases and Other Authorities on Federal Jurisdiction and Procedure* (Chicago, 1931). Lowell Turrentine had graduated from Harvard Law School in 1922. He taught at Stanford University.

5. Shattuck (see LDB to Frankfurter, 13 May 1925, n. 2), a foe of Savings Bank Life Insurance, had just been appointed treasurer of Harvard College.

To Felix Frankfurter

March 13, 1929 Washington, D.C. [Frankfurter Mss—HLS]

1. Edward P. Costigan, Counselor at Law, Denver. I haven't the street address. He returned to D. immediately on resigning from the Tariff Com[missio]n last year & has been Miss Roche's close adviser throughout.[1]

2. Of course Harlan [F. Stone] is not a "thorough"—But I see no reason why you shouldn't let him have your view direct at any time. Doubtless he would be glad to hear from you—on any subject; inter alia on the right men for the Commission.[2]

3. The C[hief].J[ustice]. is urging [William D.] Mitchell to draft a bill to submit to the extra session on the subsidiary courts without a jury.[3]

4. I read Mrs. Matthew's first articles carefully & glanced at the next. They seemed to me unworthy and I think did Eugene M[eyer] injustice.

5. Hoover made an excellent impression when we called yesterday. It is an immense relief to think that C[alvin].C[oolidge]. has passed into the discard.

6. Might it not be well to send Mitchell your Cornell article? [4]

7. O[liver].W[endell].H[olmes]. is in fine form. I said to him Monday, "By Wednesday you—true spendthrift as you are—will have your cases written & then nothing to do for nearly four weeks". He answered, "I mean to enjoy myself, reading metaphysics."

8. Lowell must be squirming a bit, despite his thick hide.[5]

9. I had not heard of A. A. Young's death.[6]

1. Josephine Roche, after long experience in social work, including the federal Children's Bureau and the Family Court of Denver, came into an inheritance which made her chief stockholder in the third-largest coal-producing mine in Colorado. She immediately began protesting against the anti-union and, as she saw it, unenlightened and repressive management of the company. Eventually she bought additional stock giving her controlling interest in the mine, the Rocky Mountain Fuel Company. She then recognized the United Mine Workers as bargaining agent for the men, and negotiated a model contract which gave the workers a decent wage scale, and incentives that made them, to some extent, cooperating partners in the firm. From the start, the Rockefeller-owned Colorado Fuel and Iron Company, which was strongly anti-union, opposed Miss Roche's policies and did all it could to undermine her work. For accounts of her work, see Josephine Roche, "Mines and Men," *Survey* 61 (15 December 1928): 341–44, and "Miners in Line," *ibid*. 65 (15 October 1930): 86.

2. The strong interest in law enforcement that President Hoover revealed in his inaugural address (see preceding letter) was demonstrated by his announcement on 9 March of the details of a high-level commission to study the problem in all of its aspects. Officially "the National Commission on Law Observance and Enforcement," the group soon became known as the Wickersham Committee after its chairman, LDB's old enemy from Pinchot-Ballinger days, George W. Wickersham. Other members of the commission included Roscoe Pound, Newton Baker, and William S. Kenyon. During the next two years the Wickersham Committee undertook a comprehensive study of the whole area of federal jurisprudence and legal administra-

tion. See *The Report of the National Commission on Law Observance and Enforcement*, 14 vols. (Washington, D.C., 1929–31). Unfortunately, the findings of the commission were largely overlooked because of the furor raised by the volume on enforcement of prohibition. The body of the report seemed to argue that prohibition legislation was not enforceable, but the commission concluded that the experiment should not be abandoned—a position calculated to draw the fire of both wets and drys. While debating the prohibition issue, the public ignored the other conclusions of the Wickersham report. See next letter.

3. On 9 March LDB wrote Frankfurter: "The C. J. is now keen on subsidiary courts without juries, & always refers to your & Landis' articles [see LDB to Frankfurter, 2 June 1925, n. 1]. . . . Harlan [F. Stone] also is for this & reforms in procedure. Wants a man to head the judicial committee. I hope they wont let their eagerness for measures submerge the pressing need for men."

4. Felix Frankfurter, "Distribution of Judicial Power Between United States and State Courts," 13 *Cornell Law Quarterly* 499 (1928).

5. "President Lowell and the Sacco Alibi," *New Republic* 58 (13 March 1929): 85–86. The article recounted an episode in the advisory committee's deliberations wherein Lowell accused two witnesses for Sacco of lying but later was forced to apologize when documentation substantiating their testimony was presented.

6. Young (see LDB to Frankfurter, 5 December 1926) died on 8 March.

To Felix Frankfurter

March 17, 1929 Washington, D.C. [Frankfurter Mss—HLS] *Confidential:* The President sent for me & I had a long talk with him [*] about his Law Commission, which he is taking very much to heart.[1] He discussed with me the human material (only lawyers) and I had a chance to suggest Judge Andrews, Bikle, and Monte Lemon [*sic*].[2]

What he needs & so far has failed to think of is a man for chairman—someone, who besides other qualities, can dramatize the situation. If you can think of the right man, wire me.

1. See preceding letter, n. 2.

2. Perhaps William Shankland Andrews (1858–1936), who was judge of the Supreme Court of New York from 1900 to 1917, at which time he went to the Court of Appeals. For Bikle see LDB to Frankfurter, 21 February 1929, n. 11. Monte M. Lemann (1884–1959), a Harvard Law School graduate of 1903, practiced law in New Orleans and was a professor at Tulane Law School. Lemann was appointed to the Wickersham Commission.

To Felix Frankfurter

April 3, 1929 Washington, D.C. [Frankfurter Mss—HLS]

1. Now that the gasoline tax has become universal, it occurs to me that it might be well to provoke a state excise tax on intrastate gross receipts of all street-using (including street crossing) light, power & telephone companies—and that, with adequate knowledge & ingenuity, some tax could be devised which would have a tendency to take some of the swollen earnings out of these companies. My thought is (a) to hitch an able economist with an able young graduate of yours & have them explore factually & legally the situation in each of the states & (b) to have Ben Flexner drawn in for consultation. To be effective the thing must be both comprehensive and intensive.

2. B. F. Goldstein turned up after his visit to you.[1] He is a vigorous person, has shown a fine instinct in his proposal for H[arvard].L[aw].S[chool].—and there should come good things from him if duly tended.

3. [William G.] McAdoo wont do [2]—as Hoover is steering clear of politics & wants no pronounced partisans on the prohibition question. He is thinking most broadly on law enforcement.

1. Benjamin Franklin Goldstein (b. 1895) graduated from Harvard Law School in 1917. After military service, he set up practice in Peoria, Illinois, and after 1920, in Chicago. He was active in Harvard Law School alumni affairs.

2. As head of the newly forming crime commission (see LDB to Frankfurter, 13 March 1929, n. 2 and preceeding letter).

To Morris Llewelyn Cooke

April 10, 1929 Washington, D.C. [Cooke Mss]

MY DEAR COOKE: The greatest of American wastes—except unemployment—is the the [sic] heavy cost of soliciting life insurance, the lapses resulting from over persuasion, and other extravagant expenditures of the private companies.

In June of this year, the Savings Bank System in operation will close its twenty first year. Enclosed memo of March 13/29 prepared by Miss Grady shows what has been achieved.[1] You will find in the insurance address,[2] in my "Business A Profession" its origins etc.

Organized labor, which helped us enact this measure, has given us no help in the many years of fighting for life, against the combined forces of the private companies, their soliciting agents and the bankers. We have just closed another successful campaign in which we defeated the enemy's bill to limit the amount of our insurance on any one life to $5,000.[3]—and passed our bill by which we shall gradually relieve the State from even the small expense of administration ($30,000) borne by it heretofore.[4]

Couldn't you get the Federationist to come out strong for Savings Bank Ins.? Look at April 13th "Labor" & see what the railroad men are doing.[5]   Cordially,

1. At the close of SBLI's twentieth year, ten banks were in the system; $57.8 million worth of insurance was in force, representing over seventy thousand policies.

2. See LDB to Adolph Brandeis, 10 October 1905, n. 1.

3. Senate Bill 132 was defeated on 30 January.

4. This bill, on a petition from Miss Grady's Savings Bank Life Insurance Division, was passed on 21 February.

5. The *American Federationist* did not take up the matter of savings bank insurance.

To Willis VanDevanter

April 17, 1929 Washington, D.C. [VanDevanter Mss]

MY DEAR VANDEVANTER: Throughout long years you have rendered to our Country and the Court devoted service of great value.

This day must not pass without the expression of my very high appreciation.

With every good wish.[1]   Cordially,

1. This date marked Justice VanDevanter's seventieth birthday.

To Felix Frankfurter

April 21, 1929 Washington, D.C. [Frankfurter Mss—HLS]

1. We like your Davison much. Hope he will take the job here if you can spare him.[1]

2. Fosdick is silly about Miss Roche's "persecution complex". I suggest that you write Costigan confidentially & ask him to tell you precisely what the Col. F & I. Co have done & what he would like to have them do.[2]

3. The C[hief].J[ustice]. told Thatcher [*sic*] with much emphasis that he ought to stick to his District Court job.[3] Van-[Devanter] and Harlan [F. Stone] agree. Those 3 C[ircuit]. C[ourt]. judges seem to have no conception of the mess they have allowed the Southern District of N.Y. to get into.

4. The Pres[iden]t's Law Com[missio]n seems to make urgent that series on Business of the Federal District Courts for which you have sketched the picture in the Cornell article and this week's N[ew]. R[epublic].[4]

5. Mrs. Holmes turned seriously ill Tuesday, I judge.[5] O.W.H. was absent from Court that day—has attended since. But yesterday at Conference he seemed crushed, and fully twenty years older than he has been for months—actually the old man. But he has done this week two opinions which I hope he will deliver tomorrow.[6]

When the time comes, Lockwood should be told to insist on staying with O.W.H. substantially all summer.[7] He is needed as no Secretary ever has been, & is evidently much beloved by O.W.H.

1. James Forrester Davison (b. 1902) graduated from Harvard Law School in 1929 and did take a job in Washington, D.C.—teaching law at George Washington University.

2. See LDB to Frankfurter, 13 March 1929, n. 1.

3. Thomas D. Thacher (see LDB to Frankfurter, 16 July 1926, n. 5) had been mentioned in connection with the crime commission.

4. "The Federal Courts," *New Republic* 58 (24 April 1929): 273–77. For the Cornell article, see LDB to Frankfurter, 13 March 1929, n. 4.

5. Fanny Dixwell Holmes was near death, and she finally died on 30 April. To Pollock, Holmes wrote: "We have had our share. For sixty years she made life poetry for me. . . ."

6. See next letter.

7. John Edwards Lockwood (b. 1904), Holmes's law clerk, did live with Justice Holmes during the summer of 1929. He then moved to New York City and went into private practice. During World War II Lockwood worked in various capacities for the federal government.

To Felix Frankfurter

April 22, 1929 Washington, D.C. [Frankfurter Mss—HLS]

Only a word to tell you that O[liver].W[endell].H[olmes]. turned up at Court with a smile &, as you saw, delivered his two opinions.[1]

He wrote yesterday his Saturday P.M. assignment.

He is not yet at his normal, but had gone a long way in pulling himself together.

1. See preceding letter. The two opinions Holmes delivered were both short and for a unanimous court, *Weiss* v. *Weiner*, 279 *U.S.* 333, and *Roschen* v. *Ward*, 279 *U.S.* 337.

To Felix Frankfurter

April 28, 1929 Washington, D.C. [Frankfurter Mss—HLS]

1. I assume you will not further R[oscoe].P[ound]'s ambition. It would be a disservice to the President.[1]

2. Yes. Hutchins will be a great loss to Yale L[aw].S[chool]. men, but it should give us a good law school at U. of C. & a liberalized University.[2]

3. Richards' death opens the way to improving Wisconsin.[3] I have advised Phil LaFollette (an extraordinarily promising man) to consult you about a Dean.

4. Tell Whitehead that "The Aims of Education" I could understand.[4] It is an admirable piece.

5. O[liver].W[endell].H[olmes]. is making a grand fight. But it is a very hard one.[5]

6. Glad Al Smith is coming to dine with the Harvard 40.[6]

Bill Rice is being considered for Dean at Wisconsin. Despite his mental limitations he may be the best man available for Wisconsin, as fitting their special needs—whether he has the executive ability, including tact in dealing with men—Phil LaF. will know much better than we. He has proved his courage, liberal attitude and devotion to public interests; and with Phil behind him might enable the State to make the most use of the School as an instrument of social & political development.[7]

Charles Eliot's father-in-law Dodge has just been in.[8] He is a friend of Ed Costigan & Miss Roche & opened his talk with me by speaking of his desire to get Rockefeller to take a friendly attitude. I suggested that he see you when he goes to New England.[9]

1. Apparently Dean Pound had asked Frankfurter's support in gaining a position on the national crime commission. Eventually, Pound was appointed to the commission.

2. Robert Maynard Hutchins (1899–1977) had just left his position as dean of the Yale Law School to assume the presidency of the University of Chicago. His twenty years at Chicago were notable for dramatic experimentation and the creation of a first-rate liberal university. He left the university in 1951, and after 1954 he was the director of the Center for the Study of Democratic Institutions.

3. Harry Sanger Richards (1868–1929) had been dean of the Law School at the University of Wisconsin since 1903.

4. Alfred North Whitehead, "The Aims of Education," *New Republic* 58 (17 April 1929): 244–46.

5. See preceding two letters.

6. On 15 May, Smith attended a dinner given by the forty Harvard professors who had endorsed his candidacy in 1928.

7. Rice did not receive the appointment.

8. Clarence Phelps Dodge (1877–1939) was a Colorado publisher and at one time a progressive politician. His daughter, Regina, had married Charles W. Eliot, II, the son of the former president of Harvard.

9. See LDB to Frankfurter, 13 March 1929, n. 1.

To Felix Frankfurter

May 11, 1929 Washington, D.C. [Frankfurter Mss—HLS]

1. I saw O[liver].W[endell].H[olmes]. a week ago today. He took the bait—telephoned me himself Wednesday asking me to come to see him & read me his piece—which is fine.[1]

Yesterday we had a Conference. I asked the C[hief].J[ustice]. to give him some opinions to write, one each week. Instead he gave OWH 3, with a promise on the donee's part not to write more than one a week. He is in fine form again, working as of old.[2]

2. Dean Bates was in Thursday. I assume he is remaining at Ann Arbor.[3] I told him earnestly our views as to what a state Law School & its Law Journal should do for its Judiciary.

3. Learned Hand, Alfred Bettman and Prof. [Joseph H.] Beale are looked for this afternoon.

4. Tomorrow I am to see Josephine Roche.[4] I suppose you take "Labor" & have seen in the last two numbers the progress they are

making with public opinion. Notably the 2 to 1 vote of commend by the State Industrial Commission.[5]

It was good to have had such talks last week. At all events, Thatcher [sic] stays put.[6] But how a well-meaning Bar Com-[mit]tee could entrust the Bankruptcy Cleansing job to [William J.] Donovan is beyond comprehension.[7]

1. Perhaps a part of the memorial service held at the Justice's home a few weeks after Mrs. Holmes's death. See preceding three letters.

2. On 16 May, LDB wrote to Frankfurter: "OWH. said today, he wouldn't object to carrying on as a judge until he was 90. I told him I wanted him to complete his 50 years as judge. He had a bit of a cough Monday & has some throat trouble still. But his main trouble is the many odds & ends he is bothering himself with. Still he is calm—for him at this season." Holmes had become a judge in 1882.

3. Henry M. Bates remained dean at the University of Michigan Law School until 1939.

4. See LDB to Frankfurter, 13 March 1929, n. 1.

5. *Labor* carried articles on the Rocky Mountain Co. in its issues of 4 and 11 May 1929. Workers in other mining companies demanded the same rights as those in the Rocky Mountain Co., and the Colorado State Industrial Commission, by a majority vote, granted their request.

6. See LDB to Frankfurter, 21 April 1929.

7. See LDB to Frankfurter, 4 February 1929.

To Felix Frankfurter

June 15, 1929 Chatham, Mass. [Frankfurter Mss—HLS]

1. In our talk yesterday we mentioned as subjects of investigation the police methods generally and third degree specifically. I assume you are making a large head, of the use of detectives & their methods, their effect on crime-making and their efficacy as means of conviction.

2. Also as a more general head the growing tendency to rely upon the police for media of proof. A great war can't be won by an exclusively mercenary array.

3. Also the fundamental enquiry (excluding in this connection liquor) to what extent criminal law has been overworked; that is to what extent court remedies and preventive administration should be substituted in dealing with mala prohibita.[1] Such subjects should tempt able investigators to enter the service. A worthy

report on any one of these (or a score of other subjects) would alone justify years of the Commission's efforts.

The thing Wick.[2] should impress upon the President is that "one bad oyster (in appointment of judge or U.S. att[orne]y) will spoil the stew."

1. "Evils prohibited by law." See LDB to Frankfurter, 2 July 1926.

2. George W. Wickersham's appointment as head of the crime commission (see LDB to Frankfurter, 13 March 1929, n. 2) was announced on 21 May.

To Felix Frankfurter

July 21, 1929 Chatham, Mass. [Frankfurter Mss—HLS]

1. The N[ew].R[epublic]. might appropriately comment on the I[nterstate].C[ommerce].C[ommission]'s recent action in ordering that the practice of hauling private cars for the officials of other R[ail]R[oads] & their families cease. This is one of the abuses uncovered in the Second Advance Rate Case (1913–14). It took 15 years to get the practice stopped. (See U.S. Daily July 19/29)

2. You made the situation clear to Chas. E. Clark. I talked to [Walton H.] Hamilton to the same effect when he was here, and had done so earlier. He is entirely of that view now; & agrees that the thing to do is to be keen in discovering & securing the unattached young [for Yale Law School faculty].

3. Paul, Elizabeth & Walter arrived yesterday in good form. They have already expressed the hope of seeing you here soon.

4. I will hold Richard W. Hale's books awaiting your coming.

5. A. N. Holcombe was here yesterday to see Auntie B. Later I had a talk with him. Does he represent the Political Science Department at Harvard?!!

To Felix Frankfurter

August 27, 1929 Chatham, Mass. [Frankfurter Mss—HLS]

1. Campbell, the N.Y. prohibition Com[missione]r, seems to be already acting on the Wick. letters and today comes Washington confirmation.[1]

2. And today comes also Hoover's states rights public land declaration. It looks like fighting all along the line.[2]

3. I fear that Weizmann-Lipsky policies & actions have a large part in the Palestine disaster—indirectly.[3]

4. Snowden's firmness is encouraging.[4]

5. I am glad you were so favorably impressed with Hutcheson. He should prove a great force for good in judicial matters.

6. I had a call from Butzel of Detroit, a newly appointed judge who did not make personally a good impression, & disclosed a pretty low in sphere of state judiciary.[5] He tells me that Isidor Levin [sic] will become practically head of the forum.

7. I understand from your telephone via Elizabeth that Powers of the Globe is to [be] here Saturday noon, Sept. 7.[6]

8. Re Rocky Mt Fuel Co enclosed reports.[7] I suppose the N[ew].R[epublic]. will already have set up some mention. But it should not fail to discuss fully the significance of this use of organized labor's purchasing power—the most neglected of social forces. Now that the employer-financial world has learned that high wages & the spending of them is essential to their own prosperity, and is voluble on "cooperation", labor should be taught that the spending must be primarily for the product of those who are friends, & it is easy enough to do so without getting enmeshed with the courts.

1. Wickersham had presented, on 17 July, his own plan for prohibition enforcement: Let the federal government be responsible for interstate violations and state governments for local ones. The text of his letter can be found in the *New York Times*, 17 July 1929. On 26 August, Maurice Campbell (1868–1942), the Federal Prohibition Administrator for the Eastern District of New York, issued a statement calling for the transfer to state jurisdiction of cases involving New York speakeasies. Campbell, who had a varied career in many fields of endeavor, resigned his post in 1930 calling for the repeal of the prohibition law. He edited *Repeal*, a monthly magazine advocating prohibition reform on the grounds that prohibition could not be enforced. For the extent to which the Wickersham position harmonized with LDB's own views, see LDB to Frankfurter, 7 February 1925.

2. Hoover suggested turning over 200,000,000 acres of federal lands to the states.

3. A series of violent riots by Arab mobs in Palestine had erupted on 23 August. The incidents left more than a hundred Jews dead and many wounded. Protests from all over the world (15,000 Jews marched on the British Embassy in New York City on this date) followed the clashes, and

both Weizmann and Lipsky seemed unable to influence British policy to take a firmer stand on behalf of Jewish settlements. See next letter.

4. Philip Snowden (1864–1937), a leading socialist writer and polemicist, was Chancellor of the Exchequer in Ramsay McDonald's first Labour government.

5. Henry Magnus Butzel (1871–1963) had just been appointed to fill an unexpired term on the Michigan Supreme Court. He was reelected frequently and served several terms as chief justice.

6. James H. Powers was a reporter for the *Boston Globe*.

7. When the Rockefeller interests cut wages 16 to 20 percent at its mines in Colorado, the union members in the Rocky Mountain Company, owned by Josephine Roche (see LDB to Frankfurter, 13 March 1929), had voluntarily taken a wage cut, and then had gone out to help sell the company's product to sympathetic consumers in order to help the owner withstand the increased competition from Rockefeller.

To Felix Frankfurter

September 6, 1929 Chatham, Mass. [Frankfurter Mss—HLS]

1. George Young [1] was brought here by Charles Crane this AM— obviously in order that Y. might talk with me, or rather have me talk with him, on the Palestine situation.[2] Crane immediately left us alone, and went into the next room to Alice, Eliz[abeth]. and Paul. And pretty promptly Young, as adviser of the Labor Party asked me about Palestine etc.—the past and the future. There was no option; but I was not sorry to do so. I told him fully and frankly my view—will tell you the details Monday. I was emphatic in my opposition to Great Britain's relinquishment of the Mandate (which he suggested) and against any material change in the fundamentals of the government;—insisting that there should be merely an avoidance of the British blundering largely responsible; and that we must start over & traverse the ground with a view to avoiding the same mistakes. i.a. that the Zionist Palestine Executive should be abolished etc. I told him that you, Mack & I agreed & why we kept silent. I told him that because of judicial office there were additional reasons governing me. He thought you might at the proper time help much, saying that "our people have confidence in him", and he wondered whether you could get leave from the [Harvard] Law School. He asked who among the English Jews might help in the present situation.

I suggested Sir Herbert Samuel. He then named Reading and I told Y. of my work with R. in 1920. I told him I thought Samuel, who knew the country, could help more. Young leaves America in Oct.

He said, unless something was done, it would not be surprising if in 2 or 3 years Great Britain surrendered her Mandate—that is [if] the views of some I[ndependent].L[abour].P[arty]. men might prevail.

I told him what I thought of Gabriel & he left me the impression that he had no better opinion of Gabriel [3] (see p. 2 for addition).

2. Morris Leeds' report to the Friends on unemployment,[4] quotes Whiting Williams [5] on the demoralization incident to irregularity and lack of employment and adds: "It is easy for those who are thus disheartened and embittered to turn to careers of crime"

Dr. Jastrow at Yale spoke of the relation of misery to crime.[6] Before the President's Com[missio]n makes its report, it should have made a thorough investigation of this subject.

3. Kenyon's letter is encouraging. I shall of course, be glad to talk with him; and also with Farrand if there is occasion. The letter to the C[hief].J[ustice]. should yield interesting [*].

4. And Gold [*]'s letter shows awakeness.

5. I fear the C.J. is less well than he was when the Term closed & that he is suffering still from his post term-Cincinnati excess. Nothing from him; but this is from one who saw him at Murray Bay.[7]

1. (continued) I put strongly the error of British in making it impossible for Jews to serve in the police & in the civil service and that in the future this should be corrected. Also that now that speech can be had with a few powerful Jewish leaders represented by the [Jewish] Agency, it would be possible to develop means by which Jews could help with men and money, without placing greater burden on the British in their own time of need.

Please have 1. copied and send one copy to Mack to be kept strictly confidential and one to me.

1. Probably Sir George Young (1872–1952), a Labour Party intellectual, authority on the Middle East, and frequent visitor and teacher in the United States.

2. See preceding letter, n. 3.

3. Edmund Vivian Gabriel (1875–1950), then in the United States, had been financial adviser and assistant administrator in Palestine in 1918 and 1919. See LDB to Julian W. Mack, 9 October 1929.

4. Leeds (see LDB to Frankfurter, 1 October 1928, n. 4) was a member of the Friends himself.

5. Whiting Williams (1878–[?]) was a lecturer, author, and consultant on labor problems.

6. Perhaps Joseph Jastrow (1863–1944), a prolific social psychologist and frequent university lecturer.

7. Murray Bay, Quebec, where the Tafts had a cottage. The Chief Justice's health had been failing steadily. He did appear at the opening of the October 1929 term and read an opinion on 25 November. By January, however, he was asking Van Devanter to read his opinions. By the end of that month he was convinced that he would be unable to continue and on 3 February he sent Hoover his resignation. Taft died on 8 March 1930.

To Felix Frankfurter

September 20, 1929 Washington, D.C. [Frankfurter Mss—HLS]

1. I had not thought it important that I should see MacDonald.[1] But I think it very important that you should. And if it proves that I am to see him, I want you present.

2. The most far reaching demand that we have to make is no discrimination and actual equal opportunity; that means, i.a. equal opportunity in every branch of the government service and under every government contract. Equal with Arabs and equal with British—with a few excepted positions.

I have faith that there are, or will be, in Palestine Jews who can, from the highest to the lowest positions, win out against the Arab in service. We should expect our Jews to do so; and our Jews should understand that no coddling [is] allowed.

For some of the tasks, for which Ashkenazim and Sephardim are not suitable, the Yemenites are. And even for the low-waged positions it should be possible, with the aid of workingmen's plots a la [Emanuel N.] Mohl, to get subsidiary family earnings which will, with Jewish intelligence & persistence, enable even Ashkenazim and Sephardim to take jobs at as low wages as Arabs. For the general cultural advantage & social services will be furnished them, in any event, by Jewish philanthropists, in a way not to pauperize, I hope.

Talk over such extension of the housing projects with B[ernard]. F[lexner]. when he is with you Wednesday.

3. Jews must not, after the present emergency is over, be denied the opportunity of defending themselves.[2] As against the Bedouins, our pioneers are in a position not unlike the American settlers against the Indians. I saw myself the need of their self-defense in 1919 in Poreah, with our Shomer,[3] on guard mounted on the hill top, and the blacktented Bedouins below who had peaceably but with ever robber purpose, crossed the Jordan. As to other Arabs, the position is not different in essence, of course. Most Arabs will have guns, or at least knives, concealed, if possession is prohibited. Of course, Jews should be adequately represented in an adequate police force. But under Palestinian conditions, no police force can be adequate if the Jews are kept defenseless.

4. We must make it clear to the British that our demand is for personal safety and opportunity—and try tactfully to have them forget about reparations,[4] or rather to let "reparations" mean reparation by wrongdoing Arabs, not by the Government.

Let me have your thoughts on the above & other matters in your mind.

5. B[ernard].F[lexner] will report fully to you on the [Felix] Warburg interview.[5] W. could not have behaved better. I think Kirstein had no small part in convincing W. he should call on me.

6. Kenyon (Sept 5 letter) learned his lesson well.

7. I had a line from Hutcheson that he expects to call on me here.

8. The Herald roast of Nichols is well done.

9. Likewise your answer to W[alter].L[ippmann]'s preposterous editorial.

10. As to the Katz fellowship.[6] My thought had been to pay the amount to the Law School to be applied to that specific purpose. If for any reason you think that would be undesirable, I will pay the amount into your special account and have you make the payment to him from time to time as is common on fellowships.

My thought had been to make the first payment Oct 1. ($625), and quarterly thereafter—if payment in that way accords with your wishes.

11. As to distributing "Labor Injunctions".[7]

    (a) I do not think of any designation of the donor more clearly innocuous than "a friend of the Harvard Law School". Of course you will send out many personally,

Oliver Wendell Holmes, Jr.

The United States Supreme Court in 1929

Franklin Delano Roosevelt

Felix Frankfurter

LDB and Alfred Brandeis

Solomon Goldman

Robert Szold

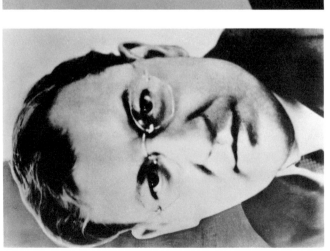

Emanuel Neumann

LDB and Fannie Brandeis

LDB, Alice Brandeis and their grandchildren

LDB at Chatham, 1931

Paul, Walter, and Elizabeth Raushenbush

and among these the Senators, Representatives and Judges with whom you have had personal relations on the subject. Please send a copy to Jacob H. Gilbert, 42 Broadway. A copy should go to Furuseth and to Dr. George L. Knapp of Labor.[8]

12. I do not think it wise to distribute copies generally to Senators and Representatives. But all legal periodicals should have copies; and so far as you can identify those who act as counsel for labor unions as "desirable citizens" the free instruction might be helpful.

13. AF of L News Sept 14.

14. Enclosed from the C[hief].J[ustice]. looks pretty bad.[9] Yes, he was more precise than usual about L.M.

1. James Ramsay MacDonald (1866–1937), one of the founders of the British Labour Party and its first prime minister, had just won his second election to that office. MacDonald had announced his intention to visit the United States in July, and he arrived in America (where one of his central purposes was the negotiation of a naval treaty) on 5 October. Naturally the visit provided an opportunity for American and Canadian Zionists to speak with MacDonald on conditions in Palestine under the Mandate, particularly after the recent riots (see LDB to Frankfurter 27 August 1929, n. 3). Finally LDB did meet with MacDonald (see LDB to Julian W. Mack, 9 October 1929 and to Frankfurter, 10 October 1929).

2. The British marines, rushed to Palestine from Egypt on 25 August, disarmed the Jewish population. See *New York Times*, 27 August and 1 September 1929.

3. a guard or watchman.

4. On 28 August the World Zionist Organization demanded reparations from the British government for losses of life and property in Palestine.

5. See LDB to Frankfurter, 23 September 1929.

6. See LDB to Frankfurter, 6 March 1929. Wilber Griffith Katz (b. 1902) graduated from Harvard Law School in 1926. After a period of private practice, he began a long association with the University of Chicago Law School in 1930, serving as dean from 1939 to 1962. He then moved to the University of Wisconsin.

7. See LDB to Felix Frankfurter, 20 December 1927, n. 2. Frankfurter and Nathan Greene published *The Labor Injunction* in 1930.

8. George Leonard Knapp (1872–19[?]) edited *Labor* between 1925 and 1934. He wrote a number of books, many of them for children, on military and patriotic topics.

9. See preceding letter, n. 7.

To Julian William Mack

September 20, 1929 Washington, D.C. [R. Szold Mss]

J.W.M.: 1. I am relying upon you to give to DeHaas a full account of all that has transpired with us from your first telephone to me after the commencement of the massacres [1] to and including my interview with Warburg yesterday.

2. I do not know when the Hadassah convention is to be held;—and I assume that the status of the Hadassah has been left unaffected by Congress and Agency Agreement.[2] B[ernard].F[lexner]. will probably be consulted about Hadassah affairs. The following may not be imminent, but I want you, Ben F., Felix and DeHaas to know the advice I gave Zip [Szold] and Pearl Franklin.

I think the persisting controversies between Hadassah and the Palestinians [3] should be adjusted, or minimized by action on the following lines:

1. So far as the health obligations can be satisfactorily taken over by the government, they should be.

2. The large portion of Hadassah's activities which cannot be taken over by the government, should by a persistent process of devolution, be turned over to the respective communities so far, and as quickly as, this can be reasonably done. The several communities (other than Jerusalem) must be made to assume the obligations incident to their local hospitals—Hadassah should give to those lopped off a gradually reducing subsidy. And each local should be left free to raise—in America—funds for this local institution by its own committee, etc. Hadassah should have one member on the local, so that it may know what is happening, but the local governing body must be left with the responsibility. Hadassah should keep the Jerusalem Hospital, and there work to establish and maintain the highest possible standard in connection with the University Medical faculty. Besides that it should do only the work which cannot be transferred to the Government or to the localities. That unescapable work would include the ever-coming new work of [   ] [4] undertakings. This irreducible minimum will be amply large to occupy all the time of the very competent Hadassah management. And all concerned must, with the high standard set by the Jerusalem Hospital, assume that the several communities

will insist upon competent local management. If the local folk let this hospital run down, they should bear the penalty of their inefficiency.[5]

I suppose DeHaas will want to come here soon. Tell him Tuesday the 24th—and either the 25th or 26th are fully occupied. Monday is free, and so will be days later in the week, for a session beginning 9 a.m.

1. See LDB to Felix Frankfurter, 27 August 1929, n. 3.

2. Article 6 of the Mandate stipulated that British administration of Palestine should include "cooperation with the Jewish Agency," and article 11 provided that the mandatory and the Jewish Agency could embark upon a series of cooperative endeavors in building the country. The Agency was to be representative of world Jewry, and until such an organ was established, the Mandatory could recognize the World Zionist Organization in that role. See LDB to Jacob deHaas, 14 February 1924, for the first steps in Weizmann's plan to create an enlarged and more representative Jewish Agency.

3. Hadassah had encountered numerous problems in establishing modern medical and hygienic standards in Palestine—both old-time Jews and Arabs opposed such measures as milk pasteurization. Moreover, the British administrators proved unwilling to cooperate with Hadassah in a number of programs.

4. There is a blank space in the copy.

5. See LDB to Zip Szold, 3 August 1930.

To Felix Frankfurter

September 23, 1929 Washington, D.C. [Frankfurter Mss—HLS]

1. Ben Flexner is to be here Saturday, again. Meanwhile he will submit to you the minutes of the Warburg interview and the draft of a formula of what Warburg may say publicly as to the extent of my participation in his management.[1] I am not sure that Ben realizes fully, as you do, the severe limitations which judicial office and my small vitality impose & I shall rely upon you to thresh this out with him, so that when he comes here Saturday (with others) there will be little to say on that subject.

During the four vacation months there will be ample time at Chatham for conferences and thinking, and that study of current facts on which thinking and judgment must be based if they are to be valuable.[2] But during the eight months of the Term the situation is very different. About half of that, which is devoted to arguments and conferences is practically a closed season. And the recess period may not be heavily invaded by either conferences or study of things Palestinian.

I had hoped that Warburg would be satisfied with my confining my functions strictly to thinking and the exercise of judgment, with the results communicated to him privately without its being publicly known that I was advising. He seems to think that this will not suffice, and that even public knowledge that he had advised with and consulted me would not be enough. I, of course, want to avail, so far as may be, of this opportunity of rescuing the Zionist movement from its aberrations and making prevail the policies which seem to us essential. But the difficulty, in view of my severe limitations, of utilizing not only my thinking and judgment, but such prestige as I have with the Jewish public, presents a problem which may be insoluble. And it may be necessary to very regretfully answer "non possumus" [3] to that.

Needless to say Warburg is entitled to all the help we can give him. And we want to help one who apparently is eager to go our way. I think he does not realize how much he will gain in support if, without any publicity as to my participation, only our small group are with him. For if we are with him, the forces of discontent aroused by deHaas and others will be at least quiescent. And the published participation of the other members of our group will lead to the assumption that I too approve etc.

2. The Bardo disclosures as to the shipbuilders lobbying on the Cruiser bill and the Merchant Marine,[4] should make it possible now to secure Congressional legislation requiring registration of legislative agents, and legislative counsel, with publication of expenses, on the general lines of the Mass[achusetts]. law long in force. The Federal law should be far more comprehensive. It should include all publicity men, require the filing of all contracts, monthly filing of expenditures and also as exhibits filing of all publicity matter etc. The Legislative Drafting Bureau counsel ought to be set to work promptly to draft a model bill and when it is introduced the N[ew].R[epublic]., Nation, N.Y. World et al. should give heavy support.

Wont you write on this, to the Senator most fit for the job?

3. The Senate's action in requiring the data from the tariff favors applicants and the formation of a women's consumers com-

[mit]tee, show that some progress has been made since my futile effort to secure, as counsel for the Young Men's Democratic Club, leave to crossexamine witnesses.

4. I hear that Bardo, formerly V.P. of the New Haven, was a very bad actor there.

1. The fall of 1929 saw the cautious and gradual reentry of LDB into public Zionist affairs. Felix Warburg, head of the Jewish Agency since Louis Marshall's death two weeks earlier, was approached by Bernard Flexner to explore the possibilities of cooperation between the non-Zionists and the Brandeis-Mack wing of the American Zionist movement. Warburg was more than anxious. He suggested that LDB leave the Supreme Court and assume the leadership of American Jewry. LDB refused, but did agree to come out in the open (see LDB to Frankfurter, 5 October 1929), promising to say a few words at a meeting Warburg would arrange on 24 November 1929. That meeting was to be a symbol of peace between the Brandeis-Mack wing and the wealthy non-Zionists. The attitude of the Zionist press at LDB's reentry could be summed up by the title of an article by Louis I. Newman: "The Return of the Pilot." With LDB's prestige now thrown openly into the balance, Louis Lipsky's defeat as leader of the Zionist Organization was inevitable.

2. See LDB to Joshua Bernhardt, 9 July 1930, n. 2.

3. "Not possible."

4. In a set of widely publicized hearings, commented upon even by President Hoover, the Senate's Naval Affairs Committee was uncovering a major scandal. It was revealed that a group of large shipbuilders had financed an expensive lobby, headed by William B. Shearer, to destroy the disarmament conference of 1927 in Geneva and to propagandize for the Merchant Marine Act of 1928. Clinton Lloyd Bardo (1867–1937), formerly a railroad executive, had assumed the presidency of the New York Shipbuilding Co. in 1928. He testified before the committee on 21 September, revealing the amounts paid to Shearer but stating that nothing improper had been done.

To Joseph Rauch

September 23, 1929 Washington, D.C. [Brandeis Mss, M 4–6]

MY DEAR DR. RAUCH: From our talk and the letters, you know my purpose in establishing the several libraries.[1] During the five years which have elapsed since the work was begun, the preliminary task of fashioning the instrument for development of the University and the people has been persistently pursued. These, in this rudimentary form, have been substantially completed and are ready for use. The books and papers have been collected and have been classified into the several libraries. They have been found, catalogued and shelved. And co-incident with the completion of this preliminary task, comes happily a new President, who, I am told, appreciates what has been done and is eager for our aid in developing the University.[2]

The time seems ripe for entering upon the second stage of our undertaking. We have now to use these instruments as the means of interesting the several sections of the community in the University and the University in them. I suggest, as a first step, that a series of functions, carefully planned and prepared for, be arranged through which persons having the special interest may be introduced to the particular library. My further suggestion is that the recent occurrences in Palestine [3] may make it desirable to inaugurate the series with the function on the Judaica-Palestine library, as American Jewry appears, for the moment at least, to be deeply stirred and unified. At that function it would be very helpful to have present Bernard Flexner. He has had a large part in the development of Palestine; and bids fair to have a much larger in the near future. He makes occasional visits to Louisville; and if he has ample notice of the desire to have him, would doubtless endeavor to so arrange his next visit, so as to attend your function.

Whether it is wise to begin with the Judaica-Palestine function you and Fanny Brandeis will know. And also, in what order the others should be held. If the J.-P. comes first, perhaps the Cooper collection on the Art Library should come next, and after those, the William N. Hailmann collection, in view of the restoration of Germany to public favor. My thought is that for each collection a small special committee of interested persons might be formed who could be relied upon for some effort to further the particular collection. And, of course, cooperation must be received from that section of the faculty especially interested.[4]

Cordially,

I assume that before any other action is taken you will have a full talk with President Kent.

1. At the University of Louisville.

2. George Colvin, whose stormy administration of University affairs (see LDB to Alfred Brandeis, 23 January 1927, n. 2) had effectively blocked the Brandeis family's projects, died in July 1928. He was succeeded by Dr. Ray-

mond Asa Kent (1883–1943). Kent had taught school throughout the Middle West and had served as a school superintendent. From 1923 to 1929 he was dean of the College of Liberal Arts at Northwestern University. Kent retained the presidency at Louisville until his death.

3. See LDB to Frankfurter, 27 August 1929, n. 3.

4. See LDB to Rauch, 13 October 1929.

To Edwin Francis Gay

September 25, 1929 Washington, D.C. [SBLI]

MY DEAR PROFESSOR GAY: [1] Through membership in the Massachusetts Savings Insurance League you helped to establish the System of Savings Bank Insurance. The results achieved in the twenty-one years of operation make me think that you may care to call to the attention of Harvard's Teaching Staff the opportunity which it offers of saving in the cost of this necessary of life.

Life insurance unsurpassed in quality is furnished by it at a net cost 26 per cent lower than that of the insurance companies. Beginning Nov. 1, 1929, the Boston Five Cents Savings Bank, the largest in the Commonwealth, and two others will open insurance departments. This raises the amount of insurance issuable on a single life from $10,000 to $13,000 and the annuities to $2,600.

The volume of business is increasing rapidly. For the 10 months ending Aug. 31/29 the premium receipts were over 30 per cent above those of the preceding year. In the month of August the increase was more than 34 per cent. The enclosures give details.

The Cambridge Savings Bank is an agency.   Cordially,

1. Edwin Francis Gay (1862–1946) had taught at Harvard since 1902; from 1908 to 1919 he was dean of the Graduate School of Business Administration. In 1936 he became a member of the research staff at the Huntington Library in San Marino, California. During the war, Gay was director of the Division of Planning and Statistics for the War Industries Board.

To Edward Francis McClennen [Extract]

September 25, 1929 Washington, D.C. [SBLI]

Those opposed to the establishment of the Savings Bank Insurance System claimed that even if some persons *should* apply for life insurance in the savings banks, they would soon allow their policies to lapse and become forfeited for non-payment of premiums, because the experience of the [commercial insurance] companies had seemed to show that men would not pay their life insurance premiums except under the spur of the persistent persuasion of the insurance agent.

The answer to this is that the lapse ratio of the policies written by the savings banks is now less than 1 per cent of the number written. This is an accomplishment unequalled by any commercial company doing business in the United States, or, so far as we know, in the world. In 1927 the average lapse ratio of the policies written by the life insurance companies was more than 27 per cent on their ordinary policies, and more than 58 per cent on their weekly premium policies. In other words, the lapse ratio of the policies written by the insurance companies in their ordinary department was 27 times as great as that of the policies written by the insurance departments of the savings banks, and the lapse ratio of the policies written by the insurance companies in their weekly premium department was 58 times as great as that of the policies written by the insurance departments of the savings banks.

Not only have the people voluntarily applied for insurance and continued to pay their premiums during their residence in Massachusetts, but they have taken their policies with them to other parts of the United States, and to nearly every country in the known world, and still continue to pay their premiums from their new homes.

To Felix Frankfurter

September 26, 1929 Washington, D.C. [Frankfurter Mss—HLS]

1. Re Katz.[1] The $625 check to your special account has been signed (Oct 1) and you should receive notice thereof (as of the $1500 deposit) on October 2. Please call up 161 Devonshire if you do not. I assume from your silence that quarterly payments are o.k.

2. It's fine to know that the students are flocking to the seminar. Not surprising.

3. I rather think [Ramsay] MacDonald wont want to see either of us; and perhaps, with his other absorptions, official and social,

it will be as well. I had to decline the invitation to luncheon at the British Embassy October 5, i.a. because of my declination of all White House and Canadian minister invites. I shall probably meet MacDonald for a moment when he calls that day on the C[hief].J[ustice]. at the Capitol.[2]

4. Max [Lowenthal] probably told you of his and Monte [Lemann]'s call Monday.

5. When I wrote you about a bill for lobby registration, I didn't know that Carraway [*sic*] had gotten something of the sort through as a joint resolution at the last session & that it was stalled in the House.[3] Probably the Carraway resolution was wholly inadequate.

6. Thanks to Schlesinger,[4] Fox [5] and Greene [6] of the Amer. Historical Association were here Tuesday for a Conference with Vance (2 hrs),[7] in which the whole subject of (a) colonial legislation, (b) colonial judicial systems and unwritten law, with a [view] to gathering the source material and editing it and alternately (c) writing American Legal History. The subject was fully & sympathetically discussed.

7. Fox and Greene were eager, and Greene (who impresses me as a person of rare quality) volunteered that he would write you.

Greene said they would try to get together promptly for conference six to twelve of the historians most likely to know & be interested; would then take it up at their Nov. Exec. Com[mit]tee meeting, with a view to bringing it up at the Annual Conference (which I think is at Durham, North Carolina Christmas week).

8. I think I made clear to them that what we need is high class scholarship, directed to this field; and that, if the comprehensive plan is well conceived and a worthy sample product can be fashioned and exhibited, there will be no obstacle to their getting from some sources, the essential financial aid. Greene, I think, appreciates this fully.

9. Also that they should seek cooperation from the several law schools and the historical societies etc in the several states, but (at least at this stage) should not get entangled with, or look for help from, either the American Bar Ass[ociatio]n or the American Law Institute.

I mentioned Cardozo as among the few judges who might be interested—and if interested, help much.

10. If this thing shapes up well, and in time, you may think it

wise to say something on the subject at your U.C. talk on Research. But there is so much that we want the Law Schools to do in fields other than early history, that perhaps we had better leave this to the historians, at the present stage.

11. Not knowing the lay of the land, I thought it unwise to mention Notestein [8] to Fox and Greene. But I did speak to [Walton H.] Hamilton in July on this subject. He is the kind of historian whose studies should be directed to the colonial law.

12. Gregory (T[homas].W.) was here yesterday. He explained the Texas political flap.[9] Says it is wholly anti-Catholic, and thinks (as the Democrats wont nominate a Catholic again), the State is safely Democratic. He says Colquet [sic] (the only Texan selected by Hoover for high office—i.e. R[ail]R[oad]. Labor arbitrator) is a very, very bad egg, who should be very closely watched.[10]

1. See LDB to Frankfurter, 6 March and 20 September 1929.

2. See LDB to Julian W. Mack, 9 October 1929 and to Frankfurter, 10 October 1929.

3. See LDB to Frankfurter, 23 September 1929. Thaddeus Horatius Caraway (1871–1931) had represented Arkansas in the House from 1913 to 1921. He was elected to the Senate in 1920 and remained there until his death. His resolution on lobbying was S. Res. 197.

4. Arthur Meier Schlesinger, Sr. (1888–1965), had been a professor of American history at Harvard since 1924. His many books covered the whole range of United States history and, in several instances, offered striking and provocative new approaches. See his autobiography, *In Retrospect: The History of a Historian* (New York, 1963). LDB had met Schlesinger through Frankfurter. For Schlesinger's view of LDB, see "A Note to Volume V," above, p. xv.

5. Dixon Ryan Fox (1887–1945) was another leading American historian. He taught at Columbia from 1912 to 1934, when he accepted the presidency of Union College. Fox's interests were also broad, but his most memorable work centered on New York before and during the American Revolution. He was coeditor (with Schlesinger) of the authoritative thirteen-volume History of American Life series.

6. Evarts Boutell Greene (1870–1947), another leading colonial and revolutionary historian, taught at the University of Illinois until 1923, when he moved to Columbia.

7. John Thomas Vance (1884–1943) was the Law Librarian at the Library of Congress.

8. Wallace Notestein (1878–1969) taught English history at Cornell before moving to Yale in 1928.

9. The Democratic Party in Texas split down the middle during the 1929 gubernatorial race, one candidate running explicitly against Al Smith. See *New York Times*, 1 September 1929.

10. Oscar Branch Colquitt (1861–1940) was an old-time Texas politico and oilman. He had served as governor of the state from 1911 to 1915.

To Felix Frankfurter

September 29, 1929 Washington, D.C. [Frankfurter Mss—HLS]

1. J[ulian].W.M[ack]. or B[ernard].F[lexner]. have doubtless told you of the plan agreed upon at yesterday's Palestine conference.[1]

2. If Warburg accedes, it will be just as well not to have any session with [Ramsay] MacDonald; or if we have one, to limit its scope.[2]

    3. As to you appearing at the N.Y. Com[missio]n Enquiry:[3]
    If the invitation comes in due form, I think
    (a) that it is wise to respond
    (b) that it will be best to talk on the ineffectiveness of regulation of the present sort—the great superiority of regulation by means of a contract, and therefore of the importance of the state's retaining its power etc.
A clear compact argument, inviting cross-examination.

4. [Harry] Schulman [*sic*] is here & enters upon the job with the promise of his being both helpful & an enjoyable associate.

5. [Irving B.] Goldsmith left yesterday, with, I think, a determination to make good in practice & life.[4]

1. For details of the conference, see LDB to Frankfurter, 5 October 1929.
2. See LDB to Julian W. Mack, 9 October 1929 and to Frankfurter, 10 October 1929.
3. Perhaps Frankfurter was anticipating an invitation to testify before the New York State Crime Commission, which was holding public hearings in late September and early October.
4. See LDB to Frankfurter, 7, 12, and 15 October 1928.

To Julian William Mack

September 29 and October 1, 1929
Washington, D.C. [Brandeis Mss, P 36–2]

J.W.M.: To overcome the Pro-Arab distortion of public opinion, we shall need a competent corps of writers, with access to the press, who will be ever vigilant and ready to meet the attacks. Wont you take this up with Ben [Flexner] and [Jacob] deHaas?

10/1/29

J.W.M.: Re yours of 30th.

In connection with publicity this should be taken up by deHaas and Ben F. DeHaas mentioned that the Jewish colonies were practically immune from attack;[1] that the casualties in Hebron, Safed, Jerusalem, were of the religious largely.

I too got that impression; and also that there was a very large percentage of Sephardim, or, at all events, of native Palestinian Jews.

If a careful check of figures etc. bears this out, it will be important, in its bearing on American and British public opinion to show:

1. That it is the religious bigotry, not economic competition, which caused uprising.

2. That native Palestinians are the victims pre-eminently.

And as bearing on the right of arming in self-defense,[2] it should impress the British that those communities which were prepared to defend themselves were left alone.

Nothing British seems to me so stupid as its prohibition of having arms.

1. In the late Palestinian riots (see LDB to Frankfurter, 27 August 1929, n. 3).

2. See LDB to Frankfurter, 20 September 1929, n. 2.

To Felix Frankfurter

October 5, 1929 Washington, D.C. [Frankfurter Mss—HLS]

1. Since writing you yesterday, I have, from Mack, yours of 3rd to J.W.M. & deH[aas] with accompanying memo.

As I entered the Conference on Sat. Sept 28,[1] my impression was in accord with your view, although deH. had outlined to me his view the day before. The conference, which was a real one, in which no words were wasted, led me to the conclusion that the decision arrived at was the wisest one.

It was helpful in clearing my mind.

(a) I am convinced that present situation requires some public action on my part—to satisfy not only American Jewish public opinion, but British officialdom and my own peace of mind. On the British official attitude, DeHaas' talk with Passfield & the undersecretary at P's residence was illuminating.[2]

(b) I was also convinced that a few words spoken at [Felix] Warburg's meeting would be the least taxing & least embarrassing of any public action suggested; and probably less so than a statement by Warburg of my participation would be.

(c) The Washington conference Nov. 3. is not within the realm of the controversial. Warburg is to call it personally. Neither rabbis, nor Jewish poli[ti]cians, nor American dignitaries, are to be present. I shall say literally only a few words—and I think my appearance there will not interfere with my otherwise universal "preclude",[3] just as my limited Zionist appearances prior to 1921 left me otherwise unembarrassed.

Abstinence at this time on my part would naturally be interpreted as loss of faith.

I think if you had been present at the Conference you would have reached the same conclusion.

2. Enclosed re Kelley, seems to close the chapter of the 4 responsible for the Wan case. Two died. Burlinghame got his show last spring and now Kelley.

Mail may reach me more promptly if addressed to P.O.B. (without number) U. (You) Street Station. Poindexter calls for my mail.

1. The conference was held to discuss, among other things, LDB's role in American Zionism during the next months. See LDB to Frankfurter, 23 September 1929, n. 1.

2. See LDB to Rennie Smith, 29 October 1930, n. 2.

3. LDB's standard method of avoiding invitations was to state "Judicial office precludes . . ." For example, see LDB to W.E.B. DuBois, 10 January 1929.

To Julian William Mack

October 9, 1929 Washington, D.C. [R. Szold Mss]

J.W.M.: Private. 6:20 PM.[1]

I had adequate time with MacDonald alone [2] to present to him these points, introducing them by saying that he knew Palestine probably better than I:

1. That American Jews, the four & a half millions were practically united in their determination—having gained in recent years (a) the labor-Hebrew trades [and] (b) the rich & potent who had not been with us in the days of the Balfour Declaration.

2. That American Zionists had in the letter of Feisal to F.F.[3] special assurance of friendly cooperation from the Arabs, which should completely answer the Arab claim of a promise in 1915 etc.[4]

3. That Jews wanted the opportunity of self-defense, & equitable participation in all governmental positions & that they had by tests shown their fitness etc.

4. That Americans wanted the assurance that in the important undertaking they were planning (Dead Sea [5] & otherwise) they would not be confronted with obstacles. Among other things there should be no restriction on immigration, as there are now no unemployed Jews in P., & reconstruction of the damaged & destroyed properties & erection etc. of the new would make a call for many laborers etc.

5. That there were some local officials who were anti-Jewish & that especially those with Eastern and Indian experience couldn't understand our Jews & that such should be removed as Balfour caused [Edmund V.] Gabriel's removal in 1919.[6]

He then spoke of the Com[missio]n of Enquiry [7] whose report they must await & the provision for counsel representing the Jews, the Arabs & the government. Said that in England they had had no intimation of any danger (I told him the local government should have had—that I had heard enough to make preparedness essential & of course the local officials must have heard many times as much and disregarded the communications).

He ended with the assurance that his Government would live up to the obligations its predecessors had assumed & had no thought of making any change in the terms & nature of this obligation & that we Americans could rest assured that we would have the opportunity to carry forward our work.[8]

1. LDB had met with MacDonald (see next note) at 5:30 P.M.

2. On 6 October, LDB wrote Mack: "Yesterday . . . I had a telephone from the British Embassy asking whether I would come to tea with MacDonald on Wednesday next at 5:30. This I think is the result of Felix' cables to Harold [Laski]. I said Yes to the invitation. I don't know whether I shall be alone with MacD. Let me have any suggestions from you and deHaas." LDB also wrote Frankfurter for suggestions.

3. One of the crucial documents in the ever-sharpening debate between Jews and Arabs over Palestine was the famous letter written by King Feisal (1885–1933) to Felix Frankfurter on 3 March 1919. The key passage of the Feisal letter read: "We Arabs, especially the educated among us, look with the deepest sympathy on the Zionist movement. . . . [W]e will wish the Jews a most hearty welcome home." Earlier, in January 1919, Feisal had concluded a similarly cordial agreement with Chaim Weizmann. In a second letter of this date to Mack, LDB wrote: "Have Felix send a copy of the Feisal letter, through Harold, to the Government, as MacDonald appeared not to have heard of it."

4. Just as the Jews based their claim to building a homeland in Palestine under British rule upon the Balfour Declaration, the Arabs presented a similar claim based on the so-called McMahon promise. In an exchange of letters between Sir Henry McMahon and the Sherif Hussein in 1915, the British held out the hope of a greater united Arab kingdom of Hedjaz, under Hussein's rule, provided the Arabs joined with the World War I Allies in their fight against Turkey. After the early riots in Palestine, Arab nationalists argued that the McMahon pledge included all of Palestine within the boundaries of Arab rule. McMahon and other members of the wartime British government denied this claim, maintaining that cis-Jordanian Palestine had been explicitly excluded from Arab control. Later historical studies have upheld this latter view; the most definitive treatment can be found in Isaiah Friedman, *The Question of Palestine, 1914–1918, British-Jewish-Arab Relations* (New York, 1973).

5. See LDB to Mack, 22 November 1925, n. 1.

6. Gabriel (see LDB to Felix Frankfurter, 6 September 1929, n. 3) had long experience in India before coming to Palestine.

7. The British Inquiry Commission sailed for Palestine on 13 October. The Shaw Commission, as it was called after its chairman, Sir Walter Shaw, took testimony in Jerusalem and issued its findings in March 1930. The majority report blamed the riots on the conflict between Jewish and Arab national aspirations and on confusing British policies. It recommended slowed immigration of Jews and a clear divorce between government in Palestine and the Zionist organization. In general, Arabs praised the report and Jews

regarded it as an exoneration of the rioters. See LDB to Mack, 5 April 1930 for LDB's reaction to the report.

8. See next letter; see also LDB to Felix Frankfurter, 29 November 1929.

To Felix Frankfurter

October 10, 1929 Washington, D.C. [Frankfurter Mss—HLS]

1. B[ernard].F[lexner]. will send you copy of my memo to him of the interview with MacDonald, and will also transmit my suggestion that a copy of Feisel's [sic] letter to you be sent through Harold [Laski] to Passfield.[1]

2. MacDonald was entirely friendly. Said he was glad we had met at last, but I am not sure that much of what I said to him will stick. He tried to listen. We were alone in the front embassy room, seated on the sofa, out of sight even, while we talked, of all others at the tea. And there were none but the Embassy folk there except Borah and Swanson and their wives.[2] MacD. had talked to Borah before he did to me, while he was taking copiously of tea and cakes. (As he came in I had said to him in a low voice that I wanted a little talk with him.)

But MacDonald look[ed] very distracted. Alice thought alarmingly so. She heard at the Ishbel luncheon [3] that he had been up till 4 A.M. with his Secretary after the Tuesday function at the Embassy and that he was up again at 7 A.M. to attend the Breakfast with 18 labor men at Sec[retar]y Davis'.[4]

All that looks like a repetition of his earlier conduct as P[rime].M[inister].

Mark Sullivan who was in last evening with the O'Briens & Col. Ritchie, of the British Army [5] (Harold [Laski]'s friend) said MacD. had unquestionably made an excellent impression.

Nevinson [6] says MacD's impromptu N.Y. speech was the best he ever made.[7]

You and [Edwin F.] Gay will know what it is best to do about promoting Savings Bank Insurance among faculty members. I suppose [Arthur M.] Schlesinger would be glad to help. If a circular is decided upon, please send me a copy when issued.

1. See preceding letter. Lord Passfield was Sidney Webb.
2. Senator Borah was the chairman of the Senate Foreign Relations Com-

mittee. The ranking Democrat on that committee was Claude Augustus Swanson (1862–1939). Swanson, a former Virginia Congressman and governor, served in the Senate from 1910 until he resigned to become Franklin Roosevelt's Secretary of the Navy in 1933.

3. Ramsay MacDonald was accompanied by his daughter Ishbel.

4. James John Davis (1873–1947) was a Welsh immigrant who began as an ironworker and went on to serve as Secretary of Labor for Harding, Coolidge, and Hoover. Davis resigned in 1930 to enter the Senate from Pennsylvania. He served there until 1945.

5. Perhaps Lt. Col. Thomas Fraser Ritchie (1875–1931).

6. Henry Wood Nevinson (1856–1941) was a distinguished liberal journalist with vast experience and a wealth of American contacts. He was covering the MacDonald visit for the *Manchester Guardian* and had dined earlier in the week with LDB.

7. Probably his remarks upon arriving in the city, 5 October.

To Felix Frankfurter

October 13, 1929 Washington, D.C. [Frankfurter Mss—HLS]

1. The C[hief].J[ustice]. has abandoned the practice of taking as law clerk a Yale graduate. Instead, he has taken as permanent assistant Robertson, former Ass't Clerk. The man who wrote the book on L[ower].C[ourt]. jurisdiction.[1] In view of the C.J.'s health,[2] this is fortunate & should greatly facilitate his work, on certioraris, statements of jurisdiction & otherwise. (Besides, I guess, the C.J.'s choice last year of Parsons, against the advice of the faculty, was not a happy one.) The C.J. seemed pretty ragged at Conference yesterday.

2. The C.J. submitted to the Council, at my suggestion, the project of increasing to 5 the number of judges on C[ir-cuit].C[ourt of].A[ppeals] & District C. of Appeals—the submission being for discussion & consideration now & during the year; & for action next year. Dennison[*sic*][3] and Manton[4] are for it. The others reserved their opinions. My suggestion was that the 5 be made up by calling in, where necessary, district judges. The argument in favor: (a) there should be an opinion, & adequate ones, in every case. If C.C.A. decision final, for that reason. If not final, to aid Counsel in determining whether to appeal & to help us. (b) To secure benefit of more minds at argument. (c) To secure benefit of more minds in Conference.

I think it would be well to start discussion of this project in the law reviews. You will recall [George W.] Anderson and B. Hand are for it.

3. My impression is that Shulman is too good in mind, temper, and aspirations to waste on a New York or other law offices. ("Lass den [*]"). Can't you land him somewhere in a law school next fall? You will recall that Yale needs men; and [Walton H.] Hamilton thinks that the right man there would find no opposition on the score of anti-Semitism.[5]

4. It seems to me that a great service could be done generally to American law and to the Jews by placing desirable ones in the law school faculties. There is in the Jew a certain potential spirituality and sense of public service which can be more easily aroused and directed, than at present is discernible in American non-Jews. And the difficulty which the Law Schools now have in getting able men may offer opportunities, not open in other fields of intellectual activity. The satisfaction I had in having Page and Friendly with me is a good deal mitigated by the thought of their present activities.[6] Of course it is possible that they, or at least Friendly, may reform and leave his occupation.[7]

It would have been possible to divert [Irving B.] Goldsmith from the private practice, but he lacked the qualities which would have made him desirable in a law school, or in any important public service. He is in the [Samuel H.] Maslon class.

5. That's an admirable statement by Sheldon Glueck re uniform definition of crimes.[8]

1. Reynolds Robertson, *Appellate Practice and Procedure in the Supreme Court.* . . . (New York, 1928).

2. See LDB to Frankfurter, 6 September 1929, n. 7.

3. Arthur Carter Denison (1861–1942) had been circuit judge for the Sixth Circuit since 1911.

4. Martin Thomas Manton (1880–1946) had been circuit judge for the Second Circuit since 1918.

5. Harry Shulman (see LDB to Frankfurter, 12 October 1928, n. 1) did in fact go to Yale after leaving LDB.

6. Both Robert Page (see LDB to Frankfurter, 9 November 1926, n. 2) and Henry J. Friendly (see LDB to Frankfurter, 14 March 1926, n. 11) were in private practice.

7. For LDB's own decision to reject teaching and go into private practice, see LDB to Charles Nagel, 12 July 1879 and to Adolph Brandeis, 30 May 1883.

8. Sheldon Glueck (b. 1896) taught criminology and criminal law at Harvard until 1963. He wrote dozens of books and articles on various facets of the subject and advised Justice Robert Jackson regarding the definition of war crimes. He was particularly expert, however, in the study of juvenile delinquency.

To Joseph Rauch

October 13, 1929 Washington, D.C. [Brandeis Mss, M 16–1]

MY DEAR DR. RAUCH: Replying to yours of 8th:

First: I accept, of course, your judgment (in which I understand Fanny Brandeis concurs) that the Fine Arts Library should be the subject of the first function.[1]

I add, that order of the later ones is entirely immaterial to me. Our purpose in establishing the several libraries was to create tools which might be employed to raise the level of the intellectual and spiritual life of the community and to develop the University in so doing. The plan of separate libraries was adopted because it was believed that thereby it would be easier to interest the various classes and sections of the population, through making the special appeals. The libraries were made memorials to individuals who had made cultural contributions to the city, because it was believed that thereby the general purpose could be furthered. Those who use the tools must decide how and when they shall be employed.

Second: For me to write Dr. [Raymond A.] Kent to come here for a conference would be sure to mislead him. He would interpret the invitation as the expression of an intention to continue, or even increase, my gifts to the Library. To do, at present, more than complete the cataloguing and binding of the material already sent, would tend to defeat my purpose. The community and the University can, in my opinion, be worthily developed only through their own efforts. In providing the tools, I thought they would have at hand the means of helping themselves. This presupposes, of course, that there will be sought out some individuals, in the faculty and outside of it, who really care; and that these will prove that they care by taking trouble—and, among other things, thinking.

I made my ideas as to this very clear in my early letters—to

Adele Brandeis in 1924, at whose instance my first contributions were made; and, before any action was taken by me, I secured, on behalf of the department then involved, Norman Ware's assurance. I had on this subject later a full understanding with President Ford. And following that, a committee was formed which included members of the faculty representing several departments. Then came Ford's death and the blight of the Colvin administration.[2] I had faith that there would be a brighter day, so I concluded to go forward and complete the tools which I had devised. Now they are about completed. And the brighter day appears to have come. I am convinced that Louisvilleians, in and out of the faculty, must now take the initiative, and use the tools energetically, if anything worthwhile is to be accomplished.

Third: Since Fanny Brandeis' conference with you, she has received a very cordial letter from Dr. Kent, which you and she may think opens the way to her taking up with him the proposed functions and securing an invitation for you. Moreover, the situation within the Board of Trustees may be more favorable than you assumed. Robert N. Miller wrote me recently, after a visit to Louisville and talks with Mr. Seligman[*sic*][3] and Dr. Kent: "It looks as if his (Dr. Kent's) coming changes the air sufficiently so that people interested in the University will be able to unite in helping him along and there are signs that this is likely to happen." I may add, that Dr. Kent expressed to Miller a desire to talk with me and that when he had to come East, he would stop in Washington; but could not do so "for awhile". Mr. Gentry's recent talk with Fanny about Dr. Kent's attitude toward the Library is also significant.

Fourth: The gifts which I made to the Library of the Law School have led to considerable activity on its behalf in the faculty and among the bar. Despite the fact that lawyers constituted so potent a factor in Colvin's support, the function inaugurated in connection with the Law School gifts appears to have produced the result contemplated.

As you see, I continue to take a hopeful view.   Cordially,

1. See LDB to Rauch, 23 September 1929.
2. See LDB to Alfred Brandeis, 23 January 1927, n. 2, and to Rauch, 23 September 1929.
3. Alfred Selligman (1871–1933), a Louisville attorney, was a member of the Board of Trustees for the University of Louisville.

To Robert D. Kesselman

October 20, 1929 Washington, D.C. [Kesselman Mss]
MY DEAR KESSELMAN: 1. Your letter is the best of birthday presents.[1] I have such faith in Jews and Palestine, that I believe the Arab outlook will prove a blessing ultimately. It will strengthen the determination of the Palestinians; unify the Jews elsewhere; and open the eyes of the British. Much in these lines has already been accomplished.

2. DeHaas will tell you of the more active participation of our group.

3. I am glad you have been at Aden, and have gained a wider knowledge of the Arabian Jews. The Yemenites should prove an important factor in Palestinian development—particularly in connection with the Dead Sea project;[2] and your knowledge will prove helpful.

4. I am glad also of what you write concerning Mrs. Kesselman's activity. I have advised the Hadassah to proceed as rapidly as possible with the devolution of its Palestinian functions, with few exceptions.[3]

It is a great satisfaction to us to know that you and [Emanuel N.] Mohl, and a few others from America, are on the firing line. With every good wish,

1. On 13 November LDB would be seventy-three.
2. See LDB to Julian Mack, 22 November 1925, n. 1.
3. See LDB to Mack, 20 September 1929.

To Julian William Mack

October 20, 1929 Washington, D.C. [R. Szold Mss]
J.W.M.: Confidential
Re yours of 17.
Of course, you must not neglect your C[ircuit]. C[ourt] of A[ppeals]. & D[istrict]. C[our]t. work. There is very much can be done for Palestine now. But with [Felix] Warburg and [Bernard] Flexner deeply interested and involved, I think you can, with an easy mind lessen your activity, provided it can be brought about that they take deH[aas]. into their entire confidence—recognizing his limitations and appreciating his un-

equalled knowledge, complete devotion & his resourcefulness. I am convinced that if what he can contribute is treated by them as material for use, no one can be of greater service. Warburg and F. as the dominant statesmen ought to make up their minds to this.[1]

I have had from Flexner since Oct. 1 only the one letter of which he sent you copy.

1. LDB made directly to Felix Warburg the suggestion that deHaas be taken on as an assistant, but Warburg politely declined. Shapiro, *Leadership of the American Zionist Organization*, 240. To Frankfurter on 22 October LDB added: "DeH. has the qualities of a most valuable aid. He was to Herzl. He was to me. He has been during the past two years to J.W.M[ack]. I am sure B.F. and Warburg would have a like experience with him, if they secured him as aid." See LDB to Mack, 7 and 13 February and 12 July 1930.

To Julian William Mack

October 20, 1929 Washington, D.C. [Brandeis Mss, Z 36–2]

J.W.M.: Re yours of 16th

1. Of course, I agree with you that the immediate need is large investment funds; among other things, in order to require for its employment immigration on a large scale. We must increase our numbers and we must consolidate our colonies, to as few as possible territorially by buying land in between and by building workmen's settlements. We can best live in amity with the Arabs by not living too near them. That is a common experience among blood relations.

2. The new Arab propaganda needs resolute persistent attention on our part, as the N[ew].R[epublic]. (Oct. 23d) and the coming Survey further evidence.[1] These attacks may be made to our benefit, if through them, we can arouse pro-Palestine activity.

3. Paul Kellogg sends me today the MacCullum article. I am writing him that as it is already in the stone and comprehensive changes are impossible, I refrain from any suggestions.

4. I think we must go slow on hitching up with Jabo[tinsky].[2] We must be strongly pro-British and as such hold them up to a policy best for them and for us. He is not in sympathy with the British au fond. We must win [Felix] Warburg completely.[3]

5. I am enclosing letter and enclosures from Kesselman which please show deH[aas]. and have returned to me after others of the group have seen them.

6. Have you seen the memo to British Labor Party submitted by DosHos? You and deH. should.

7. Since writing the above, I have yours special delivery.

    a. I agree that Felix [Frankfurter] would be the best man if he has the time to prepare and attend, and if not, that DeH. should be selected.

    b. I agree also that it is much better to wait until Jan. 3d. for the F.P.A. meeting.[4]

8. Am writing DeH. re [Israel B.] Brodie.

1. George C. Young, "The Labor Government and the Near East," *New Republic* 60 (23 October 1929): 260–62. "It seems likely that unless the imported Zionists can soon settle down on as friendly terms with the Arabs as the local Jews, the Labor party will begin to consider substituting direct administration by the League of Nations for the British mandate. . . . If Zionism is to realize its ideal, it must sever its association with British imperialism." Elizabeth P. MacCallum, "An Arab Voice," *Survey* 63 (1 November 1929): 130ff. The article is an exposition of the political and cultural views of a westernized Arab, Ameen Rihani; there is almost no mention of Zionism and Palestine in the MacCallum piece.

2. Vladimir Jabotinsky (see LDB to Jehial Tschlenow, 5 May 1915) was already well embarked upon the course of Zionist Revisionism and anti-British agitation that resulted, in 1930, in Great Britain's cancelling his visa and denying him access to Palestine for the rest of his life. For the Revisionist movement, see LDB to Mack, 20 July 1930.

3. See LDB to Felix Frankfurter, 23 September 1929, n. 1.

4. The Foreign Policy Association, in both Philadelphia and New York, scheduled debates on the question of British policy in Palestine; the Zionists were considering who might make the best presentation.

To Elizabeth Brandeis Raushenbush

November 13, 1929 Washington, D.C. [EBR]

DEAREST ELIZABETH: My thanks to you all for the birthday greetings, and for the Norman Ware which I am glad to have.[1] From the Susan family comes also a happy letter.

Susan is off today for the Hadassah Convention at Atlantic City, where there will be much of anxiety and talk.

I guess George Young is "slipping".[2] He seemed very wise in the old days of new Europe. Or perhaps it was that we knew so little then that he could impose upon us.

I think a general business depression is beginning.[3] The speculation has been so widespread that it affects directly a much larger percentage of the population than any earlier era; and luxuries have formed a much larger percentage of the total expenditures than ever before. Moreover, our productive capacity has never before exceeded so largely our capacity to consume. And the percentage of our exports is bound to shrink with the European recovery and development.   Lovingly,

1. Norman J. Ware, *The Labor Movement in the United States, 1865–1895; A Study in Democracy* (New York, 1929).

2. See preceding letter.

3. The stock market crash, two weeks before this letter, reached its low point on this date, the *New York Times* index standing at 224 (compared to 452 on 3 September). The market began a painful rise through early 1930, but before spring it lost momentum and plunged lower and lower. For the process by which the crash led into the depression that LDB here forecasts, see John K. Galbraith, *The Great Crash: 1929* (Boston, 1954).

To Felix Frankfurter

November 15, 1929 Washington, D.C. [Frankfurter Mss—HLS]

1. Many thanks for the birthday greeting. Throughout long years you have done very much to make them useful and joyous.

2. Max has handled the crisis with consumate skill.

3. I notice (U.S. Daily Nov. 15/29, p. 11) that [Thomas R.] Powell is to speak at the Tax Conference on Nov. 21. Could he not take occasion to give currency to the project of having Congress pass a law, which will (by authorizing state taxation that does not discriminate against interstate commerce etc.) prevent the Commerce Clause from operating to create tax discrimination against intrastate commerce in favor of interstate. It may be that there would be most chance of passing it by a simple bill applying only to the Gasoline tax.

4. Ned McClennen, who is a trustee of the Cambridge Savings B[an]k, is trying to get his Bank to establish an Insurance De-

partment. If Prof. [Edwin F.] Gay should (without mentioning Ned or me) go into the Bank & indicate to the Pres[iden]t. et al his interest in promoting Savings Bank Ins[urance]. it might be useful.

5. I suppose you have seen the Vanguard Press vol. of O[liver]. W[endell].H[olmes].'s dissenting opinions.[1] He seemed a little guilty the other day at not having discouraged the publication, but is undoubtedly glad that it is out—as I am.

6. Who is James J. Robinson, the Research Fellow who wrote me a nice birthday letter? [2]

7. Jewish Daily Bulletin Nov. 14/ quotes from "New Palestine" an article by Sidebothom strongly criticizing the British administration.[3]

1. Alfred Lief, ed., *The Dissenting Opinions of Mr. Justice Holmes* (New York, 1929).

2. James Jacquess Robinson (b. 1893) graduated from Harvard Law School in 1919. After some private practice and some teaching at the University of Indiana Law School, Robinson returned to Harvard in 1929 as a research fellow, after which he again taught law in Bloomington until 1941. In the next thirty years, Robinson accepted a number of special assignments, many of them outside the United States—from 1954 to 1969 he was a justice on the Supreme Court of Libya.

3. Herbert Sidebotham (1872–1940) was a British journalist who, throughout a long career, remained consistently pro-Zionist and critical of the British administration in Palestine.

To Pauline Goldmark

November 15, 1929 Washington, D.C. [Goldmark Mss]

MY DEAR "GESCHWESTER": [1]

Your loving birthday greetings came duly—also the Jefferson which we are very glad to have. It will be a great addition to our Chatham collection, and a special joy to me because of the book making. Jefferson has been properly painted for many achievements and qualities—without enough emphasis on the fact that he was the most civilized of our presidents.

Excellent Mr. Hoover must be having now a very bad time— the stockmarket collapse following the tariff law debacle [2] is verily a heaping of Pelion upon Ossa.[3] I rather think that in announcing the proposed tax reduction [4] & the reduction of the Reserve Banks rate,[5] in conjunction with Rockefeller's offer to buy S[tandard].O[il]. stock,[6] the powers that be have played all their high trumps.

It looks as if economic laws would again hold sway.

1. "Sister."

2. The Senate, ignoring urging from the White House, was torn in hopeless debate over a new tariff measure. The bitter struggle between agricultural and manufacturing interests made an early agreement impossible, and, after weeks of effort, no tariff law was in sight. Actually, the Smoot-Hawley tariff, a highly protective measure that passed despite much criticism and the opposition of economic experts, did not become law until 17 June 1930.

3. Two mountains in Greece which, according to legend, the Giants piled upon one another in order to invade Olympus and unseat Zeus.

4. Secretary Mellon, on 14 November, announced a 1% cut in income taxes for corporations and individuals.

5. The rediscount rate, which was cut from 6% to 5% on 1 November, was cut again to 4.5% by New York (other cities following within three weeks) on 15 November. The move was interpreted as a desperate attempt to encourage borrowing in order to save the stock market and avoid a general business depression.

6. On 14 November a bid for a million shares of Standard Oil was made, supposedly by John D. Rockefeller, in a move to peg the price of the stock. See *New York Times*, 14 November 1929.

To Elizabeth Brandeis Raushenbush

November 28, 1929 Washington, D.C. [EBR]

DEAREST ELIZABETH: 1. Re bonds.[1] It was not mother's and my purpose to interfere in any manner with you [*sic*] and Paul's purpose to live on your joint income or to influence your expenditures. Our purpose was to impose upon you responsibility for the care of property, which would, in any event, naturally go to you some day, and for the proper disposition of the income, whether by investing or spending it. Judgment in such things, as in others, is aided by experience.

2. Re colds: (a) see U.S. Daily Nov 27, p. 1, Column b.

(b) I agree with you that the cost of V.E.M. is excessive.[2] The cause is subjecting the buyer to the unnecessary expense of a diminutive package—a common evil. Dont you think that being an economist, you have the obligation to write the proprietor protesting and asking for the opportunity of buying in larger packages?

(c) even so—I, as efficiency expert, declare that V.E.M. is an economy in dollar bills. Our President's Secretary of Commerce will tell you on demand how many millions are wasted annually by not using it twice each day.   Lovingly,

1. LDB had signed over some bonds to his daughter, who had expressed some hesitation about how the new income would disrupt living standards. See also LDB to Elizabeth B. Raushenbush, 3 June 1931.

2. V.E.M. was apparently a patent cold remedy which LDB was using and which he recommended to his daughter.

To Felix Frankfurter

November 29, 1929 Washington, D.C. [Frankfurter Mss—HLS]

You know how reluctant I was to come out publicly re Palestine.[1] I am glad you thought well of the talk. Magnes' characteristic performance made plain, confident talk seem desirable.[2] It will be difficult to ward off demands and statements. But it seemed necessary to speak out in view of the emergency. And people seem to think it has done good.

As you were responsible for my seeing [Ramsay] MacDonald, I think you ought to know that O[liver].W[endell].H[olmes]. told me Harold L[aski] had written him—that MacDonald had said "He had been more impressed by me than by anyone he had met in America". That opinion may be of some service hereafter.

O.W.H. is in fine form—joyous & enterprising.

1. LDB's long-awaited public remarks came at a meeting of Jewish leaders—both Zionists and non-Zionists—on 24 November. He spoke briefly, reaffirming his belief in the viability of a Jewish state in Palestine, praising the settlers for their courage in meeting present difficulties, and urging continued support for the Zionist ideal. His talk is reprinted in full in the *New York Times*, 25 November 1929.

2. Magnes had issued a series of statements regarding Jewish-Arab relations in Palestine. The "performance" LDB mentions here was probably

Magnes's long cablegram to the *New York Day*, a Yiddish daily. (The text of the message was reprinted in the *New York Times*, 24 November 1929.) Magnes urged a spirit of cooperation and conciliation and the creation of a genuinely binational state in Palestine.

To Felix Frankfurter

December 2, 1929 Washington, D.C. [Frankfurter Mss—HLS]

1. I have heard no members of the Court say a word about the Survey of 1928 Term.[1] My guess is that Knaebel's suggestion is the result rather of his own timorousness.[2]

2. Upon receipt of yours re Joe Eastman, I talked again to Harlan [F. Stone] & he arranged immediately to see H[erbert] H[oover] this afternoon, & I saw him landed at 1 p.m. at the Executive Office. I made clear to him what refusal to appoint would bring in Western attacks. Also talked to G.W. Anderson who is to call up J[ames]. L. Richards this evening to stir up Massachusetts friends. (J.L.R. who was here a few weeks ago thought E. was practically safe.) Tom Woodward was in.[3] He has been busy this past 3 weeks getting signatures for E. from the I[nterstate]. C[ommerce]. C[ommission]. bar—& told me he had about 160 & had deposited these at the White House today.[4]

3. Drew Pearson[5] was in today with Dick Boekel.[6] I had a thought of saying something about the Joe Cotton article, but concluded it was wiser not to do so.

4. Dont let Ben F[lexner]. get tired re Palestine.

5. Senator Shipstead asked me Saturday what to read on Equity Practice. I told him he should waste no time, but get, as soon as you could give it, your book or articles on Injunctions.[7] You may already have heard from him. He has not got his strength back yet.

6. You will be interested in No. 60. which goes under another cover.[8]

7. C.C. B[urlingham]. probably told you he tried for me also.

1. Felix Frankfurter and James M. Landis, "The Business of the Supreme Court, at October Term, 1928," 43 *Harvard Law Review* 33 (1929).

2. Ernest Knaebel (1872–1947) was the court reporter for the Supreme Court from 1916 until his retirement in 1943.

3. Thomas Mullen Woodward (1884–1975) was a Washington attorney specializing in transportation law. He had extensive experience with the Interstate Commerce Commission. In the 1930s Woodward worked on many important New Deal agencies.

4. Joseph B. Eastman, LDB's old friend from Public Franchise League days, was reappointed to the Interstate Commerce Commission on 18 December and on 19 December his appointment was confirmed.

5. Drew (Andrew Russell) Pearson (1897–1969) was a young but already experienced reporter, currently on the staff of the *United States Daily*. He developed into one of the country's most colorful and controversial Washington correspondents. Most famous for his exposures of political figures and for his column, "Washington Merry-Go-Round," Pearson built a loyal following despite periodic criticisms of his methods and judgments.

6. Richard Martin Boeckel (b. 1892), another experienced Washington correspondent, had worked for a number of newspapers and magazines. In 1923 he founded and was editorial director of *Editorial Research Reports*, a news service to dozens of newspapers around the country.

7. See LDB to Felix Frankfurter, 20 September 1929, n. 7.

8. No. 60 was *Railroad Commission of California et al.* v. *Los Angeles Railroad Corporation*, 280 *U.S.* 145 (1929), a rate case. LDB, Holmes, and Stone all dissented separately—Holmes and LDB on jurisdictional grounds. The case was decided on this date.

To Felix Frankfurter

December 17, 1929 Washington, D.C. [Frankfurter Mss—HLS]

1. Thanks for your special delivery. I have declined to approve the Geller—Peel project.[1]

2. I hope Buxton is right about Eastman,[2] but here there is still great alarm—e.g. on Bob Wool[l]ey's part, who was in yesterday & said he had been working 3 weeks almost exclusively on this—to get support from different parts of the Country into line. I feel, personally, less confident of H[erbert]. H[oover]., since his performance re judges (where he lacked all personal prejudice). I fear he resembles Taft politically, in his lack of resoluteness and political sense.

3. O[liver]. W[endell]. H[olmes]. talked to me about Hiss' marriage the other day. I think you had better exact from his next secretary a vow of one year's celibacy.[3]

4. [Louis E.] Kirstein brought David Sarnof [*sic*] in—a man of rare intelligence, perception & engaging qualities. If you have

not met him, let K. bring him in. I regret his association with Owen Young.[4]

5. Max seemed really troubled last week.

1. Max A. Geller and Roy V. Peel, two professors of government at New York University, proposed collecting LDB's dissenting opinions for publication in book form. They had written asking for LDB's approval of the project.

2. See preceding letter. Frank Buxton was editor of the *Boston Herald* and a friend of Frankfurter.

3. Holmes's law clerk for the year was Alger Hiss (b. 1904), a bright and attractive young graduate from Harvard Law School. Hiss went into public service in Washington in 1933, and after 1936 he held high positions in the State Department. On 3 August 1948, Whittaker Chambers, an editor of *Time* and a former member of the Communist underground accused Hiss of passing secret information to the Soviet Union. Hiss was finally convicted, in 1950, of perjury and served in prison until 1954. He always protested his innocence of the charge and the Hiss case still remains a matter of controversy. Hiss had just married Priscilla Hobson. On 11 December, LDB had written to Frankfurter: "Obedient to your telegram I called on O.W.H. Hiss was still there. The Justice was in the best of form, rollicking, playful in spirit & evidently without worry of any kind. I concluded he needed no assurance about Hiss."

4. David Sarnoff (1891–1971) was a Russian immigrant who rose from errand boy and wireless operator to become a powerful corporation executive, most notably with the National Broadcasting Company and as chairman of the board of the Radio Corporation of America. Owen D. Young (see LDB to Alfred Brandeis, 26 March 1925) was connected with Sarnoff both in NBC and RCA.

To Julian William Mack

January 29, 1930 Washington, D.C. [Brandeis Mss, Z 42–1]
J.W.M.: Confirming our talk of this morning:

I deem it of supreme importance that the task of building working-men's houses, rural and urban, be undertaken on a large scale at an early date; and that the work be entrusted to the P[alestine].E[conomic].C[ouncil]. If your Committee will raise for that purpose two million, five hundred thousand dollars of new money (that is, in addition to the sums which B[ernard]. F[lexner]. expects to get from the Emergency and other funds already raised), I shall be glad to contribute one (1) percent thereof in exchange for new stock of the P.E.C. at par—and turn over the stock to the P[alestine].E[ndowment].F[und].—my payments to be made as follows: —Ten thousand dollars ($10,000) when there shall have been so raised and received in cash Nine hundred and ninety thousand ($990,000) dollars; a second ten thousand dollars ($10,000) when there shall have been raised and received in cash the further sums of Nine hundred and ninety thousand ($990,000) dollars; and the remaining Five thousand dollars ($5,000) when there shall have been raised and received in cash the remaining Four hundred and ninety-five thousand dollars ($495,000). All sums to be received and paid within the Calendar Year 1930. My payments will be made to the P.E.F. for disposition as above.[1]

Please send me a copy for my files.

1. By virtue of this project and several others of large magnitude, LDB dramatically increased his contributions to the Zionist movement. In the period 1925–1929, LDB's contributions totalled $33,197. But in 1930 alone, he gave $38,434 (the figures are from Mason, *Brandeis*, 692). A week later (7 February), LDB wrote Mack to rebuke him and Flexner for "such meager plans and hopes." He urged them to shoot for the sum of $50 million rather than the $\frac{1}{20}$ of that sum they announced to be the goal over the next three years.

To Julian William Mack

February 7, 1930 Washington, D.C. [Brandeis Mss, Z 42-1]

J.W.M.:—Confidential

I spoke to B[ernard.]F[lexner]. as you suggested about deH— asking him specifically what is to be done with and for DeHaas. He said definitely and definitively: "I don't know"—in a way that made me feel that it was useless to go further. Then he went on to say that Warburg and his entourage do not like DeH., etc., etc.[1]

I think it would be a disaster to lose his continuous services— indeed, we need many such aids if we are to do our task adequately.

I understood from you that several of those now contributing to the $1200 a month for his salary, stenographer and office expenses, have pledged themselves only for three months and that this arrangement ends with this month.

I am prepared to continue my contribution of $400. a month if you will undertake to raise the balance necessary to satisfy deHaas' needs.[2]

1. See LDB to Mack, 20 October 1929.
2. See LDB to Mack, 13 February and 12 July 1930.

To James Henle

February 10, 1930 Washington, D.C. [Brandeis Mss, M 5–1]

DEAR MR. HENLE: [1] The book is to be Mr. Lief's [2] interpretation of my economic views as gleaned from my written opinions. It seems to me better, therefore, that I should not see the manuscript.

You and Mr. Lief may care to examine in this connection my "Business—A Profession" (2d ed. Hale Cushman & Fleet, Boston) and "Other People's Money" (Fred A. Stoke Co).   Cordially,

1. James Henle (1891–1973) was president of the Vanguard Press, the prestigious publishing house. Henle was also a Louisville native, related by marriage to Bernard Flexner. He had written to ask LDB to review a manuscript by Alfred Lief (see next note) that Vanguard was about to publish: *The Social and Economic Views of Mr. Justice Brandeis* (New York, 1930).

2. Alfred Lief (1901–1972) had compiled the dissenting opinions of Holmes (see LDB to Frankfurter, 15 November 1929) as well as the opinions of LDB. He also wrote other books including a biography of George W. Norris and a full-length study of LDB, *Brandeis: The Personal History of An American Ideal* (New York, 1936).

To Julian William Mack

February 13, 1930 Washington, D.C. [Brandeis Mss, Z 42–1]

J.W.M.: Re yours of 10th and 12th re deHaas.[1]

Whether the P[alestine].E[conomic].C[orp]. should authorize selling stock on commission is, of course, a matter for its Board of Directors. But I think it would be an indignity to deHaas and a disgrace to our group to permit him to be put in a position of having to sell on commission in order to save the Jewish Cause. It is of the highest importance to us, as it is to him, that his efforts for the corporation and the Cause, should not be sullied by the commission lure.

Of course, he is often tactless and unwise in statement, but no one has rendered and is rendering such service to the Cause.[2]

1. See LDB to Mack, 20 October 1929 and 7 February 1930.
2. See LDB to Mack, 12 July 1930.

To Israel Benjamin Brodie

February 16, 1930 Washington, D.C. [Brodie Mss]

MY DEAR BRODIE: Referring to our talk at Chatham about getting high class Americans to settle in Palestine.

I was told yesterday by one who purported to know that Leo Wolman [1] would be willing to go, at least for some years, if asked to do so by the P[alestine].E[conomic].C[orporation].

1. Leo Wolman (1890–1961) was a distinguished labor economist who taught at Columbia University between 1931 and 1958. He was involved in a wide variety of public-service assignments, from advising labor unions, to working with the American delegation to Versailles in 1919, to taking a prominent part in the National Recovery Administration. He never settled in Palestine.

To Robert D. Kesselman

February 16, 1930 Washington, D.C. [Kesselman Mss]

MY DEAR KESSELMAN: Miss Emily G. Balch, some time professor of Political and social sciences at Wellesley, and in recent years active in the cause of peace, called recently to tell me that she plans soon to go to Palestine, and suggested that I might care to give her letters. I am very glad to do so, both because I value her very highly, and I fear she may be misled by her friend Dr. [Judah L.] Magnes and her own liberal opinions into views as to the proper Zionist policy, which are unwise and unsound.

I have accordingly given her letters to Bernard Joseph [1] and to you. In my letter to you I said that I knew you would be glad to aid her, which, of course means bringing her into touch with others whom she should meet.   With every good wish,

1. Bernard (Dov) Joseph (b. 1899), a Canadian Jew, joined the Jewish Legion and in 1921 settled in Jerusalem where he practiced law until 1948. He took an important part in Israeli politics from his work with the United Nations in 1947, to his influencing a favorable vote on the partition of Palestine, to his service in the early Knessets (from 1949 to 1959) and in various Cabinet positions. Joseph was the military governor of Jerusalem during the siege of 1948 and 1949.

To Julian William Mack

March 9, 1930 Washington, D.C. [R. Szold Mss]

J.W.M.: 1. Under date of 6th Ratnoff, Goldstein & Freiberger, as "Comtee appointed by Administrative Comtee of Z.O.A." asked for interview "Regarding the possibility of establishing a united front in American Zionism".[1] I wired interview impossible until after March 17th & then I should arrange for some time which would enable you, B[ernard]. F[lexner]. & deH[aas]. to be present. I told deH. of this yesterday forenoon, B.F. yesterday afternoon.

As soon as I know when our Court will recess, I will let you know & ask you to arrange with B.F., deH., and the Comtee for a date. Consider with B.F. & deH. whether anyone else should be present.

My thought [is] that we three should then have a session alone in the A.M. & fix a time for the Comtee in the P.M.

I have asked deH. to prepare preliminarily a memo of indispensables.[2]

2. From what B.F. told me of recent cable re Rosenbloom building, I think it may not be necessary for you to answer letter enclosed with yours of 5th (returned herewith) until we have had a chance to talk this matter over with B.F. & deH. If there is earlier need, let me know & I will indicate my impressions.

1. The Zionist Organization of America, now in desparate straits, appointed a high level committee to meet with the Brandeis-Mack faction and, in essence, to negotiate for return of that party to active leadership of the movement. The committee consisted of Nathan Ratnoff (1875–1947), a

Russian-born New York City physician; Israel Goldstein (b. 1896), a Conservative rabbi, a scholar, and a community worker; and, as head of the group, David Freiberger (1876–1947), a lawyer active in Zionist affairs who served as president of the American Zion Commonwealth. The group met in late March, and negotiations broke down on the issue of Louis Lipsky. LDB was adamant and immovably opposed to making any place for Lipsky in the "new" Z.O.A., and the representatives from the "old" Z.O.A. felt that banishing Lipsky in disgrace would constitute a symbolic repudiation of the last nine years of Zionist affairs. Negotiations resumed a few days before the opening of the Convention in June (see LDB to Mack, 11 June 1930).

2. See LDB to Mack, 16 March 1930.

To Charles Edward Clark

March 12, 1930 Washington, D.C. [Brandeis Mss, SC 9–3]

MY DEAR DEAN CLARK: [1] Some years ago, when I first had occasion to consider the subject, I reached the conclusion that, in view of the character of some of the questions which come before the Court, it is advisable to decline honors, as we do gifts of less valued material things. That decision is, of course, controlling.

I have written the Secretary.[2] Please express to the members of your faculty my high appreciation & to you and [Walton H.] Hamilton, who must be responsible, my special thanks.[3]

Cordially,

1. Charles Edward Clark (1889–1963) was dean of the Yale Law School from 1929 to 1939, when President Roosevelt appointed him judge for the U.S. Court of Appeals, Second Circuit. From 1954 to 1959 he served as chief judge. Clark had written to LDB to invite him to New Haven to accept an honorary Doctor of Laws degree. The degree was recommended unanimously by the faculty of the College of Law.

2. Carl A. Lohman, Secretary to the University, who officially informed LDB of the faculty's action.

3. See LDB to Stephen S. Wise, 19 January 1936.

To Julian William Mack

March 16, 1930 Washington, D.C. [Brandeis Mss, Z 42–1]

J.W.M.: 1. Re yours of 11th. Tuesday 25th which you say is available for you for the interview with the Ratnof[f] Committee will suit me.[1] If it is agreeable to B[ernard].F[lexner]. and DeH[aas]. please arrange with Ratnof[f] for that day, and ask Zip to attend if you, B.F. or DeH. deem it advisable.[2] You may select your hours as you deem best between 10 A.M. and 5 P.M., leaving free 1 P.M. to 3 P.M.

2. "By ready now" I mean this: I suppose it will be deemed best for us to say nothing at the interview—unless it be to ask for information; and to do nothing at the interview except to listen to what this Committee has to say.

3. But there is much that we should do before the interview—or after it. We should consider carefully the situation and make up our minds what, if anything, we can do—what particularly our human resources are and will be. My limitations remain what they have been. I, of course, cannot accept any office, even an honorary one. I can, in a limited way, give advice and lend moral and financial support. You are freer; but there are severe limitations upon the time you can give. [Louis E.] Kirstein is, at present, at best a hope.[3] Even if there were an unconditional surrender, we could not assume control of the Z.O.A. without men to man it. Who shall they be—considering the demands on time, character and ability?

Moreover, what are the conditions which must be agreed to by the others? I asked DeH. when here March 8th to think this out carefully and prepare a memo. Perhaps he has been in consultation with you.

4. Re yours of 14th. You have properly laid down the law to Sol Lowenstein.

5. I am returning Louis Newman's letter.[4]

1. See LDB to Mack, 9 March 1930.

2. Zip Szold (see LDB to Stephen S. Wise and Jacob deHaas, 3 May 1919, n. 2) was the president of Hadassah.

3. On 10 March LDB had written to Mack: "I told B.F. of deHaas' hopes that Kirstein could be induced to become President of the Z.O.A. He agreed that K. would be agreeable to all parties and spoke of [Felix] Warburg's faith in him. (Of course, K. or some equivalent person is an essential). It is just possible that K. might yield. He has always had a great desire to be a leader of the Jews—once limited to Boston, but I guess it goes beyond that now."

4. Louis Israel Newman (1893–1972), a rabbi, writer on Jewish topics, and Zionist activist, had been Stephen S. Wise's assistant in 1917. Newman's service with Congregation Rodeph Sholom, in New York City, lasted from 1930 until his death.

To Julian William Mack

April 5, 1930 Washington, D.C. [Brandeis Mss, Z 42–1]

1. Re yours of 3d. Kornfeld's letter returned herewith—seems reasonable.

2. That a British Commission should have made such a report is very disappointing to me.[1] Either the selection of the men must have been very unwise or defeatism has made bad inroads into the British ranks. I am most surprised that the Commission should have exculpated the Palestine Government; next that it should have so far transgressed the terms of the Mandate. Its lack of appreciation of the world Jewish situation and of the underlying purpose of the National Home Land and of the motives in making it possible is quite unworthy of British charged with world obligations. The little I have read so far of British public opinion, on the other hand, is encouraging.

3. I assume B[ernard].F[lexner]. has or will show you the cables March 31 and April 1 from [Felix] Warburg.

4. I am enclosing a batch of American clippings received from DeHaas.

5. [Boris] Kazmann was in yesterday. His limitations remain. But it was a "seelen freude"[2] to see him. He is one of the few Jews—men—whose acquaintance I made through Zionism who have grown in spiritual beauty. His face is a fine product of the spirit. And I think you may take much satisfaction in your part in making possible his striving.

1. The Shaw Commission issued its report on 31 March and it was circulating through the United States in early April (see LDB to Mack, 9 October 1929, n. 7).
2. "Joy of the soul."

To Julian William Mack

April 15, 1930 Washington, D.C. [R. Szold Mss]

J.W.M.: K's letter returned herewith.

That's an excellent letter of [Nathan] Kaplan's—sound in judgment and fine in feeling.

To me it confirms confidence in the Jewish experiment. If the Palestinians stand fast & show the spirit he describes—persistently—we shall win despite British errors in the past & the failure of the Commission to frankly condemn where condemnation is due.[1]

We must do our part in America.

I assume F.F[rankfurter]. has written you in re his talk with Howland Shaw & a consulship.[2]

1. See preceding letter and LDB to Mack, 9 October 1929, n. 7.
2. Gardiner Howland Shaw (1893–1965) had been in the State Department since 1917. He had much experience in Middle East affairs and was also involved in personnel decision-making. The Zionists were interested in securing the appointment of a "friendly" man as consul or vice-consul in Palestine.

To Morris Llewellyn Cooke

April 18, 1930 Washington, D.C. [Cooke Mss]

MY DEAR MORRIS COOKE: 1. I am very glad you broke into the Harvard Business Review with your "Shoring Up".[1]

2. The break in copper must have interested you.[2]

3. Paul Douglas was in today for 1¼ hours. I fear he & I are quite at odds as to what the Institute should do.[3]

A. He set forth seven lines of effort, for dealing with unemployment. I agreed that all were good and ought to be undertaken; but only one of them by our Institute. Swarthmore should confine its effort resolutely to Regularization of Employment if it is to achieve distinction & worthy results.

B. He proposed undertaking to regularize by convincing trade associations—for instance, the automobile manufacturers. I think that the less hopeful method of attack. It is easier to progress by taking hopeful individual concerns. Our task is not one for mass production at this time. Individual hard thinking is our need.

C. He was planning for a way to deal with some of the most difficult branches of business. I think he ought to deal first with the easiest & proceed gradually to the more difficult.

D. He suggests that there might be embarrassment in pursuing regularization because of what Morris Leed's [sic] organization is doing.[4] I think that the more separate organizations who tackle the subject & will *think*, the better.

1. Morris L. Cooke, "Shoring Up the Regulation of Electrical Utilities," *Harvard Business Review* 8 (April 1930): 316–28.

2. On 15 April the Copper Export Association announced a dramatic 4¢-per-pound drop in the price of copper (from 18¢ to 14¢). The move was attributed to anger at the way small producers were shaving the established price, and the accumulation of large surplusses in the face of much reduced world demand.

3. Cooke, at LDB's constant prodding, had persuaded the administration at Swarthmore College to establish the Swarthmore Institute on Unemployment. The Institute hired, as acting director, Paul Howard Douglas (1892–1976). Douglas, a professor of economics, most notably at the University of Chicago between 1920 and 1948, represented Illinois in the United States Senate from 1949 until his defeat in 1966. For Douglas's career as a leading liberal and labor reformer, see his autobiography, *In the Fullness of Time* (New York, 1972).

4. Leeds was associated with a number of organizations devoted to unemployment problems; perhaps LDB meant the Pennsylvania State Employment Commission, which Leeds chaired from time to time.

To Julian William Mack

April 22, 1930 Washington, D.C. [R. Szold Mss]

J.W.M.: 1. How are you and S[tephen]. S. W[ise]. getting on with counteracting the pro-Arab influence of our liberal press.[1]

2. I had a talk Sunday with Lowell Mellet[*sic*], editor of the Daily News (the Washington Scripps-Howard Paper) and Parker of N.Y., editor in chief of the Scripps-H. papers.[2] I hope that I have won their cooperation. I gave Mellet [*sic*] a copy of the Norman Angell article[3] & a clipping from the Manchester Guardian.

3. There is a movement of some well-meaning people—real Christians—to bring about an Arab-Jewish rapprochment. I told their representative that I should be willing to give him a letter to our Palestine friends & if they approve of the project would be disposed to support it here; but that I deemed it unwise for him to see anyone here or in England until the matter had been considered by these Palestinians, & unless, in a sense, it originated there. For this reason, I did not give him a letter to you; & I write

this so that you may know my views if you should be approached through some other source.

1. See LDB to Mack, 20 October 1929.

2. George Bertrand Parker (1886–1949) had worked in Oklahoma and Ohio journalism before assuming, in 1927, the post of editor in chief for the nineteen newspapers in the Scripps-Howard chain. In 1936, Parker won the Pulitzer Prize for editorial writing.

3. Angell published a pro-Zionist article in the 11 April edition of *New Palestine*.

To Robert D. Kesselman

May 15, 1930 Washington, D.C. [Kesselman Mss]

MY DEAR KESSELMAN: My thanks for yours of 21st reporting on Miss Balch's visit.[1]

There have been many untoward events in Palestine. But don't let your courage wane. It is in evil times that good deeds are done and good achievements born.   Most cordially,

1. See LDB to Kesselman, 16 February 1930.

To Julian William Mack

June 11, 1930 Chatham, Mass. [R. Szold Mss]

J.W.M.: I have yours of 9th and also copy of deH[aas]. to [Louis I.] Newman of 9th.

1. Please do not let any "Wise-Tchernowitz" or any other Com[mit]tee or delegation come here "for clarification". We have said, after much deliberation and, I think, with entire clearness, what we are willing to attempt.[1]

2. I do not see how you can safely depart an iota from the substance of what is declared in our statement;—and I have not heard suggested any ambiguity. All the suggestions I have heard of want changes in substance. Non possumus.[2]

3. Adhering to our statement, there will be six months to work in;—and through the neutral board, opportunity to secure competent & worthy officers. But it begins to look as if you were being selected for President.

1. Into the diplomatic negotiations between the Brandeis-Mack group and the Z.O.A. committee (see LDB to Mack, 9 March 1930) a new element had been injected. On 22 May a "memorandum" appeared, signed by LDB, Mack, Robert Szold, and Jacob deHaas. The article in the *New Palestine* (30 May 1930) was aptly entitled "Brandeis Defines the Terms." The 22 May memorandum demanded a new Z.O.A.—new in organization, new in leadership, new in efficiency, and with efforts directed entirely toward the economic development of Palestine (the position LDB had taken in the Zeeland memorandum [see LDB to Bernard Flexner, 15 September 1920]). According to the May document, the transition from the "old" (Lipskyite) leadership to the "new" (Brandeis-Mack), was to be managed by a neutral committee composed of people who had enjoyed no close connection with the Lipsky regime and who would serve without salary. This committee of neutrals was to have almost dictatorial power for at least six months and would be charged with reducing the debt and inaugurating businesslike methods within the Z.O.A. The memorandum was sent to the Freiberger committee, which, without comment, submitted it to the entire convention in Cleveland at the end of June. Throughout the six weeks between issuing the document and the convention, LDB maintained the position that no member of the group should attempt to clarify or interpret the memorandum. On 12 June LDB wrote to Mack: "The thing that Z.O.A. members must do, is to find themselves. That involves thinking. And perhaps they would come nearer to doing that if left to the consideration of our statement unaided by our interpretation. It would, at least, show that we are not engaged in propaganda. . . ." See Urofsky, *American Zionism*, 365 and Shapiro, *Leadership of the American Zionist Movement*, 243–45. See also LDB to Mack, 27 June 1930.

2. "Not possible."

To Nathan Kaplan

June 15, 1930 Chatham, Mass. [Brandeis Mss, Z 42–1]

MY DEAR NATHAN KAPLAN: Through Judge Mack I have seen your letter of May 20th to Dr. Wise. I am not surprised at your feeling about the British action. But I am pained to find a doubt as to the value of your remaining with your family in Palestine. There never was a time when men like you were needed there more.

Neither British, nor Arab, nor both combined, can prevent the ultimate achievement of our purpose, if the Jews on the firing line in Palestine exhibit the courage, determination, intelligence and self-sacrifice of which they are capable. It is times like these which test men's mettle—and that of people's. If we are beaten it will be because those at the fort failed to hold it.

I trust that long since your sense of discouragement has been overcome; and that the will to achieve has strengthened with the difficulties with which we are confronted.

Say this for me to any others who may care for my opinion. With every good wish   Cordially

To Julian William Mack

June 19, 1930 [Boston, Mass.] [Brandeis Mss, Z 42–1]

J.W.M.: I had my say to Lindsay—two hours and twenty minutes—as frankly as I could discuss the subject with you or anyone else.[1] He listened attentively every minute; said little and, of course, made no admissions. Will send you memo. Whether I have done any good, I, of course, can't say, but he knows we are in earnest. And—now 3½ hours later—I do not regret anything said or feel that I have omitted anything that it would have been wise to say.

Received from deH[aas]. yesterday and today letters and packages and from Felix [Frankfurter] telegram.

1. Sir Ronald Charles Lindsay (1877–1945), an experienced career diplomat, was the British ambassador to the United States from 1930 to 1939. On 19 June a meeting between Lindsay and LDB took place at the Bellevue Hotel in Boston. The topic of discussion was the British mandate (LDB had telegraphed Mack for a complete copy of the document on 13 June) and the British intentions about fulfilling the promise of the Balfour Declaration.

To Julian William Mack

June 27, 1930 Chatham, Mass. [R. Szold Mss]

J.W.M.: 1. Re deH[aas]. letter of 23rd and yours concerning same. I am telegraphing you:

"Imperative no member our group should undertake to interpret memorandum".[1]

This supplements my telegram referred to deH. letter:

"Imperative we give no assurance beyond that expressed in May twenty-second memorandum".[2]

2. I am much surprised at your saying that belief is that all members of Administrative Committee *necessarily* excluded from the 9.[3] That question was raised and disposed of in presence of Ratnoff Committee. If it does exclude them, it must be because all were recently, or are now, partisans. If so, they should be excluded.

3. I think, as I have repeatedly said, that all the talks and particularly the writing by members of our group has hurt more than helped.

4. To entertain a suggestion of doing away with the neutral period, means relinquishing most of the conditions carefully worked out, would bind us (you) to severe obligations—without having either the men or the money with which to fulfill; and without having, as now seems clear, the "effective co-operation of the body of the Zionists".

5. Please read carefully Article Second and do not minimize any one of the 5 conditions therein set forth.

Also reread my several letters on this subject.

1. See LDB to Mack, 11 June 1930, n. 1.
2. The "assurance" most wanted by delegates to the Zionist convention, of course, was that LDB himself would resume active leadership of the movement. See next letter.
3. The nine who would comprise the Lipskyite representatives to the interim "neutral committee" of administration. See LDB to Mack, 11 June 1930, n. 1. But see next letter for the final arrangement.

To Delegates to the Z.O.A. Convention

June 28, 1930 Chatham, Mass. [R. Szold Mss]

To the delegates of the Zionist Organization of America in Convention assembled: [1]

I appreciate the generous suggestion which many of you have made that I should again assume the official responsibility of leadership in the Z.O.A. When eighteen years ago I first gave serious thought to the problems of Jewry and began to search for the means of preserving the spiritual legacies of Israel as an active force in the world, I became a Zionist and a follower of Herzl. My visit to Palestine in 1919 rendered more powerful the appeal; removed any lingering doubts as to the practicability of the

undertaking; and convinced me that in carrying out the principles of the Balfour Declaration the welfare of both Jews and
Arabs would be advanced. The events since have deepened these
convictions.

Added years make it impossible for me to assume now the
official responsibilities of leadership as I did prior to 1921, but
I am ready now as then to serve the cause. Necessarily the service
to be rendered must be limited in scope to advising from time to
time when requested on questions of major policy. Such service
I am now rendering through Mr. [Felix M.] Warburg to the
Jewish Agency. Such service I can render also to the Z.O.A. In
my opinion it will be far more effective if rendered to an administration formed on the general lines of the memorandum of
May 22nd, 1930.

My warm greetings and best wishes.

1. The Cleveland convention was a tense one. Word reached the delegates that negotiations were taking place between the Brandeis-Mack faction and the Z.O.A. administration, but the negotiations turned out to be
protracted and difficult; from time to time someone would appear in the
hall to announce that no agreement had yet been hammered out. At one of
those moments, Robert Szold read this letter from LDB. It represented a
softening of the tone of the 22 May memorandum (see LDB to Julian W.
Mack, 11 June 1930), and words spoken by Szold after he had finished reading made clear to the delegates that LDB would "advise" whether or not
the assembled convention accepted the memorandum. LDB was under great
pressure to withdraw the memorandum, much of it coming from members
of his own group who had come to Chatham to plead with him to back
down. In the end, a compromise was reached (symbolized by deHaas'
and Lipsky's joining hands in public). That compromise provided for an
eighteen-member "neutral committee," six members of which would be appointed by the Lipskyites and twelve by the Brandeis-Mack group. The
neutral committee was given eighteen months to whip the organization back
into shape.

To Julian William Mack

July 4, 1930 Chatham, Mass. [Brandeis Mss, Z 42–1]

J.W.M.: 1. Bob [Szold], deH[aas]. and Brodie are to be congratulated on their handling of the Cleveland end.[1]

2. The action taken will certainly have these beneficent results:
(a) make the British realize more the potential American Jewish

strength; (b) hearten our friends in Europe and Palestine; (c) help the Allied Jewish campaign; (d) strengthen the Zionist end of the Jewish Agency.

3. Literally, every man known to have urged by writing or otherwise return of the Mack-Brandeis control ought promptly to be listed; and "Let no guilty man escape." The first call upon them to make good should be in raising money for the Z.O.A., not merely to wipe out all debts (as distinguishable from deficit), but to provide ample working capital. My guess is that the need is for $300,000. I think it would be unwise to mention the amount or the fact of the need for working capital. It is wiser to talk of deficit and debts, mentioning rarely the amount of the balance needed. But don't let this golden opportunity of afflatus pass without promptly "cashing in" while the afflatus lasts. The listing should begin July 7. All files and all memories should be searched. Each man listed should be personally appealed to and made to give as much as possible, and none permitted to escape without some giving, however small. And *after* he has given for the immediate needs, get from him a written pledge of an annual giving—all without a "drive." So far as possible, get at these men for the oral appeal; and get at them individually. Many of them would be flattered by being asked to come to your office.

4. I shall send you all telegrams and letters which come to me so that present emotion may be "cashed in" as promptly as possible. On this matter vacations are no excuse. On the contrary, the vacation period is the one which should be most prolific. My guess is that there will be [*] when they return to their businesses.

5. I am enclosing telegram of Holzman, et al. of Boston (which I have acknowledged as noted thereon.) Talk with deH as to how they may be best utilized. Also act promptly in this. These men must be made to realize that promises voluntarily made are to be kept. And "Lest we forget" the reminders should be frequent and the demands upon them serious.

6. I also enclose postal from Edward Fried; letters from [Abraham H.] Fromenson and Isaac Rosengarten.

7. All letters to me sent to you may be retained on deH.'s L.D.B. file unless marked, "Return."

1. See preceding letter.

To Julian William Mack

July 6, 1930 Chatham, Mass. [R. Szold Mss]

1. I hope Bob [Szold] will commence promptly and personally on intensive, comprehensive study of the books of the Z.O.A. with special reference to the files of correspondence and the journal entries.[1] Until that is done, you can't be sure that you are treading on solid ground, and it can't be done effectively by an expert public accountant, however trustworthy. It must be done by one who is intimate with the subject matter, including the individuals affected.

2. A like special study should quickly be made into the New Palestine accounts & activities.

3. A little later, you will have to take up the matter of efficiency and economy in the Z.O.A. office. There probably is dreadful waste there. But the matter must be handled delicately. Probably most of those there can be made to do twice as much work as is now accomplished;—& if the vigor is applied which may be expected of the new management, there will be twice as much work for the employees to do.

4. I am enclosing letter from Kesselman; said Stix, et al.

1. The Brandeis group had been charging for years that the Lipsky administration was not only inefficient, but that it squandered money and that there was a very large hidden debt. Szold's examination of the Z.O.A.'s accounts confirmed that the situation was even worse than the Brandeisists had feared. In addition to the $150,000 debt acknowledged by the Lipskyites, another $300,000 worth of hidden notes were uncovered, including a number of loans from Z.O.A. funds to Lipsky's cronies.

To Chaim Weizmann

July 8, 1930 Chatham, Mass. [Weizmann Mss]

MY DEAR DR. WEIZMANN: It was good of you to send me the message.[1]

We shall try to develop in the American Organization the needed strength.   Cordially,

1. Weizmann had cabled from London: "Your generous attitude enabled American Zionists create united front and what I feel certain will be future harmony so necessary at this critical stage of our common endeavors."

To Joshua Bernhardt

July 9, 1930 Chatham, Mass. [Brandeis Mss, Z 42–1]

DEAR DR. BERNHARDT: [1] 1. I received from you under date of August 9, 1929, a condensed financial statement as of June 30, 1929, for the Hedera Settlement. I shall be glad to have, as soon as received, the statement for the year ending June 30, 1930, and in connection therewith to learn specifically how the instalment payments have been met and generally how the residents have fared during the year thus closed. You sent me September 27/29 a memo.

2. Under date of July 18, 1929, you sent me the Bulletin containing Mr. Viteles' report on the Cooperative Movement [in Palestine], and I should be glad to have a report of the operations since and of the present condition.

3. In yours of October 23rd you enclosed a memo which stated that the Government would make in 1930 "a cumulative report" for the Agricultural Department. Kindly send me a copy if it has been received.

4. Under date of June 28, 1929, Mr. Flexner sent me the Supplement to the Second Annual Report. Kindly send me the Third Annual Report, if it has been published.

5. I should be glad to see the five year report of the Loan Bank referred to in Mr. [Emanuel N.] Mohl's letter of June 20, 1930. [2]   Cordially,

1. Joshua Bernhardt (b. 1893) was an economist and statistician, the American authority on the economics of the sugar industry. Between 1927 and 1933, Bernhardt served as secretary of the Palestine Economic Corporation.

2. LDB had written (see LDB to Jacob deHaas, 5 June 1927 and to Felix Frankfurter, 23 September 1929) that summer vacations would be the time he could best devote to considering Palestinian questions. In July and August, 1930, he sent out a flood of letters like this one, requesting information on Palestine and on the Zionist effort, both in the United States and Europe. In an effort at self-education reminiscent of his search for factual detail before undertaking a reform effort a quarter century before, LDB sought out minute statistical data on a large variety of questions: everything from dietary habits of the settlers to the data on fund collection in America, from patterns of crop rotation to the latest information on water power and irrigation, from rates of interest charged to Palestinian Arabs to judicial proceedings in the area, from the financial condition of the World Zionist Organization to the progress of the school system in Palestine. There is much evidence that LDB mastered this data and that he became one of the best

informed men in the United States about Palestinian conditions. Many letters during these months directed other Zionists to read some particular report or article as being the best available. LDB also directed that numerous
studies be undertaken by the Z.O.A. and that statistics be gathered covering questions which no report or published document had yet touched.

To Julian William Mack

July 12, 1930 Chatham, Mass. [R. Szold Mss]

J.W.M.: Re yours of 11th about deHaas.[1] Show him what you
wrote me and this letter. We all have this matter so much at
heart that we must be brutally frank with one another. And deH.
will recognize that and be ready to do as you say: "Render the
very best service if he had elsewhere a full time job, or one that
would, like Lipsky's, enable him to make his living."

We can't begin this new regime with another split in Zionist
forces. That we can't have DeH. in an important post—a full time
man—is one of the misfortunes of the situation—like the fact that
we must have Weizmann. Some day perhaps, a mercurial people
may worship him and demand his return to a commanding post.

1. Despite countless efforts on his behalf by LDB (see LDB to Mack,
20 October 1929, and 7 and 13 February 1930), deHaas was deemed too controversial and felt by many to be unfitted by his personality for a high-level,
full-time position in the new Zionist administration. This letter marks a sort
of surrender on LDB's part in his long battle to integrate deHaas again into
the movement.

To Julian William Mack

July 16, 1930 Chatham, Mass. [Brandeis Mss, Z 42–1]

J.W.M.: 1. When S[tephen]. S. W[ise]. takes up publicity with
periodicals and the press, I think he will find no material more
effective than M. Smelansky's article "Jewish Colonization and
the Fellah," which fills the special, May 15, 1930, issue of the
Palestine & Near East Economic Magazine.

2. It would be a most helpful thing if S.S.W., with his rare
eloquence, would take that article for the subject of his first

sermon-lecture of the Fall season, arranging for adequate publicity in the New York papers.

3. I should think Israel Goldberg could now be made useful; and that our group could secure his services for writing and speaking. Unlike most American Zionists, he is still capable of studying and would not rebel at the necessity of acquiring the requisite knowledge. If it should be deemed necessary, I should not object to writing him (provided if the group will indicate what is desired of Israel Goldberg;) as he has sent me the two volumes of his "Outline of Jewish Knowledge" with pleasant greetings.[1]

4. I am sending for your information (and copies) letters to Nathan D. Kaplan and A. Landau.[2]

1. Samson Benderly and Israel Goldberg, *Outline of Jewish Knowledge,* 2 vols (New York, 1929).

2. Possibly Alfred Landau (1850–1935), the noted Yiddish linguist and folklorist.

To Julian William Mack

July 20, 1930 Chatham, Mass. [Brandeis Mss, Z 42–1]

J.W.M.: When S[tephen]. S. W[ise]. comes to New York for the Political Committee meeting on July 28, I hope he will (a) bring with him [*] and (b) be prepared to stay an extra day—to have ample time for specifically and separately considering in conference the following which I deem one of the most serious and urgent tasks of the Political Committee. The blight attending the Weizmann-Lipsky regime denuded American Zionism intellectually. It removed from activity those men able and accustomed to use their minds in the solution of Zionist problems; and it prevented the normal after growth of the younger men who could be relied upon to take their places. The most urgent need now is to secure and train young, able devoted intellectuals, not merely to help build up the American organization and advance its economic projects but to help think out the solution of the international-Palestinian problems and secure the adoption of views and measures found to be wise. To do that requires the acquisition of much knowledge, Jewish, Palestinian, international;

much concentration of thought; and continuous constructive effort, ability and devotion are, of course, essentials.

I am confident that there are in abundance young Jews in America who, if properly approached, would respond to the call. They must be hand picked. Their interest as well as their Zionist efficiency must be developed. It is a matter not of numbers but of quality. The conference which I suggest should be held to enable those present to discuss the essential qualities of the men (and women) desired; and to help one another in thinking of the men to be approached. S.S.W. and J.W.M. will know who had best be called into the conference with some member or members of our group. Two years ago deHaas had great hope of a Dr. Lipshitz (a teacher of about 30) who he said was of much ability—a Galician by birth—and deep Zionist longing. Obviously you want present men who know not only the [*] but who have a wide knowledge of the Jewish young men. And you do not want to have many persons at your conference.

As to the tasks confronting the Political Committee, *First:* The urgent task is to avert the threatened worsening of the bad *status quo ante* the August disturbances. *Second:* Then we must devise ways and means to lessen the evils incident to the noxious clauses of the bad Churchill White Paper.[1] The British Home Government has sinned by placing in Palestine unsympathetic local administrators. But our faults have been even greater; both in measures and men. It was as suggested in mine of 18th, a grievous error to establish in P. a Zionist executive; among other things, because it resulted in creating the Arab Executive. It has been a [*] of persistent errors to permit Zionist interests to be represented in Palestine by men of the calibre and qualities of those there in power. It will be a very delicate task to abrogate the P.Z.E. without seeming to weaken our position vis-a-vis the British and the Arab. But I am convinced we cannot get into proper relations with the British local administration without doing so, and since Great Britain is the Mandatory, we must live in good relations with her officials. Of course, that doesn't mean yielding—it means that we must know enough, be able enough and be tactful enough to make them see what is right and what is best for both them and us. (That recent Haifa incident is instructive in this connection.)

Third: The Revisionists [2] are right in the essence of much that they ask. They are wrong *in more.* One later task will be to overcome in tactful ways serious implications of the Churchill White Paper.

Fourth: At some time Transjordania must become a part of Palestine. The how and when are matters for study and preparedness. The immediate care must always be to prevent things happening which would render more difficult or impossible the ultimate achievement.

Excellent thinking is being done by Palestinians who are not Zionist officials. And no sound thinking can be done by us without knowing what Palestinians know, think and feel. The work of upbuilding Palestine must be mainly theirs. And I have great faith in them, more by far, than I had before the August disturbances. But they need much help from America; help other than by money. They need us, because of America's prestige. They need us, because we can think like Britons; appreciate how Britons feel; approach problems from the British point of view. To this end, we need now, and shall need for a quarter of a century and more, American Zionist intellectuals of high calibre and attainments. As I said to Felix [Frankfurter] recently: "Jews learned to make bricks without straw. But they can't build a home without bricks—or an equivalent."

I suppose S.S.W. has seen in June 21/30 New Statesman the article entitled "Changing Zionism." [3]

1. The Churchill White Paper was issued by the British government in June 1922. While rejecting some Arab demands (for the abolition of the Balfour Declaration and an end to Jewish immigration), the White Paper was regarded as a softening of the Balfour doctrine. Zionist fire, of course, was not turned upon the Churchill White Paper of 1922; after the promulgation of the White Paper of 1931 (see LDB to Rennie Smith, 29 October 1930, n. 2), a far more ominous target presented itself.

2. The Revisionist movement, led by the brilliant Vladimir Jabotinsky, had arisen during the 1920s in opposition to what was considered the "minimalist" position of the Weizmann-led Zionist Organization. The Revisionists wanted to repeal the 1922 White Paper and claimed both sides of the Jordan for Jewish settlement; they demanded a greater voice in the government of Palestine by the Yishuv; and long before most other Zionists were willing to say so, Jabotinsky demanded that Palestine be made into a Jewish state. In the early 1930s, Jabotinsky was one of the prescient few who saw where Hitler's rabid anti-Semitism would lead, and much to the chagrin of many

Jewish leaders, he called for a wholesale emigration of Jews from Europe to Palestine. See Joseph B. Schechtman and Yehuda Benari, *History of the Revisionist Movement* (Tel Aviv, 1970), as well as Schechtman's two-volume *The Jabotinsky Story* (New York, 1956, 1961).

3. William Zuckerman, "Changing Zionism," *The New Statesman* 35 (21 June 1930): 326–28, noted the ascendancy of hard-headed economics within the Zionist movement, triumphing over the politics of "religious romanticism" which had once prevailed. The eastern Europeans were discredited, according to the article, and saner men were now in control.

To Zip Szold

August 3, 1930 Chatham, Mass. [Brandeis Mss, Z 42–1]

MY DEAR ZIP: Re Yours of July 30:

First: I am extremely glad to know:

(a) That the process of devolution will probably have effected by Jan. 1/31 transfer of the Tel Aviv and Haifa hospitals to the respective communities.[1]

(b) That Hadassah plans after Jan. 1/31 to act independently in fund raising.

(c) That Hadassah is willing to assume for America the raising of all funds for educational as well as health requirements, leaving to the ZOA and others the raising of funds for political and economic requirements.

This program I understand from Julius Simon's letter to Dr. Weizmann and from my talk with Dr. Hexter will have their support.[2]

Second: I am disposed to welcome the expansion of the activities of the Kuppat Holim;[3] indeed, without knowing that there was in the minds of your associates the question you discuss, I had wondered whether it might not become the instrument through which devolution could be effected in some of those places where the community itself could not take over the Hadassah hospital.

It seems to me important that so far as possible the responsibility for local health should rest with Palestinians, except so far as it should be assumed by the British Administration; that the function of the Hadassah should (in health matters) be limited ultimately to setting a high standard through the Jerusalem Hospital (in connection with the University); in maintaining through supervision and influence the highest standard possible in the local hospitals; in maintaining, so long as necessary, the other institutions noted in the Hadassah "Object in America", etc.; and in introducing new services in the borderland between health and other social activities. There would always be a residium of tasks in these fields which would tax the capacity of Hadassah management. And it clearly would be obliged to cover a large part, also, of the educational field, after it assumes to raise the American contribution in money. I realize the difficulties and dangers incident to Histadruth management. But I am deeply impressed with their ability and spirit. I should liked to have worked out some system by which Labor and other sections of the several communities and districts could cooperate through the Kuppat Holim in health work. (The Magdill agreement between the community employers and employees is suggestive).

What I have said above is to be treated merely as thoughts. Before reaching a definite conclusion, I should like to discuss the situation fully with you and some of your associates. I deem it important to get rid practically of all WZO and Palestine Executive interference and influence.   Cordially,

1. See LDB to Julian W. Mack, 20 September 1929.
2. Maurice Beck Hexter (b. 1891) was a worker in Jewish communal and philanthropic organizations. His connection with Palestinian affairs in the 1920s and 1930s was quite strong. He was a director of the Palestine Emergency Fund and a non-Zionist member of the Jewish Agency for Palestine. After the issuance of the Passfield White Paper (see LDB to Rennie Smith, 29 October 1930, n. 2), Hexter was one of those appointed to negotiate with the British Cabinet.
3. The Kupat Holim was the health insurance plan of Histradrut, the labor organization in Palestine. Founded in 1911, Kupat Holim operated through local clinics and laboratories and provided important medical services. See the article by Y. Kanev in *Encyclopedia of Zionism and Israel,* 2: 690–91 for a full description of its organization and functions.

To Julian William Mack

August 6, 1930 Chatham, Mass. [Brandeis Mss, Z 42–1]

J.W.M.: I am much relieved to know definitely that you will sail Friday—my best wishes for you and Mrs. Mack.[1]

2. I hope that between seeing [Felix] Warburg on the 15th and

the meeting on the 24th you and [Stephen S.] Wise will arrange to spend as many days as possible in private talks with Europeans and Palestinians, so as to get clear into their minds our views on the several subjects. It will take more time to gain acceptance of our views than will be afforded by the period from Aug. 24 to the end of the month.

3. It seems to me important not to have a Congress before next summer [2] and not to attack Weizmann now.

4. I assume [Maurice B.] Hexter talked with you of all matters mentioned in his letter to me—enclosed.

Please return it.

1. Mack was leaving for Berlin and the meeting of the administration committee of the Jewish Agency.

2. The next congress of the World Zionist Organization was held in Basle in July 1931. See LDB to Robert Szold, 10 June 1931.

To Harry Michael Fisher

August 7, 1930 Chatham, Mass. [Brandeis Mss, Z 42-1]

MY DEAR JUDGE FISHER: The August, 1930 financial report of the Z.O.A. shows that only $3,532 of the $103,000 pledged at the Convention toward liquidation of the deficit had been collected; and that no payment had been made by any Chicagoan except $100 by Moses B. Levin.

The political situation is very serious; and it is impossible for the Administration to take up certain projects in that connection which I deem urgent—until the Z.O.A. indebtedness has been paid.

I therefore request, in view of the urgency, that you take up with your Chicago associates immediately the collection of the $10,000 pledged; and I hope that you and they will press the matter to completion at the earliest possible moment.[1]　　　Cordially,

1. This letter was typical of many that LDB wrote in early August to Zionist leaders in large American cities.

To Jacob deHaas

August 10, 1930 Chatham, Mass. [Brandeis Mss, Z 42–1]

DEH: 1. Re yours 7th—I wrote to L[ouis].P. Rocker—requesting him to undertake the task of raising from others a substantial part of the funds needed to wipe out the deficit.[1]

2. Re yours of 8th—I am relieved to know that careful preparation is being made for "real work," about September 1st; and that you are not purposing to rely upon letters. Unless we can get Zionists to undertake personal solicitation orally—success is not possible.

3. Re yours of 8th—I can see "one or two" of the Legionaires next Friday at noon, if, in view of the following, you still think it desirable.[2]

I think it desirable that Americans of the right sort—and particularly Legionaires should settle in Palestine. But

(a) Ordinarily a rough test "of the right sort" is passed by a man who, having stakes in America, pulls them up and goes on his own to P., ready to make or break in the enterprise. The Legionaires are not of that class. Others must be chosen with at least as much care as Gideon's band. The letters which I have from them (July 24–August 4—still unacknowledged) do not indicate that they could pass an appropriate test. They indicate a willingness to leave America, where they are not happy, but I see no evidence of fitness for P. in that alone. It is about 11 years since they left P. No evidence is disclosed of a persistent, burning desire to return, which might have induced them in the 11 years to make those duty sacrifices of luxuries, comforts and pleasures, which presumably, in the prosperous Americans years, might have enabled them to raise very much more than $500. a head—to carry out their heart's desire. There is no evidence that, like the Chalutzim,[3] they have endeavored to fit themselves for agriculture. Their letter of July 24th sounds rather [un]like the noble utterances of our patriots of the Civil War, the Spanish War and the World War. We know that, whatever the reason, they were quitters when they left P. in 1919—and I have not been furnished with any data which should lead me to believe that they may not swell the already too large band of misfit emigrants from Palestine. Besides, they are no longer young.

(b) Even if I had reason to think these men hopeful—I should not be willing in 1930 to give or pledge financial aid—because my financial commitments for the calendar year are already large.

(c) Of course, I would not lend my name to their money raising campaign, as I never do that.

What has come of Avner and our other Pittsburgh friends who in 1914–1918 were such ardent Zionists? [4]

1. See preceding letter.
2. Evidently deHaas had been approached by a group of American Jews, former members of the Jewish Legion (see LDB to Jehial Tschlenow, 5 May 1915), who wished to remove to Palestine and wanted LDB's help.
3. "Pioneers."
4. Maurice Louis Avner was a Pittsburgh lawyer. He was active in the movement for a Jewish Congress and later a member of the executive committee. He was also active in Jewish philanthropic work.

To Emanuel Neumann

August 17, 1930 Chatham, Mass. [Brodie Mss]

DEAR MR. NEUMANN: re yours of the 15th. 1. I am glad to see the progress of 1929–30 over 1928–9 [1] both in gross and in expense percentage.

2. I enclose J.N.F. So. Africa report from Zionist Record, June 27, 1930. Note their cost of administration "less than 7 percent of the total receipts."

3. We must secure from American Zionists more unpaid work. No people was ever liberated, no land ever redeemed, by mercenaries. We need unpaid work not only because "a penny saved is a penny made"—important as that consideration is. We need unpaid work also because with the work comes deeper devotion; comes appetites for more knowledge of Palestine; comes thinking; and from knowledge and thinking, new achievement. For this reason, we cannot accept a money contribution, however

large, as full performance of Zionist duty. As long as some Jews suffer elsewhere, we should strive to make all American Zionists think.

4. We must secure from the paid employees more in work. This is true because they should perform their Zionist duty by doing more work than they would for the same money if engaged in a private business. Moreover, they get as compensation more than dollars—they get—or should get—the joy, the thrill, of participation in the great adventure. If they do not get that thrill, they were not wisely selected, or the leadership, the Executive, has failed to instill the appropriate spirit.

5. The closing of the doors of the United States by its restrictive immigration laws has increased the need of keeping Palestine open—and the duty of American Jews to labor to that end. And it has also increased their ability to do so. Energies necessarily devoted to taking care of newcomers here—have in large measure been released for effort elsewhere.   Cordially,

1. Of the Jewish National Fund, which Neumann headed.

To Robert Szold

August 18, 1930 Chatham, Mass. [deHaas Mss]

R.S.: Berkson was here yesterday, as you suggested.[1] The main features of the talk were:

First: He thinks, generally speaking, but with individual variations, the Kindergartens are good; the Elementary schools fair—about as good as those of N.Y. state; and the secondary schools poor.

Second: He explained the wretched system of control and supervision, with the main board selected by the coalition-party-system, which frustrates efforts at efficiency and progress; and the time consuming, obstructive action of the other boards etc. He says he is experiencing the evil effects of all we inveighed against the P[alestine].E[conomic].C[orporation]. 10 years ago.

Third: He says that (aside from about £20,000 for special schools & outside funds), the budget now is about £175,000; of which the Government supplies less than £20,000; the Pica [2] about £5,000; the Yishub about £67,000; and the Agency-WZO about £75,000. He thinks the Yishub can do no more; that the Government should, & may conceivably be led to, raise its grant-in-aid to £30,000. And he explained how the Govt. has treated, not only the efforts to get more for the Jewish Schools, but the arguments in support. It certainly is a bad story, due, at least in part (as Prof. E.A. Ross suggested), to the English custom of neglecting education in its dependencies (devoting to it only 6 (?) percent of the resources). I understand that after the last attempt made by Mr. Sacher to get more, he wrote the High Commissioner a letter setting forth the reasons.[3] I suggest that you write to the Palestine Agency Office for a copy of that letter.

I think Berkson may feel that I did much of the talking. For I thought it wise to present my views of the desirable—and cut the Gordian Knots—as follows:

1. Of local difficulties—by a process of thorough devolution as opposed to centralization of administration now practiced.
    (a) to limit the function of the director & his General Board to (1) allocating the grants-in-aid, (2) inspecting, (3) advising. But with no compulsory power except, after hearing, to withdraw a grant if not used honestly.
    (b) to put the responsibility for the manner of use and the quality of instruction upon the community or district; & let its inhabitants learn by experience. He said that, in large measure, this is what is now done with the £4,500 given to the Labour Federation which assumes responsibility for the curriculum, as well as the administration. But that in the General and the Mizrachi schools (as in Petach Tikvah), the General Board controls throughout.

Berkson says he personally is inclined to move steadily, but more slowly, on the lines of devolution; that, however, the officialdom, and also the teachers (and Miss [Henrietta] Szold) are strongly against this course. I feel strongly that functions of the Diaspora should go no farther than educational inspection & advice and allocation of the funds; and that the communities' yearning for democracy should not be denied; and that full responsibility for their acts, be assumed by the individuals with the pains & penalties of error staring them in the face.[4]

Third[sic]: I told him also that I think the responsibility of raising money for special school[s] should rest, not upon the General fund, but upon those specially interested in special schools & including i.a. Mizrachis.

I realize, of course, the supreme difficulty of making changes as suggested in Second and Third. But I think we should get our direction, & work steadily to that end. And, if the Hadassah undertakes the educational budget, it should have an adequate policy and stick to it.

Fourth: As to getting a large grant from the Government (and generally as to dealing with the Govt) I told him I thought it very important that this be not done through the Agency Executives—that men like Kisch [5] and Meyer Berlin were bound to encounter insuperable obstacles; and that so far as possible heads of Departments or Bureaus should make their appeals; and that preeminently Americans should be used for that purpose; that I realized that the Palestine Executive was dead against all this, but that he should have a private talk on the subject with Judge Mack at Berlin [6] & have him endeavor to have a start made in that direction. It is only when the Z.O. officials are in dire need of financial help, as now, that reforms can be effected.

I enclose for your information (& copy) letter to Nellie Straus Mossesohn[sic].[7]

1. Isaac Baer Berkson (b. 1891) was an educator from New York City. Deeply involved in the theory and practice of Jewish education, Berkson accepted Henrietta Szold's invitation to survey Palestinian schools in 1927. He stayed in Palestine until 1935, serving as superintendent of the Jewish schools there. He returned to the United States to teach philosophy of education at the City College of New York.

2. PICA was the Palestine Jewish Colonization Association.

3. Probably Harry Sacher (1881–1971), an English lawyer who became a Zionist and, in 1920, moved to Palestine. He was one of the founders of the Manchester Zionists, loyal to Weizmann. While in Palestine he worked both for the Zionist Executive and the Jewish Agency. In 1930 he returned to England. Sacher wrote several books on Israel and Zionism.

4. Compare with LDB's advice about medical treatment in Palestine: see LDB to Julian W. Mack, 20 September 1929 and to Zip Szold, 3 August 1930.

5. Frederick Herman Kisch (1888–1943) became a member of the Zionist Executive at Weizmann's invitation in 1922. He remained in Palestine for the rest of his life. Kisch was particularly active in the attempt to establish

friendly relations with moderate Arabs, a story he told in his *Palestine Diary* (London, 1938). He enlisted in the British army in World War II and was killed in action in Tunisia.

6. See LDB to Mack, 6 August 1930, n. 1.

7. Mrs. Mochinson was the editor of the Davar English Supplement (Tel Aviv).

To Robert Szold

August 19, 1930 Chatham, Mass. [deHaas Mss]

R.S.: 1. The multigraphed reports of Jewish Agency, etc. from London referred to in Miss Benjamin's letter of 15th, contain valuable material. I will send them to Felix [Frankfurter]. Arrangement should be made for more copies of later issues. They will be valuable to our group, and to the study clubs we hope to see founded, as proposed by I.J. Lowe,[1] and at least for Z.O.A. files, a full set of the reports from the beginning.

2. My study of the Palestine material convinces me that we have an uncommonly good case—vis-a-vis the British Administration and the Arabs, and also pro-Palestine. The evidence pro-Palestine is so strong, the arguments so persuasive, that, if properly presented, they cannot fail to secure for the Jewish development of Palestine (and Trans Jordania) support from a substantial part of any Jewish audience addressed in America—other than of Jews who are confirmed anti-Zionists. (Some of these may convert themselves.)

Our crying need is a body of competent and willing speakers and writers. Competence implies mastery of the available material, as well as educated brains and some talent for speaking and for writing—such as are possessed by, or are capable of development in, many young lawyers, sociologists, economists and political scientists. If we can get a fair number of such men to study the available material, and the current additions, I feel sure that with knowledge will come not only willingness but eagerness to present the case to groups of Jews in all parts of the country. For the case Pro-Palestine is, to a degree not commonly recognized, infinitely stronger than it was when the Zeeland Memo was prepared in 1920.[2] And it is a case with such varied material for appeal, that a discriminating penetrating speaker can reach the heart, the head and ultimately the pocket of almost any category of Jew who may be exposed, so numerous are the facets of the crystal.

A. The economic achievements of the last ten years constitute a complete answer to the main objections with which I was confronted from 1914 to 1920,—that is,

    (a) That the economic possibilities were not such that Jews could become self-supporting in Palestine, or

    (b) That the earning possibilities were not such that competent Jews would voluntarily settle there; in view of the greater allurements elsewhere.

The events establish, that despite the obstacle inherent in the British attitude and the incompetence of Zionist officials much profitable agriculture and industry has been established; able men have settled there and are enjoying in their work and life a degree of happiness not experienced elsewhere; and that the number who are eager to follow is very large.

Thus, with the detailed facts, it should be possible to overcome doubts and arguments of the worldly-wise, hard headed business man;—of the men who want to be shown.

B. The condition of Jews in the Diaspora in 1930—as compared with 1920 and 1914—has worsened to such a degree, that the belief of thinking Jews that the Jewish problem would be solved by growing enlightenment in the Diaspora must have been seriously shaken—if not shattered.

A speaker sufficiently familiar with Jewish history, could, in the light of recent events, demolish these objectors. The anti-Semitic outbreaks in Europe, the closing of the doors to immigrants by practically all the new countries, the rise of anti-Semitism even in the new countries, remove the old alternatives from consideration. The question now presented is largely Palestine—or Despair?

Not only is the argument on this score greatly aided since 1920 by the unfortunate worsening of Jewish conditions, but, thanks to J.D.B.[3] the means of illustrating the worsened condition by modern instances will be abundant. Thus pity and wisdom, emotion and judgment will support the appeal.

C. The social life and strivings of the Jews as reflected in official reports and serious economic and political discussion, and as interpreted in literary productions, affords abundant material for appeal to Jewish liberals—with or without religious faith and to idealists of any race or creed.

An intimate knowledge of the trials and sufferings of the pioneers, both early and recent, will supply abundant material for appeal to all who love adventure and heroes, all who can be stirred by talk of men and women ready to risk and give all in the service of a great cause. The aspirations and striving of the Jewish Labour Organization and the achievements should appeal mightily to our progressives.

D. Thus the material is a rich storehouse of ammunition available for attack upon Jews of any class; upon the hard-headed or the soft-hearted; upon orthodox or reform; upon believer or those of religious unbelief; upon the practical man or the idealist. One has only to know the material and to select tactfully that adapted to the particular audience. Of the speaker it will be found true that "L'appétit vient en mangeant." [4] His aim should be to speak to small groups—groups so small that all those present may feel that they can participate in the discussion;—that they are a part of it. Meetings of 15 to 25 persons would probably be most productive, at least at first, and the speaker must realize that every occasion secured is one worth while—no matter what the character of the audience. No one can tell what a person really interested by the discussion may thereafter do to help the cause. And every such meeting will help educate the speaker. It will be a long time before any speaker will do his best. There is so much to learn in knowledge and in manner of presentation.

E. Every opportunity to speak which offers, however modest or unpromising it may appear, should be availed of; and effort should be continuously and persistently made to create opportunities. Lodges, Club societies, gatherings—social or serious— should be sought—whatever their character.

Our fundamental task of getting knowledge and thinking resembles that performed by the Fabian Society. The propaganda task, resembles that performed by the British Independent Labor speakers, and their predecessors. Twenty years ago it was said that there were held every week in England two thousand meetings at which their socialist doctrine was preached. Of course many of these were no larger than small parlor meetings. We had in the early days of the Hadassah the kind of intensive educational work which laid its foundation. This we need; intimate talk by persons who know the facts and arguments within the broader sphere of our work. The Abe Goldberg type of orator is not for us. He and others of the pre-Balfour Declaration era still have their place. But the emotional orator should be supplanted now by those who, mindful of emotions, present the facts in a way to argue the cause.

The available material affords also ample evidence in support of the argument that with a proper British attitude Jews can live in harmony with the Arabs; that friendly relations are being developed in many places; and that raising of the level of Arab existence has been, and is, not only a necessary incident of the Jewish upbuilding of P.—but the Jewish desire; that the Jews recognize that raising the Arab level is essential to attain the social end which the Jewish Labor especially is seeking to serve; and which Jewish industrialists desire in order to enlarge the home market.

I enclose letter of August 16th from Judge Harry Fisher; also for your information and copies, letter from and to A. Moses Klap.

1. Isidore J. Lowe (1890–1964) was a Russian immigrant who graduated from the Harvard Law School and was practicing in Boston. At LDB's suggestion Lowe wrote numerous articles on Zionism. In 1934 he went to Washington to work for the NRA, and stayed on as a member of the staff of the Department of Agriculture.

2. See LDB to Bernard Flexner, 15 September 1920, n. 1.

3. The *Jewish Daily Bulletin* was a news survey of items relating to Palestine, Zionist affairs, and the conditions in Jewish communities in Europe.

4. "The appetite grows with the eating."

To Joshua Bernhardt

August 20, 1930 Chatham, Mass. [Brandeis Mss, M 18–1]

DEAR DR. BERNHARDT: 1. In the May 1930 Monthly Jewish Agency Report mention is made, page 20, of contemplated immigration from Yemen. At your convenience, kindly let me know the status of the Yemenites now in Palestine. Those whom I saw in 1919 impressed me as an engaging and promising body; but they appeared to have been exploited by our colonists.

2. The same report mentions among "buildings to be erected: the post office, the Rockefeller Museum, and the Building of the Town Council."—Is there any discrimination against Jews in the employment of labor on any of these buildings?   Cordially,

To Robert Szold

August 20, 1930 Chatham, Mass. [deHaas Mss]

1. Among the intellectuals who should be enlisted is Isadore Lubin—economist of Brookings Institution, Washington.[1] He visited Palestine last September and was tremendously impressed by the Halutzim.[2] He is a close friend of Leo Wolman, who should, of course, also be pressed into service.

Lubin is well thought of in Washington, and for that reason, among others, it would be very valuable to have him active.

2. Letter of 17th from Rabbi Brickner enclosed.[3] I suggest that upon his return to Cleveland, "first week in September" he be promptly prodded; and that thereafter no peace be given him until the whole deficit shall have been extinguished.

3. For your information copy of letter to Bernhardt enclosed.

4. Abe Tulin wrote me July 25 that cable reported that back numbers of Palestine & Near East Magazine had been posted July 24th. If they have arrived, please have my set sent me.

1. Isador Lubin (b. 1896) was an economist who alternated between university teaching and government service. He was at the Brookings Institution from 1922–1933. From 1933 to 1946 Lubin was United States Commissioner of Labor Statistics. He held a number of other important positions and wrote numerous books and articles.

2. "Pioneers."

3. Barnett Robert Brickner (1892–1958) was a distinguished Reform rabbi of Cleveland, Ohio. LDB had written Rabbi Brickner on 7 August, a letter similar to that sent Harry Fisher on the same date. Brickner replied that he would not be in Cleveland until "the first week in September."

To Alice Harriet Grady

August 28, 1930 Chatham, Mass. [SBLI]

A.G.H.: Prof. James M. Landis of Harvard Law School was here today. I found he had taken insurance in the Mass. Mutual and New York Life—apparently in ignorance of S[avings].B[ank]. I[nsurance]. You will remember he was my secretary. So I scolded him roundly.

Please send him

1. Your article from the Savings Bk book.[1]
2. The Cox-Evans correspondence.[2]

1. "Brief Historical Sketch of the Accomplishments of SBLI during its First 21 Years of Experience."
2. A letter of Wilmot R. Evans, President of the Boston Five Cents Savings Bank, 4 June 1930, in response to Guy W. Cox, President of the John Hancock Life Insurance Company.

To Jacob deHaas

August 31, 1930 Chatham, Mass. [Brandeis Mss, Z 42-1]

Re yours of 29th

1. I hope that before the end of October—(a) [Nathan] Ratnof[f] and Zeldin will have succeeded in getting together enough money to wipe out the deficit. (b) Zeldin et al will have laid the plans for enough money to run the Z.O.A. currently. (c) The Hadassah will have assumed the function of raising at least part of the money required for education in Palestine.

2. When these steps shall have been taken, I should urge that American Zionists be taught that their prime task is to aid in the economic upbuilding of Palestine—Industrial and agricultural; and to this end that every Zionist become a stockholder in the P[alestine].E[conomic].C[orporation]. If the pressing financial tasks can be achieved within the next two months I should think it wiser to defer calling together your Committee of 150 until that mess is out of the way and then get down to the real business—giving to your 150 an inspiring picture of what has been achieved—and the great possibilities. It would be a pity to waste

the occasion by this disheartening business of wiping out the deficit and the pettiness of current administrative expenses.

3. Whether that meeting had better be in Washington will depend upon its character and prospects. But it must be clearly understood that I will not attend or make any statement for the occasion.

It is imperative that I do not appear publicly, or quasi publicly, and that I make no further public statement. What I have said publicly and done—together with extensive private correspondence and interviews—has furnished adequate evidence of my active interest in Palestine;—and these facts, if properly used, will furnish adequate evidence of my continued interest. What little of my time and strength will remain available after the term of court begins should be devoted to necessary study and thought on Palestine matters and the few important private conferences and seeing of individuals which will be unavoidable.

I shall hope that Bob [Szold] can arrange that any conference (if any) with him and others which must be had in the near future will be held before the October term begins.

4. The men and women in Boston upon whom you should make demands are those who joined in the telegram to me promising support. Zionists must be taught to be, at least, as good as their word.

As you see, I continue to take a hopeful view.   Cordially,

To Maurice Beck Hexter

September 7, 1930 Chatham, Mass. [Brandeis Mss, Z 42–1]

My dear Dr. Hexter: Since writing you on Aug. 29, via 27 William Street, I have yours of 25th announcing your early return to Palestine.

Lord Passfield's remark about the possibilities of urban immigration is disturbing.[1] At best, it evidences lack of understanding. And it reminds painfully of a statement in the Shaw report.[2] There is a remote limit to Jewish agricultural immigration; because the supply of irrigable land and of water for irrigation is limited and the fellaheen must have their share. But the possibilities of Jewish urban immigration are practically unlimited;

because its needs for land and water are small. Palestine has about the area of Massachusetts. The commerce and industry of the Commonwealth support nearly four million people. The essentials are a sea-port, a good harbor, a good climate and a population with brains, determination and character. When Haifa's harbor shall have been made good and malaria shall have been wholly eliminated, the Jews can provide Palestine with the other essential. Moreover, Massachusetts has no natural resources comparable to the Dead Sea salts—and no cheap supply of oil, which the pipe line will bring from Mosul. Man is the great natural resource which made Athol's fine tools and Lynn's electrical products and the Gillette Safety Razor world famous. James L. Richards has shown that Massachusetts can compete even in the heavy industries. His company has been making, at a profit, pig-iron at Everett out of Swedish and Morocco iron-ore with Nova Scotia and West Virginia coal and lime from other States. And one of the company's [*] customers has its foundry at Philadelphia.

Nothing in Palestine development is more encouraging than the 1928 Census showing "3,505 producing enterprises." And happily their number is steadily growing. The new products of the "geo" and the "Lio" factories, the local production of the tins, the making of orange boxes of Hedera wood are notable events in the history of the country. We should do everything possible to promote such enterprises; to make Palestine self-sufficient; and to develop its exports of manufactured products. With the aid of these and the increasing orange production, the terrifying adverse trade balance can be overcome. The increase of £P 350,000 in the first four months of 1930 for exports and the decrease of £P 150,000 in imports is a most hopeful occurrence. The sale of £P 10,000 of artificial teeth to England is an indication of what Jewish ingenuity, courage and determination can achieve for Palestine. Even more should be possible for other Jews who are urged on by the added spur of necessity.

What all Palestinean Jews can and should do is to buy Palestine products in preference to all others. Today "made in Palestine" goods should be recognized as the "noblesse oblige". Talk with [Emanuel N.] Mohl (and such others as you and he deem advisable) as to how this movement can be promoted.   Cordially,

1. See LDB to Rennie Smith, 29 October 1930, n. 2. Hexter had sent a memorandum of a 22 August conference between Felix Warburg and Lord Passfield (Sidney Webb).

2. See LDB to Julian W. Mack, 9 October 1929, n. 7, and 5 April 1930.

To Henrietta Szold

September 8, 1930 Washington, D. C. [Brandeis Mss, Z 42–1]

MY DEAR MISS SZOLD: My thanks for your letter of August 18th and for the further information to which I look forward.

The Daganiah record is fine, both as to self-support and malaria.[1] It is perhaps a subject of congratulation that our settlers must have the ceaseless reminder that "stamina and eternal vigilance" are essentials of worthy achievement.

With every good wish,

1. Daganiah, the first kibbutz in Palestine, had been founded in 1910 by Ukrainian immigrants, along the Jordan River just below the Sea of Galilee; it became the model for all subsequent collective settlements. Among its early problems had been the prevalence of malaria, but by 1930 this problem had been largely eradicated. For LDB's interest in the problem of malaria, see LDB to Julian W. Mack and Bernard Flexner, 6 October 1921, n. 2.

To Zip Szold

September 16, 1930 Washington, D. C. [Brandeis Mss, Z 42–1]

MY DEAR ZIP: Politically-minded or unthinking Arabs are slow to admit the Jewish contribution to Arab welfare; but few who have experienced the benefits conferred by Hadassah through alleviation of pain and cure of disease would fail to remember. It occurs to me that with the growing literacy of Arabs it might be helpful, to keep before all who enter our hospitals, or who see them, ever-present evidence of our contribution to Arab well-being; and that this might be done by placing an appropriate inscription in a prominent place on every hospital or dispensary which will tell that the hospital and the service are provided by Jews for the benefit of Arabs as well as of Jews. Perhaps this has already been done. Surely Mr. Nathan Straus would like it.[1]

Cordially,

1. According to Mrs. Szold, no action was taken on LDB's suggestion.

To Robert Szold

September 17, 1930 Washington, D.C. [R. Szold Mss]

R.S.: 1. I trust the Z.O.A. Librarian will make sure that the Library contains copies of:

  (a) All the reports of the Mandatory.
  (b) All Minutes of Sessions of the Permanent Mandates Commission and of the Council and all their reports concerning Palestine.
  (c) All important documents therein referred to and not inserted in full in the above.

and that these documents be bound, so as to be more readily preserved.

2. The Minutes of the Sessions—June 3rd to 31st,—is a most interesting, as well as important, document.

The English cut an extremely bad figure.[1] The low opinion of Luke—formed during the riots and subsequently, is fully confirmed (a) His knowledge is woefully lacking (although author with Keith Roach of a Palestine Hand book).[2] (b) He is not candid. (c) He is evidently lacking backbone. Shiels[3] had an unenviable task which he didn't perform very well. Clauson[4]—who said very little—makes a better impression.

3. On the other hand—the Members of the Commission manifested a thoroughness of preparation, a depth and breadth of thought and a statesman-like quality which is most encouraging—not only for Jews, but for all who have faith in the development of the League of Nations.

4. It seems to me that our group of able lawyers would find it most interesting and educating—to make a careful study of the whole record—(a) The Shaw Report. (b) The Answers of the Agency, the Revisionists, the Va'ad Le'umi [sic], H.B. Samuels and others. (c) The Minutes of Perm. Mandates Commission (d) Their report; the British reply and (e) The Report of Hjalmar Procope, (Rapporteur) and Action of Council thereon (which I have not seen) and ultimately (f) when procured the evidence before the Commission of Enquiry.

5. I am inclined to think that, had I been on the Permanent Mandates Commission, I should have been most influenced against the British by their failure to submit copies of the evidence introduced before the Commission of Enquiry;—and by the procedure

before the Commission in having in Camera (and perhaps in part without opportunity of cross-examination) the witnesses who, in large part, were the persons complained of.

6. Ten years ago, Riegelman expressed the desire to do Zionist work—and Frank I. Schechter who has much mind—might care to take hold as an intellectual.

7. I am enclosing letter to Hyman.[5]

1. The League of Nations Mandate Commission had requested Great Britain to explain the recent disturbances in Palestine, the Mandatory government's handling of the problem, and the Shaw and Hope-Simpson reports. Although the British representatives tried to prove that they had not violated the spirit of the Mandate, which included the Balfour pledge, they did not make a favorable impression on the Commission.

2. Harry Charles Joseph Luke (1884–19[?]) and Edward Keith-Roach (1885–1954), *The Handbook of Palestine* (London, 1922); subsequent editions were published in 1930 and 1934. Roach had been assigned to Palestine at the end of the war and was district commissioner for the Jerusalem area from 1926 to 1943; he was the author of several books on the Arabs and the Middle East.

3. Sir Thomas Drummond Shiels (1881–1953), a physician, had entered Parliament as a Labour representative in 1924; in 1930 he was serving as undersecretary in the Colonial Office.

4. Albert Charles Baron Clauson (1870–1946) was a prominent justice of the Court of Chancery and a member of the British delegation to the Mandate Commission hearings.

5. Joseph C. Hyman (1889–1949) was a member of the council for the Jewish Agency and held a number of important posts in the Joint Distribution Committee.

To Robert Szold

September 18, 1930 Washington, D.C. [R. Szold Mss]

R.S.: My recent study of conditions in Palestine strongly confirms the conviction that we must resolutely oppose every British effort to slow down the pace of immigration; that we must, on the contrary, make strenuous and unceasing efforts to accelerate the pace or we shall be undone. Our pace must always, for purely practical reasons, be limited by the then absorptive economic capacity of the country. But that limit is not fixed by nature; nor should it be fixed by nature; nor should it be fixed by British political considerations. The limit at any time is subject to practically indefinite expansion—dependent only upon the will of the Jewish people—to be evidenced by their contributions of men and money. There is apparently an inexhaustible supply of men. Our crying need is for money to be wisely applied in economic enterprise—agriculture, industry and commerce. We are confronted with a race of diligence.

1. For a long period prior to 1919 the population of Palestine was practically stationary, like that of Syria and Trans-Jordania still is. Poverty and the absence of health measures resulted in a high mortality so that the death rate and the birth rate were about equal. And the lack of economic opportunity resulted in emigration, largely to America. Since 1919 the non-Jewish population of Palestine (as well as the Jewish) has been rising rapidly, the former due to four causes—which are incident to the Balfour Declaration and the Mandate.

(a) Jewish enterprise under British Administration, and the education flowing largely from Jewish example have resulted in widespread increase of Arab economic well being and thereby incidentally reduced Arab mortality. (General Gorgas said that that [sic] the most important health measure introduced by the U.S. when building the Panama Canal was high wages.)

(b) The Jewish and the British Administration have introduced important health measures and services.

(c) The better economic conditions and the British Administration in Palestine have resulted in the seeping in of non-Jewish Syrian, Transjordan and Egyptian labor and small traders; and a considerable non-Jewish body of persons from Europe.

(d) The better economic conditions in Palestine have tended to lessen the emigration; and cause re-immigration. See Minutes of Perm. Mand. Com. (1930) pp. 101, 102. Recently the arrest of emigration has been compelled by the practical closing of the doors to immigrants, not only by the United States, but by other American countries. See Minutes of Perm. Mandates Com. (1930) p. 99.

2. In the five years ending December 31, 1929 the natural increase of the population by excess of births over deaths for the

whole country was 24.64 per 1000. For the Moslems (exclusive of the 103,000 Bedouins for whom data are not available) the increase was 26.06 percent. For the Jews it was only 22.27—although the infantile mortality among Jews was only 89.78 while that for Moslems was 204.97. See report of the Mandatory for 1929 p. 84.

3. The improving economic condition and the extension of direct health measures among the Arabs is certain to reduce the infant mortality and otherwise the death rate; and it cannot be assumed that improved economic conditions will greatly reduce their birth rate, which in 1929 was 57.94 per thousand, about three times the present birth rate in the United States. See Minutes of Perm. Mandates Com. (1930) p. 116.

In Egypt, under British rule, without specific Jewish aid the population which had for centuries (and perhaps thousands of years) been practically stationary at about 6,000,000, has more than doubled in about 40 years. And the experience of India has been similar.

I am enclosing further communications from J.W.M[ack] just received from F.F[rankfurter].

To Jennie Taussig Brandeis

October 11, 1930 Washington, D. C. [Fannie Brandeis]

MY DEAR JENNIE: A glad welcome home.[1] We have followed you joyously through Europe, aided by your and Fannie's messages, richly freighted with precious memories. And already we have from Vienna reports of the pleasure your visit gave others.

The Salzkammergut, Vienna and Florence brought experiences the delight of which remains undimmed and, with your postals and letters, each day there was brought nearer. So I had a veritable voyage autour de ma chamber.[2]

Our summer was entirely uneventful, like those at Ladless which Alfred so loved. But it was a lovely summer as Alice will tell you.

We hope you three travellers are finding all well in Louisville.

1. On her trip to Europe in the summer of 1930, Alfred's widow was accompanied by her daughters Fannie and Adele, and also by her sister-in-law, Mrs. Walter Taussig.

2. "A trip within my room."

To Samuel Wohl

October 26, 1930 Washington, D. C. [Brandeis Mss, Z 42–1]

MY DEAR RABBI WOHL: [1] Re yours of 22nd.

Your thoughtful letter has gone to Chairman Szold.[2]

In your daily efforts to secure support for the Z.O.A. program, waste no time on anti-Zionists. Rouse the Zionists and the indifferent.   Cordially,

1. Samuel Wohl (1895–1972) was rabbi of the Reading Road Temple in Cincinnati from his ordination in 1927 until his retirement in 1966. He was active in numerous Zionist groups and was closely linked with the Histadrut. Wohl also played a prominent role in the national leadership of the American Reform movement.

2. Wohl had made several suggestions for action by the Zionist Organization in the light of the Passfield White Paper (see next letter), including the introduction of a Congressional resolution, gathering one million signatures on a monster petition, and convening a supreme emergency council. LDB passed the letter on to Z.O.A. leaders, but only one idea ultimately saw fruition, the creation of a Christian pro-Palestine Committee which would include members of Congress and the clergy.

To Rennie Smith

October 29, 1930 Washington, D. C. [Brandeis Mss, Z 42–1]

MY DEAR RENNIE SMITH: [1] Yours of 27th has just reached me. I am very sorry not to have seen you. The government's proposal seems to me unbelievably bad.[2] If, as I hope, you have seen Frankfurter or Robert Szold, you will know my views. Be sure to see Szold or deHaas.

It is important for the honor of Great Britain as for the welfare of the Jews that the government should recede from its mistaken policy.

With best wishes,   Cordially,

1. Rennie Smith (1888–1962) had entered government service in England as Parliamentary Secretary, and he was later appointed undersecretary for Foreign Affairs. From 1929 to 1932, as secretary of the British Group in the European Parliamentary Union, he traveled frequently in the United States lecturing on European financial affairs.

2. On 21 October 1930, the British issued simultaneously the Hope-Simpson Report and the Passfield White Paper. Following the Shaw Report (see LDB to Julian W. Mack, 9 October 1929, n. 7), the government had dispatched Sir John Hope-Simpson (1868–1961), a retired civil servant resident in India, to examine Arab complaints against Jewish immigration. Sir John spent only two months in Palestine, and listened primarily to Arab groups—refusing even to consider material submitted by Jewish agricultural experts. His estimate of available arable land was 40 percent below that held by the Jewish Agency, and thus he concluded that Palestine could support no further immigration. He went on to detail many of the Arab charges against the Yishuv and reported them as if true. Following his recommendation that all further immigration be halted, the Colonial Secretary, Lord Passfield (Sidney Webb), issued a White Paper which restricted further Jewish immigration and redefined the Balfour Declaration primarily in terms of obligations to the Arabs, severely limiting the promise of a Jewish homeland.

Naturally the White Paper caused an immediate uproar among Jews and supporters of the idea of a Jewish homeland. The government's failure to consult either with the Zionist Organization or with the Jewish Agency led Chaim Weizmann, Felix Warburg, and Lord Melchett to resign from the Jewish Agency. Prestigious Englishmen from all parties denounced the new policy as the betrayal of a solemn trust, and Zionist organizations in various countries mounted a massive anti-British campaign. Finally, on 13 February 1931, Prime Minister Ramsay MacDonald released a letter to Weizmann in which he sought to clarify the White Paper, but which in effect repealed it.

To Nathan D. Kaplan

November 10, 1930 Washington, D.C. [Brandeis Mss, Z 42–1]

MY DEAR NATHAN KAPLAN: 1. My thanks for yours of Oct. 10, the statistical abstract and the copy of the 1928 annual report on Forestry Service.

2. The pernicious Passfield White Paper has had one good effect. American Jewry is really stirred and in that respect, we are being materially aided in the rebuilding of the Z.O.A.[1] It is a long journey—but substantial progress is being made.

3. I trust that Palestine Jewry will persist in patronizing "Made in Palestine" Jewish goods; and that there will be a rapid increase

of the Jewish purchases of food products of the Jewish colonies.[2]

4. Keep me advised as to the financial condition of the Arab merchants, land owners, etc. and the effect of the White Paper proposals on them. I note the request of the Arabs for a moratorium.   Cordially,

1. See preceding letter.
2. See LDB to Maurice B. Hexter, 7 September 1930.

To Robert Szold

November 15, 1930 Washington, D. C. [R. Szold Mss]

MY DEAR BOB: 1) I hope Zionists will appreciate, as I do, your great sacrifice in assuming again the Chairmanship.[1]

2) The demands of the financial end will be increased—and there are less than 8 months before June 30—the date of your suggested release. Do take from that long period all the time and energy necessary to effect these two advances:

> (1) To bring into the Organization that body of young and able intellectuals for whom we have been longing and without whom the Z.O.A. cannot function worthily.

> (2) To bring to fruition that plan for dealing through a lawyers Committee—that steady flow of legacies— which the future could yield. (Jack Gilbert has some information on this which should be of help).

3) The press and correspondence from England repeats rumors that Hexter will come with the money-savers. He should not be allowed to leave Palestine until he is no longer needed for the 1000 family project.[2]

It was good to have your birthday greeting.[3]

1. At the Z.O.A. convention in June 1930, the Brandeis–Mack group, led by Robert Szold, had agreed to take over control of the organization for a six-month period and then decide whether to continue in power. Although the new regime had little to show, initially, for their work, other than a slight reduction in the organization's debt, Szold decided to stay with the job.
2. During the 1920s, the Palestine Economic Council financed a plan to settle one thousand new families on agricultural cooperatives in Palestine.

Under the terms of the British immigration law, there was no limit on so-called capitalist families entering Palestine, since it was assumed that they would be self-supporting. The P.E.C. aimed to help some of these families qualify for this category.

3. LDB celebrated his seventy-fourth birthday on 13 November.

To Julius Simon

November 17, 1930 Washington, D. C. [Brandeis Mss, Z 42–1]

DEAR JULIUS SIMON: I defer answering your thoughtful letter of 14th. Meanwhile, I should like you to consider with Judge Mack, Robert Szold and Dr. Bernhardt the following:

Bob told me that the P[alestine].E[ndowment].F[und]. has about $300,000 in bonds (American) yielding a low return—which are held under gifts for the Hebrew University. I suggested that these be sold from time to time, and the proceeds invested in especially choice first mortgages on urban property in Jerusalem, Tel-Aviv, or Haifa. I understand that the P[alestine].E[conomic].C[orporation]. or its subsidiary, the Mortgage & Credit Bank, hold mortgages of that character. For instance, the first series granted in 1922, on which as stated in P.E.C. Third Annual Report p. 20: "about one-half of the total indebtedness has been paid." The $300,000 now held by the P.E.F. could be used in buying these mortgages of the P.E.C.—thereby both increasing the income of the University and strengthening it incidentally by promoting Palestine development.

I had some talk with Bob on this subject on Nov. 11.

Cordially,

To Huston Thompson

November 17, 1930 Washington, D. C. [Thompson Mss]

MY DEAR HUSTON THOMPSON: Thanks for your greetings.

Yes, even the "curse of bigness" is beginning to dawn on some of our countrymen.   Cordially,

To Jacob deHaas

November 20, 1930 Washington, D.C. [Brandeis Mss, Z 42–1]

DEHAAS: You know that it has been my belief that if the positive
agricultural, industrial and social achievements of the last ten
years in Palestine could be adequately presented to American
Jewry, and the advances being made from day to day were kept
before them, financial support for Palestine enterprises would
flow naturally into those channels; there would be no need for
drives; that our efforts could be directed to furthering among our
Jews understanding of projects and information as to opportunities; and that those who were unwilling or unable to embark in
independent enterprises, would gladly entrust their funds to the
P[alestine].E[conomic].C[orporation]. as stockholders.

Yesterday Alexander Brin [1] of the Boston Jewish Advocate
called. He spoke of the recent ferment among Boston Zionists
and said that it reminded of our 1914–1915 days. I told him the
great difference between those days and these is this: That then
we had dreams and hopes. Now, we can deal with things realized.
And I told him somewhat of the progress made in agriculture and
industry; of the significant achievement of labor; of the courage
and initiative in manufacture; of the extraordinary accomplishment of [Emanuel N.] Mohl with the Labor Bank; [2] of the success of the Hedera suburb; [3] of the many projects to carry forward that experiment; of the raising of more than half a million
dollars by the Hebrew Trades Committee to meet the conditions
of my gift to the Yakhin; [4] of the conquest by [Israel] Kligler of
Malaria.[5] And I pointed out to him how all this had put a new
aspect upon appeals for support. It was not now another tale of
woe;—a seeking of relief to mitigate misery. It was opening to
American Jews the wholly new opportunity of sharing in the joy
of building a happy community; a true renaissance.

He was much interested and asked where he could get the data.
I referred him to [Israel B.] Brodie and to [Joshua] Bernhardt.
Then he said he would like to write a half dozen articles and
asked whether he might send them to me before publication, so
as to avoid the possibility of errors or of improperly quoting me.
I told him that I could not look over the articles, but that you
would, I was sure, be glad to do so, if that would satisfy him.
And he said he would like that very much.

I told him also that he must arrange at once to get the "Davar, Weekly English Supplement" and the Palestine and Near East Economic Review regularly;—and that after his articles are out, publish all economic news of interest—from week to week.

Finally he said that instead of writing for the material, he would go to New York on his return from Washington (He is here for the Care of Children Conference) [6] and would see you, Brodie and Bernhardt.

Make sure that Brin sees also Isaac Hamlin [7] and Shiplacoff [8] and gets their data.

And send to Brodie, Bernhardt, and to Hamlin a copy of this letter. Hand Brin a copy when you see him.

1. Alexander Brin (b. 1895) had purchased the *Boston Jewish Advocate* from deHaas in 1917, and he edited and published the paper for many years. He has been involved in numerous Jewish groups in New England and also served as dean of the Massachusetts Board of Education from 1949 to 1962.

2. The Histadrut, the General Federation of Labor in Palestine, had created the Bank HaPo'alim, or Workers Bank, which ultimately became the third largest financial institution in Israel.

3. Hedera, located about 40 kilometers north of Tel Aviv on the coastal road, had been founded by Russian immigrants in the 1890s. Thanks in part to American investment, the town developed several industries, including a paper mill and fruit canneries.

4. In 1926 the Histadrut had established Yakhin, a contracting office for agricultural work. The agency found work for Jewish labor on farms and orchards and later secured capital for investment in citrus industries.

5. See LDB to Julian W. Mack and Bernard Flexner, 6 October 1921.

6. The White House Conference on Child Health and Protection was then meeting in Washington, and on 22 November the conferees issued a nineteen-point program calling for, among other items: better dental and health care for children; proper diet, education, and housing; a ban on all child labor; care for the handicapped; and the creation of the necessary federal, state, and local agencies to implement these recommendations.

7. Isaac Hamlin (1891–1967) had been a leader of the Poale Zion in the United States since before World War I. In 1923, at David Ben-Gurion's request, Hamlin undertook to raise funds for the Histadrut among American labor groups. In 1955 he emigrated to Israel, and managed the American Histadrut Center in Tel Aviv until his death.

8. Abraham Isaac Shiplacoff (1877–1934) was secretary to the United Hebrew Trades and president of the International Leather Goods Workers Union. He had been the first Socialist elected to the New York State Assembly, serving from 1915 to 1919.

To Bernard Flexner

November 22, 1930 Washington, D. C. [Brandeis Mss, Z 42–1]

MY DEAR BEN: Our rights, legal and moral, seem clear. We have a compelling need. We have in the Palestinian Jews shock troops, tested and found true. We have developed through the P[alestine].E[conomic].C[orporation]. and otherwise the adequate technique. We have in Central and Eastern Europe adequate reserves of desirable immigrants. We shall succeed, provided we make sure:

    A. That no part of our rights is frittered away by concession.

    B. That, in the present emergency, we are not tripped up by lack of money and credit.

"A" was adequately discussed yesterday. "B" was only touched upon. I hope you will take up "B" with Mr. [Felix] Warburg and Dr. [Cyrus] Adler. The financial needs are:

    1. Funding existing indebtedness

    2. Money to meet the current Palestine services—especially health and education

    3. Money to effect the "consolidation of the colonies"—so as to stop current waste

    4. Money for further development,—primarily through building of workmen houses and the 1,000 settlement.[1]

As to 1, I assume progress is being made for effecting Mr. Warburg's project.

As to 2, I hope that within a relatively short time, Hadassah will be able to raise the funds for education as well as health. But obviously during the current year, it cannot raise more than a small percentage of that need from America for education. Provision must be made for the balance, lest we have a repetition of the conditions of 1926–1927, years of unpaid salaries, etc.

As to 3, I am convinced that, if we have a reasonable time for reorganization of the Z.O.A. and of bringing in the new men of character, ability and means, whom we are beginning to interest in Palestine, we shall be able to provide a large part of the aggregates needed. But there are immediate needs, like some already being met through the Emergency Fund (of which Dr. Hexter wrote me under date of October 28, 1930) that should not be suffered to wait. The loss in money and in demoralization is too great.

As to 4, I think we should put on all steam. A fully employed Jewry will be an unanswerable political argument. And it will enable us to mobilize in America, through the "new men" referred to above, a body of financial supporters of Palestine who, as stockholders in the P.E.C. or otherwise, will supply the funds needed for economic development.

The critical need of credit and money is for the current year. It is that to which I hope you will address yourself in taking up the matter with Mr. Warburg and Dr. Adler.

You will find in November 5, 1930 English "Davar" able comment on the Simpson report.[2]

1. See LDB to Robert Szold, 15 November 1930, n. 2.
2. Moshe Shertok, "The Simpson Report," *Davar English Weekly Supplement* 2 (5 November 1930): 2–3, praised the report for its optimism regarding the potential of Palestine in the future, but then attacked it for its prescriptions for realizing those possibilities. The commission had gathered enormous amounts of data, but had ignored what, to the Zionists, was the crux of the whole issue: the Jewish aspects of Palestine. The commission had tortured the terms of the Mandate to come up with a meaningful statement on Jewish-Arab rights, Shertok contended, but it had failed even to acknowledge what the development of Palestine meant for the future of Jewish life.

To Fannie Brandeis

December 10, 1930 Washington, D. C. [Brandeis Mss, M 16–1]

DEAR FAN: Re Yours of 6th.

1. I am very glad that Miss McGill[1] has been secured. That should result in a worthy booklet.

2. I suppose Judge [Robert W.] Bingham has (a) lost heavily, like so many others on the stock market—and (b) is disgusted with the break-up of the tobacco co-operative on which he worked so hard and doubtless spent much. But I think Dr. Kent should, when opportunity comes, pursue him further. Noblesse oblige.

3. I do not think that the depression is bad for our purpose. We want from Louisvillians money. But we want primarily interest in the Library. There is a better chance of getting that when they have less money to spend. And we shall gain what

we are after best, when in pursuit of an interest they curtail their unnecessary daily expenditures.

1. Probably Anna Blanche McGill, a Louisville writer and the literary editor of the *Courier-Journal* and the *Herald-Post*.

To Maurice Beck Hexter

December 15, 1930 Washington, D. C. [Brandeis Mss, Z 42–1]

DEAR DR. HEXTER: *First:* I am glad to have yours of November 28th, and I have seen through Mr. [Felix] Warburg's courtesy, your correspondence wtih Sir John [Hope-Simpson].

1. He has doubtless seen, since he wrote you, much criticism of his statement of facts, e.g. in Davar. Much of the criticism I have seen seems to me well-founded.[1]

2. Equally subject to criticism is his lack of imagination so far as the Jews are concerned. It is lamentable; and prevents understanding of his problem. Compare with his lack Wedgwood's grasp as exhibited in "The Seventh Dominion".[2]

3. What is perhaps most surprising, considering that Simpson is a Scot, is the doctrinaire quality of his proposals. Of course, the simple practical solution of the problem which engrosses him is settlement in Transjordania. There £2,500,000 would effect wonders. In Palestine it would go only a small way; would impose heavy burdens; would involve most serious obstacles; and must defer for long fruition—even if considered only from the standpoint of the Arabs. I understand political difficulties which doubtless led him to silence on this subject and on the past and present shortcomings of the local administration, and which induced him to suffer his report to be altered. But it must be remembered that he is put forward as the Expert—and from the Expert we are entitled in this serious matter, to have the truth, the whole truth and nothing but the truth. However good his intention was, the result is great unfairness to the Jewish People.[3]

Second: I am very glad that you found it possible to squeeze another £5,000 for consolidating the settlements. I hope you will find it possible to get still more. It is among the most pressing of many urgent expenditures.

I am very glad that you have seen so much of Laski. That is a great privilege. His value to any cause he espouses is significant.[4]

With best wishes,   Cordially,

1. See LDB to Rennie Smith, 29 October 1930, n. 2.

2. Josiah Wedgwood (see LDB to Jacob deHaas, 25 January 1918, n. 3) had published *Palestine: The Seventh Dominion*, in 1928, advocating a self-governing Jewish state in Palestine as a part of the British Empire; and in 1929 he formed the Seventh Dominion League to further that aim.

3. Hope-Simpson's "expertise" had been gained completely in India, where conditions were far different than in Palestine. A consistent criticism leveled by the Zionists was that Sir John had attempted to force the facts he confronted in the Holy Land into the familiar mold of Indian society and agriculture.

4. In the furor created over the Passfield White Paper, both the European and American Zionists joined in an aggressive public campaign to force the British government to retract the document. LDB, at the same time, was quietly urging Harold Laski to utilize his contacts in the Labour Party to effect the same end. See Urofsky, *American Zionism*, 383–84.

To Robert Szold

December 16, 1930 Washington, D. C. [R. Szold Mss]

R.S.: Under date of Aug. 17/30 I submitted recommendations re New Palestine. These were considered at Sept. 17 meeting of Administration Committee. Those as to format were rejected by the Special Committee. But "As to the matter of contents, the Special Committee is in complete accord with Mr. Justice Brandeis," etc.[1] See p. 3 Record. The matter was referred back to the Administrative Committee.

I do not recall whether the subject has ever been considered by the Administrative Committee since. I have made only a hasty glance at the issues of the New Palestine since that date. But I fail to find in them—with the exception of the Oct. 3 number containing Brodie's excellent paper[2]—any reference to economic progress in Palestine.

The kind of thing that would make American Jews understand what we believe in is indicated by the item "Poultry Raising up to Date" on p. 4. Davar of Nov. 26.

Of course I realize the exigencies of the Passfield White Paper troubles[3]—but "Business as usual" if we are to have bread.

1. LDB wanted *The New Palestine*, the official publication of the Z.O.A., to devote nearly three-fourths of its space to happenings in Palestine.

2. Israel B. Brodie, "Palestine's Economic Future," *The New Palestine* 19 (3 October 1930): 94–96. Actually, in the months following the return of the Brandeisists to power, more and more articles on economic topics appeared in the journal, while ideological and theoretical discussions disappeared from its pages altogether.

3. See LDB to Rennie Smith, 29 October 1930, n. 2.

To Emanuel N. Mohl

December 17, 1930 Washington, D. C. [Brandeis Mss, Z 42–1]

MY DEAR MOHL: Re your letter of Nov. 28th to Judge Mack.

I agree entirely with you that Simpson's plans and his going to Palestine would be harmful to our cause. But I am amazed at your saying: "I feel it will be useless to continue etc." The British and the Arabs may make things harder for us—But if our men are true to themselves and the cause, we shall not fail.

I think you must have been over-tired when you wrote that letter.   Cordially,

To Robert Szold

December 19, 1930 Washington, D. C. [R. Szold Mss]

DEAR BOB: 1. As you speak in yours of yesterday of B[ernard].F[lexner].'s being at home, I telegraphed you to see [Pinhas] Rutenberg's radiogram which I mailed Flexner yesterday for recoding.

2. I am sorry Warburg takes "his disappointment (as to Felix [Frankfurter] not going) personally and subjectively." [1] He should remember that (a) in things political Felix has the more experienced judgment; (b) that Felix has better understanding than any of us as to general British political considerations; (c) that Felix has constantly special reports from [Harold] Laski dealing with situation and specifically with the need for and usefulness of his coming now for a brief visit; (d) that only Felix can (with his knowledge of situation at Cambridge) judge of the extent of the sacrifice of other duties involved in his leaving.

3. I have such confidence in Felix' judgment and such appre-hension of any one undertaking a delicate task against his better judgment because of the will or judgment of others, that I should feel much troubled if he went to London at a time when he thought it unwise and probably harmful to the cause.

1. Felix Warburg wanted Frankfurter to come to London immediately, to take part in the Zionist campaign and the negotiations to have the Pass-field White Paper modified.

To Robert Szold

December 19, 1930 Washington, D. C. [R. Szold Mss]

DEAR BOB: Re Yours of 18th.

1. As to the financial situation I also wrote B[ernard]. F[lex-ner]. in the letter referred to in my telegram of today to you.

2. As to Mr. [Felix] Warburg. There has never been in my mind any thought as to Mr. Warburg's willingness to discharge his own claim for $350,000. The question was merely how much new money he would provide to tide over the present and to prevent a crash during the period which (despite his resigna-tion [1]) is his administration. For better or worse, he came in. We had nothing to do with his coming in. When he came to me with Flexner in Sept. '29 he said he could attend to the "financial" end, but needed my help at the political—and for my prestige with Zionists. We have given him the best that is in us;—and more than he expected. The difficulties which have arisen—throwing greater burdens on him are inherent in the situation—increased much by Louis Marshall's death, who would have been able to do much with American non-Zionists. I don't see how Mr. Warburg can afford to let the W.Z.O., Agency et al go into a "receiver-ship" or the like, if money which he is able to provide would save the situation. Let him pay out in cash—if need be a million or a million and a half now. Noblesse oblige. He could thus an-ticipate his Jewish obligation, if need be, for years to come. But as he has the cash, I don't see how he can make his saving the situation dependent on contributions from others.

It must be remembered also that the present plight is due to the Allied Jewish Campaign's failure to function.[2] That was conducted as Mr. Warburg wanted it conducted. We had nothing to do with it. Morally, it was his Campaign. A great financial magnate must bear losses with fortitude.[3]

2. As I have heretofore written Julius Simon,[4] I think the P[alestine].E[ndowment].F[und]. should be ready to sell American securities and buy from the P[alestine].E[conomic].C[orporation]. prime mortgages.

3. The Julius Simon report to which you refer has not yet arrived. But I have the collection of cables Nov. 8 to Dec. 18 secured today from [Joseph C.] Hyman. I do not know to what you refer about bringing P.E.C. in otherwise than as above.

1. From the Jewish Agency. See LDB to Rennie Smith, 29 October 1930, n. 2.

2. From 1925 until 1930, the various Zionist groups had merged their campaigns to raise money for Palestine into one combined effort, the United Palestine Appeal, led by Stephen S. Wise and Emanuel Neumann. In 1930 the Jewish Agency, led by Warburg, took over fund-raising and merged the Palestine Appeal and the Joint Distribution Committee into the Allied Jewish Campaign. Because of the depression, the campaign never took hold, and in 1935 the Zionists split away to revive the United Palestine Appeal. In 1939, in response to the growing Nazi persecution of European Jewry, the U.P.A. again merged with other Jewish campaigns in the United Jewish Appeal, which, despite internal differences between Zionist and non-Zionist groups, became the accepted umbrella campaign for Jewish philanthropy in the United States.

3. See LDB to Julius Simon, 27 June and 12 July 1931.

4. See LDB to Simon, 17 November 1930.

To Abraham Lincoln Filene

December 27, 1930 Washington, D.C. [SBLI]

MY DEAR A.L.: I am glad to have your note and to know that Mr. [James L.] Richards plans to spend some time on Savings Bank Insurance. What we need most now: —

1. More Savings Insurance Banks. You know my aim is 25 in the near future. We have only 16.

2. More advertising.

I am sure that Mr. Richards, with his great influence can bring us large accessions, with the aid of other officers of the League.

Best wishes for 1931.

To Robert Szold

January 10, 1931 Washington, D. C. [Brandeis Mss, Z 49–2]

MY DEAR BOB: 1. I am enclosing Bernard Harris' check for Z.O.A. dues and his letter which please return to Jack Gilbert.[1]

2. I have your letter of 8th, your telegram of 9th and copy from [Joseph C.] Hyman of [Julius] Kahn's cable of 9th that European Agency Circles and London Office are urging Wasserman[2] go to New York to help campaign and that Wasserman might accept an invitation from Agency group to do so.

In my opinion, the Palestine impending financial collapse would, if permitted to come, be politically so serious—and the American financial performance hitherto so scandalously bad—that **we** should accept the offers both of Weizmann and of Wasserman to help. They may not bring much aid, but we should be eternally damned if we fail after having rejected aid. And it is possible that they may help materially. They will, at all events, realize, if they come, what the American situation is. Unless they come, they will not be able to understand our failure.[3]

1. Jack Gilbert, LDB's son-in-law, was an active recruiter for Zionism among his friends, and it was his custom to send the initial dues check to LDB.

2. Oskar Wasserman (1869–1934), a German banker and communal leader, was chairman of the World Keren Hayesod, and also chairman of the Jewish Agency's Finance and Budget Committee.

3. Just a few days earlier, LDB had received a lengthy letter from Maurice Hexter detailing the financial plight of the Zionists. The Jewish Agency had debts of over £1,000,000, with less than £80,000 in assets. Although the Agency had adopted a budget of £545,000, £145,000 was earmarked for reduction of debt, and the most optimistic estimate of income for 1931 was under £400,000. With the full effects of the depression just beginning to be felt, there was little hope that the budget would be met.

To Robert Szold

January 18, 1931 Washington, D. C. [Brandeis Mss, Z 49–2]

MY DEAR BOB: You know how important I deem the Davar English Supplement as a political implement in Palestine and England, and as an instrument for education in America.[1] Having learned in September last that its publication would have to be abandoned unless financial aid should come from some source, I arranged through Nathan Kaplan to have [Robert D.] Kesselman make an audit. From this it appears that of the issue of 3000 copies—all but about 350 go to persons or institutions on the free list; and that in the United States there are only 60 paying subscribers. More than half of the complimentary copies go to officials in Palestine or Great Britain.

I am asking Jack Gilbert to undertake the task of developing a list of paying subscribers in America and particularly in Greater New York. In order to keep the paper going meanwhile, I have, as stated in enclosed letter to Nathan Kaplan promised $400. a month for April, May and June and will have these amounts sent the P[alestine].E[ndowment].F[und]. on the first days of March, April and May so that they may be remitted in due time. Please do not let the source of these remittances be known to Davar, Kaplan or others.

Please write Kaplan that PEF will provide the funds in monthly instalments, etc. and send me a copy of PEF's letter to him.

Kindly send me copies of this and the Kaplan letter.

1. *Davar* and its English-language supplement reflected the views of the Histadrut and the dominant Labor Zionist groups in Palestine. In 1933, this coalition rose to ascendance both in the World Zionist Organization and in the Jewish Agency, and *Davar* became the semiofficial organ of the movement. Even after the establishment of the state of Israel, *Davar* continued to be a major source of government views.

To Alpheus Thomas Mason

March 3, 1931 Washington, D. C. [Brandeis Mss, SC 10–1]

MY DEAR MR. MASON: Re yours of 2d.

It seems to me better that I should not see your article until it is published.[1] Of course, I shall be glad to advise you as to any fact about which you may be in doubt. But any such facts you would probably find (accurately reported) in Ernest Poole's Introduction to my "Business a Profession."

With thanks for your courteous letter,[2]   Cordially,

1. Mason was shortly to publish "Mr. Justice Brandeis: A Student of Social and Economic Science," 79 *University of Pennsylvania Law Review* 665 (1931). In it, Mason reviewed LDB's pre-Court career, with its emphasis on

collecting data relevant to a case, and his various articles advocating more vitality in the law.

2. A few weeks later, LDB sent a brief note to Mason expressing his satisfaction with the article and inviting him to a visit in Washington. From this introduction, Mason went on to write several articles and books on LDB, culminating in *Brandeis: A Free Man's Life* (New York, 1946).

To Robert Szold

March 3, 1931 Washington, D. C. [Brandeis Mss, Z 49–2]

MY DEAR BOB: I am very glad to hear from you fully under date of 1st.

1. I agree with [Harold] Laski that (a) transfer to Foreign Office and (b) opening of Transjordania are of paramount importance and advisable, even if Transjordania should be opened now only for Arabs.[1] It would be a step forward. But it must not be done in such a way as to throw even a cloud upon opening for Jews hereafter.

2. Like you, I view the Development Comm. with apprehension.[2] If we must have it (and pay the cost in taxes) we must make sure that we get our fair share.

3. Likewise I view [Sir John Hope-] Simpson with unabated apprehension.

4. If Felix [Frankfurter] can't go, for the April Conference, [Israel B.] Brodie would be our best man. I agree with you that Singer should not be our representative.

5. Have not yet heard from F. F. as to interview with Laski. I hope you are much better and will take good care of yourself. I seem to be restored to condition quo ante.

1. Among the proposals being explored by the Zionists and the British government were the opening of crown lands in the Transjordan to settlement, and the transfer of responsibility for Palestine from the Colonial Office (which the Zionists considered unfriendly) to the Foreign Office (which at that time seemed more responsive to Zionist goals). Neither proposal came to fruition. See LDB to Szold, 11 July 1932.

2. The proposed Development Commission would have levied special taxes in Palestine, with the proceeds devoted to economic development of the country. The Zionists opposed the idea on the basis that Jews already were putting into Palestinian development large sums of money raised in the Diaspora, and that the taxes, although elicited from both Jews and Arabs, would primarily benefit the Arabs.

To Emanuel Neumann

May 6, 1931 Washington, D. C. [Brandeis Mss, Z 49–2]

DEAR MR. NEUMANN: I am glad to have yours of 2nd with thoughtful enclosures.

Exacting demands of the Court have precluded my giving Palestinian affairs the desired attention. I hope, after this month, to do better.

I am looking forward to seeing Dr. Ettinger[1] on the 8th.

Cordially,

1. Akiba Jacob Ettinger (1872–1945), a Russian-born and -trained agronomist, was one of the architects of agricultural colonization in Palestine. From 1918 to 1925, Ettinger had headed the Land Settlement Department of the Zionist Executive, and from 1926 to 1936 he directed land acquisition for the Jewish National Fund. In 1931 he was in the United States on behalf of the J.N.F.

To Elizabeth Brandeis Raushenbush

May 7, 1931 Washington, D. C. [EBR]

DEAREST ELIZABETH: A. Lincoln Filene, who is on the Governor's Council to study unemployment insurance was in with his secretary, Edward S. Smith, to get my advice. I told them that they should apply to you for the best possible

(1) non-contributory
(2) state fund
(3) individual

You will probably get a letter of inquiry.

I am told that not much wisdom has been emitted by Chambers of Commerce, national and international.

My greetings to your husband & son,   Lovingly,

To James Lorin Richards

May 13, 1931 Washington, D.C. [SBLI]

DEAR MR. RICHARDS: My thanks for the Railroad report, to which I look forward.[1]

Our Savings Bank Insurance is prospering. With the addition of two writing banks June 1, and the recent new agency banks, we should soon reach $100,000,000 in insurance outstanding.

And I hope that before 1932 we may add five more writing banks, so as to be able to furnish $25,000 insurance to any resident of Massachusetts.   Cordially,

1. Richards had enclosed a copy of the New England Railroad Committee's "Report to the Governors of the New England States."

To Robert Szold

May 29, 1931 Washington, D. C. [R. Szold Mss]

DEAR BOB: 1. The "Summary of Deficit Fund" presents a ghastly picture of unfulfilled pledges. I hope every delinquent will receive promptly a letter setting forth his shortcomings, and that those with whom I was in correspondence will be advised of my disappointment.[1]

2. I am glad [Maurice B.] Hexter is returning to Palestine and that the 1000 family settlement will, at last, be started.[2]

3. We still plan to start for Mass. on June 1, stopping a few days at The Bellevue Hotel, 27 Beacon Street, before moving on to Chatham.

On enclosed letter to Mania Shohat[*sic*] [3]—please supply address. After May 31, please have copies of New Palestine sent to Chatham, Mass.

1. American Zionist fortunes reflected those of the world organization (see LDB to Szold, 10 January 1931); with the depression worsening, it became more and more difficult to collect pledges.

2. See LDB to Szold, 15 November 1930, n. 2.

3. Manya Wilbuschewitz-Shohat (1880–1961) had settled in Palestine in 1904 after a deep involvement with the revolutionary party in Russia. She and her husband were among the founders of the self-defense movement, first in HaShomer and later in the Haganah, and in the late 1930s and early 1940s she was active in smuggling illegal immigrants into Palestine. She traveled in the United States several times on behalf of Histadrut.

To Irving Dilliard

DEAR MR. DILLIARD: [1] Re yours of 26th.

My thanks for your generous clipping. Answering your enquiries:

I lived in St. Louis from November 1878 to June 1879; was admitted to the state and the federal bars (probably in November); and had my office with James Taussig (whose assistant I was) at 505 Chestnut St. I lived with my sister (Mrs. Charles Nagel) at 2044 LaFayette Ave.

I think my first printed brief was in the case of Martin Michael v. Joseph Locke, in the Circuit Court, City of St. Louis at the June Term 1879; later submitted to the Court of Appeals in Cement Co. v. Locke.[2]   Cordially,

1. Irving Dilliard (b. 1904) worked for the *St. Louis Post-Dispatch* from 1927 until 1960 and afterwards held various senior fellowships at both Harvard and Princeton before becoming director of the Illinois State Commission on the Aging. He edited *Mr. Justice Brandeis, Great American* (St. Louis, 1941) as well as books on Hugo Black and Learned Hand.

2. For LDB's tenure in St. Louis, see Burton C. Bernard, "Brandeis in St. Louis," 11 *St. Louis Bar Journal* 54 (1964), and LDB's letters to his family, 2 August 1878 through 1 April 1879.

To Frank Tannenbaum

DEAR FRANK TANNENBAUM: [1] Thank you for letting me see your discerning and thoughtful paper, returned herewith. I hope it will be published soon.[2]

I agree with you in the main; and specifically that there is no prospect of violent revolution in the United States. My dissent was from your general proposition that there *could* be no violent revolutions in an industrial country.   Cordially,

1. Frank Tannenbaum (1893–1969) had been jailed in 1914 for leading a labor revolt. At Sing Sing prison in Ossining, New York, he was befriended by the warden, who eventually got him into Columbia University. Tannenbaum earned a doctorate in economics at the Brookings Institute and be-

came an expert not only on Latin America, but also on social and labor conditions in the United States. From 1935 until 1961, he taught at Columbia, where he founded the influential University Seminars.

2. "Prospects of Violent Revolution in the United States," *Scribner's Magazine* 89 (May 1931): 521–25.

To Elizabeth Brandeis Raushenbush

June 3, 1931 Boston, Mass. [EBR]

DEAR ELIZABETH: As you know, mother and I have, for many years, given a large part of our income to public causes in which we took an active part; thus rendering our own work more effective. We think you and Susan may wish to do the like.

With this in view, we have transferred to each of you ten thousand (10,000) dollars face value additional bonds.[1] Miss [E. Louise] Malloch is having these registered in your names, and will send you herewith a description of the bonds.

There will be no occasion to cut any coupons before late in September so that the firm will hold the bonds for you, upon their return from the registry until you are back from your vacation.   Lovingly,

1. See LDB to Elizabeth B. Raushenbush, 28 November 1929.

To Robert Szold

June 10, 1931 Chatham, Mass. [R. Szold Mss]

DEAR BOB: Yours of 7th reached me after mine of yesterday was mailed.

The Congress is not alluring. But I have hopes that more good will come of it than now seems likely. The dire situation should bring out the better part which usually lies hidden in the Jews. And you will get a working knowledge of our fellows.[1]

I am very glad that you concluded to start so early. This will give you an opportunity for full discussion with many delegates before the day of meeting. Only after such talks can there be definite plan-making.

We agree so fully as to the desirable that I need only advise you to use your good judgment as to ways and means available.

1. The Seventeenth Zionist Congress met in Basle from 30 June through 15 July 1931. It was marked by bitter controversy over Chaim Weizmann's handling of Zionist affairs in the light of the Shaw and Hope-Simpson Reports and the Passfield White Paper. The Revisionists were particularly angered at a statement Weizmann had made that he did not regard either a Jewish state or even a Jewish majority in Palestine as essential to Zionist goals. With strong backing from the American contingent, the opposition managed to defeat Weizmann's bid for reelection, and Nahum Sokolow assumed the presidency. American power within the World Zionist Organization was further enhanced with the election of Emanuel Neumann to the Executive.

To Joshua Bernhardt

June 14, 1931 Chatham, Mass. [Brandeis Mss, M 18-1]

DEAR DR. BERNHARDT: My thanks for yours of June 2d, June 3d, June 9th & June 12th.

Some months ago, you sent me the file of the "Palestine Economic Review" covering the calendar year 1930. If you have a spare copy of the Review for 1931, kindly let me have it. During the vacation, I plan to resume my detailed study of Palestine affairs.   Cordially,

To Julius Simon

June 27, 1931 Chatham, Mass. [Brandeis Mss, M 18-1]

DEAR JULIUS SIMON: Re yours of 25th.

With the principle underlying your memorandum, I am in entire agreement. But I differ as to the scope of its application and as to some details. In my opinion:

First: Mr. [Felix] Warburg (and his associates) are in honor bound to prevent a financial collapse.[1] This moral obligation arises from their forming the [Jewish] Agency and assuming direction and control. Doing this involved the function of setting the financial house in order. The obligation remains until they shall have discharged that function. Mr. Warburg cannot be relieved of the obligation because he resigned in protest against the Passfield White Paper, or because of his past generosity. In view of his financial standing and his present financial ability, noblesse oblige. He will not live happily unless he performs that moral obligation; and the honored name of Warburg will suffer throughout the world.

Second: Setting the financial house in order implies more than honoring what you define as the obligations of the Agency. Its obligations include also the obligations of the Keren Hayesod now existing, insofar as these obligations were in existence at the time the Agency assumed control, or arose therefrom. Mr. Warburg knew, or should have known, the nature and extent of these obligations. He cannot be relieved from them because unforeseen events have prevented the expected inflow of funds which it was thought would be sufficient to discharge these obligations. You will recall what I said on this subject to Judge [Julian W.] Mack before he left for Berlin last summer and what I said in my letters to you and to Mr. [Bernard] Flexner.

Third: Obviously a fond perdue [2] of $500,000 would not enable Mr. Warburg and his associates to set the financial house in order. Much more must be provided. I am confident that if Mr. Warburg comes forward with an offer of not less than $1,000,000, his associates and the Baron [deRothschild] will make a full settlement of the indebtedness possible.[3]

Fourth: If all existing indebtedness is discharged, provision being made for paying in installments all over-due salaries as suggested by you, the Agency budget for the next fiscal year may properly be limited to the £55,000 and the business be put upon a cash basis. In that event, the invariable practice hereafter should be "pay as you go"—and literally, no debts.

Fifth: After the discharge of the indebtedness as above, the social-cultural activities should be transferred to the Knesseth Israel in co-operation with the Palestine Government and such organizations as the Hadassah and Wizo,[4] as you suggest. Adequate subsidies for this purpose can be procured from America & other countries of the Diaspora.

Sixth: Dr. Senator's [5] proposals are subject to the objections stated by you.   Cordially,

1. See LDB to Robert Szold, 19 December 1930.

2. "Secret fund."

3. See LDB to Simon, 12 July 1931.

4. The Women's International Zionist Organization, the counterpart to Hadassah among general Zionists outside the United States, supported a number of social service projects in Palestine.

5. David Werner Senator (1896–1953), a German-born social worker and scholar, had headed the European division of the Joint Distribution Committee for a number of years. He joined the Jewish Agency Executive as a non-Zionist member and was active in trying to improve Arab-Jewish relations during the 1930s.

To Maurice Beck Hexter

July 2, 1931 Chatham, Mass. [Brandeis Mss, Z 49–2]

DEAR DR. HEXTER: Your informing letter of June 16 with enclosures has just reached me.

1. Like you, I am deeply disappointed by the delay in starting the 1000 family project.[1] This undertaking has seemed to me of paramount importance politically, economically and socially. Every effort should be made to overcome obstacles and to speed carrying out of the project.

2. Next to the 1000 family project, the consolidation of the colonies is perhaps the most urgent of the undertakings before us.[2] I am relieved to know that you think the estimate of £250,000, as the sum required, grossly excessive; and your suggestion of raising special fund to be used for speedily effecting the consolidation seems to me feasible—provided: (a) the data of specific needs be effectively presented; (b) the instrument for efficiently carrying out the work be assured; and (c) the proper individuals, competent, singleminded and devoted, will undertake the tasks. If these conditions are complied with, I should be glad to make a substantial contribution to the fund.

3. I hope the High Commissioner will act on your suggestion as to legalizing the entry of Jews who enter irregularly; and that there is truth in the recent report that Jews are to get a fair share of employment in the public works.

4. I am taking the liberty of sharing your letter and enclosures with the P[alestine].E[conomic].C[orporation]. from whom you may hear in this connection.

5. I trust you have seen I. B. Brodie's admirable "Program for the Acceleration of the Absorptive Capacity of Palestine".[3]

Cordially,

1. See LDB to Robert Szold, 15 November 1930, n. 2.
2. See LDB to Julian Mack, 20 October 1929.
3. See LDB to Israel B. Brodie, 7 August 1931.

To Ray Stannard Baker

July 5, 1931 Chatham, Mass. [Baker Mss]

DEAR RAY STANNARD BAKER: I have read with much interest pp. 496–534.[1] They present well the episode, as it lies in my mind. Here, in the absence of my papers, there is nothing which I can suggest, unless it be the following:

1) Page 503. Substitute "underlying principles" for "essentials." As you state pp. 502–3: In my opinion the real curse was bigness rather than monopoly. Mr. Wilson (and others wise politically) made the attack on lines of monopoly, because Americans hated monopoly and loved bigness.[2] You may recall that in my testimony before the Clapp Committee and the Stanley Committee 1911–12 I brought out particularly "the limit of greatest efficiency" economically and socially—the thought again expressed much later in my dissent in Quaker City Cab Co. vs. Pennsylvania 277 U.S. 410[3] and meanwhile in "Other People's Money."

2) Page 502. From what was told me: I think Mr. Wilson in framing the issue in 1912—as Regulation of Competition as against Roosevelt's Regulation of Monopoly—gave particular attention to my articles in Collier's which began, as I recall, in August. Those that were signed were later collected in my "Business a Profession." But those that presented the issue most clearly were not signed, having been adopted by Norman Hapgood verbatim—as I recall for editorials.[4]

3) The Clayton Bill as passed failed to embody a number of provisions drafted by me which I deemed essential and which I think Mr. Wilson favored; and the phraseology of others were changed in committee in such a way as to render them less effective.[5]

I don't know that any of the above is important for your purpose. But these matters came to mind as I read your account. Sorry my papers are not available here.   Cordially,

1. Baker, who had published the first four volumes of his "authorized" biography of Woodrow Wilson, was then at work on the volumes covering the domestic achievements of the New Freedom. He had previously interviewed LDB on his role in the Wilson administration, and he was now checking details in the manuscript.

2. For LDB's role in the 1912 presidential campaign, see Volume II, pp. 633 ff; see also LDB to Paul Kellogg, 26 July 1912.

3. A Pennsylvania statute imposed a tax on transportation companies organized as corporations. The Quaker City Cab Company challenged the law, since its competitors, mainly individual owners or partnerships, were exempt from the tax. The Supreme Court, by a vote of 6–3, held the act unconstitutional since it denied equal protection of the law. LDB, Holmes, and Stone all wrote dissenting opinions. LDB, after carefully explaining the historical reasoning behind the statute, went on to defend it in terms reflecting his own penchant for small business. Professor Konefsky cites LDB's dissent "as an example of a judicial utterance mirroring the private notions of the man who wrote it." *Quaker City Cab Company* v. *Pennsylvania*, 277 *U.S.* 389, 410 (1928).

4. See LDB to Norman Hapgood, 4 September 1912.

5. See LDB to Robert M. LaFollette, 27 May 1913; to James C. McReynolds, 22 February 1914; and to Thomas Watt Gregory, 13 August 1914.

To Felix Moritz Warburg (Telegram)

July 11, 1931 Chatham, Mass. [Brandeis Mss, Z 49–2]

Have highest opinion of Adler's judgment but my lack of detailed information as to occurrences at Congress, & conflicting newspaper reports convince me that it would be unwise to undertake to advise Mack. He has always manifested judicial quality in passing upon Zionist problems.[1]

1. Warburg had sent an agitated telegram to LDB, conveying a cable from Cyrus Adler at the Seventeenth Zionist Congress in Basle. Adler wanted LDB and Mack to prevent the congress from adopting a resolution defining the Zionist objective as a Jewish majority within Palestine's historic borders. The resolution, which had originated with the Revisionists, did not pass because most of the delegates, although in sympathy with its aims, were aware of the political repercussions such a declaration would have.

To Julius Simon

July 12, 1931 Chatham, Mass. [Brandeis Mss, M 18–1]

Dear Julius Simon: Re yours of 9th.

I do not feel justified in advising you, not knowing how intimate your relations are with Mr. [Felix] Warburg or, exactly and in detail, what has passed between you and him in regard to the matter.[1]

My letter of June 27 was merely an answer to your enquiry. I had no thought then that it should, or might, be shown to Mr. Warburg. The original letter expresses my opinion with accuracy. I should have said as much to him if he had asked me for my opinion; and if he were my brother, or an intimate friend in whose life and happiness I had deep personal concern, I should have said as much.

Doubtless Mr. [Bernard] Flexner and Ben Cohen were in a better position than I am to judge what is advisable.   Cordially,

1. See LDB to Simon, 27 June 1931.

To Akiba Jacob Ettinger

July 15, 1931 Chatham, Mass. [Ettinger Mss]

DEAR DR. ETTINGER: Replying to yours of 13th:

1. The needs of the J[ewish]. N[ational]. F[und]. are so numerous and so varied that you can satisfy with one or the other the particular preference of any prospective giver. To him who wishes the money to go to a specified parcel, you can assure him that the money will go to the payment for some already made contract. To him who wishes that it shall be expended in completing the acquisition in a particular territory, you can give assurance that it will be so applied as soon [as] the opportunity and the adequate funds are secured. To the man of larger view who realizes the value of a free reserve fund for taking advantage of an owner's need, when the occasion arises, and who has confidence in the discretion of the J.N.F. officials, let him give to the free reserve fund. Each of these purposes is compatible with each of the others.

2. I see no objection to naming a land reserve as suggested, if the giver provides the whole fund for a particular purchase, as in the Sasson case.[1]

3. I am strongly in favor of developing through the lawyers the project of furthering bequests. On this subject, I wrote Emanuel Neumann last December; and have written and spoken frequently to Robert Szold and Jacob H. Gilbert. I suggest your conferring with them as to my suggestions.

4. I am in favor of the "Living Legacies"; but it is important that the rate of interest promised the living be not too large. It should not be more than five (5) percent; and should, if possible, be limited to four (4) percent.[2]

5. I am entirely willing that any persons be told privately that I favor the acquisition of land reserves and have contributed to a fund to be used for that purpose; and I am entirely willing to say that to any one who makes enquiry of me. But it is my invariable rule since becoming a judge not to apply to anyone for a gift to any cause; and I have been unwilling that the fact of my own gifts be given publicity.

Kindly send me a copy of this letter.   Cordially,

1. The Sasson family was one of the more prominent Jewish families in Great Britain, and well-known for their many philanthropies; probably they made a large donation to the Jewish National Fund for the purchase of a tract of land in Palestine, and in turn, had the purchase named after them.

2. A "living legacy" allowed a person to make a large donation to a particular cause, reserving to himself a specified rate of interest on the capital during his lifetime, with the entire amount reverting to the charity on his death. The device allowed the donor to enjoy the honor of the gift as well as its income during his lifetime, and yet avoid various taxes, especially estate taxes, on the amount.

To Nahum Sokolow (Cable)

July 17, 1931 Chatham, Mass. [Brandeis Mss, Z 49–2]

Best wishes.[1]

1. Sokolow had just been elected president of the World Zionist Congress; see LDB to Robert Szold, 10 June 1931, n. 1.

To Israel Benjamin Brodie

August 7, 1931 Chatham, Mass. [Brodie Mss]

DEAR ISRAEL BRODIE: Your triumph at Basle was a fitting sequel to your admirable "Program for the Acceleration of the Absorptive Capacity of Palestine." [1]

I am convinced that despite the depression—perhaps because of it—there is possible a widespread development on the lines you have blocked out. Let me talk with you further about the plans for the practical work. This can, of course, await your convenience. We expect to remain here until after Labor Day.

1. A major modification in the Balfour pledge had been the stricture in the White Paper of 1922 that immigration to Palestine would be limited to the "absorptive capacity" of that country to accept and integrate newcomers into a viable economy. By the time of the Shaw and Hope-Simpson reports, a wide split had developed between the low estimates of that capacity prepared by the Colonial Office and the much higher estimates predicted by Jewish Agency officials. The difference resulted from the British refusal to take into account potentially arable land, while Jewish agronomists held high hopes for reclaiming thousands of dunams of waste area (a dunam is ¼ acre). At the Zionist Congress, Brodie had presented a powerful address regarding intensified land reclamation in order to increase absorptive capacity.

To Stephen Samuel Wise

August 16, 1931 Chatham, Mass. [Brandeis Mss, Z 49–2]

S.S.W.: It was thoughtful of you to send me an accurate report of your effective speech.[1]

Much has been achieved. But the right to work for Palestine will not be firmly established until the Weizmann-Lipsky resurgence is crushed.[2] Much will be needed of you in September and October.

I am glad you have set apart August for a thorough rest.

1. At the Seventeenth Zionist Congress, Wise had been among the strongest speakers in his demand for Weizmann's ouster and a return to the first principles enunciated by LDB over a decade earlier.
2. Lipsky had returned from the congress angry at the role the Brandeis group had played in forcing Weizmann out, and immediately launched into an attack on the Szold administration. But after the return of the Brandeis-Mack faction the previous year, few American Zionists took Lipsky's denunciations seriously.

To Julian William Mack

September 13, 1931 Washington, D. C. [Brandeis Mss, Z 42–5]

J.W.M.: 1— Re yours of the 11th.

Answering Miss [Henrietta] Szold's letter returned herewith. I have no doubt she is doing valuable work in laying the foundation for collecting appropriate revenues.

2— I wish you would make clear to her and to other Palestinians that now is the time by tact, combined with courage, to effect a change in the relation between the Jews and the British. New men—and above all, new conditions (patricularly in view of the bad behaviour recently of the Arabs) make it possible to make ourselves recognized and accepted as the friends of the British, and as deserving of support. Our Palestine Jews should have self control, wisdom and tact sufficient to secure for us just treatment under the new National Government and we should do all we can consistently to lighten its cares.

I have noted in many reports from Palestine a less valiant bearing on the part of our Jews than in the troubled times of 1929.

To James Lorin Richards

October 13, 1931 Washington, D.C. [SBLI]

DEAR MR. RICHARDS: My thanks for a carton of Marshall apples, which must have come from you.

Since we met, Fall River Savings Bank has voted to establish an insurance department. That makes 21 writing banks. I still hope that Newton and Everett will be among the first twenty five.[1]

Cordially,

1. The Newton Savings Bank established an insurance department in March, 1937, the twenty-fourth institution to do so.

To Akiba Jacob Ettinger

November 1, 1931 Washington, D.C. [Ettinger Mss]

DEAR DR. ETTINGER: Re yours of Oct. 28th.

1. Answering the specific enquiry in your letter. I think you are wise in calling the attention of possible settlers to the low

standard of living which they must expect if they conclude to settle on the land. But I think it would be wise to send with the statement some one of the published descriptions of life on the small plantations with its worthy social joys, so that those middle-class Jews may realize that they are not being relegated to the dreary, barren life common on isolated, small American farms.

2. I have some doubt whether a man of 45 will be too old for the adventure.

3. I have also a doubt whether you should not make clearer that the $4300 [1] does not include travelling expenses or the necessary expenses incident to landing etc. in Palestine.

My best wishes,   Cordially,

1. The amount then suggested as necessary to carry a new family immigrating to Palestine until it could settle and become self-supporting.

To Solomon Dingol

November 3, 1931 Washington, D. C. [YIVO]

DEAR MR. DINGOL: [1] Re yours of Oct. 31

I shall be glad to discuss privately Jewish problems with you on Monday, Nov. 16th at 3 P.M. But this must be on the express understanding that you do not mention in print or otherwise the fact that you have seen me or talked with me recently.[2]

1. Solomon Dingol (1886–1961) had joined the Yiddish daily, *Der Tag*, in 1925 as a reporter, and he ultimately became its editor-in-chief. He was also a vice-president of the Hebrew Immigrant Aid Society.

2. Although LDB was willing to meet privately with reporters and leaders of the Yiddish-speaking community, he was still extremely sensitive that unwarranted newspaper items might damage his standing on the Court. He also feared a repetition of the 1916 encounter with the American Jewish Committee; see LDB to Hugo Pam, 21 July 1916.

To Julian William Mack

November 26, 1931 Washington, D. C. [Brandeis Mss, Z 49–5]

J.W.M.:—I have yours of 25th with Felix' letter and the telegram from DeHaas-Neumann. Regret that I may not do as you suggest.[1] Am sitting—will not adjourn until the 14th, but even in the recess it would be very unwise for me to attend any meeting—among other reasons, our recess is not for me a vacation. As you wisely reminded me, I am ten years (nearly) older than you.

I made the single departure from my rule in 1929 and attended the Warburg meeting,[2] because I deemed it very important—as if it were a war measure—to let the British know that, despite retirement of our group from the Z.O.A. management, I was still active in Zionist affairs. There was necessity of telling Americans of my active interest; and important as the organization of the Pro-Palestine Committee is, there is no emergency comparable to the 1929 situation. Moreover, I am two years older than I was then.

1. Upon a suggestion first made by Samuel Wohl (see LDB to Wohl, 26 October 1930), Emanuel Neumann had taken charge of the creation of the American Pro-Palestine Committee, which gathered support from prominent Christians for Zionist programs. Both Mack and Felix Frankfurter thought it desirable that LDB attend the organizational meeting of the group, since his prestige would draw additional supporters.
2. See LDB to Felix Frankfurter, 23 September 1929.

To Charles Warren

November 27, 1931 Washington, D. C. [Warren Mss]

MY DEAR CHARLES WARREN: I value much the birthday greeting [1] from you, who have taught me so much about our Court and the duties of its members.   Cordially,

1. LDB had celebrated his seventy-fifth birthday on 13 November.

To Moshe Shertok

December 24, 1931 Washington, D. C. [Political Dept. Records]

DEAR MR. SHERTOK: [1] Please express to the several members of the [Zionist] Executive my appreciation of their birthday greeting.

And may I add, for you personally, that I have followed with much satisfaction the reports of your political activity.

With best wishes,   Cordially,

1. Moshe Shertok (later Sharett) (1894–1965) had held a number of positions in labor Zionist groups before becoming assistant editor of *Davar* in 1925 and editor of the English-language supplement in 1929. In the reorganization following the 1931 Congress, Shertok became secretary of the Political Department of the Jewish Agency, and by the end of the decade he was the second most influential Palestinian in the Zionist movement and David Ben-Gurion's chief associate. In 1947, Shertok came to the United States to head the Zionist delegation to the United Nations, and he was the leading negotiator in securing the partition proposal. He served as Israel's first Foreign Minister from 1948 to 1956, during which time he Hebraicized his name to Sharett (literally "servant"), and from 1953 to 1955 also served as Prime Minister.

To Julian William Mack

December 29, 1931 Washington, D. C. [Frankfurter Mss—LC]

JWM: To obviate the possibility of a misunderstanding, I repeat what I said in our talk this morning.

We are committed to the deH[aas]. plan of establishing P[alestine]. D[evelopment]. Leagues in the hope of raising new forces and money through them.[1] Until that plan has been given a fair trial we have no right even to consider the B[ernard]. F[lexner]. proposal. In order that it should have a fair trial, we must give it now our wholehearted support to the extent of our available financial and moral resources.

If, after such a trial, we are of opinion that it is a failure, I am ready to consider any other plan which may seem to you, or any others of our group, to be promising of that aid in the development of Palestine which to me seems alone worthwhile. I do not exclude from such possible alternatives the plan now suggested by B.F. Indeed I know too little of its essential features to be entitled to an opinion on its merits. But I must not be understood as favoring it. In the event of the failure of the deH. plan, if I were compelled to express a decision now, I should say no.

Please send copies of this to Felix [Frankfurter], to de Haas and me.

1. The idea of local leagues had been proposed by deHaas years earlier (see LDB to Mack, *et al*. 23 October 1920) as a means of raising additional funds for Palestinian investment. LDB had earlier refused to merge the Palestine Development Council with the Jewish Agency endeavors, partly

because of his loyalty to deHaas and partly because of his suspicion of any economic program with which Weizmann would be associated. In the end, the deHaas proposal failed to work, and in the early 1930s the Palestine Development Council was quietly absorbed by the Agency-sponsored Palestine Economic Corporation, as Flexner had originally suggested.

To Julian William Mack

January 3, 1932 Washington, D. C. [Brandeis Mss, P 52–1]

J.W.M.: 1. B[ernard]. F[lexner]. doubtless sent you copy of my recent letter to him reporting my offer to [Israel B.] Brodie to provide $5000 to finance his American and Palestine bureaus, provided the P[alestine].E[conomic].C[orporation]. and the P[alestine].E[ndowment].[Fund]. contribute each a like amount, so that the total estimated requirement of $15,000 will be raised immediately. B.F. was here yesterday and says the P.E.C. is ready to contribute the $5000. I assume the P.E.F. is ready with its $5000; have written Bob to that effect and have emphasized the great importance of prompt action.

2. DeH[aas]. was here today. Reported generally on the Z.O.A. situation and i.a. expressed the opinion that our group would be turned out at the June convention—an opinion I had heard expressed by others and which accords with my view.[1] At all events, it is clear that our group cannot, under present conditions at least, make a success of the Z.O.A. and that our efforts for Palestine should be turned into other channels. My own idea is that we should work for the economic upbuilding through the Brodie scheme. P.E.C. and P.E.F., with such side lines as the lawyer-proposition (which I am glad to see is now being taken up) and the enlistment of able young intellectuals.

3. My immediate concern is about DeHaas. He seems to have no place in the projects enumerated in (2); and I think he should be prepared by you for arranging to get his living otherwise. I said nothing to him on this subject, as I have never said a word to him about a salary or allowance—since June 1929—when I closed the then pending arrangement and gave him $2200 for his and his wife's trip to Europe for the Congress. All payments since have been made through you and P.E.F.

I am willing to continue the allowance to him of $400 a month until (and including) June 30 next; and then to allow him for the following five months $300 a month—with the understanding that all allowances will cease at that time (Nov. 30, 1932). I think he should understand from you that during the next six months— while the group is in office—(as well as thereafter)—he will be free to use his time in such way as will best enable him to provide financially for his future. His loyalty to the Cause has throughout been complete; and he should be made to understand that we appreciate it and him.[2]

1. LDB's view of the situation was far too pessimistic. In November 1931, his followers had easily defeated an effort by Louis Lipsky to unseat the administrative committee headed by Robert Szold. But the Brandeis group was unable to make much headway in the light of British policies in Palestine and the worsening depression in the United States. At the 1932 convention, Szold declined to continue in office, and the Z.O.A. chose Morris Rothenberg, an old associate of both Lipsky and Weizmann, as president. Lipsky's followers immediately declared that this was a defeat for the Brandeis-Mack group; in fact, the two camps, with the exception of diehards like Lipsky and deHaas, had reconciled nearly all of their differences in the preceding three years. The Executive Committee was dominated by LDB's followers, and in 1936, Lipsky led the opposition to Rothenberg's receiving a fifth term and backed his former foe, Stephen S. Wise, a pillar of the Brandeis-Mack group.

2. Although deHaas continued to work for Zionism in the five years remaining of his life, he no longer held any positions of influence within the Z.O.A. Even his allies in the Brandeis-Mack group felt that deHaas had become a liability to them, antagonizing people when the times demanded conciliation. Within two years he became a follower of the militant Revisionists and declared their leader, Vladimir Jabotinsky, to be "the second Theodor Herzl," an accolade he had once reserved for LDB. See LDB to Mack, [December] 1934.

To Josephine Goldmark

January 8, 1932 Washington, D. C. [Brandeis Mss, M 7–2]

DEAR JOSEPHINE, I had an interesting talk with the Danish minister on Friday.[1] He has promised me material from his files and to get more comprehensive reports from Denmark.

The Danish handbook which he gave me will go to you under another cover.[2]

From Herbert Feis [3] I also expect some data.

Proceedings in and about Congress do not indicate a lessened need of educating our people.

1. Mr. Otto Wadsted.

2. See LDB to Miss Goldmark, 30 October 1932.

3. Herbert Feis (1893–1972), after teaching at several universities during the 1920s, had recently become economic advisor to Secretary of State Henry L. Stimson, with whom he served, first in State and later in the War Department, until 1947. At that time Feis began his career as a diplomatic historian, writing ten highly acclaimed books; he won the Pulitzer Prize in 1961 for his study of the Potsdam Conference.

To Oliver Wendell Holmes, Jr.

January 12, 1932 Washington, D. C. [Holmes Mss]

O.W.H.: Dec. 8, 1902—Jan. 12, 1932

"Ich habe gelebt und geliebt." [1]

I am still housed.[2]

1. "I have lived and loved," from Schiller's "Thehla's Song." On this day Holmes ended his fifty-year career as a jurist by retiring from the Supreme Court. In his letter to President Hoover, Holmes wrote: "The condition of my health makes it a duty to break off connections that I cannot leave without deep regret after the affectionate relations of many years and the absorbing interests that have filled my life. But the time has come and I bow to the inevitable." See LDB to Harold J. Laski, 28 February 1932.

2. LDB had been sick at home for several days with a bad cold.

To Louis Brandeis Wehle

January 19, 1932 Washington, D. C. [Wehle Mss]

L.B.W.: Kindly attend to the following matter for me:

In 1913, when Norman Hapgood took over (largely with C. R. Crane's money) Harpers Weekly, I wrote for the Weekly the articles later collected and published by Frederick A. Stokes Company under the name "Other Peoples Money" [1] and gave to Norman or the Weekly my copyright rights.

Although Stokes has not advertised this book and few people, even booksellers, know where it can be procured, it has not died; and every once in a while there is a demand by some one (like the Julius Haldeman [*sic*] [2] concern, or the Upton Sinclair crowd) to print a cheap edition. About two years ago Huston Thompson was eager to have Stokes publish a new edition, and he offered to write a comprehensive introduction to bring the book up to date. Stokes then stated that nothing could be done without the consent of Charles R. Crane, because he was entitled to the royalties. That was the first that I knew of this, and made up my mind that, when Norman returned from Europe and Crane from Asia, I should ask Norman to get Crane to relinquish to me his rights. Norman took the matter up with Crane, and his secretary Brodie, with the result that I received from Crane a letter of which copy is enclosed marked A, dated Jan. 4, 1932. Then I wrote Stokes asking them to send me draft of any copyright assignment which would be satisfactory to them. Under date of Jan. 13/32 they wrote me letter of which copy is enclosed marked B.

What I would like you to do is this: See Stokes, thank them for their courtesy. Arrange to have the copyright assigned to me and royalties paid to me; and that hereafter if there is an application for a cheap reprint (which I suppose would help the sale of Stokes edition), my consent (and theirs if need be) would be all that is required. And if there is a desire for a new edition and Stokes doesn't want to publish it, I can get some other publisher.

There has been in recent years far more of an interest in "Other Peoples' Money" than Stokes is probably aware of. Reviews of the book appear from time to time (about a year ago in Locomotive Engineers Journal). It is extensively discussed occasionally by broadcasting talkers. (Recently by WIBO station in Chicago.) And hardly a month passes without some enquiry coming to me as to where the book can be procured. This month one from [*] came. The present depression, the debunking of the great financial kings, and the losses of those who followed them have made men think, and i.a. realize that "Other Peoples' Money" should have been heeded.

Find out, if you can, what the sales have been.

Of course, Norman will be glad to lend aid in getting Crane's signature or otherwise. Any royalties I get will go to the Savings

Bank Ins. League, as do the royalties from my "Business a Profession." [3]

It was worth being disabled [4] to secure four hours talk from you.

1. See LDB to Alfred Brandeis, 2 September 1913, and other citations in Volume III.

2. Emanuel Haldeman-Julius (1889–1951) was the publisher of the popular "Blue Book" series, as well as the author or editor of numerous books on American life. His unusual name resulted from prefixing his wife's maiden name to his own surname at the time of their marriage in 1916.

3. See LDB to Wehle, 10 February 1932; see also LDB to Norman Hapgood, 12 March 1932, to Alice H. Grady, 2 September 1932, and to Sherman Mittell, 25 August 1933.

4. See preceding letter, n. 2.

To Robert D. Kesselman

February 5, 1932 Washington, D. C. [Kesselman Mss]

MY DEAR ROBERT KESSELMAN: Re yours of Jan 14th.

Thanks for your letter and for the final report on Davar English supplement [1] which comes via Nathan Kaplan.

It is good to know also from you of the favorable economic conditions of Palestine, relative to the rest of the world. [2] I trust this may continue, and draw from America many middle-class Jews who would be happier and more useful in Palestine.

I wish it were possible for me to go to Palestine next summer, but there is no chance of that. If you come to America, I shall, of course, expect to have a good visit from you at Chatham.

With best wishes,   Cordially,

1. See LDB to Robert Szold, 18 January 1931. The English Supplement of *Davar* was forced to suspend operations because of financial difficulties.

2. Despite the world-wide depression, Palestine was enjoying relative prosperity in 1932. This was due in part to the makeup of the so-called "Fourth Aliya," the collective name given those immigrants who arrived between 1924 and 1933. Nearly all were middle class, and they brought with them substantial amounts of capital that they used to establish and develop small industries.

To Louis Brandeis Wehle

February 10, 1932 Washington, D. C. [Wehle Mss]

L.B.W.: Re yours of 9th.

1. That's a nice letter from Stokes. I think it best to drop the Huston Thompson idea,[1] and to make simply a reprint, with a 1932 Foreword by the publishers in which the publisher will state (aided by L.B.W.) that more recent events have given added significance to the views expressed by me in 1913–1914. Perhaps you may find in Norman Hapgood's "The Changing Years" published in 1930, in the chapter "Mr. Brandeis," some passage that would be helpful in this connection.[2]

2. I think it would be better not to take up with Ralph Hale the matter of "Business—a Profession" until Stokes have agreed to the reprint of "Other Peoples Money." [3]

I am returning the R[econstruction]. F[inance]. C[orporation]. clipping. Krock treated you discreetly and helpfully.[4]

1. See LDB to Wehle, 19 January 1932.
2. Norman Hapgood, *The Changing Years* (New York, 1930), ch. 13; ultimately Hapgood wrote the introduction to the new edition of LDB's work. See LDB to Hapgood, 12 March 1932.
3. Hale had enquired into the possibility of reissueing *Business—A Profession*. See LDB to Wehle, 9 July 1932.
4. The Arthur Krock clipping was a long article from the 31 January issue of the *New York Times*, "New Finance Plan Praised by Wehle." As former counsel for the War Finance Corporation, Wehle was asked for an evaluation of the new Reconstruction Finance Corporation, the Hoover agency designed to pump new life into the staggering economy by making loans to private enterprise. Wehle thought the new RFC was no fairy godmother and certainly no cure-all, but he was convinced that the agency was a step in the right direction and that it would serve to revive many business enterprises.

To George Reed Nutter

February 15, 1932 Washington, D.C. [SBLI]

G.R.N.: It was thoughtful of you to write me after Justice Holmes resigned. The personal loss to me is great—and we might have gotten some more good law through him. But he should be happier freed from the court burdens which had grown heavy for him.

We shall hope to see you here when the Institute meets.[1]

I think you will wish to see enclosed letter of 12th from the Springfield Republican.[2]

1. The American Law Institute was scheduled to meet in Washington during the first week of May.

2. Sherman Bowles, editor of the Springfield *Republican*, had written to Miss Alice Grady on 12 February 1932. He explained that a Mr. Putnam, of the John Hancock Insurance Company, had offered to place advertising in exchange for a pledge that the *Republican* would neither condemn the commercial companies nor praise Savings Bank Insurance in editorials. Bowles promptly refused all advertising from the Hancock and told Miss Grady she could use his letter in any way she saw fit.

To Harold Joseph Laski

February 28, 1932 Washington, D. C. [Laski Mss]

MY DEAR HAROLD: My thanks for "Studies in Law and Politics", with its generous dedication.[1] I am particularly glad to have the papers which I had not seen—among them "Justice and the Law".[2] You know how great the need is also in America. But there is some ground for hope, due largely to Felix [Frankfurter]'s teaching and ever-widening influence.

And as we lose Justice Holmes, the appointment of Judge Cardozo[3] gives joy. The retirement was a serious blow. But Judge Holmes, relieved of his judicial burden, seems so much happier and resilient that I have become reconciled. At last, he has grasped the ever-eluding leisure.[4]

About conditions here Felix has doubtless kept you advised. The widespread suffering, the economic helplessness and the general dejection are appalling; and most painful the absence of any sense of shame on the part of those primarily responsible for existing conditions. But the process of debunking continues; and if the depression is long continued—which seems likely—America will gain much from her sad experience. A deficit for the current year of two billion and a half dollars now seems probable.

The Unemployment Reserve Act recently adopted in Wisconsin is our first step in grappling with irregularity of employment.[5] Possibly you saw Elizabeth's recent articles in the Survey Graphic.[6] She and Paul have had the largest part both in drafting the bill and in securing its passage.

Our best to Frieda [sic].

1. Harold J. Laski, *Studies in Law and Politics* (New Haven, 1932), was dedicated "To Mr. Justice Brandeis with affection and admiration." In the preface Laski noted that "the dedication is something more than a formal tribute. What I owe to the friendship of Mr. Justice Brandeis lies deeper than I can easily put into words."

2. The last chapter in Laski's book had originally been delivered as a lecture to the English Ethical Union, and in it he called for a far-reaching reform of the legal system in order to meet the needs of a democratic society. While not denying that some progress had been made, Laski maintained that changes in the law always lagged behind changes in the society, and that in modern times society could not afford to have a deep division between social needs and legal remedies.

3. On 15 February, much to the gratification of liberals, President Hoover had named Benjamin Nathan Cardozo (see LDB to Jacob deHaas, 25 December 1917, n. 3), the chief justice of New York's Court of Appeals, to succeed Holmes on the Supreme Court.

4. On 8 March 1931, in response to a symposium in honor of his ninetieth birthday, Holmes had said: "The riders in a race do not stop short when they reach the goal. There is a little finishing canter before coming to a standstill. There is time to hear the kind voices of friends and to say to oneself, 'The work is done.' But just as one says that, the answer comes: 'The race is over but the work never is done while the power to work remains.' The canter that brings you to a standstill need not be only coming to rest. It cannot be while you still live. For to live is to function. That is all there is in living. And so I end with a line from a Latin poet who uttered the message more than fifteen hundred years ago: 'Death plucks my ear and says Live, I am coming.'" For Holmes's "finishing canter," see Catherine Drinker Bowen, *Yankee From Olympus* (Boston, 1944), 412–17.

5. After a decade of debate, Wisconsin passed a pioneering unemployment compensation law, signed by Governor Philip LaFollette on 28 January 1932. Leading the fight in Wisconsin were Harold Groves, later a state legislator, and LDB's daughter, Elizabeth, and his son-in-law, Paul Raushenbush. The Wisconsin law required that each corporation build up its own unemployment reserves in order to take care of its own workers. The heart of the plan was an "experience rating" under which the size of the employer's contribution was determined by his own previous success in maintaining workers on the job, an idea that directly reflected LDB's longtime concern for regularity of employment. Thus, those companies with highest unemployment paid the most, while those which managed to avoid laying off workers paid the least. When the Roosevelt administration came to power,

there were a number of high officials who attempted to initiate the Wisconsin plan on a national basis. See LDB to Elizabeth B. Raushenbush, 19 September 1932 and 8 June 1934. For the origins, see Paul A. Raushenbush, "Starting Unemployment Compensation in Wisconsin," *Unemployment Insurance Review* (April–May, 1967): 17–24.

6. "Wisconsin Tackles Job Security," *Survey Graphic* 67 (15 December 1931): 295–96.

To Oliver Wendell Holmes

March 8, 1932 Washington, D.C. [Holmes Mss]

O.W.H.—March 8, 1932
Carpe diem [1]
in the well-earned, long sought, ever-eluding leisure.[2]

1. "Seize the day."
2. This note was sent to Holmes on his ninety-first birthday.

To Norman Hapgood

March 12, 1932 Washington, D. C. [Wehle Mss]

DEAR NORMAN: I am very glad you will write the introduction to the Second Edition.[1]

I dont know just which opinions you will think helpful. Will try to gather some. I suggest that, meanwhile, you look at the November, 1931, issues of Harvard Law Review, Yale Law Journal and Columbia Law Review;[2] also Alfred Lief's volume:

"The Social and Economic Views of Mr. Justice Brandeis"
all of which, I assume, you will find at the University Club.

It will be fine to see you during the Easter Recess.

1. Of *Other People's Money;* see LDB to Louis Wehle, 19 January 1932.
2. The November 1931 issues of all three law journals were dedicated to LDB in honor of his seventy-fifth birthday. 31 *Columbia Law Review* carried an introductory appreciation by Chief Justice Charles Evans Hughes, together with Walton H. Hamilton, "The Jurist's Art" and Donald R. Richberg, "The Industrial Liberalism of Justice Brandeis"; 45 *Harvard Law Review* had an introduction from the noted German scholar, Elemer Balogh, together with Henry Wolf Biklé, "Mr. Justice Brandeis and the Regulation of Railroads," and a lengthy piece by Felix Frankfurter, "Mr. Justice Brandeis

and the Constitution," together with an appendix of all the opinions written by LDB while on the bench; 41 *Yale Law Journal* featured a lead article by Max Lerner, "The Social Thought of Mr. Justice Brandeis."

To Bernard Flexner

March 27, 1932 Washington, D. C. [Brandeis Mss, M 18–2]

DEAR BEN: It was good of you to write me and to send the clipping.[1] The opinion [2] should help to stimulate thinking. We certainly need a good deal of that article in the business world.

Alice and I are very glad of the good report about Mim.

Our best wishes,

1. Flexner had sent LDB a copy of an editorial in the *New York Times* praising LDB's opinion and his judicial philosophy as expressed in his dissent in the Oklahoma Ice Case (see next note), and wishing that his opinion had been adopted by the majority of the Court.

2. LDB wrote one of his most powerful and influential dissents in *New State Ice Co.* v. *Liebmann,* 285 *U.S.* 262, 280 (1932), in which he was joined by Mr. Justice Stone (Cardozo, who had just taken his seat on the Court, did not participate in the case). An Oklahoma law required anyone entering the ice business to obtain a certificate of convenience and necessity, and the New State Company, which held such a license, sought to restrain Liebmann from entering the field without a certificate. The majority opinion, written by Justice Sutherland, declared the law unconstitutional because it fostered monopolistic situations. "The aim is not to encourage competition, but to prevent it; not to regulate the business, but to preclude persons from engaging in it."

Normally one would have expected LDB to side with an opinion which, on the face of it, opposed monopoly and sustained small business. But to LDB, the main issue in the case was not monopoly but the right of the state to exercise its police powers in innovative ways to meet a depression emergency which he termed "more serious than war." He devoted nearly five pages of the lengthy dissent to a description of the depression and its attendant problems and said that he could not "believe that the framers of the Fourteenth Amendment, or the States which ratified it, intended to deprive us of the power to correct the evils of technological unemployment and excess productive capacity which have attended progress in the useful arts."

Although LDB's dissents have been praised for their craftsmanship and legal acumen, it is generally conceded that Mr. Justice Holmes wielded a more graceful pen. But in this instance LDB's opinion concluded with an unusually eloquent statement of a philosophy of judicial tolerance:

Denial of the right to experiment may be fraught with serious consequences to the Nation. It is one of the happy incidents of the federal
system that a single courageous State may, if its citizens choose, serve as a
laboratory; and try novel social and economic experiments without risk to
the rest of the country. The Court has the power to prevent an experiment. We may strike down the statute which embodies it on the ground
that, in our opinion, the measure is arbitrary, capricious or unreasonable.
We have the power to do this, because the due process clause has been
held by the Court applicable to matters of substantive law as well as to
matters of procedure. But in the exercise of this high power, we must be
ever on our guard, lest we erect our prejudices into legal principles. If we
would guide by the light of reason, we must let our minds be bold.

To Fannie Brandeis

April 27, 1932 Washington, D.C. [Brandeis Mss, M 16–2]

DEAR FAN: Re yours of 23rd.

1. My congratulations on the Committee—and the personnel.

2. You did well in omitting Dr. [Joseph] Rauch. If he wants
to redeem his promises he can do so on the old Special Committee for J[udaica and] P[alestine]. I guess, however, that you will
have to find among the faculty some Jew of more perseverance
who has a real appreciation of the Palestine development. And I
guess it will not be hard to do that. At present Palestine has
become the major Jewish interest, pretty generally in America
as well as Europe. It is the only land in which there is no unemployment, and where there is a steady immigration (i.e. from
America); and much building.

3. I think it would be unwise for me to make any contribution
towards the salary of a cataloguer. But if the university would
raise the funds necessary to complete the work of cataloguing
and making ready for the binder by Sept. 30/32 all the material
on hand and which may come in before that date, Aunt Alice
and I will pay for binding all the material delivered to the binder
before that date, including (A) material sent by me; (B) material
collected by the Library from Government and other sources to
fill in or supplement material for the "Brandeis Libraries"; (C)
material received from others for any of those libraries (like the
periodicals in the R[ail]. R[oad]. Library which I understand

were ready for binding more than a year ago, but which were not sent to the bindery); (D) and specifically the material on Cooperation.

Incidentally this project would help to relieve somewhat unemployment in bookbinding in Louisville.

I am making the date of completion a condition because it seems unwise to make commitments for a remoter future.

Aunt Alice was so much impressed by Dr. Kent that I guess she will comply with the application for a photograph.

To Louis Brandeis Wehle

May 21, 1932 Washington, D. C. [Wehle Mss]

L.B.W.: The taxes on RRs in the several states are mostly property taxes. In view of present and prospective values of RR property, the taxes are grossly excessive. They ought to be reduced. It will be very difficult to effect this, partly because all the states are short of revenues & other property also is (to a less extent) overassessed. But the existing injustice to RRs ought to be clearly set forth by those who know; and this possible method of relief should not be neglected.

There should be at Columbia men who know, or can make the necessary studies, perhaps Prof Haig or some of his associates.[1]

If you are interested in RRs, you may care to have in your library

    1. My Scientific Management brief (1911).[2]

    2. My Second Advance Rate brief (1914).[3]

    3. My New Haven—Boston & Maine exhibit (1907).[4]

These I am sending you by parcel post.

---

1. Robert Murray Haig (1887–1953) had taught at Columbia University since 1912. A professor of business administration and political economy, Haig was active in civic affairs. His special interests were public finance and taxation.

2. LDB, *Scientific Management and the Railroads*, was published in 1912.

3. See LDB to James S. Harlan, 21 August 1913, and to Charles McCarthy, 1 August 1914.

4. See LDB to Alfred Brandeis, 2 January 1908.

To Louis Brandeis Wehle

July 9, 1932 Chatham, Mass. [Wehle Mss]

L.B.W.: Re yours "Business a Profession" of July 6th with carbons of correspondence with Hale and Norman [Hapgood]; yours of 6th with suggestions for Bonbright's [1] Introduction; and yours of 7th with carbons.

1. As to who will write the introduction: [2] (a) Obviously it should be written in time so that the third edition can be advertised & published with other Fall publications. (b) If Bonbright can't undertake it, will you return to your earlier thought of asking Edwin F. Gay. He is (as you doubtless know) back in Cambridge, 47 Holyoke House; and sent me, under date of July 5th, his article on "The Great Depression," reprint from July "Foreign Affairs," which he begins with a quotation from my Ice opinion.[3]

2. In addition to whatever else goes into the Introduction, there are two subjects which should be stressed:

(a) The obligation of the employer to provide regularity of employment. This obligation, later formulated in the much quoted statement on p. 385 of "The Social and Economic Views of Mr. Justice B", was first postulated (privately) to William H. McElwain in the spring of 1903 and led to McElwain making the changes in the conduct of his business so as to give absolute regularity of employment discussed in my address "Business a Profession." The subject had been presented by me informally about a month before the Brown [University] commencement at Gay's suggestion one evening to his students. It had been urged by me in talks to and conferences with trade unions between 1903 and 1911; and was afterwards; and I sketched a plan for encouraging regularization.[4] The recent Wisconsin Act for an Unemployment Reserve proceeds, in some respects, on these lines.[5]

(b) The other subject which should be stressed is Savings Bank Insurance. I enclose leaflets: (1) "Brief Survey 1931 Edition" (2) Miss Grady's Pittsfield address (3) "Twenty three years experience", which are the latest publications. Gay, with Felix Frankfurter and Arthur M. Schlesinger, sent a circular to the Harvard Faculty calling attention to S[avings]. B[ank]. I[nsurance]. when

the Cambridge Savings Bank opened its insurance department in
1930.

3. As to your other pregnant suggestions for the introduction
I refrain from saying anything, as I think what the introducer
says by way of opinion on my writings had better be uninflu-
enced by me.

4. As to the compensation to be paid the writer of the introduction, I think publishers would know better than either you
or I what would be reasonable compensation. (I guess your figure
of $300 is too high.) Obviously, as you suggest, no cash amount
should be paid by me or Savings Bank Insurance. A percentage
of the royalties should go to the introducer until the amount of
agreed compensation has been paid. Books with introductions are
numerous, and it should not be difficult to ascertain what may
reasonably be accepted as standard.

You will know best how to deal with Hale. He ought to pay
his share of the introducer's compensation as Stokes has agreed
to do. But if he cannot be induced to do so, I should be willing
to have it all taken out of a percentage of the royalties until the
agreed sum is liquidated. As to the amount of the introducer's
compensation, you might get some light from James by finding
out what he paid Charles A. Beard [6] for the introduction to "Social & Economic Views of Mr. Justice B.", or to [George W.]
Kirchwey for the introduction O.W. Holmes' Dissenting Opinions. Henle is a Louisville boy (of the Flexner family), a friend of
Charles Tachau.

Since writing the above Elizabeth has received & handed me
your telegram about Sliding Scale Gas.[7] The Act's Sliding Scale
was predicated upon the price for illuminating gas. The original
act (1906 c. 422) was extended from time to time. By 1926 electricity had substantially superseded gas as an illuminant and by
Act of 1926 c. 186 the 1906 Act and amendments were repealed.

I don't have any detail as to the adoption & operation of the
sliding scale elsewhere. My definite knowledge of its operation in
Boston ends with 1916, and I don't know to whom you could be
referred for such definite information. Control of the Boston gas
interest passed from Boston to Pittsburgh about two or three
years ago.

1. James Cummings Bonbright (b. 1891) taught economics at Columbia University from 1920 until his retirement in 1960. He served on numerous governmental commissions and was the author of a number of articles in both scholarly and popular journals.

2. In the end, the new edition of *Business—A Profession* contained introductory chapters by Bonbright, Ernest Poole, and Felix Frankfurter. See LDB to Wehle, 27 September 1932.

3. Edwin F. Gay, "The Great Depression," *Foreign Affairs* 10 (July 1932): 529–40; for the "Ice" opinion, see LDB to Bernard Flexner, 27 March 1932, n. 2.

4. See LDB to Abraham L. Filene, June 1911; see also LDB to J. Franklin McElwain, 18 June 1912, regarding the Brown University commencement speech.

5. See LDB to Harold J. Laski, 28 February 1932, n. 5.

6. Charles Austin Beard (1874–1948) was one of America's most influential and prolific historians. He taught at Columbia University from 1907 to 1917, when he resigned in a dispute over academic freedom in wartime. His most famous work was *An Economic Interpretation of the Constitution* (New York, 1913), which broke the pattern of historical filiopietism in American historical writing. For appraisals of Beard's work, see Howard K. Beale, ed., *Charles A. Beard* (Lexington, Ky., 1954), and Richard Hofstadter, *The Progressive Historians—Turner, Beard and Parrington* (New York, 1968).

7. See LDB to Edward R. Warren, 13 March 1905 and letters in the following year; see also LDB, "How Boston Solved the Gas Problem," *American Review of Reviews* 36 (November 1907): 594–98.

To Fannie Brandeis

July 11, 1932 Chatham, Mass. [Fannie Brandeis]

DEAR FAN: Our thanks to your mother for the photograph of the bas-relief. I hope your house harbors also the bas-relief of your great-grandfather Dembitz.

Aunt Alice and I think Franklin Roosevelt is much underrated by the Liberals.[1] The opposition of the vested interests, who have opposed him, indicated that they fear him. And the result of the Convention pleases us much. McAdoo, the ablest of the Democrats, is redivivus—that will mean much.[2]

1. Franklin Delano Roosevelt (see LDB to Louis B. Wehle, 8 July 1920, n. 1) had won the Democratic presidential nomination in Chicago at the end of June. LDB was right that not all liberals were enthusiastic about FDR. Justice Holmes characterized Roosevelt as "A second-class intellect,

but a first-rate temperament," while Walter Lippmann had recently written that Roosevelt "is a pleasant man, without any important qualifications for the office, who would very much like to be President." On 12 August, LDB wrote to Louis Wehle: "The Chicago convention had made the best available choice; . . . it was a great thing to have beaten the Smith-Raskob-Baker combine; and . . . I thought New Yorkers underrated Roosevelt."

2. At the convention, when it appeared that the delegates would come to a deadlock between Roosevelt and John Nance Garner of Texas, William Gibbs McAdoo had stepped in and swung the California delegation to Roosevelt; he also privately handled the arrangements that led to FDR's choosing Garner for the vice-presidential spot on the ticket. For details of the convention, see Arthur M. Schlesinger, Jr., *The Crisis of the Old Order* (Boston, 1957), ch. 28.

To Robert Szold

July 11, 1932 Chatham, Mass. [R. Szold Mss]

DEAR BOB: When Neumann left for Palestine, I asked him to enquire particularly in regard to Transjordan possibilities.[1] This led to two letters to me from Arlosoroff [2]—and the discussion in which you participated here. The subject was more fully discussed yesterday with Neumann, Felix [Frankfurter], [Ferdinand J.] Fohs and Ben Cohen.

Fohs suggested, independently, the importance of making a survey of the water and land possibilities in TransJordania; and it was his and Neumann's judgment that a survey, adequate for our purposes, could be made for about three thousand (3000) Dollars. It was believed that the High Commissioner would be glad to have it done and that the British resident of TransJordania would be at least not unfavorable to the project.

Neumann is to return to Palestine the end of August and will endeavor, as soon as may be, to secure the approval of the British Officials and, so far as possible, their cooperation.

I told Neumann (later when we were alone) that if he secured the necessary approval of the British, and of Abdullah [3]—that I would provide, through the P[alestine].E[conomic].C[orporation]. for the expenses up to three thousand (3000) dollars.[4]

Cordially,

1. Emanuel Neumann (see LDB to Neumann, 22 October 1920, n. 1) had moved to Palestine in 1931, and he lived there until the outbreak of World

War II. While there he undertook secret negotiations with Abdullah, the Emir of Transjordan (see n. 3), and obtained an option to purchase land east of the Jordan River for possible Jewish settlement. See LDB to Szold, 3 March 1931.

2. Hayim Victor Arlosoroff (1899–1933) was the brilliant young leader of the Histadrut and of Palestinian Labor Zionism. At twenty-four he had been elected to the Actions Committee, and he was later instrumental in establishing the Jewish Agency. A prolific writer, he was considered one of the chief theoreticians of Zionism. In June 1933 he was assassinated on the seashore near Tel Aviv, and many Zionists believed that the murder had been engineered by the rival Revisionists.

3. Abdullah Ibn Hussein (1882–1951) had been installed as king of the Hashemite Kingdom of Jordan after the British detached the Transjordan area from Palestine in 1921. During World War II he proved to be the only Arab leader who fully backed the Allies. Although he had shown himself friendly to the Yishuv in the 1920s and 1930s, Abdullah joined in the Arab attack on the newly-created state of Israel in 1948 and incorporated the West Bank of the Jordan and the Old City of Jerusalem into his kingdom. He was assassinated while entering a mosque by henchmen of the Mufti of Jerusalem, who accused him of being pro-Jewish.

4. Neumann later disclosed that during his negotiations with Abdullah he had need for an additional sum of money for out-of-pocket expenses and wired the Z.O.A. for funds. Robert Szold was leary of the idea and also did not then fully trust Neumann, who had sided with Weizmann in 1921; Szold recommended to LDB that the money not be sent. LDB overrode Szold's objection with the comment: "When building a nation, one must take chances." See LDB to Neumann, 27 January 1933.

To Stephen Samuel Wise

August 4, 1932 Chatham, Mass. [Wise Mss]

S.S.W.: Re yours of 3rd.

Sorry I cannot. Among other reasons, because I am not sure that the action is wise at this time.[1] I had hoped for a talk with you on the subject, and we must have it on your return.

With every good wish,

1. Wise was about to leave for Geneva for the planning conference that ultimately established the World Jewish Congress; he had asked LDB for a statement that might be read to the delegates. Part of LDB's hesitation was the unknown factors of Hitler's growing influence in Germany and the way hostile foreign officials might view the Congress. He later gave Wise full support in the project.

To Louis Brandeis Wehle

August 5, 1932 Chatham, Mass. [Wehle Mss]

L.B.W.: 1. My grief that the Norfolk & Southern had to seek relief in a receivership is somewhat assuaged by the notice that you are counsel for a protection com^tee. Why didn't the R[econstruction]. F[inance]. C[orporation]. come to the rescue? [1]

2. Sixty years ago tomorrow the family left Louisville for the memorable stay in Europe, sailing on Aug. 10th from N.Y. Aunt Fannie who was in the East with Jessie Cochrane et al. met us in New York.

Yours of 2d re "Business a Profession" rcd.

1. The following day Wehle responded that the R.F.C. had been unable to find sufficient security in the assets of the railroad to justify a loan. Much of its tonnage depended on lumber hauling, and the area it served had been severely denuded of trees without proper reafforestation. In addition, the stock of the company was owned wholly by American Tobacco Company interests, which should have been able to carry it.

To Alice Harriet Grady

August 6, 1932 Chatham, Mass. [Brandeis Mss, I 1–4]

A.H.G.: 1. As the spearhead argument of our campaign I suggest:

"Wage earners of Massachusetts. You can raise your wages 5 percent without its costing your employers a penny. You are paying fifty-five million dollars a year on weekly premium policies of life insurance. That is, on the average, 10 percent of your wages. You can save half of that by taking instead Savings Bank Insurance.

A dollar saved is a dollar made."

2. George L. Barnes was here yesterday a little. I put up to him the idea of a statewide company, as in 1906–7, and he approved.

3. Send for your Portuguese minister of Plymouth. See what he will do himself in the fight and whom he can get.

4. There must be Italian, French Canadian and Polish priests who can be aroused to the iniquity and who really are concerned over their flocks. The social workers should know who they are and how they can be reached.

5. I am sorry your draft resolution was not adopted at the AFL convention. An effort should be made to get it adopted by the locals, when speeches on S[avings]. B[ank]. I[nsurance]. are made to them.

6. A systematic effort should be made to get issuing banks and agencies to insert some reference to S.B.I. in every advertisement. It wouldn't cost them anything. Note clippings from July 28/32 Brookline Chronicle. It had this good S.B.I. ad & besides had another on deposits which might as well have mentioned S.B.I.

To Alice Harriet Grady

September 2, 1932 Chatham, Mass. [Brandeis Mss, I 1–4]

AHG: 1. I secured from Mr. Crane all author's royalty rights to "Other Peoples Money" before the arrangement with Mr. Hapgood for writing the new (additional) introduction was made.[1] The royalties (from the date of the assignment Jan. 1932) will go to S[avings]. B[ank]. I[nsurance]. The assignment of royalties is subject to reimbursement of Stokes for the amount ($250) paid N.H. by them for the new introduction.

2. The Protestant churches are beginning to take a determined and practical interest in the economic measures for making workable our present capitalistic system. It should be possible to interest the Mass[achusetts]. ministers in S.B.I. Your Plymouth Portuguese Methodist should be helpful in bringing this about. When we have succeeded there will be no town in Mass. without an S.B.I. policy.

1. See LDB to Louis B. Wehle, 19 January 1932.

To Robert D. Kesselman

September 2, 1932 Chatham, Mass. [Kesselman Mss]

DEAR ROBERT KESSELMAN: Re yours of Aug. 14.

Despite the regrettable falling off of income, I cannot believe that it is wise for you to abandon your profession. The need for high-class auditor service is growing, and appreciation cannot lag far behind. Your American and Palestinian friends, and particularly the Histadruth should aid your determination to restore and maintain the position which you made for yourself. Fifty one years does not suggest old age; and your daughter should prove a great help through wisely entering also a business career.[1]

With best wishes,   Cordially,

1. Two weeks later LDB wrote another letter to Kesselman, again urging him to stay in Palestine. "As to your personal affairs, don't let the defeatist mood take hold of you. Exercise your usual courage and persistence and good judgment." Kesselman did continue to live and work in Palestine.

To Elizabeth Brandeis Raushenbush

September 19, 1932 Washington, D. C. [EBR]

DEAREST ELIZABETH: I had my talk with Prest. Green [1] this afternoon. He is about what we assumed; was very nice and says he may come again. I tried to make him see clearly that the Wisconsin Act is the way to salvation, and that he should endeavor to get, so far as possible, uniform legislation of that character.[2] I think he was made to see that our aim must be to remove or lessen irregularity of employment; that we are to deal, not with the immediate emergency; that the use of the word "insurance" is to be avoided; and that the idea that irregularity is inevitable must be strenuously combatted at all points. He says it was he who secured the Ohio Workmens Compensation Act.

We are very glad that the new house promises so well and hope Walter is willing to accept its lures, and to relinquish the railroad cars.[3] Soon you will have some time for home. I am mailing you the bound volume of my 1931–2 opinions; and with them some Editorial Research Bulletins. Paul may be interested to see also the samples of Dick [Boeckel]'s Daily bulletin.

Your mother is deeply in politics, that is in converse.

Lovingly,

I suggest you send Miss Thorne a copy of the Wisconsin Act amended as Paul and you think it should be. Mr. Corrigan, the auto man, sent Walter greetings.

1. William Green (1870–1952) had risen through the ranks of the United Mine Workers to become president of the American Federation of Labor

upon the death of Samuel Gompers in 1924, and he held the position until his own death. He was active also in Democratic politics in Ohio, where he resided, and served both in the National Recovery Administration and the International Labor Organization in the 1930s.

2. See LDB to Harold J. Laski, 28 February 1932.

3. The Raushenbushes had just moved out of an apartment where their son Walter could watch the freight trains go by, and into a house at 2228 Hillington Green in Madison.

To Louis Brandeis Wehle

September 27, 1932 Washington, D.C. [Wehle Mss]

L.B.W.: "Business a Profession" re yours of 26th.

I think it inappropriate that I should write any letter that could be transmitted to Hale.[1] You know that I felt it improper to suggest, in respect to either book, what the introduction should contain & preferred not to see what was written until it had been published.[2] I did not see [Charles A.] Beard's introduction until "The Social & Economic Views" was published; did not know of the Yale Press volume until it appeared;[3] & have consistently refused to look at any of the articles on me prior to publication.

I may say to you that Hale's performance in this respect is quite in keeping with his action and inaction in respect to all other matters relating to the book.

And, I add, as already stated, that I am entirely content with Bonbright's introduction.

No doubt, with your usual tact and resourcefulness, you will put this through as planned.

Bonbright article returned herewith.

1. Hale and Cushman considered Bonbright's introductory chapter too dull (a view with which Wehle disagreed), and wanted Bonbright to deal less with LDB's ideas and more with his work on the Supreme Court. Wehle wanted to know if LDB cared to state his opinion of Bonbright's work for transmission to the publishers.

2. See LDB to Alpheus T. Mason, 3 March 1931, and to Wehle, 9 July 1932.

3. Felix Frankfurter, ed., *Mr. Justice Brandeis* (New Haven, 1932), included laudatory essays by Charles Evans Hughes, Max Lerner, Frankfurter, Donald R. Richberg, Henry Wolf Biklé, and Walton Hamilton, with an introduction by Oliver Wendell Holmes.

To Susan Goldmark

October 7, 1932 Washington, D. C. [EBR]

DEAR SUSIE: Our thanks to the Geschwester for the Nevinson.[1]
The volume came most opportunely yesterday early as Alice had
set apart the day for resting and enjoyed many hours in the
reading.

Whenever one returns to Goethe there are new revelations.
I had again the experience in reading "Wahrheit und Dichtung"
[*sic*] this summer. Writing was but an incident of his living.

The Court made its annual call on the President yesterday. He
looked very fit after two nights on the train and endless speaking.
There is marvellous exhilaration in action—and applause. We are
told that a week before, when seen here, he looked like a man
of eighty. Perhaps you heard his Des Moines speech.[2] Your radio
must have been an added comfort during these trying weeks.

Paul is due next Friday for an A.F. of L. conference on unemployment reserve legislation.

1. Henry Wood Nevinson's *Goethe: Man and Poet* (New York, 1932)
had been written for the centenary of Goethe's death.

2. Before a crowd of 10,000 in the Iowa capital, Hoover laid out a twelve-
point farm program that included the maintenance of high tariffs, development of a St. Lawrence seaway, and the use of war debts to create new
markets. Hoover warned against any attempts to cheapen money and promised to defend the gold standard. The "foundations of recovery," he declared, had already been built. For the text of the speech, see *New York
Times*, 5 October 1932.

To Josephine Goldmark

October 30, 1932 Washington, D. C. [Brandeis Mss, M 7–2]

DEAR JOSEPHINE: Early in November comes the 25th anniversary
of our entry upon the Oregon case.[1] I wish to celebrate the day
by entering upon another joint enterprise with you, which should
be no less interesting and prove equally important.

Alice tells me that you plan to come here for the birthday.
Can't you come at least a week earlier and let me talk over the
project with you, before the Court resumes its exigent sessions
on Monday, the seventh? The sooner, the better.[2]

1. See LDB to Louis B. Wehle, 10 February 1908, n. 1.

2. It is impossible to determine exactly what project LDB had in mind, but he may have been referring to his growing interest in Danish social democracy. He had earlier sent Miss Goldmark reports on the Danish system (see LDB to Josephine Goldmark, 8 January 1932), and he encouraged her to undertake some publication on the matter. The result was *Democracy in Denmark* (Washington, 1936), Part I of which was "Democracy in Action," a descriptive analysis of Danish society by Miss Goldmark. Part II was "The folk high school," by A. H. Hollman, translated from the German by Alice Goldmark Brandeis.

To Elizabeth Brandeis Raushenbush

November 2, 1932 Washington, D.C. [EBR]

DEAREST ELIZABETH: You and Paul will be interested in the enclosures on Ins[urance]. Reserve. Please return Dean Clark's letter to Felix.

The clipping will show you how the business curve is turning down.

Thanks for your letter. I am as usual, but the auto men are right. Old machines are unreliable and the maintenance cost high.

To Oliver Wendell Holmes, Jr.

December 8, 1932 Washington, D.C. [Holmes Mss]

O.W.H. S.J.C. 1882–1902
    USSC. 1902–1932 (Jan.)
"They that love him shall be filled with the Law." [1]
"And the lips of many shall tell forth his understanding." [2]

1. Sirach (Ecclesiasticus) 2:16.
2. Sirach (Ecclesiasticus) 1:21.

To Emanuel Neumann

January 27, 1933 Washington, D. C. [Neumann Mss]

DEAR EMANUEL NEUMANN: Your letter of the 9th reached me yesterday, the same day that brought through J[ewish]. D[aily].

B[ulletin]. report of the Emir's cancellation.[1] Today, I have from Bob Szold copies of his cable to you of 25th and of your reply of 26th, also copy of your letter to him of 8th.

Even if the cancellation should prove definite and final, you have, in my opinion, achieved much for the cause. The crack in the Transjordan wall which you effected will be widened, and opportunity opened for Jew and Arab by the Jewish immigration.

You have given new evidence of devotion, wisdom and resourcefulness which gives assurance of ultimate success.

Cordially yours,

1. On 17 January, Neumann and the Emir Abdullah (the Hashemite king of Transjordania) had reached an agreement whereby the Jewish Agency secured an option to lease 70,000 dunams (17,500 acres) east of the Jordan for a ninety-nine-year period (see LDB to Robert Szold, 11 July 1932). Other Arab leaders immediately objected to the prospect of settling Jews in the Transjordan and pressured the Emir into cancelling the agreement on 25 January.

To Morris Llewellyn Cooke

April 14, 1933 Washington, D. C. [Cooke Mss]

M.L.C.: That's an excellent memo on costfinding. The most glaring evidence of R[ail]R[oad] (& I[nterstate].C[ommerce].C[ommission].) shortcomings is the absence of an appropriate maintenance account. They have only the cash amounts reminiscent of the country store of 1865.

To Elizabeth Brandeis Raushenbush

April 22, 1933 Washington, D.C. [EBR]

DEAREST ELIZABETH: The year just closing has been a beautiful and useful one for you and Paul and Walter. We can wish you nothing better than another such.

It is fine to think that Chatham days are near.   Lovingly,

Public affairs are engrossing, and hopeful. But I can't believe in any inflation save through the expenditures on huge public works. Inflation is a question apart from going off gold; that is failing to sustain the dollar abroad.[1]

1. The entire nation was caught up in the ferment of the First Hundred Days of Franklin D. Roosevelt's administration, in which numerous reform measures were rushed through Congress. In order to stimulate the economy, the United States took its currency off the gold standard. The National Industrial Recovery Act included appropriations of $3.3 billion for public works. See William E. Leuchtenburg, *Franklin D. Roosevelt and the New Deal*, ch. 3.

To David K. Niles

April 25, 1933 Washington, D.C. [SBLI]

DEAR DAVID NILES: [1] Mrs. [Elizabeth Glendower] Evans quotes you as saying that Savings Bank Insurance has suffered severely during the depression and that great effort must be expended to keep the banks "going until times are better".

You will be glad to know that the contrary is true. See Richard W. Hale's letter in April 26 New Republic p. 312.[2]

And I hope you will call soon on Miss [Alice H.] Grady and let her tell you how the depression is aiding Savings Bank Insurance, in securing for it an appreciative public.

All that we need is invitations to explain the system to those who are in need of its benefits; and I hope you will make special effort to get such opportunities for our speakers.   Cordially,

1. David K. Niles (1890–1952), a figure of some mystery because of his "passion for anonymity" (see his obituary in the *New York Times*, 29 September 1952), was reputed to be an "insider" close to President Roosevelt and later to Harry Truman. A longtime progressive, who had worked for LaFollette in 1924 and for Sacco and Vanzetti, Niles was under Harry Hopkins in the WPA. He later played an important part in securing independence for the State of Israel. See John Snetsinger, *Truman, the Jewish Vote and the Creation of Israel* (Stanford, Cal., 1974), *passim*.

2. Hale's letter "Banks in the Bay State," written on the heels of the banking holiday, praised LDB, compared Savings Bank Insurance to commercial insurance, and called for "some good angel" to spread the system to other states.

To Stephen Samuel Wise

May 18, 1933 Washington, D. C. [Wise Mss]

S.S.W.: 1. Re yours of 16th & 17th to F.F.[1]

The following tends to confirm the belief that [Felix] Warburg et al were responsible for the Administration's attitude.[2]
Maurice B. Hexter was in yesterday. I put up to him the possibility of raising money from the German Jews of America. He
agreed that they are the ones who have money. "The trouble is,
there is no one to lead the movement. Warburg, Baerwald [3] and
others who have relatives in Germany dare not say anything publicly."

2. As to N[ewton]. D. B[aker].'s letter as "a non-Jew." There
are some who would be willing to bet heavily that neither he nor
his wife could stand the Hitler test.[4]

3. [Harry] Friedenwald was in last week with an encouraging
report for Baltimore.

4. He [5] did call, I am told, but through error I was not told by
the maid. She suspects he was leaving on the 4 P.M.

---

1. Wise wanted Felix Frankfurter to talk to President Roosevelt about
possible American actions to halt the increasing persecution of Jews in Germany by the recently installed government of Adolf Hitler (see note 4).
Frankfurter did see Roosevelt on 27 May 1933.

2. Wise, who had been trying to call Roosevelt's attention to the problem
of German Jewry, had discovered that the President was receiving reports
from American German-Jewish leaders that there was nothing to worry
about. It would be several years before the attitude of this group changed,
and during that time Wise had difficulty convincing the administration of
the dangers posed by Hitler.

3. Paul Baerwald (1871–1961) had emigrated from Germany in 1896 to
the United States, where he soon became a successful banker. Baerwald
had been treasurer of the Joint Distribution Committee from 1917 to 1932;
from 1932 to 1945 he headed the J.D.C.

4. Adolf Hitler (1889–1945), a painter before serving in the German
army in World War I, had gone on afterwards to lead the radical National
Socialist German Workers' Party. In 1923 he had been imprisoned for nine
months following an abortive coup to seize the Bavarian government. While
in prison, he outlined his plans for the future in *Mein Kampf*, which became
the bible of the Nazi movement. Hitler blamed Germany's defeat in the
war, as well as most of its postwar problems, on the Jews and demanded the
creation of a new Germany controlled solely by pure Aryans. After his
release from prison, Hitler molded the Nazis into a potent political force,

capitalizing on the widespread fears and frustrations and promising to lead Germany to a greater future. In 1932 he was defeated in his electoral bid to become president of the Weimar Republic, but soon afterwards the aging president von Hindenburg asked Hitler to become chancellor in January 1933. Upon von Hindenburg's death in August 1934, Hitler assumed full and dictatorial powers, and he held them to his death in 1945.

During the early- and mid-thirties, Hitler completely overhauled the German society and economy and, in violation of the Versailles Treaty, began to rearm Germany. His first real test of military prowess came when German "volunteers" fought with success against the Republicans in the Spanish Civil War. In 1938 he annexed Austria and soon after took over the German-speaking Sudetenland from Czechoslovakia. Time and again Hitler was proven right in his assumption that the Western democracies would not interfere. Finally, when he attacked Poland in September 1939, France and England felt they could no longer stand idly by and, with their declaration of war, plunged the world into a bloody and extensive war which did not end until Germany's defeat in May 1945, shortly after Hitler had taken his own life in his bunker in Berlin.

In addition to his visions of conquering Europe, Hitler also wanted to end the "Jewish menace," and soon after his rise to power he implemented a series of laws to restrict the freedom of Jews. His test for any individual's being Jewish consisted of having at least one grandparent of the faith, thus trapping many Christians whose parents or grandparents had converted from Judaism. In 1941, the Nazis began to implement their "final solution" of the Jewish problem, systematically slaughtering over six million men, women, and children in a number of concentration camps.

The literature on Hitler, the Third Reich, and the extermination of European Jewry is immense. See, among others, William L. Shirer, *The Rise and Fall of the Third Reich* (New York, 1960); Alan Bullock, *Hitler, A Study in Tyranny* (New York, rev. ed., 1962); and Raul Hilberg, *The Destruction of the European Jews* (Chicago, 1967).

5. James Grover McDonald (1886–1964) had taught history and political science before assuming the chairmanship of the Foreign Policy Association from 1919 to 1933. From 1933 to 1945 he served as League of Nations High Commissioner for Refugees, and during that time he won the friendship and respect of Jewish communities in Europe and the United States. During the second war, McDonald worked in vain to get the Roosevelt administration to provide more help for Jewish refugees. In 1948, President Truman named him as the first American ambassador to the State of Israel. See *My Mission to Israel* (New York, 1951). See LDB to Julian W. Mack, 17 October 1933.

To Harold LeClaire Ickes [1] (Telegram)

June 14, 1933 Chatham, Mass. [Brandeis Mss, G 6–1]

Answering your telegram I suggest Philip LaFollette.[2]

1. Harold LeClaire Ickes (1874–1952) had been a lawyer and civic reformer in Chicago before being named Secretary of the Interior by President Roosevelt, a position he held until 1946. Ickes also headed the powerful public works program under the National Recovery Administration. See his *Autobiography of a Curmudgeon* (New York, 1943), and *My Twelve Years with F.D.R.* (New York, 1948). In 1940, Ickes received the Louis D. Brandeis Freedom Medal, and shortly afterwards he published *Not Guilty. . . .* (Washington, 1940), in which he defended the policies of Richard A. Ballinger. See LDB to Bernard Flexner, 23 May 1940.

2. Ickes had wired LDB asking for "name and qualifications of person or persons suitable for appointment as head of proposed emergency administration of public works." In the end, the President named Ickes himself to the post.

To Oliver Wendell Holmes

July 28, 1933 Chatham, Mass. [Holmes Mss]

"Wohl dem, der seiner Väter gern gedenkt,
Der froh von ihren Thaten, ihrer Grösse
Den Hörer unterhält, und still sich freuend
An's Ende dieser schönen Reihe sich geschlossen sieht." [1]

With my greetings,

1. "Blessed is he who cherishes the memory of his fathers
    Who, proud of their deeds, their greatness
    Entertains the listener, and quietly delights
    In seeing himself included at the end of this illustrious line."
From Goethe's *Iphigenie*, I,3.

To Donald Randall Richberg

August 13, 1933 Chatham, Mass. [Richberg Mss]

DEAR DONALD RICHBERG: My thanks for the Law Review article.[1]
With you, Ickes and Lilienthal [2] in seats of power it looks really like a New Deal.

We shall hope to see you and Mrs. Richberg in September.

Cordially,

1. Donald R. Richberg, "Economic Illusions Underlying Law," 1 *University of Chicago Law Review* 96 (1933).

2. David Eli Lilienthal (b. 1899) had practiced law in Chicago during the 1920s before becoming a member of the Wisconsin Public Service Commission in 1931. On 3 June 1933, Roosevelt named Lilienthal a director of the Tennessee Valley Authority, on which board he served until 1946, the last five years as chairman. In 1946, President Truman appointed Lilienthal chairman of the newly created Atomic Energy Commission. See Lilienthal's *TVA: Democracy on the March* (New York, 1944) and the *Journals of David E. Lilienthal*, 5 vols. (New York, 1964-71).

To Sherman Fabian Mittell:

August 25, 1933 Chatham, Mass. [Brandeis Mss, G 7-3]

DEAR SHERMAN MITTELL: [1] Re yours of 23rd.

You seem to be getting on all sides deserved cooperation.

When I assented to your request for permission to publish "Other People's Money", it was my intention that you should do so without payment of royalty to any one. And it was my expectation that Frederick A. Stokes Co. would give permission without asking compensation, believing as you do that the widespread distribution of a 15 cent edition would enhance the sale of the $2. edition. As payment to Stokes of $500 is required, I think it appropriate that the charge be borne by me. I shall be glad to provide that sum for Stokes as soon as you advise me that all arrangements have been perfected by the Foundation for printing and distributing the contemplated edition of 100,000 copies.

But what is of far more importance is that you should take immediately a thoroughly restful vacation. If you act on this promptly, your health and vigor will no doubt be quickly restored. Act before it is too late.

We expect to return to Washington about Sept. 15th; and after your return from your vacation shall be glad to see you.

With best wishes,

Cordially,

I am returning herewith Stokes' letter to you of Aug. 8th.

1. Sherman Fabian Mittell (1904-1942), after graduating from Harvard, had been in the real estate business briefly before founding the National

Home Library Foundation, which specialized in inexpensive reprints of notable books. At the outset of World War II, Mittell worked as an assistant to Paul McNutt on the War Manpower Board.

To Elizabeth Brandeis Raushenbush

September 16, 1933 Washington, D. C. [EBR]

DEAR ELIZABETH: This method has occurred to me for dealing with the question of national-state provisions for "unemployment insurance." The Federal Govt should leave the providing wholly to the States; but as a "discourager of hesitancy" should lay an excise tax after a day fixed upon every employer who shall not have made provision thereupon under some adequate state law. The federal tax should go into the U. S. General revenue fund, i.e. not be specifically appropriated to unemployment compensation, lest by so doing we start national provision. But some provision will have to be made for Dist. of Columbia; so we may have to provide for it a system, e.g. the Wisconsin scheme.[1]

F. D. [Roosevelt] indicated yesterday to F[elix]. F[rankfurter]. a desire to talk with me generally on matters, before Court convenes. If he carries out his purpose, I want to discuss irregularity of employment with him. Let me have as soon as possible your & Paul's views as to the above; &, if you can, a rough suggestion for a bill.

Note enclosed clipping from AFL news.

1. See LDB to Harold J. Laski, 28 February 1932 and to Elizabeth B. Raushenbush, 19 September 1932.

To Stephen Samuel Wise

September 18, 1933 Washington, D. C. [Wise Mss]

S.S.W.: I am glad to know, from the [press] release, of your safe return.[1]

In discussion of boycott by Americans,[2] I do not recall any reference to the part played in America's struggle for independence by the boycott of British goods, prior to the Declaration of Independence.

You will find reference to Jefferson's part in the boycott in Lisitzky's "Jefferson", recently published by Viking Press, pp. 61–62, and to the action of the Continental Congress December 1774, on pp. 84–86.[3]

A fuller description of the action in the several states would doubtless reveal much dramatic material.[4]

1. Wise had just returned from Europe where he had gone on Zionist business and had also taken some of the preliminary steps that would ultimately lead to the creation of the World Jewish Congress.

2. In response to German persecution of Jews, the American Jewish Congress had spearheaded a campaign to boycott purchase of German goods. The American Jewish community was bitterly divided over the issue, with the Congress and other "activist" groups supporting the boycott, and the American Jewish Committee and its allies opposing it. For the boycott and its effects, see Moshe Gottlieb, "The First of April Boycott and the Reaction of the American Jewish Community," *American Jewish Historical Quarterly* 57 (June 1968): 516–56.

3. Genevieve (Gene) Hellen Lisitzky, *Thomas Jefferson* (New York, 1933).

4. See Arthur M. Schlesinger, *The Colonial Merchants and the American Revolution, 1763-1776* (New York, 1917), chs. 4, 5. See also LDB to Robert Szold, 24 November 1938.

To Julian William Mack

September 27, 1933 Washington, D. C. [Wise Mss]

J.W.M.: Sir Herbert Samuel called on me today. I started, at once, to talk with him on 2 Palestine problems.

1. What seemed to me unreasonably tight curb on visas. He said he would look into this on his return. Said he knew Govt. (including Wauchope)[1] were distinctly friendly—but perhaps overcautious. He spoke of the 1925 break in the boom; and I undertook to show difference in conditions.

2. Transjordania.—told him of my talk with [Lord] Reading. Samuel said on that he had very recent advice. That early in July, at his house, there was a meeting of Reading, Ruttenberg, Sir Hugo Horst, Anthony de Rothschild[2] and others of the rich about what to do in Palestine for the Germans; that the question of Transjordania was discussed; and that Ruttenberg (who was going to Palestine for a brief visit) was to look into the matter

further; that before Samuel left the end of July they had another meeting, after Ruttenberg had returned; and that this meeting was opened by a statement by Reading that Transjordania was to be dropped, for the present; that while the Emir and some sheiks were for Jewish immigration there was too much opposition now. Later things might be different.[3]

3. Samuel spoke then of the various enterprises which were discussed at the meetings. Stressed particularly an extension of the Mrs. P. printing house at Tel Aviv—that this enterprise should surely give employment to hundreds and perhaps thousands; and that they would seek to make it in this respect, another Leipsig[sic]; and take away much of the business of German publishers.

The rest of Samuel's talk related mainly to his meetings to raise funds for the [Hebrew] University.

4. Samuel says he was the first to suggest to the Govt. the Zionist project—under Britain's control.—In 1914 shortly after Turkey declared war [Chaim] Weizmann and [Nahum] Sok[olow] called on him to urge the Zionist cause. It was then assumed by the Gov. that Great Britain would win the war and Turkey lose its non-Turkish provinces. He had not, before the Weiz. Sok. call thought much on Zionism—was impressed by the project and prepared a memo which is on the files.[4]

Edwin Montague [sic] [5] opposed vigorously. Nothing was done then—Later he went out of the Govt. etc.—He depicted briefly events.

5. I hope you have seen in Sept. Labor Palestine the article "Pacifism or Passivism?" referring to Sidney Hunt's "Smoldering Peace in Palestine"—in Aug. 31 "The World Tomorrow." [6] Can you get hold of Hunt and/or the Editors.

Please send copies to S.S.W., deH., F.F. and R.S.

1. Sir Arthur Grenfell Wauchope (1874–1947), a career soldier, served as British High Commissioner for Palestine from 1931 to 1938. During his term of office the Yishuv secured large increases in population thanks to Wauchope's liberal interpretation of immigration policy. Although he tried to reconcile various interests in Palestine and hoped to use economic development as the tool to wed Arab and Jewish communities, contradictory directions from London undermined his efforts.

2. Anthony Gustav de Rothschild (1887–1961), the elder son of Sir Leopold, was prominent in hospital work in England.

3. See LDB to Emanuel Neumann, 27 January 1933.

4. See Isaiah Friedman, *The Question of Palestine*, ch. 2.

5. Edwin Samuel Montagu (1879–1924), the second son of Baron Swaythling, had entered Parliament as a Liberal in 1906. During World War I he had served first as minister for munitions and then from 1917 to 1922 as Secretary of State for India; he resigned in opposition to British refusal to give that country greater independence. Montagu, a Jew, was the chief opponent of the Balfour Declaration within high government circles. See LDB to Chaim Weizmann, 24 September 1917, n. 1.

6. The Hunt article explained the problem in Palestine in terms of a static, fatalistic Arab culture being displaced by a dynamic, optimistic Jewish culture, one that was introducing a modernistic temperament repellant to Muslim tradition. *The World Tomorrow* 16 (31 August 1933): 492–93.

To Elizabeth Brandeis Raushenbush

September 30, 1933 Washington, D. C. [EBR]

DEAREST ELIZABETH: I haven't seen F.D. [Roosevelt], but I have talked to Isador Lubin. He accepts the proposal; [1] will work on the economics; will talk to Frances Perkins; [2] & will ask the Solicitor of the Dept. [3] to work on a bill.

I was glad you had written me of his suggestion, Aug. 31.

Lovingly,

Glad your course is proving so popular. [4]

1. See LDB to Harold J. Laski, 28 February 1932, and to Elizabeth Raushenbush, 19 September 1932 and 16 September 1933.

2. Frances Perkins (Wilson) (1880–1965) had been a prominent industrial reformer in New York, closely associated with the Goldmarks. She held high state positions under both Al Smith and Franklin Roosevelt. In 1933, FDR named Madame Perkins Secretary of Labor, the first woman to hold a cabinet position. She was an ardent advocate of union rights during her twelve-year tenure in that office. See *The Roosevelt I Knew* (New York, 1946).

3. Charles Edward Wyzanski, Jr. (b. 1906), after a brilliant career at Harvard College and Harvard Law School, had clerked for both Augustus and Learned Hand before being named Solicitor of the Labor Department in 1933. In 1941 President Roosevelt appointed Wyzanski United States District Judge for Massachusetts, where he soon earned a reputation as an outstanding liberal jurist. During his tenure on the bench, Wyzanski also served as consultant to numerous international bodies.

4. This was probably a new course in American economic history, which Mrs. Raushenbush offered for many years at the University of Wisconsin.

To Julian William Mack

October 17, 1933 Washington, D. C. [Wise Mss]

J.W.M.: [James G.] Macdonald [sic] of F[oreign]. P[olicy]. A[ssociation]. was in yesterday—55 minutes. He arrived from Europe on 12th. Reported briefly on occurrences in Germany, London, Prague and Geneva—particularly on agreed High Commissionership—under League of Nations influence. Said much discussion as to nationality of Commissioner to be selected;—that an American was deemed desirable; (Cecil [1]—fine—but too old and not capable of doing necessary travelling and required Executive work.—Sanger (?) (and other Europeans persona non grata to Germans; and important not to have any such.) Said he had cabled his office to try for $50,000 from [John D.] Rockefeller for necessary administrative expenses—that he had immediately cabled to Raymond Fosdick about this and also to suggest his taking commissionership; Fosdick indicated R. would not give all but would give a substantial part; that he thought Fosdick would be fine as Commissioner but F. declined to consider it; that he has thought of Th. Roosevelt [2]—but his N. Y. Jewish friends said R. would not do.—Jewish need so great that we must have some one to whom matter would be "concern" and who would not treat Commissionership as stepping-stone to political preferment; that Fosdick had suggested him (MacDonald [sic]); and there was much said that convinced me MacDonald [sic] considered himself peculiarly well fitted.—I set forth to him at length and emphatically that I thought it would be a disaster to select any American—in view of the official attitude of the administration and commented on its shortcomings; in this respect insisted that no American ought to be selected—unless before that—(or simultaneously with it) America should adopt a policy of general admission [of Jews] and emphatic denunciation of German policy of discrimination so that the American could invite other nations to follow our lead.

He was completely surprised and evidently disappointed by this expression of opinion;—said no one in Europe, neither Neville Chamberlain,[3] Bentwich [4] or others had made any such suggestions;—that all had thought an American would be desirable i.a. to get much needed money from rich American Jews, etc.[5]

MacD. [sic] had reported earlier in our interview his talks yesterday with Hull (brief); [6] longer (and very unfavorable to Jews) with [William] Phillips; and longest with Moffat,[7] who seems to be charged with German Jewish affairs.

(I suppose you thought, when reading of the 27 complainants on whose behalf Hull is interesting himself: "Wos soll ein Jude thun auf einer Leiter") [8]

I told MacD. my views on Palestine as the hope.

1. Lord Robert Cecil; see LDB to Felix Frankfurter, 5 April 1920, n. 3.

2. Theodore Roosevelt, Jr. (1887–1944), like his father, was a well-known soldier, explorer, and naturalist. He had served with distinction in World War I, and he met his death on a battlefield in France during World War II. Roosevelt was suspect among some Jews because of the close identification of his brother, Kermit, with Middle Eastern oil interests.

3. Arthur Neville Chamberlain (1869–1940) had served in Parliament since 1918 and was Chancellor of the Exchequer from 1931 to 1937 before becoming Prime Minister. He is best remembered for his policy of attempting to appease Hitler in order to avert war. At Munich in September 1938 he gave in fully to Nazi demands for detaching the Sudetenland from Czechoslovakia and returned home to announce that there would be "peace in our time."

4. Norman deMattos Bentwich (b. 1883) was attorney general in Palestine during the 1920s and afterwards served as professor of international relations at the Hebrew University. Within a few weeks of this letter he was named deputy high commissioner for refugees, and later he was active in British efforts to alleviate the refugees' plight. Bentwich has written many books on both Palestine and Israel; see his autobiography, *My 77 Years* (Philadelphia, 1961).

5. LDB's prophecy was to be tragically borne out. McDonald was named high commissioner, and although he worked valiantly to save and rehabilitate German refugees, he was constantly hamstrung by the unwillingness of other countries to accept more than a token number of refugees, or of taking any action that might conceivably "insult" Hitler.

6. Cordell Hull (1871–1955) had represented the fourth district of Tennessee in the House of Representatives, except for one two-year term, from 1907 to 1931, before his election as Senator in 1931. Two years later Hull resigned his seat to become Roosevelt's Secretary of State, a post he held until 1944. Hull's tenure in the State Department was marked by efforts to create better relations with South America, the so-called "Good Neighbor Policy," and in the latter part of the 1930s by efforts to remain neutral as war clouds descended on Europe. During World War II he laid the groundwork for the United Nations, and he was an American delegate to the founding session of that organization in San Francisco in 1945. For his efforts to promote international cooperation, Hull received the Nobel Peace Prize in 1945. See his *Memoirs*, 2 vols. (New York, 1948).

7. Jay Pierrepont Moffat (1896–1943) was a career diplomat, and in the

early thirties he was the State Department's chief of the Western European Division. See Nancy Hooker, ed., *The Moffat Papers* (Cambridge, 1956).

8. "What is a Jew to do on a ladder?" Hull's wife was Jewish, which put him under great pressure. The Jewish groups expected him to exhibit sympathy for their problems, while Hull felt he could not appear to favor Jewish causes too much. This was a problem common to many with Jewish blood and/or relatives who were prominent, i.e., on a career ladder.

To Alfred Lief

November 3, 1933 Washington, D. C. [Brandeis Mss, SC 13–2]

DEAR ALFRED LIEF: Mr. [Norman] Hapgood has shown me your letter to him of the first, in which you say: "Justice Brandeis has authorized me to write his biography." [1]

Of course, that is not an accurate statement. What I said, in answer to yours of Sept. 25, was that it was entirely acceptable to me to have you write—a very different thing from an "authorized biography." Indeed, as you know, Alpheus Mason has just written a study (not yet seen by me) which is doubtless in large part biographical. [2]

I want to make sure that your publisher is not under the impression that yours will be "an authorized" biography. Please let me know that you and that he understand the situation, as I do.

1. Lief was at work on a biography of LDB that would appear as *Brandeis: The Personal History of an American Ideal* (New York, 1936).

2. A. T. Mason, *Brandeis: Lawyer and Judge in the Modern State* (Princeton, 1933). Seven years later, when LDB cooperated closely with Mason and gave him access to hitherto closed papers, the family would also insist that the resulting biography was not an "authorized" one. See LDB to Bernard Flexner, 7 August 1940.

To Elizabeth Brandeis Raushenbush

November 17, 1933 Washington, D. C. [EBR]

DEAR ELIZABETH: Genl. Johnson [1] came up last Friday, pursuant to our talk over the telephone at Chatham.

I put to him the Wisconsin idea & my project for Federal tax. [2] Yesterday I sent him your article obtained at great expense from N[ew]. R[epublic]. [3]

When here, the General expressed approval of the general plan;

but I guess he didn't understand overmuch. He is, however, definitely for regularization & individual reserves paid for by employer.   Lovingly,

1. Hugh Samuel Johnson (1882–1942) had been director of the draft during World War I, and then had become closely associated with Bernard Baruch. It was Baruch who recommended General Johnson to Roosevelt to head the National Recovery Administration (see LDB to Elizabeth B. Raushenbush, 22 April 1934, n. 2). Johnson's one-year tenure as head of that agency saw a paramilitary spirit converge with the latest in public relations techniques to sweep the nation into a Blue Eagle craze, with dozens of industries signing up for cooperative codes exempt from antitrust prosecution. See his *The Blue Eagle from Egg to Earth* (Garden City, N. Y., 1935).

2. See LDB to Elizabeth B. Raushenbush, 16 September 1933.

3. Elizabeth Brandeis, "Employment Reserves *vs.* Insurance," *The New Republic* 76 (27 September 1933): 177–79.

To Elizabeth Brandeis Raushenbush

November 19, 1933 Washington, D. C. [EBR]

DEAREST ELIZABETH: My thanks to you three for the birthday greetings.[1]

Curb of bigness is indispensable to true Democracy & Liberty. It is the very foundation also of wisdom in things human
"Nothing too much"
I hope you can make your progressives see this truth.[2] If they don't, we may get amelioration, but not a working "New Deal." And we are apt to get Fascist manifestations. Remember, the inevitable ineffectiveness of regulation, i.e. the limits of its efficiency in regulation.

If the Lord had intended things to be big, he would have made man bigger—in brains and character.

My "running waters" suggestion was this. My idea has been that the Depression can be overcome only by extensive public works.

(a) that no public works should be undertaken save those that would be effective in making the America of the future what it should be,

(b) that we should avail [ourselves] of the present emergency to get those public works which Americans would lack the insight & persistence to get for themselves in ordinary times.

These public works are, for every state,

(1.) afforestation

(2) running water control

(3) adult education

(4) appropriate provision for dealing with defectives and delinquents.

By "Running Water Control" I mean this:

In this country, where the rain fall is, in the main, between 35 and 50 inches, and the country largely blessed with hills or mountains, it is absurd to permit either floods or droughts, or waste of waters. We should so control all running waters, by reservoirs, etc., so

(a) as to prevent floods & soil erosion

(b) to make it possible to irrigate practically all land

(c) to utilize the water for power & inland navigation

(d) & for recreation

Every state should have its lakes and ponds galore. Doubtless, you will recall much discourse of mine on this subject.

Lovingly,

I am very glad you & Paul are doing so much talking.

1. 13 November was LDB's seventy-seventh birthday.

2. These suggestions were for consideration by a group of Wisconsin progressives, centered around Philip LaFollette, who intended issuing some sort of manifesto; the project ultimately fell through.

To Elizabeth Brandeis Raushenbush

November 20, 1933 Washington, D. C. [EBR]

DEAREST ELIZABETH: Since writing you yesterday yours of Saturday has come.

1. Phil [LaFollette] has given you very bad investment advice. Do not invest in any stock, common or preferred. Changes in the bonds should be made only if you find an opportunity for getting a safer bond. Government bonds, despite the infirmity injected by the New Deal,[1] are probably safer than most investments, if bonds are paid off.

2. If you have more income than you find yourself able to spend wisely, re-invest the surplus, so as to make good losses sure to come in some measure, through inflation or otherwise.

3. The underlying objection to investment in common stocks is, that for one with your knowledge & interests, such investment is mere speculation. The dangers of an unlisted stock are obvious. Those of the listed (and others) are not merely the inevitable risks of business. They arise from the widespread dishonesty, or low ethical standards, prevailing in officers of corporate enterprises.[2]

Lovingly,

4. If at any time you have doubt about investments, consult Miss [E. Louise] Malloch, as I do.

5. Also, as I said to you last summer—Never endorse or guarantee for anybody. You will know whether your income permits you *to give.*

---

1. The "infirmity" was the Roosevelt administration's decision to take the United States off the gold standard, and to cease paying government bonds in gold. The Supreme Court ultimately denounced the repudiation as unconstitutional and immoral but had to uphold the policy in order to avoid financial chaos. The loophole utilized was that the investor had not suffered any damages by not being paid in gold. See *Perry* v. *United States,* 294 *U.S.* 330 (1935), and John Dawson, "The Gold Clause Decisions," 33 *Michigan Law Review* 647 (1935).

2. Cf. LDB to Alfred Brandeis, 28 July 1904.

To Harry Friedenwald

November 22, 1933 Washington, D. C. [Friedenwald Mss]

DEAR DR. FRIEDENWALD: To you and Mrs. Friedenwald my thanks for the birthday greetings.

The world's unruliness is giving us all much to do. But there is some satisfaction for Zionists that their efforts for the upbuilding of Palestine were timely.

With best wishes,   Cordially,

To Stephen Samuel Wise

December 9, 1933 Washington, D. C. [Wise Mss]

SSW: I was glad to see LaGuardia,[1] though it was only for a few minutes. A wildly erring taxi driver deprived us of the precious time.

Among the many things unsaid was the following: To achieve worthy enduring results—it is essential that throughout the four years—the education of the whole population of the City in his administration's aims and accomplishments be carried on, unremittingly and thoroughly. To that end there must be organized a corp of speakers and of writers, who will be continuously in touch with the administration; and educating the educators from day to day is an indispensable part of the program. The minimum size of the corp would, I should think, be 250 speakers and 25 writers. And this work should begin Inauguration Day, and not end until after the election of 1937.[2]

1. Fiorello Henry LaGuardia (1882–1947) had just been elected to the first of three terms he would serve as mayor of New York City. A progressive reformer, LaGuardia had tackled the entrenched Tammany machine and won a seat in Congress in 1916. He went off to war as an aviator, and during the 1920s he was an implacable foe of the New York Democrats, and especially of their idol, James J. Walker. Finally, in the wake of the Pecora investigation, LaGuardia put together a winning political combination of ethnic and labor groups and began his twelve-year reign. During World War II, the "Little Flower" headed the Office of Civilian Defense. See Howard Zinn, *LaGuardia in Congress* (Westport, Conn., 1972); Arthur Mann, *LaGuardia Comes to Power: 1933* (Philadelphia, 1965); and Charles Garrett, *The LaGuardia Years: Machine and Reform Politics in New York City* (New Brunswick, N. J., 1961).
2. Cf. LDB to Henry Bruere, 20 December 1915.

To Savings Bank Life Insurance Office Force

December 17, 1933 Washington, D.C. [SBLI]

"Savings Bank Life Insurance Office Force." To each of you my belated thanks for your birthday greeting bringing renewal of the pledge to carry on the work. No greeting gave me more pleasure.   Cordially,

To Alice Park Goldmark

January 11, 1934 Washington, D.C. [EBR]

MY DEAR ALICE: [1] It was lovely of you to knit the socks, more beautiful even than their predecessors.

We had a gay Christmas with the Susan family; and Elizabeth came to usher in the New Year. Her time was spent largely on unemployment reserves—spent hopefully; and there may be some results of national significance.[2]

Of course, life in Washington now is stirring, intellectually far more so than I have ever known it. There is much noble thinking and high endeavor; sometimes impatience, sometimes a forgetting that:

"The world's wise are not wise
Claiming more than mortals know."

and that:

"Wenn man der Stein der Weisen hätte
Der Weise mangelte dem Stein." [3]

We are beginning already to think of Chatham, and we hope that nothing will interfere this year with a real visit from you three.

1. Alice Park Goldmark was LDB's sister-in-law; she was married to Charles Goldmark.

2. During her Christmas vacation of 1933, Elizabeth Raushenbush appeared at a small meeting of policy-makers in Washington, D.C. The meeting (which included Frances Perkins and Senator Wagner) was arranged by A. Lincoln Filene and held in his daughter's home. There Mrs. Raushenbush presented the basic idea of a new federal payroll tax on employers, which would give a tax credit for their contributions under approved state unemployment compensation plans (like Wisconsin's). See LDB to Harold J. Laski, 28 February 1932. See also LDB to Elizabeth B. Raushenbush, 22 April 1934.

3. "If they had the philosophers' stone, the stone would lack a philosopher." Goethe, *Faust*, II: 5063.

To David Ben-Gurion

January 25, 1934 Washington, D. C. [London Office]

DEAR BEN GURION,[1] Yours of 5th reached me to-day.[2] I agree entirely with the opinion which you express, with the reasons therefor, and that we should strive unceasingly to obtain the objective stated. I believe that this is possible.

So far as may be possible, I shall lend aid.
With best wishes,   Cordially,

1. David Ben-Gurion (1886–1973) has often been called the chief architect
of the state of Israel. During his youth in Russia he joined a Zionist group;
and he emigrated to Palestine in 1906, where he soon rose to leadership
in the Labor Zionist organization. It was Ben-Gurion who insisted that the
Poale Zion shift its emphasis from Diaspora Jewry to a Palestine-oriented
program, and that Hebrew, rather than Yiddish, be the chief language of
the movement. During World War I he came to the United States after
having spent two years studying law in Turkey. He was active in the Congress movement, and it is possible that he originally met LDB during the
agitation over a Jewish Legion.

One of the founders of the Histadrut, by 1930 Ben-Gurion was the recognized leader of the Palestine Labor Party (Mapai), and he fought against
both the leftist tendencies of socialism and the rightist agitation from the
Revisionists. Above all else, he stressed the need to develop a strong and
economically healthy Jewish settlement in Palestine. During the 1930s he
moved further and further from Chaim Weizmann, charging the Zionist
Organization president with being inconsistent and not standing up for
Jewish rights in the face of British moves to restrict the Mandate. This
brought him to LDB's attention, and the two men cooperated on several
projects during the last decade of LDB's life. It was LDB, for example, who
privately supplied Ben-Gurion with money to arm the Haganah defense
units in the late 1930s; LDB also arranged for the purchase of land in the
southern Negev which ultimately became the important port city of Eilat,
after Ben-Gurion had convinced him of that area's importance for future
Palestinian development.

During World War II Ben-Gurion took over almost undisputed control
of the Zionist movement, and from 1945 onwards he worked to prepare the
Yishuv for the armed struggle with the Arabs that he saw as the inevitable
prelude to the birth of a Jewish state. On 14 May 1948 he chaired the session of the People's Council that adopted the Israeli Declaration of Independence, a document he had in large part drafted. With the proclamation, he
assumed office as Prime Minister and Minister of Defense, offices he held
until his first retirement to Sde Boker in 1953. He rejoined the government
in 1955 as Minister of Defense and shortly thereafter also became Prime
Minister, holding both offices until his final retirement in 1963.

To Ben-Gurion goes much of the credit for the political structure of
Israel, as well as the development of the Israel Defense Forces. His was a
forceful personality that swept before it many obstacles that would have
stopped lesser men. But there were also many defects in his character that
antagonized people who would have been friends, and he could be unusually cruel to his opponents, especially to Chaim Weizmann. There have
been many books written about him, but the best source for his life is his
Israel, A Personal History (New York, 1971).

2. In a lengthy and prescient letter, Ben-Gurion reported on his recent visit to London and his analysis of the world scene. He accurately predicted that both Germany and Japan were preparing for a world war, although neither was yet ready to fight. As far as the Jews were concerned, he wrote, the only feasible solution was Palestine, and the experience of almost fifty years of agricultural pioneering proved that the land, properly utilized, could absorb many more Jews than the British were willing to admit. The only plan of action open to the Zionists, he concluded, was to continue their work in Palestine, proving even to the skeptics that a national home could be created that would absorb hundreds of thousands more Jews.

To Oliver Wendell Holmes, Jr.

March 8, 1934 Washington, D.C. [Holmes Mss]

OWH: "And the lips of many shall tell forth his understanding."
  Notre l'homme de quartre–vingt–treize who wrought without a revolution.[1]

1. Sirach (Ecclesiasticus) 1:21; Holmes was celebrating his ninety-third birthday.

To Stephen Samuel Wise

March 17, 1934 Washington, D. C. [Wise Mss]

S.S.W.: We rejoice that in this Jewish crisis you are here to lead and that you are only sixty.[1]
  With every good wish,

1. This was Wise's birthday; see LDB to Wise, 20 September 1935.

To Clarence Martin Lewis

March 21, 1934 Washington, D. C. [Brandeis Mss, M 7–4]

DEAR MR. LEWIS: [1] For purposes of reference in this letter, I have numbered the items in your list consecutively from 1 to 53.
  By Railway Express Agency, I am sending you copies of such as are available. Please guard them carefully and return them to me as soon as you conveniently can. I am sending the following:

First: No. 1. This article may be of interest because it was the earliest of mine, published (1881).[2] I should think my "Right to Privacy" published in 4 Harvard Law Review in 1890 would be of more interest to the general public and the profession. So I am enclosing also a copy of that.[3]

Second: No. 7. I have no objection to your republishing this. But would it be of general interest today? [4]

Third: No. 8 [5]

Fourth: No. 13.[6] As you are including articles of this nature—You may care to see the following sent in the express package

    (a) "The Jewish Problem. How to Solve It."

    (b) "A Call to the Educated Jew."

    (c) "Zionism and Patriotism"

    (d) "Palestine and the Jewish Democracy"

    (e) "Proposed Palestine Policy." [7]

Fifth: No. 14 [8]

Sixth: No. 21 [9]

Seventh: No. 32 (a pretty formidable document) [10]

Eighth: No. 18 [11]

Ninth: No. 30 [12]

Tenth: No. 28 [13]

Eleventh: No. 30 [14]

Twelfth: No. 47 [15]

—————

No. 13 should not be included, being a part of "Other People's Money" [16] nor No. 17, being a part of "Business a Profession." [17] The remaining 41 items would far exceed the compass of a single volume. If, after examining all, you conclude which of them you wish to select, I shall be glad to look over the list of selections to see whether reason exists why any of these should not be included. I may be able to suggest some others; and also to suggest where articles not located may be found.[18]

Cordially,

1. Clarence Martin Lewis (1882–1934), a New York attorney specializing in lease law, had begun work on a collection of LDB's writings. Less than six weeks after this letter, however, he was killed in a hit-and-run accident in front of his house. The work was completed by his friend, Osmond K.

Fraenkel, and entitled *The Curse of Bigness*. See LDB to B. W. Huebsch, 18 November 1934.

2. "Liability of Trust-Estates on Contracts Made for Their Benefit," 15 *American Law Review* 449 (1881) was used; see LDB to Otto Wehle, 1 April 1879.

3. Samuel D. Warren and LDB, "The Right to Privacy," 4 *Harvard Law Review* 193 (1890–91) was used; see LDB to Alice Goldmark, 29 November 1890, n. 6, and to Samuel D. Warren, 8 April 1905.

4. *Financial Condition of the New York, New Haven & Hartford Railroad and of the Boston & Maine Railroad* (Boston, 1907) was not used; see LDB to Alfred Brandeis, 2 January 1908.

5. *Scientific Management and the Railroads* (New York, 1912) was excerpted from LDB's testimony before the Interstate Commerce Commission in the first Advanced Rate Case (see LDB to Robert M. LaFollette, 16 September 1910); it was not used.

6. *Jewish Rights and the Congress* (New York, 1916) was not used; see LDB to Louis Lipsky, 12 January 1916.

7. *The Jewish Problem: How to Solve It* (New York, 1915) (see LDB to Stephen S. Wise, 2 March 1915); *Zionism and Patriotism* (New York, 1915) (see LDB to Jacob deHaas, 14 November 1914); "Palestine and Jewish Democracy," *The Outlook* 112 (5 January 1916): 36–40 (see LDB to Lawrence F. Abbott, 6 December 1915); and "Proposed Palestine Policy"—the Zeeland memorandum (see LDB to Bernard Flexner, 15 September 1920) were all included in *The Curse of Bigness*. "A Call to the Educated Jew," *The Menorah Journal* 1 (January 1915): 13–19 (see LDB to Jacob Billikopf, 15 January 1915) was not.

8. There were two items marked "14": "The Solution of the Trust Problem: A Program," *Harper's Weekly* 58 (8 November 1913): 18–19 (see LDB to Norman Hapgood, 15 October 1913), and "The Living Law," 10 *Illinois Law Review* 461 (1916) (see LDB to George Rublee, 28 December 1915). Both articles were included.

9. Testimony before the Senate Committee on Interstate Commerce, *Hearings on Control of Corporations, Persons and Firms Engaged in Interstate Commerce*, 62nd Cong., 2nd Sess. (Washington, 1911), part 16, pp. 1146–1291, was not used; see LDB to A. W. Russell, 7 December 1911.

10. *Revenues of Rail Carriers in Official Classification Territory* (Washington, 1914). LDB's brief in the second Advanced Rate Case (see LDB to John H. Marble, 18 July 1913) was not used.

11. Again, due to a misnumbering, two items bear the same number, "18". One referred to several excerpts from the hearings following LDB's nomination to the Supreme Court; the other was "An Essential of Lasting Peace," *Harper's Weekly* 60 (13 March 1915): 259 (see LDB to Norman Hapgood, 19 February 1915), which was included in the final volume.

12. *Consolidation of Gas Companies and of Electric Light Companies* (Boston, 1905), LDB's brief in the Boston gas fight (see LDB to Edward R. Warren, 2 May 1904), was not used.

13. Testimony before House Special Committee, *Investigation of United*

States Steel Corporation, 62nd Cong., 2nd Sess. (Washington, 1912), 2835–2872 was not used; see LDB to Paul U. Kellogg, 26 July 1912.

14. Obviously an error on LDB's part; he had already listed "No. 30."

15. "Co-operation vs. Cut-throat Competition," *Harper's Weekly* 60 (12 June 1915): 573–74, was originally a speech delivered before the National Rivers and Harbors Congress in Washington on 9 December 1914; it was included.

16. "Banker Management, Why It Has Failed: A Lesson from the New Haven," *Harper's Weekly* 58 (16 August 1913): 14–15 became ch. 9 of *Other People's Money* and was not included.

17. "Interlocking Directorates," *Annals of the American Academy of Political and Social Science* 57 (January 1915): 45–49 was reprinted in *Business—A Profession,* 320–28 and was omitted from this volume.

18. A number of additional items were selected and then grouped in seven areas: Savings Bank Life Insurance, Industrial Democracy and Efficiency, Curse of Bigness, Railroads and Finance, Zionism, Public Service, and the Law. All told, thirty-eight articles, speeches, letters, and portions of testimony were included, together with appendices listing other written material by LDB.

To Elizabeth Brandeis Raushenbush

April 20, 1934 [1] Washington, D.C. [EBR]

DEAR ELIZABETH: Paul Freund [2] was in today. Says Frances Perkins and Senator [Robert F.] Wagner are working on the President to come out for the bill; [3] that Frances Perkins will undertake to control Tugwell [4] (who has Epstein [5] proclivities) and Harry Hopkins [6] and thinks she can.

1. Although the manuscript copy is dated 20 October 1934, both Elizabeth and Paul Raushenbush, who supplied this letter, are positive that the date must have been March or April of the same year.

2. Paul Abraham Freund (b. 1908) had been LDB's clerk during the 1932–33 term, after which he joined the Justice Department where he served in a variety of positions. He joined the Harvard Law School faculty in 1939, and he has been Carl M. Loeb University Professor since 1958. Freund is widely regarded as one of the country's leading authorities on the Supreme Court.

3. See next letter.

4. Rexford Guy Tugwell (b. 1891) taught economics at Columbia University from 1920 to 1933, after which time he became involved in President Franklin D. Roosevelt's "brains trust." During the early part of the New Deal he was undersecretary in the Agriculture Department, and after 1937 he served in a variety of government posts, including governor of

Puerto Rico. He has written a number of books on the Roosevelt administration and on Latin American policy.

5. Abraham Epstein (1892–1942) was executive secretary of the American
Association for Old Age Security; he was promoting a program that would
have provided every old person in the country with a pension.

6. Harry Lloyd Hopkins (1890–1946) had been a social worker in New
York when he met Franklin Roosevelt, and he quickly became first the governor's, and later the President's closest advisor on relief matters. Hopkins
was federal administrator of emergency relief in the early days of the New
Deal, and then he headed the immense Works Progress Administration.
From 1938 to 1940 he was Secretary of Commerce, then head of Lend
Lease; and during World War II he went on numerous overseas missions
for Roosevelt. See Robert E. Sherwood, *Roosevelt and Hopkins* (New York,
1948).

To Elizabeth Brandeis Raushenbush

April 22, 1934 Washington, D. C. [EBR]

DEAREST ELIZABETH: For you, Paul and Walter, our best wishes
for the birthday, wishes for another twelve months as fruitful as
those just closing.

It is still believed that the Lewis-Wagner bill will be passed at
this session. If it is, even with the tax-rate reduced, a long step
forward will be taken; and you and Paul will have your hands
full for the next two years, at least.[1]

As you may have imagined, I see little to be joyous about in
the New Deal measures most talked about, N.R.A. and A.A.A.
seem to be going from bad to worse.[2]

Bob made a good fight on the tax bill, but, even if enacted, as
passed by the Senate, the advance will be woefully small.[3]

I am glad Paul is to have Arthur Altmyer's aid,[4] at least for a
while. A. A. would be wise if he stayed at home.   Lovingly,

1. After months of planning, the advocates of the Wisconsin system of
unemployment compensation (see LDB to Harold J. Laski, 28 February 1932,
and to Elizabeth Raushenbush, 19 September 1932 and 16 September 1933)
had developed a proposal for a national system, which was introduced in
Congress by Senator Robert A. Wagner and Representative David J. Lewis
of Maryland. The heart of the plan was an ingenious tax system devised by
LDB, a payroll tax on employers with the provision that in those states
where employers were already contributing to state funds, the amounts involved could be deducted from the federal tax. Under this system, states

could establish unemployment compensation programs without new costs to handicap industries involved in interstate commerce. There were minimum standards established, but each state had considerable leeway in which to experiment. The Wagner-Lewis bill was gaining support in Congress, much to the discomfiture of the President; see LDB to Elizabeth Raushenbush, 8 June 1934.

2. Both the National Recovery Administration and the Agricultural Adjustment Administration were products of the New Deal's first Hundred Days, in which the Roosevelt administration had attempted to act on a number of fronts. The results were often half-thought-out proposals drawn up in a sloppy manner. The NRA attempted to impose some order on industry with a variety of codes fostering cooperation, provisions for labor recognition, and exemption from the antitrust laws. It represented the resurgence during the early years of the New Deal of the New Nationalism wing of progressivism. The entire NRA was already foundering in bureaucratic mismanagement when the Supreme Court unanimously ruled it unconstitutional in *Schechter* v. *United States*, 295 *U.S.* 553 (1935). LDB, of course, opposed the NRA concept for its emphasis on bigness and consolidation and its evasion of antitrust safeguards.

The Agricultural Administration Act attempted to support farm prices by restricting production and paying farmers not to grow crops or raise livestock, and financed the plan through a tax on food processors. In *United States* v. *Butler*, 297 *U.S.* 1 (1936), the Court, speaking through Justice Owen J. Roberts, struck down the law as an unconstitutional use of the taxing power through the general welfare clause. Justice Harlan Fiske Stone, joined by LDB and Mr. Justice Cardozo, entered a powerful dissent accusing the Court of disallowing the act simply because it did not agree with Congress's interpretation of what constituted the general welfare. The major provisions of the AAA were reenacted by Congress in the Soil Conservation and Domestic Allotment Act of 1936 and the Agricultural Adjustment Act of 1938.

For the economic philosophy underlying these two acts, as well as the growing debate within New Deal circles over opposing views of recovery, see Ellis Wayne Hawley, *The New Deal and the Problem of Monopoly: A Study in Economic Ambivalence* (Princeton, 1966).

3. In the debate over revising income tax rates, Senator Robert M. LaFollette, Jr., had attempted to get the base raised from four to six percent, and the surtax range increased up to seventy-one percent. The final bill increased the base to five percent, and the upper limit on surtaxes was set at fifty-nine percent. LaFollette was more successful, however, in securing his proposal for a larger estate tax. Although known ultimately as the Wealth Tax Act of 1935, the bill was far from progressive. See William E. Leuchtenburg, *Franklin D. Roosevelt and the New Deal*, 152–54.

4. Arthur Joseph Altmeyer (1891–1972) had a long career in governmental service. Coming up through the Wisconsin system in the 1920s, Altmeyer was appointed chief of the compliance division of NRA (see note 2,

above). After 1935, he was moved from an assistant secretaryship of labor into the Social Security system. He served as chairman of the Social Security Board from 1937 to 1946. See his own book, *The Formative Years of Social Security* (Madison, Wisconsin: 1966).

To Frank Albert Fetter

May 24, 1934 Washington, D. C. [Fetter Mss]

DEAR PROFESSOR FETTER: [1] I hope you have already started on the book.[2]

As bearing upon the efficiency of small units, the enclosed story of Savings Bank Insurance will interest you. Last year the system had a larger gain in "insurance in force" than any company's Massachusetts business. The Metropolitan wrote probably 50 times as much business, but was second in gain in "insurance in force."

Sometimes "the race is not to the swift." [3]   Cordially,

1. Frank Albert Fetter (1863–1949), after retiring as chairman of the department of economics and political science at Princeton University, had gone to the University of Illinois. He wrote on numerous economic problems.

2. Fetter was then at work on *Democracy and Monopoly* (Princeton, 1939).

3. ". . . nor the battle to the strong." Ecclesiastes 9:11.

To Elizabeth Brandeis Raushenbush

June 8, 1934 Boston, Mass. [EBR]

Strictly Confidential

DEAR ELIZABETH: Don't be discouraged by the President's message.[1]

He summoned me yesterday & when I reached him at 4:45 P.M. he had in his hand his message & started in to read it to me. When he came to the part on social insurance, I stopped him, told him it was all wrong, & for about ¾ hours discussed that question & I think convinced him of the error. He said the message had already gone to the Capitol & it was too late to change that; but it would not commit him as to means, etc. I have left some efficient friends in Washington, who are to work for the true faith during the summer.[2]

Trip good & weather fine here.

From small clipping enclosed it looks as if the Walker-Lewis [sic] bill has passed in the House.[3]

1. With sentiment in both houses of Congress growing in favor of both an old-age assistance program as well as some form of unemployment compensation, and since the Wisconsin advocates had the only plan already in operation, there was pressure to adopt it on a national scale. Many critics of the Wisconsin plan, however, felt that a larger pool was necessary, and that unemployment compensation should be established as a general insurance program. Among the critics were Paul Douglas of the University of Chicago (see LDB to Morris L. Cooke, 18 April 1930, n. 3), who argued that mass unemployment, created by conditions beyond the control of a single company, required a comprehensive approach. Although President Roosevelt had by now tentatively endorsed the Wagner-Lewis bill (see LDB to Elizabeth Raushenbush, 22 April 1934), he still had his doubts, and rather than be pushed into this plan, he asked Congress on 8 June to delay further action until the fall, and then to combine unemployment compensation with a sweeping program to provide for "the security of the men, women and children of the nation." He proposed three areas for action: housing, land and water use, and social insurance against unemployment and old age. The latter would be national in scope, with the states meeting a large share of the management costs and the federal government investing, maintaining, and safeguarding the reserves. The full text of the President's speech is in the *New York Times*, 9 June 1934.

2. Three weeks after delivering his message, Roosevelt appointed a Cabinet Committee on Economic Security, chaired by Secretary of Labor Frances Perkins, and charged the members to come up with a program prior to the reconvening of Congress at the beginning of December. This committee heard a number of proposals, and defenders of the Wisconsin plan argued their case forcibly. For details of their work and the resulting Social Security and unemployment programs, see Arthur M. Schlesinger, Jr., *The Coming of the New Deal* (Boston, 1958), 301–307.

3. The Wagner-Lewis bill did not pass the House.

To Stephen Samuel Wise

June 13, 1934 Chatham, Mass. [Wise Mss]

S.S.W.: Yours dated May 29, postmarked June 6, reaches me here.

1. The Bernstein views show how deeply perverted is German Jewish judgment.[1] I hope Palestine will purify the refugees.

You evidently made some impression on B. Jacques Loeb[2] said he favored assimilation; and, in answer to my enquiry as to how long it would take, answered: "10,000 years." I told him we couldn't wait so long. I hope the purification of the German Jews won't take so long.

2. Compare with Father Coughlin's[3] talk the praise of Jews by Cardinal McConnel [sic][4] of Mass. at his 50th anniversary ceremonies.

3. I am glad Jerome Michael has talked to [*]. Give him my greetings.

4. Even Neville Laski[5] and Montefiore[6] are seeing the light.

1. See LDB to Stephen Wise, 21 November 1935.

2. Jacques Loeb (1859–1924), the head of physiological studies at the Rockefeller Institute, had arranged for LDB to meet with Albert Einstein during the Wiezmann-Brandeis controversy in 1921. See LDB to Regina Wehle Goldmark, 1 March and 27 April 1921.

3. Father Charles Edward Coughlin (b. 1891), whose rise to fame rested on his demagogic appeals to the poor over the radio, had been growing increasingly anti-Semitic. See Charles J. Tull, *Father Coughlin and the New Deal* (Syracuse, N.Y., 1965).

4. LDB probably meant Bishop Francis John McConnell (1871–1953) of the Methodists, who had served as a minister in various Massachusetts parishes until his election as a bishop in 1912.

5. Neville Jonas Laski (1890–1969), Harold's brother, was a lawyer and judge in Great Britain. Long active in Jewish affairs, he was president of the Board of Deputies of British Jews from 1933 to 1939 as well as chairman of the administrative committee of the Jewish Agency.

6. Claude Joseph Goldsmid-Montefiore (1858–1938), a biblical scholar and philanthropist, had been heavily influenced by two of his teachers, Benjamin Jowett of Balliol College, Oxford, and Solomon Schechter. Montefiore was active in promoting Reform Judaism but did not take any part in Zionist affairs.

To Huston Thompson

June 23, 1934 Chatham, Mass. [Thompson Mss]

DEAR HUSTON THOMPSON: It is good to get your letter. But bear in mind that in canoeing I have enjoyed not only floating down streams. Paddling up them was also a feature.

Cape Cod has no water power needing protection. But its power of attraction is such that we shall hope to see you and Mrs. Thompson here some day.   Cordially,

To Henrietta Szold

June 24, 1934 Chatham, Mass. [H. Szold Mss]

DEAR MISS SZOLD: Among things Palestinian which give concern are reports of a growing tendency on the part of a few to luxurious living and ostentation.

Observance of the simple life should, of course, be among those "unwritten ordinances" the transgression of which bring, as Pericles said, "admitted shame."

The transgressions are said to be most frequent among newcomers. Doubtless you, with the co-operation of others like minded, could make the transgressors realize that, as the British say, "it isn't done." I hope you will agree that the effort would be worthwhile.[1]   Cordially,

1. This unsolicited advice brought the following reply from Miss Szold, who had just returned from Germany where she had undertaken a project to resettle Jewish children in Palestine: "The tendency toward luxuriousness may well, as you write, cause us concern. Unfortunately, it is not the only cause for concern. . . . Many of us have long been unhappy. We are disappointed in ourselves, that we have not risen above the level of these parlous times. And we have no prophets. . . . And of me you expect such influence upon 'transgressors' as will make them mend their ways. I can see myself doing nothing but what I have been doing all along—keeping at the tasks my life here has set me and performing them as best I can. . . . Beyond that circle—it is a contracted circle—my voice does not reach. I am grateful for your note with its assurance that your great heart and mind are ever with our people. Why shouldn't *you* speak to their conscience publicly as you write to me personally?"

To Julius Simon

July 5, 1934 Chatham, Mass. [Brandeis Mss, M 18–1]

DEAR JULIUS SIMON: Re yours of 2d.

First: I answer "No" to the several proposals;[1] and with a conviction even stronger than when we discussed the matter two years ago, because of present conditions.

1. The present high cost of building makes any loan perilous unless the increased cost of building is compensated for by an equivalent decrease in the percentage loaned on the property. That is, you ought not to loan now more than 45 percent of the cost, on a project on which before the building boom and labor shortage you would have been willing to lend 60 percent.

2. I think your aim should be rather to make loans at a lower rate of interest than to increase the volume of your loans, however desirable increase in volume is. The prevailing high rate of interest, like the present high building costs, are apt to prove disastrous. That is, if on your loans you can, by insisting upon a large equity provided from the borrower's own funds, get such good security that you can afford to lend at a cost to the borrower of say 5½ percent, you would render a great service to all Palestine. I think you should also introduce, if not already done, the practice of monthly payments, not only of interest but in reduction of principal. The P.E.C.'s function should remain, as it has been, primarily educational.

3. I think the P.E.C. should not borrow, or give preference to any money of others; that it can and should confine itself to the administration of American (or Palestinian) money; that it should avoid loans for construction of industrial buildings; and should not aid in the erection of apartment houses—a regrettable form of housing. The P.E.C. should confine its house building aid to the construction of workingmen's houses, modest in character, located on land sufficient in quantity for the growing of their own vegetables, etc, and this should be true of urban (and suburban) as well as rural homes.

4. There may be justification in requiring life insurance as added security; but when it is done, the insurance should be of the cheapest form; that is straight life or even term insurance. Endowment insurance is an unduly heavy burden. Instead there should be installment payments as suggested above.

Second: Morrison made a good impression. His varied experience here and his legal training should prove of distinct value; and the desire to settle in Palestine, in spite of adequate occupation here, is distinctly in his favor.   Cordially,

---

1. One of the purposes of the Palestine Economic Corporation was to finance mortgages on residential and commercial property in Palestine. The

P.E.C. loans were granted primarily on potential return for the development
of Palestine, rather than on potential for profit.

To Mark deWolf Howe

July 25, 1934 Chatham, Mass. [Howe Mss]

DEAR MARK HOWE: [1] It was good of you to write me of the Justice.[2] More recently, comes the report from Prof. Morris Cohen
of his talk with you, which gives assurance that the well-being
has continued.

Please give the Justice our love. Tell him that with us all goes
well despite an endless inflow of certioraries; and also that our
efforts to improve the mind do not exceed the limits set by his
own sweet reasonableness.

With every good wish,   Cordially,

1. Mark deWolfe Howe (1906–1967), the son of the famous Boston biog-
rapher, had just served as secretary to Justice Holmes; he would later be
professor and dean at the Buffalo University Law School and, after 1945,
professor of law at Harvard. His most lasting contributions, however, were
in his work on Holmes. He edited the *Holmes-Pollock Letters*, 2 vols. (Cambridge, 1941), the *Holmes-Laski Letters*, 2 vols. (Cambridge, 1953), and the
Civil War diary. He had completed two volumes of a definitive biography
of Holmes before his own death.

2. Although Holmes had originally protested to Frankfurter that it made
no sense for the professor to continue sending secretaries to him after his
retirement from the bench, Frankfurter had persisted in doing so; and
after the death of Mrs. Holmes, the elderly justice welcomed the company
of the younger men, who read to him and assisted in his correspondence.

To Stephen Samuel Wise

August 9, 1934 Chatham, Mass. [Wise Mss]

S.S.W.: 1. Since writing you, yours of 29th from Geneva has
come.[1] It shall go to J.W.M[ack]. and copies to Felix [Frank-
furter] and your children, as requested.

2. Your session with the potentates should prove definitely
helpful. Pressure wisely applied will, if persistent, overcome the
obstructions; and pressure from distinguished freedom-enjoying
Americans who are fully informed and care much must make a
deep impression.

3. I am very glad you urged the opening of Tranjordania.[2]

4. Yesterday's J[ewish]. D[aily]. B[ulletin]. report that 55 percent of the German Jews who entered Palestine during the last year were of the Capitalist class, is a strong argument for granting many visas to workers.[3]

5. The Algeria incident re-inforces (if the report of what motivated the act of a drunken Jewish soldier is true) the need of every Jew's recognizing that his wrongdoing is apt to injure the whole Jewish people.[4] We must make all see that each is constantly in the show-window; and that because of existing prejudice each must act as trustee for the whole people. Of course, this imposes an unduly heavy burden upon the individual Jew. But that burden has become inevitable for Jews. Perhaps in private talks you may have a chance in pressing this upon our European friends. Best wishes.

1. Wise was in Geneva for one of the three preliminary conferences that would ultimately lead to the establishment of the World Jewish Congress in 1936. The organization, which Wise led until his death in 1949, replaced the Comité des Délégations Juives created at the Paris Peace conference in 1919, and it had representatives from more than thirty countries.

2. Various Jewish organizations, including the Zionists, were urging Great Britain to rescind orders prohibiting Jewish settlement east of the Jordan; see also LDB to Emanuel Neumann, 27 January 1933.

3. British restrictions on immigration following the furor over the Passfield White Paper (see LDB to Rennie Smith, 29 October 1930) allowed for unhindered entry of so-called "capitalists" who owned property or had cash of a certain value. The Zionists argued that such "capitalists" created the economic conditions that would absorb and support additional workers beyond British quotas.

4. On 6 August rioting had broken out in Constantine, Algeria, which left one hundred people dead and over three hundred injured. The trouble began when a drunken Jewish soldier named Eli Kalifa allegedly staggered into a mosque at prayer time and started cursing the worshippers. Bands of Muslims then swept into the Jewish quarter, and Jewish groups fought back.

To Leila E. Colburn

August 22, 1934 Chatham, Mass. [SBLI]

DEAR MISS COLBURN: Please advise Mr. Talmage Grady:

1. I have examined all of the papers in Miss Grady's correspondence cabinets and have destroyed all the confidential let-

ters; [1] and, with few exceptions, all her letters and most of mine, preserving only such as seemed to contain matter appropriate for S[avings].B[ank].I[nsurance]. files or memos for S.B.I. use.

2. There are many enclosures—papers sent by Miss Grady to me or by me to her—which, not being confidential, ought to be preserved. These I sent you yesterday by Mr. [Judd] Dewey. And I also sent by him all of the Cabinets.

3. I have retained some memos as to which I will write you later in connection with S.B.I. work.

4. I have also retained some S.B.I. clippings which I sent Miss Grady for the scrapbook. These I will have inserted in the scrapbooks which you sent me in May.

5. I am glad to hear from Mr. Dewey that the moving was done yesterday. My best wishes for the new Offices.

6. When will you leave on your vacation & when do you plan to return?

1. LDB's longtime private secretary and lieutenant on Savings Bank Insurance matters, Alice H. Grady, had died on 19 April 1934. She left instructions that her correspondence with LDB be destroyed; but before carrying out that wish, her brother Talmage Grady thought it best to have LDB look through the papers and save those he thought worth preserving. LDB undertook this task during the summer, while at Chatham.

To Arthur W. Sampson

September 6, 1934 Chatham, Mass. [SBLI]

DEAR MR. SAMPSON: [1] Re your weekly report of Sept 4.

1. Your report on speaking engagements is encouraging. I am convinced that the plan of getting into personal touch with officers and influential members of trade organizations will bring large results if persisted in. None should escape us.

2. In connection with the first chapter of the book, Mr. Stoddard [2] will be amused by enclosed copy of letter of Walter Wright to me, May 22, 1906, which suggests that the early volumes of the insurance trade journals may furnish much by way of prophecy which would be interesting.

3. You doubtless noticed in Sept 1st Boston Herald (Report of First Natl B[an]k bulletin) that July/34 ordinary life insurance

written in New England was 4 percent less than July/33. The
S[avings]B[ank]I[nsurance] writing was over 50 percent more
in July '34 than in July '33 (Miss [Leila E.] Colburn can give
you the data.) Isn't that "news"?

4. I am to be in Boston next Tuesday on my way to Washington;
and shall be glad to see you, Mr. Stoddard and Mr. Fellows [3] at
the Bellevue at 3 P.M. if convenient.   Cordially,

1. Arthur W. Sampson was the Executive Secretary of the Savings Bank
Insurance League.

2. William Leavitt Stoddard (1884–1954) combined careers in business
(chiefly public relations) and writing. A close associate of both A. L. Filene
and Arthur W. Sampson, Stoddard also served as Executive Secretary of
the Savings Bank Insurance League. He had talked about writing a book on
Savings Bank Insurance. The book never appeared, possibly because there
was little need after Alpheus T. Mason's full study of the Massachusetts
system, *The Brandeis Way*, appeared in 1938.

3. J. William Fellows was treasurer of the Massachusetts Savings Bank
Insurance League.

To Robert Szold

October 7, 1934 Washington, D.C. [R. Szold Mss]

DEAR BOB: With a view to a partial solution of our American
problems, I want to give to a non-Jewish friend in the Agricultural Department a picture of the social economic life and institutions of the Palestine agricultural colonies; and particularly of
the part played by small land owners, the co-operative societies,
workingmen's semi-subsistence home-steads etc. & the aim of converting every laborer into a self-employer.

A student could pick it out of The New Palestine; but there it
is too involved with the Jewish Question, etc.

Can you send me some literature which will serve?

In any event, send me a copy of the Manchester Guardian supplement. Isaac Hamlin of [the League for] Labor Palestine,
Bouckstein, the J[ewish]. N[ational]. F[und]. or Hadassah all
may be able to make suggestions.

To Benjamin W. Huebsch

November 18, 1934 Washington, D. C. [Huebsch Mss]

DEAR MR. HUEBSCH: [1] Your courteous letter and the books have come.

You and Mr. Fraenkel have done your parts uncommonly well. I hope the sales will not prove disappointing.[2]   Cordially,

1. Benjamin W. Huebsch (1876–1964) had been publisher of *The Freeman* before establishing his own publishing house, the Viking Press.
2. Upon the death of Clarence Lewis in May 1934, Osmond Kessler Fraenkel (b. 1888) had completed the editing of *The Curse of Bigness*. See LDB to Lewis, 21 March 1934.

To Arthur W. Sampson

December 7, 1934 Washington, D.C. [SBLI]

DEAR MR. SAMPSON: 1. I note with satisfaction matters reported under date of Dec 4.
2. Special effort should be made through intercession of members of the Exec. Com[mit]tee to gain favorable entrance into the leading printing Establishments, e.g.

Riverside Press
Norwood Press
Little Brown & Co. — Atlantic Monthly.

4. [*sic*] Say to Mr. [A.L.] Filene and Mr. [W.L.] Stoddard that in a recent talk with a Fera man [1] of consequence, I learned that the Federal relief in Mass. (which is one of the 3 States in which the Government acts directly through its own officers & agents) is so badly administered that a special investigation is being made. By getting in touch with the proper person, there is a good chance of putting a stop to waste of welfare funds in Industrial Insurance.

1. The Federal Emergency Relief Administration (FERA) was established in May, 1933, to make grants to states and cities. Harry Hopkins administered the agency.

To Julian William Mack

[December 1934] Washington, D. C. [Wise Mss—AJA]

I consider DeH[aas]. the maker of American Zionism. You will recall that I felt it so strongly in the past that when in Jan. 1919, there came the clamor abroad for Americans and I feared the effect here of losing DeHaas and others, I thought he, as the pre-eminent maker of our institution ought to have the right to over-ride my judgment and imperil it, if he was strongly of opinion that he was more needed abroad. I also considered that DeHaas has served the cause with extraordinary single-mindedness and devotion, and that his thinking has been extensive and deep and right in a large percentage of instances. [Bernard] Flexner, I think, underrates his past service, and this largely because he has seen him intimately only during a period when he was not at his best. The hostility developed during the past two years has, par-ticularly in the past twelve months, impaired the value of his ser-vice, partly in paralysing effort, partly in deflecting his judgment.

I consider DeH. still a very valuable man, and find difficulty in seeing, even with a much reduced organization, how the machine will run well without his all-round helpfulness, particularly with Flexner away. But I realize also that a high degree of hostility to DeHaas in the organization would render him ineffective and might make him more of a disadvantage than advantage. Naturally the hostility, involving as it does ingratitude and in many cases real disloyalty to the cause, has irritated DeHaas and has made him irritate others even more than before.

If DeHaas wants to go to Palestine as a private citizen and he and his family are willing to go there and live simply, I shall be glad to contribute liberally to a modest capital to enable him to do so. I deem the living simply of himself and family a necessary condition because I consider it an essential of personal success and an essential of those conditions of living under which alone we can establish a worthy self-supporting community there.[1]

Please show this to Flexner, [Stephen S.] Wise, Felix [Frank-furter] & [Robert] Szold, unless you see reason to the contrary.

1. See LDB to Mack, 3 January 1932; despite repeated talk of moving to Palestine, deHaas remained in the United States.

To E. J. Schneider

February 11, 1935 Washington, D. C. [Brandeis Mss, M 16–2]

DEAR MISS SCHNEIDER: There has been such an accumulation since last summer of material which should be made promptly available to the faculty and to the students (New Deal, Germany, Palestine, etc.) that I am sending you today 4 cartons by railway express.

Kindly acknowledge receipt and notify Miss [Fannie] Brandeis.
Cordially,

To Arthur W. Sampson

February 12, 1935 Washington, D.C. [SBLI]

DEAR MR. SAMPSON: I am glad to hear that the Feb 7th meeting was promising and, among other things, that a drive in the Colleges is in contemplation.

Please let me know, as of March 1 —
1. How many colleges (or universities) there are in Mass.
2. How many have opened their doors to S[avings].B[ank]. I[nsurance].
3. How many you have secured since Sept 1/34.
Cordially,

To Hattie Bishop Speed

February 27, 1935 Washington, D. C. [Speed Mss]

DEAR MISS HATTIE: Alice and I are sending you two albums which may be of interest to the Museum. One is by Max Band of Paris, whose paintings secure much favorable comment; [1] the other, drawings by Hiam Lipschitz [sic] of Palestine.[2]

Our best wishes for you and Jenny.   Cordially,

1. Max (Mordecai) Band (b. 1900), a Lithuanian-born artist, was then living in Paris; he later took up permanent residence in California. Band's best-known works are portraits of Holocaust survivors, especially Jewish children. Band had personally inscribed a copy of Paul Fierens, *Max Band* (Paris, 1935), to LDB and Mrs. Brandeis, "with deep admiration and in happy remembrance of my visit to their home."

2. The gift consisted of twenty-seven unbound black-and-white reproductions of paintings by Haim Lifshitz on the Book of Job.

To Stephen Samuel Wise

March 19, 1935 Washington, D. C. [Wise Mss]

SSW: I am very glad you spoke on Jabotinsky and spoke as you did. It should serve to clear the air.[1]

You will care to have, if you have it not, the following quotation selected as the motto for [Jan] Smuts' Rectorial Address at St. Andrews (Oct. 17, 1934):

"We fight not for glory, nor for wealth, nor for honor, but for that freedom which no good man will surrender but with his life"

(From the Arbosath Manifesto sent by the nobles and commons of Scotland to the Pope in 1320)

I am glad, too, that you resumed your natural position as President of the American Jewish Congress.[2]

1. Beginning the previous fall, Wise had become an outspoken critic of Vladimir Jabotinsky's Revisionist Zionist program (see LDB to Julian W. Mack, 20 July 1930, n. 2) which Wise claimed was essentially fascist and alien to the democratic spirit of Judaism and of Zionism. See, for example, Wise to Jabotinsky, 29 October 1934, Wise Papers–AJA.

2. Wise had resigned as head of the American Jewish Congress in 1929 in order to give some of the younger men an opportunity for leadership. As the Nazi menace increased, there arose a demand that he once again take charge; and he was reelected president of the Congress on 17 March (which was also his birthday) and retained the office until his death in 1949.

To Hattie Bishop Speed

March 20, 1935 Washington, D.C. [Speed Mss]

DEAR MISS HATTIE: Alice and I are sending you for the Museum, under another cover, an album of "Paintings and Drawings" by A. Walkowitz of New York.[1]

To you and Jennie our best wishes.   Cordially,

1. Abraham Walkowitz (1880–1965), *One Hundred Drawings* (New York, 1925); the book was inscribed from the artist to LDB.

To Elizabeth Brandeis Raushenbush

March 26, 1935 Washington, D.C. [EBR]

DEAREST ELIZABETH: Your Mother who is taking a half-day rest bids me send you enclosed picture.[1] Senator Black [2] is more bold & pertinacious than wise.

Things look none too well, here & in the country. The folly of Mr. Wallace's restriction program [3] is being seen now in the cotton price drop & development of growing elsewhere; and the cancelling of spring wheat restrictions for this year is impressive.

"But the world's wise are not wise,
Claiming more than mortals may."

Your Mother is, I think, as well as usual in spring; but constantly impatient of the limitation on the use of legs.

I guage from Tom C[orcoran]'s [4] report of talk with Witte [5] and with Ray Moley [6] (& other things) that the Social Security legislation is giving much pain; and that Madame Secretary [7] is an obstacle to concessions to lovers of the Wisconsin plan. I shall not be sorry if all unemployment legislation goes over to 1936.[8]

My greetings to your son.

1. LDB enclosed a clipping from the *New York Times* of 26 March 1935 showing him, together with Chief Justice Hughes and Mr. Justice Van Devanter testifying against a bill sponsored by Senator Hugo Black (see next note) which would have allowed appeal of injunction cases from lower federal courts directly to the Supreme Court.

2. Hugo LaFayette Black (1886–1971), an Alabama lawyer, represented that state in the United States Senate from 1927 to 1937, when he was appointed to the United States Supreme Court, where he served for thirty-four years until his death. Black created a furor at the time of his appointment when he admitted that at one time he had been a member of the Ku Klux Klan, but he went on to be one of the most liberal judges in the Court's history.

3. In an attempt to raise farm prices, Secretary of Agriculture Wallace imposed production restrictions on a number of crops. See LDB to Norman Hapgood (Excerpts), 9 August 1935 (the Hapgood excerpts begin at 15 June 1935).

4. Thomas Gardiner Corcoran (b. 1900), after graduating from Harvard Law School, clerking for Justice Holmes, and practicing law in New York City, came to Washington, D.C. in 1932. He soon became a New Deal "insider," and with Ben Cohen, drafted and helped to pass many key pieces of New Deal legislation.

5. Edwin Emil Witte (1887–1960) had served as secretary of the Wisconsin Industrial Commission and then chief of the Legislative Reference Li-

brary before being appointed to key positions on the state's Planning and Labor Relations boards in the mid-1930s. He also taught economics at the University of Wisconsin from 1920 to 1958. He was involved with the Raushenbushes in establishing unemployment compensation; see his *The Development of the Social Security Act* (Madison, 1962).

6. Raymond Moley (1886–1975) taught government and public law at Columbia from 1923 to 1954, and also contributed a column to *Newsweek* for over three decades. Moley had done some work in criminal justice, and had collaborated with Felix Frankfurter in the Cleveland study. He became a member of the Roosevelt Brains Trust; for his evaluation of the New Deal, see *After Seven Years* (New York, 1939).

7. Secretary of Labor Frances Perkins.

8. According to Mrs. Raushenbush, by late April her father was reassured that the Wisconsin plan of experience rating would survive. The unemployment compensation plan was passed as part of the Social Security Act, and signed into law by the president on 15 August 1935. See LDB to Elizabeth Raushenbush, 30 April 1935.

To Stephen Samuel Wise

April 11, 1935 Washington, D. C. [Wise Mss]

S.S.W.: 1. My congratulations to Justine [1] (and her parents) on her report.[2] Some day I hope there will be a chance of talking to you and her of the causes of our discontent (they are not the act of God or the public enemy) and "what we must do to be saved."

2. My thanks for your "As I see it." [3] Other Americans, also, have much to learn about Liberty and Democracy. As Justice Holmes used to say: "It's the obvious that most needs teaching."

4. [*sic*] Yes, I remember well the talk referred to in yours of 10th & also the Sunday telephone talk near the same time.[4] Jonah Wise [5] must have given pain to some of the die-hards of his committee. But others have been driven to see that Palestine is the only hope. I guess James Rosenberg (who called here on 8th) and George Naumberg [6] (who called on the 9th) are of that opinion. They are getting little cash.

5. Rosenberg thinks the time is now ripe for "Unity"; & I think we should make it easy for them to adopt our policies.

6. Thanks for Israel Cohen's story.[7]

1. Justine Wise Tulin Polier (b. 1903) was then an assistant corporation counsel in New York City. Later in 1935 she was named justice of the Do-

mestic Relations Court and she served there until 1962. During her tenure she was influential in reforming the court into an instrument for rehabilitation and reconciliation; from 1962 until 1973 she was a judge of the New York State Family Court. Since retirement, she has directed the juvenile justice project of the Children's Defense Fund.

2. Mrs. Tulin, as counsel to the Mayor's Committee on Relief, had written the final report and recommendations of that group, and her father had sent the document to LDB.

3. In Wise's column, "As I See It," *Opinion* 5 (March, 1935): 22, he attacked those American leaders who refused to take Hitler and Nazism seriously, believing that if left alone the danger would simply disappear.

4. In several letters written during these years, Wise recalled to LDB a dramatic conversation that took place in LDB's study on 11 March 1933. Wise, with others, had come there prior to visiting the German ambassador to express concern about developments in Germany. During the conversation, LDB said: "The Jews must leave Germany." As events conspired to substantiate fears, Wise always marvelled that LDB had enunciated that drastic position a mere six weeks after Hitler attained power.

5. Jonah Bondi Wise (1881–1959), the son of Isaac Mayer Wise, had been the successor to Stephen Wise (no relation) as rabbi for the Beth Israel congregation in Portland, Oregon, in 1906; he served there until he became rabbi of the Central Synagogue in New York in 1926. In 1931–32 he had been national chairman of the Joint Distribution Committee fund drive.

6. George Washington Naumberg (1876–1970) was a member of the well known banking family. He was active in political affairs and in philanthropy, especially child welfare. He was also a leader in Jewish philanthropy, serving as a director of the Joint Distribution Committee, and as head of the Federation of Jewish Philanthropies' finance committee.

7. Israel Cohen had issued a revised edition of *The Progress of Zionism* (London, 1935); originally published in 1929, the book would eventually go through eight editions.

To Elizabeth Brandeis Raushenbush

April 30, 1935 Washington, D.C. [EBR]

DEAREST E. Thanks for the Phil [LaFollette] speech. F.D. [Roosevelt] told a friend of ours a month ago that the Senate must amend the [Social] Security bill so as to let Wisconsin Act survive—because he had promised this to Bob.

To Elizabeth Brandeis Raushenbush

June 7, 1935 Washington, D. C. [EBR]

DEAREST ELIZABETH: It's fine you making such good progress on the book,[1] & I hope your students will pass the exam.

Tell Paul to "Stick like Spaulding's glue." [2]

I am trying through the faithful and efficient here to prevent F. D. [Roosevelt]'s [sic] from falling into social worker error.[3]

Enclosed from Lincoln Filene.

We are due to leave this P.M.   Lovingly,

1. Mrs. Raushenbush was working on her half of the third volume of John R. Commons's *History of Labor in the United States*. Her contribution dealt with labor legislation.

2. Paul Raushenbush was trying, through Senator LaFollette, to get the House-passed Social Security bill amended to permit "experience rating" in state unemployment compensation laws—a major feature of the Wisconsin legislation (see LDB to Harold J. Laski, 28 February 1932).

3. i.e., treating unemployment compensation like "relief."

Excerpts of Letters to Norman Hapgood [1]

[Roosevelt Mss]

[June 15, 1935]

If F. D. [Roosevelt] carries through the Holding Company bill [2] we shall have achieved considerable toward curbing Bigness —in addition to recent advances.

[July 4, 1935]

I am glad of your talk on F. D. R., of which the N. Y. Times brings report.[3] F. D. can have no doubt about Big Business now.[4]

[July 16, 1935]

3. "Bigness" is waning in many fields:
   a. Preeminently in agriculture, except in Russia. Reshaping Agriculture, by Wilcox (of Ohio State College), with foreword by Alvin Johnson, thinks we shall come to very small farms intensively cultivated.
   b. Some say we have built our last sky-scraper.
   c. Clearly in the railroad passenger service, the light cars and small train will dominate and in local freight.
4. As to business (Billy's comment),[5] the Government's huge

spending, coupled with six year obsolescence, must feed retail trade; and to some extent even capital goods.

[July 22, 1935]

F. D. is showing much wisdom—e.g. in what he said of corporation gifts to charity [6] and what he did re Virgin Island imbroglio . . . .[7]

You ought to have no difficulty in getting underwriting for your bet with David Lawrence.[8]

August 2, 1935

F. D. is making a gallant fight and seems to appreciate fully the evils of bigness. He should have far more support than his party is giving him; and the social worker-Progressive crowd seems blind as in 1912.

[August 6, 1935]

Lippmann's piece is worse than stupid. It, the House performance, the disclosures made in Washington, and the public's lack of indignation show how deep and widespread is the demoralization of our people and how real the need of political education.

August 9, 1935

2. Yours 3rd and 7th recd. Of course the income tax should, like the British, take in the lower brackets. But beware of Walter Lippmann.

3. F. D. gives evidence of appreciation of the irrepressible conflict with Bigness, and of growing firmness.

4. The Lobby investigation [9] is showing up the lawyers, as are the decisions on applications for rapacious fees in reorganizations.

5. It is a question whether lawyers or life insurance are nearer the needed public investigation . . . .

7. The large cotton crop and the small crop of hogs is giving Wallace additional troubles.[10]

[August 24, 1935]

2. Dorothea N.'s from Sion City, Mich. gave an impressive notion of the hideousness of the Ford irregularity of employment. An inheritance tax potent to destroy that fortune would be a ground for rejoicing, not for the tears David Lawrence is ready to shed.

3. F. D. is showing fine fighting qualities.

[November 28, 1935]

As to the political outlook:—This is certainly a period which must give concern to F. D. and his following—Liberals as well

as Democrats. Happily for F. D., it is nearly twelve months before election day.

And happily also, the enemy has neither a leader nor measures.

1. During the latter part of 1935, Hapgood corresponded frequently with
President Roosevelt, providing him with information on a variety of topics.
He also served as one conduit by which LDB advised the President on
policy matters. The following excerpts are taken from *verbatim* quotations
forwarded by Hapgood in his letters to Roosevelt; unfortunately, all of
the originals have vanished.

2. The transition from the so-called "First New Deal," which attempted
to establish Theodore Roosevelt's ideas of regulating and promoting big
business to the "Second New Deal," which followed LDB's views on
breaking up big combinations, is often dated from the introduction of the
Wheeler-Rayburn Public Utilities Holding Company Act in March 1935.
The big fight over the bill was whether or not all holding companies would
have to be disbanded by 1940, the so-called "death-sentence clause." Under
intense pressure from utilities lobbies, the Congress refused to follow the
President in his insistence that the death-sentence clause be included, and
in the end Roosevelt had to accept a compromise that would allow one
layer of holding companies above the operating plants. But he did win the
battle to eliminate "pyramiding," whereby one holding company could own
others, and all could issue stock based on no capital assets. See Arthur M.
Schlesinger, Jr., *The Politics of Upheaval*, 302–06, and Leuchtenburg, *Roosevelt and the New Deal*, 154–57.

3. Hapgood had predicted that Roosevelt would be overwhelmingly reelected in 1936. "The country does not wish to go back to the attitudes of
Harding, Coolidge and Hoover." See *New York Times*, 3 July 1935.

4. Referring to the extensive lobbying effort of the utilities to defeat the
death-sentence clause (see n. 2 above).

5. Norman's brother William had written wondering when business
would begin purchasing again; many of the industries around Indianapolis
were deferring purchases since they believed prices would have to decline
further.

6. In the debate over the new tax bill, Roosevelt had opposed a provision
that would have allowed a tax exemption of up to five percent of income
for corporate gifts to charity. The provision had the endorsement not only
of business, but of many organized charities as well.

7. Maladministration in the Virgin Islands had led to a conflict between
Secretary of the Interior Ickes, who had administrative responsibility for the
islands, and the Senate Insular Affairs Committee, which exercised Congressional oversight. Both sides agreed that a personnel shake-up was necessary,
together with an extensive investigation; but they fought over who would
do it. FDR managed to find a compromise whereby he replaced a number
of local officials and got the two parties to work together in the investigation.

8. Hapgood had bet a dollar with conservative columnist David Lawrence

(1888–1973) that Roosevelt would be reelected in 1936. Lawrence, formerly a reporter for the Associated Press and then editor of the *U.S. Daily*, had founded *U.S. News* in 1933; in 1946 he started the *World Report* and the following year merged the two into one weekly news journal. His columns appeared there regularly and at one time were picked up by more than three hundred newspapers.

9. In response to the massive lobbying of the private utility companies against the Wheeler-Rayburn bill (see note 2 above), both houses of Congress had launched investigations into the lobby and its financing.

10. Henry Agard Wallace (1888–1965) was Roosevelt's Secretary of Agriculture from 1933 to 1940 and Vice-President of the United States from 1941 to 1945. At that time, moderate and conservative Democrats forced Roosevelt to take Wallace off the ticket because he was too liberal, some would even have said too radical. Wallace was a sympathizer of the Soviet Union in the early forties, and in 1948 he led a third-party campaign on the platform of peace and understanding with the Soviets. See Edward L. and Frederick H. Schapsmeier, *Henry A. Wallace of Iowa: The Agrarian Years, 1910–1940* (Ames, Iowa, 1968), and *Prophet in Politics: Henry A. Wallace and the War Years 1940–1965* (Ames, Iowa, 1971). Wallace, under the Agricultural Adjustment Act, had been attempting to secure a reduction in farm production in order to raise prices. A bumper crop nearly destroyed the program, and in the end Wallace restored to a wholesale slaughter of of young pigs in order to keep them from flooding the market the following spring, an action that evoked much ridicule from New Deal opponents.

To Robert Szold

June 23, 1935 Chatham, Mass. [Wise Mss]

DEAR BOB: —When I saw Ben Gurion in May, he told me, in a few words, of the Akaba project, and was to see me again with details.[1] I told him that I agreed that such a project is important and that I would contribute "a substantial amount". I have heard nothing from him since. S.S.W[ise]. wrote me recently enquiring (with a view to telling Ben Gurion) what amount I had in mind; and I answered that I thought it wiser not to fix the amount until I heard further from Ben Gurion as to details. Yesterday, I received from Felix [Frankfurter] the "secret" memo. of "New York June 4/,35" (9 pages) which you have doubtless seen.

You may say to Ben Gurion (or Ussischkin) that I will give for this purpose Twenty thousand (20,000) Dollars to the P[alestine].E[ndowment].F[und]. provided before Oct. 1, 1935, there is raised for this purpose in cash from others Eighty thousand (80,000) Dollars, so as to make up the full sum of the One hundred (100,000) Dollars named in the memo. of June 4, the title to the land to be in Jewish National Fund.

If you can get a copy of this letter to S.S.W. before he sails, please do so; if not possible, send him a copy to Palestine.

1. Ben-Gurion was among the first Zionist leaders to recognize the importance of the southern part of Palestine, together with a port on the Red Sea, to the future development of the Jewish homeland. He had been unable to get backing in this regard from the regular Zionist agencies, such as the Jewish National Fund, because they were putting all of their resources into purchasing arable land in the northern part of the country. Ben-Gurion convinced LDB of the necessity for a port in the south, and LDB made funds available for the purchase of land near the port of Akaba; subsequently, Ben-Gurion's vision was proven correct, and the port city of Eilat rose on the land acquired. See LDB to Stephen S. Wise, 4 September 1936.

To Arthur W. Sampson

August 2, 1935 Chatham, Mass. [SBLI]

DEAR MR. SAMPSON: Re your reports of July 23rd & 31st.
1. I am glad to note the [Savings Bank Insurance] League's greater activity, i.a. in connection with Labor Unions.
2. I hope you and Mr. [W.L.] Stoddard will arrange to be present at some of the meetings at which Mr. [Judd] Dewey, and others speak, and that soon both of you and Mr. Clark will begin to address meetings. As you know, thorough familiarity with S[avings].B[ank].I[nsurance]. and other insurance facts is essential to your full usefulness as League representatives; and nothing teaches a man as much as having not only the ability to tell the story but also that of answering, on your feet, the questions put.
3. Hope you will have good weather in Maine for your few day's vacation.   Cordially,

To Felix Frankfurter (Telegram)

September 13, 1935 Washington, D. C. [Brandeis Mss, SC 15–3]

I think highly of Fahey.[1] He exhibited in matters in which I had opportunity to observe him both fine public spirit and good judgment. He has been much educated by contacts in Chamber of Commerce and Public Franchise League as well as his own business.

1. Frankfurter, through Thomas G. Corcoran, had requested LDB's evaluation of John Fahey (see LDB to Fahey, 22 December 1910), then on the boards of directors of the Home Owners Loan Corporation and of the Federal Savings and Loan Insurance Corporation. While Fahey may have been under consideration for another federal position, he did not receive a new appointment until 1942, when he became commissioner of the Federal Home Loan Banking Administration.

To Elizabeth Brandeis Raushenbush

September 19, 1935 Washington, D. C. [EBR]

DEAREST ELIZABETH: You and Paul were wise in declining the Washington post.[1] "In die Beschränkung zeigt sich erst der Meister."[2]

I have sent Walter a map of the middle states found among my treasures. Now I am enclosing an envelope of stamps to be given him when you think it time to begin a stamp album. With his love of geography and of numbers it should come soon.

For Paul I am sending the quotation from Collier's of which I spoke.

You and he may be interested in the enclosed letter of President [Charles W.] Eliot.

Yesterday it was a fortnight since we left Chatham. It seems an age. At all events it seems as if we had always been here.

It's good to know that the index is so well advanced.[3] I might send you and Paul Eddie Berman's Bulletin No. 615,[4] but compassionately I refrain.   With love,

1. Arthur Altmeyer (see LDB to Elizabeth B. Raushenbush, 22 April 1934, n. 4), on behalf of the Social Security Board, had offered Paul Raushenbush a position in Washington, coordinating state unemployment compensation legislation. Mr. Raushenbush, who was running the Wisconsin program, remained in Madison.

2. "One must first show oneself the master of limited things." One of LDB's favorite quotations from Goethe, *Was Wir Bringen* (1802).

3. See LDB to Elizabeth B. Raushenbush, 7 June 1935, n. 1.

4. Edward Berman (1897–1938) was an economist with the Bureau of Labor Statistics; he had just written *The Massachusetts System of Savings-Bank Life Insurance*, United States Bureau of Labor Statistics Bulletin #615 (Washington, 1935). This document was later expanded into a book; see LDB to Bernard Flexner, 19 May 1936.

To Stephen Samuel Wise

September 20, 1935 Washington, D. C. [Wise Mss]

S.S.W.: Re yours of 9th.

It would be fine to see you Sunday the 29th at 9 A.M., or later in the forenoon. But you have many unavoidable tasks for the immediate future—and I want to be sure that you do not overburden yourself. My eagerness to see you will not grant less. We can have our talk at some later and more convenient date.

Take very good care of yourself.[1]   With best wishes.

1. See LDB to Wise, 17 March 1934.

To Edward Berman

October 13, 1935 Washington, D.C. [Berman Mss]

DEAR DR. BERMAN: The N[ew]. R[epublic]. article,[1] like No. 615,[2] is very effective. I am looking forward eagerly for the book.[3]

These figures, which Caldwell has just dug out, will interest you.

Net rate of interest earned in 1934:

	Total	Excluding Policy Loans
Equitable (N.Y.)	3.64%	3.13%
Mass. Mutual	3.82%	3.24%
John Hancock	3.64%	3.26%
Metropolitan	4.06%	3.79%
Savings Bank Insurance	4.53%	4.45%

With best wishes,   Cordially,

1. "Savings Bank Life Insurance," *The New Republic* 84 (16 October 1935): 263–65.
2. See LDB to Elizabeth Brandeis Raushenbush, 19 September 1935, n. 4.
3. See LDB to Bernard Flexner, 19 May 1936.

To Stephen Samuel Wise

November 21, 1935 Washington, D.C. [Wise Mss]

S.S.W.: First, let me thank you for your generous birthday greeting.[1]

Re yours of 20th. I saw Bruno Weil,[2] at Jacob Landau's[3] request. (Mrs. Weil, who speaks English somewhat better, was with her husband.) Weil made a most unfavorable impression on me. I did not suspect his motives. But I felt that he possessed the qualities and obtuseness of the German Jews, to the highest degree without any redeeming or relieving feature. I think of him as the strongest evidence of the German Jewish policy of assimilation.[4] Him, it has affected internally, no external evidence.

I am sure he had a most unpleasant time with me, as I told him frankly what I think about the folly of the German Jews & think there is no hope for anyone who does not emigrate. I can't say that he "took up" anything with me, with "Erstens etc,"[5] what he thought and hoped for. I listened, perhaps with patience, and then, for about 10 minutes, told him what I thought.

1. On 13 November 1935, LDB was seventy-nine years old.
2. Bruno Weil (1883–1961) was a Berlin lawyer and vice-president of the Centralverein. In 1932 he had been the only Jewish candidate for the Reichstag, and was defeated by Paul Josef Goebbels. In 1935 he was still advising German Jewry not to leave the Fatherland; by 1937 he had changed his mind and began a quest to seek sanctuaries for his compatriots. He was in France at the outbreak of World War II, and he came to the United States in 1940. He established the Axis Victims League, which after the war sought indemnity for confiscated or destroyed Jewish property.
3. Jacob Landau (1892–1952) was the founder and director of the Jewish Telegraphic Agency. In 1940 he would join with several American sponsors to create the Overseas News Agency.
4. See LDB to Wise, 13 June 1934.
5. "in the first place, etc."

To Edith Bolling Wilson

November 24, 1935 Washington, D. C. [Wilson Mss]

MY DEAR MRS. WILSON: It was lovely of you to let us know that you remembered the birthday.

Won't you let us have soon the chance for the talk we did not have on that day? Cordially,

To Paul Raushenbush

December 2, 1935 Washington, D.C. [EBR]

DEAR PAUL: My very best to you. Ernest Draper [1] asked what I thought of the Security legislation. I spoke of its heresies, and he agreed.[2]

I spoke to [Isador] Lubin about some compilations desirable to show the delinquencies of the Big Ones, in a way that would enable the ordinary man to appreciate the iniquities perpetuated. Perhaps we shall get the presentation.

Meanwhile, you are making the best possible use of your time in perfecting the Wisconsin implement.[3]

1. Ernest Gallaudet Draper (1885–1951), a food processing executive, served as assistant secretary of commerce from 1935 to 1938, after which he was named to the Board of Governors of the Federal Reserve System. In the early 1930s he had been active in New York on several programs dealing with the unemployed.

2. See LDB to Elizabeth Brandeis Raushenbush, 8 June 1934.

3. See LDB to Elizabeth Brandeis Raushenbush, 7 June and 19 September 1935.

To Stephen Samuel Wise

January 19, 1936 Washington, D. C. [Wise Mss]

S.S.W.: 1. In view of F[elix]. F[rankfurter].'s memo annexed (which please return) I must decline the proposed Hebrew University degree.

I thought (and still think) that the difference between taking American degrees and one from Palestine and the reasons for refusing the American ones are so clear that no one in America could feel hurt. But it is enough that F. F. thinks otherwise. We must run no risk of raising another groundless ground for Anti-Semitism. You will understand my appreciation of your wanting me to have the degree, and will, in due time, make your associates understand. The number of American degrees, east and west, which I have declined are many; & it would be impossible to reach all those whom F. F. thinks might misunderstand.[1]

2. It's fine that you had a good talk with F. D. [Roosevelt] I hope the southern trip was satisfactory.

1. Hebrew University officials had proposed an honorary degree to be presented on LDB's eightieth birthday, 13 November 1936. See LDB to Charles E. Clark, 12 March 1930.

To Raymond Asa Kent

January 27, 1936 Washington, D. C. [Brandeis Mss, M 15–1]

DEAR DR. KENT: Dean McClain wrote me recently that you expect to start work on the Law School building in the Spring. Last year when you and he called, you graciously said that you would like to give the building my name. As since then, the Supreme Court has come much into political discussion, it would be unwise to do so.[1]

Fine reports come to me of the School's development.[2]

1. Much of the controversial legislation enacted during the early New Deal had been challenged in the courts, and appeals had carried the cases to the Supreme Court. There, in a series of decisions often decided by five-to-four votes, conservatives had struck down the Agricultural Adjustment Act, the National Recovery Act, the Railroad Pension Act, and other bills that had much popular support, including a number of progressive state measures. The resentment generated against the Court would ultimately surface in Roosevelt's court-packing plan. See LDB to Henry J. Friendly, 1 April 1937.

2. See LDB to Bernard Flexner, 5 March 1938.

To Arthur W. Sampson

February 27, 1936 Washington, D.C. [SBLI]

DEAR MR. SAMPSON: 1. This clipping reminds me of the favorable notices we used to get from the B[oot] & S[hoe]. Recorder.[1] The trade papers rarely have insurance advertising & connections. Wouldn't it be wise to make a list of all the trade papers published in Mass. & see whether you can't arrange to get favorable notices from them. Mr. Harding could doubtless help.[2]

2. The 3 months (to Jan 31/36) S[avings].B[ank].I[nsurance]. statement of business written shows $4,000,896 as compared with $2,127,152 for the 3 months ending Jan 31/34.

Let Miss [Leila E.] Colburn give you the figures for the companies writing in Mass[achusetts] for the same 3 month periods—ordinary business.   Cordially,

1. LDB had enclosed an obituary of William L. Terhune (1850–1936), a pioneer in trade journalism. Terhune had founded the *Boot and Shoe Recorder* in 1882, and ran it until turning it over to his son in 1909.

2. Richard B. Harding was Secretary of the Committee on Savings Bank Life Insurance for the Associated Industries of Massachusetts.

To Arthur W. Sampson

March 15, 1936 Washington, D.C. [SBLI]

DEAR MR. SAMPSON: I note the failure to get the Berman Exhibit into the Central Boston Public Library.[1] But there are many branch libraries and I am sure that you could be as successful at each of them as you have been at Hyde Park, if you find the right man to help you in each district. Tell me through, and with whom you are working at each of the branches.

Cordially,

1. The Berman exhibit was a travelling array of photographs, charts, and other literature designed to state the case for Savings Bank Insurance. It was put together by Edward Berman (see LDB to Elizabeth Raushenbush, 19 September 1935, n. 4).

To Hyman Parker

April 17, 1936 Washington, D. C. [Parker]

DEAR MR. PARKER: [1] Re yours of 14th.

The need of good lawyers—learned, diligent, devoted to their clients and to the public, was never greater than it is today. The fact that one is a Jew and "without connections" is no bar to success. Be scrupulously honest; live simply and worthily; work hard; have patience and persistence; and don't measure success by the number of dollars collected. Waste neither time nor money.[2]

With best wishes,   Cordially,

1. Hyman Parker (1913–1975) was in 1936 a struggling law student; he ultimately went on to a distinguished career in labor law and rose to the directorship of the Michigan Employment Relations Commission.
2. See LDB to Parker, 23 April 1936 and 18 February 1938. The editors wish to thank Mr. Philip Slomovitz for his kindness in calling these letters to our attention and his diligence in uncovering the identity of their recipient.

To Willis VanDevanter

April 17, 1936 Washington, D. C. [VanDevanter Mss]

DEAR VAN: With my good wishes must again go a word of appreciation of your long years of service to our country and the Court.[1]

1. This was VanDevanter's seventy-seventh birthday. Although he and LDB were ideologically opposed on many legal issues, there seems to have been a special bond of friendship and respect between the two men.

To Arthur W. Sampson

April 22, 1936 Washington, D.C. [SBLI]

DEAR MR. SAMPSON: Re Mr. [W.L.] Stoddard's of 21st & your report of 17th.

1. If Mr. [A.L.] Filene and Mr. [Judd] Dewey agree, would it not be desirable to suggest Clement A. Norton for membership on the Board of Directors? [1]

2. I am glad to note speaking engagements made.

3. I trust that in the Chamber of Commerce Bldg. you will make many opportunities for converting your neighbors to S[avings].B[ank].I[nsurance].

4. I have noted in the past many instances of organizations which answered that their "program is filled". Would it not be desirable to make now a list of all trade, professional, educational, & similar associations which hold annual meetings & get the approximate date of such meetings with a view to getting in our request before the program is made up?   Cordially,

5. Has anything been done about getting Berman Exhibit into Cambridge libraries, or those of other suburban municipalities? [2]

1. Clement A. Norton was a member of the Boston City Council.
2. See LDB to Sampson, 15 March 1936, n. 1.

To Hyman Parker

April 23, 1936 Washington, D. C. [Parker]

DEAR MR. PARKER: Re yours of 21st.[1]

"Poor Jewish boys" have a great inheritance—the ability to pursue courageously a high ideal, patiently and unswervingly bearing the incidental hardships with confidence and resourcefulness.

Of course, "if your heart fails you, do not climb at all." [2] But that would be unworthy of your inheritance.[3]   Cordially,

1. Parker had written back (see LDB to Parker, 17 April 1936) that he thought there were extra handicaps in the career world facing "poor Jewish boys."
2. Attributed to Queen Elizabeth I, who wrote the words on a window pane immediately following an inscription by Sir Walter Raleigh: "Fain would I climb, yet fear I to fall."
3. See LDB to Parker, 18 February 1938.

To Stephen Samuel Wise

April 29, 1936 Washington, D.C. [Wise Mss]

S.S.W.: Re yours of 27.

1. You are indispensable here. Stay at your post.

2. I am delighted to learn from Rubashow [1] that the response is generous to the Emergency Call.

3. I told him that I could not attempt to influence F[elix]. F[rankfurter]. unless I know definitely the obstacles & was asked by him for advice.

3. I am glad to learn (from J[ewish]. T[elegraphic]. A[gency].) of Tel-Aviv's determination to build 1000 houses to house Jaffa refugees. It would be a great lesson if the Jaffa Arab leaders were left without tenants; the government offices established at Tel-Aviv; and a harbor for Tel-Aviv constructed.

---

1. Sh'neur Zalman Rubashow (later Shazar) (1889–1974), the product of a Russian Hassidic background, had been a journalist and poet, and in 1924 settled in Palestine, where he edited the influential *Davar* from 1925 to 1949. He was also active in Palestinian politics and in 1948 became Israel's first minister of education and culture. In 1952 he moved over to the Jewish Agency and in 1956 became its head. Seven years later he was elected to the first of his two terms as President of Israel, a post he held at his death. His writings include several volumes of essays and poetry as well as the autobiographical *Morning Star*, translated by Sulamith Nardi (Philadelphia, 1967).

To Arthur W. Sampson

May 3, 1936 Washington, D.C. [SBLI]

DEAR MR. SAMPSON: 1. I enclose check, $44.85 endorsed by me to [Savings Bank Insurance] League (the 1935 royalties—"Other People's Money"). I should like to have this sum applied to such advertising as Mr. [Judd] Dewey deems most advisable.

2. Wouldn't Mr. Forbes [1] help you to get the Berman Exhibit into the New Bedford public libraries? [2]

3. I was disappointed not to find in your Apr. 24 Report any new speaking engagements among labor unions. Would it not be desirable to prepare a list of all all [*sic*] unions in Mass[achusetts].—International, Central Labor Unions, and independent Unions; check off against the list those in which speaking engagements have been secured and set before yourselves the task ahead?

"Let no guilty man escape."   Cordially,

1. Probably Arthur Whitton Forbes (1868–1946), a New Bedford manufacturer and member of the Board of Directors of the Savings Bank Insurance League.

2. See LDB to Sampson, 15 March 1936.

To Bernard Flexner

May 19, 1936 Washington, D.C. [Brandeis Mss, I 7–1]

MY DEAR BEN: Do not fail to get—and read—promptly "Life Insurance, A Critical Examination" by Prof. Edward Berman of the University of Illinois—a thrilling book.[1] And tell of it to your financier associates (who run, but do not read).

The Equitable's return on investments in 1935 (excluding policy loans) was 3.07%.

S[avings]. B[ank]. I[nsurance]. 3.92%

S.B.I.'s April '36 writing was 30.07 percent over April '35.

1. The book was an expansion of the study Berman had done for the government; see LDB to Elizabeth Brandeis Raushenbush 19 September 1935, and to Berman, 13 October 1935.

To Paul Underwood Kellogg

May 24, 1936 Washington, D. C. [Kellogg Mss]

DEAR PAUL KELLOGG: Re yours of 23rd.[1]

I think your plan of treatment is fine; and agree William Hard would be the best man for the article and September or October the time for publication. Also, to Felix' suggestion of Judd Dewey, Lincoln Filene & James L. Richards (if you can get him) and Parkinson for the symposium. Bob Watt [2] of the Mass[achusetts]. AF of L would probably be the best labor man. By all means, get some one from one of the industrial companies also.[3]

As Judd Dewey is to be in the symposium, I should think Grossman would be preferable for the earlier review of the Berman book.[4]   Cordially,

1. Kellogg had written requesting LDB's advice on a plan suggested by Felix Frankfurter for a full-dress symposium on savings bank life insurance, featuring a major article with commentary by several noted authorities.

2. Robert J. Watt (1894–1947) came to the United States from his native Scotland in 1912. He soon became involved with labor organization, and for many years was secretary-treasurer of the Massachusetts State Federation of Labor. He also represented American unions in a number of conferences sponsored by the International Labor Organization.

3. In the end, the symposium failed to appear. Instead, Kellogg ran a major article by Beulah Amidon, "Other People's Insurance: Massachusetts' Savings Banks," *Survey Graphic* 25 (November 1936): 598–602. See LDB to Leila E. Colburn, 2 August 1936.

4. William L. Grossman, a journalist who had previously written on savings bank insurance for the *American Mercury*, did not review Edward Berman's book, *Life Insurance: A Critical Examination* (New York, 1936) for the *Survey*.

To Fannie Brandeis

May 27, 1936 Washington, D.C. [Brandeis Mss, M 4–5]

DEAR FAN: 1. Make sure whether the Library has the reports of the N[ational]. R[ecovery]. A[dministration]. "Division of Review." Those are the set of posthumous reports, embodying the results of the work of the N.R.A. & (to some extent) the effects of its discontinuance. These reports are not printed, they come in mimeographed form and are not distributed freely. But, I guess, a beguiling letter from you to Prof. L.C. Marshall [1] who is (or until recently was) "Director, Division of Review" may secure them. I sent one volume to H.B. Doury on the Ice business in the law shipment. And I will send one more, "Restriction of Retail Price Cutting etc" by Mark Merrill (nearly 450 pp) in the supplementary carton, which I plan to send Miss Schneider before we leave for Boston next week. You had better see these two volumes before you write Prof. Marshall; but write him promptly thereafter.

2. When Prentiss Terry was here recently he discussed with me plans for the Centennial celebration & projects for raising funds. I mentioned to him the proposal (discussed from time to time with you) of reaching the several sections of Louisville's population interested in the University by showing, through the Library Collections, the University's interest in them; and to that end holding on separate days, receptions, at the Library for the different groups. The suggestion appealed to him strongly, and he thought the first reception should be held early in 1937.

As a preparation for them, I think that all bindable material ought to be bound in some form (much inexpensive in boards, etc.); but it ought to be in form to be impressive, where it can be exhibited and its extent expressed in figures.

I suggest that, this summer, the Library force go over all the material to this end. I should be disposed to pay for the binding of such of the material as appears ready for binding before the fall term begins.

I hope you had happy times in Michigan.

1. Leon Carroll Marshall (1879–1966) had held a professorship in political science as well as two deans' positions at the University of Chicago from 1907 to 1928, after which he became visiting professor at several schools as well as a private consultant. During 1935 and 1936 he headed the National Recovery Administration's internal review program.

To Stephen Samuel Wise

June 2, 1936 Washington, D. C. [Wise Mss]

S.S.W.: Re yours of May 29th. In my opinion:

1. Magnes is wholly wrong.[1] We have in Ben-Gurion and Shertok practical leaders of great ability, men of understanding, vision and wisdom rare in government. We should give them unqualified, ardent support.

2. Melchett[2] is right in stressing the importance of a harbor at Tel Aviv. My thought is that we should assume we are getting one; and stress its development.

3. I do not think we should stress its development to the exclusion of other objectives. Among other things, the drive to transfer the two million Jews, to which he refers, should be persisted in—of course in such ways as seem wise, as he suggests.

4. What Dizengoff[3] said the other day about the Jaffa harbor workers is of general application. The Arab workers must be taught, whether it be harbor workers at Jaffa, or plantation workers in the colonies, or produce farmers, that it is only through cooperation with the Jews that the golden stream can be secured. When they learn that; when Arab landlords are tenantless; and employees of the government find subsidies and salaries ending through their own malfeasance, the way to peace & cooperation will be found.

Ed. Kaufmann [4] was in on 29th. He got no satisfaction. We plan to leave for Boston & Chatham June 4. Your letter goes to Felix [Frankfurter].

1. Judah Magnes, then chancellor of the Hebrew University, had over the previous decade become increasingly worried over tensions between Arabs and Jewish settlers in Palestine. In 1929 he had founded the controversial B'rit Shalom, which sought peace between the two groups and advocated the creation of a binational state in Palestine. More recently Magnes had criticized some of the younger Palestinian leaders who were urging greater self-reliance and a tougher stance against Arab depredations. Among those he attacked were David Ben-Gurion and Moshe Shertok.

2. Henry Melchett, the second Baron Melchett of Landford (1898–1949), was a British industrialist who shared his father's Zionist sympathies. After the rise of Hitler, he formally adopted Judaism as a personal faith in practice, and he became active as chairman of the Council of the Jewish Agency.

3. Meir Dizengoff (1861–1936) had settled in Palestine early in the century after representing Russian industrial interests there. He became active in Tel Aviv municipal government, and in 1921, when the city was granted independent municipal status, he was chosen as its first mayor, a position he held almost continuously thereafter until his death. Much of the credit for Tel Aviv's growth and prosperity could be traced to the plans laid down by Dizengoff in the late twenties and early thirties.

4. Edmund Isador Kaufmann (1886–1950) was a businessman who had been introduced to Zionism by LDB and Stephen Wise. In 1940 he was elected president of the Zionist Organization of America, but the demands of the time proved greater than his abilities. He was also a cofounder of the United Jewish Appeal, and he served as its national chairman.

To Leila E. Colburn

June 3, 1936 Washington, D.C. [SBLI]

DEAR MISS COLBURN: 1. From my talks with individual S[avings].B[ank].I[nsurance]. policy holders whom I meet, from time to time, I find them quite ignorant of the progress being made by S.B.I.—and, indeed, of the relative advantages of S.B.I. over company insurance; and I am sure we don't get the full benefit of "satisfied customers." I wonder whether it would not be profitable to send to each individual who is a policy-holder, making sure that no person gets more than one however many policies he has, some publications—i.e. the 1936 Brief Survey or something else, which will make him understand; and presumably talk to others about S.B.I.

I assume we could arrange to have this done without added cost for postage, by putting the publication with the single check for the year's dividends which is in contemplation.

If Mr. [Judd] Dewey, Mr. Casady [1] & the actuaries approve of the suggestion, the cost can, of course, be readily figured.

If the policyholder has the requisite minimum of knowledge of S.B.I. & is told of its present rapid growth, a very few words should suffice to induce him "to cooperate".

2. Say to Mr. Dewey that I had on May 30 a talk with our old friend (and policyholder) John Lambert which may bear fruit.

3. Also that I have sowed some seed in Congressional & Executive quarters which may sprout into an irresistible demand for an investigation of Industrial insurance after Jan 1/37.[2]

3. [sic] Ask Mr. Casady to let me know to what extent banks have called the attention of their depositors to S.B.I. by slips in passbooks; and with what result so far as tried.

4. Tell Mr. Dewey & Mr. Casady that I had a talk with Mr. John H. Fahey yesterday, with a view to his having his Worcester paper undertake a definite campaign on S.B.I. to continue until some Savings Bank at Worcester established an Insurance Department. My suggestion was that it should begin with a review of the Berman book,[3] followed regularly with more ideas; that to this end Mr. Casady should see his editor, arrange the campaign, & keep in constant touch with him. Mr. Fahey approved of the idea, said he expected to be in Mass. within 10 days or a fortnight, wanted to see Mr. Casady first, and asked that Mr. Casady write him to his residence here (The Shoreham Hotel) his home address & house telephone so that he could be reached other than in office hours. This had better be done promptly to clinch the matter.

Hope to see you Friday.

1. Clyde S. Casady was the Supervisor of Agencies for the Savings Bank Insurance system.

2. There seems to have been no significant federal investigation of industrial insurance, as LDB predicted.

3. See LDB to Elizabeth Raushenbush, 19 September 1935, n. 4, and to Bernard Flexner, 19 May 1936.

To Israel Benjamin Brodie

July 10, 1936 Chatham, Mass. [Brodie Mss]

DEAR ISRAEL BRODIE: My thanks for your letter of the 7th with enclosures.

Yes, Palestine Jews are behaving finely; and the Administration very badly. We must help all we can. My confidence is unshaken.[1]

That was a fine letter of Naomi's.[2]

1. Following the Mufti's call for a general strike in Jerusalem, there had been a rash of riots incited by the Arab Higher Committee. The Mandatory government initially seemed confused over what course of action to follow, but eventually the High Commissioner called in an additional 20,000 British troops and quelled the disturbances. His Majesty's Government then suspended all immigration into Palestine pending further investigation (see next letter and LDB to Stephen S. Wise, 4 September 1936.

2. Naomi Brodie Daskow was one of Brodie's daughters.

To Julius Simon

July 31, 1936 Chatham, Mass. [Brandeis Mss, M 18–1]

DEAR JULIUS SIMON: 1. Welcome to America, but I hope you will be able to return soon to Palestine where you are needed. In proceedings before the Commission,[1] America's deep interest, the home of the greatest body of Jews in any country of the world, must be borne in upon the Commission. I have talked with Bob Szold and Brodie of this & what we ought to do. And I am writing Bob further on this subject.[2]

2. My thanks for yours of 30th with enclosures. As Bob has doubtless told you, I have great confidence in Ben Gurion, and also in Shertok as his associate. You will recall that I had occasion to observe the operation of Shertok's mind when he was editing the English Davar, which I am anxious to have continued[3]

3. I am very glad that [Nehemiah] DeLieme feels so strongly against any agreement to limit immigration other than that of the "absorptive capacity." And the more I have studied Jewish performance, present and past, the more inclined I am to accept Ben Gurion's "faith in the Jewish people which will overcome seemingly insurmountable difficulties."

1. In the wake of Arab rioting (see preceding letter), the British government sent still another investigating commission to Palestine. See LDB to Robert Szold, 12 July 1937.

2. See LDB to Robert Szold, 5 September 1936.

3. See LDB to Bernard Flexner, 22 November 1930 n. 2, and to Robert Szold, 18 January 1931, n. 1.

To Leila E. Colburn

August 2, 1936 Chatham, Mass. [SBLI]

DEAR MISS COLBURN: Please tell Mr. [Judd] Dewey:

1. Beulah Amidon, associate editor of the Survey Graphic, who is preparing the article on S[avings].B[ank].I[nsurance]., was here yesterday & Friday for conferences. I have told her to see Mr. Dewey and others at the office. She had already familiarized herself with much of our literature.[1]

2. Sidney E. Wolf [*sic*] is a New York cotton broker, friend of Jack's & Susan's, has visited them with his wife, from time to time, in Chatham. I talked S.B.I. to him & sent him literature. He told me on July 26 that he had concluded to form a League to secure a law in N.Y. I did not discourage him, because, as I wrote you recently, I think it may be helpful in Mass[achusetts]. to have agitation in other States. But Wolff has no conception of the difficulties in his path. He wrote to the League asking whether it could help him. [W. L.] Stoddard sent me copy of the letter. I wrote to [Arthur W.] Sampson that the League should answer that it can not aid in securing legislation in another State, but to tell Wolff that he should come to Boston and confer with you and others. Also not to discourage him, but to say nothing to him except what may be said to any insurance company man; that while I consider him absolutely honest & public spirited in the matter, he is so inexperienced and innocent of [insurance] company wiles that an insurance man might get from him any thing he knows.[2]   Cordially,

1. Beulah Amidon, "Other People's Insurance: A Social Invention of Louis D. Brandeis," *Survey Graphic*, 25 (November 1936): 598–602. See LDB to Paul U. Kellogg, 24 May 1936.

2. Sidney E. Wolff (d. 1951) did, in fact, move quickly to establish the

Savings Bank system in New York. By 1940, LDB was calling Wolff "the man chiefly entitled to credit" for the New York adoption of the scheme (see LDB to Paul A. Palmer, 26 January 1940).

To Stephen Samuel Wise

September 4, 1936 Chatham, Mass. [R. Szold Mss]

SSW: Your letter of the 1st and two letters of second have come.

1) You have performed a marvellous feat—nothing more important for us has happened since the Mandate, perhaps nothing so important as to make clear to Great Britain America's deep interest and particularly F. D. [Roosevelt]'s and Hull's views. I hope it will be possible to have these embodied promptly in an aide memoire or otherwise in conformity with diplomatic practice and submitted in that form to the British government. It will show that F. D.'s administration "means business"; and will be a record for the future.[1]

2) Felix telephoned me about counsel. I think he is right in not taking the risk. If it can be made clear to the British what F. D. thinks, that will have more effect with the British government than the most emphatic legal opinion of all American lawyers.

3) The letter to P[alestine].E[ndowment].F[und]. with the $5,000. check had been mailed to P.E.F. before your letters arrived. As I wanted New York to be in a position to send funds promptly to support confidence (in case of adverse action in London). As soon as I got your letter of the 2nd I wired to P.E.F. to hold the proceeds subject to your order. Do not hesitate to call on me for further funds if there is need.

4) Ussishkin's consuming zeal to corral all funds for J[ewish].N[ational].F[und]. is most commendable; with that zeal should naturally go disappointment at not getting the $20,000. But he was not entitled to be angry. Money was sought by Ben Gurion for Akabah.[2] It was given with the understanding that only part of the 100,000. would go into the land and that much of it would be fond perdu.[3] When Akabah became impossible, it seemed to me that the cause demanded that the funds be put at Ben Gurion's disposal. If, as we hope, the way is clear, the Akabah project is revived, I shall be glad to consider a gift specifically to

help that project; and so far as money goes into land, it will of course be Jewish Natl. Fund.

5) I hope you will be able to snatch a few days of rest. Will write you to New York of other matters.

6) We plan to leave here Wednesday the 9th, to be in Boston at the Bellevue on the 10th and 11th and are due in Washington on the 18th.

7) I could see Max, Prof. Kelsen in Washington.[4] But the schedule in Boston is already filled.

Bob Szold writes that he understands the telephone to [Ambassador Robert W.] Bingham was "that the American government would regard suspension of immigration as a breach of the Mandate." Your letters do not say that. I hope Bob is right. If so, the aide memoire should embody that statement.

1. Wise had been in Europe when he heard about the suspension of immigration into Palestine (see LDB to Israel B. Brodie, 10 July 1936, n. 1), and he had hurried to London to join other Zionist leaders protesting the decree. Upon his return he had secured an interview with President Roosevelt, and he persuaded him to intervene with the British. After consultation with Secretary of State Hull, the President directed the State Department to inform the British that the United States "would regard suspension of immigration as a breach of the Mandate." Prime Minister Stanley Baldwin realized that by a small gesture he could placate both the Zionists and the American government and, the day before the scheduled suspension was to go into effect, announced that until the Peel Commission submitted its report (see LDB to Robert Szold, 12 July 1937), there would be no change in Palestinian policy.

2. See LDB to Robert Szold, 23 June 1935.

3. "secret fund."

4. Hans Kelsen (1881–1973) had been professor of law at the University of Vienna from 1911 to 1929 and afterwards had held appointments at the universities of Cologne and Prague until forced out by the Nazis. He eventually came to the United States, first as Holmes Lecturer at the Harvard Law School, and then as professor of political science at Berkeley from 1942 until 1952. Kelsen was a widely recognized authority on international law.

To Robert Szold

September 5, 1936 Chatham, Mass. [R. Szold Mss]

DEAR BOB: *First:* In preparing the American case [1] you and Brodie should develop fully the following:

America's deep interest does not rest only upon the fact that:

(a) U. S. has the largest Jewish population of any country.

(b) U. S. has large investments in Palestine.

(c) U. S. has expended there vast sums, particularly in the early formative period, in fonds perdus.

The intensity of America's interest and its depth of feeling about British action is due in part to the fact that:

(1) we gave support to the proposed Balfour Declaration in advance, at British solicitation;

(2) we gave support, largely at British solicitation, to the appointment of Britain as Trustee (as then called) of Palestine.

Gather the support for these two propositions which must be in the files of F[elix]. F[rankfurter]., S[tephen]. S. W[ise]., [Jacob] deHaas, Provisional Zionist Com[mit]tee, American Jewish Congress. Possibly also J[ulian]. W. M[ack]. files. There are papers on the subject also in my Palestine files of (1917 to 1922) which have been deposited with the Library of the University of Louisville (where I established a Palestine-Judaica Library and which has most of my Zionist books and documents) the files not to be examined except with my consent during my lifetime. Wise's associate, Rabbi Morton Berman,[2] asked permission, last spring, to examine my files in preparation of a history of Zionism in America. I referred him, in the first instance to deHaas, who has more of my letters than anyone else. The Rabbi expressed a readiness to go to Louisville to examine my files. If he does so, he can make the search there for you. But I should think files available in the East would furnish you adequate confirmation of the correctness of the propositions. Surely F. F., S. S. W., deH and J. W. M. will recall (i.a.) the extent to which our Zionist communications came through the British diplomatic bags and wire facilities; and how extensively we acted in cooperation with them.

Second: A special feature of the preparation for a special purpose is the following:

A full, and fully supported, statement should be prepared of the losses to American investors and American institutions in Palestine—and of personal injuries suffered by Americans, if any —in the course of Arab riots and revolt.[3] This should be done with a view to presenting, at the proper time, the claims through the Department of State by the usual diplomatic procedure. The liability to make compensation to foreigners, victims of riots, is so generally recognized that this obligation can hardly be questioned, particularly as the Jews were denied leave of self defense; and the opening which Wise has marvellously secured for us should enable us to act promptly when once the data are at hand. Britain should be made aware through every legitimate means of the shortcomings of the local administration.

The failure of the British to make prompt compensation to the Palestinians seems to me even more reprehensible than its failure to suppress the incipient & developing revolt. Fear, and a supposed unpreparedness, coupled with bad judgment, may account largely for its failure to give protection. But its failure to make compensation—despite the bulging treasury of the Mandatory— has been not only unfair but mean and perhaps worse. Of course, the failure to make compensation may have been due also to fear. I hope there was no element in it of desire to weaken the Jewish economy and to break the Jewish spirit. Certainly, the attitude of the Mandatory in its refusal to take care of the refugees to Tel-Aviv and Jerusalem—many of them from places ordered evacuated,—the exactions made as a condition of appointing Jewish guards, and its attitude in regard to other financial burdens, afford evidence of an attitude in painful contrast to its generous treatment of the Arabs.

Third: Let S. S. W. tell you particulars of the interview referred to in memo of March 2/19, Exhibit A. annexed. My recollection is that it was deemed important in Paris that we should get then a public expression of opinion from President Wilson. (You will recall how brief was his stay here). F. F. can doubtless tell you about the Paris end. See Exhibit B. annexed, from his letter of March 3/19. The Feisal-Frankfurter letter shows also that America was not "a mere passenger." [4] As recalling the condition of the country in 1918 let F. F. show you Ormsby Gore's letter to him of April 24, 1918. And generally as to Ormsby Gore's ideas, let deHaas show you Gore's address to the London Political Committee on August 16, 1918.

Fourth: The following has no special bearing on America's case. You have doubtless noticed recently the several instances in which Palestine Courts have acquitted defendants because of what the Court said was inadequate preparation of the case by the Arab prosecutor. It might well have been desirable not to have Jews as prosecutors; or even British as the sole prosecutors. But to have employed only Arabs—in spite of the declarations of the Arab officials in their formal communications to the Mandatory is another of the administration's amazing acts. It may come [in] handy some day to have available the data as to the cases in which the Court criticized the preparation.

Please send S. S. W. and F. F. a copy of this letter.

A.

In a memo. of Dr. Wise on an interview Mar. 2, 1919 with President Wilson at the White House, Sunday afternoon March 2, 1919—(at which Louis Marshall, and B. G. Richards were present) appears the following:

The President: You may quote me as having said: 'As for your representations touching Palestine, I have before expressed my personal approval of the declaration of the British government regarding the historic claims of the Jewish people in regard to Palestine. I am, moreover, persuaded that the Allied Nations, with the fullest concurrence of our own government and people, are agreed that in Palestine shall be laid the foundations of a Jewish Commonwealth.'

B.

On March 3, 1919, Felix wrote me of the session "before the Council of Ten—the Big Five" on the preceding Thursday (while Felix was in London)—that the following occurred while Weizmann was presenting the main argument:

"*Secretary Lansing:* Perhaps you can tell us, Dr. Weizmann, what you mean by Palestine as a National Homeland of the Jewish people.

Dr. Weizmann: I mean the creation of such conditions,—governmental, economic and social—as will result in the immigration of some 50,000 Jews into Palestine year by year, who should settle on the land to work the land and to become self supporting so that in course of time and by the inevitable process of natural development there will be such a culture, such a Jewish Life in Palestine as to make Palestine as distinctively Jewish as England is English or France is French. Have I made myself clear?

Secretary Lansing: Perfectly, Dr. Weizmann, perfectly."

1. For presentation to the British commission investigating the Arab riots in Palestine, see LDB to Israel B. Brodie, 10 July 1936 and to Szold, 12 July 1937.

2. Morton Mayer Berman (b. 1899) served as assistant rabbi to Stephen Wise at the Free Synagogue from 1929 to 1937, during which time he was also director of field services for Wise's Jewish Institute of Religion; from 1937 to 1957 Berman was rabbi of Temple Isaiah Israel in Chicago. He then moved to Israel, where he headed the department for English-speaking countries of the Keren Hayesod until his retirement in 1967. He did not write a history of American Zionism.

3. These points were all incorporated into *Memorandum Submitted to the Palestine Royal Commission on American Interests in the Administration of the Palestine Mandate* (New York, 1936), which was signed by all of the major American Zionist organizations.

4. See LDB to Julian W. Mack, 9 October 1929, n. 3.

To Stephen Samuel Wise

September 5, 1936 Chatham, Mass. [R. Szold Mss]

SSW: 1) The following (in which Hadassah has a special interest) will doubtless be taken up in due time by our friends in Palestine and London; but I think some action on your part may at the proper time be desirable. See Chairman Youth Aliyah [1] p. 4 of Shertok's interview with H[igh]. C[ommissioner]. [2] August 7, 1936. Note that already in March His Excellency had in mind limiting the Aliyah, that is before terrorism and riots began. [3] Surely immigration of the children was not to be limited on grounds of "absorptive capacity" and there were then no disturbances. On what grounds could he legally limit or stop the immigration of youth who are guaranteed not to become public charges?

2) The visit of the three senators to Palestine would seem to have been peculiarly opportune; and Copeland's announcement that they would prepare a report to be submitted to Congress

important.[4] I presume you will see him on his return and also Isaac Don Levine.[5] I have never taken up with Levine specifically Palestine matters, but in talks with him on American subjects he left a distinctly favorable impression.

3) I suppose you will, when time serves, see the Levin-Kaplan brothers,[6] as to whose non-action Dr. [Israel] Goldstein has doubtless reported to you. I add merely that when Kaplan saw me in Washington February it was agreed that he would see me in Chatham for a full report. I have never heard from him since his visit to Palestine.

1. In 1933, Recha Freier (b. 1892) inaugurated a program to remove German Jewish children to Palestine. Within a short time, Henrietta Szold became interested in the idea, and then Hadassah became the official sponsor of Youth Aliyah in the United States. Through the efforts of this organization, twenty thousand children were saved from Hitler's death camps. The program continued long after the defeat of the Nazis, however, and Youth Aliyah has been responsible for transporting, training, and rehabilitating over 135,000 children since its inception. See Marlin Levin, *Balm in Gilead* (New York, 1973), ch. 10.

2. Sir Arthur Grenfell Wauchope.

3. See LDB to Israel B. Brodie, 10 July 1936.

4. Three United States senators—Royal Samuel Copeland of New York, Warren Robinson Austin (1877–1963) of Vermont, and Daniel O. Hastings (1874–1966) of Delaware—had sailed for Palestine in early August at the invitation of Jewish authorities to examine conditions in the Holy Land. Upon their return in late September, they praised Jewish efforts to reclaim the land and urged Great Britain to provide more support to the Yishuv; they did not, however, file any formal report.

5. Isaac Don Levine (b. 1892), a Russian-born journalist, wrote many articles and books on Russia; he arranged and guided the senatorial tour (see preceding note).

6. Two half brothers, Maurice Levin and J. M. Kaplan, had jointly pledged $50,000 to the United Palestine Appeal in May 1936; evidently they had not yet fulfilled their pledge, or had failed to do further work requested of them by LDB.

To Robert Szold

October 5, 1936 Washington, D.C. [R. Szold Mss]

DEAR BOB: I have written Dr. [Stephen S.] Wise that, in view of the present emergency, I have concluded to cumulate my Palestine gifts and send thirty thousand (30,000) during the next three months, which is probably the crucial period, sending $10,000 a month to the Jewish Agency.

I am enclosing check for $10,000 and will probably send the balance soon if funds can be made available.[1]

Please hold the proceeds until I hear from Dr. Wise whether special disposition is desirable. Cordially,

Has Dr. Wise decided disposition of the $5000 sent in September. My thanks for the good wishes.

1. According to Professor Mason, LDB gave nearly a quarter million dollars to Zionist activities from 1935 to 1939. See LDB to Szold, 4 March 1937.

To William Allen White

October 13, 1936 Washington, D. C. [White Mss]

DEAR WILLIAM ALLEN WHITE: I may not delay telling you that your letter means very much to me.[1] Cordially,

1. In anticipation of LDB's eightieth birthday, 13 November 1936, White had written: "It is just a word to tell you how much you have meant to me and to millions of your fellow Americans. You have built your life into the structure of our government. You have built your ideals into the hearts of your countrymen, and your work will live for a long time, in years, in decades, and I hope in generations, an inspiration to youth and a comfort to all who love freedom institutionalized into law."

To Henrietta Szold

November 8, 1936 Washington, D. C. [H. Szold Mss]

DEAR MISS SZOLD: It was good of you to send greetings. My thoughts are much at the front, confident that you and the 400,000 will win the day.

With best wishes, Cordially,

To Franklin Delano Roosevelt

November 13, 1936 Washington, D. C. [Roosevelt Mss]

DEAR MR. PRESIDENT: We deeply appreciate your and Mrs. Roosevelt's kind greetings.[1]   Most cordially,

1. The President had written: "On the occasion of your eightieth birthday you will doubtless indulge in many reflections on your rich experience of public life and affairs. But these reflections will be incomplete if you do not also feel near your heart the affection of a thousand friends, among whom Mrs. Roosevelt and I are proud to feel we are numbered. I congratulate you, Mr. Justice, on your years, your wisdom and your noble service."

To Edward Albert Filene

December 5, 1936 Washington, D. C. [Filene Mss]

MY DEAR E. A.: Let me thank you for your generous birthday greeting. I think often of the years we worked together in public causes and of the much I learned from you; and always will regret of the essential differences in our views, to which you refer, which prevented our cooperating in the later period. But those differences never lessened my appreciation of your public spirit.[1]

With every good wish.   Cordially,

1. Filene had become an advocate of bigness in industry, a position at variance with LDB's philosophy.

To Morris Leopold Ernst

December 24, 1936 Washington, D.C. [Ernst Mss]

DEAR MORRIS ERNST: [1] My thanks for the birthday greeting, and my regrets that I could not see you when you were here. Let me know when you are next here during a recess of the Court.

You will be interested in the latest Savings Bank Insurance figures. The fiscal year ends Oct. 31. For the latest year, these are the gains as compared with that preceding: the lapse ratio dropped from 2.23% to 1.25%; the surrender ratio dropped from 2.56% to 1.94%; the insurance in force rose 11.48%; and the increase over the preceding year in insurance written was 24.65%.

All the banks will declare the same dividends as last year.

Cordially,

Insurance in force Nov. 30—$123,798,804

Insurance gain in November $1,106,575

I am sending you "Democracy in Denmark"[2] which points the way.

1. Morris Leopold Ernst (1888–1976), a New York attorney, had worked for Governor Herbert H. Lehman in drafting banking and insurance legislation. During World War II he served as a special representative of President Roosevelt on several foreign missions. He wrote a number of books on law and public policy.

2. See LDB to Josephine Goldmark, 30 October 1932.

To Elizabeth Brandeis Raushenbush

January 25, 1937 Washington, D.C. [EBR]

DEAREST ELIZABETH: Re yours 22d.

1. Lionberger Davis was here 10 days ago. According to schedule, he & his wife must now be on the Atlantic en route to Rio Janeiro.

2. Call on evening telephone Charles Ross[1] of St. Louis Post Despatch [sic]. Make him see that the paper should make a great campaign for unemployment reserves. Induce him to come quickly to Madison to investigate Wisconsin results & put him in touch with Wisconsin manufacturers and labor men.

I have reason to know that he is anxious (& his employer Pulitzer is) to boost his paper, after the bad slump that its defection from F.D. [Roosevelt] brought.

At Post Despatch [sic] is a younger man. Irving Dilliard, who is also a good friend of Felix & mine & can be relied on if Charles Ross permits.

3. Get in touch with Irving Brant,[2] editor of the St. Louis Times-Star. He is man who wrote "Storm over the Constitution"[3] and put Post Despatch [sic] to shame. He is very intelligent, much more to the left & probably ignorant of unemploy-

ment reserves but could learn. He has been a strong supporter of me generally.

4. Despite Frances Perkins, A.F. of L. and others (who you would call "dumb") the situation is by no means hopeless. Com^r Miles [4] was in yesterday (postponed a trip to N.Y. in order to do so) was so much impressed with what I told him last year. He said he brought up question with A.F. of L. & ran up against a stone-wall. But I am keeping him thinking & shall send him copy of Wall St. Journal McElwain articles of which I told him.

5. Please send me some more U.B.C. Advisors Circulars.

6. Write articles.

Tell Walter, for me: "Arithmetic is the first of sciences and the mother of safety." [5]

1. Charles Griffith Ross (1885–1950) had been chief Washington correspondent of the *St. Louis Post-Dispatch* from 1918 to 1934, after which he took over the editorial-page duties. He won a Pulitzer Prize in 1932, and in 1945 he became President Harry S. Truman's press secretary.

2. Irving Newton Brant (b. 1885) was a reporter and editorial writer for the *St. Louis Star-Times* from 1918 to 1938. He later began a career as an historian, and he is best known for his six-volume biography of James Madison (Indianapolis, 1941–1961).

3. Irving Brant, *Storm over the Constitution* (Indianapolis, 1936).

4. Vincent Morgan Miles (1885–1947), a lawyer from Little Rock, Arkansas, had been a regional advisor to the Federal Emergency Administration, and then he became chairman of District Six of the Social Security Board. He would later hold legal positions in both the Justice Department and the Post Office.

5. See LDB to Norman Hapgood, 25 September 1911.

To Robert Szold

March 4, 1937 Washington, D. C. [R. Szold Mss]

DEAR BOB: The recrudescence of terrorism must make heavy calls on the Emergency Fund. It, therefore, seems wise to send enclosed check for $10,000, proceeds to go to Palestine for disposition as Ben Gurion may direct, as with earlier remittances provided.[1]

1. See LDB to Szold, 5 October 1936.

To Robert Szold

March 7, 1937 Washington, D.C. [R. Szold Mss]

DEAR BOB: I enclose Mrs. deHaas letter of the 5th, and have written her: "Yours of 5th have sent to Bob Szold with the request that he give such aid as may hasten Jack's recovery."

I am burdening you with determining what should be expended, because even in ordinary times Mrs. deHaas has not seemed thrifty; and I deem this a P[alestine]. E[ndowment]. F[und]. obligation. Let me know when you want a check, and the amount.[1]

I am enclosing for your information also a letter from A. Chankis (of whom I know nothing) received also yesterday.

1. See next letter.

To Robert Szold

March 11, 1937 Washington, D.C. [R. Szold Mss]

DEAR BOB: Re yours of 10th

It is sad to hear that there is no chance of recovery.

Of course I accept Dr. Poll's & your judgment against a private room.

I should think Dr. Poll's advice that "after a few days" go home the best solution for all concerned.[1]

I assume you have seen Mrs. deHaas, as proposed.

Let me know when a check is needed. Has Judge Mack decided as to Hechalutz?

1. Jacob deHaas died in Mt. Sinai Hospital in New York City on 21 March 1937 from cancer.

To Henry Jacob Friendly

April 1, 1937 Washington, D. C. [Friendly]

DEAR HENRY FRIENDLY: Re yours of 31st.

Don't let the incident give you concern. I have heard of it only from you, and cannot believe anything you may have said will do any harm.[1]

I delayed acknowledgment of your generous birthday greeting (and also of the notice of your admission to the firm), hoping there would be a chance for a talk.[2]

Let me see you when you come to Washington, or to Cape Cod later.   Cordially,

1. The "incident" concerned a public debate between Friendly and Dean Charles E. Clark of the Yale Law School, in which Friendly criticized the plan recently submitted by President Roosevelt to enlarge the Supreme Court. The "Court-packing" plan, as it was soon called, stemmed from Roosevelt's frustration over the Supreme Court's continuing invalidation of key New Deal pieces of legislation (see LDB to Raymond A. Kent, 27 January 1936). Following his landslide electoral victory in 1936, Roosevelt felt he had a mandate from the people to act, and that some means of neutralizing the Court's opposition would receive popular support. Instead of forthrightly stating the real purpose of his plan, Roosevelt on 5 February 1937 submitted a bill to Congress for the "addition of younger blood" to the Court, by which one additional judge, up to a maximum of six, could be appointed for every justice who, having passed the age of seventy and already having served ten years, did not retire. Opponents to the New Deal, demoralized after the 1936 election, suddenly found they had an issue to rally around, and Roosevelt was subjected to an unexpected storm of criticism.

Although he pushed the plan vigorously, the President found Congress extremely reluctant to approve the bill in the face of widespread popular opposition to tinkering with the Court. The plan finally foundered after Chief Justice Hughes, with the concurrence of LDB (representing the liberal wing of the Court) and Justice Van Devanter (representing the conservatives), sent a letter to the Senate Judiciary Committee refuting Roosevelt's main argument, that the Court had fallen behind on its work. In the end, Congress passed a modified bill that left the Supreme Court intact, but allowed for more favorable financial conditions upon the justices' retirement. Ultimately, however, although Roosevelt lost the battle, he won the campaign. Within a short time, Justices Van Devanter, Sutherland, and Butler retired, allowing the president to create a liberal, pro-New Deal majority on the bench.

Throughout the debate, LDB maintained a discreet silence, despite many opportunities to speak out. Willard Hurst, his clerk, never heard LDB express an opinion on the plan (Mason, *Brandeis*, 625). Yet some evidence does exist that indicates LDB's opposition, including a conversation with Arthur M. Schlesinger, Sr.: "Brandeis . . . expressed the view that the conservative mentality is a product of genes rather than of years, that in fact age, with its accompaniment of financial security, tends to emancipate judges from the economic pressures and illiberal predilections which may have conditioned their previous thinking." (*In Retrospect*, 125.)

Friendly was among many who opposed the Court-packing plan, but he was horrified to discover on the day following the debate that newspapers had carried the story under the lead "Brandeis' law clerk attacks court plan."

2. Friendly had just been made a partner in the powerful law firm of Root, Clark, Buchner & Ballantine, with which he had been associated since 1928.

To James Marsh Douglas

May 11, 1937 Washington, D. C. [Douglas Mss]

DEAR JUDGE DOUGLAS: [1] Your promotion to the Supreme Court would have given your father great happiness.

My best wishes,   Cordially,

1. James Marsh Douglas (b. 1896), the son of LDB's law school roommate, had just been appointed to fill an unexpired term on the Missouri Supreme Court. He was elected to the post in his own right in 1938, and he served until 1949 when he reentered private practice. Douglas, chief justice of the court from 1943 to 1945, was also active in numerous legal and public service groups.

To William Gorham Rice, Jr.

May 25, 1937 Washington, D.C. [Rice]

MY DEAR RICE: Thanks for the article on Canada's powers.[1] You have doubtless heard from your dean (treat as confidential, if you have not) that Willard Hurst,[2] my current law clerk, is to be appointed at your school. It is, in every respect, an admirable selection, and you will have much satisfaction from the association.   Cordially,

1. "Can Canada Ratify International Labor Conventions?" 12 *Wisconsin Law Review* 185 (1937).
2. James Willard Hurst (b. 1910) graduated from the Harvard Law School in 1935, stayed on for a year as a research fellow, and then clerked for LDB. In 1937 he began his distinguished career as a legal historian at the Wisconsin Law School. One of his most important books is *The Growth of American Law* (Boston, 1950).

To Edward Albert Filene

[June] 1937 Chatham, Mass. [Filene Mss]

DEAR E.A.: Yours of the 19th re E.R. Warren's letter shows that, like the leopard, he does not change his spots.[1] His letter I am returning, as it may be the original.

George Anderson's health seems much better than last year— physically he is much more vigorous. Prof. [William Z.] Ripley writes me that at cards he exhibited "his old audacity."

I hope all goes well with you.   Cordially,

1. Filene had written of an exchange he had with Edward Ross Warren, who had been associated with Filene and LDB in the Public Franchise League until Warren resigned in a dispute over the sliding scale (see LDB to Warren, 13 March 1905, and to Edward H. McClennen, 14 March 1916). On 13 June Filene had received a short note from Warren: "Dear Filene: It is unpleasant to associate your name with the Constitution of the United States. Sincerely yours." When Filene called Warren to find out if this outburst had anything to do with a display concerning the Constitution in the Filene department store Warren only said: "I don't want to talk to you— you're wrong about everything." Filene reported this exchange to another old associate from the Franchise League, George Anderson, complaining mildly that Anderson and LDB, both liberals, tended to criticize him because of his support of big business (see LDB to Filene, 5 December 1936). And now, Filene said, the conservatives were also against him.

To Robert Szold

July 12, 1937 Chatham, Mass. [R. Szold Mss]

DEAR BOB: 1. Rabbi [Samuel] Wohl, who leaves Cincinnati on the 15th and is to sail on the 21st, wanted to come here. I wrote him that I could not see him this week; that he should see you on arrival in New York; and that he should let me have his N.Y. address, as it may prove that I can see him on the 19th. If you and he think it desirable, I can probably arrange for one hour on the 19th. But it is a long journey & doubtless he can get from you all he needs. Of course Isaac Hamlin will know how you can reach him.

Of course you must accompany [Stephen S.] Wise.

2. At the proper times and places, you will, of course, make clear that abolition of the Mandate and partition was not only a recommendation beyond the delegation to the Commission [1] (a

defect which might be remedied by ratification), but that this fundamental issue was decided without a hearing of the Jews. So far as I have heard the subject was never publicly mentioned, at any hearing. There was only a little private talk with Weizmann. Am I right as to my assumption of the facts?

1. Following the Arab riots of 1936 (see LDB to Israel B. Brodie, 10 July 1936, n. 1), the British had appointed a commission headed by Viscount Peel to ascertain the underlying causes of the discontent and to recommend means of removing them. According to Chaim Weizmann, the Peel Commission was "by far the most distinguished and the ablest of the investigatory bodies ever sent out to Palestine." The report, issued on 7 July 1937, came to over four hundred pages; it was critical of the British administration of Palestine and sympathetic to Jewish aims and achievements. The commission declared that had His Majesty's Government started out from the beginning with a firm intention to honor the Balfour Declaration, much of the trouble might have been avoided. Instead, the British had tried to appease all factions, leading the Arabs to believe that if they objected strenuously enough to Jewish plans, the British would back down.

The commission, in its most controversial recommendations, suggested that it would be impossible to satisfy both Arabs and Jews under the Mandate; a partition of the country into a Jewish state, an Arab state, and an international zone around Jerusalem administered by Great Britain, all bound together economically, might be the answer. The proposed Jewish state, based on the areas then under control of the Yishuv, amounted to 1,554 square miles, and the territory comprised the Galilee, the Jezreel valley, the Sharon plain, and an area south from Tel Aviv to Ashdod. The Jews strenuously objected not only to the size of the area, which excluded the Negev and Judea, but also to the idea of setting up a Jewish state without Jerusalem. The Arabs condemned the plan out of hand. *Palestine Royal Commission Report*, Cmd. 5479 (London, 1937). See LDB to Szold, 2 and 16 January 1938.

To Edward Albert Filene

September 23, 1937 Washington, D. C. [Filene Mss]

MY DEAR E. A.: I am sorry to learn from the morning papers of your illness. Of course, the physicians will take the best possible care of you. Do follow suit when once you are out of their hands.[1]   Most cordially,

1. Filene, on a visit to Europe, had fallen ill with pneumonia; he entered the American Hospital in Paris, where he died on 26 September. According to a notation on the manuscript, this letter reached Paris after Filene's death.

To Bernard Flexner

November 11, 1937 Washington, D. C. [Brandeis Mss, I 9–1]

DEAR BEN: Yours of 10th & the copies of correspondence with [Raymond A.] Kent, which came yesterday, bring much good news.

1. It is fine that Mim is back better & is thinking of a trip here. We shall hope to see you and Mim during the next recess of the Court, which begins on the afternoon of Nov. 22d.

2. It will give great joy to many interested in S.B.I. if Mason is released for the second half of this academic year, as you and Abe [Flexner] are planning. Early publication of his book would help much in several states.[1]

In Mass. S.B.I. is going very well. In September '37—its writing was 94.46% more than in Sept. '36. The [commercial insurance] companies' writing in September '37 was 15 per cent less than in September '36—and only 48 per cent of what it was in September '30.

3. I am very glad you are taking up Anti-partition publicity with [Julian W.] Mack et al.[2] P[alestine].E[ndowment].F[und]. has funds from which can be used for that purpose; but my hope has been that the amount raised here from other sources would leave my contributions largely for Palestinian needs, which are great.

1. Professor Alpheus T. Mason was then at work on *The Brandeis Way: A Case Study in the Workings of Democracy* (Princeton, 1938), an examination of how the savings bank life insurance program had been established. He had begun work on the study at the specific urging of LDB.

2. See LDB to Robert Szold, 12 July 1937 and 2 January 1938.

To Fola LaFollette

December 30, 1937 Washington, D. C. [F. LaFollette]

MY DEAR FOLA: Re yours of 28th.

You are a very good reporter. The notes may be made "a part of the permanent record," as you suggest.[1]

The only correction I suggest is this. Alfred [Brandeis]'s appointment was by Hoover on the Enforcement Division of the Food Administration.

Our best to you and Mid.[2]

We hope to see you very early in 1938.

1. Miss LaFollette was then at work on the biography of her father, Senator Robert M. LaFollette, which had been begun by her mother. She had interviewed LDB regarding his collaboration with LaFollette during the progressive era. LDB later made a special gift to enable her to continue the work (see LDB to Bernard Flexner, 15 May 1941, n. 2). See Belle Case LaFollette and Fola LaFollette, *Robert M. LaFollette*, 2 vols. (New York, 1953).

2. George Middleton, Fola's husband.

To Robert Szold

January 2, 1938 Washington, D. C. [Brodie Mss]

DEAR BOB: — With Great Britain's present abandonment of reason & obligations & [Chaim] Weizmann's untrustworthiness, as reported, any decision is perilous.

But I should stand firm against partition [1] and for the Mandate with the provision for temporary adjustment on immigration which we have discussed, and take my chances.

Nothing else is right — (or in accord with the vote of Z.O.A. convention.)

I suggest that you talk to Felix [Frankfurter] if he has not already been communicated with.

I am sending F.F. enclosures in yours of 30th.

1. See LDB to Szold, 12 July 1937, to Bernard Flexner, 11 November 1937, and next letter.

To Robert Szold

January 16, 1938 Washington, D. C. [Brodie Mss]

DEAR BOB: — Re yours of 13th.

1. Under no circumstances should I be willing to relinquish the mandate or to agree to a permanent minority status.[1]

2. As heretofore indicated to you, I should be willing to agree

to a limitation upon immigration for a temporary period—say for 5 or not exceeding 10 years—the limitation to be expressed, preferably, not in the number to be admitted each year, but that by the end of the period the number of Jews in the country should not exceed 45% (40%) of the total population—the country (that is Palestine) to include Transjordania.

3. The above, as I understand, is your view, & that the "Memorandum" items are consistent with it.

If you and I are agreed, I have no objection to your writing [Julius] Simon definitely what you would agree to & that I agree with you. But as Bernard Joseph is due the end of this week it would doubtless be wiser to hear what he has to say before you write Simon. Of course, [Menahem] Ussishkin must be in the conference.

4. My lack of faith in [Judah L.] Magnes' judgment continues and I have none in Hyamson's [2] or Herbert Samuel's. But I would not reject the proposition merely because they are cooperating.

I assume you have conferred on this with Ben Cohen and S.S.W[ise].

1. See preceding letter.
2. Albert Montefiore Hyamson (1875–1945) was an authority on Palestine (see LDB to Jacob deHaas, 13 September 1917). He had served as director of immigration in the Palestine administration from 1926 to 1934; his service proved a bitter disappointment to the Jews, for he zealously carried out the restrictionist British policy. During the thirties Hyamson was actively associated with Judah Magnes in trying to create a binational state, one that would give parity of numbers to both Jews and Arabs.

To Louis Edward Levinthal

January 30, 1938 Washington, D. C. [Levinthal Mss]

DEAR JUDGE LEVINTHAL: [1] Re yours of 27th.

The name may be used if you think it will be helpful.[2]

Cordially,

Let me talk with you on Palestine when you are next in Washington.

1. Louis Edward Levinthal (1892–1976) was a long-time judge of the Court of Common Pleas in Philadelphia and active in a variety of Jewish

and Zionist activities. During the crucial years 1941 to 1943 he served as president of the Z.O.A. and also as chairman of the executive committee of the Zionist Emergency Committee.

2. Levinthal was organizing a group of Jewish lawyers in Philadelphia, hoping to interest them in Zionist affairs, and wanted to name the group after LDB.

To Hyman Parker

February 18, 1938 Washington, D. C. [Parker]

DEAR MR. PARKER: Re yours of 14th.

I am sorry your life has been so hard a one.[1] But do not despair. There is much that is grimy in most occupations. But to live nobly is not impossible. With persistent hard work, patience and unwavering courage, and simple living, happiness is attainable, whatever the character of the work you engage in.

With best wishes,　　Cordially,

1. See LDB to Parker, 17 and 23 April 1936.

To Bernard Flexner

March 5, 1938 Washington, D. C. [Brandeis Mss, M 15–1]

DEAR BEN: Re yours of 3rd.

It is grand to know that the digging has begun [1] — Your doings.

Dr. [Raymond A.] Kent has a good chance of getting Justice Reed.[2]

Governor Lehman [3] should prove persuasive — Despite insurance company wiles.[4]

1. For the University of Louisville Law School building.

2. Kent had invited Stanley Forman Reed (b. 1884) to speak at the cornerstone ceremony. Reed, a native of Louisville, had recently been appointed to the Supreme Court to fill Justice Sutherland's position; before that he had served as Solicitor General of the United States. On 12 March, LDB informed Flexner that Reed would accept the invitation.

3. Herbert Henry Lehman (1878–1963), after spending a number of years in the family banking firm, had entered politics in the 1920s as a supporter of Al Smith. In 1928, as Franklin Roosevelt's running mate, he was elected lieutenant governor of New York; and in 1932 he was elected to the first

of his five terms as governor. When the United States entered World War II, Lehman resigned to head the United Nations Relief and Rehabilitation Agency, which provided food, shelter, and training for millions of refugees. In 1949, Lehman was elected United States Senator, and during his one term in the Senate he was an outspoken critic of Joseph McCarthy. Lehman was active in Jewish affairs, including the Joint Distribution Committee and the American Jewish Committee; while not a Zionist, he proved to be a warm friend of Israel. See Allan Nevins, *Herbert H. Lehman and His Era* (New York, 1963).

4. On 28 February 1938, Lehman had proposed savings bank life insurance for New York; see next letter and LDB to Charles Warren, 30 March 1938.

To Charles Goldmark

March 17, 1938 Washington, D.C. [EBR]

DEAR CHARLES: The S[avings]. B[ank]. I[nsurance]. bill has been enacted,[1] a good first step, a necessary wee little one. The real task lies ahead, to make the act operative. That will require, for many years, much work in which I hope you will have a large part.   Best wishes,

1. After a short but bitter fight led by the insurance companies against the scheme, the legislature accepted Governor Lehman's proposal and established a savings bank insurance plan, with a limit of $3,000 per policy. See LDB to Charles Warren, 30 March 1938 and to Herbert Lehman, 10 April 1938.

To Robert Szold

March 17, 1938 Washington, D. C. [Kesselman Mss]

DEAR BOB: When Isaac S. Heller [1] of New Orleans (whom I think well of) was here recently, I spoke to him of the necessity of building up a small group of men of competence & knowledge who will think as statesmen of the Jewish problems—and told him of you, Ben Cohen, J. J. Kaplan [2] and Jonas [Friedenwald]. He said the best men he could think of were Monte Lemann (whom it would be impossible to get) and Edgar Stern [3] of N.O. whom he thought we might get, as he had been in Palestine recently and was very enthusiastic. (Stern is of the old rich N.O.

family. His father was partner of the father of Gov. [Herbert H.] Lehman in the cotton business. Stern married a daughter of Julius Rosenwald. He is a man in the early fifties.) Heller spoke of him as one of the ablest men—if not the ablest—he knew and that he has freed himself from business. So I told him to have Stern call on me. Stern was in today.

I talked over the situation with him. He is going to New York and hopes to be able to see you Saturday A.M. Will communicate with you. He has not committed himself; but, I think, left me strongly inclined to accept the invitation—and do the heavy work necessary to fit himself for the job.[4]

While abroad with his family during the past year—he went to Warsaw & to the Russian colonies & then to Palestine—came back deeply moved & convinced that the children of Julius Rosenwald ought to do all possible to improve the position of the Jews. He was urged by his brother-in-law William[5] to take up J.D.C. work—also Amer. Jewish Com[mit]tee work. But neither appealed to him, nor any work of that character.

I think if we can get him, he may be able to get Monte Lemann to join us.

1. Isaac Schenck Heller (b. 1893), after graduation from the Harvard Law School, had entered practice in his native New Orleans. The son of Rabbi Maximillian Heller, he too became active in local Zionist and Jewish affairs, and was president of the Z.O.A. district organization.

2. Jacob Joseph Kaplan (1889–1960) had joined the Brandeis firm in 1910 after graduation from Harvard Law School. He was a director of Filene's department store and sat on the boards of several Boston banks. Kaplan was active in Jewish work in Boston, and he served for a period as president of the Associated Jewish Philanthropies of Boston.

3. Edgar Bloom Stern (1886–1959), a businessman, was on the boards of many companies, including Sears, Roebuck; he was also active in a variety of charitable causes, none of them specifically Jewish.

4. Stern did not get involved in Zionism.

5. William Rosenwald (b. 1903), the younger son of Julius, was a philanthropist and financier who was extremely active in Jewish agencies. He served as chairman of the United Jewish Appeal and as vice-chairman of the Joint Distribution Committee, the American Jewish Committee, and the Hebrew Immigrant Aid Society.

To Charles Warren

March 30, 1938 Washington, D. C. [Warren Mss]

DEAR CHARLES WARREN: My thanks for your letter.

Yes, the victory in New York is encouraging.[1] To secure to its people the benefits of the law will require much more work, and the high devotion to public service exhibited by the staff in Massachusetts.

You may care to see enclosed sheet of comparative costs there of ordinary insurance in 1938.   Cordially,

1. The passage of savings bank insurance; see also next letter.

To Herbert Henry Lehman

April 10, 1938 Washington, D. C. [Lehman Mss]

DEAR GOVERNOR LEHMAN: It was good of you to write me. Those who had part in the thirty year struggle in Massachusetts can appreciate how glorious was your victory.

I am glad you are only sixty years old.

With best wishes,   Cordially,

To Edward Patrick Boland [1] (Telegram)

April 14, 1938 Washington, D. C. [Brandeis Mss, I 10–1]

Answering your telegram.[2] In my opinion the proposed limitation of the amount savings bank life insurance purchasable wholly unjustified. Amendment should be defeated as impairing the interests of the people of Massachusetts.

1. Edward Patrick Boland (b. 1911) was a member of the Massachusetts legislature; in 1953 he was elected to the United States House of Representatives, in which body he has served since.

2. In the wake of the New York bill establishing a $3,000 limit per policy, Massachusetts insurance companies attempted to have the legislature establish a similar limit on policies sold in that state. Boland, who was chairman of the committee considering the limitation, had telegraphed LDB, whom he called "the father and champion of Savings Bank Life Insurance of Massachusetts," to solicit his opinion. Following LDB's response, the measure was killed.

To Robert Szold

April 14, 1938 Washington, D.C. [R. Szold Mss]

DEAR BOB: Your 2 letters of 13th recd, very sorry to hear of the back.

1. Make dead sure that no relative or friend of [Louis] Lipsky is employed by the political bureau; S[tephen].S.W[ise]. does not support L.L.

2. The last words I said to S.S.W. on the 13th (after he had discoursed on Weizmann's trustworthiness) was "Beware of his associate Lipsky & ilk." [1]

3. As to the Julius Simon letter returned herewith, I agree with you and S.S.W. that I had better say nothing.

4. Col. [Josiah] Wedgwood was in yesterday. He is fine. I hope you have talked with him, a man of courage and rectitude and common sense.

I assume you will let me know when money is needed.

---

1. In the face of the rising danger from Hitler in Europe, Stephen S. Wise was trying to make peace between the Brandeis and Weizmann factions, but to no avail. Despite public statements of the need for unity within Zionism, both men continued to mistrust the other, and LDB in particular opposed Weizmann's American lieutenant, Louis Lipsky.

To Frederick A. Stokes

May 7, 1938 Washington, D. C. [Brandeis Mss, M 12-2]

DEAR MR. STOKES: I am glad to have yours of the 4th.[1] The numerous letters about "Other People's Money" which continue to come convince me that there is a large potential market for the book. The very small check for the 1937 royalties received from your Company on the 4th convinces me that an edition much cheaper than yours is needed. For many of those who wrote me did so to enquire where the book could be secured. I gave them your address, and evidently they did not buy it.

The proposed 5000 copies by the Blue Ribbon Books, Inc. seems very small as compared with the 100,000 copies which the National Home Library Foundation sold in 1933. At what price are these Blue Ribbon books sold at retail?

I was told that the Foundation would like to publish another edition of at least 100,000 copies, to be sold at 25 cents at retail. If, as I think, a fair royalty could be secured, they would give you more in royalty—and an arrangement with them would ensure the large distribution which I desire. What do you say? Is there a chance of your being in Washington soon? [2]

Cordially,

1. Stokes had reissued *Other People's Money* in 1932, and the following year the National Home Library Foundation had issued a cheap reprint, which seriously cut into the sales of the more expensive edition. Stokes wanted to know if LDB would consent to having an inexpensive edition handled by "Blue Ribbon Books," which imprint Stokes owned. The edition, however, would still be more costly than the National Home Library issue.

2. In the end, no new edition of *Other People's Money* was brought out until 1967.

To Alice and Charles Goldmark

June 16, 1938 Chatham, Mass. [EBR]

DEAR ALICE PARK AND CHARLES: To Boston Do sent us the report of Jonathan's honors; and we share in your joy—with great hopes for the long future.

Here Do and the lovely socks welcomed us, as Jack brought us from Yarmouth.

Susan is due tomorrow, returning from a meeting of the Regents; [1] and sunny days are long overdue here.

We trust all is going well with you.

1. Susan Brandeis Gilbert had been appointed to the Board of Regents of the University of New York, which was the overall governing body for all educational institutions in New York State.

To Bernard Flexner

June 18, 1938 Chatham, Mass. [Brandeis Mss, M 18–1]

MY DEAR BEN: We are sorry that your plans for the Cape had to be abandoned.

[Sherman F.] Mittell wrote under date of June 3rd, of his talk with you; that [Alpheus T.] Mason expects to finish the book in

August; and that upon Abe [Flexner]'s return this month there is to be a conference at Princeton about publication.[1] The recent attempt of the companies to secure in Massachusetts restrictive legislation (note enclosure) shows the urgent need of intensive widespread education.[2] Never before had the insurance lobby been so determined, and apparently so well equipped with ammunition.

Our best to Mim.

Fanny B[randeis]. writes that Stanley Reed's address was fine and the occasion impressive.[3]

1. See LDB to Flexner, 11 November 1937.
2. See LDB to Edward P. Boland, 14 April 1938.
3. See LDB to Flexner, 5 March 1938.

To Bernard Flexner

July 8, 1938 Chatham, Mass. [Brandeis Mss, M 18–2]

DEAR BEN: Re yours of 1st to Fan. I suppose there are in Washington some of Al's letters, of which no copies are in Fan's possession.[1] If you think they may be of value I will try to locate them.[2]

The British military & police are making a pretty spectacle in Palestine.[3]

1. Flexner was gathering material for *Mr. Justice Brandeis and the University of Louisville* (Louisville, 1938), which detailed LDB's involvement with the University and his philosophy of community participation in building the school.
2. According to his daughter, after his retirement from the Court, LDB reread all of the correspondence between himself and his brother and destroyed most of the letters. Elizabeth Brandeis Raushenbush managed eventually to stop him, arguing that although LDB saw the letters primarily as personal, "trivial" items, historians might view them in a different light.
3. The Arab boycott, which had started two years earlier, was still flaring up occasionally, and, despite an influx of 20,000 additional troops, the British command proved unable to control unruly Arab and Jewish groups.

To Bernard Flexner

September 21, 1938 Washington, D. C. [Brandeis Mss, M 18–2]

DEAR BEN: Re yours of 20th.

It will be grand to see you and Mim Wednesday the 28th at 5 P.M.

Although England and France will doubtless do their worst,[1] we shall ultimately win in Palestine if Jews do their best.

1. During September, Adolf Hitler's strident demands that the Czech Sudetenland be ceded to Germany caused fears of war all over Europe. Britain and France, bound by treaty to aid Czechoslovakia in case of attack, stumbled all over themselves trying to find some way to avert disaster. Finally, Hitler agreed to meet with Prime Minister Neville Chamberlain and Premier Edouard Daladier of France at Munich on 28 September together with Benito Mussolini of Italy. There the fascists browbeat the Western leaders into meeting all of Germany's demands. Czech independence and freedom were sold in return for what Chamberlain called "peace in our time."

To Bernard Flexner

October 12, 1938 Washington, D. C. [Brandeis Mss, M 18–2]

DEAR BEN: Re yours of 11th.

Yes, Partition, the stupid, ignoble action proposed, seems dead.[1]

The expression of American opinions in today's paper is, I trust, only the beginning.[2]

I am very glad you are guiding [Sherman F.] Mittell.

1. Following the Peel Commission's recommendation that separate Jewish and Arab states be created in Palestine, His Majesty's Government appointed a commission headed by Sir John Woodhead to look into the feasibility of the idea This commission report, issued the week of this letter, indicated the near impossibility of agreeing on a partition plan. The report contained three different plans, each one backed by a minority in the commission. Although the British government did not finally reject a partition scheme until November, it was clear from the lack of decisive support for any of the three Woodhead plans that partition was dead. See LDB to Robert Szold, 11 November 1938.

2. Senator Robert F. Wagner of New York, together with a number of other Congressmen, was planning to see President Roosevelt to discuss British plans for stopping Jewish immigration into Palestine. In addition, a

group of thirty Christian church and lay leaders made public a telegram to Chamberlain deploring British policy in Palestine; other Christian groups, prodded by the Zionist-sponsored Pro-Palestine Federation, joined in the campaign.

To Felix Frankfurter (Fragment)

October 16, 1938 Washington, D. C. [Wise Mss]

F. D. [Roosevelt] went very far in our talk in his appreciation of the significance of Palestine—the need of keeping it whole and of making it Jewish.[1] He was tremendously interested—and wholly surprised—on learning of the great increase in Arab population since the War;[2] and on learning of the plenitude of land for Arabs in Arab countries, about which he made specific inquiries. Possible refuges for Jews elsewhere he spoke of as "satellites", and there was no specific talk of them.

1. The previous weekend, Felix Frankfurter had met with President Roosevelt to protest British policy in Palestine. According to a letter from Robert Szold to LDB, 13 October 1938, Frankfurter reported that "the President has been 'miseducated,' particularly as to the absorptive capacity of Palestine; that the miseducation has gone to the extent that Felix was unable completely to overcome it; that Felix therefore spoke of the significance of Palestine as a symbol, and to this apparently F.D.R. agreed."

2. Although there was much information available, most of it broadcast by the Zionists, regarding the increase in the Jewish population of Palestine, a lesser-known fact was the doubling of the Arab population of the Holy Land between 1917 and 1947. The economic prosperity generated by the Yishuv attracted many Arabs to Palestine.

To Robert Szold

November 11, 1938 Washington, D. C. [R. Szold Mss]

DEAR BOB: Re: Your two letters of 10th.

1. It is a source of rejoicing for us (and should be of deep humiliation for the British) that the Government has reversed itself on partition and recognized the Mandate as binding it.

2. Its proposal to call in representatives of several Arab countries is as stupid (and craven) as its past proposal of partition—and action throughout the years.[1]

3. As I wrote to S.S.W[ise]. last week—I think nothing should be done in the way of proposing plans for future Arab-Jewish-British relations until order has been restored.

A. Because until there is a reign of law & order, British judgment (and probably also Jewish) will inevitably be unsafe and probably bad, that is, will be influenced by considerations which have no place in the adjustment to be made.

B. Any plan, except that of honestly & rigidly carrying out the provisions of the Mandate will be regarded by the Arabs (like the partition) as a concession to them, obtained by their terrorism.

My own conviction is, that if once the terrorists are beaten—soundly beaten—we can arrange to get along with the other Palestinian Arabs, but not until then. And that we must divorce Palestinians from all other Arab populations in the settlement of the Palestinian problem.

4. S.S.W. doubtless told you that he had me see on the 9th Marks [2] and [Harry] Sacher. I made very clear to them, I hope, the above views.

5. The Jewish Agency action on the Report, etc., (so far as it is in accord with the above views) seems to me commendable, though it might have been better to wait a few days until the Arabs had protested.[3]

6. I suppose you saw the Report of the luncheon of Weizmann, Ben Gurion, and Wingate,[4] at Lord Lloyd's[5] on October 28th. It shows clearly (a) amazing ignorance of Lord Lloyd, and (b) that what the British are thinking of is not settling the Palestine problem, but possible troubles with other Arabs in the Near East (due to British past stupidity).

7. London Times seems to recognize the folly of calling in representatives of the foreign (Arab) powers.

1. Following its rejection of the Woodhead Commission's report (see LDB to Bernard Flexner, 12 October 1938), the British government declared it would make still another effort to secure agreement between Jews and Arabs, and called for a conference on the future of Palestine to convene at St. James's Palace on 7 February 1939. Many commentators believe that the British knew the conference would fail but wanted to use it as a facade before issuing their own plan on Palestine. See LDB to Neville Chamberlain, 26 February 1939.

2. Sir Simon Marks, 1st Baron Marks of Broughton (1888–1964) was chairman of the board of the well-known English department store, Marks

& Spencer, Ltd., founded by his father, an immigrant from Poland. Marks had been introduced to Zionism by Chaim Weizmann and was a member of the Manchester group that proved so effective in working with Weizmann during the war. He and his family made large and significant contributions to various Zionist projects, especially the Weizmann Institute of Science.

3. In response to the Woodhead Commission Report, the Jewish Agency declared that it would reject any solution that condemned Jews to the status of a permanent minority in Palestine or deprived them of the right to establish a national home there.

4. Orde Charles Wingate (1903–1944), a British career military officer, had been posted to Palestine in 1936. While there, he trained the Special Night Squads, composed of Jewish volunteers, on how to combat Arab marauders. Within weeks after his arrival in Palestine, Wingate had become an ardent Zionist, much to the embarrassment of his superiors. The Yishuv, which had originally mistrusted him, soon came to believe implicitly in him and his methods. During World War II, Wingate wanted to head a Jewish army composed of Palestinian volunteers, but instead he was sent to the Asian theatre where he died in a plane crash.

5. David Lloyd George.

To Franklin Delano Roosevelt

November 14, 1938 Washington, D.C. [Roosevelt Mss]

DEAR MR. PRESIDENT: Let me thank you for the generous birthday greeting transmitted through Dr. Kent.[1]   Cordially,

1. On 9 November, Roosevelt had written to Raymond A. Kent: "The passing of another year in Justice Brandeis' eventful and useful life serves to remind every citizen of the magnitude of his contribution to our Judicial literature. Many years ago Justice Brandeis brought to the Bench the finest attributes of an advocate whose mind was geared to social change. As a Justice of our highest court he has pushed aside the curtain of legal verbiage and breathed into our jurisprudence a broad humanism.

"It is a pleasure to join with others of his admirers and to extend to Justice Brandeis on his eighty-second birthday my sincere wishes for his good health and for the continuance of that service which has so distinguished his life in the law."

To Robert Szold

November 24, 1938 Washington, D. C. [R. Szold Mss]

DEAR BOB: 1. I think that the attitude being exhibited by the country in respect to Germany makes this a favorable time for impressing upon Americans the propriety of an unofficial boycott; and that our pre-revolutionary practice affords a strong justification for resorting now to the boycott.[1]

2. Pursuant to my suggestions, Paul Freund made a detailed study of the pre-revolutionary practice and embodied the results in the enclosed paper.

3. I suggest that you, Dr. [Stephen S.] Wise and [Israel B.] Brodie undertake to get the widest possible and most varied publicity for these facts. Doubtless Henry Montor[2] could help. He got excellent publicity for the meeting at Washington last Sunday. Felix [Frankfurter] should be able to help.

4. You will note that Prof. Arthur M. Schlesinger (now of Harvard) made in 1918 an extensive study of the subject. He is a close friend of Felix. As copies of his study are not available, republication of it is under consideration. Schlesinger should know, through Felix, of the demand for a new edition, and perhaps S. should be induced to also write some shorter article on the subject now.[3]

5. Paul Freund does not wish to write anything himself or to be known generally as the source of this memo. You may recall that he was my secretary and is now in the Solicitor General's office. He is a great friend of Felix and had written Felix in an attempt to get a copy of the Schlesinger (1918) book.

Ben Cohen has just been in. I think the President's statement in today's Times should be helpful now and hereafter.[4] I asked Ben to telephone Miss Lehand[5] to say to F. D. that I thought it fine.

Chamberlain's statements[6] and Kennedy's[7] on the movie censorship[8] as disclosed in to-day's Times confirms James G. McDonald's estimate of them.

1. For earlier agitation for a boycott against Germany, see LDB to Stephen S. Wise, 18 September 1933.

2. Henry Montor (b. 1905) had entered Zionist work as assistant editor of the *New Palestine* in the 1920s. In 1930 he began his work with the United Palestine Appeal, and when that group merged with the Joint Distribution Committee into the United Jewish Appeal, Montor served as executive vice-president, raising unprecedented amounts of money during the 1940s. Montor was also one of the originators of the Israel Bond program and headed that project until 1955, when he resigned to enter private business.

3. Schlesinger (see LDB to Felix Frankfurter, 26 September 1929, n. 4)

did not write anything on the boycott for the popular press at the time, and his book on the colonial merchants was reissued in 1939.

4. Upon hearing of rumors (which turned out to be false) that immigration into Palestine would be increased, Roosevelt had issued a statement from the Little White House in Warm Springs, Georgia, that he was highly gratified at the news. Since Roosevelt's statement included the comment that he had no verification of the information, his words were interpreted as trying to pressure the British into allowing more Jews to enter Palestine.

5. Marguerite Alice "Missy" LeHand (1898–1944) was Roosevelt's confidential secretary.

6. In a suggestion that would resurface several times over the next seven years, Neville Chamberlain had proposed that Jews escaping from the Continent might be resettled either in British Guiana or in Tanganyika.

7. Joseph Patrick Kennedy (1888–1969) had made his fortune as a young man, first in banking and then as an early producer of motion pictures. In the 1930s he became involved in Democratic politics, and Roosevelt rewarded him with an appointment to the newly created Securities and Exchange Commission in 1934, and then in 1938 he was named ambassador to the Court of St. James. Jewish groups were particularly unhappy with Kennedy since they believed that he supported the Foreign Office position on Palestine and that he secretly favored Hitler. After World War II, Kennedy spent much of his energy advancing the political careers of his sons. See Richard J. Whalen, *The Founding Father* (New York, 1964).

8. At the request of the British government, Kennedy had utilized his contacts in the motion picture industry to remove excerpts of newsfilms critical of Chamberlain's handling of the Munich crisis (see LDB to Bernard Flexner, 21 September 1938) from four "March of Time" reels. Kennedy defended his action on the grounds that the footage would have been embarrassing to the British government in its negotiations with Germany.

To Robert Szold

December 4, 1938 Washington, D. C. [R. Szold Mss]

DEAR BOB: Re yours of 2d.

Mrs. Jacobs[1] three letters (Nov. 22, Nov. 25, Nov. 25) show her usual good judgment. But this should be said to her:

She is unduly depressed.

1. Of course the British action is very bad. But we cannot expect either good judgment or good moral[s] of them until law and order is restored in Palestine. Their bad judgment defers the coming of law and order. But I have confidence that ultimately it will come if the British Empire survives.

2. Of course, the rejection of Palestine's offer to take 40,000

refugees now & 60,000 more within 12 months is disappointing. But the large immigration to Palestine is inevitable. There is no other country into which mass immigration is now possible. The rising indignation over Hitler atrocities—evidenced in England e. g. by the Albert Hall meeting—and also on the Continent—will eventually compel admission of the immigrants. We must persist treating British refusals merely as unwise postponement.

3. Of course, Jewish officials are, as they have been, unwise, e. g. Ben Gurion's suggestions which Mrs. Jacobs reports. But when law and order is restored, we may expect better judgment even from them.

4. Mrs. Jacobs undervalues the influence she has in London and the service she is rendering. She must cling to the job and be as omnipresent as possible—learning all and teaching wherever possible.

1. Rose Gell Jacobs (b. 1888) had been a charter member of Hadassah and later served as its president; in 1937 she was elected honorary vice-president for life. In 1938 she was in London in preparation for the St. James conference.

To Robert Szold

December 12, 1938 Washington, D. C. [R. Szold Mss]

DEAR BOB: Re yours of 9th and 10th.

Dr. Nahum Goldman [*sic*] [1] says S. S. W[ise]. will go to London for the conference;—that Felix [Frankfurter] says he cant possibly do so until after March; and that Ben Cohen thinks he cant.

I think we must assume Felix wont go. To me it seems more important that you should go with Wise & that it is imperative. Weizmann et al. want Felix and Ben V. C[ohen]. for their supposed "prestige" and "influence". Of course it would be good to have all as Mrs. Jacobs suggests, but you are the most important & are indispensable.

I dont believe that Great Britain will fail to act unwisely or dishonorably, whoever attends. But it is of prime importance that the Jews be sane and honorable; and do not assent to any curtailment of our "rights" & that any curtailment imposed [not] be assented to, even if for the time submission is unavoidable.[2]

1. Nahum Goldmann (b. 1894) was an early leader of German Zionism and a founder of the monumental *Encyclopedia Judaica*. In 1933 Goldmann fled the Nazis and moved to Geneva. There he came into contact with Stephen S. Wise, with whom he worked over the next few years to create the World Jewish Congress. During World War II, Goldmann lived in the United States, where he served as a lobbyist for the World Zionist Organization and, as an ally of Wise and Weizmann, often came into bitter conflict with Abba Hillel Silver. See the *Autobiography of Nahum Goldmann* (New York, 1969).

2. See LDB to Neville Chamberlain, 26 February 1939.

To Robert Szold

December 22, 1938 Washington, D.C. [R. Szold Mss]

DEAR BOB: Re yours 20th as to your memorandum.

I thought you would understand that my statement that I was glad you sent it to Mrs. [Rose] Jacobs meant approval. It was an able document. I have no specific suggestions.[1]

The important thing always to be borne in mind, that no promise of the British now, before law & order are fully restored, can be relied upon; and that we cannot rely upon promises made hereafter, unless Jews are so numerous and strong in Palestine that they dare not break their promises.

Of course we must make no *offer* of any concession.

1. Szold had prepared a legal brief for the American Zionist representatives to the St. James Conference; see LDB to Szold, 11 November 1938.

To Emmet Vaughn Mittlebeeler

February 8, 1939 Washington, D. C. [Mittlebeeler]

DEAR MR. MITTLEBEELER: [1] Re yours of 3rd. If the staff of the 1939 Thoroughbred thinks it will be helpful to the University, the Yearbook may be dedicated as you so courteously propose.

With best wishes, Cordially,

1. Emmet Vaughn Mittlebeeler (b. 1915) was a member of the senior class at the University of Louisville Law School. He later took a doctorate in political science and now teaches at the American University in Washington, where he specializes in African customs and law. He had written to ask if the class of 1939 could dedicate their yearbook to LDB.

To Franklin Delano Roosevelt

February 13, 1939 Washington, D. C. [Roosevelt Mss]

DEAR MR. PRESIDENT: Pursuant to the Act of March, 1937, I retire this day from regular active service on the bench.[1]

Cordially,

1. On the same day President Roosevelt responded: "One must perforce
accept the inevitable. Ever since those days long ago, when you first took
your seat on the Supreme Court Bench, I have come to think of you as a
necessary and very permanent part of the Court—and, since 1933 as one
who would continue his fine service there until long after I had left Washington.

"The country has needed you through all these years, and I hope you
will realize, as all your old friends do, how unanimous the nation has been
in its gratitude to you.

"There is nothing I can do but to accede to your retirement. But with
this goes the knowledge that our long association will continue, and the
hope that you will be spared for many long years to come to render additional services to mankind."

LDB's daughter, Elizabeth wrote: "All the things I want to say sound
mawkish—or presumptuous from me to you. I cannot bear to use any
words at this time that do not ring true. . . . Measuring my words, I do
not see how any one person could have done more than you have done."

Amidst the floods of regretful letters and praise-filled articles and editorials, there was anxious speculation about whom Roosevelt would name
to fill the seat that LDB had occupied for nearly twenty-three years. (To
the immense satisfaction of LDB and other liberals throughout the country,
Roosevelt had named Felix Frankfurter to the Supreme Court only five
weeks earlier.) LDB was gratified when the appointment went to William
O. Douglas, chairman of the Securities and Exchange Commission.

To Jennie Taussig Brandeis

February 13, 1939 Washington, D. C. [Mason, *Brandeis*, 634]

DEAR JENNIE, My birthday greeting goes to you a bit early. But
I want you to know promptly that I am not retiring from the
Court because of ill health. Mine seems to be as good as heretofore.[1] But years have limited the quantity and intensity of work
possible, and I think the time has come when a younger man
should assume the burden.

It was fine to have the photograph of you and the grandchildren.

1. Actually, LDB's health was not good. He had been absent from the Court during nearly all of January 1939, suffering first from a severe case of grippe and then from a heart attack. According to Professor Mason, LDB had begun to show signs of physical decline as early as 1937. In that year he wrote only thirteen opinions, and the following year sixteen, compared to an annual average of well over thirty throughout the twenties and early thirties. Although there was no diminution of mental ability, he had less strength than before. His tea guests now found him sitting rather than standing, and Mrs. Brandeis made sure that dinner guests left by nine o'clock.

To Charles Warren

February 16, 1939 Washington, D.C. [Warren Mss]

DEAR CHARLES WARREN: My thanks for your generous letter. We plan to stay in Washington and shall hope to see you and Mrs. Warren soon.   Cordially,

To Charles Evans Hughes

February 18, 1939 Washington, D. C.
[Brandeis Mss, unmarked folder]

MY DEAR CHIEF JUSTICE: You and the Associate Justices are very generous.

Our friendship gives assurance that throughout the years to come we shall remain companions.[1]   Cordially,

1. On 17 February, the Court sent the customary letter to LDB noting his retirement. It said, in part: "Your long practical experience and intimate knowledge of affairs, the wide range of your researches and your grasp of the most difficult problems, together with your power of analysis and your thoroughness in exposition, have made your judicial career one of extraordinary distinction and far-reaching influence. It has always been gratifying to observe that the intensity of your labors has never been permitted to disturb your serenity of spirit and we shall have an abiding memory of your never-failing friendliness. We trust that, relieved of the pressing burden of regular court work, you may be able to conserve the strength which has been so lavishly used in the public service, and that you may enjoy many years of continued vigor."

Of the eight remaining justices, only seven signed the letter. Mr. Justice McReynolds, who had been an ideological opponent of LDB since 1916 and the only member of the Court ever to display a marked anti-Semitism, refused to sign.

To Neville Chamberlain (Cable)

February 26, 1939 Washington, D. C. [R. Szold Mss]

DEAR PRIME MINISTER: London friends advise me of the proposed intentions of His Majesty's Government with reference to Palestine.[1] Having discussed in detail the problem of the Jewish National Home in Palestine with the late Lord Balfour prior to the publication of the Balfour Declaration and the acceptance of the mandate, I cannot believe that your Government has fully considered how gravely shattered would be the faith of the people of this troubled world in the solemn undertakings of even democratic governments if Great Britain so drastically departed from her declared policy in reference to the Jewish National Home.[2] I urge you to consider the cruel plight of the Jews in the world today and not to crush their most cherished and sanctified hopes. In view of your own belief in direct communication I venture to address this to you personally.[3]   Respectfully,

1. As it became obvious that the St. James Conference would fail to secure an understanding between the Arab and Jewish communities of Palestine, rumors were rife that the British were prepared to impose their own settlement on the Palestinian problem—that, in fact, the so-called "Round Table Conference" had been a sham all along, designed only to provide, by its failure, a rationale for a radical change in the Mandatory arrangement. See Chaim Weizmann, *Trial and Error,* 406–407.

2. See LDB to Franklin Roosevelt, 4 May 1939, and to Robert Szold, 10 May 1939.

3. On 6 March 1939 the British ambassador to the United States, R. C. Lindsay (see LDB to Julian W. Mack, 19 June 1930, n. 1), responded: "I think you may know that any opinion you may entertain on the question of Palestine, when brought to the attention of my Government, commands their respectful and earnest attention. In the present instance I am to beg that whatever reports you may have heard, you will defer forming an opinion until my Government shall have issued an authoritative statement as to their attitude. Meanwhile you can rest assured that they are very mindful of their obligations with regard to the Jewish National Home under the Balfour Declaration and the Mandate." See LDB to Roosevelt, 16 March 1939.

To Robert D. Kesselman

March 16, 1939 Washington, D. C. [Kesselman Mss]

MY DEAR ROBERT KESSELMAN: I am very glad to have yours of Feb. 14th. Like you, I believe "that we will emerge out of these difficulties unscathed, as long as we do not remain idle and apply ourselves with our might and strength to our tasks." Make every one of our Palestinians act sedulously on that belief. If they do, neither British nor Arab can prevent our realizing, in time, "the Jewish National Home."

My health is as good as heretofore. I resigned because the work of the Court necessitated a strain unwise in view of my years.

Cordially,

To Franklin Delano Roosevelt

March 16, 1939 Washington, D. C. [Roosevelt Mss]

DEAR MR. PRESIDENT: You will recall the letter of March 6 from Ambassador Lindsay,[1] which I showed you, in which the Ambassador indicated that he had been instructed to assure me that His Majesty's Government "are very mindful of their obligations with regard to the Jewish National Home under the Balfour Declaration and the Mandate."

Today word comes to me of decisive import showing clearly a contemplated course of British action which is wholly inconsistent with the Balfour Declaration and Mandate. In order to save your time I am writing you instead of troubling you with a visit.

These are the essentials of the contemplated British action:

1. An independent state, after an interim of probably not more than ten years, which would practically crystallise the present minority status of the Jews in Palestine.

2. Restriction of immigration during the next five years to 10,000 a year, with no assurance of further immigration without Arab consent.

3. Restriction of land purchases so as practically to make land acquisition by Jews largely impossible.[2]

In a private talk with Mr. Chamberlain he admitted to Dr.

Weizmann that he did not blame Dr. Weizmann for refusing to cooperate on the basis of the British proposals. Mr. Chamberlain added that his personal feeling is friendly towards the Jews, but that he is not free to disregard the recommendations of his advisors.

As the formal action of the British Government is not to be announced until early next week, I am wondering whether you would not feel that a word from you to London may yet be in time to avert the folly and injustice of the British proposals.[3]

Yours sincerely,

1. See LDB to Neville Chamberlain, 26 February 1939, n. 3.

2. The outline bore a striking resemblance to the final British plan, presented in the MacDonald White Paper on 17 May 1939. That document predicated the establishment of an independent Palestinian state, closely tied to Britain, within ten years; immigration would not exceed 75,000 additional Jews over a five-year period; and land transfers were restricted to an area comprising less than five percent of Palestine.

3. On 23 March, Roosevelt responded: "All I have been able to do so far has been to postpone any British announcement until next week. I am trying to put it off still further. Apparently the British are very much worried by German and Italian incursions into the whole Mohammedan area." See LDB to Roosevelt, 17 April 1939.

To Stephen Samuel Wise, Robert Szold, and Solomon Goldman

March 27, 1939 Washington, D. C. [R. Szold Mss]

FOR S. S. W. AND R. S. AND S. G.: [1] Myron Taylor [2] was in over an hour. In first 50 minutes he told, without interruption, doubtless, in the main, what he told your Committee on Friday. Then he handed me copies of the 3 documents; (letter to him of March 17th; "Objects"; and Feb. 17/39 "Plan for the Emigration of Non Aryans from Germany") [3] and said he hoped I would help along the formation of the corporation etc. I told him that my relations with the rich German-American Jews rendered that impossible because of their attitude toward Palestine (and that most of those he had in mind I did not even know); that if they wish for my advice I should, of course, be glad to see them, etc.

He said this plan does not exclude Palestine. I answered "Yes" but unless they get over their "Zionist Phobia"—they will not call upon me. Then for about 10 minutes I told him my views as to the Palestinian possibilities.

Taylor told me that the President was unable to arrange for the interview with Ittleson [4] et al, which Taylor had hoped for for this afternoon.

I told him as he left that I hoped we should meet again. He said—"Yes, there are also other things we might talk over."

His narration included his talks in Paris, in Italy and at Monte Carlo.

1. Solomon Goldman (1893–1953), a Conservative rabbi from Chicago, served as president of the Zionist Organization of America from 1938 to 1940, and he headed the American delegation to the Twenty-first Zionist Congress later that year. See Jacob J. Weinstein, *Solomon Goldman: A Rabbi's Rabbi* (New York, 1973). Jacob Billikopf (see LDB to Billikopf, 25 January 1915), an occasional visitor of LDB during this period, recalled one such visit in a letter to Mrs. Max C. Sloss of San Francisco (28 October 1939): "Brandeis rarely uses superlatives when he speaks of persons. Very conservative in his estimate of folk. I don't recall his ever using a superlative in reference to such disciples as Julian W. Mack, Stephen S. Wise, the late Jacob deHaas or other folk, but he becomes lyrical when he talks of Rabbi Solomon Goldman of Chicago, President of the Zionist Organization of America. Lyrical is the word: He thinks that Goldman is one of the greatest, if not the greatest, find in American Jewry today."

2. Myron Charles Taylor (1874–1959), the long-time head of U. S. Steel, had been named American ambassador to the 1938 refugee conference at Evian, and he remained active in refugee matters until after the war. Later in 1939 Roosevelt named him the first American ambassador to the Vatican.

3. Following the uproar in Western countries over the *Kristallnacht* ("night of glass," an orgy of anti-Jewish destruction and looting that took place on 9–10 November 1938) and increased anti-Semitic repression in Germany, Nazi officials sought to find other less controversial means of ridding the Reich of its 600,000 Jews. In the early months of 1939, Hjalmar Schacht, head of the Reichsbank, carried on lengthy and ultimately futile negotiations with Taylor, George Rublee (appointed by Roosevelt to the Inter-Governmental Committee on Refugees), and Jewish leaders over a plan to impound one fourth of German Jewry's wealth to pay for the cost of resettling them outside of the Reich. For details of the plan and negotiations, see Henry Feingold, *The Politics of Rescue* (New Brunswick, N. J., 1970), ch. 3.

4. Henry Ittelson (1871–1948) founded the Commercial Investment Trust, the largest independent sales financing company in the nation. Ittel-

son was chairman of the board of New York's Federated Jewish Philanthropies, and active in the United Jewish Appeal and the American Jewish
Committee.

To Franklin Delano Roosevelt

April 17, 1939 Washington, D. C. [Roosevelt Mss]

DEAR MR. PRESIDENT: The American Zionist Organization has
just received from London the enclosed cable.[1] Our friends deem
it very important that no announcement be made in the near
future.

I hope that you may be able, by your wise counsel, to prevent
the making of an announcement now.[2]   Cordially,

1. According to the London office of the Jewish Agency, the British
Colonial Office was going to promulgate its new immigration policy for
Palestine on 24 April, but refused to disclose its contents; in fact, several
British officials even denied that there would be any new plan.

2. Evidently the Colonial Office was not yet ready to release the White
Paper and acceded to American requests not to limit Jewish immigration
to Palestine. See LDB to Roosevelt, 16 March and 4 May 1939.

To Fannie Brandeis

April 20, 1939 Washington, D. C. [Fannie Brandeis]

DEAR FAN: Dr. H. H. Bennett,[1] Chief of the Soil Conservation
Service (Dept. of Agriculture) was in today with Morris L.
Cooke to tell of the crying need for extending this service; and
what is now being done. 15,000 "experts" aided by 80,000 C.C.C.
boys are now working in aid of the efforts of 35 states.

I asked him about Kentucky. He said Kentucky is among the
states most needing aid, but that, for some unaccountable reason,
no substantial interest had developed and that it is not among the
35. I suggested that the Courier-Journal would surely be alive
to the need if properly approached, mentioning particularly
Barry Bingham.[2] Dr. Bennett said there had been two editorials
there, but no campaign.

I am sure you, as a farmer, will feel deeply on this matter; and

I hope you will, immediately, talk to Barry Bingham and his associates.

I wonder whether the [University of Louisville] Library has all the conservation documents. Obviously it should have all.

I have two impressive ones. U. S. Dep. Agr. Miscellaneous Publications No. 321 "To Hold the Soil," and "Conservation of the Soil—a program of Action," which I will send with the next shipment. But make sure promptly that you have all the others. Let me hear from you.

1. Hugh Hammond Bennett (1881–1960) had joined the Bureau of Soils in 1903, and he soon became one of the world's leading authorities on soil use. In 1933, President Roosevelt named him head of the newly created Soil Conservation Service, with a special charge to combat dust-bowl conditions in the Midwest. In his more than fifty years in government service, Hammond gained the title "Father of the soil conservation movement."

2. (George) Barry Bingham (b. 1906) was editor and publisher of the *Louisville Courier-Journal*, and a close friend of the Brandeis family. He was the son of Judge Robert W. Bingham (see LDB to Alfred Brandeis, 5 October 1909, n. 5).

To Franklin Delano Roosevelt

May 4, 1939 Washington, D. C. [Roosevelt Mss]

DEAR MR. PRESIDENT: Would it not be possible for you to again induce the British to postpone the threatened announcement of their Palestine policy? [1]

The enclosed leaflet published by the Christian Friends of Palestine,[2] of which Bishop Freeman [3] is the president, lends strong support to your view.   Cordially,

1. Although the President had successfully interceded with Great Britain twice before (see LDB to Roosevelt, 16 March and 17 April 1939), this time his efforts proved futile. Roosevelt did ask the State Department to do what it could, and in a private memorandum to Secretary of State Hull on 10 May he stated that he thought any announcement on Palestine at the time would be a mistake. On 11 May, Roosevelt assured LDB that everything possible was being done, and on 12 May he sent him a memorandum reporting that the British were contemplating delaying action. But pressure from the Arabs, and the worsening situation on the Continent, finally led to the issuance of the White Paper on 17 May (see LDB to

Roosevelt, 16 March 1939, n. 2). For details of the Jewish reaction to the White Paper, see Weizmann, *Trial and Error*, ch. 38, and Walter Laqueur, *A History of Zionism* (New York, 1972), 528–33.

2. There were a number of Christian organizations, most of them sponsored to some extent by the Zionists, that worked on behalf of Jewish immigration into Palestine. For details of their activities, see Samuel Halperin, *The Political World of American Zionism* (Detroit, 1961), ch. 7. The pamphlet may have been *Memorandum in Behalf of Jewish Immigration Into Palestine* (New York, n. d.), published by the Committee of Christian Leaders, Clergymen and Laymen.

3. James Edward Freeman (1866–1943) was Episcopal bishop of Washington, D.C.

To Robert Szold

May 10, 1939 Washington, D. C. [R. Szold Mss]

DEAR BOB: I assume you are receiving direct, from [Solomon] Goldman or from others the many cables indicating that our Palestine leaders have become panicstricken.[1] Most of the things asked are either impossible of attainment or very unwise suggestions.

Today's J[ewish]. T[elegraphic]. A[gency]. indicates that the contemplated Hashomer Hatzair settlement near Ein Hashofet has been started—and [Joshua] Leibner's letter of April 16 indicates that Ein Hashofet will not need money from us in the near future.[2]

What would you say to our sending an additional $5000. to Keren Hashomer Hatzair for the settlement announced by J.T.A. —if you find that fact confirmed? Such action might help to make them understand where our faith lies.

1. Over the imminent announcement of the White Paper.

2. Beginning in 1937, LDB had privately and quietly donated $50,000 to establish a kibbutz in Samaria that would be populated primarily by Americans. Ultimately named Ein HaShofet (Spring of the Judge) after LDB, the kibbutz was affiliated with the federation HaShomer HaTza'ir. HaShomer HaTza'ir was a Zionist youth movement formed in 1913 in Poland, which prepared Jewish youth to settle on kibbutzim in Palestine. After 1919, the movement also included the federation of kibbutzim in Palestine dedicated to Labor Zionist principles. Part of its educational work involved sending missionaries to Jewish communities in the Diaspora to recruit new settlers. See *Encyclopedia of Zionism and Israel*, I: 463–65.

To Robert Szold

May 23, 1939 Washington, D. C. [R. Szold Mss]

DEAR BOB: 1. By Railway Express I am sending you all the papers received from Mrs. [Rose] Jacobs, except those heretofore sent to Mr. Jacobs or to you. Express receipt enclosed.

2. Dr. [Stephen S.] Wise was in today, after the days operations with Congressmen, Senators & the State Department; and had some hope that [Cordell] Hull might make known the American view by direct communication with Halifax.[1]

3. S.S.W. mentioned to me the matter of inviting (?) Weizmann to come to America for his supposed influence on the members of the Lasker[2] etc. Com[mit]tee & securing large sums for Palestine. I told him emphatically (a) that we should not have any part in the responsibility for W's coming to America, if he does come, (b) that I saw no reason to believe that W—the pronounced Zionist—would have any favorable influence on the Committee.

4. I also told him emphatically that I thought he ought not to favor the British Guiana project[3] as it is a clear fraud on Britain's part and that of some anti-Zionists, designed to divert the pressure for opening Palestine.

5. I assume you have not yet learned what has been done with the birthday money.

6. The landing of the 308 "illegal" immigrants was a dramatic event, coming at this time.[4]

7. We plan to leave Washington for Boston Monday, June 5.

8. E. A. Norman[5] has asked to see me Friday next. I fixed 3 P.M.

1. Edward Frederick Lindley Wood, First Earl of Halifax (1881–1959) had entered Parliament in 1910 and in the 1920s earned high marks for his work as viceroy of India. During the 1930s he was among many in high government positions who trusted Hitler, and in 1938 he was named Foreign Secretary after Anthony Eden had resigned that office in protest over the Munich settlement. In 1940, upon the sudden death of Lord Lothian (see LDB to Szold, 7 December 1939 n. 7), Halifax became ambassador to the United States, and he served in that office until 1946. See his memoirs, *Fullness of Days* (London, 1957).

2. Albert Davis Lasker (1880–1952) was a pioneer in the American advertising industry and prominent in numerous Jewish groups. See John

Gunther, *Taken at the Flood: The Story of Albert D. Lasker* (New York, 1960).

3. See LDB to Szold, 24 November 1938, n. 6.

4. In protest against British immigration policies, the Haganah had begun a series of operations to rescue Jews fleeing Hitler and to bring them into Palestine despite the White Paper quota. One of the first boatloads of this so-called "Aliyah Bet" had landed at the time of this letter, and the movement continued until the establishment of the Jewish state in 1948. For details, see Ehud Avriel, *Open the Gates!* (New York, 1975).

5. Edward Albert Norman (1900–1955) had worked for *Survey* and the Cooperative League in the 1920s before assuming responsibilities for his family's extensive financial holdings. Although a non-Zionist, he was very much interested in Palestine and he became a member of the Jewish Agency Executive. In 1939 Norman was head of the American Economic Commission for Palestine, and he would soon establish the American Fund for Palestine Institutions, which later became the American-Israel Cultural Foundation.

To Robert Szold

June 28, 1939 Chatham, Mass. [R. Szold Mss]

DEAR BOB: And J.W.M[ack]., B[ernard]. F[lexner]., S.S.W[ise]., Mrs. [Rose] Jacobs and Solomon Goldman.

1. For nearly four weeks illness has prevented my considering the important problems presented by your letters, those of others, and many reports. Much of the material has not been examined.

2. But it is clear that in the months to come much money will be needed, and Dr. Goldman's visit to Palestine and Poland may develop some smaller needs which P[alestine].E[ndowment]. F[und]. should be able to satisfy in part. I am therefore, enclosing check to P.E.F. for $13,500. to be applied (after paying the $250. July 1 to Miss Szold & the price of the $5000. P[alestine].E[conomic].C[orporation]. bonds) to the suggested, or other, Palestine purposes as we may determine.

3. I hope that Chatham may soon bring reinvigoration, that I can see Goldman before he sails.

P.S. Re: yours of 26th. I have not yet read yours of 10th. Let me have your recommendation, if not already fully given.

To Bernard Flexner

July 12, 1939 Chatham, Mass. [Flexner Mss]

DEAR BEN: Re yours of 1st July; May 30; & June 8. Julius Simon's of June 15. Mr. Leavitt's of June 7th and 12th.

First: The time has happily come when I can begin to think of work and my first essay was to examine your Annual Report.[1] It deserves Cyrus Adler's praise, and I hope his followers will subscribe quickly to the bonds. Surely P[alestine]. E[conomic]. C[orporation]. directors etc. should come forth promptly.

Second: I think we may feel well satisfied with the arrangement made by Solomon Goldman alone representing America,[2] after his information-seeking stay in Palestine and S.S.W[ise]. and R.S[zold]. in control of the American end.

Third: I hope you had a full talk with Goldman.

Felix [Frankfurter] writes that he has found no friend of the White Paper in England, and that all his friends expect war.

I hope you and Mim will read "You and the Refugee," a Penguin book, by Norman Angell and Dorothy Frances Buxton.[3]

1. See LDB to Stephen S. Wise, 24 October 1939.
2. Goldman was in charge of the American delegation to the Twenty-First Zionist Congress in Geneva scheduled for the following month.
3. Norman Angell and Dorothy Frances Buxton, *You and the Refugee: The Morals and Economics of the Problem* (Harmondsworth, England, 1939).

To Israel Binyamin Rosov

July 14, 1939 Chatham, Mass. [Brodie Mss]

DEAR ISRAEL ROSOV: Your greeting transmitting carbon of your spirited letter of May 28th to the General Officer Commanding tells me of your continued activity in Jewish affairs.

I hope you will use all your influence to discourage and prevent outbreaks of violence or terrorism on the part of Jews.[1] Our path to victory lies in peaceful, courageous, constructive work. That will afford opportunity for the expression of the best that is in us—spiritually, intellectually, in character and in ability.

Cordially,

I hope you will have a full talk with Dr. Solomon Goldman of whose character and abilities I have a very high opinion.

1. Throughout the 1930s there had been a growing discontent on the part of some Palestinian Jews with the policy of *Havlagah* (restraint) practiced by the Haganah and the Jewish Agency in the face of increased Arab terrorism. The focus of this resentment was the Irgun Tz'vai L'umi, popularly called Etzel, which was headed by militant Revisionists. Until May 1939, Etzel played a relatively low-key role in Palestine, but with the publication of the White Paper, it launched an all-out campaign to harass the Mandatory officials, while at the same time organizing a massive illegal immigration (Aliyah Bet) to circumvent British restrictions. The Etzel campaign often followed the dictum of "an eye for an eye," and British soldiers were abducted, and on occasion executed, in retaliation for British activities against Jews. The Jewish Agency and the Zionist Executive, as well as most of the Yishuv, opposed and condemned Etzel's activities, but the organization provided the one active outlet for Jewish frustration with Great Britain. Rosov (see LDB to Alice G. Brandeis, 1 August 1919, n. 1) was a member of the Revisionists.

To Robert Szold

August 2, 1939 Chatham, Mass. [R. Szold Mss]

DEAR BOB: I have yours of July 29th.

1. Mrs. [Rose] Jacobs was here yesterday and will report fully to you.

I think she will follow my advice and consent to serve.

Her complaint of lack of support from Hadassah [1]—and of refusal of the Executive to respect American opinion seems to me justified and should be guarded against—so far as possible.

I suggest that you come here as early as possible next week, so that there will be ample time to have your letter embodying our views reach [Solomon] Goldman in due time.

Please wire on receipt of this what day will suit you best.

2. Felix [Frankfurter] was here Sunday. He says in Government circles no one is "thinking of Palestine"—but that the prevailing opinion is that the Mandates Commission will settle the matter by declaring against the White Paper [2]—and that the one important thing for us is not to antagonize the military arm.

Felix will go to Alfred Cohen's at Milford as soon as Marion is able to do so, and will ask you to come there for a talk.

3. Please show Mrs. Jacobs enclosed letter from [Israel Jacob] Kligler & return it to me. Also let me know his American address. Can you furnish a translation of enclosed letter from Mr. Goldman of Roxbury?

1. Hadassah consistently avoided getting involved in the political disputes that frequently racked the Zionist organization, and eschewed tackling any problems other than its own medical and social works in Palestine. Mrs. Jacobs was a member of the Hadassah Executive at the time, and she got caught up in the negotiations to rescind or alter the White Paper. Perhaps she felt that in this instance Hadassah could have been more involved.

2. The majority of the Permanent Mandates Commission of the League of Nations declared that the White Paper violated the terms of the Mandate conferred upon Great Britain. Before the full League could meet to discuss the issue, however, World War II broke out.

To Bernard Flexner

October 4, 1939 Washington, D. C. [R. Szold Mss]

DEAR BEN: Nelson Glueck was in today—an uncommonly attractive person.[1] You would not recognize him as a Jew (see Who's Who); and, I guess, most of the Arabs with whom he came in contact in Palestine and Trans-Jordan did not.

1. The most urgent matter about which Julius Simon wanted him to talk with us, is that set forth in Simon's letter to Glueck of Sept. 8/39, to be returned to Glueck with my letter enclosed, as soon as your secretary has made a copy for your files.

2. Glueck knows the region well and is enthusiastic for the project.[2]

3. Most of the time was consumed in his answering my questions about Arab conditions & their relations to the Jews prior to the declaration of war.

(a) The economic condition of the Arabs has become indescribably bad, worsening almost continuously since the rioting began.

(b) Among the common people the view has been steadily spreading that there are enough Jews in Palestine; and that in Trans-Jordan there should be none.

(c) This hostility to Jewish immigration is, of course, attributable in part to German and Italian propaganda, mostly German in Palestine, mostly Italian in Trans-Jordan; partly by direct gifts of money to individuals.[3] But the original source and main cause are the attitudes and activities of the British civil authorities. They poison all non-Jewish comers, whatever their nationality. Of course, Consul General Wadsworth[4] is also poisonously hostile, and in Trans-Jordan, Cox.[5] And the Arab graduates of the American School at Beirut.

(d) I have met no one so emphatic in denunciating the attitude and action of the British Civil authorities. He deems it perfectly clear that the so-called "escape" of the Mufti[6] was furthered by the British; that his commanding terrorists were allowed to come and go; and that, at anytime, the British could have put an end to the terrorism. Conditions under MacMichael[7] are definitely worse than under Wauchope.

(e) As to the views of the common people, I think Glueck is a better witness than any I have seen. He cannot be recognized as a Jew; had no Jewish associates when in the field; refuses to take a consort; has no communication while in the field with any Jew; and has known the region off and on for ten years.

(f) He says the behavior of the Palestine Jews prior to the White Paper was amazingly good.

(g) Thinks the Arabs consider their chances under British better than they would be under Hitler.

(h) Says many Jewish constables went with British soldiers to guard Suez, etc. & that the military's attitude toward Jews is good.

4. For the sake of his position in archeological work, Glueck has been careful to keep out of all political and Jewish matters, and care must be taken not to embarrass him here by any disclosures made here.

5. He is to deliver lectures before Universities & Societies on the archeological work. He expects to come east before the end of the month, & to get to Boston and New York. I asked him to keep me advised.

1. Nelson Glueck (1900–1971) had taught archaeology at Hebrew Union College since 1928 and would become president of the seminary in 1947. He directed numerous excavations in Palestine, and he popularized many of his findings in *Rivers in the Desert* (New York, 1959).

2. Several commercially useful projects resulted from Glueck's explora-

tions; one of them was the discovery and reopening of the so-called King Solomon's copper mines at Timna, about fourteen miles north of Eilat.

3. With the outbreak of the world war at the beginning of September 1939, Axis propaganda aimed at disaffecting the Arabs from the British increased enormously. A major theme was the exploitation of anti-Jewish sentiment among the Arabs, with the promise that the fascists would eliminate the Jews from Palestine.

4. George Wadsworth (1893–1958) was a career foreign service officer who had spent many years in the Middle East. Wadsworth headed the Jerusalem consulate from 1936 to 1940; he would later serve as ambassador to Iraq, Turkey, and Saudi Arabia. The Zionists considered him pro-Arab and worked for his removal; see LDB to Stephen S. Wise, 8 November 1939.

5. Sir (Charles) Henry (Fortnom) Cox (1880–1953) was the British resident in Transjordania from 1924 to 1939.

6. Hajjamin Al-Husayni (b. 1893), the Mufti of Jerusalem, had been a prime force behind the anti-Jewish riots in Palestine in the 1930s. In 1937 he escaped to Lebanon and in October 1939 went on to Baghdad, where he led an unsuccessful coup to install a pro-German government in Iraq. During the war he was a guest of Hitler in Germany, and for a while in the 1940s he played a major role in fomenting anti-Israeli activities. At last report, he was living in Saudi Arabia, a pensioner of the government.

7. Sir Harold MacMichael (1882–1969) was British High Commissioner of Palestine from 1938 to 1944. Unlike his predecessor, Sir Arthur Wauchope, MacMichael had little sympathy with the Zionists, and he attempted to enforce the provisions of the White Paper rigidly. On the eve of his departure from Palestine in 1944, an abortive attempt was made on his life, indicating the extent to which he was held personally responsible for British harshness in the Holy Land.

To Elizabeth Brandeis Raushenbush

October 14, 1939 Washington, D. C. [EBR]

DEAR ELIZABETH: You, Paul and Walter may care to see enclosed clipping.

Through Sherman Mittell, Mr. McNutt [1] and Fowler Harper,[2] his General Counsel, came in on Thursday & I subjected them to a long discourse on the heresy of the prevailing unemployment compensation system. McNutt as well as Harper were quite knowing; McNutt said definitely that he agreed with me; and both agreed to my statement that, in presenting the option to the several states, the Social Security officials have not done so fairly. McNutt remarked, "Of course, it would have been much easier to have prevented the [*] than to cure it."

We can't expect anything to result immediately, but it is worthwhile to have them understand & to be really sympathetic.

Mr. Harper said he had on his desk my 1911 memo to Lincoln Filene.[3] I suppose Mary Switzer [4] gave it to him. Wouldn't it be worthwhile for you to send Mary Paul's "Experience Rating memo." She would probably hand it to Mr. Harper.

I thought it wise for me not to give them a copy.

1. Paul Vories McNutt (1891–1955), an Indiana law professor, had been governor of that state from 1933 to 1937, and then held a number of top-level diplomatic and government assignments in the Roosevelt administration. From 1939 to 1945 he headed the Federal Security Administration.

2. Fowler Vincent Harper (1897–1965), on leave from the Indiana University Law School, was serving as counsel for the Federal Security Administration, and would later serve in other government posts. In 1947 he joined the Yale Law School, where he taught until his retirement.

3. See LDB to A. L. Filene, June 1911.

4. Mary Elizabeth Switzer (1900–1971) was a close friend of Elizabeth Brandeis, who had worked with her on the District of Columbia Wage Board in 1921. Miss Switzer continued to work for the federal government, and from 1934 to 1939 she was in the public health division of the Treasury Department. From 1939 to 1950 she served as assistant to the administrator of the Federal Security Agency, at which time she became commissioner of the Vocational Rehabilitation Administration, one of the highest-ranking women in the government.

To Shlomo H. Bardin

October 20, 1939 Washington, D. C. [R. Szold Mss]

DEAR DR. BARDIN: [1]—Re: Yours of 19th.[2]

I remember well your and Mr. Jonas' [3] visit at Chatham, some years ago, and my remark which you quote. It is probable that I reported fully to Robert Szold, as it is my custom to consult him on gifts to be made by Palestine Endowment Fund. But I have no recollection of having said to anyone that "Bardin should not be helped, his father-in-law should take care of him".

That is not my view as to the Technical High School or Haifa Nautical School, or the proposed Fishermen's School. Such technical education is highly desirable, and if, as I assume, the work is being well done at the schools of which you are the principal, Jewry is to be congratulated; and the schools should receive all possible support, regardless of Mr. Jonas' failure to contribute.

The first consideration of the Nautical School that I recall was in June 1938, when Robert Szold sent me your memorandum. No mention was then made of your connection with Mr. Jonas; the work being done was commended; and a contribution was refused solely on the ground that the money available was thought to be more urgently needed for other Palestinian purposes.

I assume you will again see Robert Szold. Of the value of nautical training and of the development of fishermen I am fully convinced. But when you come to Washington it will be a pleasure to hear of your work done and in prospect.

I am sending your letter and mine to Robert Szold.[4]

Cordially,

1. Shlomo H. Bardin (1898–1976) had founded both the Haifa Technical and the Haifa Nautical high schools in the 1930s. In 1941 he began his long career as head of the Brandeis Camp Institute in California.

2. Bardin had written protesting that the Palestinian schools were not receiving help from American sources, particularly from the Palestine Endowment Fund, and he believed that this was true because everyone assumed that his wealthy father-in-law (see next note) was providing the backing.

3. Ralph Jonas (1879–1952), a Brooklyn lawyer and a founder of Long Island University, was involved in a number of educational organizations. Aside from the Brooklyn Jewish Hospital, however, Jonas apparently did not interest himself in Jewish causes.

4. The P.E.F. later did make a small contribution to the Haifa schools.

To Bernard Flexner

October 23, 1939 Washington, D.C. [R. Szold Mss]

DEAR BEN: Re yours of 21st.

1. Dr. Leo S. Rowe of the Pan-American was in yesterday and reported to me confidentially on the Panama conference.[1] He says that the relations of the Latin American countries toward the United States are better perhaps than ever before, certainly are very good and that Sumner Welles [2] did his part admirably.

(a) But that the attitude of all the countries (except San

Domingo) are definitely adverse to Jewish refugee immigration. At best a few countries are willing to admit a few selective agricultural immigrants; but all are definite[ly] opposed to immigration of professional or businessmen, at present.

(b) As to San Domingo, he says the Government declares itself favorable; but it is very doubtful whether prospects of successful immigration are present. The only agricultural products are coffee and ?, and whether the soil etc. is fit for other agricultural products has not been ascertained, and that, in any event, the aggregate number of refugees who could find adequate living there is very limited.

(c) The proposal for settlement in Lower California must be rejected for political reasons. No Mexican administration could hold office which advocated it; and the coming year, involving a presidential election, is not a time when such a proposal could even be considered. It would be charged with being a subtle attempt of the United States to secure the peninsula.[3]

2. You will be interested in the enclosed letter of the 18th from Katherine E. Brand [4] and the Division of Manuscripts report. Of course, I wrote them that my papers had been deposited in Louisville.

3. I suppose you will read Charles Fairman's Life of Justice Miller.[5] On p. 118 you will find that James Speed, Atty General, was deemed a man without ability & a very poor lawyer. Did you ever hear that view expressed in Kentucky? [6]

4. Ben Cohen doubtless told you that I am to see the President tomorrow at 5 P.M.[7] I shall hand him a copy of your report, and see whether it is possible to get Palestine talked about now.

5. Look at "Palestine Opens its Doors" p. 5 of October Jewish Frontier.

6. I have reread [Solomon] Goldman's Convention address, now reprinted as "Land and Destiny," an admirable document.

7. It is fine to know that you and Mim plan to leave for Louisville on the 27th & to be here Nov. 3rd. The hour you suggest 10:30 A.M. Nov 3rd will suit me.

1. Following the eruption of war in Europe, the Roosevelt administration moved swiftly to strengthen the defenses of the western hemisphere against Axis intrusion. The ministers of the American republics met in Panama City on 23 September and quickly agreed upon common neutrality regulations, and on mutual consultation regarding potential transfer of territory

from one European power to another. In the Declaration of Panama, they marked out a zone three hundred miles wide around the Americas, excluding Canada and territorial possessions, into which the belligerents were forbidden to go.

2. Sumner Welles (1892–1961), a career foreign service officer, had represented the United States at the Panama conference, in his capacity as undersecretary of state. Welles was one of the few careerists in the State Department sympathetic to Zionism, and he later became an ardent advocate of the movement; see his *We Need Not Fail* (New York, 1948).

3. For the various settlement schemes proposed, but not adopted, to help Jewish refugees from fascism, see Henry L. Feingold, *The Politics of Rescue.*

4. Katherine Edith Brand was the long-time curator of manuscripts in the Library of Congress; she was primarily responsible for building up the immense Woodrow Wilson collection there.

5. Charles Fairman, *Mr. Justice Miller and the Supreme Court, 1862–1890* (Cambridge, Mass., 1939). Samuel Freeman Miller (1816–1890) was appointed to the Court by President Lincoln; his most memorable decision was in the Slaughterhouse Cases, 16 Wallace 36 (1873), against which Mr. Justice Field entered his dissent that ultimately extended the due process clause of the 14th Amendment to cover property as well as legal rights.

6. Flexner replied on the 25th that he had never heard that James Speed (1812–1887), whom Lincoln had appointed attorney general in 1864, was anything but an extremely competent lawyer.

7. See next letter.

To Stephen Samuel Wise

October 24, 1939 Washington, D. C. [R. Szold Mss]

SSW: Re yours of 23rd

I had my talk with F. D. [Roosevelt] as arranged: was there about thirty-five minutes: found him as sympathetic as in the past; and as interested in all I was able to tell him about the present in Palestine. There is reason to hope that he will say something about Palestine: also that he will do something about the Consul General situation.[1] Miss LeHand was present, and he had her take down what he wants to consider and to talk to Sumner Welles and to Lord Winterton.[2]

I handed him the P[alestine].E[conomic].C[orporation]. 12th Annual Report which he glanced at in my presence.

Please telephone Ben Flexner and Bob [Szold] the above and send me a copy.

Take very good care of yourself.

1. See LDB to Bernard Flexner, 4 October 1939 and next letter.

2. Edward Turnour, Sixth Earl of Winterton (1883–1962) had spent part of World War I stationed in Palestine, and during the 1920s he was undersecretary for India. From 1938 to 1945 he served as the British representative, as well as chairman, of the Intergovernmental Committee on Refugees. During that time he refused to budge from the official position that Palestine could not be opened to further immigration.

To Stephen Samuel Wise

November 8, 1939 Washington, D.C. [Wise Mss]

S.S.W.: 1. Messersmith [1] called on me yesterday. He stated positively that Consul General Wadsworth would be promptly transferred and that we should have, in his stead, a proper man. The substitute has not yet been selected. M. understands the situation fully. F.D. [Roosevelt] took up the matter with [Cordell] Hull the day after my visit.[2]

2. I am to see Duff Gordon Nov. 14th, 5 P.M. Please tell B[ernard]. F[lexner]. and Bob [Szold] and Mrs. deSola Pool.

I hope the bust is a good one.

1. George S. Messersmith (1883–1960) was a career foreign service officer who had represented the United States in a number of consulates and embassies. From 1937 to 1940 he was assistant secretary of state, and afterwards he served as ambassador to Cuba, Mexico, and Argentina.

2. See preceding letter, LDB to Bernard Flexner, 4 October 1939, and to Robert Szold, 22 October 1940.

To Henry Hurwitz

November 29, 1939 Washington, D. C. [Hurwitz Mss]

DEAR HENRY HURWITZ: My thanks for the birthday greeting.[1] Americans may realize the plight of the Jews in Central and Eastern Europe; but their achievements in Palestine are certainly not appreciated. These seem to me the most encouraging exhibition in a dismal world.

The significant thing is not the extraordinary material success under most adverse circumstances; but the fact that success has been possible because of the spiritual elevation of masses of common young men and women. That this heroism should not have thrilled, by its adventurous quality, the young American intellectuals is amazing.

The Menorah should tell the story. Adequately told it may be irresistible.[2]   Cordially,

1. LDB had recently celebrated his eighty-third birthday.

2. See LDB to Robert Szold, 13 December 1939, and to Hurwitz, 14 March 1941.

To Franklin Delano Roosevelt

December 4, 1939 Washington, D. C. [Roosevelt Mss]

DEAR MR. PRESIDENT: Secretary [Henry] Wallace brought me recently a report (marked confidential) on "Jewish Colonization in Palestine" by Dr. Lowdermilk,[1] Chief of Research, Soil Conservation Service. He states, i.a.: "The findings of Jewish agricultural colonization are fraught with significant consequences for the world at large, and for the United States in particular."

I hope you will ask Secretary Wallace to send you a copy of the report.[2]   Cordially,

1. Walter Clay Lowdermilk (b. 1888) was assistant chief of the Soil Conservation Division in the Department of Agriculture. He had just returned from a survey mission to Europe, Africa, and the Middle East. Lowdermilk's report, published by the Zionists in 1944 as *Palestine: Land of Promise*, praised Jewish efforts in the Holy Land, and set forth the idea of a Jordan Valley Authority, similar to the T.V.A., which would harness the waters of the river for both power and irrigation. Lowdermilk later became an ardent supporter of Israel and spent a number of years there as special consultant on water and soil. A special department was established at the Haifa Technion to develop his ideas, and he was its first head from 1954 to 1957.

2. The President replied on 16 December that he had received a copy of the report and was most interested in its findings, "especially in the devotion to the land which colonists, young and old alike, are demonstrating." He asked LDB to see him soon so they could discuss it. See LDB to Roosevelt, 20 December 1939.

To Robert Szold

December 7, 1939 Washington, D. C. [R. Szold Mss]

DEAR BOB: Dec. 1. You wrote (answering a paragraph in my letter):

"1. There is considerable stir (I would not call it a movement) at 111 Fifth Avenue against Dr. [Solomon] Goldman" etc.[1]

You treat lightly a matter which seems to me very serious in view i.a. of the following:

1. On Nov. 22 Kurt Blumenfeld,[2] who called, remarked, in passing, that Dr. Goldman is not to be re-elected (of course a statement which had been made to him at 111).

2. On Nov. 13 Dr. Goldman (who called on that day) had said in substance:

"It is clear that we shall have to fight the old guard in control at 111. Many of them must go—i.e. Abe Goldberg. (He had mentioned long before Margolies and others). And we must prepare for the fight. I want to arrange for a conference with you, Dr. [Stephen S.] Wise and Szold on this subject.["] He expressed confidence that he could beat the crowd (told me of Elihu Stone's attack).[3] And also told me that his wife had reminded him of the remarks I had made on the subject when they called on me in 1938—after his election and before he started for Palestine. (I characterized the 111 crowd as a "Tammany Gov." that he must meet and overcome).

3. I have not seen or heard directly from Goldman since Nov. 13.

4. Nov. 24. Mrs. Poole [sic] saw me 10 A.M. and again at 2:40. When she was in I told her of my talk with Dr. Joseph M. Cohen [5] who called with Breslau [6] re [Chaim] Weizmann on Nov. 20. At the 10 A.M. visit we spoke of Weiz. arriving Dec. 4. At the 2:40 visit she said she had seen Goldman (who was here with Wise and [Louis] Lipsky to see Lothian) [7] and that a cable had been received saying that W. had postponed his visit to early January.

I had not known that Goldman, Wise & Lipsky were to be here & heard nothing direct from them. Mrs. Poole [sic] told me that G. had to fly back to Chicago;—and that they concluded "not to trouble me". I supposed it was because Lipsky was with them.

5. On Nov. 28 Breslau called, and told me of a talk here between Goldman, Wise and Lipsky, at which Lipsky had talked of the importance of "rotation in office"; and Goldman had said definitely he would not run again for the Presidency.

6. Yesterday (Dec. 6) Breslau called (at my request on other matters) told me of the occurrences at the meeting in New York last Sunday (at which I understand you were present); of his talk with Goldman who reiterated that he would not run again; also of his talk with G. about Weizmann.

Naturally Goldman does not care to be President of Z.O.A. if he is not wanted & would rather not enter into a fight. But, obviously, the cause demands that he should make the fight & enter upon it at once. S.S.W. must recognize that neither Lipsky nor Weizmann will or can "change his spots". Weizmann will subtly use his influence to stop Goldman.

I understand Breslau, to whom I expressed frankly and fully my views, expects to see Goldman in New York (?) this week end. I hope you will see Breslau and before then talk with S.S.W[ise].; and thereafter you two will take this matter up with Goldman.[8]

It would be abvisable to see Mrs. Poole [sic] and have her tell you of our talk about Weizman [sic].

[Henry] Montor has sent me complete set of the audited reports of K[eren].K[ayemeth]., K[eren].H[ayesod]., Jewish Agency, and the Central Bureau for the settlement of the German Jews of the Jewish Agency. I will send you these copies (which came by air mail to N.Y.C.) unless you have them.

1. With the outbreak of the war, a number of old Zionist controversies had flared up again. Weizmann's American followers, out of power for most of the decade, now demanded that there be "unity" and total allegiance to the London office, and American Zionist headquarters saw a brief renewal of the old Brandeis-Lipsky alignments.

2. Kurt Yehuda Blumenfeld (1884–1963), until the rise of Hitler led him to flee Germany, had been president of the Zionist organization in that country for many years. Although Blumenfeld had settled in Palestine, he spent the war years in the United States on behalf of the Keren Hayesod.

3. Elihu David Stone (1888–1952), a Boston attorney, was the long-time Zionist leader of the New England region.

4. Tamar deSola Pool (b. 1894), the wife of Rabbi David deSola Pool, was an active Zionist and president of Hadassah from 1939 to 1943; she

later served as Hadassah's representative on a number of world committees within the Zionist organization.

5. Joseph M. Cohen, an Englishman, frequently served as an aide to Chaim Weizmann in the late thirties and early forties.

6. In 1939 Rabbi Isadore Breslau was an active Zionist in the Washington area. Later he was executive director of the Zionist Organization of America and a member of the executive boards of the Jewish Agency and United Jewish Appeal. During World War II he served as a chaplain in the army; he was with the first group to enter Berlin in 1945.

7. Philip Henry Kerr, Eleventh Marquess of Lothian (1882–1940) had recently become British ambassador to the United States, a position he held until his sudden death in December 1940.

8. Goldman was reelected and served as president of the Z.O.A. until the end of 1940.

To Louis Edward Levinthal

December 12, 1939 Washington, D. C. [Levinthal Mss]

DEAR JUDGE LEVINTHAL: My thanks for the birthday greeting.

In your efforts to make Philadelphians do their part toward the upbuilding of Palestine, I hope you will make the young intellectuals realize that, in the whole world, nothing finer—nothing nobler—is being achieved than by the young men and women in the agricultural settlements.   Cordially,

To Robert Szold

December 13, 1939 Washington, D. C. [Szold Mss]

DEAR BOB: Early this month I had occasion to write Henry Hurwitz and added as a qualifier the enquiry why the Menorah Journal should not, or did not, make clear to our intellectual youth, the extraordinary achievements of the young men and women in Palestine.[1] As a reply came enclosed letter from him of Dec. 4th and his visit here today.

He says he is eager to tell the story; has the writers & translators who could do it effectively; but hasn't the money; spoke of hostile attitude of Zionists to the Journal; and the difficult position it had been in financially; that he wouldn't undertake money raising, but if money was provided was eager to undertake the job. I told him that if anything was done by us, it would be through P[alestine].E[ndowment].F[und]., and suggested that he talk the matter over with you, which he said he would do.

I know nothing of the Journal's circulation or its finances or its supporters, except that Chief Judge [Irving] Lehman still befriends it. Nor do I know to what extent articles in the Journal might help. If it seemed promising, etc., it would be worthwhile providing some funds.

I had not seen H.H. for many years. I do not think that years had improved him as a human being.

You have not answered my question, whether you have the copies of the financial statements [Henry] Montor sent me & which I offered to send you.

1. See LDB to Henry Hurwitz, 29 November 1939.

To Franklin Delano Roosevelt

December 20, 1939 Washington, D. C. [Roosevelt Mss]

DEAR MR. PRESIDENT: I am very glad to have your letter of the 16th and await your convenience.[1]   Cordially,

1. See LDB to Roosevelt, 4 December 1939. On top of the letter the President had noted that he wanted to see LDB "right after the New Year."

To Bernard Flexner

January 18, 1940 Washington, D. C. [Flexner Mss]

DEAR BEN: Alpheus Mason wrote me on the 11th of his talk on the 10th with you. Yesterday he was here, and today I have sent him a letter to Miss Malloch, as he wants to talk with her, and look into things Bostonian, before he starts for Louisville.[1]

I understand that he will keep in touch with you and that you, or he, will let me know what further if anything, you want from me before he goes to Louisville or later.[2]

Alice thinks you will care to have enclosed letter of the 9th from Lott to her.

1. Professor Mason had begun work on what would become the standard and authoritative biography of LDB, *Brandeis: A Free Man's Life* (New York, 1946). See LDB to Flexner, 2 July and 7 August 1940.

2. LDB had, for some time, been in the process of transferring all of his private papers to the University of Louisville (see LDB to Flexner, 23 October 1939), where they would ultimately be housed in a special room in the law school. When Mason began work on the Brandeis biography, he hired a young Louisville woman as his research assistant to sort out and transcribe letters. Pearl von Allmen stayed on to become curator of the Brandeis collection as well as librarian of the law school until her death in 1974.

To Paul A. Palmer

January 26, 1940 Washington, D. C. [Palmer Mss]

DEAR MR. PALMER: [1] Re yours of 24th.

1. I must adhere to the rigid rule "not to write an article, give an interview, or authorize a statement."

2. Your memo returned herewith, shows that you have gotten my idea. I have in pencil suggested certain corrections as to matters of fact. Please let me have this memo, with my corrections, as soon as you have taken note of them for the clean copy to go to your associates.[2]

3. The man chiefly entitled to credit for the introduction of Savings Bank Insurance in New York is Sidney L. Wolff, 60 Beaver St., New York City, a cotton broker.   Cordially,

1. Paul A. Palmer (1906–1948), a political scientist trained at Harvard, eventually headed the government department at Kenyon College. He was a frequent contributor to several scholarly journals.

2. Palmer was seeking information for an article on savings bank life insurance.

To Yehoshua Heshel Farbstein

March 17, 1940 Washington, D. C. [R. Szold Mss]

DEAR MR. FARBSTEIN: [1] Re yours of 15th.

The last sentence in your letter does not state my position with entire accuracy. Please note: I am clearly of opinion that Palestine needs one or more small banks, with adequate capital, prepared to make to individuals of the middle class worthy of credit small loans required to enable them to engage in business or to strengthen an existing business. But as I am not familiar with the assets of the Mizrachi Bank, or with its personnel, I cannot know whether, with the additional capital now sought, its capital will be adequate or whether the personnel is competent and trustworthy.

With best wishes,   Cordially,

1. Yehoshua Heshel Farbstein (1870–1948), a leader of the Mizrachi, was also vice-president of the Actions Committee of the World Zionist Organization. He had settled in Palestine in 1931, and for a number of years he was head of the Jerusalem Jewish Community.

To Bernard Flexner

April 8, 1940 Washington, D.C. [R. Szold Mss]

DEAR BEN: Re yours of 5th.

On general principles, we should promote Arab stockholding in Jewish enterprises and proportionate employment of Arab labor, but never more than such proportionate employment and never for the purpose of employing labor at lower rates.

The particular project of shoe manufacturing with machinery from Czechoslovakia should not be touched until after very careful investigation. It has the smell of a Bata enterprise,[1] as to which there is much stir at present here, in connection with its Maryland factors and some 79, or more, retail stores in Chicago & elsewhere. The outfit is said to be stealthily violating many U.S. laws, and to be working under an arrangement with Hitler. Senator Tydings [2] is said to have acted for the Czechoslovakians.

The facts, or alleged facts, of transgression can be obtained from Goodman of the Shoeworkers union. His address can be obtained from Gardner Jackson, whom you doubtless know. He worked with Felix [Frankfurter] in the Sacco-Vanzetti case.

1. On 7 June 1939, Jan A. Bata, head of a Czechoslovakian shoe manufacturing company, had received special permission for one hundred aliens to enter the country in order to teach American workers the special techniques involved in Bata's allegedly unique process. Following that, Bata

built up a multimillion-dollar business rapidly, but he was constantly running afoul of the immigration laws. It turned out that the processes were far from unique, and the attorney general's office believed that Bata, despite his claim of having been stripped of his Czech properties, was actually working with the German government. Bata was also hauled into court several times for violating the child labor provisions of the 1938 Fair Labor Standards Act.

2. Millard Evelyn Tydings (1890–1961), a Maryland lawyer, had been elected to Congress in 1922, and then to the Senate in 1926, where he served until 1951. Despite his powerful position as chairman of the Senate Armed Services Committee, Tydings lost the 1950 election because of smears from Senator Joseph McCarthy that he was soft on communism.

To Robert Szold

April 10, 1940 Washington, D. C. [R. Szold Mss]

DEAR BOB: — Re Yours of 9th

When Dr. [Solomon] Goldman was here after the Baltimore victory, and on another occasion, when he seemed determined to carry on the fight against the [Louis] Lipsky crowd and to become President of the Z. O. A. for another year,[1] I told him to call on you for money if needed. And you are authorized to pay from any balance with P[alestine].E[ndowment].F[und]. what is needed for expenses incurred by him. But I am greatly disturbed by your statement: "Goldman leads me to believe he is definitely out of question". If that means that he will not become President for another year, I am not interested in the fight and do not want to be held for any of the expenses to be hereafter incurred. For I know no one who would be competent and willing to clean out the Lipsky gang and to worthily represent American Zionism.[2]

Please send me a memo. showing payment, commitments and balance of funds contributed by me to P.E.F.

I assume you will write concerning Hashomer Hatzair request as soon as you are able to make your recommendation.

1. See LDB to Szold, 7 December 1939, and next letter.
2. See LDB to Szold, 2 and 5 July 1940.

To Robert Szold

Washington, D. C. April 10, 1940 [R. Szold Mss]

DEAR BOB: 1. Re Yours of 9th as to war claims. I have no sympathy with Jewish Reclamation Claims. If the Germans are defeated, they will be unable to pay any claims; and even if they promised to do so, would not perform. Our interest is primarily in making possible a Jewish future.[1] It would, however, be desirable to have collected, so far as possible, an accurate account of the extent of the savagery perpetrated by the Germans upon the Jews, the robbery and destruction of property, the killing, maiming, etc. and the denial of civil rights. Those facts should be preserved.[2]

2. Re Yours as to Weizmann's coming. [Isadore] Breslau will have told you today of our talk yesterday. I am strongly against [Solomon] Goldman, and anyone else who has a soul, joining with the [Louis] Lipsky crowd.[3]

No "appeasement" for me.

1. The idea of making the Germans pay reparations to the Jews for stolen property was discussed among a number of groups early in the war, but many Jews lost interest in such measures when the full extent of the Holocaust became known. At that time, immediately after the war's end, the general sentiment was that no "blood money" could atone for the murder of six million people. As time passed, however, Nahum Goldmann and the World Jewish Congress revived the idea for two reasons: one, to help individuals who had survived the war, and, more important, to help the state of Israel. On 18 March 1953, the governments of Israel and West Germany signed an agreement under which the Federal Republic of Germany would, in the course of twelve to fourteen years, pay in cash or goods a sum of nearly one billion dollars. Of this, $107,000,000 would be turned over to the Conference on Jewish Material Claims against Germany, representing twenty-three organizations, for distribution to individuals. In the first ten years of the agreement, German payments covered nearly one-fifth of Israel's important needs.

2. Such a center for documentation was established in Israel by act of Knesset on 19 August 1953. Yad Vashem consists of a memorial to slaughtered Jews, an enormous library on the Holocaust period, and an archive which has become the world's center for Holocaust studies.

3. See LDB to Szold, 7 December 1939, n. 1.

To Bernard Flexner

April 20, 1940 Washington, D. C. [R. Szold Mss]

DEAR BEN: John Lord O'Brian [1] came to see me this A.M. to enquire about Dr. Kent. He said that as Secretary it was Horner's duty to call to the Board's Committee possible men as Commissioner; [2] that he had heard somewhere of Kent as a desirable man; that he had secured letters from a number of persons, including some in Louisville, who were eager to keep Kent there etc. O'Brian said, "Of course, letters are an entirely unsatisfactory source of information; and that Owen Young had suggested that he call on me to get my views."

I told O'Brian that, like the Louisvillians, I was prejudiced, because Kent had done an uncommonly good job there; and we wanted to keep him. I told him, in a few words, of the conditions before Kent came; what he had done; the recent developments; and that I thought it would be a distinct loss to Louisville and to rising culture in that region if he should leave.

I told him, also, that of his qualifications for the New York job I, of course, knew nothing; but that I doubted whether he would be happy at it, or in New York; that he and his wife "fitted" in Louisville; and that I doubted whether Mrs. Kent would be as happy in New York.

O'Brian said he did not think any suggestions had been made to Kent—or, indeed, that Kent knew that he had been proposed or suggested. [3]

I assume you and Mim are still planning to leave for Louisville on the 23rd.

We were glad to learn of the $100 sent in memory of Judge Mack's mother.

1. John Lord O'Brian (1874–1973) was a well known New York and Washington, D.C. lawyer. He held a number of governmental jobs (see, for example, LDB to Alice G. Brandeis, 16 October 1917), and was active in civic and political work.

2. Probably Harlan Hoyt Horner (1878–19[?]), a New York educator involved in various educational organizations. He was New York's associate commissioner of education from 1937 to 1939 and vice chairman of the American Council for Education. Perhaps he was interested in securing President Raymond A. Kent of Louisville for one of those organizations.

3. Kent remained in Louisville.

To Bernard Flexner

May 23, 1940 Washington, D. C. [R. Szold Mss]

DEAR BEN: Re yours of 22d—Ballinger-Ickes.[1]

1. On Ickes' part, the primary cause is a crazy and crazing lust for power, and hate of those who have frustrated his efforts for dominion. Transfer to the Interior of the Forestry from Agriculture; transfer of T[ennessee]. V[alley]. A[uthority]., now independent; and transfer of Rural Electric Authority, also independent. Pinchot is the chief villain in Ickes' eyes, as it was Pinchot who defeated Ickes' efforts through his friends in the Senate, and particularly Senator [George W.] Norris.[2]

I am told Ickes & Norris are no longer on speaking terms; that Ickes has been saying the vilest things of Slatterly [sic],[3] Pinchot's aid 30 years ago & recently Ickes' assistant, then undersecretary.

2. My thought has been: "Who has been behind Ickes?" The only persons who could be rationally interested in attacking the Ballinger disposition are the Taft family or friends. Of course, Taft and [George W.] Wickersham are, in the ante-dating of the Wickersham report, guilty of the worst act ever done by any president.[4]

3. While writing the above, your letter of the 22d enclosing the editorial has come. I am entirely content that Mason should publish now his article in the Post or elsewhere. If the Post won't take it, possibly Colliers might.[5] Friends of Bob Taft might use influence against its publication there.

4. Pinchot knows much about the talk on Ickes. I understand that he is leaving Washington tomorrow for his summer home at Milford, Pike Co., Pa. Sherman Mittell also spoke as if he knew much.

5. I have heard nothing from Ickes; I have read the editorial, but not the article. Enclosed letter just received (anonymous from Philadelphia), indicates what the tone of the article must be.[6]

---

1. Secretary of the Interior Harold Ickes had reopened the Pinchot-Ballinger controversy with an article entitled "Not Guilty! Richard A. Ballinger—An American Dreyfus," *Saturday Evening Post* 212 (25 May 1940): 9 ff. Shortly afterwards he issued a more formal and detailed justification, *Not Guilty, An Official Inquiry into the Charges Made by Glavis*

against Richard A. Ballinger, Secretary of the Interior (Washington, 1940). In both the article and the book, Ickes attacked Gifford Pinchot and Louis R. Glavis as political opportunists and spoilers who resented Ballinger less for his allegedly anticonservation policies than because he would not support their political ideas. Although Ickes did not attack LDB directly, he did cast aspersions upon the entire proceedings which LDB had directed. In a later article, Ickes went out of his way to say that LDB's only sin lay in his taking at face value the charges made by Pinchot and Glavis. See LDB to Norman Hapgood, 8 January 1910 and following letters in vol. 2.

2. Following the 1936 election, President Roosevelt had set out to streamline the executive branch of government, abolishing some agencies, merging others, and transferring some from one jurisdiction to another. Among the proposals was one involving shifting the Forestry Service from Agriculture to Interior. Gifford Pinchot had aroused his friends to defeat this plan, which would have added considerable power to Ickes's ability to influence national conservation policy. See Richard Polenberg, *Reorganizing Roosevelt's Government, 1936–1939* (Cambridge, Mass., 1966), especially ch. 5.

3. Harry Slattery (1887–1949) had been special assistant both to Gifford Pinchot and, later, to Secretary of the Interior Franklin K. Lane; during the 1920s he was active in a number of conservationist groups. In 1933 he rejoined the government as special assistant to Ickes, and he later served in a number of administration positions.

4. See LDB to Knute Nelson, 21 March 1910, and to James R. Garfield, 26 April 1910.

5. Instead of publishing an article, Mason eventually expanded his refutation of Ickes and defense of LDB into a book, *Bureaucracy Convicts Itself;* see LDB to Flexner, 2 July 1940.

6. Signing herself "A sorrowing woman," the anonymous author wrote: "It is too bad that the decent lawyers of New England who opposed your appointment to the Supreme Court are not now alive to know that their opposition has been vindicated, and that every American who reads the Saturday Evening Post feels just anger that such a character like you got by. . . . I cannot see how you can face decent Americans."

To Franklin Delano Roosevelt

June 14, 1940 Washington, D. C. [Roosevelt Mss]

DEAR MR. PRESIDENT: We are leaving today for our Chatham summer. You will be very much on our minds with our best wishes.[1]   Cordially,

1. On 18 June, the President responded: "I do wish I could have seen you before you left but our friends tell me you are well. Do continue to take good care of yourself. I fear that you and I have the same feeling of futility in these daily events—but both of us must keep up our spirits and our hopes."

To Bernard Flexner

July 2, 1940 Chatham, Mass. [R. Szold Mss]

DEAR BEN: I am glad to know from yours of June 26th, and Mason's of June 29th, that you have decided the [Richard A.] Ballinger study should appear as a book and that you expect to offer it to a publisher soon.[1]

I have written Mason that I shall be glad to see him here (on other matters) [2] soon.

1. Alpheus T. Mason's study of the conservation battle, and the response to Ickes's charges (see LDB to Flexner, 23 May 1940), appeared as *Bureaucracy Convicts Itself: the Ballinger-Pinchot Controversy of 1910* (New York, 1941). The book was published by Viking Press.
2. Mason's biography of LDB.

To Robert Szold (Telegram)

July 2, 1940 Chatham, Mass. [R. Szold Mss]

Congratulations to you, Goldman, Kaufman [*sic*].[1] Now take a good rest.

1. At the 1940 convention, the Z.O.A. elected Washington businessman Edmund Kaufmann as president to succeed Solomon Goldman. Goldman was chosen as a vice-president. Kaufmann, although a supporter of the Brandeis-Mack group, proved to be a weak president. In any event, power within American Zionism was already shifting to the newly created Emergency Committee for Zionist Affairs (see next letter).

To Robert Szold

July 5, 1940 Chatham, Mass. [R. Szold Mss]

DEAR BOB: My yesterday's letter was mailed before [Louis I.] Newman arrived. What he told me increased my uneasiness:

1. The composition of the Board [1] is much worse than I realized.—Clearly you must make every effort to win for us all, or most, of the possible additional five.[2] And should not our nominees be of the young men who fought resolutely against the Lipsky-Wise [3] contingent?

2. The Eliezer Kaplan [4] participation is very disturbing. Clearly Weizmann and the Palestinians and Nahum Goldman[n] must be made to keep their hands off American affairs. Of course, they should be heard on international matters. But "states rights" must be observed.[5]

(I suppose [Isadore] Breslau told you of my emphatic talk to Kaplan.)

3. The fight to clear ZOA of "the gang" must evidently be begun at once, and we must bring in the "4000" New Yorkers Dr. [Solomon] Goldman contemplated, as soon as possible, and as many more throughout the United States as possible.

Lipskyites must be made to see each day that we are in to build a worthy ZOA and that none of his gang are to be fed by ZOA.

4. The New Palestine should be published in and from Washington.[6]

1. Of the Emergency Committee for Zionist Affairs. Since the Committee was to function as the chief agency for Zionism, it had a very heavy contingent of Weizmann followers on it, together with several representatives of European-based groups. Although the Brandeis contingent had a sizeable representation, they could not control a majority of the Committee.

2. The board was authorized to co-opt an additional five members.

3. Stephen S. Wise had been among the first of LDB's followers to make his peace with the Lipsky group, and in the early 1940s he also was reconciled to Chaim Weizmann. At several points during the war, Wise's desire for unity among various Jewish factions led him to oppose the militant position of the Szold group.

4. Eliezer Kaplan (1891–1952), a Russian-born and trained engineer, had settled in Palestine in 1923, where he became a leader of Histadrut. In 1933 he became a member of the Jewish Agency Executive in charge of financial affairs, and in 1948 became Minister of Finance for the new State of Israel. Kaplan was a staunch supporter of Chaim Weizmann.

5. A constant source of irritation during the war was the resentment of American leaders, especially Abba Hillel Silver, at the alleged meddling of the European faction. Weizmann had Nahum Goldmann set up an office in Washington in order to lobby for Zionist interests, and Goldmann rarely bothered consulting with the Silver group. As a result, the Silver group was often embarrassed at not knowing what had happened, or finding that Goldmann had made a commitment without telling them. In the end, Silver resigned in protest, and he came back only when Weizmann promised to rein Goldmann in, a promise he proved unable to keep.

6. The New Palestine continued to be published in New York.

To Robert Szold

July 17, 1940 Chatham, Mass. [R. Szold Mss]

DEAR BOB: Re yours of 15th.

1. If there is any taint of "communism" in Avukah,[1] we should not, in any way, aid in their financing. Men may think what they will as to economics or politics. But renunciation of the fundamental moral law on the theory that "the end justifies the means" may not be tolerated.

2. Enclosed is letter of 14th from Mrs. Lindheim. Has she talked to you or to any of the Hadassah folk about this; or has Judge Mack talked with you about it?[2]

3. I am glad [Isadore] Breslau appears to be tied to [Edmund] Kaufman [sic].

4. My best wishes to Eliezer Kaplan on his journey. It is fortunate that he is leaving us. And I hope he has learned something about America's needs & its possibilities.

1. Avukah was an American student-Zionist group, established in 1925, that flourished throughout the 1930s. It included among its members Arthur Goldberg (later Secretary of Labor, justice of the Supreme Court, and ambassador to the United Nations), Philip M. Klutznik (later president of B'nai B'rith), and Shim'on Agranat (chief justice of Israel). There was little communism in Avukah, but it did sponsor a number of summer camps based on communal ideas similar to the kibbutz movement. Avukah closed down in 1943 after a majority of its membership had enlisted or been drafted into the armed forces.

2. Irma Lindheim (see LDB to Julian W. Mack, et al., 23 October 1920, n. 1.), a past president of Hadassah, had moved to Palestine in 1933 and was currently in the United States to lecture for the Jewish National Fund. She was in a difficult financial situation, since her husband had left her very little money, and much of that was invested in Palestine Economic Corporation stock, which had no market. She appealed to LDB to find her a salaried position within the Zionist movement so that she could continue to work for the cause.

To Alice and Charles Goldmark

August 1, 1940 Chatham, Mass. [EBR]

DEAR ALICE PARK AND CHARLES: That is indeed a great achievement of Johnnie's.[1]

He is so understanding, and handles himself so well, that he doesn't need suggestions. But I hope that, during the next year, he will feel that he can work less hard, and not risk impairing his excellent health.

To you and him our congratulations.

1. The Goldmarks' son Jonathan was then a student at Harvard.

To Bernard Flexner

August 7, 1940 Chatham, Mass. [Flexner Mss]

DEAR BEN: Alice calls attention that in the Viking Press letter (returned to you) [Alpheus T.] Mason's biography is referred to as "official". Of course, it is to be in no sense "official" and care must be taken that it be not referred to as such.[1]

1. Cf. LDB to Alfred Lief, 3 November 1933.

To Chaim Weizmann

October 10, 1940 Washington, D. C. [Weizmann Mss]

DEAR DR. WEIZMANN: My thanks for the New Year's greeting. We have good reason for hope.[1]   Cordially,

1. In his quest for support in the United States, and realizing the terrible plight facing world Jewry, Weizmann made a number of efforts to close old wounds. He sent (Jewish) New Year's greetings to LDB and would soon meet with him. Although these efforts did little to eradicate the personal animosity between the two men, they had the necessary public relations effect in showing that all groups within Zionism were closing ranks to fight Hitler and the White Paper.

To Robert Szold

October 22, 1940 Washington, D. C. [R. Szold Mss]

DEAR BOB: 1. Re Yours of 14th.

Yes [Henry] Montor had sent me copy of the talk with Norman Davis [1] et al. Your copy returned herewith. We have had no active friend among the higher-ups of the State Department except [George S.] Messersmith and his leaving for Cuba evidently resulted in setting aside his arrangement for removing [George] Wadsworth to another sphere.[2] Messersmith (whom I saw on the day of his departure for Cuba) thought the Wadsworth removal had been settled. (He had told me it would involve 12 changes in positions).

2. Yours of 17th and encl. noted.

3. Ben Gurion was most reasonable in his talk with me.[3]

1. Norman H. Davis (1878–1944), a businessman, had become involved in foreign affairs as a special adviser to Woodrow Wilson at the Paris Peace Conference. Over the next two decades he represented the United States at numerous international meetings. Davis was also chairman of the American Red Cross.

2. See LDB to Bernard Flexner, 4 October 1939, and to Stephen S. Wise, 8 November 1939.

3. David Ben-Gurion was then in the United States trying to create official interest in a Jewish army, a proposition that generated mixed feelings among Zionist leaders. In a letter to Szold on 29 October 1940, LDB wrote this about Ben-Gurion's visit: "Ben-Gurion spent only a few minutes on the Jewish Army. He mentioned incidentally intending to secure recruits in America, but immediately agreed (a) that nothing should be said about a Jewish Army until after election and (b) that nothing should be said at any time without first securing the consent of the American authorities. I am clear that he should say nothing about getting recruits here; but I did not discuss that subject, as he had agreed not to talk at all for the present."

To Frank Albert Fetter

November 15, 1940 Washington, D. C. [Fetter Mss]

DEAR PROFESSOR FETTER: Re yours of 12th.

I have ceased to know the law. But I shall be glad to see your paper to let you have my suggestions, if any.[1]   Cordially,

1. Fetter was putting together a paper on the restraint of trade, and he wanted LDB's opinion on it. See LDB to Fetter, 26 November 1940.

To Bernard Flexner

November 16, 1940 Washington, D. C. [Flexner Mss]

DEAR BEN: To you and Mim our thanks for the birthday greeting.[1]

The National Home Library Foundation (with Carnegie aid) published on the day, dedicated to me, a fine edition of Albert Jay Nock's "Jefferson"—the worthiest account of our most civilized American and true Democrat.[2] [Sherman F.] Mittell has sent you a copy.

A large number of copies have been placed at my disposal. I propose that one copy shall go to every high school (and similar institution) in Kentucky. So far as teachers and students may be led to read the book something important may be done for the education—the culture—of the State; and the gift of the book may stimulate or develop the school library.[3]

If it meets with your approval and that of President Kent, I suggest that the gift of the book and its distribution to the several schools be made by the University in its name. That may develop relations between the University and the Schools which will be helpful to both.

If you and Dr. Kent approve of the project, let me know the number of the schools and I will have that number of copies of the "Jefferson" sent to the University Library or to Dr. Kent as he may prefer.

1. 13 November was LDB's eighty-fourth birthday.
2. The original commercial edition had been published in 1926. See LDB to Felix Frankfurter, 6 December 1927.
3. Cf. LDB to Alfred Brandeis, 3 and 11 January 1914.

To Frank Albert Fetter

November 26, 1940 Washington, D. C. [Fetter Mss]

DEAR PROFESSOR FETTER: Re yours of 21st.

As I wrote you, I do not know the law. But I have read all of the paper with interest; and I do not suggest any change.[1]

But I wonder whether it would not be worth while to take this opportunity of saying emphatically that there could be no monopoly without "bigness"; that bigness was not inevitable, not merely man-made, but authorized by our corporation laws; and that which is man-made can be unmade.

As Machiavelli said: "Fate is inevitable only when it is not resisted."

The paper goes to you with my thanks, by express. Receipt enclosed.   Cordially,

1. See LDB to Fetter, 15 November 1940; Fetter's article, originally planned for the *Yale Law Journal*, did not appear there.

To Hattie Bishop Speed

December 21, 1940 Washington, D. C. [Speed Mss]

DEAR "MISS HATTIE": It was lovely of you to send the birthday greeting.

From Jennie Brandeis we heard much at Chatham of your continuous work at the Museum; and from its notices we learn with great satisfaction of its increasing activity. The City is learning to appreciate what you have done for it.

With every good wish for you and Jenny Robberts.

To Henry Hurwitz

March 14, 1941 Washington, D. C. [Hurwitz Mss]

DEAR HENRY HURWITZ: Re yours of 11th.[1]

I am very sorry for what you write of Menorah finances—and that I may not help.

More than 25 years ago, when I entered upon the Jewish work, I concluded that my contribution, financial and otherwise, should be concentrated on Palestine. Later, I concluded that the financial contributions should be made to the Palestine Endowment Fund Inc. The rule thus established has been strictly observed and has necessarily prevented my aiding several Jewish causes which I deemed very deserving.[2]

With best wishes—   Cordially,

1. Hurwitz had asked LDB for a contribution to help sustain the *Menorah Journal*, which was in difficult straits. Everyone recognized the value of the *Journal* (see LDB to Hurwitz, 29 November 1939) and wrote for copies, but few students could afford even the modest three-dollar subscription rate.

2. See next letter.

To Henry Hurwitz

March 20, 1941 Washington, D. C. [Hurwitz Mss]

DEAR HENRY HURWITZ: Re yours of March 19th.[1]

Of course, I am perfectly free to change, in whole or in part, my long established plan for donations to the Jewish Cause; but it seems to me unwise to do so. Of course, my judgment may be unsound. My refusal to contribute financially to the support of the Menorah should not dishearten you. I have never done so, although I considered it a valuable publication; and do now.

I am not contributing to the Conference on Jewish Relations.[2] The small contribution which I made was for personal reasons.

Cordially,

1. Hurwitz had responded strongly to LDB's refusal of his earlier request for money (see preceding letter) and chided him for his failure to support a journal that had given help to Zionism. At the same time, Hurwitz charged, LDB had been inconsistent, having contributed to a non-Zionist cause (see next note).

2. Shortly after the rise of Hitler, Morris Raphael Cohen and Salo Wittmeyer Baron had conceived the idea of amassing data that would give an accurate picture of Jewish conditions in the world. The Conference on Jewish Relations did not get started until 1936, when it began publication of the journal *Jewish Social Studies* under the nominal patronage of Albert Einstein and Harold Laski. In 1955 the name was changed to Conference on Jewish Social Studies.

To Pauline Goldmark

April 25, 1941 Washington, D. C. [EBR]

DEAR PAULINE: It is too bad we could not have you and Do here with Elizabeth, but grand to hear from Jack [Gilbert] that you two were at (or after) the Consumers' League dinner. We shall hope to see you two here in May.

LaGuardia's willingness to run again is fine.[1] Also C[harles]. C. B[urlingham].'s activities.[2] Thanks also for the Metropolitan bulletin.

1. During 1940 there had been several rumors that New York Mayor Fiorello H. LaGuardia had his eye on a higher national office, possibly even as running mate to Roosevelt. Nothing had come of this, however,

and LaGuardia decided to run for a third term as mayor, an election that he easily won.

2. Burlingham was an active supporter of LaGuardia, and a few days before the election announced that LDB (who by then had died) favored LaGuardia. To buttress this assertion, Burlingham produced a note from LDB dated 19 August 1941 which said, in part: "It was good to hear from you . . . i.a. that you feel confident that LaGuardia will be re-elected." Burlingham produced this "evidence" because LaGuardia's opponents were claiming that LDB had not favored him; their proof was that LDB's daughter Susan had made several speeches for William O'Dwyer, the mayor's opponent.

To Franklin Delano Roosevelt

April 26, 1941 Washington, D. C. [Roosevelt Mss]

Dear Mr. President: I must trouble you because of very serious information that comes to me regarding the danger threatening the Jewish Community in Palestine, in view of potential eventualities.[1] I shall not burden you with details, but merely venture a specific suggestion.

A word from you to the British manifesting your desire to be assured that the Jews in Palestine will be afforded the necessary means for self-protection would be of the greatest help. Nor would it be irrelevant to suggest that such a measure would help the British.

You will know best whether such word should be sent by you through the British Ambassador or by direct representation to Mr. Churchill [2] through our Ambassador.[3]

With every good wish.   Cordially,

1. With the German armies sweeping across North Africa, Zionist leaders were in consternation over the British refusal to allow the Yishuv weapons for self-defense, or to enroll all the Jewish men in Palestine who wanted to fight against the Nazis. This letter was drafted by Felix Frankfurter, who sent it to LDB in February.

2. Winston Leonard Spencer Churchill (1874–1965), after being a constant critic of the Chamberlain policy of appeasing Hitler during the 1930s, had been recalled to the British cabinet as First Lord of the Admiralty at the outbreak of the war. In 1940 he took over as Prime Minister, a role in which he would lead Great Britain through her finest hour. In addition to politics, Churchill also emerged as a major historian and won the Nobel

Prize for Literature in 1953 for his multivolume works on the world wars, several of his ancestors, and the English-speaking peoples.

3. President Roosevelt had passed LDB's letter to the State Department for advice. On 2 May Sumner Welles responded: "The danger of arming of Jews unless the still greater Arab population is armed undoubtedly would be a considerable factor in any decision that British might make." On 5 May Roosevelt wrote to LDB: "We have made sure that your suggestion has been passed on to the British Government." Eventually the problem was resolved by recruiting Palestinians into the British army, although a separate Jewish group was not allowed until later in the war. The Nazi threat to Palestine ended after the battle of El Alamein the following year.

To Bernard Flexner

May 15, 1941 Washington, D. C. [R. Szold Mss]

DEAR BEN: 1. Re yours of 13th—Nelson Glueck—I shall be glad to join you in giving $250.00 to make possible 6 months Nelson Glueck work at Princeton.[1] It should prove very helpful to our Palestine endeavors. Let me know when you are ready for the money.

2. Re yours of 12th—Washington [Flexner]'s trip to Louisville should be very helpful.

3. Re yours of 13th—very sorry for the Rockefeller decision re Fola La Follette.[2]

1. Flexner had brought several men together to create a fund for Glueck's leave of absence see LDB to Flexner, 4 October 1939.

2. Flexner passed on the news from Raymond Fosdick that the Rockefeller Foundation had turned down Fola LaFollette's request for financial assistance to complete her biography of Robert LaFollette. Shortly thereafter, LDB and his wife personally made their second financial gift to Miss LaFollette, to mark their fiftieth wedding anniversary.

To Franklin Delano Roosevelt

June 13, 1941 Washington, D. C. [Roosevelt Mss]

DEAR MR. PRESIDENT: For the Court and for our Country the nomination for Chief Justice is the best conceivable.[1]

We leave for Chatham today. You will be much in our thoughts.[2]   Cordially,

1. President Roosevelt had named Harlan Fiske Stone to replace retiring Chief Justice Charles Evans Hughes. "Aren't you delighted with what the President has done in elevating Justice Stone to the Chief Justiceship?" LDB inquired of a visitor in the summer of 1941. "No other President has performed such a signal service." When reminded that President Taft, a Republican, had promoted White, a Democrat, to be head of the Court, he replied; "But White cannot be compared to Stone." (Mason, *Brandeis,* 635.)

2. On 16 June, Roosevelt responded: "I had counted on seeing you before you left Washington, but I am laid up in bed with a sort throat. I do hope you will have a pleasant summer, and I look forward to seeing you when you return."

To Bernard Flexner

July 10, 1941 Chatham, Mass. [Flexner Mss]

DEAR BEN: Re yours of 8th

1. Please give Mason my very best wishes. I do not write him, as I assume he must refrain from unnecessary use of the eyes.[1]

2. Thanks for the New Republic review.[2] You are right that no answer should be made by Mason to unfair reviews. Others, if inclined, may engage in such occupation.[3]

3. Your concern about the use of the New Haven ms. is well founded.[4]

1. Alpheus Mason had entered Willis Hospital in Philadelphia for an operation to resolve difficulties he had experienced with his eyes for several months. Although the operation was expected to be successful, Mason's use of his eyes was restricted for several months.

2. Leonard Boudin, in reviewing *Bureaucracy Convicts Itself,* wrote: "Professor Mason has won the battle. His publishers ought to make the Ickes article an insert of Mason's scholarly refutation, for the two polemics make an exciting debate in which the Secretary enjoys the novelty of defeat." *The New Republic* 104 (23 June 1941): 865.

3. Flexner had informed LDB that Ickes had written a particularly nasty review of Mason's book (50 *Yale Law Journal* 1303), and Bruce Bliven had offered Mason space in the *New Republic* if he wanted to answer Ickes.

4. Mason had already worked up a small monograph on the New Haven controversy and was considering publishing it separately. In the end, Mason utilized it as the basis for chapters 12 and 13 of the Brandeis biography; he returned to the subject later on and together with Henry Lee Staples published *The Fall of a Railroad Empire: Brandeis and the New Haven Merger Battle* (Syracuse, N. Y., 1947).

To Robert Szold

July 13, 1941 Chatham, Mass. [R. Szold Mss]

DEAR BOB: Re yours of 11th and Miss Lippner's [1]

1. I highly approve of Judge [Louis E.] Levinthal as President of Z.O.A. Every effort should be made to get him.[2] Of course, I shall be glad to see him here.

2. C. W. now has it "black on white".[3]

3. I hope you will manage to get some real vacation days.

1. Miss R. A. Lippner was Szold's secretary.

2. See next letter.

3. Chaim Weizmann, just prior to returning to England, had addressed a meeting of the Office Committee of the Z.O.A. in which he had called for unity in action and a revivified leadership. He admitted that it would be best if the Z.O.A. could get leaders like LDB, Felix Frankfurter, and Ben Cohen, but since they were not able or willing, then they would have to rely on Louis Lipsky. This brought an immediate reaction from a number of Zionist leaders allied with Robert Szold, who made it plain to Weizmann that he was totally misreading the American situation. It was not just that the Lipsky leadership, in their eyes, had proven itself incapable of doing the job, but that the demands of American Jews were still incomprehensible to Weizmann and the Europeans. What was needed was a sense of purpose, something other than the spirit of continued accommodation that had marked Weizmann's leadership of the movement. Whether Weizmann, in fact, understood their point is questionable.

To Bernard Flexner

September 17, 1941 Washington, D. C. [Flexner Mss]

DEAR BEN: Thanks for yours of 7th & 15th.

1. The excessive heat which we struck on our return here knocked me out for a few days; but I am now, happily, "as usual".

2. Yes, Bob did a fine job for the Z.O.A. and we should now see marked improvement.[1]

3. It will be fine to see you and Mim end of the month.

4. That Mason is "improving steadily" is encouraging.[2]

1. At the Z.O.A. convention, Robert Szold had engineered the election of Louis Levinthal as president, and the Philadelphia judge proved to be an

able leader during his two-year term. In addition, the Executive Committee now consisted primarily of those allied with the Szold-Brandeis philosophy.

2. See LDB to Flexner, 10 July 1941.

To Robert Szold

September 24, 1941 Washington, D. C. [R. Szold Mss]

DEAR BOB: Re yours of 23rd.

I shall be glad to see you for a little at 9 A.M. Sunday.—Have an engagement later.[1]

1. Shortly after this meeting, LDB's health began to decline. On 1 October, after taking a drive through Rock Creek Park, LDB suffered another heart attack. On Sunday, 4 October, he sank into a coma and passed away at 7:15 P.M. on 5 October 1941. The next day, about fifty of LDB's close friends and associates gathered at the family's apartment. A violin quartet played Beethoven selections. Former law clerk Dean Acheson spoke for all of LDB's aides, saying: "Throughout these years we have brought him all of our problems and all our troubles, and he had time for all of us. A question, a comment, and the difficulties began to disappear; the dross and the shoddy began to appear for what it was, and we wondered why the matter had ever seemed difficult. . . . But to him truth was less than truth unless it was expounded so that people could understand and believe. During these years of retreat from reason, his faith in the human mind and in the will and capacity of people to understand and grasp the truth never wavered or tired. In time of moral and intellectual anarchy and frustration, he handed on the great tradition of faith in the mind and spirit of man which is the faith of the prophets and poets, of Socrates, of Lincoln." (Acheson's remarks are reprinted as "Mr. Justice Brandeis," 55 *Harvard Law Review* 191 [1941].) The service concluded with brief remarks from Felix Frankfurter, who compared LDB to Bunyan's Mr. Valiant-for-Truth and quoted from the Bible: "The law of truth was in his mouth, and unrighteousness was not found in his lips; he walked with me in peace and equity, and did turn many away from iniquity."

LDB's body was cremated, and on the first anniversary of his death the urn containing his ashes was interred beneath the porch of the University of Louisville Law School; when Mrs. Brandeis died four years later, her ashes were laid to rest next to his.

To Alfred Brandeis

May 19, 1881 Boston, Mass. [Jean Tachau]

DEAR AL: Your letter of Sunday morning including buttons received. Am delighted to hear that business is good, hope that you will be let off easy on "hot corn"—and that it may go off like "hotcakes" and that this year may show up five thousand for each of you.

The other matter mentioned[1] pained me very much and I can't understand it except for the reason that women are very strange people. However, I think still that you were right in trying and it may be some consolation to remember that it is the result of the world's experience that a woman can't always say no.[2]

Don't think of bachelorhood for yourself. Some one in our family will have to keep up the name besides Dick and Fred B.[3] and I don't see any chance of my launching out into matrimony for the next ten years.[4] As far as I can see my only equipment is the Insurance Policy.

There is nothing going on here with me that is new. My Maine Railroad Opinion is interesting but will not be very remunerative, I think. Nothing new from Cambridge as yet.[5]

We have had a North Easter on for five days and the world looks gloomy enough.

Saw Tina Goldmark[6] for a few moments Tuesday. She came on to look for a summer resort for the family on the North Shore. It is like buying an Ulster with the thermometer at 101° in the shade.

Sam [Warren] is well and sorry to hear you won't come on this summer. Davidson will be in tonight.   Goodbye,

Rec'd Ma's Sunday letter—expect to write her a long one soon.

1. Alfred had been courting Jennie Taussig for several years, and she had consistently turned down his proposals of marriage; see LDB to Alfred Brandeis, 11 September 1880.

2. Miss Taussig finally yielded, and married Alfred on 10 September 1884.

3. The sons of LDB's uncle, Samuel Brandeis.

4. See LDB to Walter Bond Douglas, 1 October 1890, and notes to Alice Goldmark, 15 September 1890 ff.

5. Professor James Bradley Thayer was due to take a leave of absence from the Harvard Law School the following fall, and had invited LDB to teach the course in Evidence. Because of a shortage of funds, however, Thayer's leave was postponed. The following year, President Eliot himself invited LDB to give the course during 1883–84, two lectures a week for $1,000. See LDB to Adolph Brandeis, 30 May 1883.

6. LDB's second cousin, Christina Goldmark, daughter of Dr. Joseph Goldmark.

To Alfred Brandeis

November 19, 1898 Boston, Mass. [Fanny Brandeis]

MY DEAR AL: We learn from Mother that Jean has been quite sick and is better—we hope very much better by this time. She is so robust that the progress should be very rapid. But I know how anxious you and Jennie must be from my own disquiet when our daughters have the slightest cold. I have no doubt you are much worse than Jennie, and I confess I am more unreasonable than Alice; but then you know Alice is very reasonable. I say this because she will probably want to know what I have written you.

We had purposed to go out of town. But the rain has descended, to the point where not only ardor but even hope became dampened. So we have been reading Worcester's Philippines which Felix [Adler] sent me.[1] One doesn't mind the rain there, I am told.

I don't know when we shall get our holidays together. The Milwaukee trip has been adjourned from time to time, which was fortunate enough in one way, as the cases requiring attention here have been very urgent. But quite a number have been worked off and I feel quite light-hearted over the "disposed ofs."

The Kipling, from Louisville I assume came from you. Alice insists it is very appropriate. Why she will doubtless tell you herself, as I know only the boys' play.   Good night,

Don't fail to read Father the Deland essay on Imagination in Business.

1. Dean C. Worcester, *The Philippine Islands and Their People* (New York, 1898).

To Alfred Brandeis

DEAR AL: Your Cin[cinna]ti banker expresses just my view of the situation. The panic is over and hard times is upon us. I believe that the optimistic newspaper clamor is largely manufactured.[1]

I am greatly distressed at the death of my friend McElwain, at the age of 40.[2] He was in my opinion really the greatest man of my acquaintance—and the greatest loss to the Commonwealth—possessing the rare charm of great ability, courage, high character and personal charm. As yet he had devoted these high qualities almost exclusively to building up his business organization, so that he was probably the largest shoe manufacturer in the world, having started with nothing. For about five years he had been overworked. But I think had he lived, he would have emerged from business into the field of his higher ideals and become a commanding figure in the Commonwealth. His death followed an appendicitis operation (which had been successful), but I feel he was really a sacrifice to overwork—to the perfecting of his business organization—for he had no love or even respect for money as such.

He leaves a fine family too, wife two girls and two boys. The older girl is a friend of Susan's.

1. Actually, the aftermath of the Bankers' Panic of 1907 was relatively mild and short-lived.
2. See LDB to William Howe McElwain, 18 June 1902. LDB eulogized McElwain and his business practices in the important speech he gave at the Brown University commencement in 1912, later published as "Business—A Profession"; see LDB to J. Franklin McElwain, 18 June 1912.

To Alfred Brandeis

DEAR AL: We had a nice visit from Amy & Dorothy. Sorry Amy can't stay longer.

Charlie N[agel]. seems to have his opportunity at short stop now & I suppose doesn't like it much.[1] I note your views on corp[oration]s & politics with interest.

The N. Haven Report shows 5⅝ percent earned & 8 percent paid. Have not seen full report, but think even these figures fail to show true deficit.[2]

1. Nagel, LDB's brother-in-law, was active in Republican politics and in the Taft presidential campaign. It was expected that if the Republicans won, Nagel would receive a major appointment; he was, in fact, named Secretary of Commerce and Labor.

2. See LDB to Alfred Brandeis, 22 February 1909, for a fuller analysis of the New Haven figures.

To Jennie Taussig Brandeis

August 14, 1910 South Yarmouth, Mass. [Jean Tachau]

MY DEAR JENNIE: Our thoughts have been much at Jamestown, and we have shared with you and yours these weeks of anxiety.[1]

I have found myself constantly recurring to some of my many meetings with dear Aunt Adele, commencing with that semi-mythical "Begegnung"[2] at Niagra [sic] in 1865, about which Alfred must have spoken often.

But it was the visit in Louisville in 1870 when your Mother made the great impression upon all of us. Her rendering of the Shubert [sic] and Schumann songs revealed them to me, and I can never hear the "Erlkönig" or the "Leiermann"[3] without thinking of her singing accompanied by Father's and Mother's tears. She really sang herself into our lifes [sic], of which she later became so much a part in many ways. Please give her and your dear Father much love from me.

We have been here nearly a fortnight, that is Alice and the girls. We cannot reconcile ourselves yet to the thought of living without some Louisville Brandeises. Alice would have written you but for three bad days, which I hope will soon be over.

1. Jennie's mother, Adele Taussig, had been stricken with a massive stroke while vacationing at Jamestown, R.I.

2. "Encounter."

3. Both were Schubert lieder, "Erlkönig" composed in 1821 and "Leiermann" in 1827.

Cumulative Index

Numbers in italics indicate letters addressed to the person named.
Asterisks (*) indicate page on which note identifies the person named.

Aaronsohn, Aaron II: 537*; III: 117, 128, 155, *157*, 398, 434, 473; IV: 322, 325-28, 331, 334, 336-37 360, 369, 395, 417; V: 37-38; LDB on, I: 537
Aaronsohn, Alexander III: 603*, 613, 619
Aaronsohn, Sarah III: 603
Abbot, Edwin H. I: 174, *203*, 344; II: 47; IV: 97
Abbot, Philip S. I: 105*
Abbott, Ernest H. II: 701*
Abbott, Frank F. cited, IV: 308
Abbott, Grace V: 142*, 166, 255
Abbott, Lawrence F. I: 590*; II, *3, 106, 191, 371, 433*; III: 393, 657
Abbott, Lyman I: 148
Abbott, Myrtle II: 461*, 466, 476, 479, 490-94, 515-16
Abbott, Nathan I: 117*
A. B. Dick Co. II: 615-16
Abdullah, Emir IV: 492; V: 514, 522
Abel, Mr. IV: 5
Abelson, Paul II: 484*, 487; III: 429-30
Abrahams, Henry I: 503*, *531, 538*, 548; II: *59*, 81, 118, *125, 175*
Abrahams, I. A. III: *433*, 648
Abramov, S. Z. cited, III: 293
Abramowitz, Rabbi III: 533
Abrams, Mr. III: 246
Abrams, Richard M. cited, I: 139, 140, 144, 375, 376, 525, 585; II: 95, 128, 293, 441, 548; III: 144, 165
Abrams v. U.S. IV: 451
A. Brandeis & Son IV: 40, 169; V: 350
Acheson, Dean G. IV: 439*, 451, *476*, 510, 538, 554; V: 12, 79, 83, 655; LDB on IV: 510

Achoosa movement III: 469, 475
Actions Comite III: 291, 322-29, 426, 449-50, 461, 470, 511-12, 561, 569, 606, 627-28, 666; IV: 85, 109, 135, 159, 161, *184*, 189, 190, 419-21, 437
Acton, Amy F. I: *280*
Adair v. U.S. II: 679; III: 63
Adams, Alva B. II: 724*
Adams, Brooks II: *113**
Adams, Charles F., II I: 533*; II: 48, 51, 71, 88, 99, 108, 112, 506; III: 342
Adams, Charles H. II: *144**
Adams, Elbridge L. cited, I: 303
Adams Express Co. III: 24; V: 274
Adams, Francis I: 259
Adams, Graham Jr. cited, II: 536; III: 77, 88
Adams, Henry C. II: 68*, *93, 193;* III: *5*
Adams, John D. II: 245*
Adams, John Q. V: 229
Adams v. Tanner IV: 299
Adamson eight-hour law IV: 266
Addams, Jane II: 386*, 390, 392, 523, 535, 564, 699, 700; III: 432, 597; IV: 154; V: 107, 143, 355
Addystone Pipe & Steel Co. v. U.S. II: 541
Adee, Alvey A. IV: 145*, 148
Ades, Moses III: 353*, *639, 671;* IV: 3, 5
Adkins, Jesse C. III: 211*, 227, $\overline{245}$; IV: 187; V: 23, 326
Adkins v. Children's Hospital V: 89, 125
Adler, Cyrus III: 409, 544*, *551, 555, 566*, 571, 574, 577, 619, 634; IV: 220; V: 465, 483, 621

Adler, Edward A. I: *175**, 183, *185,* *187, 188,* 207, 210, *222*(2), *224, 225, 231*

Adler, Felix I: 25, 91**, 98-99, 408, *554;* II: 577; III: 272, 307, 503, 541, 547, 562; IV: 26, 384; V: 657

Adler, Helen G. I: 91; III: 272, 503

Adler, Isaac IV: 7*

Adler, Joseph cited, III: 156

Adler, Margaret III: 503*

Adler, Mortimer IV: 7*

Adler, Ruth III: 271*

Adler, Selig cited, IV: 282

Adler, Simon III: 509*

advanced freight rate cases, LDB and II: 306-307, 370, 373-74, 382-83, 387-88, 393-96, 400-401, 407, 411-12; III: 12-13, 49, 78-80, 142-43, 162-65, 192, 202-203, 210-11, 245, 288-89, 295, 330-31, 334, 337, 345-46, 372, 383-86, 399-400, 410-11, 484, 502-503; IV: 46-47, 63, 113, 141, 145, 147, 149; V: 381

advertising, LDB on III: 239; V: 70, 92, 342

Agassiz, Elizabeth C. I: 105

aging, LDB on his own V: 288-89, 291, 429-30, 452, 489, 513, 610

Agranat, Shim'on V: 645

agriculture, LDB on III: 29, 151, 272-73; IV: 326, 487, 521, 548; V: 7, 10, 20, 21, 24, 26, 28-29, 35, 91-92, 135, 203-204, 206, 209, 214, 251, 289

Agricultural Adjustment Administration V: 537, 538, 558, 564

Agricultural experiment stations III: 26, 469

Agudath Israel V: 36

Aguinaldo, Emilio I: 150, 152, 154

Ahasuerus, King IV: 400

A.J.C.: see American Jewish Committee

A.J.R.C.: see American Jewish Relief Committee

Akaba V: 558, 576

Akers, M. L. II: 116*

Alabama I: 582

Alaska II: 307, 312, 340, 386, 398, 460-64, 467-81, 486-94, 499, 508, 513, 612-13, 618, 641; LDB on II: 468-74; see also Pinchot-Ballinger conservation controversy

Albee, George H. III: 12

Albertson, Ralph II: 343*

Albrocchi, Rudolph V: 276

Alcock, John IV: 402*

Alderman, Edwin A. V: 127*

Aldrich, Martha II: 18

Alexander & Greene IV: 51

Alexander, Edward R. II: 177

Alexander the Great IV: 200

Alexander, W. W. II: 201*, 286

Alexandria, Egypt IV: 235, 337, 410

Alger, George W. V: 338

Algeria V: 545

Al-Husayni, Hajjamin: see Mufti of Jerusalem

Alice: see Brandeis, Alice G.

Alinsky, Saul cited, IV: 560

All Russian Central Union of Consumer Societies IV: 388

Allen, Arthur D. V: 262*, 314

Allen, Frank G. V: 363*

Allen, Frederic L. cited, I: 595; IV: 471

Allen, Gay W. cited, III: 414

Allen, Henry J. V: 76*

Allen, R. M. I: 542

Allen v. Woonsocket I: 53-54; IV: 58

Allen, Watson II: 311

Allenby, Edmund H. H. IV: 360, 400, 408*, 408-20; LDB on IV: 416

Allied Jewish Campaign V: 471

Allied powers IV: 206, 281, 305, 317, 345, 387, 399, 434, 446, 456, 458, 462, 521

Alpha Portland Cement Co. v. Massachusetts V: 172

Alsace-Lorraine IV: 317

Alsberg, Henry IV: 304*

Altgeld, John P. I: 211

Altman, Benjamin III: 199*

Altmyer, Arthur J. V: 537*, 560

Alumni Association of Harvard Law School I: 69

Amalgamated Clothing Workers' Union IV: 511, 562; V: 185

Amalgamated Copper Co. II: 70

Amalgamated Sheet Metal Workers' Union I: 499, 501, 503

Amberg, Julius H. V: 124*

American Anti-Imperialist League I: 101, 148

American Association for Labor Legislation II: 32, 287, 310, 400, 417, 576

American Association of University Professors V: 83, 269, 307

American Bar Association I: 338-39; IV: 65, 118; V: 122, 184, 191, 337, 353, 395

American Bar Association Journal V: 276, 281

American Civil Liberties Union V: 287, 303

American Column & Lumber Co. et al. v. U.S. V: 42

American Defense Society III: 629

American Dentral Trade Association III: 559, 592

American Economic Association II: 535

American Express Co. III: 23, 49

American Fair Trade League III: 94; IV: 35, 169

American Farm Bureau Federation IV: 521; V: 137

American Federation of Labor I: 503, 506, 511, 531, 539, 553; II: 14, 113; III: 88, 212; IV: 562; V: 281, 334, 387, 509-12, 520, 569, 586

American Federationist II: 14, 198; V: 376

American [Zionist] Forestry Unit IV: 434

American Friends of Hebrew University IV: 438

American Hide and Leather Co. II: 203; IV: 89

American Historical Association V: 395

American Investment Bankers' Association III: 342

American Iron and Steel Institute II: 543, 545

American Jewish Committee III: 294, 309, 315, 324, 362, 387, 408, 434, 483-84, 491, 536-37, 544-45, 551-54, 564-80, 604, 621, 625, 634-35, 640, 651-56, 675-76, 681; IV: 9-12, 17, 56, 108, 151, 155, 180, 197, 200, 220, 236, 243, 246, 250-52, 277, 323, 330, 343, 351, 399, 435, 507; V: 116, 521, 597

American Jewish Congress movement, LDB and III: 408-409, 544-45, 551-58, 564-82, 587-88, 591-92, 605, 607-609, 619-25, 631, 634-36, 640-41, 645-46, 651-56, 681-82; IV: 10, 17-18, 56, 102-104, 116-17, 133-38, 170-75, 184-86, 197-205, 242, 250-54, 312

American Jewish Congress (after October, 1917) IV: 319, 366, 374, 392, 396, 435, 457, 541-42, 545, 553, 565; V: 521, 551, 578

American Jewish Emanicipation Committee III: 535, 538

American Jewish Relief Committee III: 341, 352, 359, 362, 366-67, 382, 387, 397, 403, 408, 414, 421-24, 436-37, 461, 472-74, 481-84, 504, 545, 547-50, 578, 582-83, 589, 604, 607, 621, 632, 641-42, 654, 665, 678-79; IV: 20, 95, 129, 146, 149, 155, 190, 205, 211, 218, 234, 253, 277, 296, **298**

American Judicature Society III: 167

American Law Institute V: 110, 395, 497

American Law Review I: 8, 49

American League to Limit Armaments III: 419

American Legion IV: 542; V: 3

American Magazine II: 351, 359, 389, 390, 453, 489-90

Amercian Medical Association IV: 187

American Palestine Co. III: 159, 186, 226; V: 18

American Peace Society I: 148

American Political Science Association II: 287

American Pro-Palestine Committee V: 489, 603

American Railway Express Co. v. Kentucky V: 274

American Social Science Association I: 233, 236

American Society of Jurisprudence III: 10

American Steam Gauge Co. IV: 68

American Tobacco Co. II: 289, 495, 503, 519, 521, 556, 664, 690, 715; III: 35, 39, 523; V: 508

American Zion Commonwealth IV: 194, 449

American Zionist Medical Unit IV: 340-41, 349, 376, 391, 424-26, 434, 438, 440, 466-69, 473, 478, 481, 489, 530, 561; V: 8, 19

"Americanization," LDB on III: 676

Amery, Leopold C. M. S. V: 249*

Ames, Butler II: 68*

Ames, James B. I: 8*, 10-11, 18, 147-48, *152, 156,* 159, *280,* 367, 436; III: 86; cited, I: 156; LDB on I: 8, 10-11

Ames, William H. I: *302**

Amicis, Edmondo de I: 68

Amidon, Beulah IV: 43*, 177; V: 570, 575

Amidon, Charles F. II: *632**; IV: *43, 177;* V: 103, 111; LDB on IV: 43

Amory, Arthur I: 342*, 344-45; IV: 97

Amos, Percy M. M. IV: 416*

Amram, David W. IV: 347*, 429; V: 36, 278

Anderson, George W. I: 271*, *286,* 290, 294, *297,* 301, 307, *317,* 399, *419, 423, 425,* 512, *515,* 516; II: 81, 507; III: *109,* 129, 150, 172-73, *177,*

191, 195, *218,* 244, *245*(3), *264, 276*(2), 277, 297, 392, 560; IV: 27, 29, 47, 56, 66, 71, 73, 76-77, 80, 85-87, 92-95, 100, *104,* 113, 117, 121-24, 127, 183, 368; V: 4, 183, 234, 303, 339, 346, 352, 404, 414, 590; LDB on II: 507; III: 297

Anderson, Warwick M. V: 138*, 198, 202, 208, 214, 223, 256, 268, 308

Andrews, John B. II: *310*, 400, 417;* V: 298, 329

Andrews, William S. V: 374

Andrist, Charles M. IV: 228*

Angell, Ernest V: 94*

Angell, Montgomery IV: *219**

Angell, Mrs. III: 229

Angell, Norman V: 425, 621

Angell, Walter F. III: 43

Anglo-Jewish Association III: 404, 625

Anglo-Palestine Bank III: 299, 413, 416, 418, 431, 469, 639; IV: 13, 110, 134, 139, 146-49, 178, 193, 216, 227, 335, 354, 379, 493, 508

Anna, Miss I: 57

Annable, H. W. I: 573

Ansonia Sentinel IV: 88-91

Antaeus V: 89

Anti-Defamation League (B'nai Brith) III: 373

Anti-imperialist movement, LDB and I: 147-59, 161-62

Anti-malaria campaign for Palestine IV: 426, 436, 440, 469; V: 19, 463

Anti-Merger League: see Massachusetts Anti-Merger League

Anti-Patronage bill I: 222

Anti-Saloon League IV: 106

antisemitism, LDB on III: 331, 349, 381; IV: 536-37

Anti-Stock-Watering Act (1894) I: 291

Antitrust legislation: see Sherman Antitrust Act and Clayton Antitrust Act; LDB on II: 100-101, 455-57, 495-96

antitrust movement and "the curse

of bigness," LDB and I: 68, 276-77;
II: 25, 99-101, 369-70, 380-81, 407,
410-13, 435-39, 442-43, 453-57, 481-
82, 495-96, 510-12, 519, 521, 523,
525, 530, 538, 540-41, 561, 564-66,
602-603, 615-16, 651-55, 663-66, 669-
76, 683-701, 707-10, 721-22, 726-27,
730; III: 4, 11-12, 25-26, 35, 39, 41,
48-49, 100-103, 116-17, 171, 187-88,
195, 218-21, 234-37, 247-60, 290, 440,
523, 592-95; V: 333, 463, 482, 527,
648

Arabs III: 32; IV: 164-65, 410-13,
415-17, 420, 455-56; V: 220, 382,
385, 397-98, 400, 407-408, 413, 425,
427, 446, 449, 454, 461, 469, 474,
487, 514, 568, 571, 574, 578-80, 586,
601, 603-604, 612-13, 637; LDB on
V: 386

Arab Higher Committee V: 574

Arbeiter Ring III: 588

Arbosath manifesto (1320) V: 551

arbitration, mediation, conciliation,
etc., LDB on I: 450-51; II: 540;
III: 25, 55, 184-85

architecture, LDB on I: 15-17, 20,
127, 480

Argentina III: 493; IV: 385, 547

Argentine Railway Co. III: 493

Argus Press Clipping Bureau I: 487

Arkansas V: 88

Arlors, the IV: 400

Arlosoroff, Hayim V. V: 506*

Armstrong, Anne W. V: 338

Armstrong, Captain IV: 423

Armstrong, Harold V: 141

Armstrong Insurance Committee
(New York) I: 363, 398-99, 448,
541, 546, 550; II: 76, 591; IV:
51

Armstrong, J. B. I: 553; II: 90

Armstrong, William W. I: 340*

Armstrong, William B. II: 281*

Arnauld, Antoine V: 184

Arnold, F. I: 20

Arnold, Horace D. II: 192*, 195,
212, 227, 301

Arnold, Matthew I: 104, 423; quoted,
I: 94

Arnold, W. B. IV: 89

Artaud, Mr. III: 384

Ashbrook, William A. II: 436*, 439,
440

Ashurst, Henry F. V: 131*

Ashinsky, Aaron M. III: 323*

Ashley, H. W. III: 229, 239

Ashley, R. Eugene II: 292

Asia, LDB on V: 33-34; see also
China and Japan

Associated Advertising Clubs III: 111

Associated Board of Trade: see Massachusetts Associated Board of
Trade

Associated Press III: 225; IV: 130

Association of National Advertising
Managers III: 94

Atkinson, Edward I: 161*, 352

Atkinson, Roy IV: 23*

Atlanta, Georgia IV: 148

Atlantic Coast Line III: 9

Atlantic Coast Line Co. v. North
Carolina Rrd Commission II: 10

Atlantic Monthly V: 141, 272, 278,
337, 548

Atlantic National Bank (Providence)
III: 161

Atlee, Clement IV: 142

Attorney-General v. New York,
New Haven & Hartford Rrd Co.
II: 238, 255

Attorney-General v. Williams IV: 93

Attwater, Jessie F. III: 659*

Atwood, Albert W. III: 267*, 271

Auerbach, Jerold S. cited, II: 374,
574; IV: 396, 559

Auerbach, Junius T. I: 320*; II: 117,
141, 251

"Auntie B.": see Evans, Elizabeth G.

Aurelius, Marcus quoted, II: 82

Austin, Calvin II: 131*, 168

Austin, James W. II: 54*

Austin, Warren R. V: 582*

Australia II: 477, 535; IV: 309, 547;
V: 141

Austria (Austria-Hungary) II: 209, 235; III: 291, 330, 345, 481, 500, 519; IV: 315-16, 405, 538, 546; V: 27

Austro-Hungarian Zionist Association III: 560, 585

automobiles, LDB on I: 410; III: 488-89

Avery, Susan L. III: 280*

Avner, Maurice L. V: 442*

Avriel, Ehud cited, V: 620

Avukah V: 645

Ayer family I: 171

Ayres, William A. IV: 169*

Babson, Thomas M. I: 267*, 269, 271-73, 298, 302, 313, 318, 426; IV: 120

Bacon, Edwin M. I: 90*

Bacon, Francis V: 326

Bacon & Burpee Co. IV: 61

Baedecker guidebook I: 20

Baer, Boris III: 403

Baer, George I: 209

Baerwold, Paul V: 516*

Bagby, Wesley cited, IV: 471

Bailey, Hollis R. I: 163*; IV: 68-72, 140

Bailey v. Drexel Furniture Co. V: 53

Baker, Captain II: 370, 660; III: 280

Baker, Frank E. V: 83*

Baker, James M. IV: 226*

Baker, Liva cited, II: 351; V: 205

Baker, Newton D. II: 350*, 651; IV: 334, 456; V: 152, 209, 251, 373, 506, 516; quoted, II: 668; LDB on V: 209

Baker, Ray S. II: 357*, 359, 389, 390, 401, 562; III: 394, 581; IV: 25, 177, 186, 529; V: 234, 482; cited, II: 490, 635, 661; III: 235

Bakewell, Miss I: 409

Bakhmet'ev, Boris A. IV: 303*

Bakhmet'ev, George III: 375; IV: 303*

Balch, Emily G. II: 403*, V: 419, 426

Balch, Francis N. I: 234*

Balch, Mr. II: 194

Baldwin, F. F. I: 561

Baldwin, George S. I: 452*, 464

Baldwin, Judge II: 254

Baldwin, Roger N. V: 12*

Baldwin, Simeon E. IV: 118*

Baldwin, Stanley V: 150, 577

Balfour, Arthur J. IV: 283*, 283-91, 310, 321, 375, 397, 405-10, 420-22, 455, 468, 495, 499; V: 44, 310, 400, 612

Balfour Declaration III: 23, 296, 317, 327, 520, 665; IV: 279-96, 310-12, 316-23, 329, 331, 338, 343, 346, 355, 369, 382, 404, 409, 420, 434, 439, 443, 446, 455, 457, 465, 495; V: 400, 428, 430, 437, 449, 456, 457, 460, 486, 522-23, 578, 591, 612-13; LDB and IV: 277-92, 295, 310-12, 316-23, 327-28, 331, 355-56, 369; V: 577-81, 612

Balfouriya IV: 499, 530

Ballantine, Arthur A. IV: 181*

Ballard, Bland V: 231

Ballard, Samuel T. III: 89*, 237

Ballard, Mrs. Thruston III: 244; V: 223

Ballinger, Richard A. II: 307*, 313-16, 320-22, 325-27, 331-35, 338-40, 344-53, 362-64, 371, 376, 386, 396-98, 401, 415, 424, 458-59, 463-64, 467, 475, 491, 493, 497; III: 33, 296, 394, 464; IV: 63, 130, 171; V: 116, 518, 641, 643; see also Pinchot-Ballinger conservation controversy

Baltimore III: 633, 637; IV: 82-83, 280

Baltimore & Ohio Rrd. II: 318; III: 266, 268; V: 266

Baltimore & Ohio Rrd. v. Goodman V: 311

Baltimore Evening Sun IV: 130

Balogh, Elemer V: 499

Bancroft, Edgar A. III: 232*

Bancroft, Hugh II: 516*

Bancroft, William A. I: 130*, 132, 427; IV: 96

Band, Max (Mordecai) V: 550*

Bang, Mr. V: 311

Bangs v. Atchison, Topeka & Santa Fe IV: 67

Bank Clerks' Association I: 239

Bank HaPo'alim V: 464

Bank Insurance League III: 263

"Banker-Management; Why It Has Failed: A Lesson from the New Haven" (1913) III: 147, 168, 184, 284, 344; V: 534-36

Bankers & Tradesmen II: 16

Bankers' Magazine II: 16

Bankhead, John H. III: *411**

banks and bankers (the "money power"), LDB on II: 408-13, 487; III: 113-15, 168, 179, 187, 189, 202, 266, 342-44, 416; IV: 15, 518; V: 29, 360, 637

Bannister, Robert C. cited, II: 357

Barbour, William II: *429**

Bardin, Shlomo H. V: *626**

Bardo, Clinton L. V: *390**

Barford, Einar III: 445

Bar-Ilan, Meir: see Berlin, Meyer

Barker, Charles cited, I: 82

Barker, Forrest I: 411

Barnard, Harry cited, IV: 532

Barnes, George L. I: 314, 316, *318**, *443*, *465*, *544*, *559*, 560; II: *80*, *85*, *88*, 89, *90*, *105*, *109*, *117*(2), *121*, *123*, *126*, *135*, *141*, *147*(2), *154*, *166*, 179, 281, *620*; IV: 62, 124, 127; V: 319, 332, 339, 508

Barnes, Julius H. IV: *308**, 403, 444, 548

Barnes, William Jr. III: *611**

Barnet, Philip III: *332**, *484*

Barnett, Lincoln cited, IV: 537

Barnett, Maurice III: 97

Barnum, Miss I: 263

Barnum, Richard L. II: *418**

Baron, Maximilian G. III: *585**, 615, 648

Baron, Salo W. V: 650

Barondess, Joseph III: *313**, 323, *488*, *545*, *579*; IV: 11, *132*

Barowsky, J. L. III: *585*

Barr, John W. V: 231, 266*, 269

Barr, William W. II: *320**

Barret, Alexander G. III: *240**

Barrett, Charles S. V: 35*

Barrett, John C. III: *442**

Barrett, Robert E. IV: *274**

Barringer, Mr. IV: 94

Barron, Clarence W. IV: *47**, 52, 58, 76, 84, 111, 113, 151, 182

Barron, Gloria J. cited, II: 522-23

Barrows Co. et al. v. Higgins et al. I: 251

Bartlett, Francis I: *500**

Bartlett, Ralph W. II: *538**

Baruch, Bernard M. II: *622**; IV: 334, 344, 358, 522; V: 120, 527

Basch, Victor G. IV: *18**, 34

the Basle [Zionist] program III: 303, 575, 598; IV: 159, 362, 393, 525

Bass, John F. II: *347**

Bass, Robert P. II: *347**, 362; III: 244, 246, 503; IV: 381

Bassett, J. Gardiner I: 589, 591; II: *8*, 11

Bata, Jan A. V: *637**

Batchelder, Wallace III: *439**

Bates, Henry M. III: 288*; V: 380

Bates, John L. I: *190**, *208*, 222, 230, 334, 490, 526, 530, 535; II: 152

Baston, George W. II: *186**

Bauer, Mrs. IV: 280

Bauer v. O'Donnell III: 100, 103, 105, 113, 120-21, 127, 170, 196

Bausman, Frederick IV: *248**

Bayard, Mabel I: *90**

Bayard, Thomas F. Jr. I: 89*

Bayard, Thomas F. Sr. I: *89**

Beale, Howard K. cited, V: 505

Beale, Joseph H. III: *13**, 18; IV: 27; V: 146, 155, 379

Beaman, Charles C. I: *125**

Beard, Charles A. V: 84, 504*, 511

Beard, Mr. V: 348

Beatson, J. W. I: *259**, *265*, 266; III: 260, *281*; IV: *223*; V: 341

Beatty v. Gillbanks V: 318

Beauvais, Alfred T. II: *420**

Beaver, Daniel R. cited, III: 350
Beck, James M. IV: 559*; V: 161
Beck, Joseph D. II: 209*
Beckden, Mr. V: 5
Becker, Carl L. V: 196*, 197, 198
Becker, James H. V: 104*, 253
Becker, Miss II: 101
Beckham, J. C. W. I: 581*; III: 383
Bedford Cut Stone Co. v. Journey-men Stone Cutters' Association V: 279, 281
Beeks, Gertrude B. II: 12*, 128
Behrens, Adolph II: 328*
Bein, Alex cited III: 156, 303
Belgium III: 412, 431-32; IV: 300, 512; V: 213
Belknap, Morris B. V: 223
Belknap, William B. V: 202*
Bell, Stoughton V: 241*
Bellom, Maurice I: 446
Belmont, August II: 632; qouted, I: 304
Belnap, Hiram W. III: 109*, 122, 124, 141
Bement v. National Harrow Co. I: 431
Bemis, Edward W. I: 349*; III: 211, 518; IV: 220
Bemis, Samuel F. cited IV: 457
Benari, Yehuda cited, III: 520; V: 438
Benderly, Samson IV: 522*, 532, 561, 564; V: 39, 435
Benedict v. Ratner V: 173, 174
Benedikt, Edmund V: 134*; quoted, V: 328
Benes, Eduard cited, IV: 315
Ben-Gurion, David III: 328; IV: 357; V: 490, 531*, 558, 571, 574, 576, 586, 604, 608, 647; LDB on, V: 571
Benjamin, Miss V: 446
Ben Jehuda, Eliazar III: 355
Bennett, Frank P. IV: 99*
Bennett, Hugh H. V: 616*
Bennett, March G. I: 544, 560
Bennington Street Railway Co. II: 240

Bentley, James R. I: 475
Bentwich, Norman deM. V: 524*; cited, III: 193; IV: 474
Berenson, Bernard I: 73*
Berenson, Mr. V: 309
Bergengren, Roy F. V: 340*
Berger, Julius III: 322*, 422-23; IV: 141
Berger, Sophia III: 662
Bergson, Henri L. IV: 346*
Berkshire County Savings Bank II: 595
Berkson, Isaac B. V: 443*
Berle, Adolph A., Sr. II: 91*, 105, 152, 161, 245; IV: 36
Berle, Adolph A., Jr. IV: 36*; V: 101
Berlin, Meyer III: 504*, 510, 533, 561, 569; IV: 5, 38, 173, 174, 181, 187, 193, 217, 342, 393, 438; V: 445; see also Mizrachi
Berlin, Treaty of III: 304, 404
Berliner, Emile IV: 330*, 438, 499, 553, 561; V: 36
Berlis, Mendel V: 44
Berman, Edward V: 560*, 561, 565, 567, 568, 569, 573
Berman, Hyman cited, II: 366
Berman, Morton M. V: 578*
Berman, William III: 427*, 484
Bernard, A. IV: 89
Bernard, Burton C. cited, I: 26; V: 477
Bernhardt, Joshua V: 433*, 449, 450, 462, 463, 479
Bernheim, Isaac W. III: 354*, 454; IV: 388
Bernheim, Lee S. I: 478*, 558, 571
Bernstein, Herman III: 400*, 431, 643-44, 648; IV: 282
Bernstein, Irving cited, V: 323
Bernstein, Mr. V: 541
Berry v. Donovan I: 360-62
Bethel, Richard IV: 451*
Bettman, Alfred V: 212*, 379
Beveridge, Albert J. I: 520*; V: 52, 76, 284

Beveridge, William H. V: 337*
Beyer, Otto S. V: 266*, 366
Bickel, Alexander M. cited, V: 47, 59
"Big Business and Industrial Liberty" (1912) II: 544
"Big Men and Little Business" (1914) III: 89, 184, 189, 232
Bigelow, A. S. I: 242
Bigelow, Herbert S. III: 375*
Bigelow, Melville M. I: 7, 367*
bigness, monopoly, trusts, etc., LDB on I: 276, 405, 407, 420-22, 541, 585, 592-95; II: 25-26, 70, 76, 90, 99-101, 125, 190, 299, 332-33, 380-81, 412-43, 481, 510-12, 521-22, 527, 530-31, 626, 666, 670-71, 684, 686-96, 701; III: 113-15, 124, 151, 218-21, 559; IV: 528; V: 17, 68, 84-85, 482, 527, 555-56, 648
Bikle, Henry W. V: 368*, 374, 499, 511
Billard, John L. II: 198*, 199, 251, 253-56, 259-65, 272-75, 278-81; III: 167, 175, 266, 284
Billikopf, Jacob III: 412*; IV: 32, 223, 309, 312; V: 615
Billings, Edmund I: 237, 238*, 241, 253, 270, 284, 368, 369, 373, 375, 376(2), 432; II: 283; III: 170
Billings, Warren K. IV: 399*
Bingham, G. Barry V: 616*
Bingham, George H. III: 53*
Bingham, John cited, I: 405
Bingham, Robert W. II: 290*; V: 179, 254, 265, 466, 577
Birch, Stephen II: 475*
Bird, Anna Child II: 348; V: 34*, 35, 233
Bird, Charles S. II: 642*; III: 79, 125, 596; V: 34, 233
Bird, George E. III: 439*
Birkenhead, Earl of V: 153
Birkenheim, Alexander IV: 388
Bisbee deportations V: 285
Bishop, Elias I: 543
Bishop, Everett I: 24, 34
Bishop, Frank S. II: 278*

Bishop, George W. III: 192
Birmingham, Stephen cited, I: 337
Biskind, Israel J. III: 349*, 375
Bismarck, Otto II: 210; III: 404
Bisno, Abraham II: 616*
Black & White Taxi Co. v. Brown & Yellow Taxi Co. V: 335, 337
Black, Hugo, L. V: 552*
Black, Morris A. II: 460*
Black v. Delaware & Raritan Canal Co. II: 253
Blackstone, William E. IV: 167*, 196, 271, 278, 289, 290, 296, 327
Blackwell, Henry B. II: 118*, 125
Blackwell, Alice S. III: 319*, 597
Blaine, James G. IV: 167
Blaine, John J. III: 383; V: 322*, 352
Blanchard, Frank L. IV: 23*
Blair, Francis P. V: 327*
Blaney, W. O. I: 183
Blankenburg, Rudolph III: 179*
Bley, Joseph L. V: 331
Bliss, Elmer J. II: 98*, 105, 204, 205, 275, 553; III: 223-24; IV: 89
Bliss, William H. II: 198*
Bliven, Bruce V: 96*, 339, 653
Bloch Publishing Co. III: 386
Block v. Hirsch IV: 550
Bloom, Dr. III: 671
Bloomfield, Meyer I: 553*; II: 195, 367, 387, 427, 444, 460, 502; IV: 231
Blue Ribbon Books, Inc. V: 599
Blue, Rupert IV: 276
Bluestone, Joseph I. III: 651*; IV: 174
Blum, John M. cited, III: 77
Blumenfeld, Kurt Y. V: 632*
Blumgart, Hermann V: 156*, 185, 232, 347
B'nai Brith III: 365, 369, 373, 564, 571, 573, 585; IV: 148, 195, 352, 426
B'nai Zion Educational Society IV: 126
Bobbs Merrill Co. v. Straus III: 120
Bodenheimer, Max I. IV: 154*
Bodley, Temple V: 264*
Boeckel, Richard M. V: 414*, 510

Boer Rebellion IV: 415, 474
Bohlen, Francis H. V: 226*
Bohn, Frank III: 87*, 98, 104
Bohn, William E. III: 98*
Boit, Robert A. I: 138*, 139
Boland, Edward P. V: 598*
Bolsheviks IV: 304, 399, 450, 463, 507, 546
Bonaparte, Charles J. II: 132*, 134, 168, 186, 241
Bonbright, James C. V: 503*, 511
Bond, Frederic D. III: 266
Bondy, Joseph IV: 80*
Bondy, William V: 368*
Bonham, Scott II: 539*
Boni, Albert V: 367*, 369
Bonsall, Ward II: 704*
Bookwalter, Alfred G. I: 542*
Boot & Shoe Club I: 225-29; II: 68
Boot & Shoe Recorder V: 565
Boot & Shoe Workers' Union I: 248, 298
Borah, William E. II: 543, 620*; IV: 17; V: 32, 126, 130, 285, 362, 402
Borchard, Edwin M. IV: 44*
Borglum, Gutzom III: 272*
Borglum, Mary cited, III: 272
Bosley v. McLaughlin III: 364, 381, 392, 400, 444
Bosnia II: 209
Boston, LDB on I: 43; II: 379, 425, 498
"Boston—1915" II: 236, 245, 246, 267, 272, 289, 294, 296, 379, 426
Boston Advertiser I: 385; II: 19, 144, 152, 156, 523, 729
Boston Aldermanic Association I: 229-30, 375
Boston American I: 322, 388, 459; II: 65, 88, 113, 220, 251, 409, 529, 724; III: 3, 53, 72, 181, 509; IV: 120
Boston & Albany Rrd II: 143, 626, 723; III: 172
"Boston & Maine Pensions" (1909) II: 268-71; III: 198
Boston & Maine Rrd: see New York, New Haven & Hartford Rrd. and

Brandeis, Louis D., and proposed merger . . .
Boston & Philadelphia Steamship Co. II: 49, 132
Boston Art Club II: 93
Boston Assessing Department I: 226
Boston Associated Board of Trade I: 138-39, 141-43, 145, 160, 167, 171-74, 177-83, 186-90, 193-99, 206-207, 210, 239, 271, 276, 291, 296, 424, 553
Boston Bar Association I: 140, 210
Boston Bank Presidents' Association II: 79
Boston Beacon I: 191
Boston Board of Aldermen I: 120, 231, 233, 253
Boston Board of Health I: 67
Boston Board of Schoolhouse Commissioners I: 158, 174
Boston Book-Binding Co. II: 202
Boston Central Business Organization II: 95, 101
Boston Central Labor Union I: 210, 279, 282, 499, 501, 560; II: 14, 59, 66, 113, 418; V: 342, 568
Boston Chamber of Commerce II: 83, 109, 120, 122, 123, 127-28, 135, 170, 216, 286, 288, 299, 370, 379, 425, 517, 622, 628, 644; III: 53, 61, 79, 86, 194-95, 223-24
Boston City Charter II: 83, 219, 222, 244-45, 283, 293
Boston City Club II: 45, 46, 67, 96, 246; IV: 260
Boston City Council I: 160
Boston Committee on Metropolitan Affairs I: 180
Boston Common II: 343, 404, 428, 504; III: 80, 104
Boston Consolidated Gas Co.: see Brandeis, Louis D. and consolidation of the Boston gas utility and development of the "sliding scale" and Richards, James L.
Boston Creditmen's Association II: 86

Boston Crime Survey V: 205, 210, 225, 238, 241, 300

Boston Disinfecting Co. I: 68

Boston Dock Commission II: 516

Boston Edison Illuminating Co. I: 229, 467, 516

Boston Elevated Railway Co. I: 128-32, 135, 138-39, 141-45, 160-203, 210, 222-25, 245, 306, 330, 389, 405, 416-19, 423-24, 512, 592; II: 62, 94, 211, 224, 254, 457, 464, 465, 480-85, 650, 666; III: 163; IV: 66, 88, 94, 97, 104, 120; see also Brandeis, Louis D., and public franchise, utility and traction contests

Boston Evening Transcript I: *128*, 459; II: 25, 61, 79, 84, 105-107, 117, 143, 158, 164, 378, 406, 409, 485, 520, 583, 645; IV: 104, 166; IV: 110, 464; V: 223, 240, 283, 284

Boston Evening Traveler II: 498; III: 61

Boston Finance Commission II: 31, 83, 219, 222, 245, 293; III: 162, 200

Boston Five Cents Savings Bank IV: 461; V: 341, 346, 348, 393

Boston Fruit & Produce Exchange II: 83, 105, 631, 644; III: 66, 70-73

Boston Garment Workers' Union III: 669-71

Boston gas bill I: 322

Boston Globe II: 164, 190, *517;* V: 244, 339, 382

Boston, Henry & Sons Ltd. IV: 89

Boston Herald I: 66, 459; II: 33, 64, 133, 158, *163,* 166, 167, 257, 273, 288, 410, 428, 557; IV: 88, 95; V: 270, 276, 283-85, 320, 330, 348, 386, 546

Boston Jewish Advocate IV: 95, 345; V: 463

Boston Journal II: 145, 154, 376, 677, 684, 687, 724, 726, 730

Boston Merchants' Association I: 171, 278; II: 216, 234, 246, 259, 264, 268

Boston News Bureau II: *63,* 84, 110, 516; III: 181, 191; IV: 47, 76, 88

Boston Paper Trade Association I: 486, 496

Boston Police Department I: 235

Boston Police strike IV: 142, 450, 471

Boston Post I: 90, 97, 173, 457-59; II: 25, 79, 84, 145, 154, 155, 163, 241, 376, 379, 482, 495-96, 502; III: 83, 90, 93, 124; IV: 23, 125; V: 329; LDB on I: 457-59

Boston Press Club II: *394*

Boston Public Library I: 127, 480; V: 565

Boston Public School Association I: 178

Boston Rrd Holding Co. III: 55, 266

Boston Record II: 158

Boston School Board I: 174; II: 99, 264

Boston Schoolhouse bill I: 167

Boston Symphony Orchestra I: 309, 328, 334

Boston Terminal Co. II: 42, 55

Boston Transportation Co. I: 296

Boston Tribune I: 532

Boston Typographical Union I: 247, 249-50, 532; III: 10

Boston Typothetae I: 246, 247, 249, 259, 357; II: 319

Boston Union Club V: 276

Boston University I: 86; V: 120

Boston Young Men's Hebrew Association III: 85

Bothwell et al. v. Buckbee Mears Co. V: 315

Bottomly, Robert J. II: *244**

Bouckstein, Mr. V: 547

Boudin, Leonard V: 653

Bourne, Edward G. I: 148, 153*, 156

Bourne, Jonathan Jr. II: 403*, 406, 413, *432,* 455, 622

Bowden, William T. III: 402

Bowditch, Alfred IV: 66*

Bowditch, Henry P. I: 183; IV: 127*

Bowen, Catherine D. cited, V: 498

Bowers, Claude V: 306; cited, I: 521

Bowles, Samuel I: *319**, *365, 458, 525;* II: *271*

Bowles, Sherman V: 497

Bowman, Arthur R. II: 312, 317*, 338

Boyd, John T. I: *206**, 207, 553, 555

Boyden, Roland W. I: *296**

Boyden, William C. II: 362*

Boyle, John V: 231

Boylston National Bank (Boston) I: 23

Brackett, John Q. A. I: 102*

Bradley, Charles S. I: 10*, 19, 24-27, 36, 47, 53; IV: 57, 339; LDB on I: 10-11; IV: 339

Bradley, Jerry P. I: 174

Bradley, Richards M. I: *501**, *533*

Bradley, William M. III: 439*

Brady, James B. III: *129**, 133

Bragdon, Henry W. cited, II: 635

Bragdon, W. T. IV: 169

Brailsford, H. N. V: 330

Braintree Bee IV: 88

Brand, Katherine E. V: 628*

Brandeis, Adele I: 5, *75**, 409; II: 199, 250, 334; III: 37, 165; V: 24, *138, 140,* 145, *162,* 176, *198,* 256, 264, 405, 459

Brandeis, Adolph I: *3**, 20, 24-25, 40, 60, *65, 68,* 72, *81, 82, 83, 84,* 94, 245, *262, 334, 335, 336, 337, 338, 339, 340, 346, 351, 352,* 354, *355,* 356, 358, 359, *362, 364, 371, 386, 387, 392,* 411, 415, 553-54; II: 191, 235, 240, 393, 662; III: 85, 443; IV: 39, 40, 315, 413, 547, 548; V: 12, 128, 129, 136, 163, 169, 192, 214, 345, 350, 657, 659

Brandeis, Albert I: 12, 15, 459; II: 368; III: 400

Brandeis, Alfred I: *3**, 6, 15, 17, 20, 23, *25, 26, 27,* 34, 40, *44, 48,* 54, *55,* 60, *63, 66*(2), 67, *72*(2), 74, 77, *78, 79*(2), *80,* 88, *90, 116,* 127, 221, 242, 245, *262,* 268, 287, 355, 356, *358, 359*(2), 363, 387, *406, 407, 408, 409* (2), *411, 413, 415,* 427, 428, 436,

438, 439, 441, 442, 449, 459, 477, 478, 480, *498, 503, 510, 511, 513, 514, 516, 530, 533, 581, 582*(2), *584*(2), *585, 586, 590;* II: *9, 12, 17*(2), *18, 31, 61, 68,* 77, *85, 96, 110, 115, 139, 155, 175, 185, 191, 194, 198, 199,* 200, *206,* 207, 208, 209, *213*(2), 221, 230, 235, 240, *249*(2), 250, 258, 276, 279 (2), *280,* 282, 284, 287, 288, *289,* 291, 292, 294, 298, 305, *306*(2), *315, 317, 318*(2), 320, 324, 326, 327, *329, 330, 331*(2), *332, 333, 334, 335, 343, 344, 348,* 356, *358, 363, 364, 365, 368,* 370, *392, 393, 405,* 452, *464, 466,* 536, 537, *611, 615,* 638, 642, 650, 652, 653, 654, *660*(2), *662,* 673, 676, 700, *703,* 706, *710, 718, 724,* 727, *728*(2), *729;* III: 37, *42, 58, 85, 110, 127, 143, 164, 165,* 229, *231, 236, 244,* 246, *262, 264, 271,* 280, *310, 330, 331, 334, 339, 340, 345*(2), *353,* 368, *381, 383*(2), 387, *399, 420* (2), *443, 444, 465, 484, 488,* 503, 508, *513, 565,* 617, *661;* IV: 7, 25, 39, 40, 54, 169, 225, 276, 284, 294, 297, *308*(2), 313, *315,* 324, 326, 329, 332, *385,* 387, *402,* 408, *415, 416, 432,* 458, *470,* 477, *480, 487, 488, 512, 518, 519,* 527, 529, 532, 535, 539, *543, 546*(2), 548, *551, 557*(2), *566;* V: *6*(2), *10*(2), *13, 14,* 20, 21, 22, 23, 24, 26, 28, *32,* 34, 35, *82, 96, 107, 128, 134, 135, 136, 139, 142, 162, 168, 169,* 175, *176, 183,* 187, 202, 206, 212, 213, 220, 221, *222*(2), *232, 234, 236,* 240, 242, *254, 255, 260, 261*(2), 267, 270, 279, 282, 288, *289, 295,* 301(2), *303, 304, 306, 307, 308, 314,* 349, 350, 367, 458, *592,* 601, *656, 657, 658*(2), 659; LDB on V: 349-50

Brandeis, Alice G. I: *91**, *92-101,* 103, 110, 112, 118-20, 127, 135, 165, 242, 245, 287, 339, 346, 356, 364, *371,* 407, *409-11, 436, 439, 442,* 530, *582;* II: *9, 17,* 140, *186,* 199, 208, 230, 249, 291, 305, 328, 331, 348, 364,

370, 407, 577, 650, 653, 702, 706;
III: 40, 203, *221, 222, 223, 224, 227,
228, 229,* 231, *234, 236, 237, 238*(2),
244, 246, *259,* 262-63, 271, 339-40,
344-45, 378, 381, 387, 420, 444, 503,
513, 562, 565; IV: 54, 107, 150, 176,
210, 224, 238, 249, 257, 266, 267,
268, 274, 275, 276, 293, 295, 297,
314, *315, 317,* 363, *367*(2), *368,* 370,
*371, 385, 398, 400, 401, 403, 405,
406, 407, 409,* 411, *412, 416, 417,
419, 421, 422*(2), *424,* 441, 443, 445,
449, *458,* 468, 470, 471, 480, 487,
488, 527, 529, 539, *554;* V: 5, 6, 14,
21, 64, 76, 82, *87,* 90, *93,* 96, 97,
99, 103, 114, 118, 119, 136, 144,
150, 151, 152, 161, 162, 163, 172,
184, 187, 190, 191, 192, 195, 202,
214, 220, 222, 223, 233, 234, 235,
237, 242, 248, 252, 255, 256, 264,
268, 273, 278, 283, 288, 294, 299-304,
326, 327, 330, 349, 350, 355, 365,
383, 402, 412, 458, 500, 505, 512,
513, 550, 552, 611, 635, 646, 655,
657, 659; LDB on I: 95, 101, 110
Brandeis, Amelia IV: 56
Brandeis, Amy (LDB's sister): see
Wehle, Amy B.
Brandeis, Amy (LDB's niece): see
McCreary, Amy B.
"Brandeis and Brandeis: The Reversible Mind of Louis D. Brandeis,
'The People's Lawyer' " IV: 76
"Brandeis and the Coupon Evil"
(1916) IV: 23
Brandeis family I: *59*
Brandeis, Fannie (LDB's sister): see
Nagel, Fannie B.
Brandeis, Fannie (LDB's niece) I:
75*, 408; II: 9, 18, 96, 298, 348, 356;
III: 443; IV: 519, 527; V: 82, 139,
144, 161, 162, 176, *190,* 222, 223,
236, 252, 254, 256, 264, 304, 350,
392, 405, 458, *466, 501, 505,* 550,
570, 601, *616*
Brandeis, Frederick V: 256*
Brandeis, Frederika D. I: *3*, 20, 21,

24, *26, 41,* 45, 54, 60, 63, 65, 72, 74,
75, 81, 103, *118,* 175, 371; II: 235,
240, 718; IV: 265; V: 32, 134,
136, 350, 656, 657, 659; LDB on I:
75
Brandeis, H. L. II: 96
Brandeis, Jean: see Tachau, Jean B.
Brandeis, Jennie T. 26, 34, 41, 57, 67,
72, 74, 77, 91, 222, *479;* II: 198, 199,
230, 250, 305, 356, 370, 650, 728;
III: 354, 381, 444, 484; IV: 54, 147,
225, 269, 276, 367, 433, 470, 520,
527; V: 108, 137, 145, 163, 206, 235,
303, 304, 307, *349, 350, 458, 610,*
649, 656, 657, *659*
"Brandeis on the Labor Problem"
(1913) III: 61
Brandeis, Louis D., and: student days
at Harvard Law School I: 5-25;
IV: 45, 107-108, 224-25; later relations with Harvard Law School I:
64-65, 69-71, 84-89, 92-93, 105-106,
113-17; II: 712; III: 13, 18-19, 134-
36, 209, 240, 288; IV: 134, 142, 339,
395-96, 400-401, 459, 463-64, 558-
59, 564; V: 11, 43-44, 50-51, 78,
80-81, 90, 109-10, 142-44, 146-47,
155-56, 159, 187, 191, 195-97, 243-
44, 248, 276, 278, 288, 320, 327-
34, 355-56, 394, 411, 656-57; practice in St. Louis I: 26-34; V: 477;
early legal practice in Boston I:
34-46, 49-58, 61, 63-64, 67-68, 72-
73, 75-78, 80, 83, 89, 93, 95, 98-99,
106-10, 124-26; III: 62-63; IV: 33-
34, 48-53, 56-59, 65-70, 74-76, 78-
79, 104-107, 113; donation of legal
services for public causes I: 206,
210-12, 452; II: 44, 50-51, 64, 92,
388, 409, 508, 631, 675; III: 70, 96-
97, 105, 138, 145, 198; IV: 51; public franchise, utility and traction
contests in Boston I: 100, 128-35,
138-46, 160-210, 220, 244-46, 257-58,
264-65, 278, 282, 295-97, 329-33,
347-49, 388-90, 405-406, 416-20, 423-
26, 467-77, 512, 516-17; II: 10, 23,

Brandeis, Louis D. (*continued*)
26, 71-72, 94, 211-12, 224, 288-89, 396-97, 419-20, 432, 465-66, 480, 482-83, 485-86, 540; IV: 68, 88, 94, 97, 104; see also Public Franchise League and Brandeis, Louis D., and consolidation of the Boston gas utility; anti-imperialist movement I: 147-59, 161-62; labor, conditions of employment, relations with capital, and arbitration efforts I: 232, 236-38, 244-51, 257, 259-64, 268, 279, 282-84, 286, 288-89, 298, 309, 326-29, 334, 350-51, 357-62, 373, 397, 408, 447, 450-51, 461-62, 513, 519-21, 572-73, 576-77; II: 32, 209-211, 268, 287, 296-300, 314-15, 359-60, 403, 415, 444-51, 507-508, 517, 519, 522-23, 527-28, 531-36, 542-49, 562-68, 575-76, 580, 586-89, 614-15, 620, 628-29, 639-40, 646-51, 676-83, 707; III: 10-11, 25, 55-56, 74; V: 56-62, 333-35, 424-25, 503; see also National Civic Federation, and Brandeis, Louis D., and New York garment workers' strike and arbitration; coal strike of 1902 I: 208-221, 223; "good government" and the battle against political corruption in Boston I: 174, 178-79, 204-208, 222-42, 248-53, 256, 268-70, 273-74, 277, 281, 300, 333-34, 351-54, 356, 368-69, 373-80, 385-91, 414-15, 432-33, 466, 586; II: 83, 219, 222-23, 244-45, 267-68, 272, 283, 294-96, 378, 416; see also Good Government Association and "Boston—1915"; consolidation of the Boston gas utility and development of the "sliding scale" mechanism I: 252-56, 267-76, 279-80, 285-334, 349-68, 398-403, 410-12, 419-28, 431-43, 452-54, 466, 588, 590; II: 3-5, 24, 378, 579; III: 69, 166, 276-80, 375-76, 509-10; IV: 113, 119, 123, 127; V: 504; uniform legislation movement I: 156, 280-81, 347,

358-59, 364, 367, 398, 401, 433-36; savings bank life insurance, the struggle to implement (to June, 1907) I: 340-46, 351, 362-70, 380-84, 388-99, 404-409, 437-38, 443-49, 452-65, 473-511, 514-19, 524-71, 574-91; V: 332, 339, 565; savings bank life insurance after June, 1907 II: 5-24, 47, 60-61, 72-76, 79-80, 114, 128-29, 176-77, 191-98, 201-206, 214-30, 234-37, 241, 252, 283-86, 300-305, 319, 389, 433-35, 442, 566-67, 589-600; III: 8, 411, 457-58; IV: 44, 229-30, 460-61; V: 89-90, 216-17, 302, 311, 319-20, 338-43, 346, 348, 356-58, 375-76, 393-94, 402, 410-11, 451, 471, 476, 487, 497, 508-509, 515, 530, 545-48, 550, 559-62, 565-76, 584-85, 598; in New York I: 482-84, 491-92, 506-507; V: 575, 595, 598; proposed merger of the New York, New Haven & Hartford Rrd with the Boston & Maine Rrd I: 582-84, 591-96; II: 23-24, 27-58, 61-92, 98-99, 104-195, 198-99, 204-206, 221-23, 230-34, 237-46, 251-67, 272-83, 286, 329-30, 500-502, 506, 520, 580-85, 620-28, 631, 635-36, 644, 647, 675, 700, 722-26, 728-29; III: 3, 12-16, 20-25, 49-50, 53-55, 58, 66-73, 106-109, 123-24, 127-35, 141-50, 153-54, 164, 171-81, 186, 188-95, 204, 244-45, 264-71, 274-77, 282-87, 306-307, 560, 590; IV: 8, 47-48, 57-58, 71, 76, 81, 84, 87, 92, 150, 153, 214; V: 659; conservation I: 519-20; II: 355-56, 392, 398, 400, 414, 451-52, 458-79, 490-98, 513-16, 612-13, 618-19, 660, 685, 713, 715-16, 723-24; III: 6-9, 59-60, 67; V: 133, 348, 527-28; see also Brandeis, Louis D., and Pinchot-Ballinger conservation controversy and Alaska; Pinchot-Ballinger conservation controversy II: 306-64, 379-80, 386, 396, 401-402, 414, 457-59, 475; III: 246, 394, 464; IV: 63, 68,

70, 73, 84, 86, 92, 101, 119, 129, 150, 171; V: 116, 126, 641-43, 653; New York garment workers' strike and arbitration, and the 'protocol of peace' in the garment industry II: 365-73, 381-82, 386-87, 390-92, 406-407, 417, 459-60, 483-89, 497, 500-503, 508, 518-19, 524, 569-72, 586, 616-18; III: 6, 9, 27-28, 52, 57, 73-74, 81-82, 104-105, 208-215, 401-402, 428-30, 524-25, 547, 562, 650-51, 669-73; IV: 9-10, 25-26, 263-64; V: 166; scientific management and efficiency movement II: 25, 383-91, 394-95, 398, 407, 418, 543, 586-89, 655-56; III: 16-20, 49-50, 78, 142-43, 240-41, 584, 618; advanced freight rate cases II: 306-307, 370, 373-74, 382-83, 387-88, 393-96, 400-401, 407, 411-12; III: 12-13, 49, 78-80, 142-43, 162-65, 192, 202-203, 210-11, 245, 288-89, 295, 330-31, 334, 337, 345-46, 372, 383-86, 399-400, 410-11, 484, 502-503; IV: 46-47, 63, 113, 141, 145, 147, 149; V: 381; United Shoe Machinery Co. I: 428-31, 470-72, 508-509; II: 104, 376, 410-11, 428-32, 464, 551-60; III: 42, 224, 369, 592-95; IV: 60-61, 76, 78, 81, 97, 150; antitrust movement and "the curse of bigness" I: 68, 276-77; II: 25, 99-101, 369-70, 380-81, 407, 410-13, 435-39, 442-43, 453-57, 481-82, 495-96, 510-12, 519, 521, 523, 525, 530, 538, 540-41, 561, 564-66, 602-603, 615-16, 651-55, 663-66, 669-76, 683-701, 707-710, 721-22, 726-27, 730; III: 4, 11-12, 25-26, 35, 39, 41, 48-49, 100-103, 116-17, 171, 187-88, 195, 218-21, 234-37, 247-60, 290, 440, 523, 592-95; V: 333, 463, 482, 527, 648; price maintenance on trademarked goods II: 615-16; III: 31-32, 89-90, 93-105, 111-13, 118-22, 125-27, 131-34, 138-39, 146-47, 152, 169-70, 173-74, 216-18, 225-27, 434, 446-48, 539-40, 559-60, 592, 618-19;

campaign of 1912 II: 526-29, 536, 539, 542-46, 550-51, 561, 568-69, 572, 576-77, 585-86, 600, 611-14, 623-25, 632-35, 639-45, 648-706, 709-10, 713-18, 726-27; III: 4; V: 234, 556; possible appointment to Wilson's cabinet II: 715; III: 32, 35-41, 44-45, 129-30; IV: 89-91; nomination to the Supreme Court and the struggle over confirmation IV: 25-36, 41-132, 139-54, 165-66, 169-72, 175-77, 182-84, 192, 196, 198, 209-16, 219-33, 240-41, 249, 264-65; V: 308; work on the U.S. Supreme Court IV: 258, 264, 267-69, 273-74, 299, 315-16, 367-69, 423, 450-52, 509-10, 517, 520-22, 540-42, 550-51, 554, 559; V: 40-41, 47-53, 56-59, 63-64, 74-75, 78-88, 91-99, 104-106, 116-20, 124-32, 137-38, 154, 159-60, 165-76, 185, 188-89, 192, 200-201, 204, 208-13, 221, 225-28, 235-39, 243-44, 247-48, 254, 272-76, 279-81, 284-86, 290-96, 303-18, 322-25, 328-37, 345-46, 350-52, 358-61, 364, 368-73, 376-80, 397, 403-404, 414-15, 482-83, 496-97, 500-501, 512, 564, 566, 587-89, 610-11, 652-53; see also specific cases; Mexican arbitration (1916) IV: 254-56; World War I and war mobilization IV: 271-76, 292-93, 300-301, 306-309, 314, 317, 324, 326, 332-34, 362-63; University of Louisville V: 138-41, 144-50, 153-54, 158, 161-65, 168-69, 175-82, 187-90, 197-98, 201-202, 207-208, 212, 217-19, 223, 229, 231-32, 236-37, 241-43, 253-58, 261-69, 282, 304-308, 314-17, 343-44, 391-93, 405-406, 466-67, 501-502, 550-51, 564, 570-71, 592, 594, 601, 617, 640, 648-49; the New Deal V: 505-506, 510, 514-15, 518-20, 523, 526-28, 531, 536-40, 552-60, 563, 570-71, 585-86, 616-17, 625-26; Zionism and Jewish affairs I: 386-87; II: 402, 611, 659; III: 4, 22-23, 64-66, 77-78, 141, 147-48,

Brandeis, Louis D. (*continued*)
158-59, 174-75, 192-93, 226, 291-341, 344, 349-83, 386-89, 393-592, 595-682; IV: 3-21, 24, 34, 38-41, 79-86, 95-98, 102-104, 108-10, 115-17, 126, 129, 132-42, 145-75, 178-81, 184-90, 193-224, 227-28, 231-37, 240-63, 269-72, 277-362, 365-474, 477-509, 513-19, 522-27, 530-38, 541, 544-45, 549-56, 560-68; V: 3-4, 8-9, 12, 14, 18-19, 25-31, 36-39, 44, 51, 73-74, 90, 100-18, 182, 191-92, 195-96, 219-20, 249-53, 258, 271-75, 291-95, 300, 309, 330, 336, 343, 347-48, 386-90, 397-99, 407-409, 413-14, 417-43, 451-52, 459, 461-92, 507, 541, 544-45, 549-54, 567-68, 577-83, 587, 590-91, 594-99, 605-609, 619-23, 632-35, 638-39, 643-55; American Jewish Congress movement III: 408-409, 544-45, 551-58, 564-82, 587-88, 591-92, 605, 607-609, 619-25, 631, 634-36, 640-41, 645-46, 651-56, 681-82; IV: 10, 17-18, 56, 102-104, 116-17, 133-38, 170, 172-75, 184-86, 197-205, 242, 250-54, 312; development of Palestine II: 537; III: 117, 155-59, 186, 206, 226, 235-36, 312-13, 317-18, 336-37, 354-56, 372-73, 416-18, 421-25, 427-28, 452-53, 468-77, 492, 495-501, 513-17, 520-22, 580, 607-11, 638-39, 674-75, 678-80; IV: 83, 109-10, 178, 334-36, 356, 417-20, 435-36, 446-47, 469, 495; V: 8, 16, 19-20, 36-39, 44, 48, 54-56, 112, 148, 182, 194-95, 220, 313-14, 382-89, 397-403, 407-408, 411, 416-17, 423-24, 427-28, 433, 436-37, 443-81, 484-92, 495, 506-10, 513-14, 521-26, 529-33, 542-44, 547, 558-59, 571-83, 586, 590-94, 602-609, 612-31, 636-37, 645, 651-52; the Balfour Declaration IV: 277-92, 295, 310-12, 316-23, 327-28, 331, 355-56, 369; V: 577-81, 612; trip to Palestine (1919) IV: 391-92, 394, 396-424; Hitler and Nazism V: 516-17, 520-21, 524-26, 531-33, 541, 553-54, 562, 599, 602, 605-608, 614-16, 619-20, 627-28, 638, 646; financial contributions to family I: 79, 438; II: 280, 729; III: 369; IV: 488, 533, 543, 557; V: 13; financial contributions to public causes I: 229, 509, 512, 522-24, 565, 567-68, 586; II: 5-6, 44, 54, 59, 205-206, 216, 246, 252, 283, 289, 292, 349, 397, 432, 466, 527, 571, 576, 698; III: 12, 43, 75, 80-81, 224, 263, 274, 288, 433, 539, 602; IV: 61-62, 92-93, 134, 168; V: 80, 231-32, 257, 304, 386, 478; financial contributions to Zionism and Jewish causes II: 402, 611; III: 65, 85, 295, 381-82, 406, 416, 478, 495, 530-31, 539, 551, 563, 603-604; IV: 62, 115, 180, 251, 347, 355, 377, 472, 491, 496; V: 25, 37-38, 252, 416-17, 491, 506, 558, 576, 582-83, 586, 618, 620, 652
—opinions on and evaluations of: Aaronsohn, Aaron II: 537; Acheson, Dean IV: 510; advertising III: 239; V: 70, 92, 342; aging, his own V: 288-89, 291, 429-30, 452, 489, 513, 610; agriculture III: 29, 151, 272-73; IV: 326, 487, 521, 548; V: 7, 10, 20, 21, 24, 26, 28-29, 35, 91-92, 135, 203-204, 206, 209, 214, 251, 289; Alaska II: 468-74; Allenby, Edmund H. H. IV: 416; the American Legion V: 3; "Americanization" III: 676; Ames, James B. I: 8, 10-11; Amidon, Charles F. IV: 43; Anderson, George W. II: 507; III: 297; anti-semitism III: 331, 349, 381; IV: 536-37; see also Hitler and Nazism; antitrust legislation II: 100-101, 455-57, 495-96; Arabs V: 386; arbitration, mediation, conciliation I: 450-51; II: 540; III: 25, 55, 184-85; see also New York garment workers' strike and arbitration; architecture I: 15-17, 20, 127, 480; Asia V: 33-34; automobiles I: 410; III:

488-89; Baker, Newton D. V: 209; banks and bankers ("the money power") II: 408-13, 487; III: 113-15, 168, 179, 187, 189, 202, 266, 342-44, 416; IV: 15, 518; V: 29, 360, 637; Barrett, Charles S. V: 35; Ben-Gurion, David V: 571; Berenson, Bernard I: 73; "bigness," monopoly, trusts, etc. I: 276, 405, 407, 420-22, 541, 585, 592-96; II: 25-26, 70, 76, 90, 99-101, 125, 190, 299, 332-33, 380-81, 412-13, 442-43, 481, 510-12, 521-22, 527, 530-31 626, 666, 670-71, 684, 686-96, 701; III: 113-15, 124, 151, 218-21, 559; IV: 528; V: 17, 68, 84-85, 482, 527, 555-56, 648; Black, Hugo V: 552; Boston I: 43; II: 379, 425, 498; Boston police I: 235; *Boston Post* I: 457-59; Boston University Law School I: 86-87; Bradley, Charles S. I: 10-11; IV: 339; Brandeis, Alfred V: 349-50; Brandeis, Alice G. I: 95, 101, 110; Brandeis, Fredericka D. I: 75; Brant, Irving N. V: 585-86; Brown, H. LaRue III: 85-86; "bucket shop" transactions II: 103, 124; Bulkeley, Robert J. III: 289; Byrnes, Timothy E. II: 111; capital v. labor I: 121, 247, 298, 335, 397, 447, 504-505, 572-73, 576-77, 584, 587; II: 299, 483-84, 519, 522, 548-49, 587, 676-83, 707-708; III: 25, 210, 218-21, 407, 428-29, 545-46; IV: 238, 521; V: 59-62; capitalism II: 70, 76, 280, 332-33, 342, 468-74, 481, 516, 522, 529, 548-49; IV: 335; V: 66-68, 91-92; Cardozo, Benjamin N. V: 258; Charlottesville, Virginia V: 301-302; Child, Walter IV: 519-20; V: 295; Chilton, William E. V: 308; China V: 277; church and state I: 521-22; Cincinnati V: 26; civil service II: 414, 416; clergymen V: 343, 347; Cleveland crime survey IV: 528; V: 17-18; Colvin, George V: 268; Commons, John R.

V: 100; communism V: 645; complacency V: 324; compulsory retirement II: 264-65; conservation II: 342, 451-52; IV: 335; V: 527-28; consumer movement 62, 66, 68-70, 91-92, 207, 382; Coolidge, Calvin IV: 470; V: 238, 270, 272-73, 324-25, 326, 330, 373; cooperative movement II: 529-31; V: 66-67, 364; Cotton, Joseph P. III: 393; Creel, George III: 543; Croly, Herbert V: 72, 188-89; Davis, Charles H. II: 404; Davis, John W. IV: 272; Dedham, Mass. I: 80; deHaas, Jacob II: 660; IV: 152, 373-74, 401, 453; V: 27-28, 148, 300, 407-408, 418-19, 434, 491-92, 549; Delano, Frederick A. III: 282; Dembitz, Louis N. V: 219; democracy I: 407; II: 332-33, 342; III: 428, 566-68; IV: 20-21, 254, 300, 477; V: 45-46; development of local culture IV: 497-99, 520, 525-29; V: 162-65, 168-69, 204-205; see also Louisville, University of; diversity of citizenship jurisdiction V: 170, 330; domestic spying IV: 510; V: 45-46, 60, 200, 203, 224-25, 310, 380; Douglas, Walter B. I: 27; duties of citizenship I: 233; V: 45-46; Eastman, Joseph B. I: 519; III: 392-93; Egypt IV: 410-16; Einstein, Albert IV: 554; Election of 1880 I: 57; Election of 1896 I: 123-24; Election of 1908 II: 213; Election of 1912 II: 709-10; see also Brandeis, Louis D., and campaign of 1912; Election of 1922 V: 76; Election of 1924 V: 134, 136, 151-52; Election of 1926 V: 240-41; Election of 1928 V: 327, 344, 348, 352, 354-55, 360-64; Elliott, Howard III: 153; Emerton, Ephraim V: 295; England I: 73-74; IV: 423, 477; V: 122, 183, 192; equal justice II: 342; Fahey, John H. V: 559-60; Federal Trade Commission III: 339,

Brandeis, Louis D. (*continued*)
381, 581; Ferber, J. Bernard II: 19;
Filene, Edward A. III: 61; V: 339,
584; Fish, Stuyvesant II: 110; Fitzgerald, John F. I: 378, 389; Flexner,
Simon IV: 470; football I: 387;
foreign trade V: 10, 15-16, 97; Fosdick, Raymond V: 192; Foss, Eugene N. II: 504-506; Frankfurter,
Felix III: 146; IV: 265, 344; V:
123, 183, 187, 364, 469-70, 497; freedom V: 45-46, 117; freedom of the
press I: 319; freedom of speech IV:
501-502, 517, 558; V: 229, 248, 286,
318, 352; Frothingham, Louis A. I:
372; II: 504; furnishings I: 60;
Germany IV: 372-73; gift coupons
III: 618-19; Glavis, Louis R. II:
315; Glueck, Nelson V: 623-24;
Goethe, Johann W. V: 512; Goldman, Solomon V: 615; Goldmark,
Henry V: 128, 130; Goldmark,
Josephine C. II: 381; Goldsmith,
Irving B. V: 358-61, 397; Grady,
Alice H. V: 89, 216, 307, 331;
Gray, Horace I: 38; Hailmann,
William N. V: 242-43; Hamlin,
Charles S. III: 47; Hapgood, Norman III: 243; Harding, Warren G.
IV: 470, 540; V: 89; Harvard Law
School I: 6, 89; V: 142-44, 146-47,
156, 276; Hast, Louis H. V: 223;
higher education V: 153-54, 215-16;
holding companies II: 602-603;
Holmes, Oliver W. III: 176; IV:
450; V: 17, 49, 50, 73, 83, 102, 123,
131, 172-73, 183-84, 204, 209, 212,
275, 310, 321, 325, 333, 364, 373,
377-79, 413, 496-97, 544; honorary
degrees V: 421, 563-64; Hoover,
Herbert IV: 300, 308, 448, 536,
539-40, 557; V: 10, 22, 75, 373, 415,
512; hours of labor I: 513; II: 78,
296-98, 359-60; III: 545; House,
Col. Edward M. IV: 470; Hughes,
Charles E. II: 68-69; V: 32-34, 321,
366; Hurwitz, Henry V: 635;

Ickes, Harold L. V: 641; immigration restriction III: 389, 506-507;
IV: 100, 272; incorporation of
trades unions I: 232-33; V: 56-58;
industrial accidents II: 319, 359-60,
377, 566-67; industrial democracy
I: 247-447; II: 548-49, 566-67, 587,
588-90, 630, 675, 707-708, 711; III:
97, 210, 216, 218-21; V: 45-46; insurance I: 342-43, 351, 362-64,
381-84, 445, 448-49, 480-84, 508,
540-41, 546; II: 222, 433-34, 590;
III: 8; V: 68, 375-76, 393-94, 601;
interlocking directorates III: 49,
79-80, 243, 247; investments I: 262-
63; IV: 241-42; V: 412, 528-29;
Ives, David O. III: 194-95; Japan
V: 34; Jay, Pierre II: 79-80; Jefferson, Thomas V: 302, 411; Jewish
fraternities IV: 496-97; Johnson,
Tom L. IV: 528; Jones, Charles H.
II: 622; Judaism and Jewry I: 386;
III: 399, 534-35, 625-27; IV: 356,
468; V: 182, 297, 545, 574; the judiciary II: 375, 421-25, 427, 509-10,
603-11, 646-47, 655-56; III: 109, 181,
242, 281, 378-79, 632-33; IV: 272;
V: 83, 227-28, 324-25, 326, 367-68,
371, 403-404, 501; Kazmann, Boris
V: 423; Kent, Raymond A. V:
640; Kligler, Israel J. V: 19; Ku
Klux Klan V: 3; labor injunctions
I: 283-84; II: 210-11; V: 60; labor
legislation II: 482, 527-28, 576, 639-
40, 707; III: 56, 442-43; V: 53, 56-
58, 131; LaFollette, Robert M. II:
489-90, 505, 539, 573, 585; V: 24,
169; the law I: 62; Lawrence
strike (1912) II: 562-64; legal education I: 6, 14, 39, 111, 117, 160,
221; II: 619, 637, 656; III: 62; V:
44, 48, 50-51, 78, 142, 284, 381; see
also Harvard Law School; the
legal profession I: 106-109, 124-26,
321-22; II: 340-41, 646-47, 655-56,
708-709; III: 62-63, 682-83; V: 49,
111, 311, 367-68, 404; Lewin-

Epstein, E. W. IV: 341-42; Lindbergh, Charles A. V: 287; Lippmann, Walter V: 124, 190-91; Lipsky, Louis IV: 294, 490, 506; V: 347, 599; Lloyd, Henry D. I: 121-22; lobbying legislation V: 390; London, England IV: 403-404; luxury, materialism, fashion, etc. I: 95, 100; III: 330-31; IV: 401, 459; V: 7-8, 97, 199, 206, 214, 251, 282, 410, 542; MacDonald, J. Ramsay V: 402; Mack, Julian W. III: 180; IV: 542; Magnes, Judah L. IV: 442; Magruder, Calvert IV: 454; Marshall, Louis IV: 354; McCarthy, Charles II: 673; McElwain, William H. II: 629-30; V: 658; McReynolds, James C. III: 35; Mellen, Charles S. II: 31, 405, 500-501; misrepresentation by the press II: 546; III: 83; IV: 88-89; Mitchell, William D. V: 370-71; Nagel, Charles II: 327; National Civic Federation II: 13; the New Deal V: 531, 537, 552, 555; the *New Republic* IV: 515; V: 62-63; old age pensions and annuities I: 565-67; II: 129, 176-77, 191-93, 196, 212, 246-48, 269-71, 277-78, 589-90; III: 28; IV: 272; Palestine IV: 248, 417-20; Perkins, George W. II: 666, 700-701; Philipson, David III: 334; philosophy, the study of V: 260; political corruption I: 204-205, 268, 369; Pound, Roscoe IV: 27, 395-96; V: 281; preferential union shop v. closed or open shop II: 368-69, 371-72, 417, 562-63, 588; III: 10-11; price control IV: 308; Price, George M. III: 74; price maintenance of trademarked goods III: 99, 101, 103, 113, 120-21; prohibition and its enforcement IV: 104-107; V: 65, 91, 103, 160-61; Public Franchise League II: 288-89; public office for himself I: 92; II: 26, 31, 642, 651, 673, 699, 715, 725; III:

37-38, 44-45, 129, 130; V: 319; public opinion I: 97, 226; 192-93; public ownership I: 438-41, 590; II: 618-19; III: 132; V: 4, 67, 360; Pujo Committee III: 184, 187; Raushenbush, Paul A. V: 184; Reading, Lord IV: 309; "red scare" IV: 441, 445, 477, 510; Reed, Warren A. I: 554-55; regularity of employment I: 213; II: 444-50, 575, 580, 630; III: 230, 390; IV: 22-23, 343; V: 20, 133, 329, 335, 424-25, 497-98, 510; respect for law II: 148-52, 340-42, 531-36, 646, 655-56, 718-19; V: 227-28, 345-46; Rice, William G. V: 378; Roman history, study of V: 185, 251; Roosevelt, Franklin D. V: 505, 556; Roosevelt, Theodore II: 68, 341-42, 568, 662; Ross, Denman V: 295; Ruppin, Arthur IV: 304-305; Russian Revolution IV: 276-77; Rutenberg, Pinhas, III: 575-76, 620-21; Sacco and Vanzetti case V: 280-81, 283, 300; San Francisco earthquake (1906) I: 427; Sarnoff, David V: 415-16; Schiff, Jacob H. IV: 116; Schurz, Carl I: 93; scientific management and the efficiency movement II: 125, 374, 383-85, 387-88, 395, 398, 548-49; III: 11, 49-50, 86-87, 151; V: 71; Scott, Sir Walter I: 103-104; self-reliance II: 74-75, 709; Sherman Antitrust Act II: 495-96; Shertok, Moshe V: 571; the "single tax" III: 151, 489; the "sliding scale" mechanism I: 438-41; III: 69, 166, 278-80, 509-10; Smith, Alfred E. V: 212; Smythe, William E. IV: 222; social experimentation III: 19-20; V: 16-17, 64, 127, 501; social legislation II: 586-88, 601-11, 639-40, 707; III: 19-20; socialism II: 152, 288, 481, 550; III: 210; V: 45-46, 66-68; Speed, Hattie B. II: 700; Stanley, Augustus O. II: 654; III: 311; state prerogatives

Brandeis, Louis D. (*continued*)
V: 91, 98, 247, 500; Steffens, Lincoln V: 42-43; Stone, Harlan F. V: 652-53; Storrow, James J. II: 295-96; V: 209; strike insurance IV: 517-18; Taft, William H. II: 191, 213, 322-25, 327, 334, 459; V: 167-68; the Talmud V: 253; the tariff II: 191, 657-59; IV: 547; Taussig, Adele V: 659; taxation IV: 528; V: 67, 84-85, 104-105, 247, 344, 375, 410, 502, 520, 556; teaching I: 39; V: 99, 153-54; Teapot Dome scandal V: 120, 122, 123, 327; *The Three Musketeers* I: 79-80; thrift I: 564, 568-69; II: 74-75, 709; Thurmin, Israel N. V: 102; Torrey, Henry W. I: 27; U. S. Supreme Court IV: 423; V: 64, 75, 93, 160, 292-93; U. S. Supreme Court, his own appointment to IV: 25-26, 40-42, 44-45, 53-54, 91, 114, 182, 239-40; VanDevanter, Willis V: 376; Walsch, David I. III: 611-13; Warburg, Felix M. V: 470-71, 479-80; Warren, Charles V: 52, 54; Warren, Samuel D. I: 38, 42, 44; water rights III: 6-7, 146; Wedgwood, Josiah V: 599; Wehle, Louis B. I: 165; IV: 488, 543; V: 35; Weil, Bruno V: 562; Weizmann, Chaim IV: 325, 331, 404, 443-44, 530, 534, 552-53; V: 271; Weyl, Walter III: 208; White, Herbert I: 513; II: 85; V: 214-15; White, Norman I: 498; Whitlock, Brand III: 229; Whitman, William C. III: 34; IV: 214; Wickersham, George W. II: 329, 352-55; Wilson, Woodrow II: 661, 663, 667, 669-71, 713, 716-17, 727; IV: 256, 398; V: 45, 113, 127-28; Wisconsin, University of V: 99-100; Wise, Stephen S. V: 533, 567; Wolff, Sidney E. V: 575; women's suffrage I: 66, 280; III: 48, 319, 535-36; IV: 363; World War I.

and war mobilization III: 307; IV: 300, 304, 308, 324, 332-34; V: 148-50, 226, 229; the "worthwhile" in life I: 93-94; V: 31, 243, 566, 595; Zionism II: 402, 611; III: 174, 357, 412-13, 455-56, 485-86, 513, 534-35, 546, 575, 587; IV: 20-21, 178, 224, 329; V: 115, 129, 195-96, 246, 429-30, 446-49, 621, 630-31; Zionist unity IV: 525-26

—speeches and writings: "Banker-Management; Why It Has Failed: A Lesson from the New Haven" (1913) III: 147, 168; V: 534-36; "Big Business and Industrial Liberty" (1912) II: 544; "Big Men and Little Business" (1914) III: 89; "Boston & Maine Pensions" (1909) II: 268-71; III: 198; "Brandeis and the Coupon Evil" (1916) IV: 23; "Business—A Profession" (1912) I: 261; II: 520, 623, 629-30, 634, 641, 643, 701-702, 712, 720; V: 503, 658; *Business—A Profession* (1914) I: 205, 233, 247, 261, 322, 363, 397; III: 199, 230, 233, 238, 260, 263, 283, 390, 451, 489; IV: 51, 67, 118, 120, 153, 169, 238; V: 119-20, 234, 376, 473, 482, 494-95, 496, 503-505, 508, 511, 534; "A Call to the Educated Jew" (1915) III: 413, 637-38; IV: 6, 303; V: 534; "Campaign Speech for Louis Frothingham" (1905) I: 379-80, 385-86; campaign speeches for Woodrow Wilson (1912) II: 665, 667, 697-98, 702-704, 706; "Consolidation of Gas Companies and of Electric Light Companies" (1905) I: 293, 332; "The Constitution and the Minimum Wage" (1914) III: 364, 443; *The Curse of Bigness* (1934) I: 46, 226, 445, 496; V: 533-36, 548; "Cutthroat Prices: The Competition that Kills" (1913) III: 125, 128, 137, 170, 196, 233; IV: 169; V: 534-36; "Democracy in Palestine"

(1915) III: 658; "Don't Condone the Crime" (1908) II: 154-55; "An Economic Exhortation to Organized Labor" (1905) I: 282; "Efficiency by Consent" (1915) III: 618; "Efficiency and the One-Price Article" (1913) III: 125; "The Employer and Trades Unions" (1904) I: 246-47, 250, 259; "An Essential of Lasting Peace" (1915) III: 436; V: 534-35; "The Experience of Massachusetts in Street Railways" (1902) I: 220, 223-24, 469; II: 419; "The Financial Condition of the New York, New Haven & Hartford Rrd and of the Boston & Maine" (1907) II: 61, 63, 81, 93, 113, 145, 193-94; III: 106; IV: 88; V: 502, 534-35; "The Greatest Life Insurance Wrong" (1906) I: 495-96, 499, 511, 547; "The Harvard Law School" (1889) I: 8, 90; "Hours of Labor" (1906) I: 391, 397; "How Boston Solved the Gas Problem" (1907) I: 253, 294, 397; II: 24, 579; III: 69, 166, 233, 259, 375; IV: 120; V: 504-505; "How Europe Deals with the One-Priced Goods" (1915) III: 125; "An Illegal Trust Legalized" (1911) II: 504, 521; "The Incorporation of Trades Unions" (1903) I: 232-33, 236, 244; "Interlocking Directorates" (1915) V: 534-36; "Is the Closed Shop Illegal and Criminal?" (1904) I: 259; "The Jewish Problem—How to Solve It" (1915) III: 455, 526, 543, 591, 600, 637-38; IV: 6, 103, 303, 369, 385; V: 119, 534; "Jewish Rights and the Congress" (1916) IV: 12, 103, 303; V: 534-35; "Jewish Unity and the Congress" (1915) III: 675; IV: 21, 103; "Labor and the New Party" (1912) II: 673-74, 676-83, 687; "The Law of Ponds" [with S. D. Warren]

(1888) I: 78; IV: 33; "The Legal Rights of Public Franchise Companies in Our Streets" (1904) I: 244-46; "Liability of Trust-Estates on Contracts Made for Their Benefit" (1881) I: 34; IV: 33; V: 534-35; "Life Insurance: The Abuses and Remedies" (1905) I: 362-63, 365, 370, 380, 390, 395-96, 405, 482, 502; II: 76, 228; IV: 97; "The Living Law" (1916) I: 46; III: 682; IV: 15-16; V: 119, 534-35; "Massachusetts' Substitute for Old Age Pensions" (1908) II: 201, 214; III: 216; "The New Conception of Industrial Efficiency" (1911) II: 418; "The New England Railroad Situation" (1912) II: 730; "The New England Transportation Monopoly: The Proposed Merger" (1908) II: 65, 81-85, 90-91, 106, 109, 624; "The New Haven—An Unregulated Monopoly" (1912) II: 724; 726, 730; III: 129; "New York, New Haven & Hartford Rrd Company Financial Primer" (1909) II: 243, 278; "On Maintaining Makers' Prices" (1913) III: 89, 94, 101; "Opportunity in the Law" (1905) I: 267, 321-22, 325-26, 338-39; II: 350; III: 682; "Organized Labor and Efficiency" (1911) II: 418; *Other People's Money* (1914) I: 595; III: 49, 60, 146-47, 165, 168, 171, 179, 183, 187, 188-90, 195, 204-205, 207, 211, 216, 219-21, 232, 238, 272-73, 280, 284, 344, 440, 451; IV: 511; V: 482, 493-95, 496, 499, 509, 519, 534, 568, 599; "Our Financial Oligarchy" (1913) III: 169, 187; "Our New Peonage: Discretionary Pensions" (1912) II: 652; "Palestine and the Jewish Democracy" (1916) III: 657, 659; IV: 6; V: 534; "Peace with Liberty" (1905) I: 304; "The Preferential Shop: A Letter from LDB"

Brandeis, Louis D. (*continued*)
(1912) II: 587-89; "Price Fixing and Monopoly" (1913) III: 101; "The Right to Privacy" [with S. D. Warren] (1890) I: 101, 302-304, 306; IV: 33; V: 534; "The Road to Social Efficiency" (1911) II: 433-34, 442, 575, 590; III: 390, 489; "Savings Bank Life Insurance for Wage Earners" (1907) I: 486; II: 14-15, 600; "Savings-Insurance Banks" (1906) I: 491, 511; II: 17; *Scientific Management and the Railroads* (1912): II: 542-43; III: 47; V: 502, 534-35; "Serve One Master Only" (1913) III: 247; "Shall We Abandon the Policy of Competition?" (1912) II: 504, 521; *The Social and Economic Views of Mr. Justice Brandeis* (1930) V: 418, 499, 503, 511; "The Solution of the Trust Problem: A Program" (1913) III: 102, 195, 219; V: 534-35; "Speech to the Boot & Shoe Club" (1903) I: 225-29; "Speech at the Cooper Union" (1905) I: 257-58, 406; Speech to Jewish leaders (1929) V: 389-91, 397-99, 413-14, 489; "Testimony before the House Committee on Interstate and Foreign Commerce" (1915) III: 217; "Testimony before the House Committee on Patents" (1912) III: 89, 99, 101, 103, 170; "Testimony before the Senate Committee on Interstate Commerce" (1911) III: 12, 27; V: 482, 534-35; "Testimony in the U. S. Steel Investigation" (1912) III: 25; V: 482, 534-36; "Trade Unionism and Employers" (1905) I: 279, 282-83; "True Americanism" (1915) III: 540; V: 119; "Trusts, Efficiency and the New Party" (1912) II: 664, 671-72; "Trusts, the Export Trade and the New Party" (1912) II: 664-65,

671-72, 683-84, 695-96; "The Twin Evils of the Literacy Test" (1915) III: 506; "Wage-Earners' Life Insurance: A Great Wrong and a Remedy" (1906) I: 364, 444-46, 448-49, 453, 457-58, 460-61, 463, 465, 469, 480, 484-85, 489, 493, 499, 502-503, 547; "Wage Earners' Life Insurance and Old Age Annuities" (1907) I: 485; "The Watuppa Pond Cases" [with S. D. Warren] (1888) I: 78; IV: 33; "What to Do" (1922) V: 59-62; "Where the Banker Is Superfluous" (1913) III: 261; V: 67; "Why I Am a Zionist" (1914) III: 308; "Wilson and the New Party" (1912) II: 676; "Wilson the Progressive" (1912) II: 676; *Women in Industry* (1908) I: 166; "Zionism and Patriotism" (1915) III: 356, 358, 371, 412, 416, 492, 543, 637, 638; IV: 6; V: 534
Brandeis Research Fellowship V: 244-45, 246, 248, 411
Brandeis, Richard V: 656*
Brandeis, Robert I: 428*; II: 287, 293
Brandeis, Rosa I: 3
Brandeis, Rudolph II: 729
Brandeis, Samuel I: 3*, 13, 91, 428, 459; IV: 39; V: 656
Brandeis, Susan: see Gilbert, Susan B.
Brandes, Joseph cited, IV: 301
Brandt, Raymond P. V: 362*
Brant, Irving N. V: 585*
Braucher, H. S. I: 510
"Breaking the Money Trust" III: 165, 211, 216
Breckenridge, John V: 231
Brenner, Carl C. II: 642*; V: 145, 304
Breslau, Isadore V: 632*, 639, 644, 645
Bressler, David M. III: *414*, 548, 641
Brett, George P. III: 89*
Brewer, David J. II: 78
Brewster, Frank I: 114*, 116-18, 141
Brewster, Mr. V: 275

Brewster, Ralph O. V: 248*
Briand, Aristide V: 249*
Brickner, Barnett R. V: 450*
Bridgewater Savings Bank II: 5, 8, 11, 114
Briggs, Alton E. II: 631*, 644; III: 70, 71-73
Brigham, G. R. I: 181*, 183
Bright, Louis V. IV: 224*
Brinsmade, Chapin III: 305*
Brisbane, Arthur II: 442; IV: 175*
Bristow, Benjamin H. I: 47*
Bristow, Joseph L. II: 440*, 618, 622; V: 22
B'rit Shalom V: 572
Britain: see England
British Aliens' Commission IV: 11
British Guiana V: 607, 619
Brockton Board of Trade II: 86
Brockton Independent IV: 88
Brockton Last Co. IV: 89
Brockton Shoe Manufacturers' Association IV: 89
Broderick, Francis L. cited, V: 366
Brodie, Israel B. III: 633*; IV: 24, 563; V: 309, 314, 409, 419, 430, 463, 468, 474, 481, 485, 491, 494, 574, 577, 606
Brodsky, Randolph T. II: 567*
Brody, David cited, IV: 432
Brody, Joseph I. III: 359*
Broesamle, John cited, II: 668; III: 509
Bromberg, Edward J. III: 485*; IV: 126
Brookings Institution V: 225, 325, 450
Brookline Chronicle V: 509
Brookline Gas Co. I: 315, 324
Brooklyn Rapid Transit Co., III: 689
Brooks, John G. I: 232*, 495, 497, 499; III: 87, 98, 104; V: 303-304
Brooks, Lawrence G. V: 303*
Brotherhood of Locomotive Engineers I: 288-89
Brougham, Herbert B. IV: 9*, 392, 35
Brown, Arthur IV: 402*

Brown, Arthur L. III: 43*, 53-54
Brown, Ashmun N. II: 492*
Brown, Benjamin H. I. II: 711*
Brown, Charles III: 562
Brown, Charles H. II: 108, 620
Brown, David F. III: 108, 167
Brown, Dorothy IV: 371
Brown, Frank S. II: 628*
Brown, George N. III: 54*
Brown, George W. II: 285*
Brown, H. LaRue II: 518*, 620; III: 85, 175, 222-23, 287; IV: 33, 47, 61; LDB on III: 85-86
Brown, John M. V: 169
Brown, Philip M. IV: 336*
Brown University, LDB's commencement address of 1912: see "Business—A Profession"
Brown, Mrs. Ward IV: 369
Brown, William C. II: 383*, 564; III: 5
Browning, Robert I: 104
Bruce, Helm III: 383*; IV: 28; V: 175, 258, 266
Bruere, Henry III: 152*, 562, 671; IV: 26, 225
Bruere, Robert W. IV: 224*; V: 45, 114, 133, 273, 355
Bryan, William J. I: 123*; II: 214, 632-35, 638, 641, 643, 648, 663, 698, 700; III: 38, 42, 44, 48, 56-57, 65, 115, 239, 304, 330, 354, 418, 455, 465, 495, 610; IV: 388, 547
Bryce, James B. IV: 356*
Bryn Mawr College IV: 480
Bublick, Gedalia IV: 174*, 513, 564
Buchanan, James II: 371
Buchanan, John G. V: 371*
"bucket shop" transactions, LDB on II: 103-104, 111, 124
Buckland, Edward G. II: 138*
Buckley, Thomas H. cited, V: 32
Buchner, Andreas I: 28*
Buckner, Mr. II: 392
Buckner, Emory R. IV: 286*, 191; V: 159, 160, 165, 191, 200, 210
Buder, Stanley cited, III: 25

Buell, Katharine III: *281**, *283*
Buell, Raymond L. V: 63*
Buenos Aires IV: 386
Buenos Aires Pacific Rrd III: 493
Buenos Aires Western Rrd III: 493
Buff, Louis F. II: 70*
Buffalo, New York IV: 7; see also Zionist Convention of 1920 (Buffalo)
Bufford v. Keokuk Northern Line Packet Co. I: 31
Builders' Iron Foundry II: 574
Buley, R. Carlyle cited, I: 398
Bulgaria II: 208
Bulkley, Robert J. II: 474*, 273, 289; LDB on III: 289
Bullard, F. Lauriston V: 285, 345*
Bullitt, Ernesta D. IV: 370*
Bullitt, William C. IV: 366*, 369
Bullitt, William M. II: 729*; V: 367
Bullivant, William I: 577
Bullock, Alan cited, V: 517
Bullock, Harry A. II: *480**; III: *32*
Bullock, Rufus A. I: 42*, 575
Bundy, McGeorge cited, II: 309
Bunn, Charles, IV: *230**
Bunting v. Oregon IV: 143
Bunyan, John V: 655
Burba, George F. cited, II: 508
Burckhardt, Jacob I: 28*
Burdeau v. McDowell V: 227
Burdette, Everett W. II: 10
Burgesses, the I: 49
Burleson, Albert S. III: 9*, 338; IV: 498, 542
Burling, Edward B. II: 360*; III: 600; IV: 371; V: 28
Burlingham, Charles C. I: 480*; II: *79, 335, 667;* III: *68, 150;* IV: 27, 423; V: 122, 281, 284, 367, 371, 414, 650
Burlinghame, Mr. V: 399
Burner, David M. cited, V: 77
Burnett bill III: 506; IV: 100-101
Burnett, John T. I: *165**; III: 138
Burns Baking Co. v. Bryan V: 127
Burns, James M. cited, IV: 475
Burns, William J. V: 131, 310, 312

Burton, Theodore E. V: 24*
Bush, Mrs. I: 61
"Business—A Profession" (1912) I: 261; II: 520, 623, 629-30, 634, 641, 643, 701-702; 712, 720; III: 126, 170, 196, 199, 230, 233, 238, 260, 263, 283, 390, 451, 489, 541, 618, 683; V: 503, 658
Business—A Profession (1914) I: 205, 233, 247, 261, 322, 397; II: 200; III: 199, 230, 233, 238, 260, 283, 390, 451, 489; IV: 51, 67, 118, 120, 153, 169, 238; V: 119-20, 234, 376, 473, 482, 494-96, 503-505, 508, 511, 534
Business Men's Merger League II: 128, 141, 157, 260
Butler, Benjamin V: 312
Butler, Geoffrey IV: 293
Butler, Margaret I: 57
Butler, Nicholas M. IV: 266*; V: 83-94
Butler, Pierce V: 79, 83*, 106, 127, 181, 238, 588
Butler, William M. V: 238*, 240, 241
Button Hole Makers' Union II: 586
Buttrick, Allan G. I: 544*, 549, 556, 575; II: 133, 156
Butzel, Henry M. V: 382*
Buxton, Dorothy F. V: 621
Buxton, Frank V: 283, 415
Byrnes, James W. V: 5
Byrnes, Timothy E: II: 34*, 36-38, 44, 46, 53, 66, 72, 75-76, 111, *115*, 116, 118-19, 122, 127, 131-32, *137*, 140, 161, 167, 170, 181, 582; LDB on II: 111
Byron, Lord quoted, I: 61

Cabot, Charles M. II: 574*; III: *545*
Cabot, Philip I: *263**
Cabot, Richard C. IV: 510*
Cady, George L. IV: 92*
Caesar, Julius IV: 413; V: 224
Cahan, Abraham IV: 330*
Cairo, Egypt IV: 412, 417, 419
Calder, William M. V: 76*
Caldwell, Mr. V: 561

California II: 573, 600, 613, 700, 710, 713; III: 7, 222; IV: 129, 147, 356, 417-18, 433; V: 279, 282, 284, 286

California Alien Land Act (1920) V: 106

California Eight Hour law: see *Bosley v. McLaughlin*

California v. Rolph V: 117

Calkins, Grosvenor III: 132*

Call, Joseph H. III: 31

Call, Malcolm L. V: 366

"A Call to the Educated Jew" (1915) III: 413, 637-38; IV: 6, 303; V: 534

Callahan, Mr. I: 585

Callahan, Lee II: 368; III: 271

Callahan, Patrick H. V: 282*

Callender, Edward B. I: 179, 205*, 389

Cambridge Electric Light Co. I: 245

Cambridge Gas Co. I: 246

Cambridge Savings Bank V: 346, 393, 410, 504

Cambridge Street Subway I: 201, 417-18, 423-24

Cambridgeport Savings Bank IV: 461

Cameron, Charles J. I: 45*

Cameron, Donald A. I: 135

Cameron, William H. II: 602*

Campaign of 1912, LDB and II: 526-29, 536, 539, 542-46, 550-51, 561, 568-69, 572, 576-77, 585-86, 600, 611-14, 623-25, 632-35, 639-45, 648-706, 709-10, 713-18, 726-27; III: 4; V: 234-556

"Campaign Speech for Louis A. Frothingham" (1905) I: 379-80, 385-86

campaign speeches for Woodrow Wilson (1912) II: 665, 667, 697-98, 702-704, 706; see also Brandeis, Louis D. and campaign of 1912

Campbell, Benjamin III: 337*

Campbell, Charles F. F. IV: 44*

Campbell, Douglas I: 119

Campbell, Maurice V: 381*

Campbell, Thomas cited, I: 45

Campbell v. City of New York V: 296

Canada II: 220, 457, 499, 535, 598; III: 591; IV: 110, 227-28, 285, 531, 547; V: 5-6, 141, 589, 629

Canadian Club II: 87

Canadian Law Times IV: 142

Cannon, James Jr. IV: 106*

Cannon, Joseph G. II: 68*, 116; III: 611

Capek, Karl cited, IV: 315

capital v. labor, LDB on I: 121, 247, 298, 335, 397, 447, 504-505, 572-73, 576-77, 584, 587; II: 299, 483-84, 519, 522, 548-49, 587, 676-83, 707-708; III: 25, 210, 218-21, 407, 428-29, 545-46; IV: 238, 521; V: 57-62

capitalism, LDB on II: 70, 76, 280, 332-33, 342, 468-74, 481, 516, 522, 529, 548-49; IV: 335; V: 66-68, 91-92

Capone, Al V: 45

Caraway, Thaddeus H. V: 395*

Cardozo, Benjamin N. II: 350; III: 145; IV: 330*, 558; V: 205, 235, 258, 273, 295, 352, 395, 497, 500, 538; LDB on V: 258

Carey, Charles H. I: 525

Carleton, A. C. IV: 154*

Carlinger, Jacob III: 652*

Carlyle, Thomas IV: 554; quoted, IV: 401

Carmalt, James W. III: 210*, 305, 330; IV: 33, 46

Carnegie, Andrew II: 214*, 561

Carnegie Foundation V: 325, 648

Carpenter, Fred W. IV: 130*

Carr, Don M. II: 313, 319*, 492

Carr, John F. III: 4*

Carr, Wilbur J. III: 495*

Carrigan, Mr. I: 82

Carroll, Bertha II: 294*

Carroll, Francis M. III: 200*

Carroll, Thomas I: 528*

Carter, James C. I: 69*

Carter, James R. I: 138*, 160, 163, 168, 171, 174, 177, 179, 181, 195, 229, 288, 296, 523-24, 553, 593

Carver, Mary cited, II: 643

Carver, Thomas N. II: 535

Casady, Clyde S. V: 573*
Case, Herbert A. I: 536
Casey, Robert J. cited, III: 272
Casey v. U.S. V: 318
Catchings, Waddill II: 161; IV: 83*
Catherine II of Russia III: 158
Catron, B. L. II: 549*
Catt, Carrie C. III: 597*
Cattell, James M. V: 84
Cavour, Camillo quoted, V: 170
Cecil, David V: 259
Cecil, Robert V: 525
Celano, Thomas A. quoted, V: 124
Cellar, Emanuel V: 250
Cement Manufacturers' Protective Association v. U.S. V: 175
Cement Co. v. Locke V: 477
Central Argentine Rrd III: 493
Central Cardoba Railway Co. III: 493
Central Conference of American Rabbis IV: 349
Central Jewish Institute IV: 204
Central Jewish Relief Committee for War Sufferers III: 359, 474, 512, 583, 589, 632, 641, 654, 665
Central Law Journal IV: 141
Central Zionist Bureau III: 309, 320, 518; IV: 402
Chadbourne, Thomas L. IV: 568*; V: 30
Chafee, Zechariah Jr. II: 574*; IV: 339, 451, 459, 517, 541, 558, 559, 561, 564; V: 11, 41, 130, 142, 224, 285, 326, 348, 354; quoted, V: 286
Challener, Richard cited, III: 44
Chalukah IV: 380, 440
Chamberlain, A. Neville IV: 424; V: 524*, 602, 603, 606, 612, 613, 651
Chamberlain, Edson II: 628*, 725
Chamberlain, George E. II: 622, 624*
Chamberlain, Lloyd I: 292, 323*, 326; II: 117; IV: 121, 124
Chamberlin, Frederick III: 95*
Chambers, Frank T. V: 35*
Chambers, Whittaker V: 416

Chandler, Edward H. I: 295; II: 45
Chandler, F. Alexander II: 96*
Chandler, William E. II: 63*, 71, 199, 211
Chankis, A. V: 587
Chantland, William T. III: 169*; IV: 46
Chapin, Mr. II: 240
Chapman, John J. II: 674*
Charleston [West Virginia] Gazette V: 308
Charlottesville, Virginia V: 301-302
Chase, Harrie B. V: 368*
Chase, Harvey S. I: 227, 228, 315, 575
Chase, Stuart V: 92*
Chastleton v. Sinclair V: 127
Chaucer, Geoffrey I: 27; quoted, V: 3
Chaytor, H. J. V: 186
Chazenovitch, Leon III: 330*
Chentang, Liang C. I: 585*
Cherbuliez, Victor quoted II: 501; V: 586
Chesapeake & Ohio Rrd III: 5; V: 229
Chibbath Zion III: 156
Chicago I: 295-96; II: 386-87, 390, 407, 508; III: 314-16, 332, 353, 357, 359-60, 368-70, 374, 405, 614-17, 673; IV: 15-16, 20-21, 48, 167, 212, 218-19, 312, 326-27, 536; V: 440
Chicago & Alton Railway Co. III: 22
Chicago, Burlington & Quincy Rrd Co. v. Drainage Commissioners II: 559
Chicago Evening Post IV: 88
Chicago garment workers' strike II: 386-87, 390, 406-407; III: 673
Chicago Great Western Rrd III: 50
Chicago Junction case V: 118
Chicago Railways Co. II: 419
Chicago Tribune II: 134, 299, 364; III: 368, 371
Chicago, University of III: 645; IV: 177, 264, 276; V: 95, 181, 379
Chicago Zionist Bureau IV: 195
Child, Anna: see Bird, Anna C.

Child, Francis J. I: 27*
Child, Richard W. I: 269*; III: 125; IV: 519; V: 258
Child, Walter I: 60*, 64; II: 111, 617; IV: 519-20; V: 232, 295; LDB on IV: 519-20; V: 295
Chilton, William E. IV: 27*, 72, 90, 125, 128, 141, 171, 176; V: 308; LDB on V: 308
China I: 336-37, 360, 585; III: 57, 523; IV: 222, 557; V: 21, 23, 29, 33, 34, 96, 270, 277, 303; LDB on V: 277
Chinitz, Sam Z. cited, IV: 434-35; V: 116
Chipman, Frank E. V: 74
Choate, Charles F. Jr. II: 54*, 65, 68, 72, 75, 132, 134, 136, 138, 142, 143, 144, 146, 150, 157, 162, 178, 179, 182; III: 72, 79; V: 116
Choate, Joseph H. III: 382; IV: 119
Christian Friends of Palestine V: 617
Christian Science Monitor II: 425; IV: 242
Christie, Loring C. IV: 455*; V: 33, 141, 186, 324
Church, Walter L. IV: 49
church and state, LDB on I: 521-22
Churchill & Alden Co. IV: 89
Churchill, Thomas W. III: 391*
Churchill White Paper V: 436, 486
Churchill, Winston I: 542*
Churchill, Winston S. V: 192, 651*
Cicero I: 338*; V: 185; quoted, IV: 231
Cincinnati III: 147, 316, 338, 345, 353, 370, 405, 415, 426-27, 430, 438-39, 441, 454, 464-65, 613-14, 619, 674; IV: 3-7, 40; V: 26; LDB on V: 26
Cincinnati, Hamilton & Dayton Rrd III: 264, 266
Civic Federation of New England I: 277, 328, 334, 450, 462, 672-73
civil service, LDB on II: 414, 416
Civilian Conservation Corps V: 616
Clapp, E. J. cited, V: 16
Clapp, Moses E. II: 455*, 525, 536, 551, 561, 611, 622, 625, 669, 670,

672, 683, 709, 721, 730; III: 39, 224; V: 482
Clapper, Raymond V: 211
Clark, Benjamin Preston IV: 73*, 314
Clark, Charles E. V: 381, 421*, 513, 588
Clark Distilling Co. v. Western Maryland Rrd Co. V: 99
Clark, E. E. cited, I: 209
Clark, Edward I: 526*
Clark, Evans V: 321*
Clark, Henry A. I: 22*
Clark, James B. ("Champ") II: 440*, 612, 632, 635, 648
Clark, Louis M. I: 240
Clark, Mr. IV: 145; V: 559
Clark, Robert F. I: 377*
Clark, Ronald cited, IV: 537
Clark, Walter E. III: 69*
Clarke, Albert II: 44*, 46, 67
Clarke, James P. III: 434*, 446, 467
Clarke, John H. IV: 300, 367*, 369, 521, 542; V: 47, 72, 154
Clarke, W. J. V: 186
Clauson, Albert C. B. V: 455*
Clay, Henry V: 306
Clayton Antitrust Act III: 25-26, 84, 100-103, 188, 247-59, 290, 310, 592-95; IV: 32, 521, 551; V: 40, 176, 482
Clayton, Gilbert F. IV: 410*
Clayton, Henry D. III: 195*, 260
Clement, Edward H. I: 142*, 206, 294, 305; IV: 106, 122
Clements, Judson C. III: 140*, 143; IV: 29, 145, 213
Cleopatra IV: 273
clergymen, LDB on V: 343, 347
Cleveland II: 459-60, 487, 500, 502, 703; III: 311, 318-19, 349, 584; IV: 528; V: 450
Cleveland Athletic Club II: 703
Cleveland Crime Survey IV: 523, 528; V: 3, 11, 17, 205, 553; LDB on IV: 528; V: 17-18
Cleveland garment workers' strike II: 459-60, 487-88, 500, 502

Cleveland, Grover I: 149, 341*, 349; II: 213, 642; IV: 51
Cleveland Municipal Court III: 181
Cleveland, Treadwell I: 125*; II: 722, 726; III: 60, 80, 119, 120, 370, 467
Clifford, Charles W. II: 646*, 649, 652
Cloak, Suit & Skirt Manufacturers' Protective Association II: 366, 373, 391-92, 407, 483-84, 508
coal strike of 1902, LDB and I: 208-21, 223
Cobb, Andrew J. I: 303*, 306
Cobb, C. K. II: 49
Cobb, Frank I. V: 83*, 125
Cobb, John C. II: 32*, 35
Cobbett, William quoted V: 227
Coben, Stanley cited, V: 122
Coburn, Frederick W. II: 16*, 21, 22, 25, 166, 269, 453; cited, II: 32
Cochran, Mr. V: 288
Cochran, Helen I: 14*, 15, 61, 73
Cochran, Jessie I: 14*, 17, 20, 45, 53, 61, 73, 263; II: 364; IV: 297-98; V: 220, 508
Cochrane: see Cochran
Cochrane, J. Eugene I: 450*, 451
Cochrane, Robert C. V: 4
Cochrans, the I: 14, 17, 19, 43-44, 49, 53, 60
Codman, Edmund D. III: 21*
Codman, Julian I: 301*
Coffee, Rudolph I. II: 451*; IV: 178, 195
Coffin, Howard E. IV: 276
Coffin, Rufus I: 59*, 63
Cogswell, Walter C. IV: 68*
Cohen, Abraham B. III: 430*
Cohen, Alfred M. V: 94*, 187, 232, 364, 622
Cohen, Benjamin V. IV: 371*, 381, 430, 455, 457, 460, 464, 466, 473, 519, 542, 552, 553, 563, 565; V: 16, 108, 484, 506, 552, 594, 596, 606, 608, 628, 654
Cohen, Edward I: 587*; II: 14, 59, 71

Cohen, Edward J. III: 485
Cohen, Mr. III: 465
Cohen, Ephraim: see Cohn-Reiss, Ephraim
Cohen, Israel III: 358*; V: 553
Cohen, Joseph L. III: 516, 531
Cohen, Joseph M. V: 632*
Cohen, Julius H. II: 366*, 367, 368, 373, 381, 390(2), 391, 407, 417, 503, 518, 570; III: 6; IV: 142, 263
Cohen, Morris R. I: 325*; V: 159, 193, 277, 285, 288, 544, 650
Cohen, Naomi W. cited, III: 313
Cohn-Reiss, Ephraim III: 397*, 434, 496, 575, 580; IV: 253
Coit, Margaret cited, III: 623
Coke, Sir Edward I: 8*
Colburn, Leila E. V: 342*, 545, 547, 565, 572, 575
Colby, Bainbridge I: 490; IV: 457*, 568; V: 30, 36, 47
Colby, Everett I: 374*, 455, 499, 506
Colby, Gerald cited, V: 202
Colby, John I: 174
Cole, G. D. H. V: 227
Cole, John N. I: 297*, 443, 593; II: 46
Cole-Lodge Antimerger bill I: 593-94
Cole, William I: 237
Coleman, George W. IV: 227*
Coleman, Greta II: 345
Coletta, Paolo E. cited, I: 124; III: 44
Colgate University V: 193
College Settlements Association I: 146, 161
Collier, Robert J. I: 396*; II: 290, 308, 309, 316, 328, 345, 355, 356-62, 363, 379, 665, 697, 705, 706, 711, 712, 714, 719; IV: 64, 85-86, 150
Collier's Weekly I: 396, 587; II: 76, 92, 112-13, 177, 210, 217, 289, 300, 308, 309, 319, 323, 336, 338, 346, 354, 360, 452, 462-63, 485-86, 492, 547, 590, 600, 663, 670, 671, 673, 683, 696-97, 704-708, 711, 714, 719-20; III: 33, 176, 199, 243; IV: 63, 73, 85-87, 92, 275; V: 119, 166, 234, 482, 560, 641

Collins, Frederick L. III: 31*, 47, 128, 138, 176

Collins, Patrick A. I: 183, 185*, 186-87, *188*, *192*, *194*, *195*, 198, *199*, *200*, *202*, *203*, 228, 242, 271, 273, 298, 302, 307, *308*, 311, 418

Collins, Peter W. II: 442

Colorado II: 601-610; V: 373, 377, 380, 383

Colorado Fuel & Iron Co. V: 373, 377

Colorado River Commission V: 76

Colorado State Industrial Commission V: 380

Colorado Supreme Court II: 601

Colquitt, Oscar B. V: 396*

Colston, William A. III: 280*, 381

Colter, S. J. II: 313

Columbia Conserve Co. IV: 293

Columbia Law Review IV: 383; V: 499; cited, IV: 330

Columbia University I: 88; III: 304; V: 83-84, 502

Columbia University Menorah Society III: 401

Columbia University Law School V: 284, 326, 334

Colver, William B. II: *435**, 442, 461, *463*, *465*

Colvin, George V: 252*, 253-55, 261, 268, 305-308, 343, 392, 406; LDB on V: 268

Coman, Katherine I: *151**, *442*

Comins, George A. I: *225**

Commager, Henry Steele IV: 353

Commerce Court III: 126, 280, 400

Commercial and Financial Chronicle V: 93

Commercial Club (Boston) I: 276, 363, 365, 370, 380, 390, 405

Commercial Travellers' Association III: 340

Commission on Public Ownership I: 467

Commission on Uniformity of Laws I: 347, 359, 364-67, 371, 391, 398, 401, 433-37

Committee of Commercial Organizations II: 306, 370

Committee of Jewish Musicians III: 485

Committee on Insurance (Massachusetts House of Representatives) I: 66, 391, 398-99, 405-406, 433-36, 465, 526, 530, 538, 543, 549, 551, 555-63, 566, 574, 577

Committee on Liquor Laws (Massachusetts House of Representatives) IV: 106

Committee on Metropolitan Affairs (Massachusetts House of Representatives) I: 141, 144, 162, 165, 166

Committee on Prisons I: *521*

Committee on Public Lighting (Massachusetts House of Representatives) I: 291, 293, 314-16, 320, 323, 390, 432

Common Counsel Club III: 239

Commons, John R. III: 88, *99**, 227; IV: 267; V: 100, 159, 297, 555; cited, I: 136; LDB on V: 100

Commonwealth Foundation V: 41, 232, 298

Commonwealth Shoe & Leather Co. II: 202, 429, 553, 622; IV: 89

Commonwealth Steel Co. V: 334-35

Commonwealth v. Hamilton Manufacturing Co. I: *521*

communism, LDB on V: 645

complacency, LDB on V: 324

compulsory retirement, LDB on II: 264-65

Comstock, Ada L. V: 114*

Conference of Mayors (1914) III: 96

Conference on Child Health and Protection (1930) V: 464

Conference on Jewish Relations V: 650

Congress movement: see Brandeis, Louis D. and American Jewish Congress Movement

Congress Organizing Committee (American Jewish Congress) III: 409, 587, 604, 621, 624, 635, 640,

Congress Organizing Com. (*cont.*)
645, 651, 656; IV: 56, 173, 185, 243,
246, 250, 252, 253
*Connally v. General Construction
Co.* V: 296
Connecticut II: 190, 207, 213, 273, 275
Connecticut Railway & Lighting Co.
II: 29, 43
Connolly, Christopher P. II: 481*;
III: 44, 199
Conrad, Sidney S. III: *501**; IV: 13
conservation, LDB and I: 519-20; II:
355-56, 392, 398, 400, 414, 451-52,
458-79, 490-98, 513-16, 612-13, 618-
19, 660, 685, 713, 715-16, 723-24;
III: 6-9, 59-60, 67; V: 133, 348, 527-
28; see also Pinchot-Ballinger con-
servation controversy and Alaska;
LDB on II: 342, 451-52; IV: 335;
V: 527-28
*Consolidated Gas Co. v. City of
New York* I: 581
Consolidated Railway Co. II: 38, 40,
56, 149, 238, 242; III: 93
"Consolidation of Gas Companies
and of Electric Light Companies"
(1905) I: 293, 332
Constantinople IV: 134, 179, 235-36,
375
"The Constitution and the Minimum
Wage" (1914) III: 364, 443
Continental and Commercial Trust
Co. (Chicago) V: 21-22, 29
Continental Congress (1774) V: 521
Continental Insurance Co. II: 430
*Continental Wall Paper Co. v. Louis
Voight & Sons* II: 556
Cook, H. W. IV: 89
Cook, J. Morgan IV: 242; V: 321,
348
Cook, Samuel A. II: 375
Cook, William W. cited, II: 257
Cooke, Morris L. II: 390*; III: 142,
179, 349, 376, 393, 396; IV: *253,*
302, 512; V: 133, 355, *375, 424, 514,*
616
Cooley, Alford W. II: 68*

Coolidge, Calvin III: 350, 458, 629;
IV: 232, 258, 470*, 476, 540; V:
103, 116, 124-25, 129, 132, 141, 151,
154, 155, 167, 171, 174, 203, 207,
210, 212, 222, 238, 240, 250, 251,
259, 270, 272, 277, 287, 289, 324,
326, 327, 330, 352, 353, 368, 372,
373, 557; LDB on IV: 470; V: 238,
270, 272-73, 324-25, 326, 330, 373
Coolidge, Harold J. II: 257*
Coolidge, John V: 353*
Coolidge, J. Randolph II: *82**, *125,
183;* III: 221
Coolidge, Louis A. II: 431*
Cooper, Albert B. II: 550*
Cooper, Mr. I: 427
Cooperative British Wholesale So-
ciety III: 151
Cooperative League of America III:
139
cooperative movement, LDB on II:
529-31; V: 66-67, 364
Copeland, Charles T. I: 88*
Copeland, Royal S. V: 77, 362*, 581
Copley, Frank B. cited, II: 391
Coppage v. Kansas II: 679
Corbin, Austin IV: 57*, 66, 74, 127
Corcoran, Thomas G. IV: 372; V:
552*, 560
Corey, Lewis cited, V: 322
Cornaro, Luigi V: 56*
Cornell University III: 677; V: 284
Cornwell, John J. IV: 515*
Corona Kid Co. IV: 89
Corrigan, Mr. V: 510
Corwin, Edward S. cited, V: 239
Cosmos Club IV: 227, *249*
Cosson, George IV: 28*
Costigan, Edward P. V: 124*, 152,
201, 372, 377, 378
Cotter, James E. I: 399*, 403, 432;
IV: 120
Cottier, Alonzo E. I: 218
Cotton Garment Manufacturers' As-
sociation III: 86, 213
Cotton, Joseph P. Jr. II: *309**, 314,
316, 322, 338, 344, 380, 399; III:

183, 393, 496; IV: 27, 63, 118, 140, 317, 326; V: 120, 414; LDB on III: 393

Coughlin, Charles E. V: 541*

Coulthurst, John I: 272*, 275, 320

Council of Constance (1414) IV: 452

Court-packing plan (1937) V: 564, 587-88

Covington & Lexington Road Co. v. Stanford I: 312

Cowan, Charles A. III: 426*; IV: 135, 137, 152, 377, 381, 384, 385, 387, 400, 509

Cowen, Joseph III: 326*, 418, 678; IV: 13, 216, 287, 508

Cowper, William quoted, I: 260

Cox, Sir C. Henry F. V: 624*

Cox, Charles M. I: 230*, 287, 523, 557, 578; II: 205, 272; III: 268, 277

Cox, George H. II: 306*

Cox, Guy W. I: 479*, 544, 560; V: 451

Cox, James M. IV: 474*, 494

Cox, Roland III: 446*

Craig v. Hecht V: 106

Crane, Charles R. II: 290*, 406, 505, 510, 536, 642, 658, 660, 695, 702, 705, 713, 727; III: 8, 18, 20, 31, 38, 51, 75, 110, 176, 238, 306, 375, 378, 383, 503, 558, 565, 600, 622, 673; IV: 171, 186, 190, 210, 258, 276, 288, 293, 397, 416; V: 383, 493, 509

Crane Co. III: 184

Crane, Richard T. III: 619*; IV: 167, 295

Crane, Winthrop M. I: 171*, 172, 180, 188, 189, 193, 194-95, 377, 378, 385-86, 389, 418; II: 89, 101, 148, 149, 491, 552, 633, 651; IV: 70, 93

Crapsey, Algernon cited, II: 451

Crawford, Charles W. I: 5

Credit Union National Association V: 340

Creel, George III: 433, 542*; LDB on III: 543

Crest, Miss I: 64

Crittenden, John J. V: 231

Crocker, George G. I: 202*, 203; II: 48, 51, 57, 71, 88, 99, 107, 112, 153, 167; cited, I: 203

Crocker, George U. I: 227*, 229

Croly, Herbert II: 654*; III: 208, 209, 222, 402; IV: 37, 45, 266, 363, 367, 398, 510, 516, 517, 520, 523, 538, 549; V: 72, 166, 171, 188, 249; LDB on V: 72, 188-89

Cromwell, Oliver IV: 462

Crowder, Enoch H. IV: 339*

Crozier, James R. II: 49, 88, 99, 112, 126, 197, 205

Crozier, William III: 244*

Cuff, Robert D. cited, III: 623; IV: 334

Culberson, Charles IV: 171, 183, 192

Cumberland Street Railway Co. II: 56

Cummings, Edward I: 523*; II: 152

Cummings, Homer S. II: 667*

Cummins, Albert B. I: 405*; II: 523, 622, 670; IV: 50, 84, 111, 115, 141-49; V: 111, 326

Cunningham claims: see Pinchot-Ballinger conservation controversy

Curley, James M. I: 226*, 240, 253

Curley, Thomas F. I: 226, 575

Currall, Mr. V: 162

Currier, Guy W. I: 172*

The Curse of Bigness (1934) I: 46, 226, 445, 496; III: 61, 89, 102, 183-84, 196, 356, 364, 407, 436, 456, 658, 675, 683; V: 533-36, 548

Curti, Merle cited, II: 387

Curtin, John II: 204*, 208

Curtis, Charles P. Jr. I: 377*

Curtis, George T. I: 24*

Curtis, James F. III: 86*

Curtis, Lionel V: 141, 189*

Curtis, Rennselear III: 160*

Curzon, Lord IV: 447

Cushing, Grafton I: 379*, 544, 551

Cushing, William E. I: 437*

Cushman, Mr. V: 511

Cutler, James H. II: 724

Cutler, Harry III: 651*, 312

"Cutthroat Prices: The Competition that Kills" (1913) III: 125, 128, 137, 170, 196, 233; IV: 169; V: 534-36

Cutting, Alfred L. II: 276*

Cutting, R. Fulton II: 101

Czechoslovakia IV: 315-16, 351-52; V: 525, 602, 637

Daledusky, Mr. IV: 506

Dalmany, Lord IV: 414

Daladier, Edouard V: 602

Dana, Richard H. I: 100*, 127, 136, 177, 419; II: 414; cited, I: 127

Dana, William F. I: 256*

Daniels, Josephus II: 663*, 668; III: 421, 465; IV: 274, 334

Daniels, Winthrop M. IV: 29, 145

Dannenbaum, Harry III: 365*, 369; IV: 324

Dante, A. quoted, I: 30; V: 274

Danziger, Ida S. III: 662; V: 8

D'Arcy, Henry I. I: 29*

Darrow, Clarence S. I: 210*, 212(2), 213, 214, 218, 223; cited, I: 296; II: 517

Daskow, Naomi V: 574

Daugherty, Harry M. V: 41*, 122, 124, 131, 203, 235, 238, 310, 327, 354

Davar V: 446, 464, 466, 467, 468, 472, 490, 495, 568, 574

Davidson, John W. cited, II: 635, 661, 686

Davidson, Mr. V: 656

Davies, George II: 358

Davies, Joseph E. III: 116*, 174, 210, 394, 447, 600; IV: 55; V: 124

Davis, Allen F. cited, I: 374

Davis, Arthur P. II: 322*

Davis, Charles H. I: 459*; II: 139, 287, 404, 406, 526, 676, 700, 716; LDB on II: 404

Davis, Charles S. I: 273*

Davis, D. D. III: 425

Davis, James III: 376*, 377

Davis, James J. V: 334, 402*

Davis, John IV: 15*

Davis, John W. IV: 258*, 273, 369-70; V: 72, 122, 123, 126, 135, 136, 141, 151, 272, 368, 370; LDB on IV: 272

Davis, Lionberger V: 585

Davis, Lucy I: 459

Davis, Mr. V: 301

Davis, Norman H. V: 656*

Davis, Oscar K. III: 4*

Davis, Phillip IV: 154*

Davis v. Henderson V: 192

Davison, Charles S. III: 35*

Davison, Gideon M. I: 410

Davison, Henry P. III: 559

Davison, J. Forrester V: 125, 376*

Dawes, Charles G. V: 94, 167, 250

Dawson, John cited, V: 529

Dawson, Miles M. I: 437

Day Light Savings bill IV: 308

Day, William A. IV: 51*

Day, William R. IV: 516; V: 229

Dean, Charles I: 559*, 560-63, 578

Dearborn Independent IV: 507; V: 296

deArnaud, Charles V: 170

Debs, Eugene V. I: 211, 310; II: 511, 709; V: 41, 72

deCourcey, Charles A. IV: 27*

Decter, Midge cited, III: 300

Dedham, Massachusetts, LDB on I: 30

Deedes, Sir Wyndham H. IV: 473*; V: 75

DeForest, Henry W. I: 506*

deHaas, Fannie IV: 398

deHaas, Jacob II: 402, 659*, 660; III: 64-65, 155, 186, 206, 226, 292, 308, 314, 319, 335, 338, 355, 356, 358, 382, 388, 406, 414, 417, 456, 462-63, 472, 474, 504, 525, 527, 564, 575, 584-85, 603, 620, 625, 644, 666, 681; IV: 11, 96, 102, 116, 137, 152, 172, 178, 190, 193, 199, 216, 220, 222, 242, 244, 250, 252, 257, 261, 269(2), 270(2), 271, 272, 277, 278, 279, 280, 281, 282, 283, 284, 284, 285, 286(2), 287, 288, 290(2), 291, 294, 295, 296, 298(2),

301, *302*(2), *303*(2), *304*, *305*, *307*, *309*, *310*, *312*(2), *316*, *318*, *320*, *321*, *322*, *324*, *325*, *326*, *327*, *328*, *329*, *331*, *335*, *336*(2), *337*, *338*(2), *339*, *340*, *342*, *343*, *344*(2), *345*, *346*, *347*, *348*, *350*(2), *351*, *353*, *354*, *355*, *358*(2), *359*, *360*, *361*, *366*, *371*, *373*, *374*, *375*, *377*, *378*, *381*, *383*, *387*, *388*, *389*, *391*, *392*, *394*, *396*, *398*, 400, 401, 414, 417, 419, 424, *425*, *426*, *428*(2), *429*, *430*, 431, *432*, *433*, *435*, *437*(2), 439, 440, 442, 447, *452*, *453*, 455-57, *458*, *459*, *461*, *463*, *464*, *465*, *468*(2), 473, 478, *481*, 482, 483, *484*(2), *486*, 487-90, *492*, *496*, *500*, 501-509, 513, 518, *522*, *524*, *526*, *530*, *533*, 537, 542, *544*, 549, 553, *554*(2), *556*, *560*, *563*, *565*, *566*; V: 3, *8*, *14*, *18*, 27, 30, *36*, *38*, 44, 55, 90, 100, 103, *106*, 109, 110, 112, *115*, 116, 148, 271, *291*, *293*, 294, *300*, 301, 309, 314, 330, 336, 347, 388, 398, 399, 407, 409, 417-23, 426-31, 434, 436, *441*, *451*, 459, *463*, 488, 490-91, 522, 549, 578, 587, 615; cited, IV: 12, 153, 483; LDB on II: 660; IV: 152, 373-74, 401, 453; V: 27-28, 148, 300, 407-408, 418-19, 434, 491-92, 549
deHaas, Lillian E. IV: *345*, 394, 401, 468; V: 587
Deinard, Benedict S. V: *130*
Deland, Lorin F. I: *81*, 101, *121*, 371, 409-10; V: 657
Deland, Margaret W. I: *75*, 80, 101, *112*, 371, 409; V: 657
Delano, Frederic A. III: *89*, 194, 282, 343; IV: *293*; V: 26, 28, *175*; LDB on III: 282
Delano, Laura IV: *293*
De LasCasas, William B. I: *353*
Delffs, Sophie cited, I: 30
deLieme, Nehemiah IV: 466, *524*, 537, *552*, *567*; V: 574
Dembitz, A. Lincoln II: *717*; IV: 553; V: 13
Dembitz, Annette V: 13
Dembitz, Emily I: *439*; V: *217*

Dembitz, Fannie W. I: *3*
Dembitz, Lewis N. I: *3*, 8, 47-49, 439; II: *659*; V: 107, 163, 219; LDB on V: 219
Dembitz, Sara IV: 533; V: 13
Dembitz, Sigmund I: *3*
Dembitz, Stella I: *3*; V: *217*, 222
Dembitz, Wilhelmine W. I: *3*, 438
Dembitz, William II: 140
DeMille, Cecil B. III: 200
Deming, Horace E. I: *329*, 369
democracy, LDB on I: 407; II: 332-33, 342; III: 428, 566-68; IV: 20-21, 254, 300, 477; V: 45-46
"Democracy in Palestine" (1915) III: 544, 658
DeMohrenschildt, Ferdinand IV: *286*
Demosthenes V: 189
Denison, Arthur C. V: *403*
Denison House I: 137, 143, 161
Denison, Winfred T. II: *521*; III: 126, *134*, 262
Denman, William IV: *29*
Denmark V: 28, 492, 513, 585
Dennett, Fred II: 312, *335*, 353, 458
Dennison, Henry S. III: *228*; V: 342
Depew, Chauncy M. I: *336*, 338
DeRan, H. C. II: *542*
Derby, Haskett I: *23*
deRothschild, Anthony G. V: *521*
deRothschild, Edmond III: 477, *498*, 622; IV: 285, *302*, 310, 320, 343, *357*, 406, *436*, 447; V: 480
deRothschild, James A. IV: *284*, 287, 292, 293, 303, 436, *288*, 473, 508, 522, 524, *294*, 532, 533
deRothschild, Lionel W. IV: 283, *321*
Des Chutes River Rrd Co. II: 313
deSola, Clarence I. IV: *227*, 285
deSoto, Hernando IV: *142*
Destler, Chester M. cited, I: 123, 209
Detroit III: 584
Detroit Times II: 540, 651
Deutsch, Gotthard V: *26*

development of local culture, LDB on IV: 497-99, 520, 524-26; V: 162-65, 168-69, 204-205

Devens, Charles Jr. I: 47*

Devine, Edward T. II: 577*, 652

Dewey, Davis R. III: 203*

Dewey, Henry S. I: 371*, 377-78, 385, 389

Dewey, John III: 673; IV: 353*; V: 50, 312

Dewey, Judd II: 424; III: 458; V: 332, 346, 546, 559, 566, 568, 569, 573, 575

Dewey, Mary H. III: 203*

Dexter, Mr. I: 164

Dexter, Philip IV: 66*

Diamond, William cited, II: 635

Dickens, Charles quoted, III: 306

Dickinson, John V: 226*, 286, 334

Dickinson, O. L. II: 387*

"Dick-to-Dick letter" II: 462-63, 467, 475, 491-96, 515-16

Dieckmann v. St. Louis I: 30

Diggs, Annie L. II: 28*

Dilliard, Irving V: 477*, 585; cited, II: 655

Dineson, Jacob IV: 158*

Dingley tariff II: 657; IV: 98

Dingol, Solomon V: 488*

Dinnerstein, Leonard cited, III: 374

Diocletian IV: 308

diversity of citizenship jurisdiction V: 322, 327, 330, 335, 337, 368; LDB on V: 170, 330

Dixon, Edward W. I: 575

Dizengoff, Meir V: 571*

"Do"; see Goldmark, Josephine C.

"The Document" IV: 568; V: 30, 36, 46

Dodd, Mr. V: 154

Dodd, William E. cited, II: 635; III: 235

Dodge, Clarence P. V: 378*

Dodge, Cleveland H. II: 51*

Dodge, Frederic III: 160*; IV: 27; V: 187

Dodge, James H. I: 228*

Dodge, James M. III: 241*

Dodge, Robert E. N. V: 116*

Dodge, William W. I: 236*

Doherty, Philip J. I: 79, 379*

Dole, Charles F. I: 500*; II: 152, 211

domestic spying, LDB on IV: 510; V: 45-46, 60, 200, 203, 224-25, 310, 380

Donald, Malcolm IV: 97*

Donaldson, William T. III: 184*

donation of legal services for public causes, LDB and I: 206, 210-12, 452; II: 44, 50-51, 64, 92, 388, 409, 508, 631, 675; III: 70, 96-97, 105, 138, 145, 198; IV: 51

Donnelly, John V: 338*

Donnelly v. U.S. V: 338

Donovan, Edward J. I: 377*

Donovan, Joseph I: 566, 569

Donovan, William J. V: 370*, 380

"Don't Condone the Crime" (1908) II: 154-55

"Mr. Dooley" II: 358

Doran, E. J. IV: 452

Dorchester [Massachusetts] Beacon IV: 88

Dorchester Mutual Fire Insurance Co. II: 234

Dorchy v. Kansas V: 237

Dorf, Samuel III: 438*

Doten, Carroll W. III: 228*

Douglas, James M. V: 589*

Douglas, Paul H. V: 424*, 540

Douglas, Walter B. I: 18*, 21, 27, 36, 63(2), 91; IV: 45, 232; V: 589; LDB on I: 27

Douglas, William L. I: 268*, 290, 347, 358, 364, 367, 401, 432, 490, 494, 498, 504, 516, 526, 535, 551; II: 14, 24, 49, 58, 71, 87, 99, 112, 192, 195, 206

Douglas, William O. V: 610

Doury, H. B. V: 570

Dowling, Noel T. V: 99

Downes v. Bidwell I: 156

Doyle, Andrew I: 561*, 570

Drake, George L. I: 370*

Drake, Thomas E. I: 398*, 517

Draper, Charles M. I: 377*

Draper, Eben S. I: 240, 560; II: 153*, 176, 181, 250, 258, 259, 269, 272, 274-82, 286, 293

Draper, Ernest G. V: 563*

Draper, George O. I: 477*

Drew, Fred IV: 89

Dreyfus, Alfred III: 156, 373*; IV: 18, 66; V: 270

Driscoll, Dennis I: 278, 279*, 531, 537-39, 548; II: 59

Dr. Miles Medical Co. v. Park & Sons Co. III: 120

Drob, Max IV: 13*

Droppers, Garrett II: 58*, 506; III: 56

Drummond, James E. IV: 283*, 288, 290, 292, 293, 319

Drury, Horace B. III: 240*

Drury, J. B. IV: 39

Dryden, John quoted, I: 287; II: 601

Dryden, John F. I: 494*

Dubnow, Simon M. III: 307, 537, 541

DuBois, W.E.B. V: 365*; cited, III: 308

Dudden, Arthur P. cited, III: 551

Dudley, Helena S. I: 138, 146, 161

Dudley, John V: 22, 180, 214

Duff, Jeanette I: 240

Dugdale, Blanche cited, IV: 284

Duquit, Leon cited, IV: 450

Duker, Abraham G. cited, IV: 339

Dumas, Alexander I: 80

Dunbar, Mrs. IV: 71

Dunbar, William H. I: 77*, 83, 106, 83, 106, 124, 146, 236, 238, 582; II: 431, 523, 650; IV: 59, 71, 211, 558

Duncan, James I: 286; II: 418*

Duncan Phillips Gallery V: 275

Dunham Brothers IV: 89

Dunn, Nellie II: 410*

Dunn, Robert IV: 510*

Dunne, Edward F. III: 673*; IV: 22

Dunne, Finley P. II: 358*, 379

Duplex Printing Co. v. Deering IV: 520; V: 40

Dupont, Ethel B. V: 202*

DuPuy, William A. V: 25

Durant, Will V: 260

DuRelle, George IV: 45*

Durland, Kellogg I: 218*

Duruy, Jean V. V: 185, 205

Dushkin, Alexander M. IV: 12*

duties of citizenship, LDB on I: 233; V: 45-46

Dwyer v. Fuller I: 73

Dyche, John A. II: 366*, 367, 459, 489, 497, 616; III: 82, 428

Easley, Ralph M. I: 259*, 277, 282, 304, 328, 356, 357, 362, 365, 395, 462, 488, 493; II: 12, 47, 214, 394; III: 228

East Boston Tunnel I: 201, 330, 418, 424

Eastern Council of Reform Rabbis III: 454, 579

Eastern Steamship Co. II: 120, 168, III: 204, 560

Eastman, Joseph B. I: 406, 419*, 423, 467, 512, 515, 516, 522, 523; II: 10, 23, 26, 62, 219, 224, 228, 289, 349, 396, 457, 465; III: 21, 54, 75, 133, 162, 222, 276, 287, 392, 397, 613; V: 244, 266, 356, 366, 414, 415; quoted, I: 173; cited, I: 167; III: 192; LDB on I: 419; III: 392-93

Eastman, S. Alden II: 273

Eaton, Amasa I: 391*, 398, 433, 435, 492

Eaton, Robert K. IV: 94*

Economic Club (Boston) I: 259, 380, 488, 494; II: 110; IV: 223

"An Economic Exhortation to Organized Labor" (1905) I: 282

Eddy, Arthur J. 559

Edgerton, Henry W. V: 316*

Edelman, Samuel III: 454*

Edison, Thomas A. III: 200; IV: 330; V: 161

Editor and Publisher IV: 23

Editorial Research Reports V: 306, 510

Edmunds, George F. I: 148*

Educational Alliance of New York City IV: 133

Edwards, Mrs. I: 410

Edwards, Seeber III: 42*

Edwards, Stephen O. III: 489*

"Efficiency and the One-Price Article" (1913) III: 125

"Efficiency by Consent" (1915) III: 618

"Efficiency in the Administration of Justice" III: 281

Efficiency movement: see Brandeis, Louis D., and Scientific management and the efficiency movement

Efficiency Society of New York III: 20

Egypt I: 135; II: 451; IV: 235, 337, 400, 409, 415-19, 443; V: 49, 457; LDB on IV: 410-16

Ehrenreich, Mr. IV: 13

Ehrlich, Eugen III: 288*, 382

Ehrmann, Herbert B. V: 306*

Eichholz, A. III: 600

Eichler, Menehem M. IV: 350*

Ein Hashofet V: 618

Einstein, Albert IV: 536*, 554, 555, 556; V: 650; LDB on IV: 554

Eisner, Henry R. IV: 352*

Ekern, Herman L. V: 216*

Elath, Eliahu cited, IV: 474

Election Laws League I: 281, 388, 586

election of 1880, LDB on I: 57

election of 1896, LDB on I: 123-24

election of 1908, LDB on II: 213

election of 1912, LDB on II: 709-10; see also Brandeis, Louis D. and the campaign of 1912

election of 1922, LDB on V: 76

election of 1924, LDB on V: 134, 136, 151-52

election of 1926, LDB on V: 240-41

election of 1928, LDB on V: 327, 344, 348, 352, 354-55, 360-64

Eliot, Charles W. I: *111**, 112, *113*, *116*, *117*, 304; II: 291, *309;* III: 52, 77, 332; IV: 192; V: 123, 154, 560, 657; quoted V: 302

Eliot, Charles W. II V: 378*

Eliot, George I: 62

Eliot, John II: 276*

Eliot, Regina D. V: 379

Elizabeth: see Raushenbush, Elizabeth B.

Elkins, Davis IV: 557*

Elkins, Stephen B. IV: 557*

Elkus, Abram I. II: 659*; III: 579; IV: 295, 301, 304, 313, 319, 336, *469*, 524

Elliott, Howard III: 143*, 153, 172, 221, 223, 231, 265, *346*, 385, 560, *590;* IV: 127; LDB on III: 153

Ellis, David A. II: 35, *98**, *104*, *108*(2); IV: 105

Ellis, George H. I: 357*

Ellis, Lewis E. cited, II: 457

Ellis, William D. I: 99*, 102; IV: 104-107

Ellison, E. H. IV: 89

Elman, Philip cited, II: 351

Elmore, Samuel D. I: 578*

Elms, E. E. IV: 89

Elwell, Fred S. I: *390**; II: 72, *222;* V: 332

Ely, Robert E. II: 418*, 535

Emergency Zionist Fund IV: 3, 11, 14, 16, 38, 82, 110, 129, 132, 173, 189, 190, 209, 217-19, 227-28, 240, 244, 247, 260

Emerson, Harrington II: 384*, 386, 543; III: 142, 241, 584; IV: *128*

Emerson, Ralph W. I: 12, 93

Emerton, Ephraim I: 19*, 45, 53, 59, 62, 135; II: 356; V: 295; LDB on V: 295

Emerton, Mrs. I: 94

"The Employer and the Trades Unions" (1904) I: 246-47, 250, 259

Endicott, Henry W. II: 240*; IV: 61, 89
"The Endless Chain: Interlocking Directorates" (1913) III: 183, 310
Engeln, John I: 32, 340
Engineering Magazine II: 384, 543
Engineering News II: *684*
England I: 73-74, 334, 340, 399, 403, 526-27; II: 196, 201, 202, 210, 212, 535, 567, 682; III: 139, 183, 291, 306, 345, 417, 539, 591; IV: 274, 279, 281-89, 293, 313, 319, 322, 324, 328, 335, 373, 403-406, 408, 423, 430, 434, 455, 458-60, 462, 468, 495, 527, 547; V: 10, 32, 37, 49, 122, 141, 183, 213, 281, 288, 517, 608; LDB on I: 73-74; IV: 423, 477; V: 122, 183, 192
England's administration of Palestine IV: 410, 420, 446-47, 455-57, 461-62, 495-96; V: 56, 220, 383-86, 398, 400-401, 422-24, 427-28, 436-37, 452, 455-60, 467-70, 474, 487, 521-22, 574-81, 590-94, 601-605, 607-609, 612-22, 651-52
English Federation of Zionists III: 504; IV: *393, 509*
Enterprise Steamship Co. II: 621
Enterprise Transportation Co. II: 76, 119, 127-28, 131-32, 168
Epstein, Abraham V: 536*
Epstein, Benjamin III: 317*, 326, 476
Epstein, Jacob IV: 522*
Epstein, Melech cited, III: 82
Equitable Life Assurance Society I: 337, 341, 351, 363, 409, 473, 540; II: 285; IV: 97, 99; V: 561, 569
Equitable Policyholders Association II: 64; IV: 51, 52, 53, 97, 99-100
Erie Railway Co. I: 212-14; III: 342
Ernst, George A. I: 167*
Ernst, Harold C. I: *386**; II: 27
Ernst, Morris L. V: 584*
Ernst, Richard P. V: 240*
Erskine, Mr. II: 87, 214
Erving, Emma V: 3, 118, 136, 364
Erving, Selma V: 3

Esch-Cummins Transportation Act (1920) V: 4, 86-88, 111, 326
Esch, John J. V: 326*
"An Essential of Lasting Peace" (1915) III: 436; V: 534-35
Estabrook, Arthur F. III: 177*
Estabrook, Charles E. I: 493*
Etkes, Mr. IV: 323
Ettinger, Akiba J. V: 475*, *484*, 487
Ettor, Joseph II: 636*, 645-50
Etzel V: 622
Euripides II: 479-80; V: 141; quoted, II: 272; IV: 362-63
Evans, Daniel I: 500*; II: 152, 164
Evans, Elizabeth G. I: 73*, 82, 92, 101, *102, 106, 110, 111, 123, 150*, 260, 371, 436, 498, 528; II: 250, 305, 441, 451, *527*, 576-77, 660, 702; III: 231, 259; IV: 458; V: 6, 21, 90, 114, 136, 200, 222, 241, 251, 281, 297, 299, 365, 381, 515
Evans, Glendower I: 74
Evans, Henry II: 430*
Evans v. Gore V: 85
Evans, Wilmot R. Jr. I: *462** 534; V: 451
Evatt, Herbert V. cited, IV: 309
Evelina deRothschild School III: 405, 679
Everett, Arthur G. I: 138*, 142-43
Everybody's Magazine II: 69, 102, 203-204, 364
Ewing, Thomas III: 127*
Exchange Club (Boston) IV: 260
"The Experience of Massachusetts in Street Railways" (1902) I: 220, 223-24, 469; II: 419
Ezra, Nissim E. B. III: *523**

Fabian Society III: 538; V: 448
Fagan, James O. II: 418*
Fahey John II: *396**, 516; III: 61; V: 332, 338, 342, 559, 573; LDB on V: 559-60
Fahy, Bartholomew J. I: 226
Fairbanks, Charles W. II: 116*

Fairbanks Co. v. Samuel S. Learnard
IV: 67
Fairbanks, Douglas Sr. V: 275
Fairchild v. Hughes V: 47
Fairman, Charles V: 628
Fall, Albert B. V: 120, 327
Fall River [Massachusetts] *Daily News* II: 173
Fall River [Massachusetts] Savings Bank V: 487
Fall River [Massachusetts] strike (1904) I: 263
Farber, J. Eugene IV: *496**
Farbstein, Y'hoshua H. IV: 157*, 161; V: *636*
Farmers' Cooperative Marketing Association V: 135-37
Farley, Vincent II: *715**
Farquhar-Pearson-Lehigh-Rock Island Syndicate II: 410
Farrand, George E. III: 320*
Farrand, Max V: 40*, 384
Faunce, William H. P. II: 619*
Faxon, William O. I: 560*; II: 141, 179
Fechheimer, S. Marcus III: 405*, 415, *438*, 442, 444, 454, 465-66, 614, 620, 666; IV: 6, 12, 243
Federal Council of Churches IV: 508; V: 46, 323
Federal Emergency Relief Administration V: 548
Federal Reserve System III: 25, 40, 48, 113-16 218; V: 97, 238, 270 412
Federal Trade Commission III: 84, 101, 218, 237, 250-59, 320, 345, 347, 370, 380, 393, 440, 447, 468, 496, 502, 523, 581, 592, 600, 680; IV: 28, 35, 197, 372, 523; V: 321, 348; LDB on III: 339, 381, 581
Federal Trade Commission v. Curtis Publishing Co. V: 81
The Federalist Papers V: 294
Federation of American Zionists II: 402, 611; III: 141, 147, 193, 313, 322-26, 338, 340, 356, 406, 417, 426, 438, 450, 456-62, 470-71, 476-85, 488, 497, 526-28, 561, 568-70, 572, 591, 606, 624, 667-68; IV: 24, 135, 193, 218, 244, 320, 430
Federation of Bessarabian Jews III: 624
Federation of Rumanian Jews III: 572
Federation of Russian Polish Jews III: 624
Federation of Zionist Societies of Canada IV: 228
Feiker, Frederick M. III: *392**
Feinberg, Mr. I: 537
Feingold, Henry cited, V: 615, 629
Feinstein, Leah IV: *19**
Feinstein, Marnin cited, IV: 168
Feis, Herbert V: 493*
Feisal, King IV: 417; V: 400*, 402, 579
Feldman, Marcus B. IV: 548
Fellows, J. William V: 547*
Fels, Joseph III: 235*, 551
Fels, Mary III: 551*; IV: *247*, 303, 338, 348, 394, 399, 423; V: 43-44
Fels, Samuel S. III: 406*, 514, *638;* IV: 96
Ferber, J. Bernard I: 561, 574, 575, *579;* II: *19;* LDB on II: 19
Ferber, Edna V: 235
Fernandez, Alice B. IV: 510
Ferrero, Guglielmo V: 186
Fetter, Frank A. V: *539*, *647 648*
Fewster, J. Donald cited, V: 322
Fidelity Trust (Louisville) II: 365
Field, Fred F. Co. IV: 89
Field, George P. I: 342*
Field, Walbridge A. I: 101*
Fields, Annie I: 44*; II: 364
Fierens, Paul V: 550
Fifield, J. J. II: 71
Filene, A. Lincoln I: 237*, 560, 578; II: 17, 81, 90, *268*, 365, 367, 387, 390, 427, *444*, 460, 630; III: *52*, 428, 609, 622, 650; V: 339, 342, *471*, 475, 531, 547, 548, 555, 569, 626

Filene Cooperative Association I: 447; II: 196, 202

Filene, Edward A. I: 145*, *164*, *169*, 181-83, *184, 185*, 205, 222, 229, 237-38, *275*, 286, *298*, 301, 307, *327*, 369, *373*, 399, *410*, 423, *447*, *591*; II: 21, 45-46, *62*, 90, *92 95*, 101, 106, 166, 173, *216, 234, 236, 245*, 257, *259*, 268, 289, 296, 349, 365, 379, 506, 516, 523, 561, 630; III: 61, *382*; IV: 77, 123, 192, *361*; V: 161, 245, *246*, 337, 339, *584, 590, 591*; LDB on III: 61; V: 339, 584

Fillebrown, Charles B. I: *468*, *472*, *473*, *476*

Filson Club (Louisville) V: 265

"Financial Condition of the New York, New Haven & Hartford Rrd and of the Boston & Maine Rrd" (1907) II: 61, 63, 81, 93, 113, 145, 193-94; III: 106; IV: 88; V: 502, 534-35

financial contributions to family, LDB and I: 79, 438; II: 280, 729; III: 369; IV: 488, 533, 543, 557; V: 13

financial contributions to public causes, LDB and I: 229, 509, 512, 522-24, 565, 567-68, 586; II: 5-6, 44, 54, 59, 205-206, 216, 246, 252, 283, 289, 292, 349, 397, 432, 466, 527, 571, 576, 698; III: 12, 43, 75, 80-81, 224, 263, 274, 288, 433, 539, 602; IV: 61-62, 92-93, 134, 168; V: 80, 231-32, 257, 304, 386, 478

financial contributions to Zionism and Jewish causes, LDB and II: 402, 611; III: 65, 85, 295, 381-82, 406, 416, 478, 495, 530-31, 539, 551, 563, 603-604; IV: 62, 115, 180, 251, 347, 355, 377, 472, 491, 496; V: 25, 37-38, 252, 416-17, 491, 506, 558, 576, 582-83, 586, 618, 620, 652

Findley, Oscar III: 271

Fink, Gary M. cited, V: 10

Fink, Reuben IV: 385

Finkelstein, J. J. III: *591*

Finley, David E. II: 440*

Finney, Edward C. II: 314, 322*; IV: 130

First National Bank (Boston) II: 429

First Universal Races Congress III: 307

Fischbein, Louis II: 245*

Fischel, Harry III: 363*; V: 108

Fischer, Jean IV: 13*

Fish, Frederic P. I: 370*; IV: 94

Fish, Stuyvesant I: 409*; II: 110, 190; IV: 84; LDB on II: 110

Fish, Walter C. II: 285*

Fisher, Boyd III: 29*, 98

Fisher-Ellis bill III: 275-77, 282-83, 285

Fisher, Harry M. IV: 28*; V: *440*, 449

Fisher, Horace I: 174

Fisher, Irving V: 189*

Fisher, Jerome II: 703*

Fisher, Laura I: 438

Fisher, Robert C. III: 160*

Fisher, Walter L. I: *295*, 509; II: *320, 325, 362, 415*, 458, 463, 467, *508*, 513, 569, 715; III: 8, 23, 44; V: 230

Fisher, Walter T. V: 229*

Fishman, Jacob IV: 500*

Fiske, Haley I: 545*; II: 591

Fiske, John I: 104

Fitch, Mr. I: 49

Fitch, John A. II: 535, 544*; III: 673; IV: 463; cited, II: 544

Fitch v. Harrington I: 76

Fite, Gilbert C. cited, III: 272; V: 340

Fitz, Eustace C. IV: 75*

Fitzgerald, John F. I: 376*, 389, *414*, 466, 470, 571; II: 31, 60, 262, 296, 651; III: 162, 200; LDB on I: 378, 389

Fitzgerald, William F. I: *242*; IV: 48-50, 113, 127

Fitzpatrick, Edward cited, II: 416; III: 409; IV: 327

Fitzpatrick, F. W. I: *503*

Fitzpatrick, Thomas B. I: 494*, 569; II: 9

Flagler, John F. II: 530

Fleischer, Charles II: 152

Fleishner, Otto III: 37

Fleming, Matthew C. I: 276*, 399, 480, 494

Fletcher, Duncan U. II: 452*; IV: 73, 87, 141, 150

Fletcher, Robert V. V: 124

Flexner, Abraham I: 438*; III: 508; IV: 431; V: 7, 110, 187, 236, 277, 592, 601

Flexner, Bernard I: 439; III: 565*; IV: 353, 365, 378, 381, 384, 389, 397-98, 404, 423, 425, 426, 427-32, 438-40, 457, 468, 471, 473, 478, 480, 482, 483-85, 489-90, 492, 499, 501, 508-509, 513, 518, 522, 524, 530, 533, 537, 544, 550, 554, 555, 559, 561-65; V: 3, 9, 19, 75, 100, 108, 195, 208, 220, 236, 249, 321, 363, 375, 385, 388, 389, 392, 397, 398, 402, 407, 414-23, 433, 465, 469-70, 480, 484, 490-91, 500, 549, 569, 592, 595, 600, 601, 602(2), 620, 621, 623, 627, 629, 630, 635, 637, 640, 641, 643, 646, 647, 652, 653; 654; cited, V: 140, 223

Flexner, Miss V: 207, 208, 236, 500, 592, 601, 602, 621, 628, 640, 647, 654

Flexner, Robert E. cited, III: 317

Flexner, Simon IV: 470, 471*; V: 236; LDB on IV: 470

Flexner, Washington V: 4*, 652

Flint, Perley G. II: 110*

Florance, J. Esdaile II: 478*

Foerster, Robert F. III: 34*

Fohs, Ferdinand J. IV: 468*, 500; V: 74, 506

Folk, Joseph W. II: 115*

Folsom, Charles E. I: 226*

Folsom, Charles F. I: 165; II: 17*

football, LDB on I: 387

Foraker, Joseph B. II: 207*

Forbes, Arthur W. V: 568*

Forbes, Frederick F. III: 78*

Forbes-Lindsay, C. H. cited, II: 130

Forbush, Ada I: 97

Forcey, Charles B. cited, II: 654; III: 88, 208

Ford, Arthur Y. V: 169*, 175-76, 179-81, 187, 190, 198, 217, 406

Ford, Henry III: 230*, 294; IV: 365, 487, 507; V: 25, 44, 69, 71, 296, 556

Ford, Henry J. V: 47*

Ford, Jeremiah D. I: 149*

Fordney-McCumber tariff IV: 547

Foreign Policy Association V: 409

foreign trade, LDB on V: 10, 15-16, 97

Forster, Rudolph II: 138*

Fortescue, John quoted, V: 230-31

Fosdick, Harry E. V: 182*

Fosdick, Raymond IV: 524; V: 72*, 75, 187, 192, 376, 524, 652; LDB on V: 192

Foss, Edward cited, I: 12

Foss, Eugene N. I: 576; II: 293, 441*, 457, 464, 504-506, 516, 517, 580, 585, 624, 626, 651, 659; III: 58, 67, 86, 172, 182, 191, 195, 245; IV: 68, 70; LDB on II: 504-506

Foster, Frank K. I: 532*

Foster, John W. III: 610

Foster, Reginald II: 72*

Foster, Roger S. V: 273*

Foster, William Z. V: 72*

Foulke, William D. II: 539*

Fourier, Francois M. II: 481

Fowler, Nathaniel C. Jr. II: 245*

Fox, Austin G. IV: 60*, 77, 84, 86, 99, 125, 128, 133, 144, 151, 176, 177, 182, 558, 561

Fox, Charles K. I: 589; II: 9*, 114

Fox, Dixon R. V: 395*

Fraenkel, Osmond K. V: 534-35, 548*

Fram, Harry III: 426*

France III: 306, 340, 360; IV: 279, 286, 289-93, 311, 324, 405-408, 411-12, 446, 447, 457-58, 462, 495, 498;

V: 36, 121, 213, 221, 231, 517, 602

Frank: see Taussig, Frank W.

Frank, Eli IV: 28*

Frank, Glenn V: 187*

Frank, Leo M. III: 373*, 383, 633; V: 131

Frankel, Lee K. II: 218*, 284; III: 228

Frankenstein, Lina H. IV: 95*

Frankfurter, Emma W. IV: 265*, 344; V: 316

Frankfurter, Felix I: 36, 71; II: 350*, 352, 412, 512, 521, 577, 648; III: 18, 19, 38, 88, 134-36, 144, 146, 203, 209, 236, 242, 262, 288, 296, 373, 428, 454 460, 467, 487, 516, 544-45, 555, 577, 613, 643, 651; IV: 29, 37, 118, 129, 140, 142, 149, 153(2), 171, 210, 216, 221, 236, 258, 261, 264-65, 266(2), 268, 280-87, 291, 296, 302, 303, 305, 310, 314, 318, 322, 330, 335, 337, 340, 344, 345, 352-53, 365-67, 370-74, 377-78, 381, 384, 394, 395, 396, 397, 398-400, 404-406, 412, 420, 423-25, 427, 429, 430, 431, 432-33, 438, 439, 441, 443, 444, 445-47, 448, 449, 451, 454, 455, 457-58, 473-75, 478, 481-82, 483, 484, 485, 487, 489, 492-94, 498, 500-501, 505, 509, 510, 513, 514, 516, 517(2), 518, 520(2), 522, 523, 524, 528, 530, 533, 537, 540, 541, 542, 544, 547, 549, 550, 552, 553, 554, 555, 559, 560, 563, 564, 565; V: 3, 7, 8, 11, 15, 16, 17, 18, 27, 30, 33, 40, 43, 45, 48, 49, 50(2), 52, 56, 59, 62, 63, 64, 65(2), 71, 73, 74, 78, 83, 84, 88(2), 90, 93, 95, 98, 100, 102, 104, 106, 108, 109, 110, 116, 119, 120, 121, 123, 126, 128, 130, 131, 136, 137, 141, 143, 146, 150(2), 153, 154, 155, 159, 160(2), 165, 167(2), 169, 170, 171, 172, 174, 176, 182, 183, 184, 185, 187, 188, 190, 192, 195, 196, 199, 200, 203, 205, 207, 209, 212, 215, 221, 222, 224(2), 225, 227, 229, 230, 232, 235, 237, 241, 243, 245, 247, 249, 251, 255, 258, 259, 260, 270, 271, 272, 275, 276, 277, 279, 280 282, 283, 284, 285, 287, 290, 292, 294, 295, 297(2), 298, 299, 300, 303, 305, 308, 309, 312, 315, 316, 317, 318, 319, 321, 322, 323, 325, 326, 329, 333, 335, 336, 344, 348, 350, 352, 353, 354, 355, 358, 359, 360, 361, 362, 363, 364, 366, 367(2), 370, 371, 372, 374, 375, 376, 378(2), 379, 380, 381(2), 383, 385, 388, 389, 394, 397, 398, 400, 402, 403, 409, 410, 413, 414, 415, 424, 428, 437, 446, 458, 459, 469, 474, 490, 497, 499, 503, 506, 511, 513, 516, 520, 522, 544, 549, 553, 558, 559, 563, 567, 569, 572, 576, 578, 585, 593, 603, 606, 608, 610, 621, 622, 637, 651, 654, 655; LDB on III: 146; IV: 265, 344; V: 123, 183, 187, 364, 469-70, 497

Frankfurter, Marian D. IV: 459, 463, 483, 490, 499, 517, 538; V: 12, 33, 41, 44, 49, 51, 52, 74-75, 83, 88, 90, 100, 103, 123, 144, 151, 155, 165, 169, 170, 172, 186, 187, 197, 241, 245 258, 283, 296, 297, 299, 300, 309, 312, 320, 323, 337, 364, 622

Frankl, Ludwig A. V: 129*

Franklin, Benjamin V: 184, 302

Franklin, Edwin A. I: 328*

Franklin, Pearl V: 330*, 388

Franzos, Karl E. I: 74; cited I: 75

Frederick, Peter J. cited, I: 138

Freedman, Max cited, II: 350

freedom, LDB on V: 45-46, 117

freedom of the press, LDB on I: 319

freedom of speech, LDB on IV: 501-502, 517, 558; V: 229, 248, 286, 318, 352

Freeman, James E. V: 617*

Freeman, Jonathan V: 144

Freiberger, David V: 420*, 427

Freidel, Frank cited, IV: 475

Freier, Recha V: 581*

French, Asa P. I: 582*; II: 18, 153, 168

French, Edward V. II: *434**

French Revolution IV: 387, 463

Freud, Sigmund IV: 366

Freund, Ernst II: 299*; IV: *15*, 140, 145; V: 40, 79, 124

Freund, Paul A. V: 536*, 606

Frey & Son v. Cudahy Packing Co. IV: 550

Frick, Henry C. I: 341*, 409

Frick v. Webb V: 106

Fricke, William A. I: 462*

Fried, Edward V: 431

Friedenburg, Ferdinand II: 566*

Friedenmann, Adolf IV: 6, 253

Friedenwald, Edgar B. III: *645**; V: 113

Friedenwald, Harry III: 302*, 323, *356*, 472, 531, 545, 567, 572, 575, 579, 591, *635*, 646; IV: *24*, 203, 205, 211-13, *220*, 237, 248, *259*, 269, 271, 280, *325*, 352, 375, 381, 410, 417-20, 422, 484, 555, 563; V: 112, *246*, 516, *529*

Friedenwald, Jonas S. IV: *248**, 555; V: 321, 596

Friedlaender, Israel III: *445**, 517, 522, *536*, *541*, 545; IV: 79, *170*, 340, 345, 376, 387, 389

Friedman, Elisha M. IV: 245*, 318, 323

Friedman, Isaiah cited, IV: 279, 282, 311, 321, 458; V: 401, 523

Friedman, Mr. III: 160*

Friedman, M. IV: *178**

Friendly, Henry J. V: 210*, 238, 244, 310, 322-24, 327, 330, 350, 354, 358, 404, *587*; cited V: 170

Friesel, Evyatar cited, IV: 439

Fries, Alfred A. V: 248

Friess, Horace L. III: 272

Fritch, L. C. III: 50

Fritz, Robert V: 273

Fromenson, Abraham H. III: 352*; IV: 3, 299, *488*, 513; V: 431

Frost, Mr. V: 339

Frothingham, Louis A. I: 172*, 178-79, 371-73, 376-80, 386, 389-90, 409; II: 27, 45, 293, 504; LDB on I: 372; II: 504

Frothingham, Paul R. II: 27*

Froude, James A. cited, I: 105

Fuess, Claude M. cited, I: 419; IV: 471

Fulda, Ludwig V: 235*

Fuller, Alvan T. V: 282, 284, 288*, 290, 294, 297, 299 313, 353, 356, 363

Fuller, Frederick T. III: 79*

Fuller, Melville W. IV: 168, 183; V: 173

Fulton, Charles W. II: 290*

Furness, Ruth V: 285, 287

furnishings, LDB on I: 60

Furtwängler, Adolf V: 190*

Furuseth, Andrew I: 257*; III: 464; V: 186, 287, 322, 387

Gabriel, Edmund V. V: 384*, 400

Galbraith John K. cited, V: 410

Galicia III: 518, 524, 539; IV: 170, 179

Galician Verband III: 606

Galena Signal Oil Co. III: 210

Gallinger, Jacob H. III: 320*, 440

Galloway, Herman J. V: 335*

Galsworthy, John III: 307

Gandhi, Mahatma IV: 309

Gans, Bird S. S. IV: 384*

Gans, Howard S. IV: 378*, 384, 397, 423, 429, 438, 441

Gantt, Henry L. II: 384*, 386, 543, *674*; III: 241

Gara, Mr. IV: 323

Garceau, Albert I: 377*

Garcelon, William F. I: 543, 578*; II: 181

Gardiner, Edward I: 82*, 83, 112

Gardner, Augustus P. IV: 272*

Gardner, George I: 364*, 367, 371, 401, 436

Gardner, Gilson II: 436*, 465, 466, 476, *479*, 494, 515, *722*; III: *39*, 467, *581*, *596*; IV: 119; V: 135; cited II: 499

Gardner, Henry I: 408
Gardner, Isabella S. I: 371*
Gardner, Rathbone I: 489*
Garfield, Harry A. IV: 317*
Garfield, James A. I: 57*
Garfield, James R. II: 327, *332**, 351, 355, 359, 399, *459*, 468, 476, *500*, 502; IV: 318
Garner, John N. V: 506
Garraty, John A. cited, I: 595; II: 46, 95, 525
Garretson, Austin B. IV: 171*
Garrett, Charles cited V: 530
Garrett, Garet III: 202*
Garrett, Robert III: 267*
Garrison, Lindley M. III: 144, 146*; IV: 449
Gary, Elbert H. II: 221, 545*, 561, 575; III: 310; IV: 432, 559
Gascoyne-Cecil, Edgar A. IV: 455*
Gaskill, Nelson B. cited, III: 259
Gaston, William A. I: 207*, 267, *281*
Gastano, Icipione I: 28*
Gay, Edwin F. III: 122*; V: *393*, 402, 411, 503
Gay, Richard L. I: 183*, *285*, *586*
Gearharts, the IV: 370
Geiger, Abraham III: 386
Geller, Max A. V: 415*
Gellhorn, Edna F. I: 408*
General Electric Co. II: 101; III: 205
Gentry, Mr. V: 406
George, Alexander cited, III: 106
George, David Lloyd II: 567; IV: 283, 289*, 310, 414-15, 423, 446, 474, 509; V: 604
George E. Keith Co. IV: 89
George, Henry I: 82*, 211, 455; III: 133, 236, 490
George, Juliette cited, III: 106
George, Samuel W. I: 411*, 420-23, 426, 527
Georgia I: 582; V: 311
German Armistice Commission IV: 159

German Club (Boston) I: 59
German National Bank v. Engeln's Committee I: 32
Germany I: 334, 340, 352, 394-95, 408; II: 74, 201-203, 210, 215, 451, 566-67; III: 74, 197, 291, 305, 345, 381, 417, 431-42, 460, 500, 539; IV: 156, 205, 233-36, 259, 272, 274, 281, 305, 308-309, 324, 365-66, 372-73, 387, 444, 521, 544, 547, 557; V: 24, 110, 204, 242, 516-17, 521, 524, 533, 542, 562, 602, 605, 614-15, 639
Gibbons, James C. III: 203*
Gifford, Hardinge S: IV: 540*
Gilbert v. Minnesota IV: 517, 550
Gilbert and Sullivan I: 101; IV: 108, 386
Gilbert, Jacob H. I: 111*; V: 137, 197, 233, 235, 246, 299, 307, *336*, 386, 461, 472, 473, 484, 575, 600, 650
Gilbert, Louis B. V: 241*, 246, 258, 307
Gilbert, Susan B. I: 60, 110*, 112, 119, 127, 135, 242, 245, 340, 346, 359, 364, 407, 409, 411, 436, 439, 581, 585; II: 9, 18, 207, 209, 249-50, 276, 287, 305-306, 343, 345, 381, 464, 650, 660, 724; III: 111, 246, 339, 354, 381, 387, 420, 503, 513, 565; IV: 43, 177, 258, 297, 314, 329, 332, 363, 394, 399, 400, 401, 404, 411, 419-22, 480, 512, 516; V: 5-6, 10-11, 14, 20-21, 24, 29, 32, 49, 100, 137, 181, 197, 233, 241, 299, 307, 342, 409, 478, 531, 575, 600, 651, 658
Gilbert, William B. V: 83*
Gilbreth, Frank B. II: 478*; III: 241
Gilder, Richard W. I: 159*
Gillespie v. People II: 679
Gillette, Frederick H. I: *519**; II: 124, 129
Gillette, King C. II: 236*; IV: 89
Gilmore, Edward I: 534*
Gilson, Frederick H. II: *319**
Ginn, Edwin I: 576*

Ginsburg, Asher Zvi: see Ha-Am, Ahad

Giovanetti, Arturo II: 636*, 645-47, 649-50

Gittell, Marilyn cited, III: 391

Glad, Betty cited, I: 321

Glad, Paul cited, I: 124

Glasser, Mr. II: 537

Glass, Carter III: 115*; V: 122

Glass-Willis plan III: 115

Glavis, Louis R. II: 307, 311, 314, 315*, 316-17, 320-21, 326, 334, 335, 338, 342, 347, 352, 400, 457, 468, 475, 478; III: 33, 238-39; IV: 63, 73, 87, 92, 150; V: 312, 642; LDB on II: 315

Glazbrook, Otis A. III: 495*; IV: 146, 320

Glenn, John M. II: 297*

Gloucester Water Supply Co. v. Gloucester I: 255

Gluck, Elsie cited, I: 212

Glueck, Nelson V: 623*, 652

Glueck, Sheldon V: 404*

Gluskin, Z'ev III: 549*, 677; IV: 5, 148, 194, 337

Godkin, Edwin L. I: 303*

Goethe Johann W. I: 22, 45, 104; V: 184, 512; quoted, II: 424-26, 578; IV: 417; V: 142, 282, 518, 531, 560; LDB on V: 512

Going, Charles B. III: 240*

Goldberg, Abraham IV: 135*, 137, 139, 188, 501, 509; V: 449, 632

Goldberg, Arthur V: 645

Goldberg, Boris (Dov) IV: 194*, 303, 534

Goldberg, Israel V: 291*, 435

Golden, John I: 561, 566*, 569, 586; 14, 81, 277, 528

Gol'denveizer, Aleksandr S. V: 238*

Goldenweiser, Emanuel A. V: 238*

Goldfarb, Israel IV: 201*

Goldfogle, Henry M. III: 348*

Goldman, Julius III: 514*

Goldman, Mr. V: 623

Goldman, Solomon V: 614*, 618, 620-22, 628, 632, 638-39, 643-44; cited, III: 175; LDB on V: 615

Goldmann, Nahum V: 609*, 639, 644

Goldmark, Adolf V: 305

Goldmark, Alice: see Brandeis, Alice G.

Goldmark, Alice P. V: 530*, 600, 645

Goldmark, Charles J. IV: 315*, 316, 363, 441; V: 531, 596, 600, 645

Goldmark, Christine: see Openhym, Christine G.

Goldmark, Clara V: 114

Goldmark, Emily II: 186*, 282

Goldmark, Godfrey V: 305*

Goldmark, Helen I: 25, 92

Goldmark, Henry I: 12*, 24, 91; II: 207, 291; IV: 221; V: 128, 130; LDB on V: 128, 130

Goldmark, James I: 25, 287*; IV: 398, 425

Goldmark, Jonathan IV: 441*; V: 600, 645

Goldmark, Joseph I: 24*, 121; V: 278

Goldmark, Josephine C. I: 4, 166*; II: 186, 207, 291, 297, 299, 306, 381, 395, 650; III: 63, 154, 168, 227, 237, 513; IV: 142, 371, 398; V: 167, 246, 492, 512, 600, 650; cited I: 4, 25, 91; II: 78; IV: 538; LDB on II: 381

Goldmark, Karl V: 82*, 330

Goldmark, Nellie I: 24

Goldmark, Pauline D. II: 207, 249*, 250, 364, 650, 706; IV: 171, 364, 537; V: 76, 114, 411, 650

Goldmark, Regina W. I: 24-25, 120*, 371; II: 186, 282, 325, 396, 706; IV: 329, 363, 421, 536; V: 119

Goldmark, Ruth IV: 315*

Goldmark, Susan I: 118*, 126; IV: 419, 441; V: 33 76, 129, 223, 306, 350, 512

Goldmark, Thelda IV: 398

Goldmark, Tiny I: 24

Goldpflamm, Dr. IV: 157

Goldsmid-Montefiore, C. J. V: 541*
Goldsmith, Irving B. V: 320*, 322, 358-61, 397, 404
Goldsmith, N. F. IV: 67*
Goldsmith, William cited, I: 253
Goldstein, Benjamin F. V: 375*
Goldstein, Dora III: 353
Goldstein, Israel V: 420*, 582
Goldthwait, Joel E. I: 138*, 142
Gompers, Samuel I: 232*, 244, 258, 283, 304, 328; II: 14, 198, 365, 517, 566; III: 464, 633; IV: 511; V: 63, 511; cited, I: 284
Gonikman, Isaac IV: 117*
Gooch, Mr. V: 278
"Good government" and the battle against political corruption in Boston, LDB and I: 174, 178-79, 204-208, 222-42, 248-53, 256, 268-70, 273-74, 277, 281, 300, 333-34, 351-54, 356, 368-69, 373-80, 385-91, 414-15, 432-33, 466, 586; II: 83, 219, 222-23, 244-45, 267-68, 272, 283, 294-96, 378, 416; see also Good Government Association and "Boston—1915"
Good Government Association I: 238, 248, 270, 368-69, 373, 375-77; II: 26, 31, 283
Good Housekeeping Magazine II: 725
Goodman, Paul IV: 358, 401
Goodman, Mr. V: 637
Gordon, Duff V: 630
Gordon, George A. V: 281*
Gordon, Harry A. III: 27*
Gordon, Peyton V: 326*
Gordon, Thomas R. IV: 28*
Gordon, William S. I: 304
Gore, Thomas P. II: 622, 624*
Goren, Arthur A. cited, III: 193
Gorgas, William C. V: 457
Gorham, Mr. IV: 140
Gottheil, Richard J. H. III: 155*, 296, 299, 302, 309, 312, 314, 339, 341, 344, 360, 374, 378, 400, 403, 404, 428, 446, 456, 460, 471, 490,

517, 522, 527, 532, 533, 537, 555, 578-79, 644, 677; IV: 4, 18, 79-82, 86, 102, 116, 216, 259, 280, 340, 345, 376, 388, 398
Gottlieb, Leo V: 191*
Gottlieb, Moshe cited, V: 521
Gottschalk, Louis V: 198*, 269
Gould, Arthur R. V: 248*
Goulston, Ernest II: 165*
Gove, William H. I: 230*, 231
Governors' Conference on Law Enforcement (1922) V: 79-80
Grabau, Mary Antin IV: 4*
Grady, Alice H. I: 437, 478*, 535-36, 543, 557, 583; II: 396, 538, 545, 600, 724; III: 223, 232, 238, 259, 263, 362; IV: 45, 199, 216, 275, 297, 460, 487; V: 4, 89, 119, 168, 183, 216, 223, 232, 234, 240, 248, 283, 287, 302, 307, 311, 319, 321, 328, 331(2), 338, 340, 341, 342, 344, 346, 348, 356, 366, 375, 451, 497, 503, 508, 509, 515, 545; LDB on V: 89, 216, 307, 331
Grady, Talmadge V: 223*, 307, 332, 545
Graebner, Norman cited, III: 44
Graham, George F. III: 295*
Graham, Howard S. III: 342*
Graham, James M. II: 371*, 460, 463-65, 466, 497, 513, 515; IV: 101, 150
Graham, Mr. III: 112, 119
Grahame, Kenneth I: 135
Grain Marketing Co. V: 135-37
Grand Duke Michael (Russia) IV: 276
Grand Rapids, Michigan IV: 463, 497
Grand Trunk Line II: 621-22, 625-26, 722-25
Grant, Robert V: 290*
Graves, Edward G. II: 26*
Gray, Horace I: 36*, 38, 42, 44, 47-49, 60, 64, 77; LDB on I: 38
Gray, John C. I: 8*, 13, 18, 71
Gray, John H. I: 442*

Gray, Reginald I: 57*
Grayson, Cary T. IV: 25*
Grayson, S. IV: 39*
Great Britain: see England
Great Northern Paper Co. I: 462
Great Southern Rrd III: 493
Greater Boston Committee III: 383
"The Greatest Life Insurance Wrong" (1906) I: 495-96, 499, 511, 547
Green, Andrew H. I: 346*
Green, Bernie F. III: 419*; IV: 113
Green, Marguerite cited, I: 259
Green v. U.S. V: 345
Green, William V: 510*
Green, William R. V: 324*
Greene, Evarts B. V: 395*
Greene, Nathan V: 317, 338, 387
Greenfield [Massachusetts] Recorder II: 7
Greenman, Frederick F. IV: 180*
Gregory, Stephen S. IV: 28*
Gregory, Thomas T. IV: 539*
Gregory, Thomas W. III: 105*, 150, 167, 175, 182, 188, 190, 204, 221-24, 228, 245, 276, 285, 290(2), 297, 321, 338, 439, 560; IV: 8, 21, 25, 29, 43, 76-77, 89, 114, 150, 165, 166, 177, 209, 210, 274, 317, 325, 365, 369; V: 154, 310, 326, 396
Grey, Sir Edward II: 551; IV: 439*
Grier, Mr. III: 661
Griffin, F. A. III: 440*
Griffin, Solomon B. I: 400*
Griffith, Mr. I: 45, 46
Grillparzer, Franz I: 14, 22
Grimes, John W. I: 566*, 569, 578
Grinstead, James F. II: 293
Grinstein, Hyman B. cited, III: 653
Grissom, D. H. II: 19*
Griswold, Erwin N. quoted, II: 299
Griswold, William E. S. II: 411*
Groesbeck, Glendenning B. I: 366*
Gross, Charles IV: 180*
Gross, Mrs. V: 289
Gross, Theodore L. cited, III: 17
Grossman, Louis III: 441*, 465

Grossman, William L. V: 569*
Groves, Harold V: 498
Grozier, Edwin A. I: 173*, 190, 305, 431, 434, 457, 458, 486, 501, 540, 566, 568, 571, 577; II: 79, 84, 143, 145, 241, 442, 482, 495, 501; III: 140
Gruening, Ernest V: 142*
Grundy, William I: 261*
Guaranty Trust & Co. IV: 337
Guggenheim, Daniel III: 514*, 622; IV: 148
Guggenheim, Ida III: 662
Guggenheims, the II: 307, 319, 323, 326, 338, 462, 468, 475, 493
Guild, Curtis Jr. I: 388*, 397, 401, 404, 410, 420, 423, 426, 432, 433, 434, 436, 438-39, 491, 513, 515, 526, 551, 571, 583-84, 587, 588, 590, 591, 593; II: 7, 8, 11-14, 19-20, 59, 71, 82, 110, 149, 154, 162, 197, 204; IV: 106

Guild, Edith: see Taussig, Edith
Gunther, John cited, V: 619-20
Gunton, Mrs. I: 473*
Guthrie, William D. V: 93*, 109, 144
Gwinn, William R. cited, II: 70

Haaglund, Joel E. III: 632*
Ha-Am, Ahad III: 303, 446, 541*, 578; V: 297
Habakkuk quoted, I: 71, 122
Haber, Samuel cited, I: 335; II: 391
Hadassah III: 300, 463-64, 470, 477, 488, 495, 526, 622, 667; IV: 115, 256, 269, 340, 346, 392, 427, 466, 493; V: 8, 82, 291, 347, 388, 407, 409, 422, 438, 444, 449, 451, 454, 465, 480, 547, 581, 608, 622, 645
Haddleston, John H. II: 397*
Hadley, Arthur T. I: 265*
Haganah III: 513, 520; V: 620, 622
Hagen, Johannes G. V: 140*
Hagerman, Frank IV: 28*
Hagerman-Riker combination II: 529
Hagerty, A. G. IV: 46*

Haifa Nautical School V: 626
Haifa Technical High School V: 626
Haifa Technicon III: 515
Haig, Robert M. V: 502*
Hailmann, William N. II: 365; V: 242*, 392; LDB on V: 242-43
Haines, Charles G. V: 129
Haines, Lynn III: 43*, 81
Halbert, Hugh T. II: 356*
Haldane, Richard B. IV: 540*
Haldeman-Julius, Emanuel V: 495*
Hale & Kilburn Manufacturing Co. II: 408
Hale, Clarence IV: 28*
Hale, Edward E. I: 50*, 66, 121
Hale, Matthew II: 526*; III: 229; IV: 150
Hale, Ralph T. III: 232*; V: 496, 503, 511
Hale, Richard W. I: 138*, 161; IV: 460; V: 354, 381, 515
Hale, Robert L. V: 199
Hale, William B. III: 30*
Halifax, Earl of V: 619
Hall, Alfred S. I: 297
Hall, Charles P. I: 398*, 399, 401, 432, 446, 452, 461, 479, 491, 509, 543, 553, 567, 568, 577, 588; II: 6, 77, 81, 90, 105, 153, 203; III: 245; IV: 89, 113, 120-23
Hall, George H. IV: 543
Hall, G. Stanley quoted, V: 243
Hall, Henry C. III: 195, 264*, 444; IV: 29, 145
Hall, Henry N. IV: 346*
Hall, Mrs. Charles P. V: 119
Hall, James P. cited, II: 421; IV: 264*
Hall, Prescott I: 314; III: 506*; IV: 122
Hall, Walter P. II: 73*, 142, 288
Halleck, Reuben P. II: 176*
Halperin, Samuel cited, V: 618
Halpern, Charles IV: 228*
Halprin, Rose IV: 115
Halvosa, Philip J. III: 355*

Hamilton, Alexander IV: 544; V: 302
Hamilton, Andy I: 411
Hamilton, Charles A. IV: 221*
Hamilton, Frederick W. II: 152
Hamilton, Walton H. V: 101*, 116, 118, 132, 154, 216, 296, 317, 325, 381, 396, 404, 421, 499, 511
Hamlin, Charles S. II: 295, 701; III: 47, 140, 148, 227, 241, 509; LDB on III: 47
Hamlin, Isaac V: 464*, 547, 590
Hammer v. Dagenhart I: 521; V: 53, 58
Hammond, Barbara V: 100, 216
Hammond, John L. V: 100, 216
Hammond, Mr. III: 172
Hammond, Mrs. I: 74
Hammond v. Farina Bus Line V: 312
Hammond v. Schappi Bus Line V: 312
Hampden Rrd III: 187, 190
Hampton, Benjamin B. II: 340*
Hampton's Magazine II: 340, 364, 376, 408, 410, 428, 476
Hand, Augustus N. IV: 558; V: 155*, 161, 191, 200, 204
Hand, B. Learned II: 654*; III: 467; IV: 27, 37, 372, 445, 459; V: 85, 155, 173, 251, 285, 322, 366, 379, 404
Handlin, Oscar cited, V: 77
Hanger, G. W. W. II: 519*
Hanna, Mark V: 131
Hannan, John J. II: 410*, 505; III: 237
Hansen, Elisha III: 467*
Hantke, Arthur M. III: 322*, 421, 486, 605, 623
Hapgood, Elizabeth IV: 293
Hapgood, Hutchins IV: 293
Hapgood, Norman I: 396*, 439, 445, 448, 453, 587; II: 130, 140, 210, 271, 290, 307, 319, 320, 321, 372, 379, 386, 408, 412, 424, 426, 428, 442, 451, 457, 461, 465, 481, 485, 486,

Hapgood, Norman I. (*continued*)
500, 547, 550, 578, *625, 633, 654,
655, 657, 663, 671, 672, 673, 683,*
685, 686, *694, 696,* 702, *704,* 706,
711, *712,* 714, 719, 720; III: *4, 20,*
31-32, 38, *43, 46, 47,* 51, 75, *104,*
110, *117, 125, 128, 137, 144, 146,*
169, *176, 183, 191, 195, 199, 205,*
211, 215, 223, *224,* 232-33, 243, *260,*
266, 303, 305, 306, *310, 384,* 392,
393, *436, 440, 451, 457, 493,* 539,
540, 542, 576, 597, 601, 618, *643,*
682; IV: 25, 27, 31, *32,* 43, 86, 91,
118, 127, 145, 169, 176, 182, 186,
190, 192, *210,* 264, 267, *292, 300,*
351, 487, 540; V: 11, 42, *55,* 76, 83,
127, *161,* 222, 232, 234, 305, 306,
310, 312, 482, 493, 496, *499, 503,*
509, 526, *555;* quoted, III: 304;
cited, II: 308, 314, 347; V: 77; LDB
on III: 243
Hapgood, Ruth III: 176; IV: 191,
267*, 293
Hapgood, William P. IV: 292*; V:
555
Hapsburg dynasty IV: 315
Harbaugh, William H. cited, IV:
259; V: 124
Hard, William II: 203*, 575, 577,
586; III: *217;* IV: *198, 226,* 350,
452, 561; V: 157, 569; cited IV:
523
Harding, Richard B. V: 565*
Harding, Warren G. III: 99; IV:
456, 470*, 474, 494, 519, 529, 532,
540, 544, 546, 547, 559, 561: V: 4,
11, 13, 32, 41, 62, 76, 80, 89, 91,
120, 123, 235, 238, 328, 352, 557;
LDB on IV: 470, 540; V: 89
Harding, Mrs. Warren G. V: 13
Hardison, Mr. II: 60
Hardison, Robert V: 34*
Hardy, Charles O. V: 248
Hardy, Frank O. I: 559; II: *246**
Harlan, James S. III: *107*, 140, *163,*
164, *165, 192,* 201, 237, 305, 331,
339, 381, 383, *385, 484, 502;* IV: 145

Harlan, John M. I: 47*; II: 683; V:
231
Harley, Herbert L. III: *166**
Harmon, Judson II: 648*
Harper, Fowler V. V: 625*
Harper, Robert N. II: 717*
Harper, Samuel N. III: 490*; IV: 4
Harper's Weekly II: 501, 705, 712;
III: 4, 31, 46, 49, 51, 75, 104, 117,
138, 144-47, 160, 165, 168-69, 176,
183-84, 189, 211, 216, 224, 230-31,
234, 239, 242, 273, 280, 285, 306,
393, 436, 458, 493, 540, 542-53, 577,
618, 643, 645; IV: 5, 119, 144, 168,
169, 182, 186, 191; V: 493
Harrigan, Mr. V: 205
Harriman, Edward H. II: 110*, 159,
164, 190, 251, 262, 266, 279, 417;
III: 207, 220, 267; IV: 58, 84, 358
Harriman, Florence J. H. III: 29*,
51
Harriman, H. R. II: 612, 618, 641
Harriman, Mrs. J. Borden III: 88,
119, 222, 236-37, 239
Harris, Albert H. III: 5*
Harris, Bernard V: 472
Harris, Robert O. III: 160*
Harrison Anti-Narcotic Act (1914)
V: 318-19
Harrison, Benjamin III: 304, 439;
IV: 167, 196, 207
Harrison, Francis B. II: 344*; IV:
130
Harrison, Leon III: 405*
Harrison, Pat V: 126
Harrison, W. B. V: 307
Hart, Albert B. I: 148*, 152, 156,
159
Hart, B. H. Liddell cited, IV: 417
Hart, Schaffner & Marx III: 260
Hart, Thomas N. I: 145*, 163, 167,
174, 185
Hartman, E. T. II: 672*
Hartman, Gustave III: 534*
Harvard Board of Overseers I: 88;
IV: 558
Harvard College and Law School I:

6-13, 41, 46, 65, 69-71, 84-90, 92, 97, 113-17; II: 299, 657, 712; III: 13, 18, 135, 209, 240, 288; IV: 68, 107, 118, 128, 134, 141, 142, 216, 224, 268, 271, 339, 395-96, 399, 400, 452, 459, 463, 558, 564; V: 11, 30, 43-44, 48, 50, 78, 80, 94, 98, 109, 142, 143, 146, 155, 195, 196, 201, 225, 243-46, 256, 273, 276, 278, 288, 320-24, 327, 334, 375, 386, 656; LDB on I: 6, 89; V: 142-44, 146-47, 156, 276
"The Harvard Law School" (1889) I: 8, 90
Harvard Law School, LDB's student days at I: 5-25; IV: 45, 107-108, 224-25
Harvard Law School, LDB's relations with after graduation I: 64-65, 69-71, 84-89, 92-93, 105-106, 113-17; II: 712; III: 13, 18-19, 134-36, 209, 240, 288; IV: 134, 142, 339, 395-96, 400-401, 459, 463-64, 558-59, 564; V: 11, 43-44, 50-51, 78, 80-81, 90, 109-10, 142-44, 146-47, 155-56, 159, 187, 191, 195-97, 243-44, 248, 276, 278, 288, 320, 327-34, 355-56, 394, 411, 656-57
Harvard Ethical Society I: 321, 326, 333, 338
Harvard Lampoon IV: 450
Harvard Law Review III: 13; IV: 33-34, 230, 330, 558; V: 43, 94, 129, 204, 225, 226, 235, 277, 306, 315, 424, 499
Harvard Law School Association I: 69; II: 353, 712
Harvard Law Society III: 503
Harvard Menorah Society III: 340, 357, 398; IV: 180
Harvard Studies in Administrative Law V: 285
Harvard Zionist Club III: 332, 381, 427-28, 460; IV: 81
Harvester trust case III: 171
Harvey, George II: 635
Hashomar III: 511

Hashomer Hatzair V: 618, 638
Haskins, Henry S. III: 419*
Hast, Louis H. I: 15; V: 223*; LDB on V: 223
Hastings, Daniel O. V: 582*
Hastings, Paul III: 383
Hatfield, Charles E. I: 536*
Hauser, Mr. IV: 275
Haven, Franklin I: 144
Haven, George I: 79*
Haverhill [Massachusetts] gas case IV: 121
Hawkins, William W. II: 333*
Hawley, Ellis W. cited, IV: 476; V: 538
Hawley v. Walker II: 543; III: 237
Hay, John I: 147, 335*; II: 304; IV: 207; V: 273
Hayes, Alfred III: 633
Hayes, Rutherford B. I: 12-13
Hayes, William P. I: 544, 556; III: 154*
Hays, Charles M. II: 628*
Hays, Samuel P. cited, II: 308
Hays, William H. IV: 561*; V: 41, 327
Hays, Judge William H. V: 231
Hayward, Fred P. IV: 94*
Hayward, William III: 518*
Haywood, William ("Big Bill") III: 633
Head, James M. II: 245*; IV: 171
Head, William O. II: 293
Hearst, William R. II: 113; III: 3*, 53, 222
Hearst's International Magazine V: 42
Heaton, James P. II: 646, 650
Heaton Peninsular Co. v. Eureka Specialty Co. I: 431
Heber, Reginald quoted, V: 22
Hebrew Institute (Chicago) IV: 20
Hebrew Press Association III: 586
Hebrew Sheltering and Immigrant Aid Society IV: 237
Hebrew Trades Association IV: 304; V: 463

Hebrew University IV: 340-42, 346-47, 351, 356, 380, 434, 438, 440, 537, 554-56; V: 36, 38, 182, 220, 253, 388, 438, 462, 522, 563

Hecht, Jacob I: 60*, 78

Hecht, Mrs. Jacob II: 47

Hedera V: 463

Hegeman, John R. I: 494*

Hegman, Yetti V: 305

Heilborn, Walter S. I: 404*

Heine, Heinrich quoted, V: 205

Heineman, Charles III: 524*

Heller, Bernard III: 602*; IV: 269

Heller, Isaac S. V: 597*

Heller, James G. III: 637*

Heller, Maximillian III: 314*, 359, 430, 439, 636; IV: 349; V: 343

Heller, Mrs. Maximillian III: 636

Hely-Hutchinson, Maurice R. III: 343*

Hemenway, Augustus I: 81*

Hemenway, Alfred I: 339*

Hemenway Gymnasium I: 65

Hemphill v. Orloff V: 331

Henderson, Charles R. I: 526*

Henderson, Florence I: 508

Henderson, Gerard C. II: 538*

Henderson, Mary V: 34

Hendrick, Burton J. II: 635; cited, I: 392; II: 214

Hendricks, Francis I: 336*, 341

Heney, Francis J. I: 475; II: 293*, 295, 435, 438, 455, 642, 669, 684; III: 33, 222; IV: 55

Henle, James V: 418*, 504

Henry, Alice III: 26*

Henry, John S. I: 9*

Henry Segal Co. II: 202

Henry v. A. B. Dick Co. II: 615

Hepburn Act II: 200

Hepburn, William P. II: 99, 103*, 111, 124

Hercules V: 89

Hermann, Henry I: 7

Hermann, Mr. III: 332

Herodotus quoted, V: 294

Herrick, Robert F. I: 479; II: 430*

Hertzberg, Arthur cited, III: 23

Herzegovina II: 210

Herzl, Theodore II: 659; III: 155*, 293, 296, 303, 327-29, 374, 404, 519, 523, 527, 530, 541, 564, 650, 662, 680; IV: 6, 11, 14, 103, 136, 139, 167, 196, 253, 285, 295, 361, 389, 449, 452, 525; V: 39, 219, 300, 312, 408, 429, 492

Herzliya High School IV: 194, 391

Hexter, Maurice B. V: 438*, 440, 452, 461, 465, 467, 472, 476, 481, 516

Hibbard, Caroline I. III: 48*

Hibbard, George A. II: 54*, 58, 60

Hickman, Mr. I: 76

Higgins, Alice L. I: 482*

Higgins, Francis W. I: 340*

Higgins, Henry B. V: 141, 286*

Higgins, James H. I: 484*

Higgins, John J. I: 443, 578*; II: 106, 117, 280

Higgins, Martin P. I: 250-5

Higgins, Milton P. I: 559*

Higgins, William E. III: 166*

Higginson, Francis L. I: 131*, 141-45, 183, 500

Higginson, Henry L. I: 131*, 163, 309, 408; II: 113; III: 38, 143-44

Higginson Over-the-counter bill I: 533, 558, 563

Higham, John cited, III: 389

higher education, LDB on V: 153-54, 215-216

Hilberg, Raul cited, V: 517

Hildreth, Horace E. II: 628*

Hill, Arthur D. V: 306*

Hill, Isaac V: 327*

Hill, James J. I: 554*; III: 49

Hill, Joe III: 632*

Hill, Josiah F. II: 125, 160, 168, 183

Hill, Louis W. III: 49*

Hill, William H. I: 56*

Hill, W. S. V: 331

Hillenkamp, Frank IV: 35

Hilliard, J. S. & Son I: 573

Hillman, Sidney IV: 561*; V: 184, 216

Hillquit, Morris II: 484*, 569, 571, 572; III: 562, 617

Hillstrom, Joseph: see Hill, Joe

Hindman, Bisco I: 475*

Hines, Walker D. III: 502*; V: 220

Hinkley, John I: 338*

Hirchbuft, Mr. I: 3

Hirsch, Emil G. III: 315*, 368, 405, 439, 645

Hirsch, Maurice III: 499

Hirschman, Rabbi III: 648

Hirst, David cited, II: 635

Hirst, Francis W. IV: 424*; V: 209

Hiss, Alger V: 415*

Hiss, Priscilla H. V: 416

Histradrut V: 439, 464, 473, 507, 510

Hitchcock, Charles C. II: 10*, 226

Hitchcock, Gilbert M. II: 622

Hitchcock, William H. V: 171*

Hitler, Adolf IV: 159, 277, 537; V: 437, 507, 516*, 525, 554, 582, 599, 602, 608, 620, 624, 637, 646, 560, 651

Hitler and Nazism, LDB and V: 516-17, 520-21, 524-26, 531-33, 541, 553-54, 562, 599, 602, 605-608, 614-16, 619-20, 627-28, 638, 646

Hitts, William IV: 171

Hitz, William V: 310*, 326, 366

Hoar, Roger S. II: 421*

Hobbs, Franklin W. IV: 99*

Hobbs, William J. III: 177*

Hobson, John A. IV: 423*; V: 142

Hodder, Mrs. V: 6

Hodge, Mrs. I: 112

Hodges, Henry G. III: 390*

Hoffman, Frederick L. II: 284*; III: 228

Hofstadter, Richard cited, I: 322; V: 84, 505

Holbrook, F. S. II: 116*, 123, 127

Holcombe, Arthur N. II: 576*, 670, 699; V: 381

Holcombe, John M. I: 380*, 390, 438

Holden, Joseph W. II: 273*

holding companies, LDB on II: 602-603

Holland I: 68

Hollis, Allen II: 630*; III: 246

Hollis, Henry F. III: 123*, 130, 206, 273, 347; IV: 46, 196

Hollman, A. H. V: 513

Holman, William A. IV: 309*

Holmes, Fanny D. V: 377, 380

Holmes, John H. I: 333*; II: 535, 704*; V: 210

Holmes, Oliver W. Sr. I: 24

Holmes, Oliver W. Jr. I: 34, 45*, 47-49, 60, 65, 105, 137, 206, 207; II: 78, 124, 504, 683; III: 64, 121, 176, 209, 223, 262, 373, IV: 58, 75, 109, 165, 210-11, 215, 300, 330, 367, 370, 373, 386, 390(2), 444, 449-51, 454, 455, 458, 463, 475, 495, 516-17, 521, 540, 542, 550-51, 559, 561; V: 17, 42, 47, 48, 49-50, 56, 72-73, 78, 79, 83-89, 93-95, 102, 106, 118-20, 121, 123, 127, 131-32, 154, 172, 173, 175, 181-84, 189, 204, 208-209, 212, 229, 238-39, 245, 259, 274, 275-76, 279, 282, 284, 288, 295, 299, 310, 316-21, 325, 333-35, 346, 353, 359, 364, 373, 377-79, 411-18, 483, 493, 496-97, 499, 500, 504-505, 511, 513, 518, 533, 544, 553; LDB on III: 176; IV: 450; V: 17, 49, 50, 73, 83, 102, 123, 131, 172-73, 183-84, 204, 209, 212, 275, 310, 321, 325, 333, 364, 373, 377-79, 413, 496-97, 544

Holmes v. Old Colony Rrd Co. I: 76

Holt, Charles S. IV: 21*

Holt, Hamilton I: 495*, 499; II: 271, 570-71, 572, 699, 708; III: 393, 402, 543; IV: 221; cited, I: 123

Holzman, Mr. V: 431

Homans, Robert I: 179, 223; II: 644*, 647; III: 79

Home Building & Loan Association v. Blaisdell III: 36

Home Market Club II: 67

Homestead strike I: 83

honorary degrees, LDB on V: 421, 563-64

Hoofien, Eliezer S. IV: 146*, 381

Hooker, Helene M. cited, II: 309

Hooker, Nancy cited V: 526

Hoover, Herbert III: 368, 401, 601; IV: 276, 300*, 308, 314, 317, 330, 366, 387, 406, 421, 444, 448, 456, 470, 512, 527, 529, 532, 536, 539, 546, 551, 557-58; V: 4, 10, 13, 22, 62, 75, 77, 95, 111, 124, 151, 154, 171, 199, 200, 222, 230, 237, 270, 344, 352, 354-55, 361-75, 378-82, 391, 411, 414-15, 496-98, 512, 557, 593; LDB on IV: 300, 308, 448, 536, 539-40, 557; V: 10, 22, 75, 373, 415, 512

Hopedale Mutual Benefit Association I: 477

Hope-Simpson Commission V: 456, 460, 466, 479

Hope-Simpson, Sir John V: 460*, 467, 469, 474, 486

Hopkins, Harry L. V: 536*, 548

Hopkins, Mary D. IV: 398

Hopkinson, Mr. IV: 511

Horace Dutton et al. v. Dickinson Paper Co. IV: 67

Hormel, Herman II: 58*

Horner, Harlan H. V: 640*

Horning v. District of Columbia IV: 516

Horseshoe Nail Co. II: 321

Horst, Sir Hugo V: 521

Host, Zeno M. I: 462*, 580

Hotchkiss, Willard E. cited, I: 296

Hough, Charles M. V: 131*, 155, 174, 280

Hough, Warwick I: 542*

Houghteling, James L. IV: 293*

Houghton, Alanson B. V: 154*, 213

Houghton, Miss I: 146

"Hours of Labor" (1906) I: 391, 397

hours of labor, LDB on I: 513; II: 78, 296-98, 359-60; III: 545

Hourvitch, Samuel H. III: 458

Hourwich, Isaac A. III: 81*, 105, 228

House, Edward M. III: 38, 77, 106*, 154, 237, 338, *393*, 610, 621; IV: *264*, 281, 301, 303, *311*, 313, 316, 319, *332*, 335, 338, *373*, 406, 421, 430, 470; LDB on IV: 470

House, Loulie H. IV: 406*

House of Truth III: 261

Houseman, Arthur A. III: 623

Houser, Walter L. II: 505*, *526*, *528*, 539, 573

Houston, David F. III: 619*; IV: 326, 521

Houston, Herbert S. III: *89*, 489

Hovey, Carl III: *199**

Hovey, Richard B. cited, II: 674

"How Boston Solved the Gas Problem" (1907) I: 253, 294, 397; II: 24, 579; III: 69, 166, 233, 259, 375; IV: 120; V: 504-505

"How Europe Deals with the One-Price Goods" (1913) III: 125

Howard, Barker B. I: 537*

Howard, Clarence H. V: *334**

Howard, Frederick B. I: 524*

Howard, Fred L. II: 85*

Howard, James B. I: 57*; IV: *107*

Howard, James R. IV: 521*

Howard, Jeremiah III: 442*

Howard, Roy W. II: 442

Howard, Sidney C. IV: 510*

Howe, Frederic C. I: 475; II: *403**, *406*, 414, 432, *544*, 574

Howe, Louis M. IV: 475

Howe, Mark D. V: *544;* cited, I: 46, 65, 106; IV: 390

Howell, Clark II: 701*

Howells, William D. III: 229

Howland, Charles P. V: 157*, 241, 243, 259

Howland, Willard I: 536*, 552

Howlitt, A. J. II: *418**

Hoyt, Henry M. II: 314, 317*

Hubbard, Adolph IV: 290*, 291

Hubbard, Charles W. I: 536*, 589; II: 9, 114

Hubbard, Preston J. cited, V: 171
Hubbert, C. H. II: *529**
Huddell, Arthur M. II: 59, 66*, 67, 126
Hudson, Manley O. IV: *539**; V: 75, 94-95, 129, 154, 197
Huebsch, Benjamin W. V: *548**
Huerta, Victoriano IV: 187
Hughes, Charles E. I: 276, *320**, 363, 399, 475, 481, 486; II: 68, 191, 286, 616, 684; IV: 215, 233, 266, 330, 445, 456, 546; V: 32-33, 58, 89, 110, 122, 126, 154, 168, 210, 239, 272, 275, 321, 324, 362, 366, 499, 511, 552, 588, *611*, 653; LDB on II: 68-69; V: 32-34, 321, 366
Hughes, James J. I: 226
Hugo, George B. I: *576**
Huies, Mr. III: 334
Huling v. Kaw Valley Railway II: 254
Hull [Massachusetts] *Beacon* IV: 88
Hull, Cordell V: *525**, 576, 617, 619, 630
Hull, G. G. III: 229
Hull, Roger B. III: *242**
Human Engineering II: 586, 590, 674
Human Life II: 453
Humphrey, Alexander P. II: 289*, 291; IV: 297; V: 175
Humphrey's Executor v. U.S. V: 239
Hungerford, Edward cited, II: 501
Hunneman, William C. I: *274**; II: 81
Hunnewell, Walter II: *276**
Hunt, William M. I: *20**
Hunt, W. Preston II: *139**
Hunt, Sidney V: 522
Hunter, Robertson G. II: 22*, *60*, 192, 195, 201, *203*, *205*, 212, *214*, *219*, *224*, 226, *228*, 241, *283*, *285*, 301
Hunter v. Louisiana V: 316
Hurley, Edward N. III: 394*, *680*, 682; IV: *35*

Hurst, J. Willard V: 588, 589*; cited, I: 322
Hurtado v. California II: 610
Hurwitz, Henry III: 193, 296*, 299, *314*, *332*, 460, *505*, 555; IV: *8*, *462*; V: *630*, 634, *649*, *650*; LDB on V: 635
Hussein, Abdullah Ibn V: 401, *506**
Husting, Paul O. IV: *213**
Hustin, James H. III: *385**
Hutcheson, Mr. V: 382, 386
Hutchins F. Lincoln III: *142**, *202*
Hutchins, Robert M. V: 285, *378**
Hutchinson, William T. cited, IV: 456
Huxley, Mr. I: 427
Hyams, Godfrey M. IV: *49**
Hyamson, Albert M. IV: 307; V: *594**
Hyde, James H. I: *341**
Hyde Park Gazette IV: 88
Hyman, Harold M. cited, V: 239
Hyman, Joseph C. V: 456*, 471, 472

Ickes, Harold L. V: 52, *518**, 556, 641, 653; cited, II: 308; LDB on V: 641
Idlesohn, Abraham Z. IV: *513**
"An Illegal Trust Legalized" (1911) II: 504, 521
Illinois II: 207
Illinois & St. Louis Rrd I: 32
Illinois Central Rrd II: 111, 159, 190, 318; IV: 84; V: 229
Illinois Law Review V: 283
Illinois Ten-Hour case: see *Ritchie v. Wayman*
Illinois Zionist Bureau III: 647
immigration restriction, LDB on III: 389, 506-507; IV: 100, 272
"The Incorporation of Trades Unions" (1903) I: 232-33, 236, 244
incorporation of trades unions, LDB on I: 232-33; V: 56-58
The Independent II: 201, 669, 708; III: 543; IV: 6, 168-69, 221

Independent Order of B'rith Abraham III: 435-38, 531, 572-74, 606, 624, 255-56

Independent Order of B'rith Sholem III: 531, 572, 606, 624

Independent Order, Sons of Israel III: 572

India V: 33, 34, 42, 458

Indiana II: 207, 703; IV: 494; V: 557

Indiana State Democratic Committee IV: 494

Indianapolis Sun II: 343, 383, 386

industrial accidents and insurance, LDB on II: 319, 359-60, 377, 566-67

Industrial Commission: see U.S. Industrial Commission

industrial democracy, LDB on I: 247, 447; II: 548-49, 566-67, 587, 588-90, 630, 675, 707-708, 711; III: 97, 210, 216, 218-21; V: 45-46

Industrial Insurance Committee (Wisconsin) II: 359

Industrial League I: 236-38, 286, 326, 366-69, 499; II: 46, 252

Industrial Relations Committee III: 407

Industrial Welfare Commission (Oregon) III: 364

"The Inefficiency of the Oligarchs" (1913) III: 183, 284, 344

Ingersoll, Charles H. III: 489*

Ingersoll, Ruth III: 111

Ingersoll v. Coram II: 67

Ingersoll, William H. III: 26*, 96, 105, 118, 120, 121, 126, 138, 144, 173, 196, 217, 225, 434, 446, 467, 490

Inner Actions Comite III: 322, 333, 394, 470, 510, 569, 588, 589, 627

Innes, Harry V: 231

In re Greene I: 431

Insular cases I: 156

insurance, LDB on I: 342-43, 351, 362-64, 381-84, 445, 448-49, 480-84, 508, 540-41, 546; II: 222, 433-34,

590; III: 8; V: 68, 375-76, 393-94, 601

Insurance Co. v. Mosely I: 11

Interborough Co. I: 264

Intercollegiate Socialist Society (Cornell) II: 550

Intercollegiate Zionist Association III: 357, 370, 460, 659; IV: 246, 248, 280, 341

interlocking directorates, LDB on III: 49, 79-80, 243, 247

"Interlocking Directorates" (1913) III: 183, 310; V: 534-36; see also "The Endless Chain"

International Association of Machinists IV: 521

International Brotherhood of Electrical Workers I: 360

International Harvester Co. II: 289; III: 51, 171, 232, 601

International Institute of Agriculture V: 214

International Jewish Emancipation Committee III: 535, 538

International Ladies Garment Workers' Union II: 367, 371-72, 386-87, 407, 483-85, 497, 500, 503; III: 81, 212; IV: 10, 26-27; V: 166

International Shoe Co. IV: 89

International Socialist Review III: 98

International Tailoring Co. V: 184

International Typographical Union I: 250, 286

International Workers of the World II: 562, 568, 588, 638, 651; III: 87-88, 98, 104, 633

International Zionist Organization III: 294; IV: 469, 479, 481-82, 485

Interstate Commerce Commission II: 31, 39-40, 51, 68, 123, 199, 200, 306-307, 327, 370-74, 377, 381-84, 387, 393, 395, 397, 412-13, 496, 514, 534, 543, 565, 584, 625, 631, 636, 644, 663, 675, 683, 698, 700, 720, 725; III: 21-25, 39-42, 47, 50, 54-55, 66, 70-73, 76, 78, 82-83, 96, 107, 110-11,

124, 130, 134, 136, 140-43, 149, 162-65, 177-81, 188, 192, 194, 196, 207, 218, 223, 228, 235-36, 241, 244-46, 263, 266, 280, 284, 287, 295, 305, 320-21, 330-31, 334, 342-43, 346, 380, 383-84, 387, 400, 444, 502; IV: 29, 46-47, 140, 145, 258, 294; V: 74-76, 88, 98, 101, 118, 132, 215, 238, 266, 272, 326, 381, 414, 514

Interstate Commerce Commission v. U.S. ex rel *Members of the Waste Merchants Association of N.Y.* V: 75-76

investments, LDB on I: 262-63; IV: 241-42; V: 412, 528-29

Iowa II: 207, 710; V: 203, 206

Ireland IV: 561; V: 49

Irgun V: 622

Irving, Sir Henry I: 66*

Irvings, the IV: 266

Isaacs, Rufus D.: see Reading, Lord

"Is the Closed Shop Illegal and Criminal?" (1904) I: 259

Israel Alliance Universalle III: 404

Italy I: 371; II: 9, 215, 284; IV: 289, 311; V: 6-7, 213, 614

Itleson, Henry V: 615*

Ives, David O. II: 299*, 306, 370, 564, 622, 625, 636, 644, 718; III: 21, 194-96, 201, 207, 218, 223, 237, 245, 287; LDB on III: 194-95

Ives, Mrs. David O. V: 7

Ives v. South Buffalo Rrd Co. II: 421, 427

Jabotinsky, Vladimir Y. III: 520*, 558, 630; IV: 420; V: 408, 437, 492, 551

Jackman, Mr. II: 22*

Jackson, Andrew V: 328

Jackson, Edith B. V: 313*

Jackson, Gardner V: 312*, 354, 637

Jackson, James F. I: 202*, 347, 413, 415, 444, 454; II: 24, 36, 38, 141, 156, 260, 306

Jackson, Robert V: 405

Jackson, W. B. I: 591; II: 11*

Jacobs, Rose G. V: 9, 607*, 609, 619-22

Jacobson, Blanche IV: 400*

Jacobson, Jeanette III: 406

Jacobson, Victor III: 353*, 422-25, 496; IV: 232, 236, 247, 359, 386, 437

Jacobstein, Meyer IV: 7*

Jaffa IV: 83, 235, 246, 280, 288, 556

Jamaica Plain Citizens' Association I: 385-86

James, Henry Jr. cited, I: 111

James, Ollie M. II: 333*, 371; IV: 150, 297

James, Thomas N. II: 453*

James, William III: 226, 412*; V: 327

Jameson, J. Franklin V: 325

January, Joe II: 662

January, Josephine P. II: 287

Japan I: 355-56, 358; II: 21; III: 96; IV: 560; V: 32-34, 533

Jastrow, Joseph V: 384*

Jastrow, Morris Jr. IV: 362*

Jay, Pierre I: 452*, 456, 461; II: 25, 38, 60, 79, 82, 205, 215, 221, 229; LDB on II: 79-80

J. B. Speed Memorial Museum V: 161-62, 164, 212, 304, 550, 551, 649

Jean: see Tachau, Jean B.

Jefferson, Thomas V: 209, 221, 301-303, 315, 411, 520, 648; quoted, II: 224; LDB on 302, 411

Jeffris, Malcolm G. IV: 257*

Jellenik v. Huron Copper Mining Co. II: 253

Jellinek, Edward L. IV: 28*

Jenkins, George I: 528

Jenkins, John J. I: 283*

Jenney, Charles F. I: 522*, 560

Jennie: see Brandeis, Jennie T.

Jerome, William T. I: 374*, 378

Jerusalem IV: 235, 329, 399, 417, 432, 456; V: 579, 591

Jerusalem Hospital V: 388, 438-39

Jessel, Sir George I: 107*

Jewish Agency IV: 323, 509; V: 109, 115-18, 196, 259, 336-384, 388, 391, 430-31, 440, 444, 446, 460, 470, 472-73, 479, 486, 490, 507, 514, 568, 583, 604, 616, 622, 633

Jewish Agricultural Experiment Station II: 537

Jewish Colonial Trust III: 313, 329, 356, 477, 589; IV: 13-14, 146, 194, 337, 347, 350-51, 355, 379, 478, 493

Jewish Colonization Association III: 498

Jewish Committee at Constantinople III: 605

Jewish Daily Bulletin V: 411, 447, 513-14, 545

Jewish Daily News III: *630*

Jewish fraternities, LDB on IV: 496-97

Jewish Frontier V: 628

Jewish Labour Organization V: 448

Jewish National Fund III: 317, 325, 328, 356, 365, 452, 461, 476-77, 501, 515, 517, 519, 551, 667, 672; IV: 14, 159, 217, 240, 380, 434-35; V: 39, 442, 484, 547, 558, 576, 645

Jewish National Labor Alliance III: 588

"The Jewish Problem—How to Solve It" (1915) III: 455, 526, 531, 543, 591, 600, 637-38; IV: 6, 103, 303, 369, 385; V: 119, 534

Jewish Publication Society IV: 115, 245

"Jewish Rights and the Congress" (1916) IV: 12, 103, 303; V: 534-35

Jewish Social Studies V: 650

Jewish Telegraphic Agency V: 568, 618

"Jewish Unity and the Congress" (1915) III: 675; IV: 21, 103

Jewish Weekly III: 644

Joffe, Mr. V: 5

Joffe, Judah A. III: 644*

John Hancock Life Insurance Co. I: 494, 541, 558; II: 591; IV: 94; V: 497, 561

Johns Hopkins University V: 237

Johnson, Alvin S. II: *421**, 535; III: 208; IV: 266; V: 206, 285, 555; cited, IV: 399; V: 286

Johnson, Henry M. II: *369**, *378*

Johnson, Herbert S. II: 152

Johnson, Hiram W. II: 683*; III: 222; IV: 266, 456, 530; V: 211

Johnson, Hugh S. V: 526*

Johnson, John I: 398

Johnson, J. F. III: 118*

Johnson, Lewis J. II: 404*, 406

Johnson, Tom L. II: 292*; IV: 528

Johnston, Sir Harry H. III: 305*

Joint Board of Arbitration (New York garment industry) II: 369, 372, 382, 391, 417, 484, 503, 518

Joint Board of Cloak & Shirt Makers' Unions II: 366

Joint Board of Sanitary Control (New York garment industry) II: 369, 392, 483, 487, 489, 500, 508; III: 73-74, 212

Joint Distribution Committee III: 316, 414, 439, 446, 481, 574, 586; IV: 132, 146, 154-60, 205, 212-13, 253, 351, 387-91, 424, 439, 469, 565; V: 18, 20, 109, 112, 220, 471, 597

Jonas, Ralph V: 626*

Jones, Arthur R. I: *544*

Jones, Charles H. I: *424**, 479, 490, 528, *545;* II: *68*, 81, 86, 97, 98, 105, 114, *130*, 133, 136, 137, 181, *183*, 205, 275, *286*, 289, 429, *545*, 553, 622; III: *132*, 246; V: 89, 332; LDB on II: 627

Jones, George I: *186*, 187, 192, *193*, *194*, 536

Jones, Horace T. II: 311, 338, 401

Jones, Jerome I: *139**, 160, 593; II: 156

Jones, Leonard A. I: *321**; V: 73

Jones, Myrta L. II: *487**

Jones, Thomas D. III: *51**

Jones, Willard N. V: 311

Jordan, Daniel P. cited, V: 10

Jose, Ernest P. III: *6**

Joseph IV: 548
Joseph, Bernard (Dov) V: 419*, 595
Joseph, Samuel III: 304
Joseph, Sarah S. IV: 39
Josephine: see Goldmark, Josephine C.
Josephson, Hannah cited, V: 77
Josephson, Matthew cited, IV: 562; V: 77
Jouett, Edward S. V: 263*, 308
Jouett, John V: 301*
Journal of Commerce V: 212
Journal of Political Economy II: 484
Jowett, Benjamin V: 541
Joy, Henry B. III: 93*, 111, 112-13, 119, 131, 188, 197, 243
Joy Steamship Line II: 126, 131, 168, 621
Joyce, Mr. II: 126, 148
J. T. Connor Co. II: 549
Judaism and Jewry, LDB on I: 386; III: 399, 534-35, 625-27; IV: 356, 468; V: 182, 297, 545, 574
judiciary, LDB on II: 375, 421-27, 509-10, 603-11, 646-47, 655-56; III: 109, 181, 242, 281, 378-79, 632-33; IV: 272; V: 83, 227-28, 324-25, 326, 367-68, 371, 403-404, 501
Jurisdictional Act (1925) V: 160, 167, 272, 306
Jusserand, Jean A. A. J. III: 341*, 360
juvenile offenders, LDB on III: 36-37

Kadimah III: 456
Kaempfer IV: 98
Kahn, Julius IV: 388*; V: 472
Kalifa Eli V: 545
Kallen, Horace M. III: 226*, 296, 314, 405, 415, 426, 427, 439, 441, 459, 530, 541, 551, 555, 598, 603, 614, 620, 646, 664; IV: 7, 9, 10, 83, 245, 280, 329, 563; V: 8, 31, 275, 352
Kallen, Jacob D. IV: 329*
Kallen, Miss V: 8, 31

Kaneko, Kentaro II: 21*
Kanev, Y. cited, V: 439
Kann, Jacobus H. III: 326*, 356, 589; IV: 13, 138, 146, 381 423-24
Kansas II: 710; IV: 543
Kansas City IV: 310
Kansas City Knife & Fork Club II: 546
Kanter, Alexander III: 357*, 616; IV: 330
Kaplan, Eliezer V: 644*, 645
Kaplan, Jacob H. IV: 3*, 6, 40
Kaplan, Jacob J. V: 597*
Kaplan J. M. V: 582
Kaplan, Nathan D. III: 313*, 314, 323, 371, 376, 407, 461, 474, 576, 599, 603, 614, 619-20, 642, 647, 658, 666, 667; V: 314, 423, 427, 435, 460, 473, 495
Kaplan, Walter III: 332
Kaplansky, Shelomoh III: 326*, 356, 452, 476
Katz, Irving cited, I: 132
Katz, Wilber G. V: 372, 386*, 394
Katzenselsohn, Nissan III: 356*
Kaufmann, Edmund I. V: 572*, 643, 645
Kaufmann, S. Walter IV: 512
Kazmann, Boris III: 456*; V: 423; LDB on V: 423
Kean, John II: 320*
Keating, Edward V: 155*, 161, 266, 355
Keeler, Mr. II: 33, 53
Keeley, James II: 508*; III: 200
Keene, Sidney B. II: 281*
Keener, William A. I: 21*
Keep, Charles A. II: 129*
Keep Commission II: 129
Kehew, Mary B. I: 151, 178
Kehillah (New York) III: 193, 430, 651; IV: 204-205
Kehler, James H. IV: 276
Keith, Benjamin F. I: 143*, 176, 177, 182, 183, 209, 229, 271
Keith, Eben S. I: 576*
Keith, George E. Co. IV: 89

Keith, Preston B. I: 525*; IV: 89

Keith-Roach, Edward V: 455*

Kelley, Charles E. IV: 86*, 91

Kelley, Florence II: 78*, 249, 395, 535; III: 228; IV: 119, 171; V: 53, 77, 166, 167

Kelley, Mr. V: 399

Kelley, Thomas A. IV: 113-14

Kellogg, Arthur P. II: 269*, 535; IV: 320

Kellogg Corn Flakes Co. case III: 96

Kellogg, Frank B. IV: 358*; V: 76, 154, 250, 270, 277, 281

Kellogg, Paul U. II: 267*, 272, 522, 530, 535, 578, 636-37, 651, 704; III: 407, 432, 433; IV: 255, 342, 461, 462, 464, 497; V: 133, 329, 408, 569; cited, II: 237

Kellogg, Vernon L. IV: 512; V: 79, 222; cited, IV: 301

Kellor, Frances A. III: 676*

Kelly, William J. IV: 27*, 57-59, 65, 74

Kelsen, Hans V: 577*

Kendall, Amos V: 327*

Kendrick, Mr. II: 36, 239

Keneseth Israel (Philadalphia) III: 388, 395

Kennedy, Andrew II: 312

Kennedy, Joseph P. V: 606*

Kent, Raymond A. V: 269, 392*, 405, 466, 502, 564, 592, 595, 605, 640, 648; LDB on V: 640

Kent, William II: 713*, 725; III: 8, 21, 32, 222, 308; IV: 25

Kentucky I: 263, 276, 356, 371, 581; III: 231; V: 10, 145, 163, 177, 208, 231, 264-65, 282, 308, 648

Kentucky tax cases IV: 297

Kenyon, William S. II: 452*, 622; IV: 92; V: 373, 384, 386

Keppel, Frederick P. IV: 371*

Kerby, Frederick M. II: 327*, 334, 337, 371, 476, 488; IV: 130; V: 122

Keren Hayesod III: 327-28; IV: 481, 491, 494, 508, 531, 534, 550, 556, 563, 566; V: 25, 39, 82, 480, 633

Keren Kayemet le-Yisroel: see Jewish National Fund

Kerensky, Alexander IV: 277

Kern, John W. II: 385

Kernwood Country Club III: 501

Kerr, Charles V: 214*, 220

Kerr, Philip H. V: 141, 632*

Kesselman, Robert D. III: 563*, 667, 668; IV: 12, 16, 18, 166, 188, 193, 216, 244, 261, 287, 384, 389, 467; V: 148, 313, 407, 409, 419, 426, 432, 473, 495, 509, 613

Kesselman, Mrs. Robert V: 407

Keynes, John M. V: 118*, 186, 192, 193; cited, IV: 387

Kidder, Clarence P. V: 339*

Kidder, Peabody & Co. III: 269

Kiefer, Daniel III: 132*

Kiefer, Jennie G. IV: 237*

Kiel, Henry W. V: 5

Kimball, Harry W. V: 341*, 342

King, Bolton I: 371

King, Clyde L. IV: 301*

King-Crane mission IV: 381, 397

King George V IV: 403

King, Henry IV: 397

King, Mr. V: 321

King, Stanley IV: 395*, 456

Kinglake, Alexander W. I: 3

Kingsley, Charles I: 104

Kingsley, Darwin P. II: 76*

Kipling Rudyard, I: 104; V: 657

Kirchwey George W. II: 636*; III: 288, 562; V: 504

Kirsh, Benjamin S. V: 49*

Kirstein, Louis E. III: 363*, 365, 501, 586, 668; IV: 206, 280, 287, 291-92, 303, 307, 312, 327, 444, 519; V: 339, 386, 415, 422

Kisch, Frederick H. V: 445*

Klap, A. Moses V: 449

Klein, Jacob I: 542*

Kligler, Israel J. V: 19*, 463, 623; LDB on V: 19

Kling, Simcha cited, III: 23, 487

Klutznik, Philip M. V: 645

Knaebel, Ernest V: 414*

Knapp, Ella A. III: *32*
Knapp, George L. V: 387*
Knauth, Nachad & Kuhne IV: 161
Kneeland, F. J. I: *253*
Knefler, Mrs. Dan II: 318
Knesseth Israel V: 480
Knifler, Mrs. I: 3
Knight-Brady bill (New York) IV: 541
Knight, F. & Son I: 573
Knights of Labor I: 553; IV: 21, 54
Knights of Zion III: 314, 462, 526-28, 599, 614-15, 619-20, 647, 658-59; IV: 9, 195, 219
Knights Templars I: 328
Knoeppel, Charles E. III: *107*
Knollenberg, Bernhard IV: 480*
Knotts, Richard W. II: 290*
Knowles, Morris IV: 255*
Kocourek, Albert V: 88
Kogan, Herman cited, III: 673
Kohler, Kaufmann III: 415*, 439
Kohler, Mr. V: 273
Kohn, George H. II: 298
Kohn, Leon A. III: 663*
Kohn, Sylvan H. IV: *40*
Kolchak, Alexander IV: 398*
Kolinsky, Abraham III: *378*; IV: 199
Kolinsky, Max IV: *199*
Kolliner, Robert S. IV: *55*
Komura, Jutaro I: 358*
Konefsky, Samuel J. cited, I: 46; II: 78, 351; III: 176; IV: 451, 517; V: 40, 64, 89, 286, 318, 483
Koomer, Manuel III: *424*
Kornfield, Mr. V: 423
Koschland, Mrs. Marcus III: 609*, 622
Kossuth, Lajos IV: 207*
Kraines, Oscar cited, II: 385
Kraus, Adolf III: 564, *570*, 572, 576, 579, *582*, 587, 591, 599, 675; IV: 32, *426*
Krauskopf, Joseph III: 387*; IV: 292
Krementzky, Johan III: *518*

Kriegshaber, V. H. III: *174*
Krock, Arthur V: 126*, 496
Ku Klux Klan V: 3, 249, 354, 552
Kuhn, Loeb & Co. III: 207, 229, 267-68, 340; V: 104
Kupat Holim V: 439
Kurtz, John A. V: 124
Kyle, William S. I: *529*, *551*, *559*

Labor, conditions of employment, relations with capital, and arbitration efforts, LDB and I: 232, 236-38, 244-51, 257 259-64, 268, 279, 282-84 286, 288-89, 298, 309, 326-29, 334 350-51, 357-62, 373, 397, 408, 447, 450-51, 461-62, 513, 519-21, 572-73, 576-77; II: 32, 209-11, 268, 287, 296-300, 314-15, 359-60, 403, 415, 444-51, 507-508, 517, 519, 522-23, 527-28, 531-36, 542-49, 562-68, 575-76, 580, 586-89, 614-15, 620, 628-29, 639-40, 646-51, 676-83, 707; III: 10-11, 25, 55-56, 74; V: 56-62, 333-35, 424-25, 503; see also National Civic Federation, Brandeis, Louis D., and New York garment workers' strike and arbitration
Labor V: 376, 379, 387
"Labor and the New Party" (1912) II: 673-74, 676-83, 687
labor injunctions, LDB on I: 283-84; II: 210-11; V: 60
labor legislation, LDB on II: 482, 527-28, 576, 639-40, 707; III: 56, 442-43; V: 53, 56-58, 131
Labor Palestine V: 522
Laboratory Kitchen II: 202
LaCombe, Emile H. I: 580*
Ladies' Tailors & Dress-makers' Union (New York) II: 489, 497, 500-503, 518, 544
LaFollette, Belle C. II: 348*, 373, *381*, 408, 442, 499, *508*, 531, *542*, 623, 639; III: 9, 169, 227, 236; IV: 233, 257; V: 10-11, 24, 34, 169, 186, 593, 652; cited, II: 330, 374, 405, 667; III: 169; IV: 314; V: 135

LaFollette, Fola II: 348, 531*; III: 45; IV: 233; V: 25, 592, 652; cited, II: 330, 374, 405, 667; III: 169; IV: 314; V: 135

LaFollette, Isabel B. V: 25

LaFollette, Marion III: 236

LaFollette, Mary II: 542; V: 25

LaFollette, Philip F. II: 374; III: 169*; IV: 38, 364; V: 25, 210, 215, 353, 378, 498, 518, 528, 554

LaFollette, Robert M. Sr. I: 91; II: 314, 329*, 333, 344, 347, 356, 361, 373, 381, 382, 400, 404, 406, 408, 410, 428, 435, 436, 438, 440, 442(2), 452, 453, 455, 459, 466, 467, 473, 474, 481, 488, 489, 495, 499, 505, 512, 513, 519, 523, 526-27, 536, 538, 539, 542, 546, 569, 573, 576, 577, 585, 600, 612-15, 622-24, 633, 638, 652, 654-56, 667, 672-73, 686, 695, 710, 714-15, 722, 726; III: 29-30, 38, 40, 45-46, 75, 100, 111, 119, 129, 133, 145, 150, 153, 154, 169, 227, 236-37, 255-56, 274, 301, 383, 420, 441, 464, 506; IV: 25, 29, 31, 32, 38, 43, 44, 92, 177, 192, 209-10, 233, 257, 268, 274, 314, 364, 459; V: 10-11, 24, 53, 63, 100-101, 111, 125, 132-36, 143, 151, 169, 186, 285, 593, 652; LDB on II: 489-90, 505, 539, 573, 585; V: 24, 169

LaFollette, Robert M. Jr. II: 330, 373*; III: 506; IV: 314; V: 25, 537, 554-55

LaFollette's Weekly II: 348, 375, 442, 638, 707; III: 101, 104, 129, 274, 506; V: 186, 311

LaGuardia, Fiorello H. V: 529*, 650

Lake Cargo cases V: 368

Lamar, Clarinda P. cited IV: 22

Lamar, Joseph R. II: 616; IV: 21*, 25

Lamartine, M. cited, IV: 44

Lamb, Roland O. I: 494*

Lambert, John V: 573

Lamont, Thomas W. II: 712*; III: 4, 21, 47, 75, 221, 230

LaMont v. Fullman I: 76

Lamport, Alexander IV: 344*

Landau, Alfred V: 435*

Landau, Jacob V: 562

Landis, James M. V: 156*, 159, 167, 174, 201, 230, 244, 290, 298, 309, 312, 327, 354, 374, 414, 451; cited I: 71

Lane, Ann W. cited, II: 721

Lane, Franklin K. II: 720*; III: 23, 40, 42-44, 127, 195, 196, 201, 218, 331; IV: 254

Lane, Frederick S. II: 94(2)*

Lane, Gardiner M. II: 109*

Lane, James cited, III: 88

Lane, Winthrop IV: 497; V: 30

Langdell, Christopher C. I: 8*, 13, 36, 84, 106, 113; V: 324

Languet, Herbert V: 123

Lanier, Alexander S. V: 294

Lanier, Mr. II: 440

Lansbury, George IV: 423*, 483

Lansing, Robert III: 330, 431, 610*, 619, 670; IV: 141, 186, 254, 282, 288, 295, 447, 449, 456, 549; V: 580

Laqueur, Walter cited, V: 618

Larrabbee, John I: 536*

Larson, Cedric cited, III: 543

Lasch, Christopher cited, II: 387

Lasker, Albert D. V: 619*

Lasker, Bruno IV: 342*, 497

Laski, Frida K. IV: 271*, 450, 455; V: 17, 49, 123, 184, 364, 498

Laski, Harold J. IV: 142*, 182, 210, 270, 395, 431, 450, 455, 458, 459; V: 16, 48, 122, 183, 193, 215, 285, 324, 361, 364, 401-402, 413, 468, 469, 474, 497, 650

Laski, Neville J. V: 541*

Lathrop, John E. II: 404*, 442, 463, 467, 475, 479

Lathrop, Judge John IV: 66*

Lathrop, Julia II: 249; V: 143, 166*, 167

Lauck, William J. III: 214*

Laughlin, J. Laurence V: 323*

Lavin, Miss V: 343
the law, LDB on I: 62; see also the legal profession, LDB on
"The Law of Ponds" (1888) I: 78; IV: 33
Law Quarterly Review V: 338
Lawler, Oscar II: 307, 323*, 327, 334-35, 339, 353, 357-58; IV: 130
Lawrence, Amory A. I: 277*
Lawrence, David V: 211, 556*
Lawrence, John S. II: 130*
Lawrence Light Guards II: 50
Lawrence, Samuel C. I: 593*; II: 34, 64, 154, 161; IV: 61, 93
Lawrence strike (1912) 547, 562, 568, 588, 636, 646, 649, 703; LDB on II: 562-64
Lawrence, T. E. IV: 360, 417*
Lawrence, Bishop William I: 507*, 535; II: *148*, 157; IV: 121, 153; V: 282
Lawrence, William B. I: 593*; II: 44, 47, 72, 75, *90*, 141
Lawson, Thomas W. I: 256*, 375; II: 69
Lazaron, Morris S. III: 636, *637**
Lea, Luke II: 710; IV: 197
League to Enforce Peace IV: 404
League of Nations IV: 450; V: 56, 73, 96, 154, 192, 197, 455, 524, 623
Leake, Stephen I: 8
Learsi, Rufus: see Goldberg, Israel
Leavitt, Ezekiel III: *546**
Leavitt, Julian III: 584*
Leavitt, Mr. V: 621
Leavitt, Peter M. IV: *262**
Lebanon IV: 260, 495
Lebow, Richard N. cited, IV: 282, 311
Leckie, W. J. IV: 89
Ledyard, Henry B. III: 24*
Ledyard, Lewis C. IV: 150*
Lee, George C. V: 209*
Lee, Higginson & Co. I: 593; II: 17, 109, 167, 269; V: 210
Lee, J. W. III: 542*

Lee, Joseph L. I: *482**, *496*; II: 45, 47, *264;* V: 354
Leeds, Morris E. V: 355*, 384, 424
Leeds, Rudolph G. II: *383**, 386
Lefkowitz, Abraham V: 248
legal education, LDB on I: 6, 14, 39, 111, 117, 160, 221; II: 619, 637, 656; III: 62; V: 44, 48, 50-51, 78, 142, 284, 381
legal practice, LDB's early law work in Boston I: 33-46, 49-58, 61-64, 67-68, 72-80, 83, 89, 93-95, 98-99, 106-10, 124-26; III: 62-63, IV: 33-34, 48-53, 56-69, 65-70, 74-76, 78-79, 104-107, 113
legal profession, LDB on I: 106-109, 124-26, 321-22; II: 340-41, 646-47, 655-56, 708-709; III: 62-63, 682-83; V: 49, 111, 311, 367-68, 404
Legal Protection Federation III: 73
"The Legal Rights of Public Franchise Companies in Our Streets" (1904) I: 244-46
LeHand, Marguerite A. V: 606*, 629
Leham, Dr. III: 615, 648
Lehman, Herbert H. IV: 30; V: 595* 596-97, *598*
Lehman, Irving IV: 27*, 200; V: 635
Lehy, Geoffrey B. II: *83**
Leibner, Joshua V: 618
Leiserson, William M. III: 364*
Lemann, Monte M. V: 374*, 395-96
Lemberg-Yassey Bahn II: 208
Lemke v. Farmers' Grain Co. V: 47
Lenin, V. I. IV: 366, 399
Lennon, John B. III: 381*
Lennox, James T. IV: 111*
Lennox, Patrick IV: 111*
Lenroot, Irvine L. II: 435, 438*, 442, 454, 455, 540, 615, 654, 656, 688; III: 255, 274; IV: 459
Leon, Eva III: 155, 378, 462; IV: 4, 7, 346, 376
Leon, Maurice III: 35*
Leopold, Richard W. cited, I: 147

Lerner, Max V: 500, 511; cited, I: 277
Lesser v. Garnett V: 47
Lessing, Gotthold I: 21
Leuchtenburg, William E. cited, IV: 475; V: 239, 515, 538
Levensohn, Lotta III: 662
Levenson, Henry H. III: *436**
Levenson, Joseph III: 295
Levi, Sylvain IV: 357*
Leviathan IV: 324
Levin, Alexandra L. cited, III: 303
Levin, H. IV: *109**
Levin, Isadore S. V: 329*, 382
Levin, Louis H. III: 466*, *468*, 474, 482, 607; IV: *243*, 374
Levin, Marlin cited, V: 582
Levin, Maurice V: 582
Levin, Moses B. V: 440
Levin, Schmarya III: 291*, 299, 313, 315, 317, 322, 324, 326, 345, 353, 355-56, 358, 369, 376, 405, 415, 417, 421-27, *448*, 471-72, 477, 482, 487, 494-95, 499-501, 516, 522, 549, 556-57, 561, 579, 588, 609, 614-16, 620, 627, 636, 642, 648, 650, 668; IV: 7, 17, 85, 271, 288, 306, 318, 320, 359, *371*, *386*, 406, 443, 538, 551
Levine, Isaac D. V: 582*
Levine, Louis V: 166, 260; cited, II: 366, 460, 485; IV: 10
Levine, Manuel III: *181**
Levinson, Benno IV: 429*
Levinthal, Louis E. V: 594*, *634*, 654
Levy, Aaron J. IV: 172*
Levy, Benjamin F. III: *638**
Levy, David W. cited, I: 322; II: 654; III: 683
Levy, Julius III: *610**
Levy, Leonard III: 439
Levy, Leonard W. cited, V: 239
Levy, Samuel J. III: 353
Lewin, Thomas I: 22, 33
Lewin-Epstein, E. W. III: 323*, 338, 354, 365-67, 418, 424, 472-74, 480, 483, 514, 520, 524, 550, 579, 596,

609, 621, 628, 663, 666, 678; IV: 5, 13, 24, 116, 129, 146, 147, 156, 161, 167, 189-90, *193*, 203, 205, 211, 213, 277, 285, 296, 298, 303, 310, 314, 318-20, 328, 335, 336, 341, 343, 349, 354, 381; LDB on IV: 341-42
Lewin-Epstein, Samuel III: 474*, 607, 678; IV: *217*
Lewis, Clarence M. V: *533**, 548
Lewis, David J. V: 537
Lewis Flanders & Co., et al. I: 572
Lewis, Harry S. III: 491
Lewis, James H. III: 6*
Lewis, John B. IV: 60*
Lewis, John L. IV: 559*; V: 23, 185
Lewis, Leon P. V: 232*
Lewis, William D. II: *718**
Lewisohn, Adolph III: 360*, *491*, 514, 531; IV: 32, 283, 355
Lewisohn, Leonard III: 360*
Lewisohn, Samuel IV: 322, 355
Lewisohn, Miss III: 623
Lezinsky, Mr. II: 487
"Liability of Trust-Estates on Contracts Made for Their Benefit" (1881) I: 34; IV: 33; V: 534-35
Libby, Charles F. I: *370**, 391, 436
Liberal League V: 94
Lichtheim, Richard III: 496*, 542, 589, 670, *672*; IV: 6, 138, 236
Liechtenstein, Prince I: 82
Lief, Alfred I: 90; V: 411, 418*, 499, *526*; cited, I: 491; III: 100, 217
Life and Labor II: 547, 551, 563, 589; III: 26, 55
"Life Insurance: The Abuses and Remedies" (1905) I: 362-63, 365, 370, 380, 390, 395-96, 405, 482, 502; II: 76, 228; IV: 97
Lifshitz, Haim V: 550
Liggett, Louis K. IV: 183*
Lilienthal, David E. V: 518*
Lilienthal, Jessee W. IV: *225**
Lilley, George L. II: 213*
Lillie, Frances C. III: *673**
Lillie, Frank R. III: 673*

Lincoln, Abraham I: 192; II: 68, 535, 718; IV: 405; V: 127, 629
Lincoln, Alice N. I: 120
Lincoln, George T. I: *491**; II: 16
Lincoln, William H. I: *234**
Lincoln [Nebraska] *Times* IV: 88
Lindbergh, Anne M. V: 288
Lindbergh, Charles A. Sr. V: 287*
Lindbergh, Charles A. Jr. V: 287*
Lindbergh, Evangeline L. L. V: 287*
Lindheim, Irma IV: 493*; V: 9, 330, 645
Lindheim, Norvin R. IV: 492*, 512, 519; V: 309
Lindsay, Sir Ronald C. V: 428*, 612, 613
Lindsay, Samuel M. I: 475; II: 577*; IV: 367
Lindsey, Almont cited, III: 25
Lindsey, Benjamin B. II: *601**, *603*, 710; III: 38, 597
Link, Arthur S. cited, II: 632, 635, 638, 661, 668, 673, 710, 721; III: 38, 41, 44, 58, 84, 116, 235, 258, 320, 581, 621; IV: 25, 26, 187, 254; V: 91
Lippmann, Walter III: 87*, 98, 402; IV: *80*, 118, 141, 176, 366, 427, 549; V: 50, 111, 118, 124, 126, 190, 237, 298, 348, 353, 354, 386, 506, 556; LDB on V: 124, 190-91
Lippner, R. A. V: 654
Lipshitz, Dr. V: 436
Lipsky, Louis III: *64**, *141, 147, 206*, 299, 306, *311*, 313, *316*, 319, 322, 335, 351, 355, *358*, 367, *387, 394, 395, 405, 408, 416*, 417, *425*, 449, 466, 470-71, 479-80, 494-95, 517, *525, 526*, 531, *551, 556, 560, 561*, 564-66, 569, 579, 585, 598, 604, *617*, 620, 625, 627, *651, 655*, 666, *681*; IV: 5, *11*, 17, 24, 83, *116, 134*, 136, 137, *139*, 148, 188, 189, *200, 205*, 207, 244, 252, 277, 290, 294, 298, 320, 335, 352, 361, 375, *381*, 384, *424, 428, 430, 435*, 439, 489, 490, 504, 506, 545, 551, 566; V: 291, 294,

336, 343, 347, 382, 391, 421, 427, 429-35, 486, 492, 599, 632, 638-39, 643, 654; LDB on IV: 294, 490, 506; V: 347, 599; cited, II: 659
Lishansky, Mrs. IV: 496*, 500
Lisitsky, Ephraim E. III: 670*
Lisitzky, Genevieve H. V: 521
Lithuania IV: 157
Little, Arthur D. III: *135**
Little, Brown & Co. V: 548
Little, John I: *547**
Little, Mr. IV: 552
Little, Stephen II: 184, 190
Littleton, Frank L. II: 703*
Littleton, Martin W. II: 653*
Littman, Lydia III: *379**
Livermore, Thomas L. I: *180*, 409; II: 152
Livesey, George I: *329**; II: 209
"The Living Law" (1916) I: 46; III: 682; IV: 15-16; V: 119, 534-35
Livingstone, John II: *409**
Llewellyn, Karl N. V: 308*
Lloyd, Henry D. I: *121**, *208*, 210-14, *218, 220, 223;* LDB on I: 121-22
Lloyd, James T. II: 440*
lobbying legislation, LDB on V: 390
Lobel, S. IV: *92*
Lochner v. New York II: 78; III: 64; V: 126
Lockwood, John E. V: 377*
Locomotive Engineers' Journal V: 494
Lodge, Henry C. Sr. I: 520, 594; II: 95*, 346, 441, 634; III: 420; IV: 70, 139; V: 152; cited, I: 387
Lodge, Henry C. Jr. V: 153
Loeb, Jacob M. IV: 312*
Loeb, Jacques II: 636*, 645; IV: 537, 554; V: 541
Loeb, William II: 134*, 138
Lowenberg, Bessie S. IV: 269*
Loftus, George S. II: 536*, *665;* IV: *228*
Lohman, Carl A. V: 421*
Lomasney, Martin I: 376

London, England IV: 317, 379, 403, 423, 438, 456; LDB on IV: 403-404

London Daily Herald IV: 484

London Daily Mail IV: 402

London Meyer II: 368*, 391, 417, 502-503, 518, 523, *524*, 570; III: *348*, 363

London School of Economics IV: 399

London Times II: 551; V: 604

London University V: 215

Long, Charles L. II: 117*

Long, John D. I: 147*

Long, Representative I: 549, 556, 570, 575, 578

Longfellow, Henry W. I: 45

Lopez, Sixto I: 149*, 152-55

Lopezzo, Anna II: 637

Lord, Everett W. V: 119*

Lorimer, William II: 452*, 456

Loring, Mr. V: 89

Loring, Mrs. I: 436

Los Angeles Times II: 517, 522; IV: 55

Lothian, Marquess of V: 632*

Lothrop, John I: 543

Lothrop, Thornton K. I: 143*

Louis: see Wehle, Louis B.

Louis D. Brandeis Zionist Club (Philadelphia) IV: 19

Louisiana V: 172

Louisville II: 369-70, 378, 380-81, 392-94; III: 639-40, 661; IV: 3, 5, 39, 199, 229; V: 301-302

Louisville & Nashville Rrd II: 675-76; III: 15-16, 28, 383, 400, 444

Louisville Board of Trade II: 393

Louisville Courier-Journal II: 348, 359; V: 616

Louisville Fidelity Trust II: 365

Louisville Herald II: 369, 380

Louisville, University of, LDB and III: 566; V: 138-41, 144-50, 153-54, 158, 161-65, 168-69, 175-82, 187-90, 197-98, 201-202, 207-208, 212, 217-19, 223, 229, 231-32, 236-37, 241-43,

253-58, 261-69, 282, 304-308, 570-71, 592, 594, 601, 617, 640, 648-49

Louisville Young Men's Hebrew Association III: 85

Love, H. K. II: 311

Love, J. W. cited, IV: 542

Lovett, Robert M. V: 312

Lovett, Robert S. III: 207*, 267

Low, Seth II: 100*, *326*, 377

Low, William G. I: 506

Lowdermilk, Walter C. V: 631*

Lowe, Isidore V: 446*

Lowell, A. Lawrence I: 80, *163**; II: 291, *352;* III: 287; IV: 60, 118, 396, 558; V: 12, 161, 278, 290, 312, 324, 352, 373

Lowell, Francis C. IV: 128*

Lowell, James A. I: *428**; III: 228

Lowell, James R. quoted, II: 578

Lowell, Percival I: 80*; III: 331; V: 161

Lowenstein, Solomon IV: 397*; V: 422

Lowenthal, Marvin IV: 245*; cited, III: 300

Lowenthal, Max IV: 367, 378*; V: 348, 395

Lowitt, Richard cited, V: 171, 271

Lowry, Edward G. III: 66*; IV: 561; V: 122

L. Q. White Shoe Co. IV: 297

Lubin, David III: *272**; IV: *356*

Lubin, Isadore IV: 514, 519; V: 450*, 523, 563

Lubschutz, Mr. V: 266

Luce bill I: 300-301, 593, 596

Luce, Robert I: *300**, 301, *460*, 593; II: *156*, 178, 281

Lucking, Alfred III: 434*

Lucullus V: 214

Ludlow Hotel (Boston) I: 83

Ludlow, James B. I: *306**

Luke, Harry C. J. V: 455*

Luncheon Club II: 86

Lusk Committee V: 93

Luther, Martin quoted, I: 21; IV: 553; V: 107

Lutz, Charles A. III: *13**, 22
luxury, materialism, fashion, etc., LDB on I: 95, 100; III: 330-31; IV: 401, 459; V: 7-8, 97, 199, 206, 214, 251, 282, 410, 542
Lyle, E. P. cited, II: 32
Lyman, Arthur T. I: *277**
Lyman, Payson W. II: *173**
Lyon, Frank IV: 33, *46**; V: 122, 215
Lyons, Joseph T. III: 321

MacArthur, Arthur I: *147**, 150
The Maccabaean II: 402; III: 416, 495, 526, 606, 617, 649, 667; IV: 13, 262, 292, 346, 394, 425, 428, 502, 506
MacCallum, Elizabeth P. V: 408
MacDonald, Ishbel V: 402
MacDonald, John F. II: *505**
MacDonald, J. Ramsay V: 123, 151, *387**, 394, 397, 400, 402, 413, 460; LDB on V: 402
MacDonald White Paper (1939) V: 614-24, 646
MacDonald, William II: *520**, *623*
MacDonald, William J. III: *228**
Macfarland, Charles S. II: *543**
MacFarland, Grenville S. II: *86**, 687; III: *3*, *53*, *62*, *172*, *274*, 277, 321; IV: 71, 269
Machiavelli, Niccolo quoted, V: 648
MacInall, Edward IV: *299**
Mack, Jessie F. IV: *392**; V: 439
Mack, Julian W. II: *577**; III: 180, 288, 296, 340, 363, 389, 415, 429, 454, 460, *487*, 514, *531*, 538, 544-45, 566-67, 572, 575, 576-77, 579, 599, 603, 609, *613*, 616, *619*, 622, 635, 639, 663, 665-66, *674;* IV: 4-8, 12, 28, *96*, *115*, 147, 206, *211*, 247, 256, *263* 299, 318, 323, 325, 327, 335, 337, 340, 343, 346, 347, *351*(2), *352*, *353*, *354*(2), *355*, *359*, 360, *365*, 371, 374, 375, *381*, *382*, *383*, 384, 385, 390-99, 425, *426*, 429, 432, 433, *434*, *435*, 436, *437*, *439*, 440, *442*(2), 443, *444*, *447*, *452*, 455, 457, 458, 460, *461*, 463, *465*, *466*, 468, *472*, *473*, *477*, 481-88, *489*, 490-91, *492*, 494, 496, 499, *500*, 501-502, *503*, *506*, *507*, *509*, *513*, *514*, 516, 518, *522*, *524*, *530*, *533*, 537, 541-42, *544*, *549*, 551-53, *555*(2), *556*, 558, 559, *562*, 565; V: 3, *8*, 11, *16*, *18*, *19*, 25, 27, 30, *36*, 37, *38*, *43*, 44, 51, 72, 74, 90, *102*, 103, *104*, 106, *107*, *108*, 111, *112*, 113-16, *134*, 152, 156, 161, *182*, *191*, 192, *194*, 195, *219*, 233-35, *244*, 245-46, *252*, 271-75, 292, 297, 308, 321, 330, 336, *343*, *347*, 383, *388*, 391, *397*, 398, 400, *407*, *408*, *416*, *417*, *418*, *420*, *421*, *423*(2), *425*, *426*, 427, *428*(2), *430*, *432*, *434*(2), *435*, *439*, 445, 458, 462, 469, 480, 483, *487*, *488*, *490*, *491*, *521*, *524*, *544*, *549*, 578, 587, 592, 615, 620, 640, 645; LDB on III: 180; IV: 542
Mack, Ruth IV: 424
Mackay & Co. II: 36
Mackenzie, Frederick W. II: *726**; III: *9*
MacLeish, Archibald cited, II: 351; V: 40
MacLeod, Frederick J. II: *291**, *507*; III: *67*, *90*, 192
MacMichael, Sir Harold V: *624**
Macnair, William M: III: *171**
MacVeagh, Isaac W. II: *524**; III: 21, 57
Madden, Eva A. II: 306
Madeiros, Celestino F. V: *283**, 306
Madero, Francisco IV: 187
Madie: see Brandeis, Adele
Madison, Edmund H. II: *322**, *401*
Magnes, Judah L. III: *192**, *296*, 298, 299, 323, 330, 338-41, *351*, *359*, 362-67, 400, 421, 466, 471-72, 474, *481*, 494, *507*, *522*, 545, *547*, 576, 577, 579, *582*, 588, *589*, 595, 597, 598, 621, 634-35, *640*, 651-53, *654*, 679; IV: 4, 10-11, 18, *19*, *108*, 133, 151, *179*, 200, 204, 211, 213, 252, 442; V: 175, 182, 253, 413, 419, 571, 594; LDB on IV: 442

Magruder, Calvert IV: 268*, 454, 459; V: 41, 281, 327; LDB on IV: 454

Maguire, John M. V: 225*

Mahaffie, Charles O. IV: 518

Mahaffy, Sir John P. V: 94, 185

Maine I: 514; II: 207; III: 264, 271, 439; V: 249

Maine Central Rrd III: 128, 177-81

Maine Steamship Co. II: 621

malaria: see anti-malaria campaign for Palestine

Malloch, E. Louise II: 32*, 33, 36 (2), 44, 49; III: 22, 263; IV: 59, 70, 87; V: 136, 290, 292, 478, 529, 635

Malone, Dana II: 133*, 144, 150, 185, 188, 242, 251, 256, 257, 265

Malone, Dudley F. III: 162; V: 234

Malone, Richard H. II: 101*

Maltbie, Milo R. I: 175*, 265; III: 384, 517

Manchester Guardian V: 425, 547

Manley, Annie L. I: 15

Manley, Basil III: 214*; V: 240, 241, 251

Mann, Arthur cited, I: 75, 138, 281, 488; III: 155; V: 530

Mannheimer, Leo III: 429*

Manning, Bishop V: 94

Mansfield, Earl of: see Murray, William

Mansfield, E. C. I: 380

Manton, Martin T. V: 403*

Manuel, Frank E. cited, IV: 397, 447

Maple Flooring Manufacturers' Association v. U.S. V: 175

Marble, John H. III: 38*, 142, 331

Marble, Joseph R. III: 145

Marble, J. Russell II: 105*

Marble, Mrs. III: 331

Mark Anthony IV: 413

Marcou, Philippe B. I: 14*, 20-23, 43-44, 49, 55-56, 60-62, 554; III: 539; V: 32

Margold, Nathan R. V: 322*, 326, 334, 337

Margolies, Moses S. III: 648*, 650

Margolies, Samuel III: 648*

Margolies, Mr. V: 632

Margolis, Max L. III: 333*

Margulies, Morris IV: 174, 294, 402*

Marks, E. Homer III: 73*

Marks, Marcus M. III: 57*

Marks, Sir Simon V: 604

Marlow, John cited, IV: 414

Marlowe, Julia I: 88*

Marmorek, Alexander IV: 361*

Marmorek, Oskar IV: 361*

Marshall, C. C. V: 278

Marshall, John I: 10*; V: 52

Marshall, Leon C. V: 571*

Marshall, Louis II: 372; III: 193, 293*, 311, 341, 366, 409, 435, 437, 491, 524, 537, 544, 574, 578, 619, 621; IV: 4, 10-12, 20, 34, 56, 108, 151, 179, 198, 201, 211, 220, 234, 251, 257, 323, 354, 399, 405, 434, 435, 438, 439, 472, 484, 493, 507, 512; V: 104, 107, 115, 258, 297, 391, 470, 580; LDB on IV: 354

Marshall, Thomas R. II: 641*, 716; IV: 209

Martin, Clarence R. S. II: 708*

Martin, Edward S. II: 335*, 702

Martin, John I: 209*, 220, 264

Martin, Selden O. III: 122*

Martine, James E. II: 622

Marx, Karl III: 617; V: 48

Masaryk, Thomas G. IV: 315*, 351

Masliansky, Avi H. III: 311*

Maslon, Samuel H. V: 98*, 100, 404

Mason, Albert J. V: 133*

Mason, Alpheus T. I: 15, 437-38; V: 187*, 473, 526, 592, 600, 635, 641, 643, 646, 653, 654; cited, I: 30, 37, 53, 83, 101, 102, 123, 131, 187, 209, 212, 233, 243, 253, 291, 294, 296, 308, 345, 360, 364, 409, 431, 443, 445, 491, 499, 508, 533, 547, 583; II: 52, 58, 61, 78, 104, 111, 216, 220, 283, 308, 366, 369, 374, 376, 402, 415, 431, 432, 457, 463, 467, 628, 635, 703, 726; III: 72, 82, 164, 181, 192, 203, 217, 263, 287, 293, 296,

386, 429, 458, 547, 566; IV: 26, 43, 45, 58, 60, 69, 76, 81, 91, 107, 112, 183, 192, 198, 216, 242, 265, 300, 301, 533; V: 46, 125, 352, 417, 547, 583, 588, 611, 653

Mason, C. E. II: 669*

Mason, Herbert W. I: 352*

Mason, John V: 243

Massachusetts Anti-Merger League II: 65, 79, 81, 85, 90, 91, 101, 117, 121, 123, 126, 135, 147, *154*, 163, 165, 171, 175, 179, 251, 257, 259, 266; III: 12; IV: 62

Massachusetts Anti-Stock-Watering Law I: 347, 412, 416, 453

Massachusetts Associated Board of Trade I: 290-92, 297-98, 305, 314, 502, 550, 555; II: 64, 117; IV: 119, 125

Massachusetts Bar Association I: *140;* II: 637, 645, 646-47, 649-50, 652; IV: 260

Massachusetts Board of Arbitration I: 552; II: 651

Massachusetts Board of Gas and Electric Light Commissioners I: 252, 256, *286, 317, 412;* III: 279, 510

Massachusetts Board of Prison Commissioners I: *354*

Massachusetts Board of Railroad Commissioners I: *133*, 135, 197, 202, 214, 224, 258, 289, 420-22, 454, 511, 594; II: *23*, 27, 36-37, 73, 97, 119, 125-26, *141*, 143, *145*, 147, 157, 164, *169*, 171, *172, 173, 178*, 179, *182*, 187, *206*, 230, 244, 250, 258, 260, 282, 288, 306, 500, 626; III: 59, 90-93, 108-109, *148*

Massachusetts Board of Schoolhouse Commissioners I: *158*

Massachusetts Bureau of Statistics of Labor I: *260;* III: 86

Massachusetts Civil Service Association IV: *260*

Massachusetts Commission on Commerce and Industry: II: 46, 48, 51, 57, 71, 87, 99, 106-109, 112, 115, 125, 153, 157, 161, 164, 166, 170, 174, 183, 231, 238, 506

Massachusetts Committee on Uniform Laws I: 156, 280-81

Massachusetts Fire Insurance Law I: 518

Massachusetts House Committee on Metropolitan Affairs I: 132, 141, 144, 160, 162, 165-69, 180, 185, 187, 194, 200, 418, 427

Massachusetts Industrial Accident Board II: 517

Massachusetts Law Quarterly IV: 539

Massachusetts Liquor Dealers' Protective Association I: 102; IV: 104-106

Massachusetts Minimum Wage Commission II: 441, 482, 518, 527, 576-77; III: 56, 86

Massachusetts Mutual Life Insurance Co. V: 451, 561

Massachusetts Peace Society III: 419

Massachusetts Public Service Commission III: 149, 172, 175, 177, *180*, 182, 190-91, 195, 196, 231, 287, 297, 392, 518, 613; IV: 87, 90

Massachusetts Real Estate Exchange II: 67

Massachusetts Reform Club I: 93

Massachusetts Savings Bank Life Insurance: see Savings Bank Life Insurance

Massachusetts Savings Bank Life Insurance League II: 64, 81, 85, 91, 598; III: 263; V: 293, 471, 494-95, 547, 559, 568, 575

Massachusetts State Branch of the A.F. of L. II: 14, 59, 113, 673-74, 676, 677-83, 687

Massachusetts State Grange II: 113

"Massachusetts' Substitute for Old Age Pensions" (1908) II: 201, 214; III: 216

Massachusetts Supreme Judicial Court II: 144, 155, 188, 559, 620, 638; V: 278, 280

Massachusetts Teachers' Association III: 28

Massies, the V: 324

Masten, Arthur H. I: 580*, 590

Master Teamsters' Association I: 573, 576

Mather, William I: 341*, 344, 346

Mathews, James A. II: 343*

Mathews, Jerry A. IV: 101*

Matthew quoted, I: 127

Matthews-Livermore bill I: 180-82, 197, 202

Matthews, Mrs. V: 373

Matthewson, Diana L. IV: 271*

Matz, Rudolph I: 508*; IV: 60

Maul v. U.S. V: 294-95

Maxwell, Arthur A. I: 143*, 144

May, Doris cited, IV: 474

May, Max B. IV: 28*

Mayberry, Representative I: 556

Mayer, Levy IV: 28*

Maynard, Laurens II: 200*

Mayo, Hamilton I: 535*, 537, 591

Mazur, Paul M. V: 308*

Mazzini, Giuseppe III: 612*

McAdoo, Nona IV: 286*, 288

McAdoo, William G. II: 667*, 687, 697, 699, 702; III: 40, 44, 47, 61, 85, 95, 106, 115-16, 138, 140, 148, 154, 160, 167, 170, 189, 509, 558; IV: 25, 197, 214, 286, 364; V: 29, 129, 261, 270, 279, 282, 375, 505; cited, III: 116; IV: 25

McAneny, George IV: 177*

McCall, Samuel W. II: 398*; III: 596

McCamant, Wallace F. V: 211*

McCarthy, Charles II: 415*, 672, 686, 726; III: 4, 29, 288, 363, 380, 409, 644; IV: 326; LDB on II: 673

McCarthy, Edward F. X. II: 91

McCarthy, Frank H. I: 278*, 282; II: 81*, 88, 89, 126

McChord, Charles C. III: 106*, 110, 122, 124, 133, 141, 186; IV: 145

McClain, Dean V: 465

McCleary, James T. II: 543*

McClennen, Edward F. I: 110; II: 18*; IV: 29, 33, 43, 47, 48, 50, 51, 53, 56, 59, 60, 61, 63, 65, 67, 70, 71, 73, 74, 76, 77, 78, 84, 86, 87, 91, 92, 93, 96, 98, 101, 110, 113, 117, 119, 123, 126, 131, 139, 143, 145, 150, 154, 165, 166, 171, 175, 177, 182, 192, 210, 215; V: 151, 215, 234, 346, 393, 410; cited, II: 44; IV: 62

McClennen, Mrs. Edward F. IV: 176

McClennen, Mary IV: 480*

McClure's Magazine II: 102, 357, 406, 484, 490; III: 31, 51, 137; IV: 168

McConnell, Francis J. V: 541*

McCook, John J. I: 125*

McCormick, Cyrus H. III: 232, 601*

McCormick, J. Medill V: 132*

McCormick, Mrs. J. Medill V: 131*

McCormick, Robert R. III: 576*

McCrea, James II: 383*

McCreary, Alfred B. IV: 487*, 519; V: 350

McCreary, Amy B. I: 75*, 359, 409, 553; II: 207, 326; III: 37, 618; IV: 386, 535, 539; V: 256, 264, 658

McCreary, James B. II: 675*, 676

McCreary, William H. III: 37*

McCreary, William B. IV: 386*, 519, 546

McCurdy, William E. V: 44*, 74, 98, 224

McDonald, Allen II: 727

McDonald, James G. V: 517*, 524, 606

McDowell, Mary E. II: 318*, 639

McElwain, J. Franklin II: 240*, 629; V: 342

McElwain, William H. I: 204*, 370, 546, 549, 561, 563, 570, 576, 591; II: 11, 113, 553, 629; III: 230; V: 503, 586, 658; LDB on II: 629-30; V: 658; see also W. H. McElwain Co.

McFarlane, Mrs. I: 22, 49

McGeary, M. Nelson cited, II: 310, 346

McGill, Anna B. V: 466*

McGinty, George B. III: 331*

McGovern, Francis E. II: 710*; III: 383

McInnis v. U.S. V: 345

McIntire, Fred I: 69*
McKay, Kenneth C. cited V: 135
McKay Shoe Machinery Co. I: 508; IV: 60, 78
McKenna, Joseph IV: 300, 451, 517, 551; V: 42, 125*, 154, 157
McKenna, Marion C. cited, II: 622
McKim, Charles F. I: 127*, 480
McKinley, William I: 147, 159, 338; II: 279; IV: 168
McLean, Angus W. IV: 543*
McLean, Edward B. V: 120*
McMahon, Sir Henry V: 401
McManmon, John J. I: 566, 569
McNamara brothers (Los Angeles dynamite case) II: 517*, 522, 531-36, 537, 703
McNary-Haugen bill V: 251
McNeill, George E. I: 281*
McNeils, the V: 281
McNutt, Paul V. V: 625*
McPherson, Miss I: 165
McPherson, John B. II: 484
McReynolds, James C. III: 35*, 39, 41, 42, 44, 53, 106, 112, 161, 180, 200, 224, 227, 231, 247, 259, 283, 288, 290; IV: 26, 274, 300, 367, 516, 551; V: 93, 106, 117, 226, 239, 611; LDB on III: 35
McSween, Angus III: 467, 618
McSween, Mr. IV: 275
McSweeney, Edward F. IV: 52*
Mead, Edwin D. I: 121*, 241, 257, 500; II: 665
Mead, Elwood V: 117*, 206, 249
Mead, Frederick S. I: 500*; II: 99, 224, 631; III: 70
Mead, George F. I: 183
Mead, George H. II: 390*
Mead, Lucia T. A. I: 241*
Means, Gardiner E. IV: 37
meat-packing industry V: 321
Medalia, Dr. IV: 376*
Medici, Cosimo II: 408
Medical Unit: see American Zionist Medical Unit
Meeker, Royal III: 402*
Meier, August cited, V: 366

Meier, Ed III: 384
Meikeljohn, Alexander V: 116*, 118, 156, 210, 237
Meir, Maurice II: 349
Meissner, Claudius I: 335
Meissner, Mrs. Claudius I: 355
Melamed, Samuel M. III: 585*
Melchett, Henry V: 571*
Meldrim, Peter W. IV: 118*
Mellen, Charles S. II: 31*, 33, 36-38, 43, 44, 48, 49, 52, 57, 61, 64-67, 107-12, 117, 126, 142, 144-50, 153, 161, 168-69, 172-75, 178, 182, 185-88, 230, 237, 245, 283, 287, 405, 425, 499, 500-502, 582, 628, 635, 722, 724-25, 728-29; III: 3, 13, 72, 123, 127-29, 133, 140-41, 143-46, 149, 178, 180-81, 190, 204, 224, 284; IV: 48, 153; LDB on II: 31, 405, 500-501
Mellen, E. J. II: 105
Mellen, James J. I: 575
Mellen, Walter B. II: 416*
Mellett, Lowell V: 285*, 287, 354, 425, 460
Mellon, Andrew W. IV: 544*; V: 105, 226, 248, 317, 412
Mencken, Henry L. V: 320*
Mendes, Henry P. III: 601*, 677; IV: 361
Menominee Indian reservation III: 23
Menorah Journal III: 398, 412, 416, 599; 638; V: 631, 634, 649, 650
Menorah movement III: 193, 357, 368, 370, 388, 395, 398, 401, 460, 505; IV: 180
Merchant Marine Act (1928) V: 390
Merchant & Miners Transportation Co. II: 132; III: 93
Merchants National Bank (Boston) I: 23
Merchants' Society of Ladies' Tailors (New York) II: 489, 497, 500, 503, 518-19
Merchants' Steamship Line II: 168
Meredith, Ernest S. IV: 264*
Meredith, George I: 101
Merhavya III: 516

Meriwether, Walter III: 32*

Merriam, Charles E. II: 642*, 654

Merrill, Bradford Jr. I: 325*

Merrill, John F. A. III: 439*

Merrill, Mark V: 570

Merritt, Walter G. V: 316*

Merz, Charles IV: 118*, 510; V: 321, 330

Messersmith, George S. V: 630*, 646

Metcalf, Edwin IV: 57*

Metcalf, Henry C. I: 286*; II: 25, 227, 284

Metropolitan Life Insurance Co. I: 66, 455, 494, 505, 545, 546, 558; II: 218, 227, 285, 591; V: 328, 539, 561

Metropolitan Magazine III: 200; IV: 350

Metropolitan Steamship Co. II: 76, 131, 287, 621

Metropolitan Street Railway Co. (New York City) I: 258, 264

Metz, Dr. V: 44

Metzger, Walter P. cited, V: 84

Mexican arbitration (1916) LDB and IV: 254-56

Mexico III: 57; IV: 187, 254-56, 269, 539; V: 126, 270, 277, 309, 628

Meyer, Balthasar H. III: 244*; IV: 29, 145

Meyer, Mrs. B. H. III: 244

Meyer, Eugene Jr. III: 538*, 555, 622, 666; IV: 8, 200, 231, 247, 285, 287, 290, 327, 330, 337, 346, 349, 371, 425, 529, 543, 551; V: 21, 32, 206, 289, 373

Meyer, Julius III: 65*, 335, 466

Meyer, Martin A. III: 586*, 598-99, 609, 665, 675

Meyer, Max II: 373*

Meyer, Walter E. III: 19*; IV: 348, 351, 354, 355

Meyers, William J. II: 720*

Michael, Jerome V: 193*, 541

Michael v. Locke V: 477

Michaels, George V: 233

Michaels, Otto V: 233

Michigan III: 32-33, 227-28

Michigan Bar Association III: 33

Middleboro Gazette IV: 88

Middleton, George II: 531*; III: 45; IV: 233; V: 24

Mikve Israel Association III: 387, 388, 395

Miles, John E. I: 288*, 289, 334, 335

Miles, H. E. II: 488*

Miles, Vincent M. V: 586*

Mill, John Stuart V: 336; quoted, V: 340

Miller, Adolph C. III: 244*; IV: 552; V: 14-15

Miller, Dickinson S. II: 702*; III: 57

Miller, Herbert A. III: 617*

Miller, John S. IV: 176*

Miller, L. C. III: 265*

Miller, Nathan IV: 541

Miller, Robert N. V: 175*, 176, 181, 187, 188, 190, 231, 241, 255, 269, 371, 406

Miller, S. F. III: 5

Miller, Samuel F. V: 241, 628*

Miller, Thomas W. V: 235

Miller v. U.S. II: 255

Millerand, Alexandre IV: 446*

Millie: see Goldmark, Emily

Mills, Ogden L. V: 151*

Milner, Viscount Alfred IV: 473*; V: 49

Milton, George F. V: 307*

Milton Research Fund V: 204, 225

Milwaukee III: 352, 353, 368-69, 374-75, 377, 407-408

Milwaukee Journal II: 710

Milwaukee Leader IV: 541, 562

Milwaukee Social Democratic Publishing Co. v. Burleson IV: 541

Milyukov, Pavel N. IV: 276*

Mingo County coal strike (W. Virginia) IV: 515, 559

Minneapolis III: 650; IV: 229

Minnesota II: 356, 666

Minnesota Law Review V: 98

Minnick, James I: 510

Minnis, James L. IV: 28*

Minot, Laurence I: 138*, 141, 143,

162, 176, *181*, *183*, 184, *204*, 207, 225, *229*, 231, 248, 253, 256, 288, 327, *380*, *385*, 530; II: 26; IV: 66

Minot, William I: 264

Mintz, Samuel V: 25*

Mirvis, Phillip IV: 166*

misrepresentations by the press, LDB on II: 546; III: 83; IV: 88-89

Missouri II: 611; III: 592-95; V: 172

Missouri, ex rel. St. Louis Brewing Association v. Public Service Commission . . . V: 305

Missouri v. Holland IV: 454

Mitchel, John P. III: *547**, 671

Mitchell, Ann M. I: *545*

Mitchell, Dr. V: 88

Mitchell, James A. I: *466**

Mitchell, John I: 210*, 213; II: *394*, *398*, 451, *488*, 568

Mitchell, John H. II: 290*

Mitchell, John K. I: 22*

Mitchell, Max II: *265**; III: *362*, 365-66, 403; IV: 338

Mitchell v. U.S. III: 305

Mitchell, William D. V: 370*, 371, 373; LDB on V: 370-71

Mitchell-Inness, Alfred III: *261**

Mittell, Sherman F. V: *519**, 600, 602, 625, 641, 648

Mittlebeeler, Emmet V. V: *609**

the Mizrachi III: 323, 505, 510, 513, 527, 557, 561, 569, 572, 624; IV: 38, 160, 173-75, 181, 188, 193, 218, 246, 280, 320, 322, 342, 348, 382, 383, 393, 435, 438, 472, 503; V: 36, 444, 637

Mochinson, Nellie S. V: 445*

Mock, James R. cited, III: 543

Moffat, J. Pierrepont V: 525*

Moffett, Cleveland L. II: 408*

Moffett, Edward A. I: *467**

Mohi, Emanuel N. V: 314, 385, 407, 433, 453, 463, *469*

Moley, Raymond IV: 37; V: 552*

Mond, Alfred M: IV: 508*

Monk, Mr. III: 467

Monod, F. IV: 344

Monroe, Thomas B. V: 231

Montagu, Edwin IV: 310; V: 522*

Montaigne, Michel V: 318

Montefiore, Sir Francis A. III: *679**

Montefiore, Moses III: 680

Monticello V: 301-302

Montor, Henry V: 606*, *633*, 635, 646

Moody Corporation II: 48

Moody, J. Carroll cited, V: 340

Moon, John A. II: 440*

Mooney, Thomas J. IV: 398*; V: 284

Moore, A. O. I: 528*

Moore, Edmund A. cited, V: 278

Moore, R. Walton V: 28*, 277, 326, 330, 337

Moore, William U. IV: *383**

Moors, John F. I: 289, 351*

Moran, John B. I: 323, 374*

Moran, Regina IV: 153*

Morawetz, Victor I: *266**; III: 236; V: 109-10, 157

Morey, Arthur T. II: *548**

Morgan, Anne III: 228*

Morgan, Edmund M. V: 225*

Morgan, J. P. I: 132, 209, 415, 480, 583, 592*; II: 46, 280, 330, 364, 462, 468, 475, 493, 525; III: 3, 9, 25, 48-49, 50, 168, 171, 204, 228-30, 267, 269, 310, 509; V: 124, 213

Morgenthau, Henry Sr. I: *482**, *491*, *506*; II: 702; III: 4, 302, 325, *336*, 418, *425*, 431, 434, 473, 496-97, 504, *542*, 595, *605*, *674*; IV: 133, *138*, 139, *145*, 148-49, 164, 286-90, 295-98, 302, 305, 320; V: 189; cited, III: 337; IV: 139

Morison, Elting E. cited, II: 356; V: 285

Morison, Samuel E. V: 296*, 363; cited, I: 89, 150; II: 277

Morley, John III: 260; V: 87*; quoted, V: 336

Morningstar, Joseph Jr. III: 272*; IV: *229*

Morningstar, Joseph Sr. III: 271*; IV: 229

Morris, Mr. III: 160*

Morris, Sophie IV: 424*

Morrison, Stuart D. B. III: 167*

Morrison, Mr. V: 543

Morrow, Dwight V: 277

Morse, Charles W. I: 592*; II: 126, 131; III: 13

Morse, George W. I: 233*

Morse, Harry P. I: 577

Morss, D. D. II: 109*

Morton, George C. II: 67*

Morton, Paul I: 341*

Mortonson, Miss IV: 370

Moseley, Harold P. I: 297, 302*

Moskowitz, Belle L. II: 372*; III: 651; V: 77, 278

Moskowitz, Henry II: 372*, 387, 406, 459, 484, 487, 489, 502, 518, 535, 547, 551, 563, 569, 572, 586, 588, 616, 653, 674; III: 9, 27, 55, 81, 104, 168, 241, 307, 402, 650; IV: 200; V: 77, 307

Moss, Ralph W. II: 464*, 465

Mosseri, Jack IV: 337, 426

Mossinsohn, Benzion III: 628*; IV: 195, 211, 212, 246, 279, 390

Mott, John R. IV: 305*

Motzkin, Leo III: 486*, 513; IV: 19, 85, 108, 151, 179, 298, 305

Mowry, George cited, I: 209; II: 70, 293, 295, 356, 684, 727

Moyer, Charles H. III: 227*

Mueller v. Engeln I: 14, 20

Mufti of Jerusalem V: 507, 575, 625*

Muller v. Oregon I: 166, 397; II: 77, 80, 92, 101, 106, 297, 299, 359, 602; III: 237, 364; IV: 521; V: 127, 512

Mumford, Charles C. III: 43*

Municipal Court (Cleveland) III: 181-82

Municipal League: see National Municipal League

Municipal Review II: 539

Munro, William B. II: 287*, 296

Munroe, James P. I: 167*, 237, 286, 369; II: 46, 86, 217, 227, 252

Munroe, John P. I: 310*

Munsey, Frank A. II: 726*

Münsterberg, Hugo IV: 259

Murchie, Guy II: 26*, 27; III: 321

Murdock, Victor III: 237*; IV: 545

Murphy, Paul cited, V: 40, 248, 279

Murray, Gilbert II: 480; IV: 362; V: 141, 230

Murray, R. H. IV: 187, 191

Murray, William I: 10*

Murray, William F. II: 518; III: 170

Muscle Shoals V: 170, 271

Musgrove, Ethel H. IV: 14*

Mussolini, Benito V: 602

Mutual Life Insurance Co. (New York) I: 363, 366, 409, 473, 475, 486, 492, 540; II: 285; IV: 94

Myers, Arthur W. IV: 443*

Myers, Frank V: 239

Myers, George H. III: 238*

Myers, Gustavus cited, I: 265

Myers, Nathaniel V: 11*

Myers v. U.S. V: 237, 244

Myrick, Herbert I: 557*; II: 197

Nagel, Alfred I: 29*, 84

Nagel, Charles I: 17*, 20, 22-23, 26-29, 32-34, 37, 43-44, 55-57, 81, 94, 147, 156, 158, 459, 510, 542; II: 96, 115, 139, 213, 230, 249, 250, 280, 299, 315, 327, 330, 427, 611, 643, 675, 700, 718; III: 42, 263, 334, 389; IV: 512, 529; V: 5, 13, 123, 124, 183, 276, 281, 304, 658; LDB on II: 327

Nagel, Fannie I: 3*, 15, 22, 24, 29, 40, 55, 58, 84, 437; II: 642, 728; V: 145, 183, 477, 508

Nagel, Hermann I: 19*

Nagel, Hildegarde I: 84*; II: 299, 326, 327; IV: 512; V: 13, 25-26, 246

Napier v. Atlantic Coast Line Rrd Co. V: 247

Napoleon I: 3; IV: 501
Napoleon III II: 299
Nardi, Sulamith V: 568
Nash, Frederick H. I: 433, 435*, 526
Nashville IV: 171
Nason, F. E. IV: 94*
Nathanson, Maurice cited, II: 390
Nathan, Jacob III: 584; IV: 238*, 256
Nathan, Paul III: 235*, 398; IV: 211
Nathenson, Stan IV: 157
The Nation I: 56, *309;* II: 353; IV: 130, 490; V: 12, 30, 83, 95, 312, 333, 352-55, 370, 390
National Association of Advertising Managers III: 89, 94
National Association of Clothiers III: 57
National Association of Jewish Social Workers III: 414
National City Bank (New York) III: 167
National Civic Federation I: 259-60, 277, 304. 356, 370, 395, 397, 488; II: 12-13, 20, 25, 32, 47, 129, 214, 377-78, 394; III: 88; LDB on II: 13
National Commission on Law Observance and Enforcement: see Wickersham Commission
National Conference of Jewish Charities III: 340
National Conference of Mayors III: 348
National Conference of Single Taxers III: 551
National Conference on Charities and Corrections II: 395, 433, 442
National Conference on Valuation of Rrds V: 101
National Conservation Association II: 310, 361, 513, 685, 716; III: 7, 59-60, 67-77
National Consumer's League II: 249, 297, 542; III: 168, 364, 443; IV: 73, 171, 267, 541; V: 53, 89, 207, 650
National Convention on Municipal Ownership I: 209, 220

National Council for the Prevention of War V: 248
National Divorce Congress I: 401
National Economic League III: 109, 281; IV: 223
National Farmers' Union V: 35
National Home Library Foundation V: 519, 599, 648
National Industrial Conference Board V: 102
National Insurance Convention I: 405
National Jewish Relief Committee III: 351, 362, 365
National Jewish Trade Council III: 621
National Municipal League I: 130-33, 328; II: 539, 573; III: 12
National Progressive Republican League II: 295, 403, 413, 432, 505, 526-27
National Recovery Administration V: 527, 537, 538, 564, 570
National Union for Jewish Rights (England) IV: 103
National Voters League III: 43, 81
National Wholesale Liquor Dealers' Association I: 542
National Women's Trade Union League II: 547, 563, 589; III: 55
National Workingmen's Committee on Jewish Rights III: 604, 651, 681; IV: 10, 17, 200, 291
Nation's Business V: 25
Naumberg, George W. V: 553*
Nay, Frank N. I: 141*; IV: 264
Nazism V: 471, 551, 554, 562, 582, 615, 652; see also Brandeis, Louis D. and Hitler and Nazism
Neale, A. D. cited, III: 594
Neall, Frank L. III: *193*
Nebbia v. New York III: 36
Nebraska II: 585, 600, 613, 710; V: 127, 206, 316
Needham [Massachusetts] *Chronicle* IV: 88

Needham, Henry B. I: *474**, 478, *502, 513, 514, 515, 519, 524*, 542; II: *45,* 47, 68, 77, *89, 99, 103, 104, 111*, 124, *133, 138*, 177, 217

Neenan, J. M. II: *566**

Neill, Charles P. II: *519**, 544, *580;* III: 52

Neilson, William A. V: *113**

Nelles, Walter R. IV: *559**; V: 213

Nelson, Knute II: *311**, *315* 316-20, *326*, 331, *344*, 354, 371, 491, *665*; III: 29; IV: 130

Nelson, John M. V: *155**, 166, 174

Nelson, Samuel I: *10**

Nerney, May C. III: *297**, 305

Nesbit, Charles F. V: *311**, 341

Nettleton, A. E. IV: 89

Netzorg, Isaac II: *551**

Neuman, Abraham A. cited, III: 545

Neumann, Emanuel IV: *491**, 545, 551, 563; V: 250, *442*, 471, *475*, 479, 484, 488, 506, *513;* cited, IV: 437

Nevins, Allan cited, V: 596

Nevinson, Henry W. V: *402**, 512

New Bedford Street Railway I: 462

New Century Club I: 386

"The New Conception of Industrial Efficiency" (1911) II: 418

New Deal IV: 372, 475; V: 505-506, 510, 514-15, 518-20, 523, 526-28, 531, 536-40, 552-60, 563, 570-71, 585-86, 616-17, 625-26; LDB on V: 531, 537, 552, 555

New England Anti-Imperialist League I: 159

New England Association of Rrd Veterans III: 198

New England Civic Federation I: 357, 397, 555, 573; II: 59, 66

New England Divisions case V: 88

New England Dry Goods Association II: 65, 79, 84, 86

New England Free Trade League II: 657

New England Gas & Coke Co. I: 299, 349, 402

New England Hardware Dealers' Association II: 113

New England Investment & Security Co. II: 30, 42, 48, 49, 52, 55, 145, 149, 238, 242

New England Mutual Life Insurance . Co. II: 73

New England Navigation Co. II: 169, 174, 239; III: 72, 91, 560

New England Railroad Conference III: 156

"The New England Railroad Situation" (1912) II: 730

New England Railway Co. II: 255

New England Shoe & Leather Association II: 86, 98, 113

New England Telephone & Telegraph Co. I: 246, 332

New England Transportation Co. II: 127

"The New England Transportation Monopoly: The Proposed Merger" (1908) II: 65, 81-85, 90-91, 106, 109, 624; III: 233, 283

New England Zionist Committee III: 435, 641

New Hampshire I: 61, 192, 379, 406-407; II: 190, 207, 363-64, 405, 710; III: 264, 271, 320, 340; V: 98

New Hampshire Public Service Commission II: 630; III: 24, 49; IV: 48

New Haven: see New York, New Haven & Hartford Rrd

"The New Haven—An Unregulated Monopoly" (1912) II: 724, 726, 730; III: 129, 233, 283

New Haven [Connecticut] *Evening Leader* II: 279

New Jersey I: 455; II: 275

New Maccabaean IV: 437, 565

New Palestine IV: 428, 552, 565; V: 411, 427, 432, 468, 476, 547, 644

The New Republic II: 654; III: 599; IV: 37, 45, 81, 119, 141, 144, 266, 267, 363, 489, 510-23, 538, 540-42, 548; V: 15, 30, 40, 50, 53, 59, 62,

64, 65, 71, 92, 95, 125, 129-31, 134-35, 141, 154, 170, 188, 203, 209-10, 213, 226, 237, 244, 248, 250, 277, 281, 287, 312, 320, 324, 333, 338, 352, 353, 361, 370, 374, 377, 381-82, 390, 408, 515, 526, 561, 653; LDB on IV: 515; V: 62-63

New School for Social Research IV: 398

New State Ice Co. v. Liebmann V: 500, 503

New Statesman V: 437

New Student V: 151

New Voters' Festival I: 241

New Willard Hotel II: *509*

New York American II: 529, 670

New York & New England Rrd IV: 56-58, 65-67, 74, 127, 131

New York Bank Note Co. II: 481

New York Board of Insurance Commissioners I: *487*

New York Central Rrd. II: 34, 582; III: 5; IV: 74; V: 118

New York City I: 235, 336-37, 396, 406; III: 671-72; IV: 9, 11, 192, 294, 506, 552, 561

New York City Bank III: 267

New York City Board of Education III: 391

New York City College III: 644

New York Consolidated Gas Co. I: 581

New York Day V: 414

New York Evening Journal II: 724; IV: 175

New York Evening Mail IV: 512

New York Evening Post II: 92, 353, 362-63, 502, 724; IV: 129

New York Financial and Commercial Chronicle II: 175, 410

New York garment workers' strike and arbitration and the 'protocol of peace' in the garment industry II: 365-73, 381-82, 386-87, 390-92, 406-407, 417, 459-60, 483-89, 497, 500-503, 508, 518-19, 524, 569-72, 586, 616-18; III: 6, 9, 27-28, 52, 57,

73-74, 81-82, 104-105, 208-15, 401-402, 428-30, 524-25, 547, 562, 650-51, 669-73; IV: 9-10, 25-26, 263-64; V: 166

New York Industrial Commission IV: 541

New York Kehillah III: 193, 430, 651; IV: 204-205

New York Life Insurance Co. I: 363, 473, 486, 492, 540; II: 77, 285; V: 451

New York, New Haven & Hartford Rrd I: 300, 334, 444, 583-84, 591-96; II: 23-58, 61, 64-68, 76-77, 80-84, 93, 98, 104-105, 108-109, 115-16, 118-19, 121-23, 131-34, 136, 140-42, 144-52, 155-58, 163, 168-75, 178, 181-85, 188-90, 193-95, 206, 221, 223, 230-44, 251, 262, 266, 278, 405, 500-502, 520, 635-36, 724-28; III: 3, 9, 13-16, 20-25, 36, 41-42, 47, 49-50, 53-55, 58, 59, 66-68, 70-73, 76, 78, 83-84, 91-95, 99, 106-10, 123-24, 127-36, 140-50, 153, 164, 167, 171-82, 186-88, 190-95, 198-201, 204, 218-22, 225, 231, 240, 244-46, 259, 264-71, 274-77, 282-87, 306-307, 342-43, 346, 385, 411, 489, 560, 590, 613; IV: 8, 47, 57-59, 65-66, 71, 76, 81, 84, 87, 92, 150, 153, 214; V: 353, 391, 659; see also Brandeis, Louis D. and proposed merger of New York, New Haven & Hartford Rrd with the Boston & Maine Rrd

"New York, New Haven & Hartford Rrd Co. Financial Primer" (1909) II: 243, 278

New York, New Haven & Hartford Rrd, and proposed merger with the Boston & Maine Rrd I: 582-84, 591-96; II: 23-24, 27-58, 61-92, 98-99, 104-195, 198-99, 204-206, 221-23, 230-34, 237-46, 251-67, 272-83, 286, 329-30, 500-502, 506, 520, 580-85, 620-28, 631, 635-36, 644, 647, 675, 700, 722-29; III: 3, 12-16, 20-25, 49-50, 53-55, 58, 66-73, 106-109, 123-24,

New Haven Rrd (*continued*) 127-35, 141-50, 153-54, 164, 171-81, 186, 188-95, 204, 244-45, 264-71, 274-77, 282-87, 306-307, 560, 590; IV: 8, 47-48, 57-58, 71, 76, 81, 84, 87, 92, 150, 153, 214; V: 659

New York, New Haven & Hartford Rrd v. Fruchter V: 94-95

New York, New Haven & Hartford Rrd v. Offield II: 253-56

New York, Ontario & Western Rrd II: 502, 520

New York Press II: 724, 726

New York Public Service Commission II: 288; III: 384, 578; V: 106

New York state I: 320-21, 482-85, 506-507, 580; II: 207, 637; III: 271, 425-26; IV: 445, 541; V: 296, 598

New York State Crime Commission V: 397

New York Sun II: 410, 412, 515; IV: 101

New York Times II: 293, 365, 386, 394, 412, 415, 418, 435, 458, 465, 480, 486, 509, 545, 546, 603, 653, 657; III: 32, *372;* IV: 34, 37, 117, 133, 134, 135, 177, 203, 204, 252, 259, 284, 388, 462, 494, 530, 559, 566; V: 22, 71, 117, 127, 135, 166, 168, 173, 200, 201, 211, 213, 236, 242, 274, 281, 284, 299, 306, 318, 321, 325, 334, 345, 348, 353, 361, 367, 382, 387, 396, 410, 412, 413, 496, 500, 512, 515, 540, 552, 555, 557, 606

New York Times Annalist III: 202, *230,* 385

New York Tribune II: 333, 339

New York Wahrheit IV: 116

New York, Westchester & Boston Rrd III: 55, 92

New York Workingmen's Compensation Act II: 421, 427, 637; V: 236

New York World I: 336, 340, 392, 459, 483, 492; II: 69, 515, 724; IV: 144, 171, 515; V: 83, 125, 127, 144, 203, 237, 248, 259, 270, 310, 333, 353, 356, 370, 390

New York Zionist Federation IV: 153

New Zealand II: 477; V: 141

Newburyport Water Co. v. Newburyport I: 255

Newell, Frederick H. III: *49**

Newhall, George I: 553*, 556

Newlands, Francis G. II: 451*, 456, 523, 622, 693; IV: 36, 209, 222

Newman, Louis I. V: 391, 422*, 426, 643

Newman, Oliver P. III: 130*

Newspaper Enterprise Association: see Colver, William and Gardner, Gilson

Newsweek V: 553

Newton, Byron R. III: 44*, 62

Newton Savings Bank V: 487

Neylan, John F. V: 213

Nicaragua II: 359; V: 259, 270, 277

Nicely, James M. V: 120*, 229, 300

Nicholas II IV: 276

Nichols, Mr. III: 565; V: 386

Nichols v. Eaton I: 23

Nichols, W. I. I: 499

Nicholson, Mrs. R. C. III: 369

Nicholson, Sadie I: 409*, 513, 514; II: 31; V: 21, 233

Nickel Plate Rrd merger V: 210

Nickerson, Mr. I: 275

Nicolay, John cited, I: 336

Nicole, Pierre V: 184

Nielson v. Johnson V: 368

Nigro v. U.S. V: 318

Niles, David K. V: 515*

Niles, Edward E. II: 631*

Nims, Harry D. III: 118*

Nixdorff, Charles E. I: 351*

Nixon v. Herndon V: 275

Noble, Ransom E. cited, I: 455

Nock, Albert J. V: 315*, 648

Noggle, Burl cited, V: 89

Non-Partisan League IV: 542-43

Nordau, Anna cited, III: 303

Nordau, Max III: 302*, 336, 341; IV: 6, 8, 361, 473; V: 200

Nordau, Maxa cited, III: 303

Norfolk III: 369

Norfolk & Southern Rrd V: 508
Norman, Edward A. V: 619*
Norris, George W. IV: 609; V: 121, 171, 270*, 322, 337, 348, 418, 641
North American Review II: 16; V: 224
North Carolina III: 46
North Carolina Railroad Commission II: 10
North Dakota II: 523, 639, 710; III: 215; V: 47, 105
North Easton Bulletin IV: 88
North, Frederick D. I: 174
North, Simon N. IV: 99*
Northern New Hampshire Rrd II: 32
Northern Pacific Rrd II: 32; IV: 33, 67
Norton, Charles D. II: 344*, 373, 492
Norton, Charles E. I: 16*
Norton, Clement A. V: 566*
Norwood Messenger IV: 88
Norwood Press V: 548
Novomeysky, Moshe V: 194*
Noxon, Frank I: 530; II: 33*, 35
Noyes, Henry T. II: 589*
Noyes, Pierrepont B. III: 139, 447*
Nutter, George R. I: 126, 351*; II: 159, 190; III: 51, 59, 81, 83, 93, 99, 114, 117, 144, 171, 175, 192, 498; V: 151, 357, 496
Nuttermilch, Dr. IV: 157

O'Brian, John L. IV: 317*; V: 640
O'Brien, Edward H. I: 561*
O'Brien, Morgan J. I: 341*
O'Brien, Robert L. I: 148, 149*, 152, 157, 530, 540; II: 84, 106; V: 333, 402
O'Brien, William II: 272*
Ochs, Adolph S. IV: 388; V: 13
O'Connell, James II: 394*
O'Connell, William H. I: 535*; II: 152, 156
O'Conner, Charles J. IV: 27*
O'Conner, Harvey cited, IV: 544
Odland, Martin cited, II: 314

Odofredus V: 121*
O'Donnell, William J. III: 10*
O'Dwyer, William V: 651
Oettinger, Julia W. I: 24*
Oettinger, Samuel I: 25
Office Committee (Zionist) III: 504, 561, 603, 625, 632, 667, 668, 670; IV: 5, 12, 79, 81, 82, 83, 85, 133, 136, 187, 189, 217, 242, 270
Offield v. New York, New Haven & Hartford Rrd II: 253
Ogilby, Charles F. R. III: 444*
Ogilby, Remsen B. II: 78*, 140; III: 444
Ohio II: 207, 703; IV: 199, 323
Ohio State University IV: 497
Ohio Supreme Court II: 609
Ohio Workingmen's Compensation Act II: 507, 542; V: 510
O'Keefe, Mr. III: 42
O'Keefe v. Somerville I: 431
Oklahoma V: 296, 368, 500
Oklahoma v. Texas V: 175
O'Laughlin, John C. II: 134; IV: 28*
old age pensions and annuities, LDB on I: 565-67; II: 129, 176-77, 191-93, 196, 212, 246-48, 269-71, 277-78, 589-90; III: 28; IV: 272
Old Colony Street Railway Co. I: 224
Old Colony Trust Co. v. Commissioner of Internal Revenue V: 368
Old Dominion Copper & Smelting Co. I: 242-43; III: 360; IV: 48-50, 68
Old Dominion Copper & Smelting Co. v. Lewisohn II: 124
Oldfield, William A. II: 616*, 652, 653, 656; III: 99, 111-12, 126
Old South Church (Boston) V: 355
O'Leary, Michael A. III: 602*
Olin, William M. I: 206*
Oliver Co. v. Mexico V: 126
Ollivant, Alfred III: 330
Olmstead v. U.S. I: 101; V: 345
Olney, Peter B. Jr. I: 235*
Olney, Richard I: 475*; II: 485

Olsho, Sidney L. III: 388*
"On Maintaining Makers' Prices" (1913) III: 89, 94, 101
Openhym, Christine G. I: 25, 436*; II: 291; V: 350, 656
Openhym, George I: 436*; II: 291
Oppenheim, Wilfred A. III: 350
Oppenheimer, Franz III: 192*, 517; IV: 6
"The Opportunity in the Law" (1905) I: 267, 321-22, 325-26, 338-39; II: 350; III: 682; IV: 271
Order of the Sons of Zion III: 323, 488, 526, 572, 688; IV: 261
Oregon II: 600, 710
Oregon Minimum Wage case: see Stettler v. O'Hara
Oregon, University of V: 114
Oregon-Washington Rrd & Navigation Co. v. Washington V: 226-27
Oregon women's hours case: see Muller v. Oregon
O'Reilly, John B. III: 155*, 157
O'Reilly, Mary B. III: 155*, 157, 235
"Organized Labor and Efficiency" (1911) II: 418; III: 233
Ormsby-Gore, Wiliiam G. IV: 404*, 410, 455; V: 72, 579
Orton, Jessie F. II: 375*
Osborn, William H. III: 189*
Oskhenaniew, Mitchell III: 23*
Osgood, Eliza V. IV: 74*
O'Sullivan, John F. I: 123*, 124
O'Sullivan, Mary K. I: 263*, 264; IV: 154*
Otash, Habib F. IV: 164*
Other People's Money (1914) I: 396, 595; III: 49, 60, 146-47, 165, 168, 171, 179, 183, 187-90, 195, 204-205, 207, 211, 216, 219-21, 232, 238-39, 272-73, 280, 284, 310, 344, 440, 451; IV: 511; V: 482, 493-95, 496, 499, 509, 519, 534, 568, 599
Otis, Harrison G. II: 517*
Ottinger, Albert V: 361*
"Our Financial Oligarchy" (1913) III: 169, 183, 187

"Our New Peonage: Discretionary Pensions" (1912) II: 652
The Outlook II: 5, 106-107, 191, 277-78, 362-63, 371-72, 375, 433, 442, 509, 575, 590, 701-702; III: 657; IV: 5, 178, 198; V: 333
Overbeck, Johannes A. I: 96, 104
Overman, Lee S. IV: 164
Owen, Robert L. II: 622; III: 115, 202*
Owens, John W. II: 579*
Owers, Frank W. II: 546*

Pacific Coast Steamship Co. II: 320
Pacific Development Corporation V: 21-23, 29
Pacific Gas & Electric Co. v. San Francisco V: 132
Packard & Field Co. IV: 89
Paderewski, Ignace J. IV: 353*
Page, Miss I: 62
Page, Robert G. V: 244*, 247, 404
Page, Thomas N. III: 17*
Page, Walter H. I: 392*; II: 722; V: 169
Paine, Horace W. III: 234*
Paine, Robert T. Jr. I: 176*, 229, 288, 294, 497; IV: 122
Paint & Oil Club II: 67, 88
Painter, Roy III: 55*
Palestina Amt III: 452, 461, 469, 472, 627
Palestine, LDB and the development of II: 537; III: 117, 155-59, 186, 206, 226, 235-36, 312-13, 317-18, 336-37, 354-56, 372-73, 416-18, 421-25, 427-28, 452-53, 468-77, 492, 495-501, 513-17, 520-22, 580, 607-11, 638-39, 674-75, 678-80; IV: 83, 109-10, 178, 334-36, 356, 417-20, 435-36, 446-47, 469, 495; V: 8, 16, 19-20, 36-39, 44, 48, 54-56, 112, 148, 182, 194-95, 220, 313-14, 382-89, 397-403, 407-408, 411, 416-17, 423-24, 427-28, 433, 436-37, 443-81, 484-92, 495, 506-10, 513-14, 521-26, 529-33, 542-44, 547, 558-59, 571-83, 586, 590-94, 602-609, 612-31, 636-37, 645, 651-52; LDB on IV: 248, 417-20

"Palestine and the Jewish Democracy" (1915) III: 657, 659; IV: 6; V: 534

Palestine & Near East Economic Magazine V: 434, 450, 464

Palestine Development Council V: 9, 16, 18, 27, 37, 74, 101, 103, 107, 111, 112, 220, 490

Palestine Development Leagues V: 26, 38, 490

Palestine Economic Corporation III: 352; V: 195, 196, 220, 416-19, 433, 443, 451, 461-65, 471, 481, 491, 506, 543, 620, 621, 629, 645

Palestine Economic Review V: 479

Palestine Endowment Fund V: 103, 220, 417, 462, 471, 473, 491, 558, 576, 587, 592, 620, 626, 634, 638, 649

Palestine, England's administration of IV: 410, 420, 446-47, 455-57, 461-62, 495-96; V: 56, 220, 383-86, 398, 400-401, 422-24, 427-28, 436-37, 452, 455-60, 467-70, 474, 487, 521-22, 574-81, 590-94, 601-605, 607-609, 612-22, 651-52

Palestine General Relief Fund III: 458, 639; IV: 338, 344, 351, 355

Palestine Jewish Colonization Association III: 499; V: 443

Palestine, LDB's trip to (1919) IV: 391-92, 394, 396-424

Palestine Restoration Fund IV: 328, 338, 341-42, 377, 428, 485

Palfrey, John G. I: 351*; II: 362; III: 223

Palgrave, Francis T. I: 104

Palmer, A. Mitchell III: 347; V: 122*, 229, 321

Palmer Cooperative Association II: 530

Palmer, Edward H. I: 578*

Palmer, Frederick cited, III: 350

Palmer, Paul A. V: 636*

Pam, Hugo III: 616*; IV: 250, 252; V: 219

Pam, Max III: 211*, 617; IV: 28, 350, 385

Panama I: 337, 346-47; III: 149; V: 457

Panama bill II: 620-22

Panama conference (1939) V: 627

Pan American Financial Conference III: 559

panic of 1907 II: 46, 221

Panitz, Esther L. cited IV: 563

Paris, France IV: 405-406, 421

Park, Clara C. II: 454*, 541

Park, Robert E. II: 455*

Parke, James I: 10*

Parker, Alton B. II: 632*

Parker, Dr. V: 89

Parker, Edmund M. I: 347*, 359, 419

Parker, Edwin B. IV: 28*

Parker, Fordis C. I: 406*

Parker, George B. V: 425*

Parker, Herbert I: 270*

Parker, Hyman V: 566*, 567, 595

Parker, Miss II: 199, 370

Parker, R. Wayne II: 336*, 354; IV: 130

Parkers, the I: 19

Parkhurst, Lewis II: 97*, 138, 143, 160

Parkinson, Mr. V: 569

Parkman, Francis V: 251

Parkman, Henry I: 534*, 565

Parlin, Albert N. IV: 57*

Parlin, Charles C. III: 116, 139

Parry, John E. I: 166*

Parsons, Charles IV: 57*, 74

Parsons, Frank I: 488*; II: 46, 81, 106

Parsons, Herbert C. II: 7*

Parsons, Mr. V: 403

Parsons, O. E. IV: 543

Parsons, Theophilus I: 8

Parzen, Herbert cited IV: 282, 294, 341, 376

Pascal, Joel F. cited II: 324

Pasha, Jemal III: 418, 431, 520

Passfield, Lord: see Webb, Sidney

Passfield White Paper V: 459, 468, 470, 479, 545

Patten, John A. IV: 186*

Patten, Simon III: 208

Patterson, Edwin W. V: 285*

Patterson, James T. cited V: 79

Patterson, John L. V: 236*, 252, 269
Patterson, Mr. IV: 85
Paul, Wesley I: 377*
Pauline: see Goldmark, Pauline
Pavesich, Paolo I: 304
Pavesich v. New England Life Insurance Co. I: 303, 306
Pawhuska v. Pawhuska Oil & Gas Co. V: 350
Payne-Aldrich tariff II: 286, 653
Payne, Henry B. I: 122*
P.C.: see Provisional Executive Committee for Zionist Affairs
P.E.C.: see Provisional Executive Committee for Zionist Affairs
Peabody, Elizabeth II: 16*; IV: 113, 307; V: 287
Peabody, Francis G. I: 418
Peabody, George F. I: 506*
Peabody, William R. I: 416, 419, 426
"Peace with Liberty" (1905) I: 304
Pearson, Andrew (Drew) R. V: 414*
Peary, Robert G. II: 358*
Pecora investigation V: 530
Peck, Mrs. IV: 265
Peel Commission V: 577, 591, 602
Peel, Roy V. V: 415*
Pegram, John C. I: 366*, 380, 392, 484, 489, 494
Peixotto, Ernest C. I: 119*
Pelham, Thomas W. V: 346*
Pember, John E. II: 73*
Penick, James L. Jr. cited, II: 308, 315; III: 33
Pennekamp v. Florida IV: 451
Pennsylvania I: 218; III: 347; V: 91
Pennsylvania Coal Co. I: 214
Pennsylvania Coal Co. v. Mahon V: 78, 83, 86
Pennsylvania Rrd III: 15, 542
Pennsylvania Rrd Co. v. U.S. Railroad Labor Board V: 86-87
Pennsylvania, University of V: 285
Pennsylvania v. West Virginia V: 93, 98, 105
Penrose, Boies III: 347, 611*; IV: 529
People v. Marcus II: 679

People v. North River Sugar Refining Co. I: 216
People v. Williams I: 521
People's League III: 29, 50-51
People's Lobby I: 474, 520, 524, 558-59, 568, 571; II: 45-46, 47, 77, 89, 101, 177, 217; III: 29
People's Municipal-Ownership League III: 133
People's Relief Committee IV: 155, 158, 205
People's Savings Bank (Brockton) II: 5, 14-15, 24, 114, 192, 195, 201, 226-28, 301, 596-98
Pepper, George W. II: 317, 321*, 327, 360; IV: 63, 87; V: 116, 124, 226
Percy, Eustace S. C. III: 20, 262, 344; IV: 233, 260, 279, 281, 284, 287, 293, 328, 331, 405-406; V: 200
Pericles quoted, V: 542
Perin, George L. II: 217*
Perkins, Dexter cited, I: 321
Perkins, Frances I: 166; V: 523*, 531, 536, 540, 552, 586, 717
Perkins, George W. II: 525*, 561, 666, 670, 673, 675, 699, 700, 727; III: 4; LDB on II: 666, 700-701
Perkins, George W. Jr. V: 41*
Perkins, Thomas N. IV: 317*, 454; V: 308
Perlstein, Benjamin III: 295*, 298, 306, 350, 361, 365, 372, 374, 406, 410, 417, 426, 445, 449, 461, 466, 470-71, 477, 478, 479, 482, 494, 503, 520, 522, 524, 525, 526, 530, 533, 536, 548, 551, 563, 569, 579, 584, 595, 598, 611, 625, 632, 635, 666; IV: 5, 16, 17, 24, 62, 129, 137, 148, 167, 188, 193, 208, 216, 263
Perry, Jarius W. I: 33
Perry, Lilla C. I: 105
Perry, Ralph B. cited, III: 413
Perry v. U.S. V: 529
Persons, Warren M. I: 578*, 579
Perth Amboy (New Jersey) IV: 464
Peters, Andrew J. III: 218*

Peters, George G. IV: 52*
Peterson, A. F. I: 385
Peterson, James A. IV: 53*
Pew, Marlen E. II: 404*, 406, *498*, 563, *568*
Pewsner, Samuel J. III: 475*, 514
Peyser, Julius I. III: 574*, 579, 584; IV: 31-32, 280, 318
Phagen, Mary III: 373
Phelan, James D. IV: 349*; V: 279
Phelps Publishing Co. II: 202
Phi Beta Kappa IV: 68, 132
Phi Epsilon Rho IV: 496, 499
Philadelphia III: 333, 349, 354, 388, 395, 595, 600; IV: 9-10, 206, 269; V: 634
Philadelphia Evening Ledger IV: 206
Philadelphia Inquirer IV: 242
Philadelphia Municipal League I: 285
Philadelphia North American II: 408; III: 113, 119, 444
Philadelphia Public Ledger IV: 9, 198, 529
Philadelphia Tageblatt IV: 451
Philadelphia v. Philadelphia Rapid Transit Co. II: 375
Philipp, Emanuel L. III: 409; IV: 459
Philippine Islands I: 147-59, 161; III: 96, 144; IV: 449; V: 657
Philipson, David III: 310, 316*, 334, 370, 405, 415, 426, 430, 438, 441, 444, 464-66, 674; IV: 4, 5, 388; LDB on III: 334
Phillips, Harlan cited, II: 351; III: 209; V: 259, 283, 297
Phillips, John S. II: 489*
Phillips, Mr. V: 311
Phillips, William III: 382*, *492*, 610; IV: 305; V: 525
Philo, E. E. IV: 13*
philosophy, LDB on the study of V: 260
Phoenix Mutual Life Insurance Co. I: 380, 390
Picot, Francois G. IV: 495

Pidgin, Charles F. I: *350**, 447
Pierce, Dante M. III: 301*
Pierce, Frank II: 335*, 353
Pierce, Myron E. II: 257; cited, I: 171
Pierce v. U.S. IV: 451
Pillsbury, Albert E. I: *131**, 186-88, 190, *191*, 202, 206; IV: 93, 96
Pinanski, Abraham E. II: *228**
Pinanski, Nathan III: *301**
Pinchot, Amos, R. E. II: 309*, 317, 344, 346, *351*, 370, *386*, *398*, *458*, *476*, *479*, *490*, *496*, 514, *515*, 546, 569; III: 347; IV: 25, *41*, 133, *239*; V: 285
Pinchot-Ballinger conservation controversy, LDB and II: 306-64, 379-80, 386, 396, 401-402, 414, 457-59, 475; III: 246, 394, 464; IV: 63, 68, 70, 73, 84, 86, 92, 101, 119, 129, 150, 171; V: 116, 126, 641-43, 653
Pinchot, Gifford I: 296, 360, 396; II: 307, 309*, 314, 317, 320, 321, 324, 337, *346*, *355*, 356, 358, 360, 386, *396*, 399, *413*, 457, *458*(2), 468, *473*, 478, 515, 569, 611-12, 625, 632, *640*, 654, *660*, 685, *715*, *723*; III: 7, *8*, 18, 33, *59*, *66*, 77, *347*; IV: 41, 63, 87, 293; V: 317, 641; cited, II: 308, 346
Pingree, Ransom C. I: 460*
Pinkett, Harold T. cited, II: 310
Pinsker, Leo III: 156
Pitney, Mahlon IV: 367*, 521; V: 40-41, 79, 86, 126
Pittsburgh II: 318, 704; III: 316
Pittsburgh Bar Association IV: 36
Pittsburgh Survey II: 543
Pittsfield Eagle IV: 94
Pittsfield Street Railway Co. II: 240
Pizzella, Frank I: 438
Plant, Thomas G. I: 369*; II: 376, 410, 428, 465, 556
Plato IV: 486
Plummer, Henry M. I: 533*, 565
Plunkett, William B. I: 561*
Plutarch II: 377; V: 141, 304

Plymouth Observer IV: 88

Poale Zion III: 323, 330, 527, 529-30, 556-57, 264, 567-70, 576, 667; IV: 98, 133, 158, 320, 322, 398

Podell, David L. V: 29*, 32

Poe, Edgar A. V: 167

Poindexter, Miles II: 376*, 513, 563, 622; IV: 209

Poindexter, Mr. IV: 480; V: 233, 324, 399

Poland III: 306, 369, 381, 431-32, 436, 456-57, 486; IV: 95, 141-42, 155-66, 170, 179, 232-33, 236, 286, 353, 385; V: 517

Polenberg, Richard cited V: 642

Polier, Justine W. T. V: 553*

Polioiketes, Demetrius V: 95*

political corruption, LDB on I: 204-205, 268, 369

Poll, Dr. V: 587

Pollock, Sir Frederick I: 105*; V: 337

Pollock, Walter W. II: 573*, 577; V: 212

Pomerene, Atlee II: 523*, 622; V: 87

Pond, Preston I: 536, 578, 589

Pond, Walter IV: 94*

Pool, David deS. III: 450*, 531, 602, 663; IV: 381, 469; V: 250, 633

Pool, Tamara deS. V: 630, 632*

Poole, Ernest II: 389*, 453; III: 233; IV: 67, 118; V: 75, 119, 473, 505

Poole, William IV: 51

Pope, Albert A. I: 410*

Pope, Alexander quoted, IV: 131

Popkin, Alice B. G. V: 342*

Porritt, Edward cited, I: 264

Portenar, Abraham J. III: 10*

Porter, Benjamin C. I: 20*

Porter, George F. III: 75*

Port Said, Egypt IV: 409, 419

Portsmouth Conference and Treaty I: 338, 354-58

Portsmouth Harbor Land & Hotel Co. v. U.S. V: 94

Posario-Mendoza Rrd III: 493

Posner, Louis S. IV: 429*

Postal Savings Banks I: 503-504, 526-27

Potter, Mark W. V: 100*, 366

Pound, Cuthbert W. V: 124, 204*, 369

Pound, Roscoe II: 299*, 613, 656, 657, 712; III: 13, 18, 50, 109, 134, 135, 209, 281, 287, 288, 373, 382; IV: 27, 91, 134, 142, 264, 270, 395, 398, 400, 451, 459, 464, 489, 498, 524, 541; V: 3, 11, 17, 52, 78, 80, 94, 102, 109, 130, 143, 146, 159, 165, 184, 187, 192, 197, 204, 259, 271, 281, 283, 323, 327, 337, 352-55, 373, 378; LDB on IV: 27, 395-96; V: 281

Powell, Thomas R. V: 97*, 123-24, 161, 174, 200, 323, 344, 410; cited, V: 89

Power, Eileen E. V: 215*

Powers, James H. V: 382*

Pow-wow Law Club I: 8; IV: 225

Poznanski, Samuel A. IV: 157*

Prang & Co. I: 83

Pratt, Harvey H. II: 86*

Pratt v. Langdon I: 76

"The Preferential Shop: A Letter from LDB" (1912) II: 587-89

the preferential union shop v. closed or open shops, LDB on II: 368-69, 371-72, 417, 562-63, 588; III: 10-11

Presby & Co. I: 573

Prescott, A. W. II: 432*

Prescott, Mr. III: 565

Price, Benjamin S. II: 20*

price control, LDB on IV: 308

"Price Fixing and Monopoly" (1913) III: 101

Price, George M. II: 483*, 487, 503; III: 74; LDB on III: 74

Price maintenance on trademarked goods, LDB and II: 615-16; III: 31-32, 89-90, 93-105, 111-13, 118-22, 124-27, 131-34, 138-38, 146-47, 152, 169-70, 173-74, 216-18, 225-27, 434,

446-48, 539-40, 559-60, 592, 618-19; LDB on, III: 199, 101, 103, 113, 120-21

Price, Overton W. II: 346*, 371 *612;* IV: 63

Prichard, E. F. cited, II: 351; V: 40

Primrose, Albert E. IV: 410*, 414

Primrose, Archibald P. IV: 410*, 414

Prince, Charles A. IV: 59, 74

Prince, Frederick H. IV: 58, 74

Prince, Morton I: 143*, *145,* 162, 169, *171, 174,* 176, *177,* 178-79, *180,* 182-83, *184, 198,* 199, *200, 223, 224,* 225, 229, *271, 272-73,* 275, 290, 292-94, 297-98, 301, *307, 326,* 419, 423, 424, 425; IV: 120; V: 241

Princeton University V: 652

Pringle, Henry cited, I: 209, 360

Printing Pressmen & assistants' Union I: 250

Prior, Emory A. I: 22*

Pritchett, Henry S. V: 110, 249*, 271

Procope, Hjalmar V: 455

Proctor, Charles W. III: 172*

Proctor & Ellison IV: 89

prohibition and enforcement, LDB on IV: 104-107, 320-21, 400, 461, 497, 559; V: 65, 91, 103, 160-61

Promboin, Jacob III: 485

"Protocol of Peace": see New York garment workers' strike and arbitration

"The Protocols of the Learned Elders of Zion" V: 365, 453, 507

Prouty, Charles A. II: 626, 631, 635, 700; III: 21, 47, 66*, 70-71, 76, 92, *108,* 123-24, 133, *136, 164,* 167, *171,* 181, 194-95, 218, 223, 245, 287, 410, 439

Prouty, Charles N. I: 578*

Prouty, William III: 76*

Providence Securities Co. II: 28, 48, 49, 52, 231, 243; III: 54, 92

Provisional Executive Committee for Zionist Affairs III: 291, 293-95, 298-303, 313, 317, 320-29, 332, 351-56,

359, 362, 365, 367, 372-76, 387, 394, 400, 408, 416, 421, 425, 433, 445, 448-49, 452-53, 459, 462, 466-90, 496-501, 507, 510-13, 517, 521-34, 537, 544-58, 578-91, 600, 603-10, 614, 623, 638-41, 648-49, 664-70, 674, 678-79; IV: 10, 11, 17, 20, 79, 108, 132, 137, 151, 173, 178, 179, 181, 190, 195, 205, 212, 216, 218, 227, 233, 236, 244, 250, 253, 257, 261, 280, 296, 298, 318, 320, 323, 337, 338, 348, 382; V: 577

Prudential Life Insurance Co. I: 505-506, 541, 558; II: 591

Prussian Aaron III: 338*

The Public III: 104

Public Franchise League I: 167, 173, 175-81, 184-89, 203-210, 220, 223-24, 229-30, 243, 252, 271-75, 278, 290-97, 300-301, 305, 312-15, 318, 327, 400, 411, 416, 420, 425-28, 432, 435, 439, 452, 467, 469, 512, 515-16, 523-24, 527, 531, 538; II: 4, 15, 23, 26, 62, 64, 89, 94, 211, 219, 224, 288-89, 349, 396, 432, 457, 465, 486, 579; III: 75, 129, 133, 191, 276, 278, 287, 613; IV: 29, 119-27; V: 157, 338, 560; LDB on II: 288-89

public franchise, utility and traction contests in Boston I: 100, 128-35, 138-46, 160-210, 220, 244-46, 257-58, 264-65, 278, 282, 295-97, 329-33, 347-49, 388-90, 405-406, 416-20, 423-26, 467-77, 512, 516-17; II: 10, 23, 26, 71-72, 94, 211-12, 224, 288-89, 396-97, 419-20, 432, 465-66, 480, 482-86, 540; IV: 68, 88, 94, 97, 104; see also Public Franchise League and Brandeis, Louis D. and consolidation of the Boston gas utility

Public Information League I: 234

Public institutions hearings (1894-95) I: 120; IV: 68; V: 273

public office for himself, LDB on II: 26, 31, 642, 651, 673, 699, 715,

public office for himself (*cont.*)
725; III: 37-38, 44-45, 129, 130; V: 319

public opinion, LDB on I: 97, 226; II: 192-93

public ownership, LDB on I: 438-41, 590; II: 618-19; III: 132; V: 4, 67, 360

Public School Association (Boston) I: 164, 178, 238-39, 240, 375

Public Service Commission (Boston) IV: 47

Public Utilities Holding Company Act V: 555

Puck Magazine I: 61; V: 83

Puffer, Loring W. I: 525*

Pujo, Arsene P. III: 48*

Pujo Committee III: 48, 84, 165, 169, 184, 187; V: 288; LDB on III: 184, 187

Pulitzer, Joseph I: 174, 209, 340*; V: 585

Pullman, George M. III: 24*

Pullman Palace Car Co. III: 24

Pullman, Raymond W. II: 346*, 375, 383, 392, 651, 685; III: 45, 80

Pullman strike II: 422

Purcell, William E. II: 523*

Purdy, Milton D. II: 68*

Pusey, Merlo cited, I: 276, 321

Putnam, Herbert II: 479*

Putnam, Mr. V: 497

Putnam, Mrs. I: 57

Quaker City Cab Co. v. Pennsylvania V: 483

Queen Elizabeth I. quoted, V: 567

Quisenbury, Smith IV: 226*

R. B. Grover Co. IV: 89

Rabinowicz, Oskar K. cited, III: 328; IV: 420

Rackemann, Felix I: 274*; II: 509

Radical Zionist Party III: 519

Raffalowich, S. III: 496

Railroad Commission of California v. Los Angeles Rrd Corp. V: 415

Railroad Holding Company bill III: 274

Railroad Securities bill III: 284

Railroad Securities Commission (Massachusetts) III: 26

Railway Business Association III: 224

Railway Labor Board V: 25

Raleigh, Sir Walter quoted, V: 567

Ralston, Samuel M. V: 77

Rand, Arnold A. I: 494*

Rand, William Jr. IV: 27*

Randall, Samuel III: 348*

Randolph Register IV: 88

Raphael I: 19

Raphael, Theophile II: 550*

Rapp, Walter II: 86

Raskin, Philip M. IV: 499*

Raskob, John J. V: 348*, 506

Rassieur, Leo V: 305*

Rassieur, Theodore V: 305

Ratcliff, Paul IV: 44

Ratcliffe, Samuel K. IV: 423*

Ratnoff, Nathan V: 420*, 421, 429, 451

Ratshesky, Abraham C. III: 366*

Rauch, Joseph V: 25*, 108, 218, 254, 264, 268, 391, 405, 501

Rauschenbusch, Pauline R. V: 279*

Rauschenbusch, Walter V: 172

Raushenbush, Elizabeth B. I: 4, 101-102, 136*, 165, 245, 346, 356, 359, 364, 407, 438-39, 442; II: 9, 18, 208, 287, 305, 343, 345, 364, 381, 531, 650, 660, 706, 728; III: 100, 111, 231, 235, 244, 246, 259, 271, 420, 503, 513, 565; IV: 45, 258, 267, 271, 274, 317, 329, 332, 363, 372, 385, 387, 400, 402, 411, 420, 422, 424, 443, 449, 458, 459, 468, 470, 471, 474, 480, 548, 567; V: 4, 5, 10, 21, 25, 26, 32, 53, 87, 88, 90, 97, 99, 113, 172, 184, 186, 210, 215, 231, 232, 240, 246, 279, 280, 297, 306, 312, 330, 345, 381, 382, 383, 409, 412, 475, 478, 498, 504, 510, 513, 514, 520, 523, 526, 527, 528, 531, 536,

537, 539, 552, 554, 555, 560, 585, 601, 610, 625, 650

Raushenbush, Paul A. I: 136; V: 172*, 184, 186, 210, 215, 231, 232, 246, 279, 280, 297, 381, 383, 412, 475, 498, 512, 513, 514, 520, 528, 537, 555, 560, 563, 625; cited, V: 499; LDB on V: 184

Raushenbush, Walter B. V: 345*, 381, 475, 510, 514, 537, 560, 586, 625

Rawle, Francis I: 339*; IV: 118

Rayburn bill III: 284

Raygorodsky, Mr. III: 585

Raymond, Robert L. I: 239*

Reading, Arthur K. V: 328

Reading, Lord IV: 309*, 388; V: 42, 384, 521; LDB on IV: 309

Reading Rrd III: 182

Ream, Norman B. III: 267*

"Rebirth of the Jewish Nation": see "Zionism and Patriotism"

reciprocity tariff II: 456, 499

Reconstruction Finance Corporation V: 496, 508

Record, George L. I: 455*

"red scare" IV: 395, 441-42, 445-46, 477, 510

Redfield, Julia W. IV: 270*

Redfield, William C. II: 658*, 661; III: 41, 42, 44, 73, 94, 102, 112, 211, 581; IV: 270

Redlich, Josef IV: 538*, 546; V: 134, 259, 327

Reed, James A. IV: 32*, 87; V: 55, 270

Reed, John V: 42

Reed, Merl E. cited, V: 10

Reed, Robert R. II: 699*

Reed, Silas W. II: 407*

Reed, Stanley F. V: 595*, 601

Reed, Thomas B. I: 159*; II: 183

Reed, Warren A. I: 278, 326, 461, 464, 498, 504, 524, 534, 535, 538, 552, 554, 561, 570, 575, 589; II: 5, 8, 11, 14, 15, 19, 109; LDB on I: 554-55

Rees, Russell I: 93

Reese, Arthur I: 59

Reform Club (Massachusetts) I: 175, 209, 264, 301, 392

Regal Shoe Co. II: 202, 205, 553; IV: 89

regularity of employment, LDB on I: 213; II: 444-50, 575, 580, 630; III: 230, 390; IV: 22-23, 343; V: 20, 133, 329, 335, 424-25, 497-98, 510

Reich, Leon V: 189*

Relief Committee of One Hundred III: 362, 365

Remick, James W. I: 484*; III: 156

Reno, Conrad I: 288*

Renshaw, Patrick cited, III: 99

respect for the law, LDB on II: 148-52, 340-42, 531-36, 646, 655-56, 718-19; V: 227-28, 345-46

Ressler, Roy E. III: 109*

Retail Dealers' Association III: 96

Review of Reviews II: 186, 579; III: 166; IV: 428

Revisionist (Zionist) movement III: 520; V: 437-38, 479, 483, 492, 507, 551, 622

Reynolds, James Brownson I: 490*, 499, 506

Reynolds, James Burton I: 520*, 558, 572; II: 45, 68

Reynolds, Mr. V: 275

Reznikoff, Charles cited, III: 294; IV: 406

Rhoades, John H. I: 507*

Rhode Island I: 484, 489

Rhode Island Suburban Co. II: 56

Rhodes, James F. I: 530*

Rhodes, Stephen H. I: 494*

Rice, William G. IV: 509*, 553; V: 100, 298, 378, 589; LDB on V: 378

Richard, Livy S. II: 404*, 406, 428, 576; III: 79, 121; IV: 206, 306

Richards, Bernard G. II: 402*, 611; III: 22, 358, 409, 604, 634, 636, 651-53, 681; IV: 116, 134, 137, 172, 188, 197, 252, 291, 312, 545, 551; V: 580

Richards, Harry S. V: 378*

Richards, James L. I: 307*, 313, 323, 362, 399-400, 424, *427*, 438, 441, 463, 588; II: 4, 269, 644; III: *69*, 166, 204, 245, 265, 276, *277, 282, 285;* IV: 94, 100, 113, 120, 124, 127; V: 319, 414, 453, 471, *475*, 487, 569

Richards, William R. I: 18*, 19, 21, 43, 45

Richardson, P. C. II: 311, 338*

Richberg, Donald R. V: 51*, 100, 161, 499, 511, *518*

Richmond, Virginia IV: 148

Ricker, E. P. III: 177*

Rickey, Harry N. II: *675*

Riddle, Judge II: 603-610

Riddle v. MacFadden I: 404

Ridgeway, Erman J. II: 69*, *203*

Riegelman, Mr. V: 456

Riggs National Bank (Washington) III: 509

"The Right to Privacy" (1890) I: 101, 302-304, 306; IV: 33; V: 534

Rihani, Ameen V: 409

Riker-Hegeman chain IV: 183

Riley, Herbert S. I: 544*, 549, 556, 578

Riley, Thomas P. III: 321*

Ripley, M. M. V: 186

Ripley, William Z. II: *184*, *189;* V: 192, 205, 207, 590

Ritchie, Thomas F. V: 402*

Ritchie v. People II: 297

Ritchie v. Wayman II: 297, 298, 299, 300, 315-18, 350, 359, 602

Ritchie, W. C. II: 297

Riverside Press V: 548

"Road to Social Efficiency" (1911) II: 433-34, 442, 575, 590; III: 390, 489

Robb, Charles H. V: 74*

Robberts, Jennie V: 551, 649

Robbins, Alexander H. IV: 141*

Robbins, Edward D. III: 175*

Robbins, Hayes I: 277*, 282, *328, 334, 360, 391, 397, 461, 473*, 555, 577; II: 59; V: 93

Robbins, Henry S. IV: 28*

Roberts, Edwin E. II: 622*

Roberts, Owen J. V: 117, 255*, 538

Roberts v. Claremont Railway & Lighting Co. I: 535

Robertson, Reynolds V: 404

Robinson, James W. I: 169

Robinson, James J. V: 411*

Robinson, Joseph T. II: 612*

Robinson, M. H. cited, II: 222

Robinson, Louis III: 579; IV: 328, 389

Roche, Josephine V: 373*, 377, 378-79, 383

Rochester, New York IV: 7-8, 463

Rockefeller Foundation V: 652; see also Flexner, Simon

Rockefeller, John D. I: 409; III: 30, 48, 433; V: 215, 373, 379, 383, 412, 524; see also Standard Oil Co.

Rocker, Louis P. V: 441

Rocky Mountain Fuel Co. V: 373, 380, 382

Roe, Gilbert E. III: 145*, 150, 154, *301*

Rogers, A. R. II: 296*

Rogers, David cited, III: 391

Rogers, Edward S. II: 226

Rogers, Lindsay V: 189*

Rogers v. Shultz I: 40, 50, 52

Rogers, Walter S. III: 21*, 184

Roland, Madame quoted, IV: 143

Roman history, study of, LDB on V: 185, 251

Romasco, Albert V. cited, IV: 301

Rome, Watertown & Ogdensburg Rrd IV: 74

Roosevelt, Eleanor IV: 475; V: 584

Roosevelt, Franklin D. II: 668; III: 30, 84, 106, 117, 119, 296, 382, 586, 601, 623; IV: 474*, 476; V: 77, 239, 361, 363, 367, 505, 514-15, 516, 520, 523, 529, 536, 539, 554, 555, 556, 557, 564, 576, *583, 585*, 588, 602, 603, *605, 606, 610, 613, 616, 617*, 628, 629, 630, *631, 635, 642*, 650, *651, 652;* LDB on V: 505, 556

Roosevelt, Kermit V: 525

Roosevelt, Theodore I: 209, 337, 355, 360, 387, 445, 502, 514-15, *517*, 520,

590; II: 18, 27, 45, 47, 68, 70, 77, 85, 99, 101-102, 111, 115, *124*, 129, *130*, 133-34, 138, 168, 186, 201, 213, 249, 307, 320, 329, 341, 346, 355, 356, 358, 361-64, 370, 376, 459, 468, 525, 542, 547, 550, 561, 568, 573, 611, 613, 633, 642, 645, 648-49, 653, 654, 662, 666, 669, 670-75, 683, 686, 694-95, 700, 703-706, 709-10, 714, 718, 727; III: 96, 107, 209, 222, 638, 676-77; IV: 26, 30, 37, 233, 519; V: 132, 211, 284 365, 482, 557; LDB on II: 68, 341-42, 568, 662

Roosevelt, Theodore Jr. V: *524**

Root Commission IV: 306

Root, Elihu I: 147*; II: 322; III: 420, 493; IV: 64, 118, 277; V: 110

Ropes Will case IV: 33

Ropke, August II: *365**

Roschen v. Ward V: 378

Roseman, Max III: *659**

Rosenbaum, Solomon G. III: *590**

Rosenberg, A. III: *669**, 670

Rosenblatt, Bernard A. II: *614**; III: *150*, *186*, 377, 454-55, *522*, 621, 652; IV: 5, 404, *448*, 455, *467*, 480, *499*, 509, 545; V: 250

Rosenblatt, Gertrude G. III: *463**

Rosenbloom, Mrs. V: 253

Rosenbloom, Solomon IV: *393**, 438; V: 9, *18*, 26, 39, 51, *54*, 73

Rosenbush, Al A. III: 403

Rosenfield, Leonora D. cited, I: 325

Rosengarten, Isaac V: 431

Rosenman, Samuel V: 49

Rosensohn, Samuel J. III: *651**; IV: 318, 322; V: 16, 195, 309

Rosenstock, Morton cited, III: 294; IV: 508

Rosenthal, Albert V: *158**

Rosenthal, Herman IV: 170*

Rosenthal, Lessing IV: 388

Rosenwald, Julius II: *537**; III: 368, 376-77, *421*, 514, 530; IV: 276, 555; V: 7, 297, 597

Rosenwald, William V: *597**

Roslindale Citizens' Association (Boston) I: 368

Rosov, Israel B. IV: *419**, 443; V: *621*

Ross, Charles G. V: *585**

Ross, Denman W. I: *16**, 20, 34, 83; V: 161, 295; LDB on V: 295

Ross, Edward A. II: *510**, 695; III: 331, 381, 507; V: 444

Ross, William A. IV: *27**

Rossetti, Dante G. I: 16

Rossiter, Clinton cited, III: 88

Rostovtsev, Mikhail I. V: 245, 251

Rotch, Arthur I: *81**

Roth, Alvin S. cited, III: 409

Rothenberg, Morris IV: 382, 545; V: 492

Rothschild, Evelina III: *679**

Rothschild, Ferdinand J. III: 680

Rothschild, Jerome J. III: *388**

Rothwell, Bernard J. II: 46, *109**, 117, *118*, *122*, *127*, 135, *156*, 178, 205, *222*, 272; V: 4, 332, 340

Rowe, Leo S. IV: *520**; V: 354, 627

Rowe, William V. IV: *27**, 221

Rubashow, Sh'neur Z. V: *568**

Rubin, David III: *357**, *381*, *395*, 427, 459-60, *528*, 584

Rubin, Samuel V: 299

Rubinoff, Jacob III: *388**

Rubinow, Isaac M. IV: *467**

Rubinsohn, Samuel L. IV: *32**

Rublee, George II: *322**, 328, 344-47, 350-52, 358, *360*, 362, 363, 379, *568*, 633, 654; III: 183, *216*, 217, 224, *226*, 236, *260*, 320, 383, 394, 434, 440, 464, *467*, *496*, *502*, 523, *539*, 581, 592, *682*; IV: 27, 36, 43, 118, 127, 140, 176, 197, 266, 317, 368; V: 26, 28, 141, 197, 309, 615; cited, III: 259

Rucker, Darnell cited II: 390

Rudy, Jacob M. III: *62**, **2*

Rugg, Arthur P. IV: *68**, 69

Ruggles, Clyde O. V: *355**

Rumania III: 304, 404; IV: 170, 207, 247, 260, 299, 351, 354

Rumely, Edward A. III: *584**; IV: 512

Rundstein, M. IV: 157

Ruport, Minnie I: 15

Ruppin, Arthur III: *303**, 312, 314, *317*, 324-26, 336, 398, 425, 434, *452*, 461, 466-72, 497, 508, 514, 550, 589, 609-10, 628; IV: 13, *304*, 423; LDB on IV: 304-305

Rural Electrification Administration V: 641

Rushmore, Charles E. IV: *273**

Ruskin, John I: 16

Russell, A. W. II: *521**

Russell, Charles E. II: 530*; IV: *41*

Russell, Charles T. I: 86*

Russell, Joseph B. II: 644*; III: 171, 245

Russell, Talcott H. I: 391*, 436

Russell, Theresa H. II: 530*

Russell, William E. IV: 104*

Russia I: 336, 338, 355; II: 210; III: 155, 291, 303-304, 306, 360, 374, 381, 431-32, 490-93, 500; IV: 19-20, 108-110, 151, 160, 170, 179, 207, 232-36, 247, 260, 276-77, 281-83, 285, 293, 303, 305-306, 348, 359, 387, 398, 507, 546; V: 128, 153, 229, 555

Russian (Zionist) Bureau IV: 19-20, 108, 151, 179

Russian Revolution IV: 276, 293, 312; LDB on IV: 276-77

Russo-American treaty (1911) IV: 207

Rutenberg, Pinhas III: 556*, 565, 575-76, 580, 620-21; IV: 280; V: 55, 112, 220, 469, 521; LDB on III: 575-76, 620-21

Ryan, Agnes E. III: *597**

Ryan, H. E. II: 226*

Ryan, John A. V: 141*, 355

Ryan, Richard S. II: 462*, 463, 467, 475, 491, 496, 513

Ryan, Thomas F. I: 336*, 341; II: 632

Sacco and Vanzetti case I: 91; V: 193, 241, 258, 272, 275-77, 280-87, 290, 294, 297-300, 305, 310, 313, 316, 318, 320, 330, 345, 352-55, 637; LDB on V: 280-81, 282, 300

Sacher, Harry V: 444*, 604

Sachs, Alexander III: 350*, *459*, 517; IV: 190, 193, 356, *385*, 400, 503, 505-506, 513, 517-18, 524, 528, *530*, *533*, 537, 542, *544*, 563, 565

Sachs, Henry III: 585*

Saffro, Joseph III: *375**

St. James Conference (1939) V: 604, 608, 609, 612

St. John, Vincent III: 98*, 104

St. Louis, Missouri I: 26-37, 44; III: 369, 405, 592-95, 614; V: 477

St. Louis, LDB's practice at I: 26-34; V: 477

St. Louis & Southwestern Rrd III: 19

St. Louis Cotton Compress Co. v. Arkansas V: 88

St. Louis Hoachooza III: 585

St. Louis Post-Dispatch II: 645; V: 362, 585

St. Louis Times-Star V: 585

Sale, Samuel III: 369*

Saltonstall, Philip L. II: 101*

Saltonstall, Richard M. II: 101*

Sampson, Arthur W. V: *546**, *548*, *550*, *559*, *565*(2), *566*, 568, 575

Sampson, George H. IV: *229**

Sampter, Jessie III: 463*, 531, 662

Samuel, Herbert IV: 443*; V: 39, 384, 455, 521, 594

Samuel, Maurice cited, III: 156

San Diego Land & Town Co. v. Jasper I: 312

San Diego Union II: 546

San Domingo V: 628

San Francisco I: 427; III: 675; IV: 245, 399

San Francisco earthquake, LDB on I: 427

San Remo Conference IV: 431, 457, 462, 468; V: 56

Sanders, Fielder III: *181**

Sanders, Leon III: 389*, 438, 572-73, 580, 585, 652-53, 655; IV: 32, 135, 200, *237*, 250

Sanders, Thomas III: 205

Sands, Mr. III: 529

Sanford, Edward T. V: 80*, 124, 181, 185, 276, 286, 308
Sanford Steamship Co. I: 56
Santogen: see *Bauer v. O'Donnell*
Sapinsky, Alvin T. III: *656**; IV: 231
Sapiro, Aaron V: 44*, 297
Sargent, Amelia H. I: 24*
Sargent, John I: 25
Sarnoff, David V: 415*; LDB on V: 415-16
Sasson family V: 485
Saturday Evening Post III: 243; V: 119, 641
Saulsbury, Willard IV: 29*
Saunders, Charles R. I: *170**, 389
savings bank life insurance, LDB and the struggle to implement (to June, 1907) I: 340-46, 351, 362-70, 380-84, 388-99, 404-409, 437-38, 443-49, 452-65, 473-511, 514-19, 524-71, 574-91; V: 332, 339, 565
savings bank life insurance, LDB's relations with after June, 1907 II: 5-24, 47, 60-61, 72-76, 79-80, 114, 128-29, 176-77, 191-98, 201-206, 214-30, 234-37, 241, 252, 283-86, 300-305, 319, 389, 433-35, 442, 566-67, 589-600; III: 8, 411, 457-58; IV: 44, 229-30, 460-61; V: 89-90, 216-17, 302, 311, 319-20, 338-43, 346, 348, 356-58, 375-76, 393-94, 402, 410-11, 451, 471, 476, 487, 497, 508-509, 515, 530, 545-48, 550, 559-62, 565-76, 584-85, 598; in New York I: 482-84, 491-92, 506-507; V: 575, 595, 598
"Savings Bank Life Insurance for Wage Earners" (1907) I: 486; II: 14-15, 600
"Savings Insurance Banks" (1906) I: 491, 511; II: 17
Sayre, Francis B. IV: 444*; V: 81
Sayre, Jessie W. IV: 445*
Sayre, Paul cited, II: 299
Sayward, William H. I: *265**
Scallon, William II: 707*
Schacht, Hjalmar V: 615
Schaefer, Peter IV: 450

Schaefer v. U.S. IV: 451, 550
Schaff, Charles E. III: 5*
Schaff, Morris I: 290*, 318, 411, 423, 434, 437
Schapiro, Israel V: 257*
Schapiro, Jacob S. III: 644*
Schapsmeier, Edward L. cited, V: 558
Schapsmeier, Frederick cited, V: 558
Schatz, Boris III: 513
Schechter, Frank I. V: 456
Schechter, Solomon III: 22; V: 541
Schechter v. U.S. V: 538
Schechtman, Joseph B. cited, III: 520; V: 438
Scheffel, Joseph V. I: 28
Schermerhorn, Charles T. II: *540**
Schick, Marvin cited, II: 655
Schiff, Jacob H. I: 336*, 337-38; II: 372; III: 207, 325, 340, 356, 421, 477, 481-82, 514, 537, 572, 574, 583-84, 589-90, 621, 645; IV: 4, 32, *34*, 102, 116, 202-205, 211, 213, 220, 234, 283, 318, 323, 382, 398, 406, 435, 439, 442, 444, 472; LDB on IV: 116
Schiff, Joseph H. III: 590
Schiller, Johann F. I: 22, *584**; quoted, V: 493
Schilling, Johannes I: *127**
Schlesinger, Arthur M. Sr. V: 395*, 402, 503, 606; quoted, V: 588; cited, V: 521
Schlesinger, Arthur M. Jr. cited, IV: 475; V: 506, 540, 557
Schmitt, Frank I: 242, 510; II: 393
Schneeberg, Mr. III: 531
Schneider, Evelyn V: 243, 550, 570
Schneiderman, Harry III: *544**
Schneiderman, Rose III: *669**
Schofield, William I: *168**, 170, 190
Schoonmaker, John H. I: *557**, *561*, 575; II: 10
Schubert, Franz V: 659
Schulman, Samuel III: 585, 603, 657*; IV: 5, 201
Schumann, Robert V: 659
Schurman, Jacob G. III: 456*

Schurz, Carl I: 93*, 148; LDB on I: 93

Schuster, Winfield I: 544*, 549, 556, 575

Schwab, Charles M. III: 310

Schwartz, Henry H. II: 312, 319*, 322, 353

Schwarz, Jordan A. cited, IV: 301

Schweitzers, the IV: 346

Scientific Management and the Railroads (1912) II: 542-43; III: 47; V: 502, 534-35

scientific management and the efficiency movement, LDB on II: 125, 374, 383-85, 387-88, 395, 398, 548-49; III: 49-50, 86-87, 151; V: 71

Scituate Herald IV: 8

Scott, Austin V: 63

Scott, Colin A. II: 217*

Scott, Edith K. II: 728*

Scott, Frank H. II: 728*; III: 222; IV: 22

Scott, John (Earl of Eldon) I: 10*

Scott, Sir Walter I: 103-104

Scripps, Edward W. II: 498*; III: 306-307

Scripps-McRea Newspapers III: 119, 157; IV: 130

Scudder, Edwin W. II: 475*

Scudder, Vida I: 138*, 161

Sears, Roebuck & Co. V: 7

Seabury, Samuel IV: 27*

Sedgwick, Ellery V: 259*, 281, 287

Seff, Joseph IV: 347*

Segal, Hyman R. III: 586*

Segal, Rabbi IV: 158

Seitz, Don C. I: 482*

self-reliance, LDB on II: 74-75, 709

Seligman, E. R. A. I: 304; II: 32, 433*, 523, 535; III: 209; IV: 388; V: 285

Seligman, Eustace II: 433*

Seligman, Isaac N. II: 32*

Seligsberg, Alice L. III: 463*, 662; IV: 340; V: 9

Selligman, Alfred V: 267, 406*

Semel, Bernard IV: 200*

Semonche, John E. cited, II: 357

Senator, David W. V: 480*

Senior, Max III: 438*, 439, 444, 464, 466, 666; IV: 388

"Serve One Master Only" (1913) III: 220, 247

Setsinger, John cited, V: 515

Seymour, Charles cited, III: 106

Seymour, Judge V: 96

Shakespeare, William I: 66-67, 89; quoted, I: 61; II: 13, 320, 699, 700-701; III: 224, 330; IV: 66, 356, 500; V: 8, 270, 321, 353, 360, 363, 364

"Shall We Abandon the Policy of Competition" (1912) II: 504, 521

Shankman, Samuel IV: 240*

Shapiro, Yonathan cited, III: 38, 293, 387, 565, 635; IV: 34, 56, 252, 312, 348, 436; V: 348, 408, 427

Sharett, Moshe: see Shertok, Moshe

Sharp, George M. I: 221*

Sharp, Malcolm P. V: 155*, 170

Shattuck, Henry L. V: 171*, 321, 366, 372

Shaw, Albert II: 186*, 440; IV: 428

Shaw, Alexander C. IV: 63*

Shaw, Arch W. III: 133*

Shaw Commission V: 400, 423, 424, 452, 455, 479, 486

Shaw, G. Howland V: 424*

Shaw, George B. III: 200

Shaw, J. F. I: 560

Shaw, S. Adele V: 144

Shaw, Sir Walter V: 401

Shaw, William B. II: 24*

Shazar, S. Z.: see Rubashow, S. Z.

Shearer, William B. V: 391

Sheffield, George I: 56*, 59, 66

Sheffield, Mrs. George I: 66, 442

Sheinkin, Menahem IV: 194*

Shepard, Harvey N. IV: 27*

Shepardson, Whitney H. IV: 406*

Sheridan, Richard B. V: 289

Sherman Antitrust Act II: 99, 107, 168, 198, 241, 352, 428, 435, 438, 442, 453, 455, 481, 495, 510-12, 521, 538, 540, 556, 615, 665, 689, 699,

701, 703, 725; III: 41, 93, 97, 220, 251, 290; IV: 8, 521; V: 58, 84, 176, 316; LDB on II: 495-96

Sherman, James S. II: 191*, 213, 345

Sherman, Philemon T. II: 377*

Sherman, Richard B. cited, II: 524

Sherry v. Perkins II: 620

Shertok, Moshe V: 466, 489*, 571, 574, 581; LDB on V: 571

Sherwood, Robert E. cited, V: 537

Shields, John K. IV: 166, 169*, 171, 197

Shiels, Sir Thomas D. V: 455*

Shiplacoff, Abraham I. V: 464*

Shipp, Thomas R. II: 346*

Shipstead, Henrik V: 77, 322, 354, 414

Shiras, George Jr. V: 170*

Shirer, William L. cited, V: 577

Shoe Manufacturers' Association III: 139

Shoe Workers' Journal I: 249, 251, 298

Shohan, Joseph III: 77*

Shulman, Harry V: 359*, 361, 397, 404

Shulman, Max III: 352*, 377, 407-408, 462, 474, 576, 585, 599, 603, 616, 620, 643, 648, 650, 658-59; IV: 181, 189, 196

Shulman, Mordecai IV: 20*

Shumway, Franklin P. I: 536*

Shuvaloff, Count I: 336

Sicher, Dudley E. III: 86*

Sidney, Frederic H. III: 198*

Sicilian Vespers V: 229

Sidebotham, Herbert V: 411*

Siegel, Henry III: 121*

Siegel, Isaac IV: 100*

Sigismund IV: 452

Siletz Indian Reservation II: 322

Silver, Abba H. IV: 490*, 492, 493, 506, 563; V: 8, 18, 27, 609, 644

Silverman, Morris R. II: 674*

Simkins, Francis B. cited, II: 63

Simmons, Furnifold L. V: 317*

Simon, Julius IV: 13, 322, 331, 389,

438, 443, 456, 466, 472, 478, 524, 526-27, 537, 552, 556, 567; V: 8, 12, 112, 117, 195, 438, 462, 471, 479, 483, 542, 574, 594, 599, 621, 623; cited, IV: 439, 473, 527; V: 9

Simonds, George W. I: 246*

Simons, Leon III: 517, 664; cited, III: 541

Sims, Thetus W. III: 229*

Sinclair, Andrew cited, IV: 456, 471

Sinclair, Harry F. V: 116, 310, 313, 328

Sinclair, Upton B. V: 310*, 494

Singer, Mr. V: 474

single tax reform I: 468, 472-73, 476; LDB on III: 151, 489

Siskin, Edgar cited, V: 104

Skeffington, Henry J. II: 87*, 275, 284; III: 129

Slater, Leonard IV: 418

Slaton, John M. III: 373*

Slattery, Charles H. I: 467

Slattery, E. I: 250*

Sleicher, John A. II: 712*

Sleman, Paul II: 329*, 344, 357, 358, 361

"sliding scale" mechanism for Boston gas (1906), LDB on I: 438-41; III: 278, 166, 276-80, 375, 509; IV: 94, 113, 120; V: 504; see also Brandeis, Louis D., and consolidation of the Boston gas utility and development of the sliding scale

Slomovitz, Philip V: 566

Sloss, Mrs. Max C. V: 615

Slouschz, Nahum IV: 286*, 289, 344

Small, Maynard & Co. II: 200; III: 233, 259, 262; IV: 453; V: 119

Smelansky, M. V: 434

Smith, Alfred E. II: 668; IV: 475; V: 76*, 210, 212, 239, 260, 278, 307, 308, 312, 325, 326, 327, 344, 348, 352-55, 361-64, 378, 396, 506; LDB on V: 212

Smith, Alice I: 60

Smith, Charles S. I: 242, 257*; IV: 49

Smith College V: 113

Smith, Courtland II: 440*
Smith, Daniel M. cited, III: 610
Smith, Dix W. III: 209*
Smith, Edward S. V: 475
Smith, Ellison D. V: 111
Smith, Frederick E. V: 152*
Smith, George S. II: 246*, 517
Smith, Gibbs M. cited, III: 633
Smith, Hoke IV: 139
Smith, Huntington I: 191*
Smith Immigration bill III: 389
Smith, J. C. B. II: 65*, 105
Smith, James I: 375
Smith, Jane IV: 107
Smith, Joseph R. III: 243*
Smith, H. Knox II: 168*
Smith, L. B. cited, I: 405
Smith, Rennie V: 459*
Smith v. Thayer McNeil IV: 67
Smith v. Wilson V: 273
Smith, William A. II: 618*
Smoot-Hawley tariff V: 411
Smoot, Reed IV: 529*
Smuts, Jan C. IV: 414*; quoted V: 551
Smyth, Constantine J. IV: 29*
Smyth, Nathan II: 317*, 322, 371, 399, 458
Smyth v. Ames V: 351
Smythe, William E. II: 561*, 573, 613, 713; III: 31, 559, 592; IV: 222, 428; LDB on IV: 222
Snow, Frederick E. I: 267*, 301, 313-20, 373; IV: 51, 124, 283
Snowden, Philip V: 382*
Social and Economic Views of Mr. Justice Brandeis (1930) V: 418, 499, 503, 511
social experimentation, LDB on III: 19-20; V: 16-17, 64, 127, 501
social legislation, LDB on II: 586-88, 601-11, 639-40, 707; III: 19-20
Social Science Research Council V: 204
Social Security Act V: 552, 554-55, 560, 563, 625

socialism, LDB on II: 152, 288, 481, 550; III: 210; V: 45-46, 66-68
Society for Jewish Rights (England) IV: 103
Society of Architects (Boston) I: 470
Society of Orthodox Rabbis III: 572
Soil Conservation and Domestic Allotment Act (1936) V: 538
Sokolow, Nahum III: 22*, 65, 158, 324, 353, 494, 497, 561, 589; IV: 278, 281, 297, 326, 343, 346, 347, 359, 360, 365, 374, 406, 457, 474, 526; V: 36, 56, 479, 485, 522
Soliday, Mr. II: 181
Solis-Cohen, Emily III: 387*, 395, 416
Solis-Cohen, Solomon III: 65*
Solomon, Barbara cited, III: 507
"Solution of the Trust Problem: A Program" III: 195-96, 219-20, 233; V: 534-35
Somers, William A. II: 573*
Sommer, Frank H. I: 455*
Sonneborn, F. IV: 259
Sonneborn, Rudolph G. IV: 418*
Sonnheim, Mark V: 152
Sonnichsen, Albert III: 139*
Sorolla y Bastida, Joaquin II: 249*
Soule, George H. V: 91*, 167, 174
South Africa I: 428; II: 477; IV: 109-10; V: 141, 442
South African Zionist Federation IV: 110
South Bay Terminal & Roxbury Central Wharf Co. II: 32
South Dakota II: 710
South End House (Boston) I: 210
South Metropolitan Gas Co. (London) I: 329; II: 209
Southern Pacific Co. v. Jensen V: 117
Southern Pacific Rrd II: 721, 722; III: 182, 207
Southmayd, Charles F. I: 125*
Spanish Inquisition IV: 442
Spargo, John IV: 508; cited IV: 457

Spaulding, Frank L. II: 338*
"Speech to the Boot & Shoe Club" (1903) I: 225-29
"Speech at Cooper Union" (1905) I: 257-58, 406
"Speech to Jewish Leaders" (1929) V: 389-91, 397-99, 413-14, 489
Speed, Hattie B. I: 24*, 582; II: 642, 700; V: 145, 161, 162, 212, 304, 550, 551, 649; LDB on II: 700
Speed, James B. I: 47*; II: 642, 700; III: 231; V: 145, 200, 231, 304, 628
Speed, Thomas I: 582
Speer, William M. I: 392*, 397, 483
Spelling, Thomas C. IV: 89*, 151
Spence, Kenneth M. IV: 126*, 144, 151, 176-77
Speyer & Co. III: 267
Speyer, James III: 267*; IV: 34
Spingarn, Joel E. III: 644*
Spinoza, Benedict V: 276
Spooner, John C. II: 327*, 358; III: 183
Sprague, Edwin L. I: 267, 270, 272, 279, 285-86, 290, 292, 297-98, 301, 323; IV: 121, 124
Sprague, Francis P. I: 143*
Spreckels, Rudolph II: 295*, 401, 713; III: 44, 489; IV: 42
Sprigge, Sylvia S. cited, I: 73
Spring-Rice, Sir Cecil A. III: 555*; IV: 328
Springfield [Massachusetts] Republican I: 71, 306, 310, 319, 365, 457-58; II: 240, 699; IV: 149; V: 343, 497
Springfield [Massachusetts] Railways Co. II: 42, 48-49, 52, 55
Squires, Fred D. L. III: 82*
Staake, William H. I: 401*
Staehlman, John K. IV: 171
Standard Oil Co. II: 207, 289, 413, 435, 456, 495, 530, 556, 602, 664, 690; III: 103, 120, 210, 373, 523; IV: 235; V: 124, 412
Standard Oil Co. v. Lincoln V: 315

Standard Oil Co. of New Jersey v. U.S. II: 496, 556
Stanley, Augustus O. II: 525*, 652-54, 686, 699; III: 25, 311; IV: 14; V: 126, 482; LDB on II: 654; III: 311
Stanley Electric Co. II: 101
Stansbury, William R. V: 182
Staples, Henry L. cited, I: 583; II: 52, 58, 111, 628; III: 287; V: 653
Starlan, Edith I: 57
Starr, Merritt IV: 176*, 177
State ex rel. Attorney General v. Standard Oil Co. I: 216
State ex rel. Zillmer v. Kreutzberg II: 679
State Industrial Board of New York v. Terry & Tench Co. . . V: 235
state prerogatives, LDB on V: 91, 98, 247, 500
State v. Julow II: 679
Steed, Henry W. IV: 315
Steed, R. E. III: 166*
Steele, H. Wirt II: 442
Steele, John A. II: 59*
Steele, John N. II: 475*
Steffens, Lincoln I: 475*; II: 101*, 115, 209, 250, 295, 300(2), 330, 357, 364; III: 87-88, 98, 104; IV: 406; V: 42; LDB on V: 42-43
Stein, Abe IV: 111*
Stein, Leonard cited, III: 328, 665; IV: 282, 285, 290, 311, 319
Steinert, William IV: 67
Steinhardt, David V: 367
Steinhardt, Laurence A. IV: 246*
Stenert, Mr. I: 428
Stephen, Henry J. I: 8
Stephens, Charles H. II: 15*
Stephens, Francis H. cited, V: 89
Sterling Coal Co. II: 311
Sterling, Henry I: 286
Stern, Adolphe IV: 260*, 299
Stern, David III: 45*, IV: 327
Stern, Edgar B. V: 597*
Stern, Mrs. IV: 346

Stern, Samuel R. IV: *42**
Sterne, Lawrence cited, I: 73
Sterzt v. Industrial Insurance Commission IV: 248
Stetson, Cushing III: *629**
Stettler v. O'Hara II: 482, 640; III: 363, *381*, 392, 442-43, 444, 682; V: 149
Steuer, Max D. V: *353**, 354
Stevens, Earnest R. III: *396**
Stevens, J. O. IV: 543
Stevens, John F. III: *14**
Stevens, Oliver I: *321**
Stevens, Raymond B. III: 84*, *123*, 217, 224, 227, 246, 340, *347*, 434, 437, 441, 467-68, 496, 539, 581, 592, 618; IV: 36, 169, 387; V: 23, 30, 192, 195, 197
Stevens, William H. III: *11**
Stevenson, Robert L. II: 306; IV: 412; V: 216
Stewart, Andrew I: 228
Stewart, John A. III: *16**
Stewart, Ethelbert V: 334*, 337
Stillman, James III: *267**
Stimson, Frederic J. I: *281**
Stimson, Henry L. II: 309*, 350, *352*, 458, 569; III: 134-35, 209, *286;* IV: 64, 558; V: 103, 260, 321
Stirling, Mr. I: *532**
Stockton, Philip I: *479**
Stoddard, William L. V: 546*, 548, *559*, *566*, 575
Stokes, Frederick III: 165, 232, 238; V: 493, 496, 504, 509, 519, *599*
Stone, Arthur K. II: *666**
Stone, Edward E. III: 172, 192
Stone, Elihu D. V: *632**
Stone, Galen L. III: *204**
Stone, Harlan F. V: 117, 124, 125*, 146, 154, 156, 175, 176, 247, 272, 308, 312, 337, 361, 367-68, 371, 372, 374, 377, 414-15, 483, 500, 538, 562; LDB on V: 652-53
Stone, Henry L. IV: *297**
Stone, Mary E. II: *296**

Stone, Mr. III: 214
Stone, Robert I: *234**
Stoner, S. N. II: 311
Storey, Moorfield III: 63; IV: 58, 65*, 66, 69, 73, 75, 77, 97, 119, 127, 131, 140
Storrow, James J. I: 137, *479**, 551, 595; II: 17, 36, 47, 99, 269, 295; V: 209, 214; LDB on II: 295-96; V: 209
Story, Joseph I: 8*, 10
Stott, W. H. I: *507**
Stotz, Mr. IV: 367
Stoughton Record IV: 88
Straight, Dorothy II: 654; III: 222; IV: 538; V: 62
Straight, Willard II: 654; III: 47, 222*; IV: 538
Strasburger, Milton IV: *318**
Stratton, Samuel W. V: *290**
Straus, Elias IV: 161
Straus, Lina G. IV: 83, *465**
Straus, Nathan Sr. III: 298*, 300; 303, 313, 361, 421, 423-24, 426, 273-74, 481, 504, *529*, 531, 577, 583, 589, 651, 666, 679; IV: 83, 127, 175, 295, 323, 325, 398, 406, 465, 563; V: *51*, 454
Straus, Nathan Jr. V: *18**
Straus, Nellie III: 662
Straus, Oscar S. III: 312*, *341*, 362, 369; IV: 32, 252, 452
Straus, William C. II: *416*
Strauss, Lewis L. IV: 266*, 405, 406, 544, 547; V: 5, 104
Strecker, Charles B. III: 61*, *402*, 406
Streeter, Frank I: 407*, 535
Streeter, John W. cited, I: 414
Streeter, Julia I: *408**
Streeter, Representative I: 549, 556, 561, 575
Stricker, Robert III: *519**
strike insurance, LDB on IV: 517-18
Stroock, Moses J. IV: *110**
Stroock, Solomon M. IV: *436**

Strout, Cushing cited, V: 196
Strull, Charles III: 353
Studley, James B. II: *540**; IV: 81, 113
Success Magazine II: 500
Sucher, Ralph G. V: 25
Sugar trust II: 350, 352; III: 94, 139
Sughrue, Michael J. I: 374*; III: 162, 201
Sullivan & Cromwell II: 159; IV: 84
Sullivan Gas bill III: 276, 277, 280, 509
Sullivan, John A. I: *519**, *520;* III: 190, 200
Sullivan, Lewis R. III: 278*
Sullivan, Mark I: 453*, *454, 457, 458, 463, 466,* 475, *478, 486, 489, 499, 506,* 510, *571, 580, 587, 588;* II: 76, *112, 217, 338, 340,* 360, 362-63, 465, *503;* III: *33, 83, 176,* 222, 243; IV: 85, 529; V: 402
Sulzberger, Arthur H. III: 340
Sulzberger, Cyrus L. III: 339*, 574; IV: 202
Summer, Will I: 64
Summers, Merle G. V: 328*, 333
Sumner, Mary B. II: 566*; cited, II: 407
Super, A. S. cited, IV: 110
The Survey II: 406, *427,* 522-23, 578, 637, 645, 646, 652; IV: 44, 119, 321, 343, 461, 497; V: 30, 53, 133, 329, 335, 408, 497, 570, 575
Susan: see Gilbert, Susan B.
Sutherland, Arthur E. cited, II: 299; IV: 559; V: 144, 278
Sutherland, George II: 322*; III: *632;* IV: 183; V: 89, 226, 310, 316, 317, 500, 588
Sutherland, William A. IV: 439*
Swacker, Frank M. IV: 8*, *65,* 88
Swallow, George A. II: *133**, *137*
Swan, Mary A. III: *36**
Swan, Thomas W. V: 189*
Swanberg, W. A. cited, III: 3
Swanson, Claude A. V: 402*

Swanwick, Anna II: 424, 426
Sweet, Harold E. II: *698**
Sweet, Thaddeus C. IV: 445
Sweetland, Cornelius S. I: 489*
Sweeney, Fred W. III: 107*
Swift, Henry W. III: 85*
Swift v. Tyson V: 335
Swinburne, Algernon C. I: 16
Switzer, Mary E. V: 626*
Sykes, Mark IV: 495
Sykes-Picot agreement IV: 276, 446, 458, 495
Symonds, John A. II: 250; IV: 542; quoted, II: 408
Symons, Mr. V: 197
Syracuse University Law School V: 298
Syria IV: 164, 431, 446-47, 495; V: 457
Syrkin, Marie cited, III: 329
Syrkin, Nachman III: 323*, 330; IV: 98
System II: 629, 641, 643, 702, 720
Szajkowski, Zosa cited, IV: 285, 313
Szold, Henrietta III: 298*, 323, 344, 365-66, 371, *463,* 467, 470-71, 480, *495,* 662; IV: 24, 115, 152, *256,* 269, 320, 340, 352, 375, *378,* 487; V: 8, 107, 192, *309,* 313, 444, *454,* 487, *542, 582, 583,* 620
Szold, Miriam IV: 392
Szold, Robert IV: 375*, 381, 392, 410, 418, 419, 420, 422, 429, 433, 466, 478, 482, 485, *524, 530, 533,* 537, *544,* 563; V: *18,* 38, 195, 291, 309, 371, 427, 430, 432, *443, 446, 450,* 452, *455, 456,* 459, *461,* 462, *468, 469, 470, 472*(2), *474, 476, 478,* 484, 486, 492, *506,* 514, *522, 547,* 549, *558,* 574, *577, 582, 586, 587*(2), *590, 593*(2), *596,* 599, *603, 605,* 607, *608, 609, 614, 618, 619,* 620, 621, *622,* 626, 629, 630, *632, 634, 638, 639, 643*(2), *645, 646, 654, 655;* cited, IV: 527
Szold, Sophia S. IV: *256**

Szold, Zip F. IV: 392*; V: 9, 330, 388, 422, *438, 454*

Taber, Harry V: 281
Tachau, Charles L. I: 5
Tachau, Charles G. V: 4, 140, 176*, *179,* 188, *197, 201,* 207, *208,* 214, 253, 256, 264, 268, 315, *343,* 504
Tachau, Emil V: 179, 235
Tachau, Emma W. I: 79*
Tachau, Jean B. I: 75*, 79; II: 9, 18, 642, 724; III: 617, 662; IV: 480, 519; V: 4, 146, 179, 188, 202, 304, 350, 657
Tachau, Nova I: 3*
Tachau, William G. V: 140, 176*, *197,* 256, 264
Tacitus V: 185
Taft, Charles P. II: 463*, 467, 491, 497
Taft, Robert A. V: 79*, 641
Taft, William H. I: 359*; II: 68, 70, 96, 129, 191, 213, 249, 290, 307, 313, 320-35, 339, 341, 345-53, 356-58, 362, 370-71, 375, 386, 458, 462-63, 466, 467, 479, 491, 495-96, 499, 504, 512-13, 519, 523, 530, *531,* 541, 542, 547, 564, 569, 573, 611, 613, 633, 641, 649, 653, 674, 703, 709, 710, 715, 718, 722, 726, 729; III: 30, 42-43, 182, 389, 464, 491; IV: 22, 25, 28, 34, 70, 118, 127-30, 370, 385, 508, 560; V: 40, 53, 58-59, 78, *81,* 83, *86,* 89, 99, 103, 106, 165, 167, 181, 185, 189, 226, 239, 240, 253, 284, 299, 308, 337, 345, 365, 367, 371, 373, 377, 379, *384,* 387, 395, 403, 415, 641, 653; LDB on II: 191, 213, 322-25, 327, 334, 459; V: 167-68
Tager, Jack, cited, II: 401
Talbot, Winthrop II: *586**
Talmud, LDB on V: 253
Tannenbaum, Frank V: *477**
Tarbell, Ida M. II: 357; cited, II: 546
Tarbox, Claude H. II: 273

Tardieu, Andre IV: 406*, 447
tariff, LDB on II: 191, 657-59; IV: 547
Tau Epsilon Rho IV: 497
Taussig, Adele I: 29*, 57; V: 659; LDB on V: 659
Taussig, Ben I: 34*
Taussig, Catherine V: 26, 349*
Taussig, Charles I: 57; III: 509*
Taussig, Dorothy II: 356
Taussig, Edith G. I: 72*, 74, 477; II: 356; V: 4, 5
Taussig, Frank W. I: 41, 67*, 68, 72, 123, *160, 268,* 477; II: 9, 199; III: 110, *523;* IV: 147, 297, 332, 406, 408; V: 14, 136, 202, 206, 214, 285, 349
Taussig, George W. I: 26*, 29, 31
Taussig, James I: 26*, 29-34, 36, 39, 57, 64; IV: 225; V: 477
Taussig, John J. I: 262*
Taussig, Louis J. IV: *225**
Taussig, Lucy II: 356
Taussig, Walter II: 199*, 349, 356; IV: *147;* V: 4
Taussig, Mrs. Walter V: 459
Taussig, William I: 29*, 72; II: 12, 156, *187,* 191, 250, 280, 349, 359; III: 127, 509
taxation, LDB on IV: 528; V: 67, 84-85, 104-105, 247, 344, 375, 410, 502, 520, 556
Taylor, Arthur O. IV: *22**
Taylor, Bayard II: 426; quoted, IV: 417
Taylor, Charles H. I: 282*
Taylor, Frederick W. II: 390*, 543; III: 241, 618
Taylor, Marion R. II: *393**
Taylor, Myron C. V: 614*
Taylor, Stevenson II: 168*
Taylor, William III: 140*, 154
Tchernowitz, Chaim V: 253*, 426
Teachers' Pension Fund (Boston) III: 28
teaching, LDB on I: 39; V: 99, 153-54

Teal, Joseph N. IV: 518*, 536; V: 34, 114

Teapot Dome scandal V: 89, 117, 120, 122-23, 235, 255, 310, 311-12, 327; LDB on V: 120, 122, 123, 327

Technicon (Haifa) III: 516; IV: 323, 399, 444

Tedcastle, A. W. & Co. IV: 89

Teeling, Richard I: 443, 556*, 575

Tel Aviv V: 522, 586, 571-72, 579, 591

Teller, Philip S. V: 331

Tennessee V: 308

Tennessee Coal & Iron Co. II: 46

Tennessee Valley Authority V: 641

Terhune, William L. V: 565*

Terry, Ellen P. I: 66*

Terry, Prentice V: 570

"Testimony before the House Committee on Interstate and Foreign Commerce" (1915) III: 217

"Testimony before the House Committee on Patents" (1912) III: 89, 99, 101, 103, 170

"Testimony before the Senate Committee on Interstate Commerce" (1911) III: 12, 27; V: 482, 534-35

"Testimony in the U.S. Steel Investigation" (1912) III: 25; V: 482, 534-35

Tetlow, Edwin I: 536

Texas III: 337, 369, 379-80; IV: 324, 326; V: 172, 396

Texas Law Review V: 129

Texas Transport & Terminal Co. v. New Orleans V: 172

Texas Zionist Association III: 379

Thacher, Thomas D. V: 229*, 377, 380

Thackeray, William M. I: 80

Thayer, Eugene V. I: 56*

Thayer, Ezra R. I: 117*; II: 619, 620, 712

Thayer, James B. I: 13, 36, 65, 92, 114-15; III: 209, 240; V: 656

Thayer, Nathaniel II: 33*, 54

Thayer, Webster V: 287*

Thayer, William R. cited, I: 336

Third Avenue Railway Co. (New York City) I: 129

Thomas A. Kelley & Co. IV: 114

Thomas, Harry D. II: 507*

Thompson, Clarence B. II: 217*, 426

Thompson, Huston III: 600*; IV: 372, 518, 523; V: 462, 494, 496, 541

Thompson, Laura A. V: 152*

Thompson Tramway Co. II: 40

Thompson, William H. III: 673*

Thompson, William G. V: 306, 312, 320*

Thomson, Elihu III: 204*

Thon, Ya'akov Y. IV: 146*, 478

Thorndike, John L. IV: 66*, 75

Thorne, Miss V: 510

Thorne, Clifford III: 164, 202*, 518; IV: 28, 33, 39, 47, 89-92, 141, 149

Thornton, Mr. I: 24-25

Thornton, Jesse E. III: 56*

The Three Musketeers, LDB on I: 79-80

thrift, LDB on I: 564, 568-69; II: 74-75, 709

Thruston, R. C. B. V: 198*, 265

Thurmin, Israel W. IV: 81*; V: 102; LDB on V: 102

Thurston, Mayor I: 425-26

Tien-yi, Li cited, III: 58

Tilden, Samuel J. I: 13, 69

Tilley, David F. II: 218*

Tillman, Benjamin R. II: 63*

Time Zionist Review (England) IV: 299

Timoleon II: 376*

Tinkham, George H. I: 230*, 231; II: 620

The Titanic II: 667

Tobacco trust III: 35, 39, 94

Tobin, John F. I: 238*, 248, 249, 257, 260, 286, 298, 370, 487, 577(2); II: 14

Todd, A. L. cited, I: 243; IV: 22, 26, 32, 34, 91, 102

Todd, George C. III: 171*, 592

Todd, Mr. II: 313

Todd, Thomas V: 231
Tolstoy, Leo V: 238
Toomey, T. G. II: 91, *171*
Torquemada, Tomas IV: 441*
Torrey, Henry W. I: 27*
Tosdal, H. R. III: 523
Touro, Judah I: 387*
Tourgueneff, Ivan I: 105
Tousley, E. M. III: 215*
Towle, Leland I: 243; IV: 49
Towne, Henry R. III: *152*
Townsend, Edward II: 280*
Townsend, Meredith IV: 414*
Townsend, Robert D. II: *277*
Towson, Charles R. II: *215*
Toynbee, Arnold J. V: 185*, 191
Trabue, Edmund F. IV: 297*
Tracy, Frank B. II: *520*
Tracy, Mr. II: 14
"Trade Unionism and Employers"
    (1905) I: 279, 282-83
Train v. Boston Disinfecting Co. I:
    68
Trani, Eugene P. cited, I: 355
Transjordania V: 437, 446, 457, 467,
    474, 506, 514, 521, 545, 594, 623
Trauerman, M. R. III: *273*
Travis, Marion IV: 355*
Treaty of Berlin II: 209
Treaty of San Stefano II: 210
Treaty of Versailles: see Versailles
    Peace Conference and Treaty
Tremont Street Subway I: 139, 141,
    160, 168, 194, 330, 424; IV: 94
Trenton v. New Jersey V: 350
Trevelyan, G. M. cited, IV: 441
Trimble, Robert V: 231
Truax v. Corrigan V: 40
"True Americanism" (1915) III: 540;
    V: 119
Trumbull, Frank III: 5*
Trumbull, Lyman IV: 30
"Trusts, Efficiency and the New
    Party" (1912) II: 664, 671-72; III:
    233, 451
"Trusts, the Export Trade and the

New Party" (1912) II: 664-65, 671-
    72, 683-84, 695-96; III: 233
Tschlenow, Jechiel III: 353*, 494,
    497, *520*, 561, 589; IV: *305*, 326
Tubular Rivet & Stud Co. IV: 89
Tuck v. Manning I: 83
Tucker & Co. II: 101
Tucker, Fred I: 237
Tucker, William A. III: 38
Tudor, Owen D. I: 22
Tugwell, Rexford G. V: 536*
Tulin, Abraham IV: 483; V: 309, 450
Tull, Charles E. cited, V: 541
Tumulty, Joseph P. III: 76*, 420
Tupper, Frederick A. III: *28*
Turkey II: 208, 210; III: 156, 158,
    312, 336-37, 345, 354, 356, 404, 417-
    18, 431-32, 470, 495-501, 513, 517,
    520-22, 542, 603, 605; IV: 133, 179,
    235-36, 260, 280-82, 288, 295-98, 331,
    335, 360, 366, 391, 409, 417, 446,
    447; V: 401
Turner, Mr. II: 333
Turner, William D. II: 526*
Turnour, Edward V: 629*
Turrentine, Lowell V: 372*
Tutein, E. G. & Co. I: 573
Tuttle, Lucius I: 277*, *288*, 328, 426,
    583
Twain, Mark I: 150*; IV: 283
Twentieth Century Club II: 46, 87,
    212
Twentieth Century Foundation V:
    339
"Twin Evils of the Literacy Test"
    (1915) III: 506-507
Twohy, George W. IV: 452
Twohy v. Doran IV: 451
Twombly, E. J. III: 73*
Tydings, Millard E. V: 637*
Tyng, Sweall T. IV: 267*

Uncle Tom's Cabin I: 121
Underwood, Herbert S. II: 726*
Underwood, Oscar II: 642; III: *34*,
    83, 196; IV: 166

Underwood-Simmons tariff III: 169, 196, 221, 263; V: 318

Uniform legislation movement, LDB and I: 156, 280-81, 347, 358-59, 364, 367, 398, 401, 433-36

Union Boat Club (Boston) I: 137; IV: 260

Union of Orthodox Jewish Congregations III: 572, 602, 624

Union Pacific Rrd II: 111, 721, 722; III: 182, 207

Unitarian Association II: 212

United Drug Stores II: 530; IV: 182

United Fuel & Gas Co. v. Public Service Commission of West Virginia V: 351

United Fuel & Gas Co. et al. v. Rrd Commission of Kentucky V: 351

United Hebrew Association v. Benshimel IV: 33

United Hungarian Societies III: 572

United Jewish Appeal IV: 277; V: 471

United Mine Workers' Union I: 209-212; II: 451; IV: 559; V: 373, 383

United Mine Workers' Union v. Cronado Coal Co. V: 57-59

United Palestine Appeal V: 471, 582

United Shoe Machinery Co., LDB and I: 428-31, 470-72, 508-509; II: 104, 376, 410-11, 428-32, 464, 551-60; III: 42, 224, 369, 592-95; IV: 60-61, 76, 78, 81, 97, 150

United Shoe Workers' Union IV: 529

U.S. Army IV: 514

U.S. Bureau of Corporations II: 693; III: 94, 210, 259, 523; IV: 307

U.S. Bureau of Labor II: 543, 545, 547, 562, 588; III: 9, 55, 208, 213

U.S. Bureau of Labor Statistics I: *260;* II: 176; III: *136,* 209, 215, 402; V: 189

U.S. Bureau of Rrd Costs III: 76, 78-80, 142

U.S. Bureau of Standards III: 219

U.S. Children's Bureau II: 577; V: 143, 153, 166

U.S. Commission on Industrial Relations II: 535, 564, 577, 639, 675; III: 30, 74, 76, 87, 89, 95, 97, 104, 119, 214, 228, 237, 239, 282, 407, 433

U.S. Commissioner of Labor II: 544

U.S. Daily V: 210, 333, 369, 381, 410, 412, 510

U.S. Department of Agriculture II: 461, 464, 465, 492-93, 537, 725; III: 137, 411; V: 641

U.S. Department of Commerce (and Labor) II: 100, 461; III: 41, 103, 210; IV: 539; V: 270

U.S. Department of the Interior II: 307, 311, 314, 318, 321, 324, 337, 340, 353, 386, 415, 461, 463, 466, 493, 724; III: 4, 7, 9, 40, 203, 239, 468; IV: 92; V: 130, 641

U.S. Department of Justice II: 456, 461, 693, 722-23; III: 41, 84, 97, 102, 106, 111-12, 131, 145, 154, 188, 201, 257, 268, 275-77, 282, 286, 290, 560, 592-95; IV: 70, 76, 452; V: 85, 122, 203, 310

U.S. Department of Labor III: 73, 214, 546

U.S. Department of the Navy III: 465, 492; IV: 275; V: 270

U.S. Department of the Post Office II: 436-37, 439; IV: 541; V: 70

U.S. Department of State III: 57, 382, 464, 492, 524, 585, 609; IV: 138, 142, 161, 186, 191, 235, 281, 295-97, 305, 340, 355, 457; V: 270, 273, 579, 617, 629, 646, 652

U.S. Department of the Treasury III: 4, 40, 161-62, 509

U.S. Department of War II: 461; III: 146, 350; IV: 332; V: 78

U.S. Employment Service IV: 370

U.S. Farm Loan Board V: 289

U.S. Forestry Service II: 324, 341; V: 641

U.S. Merchant Marine V: 390

U.S. Railroad Securities Commission II: 411

U.S.S. *Vulcan* III: 421, 424, 431, 454, 467-70, 474, 481-84, 487, 511, 514, 521, 548-50, 583, 607

U.S. Senate Committee on Interstate Commerce (Clapp Committee) II: 521, 525, 530, 536, 551-60, 564-66, 574, 652, 670

U.S. Shipping Board V: 15, 24, 31, 79, 330

U.S. Steel Corporation II: 221, 289, 525, 538, 543, 545, 547, 562, 564, 574, 588, 602, 652, 654, 664; III: 25, 310-12, 545; IV: 274, 560; V: 42, 124, 167

U.S. Supreme Court (to LDB's nomination, January, 1916) II: 10, 67, 78, 96, 102, 124, 126, 238, 242, 297, 341, 350, 413, 422, 435, 495, 504, 507, 521, 541, 543, 557, 559, 610, 615, 679, 689, 721-22, 729; III: 36, 42, 63, 99, 103, 111, 113, 120, 126, 182, 231, 237, 254, 264, 288, 305, 364, 381, 384, 392, 400, 420, 443, 539-40, 593-94, 635, 682; see also individual cases

U.S. Supreme Court, LDB's nomination and the struggle over confirmation IV: 25-36, 41-132, 139-54, 165-66, 169-72, 175-77, 182-84, 192, 196, 198, 209-16, 219-33, 240-41, 249, 264-65; V: 308; LDB on IV: 25-26, 40-45, 53-54, 91, 114, 182, 239-40

U.S. Supreme Court, LDB's work on IV: 258, 264, 267-69, 273-74, 299, 315-16, 367-69, 423, 450-52, 509-10, 517, 520-22, 540-42, 550-51, 554, 559; V: 40-41, 47-53, 56-59, 63-64, 74-75, 78-88, 91-99, 104-106, 116-20, 124-32, 137-38, 154, 159-60, 165-76, 185, 188-89, 192, 200-201, 204, 208, 213, 221, 224-28, 235-39, 243-44, 247-48, 254, 272-76, 279-81, 284-86, 290-96, 303-18, 322-25, 328-37, 345-46, 350-52, 358-61, 364, 368-73, 376-

80, 397, 403-404, 414-15, 482-83, 496-97, 500-501, 512, 564, 566, 587-89, 610-11, 652-53; see also specific cases

U.S. Supreme Court, LDB on IV: 423; V: 64, 75, 93, 160, 292-93

U.S. Tariff Commission III: 84; V: 126, 202

U.S. v. *American Livestock Commission Co.* V: 368

U.S. v. *American Railway Express Co.* V: 132

U.S. v. *American Tobacco Co.* II: 496, 504, 519, 521, 556

U.S. v. *Boston & Maine Rrd* V: 368

U.S. v. *Butler* V: 538

U.S. v. *Darby* I: 521; V: 53

U.S. v. *Kellogg Toasted Corn Flakes Co.* III: 96-97, 112, 539-40

U.S. v. *Keystone Watch Case Co.* III: 539-40

U.S. v. *Louisville & Nashville Rrd* III: 399-400, 444

U.S. v. *Los Angeles & Salt Lake Rrd* V: 274

U.S. v. *Union Pacific Rrd* II: 723

U.S. v. *U.S. Steel Corporation* IV: 274-75

U.S. v. *Weitzel* V: 226

U.S. v. *Wilson Coal Co.* II: 311

U.S. v. *Winslow* II: 560

United Stores Association II: 529

United Traction & Electric Co. (Providence) II: 48-50, 56

United Zinc & Chemical Co. v. Britt V: 94

Unity Life Insurance Co. III: 8

University Zionist Society III: 505, 532, 537-39, 555, 657; IV: 9, 81, 86, 201, 231, 280

Untermyer, Samuel III: *48**, *84*, 115, *168*, 184, *187*, 222, *416*, 666; IV: 28, 209, 246, 265

Upham, George B. I: 141*, 143, *162*, 177, 179, *182*, 185, 200, 229, 288, *418*, 424, *425*, *426*, 523, 524; II: 62

U'Ren, William S. III: 222*

Urofsky, Melvin I. cited, II: 635, 661; III: 293, 320, 683; IV: 240, 282, 344, 397, 446, 476, 563, 566, 568; V: 116, 196, 292, 348, 427, 468

Ussischkin, Manahem IV: 432, 533; V: 38*, 558, 576, 594

Utilities Bureau (Philadelphia) III: 393, 396; IV: 301

Vahey, James I: 543*; II: 293

Valentine, Robert G. II: 648*; III: 203, 262, 396; IV: 268

Valentine, Mrs. IV: 268

Van Buren, Albert A. I: 459*

Van Camp, W. J. III: 74*

Vance, John T. V: 395*

Vandenberg, Arthur H. II: 419*

Vanderbilt, William H. IV: 76

Vanderlip, Frank A. II: 695*

Van Devanter, Willis IV: 551; V: 81*, 85, 93, 171, 174, 221, 295, 308, 310, 337, 376, 377, 384, 552, 588; LDB on V: 376

Van Dyke, Henry IV: 146*

Van Etten, Edgar I: 511*

Van Hise, Charles R. II: 671*, 673, 694; III: 87, 95, 119

Van Noorden, Ezekial II: 571*

Van Tassel, Mr. IV: 89

Van Valkenburg, Edwin A. II: 408*, 442; III: 112, 237, 618

Van Vleck, William C. V: 101*, 123, 167, 224

Vare, William S. V: 227*, 344

Vaterland IV: 324

Vedem, Vladimir IV: 158*

Veech family III: 334, 340

Veiller, Lawrence T. I: 374*, 377

Venice, Italy IV: 546

Vermont III: 6-7, 264, 271, 439

Versailles Peace Conference and Treaty IV: 346, 357, 366, 369, 374, 377, 387, 388, 392, 404-407, 414, 421-23, 449-50, 550; V: 579

Vertrees, John J. II: 321*, 328, 333, 337, 342, 348; IV: 171

Vick, Walker W. III: 17*

Vigliotti v. Pennsylvania V: 91

Viking Press V: 521, 643, 646

Villard, Henry I: 245

Villard, Oswald G. II: 271, 442; V: 12*, 30, 285, 355

Vincent, Mr. I: 276

Virgin Islands V: 556

Virginia Law Register V: 294

Viteles, Mr. V: 433

Vogel, E. I. IV: 6*

Volstead Act V: 65, 91, 103, 388; see also Prohibition and enforcement, LDB on

Voltaire quoted, I: 95

vonAllmen, Pearl V: 636*

vonHeyse, Paul J. L. I: 29

vonHindenburg, Paul V: 517

vonJhering, Rudolph quoted, V: 348

Voris, Edward F. I: 22*, 27, 32

Vrooman, Carl S. II: 707*; III: 3, 410; IV: 284; V: 203, 206

Vulcan: see U.S.S. Vulcan

Wachtell, Samuel R. V: 275*, 324

Wade, Jack I: 99

Wade, Martin J. V: 316*

Wade, Winthrop H. I: 69*, 105

Wadhams, Frederick E. I: 485*

Wadlin, Horace G. I: 446*

Wadsted, Otto V: 493

Wadsworth, Mrs. I: 142

Wadsworth, George V: 624*, 630, 647

Wadsworth, James W. Jr. V: 151*

Wafd, the IV: 414

"Wage-Earners' Life Insurance: A Great Wrong and a Remedy" (1906) I: 364, 444-46, 448-49, 453, 457-58, 460-65, 469, 480, 484-85, 489, 493, 499, 502-503, 547

"Wage Earners' Life Insurance and Old Age Annuities" (1905) I: 485

Waggoner Estate v. Wichita County V: 273

Wagmeister, Mr. IV: 158

Wagner-Lewis bill V: 537-38, 540

Wagner, Richard V: 243

Wagner, Robert F. V: 368*, 531, 536, 537, 602

Wahrheit III: 625

Waite, Henry M. V: 169

Walcott, Robert I: 244*, 245

Wald, Lillian D. II: 391*, 535; III: 407, 432; cited, II: 249

Waldheim, Aaron IV: 32*

Waldo, Mr. II: 86

Waldstein, Charles I: 104

Walker, Albert H. I: 123

Walker, Francis A. I: 83*, 112

Walker, James J. V: 530

Walker, John V: 12

Walker, John B. II: 400*

Walker, Joseph H. I: 304*, 312, 559, 574, 575, 577; II: 146, 150, 153, 157, 158, 161, 163, 164, 179, 182, 190

Walkowitz, Abraham V: 551*

Wall, Joseph F. cited, II: 214

Wall, Louis H. cited, II: 721

Wall St. Journal I: 258; II: 64; IV: 48, 151; V: 586

Wallace, Hugh C. IV: 447*

Wallace, Henry A. V: 552, 556*, 631

Wallas, Graham IV: 404*; V: 283

Walpole Tire & Rubber Co. III: 160

Walsh, David I. I: 167*, 170; III: 80, 265, 392, 397, 457, 597, 603, 611-13, 629; IV: 361; V: 152, 238, 363; LDB on III: 611-13

Walsh, Frank P. III: 29*, 88, 95, 97, 380, 433; IV: 256

Walsh, John III: 601*

Walsh, Thomas J. IV: 87, 125, 127*, 141, 165, 536; V: 75, 121, 310, 322, 336, 369

Walton, John M. III: 159*, 179

Wambaugh, Eugene IV: 27*

War Finance Corporation IV: 521, 543; V: 4, 14, 22, 35, 206, 496

War Industries Board IV: 317, 332

War Labor Policies Board IV: 344, 370, 378

Warburg, Felix M. III: 339*, 341, 397, 482, 504, 548, 550, 574, 641;

IV: 146, 154, 211, 213, 218, 234, 253; V: 115, 386, 388-89, 397, 399, 407-408, 417, 422-23, 430, 439, 454, 460, 465-70, 479, 483, 489, 516; LDB on V: 470-71, 479-80

Warburg, Max M. IV: 156*, 234

Warburg, Otto III: 324*, 421; IV: 154, 160; V: 37-38, 195

Warburg, Paul M. III: 267*; IV: 317

Ward, Edmund II: 81

Ward, John W. cited, V: 288

Ward, Mrs. John I: 94

Ware, Charles E. Jr. II: 526*

Ware, Darwin E. I: 71

Ware, Norman J. V: 138*, 201, 405, 409

Ware Savings Bank II: 224, 226

Warner, Joseph B. II: 48, 51, 57*, 71, 87, 92, 99, 108, 112, 157, 158, 162, 164, 166, 273

Warner, Mr. V: 3

Warren, Charles I: 177; III: 63*, 190; IV: 226; V: 52, 54, 105, 146, 489, 598, 611

Warren, Cornelia L. I: 137*, 142, 146; II: 482; IV: 71

Warren, Edward H. IV: 141, 396; V: 144, 334*; cited, V: 334

Warren, Edward P. IV: 70*, 72, 140

Warren Edward R. I: 143*, 176, 178, 179, 181, 182, 183, 184, 185, 190, 210, 229, 232, 252, 254, 256, 270, 272, 273, 275, 278, 282, 288, 289, 292, 294, 298, 301, 305, 313, 318, 327; IV: 120-26; V: 590

Warren, Fiske I: 148*, 150, 151, 153; IV: 72

Warren, Henry IV: 72

Warren, John E. III: 289

Warren, Samuel D. I: 18*, 22, 34, 36, 38, 41-47, 53, 56, 59-62, 65, 68, 74, 75, 77, 78, 89, 101, 117, 126, 143, 148, 248, 288, 302, 352, 366, 514; II: 219, 292; IV: 34, 69, 71-72; V: 656; LDB on I: 38, 42, 44

Warren, S. D. & Co. I: 75-77; II: 68; III: 289; IV: 67, 403

Warren will case I: 192; IV: 68, 71, 78, 111, 132, 153

Warsaw, Poland IV: 156-62

Washburn bill III: 90-93, 109

Washburn, Robert M. II: 161*, 257, 273, 275, 281; III: 59

Washburn v. Hammond I: 81

Washburne, Hempstead IV: 30

Washington, Booker T. V: 366

Washington Daily News V: 425

Washington, D.C. IV: 261, 321, 350, 363

Washington, D.C., Minimum Wage Board of V: 89, 100

Washington, George II: 213; V: 272, 302

Washington Naval Conference (1921) V: 32, 33, 34, 44

Washington Post II: 439; III: 385; V: 133, 173, 353, 356

Washington Street Subway: see Boston Elevated Railway

Washington Times II: 726; IV: 130

Washington v. Dawson V: 117

Washington, W. H. IV: 171

Wasserman, Oskar V: 472*

water rights, LDB on III: 6-7, 146

Waterman, Richard II: 44, 95, 166

Watson et al. v. State Comptroller of New York V: 85

Watson, Mr. III: 222, 229, 235, 237

Watt, Robert J. V: 569*

Watterson, Henry I: 356*; II: 335, 343, 348, 351, 358, 371, 442; III: 334; V: 223

"The Watuppa Pond Cases" (1888) I: 78; IV: 33

Wauchope, Sir Arthur G. V: 521*, 581, 624

Waugh, W. Wallace I: 233*

Waugh, William L. II: 281*

Wealth Tax Act (1935) V: 538

Weaver, John I: 374*

Webb, A. L. III: 485

Webb, Beatrice P. II: 551*; V: 90, 100

Webb-Kenyon Act (1913) V: 98, 172, 275

Webb, Sidney II: 551*; V: 90, 399, 402, 452, 460

Webb v. O'Brien V: 106

Webb, William S. IV: 74*

Weber, Adna F. II: 32*

Webster & Dudley Street Railway Co. II: 238, 242

Webster, Andrew G. I: 174, 229, 296, 424, 523-24

Webster, John L. II: 613*

Webster, T. K. II: 204*

Wedgwood, Josiah C. IV: 337*; V: 468, 599; LDB on V: 599

Weed, Alonzo I: 426*, 453, 527; II: 62

Weed, Charles F. II: 432*, 465; III: 75

Weeks, John W. II: 431*; IV: 361; V: 248

Wehle, Amy B. I: 3*, 8, 13, 15, 19, 21, 26, 28, 30, 49, 52, 58(2), 60, 103, 119, 135, 165, 221, 438; II: 333; IV: 258

Wehle, Bertha V: 233*

Wehle, Fannie B. I: 26*, 49; II: 452

Wehle, Frederick I: 590; V: 140, 148*, 153, 158, 162

Wehle, Frederick Jr. V: 150*

Wehle, Frederick Jr. V: 150*

Wehle, Gottlieb V: 233*

Wehle, Harry B. II: 96, 140, 156, 209, 250, 276, 397; III: 444, 484; V: 4, 146

Wehle, Ida V: 305

Wehle, Julie I: 24*

Wehle, Louis B. I: 58*, 120, 135, 165, 192, 221, 340, 371, 387, 449, 478, 590; II: 77, 331, 333, 368, 380, 397, 416, 474, 642; III: 42, 264, 354, 444; IV: 199, 258, 268, 295, 309, 327, 385, 401, 432, 474, 488, 543; V: 14, 21, 28, 34, 35, 75, 93, 169, 222, 345, 350, 493, 496, 502, 503, 506, 508, 511; LDB on I: 165; IV: 488, 543; V: 35

Wehle, Mary IV: 199, 258, 268-69, 297, 327, 475

Wehle, Oscar II: 200*, 331

Wehle, Otto I: *5*, *9*, 13-15, 20, *21*, *23*, *26*, *29*, *30*, *33*, *47*, *48*, *50*, *54*, *55*, *56*, *58*, 120, 221; II: *156*; III: 334, 444, 484; IV: 199, 258, 324, 327, *385*, *533*; V: *13*, 22, *96*, 150, 221, 305

Weidenbach, Mr. IV: 229

Weil, A. Leo IV: *36**

Weil, Bruno V: *562**

Weil, Farrel & Co. IV: 111, 113

Weinstock, Harris III: 89*; IV: 32

Weinstein, Jacob J. cited, V: 615

Weiss, Julius III: 653*

Weiss, Louis S. IV: 383*

Weiss v. Weiner V: 378

Weissberg, Nat W. III: 353

Weizmann, Chaim III: 22, 303, *322**, *353*, 499, *500*, 519, 541, 586, 589, 598-99, *644*; IV: 154, 234, 281-93, 302, *310*, *311*, 312, *314*, 316, 318, 320, *321*, 322-23, *325*, 328, *331*, 334, 337, *341*, 343-48, *349*, 351, *353*, 359, *360*, *365*, 373, 374, *375*, 377, 381, *386*, 388, 389, 393, 398, 404, 405, *418*, 420, 423, 426-27, 433, 439, 443, 457, *465*, *467*, 473, 474, 477, 483, 487, 490-94, *508*, 514, 519, 526, 532-38, 542, 545, 549-56, 563-68; V: 9, 12, 19, 38, 104, 107, 115, 249, 252, 258, 271, 275, 292, 310, 336, 347, 382, 389, 401, *432*, 434-40, 445, 460, 472, 479, 486, 491-92, 507, 522, 532, 580, 591, 593, 599, 604, 608, 614, 619, 632, 639, 644, *646*, 654; cited, III: 329; IV: 405, 420, 434; V: 612, 618; LDB on IV: 325, 331, 404, 443-44, 530, 534, 552-53; V: 271

Weizmann Commission IV: 334-35, 341-43, 349, 354-57, 360, 380, 466

Welch, Charles W. I: *543*

Wellborn, Charles cited, III: 88

Welles, Sumner V: 627*, 629, 652

Welliver, Judson C. II: 364*, *376*, 410, 428; III: 467; V: 193

Wells, Benjamin W. I: 278*

Wells, Henry G. III: 276-77, *278**

Wells, Herbert G. III: 304*; IV: 520; V: 33, 185

Wells, Philip P. II: 346*, 360, 723; III: 7, *146*; V: 199, 248, 317

Wendt, Lloyd cited, III: 673

Wenzell, Henry B. IV: *230**

Werdenbach, Edward III: 272

Wertheim, Maurice III: 366*, 393, 395, 413, 416, 434, 473, 514; IV: 6, 12, 246

Weruse v. Illinois & St. Louis Bridge Co. I: 33

Wessel, Morris J. II: *619**

West Coast Hotel v. Parish V: 89

West End Railway Co: see Boston Elevated Railway Co.

West v. United Railways & Elevated Co. V: 350

West Virginia V: 10

Western Federation of Miners III: 227

Western Shoe Manufacturers' Alliance II: 523, 557

Western Union Telegraph Co. I: 246, 332

Westinghouse Electric Co. I: 98

Westinghouse, George I: 341*

Westminster Chambers case I: 171; II: 148, 149; IV: 93

Westmoreland Coal Strike (Pennsylvania) II: 451

Weston, Carl V: 28

Weston will case IV: 68

Weyl, Walter E. III: *208**, *401*

Weymouth, George W. I: 281*

W. H. McElwain Co. II: 202, 553, 575; III: 137; IV: 89, 528, 559

Whalen, Richard J. cited, V: 607

Whaley, Major IV: 410

"What Loyalty Demands" (1905) I: 386; III: 455

"What to Do" (1922) V: 59-62

Wheat, Alfred A. V: 324*, 326, 371

Whedon, Charles O. II: *585**

Wheeler, Burton K. V: 83, 124*, 130, 134, 136, 152, 203, 310
Wheeler, Mrs. Burton K. V: 354
Wheeler, Henry N. I: 244*
Wheeler, Harry A. III: 89*
Wheelwright, John T. III: 154*
"Where the Banker is Superfluous" (1913) III: 183, 261; V: 67
Whipple, Sherman L. IV: 110*
Whitcomb, David II: *119**, 127, *128*, 131, *132, 202*
Whitcomb, G. Henry I: 127*
White, Clarissa I: 411*, 414, 442
White, Clinton III: 192
White, Edward D. II: 616; III: 42*, 399; IV: 210, 211, *214, 241, 249, 254, 255*(2), 267, 273, 274, 276, 316, 516, 522, 551, 559, 561; V: 58, 653
White, Frederick T. I: 22
White Goods Manufacturers III: 27
White, Henry I: 411
White, Henry (1850–1927) IV: 366*, 369
White, Herbert I: 411*, 414, 442, 498, 513, 582; II: 36, 85, 195, *237*, 279, 280, 318; III: 37, 271; IV: 60, 295, 324, 518; V: 5, 23, 29, 214, 233; LDB on I: 513; II: 85; V: 214-15
White, Howard III: *25**, *242*
White, J. Harvey I: 306-307
White, James A. cited, II: 83
White, Morton cited, I: 46
White, Norman I: 412, 646*, 498, *500, 509, 511, 525, 527, 532, 534, 535, 546, 548, 550, 551, 552, 559, 560, 561, 565, 568, 569, 570, 575, 578;* II: *5, 6, 21, 22, 24, 27, 81, 85, 86,* 105, *108,* 109, *115,* 117, *120,* 158, 161, 167, *178, 179, 197,* 204, *208, 223,* 227, *234,* 237, *238,* 259, *272, 275,* 279, 281, 283, 722; III: *232, 263;* IV: 62, 453; LDB on I: 498
White, Stewart E. II: 351*
White, Susan J. IV: 67
White, William A. IV: 542; V: 79*, *365, 583;* cited, IV: *471*

White, Mrs. William A. V: 34
Whitehead, Alfred N. V: 278*, 378
Whitlock, Brand I: 475; II: 401*, *662;* III: 229; LDB on III: 229
Whitman, Charles S. III: 384*, 518
Whitman, Russell R. II: *220**
Whitman Savings Bank II: 114, 192, 195, 201, 203, 205, 227, 228, 241, 301, 596
Whitman, William C. I: 342*, 388, *404,* 408; II: 23, 44; III: 34; IV: 51, 97, 98, *214;* LDB on III: 34; IV: 214
Whitney, Anita V: 286
Whitney, E. B. V: 72
Whitney, Henry M. I: 387*, 502; IV: 104
Whitney v. California V: 213, 286
Whiton, Lucius E. II: *274**, *278*
Whitridge, Frederick W. III: 260*
Whittemore, Thomas IV: 359*
Whittier, C. A. III: *289**
Whittier, Edmund A. III: 434, 447; IV: 35, 169
Whittier, John G. I: 24
Whitwell v. Continental Tobacco Co. I: 431
Wholesale Cooperative Society (England) III: 183
"Why I Am a Zionist" (1914) III: 308
Whympers, Edward I: 127
Wickersham Commission V: 114, 373-78, 381, 384
Wickersham, George W. II: 258, *288**, 317, 326-38, 347, 352, 357-58, 362, 431, 459, 512, 602, 722, 726; III: 39, 182; IV: 118, 127, 130, 150; V: 110, 311, 373, 381, 641; LDB on II: 329, 352-55
Wickersham, James II: 461*
Wiebe, Robert cited, II: 366
Wiener, Naomi cited, III: 317
Wigglesworth, George I: 536*, 560, 589; II: 114
Wight, Carrol V: 237
Wigmore, John H. V: 87*, 282-84

Wilbuschewitz-Shohat, Manya V: 476*

Wilcox, Delos F. III: 384*

Wilcox, Professor V: 555

Wilde, Mr. III: 455

Wile, Frederick W. IV: 529*

Wile, Mrs. Frederick W. III: 535*

Wilensky, Max H. III: 348*

Wiley, Harvey W. I: 542*; II: 464, 725

Wilhelm II. IV: 415

Wilhelm, Donald V: 119*

Wilkie, Edward A. IV: 68*

Wilkins, Burleigh T. cited, V: 196

Wilkinson, Mr. and Mrs. V: 341

Will, Allen S. cited, III: 203

Willard, Daniel II: 383*, 412; III: 17, 264, 334; IV: 276; V: 366

Willcox, Mary A. III: 52*

Willcox et al. v. Consolidated Gas Co. I: 581

Willebrandt, Mabel W. V: 355*

Willert, Arthur IV: 318*

Willett, Joseph J. IV: 28*

William A. Muller & Co. II: 234

William Filene & Sons II: 196-97

Williams, Arthur II: 215*, 228

Williams, Frank H. II: 276*

Williams, George F. II: 199*; IV: 104

Williams, Gus II: 358*

Williams, John S. V: 303

Williams, Roger H. IV: 168*

Williams, S. M. III: 85

Williams v. Boston IV: 93

Williams, Whiting V: 384*

Willis, H. Parker III: 115*; cited, III: 116

Williston, Samuel V: 146*, 155

Wilmot Proviso V: 199

"Wilson and the New Party" (1912) II: 676

Wilson Coal Co. II: 311

Wilson, Edith B. V: 40, 113, 563

Wilson, Jesse E. II: 492*

Wilson, Jim V: 172

Wilson, Joseph I: 551

Wilson, Henry L. IV: 186*, 192, 293

"Wilson the Progressive" (1912) II: 676

Wilson, William B. III: 209, 239*; IV: 326

Wilson, Woodrow II: 214, 290, 329, 536, 612, 632, 633*, 637-44, 648-51, 654, 657, 658, 659-73, 676, 685, 686, 696, 699, 706, 709, 711-19, 724-27; III: 4, 8, 17-18, 27, 30-31, 36-45, 51, 56-59, 65, 67, 76, 77, 84, 87, 95-96, 97, 103, 104, 106, 113, 115-17, 127, 130, 144, 147, 170, 173, 187, 190, 194, 195-96, 201, 206, 218-21, 234-39, 252, 258, 286-90, 311, 317, 320, 338, 347, 350, 363, 371, 389, 394, 420, 429, 464, 465, 467, 468, 506, 538, 581, 601, 610, 621-23, 629, 633, 638, 673, 683; IV: 22, 25, 34-37-48, 53-55, 89, 91, 101, 115, 139, 149, 172, 182, 183, 186, 191, 196-97, 206-209, 233, 254, 255, 256, 265, 266, 269, 272, 275-77, 281, 285-89, 292, 294, 310-11, 316-19, 324, 334, 335, 344, 354-56, 362, 364-77, 381, 397, 398, 405, 423, 441, 444, 446, 447-50, 456-57, 508, 521, 546-47, 550, 558, 568; V: 30, 36, 40, 45, 46, 82, 86(2), 91, 113, 127-28, 234, 239, 365, 482, 579; LDB on II: 661, 663, 667, 669-71, 713, 716-17, 727; IV: 256, 398; V: 45, 113, 127-28

Wilson's cabinet, LDB's possible appointment to it II: 715; III: 32, 35-41, 44-45, 129-30; IV: 89-91

Winch, Harry I: 561*

Winchester Arms Co. III: 132

Wing, Daniel G. I: 551*; II: 280

Wingate, Charles F. I: 71*, 530; II: 145; V: 341

Wingate, Orde C. V: 604*

Winship, Addison L. II: 95*

Winslow, Charles H. III: 52, 55, 208*, 213, 261, 401; cited, II: 548; III: 209

Winslow, Erving I: 162, 470*, 550; II: 16

Winslow, Francis A. V: 368*
Winslow, G. H. II: 91
Winslow, John B. IV: 273*
Winslow, Sidney W. I: 508*; II: 104, 376, 428, 551; IV: 60, 78
Winsor, Robert I: 198*, 200-202, 424-25; II: 49, 62; III: 259
Winter, Nathan H. cited, IV: 523
Winterton, Earl of V: 629*
Wisconsin I: 462, 580; II: 209, 329, 344, 347, 356, 359, 375, 382, 415, 512, 573, 639, 710; III: 23, 46, 383, 409, 659-61; IV: 257, 459; V: 189, 497, 527-28
Wisconsin Central Rrd IV: 33, 60, 67
Wisconsin Industrial Commission II: 535
Wisconsin, Public Service Commission of III: 46
Wisconsin Rrd v. Price County I: 81; IV: 33
Wisconsin Unemployment Reserve Act V: 497, 503, 510, 520, 526, 531, 537, 540, 552, 554, 555, 560, 563, 585
Wisconsin, University of II: 329, 510-12, 686, 695-96; III: 87-88, 644, 659-61; V: 99, 100, 197, 237, 280, 312, 330, 378, 523, 589; LDB on V: 99-100
Wisconsin v. Illinois and the Chicago Sanitary District V: 209
Wise, Isaac M. III: 317
Wise, Jonah B. V: 553*
Wise, Otto I. III: 610, 622, 643*, 675; IV: 377
Wise, Stephen S. II: 535; III: 296*, 298, 300, 308, 309, 314, 323, 351, 360, 362, 365, 367, 374, 389, 401, 403, 415, 418, 426, 430, 439, 446, 454, 465, 471, 504, 508, 522, 531, 538, 571, 575-76, 579, 597-98, 601, 609, 614, 622, 643, 665, 668, 677, 679; IV: 5, 17, 82, 102, 108, 116, 129, 132, 133, 135, 137, 138, 146, 147, 152, 192, 207, 209, 215, 246, 250, 253, 271-72, 277, 281, 289-90, 295, 297-98, 303, 310-12, 313, 316-30, 335, 337, 351, 354, 359, 360, 363, 365, 369, 373, 374, 375, 377, 381, 384, 389, 391(2), 392, 396, 426, 431, 435, 439-43, 447, 452, 453-58, 461, 463, 466, 473, 489, 492, 494, 501, 509, 513, 514, 516, 518, 522, 524, 530, 533, 544, 553, 555, 556, 563, 565; V: 8, 18, 25, 26, 27, 36, 38, 44, 250, 273, 309, 330, 336, 425, 426-27, 434-35, 440, 471, 486, 492, 507, 516, 520, 522, 529, 533, 540, 544, 549, 551, 553, 558, 561, 562, 563, 567, 571, 576, 578, 581, 582, 590, 594, 604, 606, 608, 614, 615, 619-21, 629, 630, 632, 643; LDB on V: 533, 567
Wislezemus, Miss I: 29
Witte, Edwin E. V: 552
Witte, Serge J. I: 338*, 355
Wohl, Samuel V: 459*, 489, 590
Wolcott, Roger I: 130*
Wolcott, Roger Jr. II: 252*, 257, 262, 273; III: 264, 274
Wolf, Alexander S. III: 648*
Wolf, Horace J. IV: 7*
Wolf, Lucien IV: 103*
Wolf, Simon IV: 388
Wolfe, S. Herbert II: 590*
Wolff, Sidney E. V: 575*, 636
Wolffsohn, David III: 22, 328*
Wolfson, Harry A. III: 460*
Wolman, Leo V: 419*, 450
Women in Industry (1908) I: 166
Women's International Zionist Organization V: 480
Women's Journal III: 597
women's suffrage, LDB on I: 66, 280; III: 48, 319, 535-36; IV: 363
Women's Trade Union League III: 55
Wood, Mr. II: 116
Wood, Arthur IV: 542
Wood, Edward F. L. V: 619*
Wood, Leonard V: 201
Wood, L. Hollingsworth III: 419*
Woodhead Commission V: 604
Woodhead, Sir John V: 602

Woodlock, Thomas F. V: 210*

Woodrow Wilson's College Men's League II: 698

Woodruff, Clinton R. I: 284*, *328;* II: *573;* III: *12,* 153

Woodruff, Edwin H. I: 30

Woods, Arthur IV: 276

Woods, Charles A. V: 142*

Woods, Eleanor H. cited, I: 210

Woods, James H. V: 278*

Woods, Robert A. I: 210*, 231, *405,* *469, 482, 502,* 561; II: 523; cited, I: 167, 173, 424; II: 379

Woods, Russell A. II: 404*

Woodward, C. Vann cited, I: 13

Woodward, Thomas M. V: 414*

Woolley, Robert III: 311*; IV: 274; V: 26, 28, 122, 169, 415

Woolsey, John M. V: 372

Worcester & Connecticut Eastern Railway Co. II: 40

Worcester & Webster Street Railway Co. II: 238, 242

Worcester Board of Trade II: 137

Worcester Consolidated Co. II: 36

Worcester, Dean C. V: 657

Worcester Railways & Investment Co. II: 49, 51, 52

Works, John B. II: 622; IV: 110, 125, 132, 141, 143, 183

World Court V: 213, 249

World Jewish Congress IV: 173; V: 507, 521, 545, 639

World Peace Foundation V: 197

World Today II: 521

World Tomorrow V: 522

World War I and war mobilization, LDB and IV: 271-76, 292-93, 300-301, 306-309, 314, 317, 324, 326, 332-34, 362-63; LDB on III: 307; IV: 300, 304, 308, 324, 332-34; V: 148-50, 226, 229

World Zionist Organization III: 23, 147, 291, 327, 470, 680; IV: 406, 444, 486, 494, 503, 509, 524, 531, 535, 538, 550, 555, 563, 567; V: 135, 292, 336, 387, 389, 437, 439, 440, 444, 460, 470, 473, 479

Worthley, George H. II: 93*

the "worthwhile in life," LDB on I: 93-94; V: 31, 243, 566, 595

Wray, Arthur G. II: *648**

Wright, Carroll D. I: *244**

Wright, Elizur I: 367*, 448, 462; II: 20

Wright, Orville IV: 276

Wright, Walter C. I: *367*, 381, 393, 437, 444,* 448, 462, *492;* V: 546

Wyatt, Edith F. II: 406, 484

Wyman, Bruce III: 225*, 240

Wyzanski, Charles E. Jr. V: 523*

Xenophon quoted, V: 325, 319-20

Yad Vashem V: 639

Yager, Gedalia cited, III: 328

Yahuda, Abraham S. E. III: 341*

Yale Law Journal V: 189, 499, 653; cited, IV: 330

Yale University V: 99

Yale University Law School I: 88; V: 284, 317, 326, 360, 378, 381, 403, 421

Yale, William cited, IV: 297

Yehuda, Ben IV: 375

Yellin, David III: 366*

Yiddish Folk IV: 13, 135, 270, 292, 349, 502, 506, 513

Yoder, Jocelyn P. II: *563**

Young, Allyn A. V: 251*, 373

Young, Arthur quoted, V: 230

Young, George C. V: 383*, 409, 410

Young, James H. I: 67*

Young Judea III: 479, 488, 663, 667; IV: 40, 270

Young Men's Christian Association II: 215

Young Men's Democratic Club V: 391

Young Men's Hebrew Association III: 388, 395, 574, 580, 588, 613, 640; IV: 257

Young, Owen D. V: 169*, 367, 416, 640

Youngman, William S. I: 192*; IV: 48, 72, 140

Youngstown, Ohio IV: 13

Youth Aliyah V: 582

Zar, Isidor IV: 98*

Zeeland Memorandum IV: 482, 566; V: 446

Zeisler, Sigmund IV: 28*

Zeldin, Mr. V: 291, 451

Zhitlowsky, Chaim IV: 296*

Zikhron Ya'akov III: 622

Zimmerman v. Sutherland V: 275, 324

Zimmern, Alfred III: 599*; IV: 408, 411, 414, 417, 419; V: 33, 186

Zinn, Howard cited, V: 530

Zinoviev, Grigori E. V: 152*

Zinsser, Hans V: 278*

Zion Association of Greater Boston III: 66, 77, 622, 649; IV: 102, 219, 262, 350

Zion Association of Greater New York III: 377, 450

Zionism and Jewish affairs, LDB and I: 386-87; II: 402, 611, 659; III: 4, 22-23, 64-66, 77-78, 141, 147-48, 158-59, 174-75, 192-93, 226, 291-341, 344, 349-83, 386-89, 393-592, 595-682; IV: 3-21, 24, 34, 38-41, 79-86, 95-98, 102-104, 108-10, 115-17, 126, 129, 132-42, 145-75, 178-81, 184-90, 193-224, 227-28, 231-37, 240-63, 269-72, 277-362, 365-474, 477-509, 513-19, 522-27, 530-38, 541, 544-45, 549-56, 560-68; V: 3-4, 8-9, 12, 14, 18-19, 25-31, 26-39, 44, 51, 73-74, 90, 100-18, 182, 191-92, 195-96, 219-20, 249-53, 258, 271-75, 291-95, 300, 309, 330, 336, 343, 347-48, 386-90, 397-99, 407-409, 413-14, 417-43, 451-52, 459, 461-92, 507, 541, 544-45, 549-54, 567-68, 577-83, 587, 590-91, 594-99, 605-609, 619-23, 632-35, 638-39,

643-55; see also Brandeis, Louis D. and American Jewish Congress movement; and development of Palestine; and the Balfour Declaration; and trip to Palestine; and financial contributions to Zionism and Jewish causes

Zionism, LDB on II: 402, 611; III: 174, 357, 412-13, 455-56, 485-86, 513, 534-35, 546, 575, 587; IV: 20-21, 178, 224, 329; V: 115, 129, 195-96, 246, 429-30, 446-49, 621, 630-31

"Zionism and Patriotism" (1915) III: 355-56, 358, 371, 412, 416, 492, 543, 637, 638; IV: 6; V: 534

Zionist Bureau (Berlin) III: 291, 627

Zionist Bureau (Copenhagen) III: 627, 630

Zionist Bureau (New England) III: 405, 414, 529, 563, 566, 569, 589

Zionist Conference of 1920 (London) IV: 386, 433, 458, 466, 468-69, 476, 481-86, 490-91, 494, 501, 503, 509, 524, 526, 530, 531, 553, 556

Zionist Congress of 1897 (Basle) III: 156; IV: 159, 525; see also Basle [Zionist] Program

Zionist Congress of 1913 (Vienna) III: 147, 158

Zionist Congress of 1921 (Carlsbad) IV: 455, 567; V: 9, 12

Zionist Congress of 1931 (Basle) V: 479, 483, 485, 486

Zionist Congress of 1939 (Geneva) V: 621

Zionist Convention of 1916 (Philadelphia) IV: 199, 214, 219, 243, 247

Zionist Convention of 1917 (Baltimore) IV: 291, 294, 297-98, 325, 328, 483

Zionist Convention of 1918 (Pittsburgh) IV: 348, 492, 566

Zionist Convention of 1919 (Chicago) IV: 424, 428, 483, 489

Zionist Convention of 1920 (Buffalo) IV: 513, 542, 545

Zionist Convention of 1921 (Cleveland) IV: 439, 490, 556, 561-63, 566; V: 3

Zionist Convention of 1928 (Pittsburgh) V: 347

Zionist Convention of 1930 (Cleveland) V: 427, 430

Zionist Emergency Committee V: 595, 643, 644

Zionist Organization of America III: 528, 565, 588, 624; IV: 320, 348, 356, 362, 373-75, 382-84, 389-91, 398, 402, 423, 429-31, 435-39, 464-66, 472-73, 481-94, 501-516, 524, 532, 542, 544, 553, 556, 563, 566, 567; V: 18, 28, 51, 116, 291, 293-95, 314, 336, 391, 420-22, 426-32, 438, 440, 451, 455, 459-61, 465, 472, 489-91, 507, 572, 593, 595, 614, 616, 638, 643, 644, 654

Zionist Organization of America Delegates (1930) V: 429

Zionist Palestine Executive V: 383, 439, 445, 622

Zionist unity, LDB on IV: 525-26

Zionists of America III: 291

Zionists of Philadelphia III: 333

Zola, Emile III: 374*

Zollschan, Ignatz III: 386

Zolotkoff, Leon III: 616*, 648, 650, 659; IV: 195, 212, 218, 347-48

Zon, Raphael IV: 492*

Zuckerman, Baruch III: 529*; IV: 280

Zuckerman, William V: 438

Zueblin, Charles II: 644*, 694